Peterson's

College Guide

for

Performing Arts Majors

2007

Carole J. Everett
Former Director of Admissions
The Juilliard School

PETERSON'S

A **nelnet.** COMPANY

PETERSON'S

A (n)elnet. COMPANY

About Peterson's, a Nelnet company

Peterson's (www.petersons.com) is a leading provider of education information and advice, with books and online resources focusing on education search, test preparation, and financial aid. Its Web site offers searchable databases and interactive tools for contacting educational institutions, online practice tests and instruction, and planning tools for securing financial aid. Peterson's serves 110 million education consumers annually.

For more information, contact Peterson's, 2000 Lenox Drive, Lawrenceville, NJ 08648; 800-338-3282; or find us on the World Wide Web at www.petersons.com/about.

© 2006 Peterson's, a Nelnet company

Previous editions © 1995, 1996, 1997, 1998, 1999, 2000, 2001, 2002, 2003, 2004, 2005

Previously published as *Peterson's Professional Degree Programs in the Visual & Performing Arts*

Editor: Linda Seghers; Production Editor: Teresina Jonkoski; Copy Editors: Bret Bollmann and Pam Sullivan; Research Project Manager: Jennifer Fishberg; Programmer: Alex Lin; Interior Design: Katie Cordisco; Manufacturing Manager: Ivona Skibicki; Composition Manager: Gary Rozmierski; Client Relations Representatives: Danielle Groncki, Mimi Kaufman, Karen Mount, and Eric Wallace.

ISBN-13: 978-0-7689-2325-4
ISBN-10: 0-7689-2325-5
ISSN 1552-7751

Printed in the United States of America

10 9 8 7 6 5 4 3 2 1   08 07 06

Twelfth Edition

ABOUT THE AUTHOR

An honors graduate of Barnard College of Columbia University, an educator, and a renowned mezzo-soprano who has performed with opera companies and orchestras and on recital tours around the world, Carole Everett also holds an advanced degree from the Universita of Siena, Italy. For seven years she served as the Director of Admissions at The Juilliard School in New York City. She has also worked at the Nightingale-Bamford School, was Head of School at an independent school in St. Croix in the U.S. Virgin Islands, and currently works at St. Luke's School in Greenwich Village. Ms. Everett speaks and consults frequently on college and graduate school admissions and has taught voice, public speaking, reading, current events, and Latin at elementary through post-secondary levels. She is a native of Wellesley, Massachusetts, and lives in New York City and Spoleto, Italy, with her husband, son, and Bernese mountain dog.

Performing Arts

Contents

Performing

Arts

A Note from the Peterson's Editors

As a prospective performing arts major, you probably know where your talent lies and can see yourself becoming a dancer, a musician, or an actor one day. You are one of the lucky college-bound students who already know what they want to study and have one foot solidly on their career path. That part might have been easy. But what's usually not easy is choosing a school or a program. This guide will help you to make the right decisions.

Written by Carole J. Everett, former admissions director at The Juilliard School, *Peterson's College Guide for Performing Arts Majors* takes you step-by-step through the various stages of applying to college, provides insight into the world of performing arts education, and gives you expert advice on everything from auditioning to planning a career.

In the first section of the guide, **The College Admissions Process,** you'll learn how to assess your talent and discover your educational needs and goals—perhaps the most important step in identifying potential schools to place on your "list." The pros and cons of attending a conservatory versus a liberal arts college are explored, as are Early Decision and deferred admission. You'll discover an abundance of practical tips on campus visits, interviews, applications, and financial aid. The College Admissions Timetable sums it all up from sophomore through senior year and keeps you on track.

The guide is then divided into three sections containing in-depth information: **For Dance Majors, For Music Majors,** and **For Theater Majors.** Topics such as health issues for dancers, hiring a photographer to do head shots, and how to make an audition recording are explored. And you'll find some of the best advice available on auditions: what to expect at an audition, how to choose material, how to deal with nerves, taped versus live auditions, things you should never do at an audition, and much more. There are even sample audition evaluation forms that show you just how your dancing, acting, or musical performance will be critiqued and rated. No one who is planning a college audition should be without this invaluable information.

Performing Arts

At the end of each of the three sections you'll find essays written by current dance, music, and theater majors that contain their advice as well as a glimpse into what being a performing arts major is really like. There are checklists to keep you on track throughout the admissions process, and for those thinking ahead there is a chapter on careers in the performing arts that you might never have thought of. There is even a chapter "For Parents," which lists things that parents should do (and not do!) to help their children during the college admission process.

When it's time to get the details on individual schools and programs, turn to the **Profiles of Performing Arts Programs** section. Here you will find all the need-to-know information on accredited professional degree programs located throughout the U.S. and Canada. Some schools have provided even more information about their facilities, faculty, alumni, and special programs in *More About the School* at the end of their profile. There isn't an easier or more efficient way to explore college programs.

For those who already have specifics in mind, the **Quick-Reference Chart** lists schools by state and lets you compare programs at a glance. The **Appendixes** include additional resources, including listings of summer programs and scholarships for performing arts students. The **Indexes** let you locate schools by their majors or concentrations or alphabetically by name.

Peterson's publishes a full line of resources to help guide you and your family through the private secondary school admission process. Peterson's publications can be found at your local bookstore, library, and high school guidance office, and you can access us online at www.petersons.com.

We welcome any comments or suggestions you may have about this publication and invite you to complete our online survey at www.petersons.com/booksurvey. Or you can fill out the survey at the back of this book, tear it out, and mail it to us at:

Publishing Department
Peterson's
2000 Lenox Drive
Lawrenceville, NJ 08648

Your feedback will help us to provide personalized solutions for your educational advancement.

Remember, there is no "best" school—only the best school for you. Start examining your goals, your interests, your personality, your talents—and by all means, talk with your teachers and guidance counselors. The editors at Peterson's wish you the best of luck in your performing arts school search!

Performing

Arts

The College Admissions Process

Don't let the college admissions process intimidate you. Colleges and universities all compete for students. Choose five to eight appropriate schools, give the best audition you can, and pay close attention to your applications. You might find that the hardest part of the process will be choosing which offer of admission to accept.

Choosing Your Educational Future

PERSONAL ASSESSMENT

Choosing a college is a great challenge for every student. When you have special talent in the performing arts, the choice is even more critical and you must make some personal assessments at a rather early stage about priorities, goals, professional commitment, and direction for your future. It is important that you take the time to be brutally honest with yourself as you examine your values, strengths, weaknesses, and dreams. It is also essential that you find a college that is best for you. As a performing artist, you must begin this process early enough to prepare for any auditions required. While most students start the college admissions process in the spring of their junior year, performing arts majors should begin to explore colleges, programs, and audition requirements earlier, and no later than in their sophomore year.

Start your personal assessment by considering the following questions:

- How do I like to spend my time? What makes me happiest? What bores me to tears?

- What am I good at? Where do my academic strengths lie? What do I never want to have to study again?

- Why do I want to go to college? What do I expect to gain? What am I looking forward to?

- Do I want to stay close to home or go away? How often do I imagine myself coming home during the year?

- What kind of surroundings make me happiest? Do I thrive on the pace and opportunities in a city? Am I happiest in the country, a serene, pastoral setting? Do I enjoy suburbia? Am I sensitive to weather—do I hate the cold or heat?

- What kind of people do I like to be around?

- What values are most important to me? What do I care most about?

- What kind of person do I want to become?

- What has been the best decision I've made in the past three years? Why?

- What has been the worst decision I've made in the past three years? Why? What did I learn from that experience?

- What decision have I let others (parents, teachers, friends, etc.) make for me? Why? What was the outcome?

- How free do I feel to make my own college decisions? Do my parents generally agree with my plans for college? How important to me are the opinions of family? Friends? Teachers?

- Is there anything preventing me from enrolling in a post-secondary program (college, conservatory, etc.) right out of high school?

- What do I think of general education (liberal arts) versus specialization (conservatory training)? How does this relate to the way I want to spend my time?

- What is my favorite postsecondary program now? What characteristics make this program my favorite?

- How do I feel about the size of an institution? Do I work best in small groups? Do I prefer lots of individual attention? Do I like larger settings?

- How do I respond to competition? Do I thrive on pressure or need a more nurturing environment? Do I want a program in which I must work hard constantly, or would I prefer one in which I can obtain respectable grades without knocking myself out? How would I feel if I were in the middle or the bottom of my class? Is it important to me to be near the top of the class?

- How do I learn best? What teachers and methods of teaching have worked best for me?

- How would I feel about attending a program in which there are few requirements? How much structure is best for me?

- How have I done in high school? Where are my academic strengths? What are my standardized test scores (PSAT, SAT, ACT Assessment, SAT Subject Tests)? Is my academic record an accurate measure of any ability? Have I taken any Advanced Placement (AP) courses? What have been my scores on those? What do I consider the best measure of my potential for college work?

Once you have answered these questions and others that you, your parents, your high school counselor, and your teachers will also pose, you can begin your search for the right environment for further study. Guard against choosing the "designer-label" school of the year. Look instead for an institution where you will be able to learn, grow, have fun, make friends, and cultivate your special talents. This is an exciting time. It is also a time when you have much more control over your choices than you probably imagine. Colleges and conservatories all compete for students. If you choose eight to ten appropriate schools and if you do your best in the application, interview, and audition process, you may find yourself with multiple acceptances. You are the consumer and schools need you. You control your future.

ASSESSING YOUR TALENT

Sometimes it is difficult to know how you measure up in terms of talent. Many of you have starred in the high school play, sung solos with a glee club, danced in regular studio recitals, and perhaps even attended district or all-state band, orchestra, or chorus. Everyone in the community raves about your talent and you think you want to develop it still further at college. But how do you really know if you've got what it takes? Your answers to the following questions may help you clarify just how dedicated you are to the development of your talent.

Dancers

- Are you taking classes regularly? In ballet? In modern dance?

- Do you enjoy taking classes?

- What is the background of your teacher(s)? What feedback have you received?

- How many public performances have you done? How did you feel during the rehearsal stage? During the performance? Afterwards?

- Have you auditioned for any competitive summer programs? For regional productions? What was the outcome?

- Do you have the body type suitable for further study in dance? Have you ever had a weight problem?

- What books about dance have you read?

- What performances have you seen?

- Do you feel that you are musical or musically sensitive?

- Do you enjoy the physicality of dance?

- Are you self-motivated regarding dance?

- Do you remember sequences of dance steps well?

- Are you self-disciplined? (Ask yourself this several times.)

- Do you eat, drink, breathe, and dream dance? Are you prepared to make the sacrifices necessary to make your passion to study dance a reality?

- Is there anything else you could pursue that would make you happy? (If you answer "yes" to this, you probably should decide not to follow a full-time dance program of study.)

Musicians

- How many years of study have you had on your major instrument?

- Have you studied intensively with a private teacher? What is that teacher's background? What feedback does your teacher give you?

- Do you listen to music regularly? To recordings? To the radio? Do you attend classical concerts as well as alternative performance events?

- Have you prepared the repertoire required for auditions?

- Have you participated in musical events in your school? How did you feel during the rehearsals? During the performances? Afterwards?

- Have you auditioned and been accepted at any competitive programs? All-state programs? District programs? Youth symphonies or community choruses? Bands? Summer programs?

- Have you been a soloist? How often?

- Have you studied any music theory? Sight reading? Music history?

- How many hours a day do you practice?

- Do you have the emotional fortitude to deal with the inevitable rejection that accompanies the audition process?

- Are you realistic about the business nature of the music industry?

- Is there anything else you could pursue that would make you happy? (If you answer "yes" to this, you should probably decide not to follow a full-time music program of study.)

Actors

- Have you participated in theater productions in your school? How did you feel during the rehearsal stage? During the production? Afterwards?

- Have you taken any acting classes? Singing? Movement? Improvisation?

- Are you aware that real actor training is both physically and emotionally demanding? Are you willing to put in the dedication and concentration for the scope of training that will serve you best?

- What is the background of your principal acting teacher? Director? What feedback have you received?

- Do you know your "type"?

- Do you memorize well? Quickly?

- What kind of acting are you interested in? Film? TV? Theater?

The College Admissions Process

- Do you have the patience for the hours of memorizing and sometimes tedious rehearsals required of actors?

- Are you resourceful in thinking of ways to support yourself until you get cast as an actor? Will your ego withstand being in "rent" or "day" jobs?

- Do you have the emotional fortitude to deal with the inevitable rejection that accompanies life in the theater?

- Are you aware that show business is really just that: a business? How will you feel about dealing with the business side of the entertainment industry?

- Is there anything else you could pursue that would make you happy? (If you answer "yes" to this, you should probably decide not to follow a full-time theater program of study.)

Getting Objective Opinions About Your Talent

It is sometimes possible to arrange an "advisory" audition to help you determine your level of expertise. In dance, you might call your regional ballet company and see if they would refer you to a class where you could speak with the teacher afterwards. Does that "objective" teacher think that you are at the level of auditioning for a regional company? A conservatory program? Or, should you consider dance as an avocation?

In theater, it is virtually impossible to do an advisory audition for a selective school program. You might call a casting director or ask a working actor for some advice. It is not wise to send an unsolicited videotape or DVD of your monologues to programs in which you are interested. The admissions committee wants to see you in person or at a regional audition. Your best bet is to participate in your school and community theater group and in summer theater programs. Read lots of plays. Investigate taking private classes, too, if they are offered in your area. For your further education, the best recommendation is a liberal arts environment. Some of the best actors were English, history, or foreign language majors at liberal arts colleges who then did specific training in theater after two or four years of general education.

In classical instrumental music, it is common for well-known teachers to give advisory auditions or consultations. If you live near a conservatory or plan to visit one, write to a teacher in advance and request a consultation or lesson. Be prepared to pay for this, however. See "Researching

Teachers for Consultations and Lessons" in **For Music Majors** in this guide. If you do not live in the vicinity of a conservatory, try calling the nearest regional orchestra and asking if the principal player on your instrument is willing to hear you and give an opinion. For popular music, you might ask about sitting in with some "name" players and seeking their opinion and advice. Or you might ask if they would be willing to listen to a live or taped performance and give you an evaluation.

For singers, it is a little bit more difficult to get an objective opinion. At 17 or 18, very few singers have the physical development to reveal the true quality of their voice. While there may seem to be potential, it is usually very raw talent. Unfortunately, some voice teachers are happy to string students along as long as they are paying for regular lessons. Choir directors or directors of musical theater are usually very encouraging of young singers. However, before young singers become deluded with the sense of having a major career in opera or on Broadway, they should seek some objective assessment of their talent. Some colleges and conservatories are now requiring videotapes or DVDs for first-time college applicants as a way of pre-screening. As with theater majors, young singers should plan for at least two years of liberal arts study, including foreign languages (especially French, Italian, and German), literature, history, and economics, as well as music theory, music history, ear-training, and especially sight-singing. Because of everything from basic physical development to hormonal changes in the body, the voice is slower to develop, and so there is time for this general study.

Composers and conductors have an even more difficult time obtaining an early assessment. Composers might write in advance to ask a faculty member to evaluate copies of scores. Conductors might inquire about sending videotapes or DVDs of performances.

EDUCATIONAL CHOICES

Once you have done some self-evaluation, you will probably find that you fall into one of the following three groups:

- You are sure that you want to focus on your performing art now and will apply only to conservatory or preprofessional programs or audition for companies.

- You are not quite sure that you want to be totally focused on your performing art. You want to keep your options open and plan to apply to conservatories, joint programs, and liberal arts colleges with strong performing arts programs. You will explore

Bachelor of Arts (B.A.), Bachelor of Fine Arts (B.F.A.), and/or Bachelor of Music (B.M.) degree programs.

- You are not clear about the level of your talent, or you may think that you have talent in more than one area and want to expand your background before focusing. You think that applying to liberal arts colleges or universities is best for you at this time.

Many students do end up changing their majors. So if you are the least bit uncertain about pursuing an area within the performing arts, you should keep your options open by choosing an institution that has a good department in the area of your main interest but also has general distribution requirements. If you end up changing your major, chances are that it is because another department within the college or university offered courses that inspired you.

Whichever category best describes you, there are certain procedures in the college admissions process that are common to all programs. This guide will discuss various aspects of the entire admissions process and then focus specifically on the unique requirements for dance, music, and theater auditions and applications.

Performing

Arts

Beginning the College Search

SURFING THE INTERNET

Almost every college, university, or conservatory has its own Web site. This is a good place to begin your search. Start early in reviewing Web sites. You can read a general description of the school; determine tour information; research teachers and majors; find out about audition dates and application deadlines; and obtain audition repertoire requirements. You will sometimes find a profile of the entering class or a description of the type of student most likely to be admitted. When you analyze that profile, you may be able to get an idea of whether you are the kind of student the institution is looking for.

It is on the school's Web site that you can also usually request more information about their programs. Most students fill out an online registration form and from that get on the institution's mailing list for a catalog or view book and sometimes information about upcoming concerts.

Remember two important points regarding the Internet and college admissions.

- Do NOT use a screen name that is provocative. Such names as Partyboy@hotmail.com, hotdiva@yahoo.com, sexydancer@aol.com, staractor@gmail.com, or anything suggestive are not considered in good taste or funny. They reflect poorly on you and should be totally avoided.

- Any contact you make with a college, university, or conservatory over the Internet usually becomes part of your admissions file and is considered formal correspondence with that institution. Therefore, do NOT write in colloquial Internet language. Whether it is an e-mail to a teacher or admissions representative, contact over the school's message board, or entry on a blog, you must be extremely careful to be proper and discreet and to write in standard English.

Colleges and universities are some of the leaders in using the Internet. Some have put their entire catalog online, including the list of faculty. Others have everything from a "virtual tour" of the campus to a calendar of upcoming concerts and recitals to their student newspaper available on their Web site. It is worth your time to surf the Internet and visit the Web sites of colleges, conservatories, and universities, but remember that nothing is as memorable as your own visit to a campus to see what it is really like.

There are also interactive Web sites devoted to college search and selection. Petersons.com is a one-stop source of information on college admission. See "Searching for Performing Arts Programs and Scholarships Online" in this guide.

COLLEGE CATALOGS

Much of the information about each school can be gleaned from the college catalog This publication contains a wealth of material about the size, location, history, philosophy, calendar, costs, admissions policies, financial aid availability, faculty, and degree requirements of a school. Reading it carefully and critically will help illuminate the differences among schools. For instance, if you want to be a theater major at a liberal arts college but hate to write papers, a college that requires a written senior thesis may not be appropriate. Or, if you are a dancer and never want to take another foreign language course, a program that requires you to demonstrate proficiency in at least one foreign language may not be the one for you. Reading the catalog will help you narrow your list, come up with intelligent questions to ask your interviewer, and give you the most objective information on the policies, procedures, and climate of a campus.

VIEWBOOKS AND VIDEOS/DVDS

Because there is such great competition among schools for qualified students, many colleges have produced glossy viewbooks and professional videos or DVDs to send to prospective students. These are often written and produced by public relations or marketing specialists and include glamorous photos of the campus at its best, with the most photogenic students and the perfect view of buildings.

There is a fairly new company, Collegiate Choices Walking Tour Videos (www.collegiatechoice.com) that has nonpromotional videos of 350 colleges and universities in the United States, Canada, and the United Kingdom. While viewbooks, videos, and DVDs can give you some flavor of a campus, they should not replace your own research through a careful reading of the course catalog and a campus visit, if possible.

You can write or send a fax or e-mail to the schools that interest you for catalogs and admissions information. Be prepared to give your name, address, area of concentration, birth date, and social security number. (If you do not have a social security number, now would be a good time to get one; you'll need it for computer identification.) If you write, follow the style of the sample letter:

Sally Smith
1 Main Street
Anywhere, ST
February 15, 2007

Dear Director of Admissions:

I am currently a sophomore at Anywhere High School and am interested in learning more about (name of school). Please send me your most recent course catalog, an application, and any other admissions information. I am interested in studying dance (or theater or music—specify your instrument) further in college, so any specific information about your program in (your performing art) would be very helpful. I would also like to learn about any financial aid or scholarship information.

Thank you for your attention to this request.

Sincerely,
Sally Smith

Once you have made initial contact with a school, whether by telephone, letter, fax, or e-mail, most schools will set up a computer file on you. They will send you materials and may even deluge you with propaganda. Now it is your job to assess this information crucially and systematically.

KEEP A COLLEGE NOTEBOOK

The best way to organize your college information is to set up a "college notebook" or Excel spreadsheet. You can use it to keep track of your mailings, to make checklists for yourself, and to record your impressions of each school.

BLOGS AND OTHER INTERNET WAYS OF TRACKING YOUR REACTIONS

Some students have taken to keeping a blog about their journey through the college admission process. I highly urge you NOT to engage in this activity. Remember that a blog is open to everyone on the Internet and anybody can see what you've written. If you are writing about your reflections on College X in a blog, you just have no idea who may read your entry. It may be a friend, a teacher, a college admissions representative, employers, your Aunt Tilly. And, Web sites such as MySpace, Xanga, Facebook, LiveJournal, and Friendster are highly controversial. Some students have been suspended or expelled from summer programs or schools for what they have posted, whether it be photos or indiscreet postings. When it comes to college admission, it really is advisable to go back to the old method of pen and paper or even word-processing in a private document and keep your impressions off the Internet.

NARROWING YOUR SEARCH

After you have reviewed the Web sites, and/or read the college catalogs (some students send for twenty-five to fifty catalogs at first), you should be able to narrow your list of schools to about twelve to eighteen that seriously interest you. The list should reflect a range of selectivity, including some "reaches," "possibles," and "safeties." Other means of gathering more information about these schools before deciding to visit include:

- speaking to your high school counselor and reviewing your list;

- speaking with any students in your area who attend the college and are home on vacation;

- obtaining names of alumni in your area and speaking with them;

- talking to your current teachers about colleges and conservatories;

- attending college fairs and speaking with admissions representatives;

- meeting admission representatives visiting your high school; and

- attending any group meetings held in selected cities and towns where college and conservatory admissions representatives are available to answer your questions.

The National Association of College Admissions Counselors (NACAC) sponsors an annual series of National Performing Arts College Fairs, held in approximately fifteen cities throughout the United States. Most directors of admissions from colleges, conservatories, and universities listed in this guide attend these important fairs and provide information and answer questions. For exact dates and locations, contact NACAC at www.nacac.com, where you can view the list of college fairs, or call 703-836-2222 or 800-822-6285. The NACAC fax is 703-836-8015.

A Word about Decision Plans

Colleges and conservatories have many different policies for applying. In narrowing your list, you should also consider whether you want to play a strategy game and juggle application deadlines and decision plans. For instance, if you have decided to apply to liberal arts colleges or universities and have fallen in love with one particular college, you might consider applying by an Early Decision plan, if the college has one. This plan means that you apply early to that one school and if you are admitted, you must attend. Other plans include Early Action (you apply early and get an early reply, but do not have to make the commitment to attend right away), and some institutions have a menu of Early plans—Early Decision Plan I, Early Decision Plan II, etc. You must read the fine print about these plans very carefully and discuss your options with your college counselor. There are also Rolling Decision plans (often found at state universities, with decisions made on a first-come, first-served basis), Regular Decision plans, and others. There are strategies with deadlines and decision plans. Be a smart applicant and see if any will work for you.

If you are applying to conservatories, the traditional time to apply is in late November or early December for auditions in January through March, when most conservatories have their main auditions. Read about deadlines carefully. Since some conservatories also have later auditions, you might juggle the audition process, applying to your first choice and auditioning at the earliest audition time, usually in February or March, and attending, if admitted, but doing further auditions later, often in May, if not accepted. However, you do gamble when taking this approach, as some departments may close. For more about timing of auditions, see "Music Auditions" in **For Music Majors** in this guide.

Searching for Performing Arts Programs and Scholarships Online

Choosing a college performing arts program involves a serious commitment of time and resources. Therefore, it is important to have the most up-to-date information about institutions and their programs at your fingertips. The Internet can be a great tool for gathering that information, and one of the best sites to visit during the college selection process is Peterson's Visual & Performing Arts (VPA) channel at www.petersons.com.

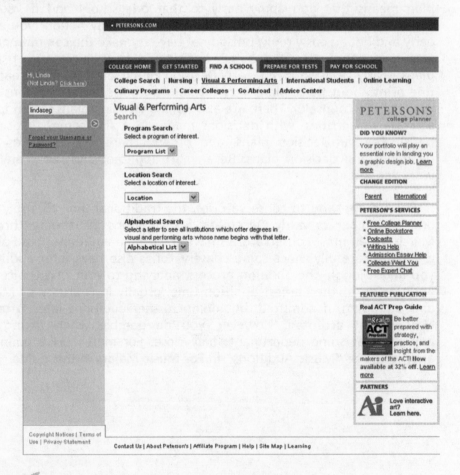

PETERSON'S VISUAL & PERFORMING ARTS CHANNEL

The VPA channel at Petersons.com is a one-stop source of information on college programs in the U.S. and Canada. Just click on <u>Visual & Performing Arts</u> to access Peterson's comprehensive database of arts programs. If you know what area of dance, theater, or music you're interested in, you can locate a school or program by clicking on the area on the Program Search pull-down menu, which gives you a list of majors or concentrations. Simply click one of these and you will get a list of schools that offer a degree program in that field. Or, if you'd like to search by location, you can access lists of schools offering art programs in any state or in Canada. Finally, if you have a particular school in mind and want to see what programs it offers, you can do an alphabetical search on the school's name and get information about their programs.

You can also request information from some schools by clicking on "Get Free Info." Within minutes, the school will receive your message and mail a catalog, an application, or information on financial aid to you. If you find the perfect school for a friend, you can even send the page to him or her with a message. There also are links to the school's Web site.

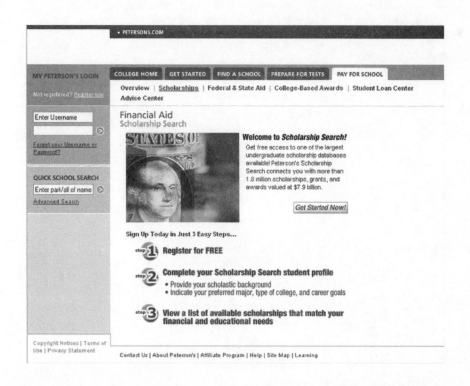

PETERSON'S FREE SCHOLARSHIP SEARCH

Petersons.com is a great site for any college-bound student. There is a wealth of information on undergraduate, graduate, online learning, and study-abroad programs and also some of the best financial aid advice available.

With Peterson's free Scholarship Search on the financial aid channel of Petersons.com (www.petersons.com/finaid), you can explore more than 1.7 million scholarships, grants, and prizes totaling nearly $8 billion and do an individualized search for awards that match your financial and educational needs. In just three easy steps, you can register; complete a customized profile indicating your scholastic and personal background, including intended major, work experience, and a host of other criteria that will allow you to access a list of scholarships that match your needs. Each scholarship is described in detail with eligibility and application requirements, contact information, and links to its e-mail address and Web site. Finding money for college couldn't be easier.

So, what are you waiting for? Log on to Petersons.com and let us help you with your college planning!

College Admissions Timetable

Below is a general outline of how to proceed and pace yourself in the college admissions process. Your actual timetable may differ slightly, depending on the deadlines at the schools you have chosen and audition schedules. Keep an up-to-date spreadsheet with deadlines and use this as a list of guideposts.

SOPHOMORE YEAR (TENTH GRADE)

September–October

- Make learning and your education a priority, along with practice in your performing art. Aim for balance.

- Take a practice PSAT in October. This is good practice for junior year, when PSAT scores count toward National Merit® Scholarships. (National Merit Scholarships are based on the scores you achieve on this test when you take it in your junior year.) Note that many schools require that sophomores take a practice PSAT, some make it optional to take, and other schools do not offer it to tenth graders at all. It can be a useful exercise to take it in tenth grade, and you should inquire in September about taking it if your guidance counselor does not have everyone register.

December

- Obtain your PSAT results. Review the answer sheet. Talk to your guidance counselor about the advisability of taking a test preparation course.

January–April

- Begin your review of Web sites for colleges and universities.

- Write for college catalogs. Read them, noting audition requirements.

- Obtain a social security number if you do not already have one.

- Investigate the National Foundation for Advancement in the Arts (NFAA or ARTS) annual scholarship competition.

- Meet with your guidance counselor. Discuss course plans—APs, honors, or additional performing arts classes—and about other plans for your future.

- Research taking and registering for any SAT Subject Tests in a subject in which you have done well and which may be required by the school you're interested in attending. Speak to your teacher first.

- Start researching financial aid and scholarship opportunities.

- Keep a file of various documents: reviews, copies of programs, photos, and any papers you have received good comments and grades on, articles you've written for the school newspaper, or stories contributed to the literary magazine.

- Attend college fairs. Find out all you can about schools you are considering.

- Plan your summer to expand your performing experience. Participate in a summer program. Remember to ask for letters of recommendation.

JUNIOR YEAR (ELEVENTH GRADE)

September

- Meet with your guidance counselor or college adviser to renew or establish your acquaintance. Review plans; register for the PSAT.

- Do well in your classes this year.

October

- Take the PSAT (again). Remember that this time it counts for National Merit® Scholarships.

- Obtain information. Surf the Internet and get catalogs and applications from all the schools you are considering.

- Continue to investigate financial aid opportunities.

- Keep your college notebook or spreadsheet up-to-date.

December

- Review your PSAT results. PSAT scores indicate what areas you need to strengthen for the SAT.

- Register for the SAT or ACT Assessment. Also consider SAT Subject Tests and the TOEFL, if appropriate. Prepare on your own or take a review course.

March–June

- Meet with your guidance counselor and parents/guardians to discuss college plans, your testing schedule, course selections for your senior year, college application essay topics, and any other related matters.

- Plan another enriching summer.

- Start your college visits.

- Take the SAT, ACT Assessment, TOEFL, and any SAT Subject Tests, if necessary.

- Attend college fairs.

July–August

- Continue your college visits and interviews over the summer.

- Continue to surf the Internet, send for applications, visit colleges, and interview.

- Start planning your audition(s).

SENIOR YEAR (TWELFTH GRADE)

September–October

- Continue your college visits and interviews. Record your reactions in your college notebook.

- Meet with your guidance counselor or college adviser. Discuss your college list and try to narrow it down.

- Consider applying Early Decision to your top-choice school. Check deadlines. November 1 and November 15 are common dates.

- Get letters of recommendation from teachers and former employees.

- Apply for the ARTS recognition scholarship through NFAA. (National Foundation for Advancement in the Arts, 444 Brickell Avenue, Miami, FL 33131; 305-377-1140; www.artsawards.org.)

- Be sure you have all application forms. Start drafting college application essays.

- Do a run-through of your audition material.

November

- Meet Early Decision deadline, if appropriate.

- Fill out college application forms. Continue to revise and perfect your essays.

- Take any additional tests: SAT, ACT, TOEFL, or SAT Subject Tests.

- Complete and submit your applications. Proofread them thoroughly and photocopy them before mailing.

- Request that your test results be sent to the colleges that require them.

- Continue practicing for your audition.

December–January

- Early Decision results are mailed. Celebrate if you were admitted and meet all deadlines for enrollment deposits. If you were deferred or rejected, submit other applications and move on.

- Obtain the FAFSA, if you are applying for financial aid. Start filling out financial aid forms and be aware of deadlines.

- Have your guidance counselor or college adviser send transcripts and test scores to the schools you've chosen.

- Last chance to take the SAT and ACT!

Performing

Arts

February–March

- Attend scheduled auditions.

- Check to make sure that all your financial aid documents are in order.

April

- Make your decision. Consider with your parents and adviser the pros and cons of each institution.

- Revisit any college if your decision to attend is not crystal clear.

- Notify colleges of your decision by May 1. If a school asks for a decision response before May 1, you have a right to request an extension until the May 1 Candidate's Reply Deadline (CRD).

May

- Be sure to notify all colleges by May 1, even if you are on the waiting list.

- Take any AP exams, if applicable.

The College Admissions Process

Campus Visits

Once you have narrowed your list further, you may want to visit a campus. There is really no substitute for seeing a campus yourself, experiencing the atmosphere, meeting students, sitting in on classes, and picturing yourself in the environment. If a school requires an interview and you are ready, you can combine the campus visit with the interview. "Drop-ins" at an admission office are not necessarily welcome. It's worthwhile to call ahead and schedule an appointment.

WHEN TO VISIT

You should visit before the application deadline, as the visit is one way for you to determine if you actually want to apply to the school. There are many things to consider when planning the timing of the visit.

Spring of Junior Year

Many students try to visit three or four colleges during spring break of their junior year. The problem with this is that many college admissions offices are at their busiest at this time, holding auditions or finalizing decisions on students who have applied. While you may be able to take a campus tour and speak to some students, this may not be a good time for your college interview.

Summer Between Junior and Senior Years

The advantage of a summer visit is that the admissions office is more relaxed and you may be given more time and personal attention. You can go on a campus tour and see the facilities, but, unless there is a summer session, you cannot get the flavor of the campus in action. You may decide that you like the school and will keep it on your list, but may need to visit again to stay overnight and sit in on classes. Your family may want to include a few summer visits to colleges as part of a vacation trip, or you may plan to visit before your summer program starts or after your summer job ends.

Fall of Senior Year

This is probably the best time to visit the colleges in which you are most interested. Just be careful not to miss so much time at your own school that you fall behind in your classes. First-semester senior-year grades are extremely important. Some high schools set aside college visiting days, and there are also the traditional fall holidays, such as Columbus Day, when many colleges are open and may have classes in session. Be sure to make appointments well in advance of your visit.

WHEN NOT TO VISIT

It is not a good idea to visit a campus when the admissions office is closed or on major holiday breaks, such as Thanksgiving, Christmas, or New Year's. Other dates to avoid include pre-exam, exam, and jury weeks (when auditions are held). While some colleges have Saturday morning interviews during the busy fall, there are seldom classes you can sit in on over the weekend.

THE IDEAL VISIT

It is best to arrive on a weekday afternoon. Take an admissions-sponsored guided tour of the campus, stay over in a dormitory with an admissions host or with a friend who attends the school, eat in the cafeteria, and observe and talk to as many students as possible. Try to attend a concert or production that evening. In the morning sit in on some classes, watch a rehearsal or coaching, and speak to faculty members. (Arrange for this in advance.) If an interview is recommended or required, have your interview, preferably after lunch.

What to Look for When You Visit

You want to gather as much information as possible during your visit. Pick up a copy of the campus newspaper, read bulletin boards to see the variety of activities announced, and look at the ride board. Are students going away every weekend? Get the calendar of events for the week or month during which you are visiting. Does it represent a variety of activities? Look through a yearbook if possible. Observe the people around you. Are they "your kind of people"? Sit in on a rehearsal. What is the level of expertise? Explore the surrounding neighborhood. Do you feel safe? Does it provide the kind of environment that makes you feel comfortable?

Questions to Ask Your Tour Guide

Here are some general questions you might ask your tour guide or student host. (Specific questions about your area in the performing arts are covered in later sections.)

- How diverse is the student body? Where are students from? Do they represent different racial, ethnic, and economic backgrounds?

- What percentage of the student body are from abroad? Which countries are represented by the most students? Are the foreign students integrated into the community?

- What do students like most about College X? What are the most frequent complaints?

- How would you describe the overall tone (attitude, morale) of the campus?

- What have been the issues or tensions on the campus this year?

- What do students do for fun?

- What do students typically do on a weekend?

- What is the role of fraternities and sororities?

- What sports teams are available?

- What extracurricular activities are strongly supported by the administration?

- Are faculty generally accessible?

- What is the workload like? How would you describe competition among students?

- What were the cultural highlights of last year? The social highlights?

- What are the housing options for freshmen? For transfers? Are there single-sex floors? Nonsmoking dorms? Quiet study facilities?

- How are roommates chosen?

- What kind of meal plans are offered? Is there vegetarian or kosher food? Must I subscribe to the meal plan if I live in college housing?

- Are student health services provided? Is a doctor, nurse, or psychologist provided at no additional charge?

- How is the library? The media center? The computer facilities? Are there any student complaints about these facilities?

- What is the relationship between the college and the surrounding town or city?

- How are the academics? Are there any outstanding faculty I should know about?

- When you register for classes, what percentage of courses that you want to take are you able to enroll in?

- Is the campus safe? What are the crime statistics? (Colleges are required to make crime statistics available to the public.)

- Are there any problems with drugs or alcohol?

- How are racial relations on the campus?

- Is there career counseling?

- What do most graduates do?

- If you have questions that your tour guide cannot answer, ask your interviewer or speak to an admissions counselor.

FOLLOW-UP TO YOUR VISIT

After your visit, it is appropriate to write a thank-you note to your interviewer. It may be just a simple, handwritten note or postcard saying that you enjoyed the conversation and look forward to applying to College X, or you may want to add something about the conversation you had. Often this note becomes part of your file, and admissions officers tend to react favorably to finding a thoughtful note among all the other information there. You should also write a note of thanks to your host, if you stayed over. A note or postcard is better than an e-mail in this case. In recent times, many colleges are using interest demonstrated in a school as one of the key factors in an admissions decision. Thus, if you are truly interested in College X, you really should be certain to write that follow-up correspondence.

The College Admissions Process

Record your impressions in your college notebook as soon as possible after you visit. Be careful not to be overly influenced by personalities on a campus. Although admissions representatives tend to be positive and perky types, anyone can have a bad day. If someone is abrupt or less than friendly, you should not let this color your view of the entire campus. Also, beware of thinking that a school seen on a perfect, sunny, crisp fall day is more appealing than another school seen on a gloomy, rainy day. Be honest with yourself, too. A prestigious school visited under ideal conditions may be seductive, but is it the right match for you?

IF YOU ARE UNABLE TO VISIT

If financial restrictions, time constraints, or other reasons make it impossible to visit a campus, you should call the admissions office and find out about alumni and current students who live near you or admissions representatives traveling in your area. Try to schedule an interview with one of these individuals for first-hand information. Also visit the Web site and request the college video or DVD if one exists. Again, if this college truly appeals to you, demonstrating your sincere interest is vitally important and you should make it clear that your inability to travel to the campus at this time is no reflection of the seriousness of your interest.

College Interviews

This is your opportunity to be more than just a stack of papers in the admissions office; it's your chance to personalize the admission process. Interviews do not usually make or break admissions decisions, but you should try to have an interview at those schools that are of real interest to you and are realistic choices.

SCHEDULING YOUR INTERVIEW

When you read the college catalog, note whether an interview is optional or required. (Let's keep this topic quite separate from auditions, which are quite another matter and discussed later.) Because of staff restrictions, travel difficulties, and financial constraints, very few colleges make the interview mandatory.

If you do decide to have an interview, never drop in. Try to plan your interviews as part of your campus visit. Don't schedule your first interview to be at your first-choice school; you'll do better after you've had some experience in an interview situation. Try to avoid making your first-choice school your last interview, also, as you want to remain fresh and spontaneous in your responses.

Schedule all interviews well in advance. And, if you cannot attend an interview appointment, be sure to call and cancel. A cancellation will not be held against, you but a missed appointment probably will be. If you get hopelessly lost en route to an interview and are running late, be sure to call.

GETTING READY

Preparing for an interview is important. Practice interviews are helpful to some students. Ask your college counselor to conduct a mock interview with you or have a family friend role-play with you.

Be sure to read the catalog and write down a list of questions that you want to ask. Take time to think about your strengths and weaknesses, and be prepared to speak about them in a positive way. College interviews are not the time for modesty and monosyllabic answers. At the same time, you do not want to sound boastful or arrogant.

Take stock of the extracurricular activities in which you have participated, your hobbies, volunteer work, and other ways that you spend your time. If there are special circumstances in your life that have affected your academic record, you may want to bring them up at an interview. For instance, if you missed a great deal of school because you had a heavy performance schedule but were able to make up the work, or if your family went through a particularly grueling year, with divorce, unemployment, or sickness, you may want to talk about it with your interviewer. Be careful not to sound as though you are making excuses for yourself, but rather adding to the college's understanding of who you are.

What to Wear

Just as there are costumes for performances, there are interview "costumes." For women, a nice skirt (not too short) or pants and a blouse, possibly with a blazer, or a simple dress is recommended, worn with low to medium heels. Men should wear nice pants with a shirt, jacket, and tie, or a turtleneck or shirt with a collar. Be neat and clean.

WHAT *NOT* TO DO AT YOUR INTERVIEW

Here are some things you should *not* do at an interview:

- smoke;

- chew gum;

- complain or make excuses;

- swear or use language that it too colloquial;

- exhibit a negative attitude (bored, arrogant, etc.);

- answer in monosyllables or one-sentence answers;

- ask questions if you have no interest in the response;

- ask for an evaluation of another school you are considering;

- bring your scrapbook of programs, reviews, articles, or term papers for the interviewer to read;

- dress in an inappropriate fashion;

- twitch, fidget, or slump in your seat; or

- pretend to be someone you are not. Be yourself!

TYPICAL INTERVIEW QUESTIONS

Every interviewer has his or her favorites questions, but there are some common areas that are covered in most interviews. These include:

- your high school experience;

- your personal traits, relationships with others, and family background;

- your interests outside the classroom–hobbies, extracurricular activities, summer vacations, movies you've seen, etc.;

- your values and goals, and how you view the world around you;

- your impressions of the college you are visiting; and

- answering your questions.

You should anticipate questions like these:

- Tell me about your high school. How long have you attended? What are the students like? Do you like your high school? What would you preserve or change about it?

- Which courses have you liked most? Which least? Which have been the most challenging?

- How well do you think your school has prepared you for your future study?

- How would you describe yourself as a student?

- Do you know what you want to major in?

- What has been your most stimulating intellectual experience?

- In what extracurricular activity have you been most involved? How much time do you devote to it?

- Do you have hobbies or special interests?

- After a long, hard day, what do you enjoy doing most? What do you do for fun? For relaxation?

- How have you spent your summer vacations? Why did you decide to spend them that way?

- How would you describe yourself in five adjectives?

- What is your family like? Describe your upbringing. How has your environment influenced your way of thinking?

- How would your friends describe you?

- Which relationships are most important to you? Why?

- Have you ever encountered people who thought and acted differently from you? What viewpoints or actions challenged you the most? How did you respond? What did you learn about yourself?

- What do your friends and family expect of you? What pressures have you felt?

- If you had a year to go anywhere and do whatever you wanted, how would you spend that year?

- What magazines or newspapers do you read regularly?

- What books have you read recently? Are there any authors you particularly like?

- What movie have you seen recently and what did you think of it?

- Who are your favorite dancers or dance companies? Why?

- Who are your favorite actors? Why?

- Who are your favorite musicians? Why?

- Who are your favorite performers? Why?

- How did you choose your particular area in the performing arts? Why do you want to pursue this art form?

- What has been your most memorable performance to date? Why?

- Have you worked with a director, choreographer, or conductor who was particularly challenging or inspirational? Describe the experience.

- Who has been your most memorable teacher? Why?

- Why do you want to go to college?

- Why have you chosen this college to investigate? What first brought us to your attention?

- What do you picture yourself doing ten years from now?

- What do you think of the National Endowment for the Arts (or some current affair in the arts)?

- What distresses you most about the world around you? If you had the opportunity to change the world, where would you start?

- Are there any outside circumstances that have interfered with your performance in school? An after-school job? Long commute back and forth to school? Home responsibilities or difficulties? Illness? Parental pressure? English not spoken at home? Problems with course scheduling? Extended absences from school due to performance schedules? (Take care not to make excuses for yourself, but to present any difficulties honestly and as positively as possible.)

- What more do you want to know about us?

This last question is your opening to ask your questions. Do not be shy about taking out your list; no one expects you to memorize a list of questions, and you want to be sure that you are learning all that you can during your visit to make the decision as to whether or not this is a campus where you could be happy. Many of the questions regarding campus life were probably answered by your tour guide or student host. Here are some other general questions you may want to ask. (Specific questions about your area in dance, theater, or music are presented later in this guide.)

- Who teaches freshmen? Transfers?

- How does registration work? Is it easy to get the classes I want to take?

- What is the advising system like? What are its strengths and weaknesses?

- Are there any changes anticipated in the curriculum?

- Are there any departments that might be cut or discontinued? What departments have been discontinued in the past two years?

- Are there any planned cutbacks in faculty? Any new appointments scheduled?

- Are there any new programs being contemplated? What are they?

- What percentage of students receive financial aid?

- Are there jobs on campus for students? What is a typical work/study job? Are there jobs in the community?

- Are there any opportunities for internships? Study abroad?

- Are financial aid decisions made separately from admissions decisions? Will applying for financial aid influence admissions decisions?

- Do you have any merit-based scholarships?

- What is your policy on fee waivers, if I cannot afford the application fee?

- What is the overall financial security of the school? Is tuition increased annually? What additional fees might I anticipate?

- What is most important in admissions decisions?

AFTER YOUR INTERVIEW

Be sure to write your impressions of the interview in your college notebook. And, most important, write the interviewer a thank-you note. Mention something specific that came up in the conversation. Three lines on nice stationery or even a postcard should be sufficient.

The Application

When you have finally narrowed your list to the eight to ten schools to which you have decided to apply, it is time to approach the applications. Application forms have several components. When you decide to apply to a school, do not go immediately to the school's Web site and fill it out online and submit it quickly. Rather, either download a copy and sit down with the print-out of the application, or if you cannot get the entire document downloaded, start to fill it out as a DRAFT and save as you go along, but do NOT hit "submit" until you have truly reviewed the entire document for completeness. (Note that many colleges now strongly prefer that you use the online application, and in recent times more than half of all applicants have applied online.)

If you are applying with hard copy via "snail mail," first, read the application carefully. Then make a photocopy of the application to fill out as your draft. It is important that applications be neat and legible, either typed or printed in black or blue ink. Never submit an application that has been filled out in pencil or an odd color ink or that has been scribbled in haste. Fill out the informational section first and then think about the essay questions, if required.

If you do apply electronically, be sure to run spellcheck and to print out your draft to proofread before sending it. Always print and save a hard copy for yourself. Some schools will ask you also to send a hard copy with the application fee.

ACADEMIC PROFILE

Colleges will require a copy of your high school transcripts(s). Be sure that you have checked your transcript for accuracy before it is sent by your high school. Many schools will also require college entrance examination scores. Some schools use standardized test scores for placement, and some use them as another indicator in your academic profile. As a performing artist, if you plan to apply to schools that require the SAT, SAT Subject Tests, or ACT Assessment and have not received scores that you think are truly representative of your ability, you should consider doing some test preparation and retaking the test to raise your score.

In analyzing your scholastic record, colleges are trying to decide if you will be able to withstand the academic rigor of their environment. Taking a full complement of challenging academic courses in high school is important. If you are applying to a conservatory, your academic profile is secondary in consideration to your demonstrated talent, but at liberal arts colleges and for joint programs, the academic profile is more important in establishing the match. If you want to leave all options open for college, the most prudent approach is to take the most challenging assortment of academic courses, including math, science, and foreign language electives. However, if you absolutely know that you are applying to a conservatory, taking an extra year of something in which you are not strong probably won't have any effect on an admissions decision. And by not taking it you may have more time to pursue work in your major or concentration area or have more time to practice. Be sure to speak to your college counselor about this and, if necessary, call a few admissions officers for opinions.

PERSONAL PROFILE

The personal profile that a college gathers on you consists largely of information that is entirely in your control. This includes your list of extracurricular activities, your recommendations, essays, and any appropriate supplementary materials you send. Let's consider each of these.

Extracurricular Activities

This term refers to any activity outside of the classroom. Many colleges will ask you to put this information in a table, showing the activity, any position of leadership, hours spent in the activity, etc.

As a performing artist, you may not have joined any clubs in your high school, focusing all your time on one activity. That's great! Do not hesitate to acknowledge such dedication. If you have participated in many activities, draft a list including school activities, any jobs you've held, hobbies, community or volunteer activities, church groups, honors, and awards. The point is to make the list comprehensive, but not exhaustive. Depth in one activity is important, so don't try to pad the list.

Recommendations

Many colleges request teacher recommendations as well as the college counselor report. You should choose teachers who know you well as a student and as a person, who like you, and who write well. You should also choose teachers who will add balance and another dimension to your application. For instance, if you are a musician who also has a passion for mathematics, consider asking your math teacher for a recommendation. When you ask a teacher to write a letter of recommendation, remember to:

- ask politely;

- give the teacher the forms (with the top part with your name, etc., filled out) well before the deadline;

- provide the teacher with stamped envelopes addressed to the colleges; and

- include a cover letter to the teacher that gives the deadlines for each school, a list of your extracurricular activities, or anything else that might be helpful to the teacher in writing your recommendation.

Guidance counselors are often also asked to fill out a counselor recommendation form that may include a checklist and narrative. If you attend a large school where the counselors have many responsibilities other than college guidance, you would do well to establish a relationship with your guidance counselor. Schedule meetings, stop by the office to ask quick questions, and, in general, make yourself known to your counselor.

Essays

While most admissions representatives say that an essay will not make or break an application, there have been applicants who essentially "wrote" themselves into acceptance. The essay is another opportunity for the admissions committee to get to know you better. Even if the essay is optional, it's a good idea to provide one. A well-written essay will make your application more memorable and distinctive.

Perhaps the hardest thing about the essay is getting started. One method that has worked well, especially with students in the performing arts, is to set your cassette recorder beside you and start talking. Then play back the cassette and transcribe what you said. Usually this technique will allow you to capture your personal voice and help you over any obstacle that you have about putting your thoughts on paper.

Plan to write several drafts of your college essay. Ask your parents, a trusted friend, your college counselor, and/or a teacher to read it and give their reactions. While some editorial help is not out of line, never allow anyone else to write your essay. Admissions counselors know when you have not submitted your own work. Also, do not allow someone to edit so much that the tone becomes stale or stilted. Do have someone proofread your final draft, however.

The best essays resonate with the personal voice of the applicant, describing ideas in very specific, reflective ways that may reveal fears, fantasies, or insecurities but are always thoughtful, fresh, and spontaneous. The worst essays present a factual, often chronological version of an experience—the orchestra's tour to Europe, for example, or a recent performance—in a way that is totally lacking in creativity or individuality. The orchestra tour to Europe essay that simply describes arriving in Paris, playing at a concert hall, and then taking a bus to the next place is hardly riveting. The same essay telling how you got lost and could not find the stage door, and how you dealt with that situation, becomes specific and says something about you.

There is no "right" essay, but there are several approaches that you should avoid. For example, do not submit a poem as an essay. If you also have talent as a poet, consider submitting a few select samples of your poetry as supplementary material instead. Also, do not use the essay to make excuses for something in your background. If you have a special situation, consider writing about it in a separate letter or asking a teacher or your guidance counselor to mention it in his or her letter of recommendation. Do not repeat information from other parts of your application, and avoid writing about trendy topics, your religious beliefs, relationships, drugs, sex or alcohol, or the importance of a college education. Do not try to impress an admissions committee with your vocabulary, revealing that you have thumbed through the thesaurus. Rather, write simply about something you really care about in a personally specific manner.

Try to limit yourself to the space provided, or type your essay on separate sheets and write, "See essay attached." In general, it is the quality, not the quantity, that counts.

Supplementary Materials

Because you are a performing artist, you will want to document your special talent with carefully chosen additional materials. A letter of recommendation from your dance, theater, or music teacher would be appropriate. You should ask colleges about sending cassettes, CDs,

DVDs, or videotapes. Some may require them for pre-screening while other schools have neither the staff nor facilities for evaluating these. Do not send:

- additional letters of recommendation from people who do not know you well: congressmen, mayors, the neighbor's uncle who attended your college choice but whom you've never met, etc. Such letters do not usually add to an understanding of who you are.

- copies of awards or honors. No scrapbooks!

- copies of lengthy reports or term papers. If a college wants a graded paper, they will specify this in the application directions.

- a pile of newspaper clippings about yourself. If you have received many positive reviews, select two or three, but do not send the entire stack and never send original copies.

- copies of programs in which you have participated. Your list of extracurricular activities or resume should reflect this.

- lots of photographs of yourself. One or two good ones, especially if you are a dancer, would be appropriate. An entire portfolio is not.

- every article you've ever written. If you write for the school newspaper, you might send a copy of one or two articles—not every issue of the paper in which one of your articles has appeared.

DEADLINES

You can do yourself and the admissions office a favor by submitting your application before it is actually due. This may also help you in getting the better audition times, if auditions are required, as some schools schedule on a first-come, first-served basis. Drama programs, in particular, but also some other programs use the deadline as one way to eliminate applicants. Remember to proofread your application before you mail or transmit it and to keep a copy of it for your files. If sent by standard mail, it is a good idea to include a postcard saying, "College X has received the application from Mary Jones. Signed by admissions: Date: __" Also watch for your canceled check to be returned. Things do get lost, and you want to be sure that your application does not go astray. And, if you are using e-mail or otherwise filing electronically, remember to print out a hard copy of whatever you transmit to save for your files, too.

College Admissions Checklist

Use this convenient checklist to remind yourself of individual college admission requirements and to record the progress of your application procedures.

	Registration Deadline	Testing Date	Registration Deadline	Testing Date	Registration Deadline	Testing Date	Registration Deadline	Testing Date
College Name								
College Address								
Application Deadline								
Application Fee								
Required Tests:								
PSAT/NMSQT								
SAT								
ACT Assessment								
Others								
Course Requirements Fulfilled								
Personal Interview Required								
Interview Date								
Audition Required								
Audition Date								
Applications Requested								
References Required								
Names/Addresses of References								
References Completed								
Application Filed								
Transcript Forwarded								
College Reply Date								
Financial Interview Required								
Required Financial Forms:								
CSS Financial Statement								
ACT Financial Statement								
Others								
Housing Deadline								
Housing Fee								
Housing Application Mailed								

Performing

Arts

INTERNATIONAL STUDENTS' CHECKLIST

Any student who is not a citizen or permanent resident of the United States is usually considered an "international" or "foreign" student (the term varies at schools). Many schools recruit abroad and most schools welcome students from abroad. The admissions procedures at most schools are the same for international students as for U.S. applicants. However, there are a few additional aspects international students should take into account.

- Begin your search extra early. International mail takes additional time and catalogues cannot be faxed at this point.

- Take advantage of the Internet and e-mail in expediting your questions, but always print a hard copy for yourself.

- Determine from each college or university whether you must take the TOEFL (Test of English as a Foreign Language), if English is not your native language. Arrange to take the test, if necessary, so that your scores can be submitted at the required time. Contact www.TOEFL.org or ETS at 609-771-7760.

- Be sure to study English intensively. There are many good English as a Second Language (ESL) programs both in the United States and abroad and many summer programs in the United States. An Internet search should help you to discover ESL programs available to you.

- Investigate the visa process early. If you must travel to the United States for an audition, many conservatories or colleges will issue you a letter to present to a consulate in order to obtain a B-2 Prospective Student Visa. An I-20 will be issued to admitted students only. Everything regarding visas does take time, so plan ahead.

- Determine a school's policy on financial aid for international students. Government or state loans are not available to students from abroad, and many schools reserve their limited scholarship funds for domestic students. Some schools will not admit a qualified international student who has applied for financial aid. Be sure to ask for the current policy, and do not hesitate to ask for clarification of the policy if you are in doubt.

- Find out whether the school requires a guarantee of financial support in advance.

- Ask about tape or application pre-screening or regional auditions in your country.

- Complete the application on your own, especially the essays. If your English is not good enough to write an acceptable essay, you probably won't be able to understand the lectures or complete the assignments at a U.S. school.

- Be sure that schools know about your academic history in terms of the grading and overall educational system in your country. For instance, if no one from your high school has ever applied to schools in the United States before, you should send a prospectus or profile of your school.

- Some colleges and universities may require that your official transcript be reviewed or translated by the World Education Service (WES). Ask about requirements of the specific schools. The URL for WES is www.wes.org.

- Find out whether it is possible for international students to work while attending the program.

- Ask whether there are quotas on the number of students from a certain country or on foreign students in general.

- Find out about advisers and other support services for students from abroad.

- Find out if the program is authorized to grant Practical Training status to international students.

Admissions Outcomes

After the application review and audition, if required, admissions committees will meet to determine whether to admit you, reject you, or place your name on a waiting list. Be aware that the weight of the letter or size of the envelope does not necessarily indicate the admissions decision.

If you are admitted to more than one school, weigh the pros and cons of each institution, perhaps visit again, ask lots of questions, and try to respond to the Office of Admissions in plenty of time before their deadline. Most institutions comply with the guidelines established by the National Association of College Admissions Counselors (NACAC) and the College Board, which set the Candidate's Reply Deadline (CRD) as May 1. If a school requires you to make a decision before that deadline or before you have heard from all of your schools, you have every right to question that institution. If, in order to make an informed decision about your college choice, you need more information, or if your financial aid package has not arrived in time to meet the deadline, call the college and request an extension on the deadline. If you do not contact the college at all by May 1, the admissions staff may assume that you have decided to attend another institution and offer your place to someone on the waiting list. Be certain to contact your college by the deadline stipulated.

If you are rejected, do not become despondent. See if you can get any feedback about ways in which you might improve before auditioning or applying again. You may want to think about applying another year as a transfer student. Speak to your college counselor about what you might do differently.

The Waiting List is a positive place to be. It means that a college realized your strengths, but due to a limited number of openings was not able to offer you admission at this time. Your initial response will probably be disappointment and irritation, but wait a few days before you do anything. Then you will be more able to make a rational decision about whether to remain active on a waiting list or to accept the offer of another college that admitted you right away.

If you want to be considered from the waiting list, now is the time to be even more proactive in demonstrating your desire to attend. Call, send an e-mail, and/or write to the college to say that you want to be considered from the waiting list. Include any new information about yourself since the review of your application. If it is true, let a college know that if taken off the waiting list, you will enroll. Talk to your college counselor about any further steps you should take, and then be patient. You should probably submit a deposit to your second-choice school to protect yourself, in the event that the first choice does not take anyone from the waiting list. If you are admitted from the waiting list, however, and intend to accept the offer of admission and enroll, be sure to immediately contact the school where you gave your deposit so that they may possibly offer your place to someone else. You should never make a deposit at more than one school, as multiple deposits are considered unethical in college admissions.

IF YOU WANT TO DEFER ADMISSION

Often a student who has been admitted will want to take a year off to travel or work. Many colleges and universities are pleased to grant a deferral of a year. They may give you guidelines about what they will allow you to do with the year. For instance, attending another college usually is not allowed, and they may give a new deadline for committing to enrollment. Some schools may ask for an account of what you have done with your time off.

Covering Your College Costs

A college education is expensive: more than $150,000 for four years at some of the higher-priced colleges and universities and more than $50,000 at many lower-cost, state-supported colleges. Figuring out how you and your family will come up with the necessary funds to pay for your education requires planning, perseverance, and learning as much as you can about the options available.

For most families, paying the total cost of a student's college education out of savings is not possible. Clearly, the more your family has saved, the better off you will be and the less you will need to earn and borrow. But paying for college should not be looked at merely as a four-year financial commitment. While some of the money you need will likely come from funds that you and your parents have managed to save, some will come from a portion of your or your parents' current income. The rest will come from future earnings, through loans you or your parents will pay off later.

If your family has not saved the total amount or does not have sufficient current income to cover the costs, you can still attend college. That's where financial aid comes in. The amount you and your family will be expected to contribute toward your college expenses will be based upon your and your family's income and assets. But if this is not enough, the rest of the expenses can be met through various financial aid programs.

FINANCIAL AID BASICS: HOW FINANCIAL AID IS AWARDED

When you apply for aid, your family's financial situation is analyzed using a government-approved formula called the Federal Methodology. The result of this is the amount you and your family are expected to contribute toward your college expenses, called your Expected Family Contribution or EFC. If this is equal to or more than the cost of attendance at a particular college, then you do not demonstrate "financial need." However, even if you don't have financial need, you may still qualify for aid since there are many grants, scholarships, and loans that are not based on financial need.

If the cost of education is greater than your EFC, then you will be eligible for "need-based" assistance. The calculation of "financial need" is very simple:

Total Cost of Attendance
− Expected Family Contribution
Financial Need

The total aid you are awarded by any one college will likely differ from the amount offered by other colleges you may be applying to because, among other things, the costs of attendance are different. Secondly, not all colleges have the same amount of funds available to offer their needy students. But, your EFC should remain about the same regardless of which college you attend. It is the goal of every financial aid office to meet the financial needs of its students and help all families find the information they need to finance the tuition, fees, room and board, and other costs.

SOURCES OF FINANCIAL AID

The largest single source of aid is the federal government, which awarded over $90 billion during 2004–05. More than 14 million people apply for financial aid each year. But the federal government is not the only source of financial aid. The colleges and universities themselves are the next-largest source of financial aid. Institutions award an estimated $24 billion to students each year. Some of this aid is awarded to students who have a demonstrated need based on either the Federal Methodology or another formula, the Institutional Methodology, which is used by some colleges to award their own funds in conjunction with other aid. Some aid is not based on need and is called merit aid. Merit-based aid is usually awarded based on a student's academic performance or specific talents or abilities, or to students the institutions most want to attract.

Another source of financial aid is from state governments, awarding more than $6 billion per year. All fifty states offer grant and/or scholarship aid, most of which is need-based, but some of which is merit-based. Most state programs award aid only to state residents attending college in their home state, although a few do allow their state aid to be "portable" from state to state.

Other sources of financial aid include private agencies, foundations, corporations, clubs, fraternal and service organizations, civic associations, unions, and religious groups that award grants, scholarships, and low-interest loans. Some employers provide tuition reimbursement benefits for employees and their families.

More information about these different sources of aid is available from high school guidance offices, public libraries, college financial aid offices, and directly from the sponsoring organizations. In addition, Peterson's offers an excellent source of scholarship leads at www.petersons.com.

APPLYING FOR FINANCIAL AID

Every student must complete the Free Application for Federal Student Aid (FAFSA) to be considered for federal aid. The FAFSA is available in your high school guidance office and many public libraries, or directly from the U.S. Department of Education. Students are encouraged to apply for aid on the Web by using the electronic FAFSA, which can be accessed at www.fafsa.ed.gov. If you apply online, you and one parent will need to obtain an electronic signature before filing. To get your Personal Identification Number or PIN, go to www.pin.ed.gov.

To award their own funds, many schools require a second application, the Financial Aid PROFILE®. The PROFILE® asks supplemental questions that some colleges and awarding agencies feel provide a more accurate assessment of the family's ability to pay for college. It is up to the college to decide whether it will use only the FAFSA or both the FAFSA and the Financial Aid PROFILE®.

The first thing you will have to do is determine whether you will need to fill out only the FAFSA or whether you will also have to complete the PROFILE®. The listings later in this book will tell you what forms are required. You should also read the schools' brochures, or speak to someone in the financial aid office to be sure. The PROFILE® contains a list of schools and agencies that require the form.

If the College You're Applying to in 2007 Requires the FAFSA

This scenario is pretty simple: Complete the FAFSA sometime after January 1, 2007, being certain to send it in before any college-imposed deadlines. (You are not permitted to send in the 2007–2008 FAFSA before January 1, 2007, which should not pose a problem because most college application deadlines are in February or March.) It is best if you wait until you have all your financial records for the previous year available, but if that is not possible, you can use estimated figures. It is critical to file by the published filing deadline. Filing late can mean the loss of thousands of dollars in assistance.

After you send in your FAFSA, either on paper or electronically, you'll receive a Student Aid Report (SAR) that includes all of the information you reported and shows your EFC. The SAR will be sent to you electronically if you provided an e-mail address. Otherwise, you will receive a paper-copy SAR in the mail. Be sure to review the SAR, checking to see if the information you reported is correct. If you used estimated numbers to complete the FAFSA, you may have to resubmit the SAR with any corrections to the data. The college(s) you have designated on the FAFSA will receive the information you reported and will use that data to make their decision. In many instances, the colleges you've applied to will ask you to send copies of your and your parents' federal income tax returns for 2006 plus any other documents needed to verify the information you reported.

If a College Also Requires the PROFILE®

Step 1: Register for the Financial Aid PROFILE® in the fall of your senior year in high school.

You can apply for the PROFILE® online at http://profileonline.collegeboard.com/index/jsp.

Registration information with a list of the schools requiring the PROFILE® is available in most high school guidance offices.

There is a fee for using the Financial Aid PROFILE® application ($23 for the first college and $18 for each additional college). You must pay for the service by credit card when you register. If you do not have a credit card, you will be billed.

Step 2: Fill out your customized Financial Aid PROFILE®.

Once you register, your application will be immediately available online and

- will have questions that must be completed by you and your parents (unless you are considered independent and the colleges or programs selected do not require parent information).

- *may* have supplemental questions needed by one or more of your schools or programs. If required, those will be found in Section Q of the application.

In addition to the PROFILE® application, which you complete online, you may be required to complete a Business/Farm Supplement in a traditional paper format. Completion of this form is not part of the "online" process. Instead, instructions about how to download and print the supplemental form are provided if it is required.

If your biological or adoptive parents are separated or divorced and your colleges and programs require it, your noncustodial parent may be asked to complete the Noncustodial PROFILE®.

Once you complete and submit your PROFILE® Application, your information is processed and sent directly to the colleges and programs that you requested.

FINANCIAL AID AWARDS

After you've submitted your financial aid application and usually after you've been accepted for admission, each college will send you a letter containing your financial aid award. Most award letters show the college's budget, how much you and your family are expected to contribute, and the amount and types of aid the college has awarded you. Most students who are eligible for aid are awarded aid from a combination of sources and programs; hence your award is often called a "package." For first-year students, award letters are often sent with, or soon after, the letter of admission.

FINANCIAL AID PROGRAMS

There are three types of financial aid: scholarships (also known as grants or gift aid), loans, and student employment. Scholarships and grants are outright gifts and do not have to be repaid. Loans must be repaid, usually after graduation; the amount you have to pay back is the total you've borrowed plus an interest charge. Student employment is a job arranged for you during the academic year. Loans and student employment programs are generally referred to as self-help aid.

The federal government has two large grant programs, the Federal Pell Grant and the Federal Supplemental Educational Opportunity Grant; a student employment program called the Federal Work-Study Program; and several loan programs, including one for parents of undergraduate students. Students who are Pell Grant-eligible and have completed a rigorous high school program may be eligible for the Academic Competitiveness Grant. Additional information on this new federal grant program is available from your college's financial aid office or high school guidance office.

The Subsidized Direct Stafford Student Loan, the Subsidized FFEL Stafford Student Loan, and the Federal Perkins Loan are all need-based, government-subsidized loans. Students who borrow under these programs do not have to pay interest on the loan until after they graduate or leave school. The Unsubsidized Direct Stafford Loan, the Unsubsidized FFEL Stafford Student Loan, and the Parent Loan (PLUS) program are not based on need, and these loans accrue interest while the student is in school.

There are also a number of federal tax–based programs that help families with incomes up to $107,000. Additional information about the Hope Scholarship and Lifetime Learning tax credits is available from the IRS. You should consult a tax adviser for other educational tax deductions.

IF YOU DON'T QUALIFY FOR NEED-BASED AID

If you are not eligible for need-based aid, or the aid you have been awarded is not sufficient, you should look into three other funding sources.

First is the search for merit scholarships, which you can start during your junior year of high school at the initial stages of the aid application process. Merit-based awards are becoming an increasingly important part of college financing plans, and many colleges award these grants to students they especially want to attract. As a result, applying to a school at which your qualifications put you at the top of the entering class may be a good idea since you may receive a merit award. It is also a good idea to look for private scholarships and grants, especially from local service and community groups.

The second source of aid is employment, during both the summer and the academic year. The student employment office at your college should be able to help you locate a job in the area, either on or off campus.

The third source is borrowing through the Unsubsidized FFEL Stafford Student Loan or the Unsubsidized Direct Stafford Student Loan, both of which are open to all students. The terms and conditions are similar to the subsidized loans. The biggest difference is that the borrower is responsible for the interest while still in college, although most lenders permit students to delay paying the interest right away and add the accrued interest to the total amount owed.

After you've secured what you can through scholarships, work, and loans, your parents will have to figure out how they will meet the balance of the college bill. Most colleges offer monthly payment plans that spread the cost out over the academic year. For many parents, the monthly payments still turn out to be more than they can afford, so they can borrow through the Federal Parent Loan for Undergraduate Students (PLUS) program, through one of the many private education loan programs available, or through home equity loans and lines of credit. This spreads the payments out over a longer period and makes the monthly payments smaller. The college financial aid office usually has a list of preferred programs that offer the best terms for students and their families.

Students and parents who are interested in more information about financing a college education and in learning more about the financial aid application process should read *Peterson's College Money Handbook.*

The College Admissions Process

For Parents

The college admissions process can be especially stressful in parent-child relations. Here are some pointers for parents of talented young people seeking admission to the best performing arts programs.

Parents SHOULD NOT:

- call or write an admissions office for the child.

- fill out the application.

- write or overly edit the essay.

- nag about deadlines.

- dictate college choices.

- ask too many questions during the campus tour. (Let your child take the lead.)

- delay filing financial aid information.

- attend the interview.

- sit in on the audition.

- serve as accompanist at the audition.

- offer too much advice about training.

- try to bribe or otherwise influence an admissions officer or teacher.

Parents SHOULD:

- be supportive.

- help to organize the college visits.

- go along on college visits, but use the time to speak with financial aid officers and placement or career counseling officers.

- submit all financial aid documents promptly.

- help set up any practice auditions that their child may decide to do at home or in a local church or auditorium.

- arrange to record on DVD, CD, or videotape any practice auditions.

- rent, buy, or borrow the best instrument within their means for their child to play.

- help their child learn how to care for him or herself best, paying special attention to nutrition, exercise, managing stress, handling rejection, and preventing injuries.

- understand if their child's performing schedule conflicts with family obligations.

- help a child deal with the tensions and frustrations of trying to excel in both academic and artistic endeavors.

The College Admissions Process

For Dance Majors

Dance programs vary greatly in terms of what is offered and what is required. If you have the passion to become a professional performer, as well as positive evaluations by your current teachers and successful aduitions for major performing institutions, a B.F.A. program may be the route to pursue.

Performing Arts

Advanced Study in Dance

AGE

Age is more of a factor in the dance world than it is in the other performing arts. If you are now a sophomore in high school, one question that you may want to ask yourself is whether it is important for you to finish your high school program. If you do decide to spend all four years in high school, be sure that you are taking regular dance classes and performing as often as possible. If you decide to finish or leave high school at the end of three years, there are other options for you.

EARLY ADMISSION

Early Admission policies apply to students who want to be admitted to college, usually during the junior year of high school. (This is not to be confused with Early Decision policies, which apply to your senior year.) You should think about Early Admission in your freshman year, or in your sophomore year, but no later than fall semester of junior year so that you will have time to plan ahead. You may approach this in one of two ways: either plan to finish the requirements for high school and graduate early, at the end of your junior year, or leave high school at the end of junior year, enroll at a college, and see if your high school will grant your diploma, pending the successful completion of your freshman year.

You may also decide that a high school diploma is not important to you and enroll at the college that admits you as an Early Admission candidate. Some students may also want to take the GED exam.

If you plan to finish high school early, you may have to take a summer course or two and take additional courses during the regular school year, too. Work carefully with your college counselor to see if this is feasible. It is usually an English or U.S. history requirement that you will need to fulfill in order to graduate early.

If you decide to leave high school and have your diploma awarded after your freshman year, be sure to get all the terms *in writing*. Does your high school require that you not only successfully complete your freshman year, but require you to take certain courses and achieve a certain grade? If your high school does not put the terms in writing, be sure that you or your parents write a letter stating your understanding, and keep a copy of this letter for your files.

CHOOSING YOUR TEACHERS

It is important that you study with someone who will inculcate the best habits in your early development and teach you a solid technique. As you investigate teachers in your area, here are some questions you might want to ask:

- Where did the teacher go to school?

- Did the teacher dance professionally? With what company?

- Does the teacher talk about placement?

- Does the teacher explain how to do an exercise as well as what to do?

- Does the teacher give corrections?

- Does the teacher save stretching for after you are warmed up?

- Does the teacher stress turnout from the hips rather than from the knees or feet?

- Does the teacher have an awareness of injury prevention?

- Is there any discussion about musicality?

- Are the dance classes focused on learning a routine for a dance concert or recital, or is technique taught regularly?

APPLICATION PHOTOGRAPHS

Often you will be asked to submit a photograph of yourself in dance attire along with your application. Unlike theater applicants trying to find the most appealing head shot, you need not go to the trouble of expensive professional photos. You should have someone take a full-length photograph of you in either color or black and white. Some schools specify an exact position they would like to see you in, and you should follow their directions exactly. When specific instructions are not given, the photograph(s) submitted should show you in a flattering pose or dance position, in appropriate dance clothing. If you have a photograph that was taken of you in a performance this would be fine, also. These photos are used for reference to remember you and should show you at your best. No provocative poses or outrageous attire should be chosen.

Dance Auditions

Most major auditions for dance programs are held in January through March, with possible late auditions in May. If you have a choice, try not to do your first audition at your first-choice school. Make sure that you have done plenty of preparation.

BEFORE YOU AUDITION

Whether it is for a company, a conservatory, or a dance department at a liberal arts college or university, you should be prepared well in advance of your audition time. Be sure to read carefully and thoroughly the catalog or any audition information that is sent to you.

Things you will need:

- your attire for a ballet class;

- your attire for a modern class;

- any other change of clothing or shoes;

- a cassette tape or CD of the music for your solo or sheet music for a piano accompaniment;

- another copy of your resume and photographs, in case they are requested; and

- any health form that is requested.

If admission is based primarily on your performance in a class or two, be sure that you arrive in plenty of time to do a complete warm-up and to get a good spot in the room. If they arrange you alphabetically for the class, you have no control, but if they arrange you according to the order in which you arrived, you may be in the front if you arrive early enough.

If you are asked to perform a solo that you have choreographed or someone has choreographed for you, be sure to choose material that accentuates your strengths. Many applicants prepare something from the standard repertoire on *pointe*, which shows the outer limits of their technique. It would be better to offer something less demanding that showcases your strengths now. Stay strictly within stipulated time regulations, as well.

Be prepared to speak about your material: the title of the piece, the choreographer, and the composer.

If for some reason you are injured before your audition, it is best to call and consult someone about postponing it. Going to the audition and saying, "I'm not allowed to jump, due to an injury," is not going to win you favor with an audition panel.

Practice

Practice ahead of time. Rehearse everything from how you will enter the room and how you will introduce yourself and your solo piece to what you need to tell the pianist (including the tempo). Go over your solo many times so that you can perform it under almost any circumstance, even a severe case of nerves. Frequently, the students who become nervous in auditions are the ones who have not lived with a piece long enough or rehearsed it enough and have some element of insecurity based on lack of preparation. Since being well prepared can help you relax, Dr. Beth Rom-Rymer, a psychologist in Chicago, says that it sometimes helps if you pretend the audition is two weeks earlier than it is to get the feeling of having gained some extra time. Try to arrange to perform for a group of your peers and for your teacher several months before the audition and record yourself; critique your performance and then do it again, at least a month before the audition. About a week before, try to get a group together and set up a mock audition situation for yourself.

Music for Your Auditions

You may be asked to perform, with music, a solo that you have choreographed or that someone else has choreographed for you. Be sure you know what player is available for you for playing the music. It would be awful to show up with a CD if there is only a cassette player. If you bring a tape, be sure that it contains only musical accompaniment for your solo and is cued to play.

If you do not bring a CD or tape, most auditions will have a pianist who accompanies the class and is available to play for your solo. If your piece is standard and not too difficult, bring the sheet music for the pianist. Be certain that it is legible, that it is assembled so that it is easy for a pianist to turn pages, and that any cuts or repeats are clearly marked. You may want to talk to the pianist ahead of time or send a copy of the music in advance. Be sure that you and the pianist communicate about the tempo before you begin your solo.

What to Wear

Schools and programs usually specify what they would like you to wear at your audition. The norm seems to be:

For a ballet class:

Black leotard, pink tights, and ballet shoes for women. White tee shirt, black tights, white socks, and ballet shoes for men. Some programs ask to see you on *pointe*. Be sure you have both ballet and *pointe* shoes with you.

For a modern class:

You can be a little more creative here, wearing a different color leotard or unitards, but usually you must be barefoot.

You should be neat and comfortable. Because dance is physical and your body is your instrument, it is important to wear proper attire and not try to hide your body. No big tee shirts or sweats. Your hair should be out of your face and nicely groomed.

WHAT TO EXPECT

When you arrive at a dance audition, check in and then go to the dressing room. (Never leave valuables in any dressing room.) At the beginning of the audition, you will be put in lines based on the order in which you arrived or in alphabetical order. Often you will be required to wear a number or your name. While you may feel that this is dehumanizing, it helps the audition panel recognize you, and you do not want to be confused with another applicant. You should also be aware that more and more dance auditions are being recorded for reference, and you should ignore the camera. Adjudicators may have your file and photos with them and compare to see that you really do look like your photograph.

During the audition, be sure to listen carefully and follow instructions precisely. Perform the material the way it is asked for, even if it is unfamiliar, and be sure to apply any corrections given to the class in general to yourself. Always be courteous to the other dancers.

Many auditions now conduct classes in ballet and modern and then have callbacks. If you do *not* receive a callback, do not assume that you are going to be rejected without confirming that this is the policy. Some schools do not call back the students who are obviously admissible.

NERVES

While a college interview may make you nervous, an audition may induce a real anxiety attack. The best defense is to be sure that you are so well prepared that you can function almost on automatic pilot. Arrive early and do a careful warm-up, including deep breathing exercises. Also, if you think of an audition as a performance, you may actually be able to develop the positive energy that you bring to the stage. It seems that the word "audition" with the connotation of judgment makes even seasoned performers nervous. Remember that the panel watching the audition really wants you to do well; so, do your best and keep your focus on performing with confidence.

WHAT *NOT* TO DO AT A DANCE AUDITION

- Do not run away after you have finished. Take your appropriate bows and then wait until you are dismissed. Many times there will be an awkward period of silence and then the adjudicators may want to ask you something. If you disappear, an opportunity may be lost.

- Do not wear inappropriate attire. Leave the big tee shirts, sweats, and tights with holes in them at home.

- Do not "play" to the judges. It is best to look a little over their heads.

- Do not choose a solo that you think the audition panel wants to see. Choose something that you love to dance and that is appropriate for your level of development.

- Do not perform a solo that is longer than the time stipulated in the guidelines.

REGIONAL AUDITIONS

Many conservatories will hold auditions in a number of different cities and sometimes in other countries as well. While doing the audition on the campus gives you an opportunity to see the facilities and probably meet with more faculty, if you have any scheduling conflicts or reasons not to travel to the campus, take the regional audition. They are usually treated as just as valid as an audition on campus, and sometimes, because you may be seen with a smaller group, may give you an advantage. Ask about who will conduct the auditions, which faculty will teach classes and evaluate the audition, and if a videotape will be made of the audition for other faculty to review.

DVD OR VIDEOTAPES VS. LIVE AUDITIONS

Some programs will accept a DVD or videotape of your dancing in lieu of a personal audition. The best advice is to use a recording only as a last resort. A live audition is always better than a DVD or videotape. Faculty members like to see applicants in person, whether at a regional audition or on campus, and you may diminish your chances of admission by submitting your audition on DVD or tape. Be sure you call the dance program for exact guidelines on length and content of the DVD or video. International students must be certain that the video is in U.S.-standard VHS format.

If you absolutely must submit a recording as your only possible way of auditioning, do not go for a glitzy professionally produced DVD or video, which will cost you a fortune in production. A well-done (hold the camera steady and have the picture in focus!) home version is fine for this, but remember you are not helping your chances for admission by not attending in person! Do not send an unsolicited recording, as it will probably end up in a pile—unwatched.

AUDITION EVALUATION CRITERIA

When you audition, the faculty and administrators in attendance will evaluate your performance in terms of certain criteria established by the school. Forms vary from school to school, but as you will note from the sample forms that follow, many similar criteria are reviewed. Some programs may give you copies of the evaluation or notes on how you might improve; other programs consider this strictly confidential.

MODERN DANCE AUDITION SHEET
ABC SCHOOL OF DANCE

Date _____   Audition No. _____

Auditioning for: Accept _____
_____ regular school only   Reject _____
_____ summer school only   Summer school to re-audition
_____ both summer school and regular school

Name: _____   Sex: M F _____

Date of Birth: _____ Age: _____ Height: _____ Weight: _____

Past Study: Years: _____ Classes/week: _____ Studios: _____

APPEARANCE

	good	fair	poor		good	fair	poor
Body tone				Turnout			
Carriage of torso				Feet			
Placement (static)				Hamstring flexibility			
Abdominal support				Hip flexibility			
Shape of leg				Lower back strength			

Comments:

TECHNIQUE

	good	fair	poor		good	fair	poor
Basic dance vocabulary				Coordination			
Torso flexibility, strength				Placement in space			
Use of upper back, arms				Learning ability			
Use of legs and feet							

Comments:

PERFORMANCE

	good	fair	poor		good	fair	poor
Use of space				Musicality			
Motivation				Projection			
Phrasing				Technical degree of difficulty			
Dynamics				Type of music used			

Comments:

Auditioner: _____

BALLET AUDITIONING SHEET
ABC School of Dance

Date _____   Audition No. _____

Name: _____ Sex: M F _____ Age: _____

Height: _____ Weight: _____ Entering grade level: _____

Past study (years): _____ Classes per week: _____ Studios: _____

	good	fair	poor	
Height				too tall/too short
Weight				overweight/underweight
Head				small/average/large
Neck				long/medium/short
Shoulders				sloping/straight/high/narrow/broad
Torso				short/medium/long
Spine				straight/curved (upper/middle/lower)
Hips (pelvis)				small/medium/wide
Legs				long/average/short
Shape of legs				(stand candidate straight with feet toward en face) straight/bowed top to bottom/bowed between knees and ankles
Knees				flat/sway back at knee joints/knees do not straighten/knock-kneed
Feet				small/large/flat/no arch/no points/no coupe de pied/stiff in ankle joints
Turnout				loose/tight/not from hips
Flexibility				
Placement (static)				shoulders up/shoulders back/lower back swayed/abdomen dropped/chest dropped/not centered
Plié demi				
Plié grand				
Extension				
Adage				good épaulé/poor épaulé/good extension/poor extension/no center
Turns en dehors				
Turns en dedens				
Turns diagonal				
Petite allegro				no speed/no turnout/no use of feet
Grand allegro				no elevation/no line/no turnout/no use of feet
Port de bras				placement of arms/correct position/incorrect positions
Quality of movement				coordination/fluidity/carriage/expression
Musicality				ahead/behind/cannot count
Schooling				correct for age/behind for age/ahead for age
Placement (in space)				
Presentation				outgoing/withdrawn/unfocused/blank/sullen
Energy				

Outstanding talent _____ COMMENTS:
Scholarship material _____
Accept _____
Further discussion _____
_____
Reject _____ AUDITIONER

THE COLLEGE OF PERFORMING ARTS
ENTRANCE AUDITION EVALUATION—FORM FOR DANCE DIVISION

Student Information	**For Dance Office Use Only**
(Computer Label)	Admit _____ Waiting List _____ Reject _____ Re-Audition _____ Scholarship Decision: _____ Audition Rating: _____ Scholarship Rating: _____ Combined Rating: _____

	Exceptional	Superior	Very Good	Good	Adequate	Possible	Unacceptable
Ballet technique							
Modern technique							
Performance							
Body Proportions							
Musicality							

Piece Performed: _____

Remarks:	Overall Rating (circle one):
	E S VG G A P U
	Accept _____ Possible _____ Reject _____
The student should be encouraged to re-audition ☐ Yes ☐ No	Scholarship Recommendations
Why?	Definitely ☐ Probably ☐ Possibly ☐
Signed: _____	
Date: _____	No ☐

Health Issues for Dancers

DEALING WITH INJURIES

If you have had an injury, be honest about it. Many colleges will require that you submit a health form or have an orthopedic evaluation prior to being allowed to take the audition. If you are not honest and a doctor reveals something about a past problem, however small, it is not a good reflection on you.

In looking at your future in dance, you must consider how injuries will influence some of your choices. All serious dancers are bound to incur some injuries. You must be brutally honest with yourself about when an injury will have to be taken into account in determining your future training. You should also be sure that you educate yourself about basic health issues, including good nutrition, basic injury prevention, and strengthening exercises, and you should read about how posture and psychology can contribute to injuries. Learn about strapping and padding techniques that support injuries, and become aware of the range of therapies available.

Although some great dancers have survived knee surgery and other injuries, every young dancer must decide whether personal injuries or physical restrictions are severe enough to interfere with career goals. The following books address the topic of dancers and health:

Arnheim, Daniel D. *Dance Injuries: Their Prevention and Care.* 3rd ed. Hightstown, NJ: Princeton Book Company/Dance Horizons Series, 1991.

Hamilton, Linda. *Advice for Dancers: Emotional Counsel and Practical Strategies.* San Francisco: Jossey-Bass, 1998.

Howse, Justin, and Moira McCormack. *Dance Technique and Injury Prevention.* 3rd ed. New York: Routledge, 2000.

Solomon, Ruth, John Solomon, and Sandra Minton. *Preventing Dance Injuries.* 2nd ed. Champaign, IL: Human Kinetics Publishers, 2005.

Spilken, Terry L., M.D. *The Dancer's Foot Book.* Princeton: Princeton Book Company/Dance Horizons Series, 1990.

Vincent, L. M., M.D., The *Dancer's Book of Health.* Hightstown, NJ: Princeton Book Company/Dance Horizons Series, 1988.

Watkins, Andrea, and Priscilla M. Clarkson. *Dancing Longer, Dancing Stronger: A Dancer's Guide to Improving Technique and Preventing Injuries.* Hightstown, NJ: Princeton Book Company/ Dance Horizons Series, 1990.

The Princeton Book Company/Dance Horizons publishers (www.dance horizons.com) also have a number of DVDs regarding dance and health. Their contact information is: 614 Route 130, Hightstown, NJ 08520; 800-220-7149 or 609-426-0602.

There are a number of Web sites that address issues of dancers' health. Some may be found as links off of ballet company Web sites. Two popular ones, however, are www.foot.com, addressing foot health and care for dancers, and the International Association for Dance Medicine and Science (IADMS) at www.iadms.org, which is dedicated to improving dancers' health.

OTHER HEALTH ISSUES

Many conservatory dance programs and also companies have recently been enforcing weight policies for young dancers. While the best dance educators consider this truly risky to both the psychology and natural physical body changes of mid-adolescence, there is an emphasis on thinness in much of the dance world. When you are looking at a college, conservatory, or company, you would be wise to ask about any weight policy.

A Dance Company vs. College

Dance company Web sites provide a wealth of information. You may learn about their educational outreach programs or summer intensives. If you are a junior or senior in high school and have the opportunity to audition for some companies, by all means take the auditions. You can learn a great deal about yourself and about a company just by auditioning. If you are admitted into the company, you must do some serious thinking about what you want to do. Review your contract very carefully. Some of the concerns you should evaluate include:

- How good is this company? How long do the dancers seem to stay with it? Where do they go from here?

- Are there any reviews of the company that you could read?

- What is the daily routine? How many classes? How many hours of rehearsal? How many performances a week?

- Will you be cast? What are the casting policies? Or are you corps de ballet?

- What do people like most about the company? What are the most common complaints?

- What is the financial profile of the company? Is payroll met regularly? Are there any problems?

- What are the plans for the near future? Any tours? What are the long-range plans?

- Where do most company members live?

Some companies that admit young dancers include the New York City Ballet, Pennsylvania Ballet, and Pittsburgh Ballet, and these companies will usually give you an indication of their interest in you very early on.

Some experienced dancers suggest that the company route is right for only a small number of dancers. These dancers point out that while dancers who join a company and those who follow a college curriculum will probably end up with the same acquired knowledge, the college route telescopes the learning time while the performing route leaves the dancer to learn by trial and error over a span of many years. These dancers also acknowledge that life after your years as a performer are much more difficult if you do not have a college education, and most directors and choreographers have attended college.

Be sure that you distinguish whether you are admitted to the *school* for a company, or to the company itself.

If you are admitted to a company, and your parents object because they want you to go to college, you should point out to them that most colleges do not have an age limit but a dance career does. If you are ready now, you might want to "leap" at the opportunity if the company meets your standards. It should be noted, however, that most modern dancers do have college degrees. In ballet, if you have no company options by age 17, college is a good choice. You might try deferring college admission or taking a year off after high school and doing a lot of auditions, or you could try to graduate from high school early and complete college in three years. By then, you would be 19 or 20 and still young enough to begin a ballet career.

If you are admitted to the school of a company, the decision about whether to enroll at a degree-granting conservatory or at a company school becomes even more difficult. Some of the company schools that you might investigate include the School of American Ballet, Dance Theater of Harlem, Alvin Ailey School, Joffrey, Pennsylvania Ballet School, San Francisco Ballet School, Boston Ballet School, Atlanta School, Graham School, Nikolais School, and Merce Cunningham School. (*Stern's Performing Arts Directory* is a good reference for these programs.) Here are some of the questions you should ask:

- What is a typical schedule for a freshman? Are there any electives?

- Is the dance department embedded within another department of the college?

- What is the reputation of the dance department within the college? Outside?

- How many dance performances are there? Fully produced concerts? Workshops?

- What is the policy on casting?

- What kind of flooring is there in the studios?

- How many studios are there? What are the facilities available to students (if you have not seen them on your campus tour)?

- Who have been the recent choreographers?

- Who has taught any recent master classes?

- What kind of technique is taught?

- What kind of repertory is studied?

- How will the audition be run?

- Who evaluates the audition?

- Is it possible to focus on ballet or modern, or do I have to be proficient in both?

- What do most graduates go on to do?

- What companies now employ graduates from your program?

- Do you help with job placement?

- What is the enrollment in the dance department? How many males? How many females? Has this been steady? Is it growing? Diminishing? How many graduate students? How many undergraduates?

- How many technical classes are required per week? In ballet? Modern? Jazz? Ethnic forms (also called international, world, or genre dance on some campuses)? Pas de deux? Pointe? Other?

- What is the difficulty level of technical classes?

- What is the length of dance classes? Size?

- Is there live accompaniment for dance classes?

- Is there an opportunity to choose faculty for specific classes?

- Do you accept DVDs or videotapes in lieu of a personal audition? If so, what special instructions should I know about? Format? Length? Do you accept DVDs or videotapes for pre-screening? Any special directions for these?

For Dance Majors

A Current Dance Major Speaks Out

PAM SOMMER
Mason Gross School of the Arts
Rutgers University

WHAT ADVICE CAN YOU GIVE HIGH SCHOOL SENIORS WHO ARE THINKING OF MAJORING IN DANCE IN COLLEGE?

The best advice I can give is that if you love it GO FOR IT. It is completely normal to have the feelings like "What am I going to do with a dance degree?" But this is the only time in your life you will have the chance to have this experience. Know that it is going to be a challenging experience, but that is worth every minute of it because rather than spending all day in lecture classes, you spend your time learning and doing what you love. I know that it is the best decision I have made. My time at Mason Gross has taught me more than just dance. I've learned valuable lessons that I will carry with me throughout my life. It's also interesting because you become a family with your class. Since you spend so much time together, you learn to love and grow with one another, which I think is so important. In school you make friends you never thought you would have.

As for choosing your school—really look into it. You have to remember that this is a place you are going to be training seriously and intensively at for four years. It is important to make sure that you love the studio, the style you will be taught, and the teachers you will be working with. Any of these things could determine how you feel about the program and influence your decision.

It is also very important to keep an open mind, since the more styles of dancing you learn, the better. So even if something doesn't appeal to you immediately, don't shut it out right away, because you could be surprised by what you will learn. It is easy to be intimidated by other people but don't be! People will ask you why you want to study dance, isn't that a hobby, what will you do with a degree in dance? All that means is they don't understand the passion in it. There are so many different fields a dancer can go into, and success isn't only measured by how much money you make, but how happy the profession makes you. So, the bottom line is, if you love to dance, don't stop. Learn as much as you possibly can and dance as hard as you can because you only live once.

Performing

Arts

HOW DID YOU PREPARE FOR BECOMING A DANCE MAJOR WHEN YOU WERE IN HIGH SCHOOL?

I took as many dance classes as I possibly could. Training is so important in the dance world. All good schools are looking for a dancer with drive, determination, and good training, so learn everything you possibly can before you get there. I also taught myself how to budget my time. A dancer's schedule isn't easy. You have to make sure that you learn to prep yourself for very long days and budget your time so that you don't overlap events or wear yourself down.

I also began to talk to people who were attending schools that I was interested in. I asked them what a day was like for them, whether they liked the school, and about the styles taught there, the teachers, and the other students. I felt that the more I knew about a school before enrolling in it, the better prepared I'd be.

I really started focusing on my school work. Honestly, I was never the best of students. I was the one who breezed my way through classes without opening a book. But I knew that wasn't going to fly once I entered college, and in order to stay in the program I would have to pass my academics with good grades. So I began to train myself to do some reading in between classes and aim for better grades. This prepared me for the loads of work and studying I was going to have to accomplish in between dance classes.

WHAT SHOULD PROSPECTIVE DANCE MAJORS LOOK FOR IN A COLLEGE?

A great faculty. To me, that is what makes or breaks the program. I have fallen in love with Mason Gross because of the teachers. They all care so much about the students and really go out of their way for us in many ways. They make class a positive learning experience instead of a place to feel belittled or insecure. They help us find confidence where we need it and really pay attention to our bodies and individual needs. I feel that I can go up to any of my teachers and talk to them about just about anything, and that is what is important. Like the other students in the class, the faculty also becomes family to you.

Also, check out the facility. Make sure that it looks like a safe and comfortable environment to dance in.

Meet some of the other dancers too. It's important to make sure that you are going to feel comfortable around the people you'll be spending time with because in this major you spend a majority of your day with the same people. Look at the academic program and make sure that it suits your needs—that it is not too easy or too hard—because although you can dance, you also have to survive academically.

I have heard from many dancers at various schools that when you walk into your school, you just know. It feels right. Go with that instinct because it's probably right.

WHAT IS YOUR TYPICAL DAILY SCHEDULE LIKE?

Busy, busy, busy is all that I can say. Expect early morning classes. I know that in my school, freshmen have an 8:10 ballet class every morning, followed by a two-hour technique class (modern), followed by two to three more classes every day, not to mention rehearsals for several hours a night and academic school work. During show season, you are usually dancing seven days a week for several hours a day. Make sure you pack a lunch, because a lot of days you won't have a break to eat. Aside from classes and rehearsal, we all know that having a social life is important in college. So the free hour or two you may have in a day is usually spent hanging out with friends. It does get hard sometimes though, when all your friends want to spend a night out and you can't because you have to wake up early and dance. But I can honestly say that you usually don't mind staying in because you enjoy going to class and don't want to be tired for it.

WHAT WAS THE BIGGEST SURPRISE YOU FOUND ONCE YOU GOT TO COLLEGE?

What I was able to accomplish on my own. I'm not going to lie, I was scared. I didn't know how I was going to survive. But you realize that if you put your mind to something, no matter what is on your plate, you can finish the job and do it well. I was surprised at how independent and self-motivating I can be and that I am capable of more than I could have ever imagined.

WHAT KINDS OF PERFORMANCES ARE YOU CURRENTLY INVOLVED IN?

I was just involved in the spring dance concert, which included all student choreography. It is such a great experience because not only do you get the chance to perform, but you get to be hands-on throughout the entire production, and that's the part I found the most exciting.

Throughout the year I also performed in faculty concerts and helped to run them. We have to take a class in dance production, and I feel it is one of the most helpful classes I have taken. I now have learned how to hook up and hang lights in a theater, design the lighting for a piece, and work backstage as a show is in progress. In this profession knowing how to do that is so important.

DO YOU HAVE A CONCENTRATION?

Modern dance is my concentration. Most dance departments now concentrate on modern dance or ballet, since they are the more classical types of training. At some schools you get to choose your concentration, and at others it is chosen for you.

WHAT CAREER PATH DO YOU HOPE TO FOLLOW?

I leave my doors open to anything. I hope to perform for a while, meet people, and let my path guide me where it may. I believe that it is important to keep an open mind and open heart to everything, and that what you are looking for will find you. But, as contradictory as this may sound, I also believe it is important to have interests in a specific field you wish to go into or something you see yourself doing in the long run. For example, I hope to one day become a dance therapist for special education. I am not limiting myself to only that, but I keep it in mind as a definite place I would like to go. All that I know is that I love what I am doing and whatever path I may choose, I know that I will never regret a moment of it because I am living my passion.

For Dance Majors

Alternative Careers for Dancers

If you decide that you do not want to pursue being a performer full-time, or if you find yourself needing to supplement your income, there are many related activities in the performing arts that you might want to consider. One recent study reported that after graduation, only 10 to 15 percent of all performance majors earn their main income from performing. The others are combining performance activities with other occupations or "temping"—working as temporary secretaries, receptionists, or assistants. Following are some examples of alternative career choices for dance majors.

Dance majors might also explore any of these career areas:

- Choreographer

- Teacher

- Director

- Dance or movement therapist

- Director of a dance school or studio

- Labanotation expert

- Model

- Cast member at a theme park or in industrial shows

Performing Arts

What to Put in Your College Notebook

You might add a page to your personal college notebook with a chart like this one, listing the areas of dance you are interested in studying.

AREAS OF DANCE TAUGHT

☐ Classical Ballet

☐ Modern Dance

    Graham-based technique

    Limon-based technique

    Nikolais-based technique

    Cunningham-based technique

☐ Other:

List: _____

☐ Repertory

☐ Jazz

☐ Tap

☐ Historical Dance

☐ Ethnic forms:

    African

    Indian

    Middle Eastern

    Spanish

    Asian

☐ Other:

List: _____

☐ Movement Techniques

    Alexander

    Feldenkrais®

    Laban movement studies

☐ Other:

List: _____

☐ Dance Composition/ Choreography

☐ Pedagogy
    (any teacher certification?)

☐ Labanotation

☐ Anatomy

☐ Music

☐ Stagecraft

☐ Acting

☐ Voice

☐ Other:

List: _____

Admissions Checklist

Here are some questions to ask yourself at various points in the admissions process.

Have I:

- reviewed the program's Web site thoroughly?

- requested catalogs and read them carefully and critically?

- requested applications and made photocopies of the ones in which I am interested?

- started a college notebook to record my impressions of colleges, audition and repertoire requirements, and deadlines?

- obtained a social security number (United States citizens and Permanent Residents)?

- registered for the PSAT?

- obtained information about the ARTS scholarships? (National Foundation for Advancement in the Arts, 444 Brickell Avenue, Miami, FL 33131; 305-377-1140; www.artsawards.org.)

- made an appointment with my guidance counselor to discuss future plans?

- looked into working with an independent counselor, if appropriate?

- talked with my current dance teacher about plans for my future?

- made arrangements to continue my dance classes?

- discussed high school courses to take?

- discussed which standardized tests to take and when?

- discussed whether tutoring for standardized tests is appropriate for me?

- discussed Early Admission possibilities?

- investigated summer programs and/or jobs and applied as necessary?

- investigated sources and policies regarding financial aid and scholarships?

- kept a file of performance programs, DVDs, or videotapes of performances, good term papers, articles, etc.?

- attended college fairs and met with college representatives who visited my school?

- finished my essays and applications and photocopied everything before mailing, or printed a hard copy before submitting online?

- registered for any standardized tests required (SAT, ACT Assessment, TOEFL, SAT Subject Tests)?

- met again with my guidance counselor?

- arranged my college visits?

- scheduled interview appointments?

- sent thank-you notes after my college interviews?

- chosen my audition material?

- narrowed my list of colleges?

- settled on decision plans?

- asked for letters of recommendation, if necessary?

- drafted my essays?

- applied for financial aid, if necessary?

www.petersons.com

- requested that official score reports be sent directly to the colleges that require them?

- done mock (practice) auditions and recorded them for my own critique?

- submitted any performance recording for pre-screening, if required?

- had photographs taken to submit with applications, if necessary?

- prepared a resume?

- requested that a copy of my transcript be sent?

- communicated regularly with my guidance counselor about my progress in the college admissions process and in school?

- kept up with all school work?

- prepared a list of extracurricular activities, if necessary?

- arranged for an accompanist for my audition, if necessary?

- checked that all financial aid documentation is complete?

- read carefully any audition or schedule information sent to me?

- prepared any necessary audition CD or tape of music for my solo piece?

- responded to colleges about any offer of admission?

- requested an extension beyond the May 1 Candidates Reply Deadline, if necessary?

- continued with my regular dance classes?

For Music Majors

Whatever program you choose, keep in mind that the vast majority of people with careers in music have extensive formal training. Music is highly structured, and theoretical studies provide the structure that puts music together. Pursuing a degree will not only make you a better, more well-rounded musician, it will also provide an automatic connection to the arts world that is much more difficult to obtain on your own.

Advanced Study in Music

BACHELOR OF ARTS VS. BACHELOR OF MUSIC

Unlike other performing arts students choosing between a Bachelor of Arts (B.A.) and a Bachelor of Fine Arts (B.F.A.) program, music students will find more differences between Bachelor of Arts and Bachelor of Music (B.M.) programs than just the proportion of courses taken in liberal arts and in applied music. Often students choosing the route of the B.A. do not want to major in music, but do want to take some music courses and continue private lessons. If you want to apply to graduate school on the master's level, it is important that at the bachelor's level you do continue your musical study; otherwise you will fall behind in both your major area of study (instrument or voice) and in music history, ear-training, and music theory.

The instrument you play has some bearing on your choice of a program. For instance, singers are encouraged to pursue liberal arts studies for at least two years before turning to more concentrated voice study. If you are a violinist or pianist, however, age seems to be more important and if you are serious about having a performing career, you may want to focus on a Bachelor of Music degree program. Age seems to matter slightly less for cellists and little for violists and double bass players, in the string family. Most wind, brass, and percussion players can also wait to pursue focused musical studies in a B.M. degree, but flutists are advised to go directly into the B.M. program. Because of the intensely competitive nature of the flute, age does matter more than on other wind instruments.

Popular music, musical theater, and jazz do seem a bit more flexible in admissions and the age factor, so whether to pursue focused musical studies at the undergraduate level or to get a more general education seems to be a matter of personal choice.

There are many well-known musicians whose choices may serve as examples. Some that come to mind immediately are cellist Yo-Yo Ma, who did his undergraduate work at Harvard while continuing his cello studies and doing music programs during the summers; he then went to Juilliard for graduate school. Pianist Emanuel Ax went to Columbia. Flutist Eugenia Zukerman attended Barnard College for two years and then transferred to Juilliard. Guitarists Eliot Fisk and Sharon Isbin did their undergraduate work at Yale. And then there are the legions of musicians who went directly to conservatories. Obviously this is a highly personal decision, and you must do what feels right to you.

Music Auditions

When you read the college catalog, take careful note of whether an audition is optional or required. All major conservatories and joint programs require auditions, as do many college music departments.

WHAT TO EXPECT

Music auditions have been portrayed in a variety of movies and plays, sometimes very accurately. *Fame*, *A Chorus Line*, and *Running on Empty* all have that hollow, disembodied voice calling out in a hall, "Thank you," often right before that fiendishly difficult passage that the auditioners have practiced so carefully and are so sure will reveal their most musical moments. To be honest, very few music auditions are pleasant experiences. It is generally conceded that music auditions are an experience unto themselves—neither a performance, nor a lesson, nor a rehearsal, nor a "woodshedding" session. After having prepared for years, you are usually given ten to fifteen minutes to demonstrate your level of achievement, talent, and potential, often in a dry, stuffy room, for a group of faculty members who are known worldwide. Sometimes the faculty members whisper amongst themselves, pass notes, argue about what repertoire to request next from you, or engage in other activities that do not relate to your performance. It can truly be an intimidating experience. If you know what to expect, however, you will be better prepared to handle even the worst situation.

Remember that you have paid for the audition and this is your time, so make every moment count and take some control of the situation yourself. Also remember that even the most jaded, tired person on the audition panel will respond to excellence, so psyche yourself up to do your best, performing music that you love.

TIMING OF AUDITIONS

If possible, plan to take your audition during the main audition period from a school, usually in January through March, though some auditions are now in November. This is when the school will be filling the greatest number of openings; any further auditions will be held to fill a limited number of vacancies that might exit after the newly admitted applicants from this main audition period have responded to the offer of admission. So, if you wait until May, some departments may be closed already and others may have only a few openings.

Performing

Arts

Schools usually set audition weeks and then contact the faculty to see which day within that week is the best for them to hear auditions. To be safe, block off the entire audition week listed in a school's catalog. You are not able to choose the day that you would like to audition; the school determines this. If you run into a major conflict, call the admissions office and see if there is any way to resolve it.

By submitting your application early, you may secure a better audition time. If you know of a conflict in advance, you might request that your audition be on a certain day, but whether or not your request is honored will be depend on faculty availability. Never try to contact faculty directly to reschedule an audition; this must go through the admissions office.

Should you need to cancel your audition or postpone it to the later audition period, be sure to call and then follow up with a letter or e-mail. Many admissions offices will take note of your phone call but consider your communication official only when put in writing. If you must cancel on the day of the audition or if you are somehow delayed, be sure to call as soon as possible. Nothing is more frustrating to an audition committee than wasting time waiting for a no-show.

Try to arrive at least one hour ahead of your audition time, but be sure to read any schedule letter sent to you by the school very carefully. Some schools have group activities or speeches you are expected to attend before the auditions start. In any event, you do want to have time to locate the audition room, check in, and find a practice room for a good warm-up. It is a good idea to do a preliminary warm-up before you leave for your audition. Practice rooms or warm-up space may be at a premium, and you may not be altogether comfortable going through your entire warm-up routine surrounded by other applicants.

WHAT TO WEAR

What you wear to an audition is important. Just as for an interview, you should have an audition outfit. Singers tend to be dressier than instrumentalists. Neatness, cleanliness, and comfort are all important, but so is the fact that you are appearing in a performance. You want to convey to the faculty that you take this audition seriously and have dressed for it appropriately. Recommendations:

Women instrumentalists: a nice skirt (not too short or too long), blouse, and a blazer, if comfortable; or a simple dress (not too frilly, flouncy, or provocative). Low-to-medium heels.

Women singers: a simple dress, neither too short nor too long. Silk, or a silk-like fabric, seems to be the most popular. No glitter, evening gowns, fancy recital dresses, plunging necklines, or outrageous stockings. If you want to make a "statement," let it be with the color, not the style. (Brown and beige are not good stage colors.) Be sure that the dress fits well so that you have plenty of room to breathe without bursting any seams, buttons, or zippers. (This happens more often than you would imagine!) Shoes should have low-to-medium heels—no spike heels.

Men (including singers): a nice pair of pants, a shirt, jacket, and tie, and loafers or nice shoes. (The traditional look of gray trousers, white shirt, tie, and navy blue blazer is very popular and appropriate.) If you want to make a "statement," let it be with your tie! A nice turtleneck is okay, too. No tuxes, tails, fancy suits, jeans, or sneakers. For singers and wind players, be sure that the shirt is large enough so that you do not have to leave the top button open or loosen your tie.

WHAT TO BRING WITH YOU

Before you leave for your audition, look at the catalog one more time and reexamine the letter sent to you with your audition schedule. Do you need to bring manuscript paper and pencils? (Conductors and composers often do.) It may also be helpful to take a look at your photocopy or hard copy print-out of the application you submitted, just to refresh your memory about what you wrote. Here are some questions to ask yourself before you leave for the audition.

- Do I have copies of the music that I am prepared to perform?

- Is the music that I am giving to my accompanist in best form? Can they read it easily? Turn pages simply? This music should NOT be stapled, should be a clean copy with all notes included and not dropped off the page.

- Do I have a copy of the schedule letter that was sent to me to glance at for reference?

- Do I have all my audition clothing? Shoes?

- Do I have all the equipment I need? This may include a music stand; sticks and brushes (percussionists); your instrument, including mouthpiece, mutes, bows, rosin, etc. (Believe it or not, a guitarist once showed up at Juilliard with his guitar case but no instrument inside!); any extra copies of your audition repertoire list just in case it is requested; tissues or handkerchiefs (for sweaty palms, to wipe the brow, or as a basic prop), and water, if you think you may need it.

REPERTOIRE CHOICES

If you do not submit the required repertoire on your application, many schools will not allow you to audition and will reject your application outright, so be sure that you are conforming to the requirements. If you have any doubts, write a letter (do not make a phone call in this case) to the admissions office and ask them if what you are planning meets with the faculty's standards. This is particularly true in piano, where the repertoire is vast and the interpretation of the word "substantial," used in several catalogs, is open to debate.

Be sure to choose music that you really love from within the repertoire requirements; this will make it much more pleasurable to perform under duress. Don't make the mistake of choosing an aria or sonata you think the audition panel wants to hear. You will do well only if you like what you have chosen to perform.

Changing repertoire may be permitted, but be sure that whatever composition you are substituting conforms with the overall requirements. You should write to the admissions office with your change of repertoire, but also announce it at the beginning of your audition. Typing a new "Audition Repertoire List" and having enough copies to distribute to the faculty at the audition is a good thing to do.

PRACTICE AUDITION

One of the best ways to prepare for the audition is to do it, under mock or concert circumstances, many, many times. Videotape or make a DVD of each mock audition and critique it yourself, as well as seeking the evaluation of others. One pianist from Texas who was admitted to several schools used her mock audition times as an opportunity for fund-raising. She would charge a modest admission, as though this were a mini-concert, and then play and discuss the performance with the audience afterwards.

When you set up these mock auditions for yourself, try out the clothing that you think you will wear. Can you breathe comfortably? Can you walk well in the shoes you have chosen? Also give yourself a number of sample rooms to audition in. While some audition rooms may be concert halls with wonderful acoustics, others are teaching studios with very dead sounds. Get used to performing under a variety of circumstances and don't let anything distract you from doing your best.

For Music Majors

BEFORE YOU AUDITION

The importance of preparation for your audition cannot be stressed enough. Classical musicians should start with the repertoire. Check your catalog or the school's Web site in your freshman and sophomore years and plan your repertoire accordingly. Usually you must perform from memory. You need to live with your selections long enough to know that you can perform them with total security technically and emotionally. By choosing repertoire early, you also allow yourself time to make a switch if you need or want to.

Popular musicians should also start early with repertoire preparation. If you are required to perform standards, get them in your blood so that you will be able to improvise easily. And, if you plan to perform any original compositions, preparing early will allow you to try out the compositions in a variety of settings and get some feedback from teachers, colleagues, and audiences.

As you read the Web site or catalog, note whether you will be required to take any additional examinations, such as an ear training, sight-reading, or music theory test. If so, be sure to do some review and familiarize yourself with the material as best you can. You may have a melodic dictation. This is usually played by an instructor at the piano. Clef and key will usually be given (e.g., A major), but not time signature or pitch. You will have to determine meter, starting note, and notate the melody correctly. You may also be asked to sight sing; do an analysis of a piece, including identifying chords with Roman numerals and indicating non-harmonic tones by type such as escape tone, appoggiatura, passing tone, upper neighbor, suspension; identify plagal, half, deceptive, or full cadences; or do harmonization with figured bass realizations. Some schools have Web-based practice tests or reviews online. Others have recommended texts. Some common texts for study are:

Music Theory

Aldwell, Edward, and Carl Schacter. *Harmony and Voice Leading.* New York: Schirmer, 2002.

Clough, John, and Joyce Conley. *Scales, Keys, Intervals, Triads, Rhythm, and Meter.* New York: Norton, 1999.

Fux, John J. *Study of Counterpoint.* New York: Norton, 1965.

Gauldin, Robert. *Harmonic Practice in Tonal Music.* New York: Norton, 1997.

Kostka, Stefan, and Dorothy Payne. *Tonal Harmony.* New York: McGraw-Hill, 2000.

Marvin, Elizabeth West, and Jane Clendinning. *Musician's Guide to Theory and Analysis.* New York: Norton, 2005.

Music History

Burkholder, J. Peter, Donald Grout, and Claude V. Paleisca. *A History of Western Music.* 7th ed. New York: Norton, 2005.

Burkholder, J. Peter, ed. *The Norton Anthology of Western Music and the Norton Recorded Anthology.* 5th ed. New York: Norton, 2005.

Fuller, Sarah. *The European Musical Heritage, 800–1750.* Revised ed. Boston: McGraw-Hill, 2006.

Salzman, Eric. *Twentieth Century Music: An Introduction.* Englewood, NJ: Prentice-Hall, 2001.

Ear Training

Fish, Arnold, and Norman Lloyd. *Fundamentals of Ear Training and Sight Singing.* Waveland Press, 1992.

Ottman, Robert. *Music for Sight Singing.* Englewood, NJ: Prentice-Hall, 2003.

Piano Literature

Dubal, David. *Art of the Piano: Its Performers, Literature, etc.* Amadeus Press, 2005.

Hinson, Maurice. *Guide to the Pianist's Repertoire.* IN: Indiana University Press, 2001.

Matthews, Denis, ed. *Keyboard Music.* New York: Praeger Publishers, 1972.

Keyboard Studies

Morris, R. O. *Preparatory Exercises in Score Reading and Figured Harmony at the Keyboard, Book I.* UK: Oxford University Press.

Once your repertoire is under control, you must begin your mental and emotional preparation for the audition. There are many parallels between music performance and sports. Just as an athlete must have tremendous powers of concentration, so should a musician. You must not allow distractions from the audition panel (often called a "jury" in music) to interfere with your performance. Learn to focus your concentration on the music and your performance of it. Walk into the audition with confidence and a positive attitude. Know the music inside and out and in retrograde inversion, but when you play or sing, perform from the heart.

Some additional tips on preparing for your audition:

- Try to avoid traveling on the day of the audition. Plan to arrive at least a day ahead, more if the location is at a higher altitude and you are a wind or brass player or a singer. Traveling can tire you out, and airplanes can dehydrate you and affect your ears.

- Get a good night's sleep the night before the audition. Do not stay up talking to friends or to other people auditioning.

- Avoid alcohol and caffeine, which can also dehydrate you. Drink lots of water.

TYPES OF AUDITIONS

Auditions are run in different ways from school to school, but there are some common types of auditions.

On-Campus for a Representative Group of the Faculty

This is the most common type of audition. You arrive at the campus and are told that the auditions for your major field of study (instrument, voice, musical theater, etc.) are being held in a certain room. You locate the room, check in with a monitor, meet your accompanist, have a few minutes to warm up and check tempi, and then are told that the faculty are ready to hear you. You walk into the room and are confronted with three to possibly sixteen distinguished faculty members. (Piano, violin, and voice seem to have the largest number of audition panel members.) One of these people usually will act as coordinator of the audition. Take your lead from this person. You might say, "Hello, my name is Sally Smith," and proceed to sit down (or stand) and wait for them to get their audition evaluation forms together and acknowledge you. If you are playing with an accompanist, the pianist should already have your music in order. Do not start until the coordinator of the audition tells you to begin. In some auditions, you may be asked some simple questions to help you relax before you play. In other auditions, the atmosphere will be very formal with many moments of silence. Then the coordinator may say something such as, "With what would you like to start today?"

Most schools let you start your audition with a piece of your choosing. You should select that piece very carefully. It need not be the most difficult piece in your repertoire, but something that you really love and that shows you off to your best. The audition panel may cut you off while you are in the midst of this piece (tapping a pencil on the table seems to be the most popular technique, but some may clap, others just speak up), but do not start with an attitude of wondering where they will stop you; this will leave your concentration unfocused. Rather, keep focused and enjoy yourself as best you can, getting "into" the music.

Usually the audition committee will ask you to perform something else from your repertoire list. Before you start that selection, be sure to take a deep breath and focus your mental energy and concentration on this new piece. If you are asked for another selection after this one, follow the same procedure.

Before you start to play or sometimes before you leave an audition, faculty may ask you a few simple questions, such as, "Where are you from?" "How long have you studied and where?" "How much do you practice each day?" "Do you make your own reeds?" "What kind of horn is that?" "What is the extent of your orchestral experience?", etc. You may or may not be asked about naming your current teacher. Whatever you do, do not be thrown by these questions and be sure to answer them honestly, thoughtfully, and completely. International students are not allowed to bring translators, so you will want to practice your responses to questions such as these prior to your audition.

Your audition is over when the faculty indicates that you may go. The length of auditions varies, but tends to be ten to fifteen minutes on average, depending on the instrument. Percussion, accompanying, organ, and jazz auditions are usually a little longer. You may feel that the faculty is being remote, detached, or unfriendly in an audition of this nature. In fact, they are trying to be objective and fair, and judge you on the quality of your music-making. You should also realize that sitting for many hours listening intently to auditions is very hard work, and people do get tired and cantankerous. If you take control of your instrument and are as pleasant and confident as possible, the image that you project will help to warm up the room.

For a Single Faculty Member

Some schools will have your audition only for the faculty member you have indicated you want to study with, or the school will have a one-person department. These auditions may be run like the audition just described or may be more like a lesson or consultation, so that the faculty member sees how you work and whether or not you are responsive to the teaching methods he or she uses. These auditions may be longer, perhaps even thirty minutes. Be prepared to be flexible.

Regional Auditions

Regional auditions, sometimes called "external auditions," held in selected cities around the country and, more frequently, internationally, are usually conducted by a member of the administration. Sometimes faculty representatives are present, but usually regional auditions are taped or videotaped, and those tapes are then played for the faculty.

If you cannot go to the campus for a personal audition, which is always preferred, a regional audition is a good alternative. Anticipate walking into the room, introducing yourself, choosing your first selection, and then being asked to play something contrasting from your repertoire list. A third selection may be requested, and you may be asked a few questions before you are dismissed.

Taped vs. Live Auditions

Some schools request that audiotapes, CDs, or videotapes be submitted with applications for a pre-screening review to see who should be invited to audition in person. Be sure that you follow the format a school requires: If audio, is it a standard cassette? A CD? If video, must it be American-format VHS? Is a DVD preferred? The audio quality of the tape should be as high as possible, and if it is a video or DVD, be sure that the camera is in focus and that the background is not distracting. (Do not bother with an expensively produced video or DVD. A good home video with high-quality audio is just fine.) You should label your recordings carefully with your name, address, instrument, and the repertoire presented, in the order in which you perform it on the tape. This information should be on the tape, CD, or DVD itself, and also on whatever packaging you send it in. If you make it past this pre-screening, you will be invited to perform in person.

Live auditions are always preferred to recordings, so you should make every effort to arrange to get an on-campus or regional audition. Sending an audiotape, CD, DVD, or videotape for your actual audition may slightly diminish your chances for admission. If you are a prize-winning performer, with many professional credits, then you may present yourself well on recording. Anyone else should really aim to perform in person.

Making an Audition Recording

Presenting your playing on an audiocassette, CD, DVD, or videotape is difficult. It is essential that you present the highest audio quality possible, while staying within your budget. One musician who has been on the orchestra committee for symphony auditions tells of reviewing tapes that were made on machines with automatic volume control, or even made on telephone answering machines! These people did not win the audition, needless to say. Other reviewers talk of students who spend money on professional videos of almost MTV quality—just not worth it.

While it is probably not worth your time and money to rent a professional recording studio, where rates are often very high and the engineers will often want to put in extra reverb or other effects, you should have good microphones and experiment with their placement. Making a good recording takes time. You will need to go through your pieces several times before you get a "take." Remember that the committee reviewing a cassette or video rarely listens to the entire set of selections, so you should put your very best pieces first. If you are working with an accompanist, set up several times to work on the recording.

Douglas Yeo, bass trombonist with the Boston Symphony, suggests the following method for making an audition tape. Buy, borrow, or rent the best equipment you can, always following the directions the school or program has given you. Set yourself up in a good-sized room, not too big and not too small. Spend one session experimenting with the microphone setup. Use high-quality tape, turn on the machine, and start playing or singing. Play every excerpt or part of a composition more than once, checking the recording set up and carefully noting what you do. Keep the tape rolling throughout this exercise.

After the session, listen to the tape on a good machine and judge the best setup from a sonic perspective. (Never send a recording that you have not reviewed! Many directors of admission tell of assembling faculty members to review tapes, only to find a few with nothing on them!) Then, the next day or even later, repeat the entire process using the setup you liked best. Play through the repertoire as best you can. Later choose your best takes and transfer them, with your very best piece first, to another tape. Listen to the finished product and if you need to, repeat the entire process until you get something you like. You should never splice an audition tape, but choosing your best rendition after several opportunities to perform it is usually permitted. After all this, it may seem even more practical, as well as to your advantage, to attend the personal audition.

DIFFICULT SITUATIONS TO ANTICIPATE

No matter how well prepared you are, you may still encounter a situation that you could not possibly have anticipated.

Faculty members who argue among themselves about your repertoire choices. You have just presented your first selection and now the coordinator asks for something else. Another faculty member does not want to hear that and speaks up. A debate ensues. You should just sit there patiently until this debate is resolved.

Lack of interest from the faculty. This may be because you are scheduled right before lunch, when the focus is on food, or right after lunch, when panel members may be sleepy, or late in the day, when they are tired. The best way to handle this situation is to be as energetic and positive as possible, and totally dedicated to the music. If they do not ask you to play a second selection, it does get a little tricky. They may have really liked you and not needed to hear more. On the other hand, if you did not do your very best on that first piece, you might tactfully try suggesting, "Well, I do have my Paganini Caprice and it's really short. Since I've only had five minutes of your time, perhaps you'd let me start this." If you do not feel comfortable with this, then stop by the admissions office and let them know what happened.

Unfortunate remarks by faculty members. Sometimes you may say the name of your teacher and there may be some history or politics involved, or someone on the audition panel may say something like, "Oh, is that person still teaching?" Do not let this throw you. You are being evaluated on the quality of your music-making, not on who your teacher is.

Faculty members who stand up and walk around, pass candies among themselves, or engage in some other sort of distracting activity. Keep your concentration. Some faculty members may move around because they cannot see your embouchure or fingerings from where they are sitting. This does not necessarily mean that they have lost interest or want you to stop. Some may have been sitting for quite a while and need to stand up and stretch.

Anything out of the blue. Perhaps the hardest thing at an audition is being asked to do something you had not expected or prepared for. For example, you might be asked to improvise, to sight-read, or to answer questions about a piece you may have studied but not prepared to play. Since this is your time, take control of the situation and present your strengths. If you have not had much practice at sight-reading and did not anticipate this as any part of your audition, you might say, "I'd be happy to give this a try, but I would love a minute or two to look it over, as I spent my time preparing the specified repertoire for this audition."

What if your accompanist plays poorly? Remember, the faculty is listening to you and is not evaluating the accompanist. Just keep going and do your best. Be sure to rehearse in advance with the accompanist and never be rude to this person.

If an audition really goes poorly, you should contact the admissions office and ask to speak with either the director or assistant director. Be very specific about what transpired. Perhaps another audition can be arranged.

PARTNERS/ACCOMPANISTS

Most schools require that classical instrumentalists play a sonata or concerto with piano accompaniment. If it is at all feasible, try to bring your own accompanist, with whom you have worked regularly. If this is not possible, call in advance (two weeks usually) and get the name of the school's accompanist assigned to your instrument. Call that person and ask if he or she would be willing to play for you. If at all possible, arrange to rehearse a day in advance. While this may cost you anywhere between $40 and $750, it is well worth the extra charge, as you will feel more at ease if you have done this extra preparation and worked out tempi in advance with the pianist. If the accompanist does not know something on your repertoire list, ask if he or she would like you to send a copy of the composition in advance or if there is someone else whom he or she might recommend.

Singers should follow essentially the same procedure as classical instrumentalists. It is best to make repertoire selections from the standard repertoire of arias and art songs if you plan to use anyone other than your own accompanist. It is also important to choose the most common editions of arias.

In musical theater, an accompanist is usually provided. Plan in advance what you want to say to the pianist about tempi. You should plan on being cut off after a limited number of measures in your songs.

Popular musicians (jazz) are often invited to sit in with a "house band," or have a rhythm section provided at their audition. Have fun!

Accompanists are usually encouraged to bring their own "partners"— usually a violinist and a singer with whom they have worked in the past.

For Music Majors

If you are unable to bring your own partners, call the school at least two weeks in advance and get the names of the people the school has assigned for these auditions. See if you can have a rehearsal the day before the audition.

Whenever collaborating with an accompanist, you must present the music in the best form possible. Arrange to have either the original score or very legible photocopies bound in a loose-leaf notebook or pasted onto cardboard. If you are taking any cuts in the music, be sure that they are marked clearly and that you point these out verbally before the audition. If your interpretation has particular nuances with tempi or dynamics, be certain to mention these verbally and have them clearly indicated in the score. An accompanist is a valuable collaborator and can really give you support during your audition. Make sure that you develop a good rapport with this person and prepare as much as possible. It is generally not advantageous to have your parent or teacher accompany you. Better to use the person assigned by the school and rehearse in advance with this person.

NERVES

Being nervous for an audition in music is de rigueur. In general, the best prescription for nerves is preparation. If you love the compositions you have chosen, focus on the performance aspect of the audition, and cancel out of your mind any sense of judgment, you may have a good time and not be nervous at all. Remember, the people listening want to like you.

Perhaps one of the most typical manifestations of nerves is a memory lapse. You'll be playing along or singing and just go blank. Stop and start up when you left off. If it really is totally gone from your mind and ear, ask the audition panel if you may start again.

Dr. Beth Rom-Rymer, a psychologist in Chicago, did a workshop with members of the Chicago Youth Symphony Orchestra, who shared their feelings about a number of topics, including nerves (*Upbeat,* Spring 1991, vol. 6, no. 2):

> *Many students related to a string player who had such bad stage fright that she had to give up after walking on stage three times, unable to play the piece she had perfected for a competition through many hours of practice. Many other students could empathize with another string player who said he sometimes gets so tense his fingers cramp up and won't move.*

To avoid anxiety before a competition, Dr. Rom-Rymer suggested meditation/relaxation exercises, including cognitive rehearsal for the expected and unforeseen event, using positive and flexible cognitive imagery. You can use your inside as a refuge for relaxing and reverse the anxiety response.

When feeling tense muscles during long hours of practice, Dr. Rom-Rymer recommended taking time off to relax the body.

Diane Nichols, head of Mental Health at the Miller Health Care Institute for Performing Artists in New York City, suggests strategies of quieting the physical and psychological symptoms of performance anxiety:

Develop a pre-performance ritual. It doesn't matter what the ritual entails as long as you do it regularly to give you a sense of comfort and security. One actor pushes against a wall before every show; a student breakfasts on cereal and bananas before taking an exam. A singer takes a shower. You could lift weights or call Mom; the choice is purely personal.

Yawn. Yawning relaxes the jaw, neck, and shoulders and releases tension. It tells the body there's no danger.

Talk to yourself. When you're fearful, you lose sight of your strengths. The next time images of hissing audiences cloud your vision, say out loud, "I don't have to be perfect," or some other verbal reminder to put the situation into perspective.

Breathe. Before stepping into the spotlight, take two slow, deep breaths. It sounds simple, but once you're in control of your breathing patterns, you'll feel more in control of the situation.

Finally, SMILE. Studies show that you can't smile and feel fear at the same time. In addition to relaxing your muscles, smiling engages the listener as your presentation begins.

AUDITION EVALUATION CRITERIA

While you are playing or singing, the faculty will usually be completing forms, evaluating you on a variety of factors. To demystify the process, copies of audition forms from a number of schools are on pages 99 to 101.

ADDITIONAL EXAMINATIONS

As part of some auditions, you will be asked to take additional examinations. These vary from school to school and are used differently: some for admissions purposes and some for placement. Be sure that you are clear about what is expected of you so that you may prepare appropriately. If you are asked to play a separate orchestral placement examination, which will include sight-reading excerpts, speak with your teacher about common excerpts so that you can look them over in advance. Music theory, music history, piano proficiency (for non-keyboard applicants), and ear training are all fairly common examinations. For applicants for whom English is not the native language, there may be an English examination. There may be a diction evaluation for singers or a foreign language proficiency examination for doctoral students. Help yourself by preparing as best you can in advance.

WHAT *NOT* TO DO AT A MUSIC AUDITION

- Dress inappropriately.

- Arrive late or forget to cancel.

- Chew gum.

- Forget to introduce yourself.

- Start playing before you are asked to begin.

- Try to talk with a particular faculty member in the audition room.

- Try to listen to other applicants' auditions.

- Make excuses for any slip you may have or curse out loud if this happens to you.

- Tell your life story in answer to a simple question intended to help you relax.

- Have to leave in the middle of the audition. If you have a tendency towards dryness, particularly as a singer or wind player, bring water into the audition room with you, and be sure you have gone to the bathroom before the audition.

- Cry.

AUDITION EVALUATION

Name: _____ ID #: _____ In person: _____ Tape: _____

Address: _____ Phone: _____

Instrument/Voice Part: _____

MAJOR IN:

☐ Piano Pedagogy   ☐ Music Education   ☐ Music Therapy   ☐ Theory/Composition

☐ Performance   ☐ Sacred Music   ☐ Conducting

☐ Music Minor with possible major in: _____

☐ First Year   ☐ Graduate   ☐ Transfer from: _____

Repertoire Performed: _____

_____

CIRCLE each characteristic from low (1) to high (10)

	unacceptable	weak	adequate	very good	outstanding
A. TONE QUALITY	1 2	3 4	5 6	7 8	9 10
B. TECHNIQUE (articulation, diction)	1 2	3 4	5 6	7 8	9 10
C. INTONATION (except keyboard)	1 2	3 4	5 6	7 8	9 10
D. RHYTHM	1 2	3 4	5 6	7 8	9 10
E. STYLE–INTERPRETATION	1 2	3 4	5 6	7 8	9 10
F. OVERALL MUSICIANSHIP	1 2	3 4	5 6	7 8	9 10
G. MUSIC READING (if checked)	1 2	3 4	5 6	7 8	9 10

Performance applicants must score 7 or higher.
Other majors and minors must score 5 or higher.

COMMITTEE RATING [_____] 1–10

COMMITTEE EVALUATION: _____

_____

_____

FACULTY RECOMMENDED: ☐ High Award   ☐ Moderate   ☐ Possible   ☐ None

EVALUATORS: _____   _____
            _____   _____
            _____   _____

For Music Majors

PETERSON COLLEGE
Conservatory of Music—General

Name: _____   ID: _____

Address: _____   Instrument: _____

_____

Telephone: _____   Audition Location: _____ Tape: _____

Application Date: _____

Wishes to Enter: _____   ASI: _____ PLI: _____

Application Type: _____   HS Grad Date: _____ Program: _____

High School: _____

    Major 1: _____   Major 2: _____

    Major 3: _____   Major 4: _____

HS Rank: _____   SAT: _____   ACT: _____

Teacher 1: _____   _____

Teacher 2: _____   _____

Teacher 3: _____   _____

Teacher 4: _____   _____

Composition 1 _____   _____

Composition 2 _____   _____

Composition 3 _____   _____

Composition 4 _____   _____

Composition 5 _____   _____

Rate the candidate in the following areas
[5 = Superior; 4 = Above Average; 3 = Average; 2 = Below Average; 1 = Poor]

Comments

Musical Talent	5	4	3	2	1
Tone	5	4	3	2	1
Intonation	5	4	3	2	1
Technique	5	4	3	2	1
Control	5	4	3	2	1
Rhythmic Accuracy	5	4	3	2	1
Interpretation	5	4	3	2	1
Contrast and Balance	5	4	3	2	1
Articulation	5	4	3	2	1
Sight Reading	5	4	3	2	1
Memory	5	4	3	2	1

Rate the audition using the 5–1 scale above
  5 4 3 2 1

On the basis of this audition do you recommend that the applicant be admitted to the conservatory?
☐ Yes   ☐ No   ☐ ?

Do you recommend that the applicant receive special talent scholarship consideration? ☐ Yes ☐ No

Faculty examiner: _____   Date: _____

Performing Arts

PERCUSSION

Name: _____   Address: _____

Performance Medium: _____   Probable Major: _____

Length of Study: Years: _____   Months: _____   Present Teacher: _____

Personal Audition: Date: _____   Time: _____   Examiner: _____

Recorded Audition: _____   Transfer: _____   College: _____

	Superior	Above Average	Average	Below Average	Poor
MARIMBA, XYLOPHONE: Composition					
Tone (touch, evenness of sound)					
Roll					
Technique and Hand Position (dynamics, phrasing)					
Contrast and Balance					
Sight Reading					
Rhythmic Accuracy					
Pitch Accuracy					
Interpretation					
SNARE DRUM: Composition					
Tone (touch, evenness of sound)					
Roll					
Technique and Hand Position (dynamics, phrasing)					
Contrast and Balance					
Sight Reading					
Rhythmic Accuracy					
Pitch Accuracy					
Interpretation					
TIMPANI: Composition					
Tone (touch, evenness of sound)					
Roll					
Technique and Hand Position (dynamics, phrasing)					
Contrast and Balance					
Sight Reading					
Rhythmic Accuracy					
Pitch Accuracy					
Interpretation					
MULTIPLE PERCUSSION: Composition					
Tone (touch, evenness of sound)					
Roll					
Technique and Hand Position (dynamics, phrasing)					
Contrast and Balance					
Sight Reading					
Rhythmic Accuracy					
Pitch Accuracy					
Interpretation					
MUSICAL TALENT					
SENSE OF METER					

In the space below please give your comments about the audition. Give special attention to the candidate's strengths and weaknesses. On the basis of this audition, do you recommend that the applicant be admitted to the conservatory?

☐ Yes   ☐ No   ☐ ?   Comments: _____

Faculty examiner: _____

Advice on Music Specialties

WOODWIND AND BRASS

Many woodwind and brass players come from a background that has focused mainly on band music. This is tremendously valuable experience, providing players a fundamental grasp of their instrument and helping them to develop a good musical sense and the ability to phrase, to be part of an ensemble, and to follow a conductor. However, it is recommended that this band training be augmented with an awareness of Western European orchestral tradition. Listen to recordings of the great orchestras, attend orchestra concerts, and learn some standard orchestral excerpts for your audition. (You should also listen to the entire piece and know the excerpt in context.) If there is a youth symphony in your area, audition and try to join this organization or investigate the community orchestra. Read the journals on your instrument.

Some specific tips: Imitate your favorite recordings. Watch DVDs or videos of your favorite soloists and orchestral players. Listen to a passage of a piece and imitate it, like a jazz musician learning a solo. Listen to articulation as well as tone. Take responsibility for teaching yourself. Your own style will come from what you want to hear. Your own point of view is important and you must know what you like. Other recommendations from woodwind and brass players include being sure that you do not warm up too much. Blowing on your chops every few minutes to check them will tire you quickly. Better to spend the time concentrating on breathing deeply and relaxing. Be sure to drink lots of water (neither too hot nor too cold) to avoid "cotton mouth," and avoid soda, tea, coffee, and certainly milk before an audition.

OBOE AND ENGLISH HORN

Very few schools will let you major in English horn; most programs require that you major in oboe and play oboe d'amore and English horn as ancillary instruments on which you develop proficiency. Most double reed players complain that very few students develop any dynamic range on the instruments; they leap into playing concerti far too soon, before they have developed a basic technique. Work diligently on your études and learn how to stop and start a note attractively. Work on your breathing. Know also that music preparation involves studying scores, harmony, and theory and having keyboard proficiency and advanced listening skills. You should also know that the politics of the oboe/English horn world often focuses on an American versus European bias and

Performing Arts

discussions about vibrato. Be sure that whatever department you are joining represents your preference and that you are aware of both camps and have an idea about your future should you choose to play in one style over another. Ask questions about this.

TROMBONE AND TUBA

Some books worth reading include *The Art of Trombone Playing*, by Edward Kleinhammer (Evanston, IL: Summy-Binchard, 1963), and *Art of Brass Playing*, by Philip Farkas (Bloomington, IN: Brass Publications, 1962). Also recommended is an article on breathing by Arnold Jacobs, which appeared in *The Instrumentalists, Brass Anthology*, and a collection of memoirs of Jacobs' students entitled *Arnold Jacobs: Legacy of a Master*. Trombonists should be acquainted with the Rochut Etude books (3 volumes); *Daily Drills and Technical Studies*, by Max Schlossberg; and the Arban book, *Blazevich Clef Studies*. They should also look at the Bach cello suites, the *David Concerto*, Kopprasch Book I and II, and orchestral excerpts. Tuba players should learn to play both the little and big tuba. Standard orchestral excerpts include *Die Meistersinger, Die Walküre (Ride of the Valkyries)*, Vaughan Williams' *Solo*, and Berlioz' *Hungarian March*.

STRINGS

In discussing auditions, preparation for auditions, and playing in general, almost every string faculty member and player talked about two things: technical facility and musical intention. It seems tremendously important to string players that you pay special attention to your bow arm, left hand position, basic sound production, vibrato, and intonation. It is also important that you think of the music musically and have definite feelings and thoughts about what you want to convey. Fast fingers without feeling, thought, and emotional involvement is vapid. You must work at all levels in order to prepare properly for an audition.

It is also important that as a string player, you perform on the best instrument available to you at this stage in your development. To present yourself positively, try to play on an instrument that will allow you to have a sound that is uniquely your own and does not stand in your way.

This brings up the whole issue of instrument dealers. You should be aware that some teachers receive large fees, sometimes very large ones, from dealers for convincing students to buy certain instruments. While you may want your teacher to evaluate an instrument for you, and you would want to compensate the teacher for his or her time, buying an instrument just because a teacher suggests it may not be wise. Stop and think about the instrument's suitability for you.

HARP

It is helpful for harpists to have a background in piano. Because harps are so expensive, some will rent the instrument before they know that they are committed to the harp, and then work to buy their own. (When you go for an audition, be sure to ask if you will be able to use the school's harp or if you need to transport your own—a rare occurrence.)

It is important to get as much playing experience as possible. Often young harpists will offer their services to the local community orchestra in order to learn the basic orchestral excerpts and to get experience playing in an ensemble. Because harpists tend to work so much on their own, it is important to try to reach out and play in ensembles, learning how to relate in chamber groups and develop an ensemble sense of rhythm. The American Harp Society holds an annual conference and has competitions every three years for all levels. There are also regional events. It is a good idea to attend or compete in these American Harp Society gatherings so that you hear other harpists and get a sense of where your level of playing stands among your peers. It should also be noted that harpists have an easier time applying to conservatories at the undergraduate level and most professional harpists have chosen the route of conservatory training.

ORGAN

Within the world of organists, there are some who are considered as "antiaquarians" and others who believe that the modern organ as it is now constructed should be the vehicle for the vast repertoire. It is probably worth your while to investigate the philosophical point of view of any department or individual teacher to be sure that you will be in harmony. Be aware that some schools require that organ applicants also audition in piano. Ask questions about the repertoire required.

PIANO

One practical suggestion offered by many faculty members is that in playing your "mock auditions," you should play on a variety of instruments so that you can play your repertoire no matter what the action or state of repair of the piano.

In speaking to piano faculty members at various institutions, the resounding piece of advice seems to be regarding the audition program. Faculty members stress that you should present what you play best and like to play, which falls within the guidelines required, and not try to play something too difficult just to be impressive. The audition program should fit together and demonstrate lyric qualities, fingers or "chops," and a full range of musical virtues: legato line, sensitivity, and technical solidity. The piano literature is vast and you should be making selections for yourself; however, the following selections are offered as a basic guideline of some repertoire that seems fairly common for auditions:

Babbitt: *Three Compositions for Piano; Partitions*

Bach: *Well-Tempered Clavier*, Books I and II–Preludes and Fugues

Barber: *Sonata*

Bartók: *Suite*, Op. 14; *Sonata*

Beethoven: *Sonatas* (excluding Op. 14, Op. 49, and Op. 79)

Bolcom: *Etudes*

Brahms: *Intermezzi; Variations on a Theme by Handel; E-flat Rhapsody; Sonatas; Variations on a Theme by Paganini*

Chopin: *Ballades; Etudes; Scherzi*

Copland: *Variations*

Corigliano: *Etude Fantasy*

Debussy: *Images; Estampe; L'isle joyeuse; Pour le Piano*

Dello Joio: *Sonata*

Ginastera: *Sonata*

Lees: *Sonatas*

Liszt: *Transcendental Etudes: Vallée d'Obermann; Après une lecture de Dante; 11th Rhapsody; Mephisto Waltz; Funerailles*

Mendelssohn: *Sonata*

Messiaen: *Vingt Regards sur l'Enfant-Jésus* or any of the *Bird Pieces (Catalogue d' oiseaux)*

Persichetti: *Poems*

Prokofiev: *Sonata #3*

Rachmaninoff: *Preludes; Etudes Tableaux; Moments Musicaux*

Ravel: *Jeux d'eau; Sonatine; Gaspard de la nuit*

Rorem: *Barcarolles; Etudes*

Schubert: *Moment Musicale; Impromptus; "little" A major Sonata*

Schumann: *8th Novelette, Abegg Variations, G minor Sonata, Papillon*

Takemitsu: *Les Yeux Clos I and II*

ACCOMPANISTS (ALSO REFERRED TO AS COLLABORATIVE PIANISTS)

Many of the most famous accompanists stress that it is most important to get your "piano chops" together first, meaning that your level of technical ability should be developed and strong. Thus, very few schools have an undergraduate major in accompanying, and most accompanists major in piano or attend a liberal arts college, keep up their private piano lessons, and then attend a graduate program in accompanying/collaborative piano.

It is important to note that some accompanying programs are only for vocal accompanying, while others are more oriented toward instrumental accompanying. While there are a handful of truly accomplished accompanists who do well in both the vocal and instrumental worlds, most have chosen an area of specialization.

Be aware that if you choose to be a vocal accompanist/coach, you should have your foreign languages and English diction in order. Study French, Italian, German, and Spanish, emphasizing both language and diction. You should have dictionaries in all these languages as part of your library, also. Study the standard vocal literature, including the "hit parade" of arias for each voice category and the song repertoire, including Brahms, Wolf, Schubert, Schumann, Fauré, Debussy, Chausson, Ravel, Italian art songs, works of Dowland and Purcell, and some of the standard American art songs, just to scratch the surface. Those wishing to pursue vocal accompanying should be attending recitals and the opera often. You should listen to recordings of the great singers and try to make arrangements to accompany lessons for a teacher with a reputable voice studio.

If you choose to specialize in instrumental accompanying, you should attend as many master classes as possible, learn as much as imaginable about the various instruments, attend solo and chamber music concerts and recitals, listen to recordings, and study the sonata and concerto repertoire. You should know how to read an orchestral score and reduce it at the piano and be able to render an orchestral accompaniment with the proper inflection to do full justice to the orchestration. You should try to accompany lessons for various teachers, too.

There have been some wonderful books written about being an accompanist. Basic recommended reading includes Bob Spilman, *The Art of Accompanying* (New York: Schirmer Books, 1985), and Gerald Moore's many books, including *Am I Too Loud? Memoirs of an Accompanist* (London: Hamish Hamilton, 1962) and *Singer and Accompanist* (London: Methuen, 1953).

SINGERS

Do not prepare repertoire that is beyond your ability at this point. For instance, young singers really should not be singing the heavy verismo arias; Mozart is much more appropriate. Be aware that if you do offer Vissi d'arte or other such heavy arias, you are increasing your chances for rejection. Faculty members will write about inappropriate repertoire, poor training, and lack of vocal understanding. Sample opera repertoire might include works of Mozart, Bellini, Donizetti, or Handel—no Verdi or Puccini! The point is not to dazzle your audition committee, but to demonstrate your ability at this time with selections that do not overtax you emotionally, but do allow you to show your personality and your languages. Lieder studies might include songs of Fauré, Schubert, Brahms, the Italian anthology, and Purcell or Dowland. If you are asked to prepare some twentieth-century repertoire, look at the songs of Ned Rorem, Richard Hundley, Benjamin Britten, Aaron Copland, Dominic Argento, or Samuel Barber, for example. Your lessons should include good vocalizes, many of which will be special exercises that your teacher devises, such as those in Nicola Vaccai's *Metodo Pratico di Canto* (Practical Singing Method), a classic book first published in 1832 of various musical matters put together in attractive ariettas with Italian texts. Other good books regarding vocal technique that may be illuminating include William Vennard, *Singing—The Mechanism and the Technic* (New York: Carl

Fischer, 1967); Johan Sundbert, *The Science of the Singing Voice* (Northern Illinois University Press, 1987); and Robert Shewen with Judith Coen, *Singing and the Brain* (NY: Roberts Wesleyan College Press, 2005).

Any teacher who says that you have a "big voice" and can handle the "large or heavy repertoire" may be hearing what your voice may become, but if you sing that heavy repertoire before you are physically, technically, or emotionally prepared, you will probably be doing damage to your vocal apparatus.

Most voice teachers with whom I spoke said it is a very rare 18-year-old who should even consider a conservatory. Most would do best studying at a liberal arts college, learning literature and several foreign languages, for at least two years, and taking private voice lessons with a reputable teacher on the side.

It is important that singers be good sight-readers. While the participation of young would-be soloists in choruses or choirs is controversial among some voice teachers, it is suggested that young singers participate in some choruses or choirs to improve their sight-reading ability and explore a variety of musical styles. Some voice teachers also recommend that singers try to participate in a summer program overseas.

CHORAL CONDUCTORS

Most choral conductors have a background as an organist or as a singer. Some have majored in music education, augmented with intensive piano studies. The best training for choral conductors seems to be in settings where there is a strong choral tradition, coupled with a good voice department, and opportunities with opera and symphony choruses as well. In the United States right now, many choral programs are in a period of transition, as some of the well-known choral conductor/teachers are retiring. Choral conductors should be as well versed in score-reading, transpositions, languages, and other musical matters, just the same as any other conductor.

ORCHESTRAL CONDUCTORS

There seems to be much debate about the best training and background for conductors. Many working conductors feel that it is essential for an aspiring conductor to work at the undergraduate level on all of the following: becoming proficient on an instrument, including piano; studying composition and analysis; gaining a background in the humanities, with special attention to literature and art history; taking as much music theory and ear-training as possible; attending as many rehearsals and concerts as possible; and learning foreign languages, including Italian, German, and French.

A common belief is that it is good training to be an assistant to an established conductor, doing an apprenticeship of sorts. While the Exxon/Affiliate Artist program is the most established way of doing this, it is highly competitive. Concentration in conducting, if desired in a school setting, should come at the graduate level. Be sure to ask how much time is spent in the classroom and how much is spent actually conducting an orchestra. Are your rehearsals recorded for your review? Will you ever have any opportunities to conduct in public? Are various art forms part of your training? Ballet orchestras? Opera? Contemporary ensembles?

In training to be a conductor, there is no substitute for time. Since the development of the conductor's ear is critical, try to sit in on orchestra rehearsals, not just in the audience, but in various sections of the orchestra. It is also important to be aware of the politics of the business and to develop an appropriate presentation of yourself. You must be extremely well organized, able to get along with everyone from the music director and administrative director, to all players in the orchestra, ladies auxiliary committees, and the coat room attendant. You must be prepared to conduct youth concerts, pops concerts, and senior citizen pre-concert lectures, and be part of an organization's sense of civic pride.

COMPOSERS

While there is some consensus about what makes for good piano playing or singing, for instance, the scope of what is considered "good" or "bad" in the composition world is very broad. It is important, therefore, in your investigation that you do careful research about composition departments. Are you comfortable with their philosophy? Do you understand and respect each other's musical idiom? Do you want your life as a composer do be more "academic," i.e. involving teaching and writing on the side, or do you intend to focus on having your music performed? What sort of facilities are available for you to use? Computer publishing programs? How often will you be guaranteed that your music will be played? With what other composers will you have contact and in what forum?

One well-known composer suggested that composition majors look for a department that is strongly oriented toward synthesis and studio technique with a willingness to be on the cutting edge of new techniques in using computers and other technology. He suggested listening to

National Public Radio (NPR), the noncommercial radio broadcast throughout the United States and parts of Canada, especially the "new sounds" of John Schaeffer's program. He also suggested that you hang out at your local music store and become acquainted with the new technology in instruments, get to know who the musicians are in your neighborhood, and go to "alternative" concerts and talk to the performers afterwards.

Other composers stress the importance of having a strong background in music theory and music history, with careful attention to analyzing scores. Learn everything from species counterpoint to the most complex analysis of music and listen to as much music as possible. One composer tells the story of a young person coming to an audition and being asked what composers he likes to listen to. The applicant responded, "Stravinsky." "What of his do you particularly like?" The applicant said, "The Rite of Spring." The professor said, "Oh, have you heard it live or do you have a favorite recording?" "No," said the applicant. "Then have you studied the score in depth?" "No, I've never looked at it," replied the applicant. Learn from this example: Study scores, listen to music of all kinds, attend as many concerts as possible, and talk to as many living composers as you can. Look at scores with an eye toward figuring out orchestration, instrumentation, transpositions, clefs, and the basic layout of the score. Learn as much about computers and their musical applications and software as possible.

At your audition in composition you will probably be asked not only to speak about your compositional choices and technique, but also given detailed questions about the music of the "masters" such as Bach and Beethoven, so prepare accordingly. Also remember that when you send your scores, you should not send the originals.

JAZZ

Jazz is now sometimes referred to as "classical jazz." Improvising, while the most natural way to make music, requires great skill in the jazz idiom. Jamey Aebersold, a nationally known saxophonist and jazz educator, once wrote in the *International Musician:*

There are several ingredients that go into making a good jazz soloist/improviser:

- Desire to improvise

- Listening to jazz via recordings and live performances

- A method of practice—knowing what and how to practice

- A rhythm section with which to practice and improvise (via live group or play-along "music minus one" recordings)

- Self-esteem, discipline, and determination

Many students of jazz wonder if they will ever be able to play on their instruments the melodies that they hear in their heads. Ms. Aebersold suggests that you begin not only by listening, but by practicing simple melodies such as "Happy Birthday," starting on one note in the middle of the register of your instrument, and then playing it starting on any of the twelve notes of the chromatic scale. This is an excellent way of conditioning your fingers and mind to work together to produce the sounds you are hearing in your head.

It is recommended that jazz musicians do a regular warm-up, which might include playing the first five notes to each chord/scale, playing the seventh and ninth chords, up and down, and variations on this, such as playing the scale up to the ninth and then coming back down the chord. This sort of warm-up conditions your mind and fingers to the scales and chords over which you will improvise.

Transcribing solos or portions of solos from recordings is also highly recommended. Analyze the solo for things like whether the soloist uses scales or bits and pieces of scales; has favorite licks that are used repeatedly; or uses chromatics or passing tones, silence/rests, or rhythmic variety—double time, for instance.

Jazz studies at the college or university level have become very sophisticated, and there are some excellent programs. Many require that you be as proficient on your instrument as any player in the strictly "classical" area. An audition is usually required, either in person or by recording. You are usually asked to perform three pieces. Be sure to offer standards and not present three of your own compositions. Play in the style with which you are most comfortable. If you are not a bebopper, do not feel compelled to present a bebop solo. You may be asked to improvise and even sit in with a house band. Listen well and be positive. Be sure that you have listened to such jazz greats as Charlie Parker, Duke Ellington, Thelonious Monk, Coleman Hawkins, Dizzy Gillespie, Sonny Stitt, and Sonny Rollins; that you have studied privately; and that you have "learned by doing"—working with a band and getting gigs.

For Music Majors

POPULAR MUSICIANS

Popular musicians vary widely in their training and range from having the most sophisticated awareness of music theory and ear-training to completely unschooled natural talent, enthusiasm, and ability.

Rock musicians have traditionally had about four years of private lessons and played in bands. Many lack reading skills, but most rock musicians have great ears and if given a passage, can repeat it with little trouble. To make the leap ahead, rock musicians should study music theory and concentrate on chord/scale relationships along with their playing ability and ensemble experience. Rock musicians would do well to be acquainted with lots of other musical styles, including jazz, R&B, the blues (people like Lightnin' Hopkins, John Lee Hooker, and Muddy Waters, for example), and country music. Also, because rock performances are almost athletic events, it is important for rock musicians to be in good physical shape.

Those who want to go on in commercial/pop music have also usually had at least three years of private lessons. Singers would do well to listen to Barbra Streisand, Ella Fitzgerald, Aretha Franklin, Frank Sinatra, Bing Crosby, Elvis Presley, and Sarah Vaughan, among others. It is also worthwhile to be exposed to a number of different styles: country music, big band, R&B, church music, folk, the blues, and rock. Diction, rhythm, and good sight-reading are very important skills to develop. Pop singers should also work hard on being as disciplined with themselves as the most focused classical musician. While there are a few good college programs for popular and commercial musicians, this is an area where you learn by doing, so performing as much as possible is vitally important, combined with some good coaching and private instruction.

MUSICAL THEATER

The best preparation for musical theater is to study voice, dance, and acting. At many auditions you will be required to sing one or two selections from musical theater. In choosing these, offer contrasting styles; one up-tempo number demonstrating your rhythm and performance pizzazz; and then another that has strong emotional content, usually a ballad. At some schools you may be asked to discuss your choices and interpretation. You may also be required to take a dance class, where you may be taught a routine and those evaluating the audition will be reviewing not just how well you move, but how well you take direction and respond to corrections. Be sure to bring appropriate clothing and shoes for this: dance attire or gym shorts or sweats are common for this part of the audition. Ask if you need tap or ballet shoes, or kneepads. Read the school's material to see if anything is specified. For the theater segment of your audition you maybe asked to present a monologue or two or to do a reading. In preparation for this multi-level audition, be sure that you have rehearsed your song with a pianist and not with the Broadway cast recording. Be prepared to be stopped after 16 measures. You should have taken both dance and acting classes and have participated in school and community productions.

In evaluating any college-level musical theater programs, be sure that the training is comprehensive in music, dance, and theater. Like singers, musical theater majors should consider acquiring at least two years of liberal arts studies. Be sure that you spend your summers wisely, however, getting as much experience as possible in summer stock.

Researching Teachers for Consultations and Lessons

Choosing the teacher with whom you would like to study is a vitally important decision. Ask your current teacher for recommendations and then do lots of investigation on your own. Read the biography of the teacher in the catalog. Has the person studied with other people who uphold a tradition that you would like to follow? What is the teacher's performing background? Is the teacher an adjudicator for major competitions? Talk to students who currently work with the person you are considering. Are they pleased with their progress? Do they have regular lessons? During those lessons do they have the teacher's undivided attention?

Because so much of the relationship between teacher and student is personal, you must be sure that the chemistry between you works. This is difficult to determine unless you are able to speak to the teacher directly or, even better, to arrange a sample lesson, often called a consultation. You should be prepared to pay anywhere from $125 to $250 for such a meeting. At that time, you will play or sing for the teacher, see if you can work together, and ask all the questions you want. Do not be intimidated about asking questions about how this person works, where he or she sees your major weaknesses now, and what direction your lessons may take. If a personal meeting is not possible, you might call, write, or send an e-mail to the teacher in care of the school and ask if you could send a recording for his or her evaluation. Then follow up with a telephone conversation.

Famous or big-name teachers are not necessarily the best. You are looking for a teacher who will be best for you at this stage of your development as a performer. While "name" teachers may help somewhat at a certain time in your development, especially with the politics of the business, they may not give you the attention that you need to make progress in your technique. Will you receive a weekly lesson from that teacher, or be taught by an assistant?

If you are assigned to a teacher and then discover that the relationship is not working out, do not despair. Still, approach this change with utmost sensitivity and care. A student-teacher relationship is a business agreement of sorts; the teacher is being paid to teach you. If you need to

Performing

Arts

make a change, most conservatories and departments of music have a procedure for this that will involve as little misery on either part as possible. You will need to have a conversation with the teacher, or perhaps write the teacher a letter. This may be difficult, but it is better that you make a change than remain trapped in a situation that is not beneficial. Remember that the music world is very small, however, and you never know when you'll encounter this person again. Will they be judging that big competition that is important for your future? Be sure you move on with tremendous good will.

For Music Majors

Questions to Ask at a Campus Visit

- What role does the audition play in my admission? Is it the major criterion, or does my high school or college record count also?

- What role do exams such as ear training play in my admission?

- Is a personal interview required? If so, who conducts the interview?

- What is the music department enrollment?

- What is the enrollment in my instrument? Is there a quota?

- What general education courses are offered? Required? Is there any cross-registration with another school?

- How many faculty members are there for my instrument? Will I have a wide enough variety of choice in case I want to make a teacher change?

- How often do students have lessons? Am I guaranteed to have lessons with my major teacher? How often do assistants teach major lessons?

- What is the policy on performance evaluations (juries)? How often are they held? Are students ever cut from the program based on a jury?

- What are the facilities like? How many teaching studios? What equipment is in them? How many performance halls are there?

- How many practice rooms are there? What is their availability? (Ask a student if there is ever a problem securing a practice room.)

- In general, how often do students perform each semester? How many fully produced concerts are there? Informal concerts? Operas? In-school performances (i.e., at a high school)? Recitals? Contemporary music concerts? Other opportunities?

Performing Arts

- Is there a program of master classes? Who has taught them recently?

- Who are some of the well-known alumni of the school?

- What sort of job-placement service does the school provide?

- What do most alumni do?

- Is there an alumni network of any sort?

- What is competition like at the school?

- What ensembles will I be required to participate in?

- How are orchestral assignments made? (Ask a student if the orchestral assignments are fair.) Is there a policy of rotation within the orchestra?

- Do you have a program for engaging guest conductors? Who have been the recent conductors?

- What is the policy for casting operas? Is the policy fair? (Ask current students.)

- What chorus requirements are there for singers?

- Is there an opportunity to get certified in music education?

- What other related courses are taught? Music engineering? Music criticism? Piano tuning?

- Is there any affiliation between the school and any other musical organization, such as the local symphony, opera, or jazz clubs?

- Are any tours anticipated?

- Are there exchange programs with any schools?

- During the auditions, are teachers informed about who has applied for them?

- Who evaluates the auditions? How are they run?

For Music Majors

- What chamber music opportunities are there? Any requirements for chamber music? Who coaches ensembles?

- Do you hold any sessions on how to audition for orchestras, companies, etc., for after graduation?

- What is the feeling at this school about regional auditions? Recorded versus live auditions?

- Do you ever defer admissions decisions?

A Current Music Major Speaks Out

NATALIA KIENIEWICZ
Applied Music in Voice (Vocal Performance)
University of Delaware

WHAT ADVICE CAN YOU GIVE HIGH SCHOOL SENIORS WHO ARE THINKING OF MAJORING IN MUSIC IN COLLEGE?

My best advice is to be prepared to make a commitment to your major: it's not for people who just don't know what else to do with themselves. There is nothing wrong with being undeclared. If you love music and think that it is what you want to do with your life, then by all means go for it. But it's not easy, and you shouldn't expect it to be. It's a lot of work and a lot of disappointment sometimes, but when your work pays off the feeling is incredibly rewarding.

WHAT SHOULD PROSPECTIVE MUSIC STUDENTS LOOK FOR IN A COLLEGE?

As a music student, it is most important to look for a teacher you can trust to point you in the right direction. A solid program at a school is a great thing, but it doesn't matter how great the program is if you are not developing your technique as a musician. At the same time, I find it important to be in an environment that is at least somewhat positive and inspiring. Backstabbing gets old fast, but at the same time, so does being surrounded by bad musicians.

HOW DID YOU PREPARE FOR BECOMING A MUSIC MAJOR WHEN YOU WERE IN HIGH SCHOOL?

I worked some on my repertoire, but mostly I tried to develop at least a concept of good singing technique so that when I was looking at colleges I could get a feel for whom I could trust. I asked people I trusted for recommendations of colleges with good teachers and good programs. I looked at the artist histories of current singers I liked to see where they studied— and it wasn't always at a conservatory. Additionally, I took language courses in high school that I knew would be beneficial. I managed to get a 4 on the AP German test and I spent a month of the summer after I graduated in Germany.

WHAT IS YOUR TYPICAL DAILY SCHEDULE LIKE?

I generally wake up around 8 a.m., though sometimes earlier if I need to get things done before class. I shower (most of the time), eat breakfast, and drink lots of coffee. It supposedly dehydrates you and is therefore not recommended for singers, but I won't sing very well if I'm falling asleep, so I don't have much of a moral crisis about it. I'm in class and rehearsal at any time from 9 a.m. until 9:30 p.m., with gaps of an hour or two or three interspersed when I eat lunch, practice, procrastinate, go to work, do homework, and/or (if I'm extremely lucky) nap. Most days I'm done by 5 or 6 p.m. and I can do something fun like yoga or bellydancing or reading. My voice lesson is usually the highlight of my week, work-wise. I take mostly music classes, but since I go to a four-year university, I also have core requirements. I actually really enjoy them, because it gets me out of the music building, and I can exercise a different part of my brain. As a music student, I take a lot of pleasure in having friends outside my department. I was on the school's Ultimate Frisbee team until the end of sophomore year when I found it impossible to make the necessary commitment without compromising my musical studies.

Another sacrifice I had to make because of the enormous commitment that music requires was a rather lucrative job as a waitress. I work 11 hours a week at the University library, which is a flexible work environment. Some semesters I can work more hours, sometimes I can't even hold onto 10 without going crazy. I'm also President of our school's chapter of Amnesty International, which is a fair amount of work but it is incredibly important to me. Additionally, although I don't believe in having a "fall-back plan" (you always end up using it), I do feel like I have garnered a great deal of experience doing this, and I could potentially look for work in the human rights world if I had to.

So when I finally do get home "for good," (sometimes around 6 or 7 p.m., sometimes at 10) I make dinner and mess around on the computer. If I have work to do that I absolutely can't put off, I take care of it. I have study groups, or do social things, I exercise, or sometimes I lie around and watch a movie. I'm often pretty exhausted when I go to bed. It used to be around 2 or 3 a.m., but these days I try to get to bed around 1. Guess I'm getting old or something.

WHAT WAS THE BIGGEST SURPRISE YOU FOUND ONCE YOU GOT TO COLLEGE?

I was really surprised to find out what I am capable of and at the same time how far I have to go.

WHAT KINDS OF PROJECTS ARE YOU CURRENTLY WORKING ON?

I recently gave my Junior Recital, which was a fantastic success after months and months of hard work. I have two competitions this weekend, and a third two weeks from now. This summer, I am participating in a summer opera program in Graz, Austria, at the American Institute of Musical Studies.

WHAT CAREER PATH DO YOU HOPE TO FOLLOW?

When I graduate, I plan to move overseas to Austria or Germany. This summer, when I am in Graz, I hope to connect with a teacher who will agree to take me on after I graduate. I am lucky enough to have the right to British citizenship, meaning that I can live and work anywhere in the European Union without having to obtain a work visa. I also speak enough German to get around. I plan to take voice lessons and work for awhile, do competitions, and apply for young artist studios at opera companies. After a year or so, I will decide if I want to apply for graduate school.

Alternative Careers for Music Majors

People trained as musicians may be found in every career from insurance to medicine to college administration. With technological advancements the nature of the music business is constantly changing. Some other related careers include:

- Arranger/orchestrator

- Music critic

- Music copyists (be sure that you know some of the computer programs, such as Finale and Sibelius)

- Recording engineer

- Music therapist

- Instrument builder or repairer

- Music publisher

- Piano tuner

- Music manager

- Music librarian

- Music administrator: schools, orchestras, choruses

- Radio announcer

- Box office manager

- Development director

- Teacher: elementary, secondary, college, or private instruction

If you do decide to teach, you should be sure that you are proficient on the piano for accompanying choruses or other ensembles. If you plan to teach in a public school, you will need certification, so be certain to take appropriate courses.

Performing

Arts

What to Put in Your College Notebook

Use the sample Music Program Rating Sheet below or one of your own design:

MUSIC PROGRAM RATING SHEET
Size of department: Enrollment _____   Teachers _____
Lessons: How often? With major teachers or assistants?
Facilities: Number of teaching studios, practice rooms
Performances: How often? Type (concerts, operas, recitals, etc.)
Master classes: Availability? Recent teachers?
Exchange Programs with other schools?
Affiliation between school and other musical organizations?
Curriculum: General education requirement? Certificate in Music Ed?
Techniques taught:
Audition workshops:
Job placement record:
Famous alumni:
Current students' opinions:
My Personal Reaction:

Admissions Checklist

Here are some questions to ask yourself at various points in the admissions process.

Have I:

- checked out the Web site for any schools or programs of interest?

- requested catalogs and read them carefully and critically?

- requested applications and made photocopies of the ones in which I am interested?

- started a college notebook with my impressions of colleges and notes about audition requirements, dates, etc?

- noted repertoire requirements?

- obtained a social security number (United States and Permanent Residents)?

- registered for PSATs?

- obtained information about the ARTS scholarships? (National Foundation for Advancement in the Arts, 444 Brickell Avenue, Miami, FL 33131; 305-377-1140; www.artsawards.org)?

- made an appointment with my guidance counselor?

- looked into working with an independent counselor, if appropriate?

- talked with my current private music teacher about plans for my future?

- made arrangements to continue my music lessons?

- discussed high school courses to take?

- been taking regular private lessons?

- participated regularly in music programs at my school or in the community?

- discussed which standardized tests to take and when?

- discussed whether tutoring for standardized tests is appropriate for me?

- investigated summer programs and/or jobs and applied and taken auditions as necessary?

- investigated sources and policies regarding financial aid and scholarships?

- kept a file of performance programs, DVDs, or videotapes of performances, good term papers, articles, etc.?

- attended college fairs and met with college representatives who visited my school?

- registered for any standardized tests required (SAT, ACT Assessment, TOEFL, SAT Subject Tests)?

- met again with my guidance counselor?

- arranged my college visits?

- scheduled any interview appointments?

- sent thank-you notes after my college interviews?

- chosen my audition material?

- narrowed my list of colleges?

- settled on decision plans?

- asked for letters of recommendation, if necessary?

- drafted any essays?

- finished my essays and applications and photocopied everything before mailing?

- applied for financial aid, if necessary?

- requested that official test score reports be sent directly to the colleges that require them?

- done mock auditions and recorded them for my own critique?

- submitted any recordings for pre-screening, if required?

- had photographs taken to submit with applications, if necessary?

- prepared a resume?

- requested that a copy of my transcript be sent to the college?

- communicated regularly with my guidance counselor or guidance adviser about my progress in the college admissions process and in school?

- kept up with all school work?

- prepared a list of extracurricular activities, if necessary?

- arranged for an accompanist for my audition, if necessary?

- checked that all financial aid documentation is complete?

- read carefully any audition or schedule information sent to me?

- prepared photocopies of piano music for my accompanist?

- made copies of any original compositions I intend to perform?

- responded to colleges about any offers of admission?

- requested an extension beyond the May 1 CDR, if necessary?

- continued with regular music lessons and ensemble opportunities?

For Theater Majors

If you're planning on hearing "break a leg" or "lights, camera, action" in your future, be prepared for a lot of competition, starting with your college applications. Keep in mind that theater programs all have their own personality and mission. You'll want to make sure that the one you choose meets your needs, talents, and professional goals.

Advanced Study in Theater

"All the world's a stage," and so many young people aspire to be in the spotlight. There is debate among actors about the best training. Some believe that years of training provide a distinct advantage; others suggest relying on natural talent and instincts. There is a school of thought that says that taking too many classes in acting develops a dependency wherein you become a professional student, rather than a professional actor, and another that says that you can never take too many classes in voice, acting, and movement, and should never stop studying. For a young actor, there are many available options.

BACHELOR OF ARTS VS. BACHELOR OF FINE ARTS

The essential difference between these two programs involves proportion in course work. In a Bachelor of Arts (B.A.) degree program, you will be expected to study a broad range of courses in the liberal arts and sciences and, at some schools, to fulfill distribution requirements. You might major in theater (called a drama or acting major at some schools) and take a certain number of credit hours in this as your major, but the proportion of liberal arts to theater courses is tilted in the direction of the liberal arts. A Bachelor of Fine Arts (B.F.A.) program is more heavily weighted on the theater side.

For certain people there is a distinct advantage to attending a liberal arts college and majoring in theater. For one thing, the number of students who change their major after freshman year is extremely high. If you were locked into a B.F.A. program, you might have more trouble changing to another major than you would in a B.A. program, where changing majors is common. Another reason to attend a liberal arts college to obtain a B.A. is just for the very breadth of learning in a wide range of subjects. When you create a role, you can call more to it if you have a background in literature and history than if you know only the theater. Finally, you are likely to encounter a more diverse student body at a liberal arts college than you would at a specialized school. This very diversity might influence you in creating a role someday.

If you do choose the liberal arts route, you must look very carefully at the strength of the theater department. In some liberal arts colleges, theater courses are taught through the English department. What is the curriculum? A liberal arts college offering a theater major that teaches only theater history, dramatic literature, and a basic acting course probably does not have the strongest theater department. How many faculty members are there? Do they also work in conjunction with a dance and/or music department? A theater department with fewer than four faculty members may not be considered a priority by the administration and may not present to you enough variety in your learning. Investigate carefully.

The B.F.A. program is for students who want to focus immediately on specific theater skills. If you know, without a doubt, that you want to pursue your major in theater and that you want that focus, a good B.F.A. program may be for you.

Most B.F.A. programs, either at conservatories or at universities, do require an audition, even if you have been admitted into the main school. Prepare thoroughly for the audition.

Note for International Students: If English is not your native language and you speak with a heavy accent, quite bluntly, your chances for admission to a theater program in a competitive U.S. conservatory or B.F.A. program are not strong. A B.A. program will be more flexible.

RESUMES FOR THEATER STUDENTS

Most theater programs ask for a copy of your resume. If you have had a great deal of experience, putting your resume together will not be a problem. Just get used to keeping it up-to-date. If your experience has been limited to high school productions and classes, this is absolutely fine. Present your background and qualifications honestly. Knowing about your previous experience may be useful to the admissions committee, but how you handle the audition will count the most.

There is no one prescribed format for theater resumes. There is certain standard background information that should appear, however, including your name, address, phone numbers (day, evening, and cell), e-mail address, height, weight, eye and hair color, and voice range, if you sing. Experience may be broken down into categories including theater or stage, musicals, summer stock, film, television, etc. A high school student might list high school productions, summer work, workshops, and master classes. Include names of your teachers. Mention any specialized skills, such as playing a musical instrument, gymnastics, stage combat, fencing, ice skating, juggling, mime, skateboarding, horseback riding, whistling, etc.

A good resume should be on 8½ × 11 paper (white bond, not colored), word-processed (easy for regular updating), and certainly be no longer than two pages; a one-page resume for theater is best. This resume should be attached to your head shot. (See pages 134 to 136 for three typical resumes: one for a freshman applicant, one for a transfer student, and one for a graduate student.)

HEAD SHOTS

Many programs will request that you submit a head shot with your resume and application. If you do not have a professional photo, do not allow this to stop you from applying or delay you in sending in your application. Instead, submit the application with a note saying that you are having the head shot done and will submit it as soon as possible.

Your application head shot should look like you and present a pleasant impression. Just as you should go for a somewhat conventional look in your dress for a college interview, you should choose a pose and overall look for your head shot that calls attention to your eyes, your face. Do not wear outrageous jewelry, pose in a provocative way, or choose a hairstyle that focuses attention on your hair rather than on you. Selective schools claim never to have admitted candidates who submitted head shots that were either in bad taste or particularly weird or inappropriate.

Finding a good photographer to take your head shot can be a challenge. If you do not live in a city, you might ask the photography teacher at your high school for a recommendation, or perhaps he or she might take it for you. Bring along some head shots you like from programs or newspapers as samples. Yearbook photographers who are experienced in photographing in black and white are also a possibility. You do not have to spend an exorbitant amount of money on your head shot. Go for quality with economy, if that is possible. *The Back Stage Handbook for Performing Artists* (Sherry Eaker, editor) has a helpful article about head shots. It suggests that you ask a prospective photographer some of the following questions:

- Have you taken head shots before? Could I see your portfolio? (When reviewing the portfolio, look at the expression in the eyes that the photographer has captured in each photograph. Is the look engaging or vacant? Is the smile genuine or tense? Does the pose capture the "best side" of the person, or just look staged? Does the skin texture look real? Does the photograph have the look of a real person or someone who has been retouched and airbrushed into a homogenized glamorous look? How is the lighting?)

- What format do you use? Digital? Film?

- Do you take Polaroids first? Could I see some before-and-after shots?

- What do you charge for head shots? (Prices generally range from $200 to $1,500.) What is included in this fee?

- How many rolls of film do you shoot? What format do you use? Do you give your clients the negatives or charge for them? Do you charge for airbrushing or retouching? Do you do the blowups and reprints yourself or will you recommend where I can get them done?

- How long will it be before I get to see the contact sheets?

- How far in advance do I need to book a sitting? How long is a typical sitting?

- Do you require a deposit? Will you refund the deposit or reshoot if I don't like the results?

- Are hair and make-up included in the price? Will you recommend a stylist?

It is very important that you feel a rapport with the photographer. When you feel comfortable during a photo session, the photographs themselves reflect this. If the chemistry just is not right between you and the photographer, find someone else.

Here are some things you should bring to your photo session:

- changes of clothing, with particular attention to your waist-up look;

- additional make-up;

- hairbrush, comb, hair spray, mousse, or gel;

- extra shaving equipment for men;

- a favorite photo of yourself done in the past;

- anything that will help you to relax, such as tapes (I've even known people to bring a favorite stuffed animal or herbal tea);

- any props that you discuss in advance with your photographer, such as glasses, a book, or a musical instrument; and

- additional jewelry, such as a change of earrings.

Once you have the contact sheets, show them to a variety of people—your parents, teachers, friends, and agent (if you have one)—and seek opinions. Keep track of these opinions on a separate piece of paper. The photographer will probably indicate his or her two favorite choices. Remember that this is a photograph that you will have to live with for probably two or three years before you update it, so choose carefully. Be sure that your head shot has your name on either the front or back, so that if it becomes separated from your resume, the photograph can still be identified.

For Theater Majors

FRESHMAN RESUME

John A. Doe
123 Main Street
Anytown, U.S.A.
(123) 456-7890

EDUCATION

A. I. Du Pont High School	Diploma anticipated, June 2006

EXPERIENCE

2006	This is a Test (Pat)	One-act play A.I. Du Pont High School
2005	Renaissance Faire	
	St. George and the Dragon (Reginald Brown)	Delaware Theater Company
2005	Cinderella, Cinderella . . . (Prince Charming)	Wilmington Drama League
2005	To Kill a Mockingbird (Townsperson)	Delaware Theater Company
2005	Baby (Father)	One-act play A. I. Du Pont High School
2005	Zombie Army (Orderly)	Film Cheapshot Productions, Inc.
2004	Get Smart (Professor Dante)	Senior play A. I. Du Pont High School

TRAINING AND EXTRA ACTIVITIES

Two years theater/acting class	A. I. Du Pont High School
One year public speaking	Carson Long Military Institute
Senior Literary Society	Carson Long Military Institute
The Art of Acting	Delaware Technical & Community College
Drama Club	
The International Thespian Society	A. I. Du Pont High School

TECHNICAL WORK

2004	Get Smart	Play. Light and makeup.

One-Act Plays

2003	This Is a Test	A. I. Du Pont High School
2002	Pink Lemonade	
2002	Drive-in	

AWARDS AND COMPETITION

Third Place, Declamation Contest	Carson Long Military Institute
Julius Caesar (Marcus Antonius)	

OTHERS SKILLS

Certified scuba diver.   Juggler.   Expert whistler.

REFERENCES AND RECOMMENDATIONS

Available upon request.

Performing Arts

TRANSFER STUDENT RESUME

MARCIA SMITH

123 4th Avenue
New York, New York 10003
212-123-4567—home

Height: 5'4"
Weight: 120
Hair: Brown
Eyes: Brown

THEATER

THANK YOU AMY	Amy	Theater in the Square
THE DINING ROOM	Ensemble	Tisch School of the Arts, NYU
NO COMMENT CAB.A.RET	Sandy	Tisch School of the Arts
VESTLESS ATTIRE	Ensemble	The Gas Station
CINDERELLA	Cinderella	Boston Children's Theater
LUDLOW FAIR	Rachel	Directing Project Williamstown Theater Festival
PARLOUR GAMES	Ensemble	Massachusetts College of Art
THIRD RAIL	Cathy	Emerson College

TELEVISION AND FILM

RAP AROUND (Four Segments)	Jessica	WBZ-TV
PUBLIC SERVICE ANNOUNCEMENT	Girl	WBZ-TV
CHILDREN AND DIVORCE		WNEV-TV
SIDEWALK	Girl	Tisch School of the Arts

SUMMER

Institute Member	2006	National Shakespeare Conservatory
Apprentice	2005	Williamstown Theater Festival
Young Critic's Institute	2004	Huntington Theater

TRAINING

Classes:	Lyric Stage, Wheelock Family Theater, Boston Children's Theater
Participant:	Oberlin Theater Institute Circle in the Square Theatre School
Currently attending: B.F.A. program	Tisch School of the Arts, New York University

AWARDS

National Foundation for the Advancement in the Arts:
   Arts Recognition and Talent Search Awardee, 2004

National Endowment for the Humanities Scholar:
   Young Critic's Institute–Huntington Theater

Presidential Scholar in the Arts:
   Semifinalist, 2004

OTHER SKILLS

Ice skate; Fencing; Mime

GRADUATE STUDENT RESUME

SARA GREEN
Height: 5'6"
Age Range: 18–24

SAG/AFTRA
AEA (Eligible)

12 EAST 90th STREET, NY, NY 10004
    cell: **2 1 2 - 6 6 6 - 1 1 1 1**
home: **2 1 2 - 3 4 5 - 6 7 8 9**

High soprano

theater
BLACK ICE	Lady Die	Kampo Cultural Center/Dean Mitchell
CRIMES OF THE HEART	Lenny	Herald Square Players/Boy Byrd

films
NEW JACK CITY	Crack Addict	Jac/Mac Prods./Mario Van Peebles
IDENTITY CRISIS	Gang Member	Block & Chip Prods./Melvin Van Peebles

television
AMAZING UNSOLVED MYSTERIES	Angelica	WWOR-TV
COSBY SHOW	Church Attendant	NBC
CHEERS	Karen (Bar Patron)	NBC
L.A. LAW	Court Stenographer	NBC
HARD BALL	Sara B (Homeless Woman)	NBC
THE LAKER GIRLS	Laker Cheerleader	CBS (Pilot)

commercials/voice overs
List Available Upon Request

training

Commercial: Reed-Sweeney-Reed—Pat Sweeney . . . On-Camera Technique
SAG & AFTRA Conservatory—Affiliated Instructors . . . On-Camera Commercial Tech. & Improv.
Hyde Hamlet Casting–Sara Hamlet . . . On-Camera Technique

Acting: Video Perspectives—Boy Byrd . . . Sitcom Workshop
Herbert Berghof Studios—Michael Beckett . . . Scene Study & Technique I, II

Dance: Broadway Dance Center—Sue Samuels . . . Jazz Technique I
Broadway Dance Center—FarnsworthàBallet Technique I
Ruth Williams Dance Studios—Ruth Williams . . . Modern Dance/Ballet

Voice: NY School of Commercial Music—Ruth DeBrow . . . Mezzo-Soprano

Education: B.A. Architecture—Syracuse University
Member of Black Filmmakers Foundation

special skills Jamaican, Southern & New York Dialects; Syracuse University, Cheerleader (3 years); Aerobics/Weight Training; Roller Skating; Double-Dutch Jumping; Scuba Diving (certified); Licensed Driver; Excellent with Children and Pets. Own Evening Gowns, Nurse Uniform, and selection of 10 Wigs and Hairpieces.

Performing

Arts

Theater Auditions

It is very important for theater students to submit applications well in advance of any deadlines. Because there are usually many more applicants to theater programs than can be accepted, one means of elimination is to observe the deadline strictly. Do not procrastinate in sending your application! And, if possible, schedule your first-choice school as your second or third audition, not your first.

WHAT TO EXPECT

Most theater auditions consist of presenting monologues of your choice from memory. Some programs may assign required monologues; ask you to improvise; sing *a cappella* (unaccompanied); participate in a movement class; do a group theater activity or "theater game"; possibly do a dance combination; or do a cold reading. Some may also ask you to write an essay while you are there for the audition. A theater audition begins right when you walk in the door of the audition location. The way you greet the receptionist and introduce yourself makes a difference. If you are rude, pushy, withdrawn, or odd, that information will be relayed. At an audition, you are *always* being observed. When you attend an audition, there may be a group warm-up. If so, use this time to make sure that your voice is working and your body is relaxed. Once you enter the audition room, be prepared to answer a few short questions from the audition panel. Questions such as "Where are you from?" or "How did you get here today?" are intended to help you relax. This is not the time to be dramatic or to relate your entire life story, but the chance for you to answer politely and normally. If the audition panel suggests that you "take a few minutes to gather yourself before you present your first monologue," do not use the time to go through your whole warm-up in front of them. Just take a few deep breaths and think about getting into character for the part you will play.

CHOOSING MONOLOGUES

Some programs will give you a list of suggested monologues. The list is just that: suggestions. You need not choose something from the list, but consider it as a guideline for the type of material the audition panel considers appropriate. Be sure to observe the time limit suggested, usually two monologues, not to exceed a total length of four minutes. Most often you are asked to present one monologue from the classical repertoire and one contemporary monologue of a contrasting nature.

Some may ask for a lighter piece. Remember that a comedic monologue is NOT a stand-up comedy act! While researching monologues on the Internet or glancing through a book of monologues may be somewhat helpful, it is critical to know the whole play and the monologue in context; some audition panels may even ask you questions about the entire play. Many programs specify no dialects or old characters, and some programs are clear in their advice about choosing a character close to your own age. Be sure to read requirements carefully and rehearse well in advance. In some audition rooms, there may be a table and some chairs should you need them. Expect to be interrupted and stopped. Do not read into this; the panel may love you and just be pressed for time. All audition panels anticipate that auditioners may be nervous, and usually the panelists are quite sympathetic. It is a good idea to bring a clearly printed copy of your monologues with you. Some audition panels may follow along and be there to prompt you should you have a memory lapse. In choosing your monologues, give some thought to your "type." Are you an ingénue? A character actor? What age range are you most comfortable playing? Some people will work from a process of elimination: "I'm not a (fill in the blank)." The best advice is to choose a monologue you are comfortable performing and that you can present with conviction. Remember, an audition is a performance.

SUGGESTED MONOLOGUES FOR AUDITIONS

In surveying various Theater/Drama departments, the following seemed to be some commonly suggested monologues:

SAMPLE AUDITION SCENES FOR WOMEN		
CLASSICAL		
Aeschylus	Agamemnon	Clytemnestra (telling how she killed Agamemnon)
Beaumont/Fletcher	The Maid's Tragedy	Aspatia, Act II, Scene 1 (line 5)
Euripides	Trojan Women	Andromache (gives up son to be killed by Greeks)
	Iphigenia at Aulos	Iphigenia
Middleton	The Changeling	Beatrice Joanna

SAMPLE AUDITION SCENES FOR WOMEN—*continued*		
CLASSICAL—*continued*		
Shakespeare	The Merchant of Venice	Portia, Act III, Scene 2 (line 149)
	All's Well That Ends Well	Helena, Act I, Scene 3 (line 197)
	King John	Constance, Act III, Scene 1, (line 43)
	Richard III	Anne, Act I, Scene 2 (line 1)
	Henry IV, Part 1	Lady Percy, Act II, Scene 3 (line 40)
	Henry IV, Part 2	Lady Percy, Act II, Scene 3 (line 9)
	Hamlet	Ophelia, Act III, Scene 1 (line 158)
	Othello	Desdemona, Act I, Scene 3 (line 249)
	Comedy of Errors	Adriana, Act II, Scene 2 (line 111)
	Midsummer Night's Dream	Helena, Act III, Scene 2 (line 195)
	The Winter's Tale	Hermione, Act III, Scene 2 (line 90)
	The Winter's Tale	Paulina, Act III, Scene 2 (line 173)
	Cymbeline	Imogen, Act III, Scene 6 (line 1)
	Henry VI, Part 3	Queen Margaret, Act I, Scene 1 (line 230)
Sophocles	Antigone	Antigone (answering Creon, daring his law)
Webster	The White Devil	Vittoria (Trial Scene)

SAMPLE AUDITION SCENES FOR WOMEN—*continued*		
CONTEMPORARY		
Anouilh	The Lark	Joan
Chekhov	Three Sisters	Irina
	Uncle Vanya	Sonya
Elder	Ceremonies in Dark Old Men	Adelaide
Giraudoux	Apollo of Bellac	Agnes
Hansberry	A Raisin in the Sun	Beneatha
McNally	Noon	Allegra
Medoff	When You Coming Back, Red Ryder	Angel
O'Neill	Beyond the Horizon	Ruth
	Mourning Becomes Electra	Lavinia
Patrick	Kennedy's Children	Carla
Polikov, S.	City Sugar	Nicola, Scene 7
Rabe	In the Boom Boom Room	Chrissie
Shange	For Colored Girls . . .	
Shaw	Heartbreak House	Ellie
	Major Barbara	Barbara
Shepard	Tooth of Crime	Becky
	Angel City	Miss Scoom
	Buried Child	Shelie
Strindberg	Easter	Eleanora, Act I
Whiting, J.	The Devils	Sister Jeanne, Act I
Williams	Summer and Smoke	Alma
	Talk to Me Like the Rain	Girl
	Cat on a Hot Tin Roof	Maggie
	Orpheus Descending	Carol

SAMPLE AUDITION SCENES FOR MEN		
CLASSICAL		
Euripides	Hippolytus	Hippolytus (speech against women, after learning of Phaedra's love)
Jonson	The Alchemist	Sir Epicure, Act II, Scene 1
	The Alchemist	Subtle, Act II, Scene 2
Middleton	The Changeling	Deflores
Shakespeare	Taming of the Shrew	Petruchio, Act IV, Scene 1 (line 191)
	Two Gentlemen of Verona	Proteus, Act II, Scene 6 (line 1)
		Val, Act III, Scene 1 (line 170)
	Much Ado About Nothing	Benedick, Act II, Scene 3 (line 7)
	Twelfth Night	Sebastian, Act IV, Scene 3 (line 1)
	Troilus and Cressida	Ulysses, Act III, Scene 3 (line 145)
	Henry VI, Part 3	Richard of Gloucester, Act III, Scene 2 (line 124)
		Richard, Duke of York, Act I, Scene 4 (line 111)
	Henry V	Henry, Act I, Scene 1 (line 259)
		Henry, Act III, Scene 1 (line 1)
	Julius Caesar	Brutus, Act III, Scene 2 (line 13)
	Othello	Iago, Act I, Scene 3 (line 338)
		Othello, Act III, Scene 3 (line 258)

SAMPLE AUDITION SCENES FOR MEN—*continued*		
CLASSICAL—*continued*		
	Richard II	Mowbray, Act 1, Scene 3 (line 154)
	King Lear	Edgar, Act III, Scene 6 (line 102)
	Measure for Measure	Claudio, Act III, Scene 1 (line 117)
	The Tempest	Ferdinand, Act III, Scene 1 (line 1)
	Henry IV, Part 2	Prince Hal, Act IV, Scene 5 (line 20 or 138)
	Pericles	Pericles, Act I, Scene 1 (line 121)
	Titus Andronicus	Aaron the Moor, Act IV, Scene 2 (line 88)
Sheridan	The Rivals	Jack Absolute
Sophocles	Antigone	Messenger's Final Speech
Webster	The Duchess of Malfi	Ferdinand, Act III, Scene 2 (line 120)
	The Duchess of Malfi	Basola, Act V, Scene 2 (line 328)
CONTEMPORARY		
Babe	Kid Champion	Kid Bullins
	In the Wine Time	Cliff Dawson
Chekhov	The Three Sisters	Andrei
	The Seagull	Treplev
Davis	Mass Appeal	Mark Dolson
Elder	Ceremonies in Dark Old Men	Mr. Bluehaven
Gordone	No Place to Be Somebody	Johnny Williams
Horowitz	The Indian Wants the Bronx	

SAMPLE AUDITION SCENES FOR MEN—*continued*		
CONTEMPORARY—*continued*		
Ibsen	Ghosts	Oswald
Inge	Picnic	Hal
O'Neill	Beyond the Horizon	Rob
	Ah! Wilderness	Richard
Peterson, D.	Does the Tiger Wear a Necktie?	Bickell
Peterson, L.	Take a Giant Step	Spencer
Rabe	Pavlo Hummel	Pavlo
	Streamers	Billy
Shepard	Tooth of Crime	Hoss
	Buried Child	Vince or Tilden
	Curse of the Starving Class	Wesley
Wilder	Our Town	George
	The Matchmaker	Cornelius
Williams	Sweet Bird of Youth	Chance
	Cat on a Hot Tin Roof	Brick
	The Glass Menagerie	Tom
Wilson, L.	Burn This	Pale

If a program specifies that the classical piece must be in verse or blank verse, some playwrights to consider are: the Greeks; Lope de Vega; Christopher Marlowe; William Shakespeare; John Ford; John Webster; Racine in verse translation; William Congreve; Richard Brinsley Sheridan. For comedic monologues, be aware that Victoria Wood and Alan Bennett are frequently chosen.

CHOOSING SONGS

Most theater auditions will include asking you to sing a song unaccompanied. You need not think that you must have had extensive vocal training. The audition panel wants to get a sense of your vocal range and the basic quality of your voice. For musical theater auditions, you may be asked to prepare two songs: usually a ballad, to demonstrate your emotional range, sensitivity to the text, and lyrical phrasing and an up-tempo song to demonstrate your rhythm and showmanship. Choose repertoire that is age appropriate. Be in character when you are singing. And remember that humor helps.

DANCE

While most theater auditions will include some sort of movement class, others, especially for musical theater, will ask you to do a dance sequence. Ask in advance what kind of shoes you need to bring: tap, ballet, jazz, knee pads, etc. Inquire about what style of dance you might expect at the audition. Pay attention and have fun in this portion of the audition. A smile helps a lot.

WHAT TO WEAR

Black seems to be the color for theater auditions: women in black dresses, leotards with a skirt, or black pants and a black turtleneck, and men in black pants and turtlenecks. If this is your color, that's fine. The bottom line for your audition is to dress comfortably so that you can move freely, and yet nicely to indicate respect for the situation. Dress for theater auditions does seem to be more casual than for classical music auditions. For the basic monologue part of the audition, women should wear a skirt (not too short) and blouse or a dress or pants and a sweater or blouse, and shoes with low to medium heels. Men should choose a turtleneck and pants or a shirt and pants. Suits, or jackets and ties, are not recommended—and neither are sweat suits! Since an actor's body is his or her instrument, it is important to wear something that gives some indication of what shape you are in. Appearance matters for actors. While you do not want to show up in costume for your audition, keeping in mind your characters for your monologues and acknowledging that in a subtle way, may be helpful. You should inquire if there is a required movement class also, and bring appropriate attire for that. For a movement class, you may be asked to remove your jewelry and any piercings. (Remember, it is best to leave valuables at home.) If there are going to be dance auditions, be prepared with tap, jazz, and ballet shoes, as needed. And, if there are callbacks, many audition panelists suggest that you wear the same clothes as you did for the first audition to aid in recognition.

BEFORE YOU AUDITION

It is important that you know exactly what will be expected of you at the audition. Will you have to write an essay while you are there for the audition, to show that you can write in English? Does the audition schedule involve callbacks? How much time should you realistically set aside for this audition? Be sure to ask enough questions so that you know what to bring with you and what to expect.

PRACTICE AUDITIONS

The best way to prepare for an audition is to practice often in a mock audition situation. Do this several months in advance and videotape yourself. Ask members of your family, your teachers, and friends to critique your performance as you watch the tape. Remember, though, that audition panels want to see your interpretation of a monologue, not something that has been coached to death and reflects a teacher's version. Be simple and truthful. Do practice auditions often, up to a week before the actual audition, so that you feel totally comfortable about your presentation. Prepare yourself mentally so that you go to every audition with the most positive mental attitude, anticipating success.

NERVES

What do you do if you walk into the audition room and your knees are shaking, you cannot get a good breath, and your voice is quaking? It helps to remember that everyone else is in the same boat and an attack of nerves is totally normal. Try deep breathing: breathing in on a count of four and out on eight. Do not be ashamed to say, "I'm so nervous," but do not let that be an excuse for yourself. Use the beginning of the audition to relax as best you can, and then to get into the character of the first monologue. If you think of the audition panel as an audience at your performance, you may get past the nerves. It is very important in your overall actor training that you learn to take care of yourself. Educate yourself about nutrition and exercise, how to manage stress, handle rejection, prevent injury, and handle nerves constructively.

AUDITION EVALUATION CRITERIA

When an audition panel watches and listens to your audition, they are looking for several things. This may include your fluency in English; sense of humor; sense of language; imagination; energy; evidence of having an open mind; intellectual and artistic curiosity; willingness to take risks; work ethic; ability to read, understand, and interpret texts; concentration and focus; your overall physical appearance: body, weight, features; and voice. The audition sheets on pages 148–150 indicate the kinds of things the audition panel are evaluating.

WHAT *NOT* TO DO AT A THEATER AUDITION

- Do not try to play something other than the core of the part. Play the character and do not get caught up in the language.

- Do not just learn the monologue. Read the entire play and know the context for the monologue.

- Never leave the room during an audition. There are some humorous yet sad stories about applicants who either wanted to make an entrance or exit, in character, for their monologue and walked out of the room, only to discover that the door would not open again. Applicants who think they may get dry should bring water in with them to the audition, so as not to need to leave the room. Also, at the end of the audition, do not leave until the faculty panel invites you to go.

- Do not drag in props or set pieces. A piece of paper for a letter scene may be fine, but anything beyond that is not appropriate. Most places will have a chair or two and a table to use as props if you need them.

- Do not even think of changing costumes between monologues!

- Do not stand too close to the audition panel.

- Do not get up on the audition table.

- Do not use the audition panel as your scene partners. It is better to play slightly above their heads.

- Do not tell the audition panel your life story if you are asked a simple question.

- Do not cry before your scene.

- Do not do your warm-up in the audition room. Walk in prepared.

- Do not take forever with your "actor focus moment" before you start your scene.

- Do not change the lyrics of a song.

- Do not offer to sing an original song.

- Do not throw things around the room.

- Do not ask on the spot if you are getting the callback.

REGIONAL AUDITIONS

Theater programs will sometimes hold auditions in chosen cities as well as on campus. They will bring along faculty and administration members and treat these auditions as being as valid as any auditions on campus. Because regional auditions are very popular, it is important that you submit your application early, before all audition openings are booked.

DVDS OR VIDEOTAPES VS. LIVE AUDITIONS

A live audition is always better than a DVD or videotape. If you absolutely must submit a recording as your only possible way of auditioning, do not go for a glitzy professionally produced DVD or video, which will cost you a fortune in production. A well-done (hold the camera steady and have the picture in focus!) home version is fine for this, but remember you are not helping your chances for admission by not attending in person! Do not send an unsolicited recording, as it will probably end up in a pile—unwatched.

ACADEMY OF DRAMATIC ARTS

Audition Notes: _____

Auditioner: _____

Date: _____

Name: _____ Program: _____ M.F.A.: _____ CERTIFICATE: _____

CONTEMPORARY: _____

    Is talking immediate:

    Are actions used:

    Is there a purpose/arc:

    Is it spontaneous:

    Is there an organic character:

    Is it personalized:

    Are there clear transitions:

    Sense of humor:

    Trainable:

CLASSICAL: _____

    Vocal quality:

    Speech:

    Physically alive:

    Phrasing:

    Sensitivity to language:

    Use of actions:

    Use of self in the circumstances:

    Spontaneity:

_____ _____ _____ _____

  TAKE   POSSIBLE   LOW   NO
                            POSSIBLE

COMMENTS:

Performing

Arts

Audition Form

XXX UNIVERSITY
Department of Drama

Audition City: _____   Audition Date: _____

Option: Acting: _____   Musical Theater: _____

_____
Last Name   First Name   Initial

_____
Street   City   State   Zip

_____
Phone   Age   Height   Weight

_____
Language studied   Years studied

Musical Theater Option ONLY:
    Can you read music? _____   Sing? _____
    Play an instrument? _____   If yes, what? _____

_____
High School or College Name   City   State

Is there a reason why you can NOT participate in a strenuous program of development?
_____

_____

TRAINING . . . outside of high school	Acting	Singing	Dancing
Years studied	_____	_____	_____
Teacher's name	_____	_____	_____

EXPERIENCE . . . list representative roles; if you have a resume, please attach.

Play	_____	_____	_____	_____
Role	_____	_____	_____	_____
Date performed	_____	_____	_____	_____
Place perormed	_____	_____	_____	_____

AUDITION	Acting (two pieces REQUIRED)		Singing (Musical Theater ONLY —two pieces REQUIRED)	
Play/Song	_____	_____	_____	_____
Character	_____	_____	_____	_____

_____ DO NOT WRITE BELOW THIS LINE _____

012   345   678   9

_____signed _____date

PETERSON'S ACTING CONSERVATORY

CITY: _____   DATE: _____

NAME: _____   YES: _____

AGE: _____   NO: _____

POSSIBLE: _____

	CLASSICAL	CONTEMPORARY	COLD READING	ADDITIONAL
SCENE				
VOICE				
SPEECH				
BODY				
PERFORMANCE				

GENERAL IMPRESSIONS

APPEARANCE:

TRAINING:

ATTITUDE:

POTENTIAL:

OTHER REMARKS:

Signed: _____

Performing

Arts

Questions to Ask at a Campus Visit

- What is the enrollment in the theater department? Males? Females? Undergraduates? Graduates?

- Is the theater department embedded within another department?

- How many faculty members are there? Full-time? Part-time? What is the student/faculty ratio?

- How many faculty members are working professionally in the theater world? How many have more of an academic background and approach?

- Do you require an audition? If so, what is required?

- What does the basic curriculum entail? What acting technique is taught?

- What is the philosophy of the program?

- Who are your resident directors?

- Who have been recent directors of your productions?

- Do you have a program of master classes or guest speakers? Who has given these in the past two years? Did students have an opportunity to get to know the guests?

- What repertoire is performed?

- How and when do you evaluate a student's progress? Do you have a "cut" after one or two years?

- How often to the students perform each semester? Which of the following types of performing opportunities are available and how frequently: Fully produced productions? Informal workshops? Workshops? In-school performances (i.e., at high schools, etc.)? Off-campus performances?

- Are student-initiated projects encouraged? Is there a budget for these? What are examples of this in the past two years?

- What performing facilities are available for students (if you have not seen them on your campus tour)?

- How many productions are presented by your theater program each year?

- What is the casting policy? (Ask a student, "Is the casting policy fair?")

- (At a liberal arts college) Is there a theater club? What is the relationship between the extracurricular theater activities and the theater department?

- Does the college have a relationship with a professional theater company or summer stock theater? If so, which one and what is the relationship?

- Does the college help students to obtain an Equity card?

- Are there any restrictions on first-year (freshman) activities in the department? In casting?

- What are the strengths and weaknesses of this program?

- (Ask a student) If you had it all to do over again, would you choose this program?

- Who are some renowned alumni?

- What do the majority of alumni go on to do?

- Do you teach auditioning skills?

- Is there any sort of alumni network?

- Is there a technical requirement? Is so, what is it?

- Does the school recruit at any Thespian Societies? Which ones? Are there any scholarships available through these?

- Does the school participate in any of the regional events of the American College Theater Festivals?

- Is the program accredited by the National Association of Schools of Theatre?

For Theater Majors

A Current Theater Major Speaks Out

ALEXIS BRONKOVIC
Theater Arts
Marymount Manhattan College

WHAT ADVICE CAN YOU GIVE HIGH SCHOOL SENIORS WHO ARE THINKING OF MAJORING IN THEATER IN COLLEGE?

I would advise high school students to make sure that they enjoy other parts of the acting profession besides the lights and the applause. Most of your time at school is spent in class and alone in your room memorizing, researching, rehearsing, and auditioning. Even if you are cast in a lot of main stage college plays, they often only run for a few nights. Therefore you have to be able to appreciate the process and not just the end result. If there is one thing that you learn at school, it's that art is a process, not a product. Be prepared to work. The students that truly take their work seriously and aren't afraid to jump in are the students who find success in their classes.

HOW DID YOU PREPARE FOR BECOMING A THEATER MAJOR WHEN YOU WERE IN HIGH SCHOOL?

I spent much of my time working on high school and community theater productions and working in local playhouses trying to gain as much experience as possible. I wanted to try anything and everything because EVERY experience is a good one. The more auditions you go on, directors you work with, people you meet, and shows you are in, the more it will help.

WHAT IS YOUR TYPICAL DAILY SCHEDULE LIKE?

This semester I have a lot of theater classes. On Mondays, Wednesdays, and Fridays I head to Times Square for dance class at 9:30 a.m. Typically I walk, because well, I'm broke. But it's great exercise! After that, I walk home to take a quick shower and head to school where I work in the admissions office. I work there from about 12:30 to 4 p.m. and then I head to either acting class or musical theater techniques class. After those classes is when I might head to the library, run errands, rehearse, etc. Then I head home to the residence hall where I can get distracted from work by my friends or else I go on duty (I'm an R.A.). Often these shifts last until 12:30 a.m. On Tuesdays and Thursdays I begin my day with

Performing

Arts

voice and speech class at 10 a.m. After that I have a break to catch up on or start my reading for my 1 p.m. class, which is theater history. We always have textbook pages and a play to read for every class. On Thursdays I take the subway to the West Village for my voice lesson, and then go home, eat dinner, and go to my 7:15–10 p.m. class.

As a theater arts student there are lots of extra hours devoted to rehearsal/lab time. It's not class time and it's not free time—yet it's some of the most important time! It is much needed in order to really get the most out of what you are studying. Be prepared for lots of time commitments to various classes and activities. My acting teacher always says that "you can be as good as want to be." The harder you work, the better you'll get.

DO YOU HAVE A CONCENTRATION?

I am a Theater Arts major with a concentration in Performance. Basically that means I am an acting major. I have a minor in Musical Theater as well.

WHAT CAREER PATH DO YOU HOPE TO FOLLOW?

I want to work professionally in the field, but I do not have specific plans. I think that when I am finished here at Marymount I would love to explore some other institutions in Europe to further my education. Many students choose to go to graduate school as well. I do not really know at the moment what I plan to do when I graduate, but I think that that's okay. Studying theater, you have to be prepared for anything. Unexpected opportunities arise all the time, and you have to be flexible and prepared to take advantage of them. I am keeping my options open and plan to follow my instinct. That's the best advice I can give. Follow your heart both in your career choices and in your stage work. It always leads you the right way.

Alternative Careers for Theater Majors

In addition to the obvious Broadway, film, and television venues, actors should expand their job search to include Off-Off Broadway, dinner theater, children's theater, theme parks, cruise lines, summer stock, industrial shows (sometimes called business theater), cabarets, and improvisation groups. Producing your own showcase, creating a one-person show, and becoming involved in museum theater are also ways to launch your career.

However, theater students develop observation, communication, analytical, and critical-thinking skills that can be transferred to a variety of other career fields. Examples of these include:

- Working in the business side of the entertainment industry as personal managers, casting directors, agents, or publicists

- Sales, including telemarketing

- Voice-overs

- Stage management

- Directing

- Technical theater

- Theater design

- Teaching

- Playwriting

- Criticism

Some actors work on the "other side" for a time, to observe the common mistakes made by other actors, and then go back on the audition circuit hoping to benefit from their business experience. It is a good idea to take some courses in these related areas as part of your actor training.

What to Put in Your College Notebook

You might want to keep a page of impressions about your theater department visit and include some of the information provided on the Theater Program Rating Sheet below.

THEATER PROGRAM RATING SHEET

Size of the department: _____
(too large, you will never be cast; too small, not enough variety)

Faculty: _____
(working pros to give realistic approach; academics; combination)

Curriculum: _____

Acting technique: _____
(Is there a specific technique taught? Elaborate.)

Do other courses offered include:

- Alexander Technique
- Dramatic Verse/Literature
- Drama History
- Masks
- Commedia dell'Arte
- Movement
- Music Studies
- Liberal Arts Courses
- Physical Comedy
- Singing
- Speech

- Stage Combat
- Stage Makeup
- Tap Dance
- Voice
- Text Analysis
- Monologue Class
- Audition Workshop
- Period Styles
- Mime
- Improvisation
- Scene Studies

- Acrobatics
- Jazz Dance
- Technical Theater (Scene Shop)
- Design (Scene, Costume, Lighting)
- Directing
- Stage Management
- Arts Management
- Other

Facilities: _____
(full range from state-of-the-art, with computerized lighting boards, trap doors, revolving stage, etc., to bare bones, learning how to cope with little)

Productions: _____
(number, quality, diversity—If they perform only Shakespeare, how will you find your experience in more modern theater?)

Current students' opinions: _____

Alumni: _____

Job placement record: _____

For Theater Majors

Admissions Checklist

Here are some questions to ask yourself at various points in the admissions process.

Have I:

- surfed the Internet and seen the Web sites for programs in which I am interested
- requested catalogs and read them carefully and critically?
- requested applications and made photocopies of the ones in which I am interested?
- started a college notebook with my impressions of colleges and notes about audition requirements, dates, etc.?
- noted any requirements about scenes or monologues?
- obtained a social security number (United States and Permanent Residents)?
- registered for the PSAT?
- obtained information about the ARTS scholarships? (National Foundation for Advancement in the Arts, 444 Brickell Avenue, Miami, FL 33131; 305-377-1140; www.artsawards.org.)
- made an appointment with my guidance counselor?
- looked into working with an independent counselor, if appropriate?
- talked with my current theater or acting teacher about plans for my future?
- participated regularly in school, community, or professional productions?
- made arrangements to continue my involvement in theater activities?

- discussed high school courses to take?

- discussed which standardized tests to take and when?

- discussed whether tutoring for standardized tests is appropriate for me?

For Theater Majors

How to Use This Guide

Peterson's College Guide for Performing Arts Majors offers detailed information on professional degree programs in Dance, Music, and Theater offered at institutions in the U.S., its territories, and Canada. The guide should be used as a first step toward identifying potential programs; students are encouraged to consult with their school counselors and arts teachers for additional guidance.

PERFORMING ARTS PROGRAMS AT-A-GLANCE

If you want to find out quickly which professional degrees are offered by a specific school, turn to the **Quick-Reference Chart.** Organized geographically, the chart provides the most basic information about each school in this guide, including:

- *Institution name and location*

- *Professional degrees offered in dance, music, and theater*

- *Total enrollment*

- *Tuition and fees for the 2006–07 or 2005–06 academic year*

- *Profile page reference*

PROFILES OF PERFORMING ARTS PROGRAMS

This guide profiles professional degree programs only. The **Profiles of Performing Arts Programs** section is organized alphabetically by institution name and divided into three sections:

- Dance Programs

- Music Programs

- Theater Programs

Each profile consists of the following elements:

Institutional control: Private institutions are designated as *independent* (nonprofit), *independent/religious* (sponsored by or affiliated with a religious group or having a non-denominational or interdenominational religious orientation), or *proprietary* (profit-making). Public institutions are designated by their primary source of support, such as *federal, state, commonwealth* (Puerto Rico), *territory* (U.S. territories), *county, district* (an administrative unit of public education, often having boundaries different from units of local government), *city, state and local* ("local" refers to county, district, or city), or *state-related* (funded primarily by the state but administered autonomously).

Student body type: Categories are *men* (100 percent of student body), *primarily men, women* (100 percent of student body), *primarily women*, and *coed*.

Campus setting: Setting is designated as *urban, suburban, small town*, or *rural*.

Degrees: Many of the degrees listed (both undergraduate and graduate) are purely professional in scope and definition. Institutions may also offer B.A., B.S., M.A., and M.S. degrees that are considered "professional" based upon the prescribed curriculum and course load within the discipline. In a professional degree program, the majority of the curriculum is made up of course work within the particular arts field, while the rest of the program involves traditional liberal arts course work. A professional degree program allows students to focus most of their studies in dance, music, or theater and emphasizes professional training and acquiring professional skills in such areas as performance, exhibition, and education.

Enrollment: This data element cites the number of matriculated undergraduate and (if applicable) graduate students at the institution, both full-time and part-time, as of fall 2005.

Student profile: Whole-figure percentages are given for the total program enrollment broken down into the following categories: *minorities, female, male, international*.

Faculty: Numbers are given for undergraduate and graduate (if applicable) faculty members teaching full-time and part-time in the respective area of study. A percentage of full-time faculty members who have appropriate terminal degrees in their field is listed, as is the ratio of undergraduate students to faculty members teaching undergraduate courses. Finally, mention is made if graduate students teach undergraduate courses in the program.

Student life: This section lists program-related organizations and campus activities in which performing arts students may participate. The availability of housing opportunities designated solely for performing arts students is mentioned here as well.

Expenses: Figures are given for the 2006–07 academic year (actual or estimated) or for the 2005–06 academic year if more recent figures were not yet available at the time of data collection. Annual expenses may be expressed as a *comprehensive fee* (this includes full-time tuition, mandatory fees, and college room and board) or as separate figures for full-time *tuition, mandatory fees, college room and board*, or *college room only*. For public institutions where tuition differs according to residence, separate figures are given for area and/or state residents and for out-of-state residents. The tuition structure at some institutions is complex in that freshmen and sophomores may be charged a different rate from that for juniors and seniors, or a professional or vocational division may have a different fee structure than the liberal arts division of the same institution. In such cases, the lowest tuition appears in the profile, followed by the notation minimum. Also, in instances where colleges report room and board costs that vary depending on the type of accommodation and meal plan, the figures given are either for the most common room arrangement and a full meal plan or for the lowest figures, followed by the notation minimum. If the institution charges special program-related fees for students in the visual and performing arts, these are listed as well.

Financial aid: This section provides information regarding any college-administered award opportunities dedicated exclusively for undergraduate students in the program. Keep in mind that while these awards are only for students in the program, program students may qualify for other financial aid opportunities at the institution as well.

Application procedures: This section indicates if students are admitted directly into the professional program when they enroll for the freshman year or if they must apply for admission into the professional program at some point during their undergraduate career. Admission application deadlines and dates for notification of acceptance or rejection into the program are given either as specific dates or as *continuous* for freshmen and transfers. Continuous means that applications are processed as they are received, and qualified students are accepted as long as there are openings. Continuous notification means that applicants are notified of acceptance or rejection as applications are processed up until the date indicated or until the actual beginning of classes. Application requirements are grouped into either *required* or *recommended*. In addition to

Performing

Arts

these requirements, an institution may indicate if *auditions* are held and where they are held (on or off campus).

Contact: Information includes the name, title, mailing address, phone number, fax number, and e-mail address of the person to contact for further information. Where applicable, a graduate contact is listed as well.

More About the School: A **Special Message** may be included for schools that wish to place additional emphasis on some aspect of their program offerings.

APPENDIXES

The **Summer Programs in the Performing Arts** appendix lists names and contact information for summer programs that can help high school students develop their talent and skills in dance, music, or theater.

Scholarships for Performing Artists contains a partial listing of private scholarships, grants & prizes awarded to college-bound dance, music, or theater students. The awards are based on data collected between January and April 2006 through survey mailings and phone interviews. Every effort has been made to provide up-to-date information. However, changes in particular program information may occur after this book is published. To make sure that you have the most current information, always contact the sponsors directly.

The **Additional Resources** appendix provide readers with lists of various performing arts education organizations that provide support to students in the arts.

INDEXES

The **Majors and Concentrations** index presents 264 major fields of study. This index is divided into three sections: Dance, Music, and Theater. The majors are listed alphabetically in each section. The terms used for the majors are the most widely used. However, many institutions use different terms for the same or similar areas. In addition, while the term "major" is used in this guide, some schools may use other terms such as concentration, program of study, or field.

The **Alphabetical Listing of Schools** index lists every professional degree-granting institution in the guide alphabetically and gives the page number(s) on which its profile can be found.

DATA COLLECTION PROCEDURES

The data contained in the college chart, profiles, and indexes were collected through *Peterson's Survey of Professional Degree Programs in the Visual & Performing Arts*. Questionnaires were sent to the more than 1,100 programs that meet the criteria for inclusion outlined below. All data included in this edition have been submitted by officials (usually program directors, department heads, or admissions personnel) at the institutions themselves. In addition, the great majority of institutions that submitted data were contacted directly by Peterson's editorial staff to verify unusual figures, resolve discrepancies, and obtain additional data. All usable information received in time for publication has been included. The omission of any items from an index or profile listing signifies either that the data were not applicable to that institution or that data were not available. Institutions that did not return a survey are listed with an abbreviated profile in order to ensure a comprehensive reference product. We have every reason to believe that the information presented in this guide is accurate. However, students should check with a specific college or university at the time of application to verify such figures as tuition and fees, which may have changed since the publication of this volume.

CRITERIA FOR INCLUSION IN THIS BOOK

Peterson's College Guide for Performing Arts Majors covers accredited baccalaureate-degree-granting institutions in the United States, U.S. territories, and Canada. Institutions have full accreditation or candidate-for-accreditation (preaccreditation) status granted by an institutional or specialized accrediting body recognized by the U.S. Department of Education or Council for Higher Education Accreditation. Recognized institutional accrediting bodies, which consider each institution as a whole, are the following: the six regional associations of schools and colleges (Middle States, New England, North Central, Northwest, Southern, and Western), each of which is responsible for a specified portion of the United States and its territories; the Association for Biblical Higher Education (ABHE); the Accrediting Council for Independent Colleges and Schools (ACICS); the Accrediting Commission of Career Schools and Colleges of Technology (ACCSCT); the Distance Education and Training Council (DETC); the American Academy for Liberal Education (AALE); the Council on Occupational Education; and the Transnational Association of Christian Colleges and Schools (TRACS). Program registration by the New York State Board of Regents is considered to be the equivalent of institutional accreditation, since the Board requires that all programs offered by an institution meet its standards before recognition is granted. A Canadian institution must be chartered and authorized to grant degrees by the provincial government, affiliated with a chartered institution, or accredited by a recognized U.S. accrediting body. There are recognized specialized accrediting bodies in over forty different fields, each of which is authorized to accredit specific programs in its particular field. This can serve as the equivalent of institutional accreditation for specialized institutions that offer programs in one field only (schools of art, music, optometry, theology, etc.).

In addition, a profiled institution must grant one or more of the following undergraduate professional degrees in art, dance, music, or theater:

Associate in Occupational
  Studies
Bachelor of Arts
Bachelor of Arts/Bachelor
  of Education
Bachelor of Arts/Bachelor
  of Fine Arts
Bachelor of Arts/Bachelor
  of Music
Bachelor of Arts/Bachelor
  of Science
Bachelor of Arts in Music
Bachelor of Church Music
Bachelor of Dance Arts
Bachelor of Education
Bachelor of Fine Arts
Bachelor of Fine Arts/
  Master of Arts
Bachelor of Music

Bachelor of Music/Bachelor
  of Music Education
Bachelor of Music/Bachelor
  of Science
Bachelor of Musical Arts
Bachelor of Music
  Education
Bachelor of Music
  Education/Music Therapy
Bachelor of Music Therapy
Bachelor of Sacred Music
Bachelor of Science
Bachelor of Science/
  Bachelor of Fine Arts
Bachelor of Science in
  Education
Bachelor of Science in
  Music Education

Many of these institutions also offer advanced degrees at the master's or doctoral level:

Honors Bachelor of Arts
Honors Bachelor of Music
Master of Arts
Master of Arts/Doctor of
  Philosophy
Master of Arts/Master of
  Fine Arts

Master of Arts/Master of
  Science
Master of Arts in Education
Master of Arts in Teaching
Master of Church Music
Master of Design
Master of Education

Master of Fine Arts
Master of Humanities
Master of Liturgical Music
Master of Music
Master of Music Education
Master of Music Therapy
Master of Music/Doctor of
    Philosophy
Master of Musical Arts
Master of Professional
    Studies
Master of Public Art
    Studies
Master of Sacred Music

Master of Science
Master of Science in
    Education
Master of Science in
    Physical Education
Master of Science in
    Teaching
Doctor of Arts
Doctor of Education
Doctor of Music
Doctor of Music Education
Doctor of Musical Arts
Doctor of Philosophy

Performing Arts

Quick-Reference Chart

Performing Arts Programs At-a-Glance

	Dance	Music	Theater	Enroll-ment	Tuition and Fees	Summer Programs	Page
Alabama							
Auburn University		BMEd, MEd, MS, PhD		23,333	$5516**		225
Birmingham-Southern College		BM, BMEd, MM		1,411	$21,055*	Music	229
Jacksonville State University		BA, MA		9,110	$4040*	Music	271
Samford University		BM, MM		4,507	$14,642*		314
Troy University		BS, MS		26,880	$4678*		327
The University of Alabama		BM, MM		21,835	$4864*		328
University of Mobile		BM, BSME		1,758	$10,560*	Music	347
University of Montevallo		BM, MM	BFA	2,999	$5664*	Music	348, 413
University of North Alabama				6,415	$4366*		350
University of South Alabama		BFA, BM		13,122	$4502*		354
Alaska							
University of Alaska Anchorage		BM		16,261	$3465*		329
Arizona							
Northern Arizona University		BA, BM, BMEd, MM		18,779	$4393*	Music	297
The University of Arizona	BFA, MA/MFA			37,036	$4498*	Dance	212
Arkansas							
Arkansas State University			BFA	10,414	$5440*	Theater	377
Arkansas Tech University		BMEd		6,842	$4700*		224
Harding University		BMEd		5,744	$11,200*		262

* Expenses for 2005–2006.   ** Estimated expenses for 2006–2007.   NR = Not reported.

	Dance	Music	Theater	Enroll-ment	Tuition and Fees	Summer Programs	Page
Arkansas—continued							
Henderson State University		BM		3,584	$4625*		263
Southern Arkansas University–Magnolia		BMEd		3,057	$4290*		320
University of Arkansas		BM, MM		17,821	$5494*	Music	330
University of Arkansas at Monticello		BMEd		2,875	NR		330
University of Central Arkansas		BM, MM		11,375	$5664*		332
California							
California Institute of the Arts	BFA, MFA	BFA, MFA	BFA, MFA	1,327	$27,725*		197, 235, 381
California State University, Fullerton		BM, MM		35,040	$2990*		237
California State University, Long Beach		BM, MM		1,344	$2864**		237
California State University, Sacramento		BA, BM, MM		27,932	$16,866**		237
Chapman University	BFA	BM, BMEd	BFA	5,732	$30,748**		198, 242, 383
Holy Names University		BM, MM		1,093	$22,710**		264
Musicians Institute		BM		650	$17,200*	Music	291
Notre Dame de Namur University		BFA, BM, MM		1,588	$23,850**		300
Pacific Union College		BM		1,518	$19,125*		306
San Diego State University		BM, MA, MM		32,936	$3155*		314
San Francisco Conservatory of Music		BM, MM			NR		315
San Jose State University		BA, BM, MA		29,975	$13,462*		316
University of California, Irvine		BA, BM, MFA		24,362	$6141**		331
University of California, Santa Barbara	BFA	BM, MM, PhD, DMA	BFA	21,016	$6993*	Dance	212, 332, 408
University of Redlands		BM, MM		2,454	$27,164*		354
University of Southern California		BM, MA, MM, MMEd, PhD, DMA	BFA, MFA	32,836	$32,008*	Theater	355, 415

* Expenses for 2005–2006.   ** Estimated expenses for 2006–2007.   NR = Not reported.

	Dance	Music	Theater	Enroll-ment	Tuition and Fees	Summer Programs	Page
California—*continued*							
University of the Pacific		BA, BM, MA, MM		6,196	$26,088*	Music	358
Colorado							
Colorado Christian University		BM		2,142	$16,740*		247
Colorado State University		BM, MM		27,133	$4562*		247
Metropolitan State College of Denver		BM, BME		20,761	$2859*		287
University of Colorado at Boulder	BFA, MFA	BM, BMEd, MM, MMEd, PhD, DMA	BFA, PhD	31,068	$5372*		213, 335, 409
University of Denver		BM, MA, MM		10,374	$28,410*		336
University of Northern Colorado		BM, BMEd, MM, DA		13,156	$3837*		351
Western State College of Colorado		BA		2,177	$3,208**		368
Connecticut							
Albertus Magnus College			BFA	2,230	$17,310*		375
Central Connecticut State University			BFA	12,315	$6164*		382
University of Bridgeport		BM		3,626	$20,595*		330
University of Connecticut		BA, BM, BS, MA, MM, PhD, DMA	BFA, MA, MFA	23,185	$8362**		335, 409
University of Hartford	BFA	BA, BM, MM, MMEd, PhD, DMA	BFA	7,260	$25,766**		213, 337, 410
Delaware							
University of Delaware		BM, BMEd, MM		20,373	$7318*		336

* Expenses for 2005–2006.   ** Estimated expenses for 2006–2007.   NR = Not reported.

Performing

Arts

	Dance	Music	Theater	Enroll-ment	Tuition and Fees	Summer Programs	Page
District of Columbia							
The Catholic University of America		BM, MA, MM, MMSM, DMA		6,130	$26,000*		240
Howard University		BM, BMEd, MM, MMEd	BFA	10,623	$12,295*		265, 388
Florida							
The Baptist College of Florida		BM, BMEd		623	$7250*		227
Florida Atlantic University			BA, MFA	25,704	$3259*	Theater	387
Florida International University			BFA	36,904	$3314*		387
Florida State University	BFA, MA, MFA	BM, BMEd, EdD, MA, MM, MMEd, PhD, DM	BFA, MFA	39,146	$3208*		201, 259, 388
Jacksonville University	BFA	BM, BMEd	BFA	2,948	$19,970*		202, 271, 391
New World School of the Arts	BFA	BM	BFA	371	$12,000*		205, 294, 395
Palm Beach Atlantic University		BM		3,171	$17,350*	Music	306
University of Central Florida			BFA, MFA	44,953	$3339*		408
University of Florida	BFA		BFA, MFA	49,693	$3094*		213, 410
University of Miami		BA, BM, BS, MM, MS, DMA	BFA	15,674	$29,020*		343, 412
University of North Florida				15,234	$3269*		352
University of South Florida	BA, BFA	BM, BS, MA, MM, PhD	BA, BFA	42,660	$3384*		218, 356, 417
Georgia							
Armstrong Atlantic State University		BMEd		6,710	$3074**		224
Augusta State University		BM		6,312	$2920*		225
Berry College		BA, BM		1,970	$18,950**		229

* Expenses for 2005–2006.   ** Estimated expenses for 2006–2007.   NR = Not reported.

	Dance	Music	Theater	Enroll-ment	Tuition and Fees	Summer Programs	Page
Georgia—continued							
Brenau University	BFA	BFA, BM	BFA	743	$16,440*	Music, Theater	196, 232, 379
Brewton-Parker College		BM		1,094	$12,684*		233
Clayton State University		BM		6,152	$3290**		243
Columbus State University		BM, MM		7,475	$2944*		249
Covenant College		BM		898	$21,850**		251
Georgia College & State University		BA, BMEd, BMT		5,659	$4142*		260
Georgia Southern University		BM, MM		16,646	$3462*		261
Georgia State University		BM, BS, MM, PhD		25,945	$4464*		261
Kennesaw State University		BM		18,556	$3044*		274
Mercer University		BM, BMEd, MOM		7,154	$23,460*	Music	286
Shorter College			BFA	967	$13,500*		404
University of Georgia		BM, EdD, MM, MMEd, PhD, DMA		33,660	$4628*	Music	337
University of West Georgia		BM, MM		10,155	$3270*		360
Valdosta State University			BFA	10,503	$3278*		419
Hawaii							
University of Hawaii at Manoa	BFA, MA, MFA			20,644	$4513*		213
Idaho							
Idaho State University		BM, BMEd, MEd	BA, BFA, BS	13,977	$11,700**	Music	266, 389
University of Idaho	BDA, BS, MSPE			12,476	$3968*		214
Illinois							
Bradley University		BM	BA, BS	6,154	$18,830*		231, 379

* Expenses for 2005–2006.   ** Estimated expenses for 2006–2007.   NR = Not reported.

	Dance	Music	Theater	Enroll-ment	Tuition and Fees	Summer Programs	Page
Illinois—*continued*							
Columbia College Chicago	BA, BFA	BA, BM	BA, BFA	10,842	$16,788**	Dance, Music, Theater	199, 248, 383
DePaul University		BM, BS, MM		23,148	$21,040*		253
Eastern Illinois University		BM, MM		12,129	$6373*		255
Elmhurst College		BM, BS		2,670	$21,600*		257
Illinois State University		BA, BM, BMEd, BS, MM, MMEd, MS		20,653	$7091*		266
Illinois Wesleyan University		BM, BMEd	BA, BFA	2,146	$29,076**		267, 389
Millikin University		BM		2,641	$21,121*		288
Northern Illinois University		BM, MM		25,208	$6439*		298
North Park University		BM, BMEd, MM		2,181	$13,960*		299
Northwestern University		BA/BM, BM, BM/BS, BM/MSJ, MM, PhD, DM		17,004	$33,559**	Music	300
Roosevelt University		BM, MM	BFA, MA, MFA	7,234	$14,430*		310, 402
Saint Xavier University		BM		5,705	$18,520*		313
Southern Illinois University Carbondale		BM, MM		21,441	$6831*		320
Southern Illinois University Edwardsville		BM, MM		13,460	$5179*		320
University of Illinois at Urbana–Champaign	BFA, MFA		BFA, MFA, PhD	41,938	$8624*		214, 411
VanderCook College of Music		BMEd, MMEd			$17,890**		364
Western Illinois University		BM, MM		13,404	$6899*		367
Wheaton College		BM, BMEd		2,932	$21,100*		371

* Expenses for 2005–2006. ** Estimated expenses for 2006–2007. NR = Not reported.

	Dance	Music	Theater	Enroll-ment	Tuition and Fees	Summer Programs	Page
Indiana							
Ball State University		BM, BS, MA, MM, DA		20,351	$6458*		226
Butler University	BA, BFA, BS	BA, BM, BS, MM	BA, BS	4,384	$23,774*	Dance	196, 234, 380
DePauw University		BM, BMA, BMEd		2,397	$27,780**	Music	254
Grace College		BM		1,275	$16,020*		261
Huntington University		BM		1,019	$18,860**		266
Indiana State University		BA, BM, BMEd, BS, MM		10,679	$5864*		267
Indiana University Bloomington	BS, BSOF, MS	BM, BMEd, BS, MA, MAT, MM, MMEd, MS, PhD, DM, DME		37,958	$7112*	Music	202, 268
Indiana University–Purdue University Fort Wayne		BM, BME, BSMT		11,795	$5067*		268
Indiana University South Bend		BM, BS, MM		7,459	$4989*	Music	269
Oakland City University		BA, BMEd		1,900	$14,220**		301
Saint Mary's College		BM		1,397	$25,580**		312
Taylor University		BA, BM, BMEd, BS		1,865	$20,746*		324
University of Evansville		BM, BS		2,836	$21,660*		337
Valparaiso University		BM, BMEd		3,864	$22,750*		363
Iowa							
Central College		BA		1,635	$20,972**		241
Coe College		BM, BMEd		1,355	$25,120**		245
Cornell College		BM, BMEd		1,179	$23,680*		251
Drake University				5,277	$21,462*		254, 385
Iowa State University of Science and Technology		BM, BMEd		25,741	$5634*		269
Iowa Wesleyan College		BMEd		849	$17,800**		269

* Expenses for 2005–2006.   ** Estimated expenses for 2006–2007.   NR = Not reported.

	Dance	Music	Theater	Enroll-ment	Tuition and Fees	Summer Programs	Page
Iowa—*continued*							
Simpson College		BM		2,035	$20,911*	Music	318
The University of Iowa	BFA, MFA	BM, MA, MFA, PhD, DMA		28,426	$5935**		214, 338
University of Northern Iowa				12,622	$5602*		352
Wartburg College		BA, BM, BMEd, BMEd/MT		1,811	$21,130*		365
Kansas							
Baker University		BMEd		916	$16,560*		226
Emporia State University		BM, BMEd, MM	BFA	6,288	$3306*		257, 386
Friends University	BFA	BFA, BM, BMEd		3,190	NR	Dance	201, 259
Kansas State University		BM, BMEd, MM		23,182	$5124*		274
Pittsburg State University		BM, BMEd, MM		6,628	$3562*		307
University of Kansas		BFA, BM, BMEd, MM, MMEd, PhD, DMA		28,949	$5413*		339
Washburn University		BM, BMEd		7,261	$4982*		365
Kentucky							
Campbellsville University		BM, MM		2,286	$16,340**		238
Kentucky Wesleyan College		BM, BME		755	$13,600**		275
Morehead State University		BM, BMEd, MM		9,062	$4320*		290
Murray State University				10,266	$4428*		291
Northern Kentucky University		BM	BFA	13,908	$4968*		298, 397
University of Kentucky			BA, BFA	25,672	$5812*		411

* Expenses for 2005–2006.   ** Estimated expenses for 2006–2007.   NR = Not reported.

	Dance	Music	Theater	Enroll-ment	Tuition and Fees	Summer Programs	Page
Kentucky—*continued*							
University of Louisville		BM, MAT, MM, MME		20,734	$5532*		340
University of the Cumberlands		BM		1,843	$13,658**		358
Western Kentucky University		BM, MA	BFA	18,634	$5316*		368, 422
Louisiana							
Centenary College of Louisiana		BM, BMEd		1,044	$18,900**		241
Louisiana State University and Agricultural and Mechanical College		BM, BMEd, MM, PhD, DMA		31,264	$4419*		280
Louisiana Tech University		BA, BM		11,691	$4375*		280
Loyola University New Orleans		BM, BMEd, BMT, MM, MMEd, MMT		5,423	$25,246*		280
Nicholls State University		BA, BMEd		7,525	$3389*		296
Northwestern State University of Louisiana		BM, BMEd, MM	BS	9,847	$3393*	Theater	299, 398
Southeastern Louisiana University		BM, BMEd, MM		15,472	$3341*		319
Southern University and Agricultural and Mechanical College		BM, BMEd		9,941	$3592*		321
Tulane University	BFA		BFA, MFA	12,691	$32,946*		212, 407
University of Louisiana at Lafayette		BM, BMEd, MM, MMEd		17,075	$3324*		339
University of Louisiana at Monroe		BM, BMEd, MM		9,056	$3402*		340
Maryland							
The Johns Hopkins University		BM, MA, MM, DMA		6,025	$34,400**		272
Towson University	BFA	BM, BS, MM, MS		18,011	$7096*		211, 327

* Expenses for 2005–2006. ** Estimated expenses for 2006–2007. NR = Not reported.

	Dance	Music	Theater	Enroll-ment	Tuition and Fees	Summer Programs	Page
Maryland—*continued*							
University of Maryland, College Park		BM, MA, MM, PhD, DMA		35,300	$7821*	Music	341
Massachusetts							
Anna Maria College		BM		1,042	$21,880*		223
Berklee College of Music		BM		4,037	$26,307*	Music	228
The Boston Conservatory	BFA	BM, MM	BFA, MM	537	$27,835**	Dance, Music	195, 230, 377
Boston University		BM, MM, DMA	BFA, MFA	30,957	$31,966*	Theater	230, 378
Emerson College			BFA, MA	4,326	$24,622*		386
New England Conservatory of Music		BM, MM, DMA		801	$29,300**		292
Salem State College			BFA	9,863	$5,284*		403
University of Massachusetts Amherst	BFA	BM, MM, PhD		25,093	$9595**		215, 341
University of Massachusetts Dartmouth		BA		8,549	$8036*		342
University of Massachusetts Lowell		BM, MM		10,666	$8166*	Music	342
Michigan							
Aquinas College		BM, MAT		2,193	$17,926*		223
Central Michigan University		BM, BME, MM		27,221	$5868*	Music	242
Eastern Michigan University	BS	BM, BME, BMT, MA		23,240	$6541*		201, 256
Grand Valley State University		BM, BMEd		22,565	$6220*		262
Hope College				3,141	$21,540*		264
Marygrove College		BM		3,591	$13,135*	Music	283
Michigan State University				45,166	$7587*		287
Northern Michigan University		BMEd		9,379	$5958*		298
Oakland University		BM, MM		17,339	$6443*		301

* Expenses for 2005–2006.   ** Estimated expenses for 2006–2007.   NR = Not reported.

	Dance	Music	Theater	Enroll-ment	Tuition and Fees	Summer Programs	Page
Michigan—*continued*							
University of Michigan	BFA	BFA, BFA, BM, BMA, BS, MA, MM, PhD, DMA	BFA, BTA	39,993	$9400*	Dance, Music	215, 344, 345, 412
University of Michigan–Flint			BFA	6,423	$6398*		413
Wayne State University		BA, BM, MA, MM	BFA, MFA, DA	33,137	$6439*		366, 421
Western Michigan University		BM, MM		26,239	$6478*	Music	368
Minnesota							
Augsburg College		BA, BM, BMEd, BS		3,508	$23,422**		225
Concordia College		BM		2,764	$20,980**		249
Minnesota State University Mankato		BM, BS, MM		14,335	$5846*	Music	288
St. Cloud State University		BA, BM, BS, MM		15,964	$5322*		312
St. Olaf College		BM		3,058	$28,200**		313
University of Minnesota, Duluth		BA, BM, MM, MMEd		10,496	$8928*		346
University of Minnesota, Twin Cities Campus	BFA		BFA, MFA	51,175	$8622*		215, 413
Mississippi							
Belhaven College	BFA			2,580	$14,774**		195
Delta State University		BM, BMEd		3,998	$4252*		252
Jackson State University		BM, BMEd, MM, MMEd		8,351	$3964*	Music	271
Mississippi University for Women		BM		2,328	NR		289
University of Mississippi		BM, MM, DA		14,901	$4320*		346
University of Southern Mississippi	BFA		BFA, MFA	15,030	$4342**		218, 416

* Expenses for 2005–2006.   ** Estimated expenses for 2006–2007.   NR = Not reported.

	Dance	Music	Theater	Enroll-ment	Tuition and Fees	Summer Programs	Page
Missouri							
Calvary Bible College and Theological Seminary		BM, BS		348	$7296*		238
Central Missouri State University		BM, BMEd, MA		10,604	$5835**		242
Culver-Stockton College		BM		840	$15,250**		251
Lindenwood University			BFA, MFA	9,076	$12,240**		393
Missouri State University				18,928	$5454**		205, 289, 395
Stephens College			BFA	824	$20,500**		406
Truman State University		BM, MA, MAE		5,803	$5812*		328
University of Missouri–Columbia		BM, BS, MA, MEd, MM, PhD		27,985	$7745*		346
University of Missouri–Kansas City	BFA	BA, BM, BMEd, IPhD, MA, MM, MME, DMA		14,310	$6819**	Music	216, 347
Webster University	BA, BFA	BM, BMEd, MM	BA, BFA	7,327	$17,210*	Music	220, 367, 421
Montana							
Montana State University		BA, BME		12,166	$5221*		289
The University of Montana–Missoula		BM, BMEd, MM	BFA, MFA	13,602	$5030**		347, 413
Nebraska							
Hastings College		BM		1,189	$17,268*		263
Nebraska Wesleyan University		BA, BM	BFA	2,016	$18,410*	Music, Theater	292, 395
University of Nebraska at Omaha		BM, MM		14,093	$4,825*	Music	348
University of Nebraska–Lincoln		BM, BME, MM, DMA	BFA, MFA	21,675	$5540*	Music	348, 414
Nevada							
University of Nevada, Reno			BFA	16,336	$3270*		414

* Expenses for 2005–2006.   ** Estimated expenses for 2006–2007.   NR = Not reported.

	Dance	Music	Theater	Enroll-ment	Tuition and Fees	Summer Programs	Page
New Hampshire							
University of New Hampshire		BM, MA		14,564	$10,401**		349
New Jersey							
The College of New Jersey		BM		6,768	$9707*		246
Fairleigh Dickinson University, College at Florham			BA	3,481	$24,904*		387
Montclair State University	BFA	BA, BM, MA		16,063	$7709*		205, 289
Rowan University		BM, MA, MM		9,762	$8607*		311
Rutgers, The State University of New Jersey, Mason Gross School of the Arts	BFA	BM, MM, DMA	BFA, MFA		NR	Theater	204, 284, 394
Seton Hall University		BA, BS		9,637	$24,720**	Music	316
Westminster Choir College of Rider University		BA, BM, MA, MM, MMEd, MVP		452	$23,470*	Music	369
New Mexico							
College of Santa Fe		BA	BFA	1,661	$22,276*		246, 383
New Mexico State University		BM, BMEd, MM		16,072	$3918*		293
University of New Mexico		BM, BMEd, MM		26,172	$4108*		349
New York							
Adelphi University	BFA		BFA	7,898	$19,720*		195, 375
American Academy of Dramatic Arts			AOS, Cert	220	$17,400**	Theater	375
Brooklyn College of the City University of New York		BM, MA, MM		15,281	$4375**		234
City College of the City University of New York		BFA, MA		12,440	$4080*		243
Five Towns College		BM, MM, DMA	BFA	1,162	$14,100*	Theater	258, 387
Hofstra University			BFA	12,890	$21,530*		388

* Expenses for 2005–2006.   ** Estimated expenses for 2006–2007.   NR = Not reported.

	Dance	Music	Theater	Enroll-ment	Tuition and Fees	Summer Programs	Page
New York—*continued*							
Houghton College		BM, MM		1,411	$19,420*		264
Hunter College of the City University of New York		B Mus, MA		20,843	$4349**		265
Ithaca College		BM, MM	BFA	6,412	$25,194*		269, 390
The Juilliard School	BFA	AD, AD, BM, BM, MM, DMA	AD, BFA	808	$24,930*	Dance, Music	203, 273, 392
Lehman College of the City University of New York		BS, MAT		10,615	$4288**		278
Long Island University, C.W. Post Campus	BFA	BM, MA, MS	BFA, MA	8,472	$23,230*		204, 279, 393
Manhattan School of Music		BM, MM, DMA		891	$29,960**		281
Mannes College The New School for Music		BM, BS, MM		366	$26,130*		282
Marymount Manhattan College	BFA		BFA	2,007	$19,638**		204, 394
Nazareth College of Rochester		BM, MS		3,120	$19,874*	Music	291
New York University	BFA, MFA	BM, EdD, MA, MM, PhD	BFA, BFA, BS, EdD, MA, MFA, MFA, PhD	40,004	$31,690*	Music, Theater	205, 295, 396
Niagara University			BFA	3,853	$19,800*		397
Nyack College		BM, BSM		3,000	$15,400**		301
Pace University			BFA	14,177	$25,388*		399
Purchase College, State University of New York	BFA, MFA	BM, MM	BFA, MFA	3,826	$5608**	Theater	207, 308, 401
Queens College of the City University of New York		BM, MA, MS		17,638	$4,377**		309
Russell Sage College			BA	838	$23,520*		403
State University of New York at Binghamton		BM, MM		14,018	$5838*		322
State University of New York at Buffalo				27,220	$6068*		322
State University of New York College at Brockport	BFA, MFA			8,484	NR		210

* Expenses for 2005–2006.   ** Estimated expenses for 2006–2007.   NR = Not reported.

	Dance	Music	Theater	Enroll-ment	Tuition and Fees	Summer Programs	Page
New York—*continued*							
State University of New York College at Potsdam		BM, MM		4,329	$5289*	Music	322
State University of New York, Fredonia		BFA, BM, BS, MM	BFA	5,432	$5441*		322, 405
Syracuse University		BA, BM, MM	BFA, BS	17,266	$28,285*	Theater	324, 406
The New School for Jazz and Contemporary Music		BA/BFA, BFA			$27,600**		293
North Carolina							
Appalachian State University		BM, BS, MM, MMT		14,653	$3918**	Music	223
Brevard College		BA, BM		597	$15,990*		232
Catawba College			BFA	1,288	$18,750*		382
East Carolina University	BFA	BM, MM	BFA	23,164	$3627*	Dance	201, 255, 385
Elon University			BFA	4,956	$18,949*		386
Mars Hill College			BA, BFA	1,378	$17,950**		394
Meredith College		BM, MM		2,168	$21,200**		286
North Carolina Agricultural and Technical State University			BFA	11,103	$3124**		397
North Carolina School of the Arts	BFA	BM, MM	BFA, MFA	827	$4306*	Dance, Theater	206, 297, 397
Queens University of Charlotte		BM		2,113	$19,450**		309
Salem College		BM		1,109	$17,190*		313
The University of North Carolina at Charlotte		BM		20,772	$3549*	Music	350
The University of North Carolina at Greensboro	BFA, BS, MA, MFA	BM, MM, PhD, DMA	BFA, MEd, MFA	16,060	$3813**		217, 350, 414
The University of North Carolina at Pembroke		BM, MA, MAT		5,732	$2980*		350
The University of North Carolina Wilmington		BM		11,653	$3695*	Music	351
Western Carolina University		BM, BSEd, MM	BFA	8,665	NR		367, 421

* Expenses for 2005–2006.   ** Estimated expenses for 2006–2007.   NR = Not reported.

	Dance	Music	Theater	Enroll-ment	Tuition and Fees	Summer Programs	Page
North Dakota							
University of North Dakota		BM, MM, PhD		12,954	$5327*		351
Valley City State University		BS		1,035	$5160*		363
Ohio							
Ashland University		BM		6,472	$21,430**		224
Baldwin-Wallace College		BM, BMEd		4,469	$21,236**		226
Bowling Green State University		BM, MM		19,016	$8560*	Music	231
Capital University		BA, BM, MM		3,901	$24,100*	Music	239
Cedarville University		B Mus, BMEd		3,113	$17,120**		241
Cleveland Institute of Music		BM, MM, DMA		409	$26,870*		244
Cleveland State University		BM, MM		15,722	$6792*	Music	245
The College of Wooster		BM, BMEd		1,846	$28,230*		247
Heidelberg College		BM		1,435	$16,134*		263
Kent State University	BFA		BFA, MFA	23,622	$7954*		204, 392
Miami University		BM, MM		16,338	$21,487*		287
Oberlin College		BM, MM, MMEd		2,864	$32,724*		302
Ohio Northern University		BM	BFA	3,542	$28,260**		303, 398
The Ohio State University				50,504	$8082*		206, 303
Ohio University	BFA	BM, MM	BFA, MA, MFA	20,396	$8235*		206, 303, 398
Ohio Wesleyan University		BM		1,976	$28,280*		303
Otterbein College		BFA, BM, BMEd	BFA	3,094	$22,518*		305, 399
The University of Akron				21,049	$7958*		212
University of Cincinnati		BM, MM, PhD, DMA	BFA, MFA	27,932	$8883*		333, 408
University of Dayton		BM, BMEd, MEd		10,572	$22,846*		336

* Expenses for 2005–2006.   ** Estimated expenses for 2006–2007.   NR = Not reported.

	Dance	Music	Theater	Enroll- ment	Tuition and Fees	Summer Programs	Page
Ohio—*continued*							
Wittenberg University		BM, BME		2,093	$29,280**		373
Wright State University	BFA	BM, MHUM, MM	BFA	16,207	$7278**		221, 373, 422
Youngstown State University		BM, MM		12,809	$6333*		374
Oklahoma							
Cameron University		BM		5,873	$3440*		238
East Central University		BS		4,571	$3566*		255
Oklahoma Baptist University		BM, BMEd		1,883	$13,846*		304
Oklahoma City University		BM, BMEd, MM		3,688	$17,613*		304
Oklahoma State University		BM, MM		23,461	$4365*		304
Oral Roberts University		BM, BMEd		4,086	$15,880*		305
Southwestern Oklahoma State University		BM, BMEd, MM		4,841	NR	Music	321
University of Oklahoma	BFA, MFA		BFA, MA, MFA	26,968	$4408*	Dance, Theater	217, 415
University of Tulsa		BM, BMEd		4,084	$20,738**		359
Oregon							
Marylhurst University		BMT		1,268	$14,220*		284
Southern Oregon University			BFA	4,977	$4986**		405
University of Oregon		BM, MA, MM, PhD, DMA		20,347	$5613*		352
University of Portland		BMEd		3,413	$24,900*		352
Pennsylvania							
Arcadia University				3,403	$25,990**		376
Bucknell University		BM		3,648	$36,002**		234
Carnegie Mellon University		BFA, MM	BFA, MFA	10,017	$34,578**	Music, Theater	239, 382
The Curtis Institute of Music		BM, MM			NR		252

* Expenses for 2005–2006.   ** Estimated expenses for 2006–2007.   NR = Not reported.

	Dance	Music	Theater	Enroll-ment	Tuition and Fees	Summer Programs	Page
Pennsylvania—*continued*							
Drexel University		BS, BS/MBA		18,466	$24,280*	Music	254
Duquesne University		BM, BS, MM		9,916	$21,480*	Music	254
Immaculata University		BM, MA		4,019	$20,575**		267
Lebanon Valley College		BM, BS		1,915	$24,860*		278
Mansfield University of Pennsylvania		BM, MA		3,390	$6408*		283
Moravian College		BM		2,030	$25,263*		290
The Pennsylvania State University University Park Campus		BM, BMA, BS, MA, MM, MME, PhD	BFA, MFA	40,709	$11,508*		307, 399
Philadelphia Biblical University		BM		1,439	$15,875**		307
Point Park University	BA, BA/BFA		BA/BFA, MFA	3,407	$16,740*	Dance, Theater	206, 400
Seton Hill University		BM		1,863	$21,990*		317
Slippery Rock University of Pennsylvania	BA	BM, BS		8,105	$6275**		210, 318
Susquehanna University		BM		1,989	$26,265*		323
Temple University	BFA, EdM, MFA, PhD			33,693	$9640*		211
The University of the Arts	BFA	BM, MAT, MM	BFA	2,277	$25,680**	Dance, Music, Theater	218, 358, 417
West Chester University of Pennsylvania				12,988	$6147**		367
Westminster College		BM		1,593	$24,325**		370
Puerto Rico							
Conservatory of Music of Puerto Rico		BM		266	NR	Music	250
Rhode Island							
Rhode Island College				8,871	$4676*		310
Roger Williams University	BA		BA	5,214	$24,066**		209, 402

* Expenses for 2005–2006. ** Estimated expenses for 2006–2007. NR = Not reported.

	Dance	Music	Theater	Enroll-ment	Tuition and Fees	Summer Programs	Page
Rhode Island—*continued*							
University of Rhode Island		BA, BA/BS, BM, MM		15,095	$7284*		354
South Carolina							
Coker College		BMEd		551	$17,952**		245
Columbia College	BFA			1,493	$19,214*		199
Converse College		BM, MM		2,176	$22,234**	Music	250
Furman University		BM		3,221	$26,352*		260
Lander University		BS		2,703	$6668*		276
University of South Carolina		BM, MM, MMEd, PhD, DMA		27,065	$6914*		355
South Dakota							
Northern State University		BA, BMEd		2,631	$4699*		298
The University of South Dakota		BM, MM		8,641	$4829*		355
Tennessee							
Belmont University		BM, MM		4,319	$17,260*		227
East Tennessee State University		BM		11,894	$4662**		256
Fisk University		BM		890	$13,180*		257
Lambuth University		BM		805	$16,380**		276
Lee University		BA, BM, BMEd, BS, MCM, MOM		3,930	$9610*		278
Middle Tennessee State University		BM, MA		22,554	$4600*		287
Southern Adventist University		BM		2,522	$14,784**		319
Tennessee Technological University		BM		9,313	$4660**	Music	325
Union University		BM		2,866	$16,450*		328
University of Memphis		BM, MM, PhD, DMA	BFA, MFA	20,465	$5084*		343, 411
The University of Tennessee		BM, MM		31,157	$5626*		356
The University of Tennessee at Chattanooga		BM, MM		8,656	$5400*		357

* Expenses for 2005–2006.   ** Estimated expenses for 2006–2007.   NR = Not reported.

	Dance	Music	Theater	Enroll-ment	Tuition and Fees	Summer Programs	Page
Tennessee—*continued*							
Vanderbilt University		BM, BM/MEd		11,481	$31,700*		364
Texas							
Abilene Christian University		BA, BM		4,685	$15,160*		222
Angelo State University		BM		6,156	$4290**	Music	222
Baylor University		BM, BMEd, MM		13,975	$22,814**		227
East Texas Baptist University		BM		1,326	$12,840*		256
Hardin-Simmons University		BM, MM		2,435	$15,626**	Music	262
Howard Payne University		BM		1,319	NR		265
Lamar University		BM, MM, MMEd		10,595	$2880*		275
Midwestern State University		BM	BA, BFA	6,279	$4566**		288, 395
Prairie View A&M University		BM		7,912	$4906*		308
Rice University		BM, MM, DMA		5,258	$23,746*		310
Sam Houston State University		BM, MM, MMEd		15,000	$3822*		314
Southern Methodist University	BFA, MFA	BM, MM, MSM	BFA, MFA	11,152	$28,630**		210, 321, 404
Stephen F. Austin State University		BM, MA, MM	BFA	11,435	$4718*		323, 405
Texas A&M University–Commerce		BM, BS, MM		8,787	$4824*		325
Texas A&M University–Corpus Christi		BM		8,227	$4516*		326
Texas Christian University	BFA			8,749	$21,320*	Dance	211
Texas State University-San Marcos		BM, MM		27,129	$5252*	Music	326
Texas Tech University		BM, MM, MMEd, PhD, DMA		28,001	$6152*	Music	326
Trinity University		BM		2,756	$21,582*		327
University of Houston		BM, MM, DMA	BA, MA, MFA	35,344	$6486*		338, 410
The University of Texas at Austin	BFA, MFA			49,696	$6972*		218

* Expenses for 2005–2006.   ** Estimated expenses for 2006–2007.   NR = Not reported.

	Dance	Music	Theater	Enroll-ment	Tuition and Fees	Summer Programs	Page
Texas—*continued*							
The University of Texas at El Paso				19,268	$5064*		357
The University of Texas at San Antonio		BM, MM		27,337	$5858*		357
University of the Incarnate Word		BA, BMEd, BMT		5,217	$18,272**		358
West Texas A&M University	BFA, MA	BM, MA, MM		8,667	$3756*	Dance	221, 370
Utah							
Brigham Young University		BM, MM	BA, BFA, MA, MFA	34,067	$5116*	Theater	233, 379
University of Utah	BFA, BFA, MA, MFA, MFA	BA, BM, BMEd, MA, MM, MMEd, PhD	BFA	29,012	$4342*		219, 359, 417
Utah State University		BM, BS	BFA, MFA	14,458	$3672*		363, 419
Weber State University		BM, BMEd		18,142	$3138*.		366
Vermont							
Johnson State College			BA	1,866	$6906**		392
Virginia							
George Mason University	BFA, MFA			29,728	$5880*		202
James Madison University		BM, MM		16,938	$5886*		272
Liberty University		BM, BS		12,458	$15,350**		279
Longwood University		BM	BA, BFA	4,289	$7020*		279, 393
Norfolk State University		BM, MM		6,096	$4670**	Music	297
Radford University		BM, MS		9,552	$5130*	Music	309
Shenandoah University	BFA, MA, MFA, MS	BM, BMT, BS, MM, MME, MMT, MS, DMA	BFA	2,998	$20,050*		209, 317, 404
Virginia Commonwealth University	BFA	BA, BM, MM	BFA, MFA	29,349	$5385*	Dance	220, 364, 420
Virginia Intermont College	BFA		BFA	1,138	$16,450*	Dance	220, 420

* Expenses for 2005–2006.   ** Estimated expenses for 2006–2007.   NR = Not reported.

	Dance	Music	Theater	Enroll-ment	Tuition and Fees	Summer Programs	Page
Washington							
Cornish College of the Arts	BFA	BM	BFA, BFA	768	$21,500*	Dance	200, 251, 385
Pacific Lutheran University		BM, BMA, BME		3,680	$22,040*		306
University of Puget Sound		BM		2,887	$28,460*		353
University of Washington				39,251	$5532*		360
Walla Walla College		BM		1,942	$19,917**		365
West Virginia							
Marshall University				13,988	$3932*		283, 394
West Virginia University		BM, MM, PhD, DMA		26,051	$4164*		370
West Virginia Wesleyan College		BMEd		1,408	$21,250*		371
Wisconsin							
Alverno College		BM		2,372	$15,418*		222
Lawrence University		BA/BM, BM		1,450	$29,598**		276
University of Wisconsin–Green Bay		BM		5,826	$5425*		360
University of Wisconsin–Madison		BM, MMA, MMEd, DMA		41,480	$6617*	Music	360
University of Wisconsin–Milwaukee			BFA	27,502	$6224*		418
University of Wisconsin–Oshkosh		BM, BMEd		10,997	$4981*		361
University of Wisconsin–Stevens Point		BM, MMEd	BFA	8,577	$5062*	Music	361, 418
University of Wisconsin–Superior		BM, BMEd	BFA	2,872	$5,188*		362, 418
University of Wisconsin–Whitewater		BM		10,750	$5080*		362
Wyoming							
University of Wyoming	BFA	BM, BMEd, MM	BFA	13,126	$3426*	Dance	219, 362, 419

* Expenses for 2005–2006.   ** Estimated expenses for 2006–2007.   NR = Not reported.

Profiles of Performing
Arts Programs

Dance Programs

Adelphi University

Garden City, New York

Independent, coed. Suburban campus. Total enrollment: 7,898. Dance program established 1938.

Degrees Bachelor of Fine Arts. Majors and concentrations: dance. Program accredited by NASD.

Enrollment 30 total; all undergraduate.

Dance Student Profile 80% females, 20% males, 8% minorities, 10% international.

Dance Faculty 2 undergraduate (full-time), 6 undergraduate (part-time). 100% of full-time faculty have terminal degrees. Graduate students do not teach undergraduate courses. Undergraduate student–faculty ratio: 6:1.

Student Life Student groups/activities include Interact Performance Club. Special housing available for dance students.

Expenses for 2005–2006 Application fee: $35. Comprehensive fee: $28,910 includes full-time tuition ($18,620), mandatory fees ($1100), and college room and board ($9190). College room only: $5990. Full-time tuition and fees vary according to course level, location, and program. Room and board charges vary according to board plan and housing facility.

Financial Aid Program-specific awards: 20 talent awards for excellent dancers ($4000–$7000).

Application Procedures Students admitted directly into the professional program freshman year. Deadline for freshmen and transfers: continuous. Required: essay, high school transcript, college transcript(s) for transfer students, 2 letters of recommendation, interview, SAT I or ACT test scores (minimum combined SAT I score of 1000), minimum 2.5 high school GPA, video or audition. Auditions held on campus; videotaped performances are permissible as a substitute for live auditions when distance is prohibitive.

Web Site http://www.adelphi.edu

Undergraduate Contact Mr. Nicholas Petron, Chair, Department of Performing Arts, Adelphi University, Post Hall, Room 4, Garden City, New York 11530; 516-877-4930, fax: 516-877-4926, e-mail address: petron@adelphi.edu

The Katherine K. Herberger College of Fine Arts

Arizona State University

Tempe, Arizona

State-supported, coed. Suburban campus. Total enrollment: 51,612. Dance program established 1937.

Belhaven College

Jackson, Mississippi

Independent Presbyterian, coed. Urban campus. Total enrollment: 2,580. Dance program established 1997.

Degrees Bachelor of Fine Arts in the area of dance. Majors and concentrations: ballet, modern dance. Program accredited by NASD.

Enrollment 63 total; 15 undergraduate, 48 nonprofessional degree.

Dance Student Profile 97% females, 3% males.

Dance Faculty 4 undergraduate (full-time), 4 undergraduate (part-time). 50% of full-time faculty have terminal degrees. Graduate students do not teach undergraduate courses. Undergraduate student–faculty ratio: 16:1.

Student Life Student groups/activities include Belhaven College Dance Ensemble, DOXA (student organization), Swing Club.

Expenses for 2006–2007 Application fee: $25. Comprehensive fee: $20,478 includes full-time tuition ($14,124), mandatory fees ($650), and college room and board ($5704).

Financial Aid Program-specific awards: 500 dance scholarships for program students ($8000).

Application Procedures Students apply for admission into the professional program by freshman year. Deadline for freshmen and transfers: July 2. Notification date for freshmen and transfers: August 8. Required: high school transcript, college transcript(s) for transfer students, minimum 2.0 high school GPA, letter of recommendation, audition, SAT I or ACT test scores (minimum combined SAT I score of 930, minimum composite ACT score of 20), letter of intent, snapshots, completed registration form, dance resume. Recommended: interview, video. Auditions held twice on campus; videotaped performances are permissible as a substitute for live auditions in special circumstances (scholarships not awarded based on video).

Web Site http://www.belhaven.edu/arts/Dance/default.htm

Undergraduate Contact Suzanne Sullivan, Director of Admissions, Belhaven College, 1500 Peachtree Street, Box 153, Jackson, Mississippi 39202; 601-968-8725, e-mail address: ssullivan@belhaven.edu

The Boston Conservatory

Boston, Massachusetts

Independent, coed. Urban campus. Total enrollment: 537 (2004). Dance program established 1943.

Degrees Bachelor of Fine Arts. Majors and concentrations: dance. Cross-registration with ProArts Consortium. Program accredited by NASM.

Enrollment 76 total; all undergraduate.

Dance Student Profile 84% females, 16% males, 30% minorities, 5% international.

Dance Faculty 7 total (full-time), 15 total (part-time). Graduate students do not teach undergraduate courses. Undergraduate student–faculty ratio: 2:1.

Student Life Student groups/activities include The Boston Conservatory Dance Theater, Boston Dance Theater. Special housing available for dance students.

Expenses for 2006–2007 Application fee: $105. Comprehensive fee: $42,155 includes full-time tuition ($26,400), mandatory fees ($1435), and college room and board ($14,320).

Financial Aid Program-specific awards: Conservatory Scholarships for those passing audition evaluations, Jan Veen Memorial Scholarships for continuing students, Ruth S. Ambrose Award for juniors, Anamarie Sarazin Award for junior ballet students.

Application Procedures Students admitted directly into the professional program freshman year. Deadline for freshmen and transfers: December 1. Notification date for freshmen and transfers: April 1. Required: essay, high school transcript, college transcript(s) for transfer students, 2 letters of recommendation, interview, audition, minimum TOEFL score of 550 for international applicants, artistic resumé, minimum 2.7 high school GPA. Auditions held throughout January, February, and March on campus and off campus in Los Angeles, CA; Houston, TX; New York, NY; Washington, DC; St. Petersburg, FL; videotaped performances are permissible as a substitute for live auditions when distance is prohibitive.

Web Site http://www.bostonconservatory.edu

Undergraduate Contact Admissions Office, The Boston Conservatory, 8 The Fenway, Boston, Massachusetts 02215; 617-912-9153, fax: 617-247-3159, e-mail address: admissions@bostonconservatory.edu

More About the Conservatory

The Boston Conservatory trains exceptional young performing artists for careers that enrich and transform the human experience. Known for its multidisciplinary environment, the Conservatory offers fully accredited graduate and undergraduate programs in music, dance, theater, and music education and

The Boston Conservatory (continued)

presents more than 200 performances each year by students, faculty members, and guest artists. The intimacy of the Conservatory's class settings provides a student-centered atmosphere that is uniquely intensive and supportive.

Since its founding in 1867, the Boston Conservatory has shared its talent and creativity with the city of Boston, the region, and the nation, and it continues to grow today as a vibrant community of artists and educators.

The Boston Conservatory Dance Division is one of the oldest degree-granting dance program in the United States. Founded in 1943 by the dance innovator and teacher, Jan Veen, the Dance Division was the first to offer ballet and modern training as a core curriculum of study. This tradition continues today with additional study in all styles of dance performance.

Daily technique classes provide professional training in ballet and modern dance. In addition, dancers study choreography, pedagogy, music, laban, jazz, tap, and ethnic dance styles.

Versatility for a dancer translates into work and performance opportunities; therefore, the Boston Conservatory curriculum requires students to extend themselves and be knowledgeable about music, literature, dance repertory, dance history, nutrition, Pilates, Alexander Technique, and anatomy. To support the inner dancer, seminars in health and wellness are scheduled throughout the academic year.

Faculty members are current or former members of some of the most prestigious dance organizations in the United States. Their artistry and professional qualifications offer students a full range of dance technique and teaching methods. Faculty members serve as mentors to a core of dancers, forming a nurturing and supportive relationship. Students are thus able to grow and achieve their dreams within a caring, artistic environment.

Performance experience is provided in both studio and mainstage concerts. The range of work performed runs the gamut of dance repertory, in addition to frequent premieres of new works choreographed by artist faculty members or guest artists commissioned by the school. Mainstage concerts are held in collaboration with the Music Division, offering a unique opportunity to interact with musicians as part of the performance preparation.

Boston is a major center of higher education in America, with more than fifty major colleges and universities. This provides a diverse student population and an endless array of courses, lectures, concerts, and social opportunities. The Conservatory is a member of the Pro-Arts Consortium, in collaboration with five area colleges (Emerson College, Berklee College of Music, School of the Museum of Fine Arts, Massachusetts College of Art, and Boston Architectural Center), offering extensive cross-registration course possibilities to all students.

On-campus housing is provided for freshmen and to upperclassmen and graduates on a space-available basis, offering brownstone-style living accommodations just a few steps from the main training and rehearsal buildings. For those students interested in off-campus housing, Boston offers a wide range of architectural styles and rent prices in neighborhoods throughout the city that are all within easy access to the school by public transportation.

The Boston Conservatory strives to meet each student's needs—musically and personally—and provides a nurturing, safe environment in which to study, learn, and grow. The supportive atmosphere of the college extends to student life areas as well. More than a dozen special-interest groups and organizations exist on campus, with new ones developing constantly as the student population grows and needs change. As part of the student services, a number of career seminars are given each year ranging from resume writing and audition anxiety to grant writing and tax laws for the performing artist. In addition, there is an active student government and a student-run newspaper.

Brenau University
Gainesville, Georgia

Independent, Small town campus. Total enrollment: 743. Dance program established 1978.

Degrees Bachelor of Fine Arts in the areas of arts management, dance performance, dance education. Majors and concentrations: dance education, dance performance. Program accredited by NASD.

Enrollment 59 total; 38 undergraduate, 21 nonprofessional degree.

Dance Student Profile 100% females, 27% minorities.

Dance Faculty 3 undergraduate (full-time), 3 undergraduate (part-time). 100% of full-time faculty have terminal degrees. Graduate students do not teach undergraduate courses. Undergraduate student–faculty ratio: 10:1.

Student Life Student groups/activities include Tau Sigma Dance Fraternity, Brenau Opera Company, Gainesville Theatre Alliance.

Expenses for 2005–2006 Application fee: $35. Comprehensive fee: $24,990 includes full-time tuition ($16,440) and college room and board ($8550). Full-time tuition varies according to class time, location, and program. Room and board charges vary according to housing facility.

Financial Aid Program-specific awards: dance scholarships for program majors ($1000–$5000).

Application Procedures Students admitted directly into the professional program freshman year. Deadline for freshmen and transfers: continuous. Notification date for freshmen and transfers: continuous. Required: high school transcript, college transcript(s) for transfer students, letter of recommendation, audition, SAT I or ACT test scores (minimum combined SAT I score of 900, minimum composite ACT score of 19), minimum 2.5 high school GPA. Recommended: minimum 3.0 high school GPA, interview. Auditions held 4 times on campus; videotaped performances are permissible as a substitute for live auditions when distance is prohibitive.

Web Site http://www.brenau.edu/sfah

Undergraduate Contact Christina White, Coordinator of Admissions, Brenau University, 500 Washington Street, SE, Gainesville, Georgia 30501; 800-252-5119, fax: 770-538-4306, e-mail address: cwhite@lib.brenau.edu

Jordan College of Fine Arts
Butler University
Indianapolis, Indiana

Independent, coed. Urban campus. Total enrollment: 4,384. Dance program established 1913.

Degrees Bachelor of Arts in the area of dance pedagogy; Bachelor of Fine Arts in the area of dance performance; Bachelor of Science. Majors and concentrations: dance pedagogy, dance performance. Cross-registration with Indianapolis Consortium for Urban Education. Program accredited by NASD.

Enrollment 71 total; all undergraduate.

Dance Student Profile 89% females, 11% males, 24% minorities, 4% international.

Dance Faculty 6 undergraduate (full-time), 4 undergraduate (part-time). 85% of full-time faculty have terminal degrees. Graduate students do not teach undergraduate courses. Undergraduate student–faculty ratio: 15:1.

Student Life Student groups/activities include Butler Ballet, senior production concerts, summer dance concert and touring.

Expenses for 2005–2006 Application fee: $35. Comprehensive fee: $31,944 includes full-time tuition ($23,530), mandatory fees ($244), and college room and board ($8170). College room only: $3980. Full-time tuition and fees vary according to program. Room and board charges vary according to housing facility.

Financial Aid Program-specific awards: talent awards.

Application Procedures Students admitted directly into the professional program freshman year. Deadline for freshmen and transfers: continuous. Required: essay, high school transcript, college transcript(s) for transfer students, minimum 2.0 high school GPA, letter of recommendation, audition, SAT I or ACT test scores, 5x7 photo in dance attire and appropriate pose (for male dancer: attitude derriére, female dancer: arabesque on pointe). Recommended: minimum 3.0 high school GPA, interview, portfolio. Auditions held 18 times on campus; videotaped performances are permissible as a substitute for live auditions when residence is outside contiguous 48 states. Portfolio reviews held on campus.

Web Site http://www.butler.edu/dance/

Undergraduate Contact Kathy Lang, Admission Representative, Jordan College of Fine Arts, Butler University, Lilly Hall - 138B, 4600 Sunset Avenue, Indianapolis, Indiana 46208; 317-940-9656, fax: 317-940-9658, e-mail address: klang@butler.edu

More About the University

Butler University is most proud of its tradition of excellence and innovation. Challenging and enabling students to meet their personal and professional goals has guided the University since 1855. Today, Butler is an independent, coeducational, nonsectarian university, with a total undergraduate enrollment of more than 3,800 students. The University is accredited by the North Central Association of Colleges and Schools.

Butler's reputation as one of the finest university dance programs in the nation continues, with a department offering the serious dance student professional-level training with a broad approach to liberal arts education. The Department of Dance was among the first in the nation to offer a dance major centered on ballet technique. Many of its graduates have gone on to prestigious professional careers as dancers, teachers, choreographers, managers, and writers.

Dance majors acquire a strong technical training based on the central focus of ballet; versatility in other techniques; the opportunity to perform extensively in a preprofessional company; broad exposure to academic subjects in dance and other arts; and skills in writing, speaking, and analysis from the humanities, mathematics, and science.

Campus and Surroundings Indianapolis, Indiana's state capital and the twelfth-largest city in the nation, boasts a variety of cultural activities, including the Indianapolis Symphony Orchestra, Dance Kaleidoscope, Indiana Repertory Theatre, the Indianapolis Museum of Art, the Eiteljorg Museum, and the world's largest children's museum. Citywide celebrations are plentiful, including ethnic festivals, art fairs, and outdoor music festivals.

Program Facilities The five dance studios in Lilly Hall are equipped with state-of-the-art resilient L'Air modular flooring, barres and mirrors, pianos, and abundant audiovisual equipment. A new performing arts complex is currently under construction. The first phase of the complex, a 47,000-square-foot addition to Lilly Hall called the Courtyard Building, was completed in spring 2003. This new building houses a choral rehearsal hall, an instrumental rehearsal hall, dance studios, a theater studio, an electronic music lab, and a percussion studio. The second phase, the 140-seat Eidson-Duckwall Recital Hall, was completed in fall 2004. The third phase is a 450-seat performance hall/proscenium theater with adjustable acoustical features.

Butler Ballet performs three-to-four productions each year on campus in Clowes Memorial Hall to a total audience of more than 20,000. Clowes Hall, the hub of performing arts at Butler, also presents an extensive array of local, national, and international companies each season.

Faculty/Alumni Butler's highly qualified teachers are artist-scholars who combine broad educational backgrounds with professional performing careers, in-depth study, choreography, and teaching in the United States, Europe, and Asia. Their diversity, expertise, and experience contribute to the scope of the program. Faculty members provide a direct link to the important developments of dance not only in America, but worldwide. They are soloists, artistic directors, certified movement analysts, principal dancers, ballet masters, and ballet mistresses. Recent graduates are performing with the American Repertory Ballet, Atlanta Ballet, Ballet Arizona, Ballet Austin, Boston Ballet, Dance Kaleidoscope, Dance Theatre of Harlem, Georgia Ballet, San Diego Ballet, *The Producers'* National Tour, and the Broadway production and national tour of *Movin' Out.*

Student Performance Opportunities The Butler Ballet is a preprofessional company offering extensive opportunities for performance. The annual presentation of *The Nutcracker* has been an Indianapolis family tradition for more than twenty years. The company also presents full-length classical ballets, such as *Swan Lake, Giselle, Sleeping Beauty, Cinderella,* or *Coppelia.*

Occasionally, the Butler Ballet produces an original contemporary full-length work such as *The Messiah* or Gustav Holst's *The Planets.* In spring 2003, the company presented the world premiere of a new full-length ballet called *The Willow Maiden.*

The company performs in Clowes Memorial Hall, the University's 2,200-seat performance hall, which is rated among the top facilities in the region. Butler Ballet performs with a number of symphonies, notably the Indianapolis Chamber Orchestra. For more than thirty years, the company has toured regionally, providing a unique experience for the students.

Special Programs Degrees in dance require 136 credit hours, including study in three areas: technique, performance, and dance academics. Butler is one of very few schools accredited to offer a Bachelor of Fine Arts degree in performance. Butler also offers a Bachelor of Arts in dance-pedagogy and a Bachelor of Science in dance-arts administration. Students may also opt to have dance as a secondary major or minor.

Cooperative Agreements Butler University has collaborative relationships with many local arts organizations, including the Indianapolis Opera. The following collaborative groups are located on campus: Dance Kaleidoscope, Indianapolis Symphonic Choir, Indianapolis Chamber Orchestra, American Pianists Association, and the Indianapolis Children's Choir.

Career Placement Services and Opportunities Graduates of the dance department excel as dancers, teachers, choreographers, and artistic directors with professional, semi-professional, and regional companies as well as on Broadway or in musical theater and film productions. Some work for universities and private studios while others combine their knowledge with other artistic disciplines to become photographers or designers of costumes, sets, and lighting. Arts management or dance research and criticism are additional career choices. Graduates qualify for a wide variety of careers due to the diverse curricula and personalized advising from Butler's faculty members. The University's Center for Career Planning and Development and the Department of Dance both play an active role in assisting dance majors with job opportunities.

California Institute of the Arts
Valencia, California

Independent, coed. Total enrollment: 1,327. Dance program established 1971.

Degrees Bachelor of Fine Arts. Majors and concentrations: dance. Graduate degrees offered: Master of Fine Arts in the areas of choreography, integrated media. Program accredited by NASD.

Enrollment 83 total; 68 undergraduate, 10 graduate, 5 nonprofessional degree.

Dance Student Profile 79% females, 21% males, 37% minorities, 13% international.

Dance Faculty 7 total (full-time), 10 total (part-time). 100% of full-time faculty have terminal degrees. Graduate students do not teach undergraduate courses. Undergraduate student–faculty ratio: 7:1.

Student Life Student groups/activities include American College Dance Festival Association. Special housing available for dance students.

Expenses for 2005–2006 Application fee: $65. Comprehensive fee: $35,422 includes full-time tuition ($27,260), mandatory fees ($465), and college room and board ($7697). College room only: $4095. Full-time tuition and fees vary according to course load. Room and board charges vary according to board plan, housing facility, and location. Special program-related fees: $475 per year for technology fee.

California Institute of the Arts (continued)

Financial Aid Program-specific awards: 30–35 Sharon Lund Scholarships for program majors ($2000–$10,000).

Application Procedures Students admitted directly into the professional program freshman year. Deadline for freshmen and transfers: January 5. Required: essay, high school transcript, college transcript(s) for transfer students, 2 letters of recommendation, audition. Auditions held 15 times on campus and off campus in New York, NY; Baltimore, MD; Dallas, TX; Houston, TX; San Francisco, CA; Chicago, IL; Hilo, HI; Minneapolis, MN; Portland, OR; San Diego, CA; San Antonio, TX; Phoenix, AZ; Atlanta, GA; Valencia, CA; videotaped performances are permissible as a substitute for live auditions with approval from the department and for international students.

Web Site http://www.calarts.edu

Contact Mr. Clyde Howell, Recruitment Specialist, School of Dance, California Institute of the Arts, 24700 McBean Parkway, Valencia, California 91355; 661-291-3046, fax: 661-253-1562, e-mail address: chowell@calarts.edu

More About the Institute

Located in Valencia in Southern California, the California Institute of the Arts (CalArts) School of Dance offers a Bachelor of Fine Arts (B.F.A.) degree in dance performance/choreography/production and a Master of Fine Arts (M.F.A.) degree in choreography. The B.F.A degree program carries with it a complete component of general studies as presented by the School of Critical Studies. An audition is required of all incoming students. Acceptance into the program is based solely on talent. Information on times, locations, and dates is available from the School of Dance office and the Office of Enrollment Services.

The B.F.A. curriculum places a strong emphasis on the individual development of each dancer through modern and ballet techniques, performance opportunities, and dance production and nurtures creative freedom through dance composition and choreography. Because of a low student-faculty ratio, equal importance is placed on studies relating to dance, such as production technology, music, dance history, anatomy, kinesiology, video, digital technologies, production crewing, Pilates, and African and Indonesian dance as electives. Interdisciplinary collaboration is encouraged on all levels, broadening the future of dance in ways that constantly challenge the imagination.

Program Facilities The CalArts Sharon Disney Lund Dance Theater is a 50-foot-by-70-foot space used exclusively for dance performances, rehearsals, and classes. This hall features wall-to-wall *L Air* sprung flooring covered with seamless black *Lonstage*. Retractable theater seating allows for many different staging configurations. Seating capacity is usually 125 persons, with a maximum capacity of 250.

In addition to the Sharon Disney Lund Dance Theater, there are three other full-time dance studios available for technique classes, composition classes, and rehearsals. The two larger dance studios measure 36-feet-by-50-feet each. Each studio has one mirrored wall and barres set into the other three walls, and is equipped with a set of eight portable barres, a piano, and power outlets for sound and video equipment. Both spaces have *L Air* sprung floors covered in seamless *Lonstage*. The third studio is 39-feet-by-23-feet and has a sprung wooded floor, a full wall of mirrors, and a chalkboard.

A fully carpeted Pilates body-conditioning studio measures 39-feet-by-23-feet. It has a mirrored wall and includes the following equipment: four Pilates studio reformers, two trapeze tables, one Wunda chair, one whale, four tumbling mats, and one Pacemaster Pro-Plus treadmill.

The School of Dance's array of digital, video, and sound equipment allows M.F.A. and upper-division B.F.A students to experiment with multi-track mixing and video editing techniques while creating movement-themed DVDs as well as Web page design. Digital video is incorporated into documenting all dance works and a variety of other classroom and production purposes.

In downtown Los Angeles, The Roy and Edna Disney/CalArts Theater, otherwise known as REDCAT, is housed as a separate entity in the stunning, new Frank Gehry-designed Walt Disney Concert Hall. REDCAT is conceived as a unique platform to showcase CalArts experimental and interdisciplinary work in dance, theater, music, the visual arts, and film/video.

Faculty and Alumni The School's faculty consists of well-known, seasoned professional artists who are continuing to pursue and explore dance while teaching. The School of Dance faculty members include Tina Yuan, Acting Dean, Clare Duncan, David Kroth, Lyndon Branaugh, Laurence Blake, Fontella Boone, David Burns, Colin Connor, John Gaydos, Kate Fox, Cheryl Montelle, Ed Groff, Francesca Penzani, Michael Roberts, Cynthia Young, Rachel Berman, and Glen Eddy.

The CalArts Dance Ensemble, formed in 1980, has created a venue for the faculty members to continue performing and choreographing on a professional level among each other, selected advanced students, guest choreographers, alumni, composers, and designers.

The School of Dance has alumni performing in dance and touring companies, choreographing, directing, and teaching. Among these include Jamie Bishton, artistic director of Jamie Bishton/Dance in New York City; Keisha Clarke, who tours with the Garth Fagan Dance Company in Rochester, New York; Qi Zhang, choreographer; Laura Gorenstein, artistic director of Helios Dance Theater in Los Angeles; Dawn Stoppiello, co-artistic director of Troika Ranch in New York City; Yuan-Yuan Wang, choreographer; Jacques Heim, artistic director of the Diavolo Dance Theater in Los Angeles; and others.

Student Performance/Exhibit Opportunities The School of Dance's performance schedule features as many as twelve student- and faculty-produced concerts each year—including the Open House Concert, two noon concerts, M.F.A. thesis concerts, the Spring Dance Concert, and the CalArts Dance Ensemble concert. The CalArts Dance Ensemble also serves as a showcase for the School's alumni, who regularly choreograph and perform with the group.

Special Programs The School of Dance has an ongoing exchange program with the London Contemporary Dance School. Each fall, two upper-division undergraduates selected by the dean and faculty enjoy the unique opportunity to study abroad for one semester.

Chapman University
Orange, California

Independent, coed. Suburban campus. Total enrollment: 5,732.

Degrees Bachelor of Fine Arts. Majors and concentrations: performance.

Enrollment 77 total; 11 undergraduate, 66 nonprofessional degree.

Dance Student Profile 87% females, 13% males, 22% minorities.

Dance Faculty 3 undergraduate (full-time), 11 undergraduate (part-time). 100% of full-time faculty have terminal degrees. Graduate students do not teach undergraduate courses. Undergraduate student–faculty ratio: 10:1.

Student Life Student groups/activities include Chapman Dance Association, American Celebration, Performing Arts Society of Chapman.

Expenses for 2006–2007 Application fee: $55. Comprehensive fee: $41,248 includes full-time tuition ($29,900), mandatory fees ($848), and college room and board ($10,500). Special program-related fees: $75 per per course for senior-level conservatory courses only; fee for individual instruction.

Financial Aid Program-specific awards: 40 talent awards for incoming students ($2000).

Application Procedures Students apply for admission into the professional program by sophomore year. Deadline for freshmen: January 31; transfers: March 15. Required: essay, high school transcript, college transcript(s) for transfer students, minimum 2.0 high school GPA, 2 letters of recommendation, audition, SAT I or ACT test scores, recent photograph, resume. Recommended: interview. Auditions held 4 times on campus;

videotaped performances are permissible as a substitute for live auditions with permission of the Senior Department Secretary.
Web Site http://www.chapman.edu/comm/td/
Undergraduate Contact Ms. Bonnie Walker, Senior Department Secretary, Theatre and Dance Department, Chapman University, 1 University Drive, Orange, California 92866; 714-744-7087, fax: 714-744-7015, e-mail address: tdoffice@chapman.edu

College-Conservatory of Music Dance Division

See University of Cincinnati

Columbia College

Columbia, South Carolina

Independent United Methodist, Suburban campus. Total enrollment: 1,493. Dance program established 1976.
Degrees Bachelor of Fine Arts. Majors and concentrations: choreography, dance performance. Program accredited by NASD.
Enrollment 100 total; 10 undergraduate, 50 graduate, 40 nonprofessional degree.
Dance Student Profile 100% females, 10% minorities.
Dance Faculty 4 undergraduate (full-time), 4 undergraduate (part-time). 50% of full-time faculty have terminal degrees. Graduate students do not teach undergraduate courses. Undergraduate student–faculty ratio: 10:1.
Student Life Student groups/activities include American College Dance Festival Association, The Power Company-Resident Professional Contemporary Dance Company, South Carolina Dancing Association (SCDA).
Expenses for 2005–2006 Application fee: $25. Comprehensive fee: $25,032 includes full-time tuition ($18,864), mandatory fees ($350), and college room and board ($5818). College room only: $3034. Full-time tuition and fees vary according to class time. Room and board charges vary according to board plan and housing facility.
Financial Aid Program-specific awards: 10 dance scholarships for program majors ($3000–$5000).
Application Procedures Students apply for admission into the professional program by freshman, sophomore year. Deadline for freshmen and transfers: continuous. Required: high school transcript, college transcript(s) for transfer students, minimum 2.0 high school GPA, 4 letters of recommendation, SAT I or ACT test scores (minimum combined SAT I score of 850, minimum composite ACT score of 21). Recommended: essay, interview. Auditions held once and by appointment on campus; recorded music is permissible as a substitute for live auditions for out-of-state applicants and videotaped performances are permissible as a substitute for live auditions for out-of-state applicants. Portfolio reviews held twice on campus.
Web Site http://www.columbiacollegesc.edu
Undergraduate Contact Ms. Patty Graham, M.A., Associate Professor, Dance Department, Columbia College, 1301 Columbia College Drive, Columbia, South Carolina 29203; 803-786-3668, fax: 803-786-3868, e-mail address: pgraham@colacoll.edu

Columbia College Chicago

Chicago, Illinois

Independent, coed. Urban campus. Total enrollment: 10,842. Dance program established 1970.
Degrees Bachelor of Arts in the area of dance; Bachelor of Fine Arts in the area of dance. Majors and concentrations: choreography, dance education, music theater, performance.
Enrollment 218 total; all undergraduate.
Dance Student Profile 95% females, 5% males, 35% minorities, 2% international.
Dance Faculty 9 total (full-time), 35 total (part-time). Graduate students do not teach undergraduate courses. Undergraduate student–faculty ratio: 5:1.

Expenses for 2006–2007 Application fee: $35. Comprehensive fee: $26,553 includes full-time tuition ($16,328), mandatory fees ($460), and college room and board ($9765). College room only: $8265. Special program-related fees: $15–$110 per course for class fees.
Financial Aid Program-specific awards: 1 Dance Africa Scholarship ($2500), 2 Dance Center Scholarships ($1500).
Application Procedures Students admitted directly into the professional program freshman year. Deadline for freshmen and transfers: continuous. Notification date for freshmen and transfers: continuous. Required: essay, high school transcript, college transcript(s) for transfer students, letter of recommendation, students with less than a 2.0 GPA may be required to see an admissions counselor for a personal interview and may be required to attend an intensive remediation program, audition and portfolio for transfer students. Recommended: minimum 2.0 high school GPA, interview, SAT I or ACT test scores. Auditions held on campus. Portfolio reviews held on campus.
Web Site http://www.colum.edu
Undergraduate Contact Mr. Murphy Monroe, Director, Office of Admissions, Columbia College Chicago, 600 South Michigan Avenue, Chicago, Illinois 60605; 312-344-7133, fax: 312-344-8024, e-mail address: admissions@colum.edu

More About the College

Columbia College is the largest and most diverse private undergraduate and graduate arts, media, and communications college in the nation. Located in downtown Chicago, Columbia sits at the heart of the Midwest's arts and communications industries. Columbia's faculty and student body comprise a widely diverse mix of cultures and backgrounds, creating a stimulating environment ideally suited to the pursuit of creative innovation. Intimate class settings (class sizes average only 16 students) facilitate personal attention and practical mentoring with a faculty of working professionals. An aggressive, wide-reaching internship program offers students the opportunity to gain on-site education in their areas of interest.

Columbia places a strong emphasis on each student's development of a professional body of work or portfolio in all disciplines across the college. Columbia's Portfolio Center is dedicated to helping graduating students present their body of work in the most professional way—the exact way employers want to see it. Faculty members work closely with students to help them refine and select appropriate pieces and samples for inclusion in their final portfolio.

The College also provides a strong liberal arts background for the developing artist or communicator. Of the required credit hours for the undergraduate degree programs, 47 are distributed among courses in the humanities and literature, science and mathematics, English composition, oral communications, social sciences, and computer applications. Creative students who enjoy a supportive but challenging environment thrive at Columbia.

The Dance Center features a nationally respected academic program and offers three different undergraduate programs designed to suit varied levels of student interest in the art of dance: the Bachelor of Fine Arts (B.F.A.) in dance, Bachelor of Arts (B.A.) in dance, and a dance minor. The curriculum focuses on developing skill, personal voice, and maturity in the dance artist—as dancer, choreographer, or teacher. Challenging technique courses across a range of styles, combined with the study of improvisation, composition, dance history and theory, music, and technical theater, provide students with essential learning and practice, preparing them for professional and graduate endeavors in dance. The Dance Center's faculty, composed of working artists, is enhanced by an array of visiting artist-teachers of national and international stature.

The core requirements are shared by both the B.A. and B.F.A. programs. However, the B.F.A. program is intended for students with professional aspirations and includes a variety of courses that, in their breadth and depth, prepare students to enter the field as young artists. At 79 credit hours, the demands of the B.F.A. program are significant. The possibility of minoring in another subject within a standard four-year course of study is greatly

Columbia College Chicago (continued)

diminished on this track. The B.F.A. is most appropriate for students who wish to make a definitive commitment to dance.

The Bachelor of Arts program is intended for students who wish to make dance the focus of their undergraduate education but who do not necessarily have aspirations to be artistic professionals in the field. The major is an appropriate choice for those who want significant exposure and proficiency in dance but who also desire the opportunity to explore other areas of interest. At 56 credit hours, the dance major provides substantial proficiency in modern dance idioms as well as solid foundations of related information, skills, and experiences. The requirements for the major allow enough time and credit hours for students to explore other fields through elective courses and minors.

The dance minor is intended for students who desire a formal course of study in dance as an adjunct to their major in another field. The dance minor provides students with practical and intellectual experiences in dance and a limited degree of physical proficiency in modern dance idioms.

Columbia's enrollment of more than 10,500 students is drawn from Chicago and its suburbs, the Midwest, across the United States, and more than forty-five other countries. The student body is almost equally divided between men and women.

Campus and Surroundings Columbia's campus is set in Chicago's dynamic South Loop neighborhood, across from Grant Park and Lake Michigan. Close to the Art Institute, Navy Pier, the Adler Planetarium, the Field Museum, the Chicago Symphony, and several other colleges and universities, Columbia's faculty members and students utilize the city of Chicago as a social, educational, and professional resource. Convenient public transportation makes all cultural and educational opportunities easily accessible.

Program Facilities Columbia College consists of eighteen campus buildings located primarily in the historic South Loop neighborhood of downtown Chicago. The centers for dance, music, and theater are conveniently located and are designed for their specific performance needs, including individual and group rehearsal and specialized performance spaces.

The College's 200,000-volume library and instructional service center provide comprehensive information and study facilities. Reading/study rooms and special audiovisual equipment are available for use in individual projects and research. As a member of a statewide online computer catalog and resource-sharing network, Columbia's library provides students with access to the resources of forty-five academic institutions in Illinois, effectively creating an information base of several million volumes.

Faculty, Resident Artists, and Alumni Many of Columbia's 1,340 full- and part-time faculty members are working professionals (artists, writers, filmmakers, dancers, etc.) with national reputations. The College is constantly seeking individuals who are both gifted teachers and talented professionals. Many faculty members work nearby in the disciplines in which they teach and share practical expertise with students in informal workshop settings and in the classroom. Interaction with faculty members who are practicing professionals provides students with invaluable access to the latest information in their fields. Students also begin developing their own professional network, as faculty members share contacts and information on how to break into the market.

Students in the dance programs at Columbia College Chicago learn in the environment of a working dance center, with accomplished faculty artists, producers, and scholars and numerous guest artists participating in short- and long-term teaching residencies. Recent guest teachers include Liz Burritt, David Gordon, Joe Goode, Millicent Hodson, Wendy Rogers, and Erica Wilson-Perkins. The Dance Center is also home to Chicago's finest and most active contemporary dance presenting series, featuring national and international companies.

Student Performance Opportunities Dance Center students have numerous opportunities to perform while they are studying dance at Columbia College Chicago. Usually they are involved directly with the choreographers in the development of new dance works—valuable experience they can take into the real world.

Concordia University
Montreal, Quebec, Canada

Province-supported, coed. Urban campus. Total enrollment: 31,042. Dance program established 1979.
Degrees Bachelor of Fine Arts. Majors and concentrations: contemporary dance. Cross-registration with any university in Quebec or other approved international institutions.
Enrollment 55 total; all undergraduate.
Dance Student Profile 4% international.
Dance Faculty 3 total (full-time), 15 total (part-time). Graduate students teach a few undergraduate courses. Undergraduate student–faculty ratio: 4:1.
Student Life Student groups/activities include Art Matters Festival, Fine Arts Student Alliance activities, year-end dance shows.
Expenses for 2005–2006 Application fee: $50 Canadian dollars. Tuition, fee, and room and board charges are reported in Canadian dollars. Province resident tuition: $1668 full-time. Canadian resident tuition: $4651 full-time. Mandatory fees: $979 full-time. Full-time tuition and fees vary according to program. College room and board: $6905. Room and board charges vary according to housing facility. International student tuition: $11,238 full-time.
Financial Aid Program-specific awards: Concordia University Entrance Scholarships for Canadian students ($2000).
Application Procedures Students admitted directly into the professional program freshman year. Deadline for freshmen and transfers: June 1. Notification date for freshmen and transfers: August 31. Required: high school transcript, college transcript(s) for transfer students, video, audition. Auditions held 3 times in April, May, and June on campus; videotaped performances are permissible as a substitute for live auditions if a campus visit is impossible.
Web Site http://dance.concordia.ca
Undergraduate Contact Ms. Jolanta Manowska, Communications Assistant, Office of Student Recruitment, Concordia University, 1455 de Maisonneuve Boulevard West, FB801, Montreal, Quebec H3G 1M8, Canada; 514-848-4772, fax: 514-848-2827.

Cornish College of the Arts
Seattle, Washington

Independent, coed. Urban campus. Total enrollment: 768. Dance program established 1914.
Degrees Bachelor of Fine Arts in the area of dance. Majors and concentrations: ballet, choreography and performance, modern dance.
Enrollment 90 total; all undergraduate.
Dance Student Profile 65% females, 35% males, 14% minorities, 4% international.
Dance Faculty 6 undergraduate (full-time), 13 undergraduate (part-time). 58% of full-time faculty have terminal degrees. Graduate students do not teach undergraduate courses. Undergraduate student–faculty ratio: 5:1.
Student Life Student groups/activities include Cornish Dance Theater.
Expenses for 2005–2006 Application fee: $35. Tuition: $21,200 full-time. Mandatory fees: $300 full-time.
Financial Aid Program-specific awards: Nellie Scholarships for new students, departmental scholarships for new and continuing students, Presidential Scholarships for continuing students.
Application Procedures Students admitted directly into the professional program freshman year. Deadline for freshmen and transfers: August 15. Required: essay, high school transcript, college transcript(s) for transfer students, minimum 2.0 high school GPA, audition. Recommended: 2 letters of recommendation, interview, SAT I or ACT test scores. Auditions held 10 times on campus and off campus in various sites in northern and southern California, Interlochen, MI; Perpich School (Minneapolis, MN); videotaped performances are permissible as a substitute for live auditions when distance is prohibitive.

Web Site http://www.cornish.edu
Undergraduate Contact Eric Pedersen, Director of Admission, Cornish College of the Arts, 1000 Lenora, Seattle, Washington 98121; 800-726-ARTS, fax: 206-720-1011, e-mail address: epedersen@cornish.edu

East Carolina University
Greenville, North Carolina

State-supported, coed. Urban campus. Total enrollment: 23,164. Dance program established 1962.
Degrees Bachelor of Fine Arts in the area of dance. Majors and concentrations: ballet, dance education, jazz dance, modern dance.
Enrollment 85 total; 70 undergraduate, 15 nonprofessional degree.
Dance Student Profile 70% females, 30% males, 4% minorities, 1% international.
Dance Faculty 6 total (full-time), 2 total (part-time). 95% of full-time faculty have terminal degrees. Graduate students do not teach undergraduate courses. Undergraduate student–faculty ratio: 25:1.
Student Life Student groups/activities include guest artists/visiting artists, day of dance, master classes.
Expenses for 2005–2006 Application fee: $50. State resident tuition: $2135 full-time. Nonresident tuition: $12,649 full-time. Mandatory fees: $1492 full-time. College room and board: $6840. College room only: $3790. Room and board charges vary according to board plan and housing facility.
Financial Aid Program-specific awards: 3 endowed scholarships for program majors ($500–$1000).
Application Procedures Students apply for admission into the professional program by sophomore year. Deadline for freshmen: March 15; transfers: April 15. Required: high school transcript, college transcript(s) for transfer students, SAT I or ACT test scores. Recommended: minimum 2.0 high school GPA, 3 letters of recommendation, audition. Auditions held once on campus.
Web Site http://www.theatre-dance.ecu.edu
Undergraduate Contact Undergraduate Admissions, East Carolina University, Wichard Building, Greenville, North Carolina 27858-4353; 252-328-6640, e-mail address: admis@mail.ecu.edu

Eastern Michigan University
Ypsilanti, Michigan

State-supported, coed. Suburban campus. Total enrollment: 23,240. Dance program established 1951.
Degrees Bachelor of Science in the area of dance. Majors and concentrations: dance performance, dance therapy, studio management.
Enrollment 22 total; all undergraduate.
Dance Faculty 3 undergraduate (full-time), 4 undergraduate (part-time). 100% of full-time faculty have terminal degrees. Graduate students do not teach undergraduate courses. Undergraduate student–faculty ratio: 15:1.
Student Life Student groups/activities include performances (on and off campus), Dance Forum.
Expenses for 2005–2006 Application fee: $30. State resident tuition: $5463 full-time. Nonresident tuition: $16,818 full-time. Mandatory fees: $1078 full-time. College room and board: $6356.
Financial Aid Program-specific awards: 2 financial aid scholarships for talent based ($1000), 1 Linda Hemmelgarn Scholarship for continuing students ($300), 5 Service Awards for continuing students ($1000).
Application Procedures Students admitted directly into the professional program freshman year. Deadline for freshmen and transfers: August 1. Required: high school transcript, college transcript(s) for transfer students, minimum 2.0 high school GPA, SAT I or ACT test scores. Auditions held 3 times on campus; videotaped performances are permissible as a substitute for live auditions.
Web Site http://www.emich.edu/dance

Undergraduate Contact Academic Admissions, Eastern Michigan University, 400 Pierce Hall, EMU, Ypsilanti, Michigan 48197; 734-487-3060, fax: 784-487-6559.

Emerson College
Boston, Massachusetts

Independent, coed. Urban campus. Total enrollment: 4,326.

Feinstein College of Arts and Sciences

See Roger Williams University

Florida State University
Tallahassee, Florida

State-supported, coed. Suburban campus. Total enrollment: 39,146. Dance program established 1965.
Degrees Bachelor of Fine Arts. Majors and concentrations: dance. Graduate degrees offered: Master of Arts in the area of American dance studies; Master of Fine Arts in the area of dance. Cross-registration with Florida Agricultural and Mechanical University. Program accredited by NASD.
Enrollment 619 total; 61 undergraduate, 18 graduate, 540 nonprofessional degree.
Dance Student Profile 92% females, 8% males, 22% minorities.
Dance Faculty 17 total (full-time), 1 total (part-time). 43% of full-time faculty have terminal degrees. Graduate students teach about a quarter of undergraduate courses. Undergraduate student–faculty ratio: 5:1.
Student Life Student groups/activities include American College Dance Festival Association, Florida Dance Association.
Expenses for 2005–2006 Application fee: $30. State resident tuition: $3208 full-time. Nonresident tuition: $16,340 full-time. Full-time tuition varies according to location. College room and board: $6778. College room only: $3600. Room and board charges vary according to board plan and housing facility.
Financial Aid Program-specific awards: 25 out-of-state tuition waivers for program majors ($2400–$3200), 8 talent and need awards for program majors ($250–$1000).
Application Procedures Students admitted directly into the professional program freshman year. Deadline for freshmen: March 3; transfers: July 3. Required: high school transcript, college transcript(s) for transfer students, minimum 3.0 high school GPA, audition, SAT I or ACT test scores, video for international applicants. Recommended: 3 letters of recommendation. Auditions held 3 times on campus.
Web Site http://dance.fsu.edu/
Undergraduate Contact Ms. Patricia Phillips, Associate Chairperson, Department of Dance, Florida State University, Room 201 Montgomery Gym, Tallahassee, Florida 32306-2120; 850-644-1023, fax: 850-644-1277.
Graduate Contact Ms. Elizabeth Patenaude, Chairperson, Department of Dance, Florida State University, Room 201 Montgomery Gym, Tallahassee, Florida 32306-2120; 850-644-1023, fax: 850-644-1277.

Friends University
Wichita, Kansas

Independent, coed. Urban campus. Total enrollment: 3,190. Dance program established 1987.
Degrees Bachelor of Fine Arts. Majors and concentrations: ballet. Cross-registration with Newman University.
Enrollment 30 total; all undergraduate.
Dance Student Profile 80% females, 20% males, 5% international.
Dance Faculty 1 undergraduate (full-time), 5 undergraduate (part-time). 50% of full-time faculty have terminal degrees. Graduate students do not teach undergraduate courses. Undergraduate student–faculty ratio: 20:1.
Student Life Student groups/activities include Wichita Ballet Theater.

Friends University (continued)

Expenses for 2004–2005 Application fee: $15. Tuition: $14,430 full-time. Mandatory fees: $170 full-time.
Financial Aid Program-specific awards: 5 Miller Scholarships for program majors ($1500), 18 departmental scholarships for program majors ($2400), 4 citizenship awards for program majors ($1500).
Application Procedures Students admitted directly into the professional program freshman year. Deadline for freshmen: August 1; transfers: August 15. Required: high school transcript, college transcript(s) for transfer students, minimum 2.0 high school GPA, interview, audition, SAT I or ACT test scores. Auditions held 4 times on campus and off campus in various locations; video-taped performances are permissible as a substitute for live auditions if a campus visit is impossible.
Web Site http://www.friends.edu
Undergraduate Contact Mr. Stan Rogers, Director, Department of Dance, Friends University, 2100 University Drive, Wichita, Kansas 67213; 316-295-5848, e-mail address: rogersst@friends.edu

George Mason University
Fairfax, Virginia

State-supported, coed. Suburban campus. Total enrollment: 29,728. Dance program established 1980.
Degrees Bachelor of Fine Arts in the area of dance. Majors and concentrations: choreography and performance. Graduate degrees offered: Master of Fine Arts in the area of dance.
Enrollment 78 total; 51 undergraduate, 8 graduate, 19 nonprofessional degree.
Dance Student Profile 95% females, 5% males, 18% minorities, 4% international.
Dance Faculty 8 total (full-time), 12 total (part-time). 88% of full-time faculty have terminal degrees. Graduate students do not teach undergraduate courses. Undergraduate student–faculty ratio: 10:1.
Student Life Student groups/activities include George Mason University Dance Company, guest artists residencies. Special housing available for dance students.
Expenses for 2005–2006 Application fee: $60. State resident tuition: $4356 full-time. Nonresident tuition: $15,636 full-time. Mandatory fees: $1524 full-time. Full-time tuition and fees vary according to course load. College room and board: $6480. College room only: $3700. Room and board charges vary according to board plan and housing facility.
Financial Aid Program-specific awards: 1 Joanne Johnson Arts Scholarship for program majors ($1000), 1 Harriet Mattusch Special Recognition Award for program majors ($2400), 4 Kevin Campbell Summer Scholarships for program majors ($500), 1 Bette Carter Scholarship for program majors ($1000), 1 Dance Faculty Talent Scholarship for incoming freshmen (renewable) ($5000), 1 Sallie Mae Fund Scholarship for program majors ($5000).
Application Procedures Students apply for admission into the professional program by freshman year. Deadline for freshmen: January 15; transfers: April 1. Notification date for freshmen: April 1; transfers: April 15. Required: essay, high school transcript, college transcript(s) for transfer students, interview, audition, SAT I or ACT test scores. Recommended: minimum 3.0 high school GPA. Auditions held 5 times on campus and off campus in New York, NY; videotaped performances are permissible as a substitute for live auditions for students living more than 500 miles from campus.
Web Site http://dance.gmu.edu
Undergraduate Contact Ms. Marjorie Summerall, Program Coordinator, Dance Department, George Mason University, MS 3D4, Fairfax, Virginia 22030-4444; 703-993-1114, fax: 703-993-1366, e-mail address: msummera@gmu.edu
Graduate Contact Mr. Dan Joyce, Graduate Program Coordinator, Dance Department, George Mason University, MS 3D4, Fairfax, Virginia 22030-4444; 703-993-1114, fax: 703-993-1366, e-mail address: djoyce@gmu.edu

The Hartt School
See University of Hartford

Indiana University Bloomington
Bloomington, Indiana

State-supported, coed. Small town campus. Total enrollment: 37,958. Dance program established 1956.
Degrees Bachelor of Science; Bachelor of Science with an Outside Field. Majors and concentrations: ballet. Graduate degrees offered: Master of Science in the area of ballet. Program accredited by NASM.
Enrollment 55 total; all undergraduate.
Dance Student Profile 82% females, 18% males, 15% minorities.
Dance Faculty 4 total (full-time), 2 total (part-time). Graduate students do not teach undergraduate courses. Undergraduate student–faculty ratio: 9:1.
Student Life Student groups/activities include dancing with Illinois Opera Theatre, teaching in Pre-College Program (ages 3-18), major ballet performances (3 per year).
Expenses for 2005–2006 Application fee: $50. State resident tuition: $6291 full-time. Nonresident tuition: $18,687 full-time. Mandatory fees: $821 full-time. Full-time tuition and fees vary according to location, program, and student level. College room and board: $6240. College room only: $3760. Room and board charges vary according to board plan and housing facility. Special program-related fees: $150 per course for ballet therapy.
Financial Aid Program-specific awards: School of Music Dean's Awards for those demonstrating musical ability and scholastic achievement, minority scholarships for those demonstrating musical ability, scholastic achievement, and financial need, University Grants for those demonstrating musical ability, scholastic achievement, and financial need.
Application Procedures Students admitted directly into the professional program freshman year. Deadline for freshmen and transfers: continuous. Required: essay, high school transcript, college transcript(s) for transfer students, minimum 2.0 high school GPA, audition, SAT I or ACT test scores. Recommended: minimum 3.0 high school GPA. Auditions held 6 times on campus; videotaped performances are permissible as a substitute for live auditions.
Web Site http://www.music.indiana.edu
Contact Music Admissions, School of Music, Indiana University Bloomington, 1201 East 3rd Street-MU 101, Bloomington, Indiana 47405; 812-855-7998, fax: 812-856-6086, e-mail address: musicadm@indiana.edu

Jacksonville University
Jacksonville, Florida

Independent, coed. Suburban campus. Total enrollment: 2,948. Dance program established 1958.
Degrees Bachelor of Fine Arts. Majors and concentrations: dance. Program accredited by NASD.
Enrollment 51 total; all undergraduate.
Dance Student Profile 58% females, 42% males, 22% minorities, 3% international.
Dance Faculty 3 undergraduate (full-time). 100% of full-time faculty have terminal degrees. Graduate students do not teach undergraduate courses. Undergraduate student–faculty ratio: 17:1.
Student Life Student groups/activities include Jacksonville University Dance Theatre, Jacksonville University Dance Ensemble, Alpha Psi Omega.
Expenses for 2005–2006 Application fee: $30. Comprehensive fee: $26,430 includes full-time tuition ($19,970) and college room and board ($6460). College room only: $3030. Special program-related fees: $15–$80 per course per semester for materials, $50 per course per semester for student choreography production fees.
Financial Aid Program-specific awards: 11 dance scholarships for those demonstrating need/talent ($1000–$5300), 1 Phillips Scholarship for those demonstrating exceptional talent ($1000).
Application Procedures Students admitted directly into the professional program freshman year. Deadline for freshmen and transfers: continuous. Notification date for freshmen and transfers: continuous. Required: high school transcript, college transcript(s) for transfer students, minimum 2.0 high school GPA,

audition, SAT I or ACT test scores (minimum combined SAT I score of 800). Recommended: essay, minimum 3.0 high school GPA, 3 letters of recommendation. Auditions held twice and by appointment on campus; videotaped performances are permissible as a substitute for live auditions if a campus visit is impossible.
Web Site http://www.ju.edu
Undergraduate Contact Miriam King, Vice President of Enrollment Management, Jacksonville University, 2800 University Boulevard North, Jacksonville, Florida 32211; 904-256-7000, fax: 904-256-7012, e-mail address: admissions@ju.edu

Jordan College of Fine Arts
See Butler University

The Juilliard School
New York, New York

Independent, coed. Urban campus. Total enrollment: 808. Dance program established 1951.
Degrees Bachelor of Fine Arts. Majors and concentrations: dance. Cross-registration with Barnard and Columbia Colleges (Columbia University).
Enrollment 88 total; all undergraduate.
Dance Student Profile 52% females, 48% males, 38% minorities, 8% international.
Dance Faculty 12 undergraduate (full-time), 13 undergraduate (part-time). Graduate students do not teach undergraduate courses. Undergraduate student–faculty ratio: 4:1.
Student Life Student groups/activities include dance performances, composers/choreographers collaboration, arts outreach program. Special housing available for dance students.
Expenses for 2005–2006 Application fee: $100. Comprehensive fee: $34,500 includes full-time tuition ($24,330), mandatory fees ($600), and college room and board ($9570). Room and board charges vary according to housing facility.
Financial Aid Program-specific awards: 82 merit and/or need-based aid for program majors ($22,985).
Application Procedures Students admitted directly into the professional program freshman year. Deadline for freshmen and transfers: December 1. Notification date for freshmen and transfers: April 1. Required: essay, high school transcript, college transcript(s) for transfer students, 2 letters of recommendation, audition, TOEFL for all non-native English speakers. Recommended: photo. Auditions held once on campus and off campus in San Francisco, CA; Dallas, TX; St. Petersburg, FL; Minneapolis, MN.
Web Site http://www.juilliard.edu
Undergraduate Contact Ms. Lee Cioppa, Associate Dean for Admissions, The Juilliard School, 60 Lincoln Center Plaza, New York, New York 10023-6588; 212-799-5000 ext. 223, fax: 212-769-6420, e-mail address: admissions@juilliard.edu

More About the School

Juilliard aims to create true contemporary dancers—trained equally in classical ballet and modern dance. By teaching dancers the great traditions and disciplines of both past and present, Julliard opens their eyes and minds to all the choreographic possibilities that lie ahead. Now in its fifty-fifth season, the Juilliard Dance Division is a groundbreaking conservatory dance program whose faculty members and alumni have changed the face of dance around the world. Established in 1951 by William Schuman during his tenure as president of Juilliard, with the guidance of founding director Martha Hill, Juilliard Dance became the first major teaching institution to combine equal dance instruction in both contemporary and ballet techniques, an idea that was considered heretical in its day. Early faculty members included renowned dance figures, such as Alfredo Corvino, Doris Humphrey, José Limón, Anna Sokolow, Antony Tudor, and Hector Zaraspe. Ms. Hill became Artistic Director Emeritus with the appointment of Muriel Topaz as Director in 1985, and she remained active at Juilliard almost until her death in 1995. In 1992, choreographer and artistic director

Benjamin Harkarvy was appointed head of the division, a position he maintained until his death in March 2002. In July of 2002, master teacher Lawrence Rhodes was appointed the new director of the Dance Division. Since his appointment, Mr. Rhodes' focus remains the students' involvement with a wide variety of dance styles and language, inviting numerous well-known and up-and-coming choreographers to create works and restage classic repertoire for the dancers. Recent choreographers include Robert Battle, Janis Brenner, Ronald K. Brown, Eliot Feld, William Forsythe, Susan Marshall, Mark Morris, and Ohad Naharin. Numerous performances each season also present the year's best work by Juilliard's own young choreographers.

The dance faculty brings to the classroom, the studio, and the stage an extraordinary background of professional accomplishment. All faculty members are active in the world of dance as coaches, adjudicators, choreographers, restagers of works, writers, guest teachers—and as dancers.

The Dance Division's four-year course of study offers students the choice of pursuing a Bachelor of Fine Arts (B.F.A.) degree or a diploma. The core curriculum requires intensive technical study and performance in classical ballet and modern dance and includes courses in repertory, pas de deux, pointe or men's class, dance composition, anatomy, acting, dance history, stagecraft, production, music theory, and elements of performing. The dancers work in an enormous variety of repertory styles and techniques. Traditional courses, such as dance composition, also benefit from guest artists and noted choreographers who work in the studios with Juilliard dancers as part of their weekly schedule. Also offered are electives such as voice and tap and jazz. All dancers are introduced to the techniques of creating new works in beginning choreography classes and are encouraged to present their own choreographed works in informal concerts and workshops showings. Also each year, a Choreographers and Composers program offers six collaborations between third-year student choreographers and student composers. A springtime concert, Senior Production, features the work of accomplished choreographers selected from the senior class in a concert produced by the senior class, with lighting design and behind the scenes production by the junior class.

In addition, in the fall, each individual class has the opportunity to work with established choreographers in premiere dances as part of the *New Dances* performances. Spring dance performances, entitled *Juilliard Dances Repertory*, give dancers the opportunity to perform in established works from contemporary repertory, in addition to those listed previously, including Lar Lubovitch and Paul Taylor. Facilities include five class and rehearsal studios as well as the Peter J. Sharp Theater and other smaller performance venues. The Juilliard Dance Division also presents programs in Lincoln Center's Clark Theater and in venues throughout the metropolitan region, including New York City public schools.

A seminar class for seniors teaches dancers how to prepare resumes, write grant proposals, and produce their own performances. Juilliard dancers also learn production techniques, how to audition, and how to focus their career ambitions.

Graduates of the division have gone on to dance with virtually every established modern and ballet company in the United States and abroad, and they are also among the directors and administrators of respected companies worldwide. Alumni include noted directors and choreographers, such as Robert Battle, Pina Bausch, Martha Clarke, Mercedes Ellington, Robert Garland, Kazuko Hirabayashi, Saeko Ichinohe, Lar Lubovitch, Bruce Marks, Susan Marshall, Ohad Naharin, and Paul Taylor.

The Katherine K. Herberger College of Fine Arts
See Arizona State University

Kent State University
Kent, Ohio

State-supported, coed. Suburban campus. Total enrollment: 23,622. Dance program established 1983.
Degrees Bachelor of Fine Arts. Majors and concentrations: dance education, dance performance. Program accredited by NASD.
Enrollment 30 total; all undergraduate.
Dance Student Profile 98% females, 2% males, 7% minorities, 1% international.
Dance Faculty 5 undergraduate (full-time), 5 undergraduate (part-time). 80% of full-time faculty have terminal degrees. Graduate students do not teach undergraduate courses. Undergraduate student–faculty ratio: 9:1.
Student Life Student groups/activities include Kent Dance Ensemble, Kent Dance Association. Special housing available for dance students.
Expenses for 2005–2006 Application fee: $30. State resident tuition: $7954 full-time. Nonresident tuition: $15,386 full-time. Full-time tuition varies according to course level, course load, degree level, location, program, reciprocity agreements, and student level. College room and board: $6640. College room only: $4040. Room and board charges vary according to board plan and housing facility.
Financial Aid Program-specific awards: 5–8 Creative Arts Awards for program majors ($1500–$3500).
Application Procedures Students admitted directly into the professional program freshman year. Deadline for freshmen and transfers: continuous. Required: high school transcript, college transcript(s) for transfer students, minimum 2.0 high school GPA, audition, SAT I or ACT test scores, 1 page resumé. Recommended: 3 letters of recommendation, interview. Auditions held 4 times on campus; recorded music is permissible as a substitute for live auditions and videotaped performances are permissible as a substitute for live auditions when distance is prohibitive. Portfolio reviews held once on campus.
Web Site http://www.dance.kent.edu
Undergraduate Contact Andrea Shearer, Dance Coordinator, School of Theatre and Dance, Kent State University, PO Box 5190, Kent, Ohio 44242; 330-672-2069, fax: 330-672-4897, e-mail address: ashearer@kent.edu

Leigh Gerdine College of Fine Arts
See Webster University

Long Island University, C.W. Post Campus
Brookville, New York

Independent, coed. Suburban campus. Total enrollment: 8,472. Dance program established 1996.
Degrees Bachelor of Fine Arts in the area of arts management. Majors and concentrations: dance.
Enrollment 32 total; all undergraduate.
Dance Student Profile 93% females, 7% males, 25% minorities, 5% international.
Dance Faculty 2 undergraduate (full-time), 8 undergraduate (part-time). 80% of full-time faculty have terminal degrees. Graduate students do not teach undergraduate courses. Undergraduate student–faculty ratio: 7:1.
Student Life Student groups/activities include lecture demonstrations, Post Concert Dance Company, American College Dance Festival Association.
Expenses for 2005–2006 Application fee: $30. Comprehensive fee: $31,930 includes full-time tuition ($22,100), mandatory fees ($1130), and college room and board ($8700). College room only: $5730. Full-time tuition and fees vary according to program. Room and board charges vary according to board plan and housing facility. Special program-related fees: $55 per technical theater for class supplies, $55 per technique class for accompanist and theater services.
Financial Aid Program-specific awards: 2 Provost's Awards for dance studies majors ($2000), 12 Post Concert Dance Company

Awards for dance studies majors ($2000), 7 freshman incentive awards for dance studies majors ($2000).
Application Procedures Students admitted directly into the professional program freshman year. Deadline for freshmen and transfers: continuous. Required: essay, high school transcript, college transcript(s) for transfer students, 2 letters of recommendation, interview, audition, SAT I or ACT test scores. Recommended: minimum 3.0 high school GPA. Auditions held 3 times on campus; videotaped performances are permissible as a substitute for live auditions when distance is prohibitive.
Web Site http://www.liu.edu
Undergraduate Contact Mr. Gary Bergman, Associate Provost for Enrollment Services, Admissions, Long Island University, C.W. Post Campus, 720 Northern Boulevard, Brookville, New York 11548-1300; 516-299-2900, fax: 516-299-2418, e-mail address: enroll@cwpost.liu.edu

Marymount Manhattan College
New York, New York

Independent, coed. Total enrollment: 2,007.
Degrees Bachelor of Fine Arts. Majors and concentrations: dance.
Enrollment 165 total; all undergraduate.
Dance Student Profile 85% females, 15% males, 20% minorities, 10% international.
Dance Faculty 6 undergraduate (full-time), 35 undergraduate (part-time). 50% of full-time faculty have terminal degrees. Graduate students do not teach undergraduate courses. Undergraduate student–faculty ratio: 26:1.
Expenses for 2006–2007 Application fee: $60. Comprehensive fee: $31,728 includes full-time tuition ($18,748), mandatory fees ($890), and college room and board ($12,090). College room only: $10,090. Special program-related fees: $15 per credit hour for technique/lab fees.
Financial Aid Program-specific awards: competitive talent awards for dance majors ($1000–$4000).
Application Procedures Students admitted directly into the professional program freshman year. Deadline for freshmen and transfers: March 25. Required: high school transcript, college transcript(s) for transfer students, 2 letters of recommendation, interview, audition, SAT I or ACT test scores, 5" x 7" photograph in first arabesque en l'air or tendu a la seconde. Auditions held 6 times on campus and off campus in San Francisco, CA; Chicago, IL; videotaped performances are permissible as a substitute for live auditions when distance is prohibitive.
Web Site http://marymount.mmm.edu
Undergraduate Contact M. J. Thompson, Recruiter, Department of Dance, Marymount Manhattan College, 221 East 71st Street, New York, New York 10021; 212-517-0610, fax: 212-517-0619, e-mail address: dance@mmm.edu

Rutgers, The State University of New Jersey
Mason Gross School of the Arts
New Brunswick, New Jersey

State-supported, coed. Small town campus. Dance program established 1981.
Degrees Bachelor of Fine Arts in the area of dance. Majors and concentrations: modern dance. Program accredited by NASD.
Enrollment 109 total; 67 undergraduate, 42 nonprofessional degree.
Dance Student Profile 85% females, 15% males, 15% minorities, 1% international.
Dance Faculty 7 undergraduate (full-time), 8 undergraduate (part-time). 90% of full-time faculty have terminal degrees. Graduate students do not teach undergraduate courses. Undergraduate student–faculty ratio: 15:1.
Student Life Student groups/activities include DancePlus Concert Series, student produced performances, University Dance Works. Special housing available for dance students.
Expenses for 2005–2006 Special program-related fees: $50 per 3-credit course for supplies for dance production, $75 per 3-credit course for performance tickets.

Financial Aid Program-specific awards: 4 University DanceWorks Awards for BFA dancers ($12,000).
Application Procedures Students admitted directly into the professional program freshman year. Deadline for freshmen and transfers: continuous. Notification date for freshmen and transfers: continuous. Required: high school transcript, college transcript(s) for transfer students, minimum 2.0 high school GPA, interview, audition, SAT I or ACT test scores. Auditions held 4 times on campus; videotaped performances are permissible as a substitute for live auditions when distance is prohibitive.
Web Site http://mgsa.rutgers.edu
Undergraduate Contact Office of Undergraduate Admissions, Rutgers, The State University of New Jersey, Mason Gross School of the Arts, PO Box 2101, New Brunswick, New Jersey 08903-2101; 732-445-3777.

Meadows School of the Arts
See Southern Methodist University

Missouri State University
Springfield, Missouri

State-supported, coed. Suburban campus. Total enrollment: 18,928.

Montclair State University
Upper Montclair, New Jersey

State-supported, coed. Suburban campus. Total enrollment: 16,063.
Degrees Bachelor of Fine Arts. Majors and concentrations: dance. Program accredited by NASD.
Enrollment 50 total; all undergraduate.
Dance Student Profile 97% females, 3% males, 3% minorities, 1% international.
Dance Faculty 2 undergraduate (full-time), 6 undergraduate (part-time). 50% of full-time faculty have terminal degrees. Graduate students do not teach undergraduate courses. Undergraduate student–faculty ratio: 7:1.
Student Life Student groups/activities include Danceworks, musicals, American College Dance Festival Association.
Expenses for 2005–2006 Application fee: $55. State resident tuition: $5581 full-time. Nonresident tuition: $10,029 full-time. Mandatory fees: $2128 full-time. College room and board: $8618. College room only: $5768. Room and board charges vary according to board plan and housing facility. Special program-related fees: $20 per class for accompanists.
Application Procedures Students admitted directly into the professional program freshman year. Deadline for freshmen: March 1; transfers: May 1. Required: essay, high school transcript, college transcript(s) for transfer students, minimum 2.0 high school GPA, interview, audition, SAT I test score only. Recommended: 2 letters of recommendation. Auditions held continuously on campus; videotaped performances are permissible as a substitute for live auditions for international students and U.S. students when distance is prohibitive.
Web Site http://www.montclair.edu
Undergraduate Contact Ms. Lori Katterhenry, Program Coordinator, Division of Dance, Montclair State University, Normal Avenue, Montclair, New Jersey 07043; 973-655-7080, fax: 973-655-7717, e-mail address: katterhenrl@mail.montclair.edu

New World School of the Arts
Miami, Florida

State-supported, coed. Urban campus. Total enrollment: 371. Dance program established 1988.
Degrees Bachelor of Fine Arts in the area of dance. Majors and concentrations: performance. Mandatory cross-registration with University of Florida, Miami-Dade College. Program accredited by NASD.
Enrollment 65 total; all undergraduate.

Dance Student Profile 69% females, 31% males, 75% minorities, 1% international.
Dance Faculty 5 undergraduate (full-time), 11 undergraduate (part-time). Graduate students do not teach undergraduate courses. Undergraduate student–faculty ratio: 2:1.
Student Life Student groups/activities include Florida Dance Association, local dance companies, Student Government.
Expenses for 2005–2006 Application fee: $0. State resident tuition: $12,000 full-time. Nonresident tuition: $17,000 full-time.
Financial Aid Program-specific awards: 4 Nations Bank Merit Scholarships for program majors ($2000), 1 Lewis Dorfman Merit Scholarship for program majors ($1000), 1 Patricia Olalde Merit Scholarship for choreography majors ($1000), 10 Dr. Betty Rowen Merit Scholarships for dance education majors ($1500), 25 Miami-Dade College Scholarships for program majors ($1500).
Application Procedures Students admitted directly into the professional program freshman year. Deadline for freshmen and transfers: continuous. Required: essay, high school transcript, college transcript(s) for transfer students, 2 letters of recommendation, audition. Recommended: minimum 2.0 high school GPA, interview, SAT I or ACT test scores. Auditions held continuously on campus and off campus in Jacksonville, FL; Dallas, TX; videotaped performances are permissible as a substitute for live auditions when distance is prohibitive.
Web Site http://www.mdc.edu/nwsa
Undergraduate Contact Pamela Neumann, Recruitment and Admissions Coordinator, Student Services, New World School of the Arts, 300 North East 2nd Avenue, Miami, Florida 33132; 305-237-7007, fax: 305-237-3794, e-mail address: nwsaadm@mdc.edu

Tisch School of the Arts, Department of Dance
New York University
New York, New York

Independent, coed. Urban campus. Total enrollment: 40,004. Dance program established 1965.
Degrees Bachelor of Fine Arts. Majors and concentrations: dance. Graduate degrees offered: Master of Fine Arts in the area of dance.
Enrollment 103 total; 75 undergraduate, 28 graduate.
Dance Student Profile 73% females, 27% males, 11% minorities, 6% international.
Dance Faculty 9 total (full-time), 15 total (part-time). Graduate students do not teach undergraduate courses. Undergraduate student–faculty ratio: 5:1.
Student Life Student groups/activities include Community Connections, The Collective, Tisch Talent Guild.
Expenses for 2005–2006 Application fee: $65. Comprehensive fee: $43,170 includes full-time tuition ($29,890), mandatory fees ($1800), and college room and board ($11,480). Full-time tuition and fees vary according to program. Room and board charges vary according to board plan and housing facility.
Financial Aid Program-specific awards available.
Application Procedures Students admitted directly into the professional program freshman year. Deadline for freshmen: January 15; transfers: April 1. Notification date for freshmen: April 1; transfers: May 15. Required: essay, high school transcript, college transcript(s) for transfer students, 2 letters of recommendation, audition, SAT I or ACT test scores. Recommended: minimum 3.0 high school GPA, interview. Auditions held continuously from November through April on campus and off campus in Chicago, IL; San Francisco, CA; Los Angeles, CA; videotaped performances are permissible as a substitute for live auditions for international applicants only.
Web Site http://dance.tisch.nyu.edu
Undergraduate Contact Mr. Andrew I. Uriarte, Director of Recruitment and Student Affairs, Tisch School of the Arts, New York University, 721 Broadway, 8th Floor, New York, New York 10003-6807; 212-998-1900, fax: 212-995-4060, e-mail address: andrew.uriarte@nyu.edu
Graduate Contact Mr. Dan Sanford, Director of Graduate Admissions, Tisch School of the Arts, New York University, 721

New York University (continued)

Broadway, 8th Floor, New York, New York 10003-6807; 212-998-1900, fax: 212-995-4060, e-mail address: dan.sandford@nyu.edu

North Carolina School of the Arts
Winston-Salem, North Carolina

State-supported, coed. Urban campus. Total enrollment: 827. Dance program established 1965.

Degrees Bachelor of Fine Arts in the area of dance. Majors and concentrations: ballet, contemporary dance.

Enrollment 84 total; 58 undergraduate, 26 nonprofessional degree.

Dance Student Profile 74% females, 26% males, 9% minorities, 5% international.

Dance Faculty 13 undergraduate (full-time), 1 undergraduate (part-time). 20% of full-time faculty have terminal degrees. Graduate students do not teach undergraduate courses. Undergraduate student–faculty ratio: 5:1.

Student Life Special housing available for dance students.

Expenses for 2005–2006 Application fee: $50. State resident tuition: $2755 full-time. Nonresident tuition: $14,035 full-time. Mandatory fees: $1551 full-time. Full-time tuition and fees vary according to program. College room and board: $5700. College room only: $3035. Room and board charges vary according to board plan and housing facility. Special program-related fees: $60 per year for injury screening fee, $135 per year for educational and technology fee.

Financial Aid Program-specific awards: 49 talent/need scholarships for those demonstrating talent and/or need ($2667).

Application Procedures Students admitted directly into the professional program freshman year. Deadline for freshmen and transfers: continuous. Required: high school transcript, college transcript(s) for transfer students, 2 letters of recommendation, interview, audition, two photos. Recommended: SAT I or ACT test scores. Auditions held by request on campus and off campus in various cities in the U.S.; videotaped performances are permissible as a substitute for live auditions for provisional acceptance.

Web Site http://www.ncarts.edu

Undergraduate Contact Ms. Sheeler Lawson, Director of Admissions, North Carolina School of the Arts, 1533 South Main Street, Winston-Salem, North Carolina 27117-2189; 336-770-3291, fax: 336-770-3370, e-mail address: admissions@ncarts.edu

Northern Illinois University
De Kalb, Illinois

State-supported, coed. Small town campus. Total enrollment: 25,208. Dance program established 1989.

The Ohio State University
Columbus, Ohio

State-supported, coed. Total enrollment: 50,504. Dance program established 1968.

Ohio University
Athens, Ohio

State-supported, coed. Small town campus. Total enrollment: 20,396. Dance program established 1969.

Degrees Bachelor of Fine Arts. Majors and concentrations: dance. Program accredited by NASD.

Enrollment 44 total; all undergraduate.

Dance Student Profile 93% females, 7% males, 9% minorities, 2% international.

Dance Faculty 8 undergraduate (full-time). 70% of full-time faculty have terminal degrees. Graduate students do not teach undergraduate courses. Undergraduate student–faculty ratio: 6:1.

Student Life Student groups/activities include The Movement (student performance organization). Special housing available for dance students.

Expenses for 2005–2006 Application fee: $45. State resident tuition: $8235 full-time. Nonresident tuition: $17,199 full-time. College room and board: $7686. College room only: $3855. Room and board charges vary according to board plan.

Financial Aid Program-specific awards: 4–5 Provost Scholarships for talented students ($1000), 1 Ruiz-Lewis Scholarship for minorities and males ($500), 1 Bailin-Stern Scholarship for talented students ($400–$500), 1 Hazeland Carr Liggett Award for talented students ($800), 1–2 Shirley Wimmer Awards for talented students ($1000–$1200), 1 Betty Milhendler Award for talented students ($500), 1 Bill Cratty Award for talented males ($500), 1 Yolanda Molnar Scholarship for talented students ($1000), 1 Margaret Schuette Scholarship for talented students ($1000).

Application Procedures Students admitted directly into the professional program freshman year. Deadline for freshmen: February 1; transfers: June 1. Notification date for freshmen: March 15; transfers: June 15. Required: essay, high school transcript, college transcript(s) for transfer students, 2 letters of recommendation, audition, SAT I or ACT test scores. Recommended: minimum 3.0 high school GPA, interview. Auditions held twice on campus; videotaped performances are permissible as a substitute for live auditions when distance is prohibitive.

Web Site http://www.dance.ohiou.edu

Undergraduate Contact Ms. Teresa Holland, Assistant to the Director, School of Dance, Ohio University, Putnam Hall 137, Athens, Ohio 45701; 740-593-1826, fax: 740-593-0749, e-mail address: dance@ohiou.edu

Point Park University
Pittsburgh, Pennsylvania

Independent, coed. Urban campus. Total enrollment: 3,407. Dance program established 1968.

Degrees Bachelor of Arts in the area of dance pedagogy; Bachelor of Arts/Bachelor of Fine Arts in the area of dance. Majors and concentrations: ballet, dance pedagogy, modern dance. Cross-registration with Carnegie Mellon University, University of Pittsburgh, Chatham College, Robert Morris College, Duquesne University, Carlow College. Program accredited by NASD.

Enrollment 215 total; all undergraduate.

Dance Student Profile 90% females, 10% males, 10% minorities, 10% international.

Dance Faculty 9 undergraduate (full-time), 15 undergraduate (part-time). 90% of full-time faculty have terminal degrees. Graduate students do not teach undergraduate courses. Undergraduate student–faculty ratio: 12:1.

Student Life Student groups/activities include Pittsburgh Playhouse Dance Company, American College Dance Festival Association, Point Park College Dance Club.

Expenses for 2005–2006 Application fee: $40. Comprehensive fee: $24,160 includes full-time tuition ($16,280), mandatory fees ($460), and college room and board ($7420). College room only: $3500. Full-time tuition and fees vary according to program. Room and board charges vary according to board plan. Special program-related fees: $395 per term for voice/piano private lessons.

Financial Aid Program-specific awards: 22 academic scholarships for those demonstrating talent and academic achievement ($2000–$7500), 24–35 dance scholarships for those demonstrating talent and academic achievement ($1000–$5000), 25 dance apprenticeships for those demonstrating talent ($500–$3500).

Application Procedures Students admitted directly into the professional program freshman year. Deadline for freshmen and transfers: May 1. Required: high school transcript, college transcript(s) for transfer students, minimum 2.0 high school GPA, 2 letters of recommendation, audition, ACT test score only. Auditions held 10 times on campus and off campus in New York, NY; Chicago, IL; Dayton, OH; Detroit, MI; Washington, DC; Los Angeles, CA; Houston, TX; videotaped performances are permissible as a substitute for live auditions if distance is prohibitive or in special circumstances.

Web Site http://www.pointpark.edu
Undergraduate Contact Mr. Joseph McGoldrick, Director of Artistic Recruitment, Conservatory of Performing Arts, Point Park University, 201 Wood Street, Pittsburgh, Pennsylvania 15222-1984; 412-392-3450, fax: 412-391-2424, e-mail address: jmcgoldrick@pointpark.edu

More About the Program

The Conservatory of Performing Arts confers Bachelor of Arts and Bachelor of Fine Arts degrees in dance, dance pedagogy, and theater arts and offers conservatory training within a liberal arts context. Students receive intense training in their concentration as well as a thorough academic education. Because the faculty members believe that performing arts majors develop best in front of a live audience, the program offers varied performing opportunities for students at the Pittsburgh Playhouse of Point Park University.

Nationally renowned, the Pittsburgh Playhouse is the performance facility for the Conservatory of Performing Arts. Here students participate in live-theater/dance experiences before a subscription audience. Consisting of three working theaters, this 70-year-old facility is fully staffed by a production team of designers and artisans who train and supervise student apprentices in building, designing, lighting, and managing shows. The front-of-house staff members as well as the box office and public relations personnel engage all students in the business aspect of running a theater. The season, which features student actors, dancers, designers, and stage managers, consists of five Playhouse Jr. shows for children and five Conservatory Company dramas/musicals.

Dance students may perform in one of five Playhouse Dance Company productions and a Playhouse Jr. Children's Dance Show as well as a public school outreach program.

The Bachelor of Arts degree in cinema and digital arts is an innovatively designed program, with an emphasis on professional education and liberal arts—both in theory and in practice. Exploring the integration of media and the arts in society as well as the impact of technology on culture, the curriculum provides practical, professional training while developing a sound foundation in the arts and humanities. Theory and aesthetics are taught as an integral part of developing communication and production skills.

In the Conservatory of Performing Arts, it is the mission to educate, train, and artistically equip students with the skills necessary to compete in the commercial media industry. The degree offered is a four-year, 120-credit Bachelor of Arts in film and electronic arts, with concentrations in cinematography, directing, editing and sound, producing, and screenwriting.

This well-rounded educational experience culminates with the annual Point Park Digital Film Festival, presented to showcase graduating senior thesis production projects. Admission to the Film and Electronic Arts program is based on self-discipline, professional attitude, and a commitment to the craft as demonstrated through an interview with the Director of Film.

The B.F.A. degree in film and video production is offered in collaboration with Pittsburgh Filmmakers. Students take their academic courses at Point Park University and their film and video requirements at Pittsburgh Filmmakers' newly built facility in the Oakland section of Pittsburgh. Both institutions work together to ensure students receive a challenging educational experience.

Conservatory faculty members are working professionals in acting, singing, dancing, writing, composing, painting, designing, choreography, and other specialties. Guest artists and master teachers in musical theater, voice and speech, and dance are regularly featured. Past guests include Chita Rivera, Michael Rupert, Jeff Shade, Rob Ashford, Sherry Zunker-Dow, Cicely Berry, Paul Gavert, Patricia Wilde, Albert Poland, Barbara Pontecorvo, Edward Villella, Maxine Sherman, Marshall Swiney, and Claire Bataille. The program also offers many workshops and collaborative efforts of an interdisciplinary nature with other University programs.

During the summer, the Conservatory offers an International Summer Dance program (open by audition) featuring renowned names in the world of dance. The International Summer Dance program offers training in jazz, ballet, Alexander, and modern dance. The program culminates in a recital performance.

The community of Pittsburgh itself is an arts and education center with the Pittsburgh Symphony, Opera, Ballet, and Dance Council and the Pittsburgh Public Theaters supplemented by eight other institutions of higher learning within a 15-minute drive. The whole city is truly the campus of the programs.

Prospective applicants must apply and be accepted by the University. An audition for and an interview with faculty members is required of all prospective majors. Scholarships/apprenticeships from $1000 to $5000 are based on either talent or academics or both. Presidential and special academic full- and part-time awards are highly competitive.

Off-campus auditions are possible at Thespian State Conferences and dance conferences in Chicago; New York; Washington, D.C.; Houston; Detroit; and Louisville, Kentucky. Videotaped auditions are acceptable; prospective students should contact the Conservatory for procedures.

Program Facilities and Features At the Conservatory of Performing Arts, facilities include ten dance studios as well as the three-theater complex at the Pittsburgh Playhouse of Point Park University, which offers performance opportunities for students in front of a subscription audience. In addition, students can take advantage of the on-site costume/set construction apprenticeships, 11 private singing and piano instructors; art and design classes; more than 100 dance classes per week, acting classes with a ratio of 1 instructor to 15 students, and the Point Park University Singers. Point Park University is central to many educational, arts, and entertainment activities, and it is within walking distance of boating, swimming, and parks.

Alumni The Conservatory has numerous graduates performing in touring companies, on Broadway, in dance companies, in movies, on TV, and in other theaters. Many more alumni are teaching in schools, on faculties, choreographing, writing, directing, and stage managing across the world. Broadway and national touring productions of *Contact, Cabaret, 42nd St.,* and *Kiss Me Kate* as well as movie and TV credits, including *Pulp Fiction, Inspector Gadget, Wonder Boys, NYPD Blue, Due South, The Guiding Light, Providence, CSI: NYC,* and *Leaving L.A.* are just a few of the vehicles showcasing Conservatory graduates of theater and dance.

Purchase College, State University of New York
Purchase, New York

State-supported, coed. Small town campus. Total enrollment: 3,826.
Degrees Bachelor of Fine Arts in the area of dance. Majors and concentrations: ballet, composition, modern dance, performance, production. Graduate degrees offered: Master of Fine Arts in the area of dance.
Enrollment 157 total; 148 undergraduate, 9 graduate.
Dance Student Profile 76% females, 24% males, 24% minorities, 7% international.
Dance Faculty 7 undergraduate (full-time), 8 undergraduate (part-time), 5 graduate (part-time). 100% of full-time faculty have terminal degrees. Graduate students do not teach undergraduate courses. Undergraduate student–faculty ratio: 19:1.
Student Life Student groups/activities include lectures/demonstrations at local schools, national and international performance tours, Purchase Dance Corps.

Purchase College, State University of New York (continued)

Expenses for 2006–2007 Application fee: $40. State resident tuition: $4350 full-time. Nonresident tuition: $10,610 full-time. Mandatory fees: $1258 full-time. College room and board: $8466. College room only: $5378.

Financial Aid Program-specific awards: 50 dance scholarships/awards ($2626).

Application Procedures Students admitted directly into the professional program freshman year. Deadline for freshmen and transfers: April 15. Notification date for freshmen and transfers: May 1. Required: high school transcript, college transcript(s) for transfer students, audition, minimum TOEFL score of 550 for international applicants. Recommended: SAT I or ACT test scores. Auditions held 9 times on campus and off campus in Miami, FL; Chicago, IL; San Francisco, CA; Los Angeles, CA; Interlochen, MI; videotaped performances are permissible as a substitute for live auditions for international applicants and applicants from Hawaii and Puerto Rico.

Web Site http://www.purchase.edu/dance

Undergraduate Contact Lisa Labeille, Counselor, Office of Admissions, Purchase College, State University of New York, 735 Anderson Hill Road, Purchase, New York 10577-1400; 914-251-6317, fax: 914-251-6314.

Graduate Contact Ms. Sabrina Johnston, Counselor, Office of Admissions, Purchase College, State University of New York, 735 Anderson Hill Road, Purchase, New York 10577-1400; 914-251-6479, fax: 914-251-6314.

More About the College

Purchase is a preeminent conservatory program from which to launch a career in dance. It offers professional, comprehensive, in-depth, personalized training in modern dance and classical ballet/performance and composition. The Conservatory of Dance curriculum in the School of the Arts has a shared emphasis for all students in performance and composition. Prospective students must audition in person, except for international students residing abroad, who may send videotapes. Scholarships are awarded based on the talent demonstrated at the entrance audition. Students in the Conservatory are from thirty-six states and fourteen other countries.

Performance credits are required for graduation. Students may perform in the Purchase Dance Corps concerts, tours, senior project concerts, M.F.A. concerts, lecture demonstrations, galas and fund-raising events, student concerts, studio showings, and workshops. Performance of a major professional repertory piece is required for the B.F.A. senior project. Purchase Dance Corps International Tours have included Amsterdam (1991); Taiwan (1992, 1995, and 2004); Beijing, China (1994); France (1995); Hong Kong (1987, 1990, and 1997); Germany (2002); and the Kennedy Center in the United States.

The four-year composition curriculum involves each student in performance of a sophomore and junior composition showing. The senior choreography project is mentored by a faculty member and monitored by the faculty senior project committee. The senior project concerts, coproduced by 3 to 4 seniors in the Dance Theatre Lab, are culminating artistic and directorial events that serve the student as a bridge to the profession.

The B.F.A. degree conservatory professional training program requires 120 semester credits to graduate: 90 credits in the professional dance curriculum, 30 credits in liberal arts, which fulfill the SUNY-mandated general education requirements. The program emphasizes modern dance technique/classical ballet technique daily, anatomy for dance, music for dance, dance history, dance production, improvisation, ballet and modern partnering, ballet or modern composition, and pointe. The M.F.A. degree is a 60-credit, two-year, residential curriculum in choreography or performance/teaching.

The Conservatory of Dance faculty members are active in the profession as choreographers, teachers, coaches, musicians, and performers. Alumni are performing or have performed in the Martha Graham Dance Company, the Merce Cunningham Dance Company, the Trisha Brown Dance Company, the Frankfurt Ballet, the Houston Ballet, the Parson's Company, the Mark

Morris Dance Group, Limon Dance Company, American Ballet Theatre, the Feld Ballets N.Y., the Paul Taylor Dance Company, Alvin Ailey American Dance Theatre, and the Bill T. Jones/Arnie Zane Company. Alumni are founders of their own companies or are freelance choreographers. An extensive listing of alumni accomplishments is available on request.

Campus and Surroundings On campus, The Performing Arts Center provides professional theaters for performances by the Conservatory students as well as an annual professional concert series of major contemporary and classical companies. Each company provides a master class for students. These have included the Miami City Ballet, Alvin Ailey Dance Theatre of Harlem, Paul Taylor, Hubbard Street, Bill T. Jones, David Parsons, and Lyon Opera Ballet.

Purchase College is 35 minutes north of New York City in a suburban setting where students have the best of both worlds. They reside on campus in residence halls or apartment complexes with students from the other arts programs and liberal arts and sciences. The ease of living in a campus setting, combined with the cultural advantages of Manhattan, informs the students' artistic stimulation and knowledge of the real challenges they are likely to face upon graduation. They travel to the city to attend concerts, take classes, go to auditions, visit museums, and absorb the rich culture. New York City is a crucial resource in the education of these future artists. It is the reality check and the constant reminder of what students work for in their programs in the Conservatory.

Facilities The award-winning dance building at Purchase College is the first specially built facility in the United States designed exclusively for the training and performance of dance. There are also nine fully equipped, light-filled studios; a 270-seat Dance Theatre Lab, and The Performing Arts Center, with four theaters, where the Purchase Dance Corps performs.

Faculty B.F.A. and M.F.A. faculty members have performed with Martha Graham, Merce Cunningham, Alvin Ailey, Jose Limon, Viola Farber, Mark Morris, New York City Ballet, and the American Ballet Theatre. They choreograph, teach, and/or set masterworks in Asia, Europe, and South America. They produce their own work in Manhattan. The faculty members teach the students daily. Musicians accompany all technique classes.

Performance Opportunities Students are required to perform. The Purchase Dance Corps, the performing company of the Conservatory of Dance B.F.A. program, for which all students are eligible to audition, presents two concerts annually of major professional repertory in the Performing Arts Center, including modern works by artists such as Paul Taylor, Merce Cunningham, and Mark Morris; ballets by George Balanchine and Robert Hill; works by stellar alumni, such as Doug Varone and Nicolo Fonte; and co-commissioned collaborations with the American Ballet Theatre Ballet Studio Company; the Nutcracker Ballet; works by international choreographers Lin Hwai Min, Shen Wei, and Robert Cohan; as well as commissioned pieces by emerging choreographers and works by faculty members, created especially for the Purchase Dance Corps. Additional performance opportunities include B.F.A. senior project concerts and M.F.A. showings and concerts in the Dance Theatre Lab, special fund-raising events and galas, and summer tours to Asia and Europe.

Special Programs Student exchange programs in dance are available in London; Amsterdam; Rotterdam; Perth, Australia; or Taipei. The College also offers an Arts Management certificate. A physical therapist is available two days per week.

For additional information, prospective students should visit the Web site at http://www.purchase.edu/dance.

Radford University
Radford, Virginia

State-supported, coed. Small town campus. Total enrollment: 9,552. Dance program established 1966.

Feinstein College of Arts and Sciences
Roger Williams University
Bristol, Rhode Island

Independent, coed. Total enrollment: 5,214. Dance program established 1972.
Degrees Bachelor of Arts in the area of dance performance. Majors and concentrations: ballet, choreography, jazz, modern dance, tap dance.
Enrollment 37 total; all undergraduate.
Dance Student Profile 51% females, 49% males, 6% minorities, 2% international.
Dance Faculty 3 undergraduate (full-time), 5 undergraduate (part-time). Graduate students do not teach undergraduate courses.
Student Life Student groups/activities include Dance Club.
Expenses for 2006–2007 Application fee: $50. Comprehensive fee: $34,759 includes full-time tuition ($22,932), mandatory fees ($1134), and college room and board ($10,693). College room only: $5569.
Application Procedures Students admitted directly into the professional program freshman year. Deadline for freshmen and transfers: continuous. Required: essay, high school transcript, college transcript(s) for transfer students, 2 letters of recommendation, audition, SAT I or ACT test scores. Auditions held by appointment only on campus; videotaped performances are permissible as a substitute for live auditions when distance is prohibitive.
Web Site http://www.rwu.edu
Undergraduate Contact Michelle L. Beauregard, Director of Freshman Admissions, Roger Williams University, 1 Old Ferry Road, Bristol, Rhode Island 02809; 401-254-3500, fax: 401-254-3557, e-mail address: admitt@rwu.edu
Graduate Contact Matthew McDonough, Director of Graduate Admissions, Roger Williams University, 1 Old Ferry Road, Bristol, Rhode Island 02809; 401-254-3500, fax: 401-254-3557, e-mail address: mmcdonough@rwu.edu

Rutgers, The State University of New Jersey
See Mason Gross School of the Arts

Ryerson University
Toronto, Ontario, Canada

Province-supported, coed. Urban campus. Total enrollment: 28,051. Dance program established 1971.
Degrees Bachelor of Fine Arts. Majors and concentrations: dance.
Enrollment 115 total; all undergraduate.
Dance Student Profile 91% females, 9% males, 5% minorities, 2% international.
Dance Faculty 5 undergraduate (full-time), 10 undergraduate (part-time). 20% of full-time faculty have terminal degrees. Graduate students do not teach undergraduate courses. Undergraduate student–faculty ratio: 6:1.
Expenses for 2005–2006 Application fee: $95 Canadian dollars. Tuition, fee, and room and board charges are reported in Canadian dollars. Province resident tuition: $4184 full-time. Mandatory fees: $527 full-time. Full-time tuition and fees vary according to course load, degree level, and program. College room and board: $7257. Room and board charges vary according to board plan and housing facility. International student tuition: $12,924 full-time. Special program-related fees: $50 per year for theater ticket voucher, $70 per year for subscription series.
Financial Aid Program-specific awards: 3 entrance awards ($2500), 1 second-year award for those demonstrating talent and academic achievement ($2000).
Application Procedures Students admitted directly into the professional program freshman year. Deadline for freshmen and transfers: March 1. Required: essay, high school transcript, college transcript(s) for transfer students, minimum 2.0 high school GPA, interview, audition, resume, photo. Recommended: 2 letters of recommendation. Auditions held on campus; videotaped performances are permissible as a substitute for live auditions for those living outside 300-mile radius. Portfolio reviews held once on campus.
Web Site http://www.ryerson.ca
Undergraduate Contact Jessie Bickerton, Admission Officer, Dance Program, Ryerson University, 350 Victoria Street, Toronto, Ontario M5B 2K3, Canada; 416-979-5000 ext. 6025, fax: 416-979-5221, e-mail address: jbickert@acs.ryerson.ca

Sam Houston State University
Huntsville, Texas

State-supported, coed. Small town campus. Total enrollment: 15,000. Dance program established 1975.

Shenandoah Conservatory
See Shenandoah University

Shenandoah Conservatory
Shenandoah University
Winchester, Virginia

Independent United Methodist, coed. Total enrollment: 2,998.
Degrees Bachelor of Fine Arts. Majors and concentrations: dance, dance education. Graduate degrees offered: Master of Arts in the area of dance; Master of Fine Arts in the area of dance; Master of Science.
Enrollment 54 total; 35 undergraduate, 8 graduate, 11 nonprofessional degree.
Dance Student Profile 93% females, 7% males, 11% minorities, 15% international.
Dance Faculty 3 total (full-time), 8 total (part-time). 100% of full-time faculty have terminal degrees. Graduate students teach a few undergraduate courses. Undergraduate student–faculty ratio: 5:1.
Student Life Student groups/activities include American College Dance Festival Association, Shenandoah Dance Ensembles on tour, Sigma Rho Delta National Dance Fraternity-Epsilon Chapter.
Expenses for 2005–2006 Application fee: $30. Comprehensive fee: $27,600 includes full-time tuition ($19,900), mandatory fees ($150), and college room and board ($7550). Full-time tuition and fees vary according to course load and program. Room and board charges vary according to board plan.
Financial Aid Program-specific awards: 40 talent and academic scholarships for program majors ($4233).
Application Procedures Students admitted directly into the professional program freshman year. Deadline for freshmen and transfers: continuous. Required: high school transcript, college transcript(s) for transfer students, minimum 2.0 high school GPA, interview, video, audition, SAT I or ACT test scores. Recommended: letter of recommendation. Auditions held 6 times on campus and off campus in various cities; videotaped performances are permissible as a substitute for live auditions if a campus visit is impossible.
Web Site http://www.su.edu
Contact Mr. David Anthony, Dean, Admissions Office, Shenandoah University, 1460 University Drive, Winchester, Virginia 22601-5195; 540-665-4581, fax: 540-665-4627, e-mail address: admit@su.edu

Simon Fraser University
Burnaby, British Columbia, Canada

Province-supported, coed. Suburban campus. Total enrollment: 20,187. Dance program established 1993.
Degrees Bachelor of Fine Arts. Majors and concentrations: dance. Graduate degrees offered: Master of Fine Arts in the area of interdisciplinary studies. Cross-registration with National Ballet School of Canada.

Simon Fraser University (continued)

Enrollment 54 total.

Dance Faculty 6 total (full-time). 66% of full-time faculty have terminal degrees. Graduate students teach a few undergraduate courses. Undergraduate student–faculty ratio: 14:1.

Student Life Student groups/activities include Off-Centre Dancers.

Expenses for 2006–2007 Application fee: $100 Canadian dollars. Tuition and fee charges are reported in Canadian dollars.

Financial Aid Program-specific awards: 5 Adaline May Clark Scholarships for program majors ($100–$500), 1 Murray Farr Award for program majors ($500), 1–2 SCA Scholarships for SCA students ($2000), 3 Bice Caple Awards for SCA students ($1000), 2 SFU Service Awards for SCA students ($250), 1 Gloria Garrett Carlton Memorial Bursary in Dance for program majors.

Application Procedures Students apply for admission into the professional program by sophomore year. Deadline for freshmen and transfers: April 30. Required: high school transcript, minimum 3.0 high school GPA, interview, audition. Auditions held twice on campus; videotaped performances are permissible as a substitute for live auditions for international applicants and those who live outside the lower mainland.

Web Site http://www.sfu.ca/sca

Undergraduate Contact Linda Hegland, Undergraduate Advisor, School for Contemporary Arts, Simon Fraser University, 8888 University Drive, Burnaby, British Columbia V5A 1S6, Canada; 604-291-3363, fax: 604-291-5907, e-mail address: ca@sfu.ca

Graduate Contact Noni Fidler, Graduate Secretary, MFA Program, School for the Contemporary Arts, Simon Fraser University, 8888 University Drive, Burnaby, British Columbia V5A 1S6, Canada; 604-291-3724, fax: 604-291-5907, e-mail address: mfagrad@sfu.ca

Slippery Rock University of Pennsylvania

Slippery Rock, Pennsylvania

State-supported, coed. Rural campus. Total enrollment: 8,105. Dance program established 1989.

Degrees Bachelor of Arts. Majors and concentrations: dance. Program accredited by NASD.

Enrollment 90 total; all undergraduate.

Dance Student Profile 95% females, 5% males, 3% minorities.

Dance Faculty 6 undergraduate (full-time), 1 undergraduate (part-time). 100% of full-time faculty have terminal degrees. Graduate students do not teach undergraduate courses. Undergraduate student–faculty ratio: 15:1.

Student Life Student groups/activities include Slippery Rock University Dance Theatre, Slippery Rock University Tour Group , Dance Express. Special housing available for dance students.

Expenses for 2006–2007 Application fee: $25. State resident tuition: $4906 full-time. Nonresident tuition: $7360 full-time. Mandatory fees: $1369 full-time. College room and board: $4796. College room only: $2688.

Financial Aid Program-specific awards: 1 freshman scholarship for freshmen ($1000), 1 transfer scholarship for transfer students ($1000), 1 Lucy I. Sack Scholarship for dance majors ($1000), 2 summer study scholarships for dance majors ($500).

Application Procedures Students admitted directly into the professional program freshman year. Deadline for freshmen and transfers: continuous. Required: essay, high school transcript, college transcript(s) for transfer students, minimum 2.0 high school GPA, interview, audition, SAT I or ACT test scores. Recommended: minimum 3.0 high school GPA. Auditions held on campus; videotaped performances are permissible as a substitute for live auditions if campus visit impossible.

Web Site http://www.sru.edu/depts/chhs/dance

Undergraduate Contact Nora Ambrosio, Professor, Dance Department, Slippery Rock University of Pennsylvania, Slippery Rock, Pennsylvania 16057; 724-738-2036, fax: 724-738-4524, e-mail address: nora.ambrosio@sru.edu

Meadows School of the Arts

Southern Methodist University

Dallas, Texas

Independent, coed. Suburban campus. Total enrollment: 11,152.

Degrees Bachelor of Fine Arts in the area of dance performance. Majors and concentrations: ballet, jazz dance, modern dance. Graduate degrees offered: Master of Fine Arts in the area of choreographic theory and practice. Program accredited by NASD.

Enrollment 78 total; 75 undergraduate, 3 graduate.

Dance Student Profile 85% females, 15% males, 19% minorities.

Dance Faculty 8 total (full-time), 5 total (part-time). 25% of full-time faculty have terminal degrees. Graduate students do not teach undergraduate courses. Undergraduate student–faculty ratio: 6:1.

Student Life Student groups/activities include American Dance Festival, Dallas Morning News Dance Festival, Dance for the Planet. Special housing available for dance students.

Expenses for 2006–2007 Application fee: $50. Comprehensive fee: $38,325 includes full-time tuition ($25,400), mandatory fees ($3230), and college room and board ($9695). College room only: $5775.

Financial Aid Program-specific awards: Meadows Artistic Scholarships for talented program majors ($1000–$5000).

Application Procedures Students apply for admission into the professional program by sophomore year. Deadline for freshmen and transfers: continuous. Required: essay, high school transcript, college transcript(s) for transfer students, letter of recommendation, audition, SAT I or ACT test scores. Recommended: minimum 3.0 high school GPA, interview. Auditions held 12 times on campus and off campus in various national venues; videotaped performances are permissible as a substitute for live auditions when distance is prohibitive.

Web Site http://www.smu.edu/meadows/dance

Undergraduate Contact Kevin Hofeditz, Associate Dean for Student Affairs, Meadows School of the Arts, Southern Methodist University, PO Box 750356, Dallas, Texas 75275-0356; 214-768-4067, fax: 214-768-3272, e-mail address: hofeditz@mail.smu.edu

Graduate Contact Jean Cherry, Coordinator, Graduate Studies, Division of Dance, Southern Methodist University, PO Box 750356, Dallas, Texas 75275-0356; 214-768-3765, fax: 214-768-3272.

State University of New York College at Brockport

Brockport, New York

State-supported, coed. Small town campus. Total enrollment: 8,484. Dance program established 1970.

Degrees Bachelor of Fine Arts. Majors and concentrations: dance. Graduate degrees offered: Master of Fine Arts in the area of dance. Program accredited by NASD.

Enrollment 110 total; 40 undergraduate, 10 graduate, 60 nonprofessional degree.

Dance Student Profile 95% females, 5% males, 10% minorities, 6% international.

Dance Faculty 10 total (full-time), 13 total (part-time). 80% of full-time faculty have terminal degrees. Graduate students do not teach undergraduate courses. Undergraduate student–faculty ratio: 3:1.

Student Life Student groups/activities include Dance Club, Scholars Day, Freshman Convocation.

Expenses for 2006–2007 Application fee: $40.

Financial Aid Program-specific awards: 2–3 Friars Foundation Scholarships for talented sophomores, juniors ($2500), 1 Pylyshenko-Strasser Award for freshmen ($1000), 1–3 Lipson Summer Study Awards for returning students ($1000).

Application Procedures Students apply for admission into the professional program by freshman year. Deadline for freshmen and transfers: March 22. Required: essay, high school transcript, college transcript(s) for transfer students, minimum 3.0 high school GPA, audition, SAT I or ACT test scores. Recommended: letter of recommendation, interview. Auditions held 3 times on

campus; videotaped performances are permissible as a substitute for live auditions for international applicants.
Web Site http://www.brockport.edu/dance
Undergraduate Contact Jacquie Davis, Undergraduate Program Director, Department of Dance, State University of New York College at Brockport, Hartwell Hall, Brockport, New York 14420; 585-395-5303, fax: 585-395-5134, e-mail address: jdavis@brockport.edu
Graduate Contact Darwin Prioleau, Graduate Program Director, Department of Dance, State University of New York College at Brockport, Hartwell Hall, Brockport, New York 14420; 585-395-2153, fax: 585-395-5134, e-mail address: dpriolea@brockport.edu

Stephens College
Columbia, Missouri

Independent, Urban campus. Total enrollment: 824. Dance program established 1958.

Sybil B. Harrington College of Fine Arts and Humanities

See West Texas A&M University

Temple University
Philadelphia, Pennsylvania

State-related, coed. Urban campus. Total enrollment: 33,693. Dance program established 1970.
Degrees Bachelor of Fine Arts. Majors and concentrations: dance. Graduate degrees offered: Master of Education in the area of dance; Master of Fine Arts in the area of dance. Doctor of Philosophy in the area of dance. Program accredited by NASD.
Enrollment 120 total; 70 undergraduate, 50 graduate.
Dance Student Profile 92% females, 8% males, 25% minorities, 7% international.
Dance Faculty 9 total (full-time), 6 total (part-time). 80% of full-time faculty have terminal degrees. Graduate students teach a few undergraduate courses. Undergraduate student–faculty ratio: 10:1.
Student Life Student groups/activities include American College Dance Festival Association, National Dance Education Organization, Congress on Research in Dance, Society of Dance History Scholars.
Expenses for 2005–2006 Application fee: $35. State resident tuition: $9140 full-time. Nonresident tuition: $16,736 full-time. Mandatory fees: $500 full-time. Full-time tuition and fees vary according to course load, location, program, and reciprocity agreements. College room and board: $7794. College room only: $5054. Room and board charges vary according to board plan and housing facility. Special program-related fees: $10–$75 per course for lab fees, accompanists, guest artists.
Financial Aid Program-specific awards: 4–6 departmental scholarships for freshmen and returning students ($500–$2000).
Application Procedures Students admitted directly into the professional program freshman year. Deadline for freshmen and transfers: March 1. Notification date for freshmen and transfers: May 1. Required: essay, high school transcript, college transcript(s) for transfer students, minimum 3.0 high school GPA, interview, audition, SAT I or ACT test scores (minimum combined SAT I score of 1000, minimum composite ACT score of 22). Recommended: letter of recommendation. Auditions held 5 times on campus; videotaped performances are permissible as a substitute for live auditions for international applicants.
Web Site http://www.temple.edu/boyer/dance
Contact Ms. Vanessa Thomas, Admissions Coordinator, Department of Dance, Temple University, 309 Vivacqua Hall, Philadelphia, Pennsylvania 19122-0843; 215-204-5169, fax: 215-204-4347, e-mail address: danceadm@temple.edu

Texas Christian University
Fort Worth, Texas

Independent, coed. Suburban campus. Total enrollment: 8,749. Dance program established 1949.
Degrees Bachelor of Fine Arts. Majors and concentrations: ballet, modern dance.
Enrollment 91 total; 65 undergraduate, 1 graduate, 25 nonprofessional degree.
Dance Student Profile 85% females, 15% males, 10% minorities, 2% international.
Dance Faculty 5 undergraduate (full-time), 6 undergraduate (part-time). 80% of full-time faculty have terminal degrees. Graduate students do not teach undergraduate courses.
Student Life Student groups/activities include Chi Tau Epsilon (honor society).
Expenses for 2005–2006 Application fee: $40. Comprehensive fee: $28,300 includes full-time tuition ($21,280), mandatory fees ($40), and college room and board ($6980). College room only: $4180. Room and board charges vary according to board plan and housing facility.
Financial Aid Program-specific awards: Nordan Awards for dance majors.
Application Procedures Students admitted directly into the professional program freshman year. Notification date for transfers: continuous. Required: essay, high school transcript, college transcript(s) for transfer students, letter of recommendation, audition, SAT I or ACT test scores. Recommended: interview. Auditions held 4 times on campus; videotaped performances are permissible as a substitute for live auditions for international applicants only.
Web Site http://www.dance.tcu.edu
Contact Ms. Ellen Page Shelton, Chair, Ballet and Modern Dance Department, Texas Christian University, PO Box 297910, Fort Worth, Texas 76129; 817-257-7615, fax: 817-257-7675, e-mail address: e.shelton@tcu.edu

Tisch School of the Arts, Department of Dance

See New York University

Towson University
Towson, Maryland

State-supported, coed. Suburban campus. Total enrollment: 18,011. Dance program established 1982.
Degrees Bachelor of Fine Arts. Majors and concentrations: dance performance. Cross-registration with other universities in Maryland. Program accredited by NASD, NCATE.
Enrollment 100 total; all undergraduate.
Dance Student Profile 85% females, 15% males, 19% minorities, 1% international.
Dance Faculty 6 undergraduate (full-time), 8 undergraduate (part-time). 80% of full-time faculty have terminal degrees. Graduate students do not teach undergraduate courses. Undergraduate student–faculty ratio: 17:1.
Student Life Student groups/activities include Dance Company, Sigma Rho Delta, dance majors performance project.
Expenses for 2005–2006 Application fee: $45. State resident tuition: $5180 full-time. Nonresident tuition: $14,114 full-time. Mandatory fees: $1916 full-time. Full-time tuition and fees vary according to course load. College room and board: $6828. College room only: $3968. Room and board charges vary according to board plan and housing facility.
Financial Aid Program-specific awards: 15 dance scholarships for program majors ($1000), 2 Dean's Scholarships for program majors ($2000), out-of-state differential scholarships for program majors ($6000).
Application Procedures Students admitted directly into the professional program freshman year. Deadline for freshmen and transfers: May 1. Notification date for freshmen and transfers: continuous. Required: high school transcript, college transcript(s) for transfer students, minimum 3.0 high school GPA, interview, audition, SAT I or ACT test scores (minimum combined SAT I score of 1100, minimum composite ACT score of 22). Recommended: letter of recommendation. Auditions held once in January and once in February on campus.
Web Site http://www.towson.edu/dance

Towson University (continued)

Undergraduate Contact Maria DeMeo, Administrative Assistant, Department of Dance, Towson University, Center for the Arts, Room 1002C, Towson, Maryland 21252; 410-704-2760, fax: 410-704-3752, e-mail address: mdemeo@towson.edu

Tulane University
New Orleans, Louisiana

Independent, coed. Urban campus. Total enrollment: 12,691. Dance program established 1940.

Degrees Bachelor of Fine Arts. Majors and concentrations: dance. Cross-registration with Loyola University.

Enrollment 310 total; 10 undergraduate, 300 nonprofessional degree.

Dance Student Profile 90% females, 10% males, 12% minorities, 8% international.

Dance Faculty 4 undergraduate (full-time), 8 undergraduate (part-time). 100% of full-time faculty have terminal degrees. Graduate students do not teach undergraduate courses. Undergraduate student–faculty ratio: 3:1.

Student Life Student groups/activities include Newcomb Dance Company (student company), Spring Arts, Young Performers (student choreography).

Expenses for 2005–2006 Application fee: $55. Comprehensive fee: $41,357 includes full-time tuition ($30,350), mandatory fees ($2596), and college room and board ($8411). College room only: $4841.

Application Procedures Students apply for admission into the professional program by freshman year. Deadline for freshmen: January 15; transfers: June 1. Required: essay, high school transcript, college transcript(s) for transfer students, letter of recommendation, audition, SAT I or ACT test scores. Recommended: minimum 2.0 high school GPA, minimum 3.0 high school GPA, interview. Auditions held by appointment on campus.

Web Site http://www.tulane.edu/~theatre/danceProg.html

Undergraduate Contact John Allen, Theatre and Dance, Tulane University, 215 McWilliams Hall, New Orleans, Louisiana 70118; 504-314-7759, fax: 504-865-6737, e-mail address: jallen1@tulane.edu

The University of Akron
Akron, Ohio

State-supported, coed. Urban campus. Total enrollment: 21,049. Dance program established 1970.

The University of Arizona
Tucson, Arizona

State-supported, coed. Urban campus. Total enrollment: 37,036. Dance program established 1984.

Degrees Bachelor of Fine Arts in the area of dance. Majors and concentrations: ballet, jazz dance, modern dance. Graduate degrees offered: Master of Arts/Master of Fine Arts in the area of theater arts (with concentration in dance). Program accredited by NASD.

Enrollment 140 total; 125 undergraduate, 15 graduate.

Dance Student Profile 89% females, 11% males, 12% minorities, 4% international.

Dance Faculty 9 total (full-time). 57% of full-time faculty have terminal degrees. Graduate students teach about a quarter of undergraduate courses. Undergraduate student–faculty ratio: 15:1.

Student Life Student groups/activities include Dancers' Consort.

Expenses for 2005–2006 Application fee: $25. State resident tuition: $4394 full-time. Nonresident tuition: $13,578 full-time. Mandatory fees: $104 full-time. Full-time tuition and fees vary according to course load. College room and board: $7460. College room only: $4100. Room and board charges vary according to board plan and housing facility.

Financial Aid Program-specific awards: 6–12 out-of-state tuition waivers for program majors ($8000), 7–14 in-state fee waivers for program majors ($2500), 18–20 dance performance scholarships for program majors ($250–$1000).

Application Procedures Students admitted directly into the professional program freshman year. Deadline for freshmen: April 1; transfers: June 1. Required: high school transcript, college transcript(s) for transfer students, SAT I or ACT test scores, minimum 2.8 high school GPA, video or audition. Auditions held continuously by appointment on campus; videotaped performances are permissible as a substitute for live auditions if a live audition is impossible.

Undergraduate Contact Michalene Cardella, Administrative Assistant, Dance Division, School of Dance, The University of Arizona, Ina Gittings Building, Room 121, Tucson, Arizona 85721; 520-621-4698, fax: 520-621-6981, e-mail address: cardella@u.arizona.edu

Graduate Contact Dr. Suzanne Knosp, Graduate Advisor, Dance Division, School of Dance, The University of Arizona, Ina Gittings Building, Room 121, Tucson, Arizona 85721; 520-621-2923, fax: 520-621-6981.

University of California, Irvine
Irvine, California

State-supported, coed. Total enrollment: 24,362. Dance program established 1965.

University of California, Santa Barbara
Santa Barbara, California

State-supported, coed. Suburban campus. Total enrollment: 21,016. Dance program established 1984.

Degrees Bachelor of Fine Arts. Majors and concentrations: choreography, performance. Program accredited by NASD.

Enrollment 68 total; 10 undergraduate, 58 nonprofessional degree.

Dance Student Profile 90% females, 10% males.

Dance Faculty 7 undergraduate (full-time), 1 undergraduate (part-time). 25% of full-time faculty have terminal degrees. Graduate students do not teach undergraduate courses. Undergraduate student–faculty ratio: 4:1.

Student Life Student groups/activities include American College Dance Festival Association, Intercampus Arts Festival.

Expenses for 2005–2006 Application fee: $40. State resident tuition: $0 full-time. Nonresident tuition: $17,820 full-time. Mandatory fees: $6993 full-time. College room and board: $10,577. College room only: $8110.

Financial Aid Program-specific awards: 1 Sherrill C. Corwin Award for seniors ($750), 1–2 M. Plaskett Scholarships for incoming males ($1000), 1 Drama and Dance Affiliate Scholarship for seniors ($200–$400).

Application Procedures Students apply for admission into the professional program by sophomore year. Deadline for freshmen and transfers: November 30. Notification date for freshmen: March 15; transfers: April 1. Required: essay, high school transcript, college transcript(s) for transfer students, minimum 3.0 high school GPA, audition. Auditions held twice on campus; videotaped performances are permissible as a substitute for live auditions if a campus visit is impossible.

Web Site http://www.dramadance.ucsb.edu

Undergraduate Contact Amy Runjavac, Undergraduate Advisor, Department of Dramatic Art and Division of Dance, University of California, Santa Barbara, Building 479, Santa Barbara, California 93106-7060; 805-893-3241, fax: 805-893-7029, e-mail address: runjavac@dramadance.ucsb.edu

College-Conservatory of Music Dance Division
University of Cincinnati
Cincinnati, Ohio

State-supported, coed. Urban campus. Total enrollment: 27,932. Dance program established 1964.

University of Colorado at Boulder

Boulder, Colorado

State-supported, coed. Small town campus. Total enrollment: 31,068. Dance program established 1948.

Degrees Bachelor of Fine Arts in the area of dance. Majors and concentrations: choreography and performance, dance performance, modern dance. Graduate degrees offered: Master of Fine Arts in the area of dance.

Enrollment 83 total; 14 undergraduate, 15 graduate, 54 nonprofessional degree.

Dance Student Profile 90% females, 10% males, 14% minorities, 2% international.

Dance Faculty 7 total (full-time), 5 total (part-time). 72% of full-time faculty have terminal degrees. Graduate students do not teach undergraduate courses. Undergraduate student–faculty ratio: 2:1.

Student Life Student groups/activities include American College Dance Festival Association, Onstage (theater and dance student group), Black College Dance Exchange.

Expenses for 2005–2006 Application fee: $50. One-time mandatory fee: $108. State resident tuition: $4446 full-time. Nonresident tuition: $21,900 full-time. Mandatory fees: $926 full-time. Full-time tuition and fees vary according to program. College room and board: $7980. Room and board charges vary according to board plan, location, and student level. Special program-related fees: $10 per course (jazz classes) for tapes and compact discs, $20 per course for guest lecturer fee, $40–$70 per course for accompanist fee (modern, ballet, music theater, African, flamenco).

Financial Aid Program-specific awards: 10–12 University Dance Awards for program majors ($250–$1000), 1–3 Redmond Scholarships for upperclass program majors demonstrating talent and academic achievement ($800–$1700), 1 Katherine J. Lamont Scholarship for program majors ($500–$1000), 1 De Castro Scholarship for program majors ($300–$500), 1 Freshman Scholarship for freshman majors ($300–$600).

Application Procedures Students apply for admission into the professional program by sophomore year. Deadline for freshmen: January 15; transfers: April 1. Notification date for freshmen and transfers: continuous. Required: essay, high school transcript, college transcript(s) for transfer students, minimum 2.0 high school GPA, SAT I or ACT test scores, letter of application to dance faculty, at least 1 semester as BA student in dance program, enrollment in or completion of beginning composition.

Web Site http://www.colorado.edu/TheatreDance

Undergraduate Contact Office of Admissions, University of Colorado at Boulder, 030 UCB, Boulder, Colorado 80309; 303-492-6301, fax: 303-492-7115, e-mail address: apply@colorado.edu

Graduate Contact Michelle Gipner, Graduate Secretary, Department of Theatre and Dance, University of Colorado at Boulder, 261 UCB, Boulder, Colorado 80309; 303-492-7356, fax: 303-492-7722, e-mail address: michelle.gipner@colorado.edu

University of Florida

Gainesville, Florida

State-supported, coed. Suburban campus. Total enrollment: 49,693. Dance program established 1975.

Degrees Bachelor of Fine Arts in the area of dance performance. Majors and concentrations: choreography and performance, dance in medicine, theater arts/drama, world dance. Cross-registration with Florida State University System.

Enrollment 23 total; all undergraduate.

Dance Student Profile 95% females, 5% males, 20% minorities, 1% international.

Dance Faculty 5 undergraduate (full-time), 4 undergraduate (part-time). 100% of full-time faculty have terminal degrees. Graduate students do not teach undergraduate courses. Undergraduate student–faculty ratio: 5:1.

Student Life Student groups/activities include Edgework Dance Company, Florida Mod Project, Agbedidi Africa. Special housing available for dance students.

Expenses for 2005–2006 Application fee: $30. State resident tuition: $3,094 full-time. Nonresident tuition: $17,222 full-time.

College room and board: $6260. College room only: $3940. Room and board charges vary according to board plan and housing facility. Special program-related fees: $15–$45 for lab fees.

Financial Aid Program-specific awards: 5 Constans Theatre and Dance Scholarships for program majors ($500), 5 Ingram Scholarships for program majors ($500), 2 Richardson Scholarships for program majors ($1000), 8 Stoughton Scholarships for program majors ($500), 3 Outstanding Senior Awards for graduating seniors ($500).

Application Procedures Students admitted directly into the professional program freshman year. Deadline for freshmen: January 7; transfers: March 1. Required: essay, high school transcript, college transcript(s) for transfer students, minimum 2.0 high school GPA, audition, SAT I or ACT test scores. Auditions held 3 times on campus; videotaped performances are permissible as a substitute for live auditions with approval from the school and in compliance with UF/School of Theatre and Dance video auditions requirements as posted on Web site.

Web Site http://www.arts.ufl.edu/theatreanddance

Undergraduate Contact Dr. Russella Brandman, Coordinator of Dance, School of Theatre and Dance, University of Florida, PO Box 115900, Gainesville, Florida 32611-5900; 352-273-5054, fax: 352-392-5114, e-mail address: drdance@ufl.edu

The Hartt School

University of Hartford

West Hartford, Connecticut

Independent, coed. Suburban campus. Total enrollment: 7,260. Dance program established 1994.

Degrees Bachelor of Fine Arts. Majors and concentrations: dance education, performance. Cross-registration with Trinity College, Saint Joseph College, Hartford Seminary, Central Connecticut State University, University of Connecticut (Hartford Campus), Capitol Community College. Program accredited by NASD.

Enrollment 37 total; all undergraduate.

Dance Student Profile 90% females, 10% males, 5% minorities, 1% international.

Dance Faculty 4 undergraduate (full-time), 8 undergraduate (part-time). 80% of full-time faculty have terminal degrees. Graduate students do not teach undergraduate courses. Undergraduate student–faculty ratio: 6:1.

Student Life Special housing available for dance students.

Expenses for 2006–2007 Application fee: $35. Comprehensive fee: $35,688 includes full-time tuition ($24,576), mandatory fees ($1190), and college room and board ($9922). College room only: $6118.

Financial Aid Program-specific awards: 20 Performing Arts Scholarships for students passing audition evaluations ($7090).

Application Procedures Students admitted directly into the professional program freshman year. Deadline for freshmen and transfers: continuous. Required: high school transcript, college transcript(s) for transfer students, minimum 2.0 high school GPA, 3 letters of recommendation, interview, audition, SAT I or ACT test scores, photo, resume. Recommended: essay, minimum 3.0 high school GPA. Auditions held 12 times on campus; videotaped performances are permissible as a substitute for live auditions when distance is prohibitive.

Web Site http://www.hartford.edu/hartt

Undergraduate Contact Director of Admissions, The Hartt School, University of Hartford, 200 Bloomfield Avenue, West Hartford, Connecticut 06117-1500; 860-768-4465, fax: 860-768-4441, e-mail address: harttadm@hartford.edu

University of Hawaii at Manoa

Honolulu, Hawaii

State-supported, coed. Urban campus. Total enrollment: 20,644. Dance program established 1965.

Degrees Bachelor of Fine Arts in the area of dance. Majors and concentrations: dance theater. Graduate degrees offered: Master of Arts in the areas of dance ethnology, dance education; Master of Fine Arts in the area of dance.

University of Hawaii at Manoa (continued)

Enrollment 62 total; 47 undergraduate, 15 graduate.
Dance Student Profile 90% females, 10% males, 70% minorities, 10% international.
Dance Faculty 5 total (full-time), 9 total (part-time). 80% of full-time faculty have terminal degrees. Graduate students teach a few undergraduate courses. Undergraduate student–faculty ratio: 14:1.
Student Life Student groups/activities include American College Dance Festival Association, Council of Dance Administrators, London Contemporary Dance School Exchange Program.
Expenses for 2005–2006 Application fee: $50. State resident tuition: $4320 full-time. Nonresident tuition: $12,942 full-time. Mandatory fees: $193 full-time. Full-time tuition and fees vary according to class time, course load, program, and reciprocity agreements. College room and board: $6690. College room only: $4232. Room and board charges vary according to board plan and housing facility.
Financial Aid Program-specific awards: 2 Department of Theatre and Dance tuition waivers for BA and BFA dance students, John Young Scholarship Fund Awards for dance majors ($2500), 7 UH Dance Ensemble tuition waivers for dance majors.
Application Procedures Students apply for admission into the professional program by freshman year. Deadline for freshmen and transfers: May 3. Required: college transcript(s) for transfer students, minimum 3.0 high school GPA, audition, SAT I or ACT test scores (minimum combined SAT I score of 1120), minimum TOEFL score of 600 for international applicants. Auditions held once on campus.
Web Site http://www2.hawaii.edu/~uhmdance
Undergraduate Contact Ms. Peggy Gaither Adams, Undergraduate Advisor, Department of Theatre and Dance, University of Hawaii at Manoa, 1770 East West Road, Honolulu, Hawaii 96822; 808-956-3264, fax: 808-956-4234, e-mail address: adamsp@hawaii.edu
Graduate Contact Mr. Gregg Lizenbery, Director and Graduate Chair of Dance, Department of Theatre and Dance, University of Hawaii at Manoa, 1770 East West Road, Honolulu, Hawaii 96822; 808-956-2464, fax: 808-956-4234, e-mail address: lgreg@hawaii.edu

University of Idaho
Moscow, Idaho

State-supported, coed. Small town campus. Total enrollment: 12,476.
Degrees Bachelor of Dance Arts; Bachelor of Science in the area of dance. Majors and concentrations: dance arts. Graduate degrees offered: Master of Science in Physical Education in the area of dance pedagogy.
Enrollment 33 total; 30 undergraduate, 3 graduate.
Dance Student Profile 90% females, 10% males, 20% minorities.
Dance Faculty 2 total (full-time), 1 total (part-time). 100% of full-time faculty have terminal degrees. Graduate students teach a few undergraduate courses. Undergraduate student–faculty ratio: 15:1.
Student Life Student groups/activities include Dance Major Club. Special housing available for dance students.
Expenses for 2005–2006 Application fee: $40. State resident tuition: $0 full-time. Nonresident tuition: $8770 full-time. Mandatory fees: $3968 full-time. Full-time tuition and fees vary according to degree level and program. College room and board: $5342. Room and board charges vary according to board plan and housing facility.
Financial Aid Program-specific awards: 1 Freshman Scholarship for dance majors ($700), 8 Bookstore Dance Scholarships for dance majors ($800).
Application Procedures Students admitted directly into the professional program freshman year. Required: high school transcript, college transcript(s) for transfer students, minimum 2.0 high school GPA, SAT I or ACT test scores. Recommended: interview, video, audition. Auditions held twice on campus; videotaped performances are permissible as a substitute for live auditions.
Web Site http://www.dance.uidaho.edu
Contact Greg Halloran, Dance Coordinator, Division arf Health, Physical Education, Recreation, and Dance, University of Idaho,

Physical Education Building, Route 101, Moscow, Idaho 83844-2401; 208-885-2184, fax: 208-885-5929, e-mail address: halloran@uidaho.edu

University of Illinois at Urbana–Champaign
Champaign, Illinois

State-supported, coed. Small town campus. Total enrollment: 41,938. Dance program established 1949.
Degrees Bachelor of Fine Arts in the area of dance. Majors and concentrations: choreography and performance. Graduate degrees offered: Master of Fine Arts in the area of dance. Program accredited by NASD.
Enrollment 74 total; 60 undergraduate, 14 graduate.
Dance Student Profile 90% females, 10% males, 9% minorities, 9% international.
Dance Faculty 8 total (full-time), 6 total (part-time). 88% of full-time faculty have terminal degrees. Graduate students teach a few undergraduate courses. Undergraduate student–faculty ratio: 7:1.
Student Life Student groups/activities include Illini Union Board Musicals.
Expenses for 2005–2006 Application fee: $40. State resident tuition: $7042 full-time. Nonresident tuition: $21,128 full-time. Mandatory fees: $1582 full-time. Full-time tuition and fees vary according to course load, program, and student level. College room and board: $7176. College room only: $2970. Room and board charges vary according to board plan and housing facility. Special program-related fees: $400 per year for equipment and educational needs.
Financial Aid Program-specific awards: talented student awards.
Application Procedures Students admitted directly into the professional program freshman year. Deadline for freshmen and transfers: continuous. Notification date for freshmen and transfers: continuous. Required: essay, high school transcript, college transcript(s) for transfer students, minimum 3.0 high school GPA, interview, audition, SAT I or ACT test scores. Auditions held 4 times on campus; videotaped performances are permissible as a substitute for live auditions when distance is prohibitive.
Web Site http://www.dance.uiuc.edu/
Undergraduate Contact Linda Lehovec, Associate Professor, Department of Dance, University of Illinois at Urbana–Champaign, 907 1/2 West Nevada, Urbana, Illinois 61801-3810fax: 217-333-3000.
Graduate Contact Ms. Kimberly Mattingly, Administrative Secretary, Department of Dance, University of Illinois at Urbana–Champaign, 907 1/2 West Nevada, Urbana, Illinois 61801-3810; 217-333-1011, fax: 217-333-3000, e-mail address: kmatting@uiuc.edu

The University of Iowa
Iowa City, Iowa

State-supported, coed. Small town campus. Total enrollment: 28,426. Dance program established 1987.
Degrees Bachelor of Fine Arts. Majors and concentrations: dance. Graduate degrees offered: Master of Fine Arts in the area of dance.
Enrollment 120 total; 14 undergraduate, 11 graduate, 95 nonprofessional degree.
Dance Student Profile 90% females, 10% males, 5% minorities, 5% international.
Dance Faculty 8 total (full-time), 2 total (part-time). 50% of full-time faculty have terminal degrees. Graduate students do not teach undergraduate courses. Undergraduate student–faculty ratio: 11:1.
Student Life Student groups/activities include American College Dance Festival Association. Special housing available for dance students.
Expenses for 2006–2007 Application fee: $40. State resident tuition: $5110 full-time. Nonresident tuition: $17,334 full-time. Mandatory fees: $825 full-time. College room and board: $6912.

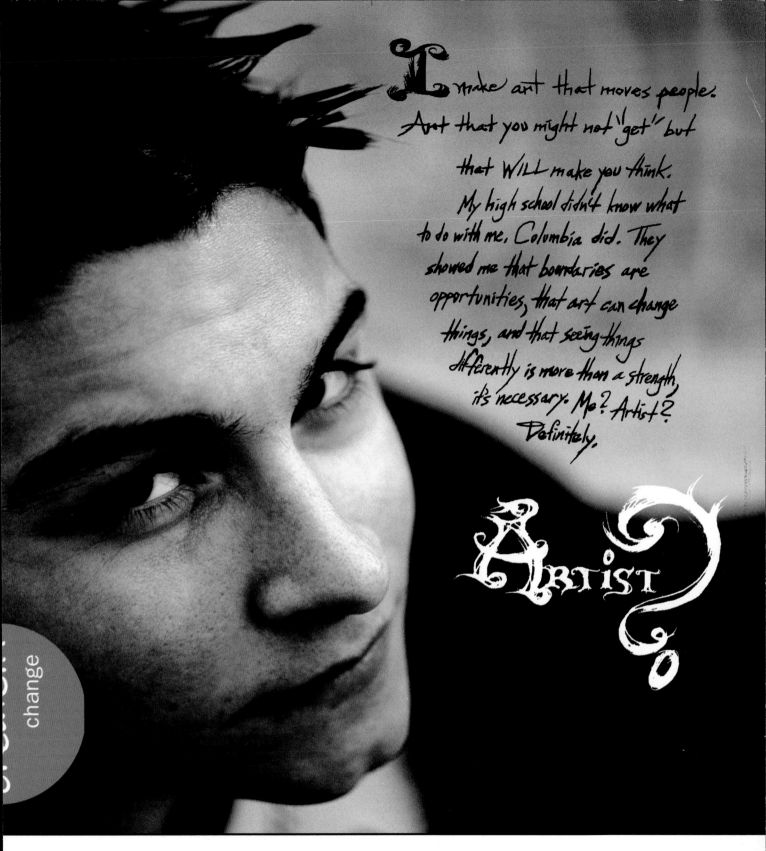

I make art that moves people. Art that you might not "get" but that WILL make you think. My high school didn't know what to do with me. Columbia did. They showed me that boundaries are opportunities, that art can change things, and that seeing things differently is more than a strength, it's necessary. Me? Artist? Definitely.

Artist?

change

Our world can be your stage.

Creativity flourishes at Roger Williams University, a leading liberal arts university in New England.

Refine your writing, visual arts skills and performance techniques, energized by our beautiful 140-acre waterfront campus in historic Bristol, Rhode Island, easily accessible from Boston and New York.

Accredited by the New England Association of Schools and Colleges, Roger Williams University draws 3,650 full-time undergraduates who benefit from a dedicated faculty and an ideal academic setting with excellent facilities, recreation, athletics, and social opportunities. The Roger Williams education produces well-rounded students who successfully bridge transitions to a rewarding career and gratifying life.

The Theatre Program
The Roger Williams Theatre Program is unique in the range and breadth of its areas of study, offering you the opportunity to major in Theatre, leading to a Bachelor of Arts degree.

Creative Writing Program
Roger Williams University is one of the few colleges and universities in the United States to offer an undergraduate major in Creative Writing, leading to a Bachelor of Fine Arts degree.

Dance Performance Studies
The University offers courses in technique, choreography, history, pedagogy, movement analysis, performance techniques, and movement theatre (we are the only dance-based university program in the country to offer this training).

Graphic Design Communications
This program consists of a contemporary blend of a liberal arts education and applied technology. Students draw on their complete educational experience to create images and visual messages that are thought-provoking, well-researched, and technically excellent.

Visual Arts Studies
Our School of Architecture, Art and Historic Preservation offers the Bachelor of Arts degree in Visual Arts Studies. You can develop your talents in one of the following disciplines: Painting/Drawing/Printmaking, Sculpture, or Photography/Digital Media.

Financial Aid Program-specific awards: 1 Iowa Center for the Arts Scholarship for incoming freshmen ($3000), 1 T. J. Myers Memorial Scholarship for male incoming freshmen ($1000), 1 dance scholarship for freshmen program majors ($1000), 2 Francoise Martinet Scholarships for program majors ($1000), 6 Dance Foundation Scholarships for program majors ($1000).

Application Procedures Students apply for admission into the professional program by sophomore year. Deadline for freshmen and transfers: May 13. Required: high school transcript, college transcript(s) for transfer students, 3 letters of recommendation, interview, audition, SAT I or ACT test scores, audition or video for placement and scholarship consideration, minimum 2.5 high school GPA. Recommended: essay, minimum 3.0 high school GPA, resume. Auditions held 4 times on campus; videotaped performances are permissible as a substitute for live auditions when distance is prohibitive or for financial reasons.

Web Site http://www.uiowa.edu/~dance

Undergraduate Contact Charlotte Adams, Associate Professor, Dance Department, The University of Iowa, E114 Halsey Hall, Iowa City, Iowa 52242; 319-335-2185, fax: 319-335-3246, e-mail address: charlotte-adams@uiowa.edu

Graduate Contact Armando Duarte, Associate Professor, Dance Department, The University of Iowa, E114 Halsey Hall, Iowa City, Iowa 52242; 319-335-2184, fax: 319-335-3246, e-mail address: armando-duarte@uiowa.edu

University of Louisiana at Lafayette
Lafayette, Louisiana

State-supported, coed. Urban campus. Total enrollment: 17,075. Dance program established 1994.

University of Massachusetts Amherst
Amherst, Massachusetts

State-supported, coed. Total enrollment: 25,093. Dance program established 1974.

Degrees Bachelor of Fine Arts. Majors and concentrations: dance. Cross-registration with Amherst College, Hampshire College, Mount Holyoke College, Smith College.

Enrollment 45 total; 30 undergraduate, 15 nonprofessional degree.

Dance Student Profile 99% females, 1% males, 1% minorities.

Dance Faculty 3 undergraduate (full-time), 1 undergraduate (part-time). Graduate students teach a few undergraduate courses. Undergraduate student–faculty ratio: 14:1.

Student Life Student groups/activities include Alive With Dance, Dance Team, Music Theater Guild.

Expenses for 2006–2007 Application fee: $40. State resident tuition: $2031 full-time. Nonresident tuition: $10,857 full-time. Mandatory fees: $7564 full-time.

Financial Aid Program-specific awards: 12 Chancellor's Talent Awards for program students.

Application Procedures Students admitted directly into the professional program freshman year. Deadline for freshmen: January 15; transfers: May 2. Notification date for freshmen: April 15; transfers: June 1. Required: essay, high school transcript, college transcript(s) for transfer students, audition, SAT I or ACT test scores. Auditions held 4 times on campus; videotaped performances are permissible as a substitute for live auditions when distance is prohibitive, if auditions are full, or in special circumstances.

Web Site http://www.umass.edu/hfa

Undergraduate Contact Ms. Mary Lou Laurenza, Director of Dance Admissions, Dance Program, University of Massachusetts Amherst, 11 Totman, Amherst, Massachusetts 01003; 413-545-6064, fax: 413-545-0220, e-mail address: mllauren@dance.umass.edu

University of Michigan
Ann Arbor, Michigan

State-supported, coed. Suburban campus. Total enrollment: 39,993. Dance program established 1929.

Degrees Bachelor of Fine Arts in the area of dance. Majors and concentrations: choreography and performance, modern dance.

Enrollment 399 total; 64 undergraduate, 10 graduate, 325 nonprofessional degree.

Dance Student Profile 90% females, 10% males, 7% minorities, 2% international.

Dance Faculty 11 total (full-time), 3 total (part-time). 90% of full-time faculty have terminal degrees. Graduate students do not teach undergraduate courses. Undergraduate student–faculty ratio: 7:1.

Expenses for 2005–2006 Application fee: $40. State resident tuition: $9213 full-time. Nonresident tuition: $27,602 full-time. Mandatory fees: $187 full-time. Full-time tuition and fees vary according to course load, degree level, location, program, and student level. College room and board: $7374. Room and board charges vary according to board plan and housing facility.

Financial Aid Program-specific awards: dance merit scholarships for incoming students.

Application Procedures Students admitted directly into the professional program freshman year. Deadline for freshmen and transfers: December 1. Required: essay, high school transcript, college transcript(s) for transfer students, minimum 3.0 high school GPA, 2 letters of recommendation, audition, SAT I or ACT test scores (minimum combined SAT I score of 1100, minimum composite ACT score of 24), written personal statement. Auditions held 5 times on campus and off campus in New York, NY; videotaped performances are permissible as a substitute for live auditions with permission of the chair.

Web Site http://www.music.umich.edu

Undergraduate Contact Ms. Laura Strozeski, Assistant Dean for Enrollment Management and Student Services, School of Music Office of Admissions and Student Services, University of Michigan, 2240 Moore Building, 1100 Baits Drive, Ann Arbor, Michigan 48109-2085; 734-764-0593, fax: 734-763-5097, e-mail address: music.admissions@umich.edu

Graduate Contact Bill De Young, Chair, Department of Dance, University of Michigan, 1310 North University Court, Ann Arbor, Michigan 48109-2217; 734-763-5460, fax: 734-763-5962, e-mail address: bdyj@umich.edu

University of Minnesota, Twin Cities Campus
Minneapolis, Minnesota

State-supported, coed. Urban campus. Total enrollment: 51,175. Dance program established 1987.

Degrees Bachelor of Fine Arts. Majors and concentrations: dance. Program accredited by NASD.

Enrollment 1,080 total; 80 undergraduate, 1,000 nonprofessional degree.

Dance Student Profile 82% females, 18% males, 12% minorities, 1% international.

Dance Faculty 4 undergraduate (full-time), 40 undergraduate (part-time). 75% of full-time faculty have terminal degrees. Graduate students do not teach undergraduate courses. Undergraduate student–faculty ratio: 4:1.

Student Life Student groups/activities include West Bank Arts Quarter Collective, Student Dance Coalition. Special housing available for dance students.

Expenses for 2005–2006 Application fee: $45. State resident tuition: $7140 full-time. Nonresident tuition: $19,670 full-time. Mandatory fees: $1482 full-time. Full-time tuition and fees vary according to program and reciprocity agreements. College room and board: $6722. College room only: $3886. Room and board charges vary according to board plan, housing facility, and location. Special program-related fees: $35 for musician accompanist fee.

Financial Aid Program-specific awards: 1 Sealy Scholarship for incoming freshman ($2500), 1 Nadine Jette-Sween Scholarship for dance majors ($1000), 1 Marion Haynes Andrus Scholarship for dance majors ($1000), 1 Advisory Council Scholarship for dance majors ($1000), 1 Tom and Ellie Crosby Scholarship for incoming freshmen or newly declared dance majors ($1000), 2 Robert Moulton Memorial Scholarships for dance majors ($1000), 1 Barbara Barker Scholarship for dance majors ($1000–

University of Minnesota, Twin Cities Campus (continued)

$2000), 1–2 Gertrude Lippencott Scholarship for incoming freshman ($6000), 1 Stefannie Valencia Kierlen Memorial Scholarship for dance majors ($1000), 1 Marge Maddux Scholarship for incoming freshman ($2500), 1 Hope-Supan Scholarship for incoming freshman ($3000).
Application Procedures Students admitted directly into the professional program freshman year. Deadline for freshmen and transfers: continuous. Required: high school transcript, college transcript(s) for transfer students, interview, audition, SAT I or ACT test scores, core subjects. Recommended: essay, minimum 3.0 high school GPA, letter of recommendation. Auditions held 3 times on campus.
Web Site http://dance.umn.edu
Undergraduate Contact Office of Admissions, University of Minnesota, Twin Cities Campus, 240 Williamson Hall, 231 Pillsbury Drive, SE, Minneapolis, Minnesota 55455; 612-625-2008.

More About the Dance Program

The University of Minnesota Dance Program provides professional technical training, fosters an intensive creative process, offers extensive performance experience, and promotes rigorous intellectual inquiry through its two degree programs: the Bachelor of Arts (B.A.) and the Bachelor of Fine Arts (B.F.A.). The goal of the University of Minnesota Dance Program is to turn out versatile dancing thinkers and thinking dancers. One administrator has called the program, which is part of the Department of Theatre Arts and Dance, "a jewel in the crown of the University." It is also a matrix for the Twin Cities dance community, providing dancers of technical distinction and powerful performing presence to the numerous dance companies based in the Twin Cities, as well as the dance community at large.

The Twin Cities has long fostered a diverse dance environment that supports a vast range of styles and aesthetics and is considered by many to be one of the most thriving dance communities in the country. Currently, there are two professional chamber ballet companies, several modern-based companies, a jazz and percussive dance company, and numerous culturally diverse companies. In addition, local presenters bring in nationally and internationally recognized companies on a regular basis. There is also a host of independent choreographers producing work and experimenting with new forms.

The Dance Program contributes significantly to this environment by employing local dance artists (many of them with

national and international reputations) to teach and choreograph students. The distinguished faculty includes veteran artists, such as Toni Pierce-Sands, formerly of the Alvin Ailey American Dance Theater; Joanie Smith and Danial Shapiro, of Shapiro & Smith Dance; Ananya Chatterjea, a noted scholar, performer, and choreographer; and Carl Flink, the program director. Emerging artists also teach classes in contemporary forms, such as release technique and contact improvisation. Each year, the program brings in celebrated teachers, scholars, and choreographers for guest residencies. Past guest artists include Merce Cunningham, Bill T. Jones, Ralph Lemon, Elizabeth Streb, Bebe Miller, Jawole Willa Jo Zollar, Tere O'Connor, and Doug Varone. Guest critics and scholars have included Deborah Jowitt, Sally Banes, and Brenda Dixon Gottschild.

Program Facilities The program facilities are state-of-the-art. The Barbara Barker Center for Dance is a building that indeed dances—from its soaring exterior to its beautifully designed studios with floor-to-ceiling windows and curved walls. The program is large enough to offer students a variety of resources, yet intimate enough to ensure that each student gets individual attention and mentoring. With its reputation for academic excellence, the University of Minnesota offers the opportunity for a well-rounded education in a volatile learning environment.

In 1999, the Dance Program moved into the Barbara Barker Center for Dance, a new award-winning facility with three large studios, a classroom, and performance space. The campus is situated in a major metropolitan area minutes from the downtown districts of Minneapolis and St. Paul. Both cities are noted for their extraordinary arts communities. Professional dance companies include Shapiro and Smith Dance, TU Dance, Zenon Dance Company, Ethnic Dance Theater, Ananya Dance Theatre, Paula Mann's Time Track Productions, ARENA Dances, and Joe Chvala's Flying Foot Forum. Directors or members of these companies teach in the Dance Program. Several of the program's current students and alumni currently perform in these and other professional companies in the area.

Faculty, Resident Artists, and Alumni The professional faculty consists of 4 full-time and 40 affiliate faculty members, many of whom are directors of their own companies. They teach a range of styles and techniques in modern dance, ballet, jazz, and world dance forms. The Cowles Chair Visiting Artists program brings in 5 to 7 nationally and internationally recognized guest choreographers, teachers, and scholars per year to work with the students, exposing them to both contemporary artistry and masterwork.

Performance Opportunities Students give nearly two dozen performances per year, including informal showings, performances in the schools, self-produced events by the Student Dance Coalition, fully produced concerts by the University Dance Theater (UDT), and an annual event in collaboration with students from the theater department. In addition, the Dance Program provides opportunities for students to perform in works by visiting choreographers in major venues. Past performances have included *The Promised Land* by Bill T. Jones, *Spectators at an Event* by Susan Marshall, and *PASTforward* with Mikhail Baryshnikov's White Oak Project.

For more information on the University of Minnesota Dance Program, prospective students are encouraged to visit the Web site at http://www.dance.umn.edu.

University of Missouri–Kansas City
Kansas City, Missouri

State-supported, coed. Urban campus. Total enrollment: 14,310. Dance program established 1907.
Degrees Bachelor of Fine Arts. Majors and concentrations: dance.
Enrollment 105 total; 55 undergraduate, 50 nonprofessional degree.
Dance Student Profile 90% females, 10% males, 5% minorities, 15% international.

Dance Faculty 4 undergraduate (full-time), 3 undergraduate (part-time). 75% of full-time faculty have terminal degrees. Graduate students do not teach undergraduate courses. Undergraduate student–faculty ratio: 13:1.
Student Life Student groups/activities include Dance Students Association.
Expenses for 2006–2007 Application fee: $35. State resident tuition: $6819 full-time. Nonresident tuition: $17,085 full-time.
Financial Aid Program-specific awards: endowed scholarships for program majors ($700–$2500).
Application Procedures Students admitted directly into the professional program freshman year. Deadline for freshmen and transfers: March 3. Notification date for freshmen and transfers: continuous. Required: high school transcript, college transcript(s) for transfer students, minimum 2.0 high school GPA, 3 letters of recommendation, audition, ACT score for state residents, SAT I or ACT score for out-of-state residents. Recommended: minimum 3.0 high school GPA. Auditions held by appointment on campus; videotaped performances are permissible as a substitute for live auditions for provisional acceptance.
Web Site http://www.umkc.edu/conservatory
Undergraduate Contact Dr. James T. Elswick, Associate Director of Admissions, UMKC Conservatory of Music, University of Missouri–Kansas City, 5227 Holmes Road, Kansas City, Missouri 64110; 816-235-2900, fax: 816-235-5264, e-mail address: cadmissions@umkc.edu

The University of Montana–Missoula
Missoula, Montana

State-supported, coed. Total enrollment: 13,602. Dance program established 1972.

The University of North Carolina at Greensboro
Greensboro, North Carolina

State-supported, coed. Urban campus. Total enrollment: 16,060. Dance program established 1948.
Degrees Bachelor of Fine Arts in the area of dance choreography and performance; Bachelor of Science in the area of dance education. Majors and concentrations: choreography and performance, dance, dance education. Graduate degrees offered: Master of Arts in the area of dance; Master of Fine Arts in the areas of performance, choreography, design. Cross-registration with North Carolina Agricultural and Technical State University, Guilford College, Greensboro College, Bennett College, Guilford Technical Community College. Program accredited by NCATE, NASD.
Enrollment 188 total; 115 undergraduate, 23 graduate, 50 nonprofessional degree.
Dance Student Profile 90% females, 10% males, 15% minorities, 3% international.
Dance Faculty 10 total (full-time), 6 total (part-time). 80% of full-time faculty have terminal degrees. Graduate students teach a few undergraduate courses. Undergraduate student–faculty ratio: 10:1.
Student Life Student groups/activities include Prime Movers (student dance association). Special housing available for dance students.
Expenses for 2006–2007 Application fee: $45. State resident tuition: $2308 full-time. Nonresident tuition: $13,576 full-time. Mandatory fees: $1505 full-time. College room and board: $5706. College room only: $3232.
Financial Aid Program-specific awards: 1–2 Virginia Moomaw Scholarships for continuing program students ($1000), 1 Feinstein Scholarship for minority students demonstrating financial need ($900), 1–3 Burns Scholarships for continuing students with career interest in musical theater and demonstrating financial need ($1000–$3000), 1 Goodman Scholarship for those demonstrating financial need ($1000), 1 Stout Scholarship for dance majors ($2000).

Application Procedures Students apply for admission into the professional program by sophomore year. Deadline for freshmen and transfers: continuous. Notification date for freshmen and transfers: continuous. Required: essay, high school transcript, college transcript(s) for transfer students, interview, audition, SAT I or ACT test scores, minimum 2.0 college GPA for transfer students. Recommended: minimum 3.0 high school GPA, letter of recommendation. Auditions held twice on campus; videotaped performances are permissible as a substitute for live auditions.
Web Site http://www.uncg.edu/dce
Undergraduate Contact Caitlin Medlock, Public Relations and Marketing Coordinator, Department of Dance, The University of North Carolina at Greensboro, UNCG Box 26170, Greensboro, North Carolina 27402-6170; 336-334-5955, fax: 336-334-3238.
Graduate Contact Dr. Jan Van Dyke, Graduate Coordinator, Department of Dance, The University of North Carolina at Greensboro, UNCG Box 26170, Greensboro, North Carolina 27402-6170; 336-334-5570, fax: 336-334-3238, e-mail address: jevandyk@uncg.edu

University of Oklahoma
Norman, Oklahoma

State-supported, coed. Suburban campus. Total enrollment: 26,968. Dance program established 1963.
Degrees Bachelor of Fine Arts in the area of dance. Majors and concentrations: ballet, modern dance. Graduate degrees offered: Master of Fine Arts in the area of dance.
Enrollment 89 total; 80 undergraduate, 9 graduate.
Dance Student Profile 90% females, 10% males, 12% minorities, 5% international.
Dance Faculty 8 total (full-time), 6 total (part-time). 67% of full-time faculty have terminal degrees. Graduate students do not teach undergraduate courses. Undergraduate student–faculty ratio: 8:1.
Student Life Student groups/activities include Drama and Dance Student Association, Student Advisory Council.
Expenses for 2005–2006 Application fee: $40. State resident tuition: $2862 full-time. Nonresident tuition: $10,755 full-time. Mandatory fees: $1546 full-time. Full-time tuition and fees vary according to course load, location, program, and reciprocity agreements. College room and board: $6361. College room only: $3355. Room and board charges vary according to board plan and housing facility. Special program-related fees: $85 per course for accompanist's salary.
Financial Aid Program-specific awards: 15–20 tuition waivers for out-of-state program students ($1500–$4000), 10–20 Barnett Foundation Scholarships for excellent dancers ($300–$800), 2–6 Everett Foundation Scholarships for male ballet majors ($1000), 4–6 fee waivers for state residents ($500–$1000), 2 Busken Scholarships for junior/senior ballet majors ($2000).
Application Procedures Students admitted directly into the professional program freshman year. Deadline for freshmen and transfers: continuous. Notification date for freshmen and transfers: continuous. Required: high school transcript, minimum 3.0 high school GPA, 2 letters of recommendation, audition, SAT I or ACT test scores (minimum combined SAT I score of 1090, minimum composite ACT score of 24), minimum SAT score of 1090 for state residents; 1170 for nonresidents, minimum ACT score of 24 for state residents; 26 for nonresidents. Recommended: college transcript(s) for transfer students, interview. Auditions held 3 times and by appointment on campus and off campus in Dallas, TX; Houston, TX; Louisville, KY; New York, NY; videotaped performances are permissible as a substitute for live auditions when distance is prohibitive.
Web Site http://www.ou.edu/finearts
Undergraduate Contact Ms. Kate O'Brien-Hamough, Staff Assistant, School of Dance, University of Oklahoma, 560 Parrington Oval, Room 1000, Norman, Oklahoma 73019; 405-325-4051, fax: 405-325-7024, e-mail address: dance@ou.edu
Graduate Contact Ms. Mary Margaret Holt, Director, School of Dance, University of Oklahoma, 560 Parrington Oval, Room 1000, Norman, Oklahoma 73019; 405-325-4051, fax: 405-325-7024, e-mail address: marymholt@ou.edu

University of Southern Mississippi
Hattiesburg, Mississippi

State-supported, coed. Suburban campus. Total enrollment: 15,030. Dance program established 1982.
Degrees Bachelor of Fine Arts in the areas of dance performance and choreography, dance education. Majors and concentrations: choreography and performance, dance education. Program accredited by NASD.
Enrollment 55 total; all undergraduate.
Dance Student Profile 85% females, 15% males, 27% minorities.
Dance Faculty 5 undergraduate (full-time). 100% of full-time faculty have terminal degrees. Graduate students do not teach undergraduate courses. Undergraduate student–faculty ratio: 11:1.
Student Life Student groups/activities include dance concerts.
Expenses for 2006–2007 Application fee: $0. State resident tuition: $4312 full-time. Nonresident tuition: $9742 full-time. Mandatory fees: $30 full-time. College room and board: $5800. College room only: $2620. Special program-related fees: $35 for course fees, accompanists.
Financial Aid Program-specific awards: 15 service awards for program majors ($300), 10 foundation awards for program majors ($500).
Application Procedures Students admitted directly into the professional program freshman year. Deadline for freshmen and transfers: August 5. Required: essay, high school transcript, college transcript(s) for transfer students, minimum 2.0 high school GPA, interview, audition, SAT I or ACT test scores (minimum composite ACT score of 16). Recommended: 2 letters of recommendation, video. Auditions held twice on campus.
Web Site http://www.usm.edu
Undergraduate Contact Ms. Stacy Reischman, Interim Chair/Director of Dance, Department of Theatre and Dance, University of Southern Mississippi, 118 College Drive, #5052, Hattiesburg, Mississippi 39406; 601-266-4151, fax: 601-266-5816, e-mail address: stacy.reischman@usm.edu

University of South Florida
Tampa, Florida

State-supported, coed. Urban campus. Total enrollment: 42,660.
Degrees Bachelor of Arts; Bachelor of Fine Arts. Majors and concentrations: ballet, choreography, dance performance, dance studies, modern dance. Program accredited by NASD.
Enrollment 75 total; all undergraduate.
Dance Student Profile 90% females, 10% males, 2% international.
Dance Faculty 6 undergraduate (full-time), 2 undergraduate (part-time). Graduate students do not teach undergraduate courses.
Student Life Student groups/activities include Honors Research Symposium, Taste of the Arts, dance productions/concerts.
Expenses for 2005–2006 Application fee: $30. State resident tuition: $3310 full-time. Nonresident tuition: $16,076 full-time. Mandatory fees: $74 full-time. Full-time tuition and fees vary according to course level, course load, and location. College room and board: $6900. College room only: $3563. Room and board charges vary according to board plan, housing facility, and location.
Financial Aid Program-specific awards: 1–5 Diversity Enhancement Awards for minority students ($150–$250), 1–4 Exceptionally Talented Black Student Award ($200–$1000), 1–6 Green and Gold Talent Scholarships for out of state students ($1500).
Application Procedures Students admitted directly into the professional program freshman year. Deadline for freshmen and transfers: April 15. Required: essay, high school transcript, college transcript(s) for transfer students, audition, SAT I or ACT test scores. Recommended: 3 letters of recommendation. Auditions held 4 times on campus; videotaped performances are permissible as a substitute for live auditions.
Web Site http://www.arts.usf.edu/cvpa/theatredance.html
Contact Ms. Merry Lynn Morris, Academic Advisor, Advising/School of Theatre and Dance, University of South Florida, 4204 East Fowler Avenue, FAH 110, Tampa, Florida 33620; 813-974-1739, fax: 813-974-4165, e-mail address: mmorris@arts.usf.edu

The University of Texas at Austin
Austin, Texas

State-supported, coed. Urban campus. Total enrollment: 49,696. Dance program established 1938.
Degrees Bachelor of Fine Arts in the area of dance. Majors and concentrations: dance. Graduate degrees offered: Master of Fine Arts in the area of performance/dance. Program accredited by NASD.
Enrollment 25 total.
Dance Student Profile 97% females, 3% males, 10% minorities.
Dance Faculty 7 total (full-time), 2 total (part-time). 75% of full-time faculty have terminal degrees. Graduate students do not teach undergraduate courses. Undergraduate student–faculty ratio: 7:1.
Student Life Student groups/activities include Dance Repertory Theatre, community outreach programs.
Expenses for 2005–2006 Application fee: $60. State resident tuition: $6972 full-time. Nonresident tuition: $16,310 full-time. Full-time tuition varies according to course load and program. College room and board: $7638. Room and board charges vary according to board plan, housing facility, and location. Special program-related fees: $115 per semester for performance and production fee.
Financial Aid Program-specific awards: 2 McGriff Scholarships for program students ($2000), 3 Danielian Scholarships for program students ($2000).
Application Procedures Students admitted directly into the professional program freshman year. Deadline for freshmen: February 1; transfers: March 1. Notification date for freshmen and transfers: continuous. Required: essay, high school transcript, college transcript(s) for transfer students, 3 letters of recommendation, audition, SAT I or ACT test scores. Auditions held 3 times on campus; videotaped performances are permissible as a substitute for live auditions for out-of-state applicants with permission from the faculty.
Web Site http://www.utexas.edu/cofa/theatre
Undergraduate Contact Jun Hurt, Academic Advisor, Department of Theatre and Dance, The University of Texas at Austin, 1 University Station D3900, Austin, Texas 78712-0362; 512-471-5793, fax: 512-471-0824, e-mail address: jhurt@mail.utexas.edu
Graduate Contact Andrew Johnson, Graduate Program Coordinator, Department of Theatre and Dance, The University of Texas at Austin, 1 University Station D3900, Austin, Texas 78712-0362; 512-475-7336, fax: 512-471-0824, e-mail address: arjohnson@mail.utexas.edu

The University of the Arts
Philadelphia, Pennsylvania

Independent, coed. Total enrollment: 2,277. Dance program established 1947.
Degrees Bachelor of Fine Arts in the areas of dance, dance education, modern, ballet, jazz/dance. Majors and concentrations: ballet, dance, dance education, jazz dance, modern dance.
Enrollment 270 total; all undergraduate.
Dance Student Profile 56% females, 44% males, 17% minorities, 3% international.
Dance Faculty 8 undergraduate (full-time), 20 undergraduate (part-time). 33% of full-time faculty have terminal degrees. Graduate students do not teach undergraduate courses. Undergraduate student–faculty ratio: 9:1.
Student Life Student groups/activities include Student Government. Special housing available for dance students.
Expenses for 2006–2007 Application fee: $60. Tuition: $24,730 full-time. Mandatory fees: $950 full-time. College room only: $6300.
Financial Aid Program-specific awards: 25 merit scholarships for incoming students ($500–$8000).
Application Procedures Students admitted directly into the professional program freshman year. Deadline for freshmen and transfers: continuous. Notification date for freshmen and transfers: September 1. Required: essay, high school transcript, college transcript(s) for transfer students, minimum 2.0 high school GPA, letter of recommendation, audition, SAT I or ACT

test scores, resume. Recommended: minimum 3.0 high school GPA, interview, photo. Auditions held 9 times on campus and off campus in various locations in California; videotaped performances are permissible as a substitute for live auditions if student lives more than 200 miles from Philadelphia.
Web Site http://www.uarts.edu
Undergraduate Contact Susan Gandy, Director of Admission, The University of the Arts, 320 South Broad Street, Philadelphia, Pennsylvania 19102; 800-616-ARTS ext. 6049, fax: 215-717-6045, e-mail address: admissions@uarts.edu

University of Utah
Salt Lake City, Utah

State-supported, coed. Urban campus. Total enrollment: 29,012. Dance program established 1951.
Degrees Bachelor of Fine Arts in the area of ballet. Majors and concentrations: ballet. Graduate degrees offered: Master of Arts in the area of ballet; Master of Fine Arts in the area of ballet.
Enrollment 312 total; 110 undergraduate, 8 graduate, 194 nonprofessional degree.
Dance Student Profile 90% females, 10% males, 10% minorities, 5% international.
Dance Faculty 7 total (full-time), 10 total (part-time). 43% of full-time faculty have terminal degrees. Graduate students teach a few undergraduate courses. Undergraduate student–faculty ratio: 15:1.
Student Life Student groups/activities include collaborative concerts, student guest artist opportunities, senior concert. Special housing available for dance students.
Expenses for 2005–2006 Application fee: $35. State resident tuition: $3672 full-time. Nonresident tuition: $12,860 full-time. Mandatory fees: $670 full-time. Full-time tuition and fees vary according to course level, course load, degree level, and student level. College room and board: $5422. College room only: $2704. Room and board charges vary according to board plan and housing facility. Special program-related fees: $5–$15 for live accompanists, $10 for hydrostatic weighing of students.
Financial Aid Program-specific awards: 6 Willam F. Christensen Scholarships for resident incoming program students ($2000), 25–40 departmental scholarships for program students ($600–$6000), 1–2 Honors at Entrance/Presidential Scholarships for ballet majors demonstrating high academic achievement ($2280–$7000), 1 Fine Arts Advisory Board Award for juniors or seniors ($2000), 1 Kennecott Award for juniors/seniors ($2000).
Application Procedures Students admitted directly into the professional program freshman year. Deadline for freshmen and transfers: March 1. Notification date for freshmen and transfers: May 31. Required: high school transcript, college transcript(s) for transfer students, minimum 2.0 high school GPA, 2 letters of recommendation, audition, SAT I or ACT test scores, 2 photographs in ballet poses - women on pointe, application form (ballet majors). Recommended: essay, minimum 3.0 high school GPA. Auditions held twice on campus; videotaped performances are permissible as a substitute for live auditions when distance is prohibitive or time constraints exist (request instructions).
Web Site http://www.ballet.utah.edu
Undergraduate Contact Ms. Valerie Horton, Administrative Assistant, Ballet Department, University of Utah, 330 S 1500 E, Room 112, Salt Lake City, Utah 84112-0280; 801-581-8231, fax: 801-581-5442, e-mail address: v.horton@utah.edu
Graduate Contact Prof. Sharee Lane, Graduate Advisor, Ballet Department, University of Utah, 330 S 1500 E, Room 112, Salt Lake City, Utah 84112-0280; 801-587-3794, fax: 801-581-5442, e-mail address: sharee.lane@utah.edu

University of Utah
Salt Lake City, Utah

State-supported, coed. Urban campus. Total enrollment: 29,012. Dance program established 1940.
Degrees Bachelor of Fine Arts. Majors and concentrations: modern dance. Graduate degrees offered: Master of Fine Arts in the area of modern dance.

Enrollment 100 total; 80 undergraduate, 20 graduate.
Dance Student Profile 90% females, 10% males, 10% minorities, 5% international.
Dance Faculty 10 total (full-time), 2 total (part-time). 90% of full-time faculty have terminal degrees. Graduate students do not teach undergraduate courses. Undergraduate student–faculty ratio: 6:1.
Student Life Student groups/activities include American College Dance Festival Association, Associated Student Organization, Student Dance Company. Special housing available for dance students.
Expenses for 2005–2006 Application fee: $35. State resident tuition: $3672 full-time. Nonresident tuition: $12,860 full-time. Mandatory fees: $670 full-time. Full-time tuition and fees vary according to course level, course load, degree level, and student level. College room and board: $5422. College room only: $2704. Room and board charges vary according to board plan and housing facility. Special program-related fees: $8–$15 per class for equipment use fee, musicians.
Financial Aid Program-specific awards: 3 Hayes Scholarships for state residents, 15 departmental scholarships for program students.
Application Procedures Students admitted directly into the professional program freshman year. Deadline for freshmen: August 25; transfers: April 1. Required: high school transcript, college transcript(s) for transfer students, minimum 3.0 high school GPA, audition. Auditions held 3 times on campus and off campus in various cities; videotaped performances are permissible as a substitute for live auditions.
Web Site http://www.dance.utah.edu
Undergraduate Contact Department of Modern Dance, University of Utah, 330 S 1500 E, Room 106, Salt Lake City, Utah 84112-0280; 801-581-7327, fax: 801-581-5442.
Graduate Contact Mr. Steve Koester, Director of Graduate Studies, Department of Modern Dance, University of Utah, 330 South 1500 East, Room 106, Salt Lake City, Utah 84112-0280; 801-581-7327, fax: 801-581-5442, e-mail address: stephen.koester@utah.edu

University of Wisconsin–Milwaukee
Milwaukee, Wisconsin

State-supported, coed. Urban campus. Total enrollment: 27,502.

University of Wyoming
Laramie, Wyoming

State-supported, coed. Total enrollment: 13,126. Dance program established 1972.
Degrees Bachelor of Fine Arts in the area of dance. Majors and concentrations: ballet, jazz dance, modern dance.
Enrollment 65 total; 40 undergraduate, 25 nonprofessional degree.
Dance Student Profile 90% females, 10% males, 15% minorities, 1% international.
Dance Faculty 12 undergraduate (full-time), 1 undergraduate (part-time). 90% of full-time faculty have terminal degrees. Graduate students do not teach undergraduate courses. Undergraduate student–faculty ratio: 10:1.
Student Life Student groups/activities include Associated Students of the Performing Arts.
Expenses for 2005–2006 Application fee: $30. State resident tuition: $2760 full-time. Nonresident tuition: $9150 full-time. Mandatory fees: $666 full-time. Full-time tuition and fees vary according to course load, location, program, and reciprocity agreements. College room and board: $6240. College room only: $2709. Room and board charges vary according to board plan and housing facility.
Financial Aid Program-specific awards: 21 departmental awards for program majors ($2575).
Application Procedures Students admitted directly into the professional program freshman year. Deadline for freshmen and transfers: August 31. Required: high school transcript, college transcript(s) for transfer students, SAT I or ACT test scores, audition for scholarship consideration, minimum 2.5 high school

University of Wyoming (continued)

GPA. Recommended: letter of recommendation, interview, audition. Auditions held twice on campus and off campus in Rocky Mountain Theatre Association Festival locations; videotaped performances are permissible as a substitute for live auditions if a campus visit is impossible.
Web Site http://www.uwyo.edu/th&d/homepage.htm
Undergraduate Contact Dr. Rebecca Hilliker, Head, Department of Theatre and Dance, University of Wyoming, Box 3951, Laramie, Wyoming 82071-3951; 307-766-2198, fax: 307-766-2197, e-mail address: hilliker@uwyo.edu

Virginia Commonwealth University
Richmond, Virginia

State-supported, coed. Urban campus. Total enrollment: 29,349. Dance program established 1981.
Degrees Bachelor of Fine Arts in the area of dance and choreography. Majors and concentrations: modern dance. Program accredited by NASD.
Enrollment 80 total; all undergraduate.
Dance Student Profile 80% females, 20% males, 30% minorities, 2% international.
Dance Faculty 7 undergraduate (full-time), 14 undergraduate (part-time). 65% of full-time faculty have terminal degrees. Graduate students do not teach undergraduate courses. Undergraduate student–faculty ratio: 12:1.
Student Life Student groups/activities include public performances, dance festivals.
Expenses for 2005–2006 Application fee: $30. State resident tuition: $5385 full-time. Nonresident tuition: $17,440 full-time. College room and board: $7042. College room only: $4102. Room and board charges vary according to board plan. Special program-related fees: $30 per course for dance course fees, $75–$265 per semester for School of the Arts major fees.
Financial Aid Program-specific awards: Oates Dance Education Scholarship for full-time students who wish to teach dance (K-12), Carpenter Foundation Scholarship for full-time students, School of the Arts Scholarship in Dance for incoming freshman.
Application Procedures Students admitted directly into the professional program freshman year. Deadline for freshmen and transfers: continuous. Notification date for freshmen and transfers: continuous. Required: essay, high school transcript, college transcript(s) for transfer students, minimum 2.0 high school GPA, 2 letters of recommendation, audition, SAT I or ACT test scores (minimum combined SAT I score of 850). Recommended: interview. Auditions held 4 times on campus; videotaped performances are permissible as a substitute for live auditions when distance is prohibitive.
Web Site http://www.vcu.edu/artweb/dance/
Undergraduate Contact Ms. Martha Curtis, Chair, Department of Dance and Choreography, Virginia Commonwealth University, 1315 Floyd Avenue, Box 843007, Richmond, Virginia 23284-3007; 804-828-1711, fax: 804-828-7356, e-mail address: mcurtis@vcu.edu

Virginia Intermont College
Bristol, Virginia

Independent, coed. Small town campus. Total enrollment: 1,138.
Degrees Bachelor of Fine Arts. Majors and concentrations: dance. Cross-registration with King College.
Enrollment 14 total; all undergraduate.
Dance Student Profile 90% females, 10% males, 30% minorities, 10% international.
Dance Faculty 1 undergraduate (full-time), 2 undergraduate (part-time). 100% of full-time faculty have terminal degrees. Graduate students do not teach undergraduate courses. Undergraduate student–faculty ratio: 8:1.
Student Life Student groups/activities include American College Dance Festival Association, Visiting Artists Workshop, Tennessee Dance Association.
Expenses for 2005–2006 Application fee: $15. Comprehensive fee: $22,200 includes full-time tuition ($15,500), mandatory fees

($950), and college room and board ($5750). College room only: $2750. Full-time tuition and fees vary according to class time and program. Room and board charges vary according to housing facility. Special program-related fees: $400 per semester for instruction fee.
Financial Aid Program-specific awards: room grants for program majors ($1800), departmental awards for program majors ($1200), performance scholarships for program majors ($500–$1500).
Application Procedures Students admitted directly into the professional program freshman year. Deadline for freshmen and transfers: continuous. Notification date for freshmen and transfers: continuous. Required: high school transcript, college transcript(s) for transfer students, minimum 2.0 high school GPA, letter of recommendation, interview, video, audition, SAT I or ACT test scores. Recommended: portfolio. Auditions held twice and by request on campus; videotaped performances are permissible as a substitute for live auditions. Portfolio reviews held on individual basis on campus.
Undergraduate Contact Mr. Craig Wesley, Vice President for Enrollment Management, Virginia Intermont College, Box D-460, Bristol, Virginia 24201; 276-466-7856, fax: 276-466-7855, e-mail address: viadmit@vic.edu

Leigh Gerdine College of Fine Arts
Webster University
St. Louis, Missouri

Independent, coed. Suburban campus. Total enrollment: 7,327. Dance program established 1970.
Degrees Bachelor of Arts; Bachelor of Fine Arts. Majors and concentrations: dance. Cross-registration with various colleges in St. Louis.
Enrollment 40 total; all undergraduate.
Dance Student Profile 93% females, 7% males, 5% minorities.
Dance Faculty 2 undergraduate (full-time), 5 undergraduate (part-time). Graduate students do not teach undergraduate courses.
Student Life Student groups/activities include Dance Club, Fine Arts Club.
Expenses for 2005–2006 Application fee: $25. Comprehensive fee: $23,947 includes full-time tuition ($17,210) and college room and board ($6737). College room only: $3586. Full-time tuition varies according to program. Room and board charges vary according to board plan and housing facility.
Application Procedures Students admitted directly into the professional program freshman year. Deadline for freshmen and transfers: May 1. Required: essay, high school transcript, college transcript(s) for transfer students, letter of recommendation, audition, SAT I or ACT test scores. Recommended: minimum 2.0 high school GPA. Auditions held 8 times on campus; videotaped performances are permissible as a substitute for live auditions when distance is prohibitive.
Web Site http://www.webster.edu
Undergraduate Contact Jennifer Andonoff, Auditions Coordinator, Office of Admissions, Webster University, 470 East Lockwood Avenue, St. Louis, Missouri 63119-3194; 314-968-7001, fax: 314-968-7115.

Western Michigan University
Kalamazoo, Michigan

State-supported, coed. Urban campus. Total enrollment: 26,239. Dance program established 1972.

Sybil B. Harrington College of Fine Arts and Humanities
West Texas A&M University
Canyon, Texas

State-supported, coed. Small town campus. Total enrollment: 8,667. Dance program established 1984.

Degrees Bachelor of Fine Arts. Majors and concentrations: dance. Graduate degrees offered: Master of Arts in the area of interdisciplinary studies.
Enrollment 14 total; 13 undergraduate, 1 graduate.
Dance Student Profile 60% females, 40% males, 16% minorities, 1% international.
Dance Faculty 1 total (full-time), 1 total (part-time). Graduate students teach a few undergraduate courses. Undergraduate student–faculty ratio: 10:1.
Student Life Student groups/activities include American College Dance Festival Association, Dance for the Planet, community outreach performances.
Expenses for 2005–2006 Application fee: $25. State resident tuition: $2760 full-time. Nonresident tuition: $11,040 full-time. Mandatory fees: $996 full-time. College room and board: $4916. College room only: $2300.
Financial Aid Program-specific awards: 10 Endowed Scholarships for dancers ($1000).
Application Procedures Students admitted directly into the professional program freshman year. Deadline for freshmen and transfers: August 1. Notification date for freshmen and transfers: August 1. Required: high school transcript, college transcript(s) for transfer students, minimum 2.0 high school GPA, audition, SAT I or ACT test scores, minimum 2.5 high school GPA for out-of-state students. Recommended: essay, 2 letters of recommendation, interview. Auditions held at various times on campus; videotaped performances are permissible as a substitute for live auditions when distance is prohibitive.
Web Site http://www.wtamu.edu/academic/fah/mus
Contact Mr. Edward Truitt, Director of Dance, Department of Music and Dance, West Texas A&M University, Box 60879, Canyon, Texas 79016-0001; 806-651-2820, fax: 806-651-2779.

Wichita State University

Wichita, Kansas

State-supported, coed. Urban campus. Total enrollment: 14,076. Dance program established 1978.

Wright State University

Dayton, Ohio

State-supported, coed. Suburban campus. Total enrollment: 16,207.
Degrees Bachelor of Fine Arts. Majors and concentrations: dance.
Enrollment 40 total; all undergraduate.
Dance Student Profile 90% females, 10% males, 5% minorities.
Dance Faculty 3 undergraduate (full-time), 4 undergraduate (part-time). 66% of full-time faculty have terminal degrees. Graduate students do not teach undergraduate courses. Undergraduate student–faculty ratio: 13:1.
Student Life Student groups/activities include Dayton Ballet II Company, Dayton Contemporary Dance Company II.
Expenses for 2006–2007 Application fee: $30. State resident tuition: $7278 full-time. Nonresident tuition: $14,004 full-time. College room and board: $7180. Special program-related fees: $190 per quarter for private voice lessons.
Financial Aid Program-specific awards: Wright State/Dayton Ballet, Dayton Contemporary Dance Company II Awards for program majors ($1000–$2000), Faculty Academic Scholarships ($6400), Jon Rodriguez Scholarship ($500–$1000), Arts Gala Award ($500–$2000).
Application Procedures Students admitted directly into the professional program freshman year. Deadline for freshmen and transfers: continuous. Notification date for freshmen and transfers: April 19. Required: high school transcript, video, audition, SAT I or ACT test scores, dance photograph. Auditions held by appointment on campus; videotaped performances are permissible as a substitute for live auditions when distance is prohibitive.

Web Site http://www.wright.edu
Undergraduate Contact Ms. Victoria Oleen, Managing Director, Department of Theatre Arts, Wright State University, 3640 Colonel Glenn Highway, T148 CAC, Dayton, Ohio 45435; 937-775-3072, fax: 937-775-3787, e-mail address: victoria.oleen@wright.edu

York University

Toronto, Ontario, Canada

Province-supported, coed. Urban campus. Total enrollment: 49,496. Dance program established 1970.
Degrees Bachelor of Fine Arts in the areas of dance performance, composition. Majors and concentrations: ballet, composition, modern dance. Cross-registration with University of Chichester (United Kingdom).
Enrollment 250 total; 194 undergraduate, 56 nonprofessional degree.
Dance Student Profile 98% females, 2% males, 2% international.
Dance Faculty 17 total (full-time), 12 total (part-time). 92% of full-time faculty have terminal degrees. Graduate students teach a few undergraduate courses. Undergraduate student–faculty ratio: 7:1.
Student Life Student groups/activities include Dance Students Association, Creative Arts Students Association.
Expenses for 2005–2006 Application fee: $90 Canadian dollars. Comprehensive fee: $10,981 includes full-time tuition ($4862) and college room and board ($6119). College room only: $3719. Full-time tuition varies according to course load, degree level, and program. Room and board charges vary according to board plan and housing facility. International student tuition: $14,862 full-time. Special program-related fees: $20 per year for studio/conditioning equipment/lockers.
Financial Aid Program-specific awards: 2 talent awards for applicants with outstanding auditions ($1000), 5 Harry Rowe Bursaries for those demonstrating achievement or potential in artistic or scholarly work ($2000), 20 Fine Arts Bursaries for academically qualified students demonstrating financial need ($200–$700), 1 Spedding Memorial Award for applicants showing excellence in choreography and demonstrating need ($550), 2 Nirvan Bhavan Foundation Scholarships for 3rd- and 4th- year students enrolled in courses dealing with Indian studies ($3000), 1 Manorama Thakkar Award in Indian Dance for those demonstrating academic/artistic excellence and achievement in Indian dance studies ($500), 3 Dance Department Awards for those demonstrating exceptional talent and need ($500), 1 Menaka Thakkar Award for 3rd- or 4th- year students demonstrating excellence in world dance ($500), 21 IMASCO Performing Arts Awards for 2nd- or 3rd-year students demonstrating outstanding ability and sound academic standing ($3000).
Application Procedures Students admitted directly into the professional program freshman year. Deadline for freshmen and transfers: February 1. Notification date for freshmen: June 16; transfers: continuous. Required: essay, high school transcript, minimum 3.0 high school GPA, interview, audition, 2 letters of recommendation and video if applicant cannot audition in person. Recommended: 2 letters of recommendation. Auditions held 10 times on campus; videotaped performances are permissible as a substitute for live auditions when distance is prohibitive.
Web Site http://www.yorku.ca/finearts/dance/
Undergraduate Contact Pamela Persaud, Manager, Student and Academic Services, York University, 201 T Goldfarb Centre of Fine Arts, 4700 Keele Street, Toronto, Ontario M3J 1P3, Canada; 416-736-5135, fax: 416-736-5447, e-mail address: ask_ffa@yorku.ca

Music Programs

Aaron Copland School of Music
See Queens College of the City University of New York

Abilene Christian University
Abilene, Texas

Independent, coed. Urban campus. Total enrollment: 4,685.
Degrees Bachelor of Arts in the areas of vocal music, piano, instrumental music; Bachelor of Music in the areas of voice performance, piano performance, vocal music education, instrumental music education. Majors and concentrations: instrumental music, piano, vocal music. Cross-registration with Hardin-Simmons University. Program accredited by NASM.
Enrollment 75 total; all undergraduate.
Music Student Profile 57% females, 43% males, 5% minorities, 7% international.
Music Faculty 12 undergraduate (full-time), 12 undergraduate (part-time). 60% of full-time faculty have terminal degrees. Graduate students do not teach undergraduate courses. Undergraduate student–faculty ratio: 17:1.
Student Life Student groups/activities include Children's Theater, Sing Song, Homecoming Musical.
Expenses for 2005–2006 Application fee: $25. Comprehensive fee: $20,830 includes full-time tuition ($14,610), mandatory fees ($550), and college room and board ($5670). College room only: $2750. Full-time tuition and fees vary according to course load. Room and board charges vary according to board plan and housing facility. Special program-related fees: $90–$225 per credit hour for private lessons.
Financial Aid Program-specific awards: 40 budgeted awards for musically qualified program majors ($1500), 10 endowed awards for program majors ($1000).
Application Procedures Students admitted directly into the professional program freshman year. Deadline for freshmen and transfers: August 5. Required: high school transcript, college transcript(s) for transfer students, 2 letters of recommendation, audition, SAT I or ACT test scores. Recommended: interview. Auditions held once in February and by appointment on campus; recorded music is permissible as a substitute for live auditions when distance is prohibitive and videotaped performances are permissible as a substitute for live auditions when scheduling is difficult.
Web Site http://www.acu.edu/music
Undergraduate Contact Kara Taylor, Recruiting Supervisor, Music Department, Abilene Christian University, ACU Station, Box 28274, Abilene, Texas 79699; 325-674-2197, fax: 325-674-2608.

Acadia University
Wolfville, Nova Scotia, Canada

Province-supported, coed. Small town campus. Total enrollment: 3,856. Music program established 1926.

Adams State College
Alamosa, Colorado

State-supported, coed. Small town campus. Total enrollment: 5,578. Music program established 1930.

Alcorn State University
Lorman, Mississippi

State-supported, coed. Rural campus. Total enrollment: 3,544.

Alma College
Alma, Michigan

Independent Presbyterian, coed. Small town campus. Total enrollment: 1,284. Music program established 1886.

Alverno College
Milwaukee, Wisconsin

Independent Roman Catholic, Suburban campus. Total enrollment: 2,372.
Degrees Bachelor of Music in the area of music therapy. Majors and concentrations: music therapy. Program accredited by NASM.
Enrollment 28 total; all undergraduate.
Music Student Profile 100% females, 38% minorities.
Music Faculty 3 undergraduate (full-time), 14 undergraduate (part-time). 100% of full-time faculty have terminal degrees. Graduate students do not teach undergraduate courses. Undergraduate student–faculty ratio: 3:1.
Student Life Student groups/activities include Music Therapy Club.
Expenses for 2005–2006 Application fee: $20. Comprehensive fee: $21,628 includes full-time tuition ($15,168), mandatory fees ($250), and college room and board ($6210). College room only: $2100. Full-time tuition and fees vary according to class time and program. Room and board charges vary according to board plan and housing facility. Special program-related fees: $100–$250 per credit for private lessons.
Application Procedures Students admitted directly into the professional program freshman year. Deadline for freshmen and transfers: continuous. Required: essay, high school transcript, college transcript(s) for transfer students, interview, audition, placement assessment. Recommended: ACT test score only. Auditions held 3 times on campus; recorded music is permissible as a substitute for live auditions for out-of-state applicants and videotaped performances are permissible as a substitute for live auditions for out-of-state applicants.
Web Site http://www.alverno.edu
Undergraduate Contact Mary Kay Farrell, Director, Admissions Department, Alverno College, 3401 South 39th Street, Milwaukee, Wisconsin 53234-3922; 414-382-6100, fax: 414-382-6354, e-mail address: marykay.farrell@alverno.edu

Anderson University
Anderson, South Carolina

Independent Baptist, coed. Suburban campus. Total enrollment: 1,644. Music program established 1911.

Andrews University
Berrien Springs, Michigan

Independent Seventh-day Adventist, coed. Small town campus. Total enrollment: 3,087.

Angelo State University
San Angelo, Texas

State-supported, coed. Urban campus. Total enrollment: 6,156. Music program established 1966.
Degrees Bachelor of Music. Majors and concentrations: music education. Program accredited by NASM.
Music Faculty 13 undergraduate (full-time), 1 undergraduate (part-time). 70% of full-time faculty have terminal degrees. Graduate students do not teach undergraduate courses.

Student Life Student groups/activities include Kappa Kappa Psi, Phi Mu Alpha, Sigma Alpha Iota, Tau Beta Sigma, Pi Kappa Lau 304.
Expenses for 2006–2007 Application fee: $20. State resident tuition: $3180 full-time. Nonresident tuition: $11,460 full-time. Mandatory fees: $1110 full-time. College room and board: $5314. College room only: $3147. Special program-related fees: $20–$40 per semester for private lessons.
Financial Aid Program-specific awards: Carr Academic Scholarships for academically qualified applicants, band awards for instrumentalists, choral awards for vocalists, 5 Carr Performing Arts Scholarships ($2000), 20 Fame Scholarships ($500).
Application Procedures Students admitted directly into the professional program freshman year. Deadline for freshmen and transfers: August 5. Notification date for freshmen and transfers: August 15. Required: high school transcript, college transcript(s) for transfer students, audition, SAT I or ACT test scores. Recommended: minimum 2.0 high school GPA, 2 letters of recommendation. Auditions held continuously on campus; recorded music is permissible as a substitute for live auditions for out-of-state applicants and videotaped performances are permissible as a substitute for live auditions for out-of-state applicants.
Web Site http://www.angelo.edu/dept/artmusic
Undergraduate Contact Lorri Moore, Associate Director of Admissions, Angelo State University, HAR 101, San Angelo, Texas 76909; 325-942-2042, e-mail address: lorri.moore@angelo.edu

Anna Maria College
Paxton, Massachusetts

Independent Roman Catholic, coed. Rural campus. Total enrollment: 1,042. Music program established 1947.
Degrees Bachelor of Music in the areas of music education, music therapy, music education and music therapy, piano performance, vocal performance. Majors and concentrations: music, music education, music therapy, piano/organ performance, voice performance. Cross-registration with Worcester Consortium.
Enrollment 48 total; all undergraduate.
Music Student Profile 77% females, 23% males, 2% international.
Music Faculty 6 undergraduate (full-time), 18 undergraduate (part-time). 17% of full-time faculty have terminal degrees. Graduate students do not teach undergraduate courses. Undergraduate student–faculty ratio: 3:1.
Student Life Student groups/activities include Music Education Club, Music Educators National Conference, Music Therapy Club.
Expenses for 2005–2006 Application fee: $40. Comprehensive fee: $29,815 includes full-time tuition ($19,900), mandatory fees ($1980), and college room and board ($7935). Special program-related fees: $2000 per semester for private lessons, instrument rental.
Financial Aid Program-specific awards: 8 music scholarships for program majors ($1281).
Application Procedures Students admitted directly into the professional program freshman year. Deadline for freshmen and transfers: continuous. Required: essay, high school transcript, college transcript(s) for transfer students, minimum 2.0 high school GPA, 3 letters of recommendation, audition, SAT I or ACT test scores. Recommended: interview. Auditions held on campus; recorded music is permissible as a substitute for live auditions when distance is prohibitive and videotaped performances are permissible as a substitute for live auditions when distance is prohibitive.
Web Site http://www.annamaria.edu
Undergraduate Contact Jane Fidler, Director of Admissions, Anna Maria College, Box U, Paxton, Massachusetts 01612-1198; 508-849-3365, fax: 508-849-3362.

Mariam Cannon Hayes School of Music
Appalachian State University
Boone, North Carolina

State-supported, coed. Small town campus. Total enrollment: 14,653.

Degrees Bachelor of Music in the areas of music education, performance, composition, sacred music, music therapy; Bachelor of Science in the area of music industry studies. Majors and concentrations: composition, music, music business, music education, music therapy, piano/organ, sacred music, stringed instruments, voice, wind and percussion instruments. Graduate degrees offered: Master of Music in the areas of music education, performance, composition; Master of Music Therapy in the area of music therapy. Program accredited by NASM.
Enrollment 476 total; 460 undergraduate, 16 graduate.
Music Student Profile 64% females, 36% males, 5% minorities, 2% international.
Music Faculty 15 undergraduate (full-time), 20 undergraduate (part-time), 24 graduate (full-time). 75% of full-time faculty have terminal degrees. Graduate students teach a few undergraduate courses. Undergraduate student–faculty ratio: 12:1.
Student Life Student groups/activities include Music Educators National Conference, Music and Entertainment Industry Student Association, music fraternities and sororities.
Expenses for 2006–2007 Application fee: $45. State resident tuition: $2221 full-time. Nonresident tuition: $11,963 full-time. Mandatory fees: $1697 full-time. College room and board: $4960. College room only: $3100.
Financial Aid Program-specific awards: 30 School of Music Awards for program majors ($750–$1000), 4 Hayes Scholarships for program majors ($1000–$5000), 1 Presser Award for program majors ($4000), 20 Appal PIE Awards for program majors ($2500), 4 White Scholarships for program majors ($3000).
Application Procedures Students admitted directly into the professional program freshman year. Deadline for freshmen and transfers: April 1. Notification date for freshmen and transfers: July 1. Required: high school transcript, college transcript(s) for transfer students, audition, SAT I or ACT test scores (minimum combined SAT I score of 900). Recommended: minimum 3.0 high school GPA. Auditions held 5 times on campus; recorded music is permissible as a substitute for live auditions when distance is prohibitive and videotaped performances are permissible as a substitute for live auditions when distance is prohibitive.
Web Site http://www.music.appstate.edu
Undergraduate Contact Ms. Cara Osborne, Receptionist, Mariam Cannon Hayes School of Music, Appalachian State University, PO Box 32096, Boone, North Carolina 28608; 828-262-3020, fax: 828-262-6446.
Graduate Contact Dr. Douglas James, Coordinator of Graduate Studies in Music, Mariam Cannon Hayes School of Music, Appalachian State University, PO Box 32096, Boone, North Carolina 28608; 828-262-6463, fax: 828-262-6446.

Aquinas College
Grand Rapids, Michigan

Independent Roman Catholic, coed. Suburban campus. Total enrollment: 2,193. Music program established 1944.
Degrees Bachelor of Music in the areas of choral supervision, instrumental supervision, liturgical music. Majors and concentrations: liturgical music, music education. Graduate degrees offered: Master of Arts in Teaching.
Enrollment 42 total; 28 undergraduate, 14 nonprofessional degree.
Music Student Profile 66% females, 34% males, 10% minorities, 1% international.
Music Faculty 3 total (full-time), 22 total (part-time). 33% of full-time faculty have terminal degrees. Graduate students do not teach undergraduate courses. Undergraduate student–faculty ratio: 12:1.
Student Life Student groups/activities include Music Educators National Conference, National Association of Teachers of Singing, National Pastoral Musicians.
Expenses for 2005–2006 Application fee: $0. Comprehensive fee: $23,750 includes full-time tuition ($17,926) and college room and board ($5824). College room only: $2690. Full-time tuition varies according to course load. Room and board charges vary according to board plan and housing facility. Special program-related fees: $225 per semester for private lesson fee.
Financial Aid Program-specific awards: 2 departmental awards for students taking private lessons ($175–$350), 24 Audrey E.

Aquinas College (continued)

Mohler Awards for music education majors ($500–$3000), 1 Dr. R. Bruce Early Award for undergraduate jazz students ($600), 1 Sisters Emmanuel and Evangelista Award for private piano students ($600), 3 Ernest "Bud" Kretschner Awards for private lessons students ($400), 2 Benny Carew Awards for jazz ensemble and/or vocal jazz members ($350), Sr. Henry Suso Lerczak Award for freshmen music majors, 1 Margaret Bailey Osborn Award for junior or senior music majors ($500), 2 Mary Jane Kirchgessner Awards for band or chorus members ($500), 4 Darlene Gray Scholarships for continuing education music students ($250–$500).

Application Procedures Students admitted directly into the professional program freshman year. Deadline for freshmen and transfers: continuous. Notification date for freshmen and transfers: continuous. Required: high school transcript, college transcript(s) for transfer students, letter of recommendation, SAT I or ACT test scores, video or audition for scholarship consideration. Recommended: essay, minimum 3.0 high school GPA, video. Auditions held 3 times on campus; recorded music is permissible as a substitute for live auditions if unable to visit campus prior to the February 1 scholarship application deadline and videotaped performances are permissible as a substitute for live auditions.

Web Site http://www.aquinas.edu

Undergraduate Contact Ms. Paula Meehan, Dean of Admissions, Aquinas College, 1607 Robinson Road, SE, Grand Rapids, Michigan 49506; 616-459-8281 ext. 5205, fax: 616-732-4435.

Graduate Contact Dr. Michael R. Williams, Dean of School of Education, Aquinas College, 1607 Robinson Road, SE, Grand Rapids, Michigan 49506; 616-459-8281 ext. 5422, fax: 616-732-4487, e-mail address: willimic@aquinas.edu

Arizona State University

Tempe, Arizona

State-supported, coed. Suburban campus. Total enrollment: 51,612. Music program established 1946.

Arkansas State University

State University, Arkansas

State-supported, coed. Small town campus. Total enrollment: 10,414. Music program established 1945.

Arkansas Tech University

Russellville, Arkansas

State-supported, coed. Small town campus. Total enrollment: 6,842. Music program established 1950.

Degrees Bachelor of Music Education. Majors and concentrations: instrumental music education, vocal music education. Program accredited by NASM, NCATE.

Enrollment 134 total; 101 undergraduate, 33 nonprofessional degree.

Music Student Profile 44% females, 56% males, 5% minorities, 1% international.

Music Faculty 13 undergraduate (full-time), 4 undergraduate (part-time). 31% of full-time faculty have terminal degrees. Graduate students do not teach undergraduate courses. Undergraduate student–faculty ratio: 13:1.

Student Life Student groups/activities include Tau Beta Sigma, Phi Mu Alpha Sinfonia, Kappa Kappa Psi.

Expenses for 2005–2006 Application fee: $0. State resident tuition: $4290 full-time. Nonresident tuition: $8580 full-time. Mandatory fees: $410 full-time. Full-time tuition and fees vary according to course load and location. College room and board: $4290. College room only: $2290. Room and board charges vary according to board plan and housing facility. Special program-related fees: $20 per credit hour for applied lesson fee.

Financial Aid Program-specific awards: 130 performance scholarships for band/choir students ($3000).

Application Procedures Students admitted directly into the professional program freshman year. Deadline for freshmen and

transfers: continuous. Required: high school transcript, college transcript(s) for transfer students, minimum 2.0 high school GPA, audition, SAT I or ACT test scores (minimum combined SAT I score of 710, minimum composite ACT score of 15). Auditions held as needed on campus and off campus in Arkansas high schools; recorded music is permissible as a substitute for live auditions when distance is prohibitive **when distance is prohibitive** **when distance is prohibitive and videotaped performances are permissible as a substitute for live auditions when distance is prohibitive.**

Web Site http://www.atu.edu

Undergraduate Contact V. Andy Anders, Chair, Department of Music, Arkansas Tech University, 407 West Q Street, Russellville, Arkansas 72801-2222; 501-968-0368, fax: 501-968-0467.

Armstrong Atlantic State University

Savannah, Georgia

State-supported, coed. Total enrollment: 6,710. Music program established 1935.

Degrees Bachelor of Music Education. Majors and concentrations: choral music education, instrumental music education, music education. Program accredited by NASM.

Enrollment 60 total; 35 undergraduate, 25 nonprofessional degree.

Music Student Profile 50% females, 50% males, 20% minorities, 4% international.

Music Faculty 7 undergraduate (full-time), 14 undergraduate (part-time). 86% of full-time faculty have terminal degrees. Graduate students do not teach undergraduate courses. Undergraduate student–faculty ratio: 5:1.

Student Life Student groups/activities include Collegiate Music Educators National Conference.

Expenses for 2006–2007 Application fee: $20. State resident tuition: $3074 full-time. Nonresident tuition: $10,756 full-time. Special program-related fees: $90 per semester for applied music fee.

Financial Aid Program-specific awards: 30 departmental awards for program majors ($600).

Application Procedures Students admitted directly into the professional program freshman year. Deadline for freshmen and transfers: continuous. Notification date for freshmen and transfers: continuous. Required: high school transcript, college transcript(s) for transfer students, minimum 2.0 high school GPA, interview, audition, SAT I or ACT test scores, music theory placement test. Recommended: minimum 3.0 high school GPA. Auditions held by appointment on campus; recorded music is permissible as a substitute for live auditions for out-of-state applicants and videotaped performances are permissible as a substitute for live auditions for out-of-state applicants.

Web Site http://www.finearts.armstrong.edu

Undergraduate Contact Dr. Tom Cato, Head, Department of Art, Music and Theatre, Armstrong Atlantic State University, 11935 Abercorn Street, Savannah, Georgia 31419; 912-927-5325, fax: 912-921-5492, e-mail address: finearts@mail.armstrong.edu

Ashland University

Ashland, Ohio

Independent, coed. Small town campus. Total enrollment: 6,472.

Degrees Bachelor of Music. Majors and concentrations: music education. Program accredited by NASM.

Enrollment 45 total; 35 undergraduate, 10 nonprofessional degree.

Music Student Profile 70% females, 30% males, 5% minorities.

Music Faculty 9 undergraduate (full-time), 12 undergraduate (part-time). 78% of full-time faculty have terminal degrees. Graduate students do not teach undergraduate courses. Undergraduate student–faculty ratio: 4:1.

Student Life Student groups/activities include Music Educators National Conference, Kappa Kappa Psi.

Expenses for 2006–2007 Application fee: $25. Comprehensive fee: $29,220 includes full-time tuition ($20,666), mandatory fees

($764), and college room and board ($7790). College room only: $4184. Special program-related fees: $281 per semester for private music lessons.
Financial Aid Program-specific awards: 40 scholarships for program majors ($2800).
Application Procedures Students admitted directly into the professional program freshman year. Deadline for freshmen and transfers: continuous. Required: essay, high school transcript, college transcript(s) for transfer students, 2 letters of recommendation, audition, SAT I or ACT test scores. Recommended: minimum 3.0 high school GPA, interview. Auditions held 5 times and by appointment on campus; videotaped performances are permissible as a substitute for live auditions when distance is prohibitive.
Web Site http://www.ashland.edu
Undergraduate Contact Dr. Thomas Reed, Chair, Department of Music, Ashland University, 401 College Avenue, Ashland, Ohio 44805; 419-289-5100, fax: 419-289-5638, e-mail address: crowlan1@ashland.edu

Atlantic Union College

South Lancaster, Massachusetts

Independent Seventh-day Adventist, coed. Small town campus. Total enrollment: 473.

Auburn University

Auburn University, Alabama

State-supported, coed. Small town campus. Total enrollment: 23,333. Music program established 1935.
Degrees Bachelor of Music Education. Majors and concentrations: choral music education, instrumental music education. Graduate degrees offered: Master of Education in the areas of choral, instrumental music; Master of Science in the areas of choral, instrumental music education. Doctor of Philosophy in the area of music education. Program accredited by NASM.
Enrollment 95 total; 79 undergraduate, 16 graduate.
Music Student Profile 51% females, 49% males, 2% minorities.
Music Faculty 11 total (full-time), 8 total (part-time). 90% of full-time faculty have terminal degrees. Graduate students teach a few undergraduate courses.
Student Life Student groups/activities include Phi Mu Alpha, Kappa Kappa Psi, Collegiate Music Educators National Conference.
Expenses for 2006–2007 Application fee: $25. State resident tuition: $5278 full-time. Nonresident tuition: $14,878 full-time. Mandatory fees: $238 full-time. College room and board: $7232. College room only: $3060. Special program-related fees: $156 per hour for private lessons.
Financial Aid Program-specific awards: Hargis Scholarships for band participants, music scholarships for music education students.
Application Procedures Students apply for admission into the professional program by sophomore year. Deadline for freshmen and transfers: July 7. Required: high school transcript, college transcript(s) for transfer students, ACT test score only. Recommended: audition. Auditions held 3 times on campus; recorded music is permissible as a substitute for live auditions and videotaped performances are permissible as a substitute for live auditions.
Contact Dr. Kimberly C. Walls, Coordinator of Music Education, Department of Curriculum and Teaching, Auburn University, 5040 Haley Center, Auburn University, Alabama 36849-5420; 334-844-6892, fax: 334-844-6789, e-mail address: kim.walls@auburn.edu

Augsburg College

Minneapolis, Minnesota

Independent Lutheran, coed. Urban campus. Total enrollment: 3,508. Music program established 1922.
Degrees Bachelor of Arts in the area of music; Bachelor of Music in the area of performance; Bachelor of Music Education; Bachelor of Science in the area of music therapy. Majors and concentrations: music, music education, music performance, music therapy. Cross-registration with Associated Colleges of the Twin Cities (Hamline University, Macalester College, College of St. Catherine, University of St. Thomas). Program accredited by NASM.
Enrollment 109 total; all undergraduate.
Music Student Profile 65% females, 35% males, 1% minorities, 1% international.
Music Faculty 7 undergraduate (full-time), 25 undergraduate (part-time). 50% of full-time faculty have terminal degrees. Graduate students do not teach undergraduate courses. Undergraduate student–faculty ratio: 10:1.
Student Life Student groups/activities include receptions/dinners, concerts/recitals. Special housing available for music students.
Expenses for 2006–2007 Application fee: $25. Comprehensive fee: $30,026 includes full-time tuition ($22,900), mandatory fees ($522), and college room and board ($6604). College room only: $3396. Special program-related fees: $350–$700 per semester for lessons.
Financial Aid Program-specific awards: 40 scholarships for program majors ($200–$10,000).
Application Procedures Students apply for admission into the professional program by sophomore year. Deadline for freshmen and transfers: February 1. Required: essay, high school transcript, college transcript(s) for transfer students, minimum 2.0 high school GPA, SAT I or ACT test scores, audition for scholarship consideration. Recommended: 2 letters of recommendation. Auditions held once on campus; recorded music is permissible as a substitute for live auditions when distance is prohibitive and videotaped performances are permissible as a substitute for live auditions when distance is prohibitive.
Web Site http://www.augsburg.edu/music
Undergraduate Contact Admissions, Augsburg College, 2211 Riverside Avenue, Minneapolis, Minnesota 55454; 612-330-1001, fax: 612-330-1590.

Augusta State University

Augusta, Georgia

State-supported, coed. Urban campus. Total enrollment: 6,312. Music program established 1971.
Degrees Bachelor of Music in the areas of performance, music education. Majors and concentrations: music education, piano/organ, stringed instruments, voice, wind and percussion instruments. Program accredited by NASM.
Enrollment 91 total; 44 undergraduate, 47 nonprofessional degree.
Music Student Profile 48% females, 52% males, 23% minorities, 3% international.
Music Faculty 9 undergraduate (full-time), 16 undergraduate (part-time). 100% of full-time faculty have terminal degrees. Graduate students do not teach undergraduate courses. Undergraduate student–faculty ratio: 8:1.
Student Life Student groups/activities include American String Teachers Association, Collegiate Music Educators National Conference.
Expenses for 2005–2006 Application fee: $20. State resident tuition: $2438 full-time. Nonresident tuition: $9754 full-time. Mandatory fees: $482 full-time. College room only: $4920. Special program-related fees: $38–$68 per semester for applied music fee.
Financial Aid Program-specific awards: 12–15 Maxwell Fund Awards for program majors ($300–$600), 4–6 Church Scholarships for choir singers ($1200–$1500), 2 Mary Byrd Scholarships for students from Columbia County, Georgia ($1500), 3–4 Pamplin Scholarships for program majors ($300–$600), 1 Sweet Adelines Award for vocal majors ($800), 1 Garden City Chorus Award1 for vocal majors ($800), 8 Cleon Mauldin Scholarships for program majors ($1000).
Application Procedures Students apply for admission into the professional program by sophomore year. Deadline for freshmen and transfers: July 18. Required: high school transcript, college transcript(s) for transfer students, minimum 2.0 high school GPA, 2 letters of recommendation, SAT I or ACT test scores. Recommended: audition. Auditions held 4 times on campus and

Augusta State University (continued)

off campus in Aiken, SC; Thomson, GA; Harlem, GA; recorded music is permissible as a substitute for live auditions when distance is prohibitive and videotaped performances are permissible as a substitute for live auditions when distance is prohibitive.

Web Site http://www.aug.edu

Undergraduate Contact Dr. Angela Morgan, Chair, Fine Arts Department, Augusta State University, 2500 Walton Way, Augusta, Georgia 30904-2200; 706-737-1453, fax: 706-667-4937, e-mail address: amorgan@aug.edu

Baker University

Baldwin City, Kansas

Independent United Methodist, coed. Small town campus. Total enrollment: 916. Music program established 1858.

Degrees Bachelor of Music Education. Majors and concentrations: music education. Program accredited by NASM, NCATE.

Enrollment 35 total; all undergraduate.

Music Student Profile 55% females, 45% males, 2% minorities.

Music Faculty 6 undergraduate (full-time), 9 undergraduate (part-time). 83% of full-time faculty have terminal degrees. Graduate students do not teach undergraduate courses. Undergraduate student–faculty ratio: 8:1.

Student Life Student groups/activities include Collegiate Music Educators National Conference.

Expenses for 2005–2006 Application fee: $0. Comprehensive fee: $22,190 includes full-time tuition ($16,100), mandatory fees ($460), and college room and board ($5630). College room only: $2580. Full-time tuition and fees vary according to location and program. Room and board charges vary according to board plan and housing facility. Special program-related fees: $155 per credit for applied music fee.

Financial Aid Program-specific awards: 130 participation awards for band, chorus, and orchestra members ($1000–$3000), academic scholarships for musicians ($3000–$6000).

Application Procedures Students admitted directly into the professional program freshman year. Deadline for freshmen and transfers: continuous. Required: high school transcript, letter of recommendation, interview, audition, SAT I or ACT test scores, minimum 2.7 high school GPA. Recommended: minimum 3.0 high school GPA. Auditions held 5 times and by appointment on campus; recorded music is permissible as a substitute for live auditions when distance is prohibitive and videotaped performances are permissible as a substitute for live auditions when distance is prohibitive.

Web Site http://www.bakeru.edu

Undergraduate Contact Dr. John Buehler, Chairman, Department of Music, Baker University, PO Box 65, Baldwin City, Kansas 66006-0065; 785-594-8400, fax: 785-594-4546.

Baldwin-Wallace College

Berea, Ohio

Independent Methodist, coed. Suburban campus. Total enrollment: 4,469. Music program established 1898.

Degrees Bachelor of Music in the areas of performance, musical theater, music therapy, composition, music history and literature, music theory; Bachelor of Music Education in the area of integrated instrumental/vocal music education. Majors and concentrations: brass, classical guitar, composition, music education, music history and literature, music theater, music therapy, piano/organ, stringed instruments, voice, wind and percussion instruments. Cross-registration with Case Western Reserve University, Cleveland Institute of Music, Cleveland State University, John Carroll University, Hiram College, Lake Erie College, Ursuline College, Notre Dame College of Ohio, David N. Meyers College, and several community colleges. Program accredited by NASM, NCATE.

Enrollment 267 total; 248 undergraduate, 19 nonprofessional degree.

Music Student Profile 60% females, 40% males, 10% minorities, 1% international.

Music Faculty 26 undergraduate (full-time), 40 undergraduate (part-time). 75% of full-time faculty have terminal degrees. Graduate students do not teach undergraduate courses. Undergraduate student–faculty ratio: 4:1.

Student Life Student groups/activities include Northcoast Student Music Therapists, Ohio Collegiate Music Educators Association Student Chapter, American String Teachers Association.

Expenses for 2006–2007 Application fee: $25. Comprehensive fee: $28,210 includes full-time tuition ($21,236) and college room and board ($6974). College room only: $3406.

Financial Aid Program-specific awards: 30 Griffiths Scholarships for musicians ($2000), Conservatory Merit Awards for musicians.

Application Procedures Students admitted directly into the professional program freshman year. Deadline for freshmen and transfers: March 1. Notification date for freshmen: June 1; transfers: August 1. Required: essay, high school transcript, college transcript(s) for transfer students, 2 letters of recommendation, audition, SAT I or ACT test scores. Recommended: minimum 3.0 high school GPA, interview, minimum 2.8 high school GPA. Auditions held 6 times on campus; 6 times off-campus on campus and off campus in Tampa, FL; Seoul, Hong Kong, Bangkok, Taipei, Singapore; recorded music is permissible as a substitute for live auditions except musical theater applicants and videotaped performances are permissible as a substitute for live auditions except musical theater.

Web Site http://www.bw.edu/academics/conservatory

Undergraduate Contact Ms. Anita S. Evans, Associate Director of Admission, Conservatory of Music, Baldwin-Wallace College, 275 Eastland Road, Berea, Ohio 44017; 440-826-2367, fax: 440-826-3239, e-mail address: aevans@bw.edu

Ball State University

Muncie, Indiana

State-supported, coed. Suburban campus. Total enrollment: 20,351. Music program established 1945.

Degrees Bachelor of Music in the areas of guitar, composition, organ, piano, music technology, symphonic instruments, voice; Bachelor of Science in the area of music education. Majors and concentrations: composition, music education, music technology, performance. Graduate degrees offered: Master of Arts in the area of music; Master of Music in the areas of performance, conducting, woodwinds, piano chamber music/accompanying, music history and musicology, music education, music theory, music composition, piano performance and pedagogy. Doctor of Arts in the areas of performance, conducting, piano chamber music/accompanying, music education, music theory and composition. Program accredited by NASM.

Enrollment 575 total; 475 undergraduate, 100 graduate.

Music Faculty 54 total (full-time), 17 total (part-time). 95% of full-time faculty have terminal degrees. Graduate students teach a few undergraduate courses. Undergraduate student–faculty ratio: 10:1.

Student Life Student groups/activities include Music Educators National Conference, American String Teachers Association, Indiana Music Educators Association.

Expenses for 2005–2006 Application fee: $25. State resident tuition: $6030 full-time. Nonresident tuition: $15,790 full-time. Mandatory fees: $428 full-time. College room and board: $6680. Special program-related fees: $30 per semester for instrument rental, $40 per credit hour for applied music lesson fee.

Financial Aid Program-specific awards: 70 Young Artist Scholarships for program students ($1000), 100 general music scholarships for program students ($1000), 20 Meloy Scholarships for program students ($1000).

Application Procedures Students admitted directly into the professional program freshman year. Deadline for freshmen: April 15; transfers: June 15. Required: high school transcript, college transcript(s) for transfer students, audition, SAT I or ACT test scores. Recommended: 2 letters of recommendation, interview. Auditions held 5 times on campus; recorded music is permissible as a substitute for live auditions when distance is prohibitive and videotaped performances are permissible as a substitute for live auditions when distance is prohibitive.

Web Site http://www.bsu.edu/music

Undergraduate Contact Dr. Jeffrey Carter, Undergraduate Coordinator, School of Music, Ball State University, 2000 University Avenue, Muncie, Indiana 47306; 765-285-5503, fax: 765-285-5401, e-mail address: jcarter2@bsu.edu
Graduate Contact Dr. Kirby Koriath, Coordinator, Graduate Programs in Music, School of Music, Ball State University, 2000 University Avenue, Muncie, Indiana 47306; 765-285-5502, fax: 765-285-5401, e-mail address: klkoriath@bsu.edu

The Baptist College of Florida
Graceville, Florida

Independent Southern Baptist, coed. Small town campus. Total enrollment: 623. Music program established 1960.
Degrees Bachelor of Music; Bachelor of Music Education. Majors and concentrations: church music, music education. Program accredited by NASM.
Enrollment 58 total; 30 undergraduate, 28 nonprofessional degree.
Music Student Profile 40% females, 60% males, 10% minorities.
Music Faculty 5 undergraduate (full-time), 4 undergraduate (part-time). 80% of full-time faculty have terminal degrees. Graduate students do not teach undergraduate courses. Undergraduate student–faculty ratio: 6:1.
Student Life Student groups/activities include Spring Concert, Christmas Concert, Senior Adult Day.
Expenses for 2005–2006 Application fee: $20. Comprehensive fee: $10,820 includes full-time tuition ($6900), mandatory fees ($350), and college room and board ($3570). Full-time tuition and fees vary according to course load. Room and board charges vary according to board plan and housing facility. Special program-related fees: $20–$30 per semester for recital fee, $25 per semester for class instruction (applied), $175–$275 per semester for private lessons.
Financial Aid Program-specific awards: 7 music scholarships for music majors ($500).
Application Procedures Students admitted directly into the professional program freshman year. Deadline for freshmen and transfers: August 1. Notification date for freshmen and transfers: August 15. Required: high school transcript, college transcript(s) for transfer students, minimum 2.0 high school GPA, 3 letters of recommendation, interview, audition, SAT I or ACT test scores. Auditions held 5-6 times on campus.
Web Site http://www.baptistcollege.edu
Undergraduate Contact Mr. Chris Bishop, Director of Admissions, The Baptist College of Florida, 5400 College Drive, Graceville, Florida 32440-1898; 850-263-3261 ext. 460, fax: 850-263-7506, e-mail address: admissions@baptistcollege.edu

Barry University
Miami Shores, Florida

Independent Roman Catholic, coed. Suburban campus. Total enrollment: 9,207. Music program established 1997.

Baylor University
Waco, Texas

Independent Baptist, coed. Urban campus. Total enrollment: 13,975. Music program established 1903.
Degrees Bachelor of Music in the area of classical music; Bachelor of Music Education in the area of classical music. Majors and concentrations: classical music, music, music education, opera, piano/organ, sacred music, stringed instruments, voice, wind and percussion instruments. Graduate degrees offered: Master of Music in the area of classical music. Program accredited by NASM.
Enrollment 382 total; 295 undergraduate, 72 graduate, 15 nonprofessional degree.
Music Student Profile 48% females, 52% males, 16% minorities, 3% international.

Music Faculty 53 total (full-time), 10 total (part-time). 81% of full-time faculty have terminal degrees. Graduate students teach a few undergraduate courses. Undergraduate student–faculty ratio: 6:1.
Student Life Student groups/activities include professional fraternities and sororities, Music Educators National Conference Student Chapter, Baylor Association of Church Musicians.
Expenses for 2006–2007 Application fee: $50. Comprehensive fee: $29,939 includes full-time tuition ($20,574), mandatory fees ($2240), and college room and board ($7125). College room only: $3600. Special program-related fees: $50 per course for lab fees, $142 per credit hour for applied music fee.
Financial Aid Program-specific awards: 1 competitive scholarship for organ majors, 33 general scholarships for program majors, 65 incentive scholarships for program majors.
Application Procedures Students admitted directly into the professional program freshman year. Deadline for freshmen and transfers: continuous. Required: high school transcript, college transcript(s) for transfer students, minimum 2.0 high school GPA, audition, SAT I or ACT test scores. Recommended: minimum 3.0 high school GPA. Auditions held 4 times on campus; recorded music is permissible as a substitute for live auditions if a campus visit is impossible.
Web Site http://www.baylor.edu/~music/
Undergraduate Contact Ms. Celia Austin, Secretary, School of Music, Baylor University, 1 Bear Place, #97408, Waco, Texas 76798-7408; 254-710-7681, fax: 254-710-1191, e-mail address: celia_austin@baylor.edu
Graduate Contact Dr. David Music, Director of Graduate Studies, School of Music, Baylor University, 1 Bear Place, #97408, Waco, Texas 76798-7408; 254-710-2360, fax: 254-710-1191, e-mail address: david_music@baylor.edu

Belmont University
Nashville, Tennessee

Independent Baptist, coed. Urban campus. Total enrollment: 4,319. Music program established 1951.
Degrees Bachelor of Music. Majors and concentrations: church music, classical performance, commercial music, composition, music education, music theater, music theory, piano pedagogy. Graduate degrees offered: Master of Music in the areas of performance, pedagogy, church music, music education, composition. Program accredited by NASM.
Enrollment 490 total; 450 undergraduate, 40 graduate.
Music Student Profile 55% females, 45% males, 10% minorities, 1% international.
Music Faculty 30 total (full-time), 74 total (part-time). 59% of full-time faculty have terminal degrees. Graduate students teach a few undergraduate courses. Undergraduate student–faculty ratio: 11:1.
Student Life Student groups/activities include International Association for Jazz Education, Phi Mu Alpha, Sigma Alpha Iota.
Expenses for 2005–2006 Application fee: $35. Comprehensive fee: $25,910 includes full-time tuition ($16,360), mandatory fees ($900), and college room and board ($8650). College room only: $5300. Full-time tuition and fees vary according to class time and course load. Room and board charges vary according to board plan, housing facility, and location. Special program-related fees: $30–$100 per semester for material fees, $60–$200 per semester for applied lessons.
Financial Aid Program-specific awards: 6–16 endowed scholarships for talented applicants ($1000–$2000), 20–25 music scholarships for talented applicants ($1000–$2000).
Application Procedures Students admitted directly into the professional program freshman year. Deadline for freshmen and transfers: June 1. Required: essay, high school transcript, college transcript(s) for transfer students, letter of recommendation, audition, SAT I or ACT test scores, minimum 2.8 high school GPA. Auditions held 5 times on campus; recorded music is permissible as a substitute for live auditions if a campus visit is impossible and videotaped performances are permissible as a substitute for live auditions if a campus visit is impossible.
Web Site http://www.belmont.edu/music/
Undergraduate Contact Dr. Sharon F. Gregg, Director of Admissions, School of Music, Belmont University, 1900 Belmont Boulevard,

Belmont University (continued)

Nashville, Tennessee 37212-3757; 615-460-6408, fax: 615-386-0239, e-mail address: greggs@mail.belmont.edu
Graduate Contact Dr. Robert B. Gregg, Director of Graduate Studies, School of Music, Belmont University, 1900 Belmont Boulevard, Nashville, Tennessee 37212-3757; 615-460-6408, fax: 615-386-0239, e-mail address: greggr@mail.belont.edu

Benjamin T. Rome School of Music
See The Catholic University of America

Berklee College of Music
Boston, Massachusetts

Independent, coed. Urban campus. Total enrollment: 4,037. Music program established 1945.
Degrees Bachelor of Music in the areas of performance, music synthesis, music education, composition, contemporary writing and production, film scoring, jazz composition, music business/management, music production and engineering, music therapy, professional music, songwriting. Majors and concentrations: composition, contemporary writing and production, film scoring, jazz composition, music business/management, music education, music engineering and production, music synthesis, music therapy, performance, professional music, songwriting. Cross-registration with ProArts Consortium: Boston Architectural Center, School of the Museum of Fine Arts, Massachusetts College of Art, Boston Conservatory, Emerson College.
Enrollment 4,037 total; all undergraduate.
Music Student Profile 25% females, 75% males, 21% minorities, 24% international.
Music Faculty 229 undergraduate (full-time), 290 undergraduate (part-time). Graduate students do not teach undergraduate courses. Undergraduate student–faculty ratio: 14:1.
Student Life Student groups/activities include Berklee Cares (community action response education service), Artist Development Group, Society for World Music at Berklee. Special housing available for music students.
Expenses for 2005–2006 Application fee: $100. Comprehensive fee: $37,997 includes full-time tuition ($21,790), mandatory fees ($4517), and college room and board ($11,690).
Financial Aid Program-specific awards: 414 United States and European Scholarship Tour Awards for incoming freshmen ($4526), 165 Berklee Entering Student Talent (BEST) Scholarships for incoming freshmen ($4586), 249 Berklee Achievement Scholarships (BAS) for upperclassmen ($4966).
Application Procedures Students admitted directly into the professional program freshman year. Deadline for freshmen and transfers: continuous. Notification date for freshmen and transfers: continuous. Required: essay, high school transcript, college transcript(s) for transfer students, minimum 2.0 high school GPA, 2 letters of recommendation, interview, audition, English reference letter for international applicants, audition for scholarship consideration. Recommended: minimum 3.0 high school GPA, SAT I or ACT test scores, TOEFL score for international applicants. Auditions held 45 times on campus and off campus in domestic and international sites; recorded music is permissible as a substitute for live auditions at discretion of applicant.
Web Site http://www.berklee.edu
Undergraduate Contact Damien Bracken, Director of Admissions, Berklee College of Music, 1140 Boylston Street, Boston, Massachusetts 02215-3693; 617-747-2222, fax: 617-747-2047, e-mail address: admissions@berklee.edu

More About the College

Founded in 1945, Berklee is the world's largest accredited music college and the premier institution for the study of contemporary music. The College's 3,900 students from seventy-eight countries and more than 500 faculty members interact in an environment designed to provide the most complete learning experience possible, including all of the opportunities and challenges presented by a career in the contemporary music

industry. Using Berklee's extensive facilities, students develop musical competencies in such areas as composition, performance, and recording/production and also learn to make the informed business decisions necessary to career success.

Berklee was founded on two revolutionary ideas: that musicianship could be taught through the music of the time and that students need practical, professional skills for successful, sustainable music careers. While Berklee's bedrock philosophy has not changed, the music around has and requires that the College evolve with it. For more than half a century, Berklee has demonstrated its commitment to this approach by wholeheartedly embracing change.

Berklee continually updates its curriculum and technology to make them more relevant, and it attracts diverse students who reflect the multiplicity of influences in today's music. The College prepares students for a lifetime of professional and personal growth through the study of the arts, sciences, and humanities. Berklee is also developing new initiatives to reach and influence an ever-widening audience.

More than a college, Berklee has become the world's singular learning lab for the music of today—and tomorrow. Berklee is a microcosm of the music world, reflecting the interplay between music and culture, and an environment where aspiring music professionals learn how to integrate new ideas, adapt to changing musical genres, and showcase their distinctive skills in an evolving community. The College is at the center of a widening network of industry professionals who use their openness, virtuosity, and versatility to take music in surprising new directions.

Berklee students focus on their musicianship, on the technologies that help shape this art form, on the intricacies and realities of the business and promotion of music, or on the leading thinking in music education and music therapy.

Students at Berklee start bands of their own, participate in regularly scheduled ensembles, go on tour, and take advantage of internships throughout the industry. They record student projects, score films, write, practice, and perform.

What separates Berklee College of Music from everywhere else is the people who make it up. It is the faculty and staff members, the students, and the alumni who compose the extraordinary community. Every year, a common passion and a common spirit of innovation draw remarkable people from all over the world to Boston and Berklee.

Berklee offers a Bachelor of Music (B.M.) degree program and a four-year program leading to the professional diploma. Students may choose to major in composition, contemporary writing and production, film scoring, jazz composition, music business/management, music education, music production and engineering, music synthesis, music therapy, performance, professional music, and songwriting. The College also offers a five-year, dual-major option in which students graduate with an even more marketable education that expands their career options in the music industry.

Berklee students have the chance to work in the College's state-of-the-art music technology facilities, using some of the most sophisticated recording and synthesis equipment currently available, in addition to facilities specifically designed for the areas of composition, arranging, and film scoring. The facilities at Berklee are furnished with the instruments and equipment that are being used in the world beyond the classroom. Berklee's performance facilities include the Berklee Performance Center, a 1,200-seat concert hall hosting more than 300 concerts by students, faculty members, and others each year; four recital halls equipped with a variety of sound reinforcement systems; more than forty ensemble rooms; seventy-five private instruction studios; 300 private practice rooms; and an outdoor concert pavilion.

The personal attention students receive from teachers at Berklee guides them beyond the theoretical so that they can apply what they have learned in their next ensemble rehearsal, evening jam session, or gig. Berklee faculty members teach all instruction. The teachers are talented artists who demonstrate their commitment to music education in the classroom—and beyond. Most faculty members also write and arrange music, perform in concert halls and clubs, make recordings, or perform on television and radio—some do it all. All faculty members bring to the classroom a knowledge of music and the wisdom that comes from professional music experience.

Berklee awards $12.5 million in scholarships each year to students from all over the world who demonstrate the potential to succeed in today's music industry.

Prospective students who are ready to live, breathe, and play music on a different scale should go to http://www.berklee.edu for admissions information.

Bernice Young Jones School of Fine Arts
See Ouachita Baptist University

Berry College
Mount Berry, Georgia

Independent interdenominational, coed. Suburban campus. Total enrollment: 1,970. Music program established 1969.
Degrees Bachelor of Arts in the area of music; Bachelor of Music in the areas of music education, music business. Majors and concentrations: brass, guitar, music and business, music education, piano/organ, strings, voice, wind and percussion instruments. Cross-registration with Shorter College. Program accredited by NASM.
Enrollment 106 total; 84 undergraduate, 22 nonprofessional degree.
Music Student Profile 58% females, 42% males, 3% minorities, 1% international.
Music Faculty 8 undergraduate (full-time), 7 undergraduate (part-time). 63% of full-time faculty have terminal degrees. Graduate students do not teach undergraduate courses. Undergraduate student–faculty ratio: 10:1.
Student Life Student groups/activities include Music to the People Projects, church, local, and regional concerts, Kindermusik Program.
Expenses for 2006–2007 Application fee: $50. Comprehensive fee: $26,114 includes full-time tuition ($18,950) and college room and board ($7164). College room only: $4024. Special program-related fees: $90–$175 per semester for weekly lessons.
Financial Aid Program-specific awards: 80 music scholarships for performers/program majors ($2000), 20 performance grants for performers/program minors ($750).
Application Procedures Students admitted directly into the professional program freshman year. Deadline for freshmen and transfers: July 31. Required: high school transcript, college transcript(s) for transfer students, 2 letters of recommendation, interview, audition, SAT I or ACT test scores (minimum combined SAT I score of 1000, minimum composite ACT score of 20),

minimum 2.5 college GPA for transfers, minimum SAT verbal score of 500 and minimum SAT math score of 500. Recommended: minimum 3.0 high school GPA. Auditions held 3 times on campus; recorded music is permissible as a substitute for live auditions when distance is prohibitive and videotaped performances are permissible as a substitute for live auditions when distance is prohibitive.
Web Site http://www.berry.edu/academics/humanities/finearts/music
Undergraduate Contact Mr. Garreth M. Johnson, Dean of Admissions, Berry College, PO Box 490159, Mount Berry, Georgia 30149-0159; 800-BERRYGA, fax: 706-290-2178, e-mail address: gjohnson@berry.edu

Bethel University
St. Paul, Minnesota

Independent, coed. Suburban campus. Total enrollment: 3,857.

Biola University
La Mirada, California

Independent interdenominational, coed. Suburban campus. Total enrollment: 5,455. Music program established 1955.

Birmingham-Southern College
Birmingham, Alabama

Independent Methodist, coed. Urban campus. Total enrollment: 1,411. Music program established 1922.
Degrees Bachelor of Music in the areas of classical performance, composition, music history, church music; Bachelor of Music Education. Majors and concentrations: church music, classical music, composition, guitar, music education, music history, opera, piano/organ, stringed instruments, voice, wind and percussion instruments. Graduate degrees offered: Master of Music in the areas of composition, organ, piano, voice. Cross-registration with University of Alabama at Birmingham, Samford University, University of Montevallo. Program accredited by NASM.
Enrollment 117 total; 40 undergraduate, 75 nonprofessional degree.
Music Student Profile 60% females, 40% males, 20% minorities, 10% international.
Music Faculty 10 undergraduate (full-time), 15 undergraduate (part-time). 100% of full-time faculty have terminal degrees. Graduate students do not teach undergraduate courses. Undergraduate student–faculty ratio: 8:1.
Student Life Student groups/activities include GALA, opera productions, music theater productions.
Expenses for 2005–2006 Application fee: $25. Comprehensive fee: $28,135 includes full-time tuition ($20,425), mandatory fees ($630), and college room and board ($7080). College room only: $5000. Special program-related fees: $160–$300 per course for private lessons.
Financial Aid Program-specific awards: 2–3 music theater scholarships for program majors and minors ($3000–$8000), 7–8 music performance scholarships for program majors and minors ($4000–$15,000), 1–2 music composition awards for program majors ($4000–$15,000).
Application Procedures Students admitted directly into the professional program freshman year. Deadline for freshmen and transfers: May 1. Required: essay, high school transcript, college transcript(s) for transfer students, minimum 2.0 high school GPA, SAT I or ACT test scores. Recommended: letter of recommendation, interview, audition, portfolio for composition majors. Auditions held twice on campus; recorded music is permissible as a substitute for live auditions when distance is prohibitive and videotaped performances are permissible as a substitute for live auditions when distance is prohibitive. Portfolio reviews held once on campus.
Web Site http://www.bsc.edu
Undergraduate Contact Ms. Sheri Salmon, Associate Vice President of Admissions, Birmingham-Southern College, 900 Arkadelphia

Birmingham-Southern College (continued)

Road, Box 549033, Birmingham, Alabama 35254; 205-226-4686, fax: 205-226-4696, e-mail address: ssalmon@panther.bsc.edu
Graduate Contact Dr. Lester Seigel, Chair, Division of Fine and Performing Arts, Birmingham-Southern College, 900 Arkadelphia Road, Box 549033, Birmingham, Alabama 35254; 205-226-4952, fax: 205-226-3058, e-mail address: lseigel@panther.bsc.edu

Blair School of Music

See Vanderbilt University

The Boston Conservatory

Boston, Massachusetts

Independent, coed. Urban campus. Total enrollment: 537 (2004). Music program established 1867.
Degrees Bachelor of Music in the areas of composition, performance. Majors and concentrations: brass, composition, guitar, harp, marimba, opera, piano, saxophone, stringed instruments, voice, wind and percussion instruments. Graduate degrees offered: Master of Music in the areas of composition, choral conducting, performance, opera, music education, orchestral conducting. Cross-registration with ProArts Consortium. Program accredited by NASM.
Enrollment 313 total; 170 undergraduate, 143 graduate.
Music Student Profile 60% females, 40% males, 20% minorities, 18% international.
Music Faculty 29 total (full-time), 94 total (part-time). Graduate students do not teach undergraduate courses. Undergraduate student–faculty ratio: 1:1.
Student Life Student groups/activities include Music Educators National Conference, Phi Mu Alpha Sinfonia, Sigma Alpha Iota. Special housing available for music students.
Expenses for 2006–2007 Application fee: $105. Comprehensive fee: $42,155 includes full-time tuition ($26,400), mandatory fees ($1435), and college room and board ($14,320). Special program-related fees: $65 per year for music education lab fees.
Financial Aid Program-specific awards: merit scholarships for artistically talented students.
Application Procedures Students admitted directly into the professional program freshman year. Deadline for freshmen and transfers: December 1. Notification date for freshmen and transfers: April 1. Required: essay, high school transcript, college transcript(s) for transfer students, 2 letters of recommendation, audition, SAT I or ACT test scores, video for some programs, and portfolio for composition majors, interview for some majors, minimum TOEFL score of 550 for international applicants, artistic resume, minimum 2.7 high school GPA. Auditions held during the months of February and March on campus and off campus in Atlanta, GA; Houston, TX; Seattle, WA; Los Angeles, CA; Toronto; Interlochen, MI; and Washington, DC; recorded music is permissible as a substitute for live auditions when distance is prohibitive and videotaped performances are permissible as a substitute for live auditions when distance is prohibitive. Portfolio reviews held on campus.
Web Site http://www.bostonconservatory.edu
Contact Admissions Office, The Boston Conservatory, 8 The Fenway, Boston, Massachusetts 02215; 617-536-9153, fax: 617-247-3159, e-mail address: admissions@bostonconservatory.edu

More About the Conservatory

The Boston Conservatory trains exceptional young performing artists for careers that enrich and transform the human experience. Known for its multidisciplinary environment, the Conservatory offers fully accredited graduate and undergraduate programs in music, dance, theater, and music education and presents more than 200 performances each year by students, faculty members, and guest artists. The intimacy of the Conservatory's class settings provides a student-centered atmosphere that is uniquely intensive and supportive.

Since its founding in 1867, the Boston Conservatory has shared its talent and creativity with the city of Boston, the region,

and the nation, and it continues to grow today as a vibrant community of artists and educators.

Music students work with artist faculty members and teachers who are truly interested in working to develop students' musical abilities to their utmost potential. With more than 300 concerts being offered each year, performance experience is a core part of the curriculum. Students participate in orchestra, choral ensembles, chamber groups, and pit work for the dance, opera, and musical theater main-stage productions that are produced several times throughout the academic year.

In addition to the school's performance opportunities, the greater Boston area provides numerous playing possibilities for solo, small chamber, and orchestral musicians so that students may choose to further expand both their performance experience and knowledge of the repertory.

Boston is a major center of higher education in America, with more than fifty major colleges and universities. The city provides a diverse student population and an endless array of courses, lectures, concerts, and social opportunities. The Conservatory is a member of the Pro-Arts Consortium, in collaboration with five area colleges (Emerson College, Berklee College of Music, School of the Museum of Fine Arts, Massachusetts College of Art, and Boston Architectural Center), offering extensive cross-registration course possibilities to all students.

On-campus housing is provided for freshmen and to upperclassmen and graduates on a space-available basis, offering brownstone-style living accommodations just a few steps from the main training and rehearsal buildings. For those students interested in off-campus housing, Boston offers a wide range of architectural styles and rent prices in neighborhoods throughout the city that are all within easy access to the school by public transportation.

The Boston Conservatory strives to meet each student's needs—musically and personally—and provides a nurturing, safe environment in which to study, learn, and grow. The supportive atmosphere of the college extends to student life areas as well. More than a dozen special-interest groups and organizations exist on campus, with new ones developing constantly as the student population grows and needs change. As part of the student services, a number of career seminars are given each year ranging from resume writing and audition anxiety to grant writing and tax laws for the performing artist. In addition, there is an active student government and a student-run newspaper.

Boston University

Boston, Massachusetts

Independent, coed. Urban campus. Total enrollment: 30,957. Music program established 1872.
Degrees Bachelor of Music in the areas of performance, music education, music theory and composition, music history and literature. Majors and concentrations: brass, music education, music theory and composition, musicology, percussion, piano, stringed instruments, voice, wind instruments. Graduate degrees offered: Master of Music in the areas of performance, music education, music theory and composition, music history and literature, orchestral and choral conducting, historical performance, collaborative piano. Doctor of Musical Arts in the areas of performance, music education, music theory and composition, music history and literature, orchestral and choral conducting, historical performance, collaborative piano. Program accredited by NASM.
Enrollment 535 total; 210 undergraduate, 325 graduate.
Music Student Profile 60% females, 40% males, 25% international.
Music Faculty 48 total (full-time), 80 total (part-time). 100% of full-time faculty have terminal degrees. Graduate students teach a few undergraduate courses.
Student Life Student groups/activities include symphonic orchestra, symphonic chorus, marching band, concert band, pep band, jazz ensemble. Special housing available for music students.
Expenses for 2005–2006 Application fee: $70. Comprehensive fee: $42,046 includes full-time tuition ($31,530), mandatory fees

($436), and college room and board ($10,080). College room only: $6450. Full-time tuition and fees vary according to class time and degree level. Room and board charges vary according to board plan and housing facility. Special program-related fees for applied music fee.

Financial Aid Program-specific awards: 55 grants-performance awards for freshmen ($6000–$22,900).

Application Procedures Students admitted directly into the professional program freshman year. Deadline for freshmen: January 1; transfers: April 1. Notification date for freshmen and transfers: June 1. Required: essay, high school transcript, college transcript(s) for transfer students, 2 letters of recommendation, audition, SAT I or ACT test scores, portfolio for composition majors. Recommended: minimum 3.0 high school GPA, interview, resume. Auditions held 40 times on campus and off campus in various cities; recorded music is permissible as a substitute for live auditions when distance is prohibitive (beyond a 300-mile radius). Portfolio reviews held as needed on campus.

Web Site http://www.bu.edu/cfa

Contact Zoe Krohne, Director of Admissions, School of Music, Boston University, 855 Commonwealth Avenue, Boston, Massachusetts 02215; 617-353-3341, fax: 617-353-7455, e-mail address: cfamusic@bv.edu

More About the University

Boston University College of Fine Arts (CFA) is a small, conservatory-style school within a major university, offering outstanding professional training in music, the theater, and visual arts. The College was begun as the College of Music in 1873 and was the first college in the United States to offer a Bachelor of Music. There are currently 500 students enrolled in the School of Music.

The School offers the Bachelor of Music, the Master of Music, the Doctor of Musical Arts, the Artist Diploma, the Performance Diploma, and a certificate from the Opera Institute. The School prepares its students for careers as performers, composers, educators, and scholars. The faculty members are committed to providing outstanding opportunities for students to study, create, and perform.

Campus Surroundings Boston University—independent, coeducational, nonsectarian—is an internationally recognized center of higher education and research. The University is located in the heart of Boston, along the banks of the Charles River and adjacent to the historic Back Bay district of Boston. Boston University is perfectly situated to enjoy both the charm and beauty of the city and its cultural and recreational attractions. Boston is a city rich in music, and students have the opportunity to listen to some of the world's greatest musicians. Students benefit from the many major musical organizations, museums and galleries, and theaters that make Boston a rich and varied cultural environment.

Program Facilities The College of Fine Arts houses a 485-seat concert hall, music studios and practice rooms, a curriculum lab, recording studio and three electronic music studios. Students also perform at the 650-seat Tsai Performance Center on campus. The Boston University Symphony performs twice a year at Boston's Symphony Hall. The Opera Institute performs at the Boston University Theatre, an 850-seat proscenium house which is also the home of the Huntingdon Theatre Company.

Faculty, Resident Artists, and Alumni The faculty includes many members of the Boston Symphony Orchestra. The Muir String quartet and Allea III, a contemporary music ensemble, are in residence. Boston Baroque, America's leading Baroque Orchestra and Chorus, is the resident ensemble in support of the School's historic performance program. Notable alumni include Fred A. Bronstein, President of the Dallas Symphony Orchestra, Ikuno Mizuno-Spire, the first woman to play first violin with the Boston Symphony Orchestra; Peter Chapman, trumpet, the Boston Symphony Orchestra; Edward Atkatz, percussion, Chicago Symphony Orchestra; and opera singers Dominique LaBelle and Stephen Salters.

Student Performance Opportunities More than 400 student and faculty performances are held throughout the year. Ensembles

include the Symphony Orchestra, Chamber Orchestra, Wind Ensemble Opera Workshop, and Women's Chorale. All-University organizations include the Jazz Ensemble, Concert Band, Pep Band, and Marching Band.

Special Programs Students at the Boston University College of Fine Arts may take advantage of a wide range of academic and extracurricular activities. Through the Collaborative Degree Program (BUCOP), students may obtain a dual degree in two of the University's schools and colleges and can minor in liberal arts, communications, or business. Students may spend the fall semester of their junior year at the Royal College of Music in London.

Bowling Green State University
Bowling Green, Ohio

State-supported, coed. Small town campus. Total enrollment: 19,016. Music program established 1917.

Degrees Bachelor of Music in the areas of music education, performance, music history and literature, composition, jazz studies, world music. Majors and concentrations: brass, composition, guitar, harp, jazz, literature, music, music education, music history, piano accompanying, piano pedagogy, piano/organ, stringed instruments, voice, wind and percussion instruments, world music. Graduate degrees offered: Master of Music in the areas of music education, performance, composition, music theory, music history, ethnomusicology. Cross-registration with University of Toledo. Program accredited by NASM.

Enrollment 551 total; 430 undergraduate, 121 graduate.

Music Student Profile 52% females, 48% males, 7% minorities, 3% international.

Music Faculty 53 total (full-time), 29 total (part-time). 100% of full-time faculty have terminal degrees. Graduate students teach a few undergraduate courses. Undergraduate student–faculty ratio: 7:1.

Student Life Student groups/activities include Ohio Collegiate Music Educators Association, professional music fraternities and sororities, American Choral Directors Association. Special housing available for music students.

Expenses for 2005–2006 Application fee: $35. State resident tuition: $7314 full-time. Nonresident tuition: $14,622 full-time. Mandatory fees: $1246 full-time. College room and board: $6434. College room only: $3934. Room and board charges vary according to board plan and housing facility. Special program-related fees: $100 per year for music equipment fee, $180 per year for applied music lesson fee.

Financial Aid Program-specific awards: 115 Music Talent Awards for top musicians ($2200).

Application Procedures Students admitted directly into the professional program freshman year. Deadline for freshmen and transfers: continuous. Notification date for freshmen and transfers: continuous. Required: high school transcript, college transcript(s) for transfer students, audition, SAT I or ACT test scores, minimum 2.5 high school GPA. Recommended: essay, minimum 3.0 high school GPA, 2 letters of recommendation, interview. Auditions held 6 times on campus; recorded music is permissible as a substitute for live auditions when distance is prohibitive and videotaped performances are permissible as a substitute for live auditions when distance is prohibitive.

Web Site http://www.bgsu.edu/colleges/music/index.html

Undergraduate Contact Dr. Kathleen Moss, Coordinator of Music Admissions, College of Musical Arts, Bowling Green State University, 1031 Moore Musical Arts Center, Bowling Green, Ohio 43403-0290; 419-372-8577, fax: 419-372-2938, e-mail address: kmoss@bgnet.bgsu.edu

Graduate Contact Dr. William Mathis, Coordinator of Graduate Admissions, College of Musical Arts, Bowling Green State University, 1031 Moore Musical Arts Center, Bowling Green, Ohio 43403-0290; 419-372-2182, fax: 419-372-2938.

Bradley University
Peoria, Illinois

Independent, coed. Urban campus. Total enrollment: 6,154. Music program established 1921.

Bradley University (continued)

Degrees Bachelor of Music in the areas of composition, music education, performance. Majors and concentrations: composition, music education, performance. Program accredited by NASM.
Enrollment 105 total; 47 undergraduate, 58 nonprofessional degree.
Music Student Profile 53% females, 47% males, 8% minorities, 2% international.
Music Faculty 10 undergraduate (full-time), 19 undergraduate (part-time). 80% of full-time faculty have terminal degrees. Graduate students do not teach undergraduate courses. Undergraduate student–faculty ratio: 8:1.
Student Life Student groups/activities include Music Educators National Conference, Phi Mu Alpha Sinfonia, Sigma Alpha Iota.
Expenses for 2005–2006 Application fee: $35. Comprehensive fee: $25,280 includes full-time tuition ($18,700), mandatory fees ($130), and college room and board ($6450). College room only: $3700. Full-time tuition and fees vary according to program. Room and board charges vary according to board plan. Special program-related fees: $165 per hour for applied music fee.
Financial Aid Program-specific awards: 70 music scholarships for program majors ($1600).
Application Procedures Students admitted directly into the professional program freshman year. Deadline for freshmen and transfers: continuous. Required: high school transcript, college transcript(s) for transfer students, minimum 2.0 high school GPA, audition, SAT I or ACT test scores. Recommended: letter of recommendation. Auditions held continuously on campus; recorded music is permissible as a substitute for live auditions when distance is prohibitive and videotaped performances are permissible as a substitute for live auditions when distance is prohibitive.
Web Site http://gcc.bradley.edu/music/
Undergraduate Contact Ms. Nickie Roberson, Director of Admissions, Office of Undergraduate Admissions, Bradley University, Swords Hall, Peoria, Illinois 61625; 800-447-6460, fax: 309-677-2797, e-mail address: admissions@bradley.edu

Brandon University
Brandon, Manitoba, Canada

Province-supported, coed. Small town campus. Total enrollment: 3,524. Music program established 1963.
Degrees Bachelor of Music in the areas of music education, performance, honours music; Bachelor of Music/Bachelor of Education. Majors and concentrations: music, music education, performance. Graduate degrees offered: Master of Music in the areas of performance and literature: piano and strings, music education. Program accredited by CUMS.
Enrollment 160 total; 140 undergraduate, 20 graduate.
Music Faculty 19 total (full-time), 10 total (part-time). Graduate students do not teach undergraduate courses. Undergraduate student–faculty ratio: 7:1.
Expenses for 2005–2006 Application fee: $60 Canadian dollars. Tuition, fee, and room and board charges are reported in Canadian dollars. Province resident tuition: $3,019 full-time. Canadian resident tuition: $3018 full-time. Mandatory fees: $345 full-time. College room and board: $6270. College room only: $3614. International student tuition: $6,373 full-time. $637.26 per course for international students.
Financial Aid Program-specific awards: Vasey Memorial Scholarship ($3900), Cowan Bursary ($750), 2 Don Wright Scholarships in Music Education for instrumental/choral/vocal students ($2837), 2 Jane Vasey Memorial Scholarships ($1900), The Kay & G. R. Rowe Scholarship ($1350), Shirley Craig Scholarship ($1000), R. D. Bell String Scholarships, Helen C. Riesberry Scholarship ($1000).
Application Procedures Students admitted directly into the professional program freshman year. Deadline for freshmen and transfers: May 2. Required: high school transcript, college transcript(s) for transfer students, letter of recommendation, audition. Auditions held 8 times on campus; recorded music is permissible as a substitute for live auditions when distance is prohibitive and videotaped performances are permissible as a substitute for live auditions when distance is prohibitive.

Web Site http://www.brandonu.ca
Undergraduate Contact Heather Beesley, Administrative Assistant, School of Music, Brandon University, 270 18th Street, Brandon, Manitoba R7A 6A9, Canada; 204-727-7388, fax: 204-728-6839, e-mail address: music@brandonu.ca
Graduate Contact Dr. Art Bower, Chair, Graduate Music Department, Brandon University, School of Music, Brandon, Manitoba R7A 6A9, Canada; 204-727-7436, fax: 204-728-6839, e-mail address: bower@brandonu.ca

Brenau University
Gainesville, Georgia

Independent, Small town campus. Total enrollment: 743. Music program established 1878.
Degrees Bachelor of Fine Arts in the area of arts management in music; Bachelor of Music in the areas of performance, music education. Majors and concentrations: choral music education, piano, voice. Program accredited by NCATE.
Enrollment 25 total; 20 undergraduate, 5 nonprofessional degree.
Music Student Profile 100% females, 20% minorities, 3% international.
Music Faculty 3 undergraduate (full-time), 2 undergraduate (part-time). 100% of full-time faculty have terminal degrees. Graduate students do not teach undergraduate courses. Undergraduate student–faculty ratio: 10:1.
Student Life Student groups/activities include Opera Company, Lahier Chamber Singers, Mu Phi Epsilon. Special housing available for music students.
Expenses for 2005–2006 Application fee: $35. Comprehensive fee: $24,990 includes full-time tuition ($16,440) and college room and board ($8550). Full-time tuition varies according to class time, location, and program. Room and board charges vary according to housing facility. Special program-related fees: $150 per semester for accompanist.
Financial Aid Program-specific awards: music scholarships for program majors ($3000–$5000).
Application Procedures Students admitted directly into the professional program freshman year. Deadline for freshmen and transfers: continuous. Required: high school transcript, college transcript(s) for transfer students, minimum 2.0 high school GPA, letter of recommendation, interview, audition, SAT I or ACT test scores (minimum combined SAT I score of 900, minimum composite ACT score of 19). Recommended: minimum 3.0 high school GPA. Auditions held twice and by appointment on campus; recorded music is permissible as a substitute for live auditions when distance is prohibitive and videotaped performances are permissible as a substitute for live auditions when distance is prohibitive.
Web Site http://www.brenau.edu/music
Undergraduate Contact Dean of Admissions, Brenau University, 500 Washington Street, SE, Gainesville, Georgia 30501; 800-252-5119, fax: 770-538-4306, e-mail address: wcadmissions@lib.brenau.edu

Brevard College
Brevard, North Carolina

Independent United Methodist, coed. Small town campus. Total enrollment: 597. Music program established 1995.
Degrees Bachelor of Arts in the areas of music, music teaching; Bachelor of Music in the area of performance. Majors and concentrations: church music, composition, jazz studies, music teaching, performance. Program accredited by NASM.
Enrollment 75 total; 40 undergraduate, 35 nonprofessional degree.
Music Student Profile 55% females, 45% males, 15% minorities, 5% international.
Music Faculty 10 undergraduate (full-time), 8 undergraduate (part-time). 90% of full-time faculty have terminal degrees. Graduate students do not teach undergraduate courses. Undergraduate student–faculty ratio: 8:1.
Expenses for 2005–2006 Application fee: $30. Comprehensive fee: $21,970 includes full-time tuition ($15,620), mandatory fees ($370), and college room and board ($5980). Full-time tuition

and fees vary according to course load. Room and board charges vary according to board plan and housing facility. Special program-related fees: $100 for recital fee, $125 per credit hour for applied music fee.
Financial Aid Program-specific awards: 12–20 music audition awards for freshmen and transfers ($3000).
Application Procedures Students apply for admission into the professional program by sophomore year. Required: high school transcript, college transcript(s) for transfer students, minimum 2.0 high school GPA, audition, SAT I or ACT test scores, entrance test in theory and instrument, keyboard placement. Recommended: 1-2 letters of recommendation. Auditions held 4 times and by appointment on campus; recorded music is permissible as a substitute for live auditions and videotaped performances are permissible as a substitute for live auditions when distance is prohibitive.
Web Site http://www.brevard.edu
Undergraduate Contact Prof. S. K. Hoke, Chair, Division of Fine Arts, Department of Music, Brevard College, 400 North Broad Street, Brevard, North Carolina 28712; 828-884-8211, fax: 828-884-3790, e-mail address: music@brevard.edu

Brewton-Parker College
Mt. Vernon, Georgia

Independent Southern Baptist, coed. Rural campus. Total enrollment: 1,094. Music program established 1964.
Degrees Bachelor of Music. Majors and concentrations: church music, music education, performance. Program accredited by NASM.
Enrollment 34 total; 24 undergraduate, 10 nonprofessional degree.
Music Student Profile 62% females, 38% males, 4% minorities, 5% international.
Music Faculty 5 undergraduate (full-time), 4 undergraduate (part-time). 100% of full-time faculty have terminal degrees. Graduate students do not teach undergraduate courses. Undergraduate student–faculty ratio: 5:1.
Student Life Student groups/activities include Students Professional Association of Georgia Educators. Special housing available for music students.
Expenses for 2005–2006 Application fee: $25. Comprehensive fee: $17,504 includes full-time tuition ($11,584), mandatory fees ($1100), and college room and board ($4820). College room only: $2150. Room and board charges vary according to board plan and housing facility. Special program-related fees: $100 per credit hour for applied music.
Financial Aid Program-specific awards: 50–60 music scholarships for music majors and ensemble participants ($700–$2180), 9 endowed music scholarships for music majors ($2100–$5000).
Application Procedures Students apply for admission into the professional program by freshman year. Deadline for freshmen and transfers: continuous. Required: essay, high school transcript, college transcript(s) for transfer students, minimum 2.0 high school GPA, letter of recommendation, interview, audition, SAT I or ACT test scores, evaluation exam of musical skills and literature. Auditions held 3 times and by appointment on campus.
Web Site http://www.bpc.edu
Undergraduate Contact Stephanie Whaley, Director of Admissions, Brewton-Parker College, Highway 280, Mt. Vernon, Georgia 30445; 912-583-2241, fax: 912-583-4498, e-mail address: swhaley@bpc.edu

Brigham Young University
Provo, Utah

Independent, coed. Suburban campus. Total enrollment: 34,067. Music program established 1878.
Degrees Bachelor of Music in the areas of composition, instrumental and choral music education (K-12), elementary music specialist, performance, jazz studies, media music studies, sound recording technology. Majors and concentrations: brass, choral music education, composition, elementary music specialist, instrumental music education, jazz studies, media music

studies, organ, percussion, piano, piano/organ performance, sound recording technology, strings, voice, woodwinds. Graduate degrees offered: Master of Music in the areas of composition, conducting, music education, performance specializations. Program accredited by NASM.
Enrollment 344 total; 223 undergraduate, 51 graduate, 70 nonprofessional degree.
Music Student Profile 60% females, 40% males.
Music Faculty 52 total (full-time), 43 total (part-time). 84% of full-time faculty have terminal degrees. Graduate students teach a few undergraduate courses.
Student Life Student groups/activities include School of Music Student Association.
Expenses for 2005–2006 Application fee: $30. Comprehensive fee: $10,906 includes full-time tuition ($5116) and college room and board ($5790). Full-time tuition varies according to reciprocity agreements. Room and board charges vary according to board plan and housing facility. Special program-related fees: $315 per semester for private lessons.
Financial Aid Program-specific awards: performance scholarships for program majors, service awards for marching band students, service awards for pep band students.
Application Procedures Students apply for admission into the professional program by freshman year. Deadline for freshmen and transfers: January 15. Notification date for freshmen and transfers: June 15. Required: essay, high school transcript, college transcript(s) for transfer students, minimum 3.0 high school GPA, letter of recommendation, audition, ACT test score only (minimum composite ACT score of 25), music theory examination, keyboard diagnostic exam. Auditions held once on campus; recorded music is permissible as a substitute for live auditions if a campus visit is impossible and videotaped performances are permissible as a substitute for live auditions if a campus visit is impossible (video tape preferred).
Web Site http://cfac.byu.edu/music/
Undergraduate Contact Michael Ohman, Assistant Director, School of Music, Brigham Young University, C-550 HFAC, Provo, Utah 84602; 801-422-3149, fax: 801-422-0533, e-mail address: michael_ohman@byu.edu
Graduate Contact Dr. Thomas L. Durham, Associate Director of Graduate Studies, School of Music, Brigham Young University, C-550 HFAC, Provo, Utah 84602; 801-422-3226, fax: 801-422-0533, e-mail address: thomas_durham@byu.edu

Brock University
St. Catharines, Ontario, Canada

Province-supported, coed. Urban campus. Total enrollment: 17,409.
Degrees Bachelor of Arts. Majors and concentrations: music. Graduate degrees offered: Bachelor of Music. Program accredited by CUMS.
Enrollment 60 total; all undergraduate.
Music Student Profile 85% females, 15% males, 5% minorities, 3% international.
Music Faculty 5 undergraduate (full-time), 15 undergraduate (part-time). 100% of full-time faculty have terminal degrees. Graduate students do not teach undergraduate courses. Undergraduate student–faculty ratio: 11:1.
Student Life Student groups/activities include performances at on-campus and off-campus functions, Music Society.
Expenses for 2006–2007 Application fee: $115 Canadian dollars. Tuition, fee, and room and board charges are reported in Canadian dollars. Canadian resident tuition: $4483 full-time. Mandatory fees: $528 full-time. College room and board: $7040. College room only: $3445. International student tuition: $11,378 full-time. Special program-related fees: $50 per year for practice room rental, $1170 per year for music lesson fee for non-MusB students.
Financial Aid Program-specific awards: 1 Sir Isaac Brock Scholarship for junior and senior program majors ($475), 1 Senior Scholarship in Music I for junior program majors ($425), 1 Senior Scholarship in Music II for senior program majors ($425), 1 A. Whitmore Griffin Award in Music for junior and senior program majors ($2400).

Brock University (continued)

Application Procedures Students admitted directly into the professional program freshman year. Deadline for freshmen and transfers: June 1. Notification date for freshmen and transfers: June 30. Required: essay, high school transcript, college transcript(s) for transfer students, minimum 3.0 high school GPA, 2 letters of recommendation, interview, audition, 2 years of theory study, photograph, questionnaire. Recommended: 4 years of keyboard study. Auditions held 5 times and by appointment on campus; recorded music is permissible as a substitute for live auditions for international applicants and videotaped performances are permissible as a substitute for live auditions for international applicants.
Undergraduate Contact Natalie Fedj, Administrative Assistant, Department of Music, Brock University, 500 Glenridge Avenue, St. Catharines, Ontario L2S 3A1, Canada; 905-688-5550 ext. 3817, fax: 905-688-2789, e-mail address: music@brocku.ca

Brooklyn College of the City University of New York

Brooklyn, New York

State and locally supported, coed. Urban campus. Total enrollment: 15,281. Music program established 1963.
Degrees Bachelor of Music in the areas of performance, composition, music education. Majors and concentrations: classical music, composition, music, music education, opera, performance, stringed instruments, voice, and percussion instruments. Graduate degrees offered: Master of Arts in the area of music education; Master of Music in the areas of performance, composition. Cross-registration with City University of New York System.
Enrollment 230 total; 100 undergraduate, 110 graduate, 20 nonprofessional degree.
Music Student Profile 60% females, 40% males, 30% minorities, 30% international.
Music Faculty 17 total (full-time), 30 total (part-time). 95% of full-time faculty have terminal degrees. Graduate students teach a few undergraduate courses. Undergraduate student–faculty ratio: 5:1.
Student Life Student groups/activities include music for convocations, commencements, and community concerts, Conservatory Concert Series, Arts Council events and performances.
Expenses for 2006–2007 Application fee: $65. State resident tuition: $4000 full-time. Nonresident tuition: $8640 full-time. Mandatory fees: $375 full-time. Special program-related fees: $75 per semester for technology fee.
Financial Aid Program-specific awards: 20 music scholarships for qualified students ($300–$2000).
Application Procedures Students admitted directly into the professional program freshman year. Deadline for freshmen and transfers: continuous. Notification date for freshmen and transfers: August 15. Required: high school transcript, college transcript(s) for transfer students, minimum 3.0 high school GPA, audition, SAT I test score only (minimum combined SAT I score of 1100), minimum TOEFL score of 500 for international students, portfolio for composition students. Recommended: letter of recommendation, interview. Auditions held 4 times on campus; recorded music is permissible as a substitute for live auditions when distance is prohibitive and videotaped performances are permissible as a substitute for live auditions when distance is prohibitive. Portfolio reviews held continuously, September through May on campus.
Web Site http://bcmusic.org
Undergraduate Contact Dr. Jonathan Babcock, Deputy Chairman, Conservatory of Music, Brooklyn College of the City University of New York, 2900 Bedford Avenue, Brooklyn, New York 11210; 718-951-5846, fax: 718-951-4502, e-mail address: jbabcock@brooklyn.cuny.edu
Graduate Contact Dr. Bruce MacIntyre, Deputy Chairman, Conservatory of Music, Brooklyn College of the City University of New York, 2900 Bedford Avenue, Brooklyn, New York 11210; 718-951-5954, fax: 718-951-4502, e-mail address: brucem@brooklyn.cuny.edu

Bucknell University

Lewisburg, Pennsylvania

Independent, coed. Small town campus. Total enrollment: 3,648. Music program established 1892.
Degrees Bachelor of Music in the areas of performance, music education, music history, music composition. Majors and concentrations: composition, music education, music history, piano/organ, stringed instruments, voice, wind instruments. Program accredited by NASM.
Enrollment 49 total; 16 undergraduate, 33 nonprofessional degree.
Music Student Profile 60% females, 40% males.
Music Faculty 10 undergraduate (full-time), 16 undergraduate (part-time). 88% of full-time faculty have terminal degrees. Graduate students do not teach undergraduate courses. Undergraduate student–faculty ratio: 2:1.
Expenses for 2006–2007 Application fee: $60. Comprehensive fee: $43,368 includes full-time tuition ($35,802), mandatory fees ($200), and college room and board ($7366). College room only: $3972. Special program-related fees: $285 per semester for lessons for non-majors.
Financial Aid Program-specific awards: preferential awards for program majors demonstrating need ($2000).
Application Procedures Students admitted directly into the professional program freshman year. Deadline for freshmen: January 1; transfers: April 1. Notification date for freshmen: April 1; transfers: July 1. Required: essay, high school transcript, college transcript(s) for transfer students, minimum 3.0 high school GPA, audition, SAT I or ACT test scores. Recommended: 3 letters of recommendation, interview. Auditions held 4 times on campus; recorded music is permissible as a substitute for live auditions if a campus visit is impossible and videotaped performances are permissible as a substitute for live auditions if a campus visit is impossible.
Web Site http://www.departments.bucknell.edu/music
Undergraduate Contact Ms. Brenda Ross, Secretary, Department of Music, Bucknell University, Lewisburg, Pennsylvania 17837; 570-577-1216, fax: 570-577-1215, e-mail address: bross@bucknell.edu

Jordan College of Fine Arts
Butler University

Indianapolis, Indiana

Independent, coed. Urban campus. Total enrollment: 4,384. Music program established 1896.
Degrees Bachelor of Arts in the areas of music theory, music history, music composition, piano pedagogy, applied music; Bachelor of Music in the areas of performance, composition, piano pedagogy, music education; Bachelor of Science in the area of arts administration/music. Majors and concentrations: applied music, brass, composition, jazz studies, music education, music history and literature, music theory, performance, piano, piano pedagogy, stringed instruments, voice, wind and percussion instruments. Graduate degrees offered: Master of Music in the areas of performance, composition, conducting, music theory, music history, piano pedagogy, music education. Cross-registration with Indianapolis Consortium for Urban Education. Program accredited by NASM.
Enrollment 220 total; 175 undergraduate, 45 graduate.
Music Student Profile 58% females, 42% males, 7% minorities, 2% international.
Music Faculty 28 total (full-time), 28 total (part-time). 64% of full-time faculty have terminal degrees. Graduate students do not teach undergraduate courses. Undergraduate student–faculty ratio: 6:1.
Student Life Student groups/activities include Music Educators National Conference Student Chapter, Butler Community Arts School, music fraternities and sororities.
Expenses for 2005–2006 Application fee: $35. Comprehensive fee: $31,944 includes full-time tuition ($23,530), mandatory fees ($244), and college room and board ($8170). College room only: $3980. Full-time tuition and fees vary according to program.

Room and board charges vary according to housing facility. Special program-related fees: $170 per credit hour for one-on-one instruction.

Financial Aid Program-specific awards: audition awards for program majors.

Application Procedures Students admitted directly into the professional program freshman year. Deadline for freshmen and transfers: continuous. Required: essay, high school transcript, college transcript(s) for transfer students, minimum 2.0 high school GPA, letter of recommendation, audition, SAT I or ACT test scores, music application. Recommended: minimum 3.0 high school GPA, interview. Auditions held 5 times on campus; recorded music is permissible as a substitute for live auditions when distance is prohibitive and videotaped performances are permissible as a substitute for live auditions when distance is prohibitive.

Web Site http://www.butler.edu/music/

Contact Ms. Kathy Lang, Admission Representative, Jordan College of Fine Arts, Butler University, Lilly Hall - 138B, 4600 Sunset Avenue, Indianapolis, Indiana 46208; 317-940-9656, fax: 317-940-9658, e-mail address: klang@butler.edu

More About the University

Butler University is most proud of its tradition of excellence and innovation. Challenging and enabling students to meet their personal and professional goals has guided the University since 1855. Today, Butler is an independent, coeducational, nonsectarian university, with a total undergraduate enrollment of more than 3,800 students. The University is accredited by the North Central Association of Colleges and Schools.

As one of America's oldest music institutions, Butler's programs prepare young musicians to become outstanding teachers, solo artists, and leaders in the cultural community. Programs in performance combine quality private study, engaging classroom work, and a variety of performance ensembles. Aspiring musicians/teachers pursue diverse field experiences in their first year of study. The arts administration program prepares talented artistic students for careers in arts-related, not-for-profit organizations and in the business world. Arts administration students regularly intern at the Kennedy Center, the San Francisco Opera, Kentucky Center for the Arts, and many of Indianapolis's finest cultural institutions.

Campus and Surroundings Indianapolis, Indiana's state capital and the twelfth-largest city in the nation, boasts a variety of cultural activities, including the Indianapolis Symphony Orchestra, Indiana Repertory Theatre, Indianapolis Chamber Orchestra, the Indianapolis Museum of Art, and the world's largest children's museum. Citywide celebrations are plentiful, including ethnic festivals, art fairs, and outdoor music festivals.

Program Facilities Clowes Memorial Hall is a 2,200-seat performance hall that hosts a variety of events, from community arts groups to national and international touring companies and many University performances. A new performing arts complex is currently under construction. The first phase of the complex, a 47,000-square-foot addition to Lilly Hall called the Courtyard Building, was completed in spring 2003. This new building houses a choral rehearsal hall, an instrumental rehearsal hall, dance studios, a theater studio, an electronic music lab, and a percussion studio. The second phase, the 140-seat Eidson-Duckwall Recital Hall, was completed in fall 2004. The third phase is a 450-seat performance hall/proscenium theater with adjustable acoustical features.

Faculty/Alumni Studio instruction at Butler is always with professional members of the faculty, and classrooms are led by outstanding scholar educators. The award-winning group includes editors of definitive editions of the songs by Debussy and Schubert; nationally known composers in demand as composers-in-residence; an outstanding performing faculty; individual artists with opera companies and orchestras throughout the world; winners in the Metropolitan Opera Auditions, MacAllister

Awards, Bodky Competition, and the Van Cliburn Competition; and conductors who have given the downbeat on the podium in the world's great concert halls.

Butler's program prepares students for the future with its graduates pursuing master's programs at the Eastman School of Music, Peabody Conservatory, Boston University, Florida State University, the University of Michigan, and Indiana University.

Student Performance Opportunities In addition to numerous solo recital opportunities, students participate in a variety of large and small ensembles. Instrumental students may play in groups that range from chamber-style winds, string quartets, and piano trios to the larger Symphonic Wind Ensemble and the University's full-scale Butler Symphony Orchestra. Singers might find themselves in intimate ensembles like the Jordan Jazz or Madrigal Singers or in larger staged productions of the Butler Opera and the University Choir or Butler Chorale. Students regularly combine forces to present titan works, such as Orff's *Carmin Burana*, Beethoven's *Choral Symphony*, or Bernstein's *Candide*.

Special Programs Butler has a strong commitment to new programs, technology, and facilities, including a new recording industry studies major, in collaboration with the media arts department that places students in studios for hands-on learning experiences. Each year, more than 30 visiting artists perform on campus and interact with students. Butler music students have worked with the likes of Yo-Yo Ma, Andre Watts, Richard Stolzman, Denyce Graves, Jeffrey Kahane, Cleo Laine, Dale Warland, Marvin Hamlisch, John Holloway, H. Robert Reynolds, Karel Haus, and Suzanne Vega.

Cooperative Agreements Butler University has collaborative relationships with many local arts organizations, including the Indianapolis Opera. The following are located on campus: Dance Kaleidoscope, Indianapolis Symphonic Choir, Indianapolis Chamber Orchestra, American Pianists Association, and the Indianapolis Children's Choir.

Career Placement Services and Opporutunities Butler students sing, play, conduct, teach, and inspire. Students with undergraduate Butler music degrees continue their studies at some of the country's finest advanced-study programs, including Indiana University, the Manhattan School of Music, the Juilliard Opera Program, Florida State University, and the Eastman School of Music.

Former Butler students are on the stage and in the pit for major Broadway shows like *Les Misérables, Blast!*, and *Phantom of the Opera*. The music education program has a 99 percent placement for teachers. Butler's music education students are regularly cited as outstanding young educators by the Music Educators National Conference and hold teaching positions at public and private schools all over the country. Butler has maestros on the podium at the Warner Brothers Orchestra, Evansville Philharmonic, Ft. Smith Symphony, and on Broadway.

California Institute of the Arts
Valencia, California

Independent, coed. Total enrollment: 1,327. Music program established 1961.

Degrees Bachelor of Fine Arts in the areas of music composition, musical arts, performance, world music, jazz, music technology, performer/composer. Majors and concentrations: classical music, composition, harp, jazz, music technology, musical arts, new media, performer/composer, piano, stringed instruments, voice, wind and percussion instruments, world music. Graduate degrees offered: Master of Fine Arts in the areas of music composition, performance, world music, composition/new media, jazz, performer/composer, integrated media-music, performer/composer-African American improvisational music. Program accredited by NASM.

Enrollment 244 total; 146 undergraduate, 98 graduate.

Music Student Profile 23% females, 77% males, 25% minorities, 6% international.

California Institute of the Arts (continued)

Music Faculty 30 total (full-time), 32 total (part-time). 80% of full-time faculty have terminal degrees. Graduate students do not teach undergraduate courses. Undergraduate student–faculty ratio: 5:1.

Student Life Student groups/activities include Community Arts Partnership (CAP), off-campus performance groups, Intercultural Arts Project (ICAP). Special housing available for music students.

Expenses for 2005–2006 Application fee: $65. Comprehensive fee: $35,422 includes full-time tuition ($27,260), mandatory fees ($465), and college room and board ($7697). College room only: $4095. Full-time tuition and fees vary according to course load. Room and board charges vary according to board plan, housing facility, and location. Special program-related fees: $680 per year for technology fee.

Financial Aid Program-specific awards: CalArts Scholarships for students demonstrating talent ($2000–$22,000), Minority Scholarships ($2000–$22,000).

Application Procedures Students admitted directly into the professional program freshman year. Deadline for freshmen and transfers: January 5. Required: essay, high school transcript, college transcript(s) for transfer students, 2 letters of recommendation, audition, portfolio for composition applicants, a recorded audition for jazz applicants. Recommended: interview. Auditions held by appointment on campus and off campus in New York, NY; Chicago, IL; Interlochen, MI; Valencia, CA; San Francisco, CA; recorded music is permissible as a substitute for live auditions whenever needed and videotaped performances are permissible as a substitute for live auditions whenever sound reading is not available. Portfolio reviews held on campus.

Web Site http://www.calarts.edu

Undergraduate Contact Ms. Natalie Brejcha, Admissions Counselor, California Institute of the Arts, 24700 McBean Parkway, Valencia, California 91355; 661-255-1050, fax: 661-253-7710, e-mail address: nbrejcha@calarts.edu

Graduate Contact Ms. Natalie Brajcha, Admissions Counselor, California Institute of the Arts, 24700 McBean Parkway, Valencia, California 91355; 661-255-1050, fax: 661-253-7710, e-mail address: nbrejcha@calarts.edu

More About the Institute

The School of Music at California Institute of the Arts (CalArts) strives to create a learning environment to support the informed, creative music maker. High standards, a focus on new and experimental forms, and a respect for great musical traditions are the School's hallmark and its formula for success. In addition to cross-stylistic collaborations within the School of Music, students work with visual artists, filmmakers, animators, dancers, actors, and writers from the five other schools at CalArts.

The School of Music offers rigorous training in a unique variety of musical styles and cultures, from chamber and orchestral music to computer music, from opera to interdisciplinary performance, from jazz improvisation to the musical traditions of Africa, India, and Indonesia. With approximately 240 students, the School of Music offers one of the most intimate learning environments available. Every student works closely with a mentor, a faculty member who serves as that student's artistic and academic advisor.

Programs of Study The School of Music offers undergraduate programs that lead to a Bachelor of Fine Arts (B.F.A.) degree or a Certificate of Fine Arts. Graduate programs lead to a Master of Fine Arts (M.F.A.) degree or an Advanced Certificate of Fine Arts. Prospective students are invited to apply to the following degree programs: Composition Program (B.F.A., M.F.A.), with a specialization available in experimental sound practices for M.F.A. only; Jazz Studies Program (B.F.A., M.F.A.); Multifocus Programs in Performance (B.F.A., M.F.A.), including the Wind/Brass/String Instruments Program, the Harp Program, the Piano/Keyboard/Collaborative Keyboard Program, the Guitar Program, the Percussion/World Percussion Program, and the Voice Program; Multi Focus Music Technologies Program (B.F.A. only); Performer/Composer Program (Upper-division B.F.A., M.F.A. only), with a specialization available in African American

improvisational music; World Music Performance Program (B.F.A., M.F.A.), with specializations available in African music and dance (M.F.A. only), Balinese and Javanese music and dance (M.F.A. only), and North Indian music (M.F.A. only).

Every B.F.A. student pursues course work in three areas: the School of Music core curriculum, the critical studies undergraduate requirements, and his or her specialized program curriculum.

M.F.A. students concentrate primarily on advanced work in their respective programs. They are generally not required to take core curriculum and critical studies courses. M.F.A. students may be required, however, to take core curriculum courses to strengthen their musical skills and/or theoretical knowledge. Qualified graduate applicants may also apply to be considered for a supplemental concentration in integrated media (IM), a course of study focused on interdisciplinary work with digital media.

All B.F.A. and M.F.A. programs offered by the School of Music have their own integral curriculum. The School, however, encourages courses of study that draw on the resources of several programs. Faculty mentors guide students in designing such courses of study.

The School of Music offers more than 200 courses each semester. Music students may also take advantage of numerous elective courses offered throughout CalArts. In order to graduate, students must complete all program and course requirements and pass regular faculty member reviews of their artistic and academic progress.

Program Facilities Most large-ensemble performances take place in the Roy O. Disney Music Hall, a multipurpose space with adaptable acoustics, lighting, and sound features. This hall is used for both traditional and experimental events. Additional concerts are presented in the Walt Disney Modular Theater and the Main Gallery.

An important new addition to the School of Music's resources is the Roy and Edna Disney/CalArts Theater (REDCAT), a performance and exhibition space that opened in November 2003 in downtown Los Angeles. Housed as a separate entity in the Frank Gehry-designed Walt Disney Concert Hall complex (the new home of the Los Angeles Philharmonic Orchestra), REDCAT features CalArts student, alumni, and faculty member work as well as that of visiting artists.

The School of Music has more than twenty-five practice rooms, many with pianos, including special rooms for piano and percussion majors. All rooms are available around-the-clock when school is in session.

CalArts' sizable instrument collection features fifty pianos, three harpsichords, an organ, and a celesta; three harps; various strings, woodwinds, brass, and early European instruments; numerous orchestral and nontraditional percussion instruments; Balinese and Javanese gamelans; African drum ensembles; and sarods, sitars, tabla, and other Indian instruments.

The School of Music has extensive state-of-the-art facilities for using computers and interactive media to create, perform, record, and print music. Studios support classes in composition, synthesis, and scoring; digital recording, editing, and processing; multimedia design; telecommunications; and software and hardware development. All studios are open around the clock during academic sessions.

Faculty, Resident Artists, Alumni CalArts' faculty features innovators and leaders in each specialty—composers, performers, and producers who have distinguished themselves at the highest levels. All faculty members are practicing professionals and can prepare students for the demands of a global music community.

The School of Music regularly invites celebrated artists in a variety of specialties to share their experience and insights with students and to supplement the expertise of regular faculty members. They may perform, conduct their compositions, give master classes and workshops, and teach courses or lessons.

CalArts alumni have made their mark on every aspect of musicmaking, including professors at distinguished music schools, performing and recording artists, composers, computer musicians, and the like.

Student Performance/Exhibit Opportunities The School of Music's performance schedule features more than 250 concerts every year, running the gamut from informal noon concerts and student-organized jam sessions to formal on-campus evening events and performances at high-profile venues throughout the Los Angeles area. Faculty members play alongside students at many of these concerts.

California State University, Fullerton

Fullerton, California

State-supported, coed. Urban campus. Total enrollment: 35,040. Music program established 1960.

Degrees Bachelor of Music. Majors and concentrations: composition, piano/organ, stringed instruments, voice, wind and percussion instruments. Graduate degrees offered: Master of Music in the areas of performance, composition. Cross-registration with California State University System, California community colleges. Program accredited by NASM.

Enrollment 333 total; 46 undergraduate, 37 graduate, 250 nonprofessional degree.

Music Student Profile 55% females, 45% males, 40% minorities, 5% international.

Music Faculty 22 total (full-time), 48 total (part-time). 85% of full-time faculty have terminal degrees. Graduate students do not teach undergraduate courses. Undergraduate student–faculty ratio: 12:1.

Student Life Student groups/activities include American Choral Directors Association Student Chapter, Phi Mu Alpha Sinfonia, Mu Phi Epsilon.

Expenses for 2005–2006 Application fee: $55. State resident tuition: $0 full-time. Nonresident tuition: $10,170 full-time. Mandatory fees: $2990 full-time. Full-time tuition and fees vary according to course load. College room only: $4504. Special program-related fees: $25 per semester for instrument use fee, $25 per semester for piano maintenance fee.

Financial Aid Program-specific awards: 15–20 departmental scholarships for performers ($1000).

Application Procedures Students apply for admission into the professional program by sophomore year. Required: high school transcript, college transcript(s) for transfer students, minimum 2.0 high school GPA, audition, SAT I or ACT test scores. Auditions held 3 times on campus; recorded music is permissible as a substitute for live auditions when distance is prohibitive and videotaped performances are permissible as a substitute for live auditions when distance is prohibitive.

Web Site http://www.fullerton.edu/catalog/academic_departments/mus.asp

Undergraduate Contact Mr. David Grimes, Vice Chair, Department of Music, California State University, Fullerton, Box 6850, Fullerton, California 92834-6850; 714-278-3598, fax: 714-278-5956, e-mail address: dgrimes@fullerton.edu

Graduate Contact Dr. Katherine Powers, Coordinator of Graduate Studies, Department of Music, California State University, Fullerton, PO Box 6850, Fullerton, California 92834-6850; 714-278-3511, fax: 714-278-5956, e-mail address: kpowers@fullerton.edu

California State University, Long Beach

Long Beach, California

State-supported, coed. Suburban campus. Total system enrollment: 1,344. Total unit enrollment: 34,547. Music program established 1949.

Degrees Bachelor of Music in the areas of performance, music history and literature, composition, jazz studies, music education. Majors and concentrations: classical music, composition, jazz, music, music education, music history, opera, piano,

stringed instruments, voice, wind and percussion instruments. Graduate degrees offered: Master of Music in the areas of composition, conducting, performance, music history, music theory, opera, jazz studies. Cross-registration with California State University System. Program accredited by NASM.

Enrollment 475 total; 380 undergraduate, 65 graduate, 30 nonprofessional degree.

Music Student Profile 52% females, 48% males, 40% minorities, 5% international.

Music Faculty 21 total (full-time), 75 total (part-time). 85% of full-time faculty have terminal degrees. Graduate students teach a few undergraduate courses. Undergraduate student–faculty ratio: 20:1.

Student Life Student groups/activities include American Choral Directors Association, Music Educators National Conference, professional music fraternities.

Expenses for 2006–2007 Application fee: $55. State resident tuition: $0 full-time. Nonresident tuition: $10,170 full-time. Mandatory fees: $2864 full-time. College room and board: $6648. Special program-related fees: $25 per semester for practice room, instrument fee, locker room fee.

Financial Aid Program-specific awards: 80 music scholarships for program majors ($700).

Application Procedures Students admitted directly into the professional program freshman year. Deadline for freshmen: November 30; transfers: February 1. Required: high school transcript, college transcript(s) for transfer students, minimum 3.0 high school GPA, audition, SAT I or ACT test scores. Auditions held 4 times on campus; recorded music is permissible as a substitute for live auditions when distance is prohibitive and videotaped performances are permissible as a substitute for live auditions when distance is prohibitive.

Web Site http://www.csulb.edu/~music

Undergraduate Contact Dr. Lee Vail, Undergraduate Advisor, Department of Music, California State University, Long Beach, 1250 Bellflower Boulevard, Long Beach, California 90840-7101; 562-985-4399, fax: 562-985-2490, e-mail address: lvail@csulb.edu

Graduate Contact Dr. Kristine Forney, Director of Graduate Studies, Department of Music, California State University, Long Beach, 1250 Bellflower Boulevard, Long Beach, California 90840-7101; 562-984-4788, fax: 562-985-2490, e-mail address: kforney@csulb.edu

California State University, Los Angeles

Los Angeles, California

State-supported, coed. Urban campus. Total enrollment: 20,014. Music program established 1952.

California State University, Northridge

Northridge, California

State-supported, coed. Urban campus. Total enrollment: 33,243. Music program established 1958.

California State University, Sacramento

Sacramento, California

State-supported, coed. Urban campus. Total enrollment: 27,932. Music program established 1947.

Degrees Bachelor of Arts in the areas of music, music management; Bachelor of Music in the areas of voice, piano, organ, orchestral instruments, guitar, music theory/composition, music education. Majors and concentrations: guitar, jazz studies, music, music education, music management, music theory and composition, piano/organ/harpsichord, stringed instruments, voice, wind and percussion instruments. Graduate degrees offered: Master of Music in the areas of conducting, composition, music education, music history and literature, performance.

California State University, Sacramento (continued)

Cross-registration with University of California-Davis, Los Rios Community College District. Program accredited by NASM.
Enrollment 285 total; 200 undergraduate, 35 graduate, 50 nonprofessional degree.
Music Student Profile 59% females, 41% males, 5% international.
Music Faculty 22 total (full-time), 30 total (part-time). 100% of full-time faculty have terminal degrees. Graduate students do not teach undergraduate courses. Undergraduate student–faculty ratio: 12:1.
Student Life Student groups/activities include Music Educators National Conference, Mu Phi Epsilon, Pi Kappa Lambda.
Expenses for 2006–2007 Application fee: $55. Nonresident tuition: $13,242 full-time. Mandatory fees: $3624 full-time. College room and board: $7458. Special program-related fees: $40 per semester for music service fee.
Financial Aid Program-specific awards: 30–50 music awards for program majors ($150–$2000).
Application Procedures Students admitted directly into the professional program freshman year. Deadline for freshmen and transfers: continuous. Required: high school transcript, college transcript(s) for transfer students, minimum 2.0 high school GPA, audition, SAT I or ACT test scores, portfolio for theory/composition applicants. Recommended: essay, minimum 3.0 high school GPA, video. Auditions held 4 times on campus; recorded music is permissible as a substitute for live auditions if a campus visit is impossible and videotaped performances are permissible as a substitute for live auditions if a campus visit is impossible. Portfolio reviews held 4 times on campus.
Web Site http://www.csus.edu/music
Undergraduate Contact Mr. Mark Allen, Admissions Counselor, Department of Music, California State University, Sacramento, 6000 J Street, Sacramento, California 95819-6015; 916-278-6543, e-mail address: music@csus.edu
Graduate Contact Dr. Robert Halseth, Graduate Coordinator, Department of Music, California State University, Sacramento, 6000 J Street, Sacramento, California 95819-6015; 916-278-5091, e-mail address: halseth@saclink.csus.edu

California State University, Stanislaus

Turlock, California

State-supported, coed. Small town campus. Total enrollment: 8,137.

Calvary Bible College and Theological Seminary

Kansas City, Missouri

Independent nondenominational, coed. Suburban campus. Total enrollment: 348. Music program established 1955.
Degrees Bachelor of Music in the area of music education; Bachelor of Science in the area of church music. Majors and concentrations: church music, music education, piano pedagogy, piano performance, vocal pedagogy, voice performance.
Enrollment 25 total.
Music Student Profile 66% females, 34% males, 10% minorities.
Music Faculty 3 undergraduate (full-time), 2 undergraduate (part-time). 67% of full-time faculty have terminal degrees. Graduate students do not teach undergraduate courses. Undergraduate student–faculty ratio: 5:1.
Student Life Student groups/activities include musicals, dramas, oratorios.
Expenses for 2005–2006 Application fee: $25. Comprehensive fee: $10,996 includes full-time tuition ($6720), mandatory fees ($576), and college room and board ($3700). College room only: $1750. Special program-related fees: $50 per semester for accompanist fee, $125 per semester for private lessons.
Financial Aid Program-specific awards: 3–6 Music Department Scholarships for music majors ($700).
Application Procedures Students admitted directly into the professional program freshman year. Deadline for freshmen and transfers: July 15. Required: high school transcript, college

transcript(s) for transfer students, 2 letters of recommendation, audition, SAT I or ACT test scores. Auditions held whenever needed on campus; recorded music is permissible as a substitute for live auditions if a campus visit is impossible and videotaped performances are permissible as a substitute for live auditions if a campus visit is impossible.
Web Site http://www.calvary.edu
Undergraduate Contact Paul Vander Mey, Chairman, Music Department, Calvary Bible College and Theological Seminary, 15800 Calvary Road, Kansas City, Missouri 64147; 816-322-0110 ext. 1354, fax: 816-331-4474, e-mail address: musicdir@calvary.edu

Calvin College

Grand Rapids, Michigan

Independent, coed. Suburban campus. Total enrollment: 4,177. Music program established 1995.

Cameron University

Lawton, Oklahoma

State-supported, coed. Small town campus. Total enrollment: 5,873.
Degrees Bachelor of Music in the areas of vocal music education, instrumental music education, composition, performance, keyboard music education. Majors and concentrations: brass, composition, music education, performance, piano, voice. Mandatory cross-registration with Oklahoma University, State Board of Regents University System. Program accredited by NASM.
Enrollment 61 total; 37 undergraduate, 24 nonprofessional degree.
Music Student Profile 44% females, 56% males, 27% minorities.
Music Faculty 12 undergraduate (full-time), 7 undergraduate (part-time). 60% of full-time faculty have terminal degrees. Graduate students do not teach undergraduate courses. Undergraduate student–faculty ratio: 4:1.
Student Life Student groups/activities include Kappa Kappa Psi, Pi Kappa Lambda, Mu Phi Epsilon.
Expenses for 2005–2006 Application fee: $15. State resident tuition: $3240 full-time. Nonresident tuition: $7830 full-time. Mandatory fees: $200 full-time. Full-time tuition and fees vary according to course load. College room and board: $3014. Room and board charges vary according to board plan. Special program-related fees: $25 per credit hour for private music lessons.
Financial Aid Program-specific awards: 1 Presser Scholarship for above-average students with exceptional artistic ability ($4000), 30 McMahon Scholarships for academically qualified applicants ($1200), 3 Aldine Cash Scholarships for academically qualified applicants ($1000).
Application Procedures Students apply for admission into the professional program by sophomore year. Deadline for freshmen and transfers: continuous. Required: high school transcript, college transcript(s) for transfer students, minimum 2.0 high school GPA, audition, SAT I or ACT test scores. Recommended: essay. Auditions held twice on campus; recorded music is permissible as a substitute for live auditions when distance is prohibitive and videotaped performances are permissible as a substitute for live auditions when distance is prohibitive. Portfolio reviews held twice on campus; the submission of slides may be substituted for portfolios.
Web Site http://www.cameron.edu/liberal_arts/music/index.html
Undergraduate Contact Ms. Sandra Dunn, Secretary, Department of Music and Theatre Arts, Cameron University, 2800 West Gore Boulevard, Lawton, Oklahoma 73505; 580-581-2440, fax: 580-581-5764.

Campbellsville University

Campbellsville, Kentucky

Independent, coed. Small town campus. Total enrollment: 2,286. Music program established 1957.

Degrees Bachelor of Music. Majors and concentrations: church music, music education. Graduate degrees offered: Master of Music in the areas of music education, church music. Program accredited by NASM.
Enrollment 114 total; 64 undergraduate, 10 graduate, 40 nonprofessional degree.
Music Student Profile 48% females, 52% males, 20% minorities, 19% international.
Music Faculty 11 total (full-time), 13 total (part-time). 72% of full-time faculty have terminal degrees. Graduate students do not teach undergraduate courses. Undergraduate student–faculty ratio: 6:1.
Student Life Student groups/activities include Fall Drama, Spring Musical Drama, Children's Theater.
Expenses for 2006–2007 Application fee: $20. Comprehensive fee: $22,272 includes full-time tuition ($15,960), mandatory fees ($380), and college room and board ($5932). Special program-related fees: $130 per credit hour for applied lesson fees.
Financial Aid Program-specific awards: 3 competitive music scholarships for program majors ($2000), 85 music performance grants for program majors/minors ($1400), 50 band grants for band members ($600).
Application Procedures Students apply for admission into the professional program by sophomore year. Deadline for freshmen and transfers: continuous. Required: high school transcript, college transcript(s) for transfer students, audition, SAT I or ACT test scores (minimum combined SAT I score of 890, minimum composite ACT score of 19). Recommended: essay, minimum 2.0 high school GPA, 2 letters of recommendation. Auditions held by request on campus; recorded music is permissible as a substitute for live auditions when distance is prohibitive and videotaped performances are permissible as a substitute for live auditions when distance is prohibitive.
Web Site http://www.campbellsville.edu/music
Contact Dr. Robert Gaddis, Dean, School of Music, Campbellsville University, 1 University Drive, CPO 1314, Campbellsville, Kentucky 42718; 270-789-5269, fax: 270-789-5524, e-mail address: jrgaddis@campbellsville.edu

Capital University
Columbus, Ohio

Independent, coed. Suburban campus. Total enrollment: 3,901. Music program established 1918.
Degrees Bachelor of Arts in the area of music; Bachelor of Music in the areas of music education, composition, jazz studies, music industry, performance, keyboard pedagogy, music theater, music merchandising, music media, music technology. Majors and concentrations: composition, jazz studies, keyboard pedagogy, music education, music industry, music media, music merchandising, music performance, music technology. Graduate degrees offered: Master of Music in the area of music education with an emphasis in Kodaly. Cross-registration with Higher Education Council of Columbus. Program accredited by NASM.
Enrollment 247 total; 205 undergraduate, 42 graduate.
Music Student Profile 54% females, 46% males, 3% minorities, 2% international.
Music Faculty 27 total (full-time), 22 total (part-time). 41% of full-time faculty have terminal degrees. Graduate students do not teach undergraduate courses. Undergraduate student–faculty ratio: 4:1.
Student Life Student groups/activities include Ohio Collegiate Music Educators Association, Phi Mu Alpha/Phi Beta/Sigma Alpha Iota/Tau Beta Sigma, Music and Entertainment Industry Student Association.
Expenses for 2005–2006 Application fee: $25. Comprehensive fee: $30,444 includes full-time tuition ($24,100) and college room and board ($6344). Full-time tuition varies according to course load, degree level, program, and student level. Room and board charges vary according to board plan and housing facility. Special program-related fees: $150 per semester for group lesson, $315–$395 per semester for private lessons.
Financial Aid Program-specific awards: music scholarships for program majors ($500–$10,000), participation awards for non-music majors ($500–$1000), music grants for program majors

with exceptional talent or a needed instruments ($500–$1000), composition awards for composition majors ($500–$1000).
Application Procedures Students admitted directly into the professional program freshman year. Deadline for freshmen: April 15; transfers: continuous. Notification date for freshmen and transfers: continuous. Required: high school transcript, college transcript(s) for transfer students, letter of recommendation, audition, SAT I or ACT test scores (minimum combined SAT I score of 900, minimum composite ACT score of 18), minimum 2.6 high school GPA, minimum 2.25 college GPA for transfers, college report form for transfer students. Recommended: minimum 3.0 high school GPA, interview. Auditions held 5 times on campus; videotaped performances are permissible as a substitute for live auditions for out-of-state students only.
Web Site http://www.capital.edu
Undergraduate Contact Ms. Meagan M. Webb, Assistant Director of Admission, Capital University, 1 College and Main, Columbus, Ohio 43209; 614-236-6101 ext. 6574, fax: 614-236-6926, e-mail address: admissions@capital.edu
Graduate Contact Dr. Sandra Mathias, Professor of Music and Education, Conservatory of Music, Capital University, 1 College and Main, Columbus, Ohio 43209; 614-236-6267, fax: 614-236-6935, e-mail address: smathias@capital.edu

Carleton University
Ottawa, Ontario, Canada

Province-supported, coed. Urban campus. Total enrollment: 23,683. Music program established 1967.

Carnegie Mellon University
Pittsburgh, Pennsylvania

Independent, coed. Urban campus. Total enrollment: 10,017. Music program established 1913.
Degrees Bachelor of Fine Arts in the areas of music performance, composition. Majors and concentrations: composition, instrumental music, piano/organ, voice. Graduate degrees offered: Master of Music in the areas of composition, conducting, performance, music education. Cross-registration with Pittsburgh Council on Higher Education. Program accredited by NASM.
Enrollment 251 total; 146 undergraduate, 75 graduate, 30 nonprofessional degree.
Music Student Profile 55% females, 45% males, 4% minorities, 20% international.
Music Faculty 70 total (full-time), 20 total (part-time). 33% of full-time faculty have terminal degrees. Graduate students do not teach undergraduate courses. Undergraduate student–faculty ratio: 4:1.
Student Life Student groups/activities include Greek Sing, Carnival, Scotch 'n Soda (student-run theater group).
Expenses for 2006–2007 Application fee: $60. Comprehensive fee: $43,858 includes full-time tuition ($34,180), mandatory fees ($398), and college room and board ($9280). College room only: $5440.
Financial Aid Program-specific awards: 20–40 music scholarships for program majors.
Application Procedures Students admitted directly into the professional program freshman year. Deadline for freshmen and transfers: January 1. Notification date for freshmen and transfers: March 15. Required: essay, high school transcript, college transcript(s) for transfer students, 3 letters of recommendation, audition, SAT I or ACT test scores. Recommended: minimum 3.0 high school GPA, interview, video. Auditions held 20 times on campus and off campus in Atlanta, GA; Boston, MA; Chicago, IL; Miami, FL; New York, NY; Philadelphia, PA; Washington, DC; Los Angeles, CA; San Francisco, CA; recorded music is permissible as a substitute for live auditions if a campus visit is impossible and videotaped performances are permissible as a substitute for live auditions if a campus visit is impossible.
Web Site http://www.cmu.edu/cfa/music/
Contact Ms. Sandra Ragusa, Director of Recruitment and Enrollment, School of Music, Carnegie Mellon University, 5000

Carnegie Mellon University (continued)

Forbes Avenue, Pittsburgh, Pennsylvania 15213-3890; 412-268-4118, fax: 412-268-3222, e-mail address: sragusa@andrew.cmu.edu

The Carroll McDaniel Petrie School of Music

See Converse College

Carson-Newman College
Jefferson City, Tennessee

Independent Southern Baptist, coed. Small town campus. Total enrollment: 1,993. Music program established 1888.

Benjamin T. Rome School of Music
The Catholic University of America
Washington, District of Columbia

Independent, coed. Urban campus. Total enrollment: 6,130. Music program established 1965.

Degrees Bachelor of Music in the areas of vocal performance, instrumental performance, composition, musical theatre, general-choral music education, instrumental music education, combined general choral and instrumental music education, music history and literature. Majors and concentrations: choral music education, composition, instrumental music education, instrumental performance, music history and literature, music theater, voice performance. Graduate degrees offered: Master of Arts in the areas of music history, music theory; Master of Music in the areas of vocal performance, instrumental performance, accompanying, chamber music, pedagogy, composition, instrumental conducting; Master of Music in Sacred Music in the areas of choral music, composition, organ and voice. Doctor of Musical Arts in the areas of vocal performance, instrumental performance, accompanying, chamber music, composition, instrumental conducting, pedagogy. sacred music. Cross-registration with Consortium of Universities of the Washington Metropolitan Area. Program accredited by NASM.

Enrollment 313 total; 187 undergraduate, 125 graduate, 1 nonprofessional degree.

Music Student Profile 65% females, 35% males, 9% minorities, 6% international.

Music Faculty 17 total (full-time), 110 total (part-time). 71% of full-time faculty have terminal degrees. Graduate students teach a few undergraduate courses.

Student Life Student groups/activities include drama department productions and student-run productions, Music Educators National Conference Student Chapter, Sigma Alpha Iota.

Expenses for 2005–2006 Application fee: $55. One-time mandatory fee: $365. Comprehensive fee: $35,838 includes full-time tuition ($24,800), mandatory fees ($1200), and college room and board ($9838). College room only: $5646. Full-time tuition and fees vary according to program. Room and board charges vary according to board plan and housing facility. Special program-related fees for applied music , $35–$50 per semester for practice room fee, $50 for recital fee.

Financial Aid Program-specific awards: 110 music performance scholarships for musically qualified applicants ($1000–$13,000).

Application Procedures Students admitted directly into the professional program freshman year. Deadline for freshmen: February 1; transfers: June 1. Required: essay, high school transcript, college transcript(s) for transfer students, minimum 3.0 high school GPA, letter of recommendation, audition, SAT I or ACT test scores. Recommended: interview, SAT II. Auditions held approximately once per month on campus; recorded music is permissible as a substitute for live auditions if a campus visit is impossible and videotaped performances are permissible as a substitute for live auditions if a campus visit is impossible.

Web Site http://music.cua.edu

Undergraduate Contact Dr. Amy Antonelli, Assistant Dean, Benjamin T. Rome School of Music, The Catholic University of America, Washington, District of Columbia 20064; 202-319-5414, fax: 202-319-6280.

Graduate Contact Dr. Paul Taylor, Assistant Dean of Graduate Studies, Benjamin T. Rome School of Music, The Catholic University of America, Washington, District of Columbia 20064; 202-319-5414, fax: 202-319-6280.

More About the School

As Washington, D.C.'s only university school of music, the Benjamin T. Rome School of Music is both professionally competitive and personally supportive. The School has an excellent location and offers numerous performance opportunities both on and off campus in the city of Washington. Through its comprehensive graduate and undergraduate programs, the Benjamin T. Rome School of Music is committed to excellence and personal attention. The School of Music is a professional school within a liberal arts university.

Undergraduate students study with an outstanding full-time faculty of artists-scholars and an extensive part-time faculty, including members of the National Symphony Orchestra, Washington Opera Orchestra, Philadelphia Orchestra, Baltimore Symphony Orchestra, and the Metropolitan Opera Orchestra. Piano faculty members perform internationally in solo, chamber, and orchestra programs. Voice faculty members have performance experience or are currently performing with nationally and internationally renowned opera houses, such as the Metropolitan Opera and La Scala. Undergraduates benefit from teaching by scholars whose research includes Gregorian chant, medieval music, opera, musical theater, and twentieth-century music. In addition, many of the world's greatest performers hold master classes at the Catholic University of America, including Andre Watts, Gian Carlo Menotti, Faith Prince, Mstislav Rostropovich, Renata Scotto, and Joseph Kalichstein.

The School of Music offers the Bachelor of Music (B.M.) degree, with majors in performance (orchestral instruments, organ, piano, and voice), music education (choral, orchestral, and combined) composition, and music history and literature (honors program). Students may pursue dual degrees in music and another discipline. Students who wish to major in music without the rigorous musical training demanded in the B.M. curriculum may pursue a B.A. with a concentration in music and/or minor in music.

With a present enrollment of 350 music majors, the School schedules numerous concerts, recitals, and special events throughout each academic year. As performance is the focus of all the degree programs, more than 200 performances are presented each year. In addition to solo recitals and chamber music, the CUA Symphony Orchestra, Chorus, and Jazz Ensemble perform throughout the academic year. These concerts are highlighted by a nationally televised Christmas concert, concerto and vocal competitions, fully staged opera and musical theater productions, and a yearly week-long festival of the arts that includes symposia, films, concerts, and musical theater productions. This year, the School of Music has been invited to participate in the prestigious Prague Spring Festival. Members of the orchestra and chorus will perform Defiant Requiem, a concert drama about the Verdi Requiem at Terezin, 1943–1944, with recollections, historic film, and a full performance of Verdi's score. The production was conceived, written, and will be conducted by Murry Sidlin.

Music alumni and faculty members have won many awards and maintain high professional visibility as performers, music educators, composers, liturgical musicians, and scholars. Among those who have received national and international recognition are Grammy Award winners John Aler (opera) and Robert Shafer (choral conductor), and Emmy Award winners Marilyn Neeley (piano) and Robert Gerle (violin). Graduates of the School of Music have performed on Broadway, off-Broadway, in touring companies and regional theaters; at the Metropolitan Opera, Vienna Opera, and York City Opera; and with virtually every major symphony orchestra in the United States.

Catholic University is housed on a spacious 144-acre campus in the heart of Washington, D.C. The campus provides an impressive combination of collegiate and city life. Student life is culturally dynamic in a city that is famous for museums, monuments, and landmarks, such as Capitol Hill, the Smithsonian Institution, the Library of Congress, the National Zoo, and the John F. Kennedy Center for the Performing Arts. Most attractions are just minutes from campus via Metrorail, a modern subway system that stops adjacent to the campus.

The School of Music performance spaces include the acoustically excellent Ward Recital Hall (120 seats), Hartke Theatre (590 seats), and St. Vincent's Chapel (400 seats). School of Music performances are also held at the Basilica of the National Shrine of the Immaculate Conception on the campus of CUA, at St. Matthew's Cathedral, and at the Concert Hall and the Millennium Stage of the John F. Kennedy Center for the Performing Arts. Music students have also performed in many of the regional theaters in and around Washington.

There are numerous internships available in Washington, D.C. Music students have interned at local television stations, local theaters, the Washington Performing Arts Society, the Washington Opera, and the John F. Kennedy Center for the Performing Arts.

Cedarville University

Cedarville, Ohio

Independent Baptist, coed. Rural campus. Total enrollment: 3,113. Music program established 1887.

Degrees Bachelor of Music in the areas of church music, keyboard pedagogy, composition, performance; Bachelor of Music Education in the areas of choral music education, instrumental music education. Majors and concentrations: brass instruments performance, church music, composition, keyboard pedagogy, music education, piano/organ performance, stringed instrument performance, voice performance, wind and percussion instruments performance. Program accredited by NASM.

Enrollment 123 total; 69 undergraduate, 54 nonprofessional degree.

Music Student Profile 58% females, 42% males, 1% minorities.

Music Faculty 14 undergraduate (full-time), 16 undergraduate (part-time). 71% of full-time faculty have terminal degrees. Graduate students do not teach undergraduate courses. Undergraduate student–faculty ratio: 9:1.

Student Life Student groups/activities include Music Educators National Conference.

Expenses for 2006–2007 Application fee: $30. Comprehensive fee: $22,130 includes full-time tuition ($17,120) and college room and board ($5010). College room only: $2684. Special program-related fees: $75 per semester for lab fee, $200 per semester for practice room fee.

Financial Aid Program-specific awards: 20 music scholarships for those demonstrating musical achievement ($1000–$4000).

Application Procedures Students apply for admission into the professional program by freshman year. Deadline for freshmen and transfers: continuous. Required: essay, high school transcript, college transcript(s) for transfer students, minimum 2.0 high school GPA, 2 letters of recommendation, audition, SAT I or ACT test scores (minimum composite ACT score of 22). Recommended: minimum 3.0 high school GPA, portfolio. Auditions held 4 times and by appointment on campus; recorded music is permissible as a substitute for live auditions (video tape or signed affidavit preferred) and videotaped performances are permissible as a substitute for live auditions if a campus visit is impossible.

Web Site http://www.cedarville.edu

Undergraduate Contact Ms. Pam Miller, Administrative Assistant, Music Department, Cedarville University, 251 North Main Street, Cedarville, Ohio 45314; 937-766-7728, fax: 937-766-7661, e-mail address: millerp@cedarville.edu

Hurley School of Music
Centenary College of Louisiana
Shreveport, Louisiana

Independent United Methodist, coed. Suburban campus. Total enrollment: 1,044. Music program established 1936.

Degrees Bachelor of Music in the areas of performance, sacred music, music theory/composition; Bachelor of Music Education in the areas of vocal music education, instrumental music education. Majors and concentrations: music education, music theory and composition, piano/organ, sacred music, stringed instruments, voice, wind and percussion instruments. Program accredited by NASM.

Enrollment 62 total; 49 undergraduate, 13 nonprofessional degree.

Music Student Profile 61% females, 39% males, 11% minorities, 1% international.

Music Faculty 9 undergraduate (full-time), 17 undergraduate (part-time). 88% of full-time faculty have terminal degrees. Graduate students do not teach undergraduate courses. Undergraduate student–faculty ratio: 11:1.

Student Life Student groups/activities include Sigma Alpha Iota, Music Educators National Conference, Music Teachers National Association.

Expenses for 2006–2007 Application fee: $30. Comprehensive fee: $25,680 includes full-time tuition ($18,900) and college room and board ($6780). College room only: $3310. Special program-related fees: $125 per semester for applied music fee.

Financial Aid Program-specific awards: 50–70 Hurley Foundation Scholarships for incoming freshmen and ensemble participants ($1000–$14,000), 1–4 Mary C. White Awards for program majors ($19,100).

Application Procedures Students admitted directly into the professional program freshman year. Deadline for freshmen: February 15; transfers: continuous. Notification date for freshmen: March 15. Required: essay, high school transcript, college transcript(s) for transfer students, minimum 2.0 high school GPA, 2 letters of recommendation, interview, audition, SAT I or ACT test scores (minimum combined SAT I score of 1000, minimum composite ACT score of 21). Auditions held 4 times on campus; recorded music is permissible as a substitute for live auditions when distance is prohibitive and videotaped performances are permissible as a substitute for live auditions when distance is prohibitive.

Web Site http://www.centenary.edu

Undergraduate Contact Mr. Tim Crowley, Director of Admissions, Centenary College of Louisiana, 2911 Centenary Boulevard, Shreveport, Louisiana 71104; 318-869-5131, fax: 318-869-5026, e-mail address: tcrowley@centenary.edu

Central College
Pella, Iowa

Independent, coed. Small town campus. Total enrollment: 1,635. Music program established 1853.

Degrees Bachelor of Arts in the areas of music, music education. Majors and concentrations: brass instruments performance, composition, instrumental music education, music, percussion, piano, stringed instruments, vocal music education, voice, woodwind instruments. Program accredited by NASM.

Enrollment 35 total; all undergraduate.

Music Student Profile 60% females, 40% males, 3% minorities.

Music Faculty 8 undergraduate (full-time), 11 undergraduate (part-time). 88% of full-time faculty have terminal degrees. Graduate students do not teach undergraduate courses. Undergraduate student–faculty ratio: 5:1.

Student Life Student groups/activities include Mu Gamma Pi.

Expenses for 2006–2007 Application fee: $25. Comprehensive fee: $28,196 includes full-time tuition ($20,972) and college room and board ($7224). College room only: $3542. Special program-related fees: $190 per credit hour for private lessons.

Financial Aid Program-specific awards: music department scholarships for program majors and non-majors ($500–$2000).

Application Procedures Students admitted directly into the professional program freshman year. Required: high school transcript,

Central College (continued)

college transcript(s) for transfer students, SAT I or ACT test scores (minimum combined SAT I score of 900, minimum composite ACT score of 19). Recommended: essay, minimum 3.0 high school GPA, 2 letters of recommendation, interview, audition. Auditions held 3 times on campus; recorded music is permissible as a substitute for live auditions and videotaped performances are permissible as a substitute for live auditions.
Web Site http://www.central.edu
Undergraduate Contact Terri Snyders Crumley, Director of Admission, Central College, 812 University, Box 5100, Pella, Iowa 50219; 641-628-7604, e-mail address: crumleyt@central.edu

The Swinney Conservatory of Music
Central Methodist University
Fayette, Missouri

Independent Methodist, coed. Small town campus. Total enrollment: 781. Music program established 1927.

Central Michigan University
Mount Pleasant, Michigan

State-supported, coed. Small town campus. Total enrollment: 27,221. Music program established 1900.
Degrees Bachelor of Music in the areas of performance, music theory/composition; Bachelor of Music Education. Majors and concentrations: music education, music theory and composition, orchestral instruments, piano/organ, voice. Graduate degrees offered: Master of Music in the areas of music education, performance, composition, conducting, piano pedagogy. Program accredited by NASM.
Enrollment 564 total; 447 undergraduate, 117 graduate.
Music Student Profile 55% females, 45% males, 4% minorities, 1% international.
Music Faculty 34 total (full-time), 7 total (part-time). 76% of full-time faculty have terminal degrees. Graduate students teach a few undergraduate courses. Undergraduate student–faculty ratio: 14:1.
Student Life Student groups/activities include student ensembles, preprofessional student associations, music service fraternity and sororities. Special housing available for music students.
Expenses for 2005–2006 Application fee: $35. State resident tuition: $5868 full-time. Nonresident tuition: $13,632 full-time. Full-time tuition varies according to student level. College room and board: $6376. College room only: $3188. Room and board charges vary according to board plan, housing facility, and location. Special program-related fees: $5 per semester for locker rental, $40–$75 per semester for private lessons.
Financial Aid Program-specific awards: 69 music scholarships for program majors ($1000–$2000).
Application Procedures Students admitted directly into the professional program freshman year. Deadline for freshmen and transfers: February 26. Notification date for freshmen and transfers: April 15. Required: high school transcript, college transcript(s) for transfer students, minimum 2.0 high school GPA, audition, SAT I or ACT test scores. Recommended: minimum 3.0 high school GPA. Auditions held 4 times on campus; recorded music is permissible as a substitute for live auditions for out-of-state applicants and videotaped performances are permissible as a substitute for live auditions for out-of-state applicants.
Web Site http://www.mus.cmich.edu
Graduate Contact Dr. Daniel Steele, Graduate Coordinator, School of Music, Central Michigan University, Room 162, Mount Pleasant, Michigan 48859; 989-774-3281, fax: 989-774-3766, e-mail address: daniel.steele@cmich.edu

Central Missouri State University
Warrensburg, Missouri

State-supported, coed. Small town campus. Total enrollment: 10,604. Music program established 1920.

Degrees Bachelor of Music in the areas of instrumental music, jazz/commercial music, piano pedagogy, music technology; Bachelor of Music Education in the areas of instrumental music education, vocal music education. Majors and concentrations: jazz, music education, music technology, piano pedagogy, piano/organ, stringed instruments, voice, wind and percussion instruments. Graduate degrees offered: Master of Arts in the areas of theory and composition, history and literature, music education, performance, piano pedagogy. Program accredited by NASM.
Enrollment 192 total; 173 undergraduate, 13 graduate, 6 nonprofessional degree.
Music Student Profile 36% females, 64% males, 7% minorities, 1% international.
Music Faculty 22 total (full-time), 1 total (part-time). 91% of full-time faculty have terminal degrees. Graduate students do not teach undergraduate courses. Undergraduate student–faculty ratio: 8:1.
Student Life Student groups/activities include Phi Mu Alpha Sinfonia, Sigma Alpha Iota, Music Educators National Conference. Special housing available for music students.
Expenses for 2006–2007 Application fee: $30. State resident tuition: $5835 full-time. Nonresident tuition: $11,250 full-time. College room and board: $5109. College room only: $3406. Special program-related fees: $35 per course for music technology courses.
Financial Aid Program-specific awards: 10–12 achievement awards for program majors ($300), 30–35 Foundation Awards for program majors and minors ($500–$2000), 150–175 service awards for ensemble performers ($200–$1000).
Application Procedures Students admitted directly into the professional program freshman year. Deadline for freshmen and transfers: continuous. Required: high school transcript, college transcript(s) for transfer students, minimum 2.0 high school GPA, audition, ACT test score only (minimum composite ACT score of 21). Recommended: letter of recommendation. Auditions held at student's convenience on campus; recorded music is permissible as a substitute for live auditions if a campus visit is impossible and videotaped performances are permissible as a substitute for live auditions if a campus visit is impossible.
Web Site http://www.cmsu.edu/music
Undergraduate Contact Mr. Paul Orscheln, Director of Admissions, Central Missouri State University, Ward Edwards 1422, Warrensburg, Missouri 64093; 660-543-4290, fax: 660-543-8517.
Graduate Contact Dr. Franklin Fenley, Graduate Coordinator, Department of Music, Central Missouri State University, Warrensburg, Missouri 64093; 660-543-4974, fax: 660-543-8271, e-mail address: fenley@cmsu1.cmsu.edu

Central State University
Wilberforce, Ohio

State-supported, coed. Rural campus. Total enrollment: 1,623. Music program established 1947.

Central Washington University
Ellensburg, Washington

State-supported, coed. Small town campus. Total enrollment: 10,190. Music program established 1958.

Chapman University
Orange, California

Independent, coed. Suburban campus. Total enrollment: 5,732. Music program established 1974.
Degrees Bachelor of Music in the areas of performance, conducting, composition, music therapy; Bachelor of Music Education. Majors and concentrations: composition, conducting, music education, music therapy, piano/organ, stringed instruments, voice, wind and percussion instruments. Program accredited by NASM.
Enrollment 197 total; 185 undergraduate, 12 nonprofessional degree.

Music Student Profile 60% females, 40% males, 15% minorities, 10% international.

Music Faculty 14 undergraduate (full-time), 36 undergraduate (part-time). 70% of full-time faculty have terminal degrees. Graduate students do not teach undergraduate courses. Undergraduate student–faculty ratio: 4:1.

Student Life Student groups/activities include American Choral Directors Association Student Chapter, American Association of Music Therapy Student Chapter, American String Teachers Association Student Chapter.

Expenses for 2006–2007 Application fee: $55. Comprehensive fee: $41,248 includes full-time tuition ($29,900), mandatory fees ($848), and college room and board ($10,500). Special program-related fees: $125 per unit for private lessons.

Financial Aid Program-specific awards: 75 talent awards for talented students ($10,000).

Application Procedures Students admitted directly into the professional program freshman year. Deadline for freshmen: January 31; transfers: March 15. Required: essay, high school transcript, college transcript(s) for transfer students, letter of recommendation, audition, SAT I or ACT test scores. Recommended: minimum 2.0 high school GPA. Auditions held by appointment on campus; recorded music is permissible as a substitute for live auditions when distance is prohibitive and videotaped performances are permissible as a substitute for live auditions when distance is prohibitive.

Web Site http://www.chapman.edu/music/index.html

Undergraduate Contact Mr. Michael Pelly, Director of Admissions, Chapman University, 1 University Drive, Orange, California 92866; 714-997-6711, fax: 714-997-6713, e-mail address: pelly@chapman.edu

Chicago College of Performing Arts - The Music Conservatory

See Roosevelt University

Christopher Newport University

Newport News, Virginia

State-supported, coed. Suburban campus. Total enrollment: 4,699. Music program established 1984.

Cincinnati Christian University

Cincinnati, Ohio

Independent, coed. Urban campus. Total enrollment: 922.

City College of the City University of New York

New York, New York

State and locally supported, coed. Urban campus. Total enrollment: 12,440. Music program established 1973.

Degrees Bachelor of Fine Arts in the areas of jazz performance, classical performance, music and technology. Majors and concentrations: acoustic recording, classical music, jazz, music, performance, sonic arts. Graduate degrees offered: Master of Arts in the areas of musicology, theory, composition, performance (classical and jazz). Cross-registration with other senior colleges within City University of New York.

Enrollment 230 total; 100 undergraduate, 30 graduate, 100 nonprofessional degree.

Music Student Profile 40% females, 60% males, 70% minorities, 50% international.

Music Faculty 15 total (full-time), 20 total (part-time). 90% of full-time faculty have terminal degrees. Graduate students teach a few undergraduate courses. Undergraduate student–faculty ratio: 8:1.

Student Life Student groups/activities include Friends of Music, gospel choir.

Expenses for 2005–2006 Application fee: $65. State resident tuition: $4080 full-time. Nonresident tuition: $8640 full-time. Full-time tuition varies according to class time and program. Special program-related fees: $25 per course for technology fee.

Financial Aid Program-specific awards: 2 Friar Foundation Awards for BFA applicants passing audition evaluation ($750), 2 Rosalind Joel Scholarships for talented performers ($3000), 1 Ben Jablonsky Scholarship for jazz composers/arrangers ($750).

Application Procedures Students apply for admission into the professional program by sophomore, junior year. Deadline for freshmen and transfers: continuous. Required: high school transcript, college transcript(s) for transfer students, minimum 3.0 high school GPA, audition for performance majors. Recommended: interview, audition. Auditions held twice on campus; recorded music is permissible as a substitute for live auditions when distance is prohibitive and videotaped performances are permissible as a substitute for live auditions when distance is prohibitive.

Web Site http://www.ccny.cuny.edu/music/

Undergraduate Contact Mr. Alan Sabal, Associate Director of Admissions, City College of the City University of New York, Admissions A100B, 138th Street and Convent Avenue, New York, New York 10031; 212-650-6444, fax: 212-650-6417.

Graduate Contact Prof. Shaugn O'Donnell, MA Supervisor, Music Department, City College of the City University of New York, Shepard Hall 72, 160 Convent Avenue, New York, New York 10031; 212-650-7683, fax: 212-650-5428, e-mail address: sodonnell@ccny.cuny.edu

Claire Trevor School of the Arts

See University of California, Irvine

Clarion University of Pennsylvania

Clarion, Pennsylvania

State-supported, coed. Rural campus. Total enrollment: 6,338. Music program established 1965.

Clayton State University

Morrow, Georgia

State-supported, coed. Suburban campus. Total enrollment: 6,152. Music program established 1992.

Degrees Bachelor of Music in the areas of performance, composition, music education. Majors and concentrations: composition, keyboard, stringed instruments, voice, wind and percussion instruments. Cross-registration with all eighteen schools affiliated with The Atlanta Regional Consortium for Higher Education.

Enrollment 58 total; 30 undergraduate, 28 nonprofessional degree.

Music Faculty 7 undergraduate (full-time), 14 undergraduate (part-time). 100% of full-time faculty have terminal degrees. Graduate students do not teach undergraduate courses.

Student Life Student groups/activities include MENC, Mu Phi Epsilon, Society of Composers.

Expenses for 2006–2007 Application fee: $40. State resident tuition: $2802 full-time. Nonresident tuition: $9770 full-time. Mandatory fees: $488 full-time.

Financial Aid Program-specific awards: Spivey Scholarships for program majors.

Application Procedures Students admitted directly into the professional program freshman year. Deadline for freshmen and transfers: July 17. Notification date for freshmen and transfers: continuous. Required: high school transcript, college transcript(s) for transfer students, minimum 2.0 high school GPA, SAT I or ACT test scores (minimum combined SAT I score of 830, minimum composite ACT score of 16). Recommended: audition. Auditions held 3 times and by arrangement on campus; recorded music is permissible as a substitute for live auditions for out-of-state applicants and videotaped performances are permissible as a substitute for live auditions for out-of-state applicants.

Web Site http://www.clayton.edu

Clayton State University (continued)

Undergraduate Contact Dr. Douglas Wheeler, Head, Department of Music, Clayton State University, 5900 North Lee Street, Morrow, Georgia 30260; 770-961-3443, fax: 770-961-3700, e-mail address: douglaswheeler@mail.clayton.edu

Cleveland Institute of Music
Cleveland, Ohio

Independent, coed. Urban campus. Music program established 1920.

Degrees Bachelor of Music in the areas of piano, harpsichord, organ, voice, violin, viola, cello, double bass, harp, classical guitar, flute, oboe, clarinet, bassoon, trumpet, horn, trombone, bass trombone, tuba, percussion, audio recording, composition, music theory, eurhythmics. Majors and concentrations: audio recording technology, classical guitar, composition, eurythmics, harpsichord, piano/organ, stringed instruments, voice, wind and percussion instruments. Graduate degrees offered: Master of Music in the areas of piano, harpsichord, organ, accompanying, voice, violin, viola, cello, double bass, harp, classical guitar, flute, oboe, clarinet, bassoon, trumpet, horn, trombone, bass trombone, tuba, Suzuki violin pedagogy, percussion, composition, orchestral conducting. Doctor of Musical Arts in the areas of piano, organ, accompanying, voice, violin, viola, cello, double bass, harp, classical guitar, flute, oboe, clarinet, bassoon, trombone, bass trombone, tuba, percussion, composition, horn, trumpet, harpsichord. Mandatory cross-registration with Case Western Reserve University. Program accredited by NASM.

Enrollment 417 total; 228 undergraduate, 189 graduate.

Music Student Profile 54% females, 46% males, 13% minorities, 20% international.

Music Faculty 31 total (full-time), 72 total (part-time). 15% of full-time faculty have terminal degrees. Graduate students do not teach undergraduate courses. Undergraduate student–faculty ratio: 7:1.

Student Life Student groups/activities include orchestra, opera, chamber music. Special housing available for music students.

Expenses for 2005–2006 Application fee: $100. Comprehensive fee: $35,596 includes full-time tuition ($25,870), mandatory fees ($1000), and college room and board ($8726). College room only: $5120. Room and board charges vary according to board plan. Special program-related fees: $50 per semester for audio fee, $60 per year for accompanist fee.

Financial Aid Program-specific awards: 215 Cleveland Institute of Music Scholarships for program students ($1000–$20,000), 10 Cleveland Institute of Music Loans for program students ($1000–$2000).

Application Procedures Students admitted directly into the professional program freshman year. Deadline for freshmen and transfers: December 1. Notification date for freshmen and transfers: April 1. Required: essay, high school transcript, college transcript(s) for transfer students, 2 letters of recommendation, audition, SAT I or ACT test scores. Recommended: minimum 3.0 high school GPA, interview. Auditions held several times on campus; recorded music is permissible as a substitute for live auditions with approval from the department and videotaped performances are permissible as a substitute for live auditions with approval from the department.

Web Site http://www.cim.edu

Undergraduate Contact Mr. William Fay, Director of Admission, Cleveland Institute of Music, 11021 East Boulevard, Cleveland, Ohio 44106; 216-795-3107, fax: 216-791-1530, e-mail address: ewf3@po.cwru.edu

More About the Institute

The mission of the Cleveland Institute of Music (CIM) is to provide exceptionally talented students from around the world an outstanding and thoroughly professional education in the art of music performance and related musical disciplines. The Institute embraces the legacy of the past and promotes the continuing evolution of music within a supportive and nurturing environment. The Institute also provides rigorous training in programs for gifted precollege musicians and serves as a resource for the community with training for individuals of all ages and abilities.

A guiding principle at the Institute maintains that a liberal arts education contributes to a broad, humanistic perspective and is a vital component of the undergraduate curriculum. Equally important is the faculty's commitment to incorporating new technologies to complement and enhance the educational program.

The distinguished faculty of the Institute aims to develop the full artistic potential of all its students. Through performance and teaching, the faculty and administration are dedicated to passing along their knowledge and love for this great art and to providing the bridge to an exciting and fulfilling career.

Founded in 1920, the Cleveland Institute of Music maintains its current size of approximately 400 undergraduate and graduate students and 90 full- and part-time faculty members by controlling enrollment through carefully balanced admission policies. In admitting the optimum rather than an unlimited number of students to each performance area, CIM seeks to provide personal, individual attention for each student and to maximize performance opportunities.

The unusually intense performance environment encourages students to develop multifaceted skills that include solo, chamber, orchestral, and operatic literature. This approach leads students to focus on solo expertise as well as to develop the collaborative abilities necessary for small and large ensemble work. The key is access to faculty members and visiting artists in a challenging but supportive atmosphere of private lessons, master classes, repertoire classes, concerts, and recitals.

Orchestral studies are designed to develop and maintain the discipline and skill necessary to make the smoothest possible transition from school to professional life. Regularly scheduled sectional rehearsals and orchestral repertoire classes are conducted by principals of The Cleveland Orchestra. The Institute's two symphony orchestras present approximately twenty concerts during the academic year, including multiple performances of two fully staged operas. These ensembles also provide a vehicle through which student composers may hear and record readings of their works.

The sequence of opera courses is devoted to the principles of theory and practice of the various arts that combine to create an operatic performance. Emphasis is placed on vocal, musical, stylistic, linguistic, and dramatic techniques. Study stresses the application of these elements to role preparation for operas of different historical periods.

CIM is located in University Circle, a cultural, educational, and scientific research center situated approximately 3 miles east of downtown Cleveland. University Circle comprises more than thirty institutions that together constitute one of the largest diversified cultural complexes in the world. Located within easy walking distance of CIM are Case Western Reserve University, where CIM students have access to all facilities and liberal arts course offerings, and Severance Hall, home of The Cleveland Orchestra, the rehearsals of which are open to CIM students by special arrangement. Also easily accessible are numerous other University Circle institutions, such as the Cleveland Museum of Art, Cleveland Institute of Art, Cleveland Play House, Cleveland Museum of Natural History, Western Reserve Historical Society, and Cleveland Botanical Garden.

Program Facilities In February 2005, CIM broke ground for a $40-million expansion project to add practice, teaching, and performance space to its facility. The project will provide two major additions and will include a new state-of-the-art recital hall and new façade at its main entrance. The recital hall will seat 250 people in an acoustically outstanding space for recitals and chamber music. This portion of the project is scheduled for completion in fall 2007. Another addition at the rear of the main building, scheduled for completion one year earlier, will include practice rooms, teaching studios, audio recording and distance learning studios, administrative space, and a new student lounge, complete with outdoor patio.

Cleveland Institute of Music's main building includes a concert hall, classrooms, teaching studios, practice rooms, a library, a eurhythmics studio, an orchestra library, an opera theater workshop and studio, and a music store. Through connection of the entire facility to Case Western Reserve University's fiber-optic computer network, CIM also provides wireless Internet access as well as a Technology Learning Center that enables students to become aware of and accustomed to the ways in which music and technology go hand in hand.

The library contains 51,000 books and scores, 110 periodical subscriptions, and an audiovisual collection of 22,500 items. Through the Institute's relationship with Case, CIM students have access to additional library resources, especially those at the Case Music Department. Case holdings include more than 2,452,731 volumes, 2,524,889 microforms, and 20,768 current serial subscriptions. A shared online system with Case Western Reserve permits the viewing of Case library holdings from online public catalogs in the CIM library. Through CIM's relationship with Case, there is access to OhioLink, a statewide information network.

The residence hall, Cutter House, is adjacent to CIM's main building. In addition to the usual amenities, each room has fiber-optic computer access. Also adjacent to CIM's main building is the Hazel Road Annex, an additional facility for individual practice, chamber music, rehearsal and coaching, master classes, and class recitals.

Faculty The distinguished faculty includes the principals and many section players of The Cleveland Orchestra, with which CIM has a close relationship. All collegiate-level music instruction is conducted by CIM faculty members and not by teaching assistants. Liberal arts, music education, and music history courses are taught by the faculty of Case Western Reserve University.

Cleveland State University
Cleveland, Ohio

State-supported, coed. Urban campus. Total enrollment: 15,722. Music program established 1964.
Degrees Bachelor of Music in the areas of performance, education, composition. Majors and concentrations: composition, guitar, harp, music education, music therapy, piano/organ, stringed instruments, voice, wind and percussion instruments. Graduate degrees offered: Master of Music in the areas of performance, education, composition, history. Program accredited by NASM.
Enrollment 189 total; 111 undergraduate, 64 graduate, 14 nonprofessional degree.
Music Student Profile 56% females, 44% males, 21% minorities, 7% international.
Music Faculty 11 total (full-time), 52 total (part-time). 100% of full-time faculty have terminal degrees. Graduate students do not teach undergraduate courses. Undergraduate student–faculty ratio: 17:1.
Student Life Student groups/activities include Ohio Collegiate Music Educators Association, Mu Phi Epsilon, American Choral Directors Association.
Expenses for 2005–2006 Application fee: $30. State resident tuition: $6792 full-time. Nonresident tuition: $9216 full-time. Full-time tuition varies according to program and student level. College room and board: $6809. College room only: $4091. Room and board charges vary according to board plan and housing facility. Special program-related fees: $150–$248 per 1-2 credit hours for music lessons.
Financial Aid Program-specific awards: 81 music scholarships for program majors ($2100).
Application Procedures Students admitted directly into the professional program freshman year. Deadline for freshmen and transfers: continuous. Notification date for freshmen and transfers: continuous. Required: high school transcript, college transcript(s) for transfer students, interview, audition, portfolio for composition applicants. Recommended: minimum 2.0 high school GPA, SAT I test score only, ACT test score only. Auditions held by appointment on campus; recorded music is permissible as a substitute for live auditions when distance is prohibitive and

videotaped performances are permissible as a substitute for live auditions when distance is prohibitive. Portfolio reviews held as needed on campus.
Web Site http://www.csuohio.edu/music
Undergraduate Contact Rachael Scalf, School Recruiter, Music Department, Cleveland State University, 2121 Euclid Avenue, Cleveland, Ohio 44115; 216-687-5039, fax: 216-687-9279, e-mail address: r.scalf@csuohio.edu
Graduate Contact Dr. Birch P. Browning, Assistant Professor, Music Department, Cleveland State University, 2121 Euclid Avenue, Cleveland, Ohio 44115; 216-687-3768, fax: 216-687-9279, e-mail address: b.browning@csuohio.edu

Coe College
Cedar Rapids, Iowa

Independent, coed. Urban campus. Total enrollment: 1,355. Music program established 1920.
Degrees Bachelor of Music in the areas of performance, music education, music theory/composition; Bachelor of Music Education in the area of vocal and instrumental. Majors and concentrations: classical music, guitar, harpsichord, music, music education, music theory and composition, piano/organ, stringed instruments, voice, wind and percussion instruments. Cross-registration with Mount Mercy College. Program accredited by NASM.
Enrollment 74 total; 52 undergraduate, 22 nonprofessional degree.
Music Student Profile 57% females, 43% males, 7% minorities, 1% international.
Music Faculty 5 undergraduate (full-time), 28 undergraduate (part-time). 80% of full-time faculty have terminal degrees. Graduate students do not teach undergraduate courses. Undergraduate student–faculty ratio: 15:1.
Student Life Student groups/activities include Pi Kappa Lambda, Mu Phi Epsilon, Phi Mu Alpha.
Expenses for 2006–2007 Application fee: $30. Comprehensive fee: $31,670 includes full-time tuition ($24,830), mandatory fees ($290), and college room and board ($6550). College room only: $2990. Special program-related fees: $150–$400 per term for private lessons.
Financial Aid Program-specific awards: Bachelor of Music Full-Tuition Scholarships for program majors ($23,615), 20–30 music scholarships for program majors ($4500).
Application Procedures Students apply for admission into the professional program by sophomore year. Deadline for freshmen and transfers: March 1. Notification date for freshmen and transfers: March 15. Required: essay, high school transcript, college transcript(s) for transfer students, 2 letters of recommendation, SAT I or ACT test scores. Recommended: minimum 3.0 high school GPA, interview, audition. Auditions held twice on campus; recorded music is permissible as a substitute for live auditions when distance is prohibitive and videotaped performances are permissible as a substitute for live auditions when distance is prohibitive.
Web Site http://www.coe.edu
Undergraduate Contact Ms. Sharon Kay Stang, Recruiting Coordinator, Music Department, Coe College, 1220 1st Avenue, NE, Cedar Rapids, Iowa 52402; 319-399-8640, fax: 319-399-8209, e-mail address: sstang@coe.edu

Coker College
Hartsville, South Carolina

Independent, coed. Small town campus. Total enrollment: 551. Music program established 1908.
Degrees Bachelor of Music Education. Majors and concentrations: music education. Program accredited by NASM.
Enrollment 7 total; all undergraduate.
Music Student Profile 60% females, 40% males, 26% minorities, 3% international.
Music Faculty 3 undergraduate (full-time). 67% of full-time faculty have terminal degrees. Graduate students do not teach undergraduate courses. Undergraduate student–faculty ratio: 2:1.

Coker College (continued)

Student Life Student groups/activities include Music Educators National Conference, National Association of Teachers of Singing, Music Teachers National Association.

Expenses for 2006–2007 Application fee: $15. Comprehensive fee: $23,728 includes full-time tuition ($17,472), mandatory fees ($480), and college room and board ($5776). College room only: $2740. Special program-related fees: $15 per hour for accompanist fee (vocal only).

Financial Aid Program-specific awards: 5–10 Wilds Music Scholarships for music majors ($1000–$3000), 2 Goodson Music Scholarships for musically talented performers ($2000), 1–2 Anna White Hill Scholarships for non-music major/chorale singers ($250), 1–2 Bethea Scholarships for those demonstrating need and living in Dillon/Marion area ($500–$2000), 1 Brittain Music Scholarship for program students (piano preferred) ($3000), 1 Cottingham Music Scholarship for program students (piano preferred) ($1000), 1 Edwards Music Scholarship for program students with B average ($500), 1 McLeod Music Scholarship for program students with B average ($500).

Application Procedures Students admitted directly into the professional program freshman year. Deadline for freshmen and transfers: continuous. Required: high school transcript, college transcript(s) for transfer students, letter of recommendation, audition, SAT I or ACT test scores (minimum combined SAT I score of 830, minimum composite ACT score of 17). Recommended: minimum 3.0 high school GPA, interview, minimum 2.5 high school GPA. Auditions held by arrangement on campus; recorded music is permissible as a substitute for live auditions when distance is prohibitive and videotaped performances are permissible as a substitute for live auditions when distance is prohibitive. Portfolio reviews held by appointment on campus.

Web Site http://www.coker.edu

Undergraduate Contact Shelli Wilson, Admissions Counselor, Coker College, 300 East College Avenue, Hartsville, South Carolina 29550; 843-383-8050, fax: 843-383-8056, e-mail address: swilson@coker.edu

The Colburn School Conservatory of Music

Los Angeles, California

Independent, coed. Urban campus. Music program established 2003.

Degrees Bachelor of Music. Majors and concentrations: performance. Program accredited by NASM.

Enrollment 33 total; 17 undergraduate, 16 graduate.

Music Student Profile 61% females, 39% males, 3% minorities, 42% international.

Music Faculty 4 total (full-time), 9 total (part-time). Graduate students do not teach undergraduate courses.

Student Life Special housing available for music students.

Expenses for 2005–2006 Application fee: 100. Tuition: $0 full-time. Mandatory fees: $1200 full-time.

Financial Aid Program-specific awards available.

Application Procedures Students admitted directly into the professional program freshman year. Deadline for freshmen and transfers: January 15. Notification date for freshmen and transfers: May 1. Required: essay, high school transcript, college transcript(s) for transfer students, 2 letters of recommendation, interview, audition, minimum TOEFL score of 500 for international students. Recommended: SAT I or ACT test scores. Auditions held once on campus.

Web Site http://www.colburnschool.edu

Undergraduate Contact Ms. Kathleen Tesar, Director of Admissions and Student Affairs, The Colburn School Conservatory of Music, 200 South Grand Avenue, Los Angeles, California 90012; 213-621-2200 ext. 270, fax: 213-621-2110, e-mail address: ktesar@colburnschool.edu

The College of New Jersey

Ewing, New Jersey

State-supported, coed. Suburban campus. Total enrollment: 6,768. Music program established 1916.

Degrees Bachelor of Music in the areas of performance, music education. Majors and concentrations: accordion, music education, piano, stringed instruments, voice, wind and percussion instruments. Program accredited by NASM, NCATE.

Enrollment 167 total; all undergraduate.

Music Student Profile 61% females, 39% males, 7% minorities.

Music Faculty 12 undergraduate (full-time), 34 undergraduate (part-time). 100% of full-time faculty have terminal degrees. Graduate students do not teach undergraduate courses. Undergraduate student–faculty ratio: 5:1.

Student Life Student groups/activities include Music Educators National Conference, American String Teachers Association, Pi Kappa Lambda.

Expenses for 2005–2006 Application fee: $50. State resident tuition: $7051 full-time. Nonresident tuition: $12,314 full-time. Mandatory fees: $2656 full-time. College room and board: $8458. College room only: $6090. Room and board charges vary according to board plan.

Financial Aid Program-specific awards: 5–10 talent scholarships for those demonstrating talent ($750–$1000), 1 Hy Frank Music Scholarship for music education students (non voice/keyboard) ($1500), 1 Thomas H. Kean Scholarship for junior and senior New Jersey residents ($2500), 1 Laurenti Family Art Fund for Mercer County resident music majors ($1000), 1 Barbara Meyers Pelson Fund for music education majors ($2600), 1 Peter Nicholas Crocker Fund for sophomore, or junior music majors ($1000).

Application Procedures Students admitted directly into the professional program freshman year. Deadline for freshmen and transfers: February 1. Notification date for freshmen: April 1; transfers: April 15. Required: essay, high school transcript, college transcript(s) for transfer students, minimum 3.0 high school GPA, 2 letters of recommendation, interview, audition, SAT I or ACT test scores (minimum combined SAT I score of 1100). Auditions held 5 times on campus.

Web Site http://www.tcnj.edu/~music

Undergraduate Contact Dr. Suzanne L. Hickman, Chair, Department of Music, The College of New Jersey, PO Box 7718, Ewing, New Jersey 08628-0718; 609-771-2551, fax: 609-637-5182, e-mail address: hickman@tcnj.edu

College of Santa Fe

Santa Fe, New Mexico

Independent, coed. Suburban campus. Total enrollment: 1,661. Music program established 1992.

Degrees Bachelor of Arts. Majors and concentrations: contemporary music.

Enrollment 47 total; all undergraduate.

Music Student Profile 19% females, 81% males, 17% minorities, 2% international.

Music Faculty 3 undergraduate (full-time), 22 undergraduate (part-time). 86% of full-time faculty have terminal degrees. Graduate students do not teach undergraduate courses. Undergraduate student–faculty ratio: 8:1.

Expenses for 2005–2006 Application fee: $35. Comprehensive fee: $28,978 includes full-time tuition ($21,530), mandatory fees ($746), and college room and board ($6702). College room only: $3204. Room and board charges vary according to board plan and housing facility. Special program-related fees: $20–$125 per course for music workshops, $240 per semester hour for private lessons.

Financial Aid Program-specific awards available.

Application Procedures Students admitted directly into the professional program freshman year. Deadline for freshmen and transfers: continuous. Required: essay, high school transcript, college transcript(s) for transfer students, minimum 2.0 high school GPA, 2 letters of recommendation, interview, SAT I or ACT test scores. Recommended: minimum 3.0 high school GPA, audition, campus visit. Auditions held as needed on campus; recorded music is permissible as a substitute for live auditions

with approval from the department and videotaped performances are permissible as a substitute for live auditions with approval from the department.
Web Site http://www.csf.edu
Undergraduate Contact Mr. Jeff Miller, Dean of Enrollment, Admissions Office, College of Santa Fe, 1600 Saint Michael's Drive, Santa Fe, New Mexico 87505; 505-473-6133, fax: 505-473-6219, e-mail address: admissions@csf.edu

The College of Wooster
Wooster, Ohio

Independent, coed. Small town campus. Total enrollment: 1,846. Music program established 1872.
Degrees Bachelor of Music in the areas of performance, music theory/composition, music history/literature, composition; Bachelor of Music Education in the areas of public school teaching, music therapy. Majors and concentrations: composition, music education, music history and literature, music therapy, piano/organ, stringed instruments, voice, wind and percussion instruments. Mandatory cross-registration with Baldwin-Wallace College (music therapy courses only). Program accredited by NASM, AMTA.
Enrollment 49 total; 43 undergraduate, 6 nonprofessional degree.
Music Student Profile 61% females, 39% males, 2% minorities.
Music Faculty 9 undergraduate (full-time), 17 undergraduate (part-time). 67% of full-time faculty have terminal degrees. Graduate students do not teach undergraduate courses. Undergraduate student–faculty ratio: 5:1.
Student Life Student groups/activities include Student Music Association.
Expenses for 2005–2006 Application fee: $40. Comprehensive fee: $35,290 includes full-time tuition ($28,230) and college room and board ($7060). College room only: $3210. Full-time tuition varies according to course load and reciprocity agreements. Special program-related fees: $335 per semester for music lessons in secondary instrument only.
Financial Aid Program-specific awards: 8–15 music performance scholarships for talented musicians ($2000–$8000).
Application Procedures Students admitted directly into the professional program freshman year. Deadline for freshmen: February 15; transfers: June 1. Notification date for freshmen: March 25. Required: essay, high school transcript, college transcript(s) for transfer students, 2 letters of recommendation, SAT I or ACT test scores. Recommended: minimum 2.0 high school GPA, interview.
Web Site http://www.wooster.edu/music
Undergraduate Contact Dean of Admissions, The College of Wooster, 1101 North Bever Street, Wooster, Ohio 44691; 800-877-9905.

Colorado Christian University
Lakewood, Colorado

Independent interdenominational, coed. Suburban campus. Total enrollment: 2,142. Music program established 1914.
Degrees Bachelor of Music in the areas of music ministry, choral music education, instrumental music education, general music education. Majors and concentrations: classical music, contemporary Christian music, jazz, music, music education, piano/organ, sound recording technology, stringed instruments, voice, wind and percussion instruments. Program accredited by NASM.
Enrollment 65 total; 35 undergraduate, 30 nonprofessional degree.
Music Student Profile 55% females, 45% males, 2% minorities, 2% international.
Music Faculty 5 undergraduate (full-time), 20 undergraduate (part-time). 40% of full-time faculty have terminal degrees. Graduate students do not teach undergraduate courses. Undergraduate student–faculty ratio: 8:1.
Student Life Student groups/activities include Music Ministry in local churches, music theater productions, contemporary Christian music ensembles/chapel teams.
Expenses for 2005–2006 Application fee: $50. Comprehensive fee: $23,422 includes full-time tuition ($16,590), mandatory fees ($150), and college room and board ($6682). College room only:

$3930. Special program-related fees: $25 per semester for instrument rentals, $50 per semester for ensemble fee, $100 per semester for instrumental accompanying fee, $100 per semester for vocal accompanying fee.
Financial Aid Program-specific awards: 51 music scholarships for program students ($1500), 5 ensemble scholarships for program students ($200).
Application Procedures Students apply for admission into the professional program by sophomore year. Deadline for freshmen and transfers: continuous. Notification date for freshmen and transfers: continuous. Required: essay, high school transcript, college transcript(s) for transfer students, minimum 2.0 high school GPA, 3 letters of recommendation, audition, SAT I or ACT test scores. Recommended: minimum 3.0 high school GPA, interview, video. Auditions held 3 times on campus; videotaped performances are permissible as a substitute for live auditions if a campus visit is impossible.
Web Site http://www.ccu.edu
Undergraduate Contact Mr. Mike Moroney, Director of Admissions, Colorado Christian University, 8787 West Alameda Avenue, Lakewood, Colorado 80226; 800-44-FAITH, fax: 303-963-3201, e-mail address: mmoroney@ccu.edu

Colorado State University
Fort Collins, Colorado

State-supported, coed. Urban campus. Total enrollment: 27,133. Music program established 1937.
Degrees Bachelor of Music in the areas of music therapy, music education, performance. Majors and concentrations: composition, music, music education, music therapy, piano pedagogy, piano/organ, string pedagogy, stringed instruments, voice, wind and percussion instruments. Graduate degrees offered: Master of Music in the areas of conducting, music therapy, music education, performance. Program accredited by NASM.
Enrollment 307 total; 240 undergraduate, 67 graduate.
Music Student Profile 57% females, 43% males, 21% minorities, 5% international.
Music Faculty 20 total (full-time), 20 total (part-time). 95% of full-time faculty have terminal degrees. Graduate students teach a few undergraduate courses. Undergraduate student–faculty ratio: 12:1.
Student Life Student groups/activities include Music Therapy Student Association, Music Educators National Conference Student Chapter, Phi Mu Alpha Sinfonia. Special housing available for music students.
Expenses for 2005–2006 Application fee: $50. State resident tuition: $3381 full-time. Nonresident tuition: $14,343 full-time. Mandatory fees: $1181 full-time. College room and board: $6316. College room only: $2852. Room and board charges vary according to board plan and housing facility. Special program-related fees: $20 per semester for locker fee, $20 per semester for practice room fee, $25 per semester for instrument fee, $100 per semester for accompanists fee.
Financial Aid Program-specific awards: 1 Walter Charles Scholarship for cello majors ($1000), 1 Wendel Diebel Scholarship for pianists ($1500), 15 Sallee Performance Awards for program majors ($1000–$2500), 122 Creative and Performing Arts Awards for program majors ($1500–$3500), 2 David Knight Awards for guitar and jazz students ($1000).
Application Procedures Students admitted directly into the professional program freshman year. Deadline for freshmen and transfers: July 1. Required: essay, high school transcript, college transcript(s) for transfer students, audition, SAT I or ACT test scores. Recommended: minimum 3.0 high school GPA, 2 letters of recommendation. Auditions held 6 times on campus; recorded music is permissible as a substitute for live auditions when distance is prohibitive or scheduling is difficult and videotaped performances are permissible as a substitute for live auditions when distance is prohibitive or scheduling is difficult.
Web Site http://www.colostate.edu/Depts/Music/
Undergraduate Contact Dr. William Davis, Assistant Chair, Department of Music, Theatre, and Dance, Colorado State University, Fort Collins, Colorado 80523-1778; 970-491-5888, fax: 970-491-7541, e-mail address: mtdinfo@colostate.edu

Colorado State University (continued)

Graduate Contact Dr. William B. Davis, Director of Graduate Studies, School of the Arts, Colorado State University, Fort Collins, Colorado 80523-1778; 970-491-7384, fax: 970-491-7541, e-mail address: mtdinfo@colostate.edu

Columbia College
Columbia, South Carolina

Independent United Methodist, Suburban campus. Total enrollment: 1,493. Music program established 1854.

Columbia College Chicago
Chicago, Illinois

Independent, coed. Urban campus. Total enrollment: 10,842. Music program established 1970.
Degrees Bachelor of Arts in the area of music; Bachelor of Music in the area of music. Majors and concentrations: composition, directing, instrumental jazz, instrumental performance, jazz composition, jazz voice, voice performance.
Enrollment 278 total; all undergraduate.
Music Student Profile 32% females, 68% males, 33% minorities, 4% international.
Music Faculty 13 total (full-time), 16 total (part-time). 17% of full-time faculty have terminal degrees. Graduate students do not teach undergraduate courses. Undergraduate student–faculty ratio: 10:1.
Student Life Student groups/activities include Columbia Organization of Rap and Hip Hop Entertainment, Columbia Urban Music Association, Composer's Association Dedicated to the Reinvention of Expression.
Expenses for 2006–2007 Application fee: $35. Comprehensive fee: $26,553 includes full-time tuition ($16,328), mandatory fees ($460), and college room and board ($9765). College room only: $8265. Special program-related fees: $15–$120 per course for class fee.
Financial Aid Program-specific awards: 5 jazz studies scholarships ($12,000).
Application Procedures Students admitted directly into the professional program freshman year. Deadline for freshmen and transfers: continuous. Notification date for freshmen and transfers: continuous. Required: essay, high school transcript, college transcript(s) for transfer students, letter of recommendation, students with less than a 2.0 GPA may be required to see an admissions counselor for a personal interview and may be required to attend an intensive remediation program, audition for transfer students. Recommended: minimum 2.0 high school GPA, interview, SAT I or ACT test scores. Auditions held on campus.
Web Site http://www.colum.edu
Undergraduate Contact Mr. Murphy Monroe, Director, Office of Admissions, Columbia College Chicago, 600 South Michigan Avenue, Chicago, Illinois 60605; 312-344-7133, fax: 312-344-8024, e-mail address: admissions@colum.edu

More About the College

Columbia College is the largest and most diverse private undergraduate and graduate arts, media, and communications college in the nation. Located in downtown Chicago, Columbia sits at the heart of the Midwest's arts and communications industries. Columbia's faculty and student body comprise a widely diverse mix of cultures and backgrounds, creating a stimulating environment ideally suited to the pursuit of creative innovation. Intimate class settings (class sizes average only 16 students) facilitate personal attention and practical mentoring with a faculty of working professionals. An aggressive, wide-reaching internship program offers students the opportunity to gain on-site education in their areas of interest.

Columbia places a strong emphasis on each student's development of a professional body of work or portfolio in all disciplines across the college. Columbia's Portfolio Center is dedicated to helping graduating students present their body of work in the most professional way—the exact way employers want to see it. Faculty members work closely with students to help them refine and select appropriate pieces and samples for inclusion in their final portfolio.

Columbia College Chicago's music program combines a solid liberal arts education with a curriculum that emphasizes musicianship, professionalism, self-expression, and originality taught by an award-winning faculty of professional working musicians.

By virtue of living in Chicago, a world-class city that puts a high premium on the arts, students at Columbia are continually challenged to master and expand their artistic goals. Columbia takes an interdisciplinary approach to arts education, which means that music students interact with virtually every department on campus—Film/Video, Audio Arts and Acoustics, Theater, Arts Entertainment and Media Management, Television, Dance, and more—while learning their craft. They also have access to the internationally respected Center for Black Music Research.

The Music Department offers the Bachelor of Arts (B.A.) and the Bachelor of Music (B.M.) degrees in music composition, a B.A. in instrumental performance, a B.A. in jazz studies, a B.A. in vocal performance, and a Master of Fine Arts (M.F.A.) degree in music composition for the screen.

The Music Composition program of Columbia College Chicago combines technical training with a practical approach. Techniques learned are immediately applied in assignments that are critiqued in class. Every course in the composition program culminates in a performance of student work by a professional ensemble. The composition curriculum is designed to provide students from diverse composition backgrounds the skills necessary to compose in a variety of genres and idioms.

Instrumental performance studies emphasize professional training with a foundation in liberal arts and sciences. Practical procedures, such as working on stage, solo techniques, and ensemble techniques are emphasized. Qualified students are encouraged to audition for performances in Chicago's professional music community.

The Jazz Studies program allows for the comprehensive study of jazz from academic and performance perspectives. It offers a strong foundation in improvisation, jazz history, theory, composition and arranging, and ensemble performance. The Jazz Studies program includes instrumental performance and vocal performance. The program focuses on three areas: individual achievement fostered by private lessons, with classroom instruction by accomplished jazz musicians; performance with chamber jazz or small combos; and performance with larger jazz ensembles and orchestras.

Vocal performance studies emphasize professional training with a foundation in liberal arts and sciences. Practical procedures, such as working on stage, solo techniques, and ensemble techniques are emphasized. Qualified students are encouraged to audition for performances in Chicago's professional music community.

The M.F.A. in music composition for the screen program offers not only one of the nation's few advanced degrees in music scoring for film, television, and other visual media but a genuine point of entry to this highly competitive field. In an industry whose key figures are increasingly culled from postgraduate ranks, composers must be expected to have undergone the same kind of rigorous training as the directors, writers, and actors with whom they will collaborate. An interdisciplinary curriculum drawing upon four academic departments (Music, Film/Video, Audio Arts and Acoustics, and Television) provides instruction and mentoring at the highest professional level, and project-based interaction with students in other areas of the dramatic arts encourages the cooperative spirit that is the hallmark of great screen composers. The final semester in Los Angeles offers students a real-world experience in the creative, technical, and business areas of the craft by way of their thesis scores and direct exposure to professionals through industry internships.

Program Facilities The Concert Hall of the Music Center is an intimate 148-seat venue that provides the perfect setting for students to experience the art of music performance up close. Concert Hall workshops and open rehearsals give students the opportunity to observe preperformance preparation and to connect with and learn from accomplished artists. Recent visiting artists include Jon Faddis, Kurt Elling, Joe Lovano, Lennie Niehaus, Bill Dobbins, George Crumb, Bernard Rands, and Mario Davidovsky. The Concert Hall is equipped with professional sound and video recording capabilities, and each performance is videotaped. Students can order VHS or DVD copies of their performances as they begin compiling their portfolios.

The Music Department's Computer Music Studios and Music Technology and Teaching Lab contain eight fully operational MIDI workstations and sixteen Yamaha Clavinova Digital pianos with headphones and offer state-of-the-art equipment for digital sound editing and film music production. Equipment operates on Macintosh computers with ZIF G4 processors and Roland SC-D70 tone generators, and stations in one of the studios have extensive analog/digital audio recording capabilities using ProTools for MIDI and audio sequencing. These stations also have Digidesign SampleCell sampling cards (built into the computers) or software-based SampleCell and Mackie 1280 mixers or Yamaha 01V digital mixing panels, with built-in digital effect processors.

Faculty, Resident Artists, and Alumni The Music Department's award-winning faculty of working professional artists brings a diversity of musical experience, wisdom, and innovative approaches to the program's hands-on, minds-on curriculum. Music students become skilled artists as they learn theory from the sound designer for Steppenwolf Theater, take private lessons with artists who have toured with Ramsey Lewis and Ray Charles, or attend workshops with Jon Faddis, the Artistic Director of the Chicago Jazz Ensemble, in residence at Columbia College Chicago.

Student Performance Opportunities The Concert Hall of the Music Center presents more than 100 student, faculty, and professional performances and workshops each year.

Special Programs The Semester in Los Angeles is a 12-credit, five-week intensive course in scoring, producing, recording, and mixing music for films. Participants visit film studios and work in an on-site sound stage. In addition, their music compositions are performed and recorded by L. A. musicians at one of the best and most advanced recording studios in the country. As part of their studies, students produce a demo of their final music mix synchronized to video, with an accompanying promotional brochure based on industry standards.

Columbia Union College
Takoma Park, Maryland

Independent Seventh-day Adventist, coed. Suburban campus. Total enrollment: 1,047.

Schwob School of Music
Columbus State University
Columbus, Georgia

State-supported, coed. Suburban campus. Total enrollment: 7,475. Music program established 1969.
Degrees Bachelor of Music in the areas of performance, piano pedagogy, music education. Majors and concentrations: guitar, music education, piano pedagogy, piano/organ, stringed instruments, voice, wind and percussion instruments. Graduate degrees offered: Master of Music in the area of music education. Program accredited by NASM, NCATE.
Enrollment 192 total; 156 undergraduate, 7 graduate, 29 nonprofessional degree.

Music Student Profile 54% females, 46% males, 21% minorities, 6% international.
Music Faculty 20 total (full-time), 14 total (part-time). 60% of full-time faculty have terminal degrees. Graduate students do not teach undergraduate courses. Undergraduate student–faculty ratio: 5:1.
Student Life Student groups/activities include Music Educators National Conference Student Chapter, professional music societies, Phi Mu Alpha Sinfonia.
Expenses for 2005–2006 Application fee: $25. State resident tuition: $2438 full-time. Nonresident tuition: $9754 full-time. Mandatory fees: $506 full-time. College room and board: $5720. College room only: $3510. Room and board charges vary according to board plan and location. Special program-related fees: $82 per semester for lessons.
Financial Aid Program-specific awards: 120 Patrons of Music Awards ($2000).
Application Procedures Students apply for admission into the professional program by sophomore year. Deadline for freshmen and transfers: July 30. Notification date for freshmen and transfers: July 30. Required: high school transcript, college transcript(s) for transfer students, interview, audition, SAT I or ACT test scores (minimum combined SAT I score of 840), college preparatory curriculum. Recommended: minimum 3.0 high school GPA, 2 letters of recommendation. Auditions held 3 times and by appointment on campus; recorded music is permissible as a substitute for live auditions for out-of-state applicants and videotaped performances are permissible as a substitute for live auditions for out-of-state applicants.
Web Site http://music.colstate.edu
Undergraduate Contact Ms. Diane E. Andrae, Admissions Secretary, Schwob School of Music, Columbus State University, 4225 University Avenue, Columbus, Georgia 31907-5645; 706-649-7224, fax: 706-649-7369, e-mail address: andrae_diane@colstate.edu
Graduate Contact Dr. Deborah Jacobs, Graduate Studies Coordinator, Schwob School of Music, Columbus State University, 4225 University Avenue, Columbus, Georgia 31907-5645; 706-649-7243, fax: 706-649-7369, e-mail address: jacobs_deborah@colstate.edu

Concordia College
Moorhead, Minnesota

Independent, coed. Suburban campus. Total enrollment: 2,764. Music program established 1932.
Degrees Bachelor of Music in the areas of music education, performance, music theory. Majors and concentrations: composition, music education, music theory, piano/organ, stringed instruments, voice, wind and percussion instruments. Cross-registration with Minnesota State University Moorhead, North Dakota State University. Program accredited by NASM.
Enrollment 185 total; all undergraduate.
Music Student Profile 62% females, 38% males, 2% minorities, 2% international.
Music Faculty 31 undergraduate (full-time), 12 undergraduate (part-time). 50% of full-time faculty have terminal degrees. Graduate students do not teach undergraduate courses. Undergraduate student–faculty ratio: 5:1.
Student Life Student groups/activities include Music Educators National Conference Student Chapter, American Choral Directors Association Student Chapter.
Expenses for 2006–2007 Application fee: $20. Comprehensive fee: $26,070 includes full-time tuition ($20,980) and college room and board ($5090). College room only: $2460. Room and board charges vary according to board plan and housing facility. Special program-related fees: $50 for applied music fees use of instruments, practice rooms.
Financial Aid Program-specific awards: 40 music performance scholarships for freshmen ($10,000).
Application Procedures Students apply for admission into the professional program by freshman year. Deadline for freshmen and transfers: continuous. Notification date for freshmen and transfers: September 5. Required: high school transcript, minimum 2.0 high school GPA, audition, SAT I or ACT test scores, proficiency exams for transfer students. Auditions held 4-6 times

Concordia College (continued)

on campus and off campus in Minneapolis, MN; recorded music is permissible as a substitute for live auditions when distance is prohibitive and videotaped performances are permissible as a substitute for live auditions when distance is prohibitive.
Web Site http://www1.cord.edu/dept/music/frontpage.html
Undergraduate Contact Mr. Omar Correa, Vice President of Admissions, Concordia College, 901 8th Street South, Moorhead, Minnesota 56562; 218-299-3004.

Concordia College
Bronxville, New York

Independent Lutheran, coed. Suburban campus. Total enrollment: 649. Music program established 1975.

Concordia University
Montreal, Quebec, Canada

Province-supported, coed. Urban campus. Total enrollment: 31,042. Music program established 1975.
Degrees Bachelor of Fine Arts in the areas of jazz studies, music performance studies, music theory/composition, integrative music studies, electroacoustic studies. Majors and concentrations: electroacoustic studies, integrative music studies, jazz studies, music performance, music theory and composition. Cross-registration with any university in Quebec.
Enrollment 90 total; all undergraduate.
Music Student Profile 4% international.
Music Faculty 10 total (full-time), 53 total (part-time). Graduate students teach a few undergraduate courses. Undergraduate student–faculty ratio: 5:1.
Student Life Student groups/activities include jazz ensembles, chamber ensembles, choir.
Expenses for 2005–2006 Application fee: $50 Canadian dollars. Tuition, fee, and room and board charges are reported in Canadian dollars. Province resident tuition: $1668 full-time. Canadian resident tuition: $4651 full-time. Mandatory fees: $979 full-time. Full-time tuition and fees vary according to program. College room and board: $6905. Room and board charges vary according to housing facility. International student tuition: $11,238 full-time. Special program-related fees: $190 per 3 credits for private studies.
Financial Aid Program-specific awards: Concordia University Entrance Scholarships for Canadian students ($2000), 1 Robert D. Memorial Scholarship for full-time third year students ($585), 7 Dr. Oscar Peterson Jazz Scholarships for full-time students ($1000).
Application Procedures Students admitted directly into the professional program freshman year. Deadline for freshmen and transfers: March 1. Notification date for freshmen and transfers: June 15. Required: high school transcript, college transcript(s) for transfer students, interview, audition, portfolio, portfolio for electroacoustic studies. Auditions held 3 times in April, May, and June on campus; recorded music is permissible as a substitute for live auditions if a campus visit is impossible. Portfolio reviews held once on campus.
Web Site http://music.concordia.ca
Undergraduate Contact Ms. Jolanta Manowska, Communications Assistant, Office of Student Recruitment, Concordia University, 1455 de Maisonneuve Boulevard West, FB 801, Montreal, Quebec H3G 1M8, Canada; 514-848-2424 ext. 4772, fax: 514-848-2827.

Conservatory of Music of Puerto Rico
San Juan, Puerto Rico

Commonwealth-supported, coed. Urban campus. Music program established 1959.
Degrees Bachelor of Music. Majors and concentrations: composition, jazz, music education, performance. Cross-registration with Sacred Heart University. Program accredited by NASM.
Enrollment 298 total; all undergraduate.

Music Student Profile 30% females, 70% males, 100% minorities, 5% international.
Music Faculty 42 undergraduate (full-time), 32 undergraduate (part-time). Graduate students do not teach undergraduate courses.
Student Life Student groups/activities include community outreach activities/concerts, recruitment visits, institutional committees.
Expenses for 2005–2006 Special program-related fees: $35 per course for accompanist fee.
Financial Aid Program-specific awards: 9 Angel Matas Foundation Grants for undergraduate students ($436), 60 FSEM for undergraduate students ($166), 64 FFEL for undergraduate students ($3984), 19 Programa de becas for undergraduate students ($338), 132 Programa Ayoda Suplementaria for undergraduate students ($263), 4 Banco Popular Foundation Grants for undergraduate students ($490).
Application Procedures Students admitted directly into the professional program freshman year. Deadline for freshmen and transfers: April 15. Required: high school transcript, college transcript(s) for transfer students, minimum 2.0 high school GPA, letter of recommendation, audition, SAT I or ACT test scores, birth certificate, vaccination certificate, essay and interview for music education applicants. Recommended: interview. Auditions held once on campus; videotaped performances are permissible as a substitute for live auditions for out-of-state students.
Web Site http://www.cmpr.edu
Undergraduate Contact Eutimia Santiago, Director of Admission, Student's Affair Office, Conservatory of Music of Puerto Rico, 350 Rafael Lamar Street, Corner FD Roosevelt, San Juan, Puerto Rico 00918-2199; 787-751-0160 ext. 275, fax: 787-758-8268, e-mail address: mrajaballey@cmpr.gobierno.pr
Graduate Contact Eutimia Santiago, Director of Admission, Student's Affair Office, Conservatory of Music of Puerto Rico, 350 Rafael Lamor Street, San Juan, Puerto Rico 00918-2199; 787-751-0160 ext. 275, fax: 787-758-8268.

The Carroll McDaniel Petrie School of Music
Converse College
Spartanburg, South Carolina

Independent, Total enrollment: 2,176. Music program established 1889.
Degrees Bachelor of Music in the areas of performance (vocal, instrumental), music theory, composition, music history, music education, piano pedagogy. Majors and concentrations: music education, music history, music theory and composition, music therapy, piano pedagogy, piano/organ, stringed instruments, voice, wind and percussion instruments. Graduate degrees offered: Master of Music in the areas of performance (vocal, instrumental), piano pedagogy, music education. Cross-registration with Wofford College. Program accredited by NASM.
Enrollment 114 total; 79 undergraduate, 17 graduate, 18 nonprofessional degree.
Music Student Profile 96% females, 4% males, 12% minorities, 4% international.
Music Faculty 18 total (full-time), 11 total (part-time). 85% of full-time faculty have terminal degrees. Graduate students do not teach undergraduate courses. Undergraduate student–faculty ratio: 7:1.
Student Life Student groups/activities include Delta Omicron, Pi Kappa Lambda.
Expenses for 2006–2007 Application fee: $40. Comprehensive fee: $29,082 includes full-time tuition ($22,234) and college room and board ($6848). Special program-related fees: $1000 per year for private lessons/accompanist.
Financial Aid Program-specific awards: 1 Daniel Music Scholarship for music majors (most talented and in need) ($20,000–$28,000), 38 Petrie Honor Music Scholarships for music majors ($1000–$18,000).
Application Procedures Students admitted directly into the professional program freshman year. Deadline for freshmen and transfers: continuous. Notification date for freshmen and transfers: September 1. Required: essay, high school transcript,

college transcript(s) for transfer students, minimum 3.0 high school GPA, 2 letters of recommendation, audition, SAT I or ACT test scores (minimum combined SAT I score of 1000, minimum composite ACT score of 21). Recommended: interview. Auditions held 3 times on campus and off campus in Louisville, KY; recorded music is permissible as a substitute for live auditions when distance is prohibitive and videotaped performances are permissible as a substitute for live auditions when distance is prohibitive.
Web Site http://www.converse.edu
Contact Anne Denbow, Assistant Director of Admissions, Petrie School of Music, Converse College, 580 East Main, Spartanburg, South Carolina 29302-0006; 864-596-9759, fax: 864-596-9167, e-mail address: music@converse.edu

Cornell College
Mount Vernon, Iowa

Independent Methodist, coed. Small town campus. Total enrollment: 1,179. Music program established 1853.
Degrees Bachelor of Music; Bachelor of Music Education. Majors and concentrations: music education, performance.
Enrollment 40 total; 30 undergraduate, 10 nonprofessional degree.
Music Student Profile 60% females, 40% males, 10% minorities, 5% international.
Music Faculty 5 undergraduate (full-time), 18 undergraduate (part-time). 100% of full-time faculty have terminal degrees. Graduate students do not teach undergraduate courses. Undergraduate student–faculty ratio: 5:1.
Expenses for 2005–2006 Application fee: $30. Comprehensive fee: $30,110 includes full-time tuition ($23,500), mandatory fees ($180), and college room and board ($6430). College room only: $3010. Full-time tuition and fees vary according to reciprocity agreements. Room and board charges vary according to board plan.
Financial Aid Program-specific awards: 10 Trustees Music Scholar Awards for music majors and minors ($15,000), 4 WFK Music Scholarships for music majors and minors, Horace Alden Miller (HAMM) Award for music majors and minors ($5000).
Application Procedures Students apply for admission into the professional program by sophomore year. Deadline for freshmen and transfers: continuous. Required: essay, high school transcript, college transcript(s) for transfer students, minimum 2.0 high school GPA, letter of recommendation, audition, SAT I or ACT test scores. Recommended: interview. Auditions held once and by appointment on campus; recorded music is permissible as a substitute for live auditions if a campus visit is impossible and videotaped performances are permissible as a substitute for live auditions if a campus visit is impossible.
Web Site http://www.cornellcollege.edu
Undergraduate Contact Jonathan Stroud, Director of Admissions, Cornell College, 600 First Street West, Mount Vernon, Iowa 52314-1098; 319-895-4477, fax: 319-895-4451.

Cornish College of the Arts
Seattle, Washington

Independent, coed. Urban campus. Total enrollment: 768. Music program established 1914.
Degrees Bachelor of Music in the areas of jazz performance, classical and new music performance, composition. Majors and concentrations: classical music, composition, electronic music, instrumental music, jazz, voice, world music.
Enrollment 145 total; all undergraduate.
Music Student Profile 65% females, 35% males, 14% minorities, 4% international.
Music Faculty 13 undergraduate (full-time), 21 undergraduate (part-time). 58% of full-time faculty have terminal degrees. Graduate students do not teach undergraduate courses. Undergraduate student–faculty ratio: 4:1.
Expenses for 2005–2006 Application fee: $35. Tuition: $21,200 full-time. Mandatory fees: $300 full-time. Special program-related fees: $700 per year for private lessons (amount may vary by major).

Financial Aid Program-specific awards: Nellie Scholarships for new students, departmental scholarships for new and continuing students, Presidential Scholarships for continuing students.
Application Procedures Students admitted directly into the professional program freshman year. Deadline for freshmen and transfers: August 15. Notification date for freshmen and transfers: August 30. Required: essay, high school transcript, college transcript(s) for transfer students, minimum 2.0 high school GPA, audition. Recommended: 2 letters of recommendation, interview, SAT I or ACT test scores. Auditions held 20 times on campus and off campus in San Francisco, CA; recorded music is permissible as a substitute for live auditions when distance is prohibitive.
Web Site http://www.cornish.edu
Undergraduate Contact Eric Pedersen, Director of Admission, Cornish College of the Arts, 1000 Lenora, Seattle, Washington 98121; 800-726-ARTS, fax: 206-720-1011, e-mail address: epedersen@cornish.edu

Covenant College
Lookout Mountain, Georgia

Independent, coed. Suburban campus. Total enrollment: 898. Music program established 1964.
Degrees Bachelor of Music in the areas of applied music, church music. Majors and concentrations: church music, instrumental music, organ, piano, voice.
Enrollment 44 total; 18 undergraduate, 26 nonprofessional degree.
Music Student Profile 66% females, 34% males, 1% international.
Music Faculty 4 undergraduate (full-time), 9 undergraduate (part-time). 100% of full-time faculty have terminal degrees. Graduate students do not teach undergraduate courses. Undergraduate student–faculty ratio: 5:1.
Student Life Student groups/activities include Jazz Ensemble, College Chorale, chamber orchestra, Covenant Singers.
Expenses for 2006–2007 Application fee: $35. Comprehensive fee: $28,030 includes full-time tuition ($21,100), mandatory fees ($750), and college room and board ($6180). Special program-related fees: $250–$500 per semester for lessons.
Financial Aid Program-specific awards: keyboard scholarships for musically qualified students ($500–$5000), instrument scholarships for musically qualified students ($500–$5000), vocal scholarships for musically qualified students ($500–$5000), bagpipes scholarships for musically qualified students ($500–$1000).
Application Procedures Students admitted directly into the professional program freshman year. Deadline for freshmen and transfers: continuous. Required: essay, high school transcript, college transcript(s) for transfer students, letter of recommendation, interview, video, audition, ACT test score only, minimum 2.5 high school GPA. Auditions held by appointment and October/March special weekends on campus; videotaped performances are permissible as a substitute for live auditions when distance is prohibitive.
Web Site http://www.covenant.edu
Undergraduate Contact Ms. Karen Emerson, Secretary, Music Department, Covenant College, 14049 Scenic Highway, Lookout Mountain, Georgia 30750; 706-419-1453, fax: 706-820-2165, e-mail address: kemerson@covenant.edu

The Crane School of Music
See State University of New York College at Potsdam

Crown College
St. Bonifacius, Minnesota

Independent, coed. Suburban campus. Total enrollment: 1,304. Music program established 1980.

Culver-Stockton College
Canton, Missouri

Independent, coed. Rural campus. Total enrollment: 840. Music program established 1925.

Culver-Stockton College (continued)

Degrees Bachelor of Music in the area of music education. Majors and concentrations: music education, piano, voice, wind and percussion instruments. Program accredited by NASM.
Music Faculty 5 undergraduate (full-time), 5 undergraduate (part-time). 80% of full-time faculty have terminal degrees. Graduate students do not teach undergraduate courses.
Student Life Student groups/activities include Music Educators National Conference, Sigma Phi Zeta (honorary music fraternity).
Expenses for 2006–2007 Application fee: $25. Comprehensive fee: $21,796 includes full-time tuition ($15,250) and college room and board ($6546). College room only: $3030. Special program-related fees: $75 per hour for private instruction.
Financial Aid Program-specific awards: music grants for program majors and non-majors, William Spencer Johnson Piano Scholarship.
Application Procedures Students admitted directly into the professional program freshman year. Deadline for freshmen: May 1; transfers: June 1. Notification date for freshmen: June 1; transfers: July 1. Required: high school transcript, college transcript(s) for transfer students, minimum 2.0 high school GPA, 2 letters of recommendation, interview, audition, SAT I or ACT test scores. Auditions held as needed on campus; recorded music is permissible as a substitute for live auditions if a campus visit is impossible and videotaped performances are permissible as a substitute for live auditions if a campus visit is impossible.
Web Site http://www.culver.edu
Undergraduate Contact Ron Cronacher, Director of Enrollment Services, Culver-Stockton College, 1 College Hill, Canton, Missouri 63435-1299; 800-537-1883, fax: 217-231-6611, e-mail address: admissions@culver.edu

The Curtis Institute of Music
Philadelphia, Pennsylvania

Independent, coed. Urban campus. Total enrollment: 160 (2003). Music program established 1924.
Degrees Bachelor of Music in the area of performance. Majors and concentrations: brass, composition, conducting, harpsichord, piano/organ, stringed instruments, voice, wind and percussion instruments. Graduate degrees offered: Master of Music in the area of opera. Cross-registration with University of Pennsylvania. Program accredited by NASM.
Enrollment 158 total.
Music Student Profile 55% females, 45% males, 46% international.
Music Faculty 2 total (full-time), 86 total (part-time). Graduate students do not teach undergraduate courses.
Student Life Student groups/activities include symphony concerts, operas, chamber concerts.
Expenses for 2006–2007 Special program-related fees: $1100 per year for comprehensive fee (includes textbooks).
Financial Aid Program-specific awards: tuition scholarships for program students, supplemental financial assistance awards for those demonstrating need.
Application Procedures Students admitted directly into the professional program freshman year. Deadline for freshmen and transfers: December 15. Notification date for freshmen and transfers: April 15. Required: high school transcript, college transcript(s) for transfer students, 4 letters of recommendation, audition, SAT I test score only. Auditions held once on campus.
Web Site http://www.curtis.edu
Contact Mr. Chris Hodges, Director of Admissions, The Curtis Institute of Music, 1726 Locust Street, Philadelphia, Pennsylvania 19103; 215-893-5262 ext. 3117, fax: 215-893-0194.

Dalhousie University
Halifax, Nova Scotia, Canada

Province-supported, coed. Total enrollment: 15,528. Music program established 1967.
Degrees Bachelor of Arts in the area of music and theater; Bachelor of Music in the areas of composition, history, church music, performance, music instruction, self-directed study, contemporary musics. Majors and concentrations: brass, church music, classical guitar, music history, music instruction, music theory and composition, piano/organ, stringed instruments, voice, wind and percussion instruments. Cross-registration with Atlantic School of Theology (for church music majors only); University of Kings College.
Enrollment 101 total; 68 undergraduate, 33 nonprofessional degree.
Music Student Profile 55% females, 45% males, 6% minorities, 4% international.
Music Faculty 13 undergraduate (full-time), 19 undergraduate (part-time). 100% of full-time faculty have terminal degrees. Graduate students do not teach undergraduate courses. Undergraduate student–faculty ratio: 5:1.
Student Life Student groups/activities include Symphony Nova Scotia, Nova Scotia Choral Federation.
Expenses for 2005–2006 Application fee: $45 Canadian dollars. Tuition, fee, and room and board charges are reported in Canadian dollars. Comprehensive fee: $13,952 includes full-time tuition ($5820), mandatory fees ($632), and college room and board ($7500). International student tuition: $11,460 full-time. Special program-related fees: $850 per year for applied skills and electroacoustic classes.
Financial Aid Program-specific awards: 2 Don Wright Scholarships for music instruction students ($500), 1 Halifax Ladies Musical Club Scholarship for first-year students ($500), 18 Effie Mae Ross and Campbell Scholarships for in-course students ($600–$2750), 1 L. D. Currie Memorial Scholarship for in-course students ($750), 1 Elizabeth Meyerhof Scholarship for fourth-year students ($2000), 1 David Peters Organ Scholarship for piano or organ majors ($1000), 1 Bornoff/Gramie Memorial String Scholarship for 4th-year string students ($500), James and Abbie Campbell Incentive Scholarships for incoming students, 12 Effie May Ross Entrance Scholarships ($500–$3000), Elvira Gonnella Scholarship for 3rd-and 4th-year voice students, 2 Tietje Zonneveld Scholarship in Piano Studies for senior piano student ($500), 1 Charles and Mary Machennan Bursary in Music for in-course students ($2500), 1 Margaret Newcomb Layton Harrigan Brink Bursary for in-course students from Nova Scotia ($500).
Application Procedures Students admitted directly into the professional program freshman year. Deadline for freshmen: April 1; transfers: June 1. Notification date for freshmen: June 1; transfers: September 1. Required: high school transcript, college transcript(s) for transfer students, minimum 3.0 high school GPA, interview, audition, portfolio for composition applicants, SAT I for U.S. applicants only. Recommended: letter of recommendation. Auditions held 4-5 times from March through May on campus; recorded music is permissible as a substitute for live auditions when distance is prohibitive and videotaped performances are permissible as a substitute for live auditions when distance is prohibitive. Portfolio reviews held as needed on campus.
Web Site http://music.dal.ca
Undergraduate Contact Mr. Gary Ewer, Student Advisor, Department of Music, Dalhousie University, Room 514 Arts Center, Halifax, Nova Scotia B3H 4R2, Canada; 902-494-1826, fax: 902-494-2801, e-mail address: gary.ewer@dal.ca

Dallas Baptist University
Dallas, Texas

Independent, coed. Urban campus. Total enrollment: 4,988. Music program established 1965.

Dana School of Music
See Youngstown State University

The D'Angelo School of Music
See Mercyhurst College

Delta State University
Cleveland, Mississippi

State-supported, coed. Small town campus. Total enrollment: 3,998.

Degrees Bachelor of Music in the areas of voice, piano, instrumental performance; Bachelor of Music Education in the areas of vocal music education, instrumental music education. Majors and concentrations: piano/organ, voice, wind and percussion instruments. Program accredited by NASM.
Enrollment 84 total; all undergraduate.
Music Student Profile 49% females, 51% males, 15% minorities, 2% international.
Music Faculty 13 total (full-time), 4 total (part-time). 87% of full-time faculty have terminal degrees. Graduate students do not teach undergraduate courses. Undergraduate student–faculty ratio: 6:1.
Student Life Student groups/activities include Phi Mu Alpha, Mu Phi Epsilon, Pi Kappa Lambda.
Expenses for 2005–2006 Application fee: $15. State resident tuition: $3762 full-time. Nonresident tuition: $8950 full-time. Mandatory fees: $490 full-time. College room and board: $4272. Room and board charges vary according to board plan and housing facility. Special program-related fees: $10 for music computer lab fee, $15 for string methods and materials lab fee, $20 for keyboard lab fee, $50 per credit hour for applied fee.
Financial Aid Program-specific awards: 232 music scholarships for members of ensembles ($1600).
Application Procedures Students admitted directly into the professional program freshman year. Deadline for freshmen and transfers: continuous. Required: high school transcript, audition, SAT I or ACT test scores. Auditions held by appointment on campus; recorded music is permissible as a substitute for live auditions when distance is prohibitive and videotaped performances are permissible as a substitute for live auditions when distance is prohibitive.
Web Site http://www.deltastate.edu
Undergraduate Contact Dr. David Schubert, Chair, Department of Music, Delta State University, PO Box 3256, Cleveland, Mississippi 38733; 662-846-4606, fax: 662-846-4605, e-mail address: schubert@deltastate.edu

DePaul University
Chicago, Illinois

Independent Roman Catholic, coed. Urban campus. Total enrollment: 23,148.
Degrees Bachelor of Music in the areas of composition, jazz studies, music/business, music education, performance; Bachelor of Science in the area of sound recording technology. Majors and concentrations: brass, composition, jazz studies, music business, music education, piano, sound recording technology, stringed instruments, voice, wind and percussion instruments. Graduate degrees offered: Master of Music in the areas of composition, music education, performance, jazz studies. Program accredited by NASM.
Enrollment 389 total; 300 undergraduate, 80 graduate, 9 nonprofessional degree.
Music Student Profile 44% females, 56% males, 15% minorities, 9% international.
Music Faculty 22 total (full-time), 95 total (part-time). 88% of full-time faculty have terminal degrees. Graduate students do not teach undergraduate courses. Undergraduate student–faculty ratio: 8:1.
Student Life Student groups/activities include Music Educators National Conference.
Expenses for 2005–2006 Application fee: $40. Comprehensive fee: $29,905 includes full-time tuition ($20,900), mandatory fees ($140), and college room and board ($8865). College room only: $6507. Full-time tuition and fees vary according to program. Room and board charges vary according to board plan, housing facility, and location. Special program-related fees: $20 for music education instrument rental, $200 per quarter for vocal accompanist fee.
Financial Aid Program-specific awards: 250 music performance awards for program majors ($3000–$10,000).
Application Procedures Students admitted directly into the professional program freshman year. Deadline for freshmen and transfers: January 15. Notification date for freshmen and transfers: April 1. Required: essay, high school transcript, college transcript(s) for transfer students, letter of recommendation,

audition, SAT I or ACT test scores (minimum combined SAT I score of 1040, minimum composite ACT score of 22), minimum 2.75 high school GPA. Recommended: minimum 3.0 high school GPA, interview. Auditions held January and February on campus; recorded music is permissible as a substitute for live auditions for students outside the continental U.S. and videotaped performances are permissible as a substitute for live auditions for students outside the continental U.S..
Web Site http://music.depaul.edu
Contact Mr. Ross Beacraft, Director of Admission, School of Music, DePaul University, 804 West Belden Avenue, Chicago, Illinois 60614-3296; 800-433-7285 ext. 57444, fax: 773-325-7429, e-mail address: rbeacraf@depaul.edu

More About the School

DePaul University School of Music graduates are currently performing with the Chicago and Boston Symphony Orchestra; the Berlin Philharmonic; the Los Angeles Philharmonic; the Buffalo, Charleston, Jacksonville, Memphis, Winnipeg, and Kitchner-Waterloo Symphony Orchestras; the Metropolitan, Houston, Chicago Lyric, Berlin, Zurich, Montreal, Boston, Glimmerglass, Santa Fe, and Minnesota Opera Companies; and touring in musical theater productions across the country. Jazz studies majors have gone on to work in Chicago's commercial recording studios; recorded and toured with Maynard Ferguson, Chick Corea, Frank Mantooth, Woody Herman, Chicago Jazz Ensemble, Alanis Morissette, and Mighty Blue Kings; and released CDs for Reference, Corridor, River North, and Mesa/Bluemoon recordings.

Formed in 1923, the School of Music provides approximately 400 music majors from the United States, Canada, South and Central America, Europe, Asia, and Australia the opportunity to study with a world-class faculty. Students work with 100 full- and part-time faculty members who are members of the Chicago Symphony, the Lyric Opera, and Chicago's major chamber music ensembles and recording and jazz artists. In addition, students receive master classes with such major artists as Renee Flemming, Susan Mentzer, Phillip Glass, Elliot Carter, George Pearle, Phil Smith, Joseph Alessi, John Faddis, Bobbi Shew, and Phil Woods.

The School of Music is located on DePaul's beautiful Lincoln Park Campus in one of Chicago's most desirable neighborhoods. Students are less than 15 minutes from Symphony Center, the Civic Opera House, the Art Institute, Auditorium Theater, and literally dozens of other concert, theater, and jazz venues. Practice rooms are open from 7 a.m. until midnight, seven days a week. There are separate facilities for piano and percussion majors.

DePaul has great pride in the quality of its performing ensembles. Students have the opportunity to perform and read major repertoire with DePaul Symphony Orchestra, DePaul Chamber Orchestra, DePaul Wind Ensemble, Wind Symphony, DePaul Jazz Ensemble, Jazz Orchestra & Jazz Workshop, DePaul Opera Theater, Concert Choir, and Chamber Choir. All performance majors are also required to participate in chamber music, a very important part of music at DePaul. Student performances are given in the Lincoln Park Campus Recital and Concert Halls, Orchestra Hall at Symphony Center, and the Merle Reskin Theatre. In addition, many students perform with the Civic Orchestra of Chicago, the many regional and metropolitan orchestras, theater orchestras, jazz ensembles, and churches in the area.

The School of Music offers undergraduate degrees in Performance, Music Education, Jazz Studies, Composition, Performing Arts Administration, and Sound Recording Technology. Graduate degrees are offered in Performance, Music Education, Jazz Studies, and Composition. All applicants are required to audition. The School requires a live on-campus audition but accepts an audiotape or videotape from applicants outside the continental United States. The application deadline for freshman and transfer students is January 15. All auditions must be completed by February 28.

For more information, prospective students should contact: Mr. Ross Beacraft, Director of Admissions, DePaul University School

DePaul University (continued)

of Music, 804 West Belden, Chicago, Illinois 60614. Telephone: 773-325-7444 or 800-4-DePaul Ext. 7444 (toll-free). Fax: 773-325-7429. E-mail: rbeacraf@depaul.edu. Web site: http://music.depaul.edu.

DePauw University
Greencastle, Indiana

Independent, coed. Small town campus. Total enrollment: 2,397. Music program established 1884.
Degrees Bachelor of Music in the areas of performance, music/business; Bachelor of Musical Arts in the areas of music, music/business, music in conjunction with an outside field; Bachelor of Music Education in the areas of vocal education, instrumental education. Majors and concentrations: music and business, music education, piano/organ, stringed instruments, voice, wind and percussion instruments. Program accredited by NASM.
Enrollment 107 total; all undergraduate.
Music Student Profile 60% females, 40% males, 12% minorities, 2% international.
Music Faculty 21 undergraduate (full-time), 20 undergraduate (part-time). 54% of full-time faculty have terminal degrees. Graduate students do not teach undergraduate courses. Undergraduate student–faculty ratio: 5:1.
Student Life Student groups/activities include Music Educators National Conference, Pi Kappa Lambda, Mu Phi Epsilon.
Expenses for 2006–2007 Application fee: $40. Comprehensive fee: $35,580 includes full-time tuition ($27,400), mandatory fees ($380), and college room and board ($7800). College room only: $4100. Special program-related fees for accompanist.
Financial Aid Program-specific awards: performance award scholarships for talented students ($1000–$24,000).
Application Procedures Students admitted directly into the professional program freshman year. Deadline for freshmen: February 6; transfers: March 6. Notification date for freshmen and transfers: April 6. Required: essay, high school transcript, college transcript(s) for transfer students, letter of recommendation, audition, SAT I or ACT test scores, supplemental application to the School of Music, 2 letters of recommendation including one from music teacher. Recommended: minimum 3.0 high school GPA, interview. Auditions held 4 times or by appointment on campus and off campus in Interlochen, MI; recorded music is permissible as a substitute for live auditions when distance is prohibitive and videotaped performances are permissible as a substitute for live auditions when distance is prohibitive.
Web Site http://www.depauw.edu/music/
Undergraduate Contact Corinna Nash, Assistant Director of Music Admission, School of Music, DePauw University, Performing Arts Center, 600 South Locust, Greencastle, Indiana 46135; 800-447-2495 ext. 4100, fax: 765-658-4042.

Dorothy F. Schmidt College of Arts and Letters

See Florida Atlantic University

Drake University
Des Moines, Iowa

Independent, coed. Suburban campus. Total enrollment: 5,277.

Drexel University
Philadelphia, Pennsylvania

Independent, coed. Urban campus. Total enrollment: 18,466. Music program established 2001.
Degrees Bachelor of Science; Bachelor of Science/Master of Business Administration. Majors and concentrations: music industry.
Enrollment 135 total; all undergraduate.

Music Student Profile 30% females, 70% males, 1% international.
Music Faculty 10 total (full-time), 40 total (part-time). 100% of full-time faculty have terminal degrees. Graduate students do not teach undergraduate courses. Undergraduate student–faculty ratio: 15:1.
Student Life Student groups/activities include Drexel Players (theater group), musical ensembles.
Expenses for 2005–2006 Application fee: $50. Comprehensive fee: $34,795 includes full-time tuition ($22,700), mandatory fees ($1580), and college room and board ($10,515). College room only: $6255. Full-time tuition and fees vary according to course load, program, and student level. Room and board charges vary according to board plan and housing facility. Special program-related fees: $500 per term for private music lessons.
Financial Aid Program-specific awards: 108 Performing Arts Scholarships ($1000).
Application Procedures Students admitted directly into the professional program freshman year. Deadline for freshmen: January 15. Required: high school transcript, minimum 2.0 high school GPA, letter of recommendation, portfolio, SAT I or ACT test scores (minimum combined SAT I score of 1200). Recommended: essay, minimum 3.0 high school GPA, interview, video, audition. Auditions held by appointment on campus; recorded music is permissible as a substitute for live auditions and videotaped performances are permissible as a substitute for live auditions. Portfolio reviews held on campus; the submission of slides may be substituted for portfolios.
Web Site http://www.drexel.edu/comad
Undergraduate Contact David Miller, Director of Recruitment, Dean's Office, College of Media Arts and Design, Drexel University, 33rd and Market Streets, Philadelphia, Pennsylvania 19104; 215-895-1675, fax: 215-895-4917, e-mail address: ddm22@drexel.edu

The Mary Pappert School of Music
Duquesne University
Pittsburgh, Pennsylvania

Independent Roman Catholic, coed. Urban campus. Total enrollment: 9,916. Music program established 1926.
Degrees Bachelor of Music in the areas of performance, music technology; Bachelor of Science in the areas of music education, music therapy. Majors and concentrations: music education, music performance, music technology, music therapy. Graduate degrees offered: Master of Music in the areas of performance, sacred music, music theory/composition, music technology, music education. Cross-registration with Pittsburgh Council on Higher Education. Program accredited by NASM.
Enrollment 375 total; 276 undergraduate, 98 graduate, 1 nonprofessional degree.
Music Student Profile 43% females, 57% males, 21% minorities, 10% international.
Music Faculty 26 total (full-time), 74 total (part-time). 100% of full-time faculty have terminal degrees. Graduate students do not teach undergraduate courses. Undergraduate student–faculty ratio: 8:1.
Student Life Student groups/activities include Mu Phi Epsilon, Music Educators National Conference, Music Therapy Club.
Expenses for 2005–2006 Application fee: $50. Comprehensive fee: $29,534 includes full-time tuition ($19,721), mandatory fees ($1759), and college room and board ($8054). College room only: $4394. Full-time tuition and fees vary according to program. Room and board charges vary according to board plan and housing facility.
Financial Aid Program-specific awards: 70 School of Music Talent Awards for program students ($2000–$20,000).
Application Procedures Students admitted directly into the professional program freshman year. Deadline for freshmen and transfers: May 1. Notification date for freshmen and transfers: August 15. Required: essay, high school transcript, college transcript(s) for transfer students, minimum 2.0 high school GPA, 2 letters of recommendation, audition, SAT I or ACT test scores, theory examination, musicianship examination, compositions (for composition majors) (portfolio), piano placement exam. Recommended: minimum 3.0 high school GPA, interview.

Auditions held 12 times on campus and off campus in Washington, DC area; recorded music is permissible as a substitute for live auditions if a campus visit is impossible and videotaped performances are permissible as a substitute for live auditions if a campus visit is impossible.
Web Site http://www.music.duq.edu/
Undergraduate Contact Mr. Paul Cukanna, Dean of Admissions, Duquesne University, 600 Forbes Avenue, Pittsburgh, Pennsylvania 15282; 412-396-6222, fax: 412-396-5644.
Graduate Contact Mr. Nicholas Jordanoff, Director of Music Admissions, School of Music, Duquesne University, 600 Forbes Avenue, Pittsburgh, Pennsylvania 15282; 412-396-5983, fax: 412-396-5479, e-mail address: jordanof@duq2.cc.duq.edu

East Carolina University

Greenville, North Carolina

State-supported, coed. Urban campus. Total enrollment: 23,164. Music program established 1909.
Degrees Bachelor of Music in the areas of performance, music education, piano pedagogy, sacred music, theory/composition, music therapy, music theater, jazz studies. Majors and concentrations: jazz performance, music education, music theater, music theory and composition, music therapy, piano pedagogy, piano/organ, sacred music, stringed instruments, voice, wind and percussion instruments. Graduate degrees offered: Master of Music in the areas of accompanying, sacred music, music education, composition, performance, piano pedagogy, Suzuki pedagogy, music therapy, choral conducting, jazz performance, theory, voice pedagogy, instrumental conducting. Program accredited by NASM, AMTA.
Enrollment 304 total; 265 undergraduate, 39 graduate.
Music Student Profile 50% females, 50% males, 11% minorities, 1% international.
Music Faculty 48 total (full-time), 13 total (part-time). 94% of full-time faculty have terminal degrees. Graduate students teach a few undergraduate courses. Undergraduate student–faculty ratio: 6:1.
Student Life Student groups/activities include music sororities and fraternities, Music Educators National Conference, American Choral Directors Association.
Expenses for 2005–2006 Application fee: $50. State resident tuition: $2135 full-time. Nonresident tuition: $12,649 full-time. Mandatory fees: $1492 full-time. College room and board: $6840. College room only: $3790. Room and board charges vary according to board plan and housing facility. Special program-related fees: $30 per credit hour for applied music fee.
Financial Aid Program-specific awards: 75 music scholarships for music majors ($500–$7000).
Application Procedures Students admitted directly into the professional program freshman year. Deadline for freshmen: March 15; transfers: April 15. Required: high school transcript, college transcript(s) for transfer students, minimum 2.0 high school GPA, interview, audition, SAT I or ACT test scores (minimum combined SAT I score of 900), minimum combined SAT I score of 1000 for out-of-state applicants, musicianship test (written and aural). Recommended: essay, minimum 3.0 high school GPA, 2 letters of recommendation. Auditions held 8 times on campus; recorded music is permissible as a substitute for live auditions if a campus visit is impossible and videotaped performances are permissible as a substitute for live auditions if a campus visit is impossible.
Web Site http://www.music.ecu.edu
Undergraduate Contact Mr. Christopher Ulffers, Assistant Director, School of Music, East Carolina University, A.J. Fletcher Music Center, Greenville, North Carolina 27858-4353; 252-328-4281, fax: 252-328-6258, e-mail address: ulffersj@mail.ecu.edu
Graduate Contact Dr. Rodney Schmidt, Assistant Dean, Graduate Studies, School of Music, East Carolina University, A.J. Fletcher Music Center, Greenville, North Carolina 27858-4353; 252-328-6282, fax: 252-328-6258, e-mail address: schmidtr@mail.ecu.edu

East Central University

Ada, Oklahoma

State-supported, coed. Small town campus. Total enrollment: 4,571. Music program established 1909.

Degrees Bachelor of Science in the areas of music, music education. Majors and concentrations: music education, piano/organ, voice, wind and percussion instruments. Program accredited by NASM.
Enrollment 65 total; all undergraduate.
Music Student Profile 50% females, 50% males, 1% minorities.
Music Faculty 8 undergraduate (full-time), 6 undergraduate (part-time). 90% of full-time faculty have terminal degrees. Graduate students do not teach undergraduate courses. Undergraduate student–faculty ratio: 15:1.
Student Life Student groups/activities include Music Educators National Conference Student Chapter, Kappa Kappa Psi.
Expenses for 2005–2006 Application fee: $20. State resident tuition: $2,722 full-time. Nonresident tuition: $5,739 full-time. Mandatory fees: $844 full-time. Full-time tuition and fees vary according to course load. College room and board: $3000. College room only: $1070. Room and board charges vary according to board plan and housing facility. Special program-related fees: $3 per semester for class instrument rental fee, $10 per semester for organ rental, $36 per credit hour for private lessons.
Application Procedures Students admitted directly into the professional program freshman year. Deadline for freshmen and transfers: continuous. Required: high school transcript, college transcript(s) for transfer students, minimum 2.0 high school GPA, audition, portfolio, ACT test score only (minimum composite ACT score of 20). Auditions held continuously on campus; recorded music is permissible as a substitute for live auditions if a campus visit is impossible and videotaped performances are permissible as a substitute for live auditions if a campus visit is impossible. Portfolio reviews held on campus; the submission of slides may be substituted for portfolios when distance is prohibitive.
Web Site http://www.ecok.edu
Undergraduate Contact Dr. Mark S. Hollingsworth, Chair, Department of Music, East Central University, Box P-6, Ada, Oklahoma 74820; 580-332-8000 ext. 474, fax: 580-310-5752, e-mail address: mholling@mailclerk.ecok.edu

Eastern Illinois University

Charleston, Illinois

State-supported, coed. Small town campus. Total enrollment: 12,129. Music program established 1928.
Degrees Bachelor of Music in the areas of music education, performance, jazz studies, composition. Majors and concentrations: classical music, composition, jazz, music, music education, piano, stringed instruments, voice, wind and percussion instruments. Graduate degrees offered: Master of Music in the areas of performance, conducting, music education. Program accredited by NASM.
Enrollment 160 total; 150 undergraduate, 10 graduate.
Music Student Profile 52% females, 48% males, 7% minorities, 2% international.
Music Faculty 25 undergraduate (full-time), 2 undergraduate (part-time), 12 graduate (full-time). 60% of full-time faculty have terminal degrees. Graduate students do not teach undergraduate courses. Undergraduate student–faculty ratio: 5:1.
Student Life Student groups/activities include professional music fraternities and sororities.
Expenses for 2005–2006 Application fee: $30. State resident tuition: $4629 full-time. Nonresident tuition: $13,887 full-time. Mandatory fees: $1744 full-time. Full-time tuition and fees vary according to course load. College room and board: $6196. Room and board charges vary according to board plan and housing facility. Special program-related fees: $15 per season for marching band equipment, $30 per recital for recital recording.
Financial Aid Program-specific awards: 25 endowed scholarships for program majors ($250–$2500).
Application Procedures Students admitted directly into the professional program freshman year. Deadline for freshmen and transfers: continuous. Required: high school transcript, college transcript(s) for transfer students, minimum 2.0 high school GPA, audition, SAT I or ACT test scores. Recommended: interview. Auditions held 6 times on campus; recorded music is permissible

Eastern Illinois University (continued)

as a substitute for live auditions when distance is prohibitive and videotaped performances are permissible as a substitute for live auditions when distance is prohibitive.

Web Site http://www.eiu.edu/~music

Undergraduate Contact Dr. W. Parker Melvin, Chair, Department of Music, Eastern Illinois University, 600 Lincoln Avenue, Charleston, Illinois 61920; 217-581-3010, fax: 217-581-7137, e-mail address: cfwpml@eiu.edu

Graduate Contact Dr. Peter Hesterman, Director of Graduate Studies, Department of Music, Eastern Illinois University, 600 Lincoln Avenue, Charleston, Illinois 61920; 217-581-3611, fax: 217-581-7137, e-mail address: cfpdh@eiu.edu

Eastern Kentucky University

Richmond, Kentucky

State-supported, coed. Small town campus. Total enrollment: 16,219. Music program established 1930.

Eastern Michigan University

Ypsilanti, Michigan

State-supported, coed. Suburban campus. Total enrollment: 23,240.

Degrees Bachelor of Music in the area of performance; Bachelor of Music Education in the areas of vocal music education, instrumental music education; Bachelor of Music Therapy. Majors and concentrations: guitar, music education, music therapy, piano/organ, stringed instruments, voice, wind and percussion instruments. Graduate degrees offered: Master of Arts in the areas of performance, piano pedagogy, theory/literature, music education. Program accredited by NASM.

Enrollment 350 total; 265 undergraduate, 55 graduate, 30 nonprofessional degree.

Music Student Profile 60% females, 40% males, 5% international.

Music Faculty 34 undergraduate (full-time), 10 undergraduate (part-time). 60% of full-time faculty have terminal degrees. Graduate students teach a few undergraduate courses. Undergraduate student–faculty ratio: 10:1.

Student Life Student groups/activities include Kappa Kappa Psi, Tau Beta Sigma. Special housing available for music students.

Expenses for 2005–2006 Application fee: $30. State resident tuition: $5463 full-time. Nonresident tuition: $16,818 full-time. Mandatory fees: $1078 full-time. College room and board: $6356. Special program-related fees: $10 per course for instrument maintenance, $30–$60 per semester for applied music fee.

Financial Aid Program-specific awards: Alexander Talent Awards for music majors ($500–$3000), endowed awards for music majors ($200–$1900).

Application Procedures Students admitted directly into the professional program freshman year. Deadline for freshmen and transfers: continuous. Required: high school transcript, college transcript(s) for transfer students, minimum 2.0 high school GPA, audition, SAT I or ACT test scores, interview for music education and music therapy applicants. Auditions held 5 times and by special arrangement on campus; recorded music is permissible as a substitute for live auditions when distance is prohibitive and videotaped performances are permissible as a substitute for live auditions by special arrangement.

Web Site http://music.emich.edu

Contact Dr. David M. Pierce, Coordinator of Advising, Department of Music, Eastern Michigan University, Alexander Music Building, Ypsilanti, Michigan 48197; 734-487-1044, fax: 734-487-6939, e-mail address: david.pierce@emich.edu

Eastern New Mexico University

Portales, New Mexico

State-supported, coed. Rural campus. Total enrollment: 4,033.

Eastern Washington University

Cheney, Washington

State-supported, coed. Small town campus. Total enrollment: 10,908. Music program established 1890.

Eastman School of Music of the University of Rochester

See University of Rochester

East Tennessee State University

Johnson City, Tennessee

State-supported, coed. Small town campus. Total enrollment: 11,894. Music program established 1949.

Degrees Bachelor of Music in the areas of music education, performance. Majors and concentrations: music education, piano, voice, wind and percussion instruments. Cross-registration with Milligan College. Program accredited by NASM.

Enrollment 114 total; 113 undergraduate, 1 graduate.

Music Student Profile 45% females, 55% males, 11% minorities, 1% international.

Music Faculty 11 undergraduate (full-time), 10 undergraduate (part-time). 82% of full-time faculty have terminal degrees. Graduate students do not teach undergraduate courses. Undergraduate student–faculty ratio: 5:1.

Student Life Student groups/activities include Pi Kappa Lambda, Music Educators National Conference, Percussive Arts Society.

Expenses for 2006–2007 Application fee: $15. State resident tuition: $4032 full-time. Nonresident tuition: $14,136 full-time. Mandatory fees: $630 full-time. College room and board: $5026. College room only: $2426. Special program-related fees: $100 per credit hour for private music lessons.

Financial Aid Program-specific awards: 10 Floyd Cramer Scholarships for those passing audition evaluations ($1000), 7 Lamar Alexander Scholarships for those passing audition evaluations ($1000), 1 Theresa Bowers Endowment Award for those passing audition evaluations ($350), 70 APS Awards for above-average students with exceptional artistic ability ($2556), 7 other endowed scholarships for those passing audition evaluations ($750), 10 Powell Choral Scholarships for choir members ($750), 20 Public Performance Awards for out-of-state music students ($6000).

Application Procedures Students admitted directly into the professional program freshman year. Deadline for freshmen and transfers: continuous. Required: high school transcript, college transcript(s) for transfer students, audition, SAT I or ACT test scores (minimum composite ACT score of 19), minimum 2.3 high school GPA, TCAP results (graduates of TN high schools). Auditions held 4 times on campus and off campus in high schools in northeast Tennessee; recorded music is permissible as a substitute for live auditions if a live audition is impossible and videotaped performances are permissible as a substitute for live auditions if a live audition is impossible.

Web Site http://www.etsu.edu/music

Undergraduate Contact Dr. Mary Dave Blackman, Chair, Department of Music, East Tennessee State University, Box 70661, Johnson City, Tennessee 37614; 423-439-6948, fax: 423-439-7088, e-mail address: blackman@etsu.edu

East Texas Baptist University

Marshall, Texas

Independent Baptist, coed. Small town campus. Total enrollment: 1,326. Music program established 1912.

Degrees Bachelor of Music. Majors and concentrations: music education, piano performance, sacred music, voice performance. Program accredited by NASM.

Enrollment 190 total; 80 undergraduate, 110 nonprofessional degree.

Music Student Profile 60% females, 40% males, 5% minorities, 5% international.

Music Faculty 9 undergraduate (full-time), 9 undergraduate (part-time). 78% of full-time faculty have terminal degrees. Graduate students do not teach undergraduate courses. Undergraduate student–faculty ratio: 9:1.

Student Life Student groups/activities include Sigma Alpha Iota, Tau Beta Sigma, Kappa Kappa Psi.

Expenses for 2005–2006 Application fee: $25. Comprehensive fee: $16,713 includes full-time tuition ($12,840) and college room and board ($3873). Room and board charges vary according to board plan and housing facility. Special program-related fees: $40 for recital accompanist, $50 per credit hour for applied music fee, $125 per credit hour for applied music accompanist.

Financial Aid Program-specific awards: 35 music scholarships for program majors ($1500–$2400), 50 ensemble scholarships for ensemble players ($300–$1000).

Application Procedures Students admitted directly into the professional program freshman year. Deadline for freshmen and transfers: August 31. Required: essay, high school transcript, college transcript(s) for transfer students, minimum 2.0 high school GPA, interview, audition, SAT I or ACT test scores (minimum combined SAT I score of 860, minimum composite ACT score of 18), portfolio for scholarship consideration. Recommended: letter of recommendation. Auditions held 10 times on campus; recorded music is permissible as a substitute for live auditions when distance is prohibitive or scheduling is difficult and videotaped performances are permissible as a substitute for live auditions when distance is prohibitive or if scheduling is difficult. Portfolio reviews held 4 times on campus.

Web Site http://www.etbu.edu

Undergraduate Contact Vince Blankenship, Director of Admissions, East Texas Baptist University, 1209 North Grove, Marshall, Texas 75670; 800-804-3828 ext. 002, fax: 903-923-2000, e-mail address: vblankenship@etbu.edu

Elmhurst College
Elmhurst, Illinois

Independent, coed. Suburban campus. Total enrollment: 2,670. Music program established 1938.

Degrees Bachelor of Music in the areas of music education, music business; Bachelor of Science in the area of music business. Majors and concentrations: music business, music education.

Music Faculty 6 undergraduate (full-time), 55 undergraduate (part-time). Graduate students do not teach undergraduate courses.

Student Life Student groups/activities include Music Educators National Conference, Music and Entertainment Industry Student Association, Student Recording Services.

Expenses for 2005–2006 Application fee: $25. Comprehensive fee: $28,506 includes full-time tuition ($21,600) and college room and board ($6906). College room only: $3816. Room and board charges vary according to board plan and housing facility.

Financial Aid Program-specific awards: music scholarship/talent awards for performers, National Association of Music Merchants Scholarship for academically qualified/talented applicants, National Academy of Recording Arts and Sciences Scholarship for academically qualified/talented applicants, endowed scholarships.

Application Procedures Students admitted directly into the professional program freshman year. Deadline for freshmen: April 15. Notification date for freshmen and transfers: August 15. Required: high school transcript, college transcript(s) for transfer students, letter of recommendation, audition, SAT I or ACT test scores, minimum 2.5 high school GPA. Auditions held continuously on campus; recorded music is permissible as a substitute for live auditions for international students and U.S. students from a great distance and videotaped performances are permissible as a substitute for live auditions for international students and U.S. students from a great distance.

Web Site http://www.elmhurst.edu

Undergraduate Contact Mr. Kevin Olson, Director of Music Admissions, Music Department, Elmhurst College, 190 Prospect Avenue, Elmhurst, Illinois 60126; 630-617-3515, fax: 630-617-3738.

Emporia State University
Emporia, Kansas

State-supported, coed. Small town campus. Total enrollment: 6,288. Music program established 1925.

Degrees Bachelor of Music in the area of performance; Bachelor of Music Education in the areas of instrumental music education, vocal music education. Majors and concentrations: music education, piano, stringed instruments, voice, wind and percussion instruments. Graduate degrees offered: Master of Music in the areas of performance, music education. Program accredited by NASM.

Enrollment 104 total; 88 undergraduate, 16 graduate.

Music Student Profile 55% females, 45% males, 5% minorities, 3% international.

Music Faculty 13 total (full-time), 7 total (part-time). 13% of full-time faculty have terminal degrees. Graduate students do not teach undergraduate courses. Undergraduate student–faculty ratio: 6:1.

Student Life Student groups/activities include Collegiate Music Educators National Conference, Kappa Kappa Psi, Tau Beta Sigma/Sigma Alpha Iota.

Expenses for 2005–2006 Application fee: $30. State resident tuition: $2638 full-time. Nonresident tuition: $9990 full-time. Mandatory fees: $668 full-time. Full-time tuition and fees vary according to degree level. College room and board: $4787. College room only: $2363. Room and board charges vary according to board plan and housing facility.

Financial Aid Program-specific awards: 60 endowed scholarships for talented students ($800–$1500), 5 academic scholarships for those with a minimum 3.75 GPA ($500–$1000).

Application Procedures Students apply for admission into the professional program by sophomore year. Deadline for freshmen and transfers: continuous. Required: high school transcript, college transcript(s) for transfer students, SAT I or ACT test scores, theory skills evaluation for transfer students. Recommended: audition. Auditions held 3 times on campus; recorded music is permissible as a substitute for live auditions for out-of-state applicants and videotaped performances are permissible as a substitute for live auditions for out-of-state applicants.

Web Site http://www.emporia.edu

Undergraduate Contact Dr. Marie Miller, Chair, Department of Music, Emporia State University, Box 4029, Emporia, Kansas 66801; 620-341-5431, fax: 620-341-5601, e-mail address: millerma@emporia.edu

Graduate Contact Dr. Andrew Houchins, Director, Graduate Studies in Music, Department of Music, Emporia State University, Box 4029, Emporia, Kansas 66801; 620-341-6089, fax: 620-341-5601, e-mail address: houchina@emporia.edu

Esther Boyer College of Music

See Temple University

Evangel University
Springfield, Missouri

Independent, coed. Urban campus. Total enrollment: 1,801. Music program established 1955.

Fisk University
Nashville, Tennessee

Independent, coed. Urban campus. Total enrollment: 890. Music program established 1866.

Degrees Bachelor of Music in the area of performance. Majors and concentrations: piano performance, voice performance. Cross-registration with Vanderbilt University, Belmont University. Program accredited by NASM.

Enrollment 30 total; all undergraduate.

Music Student Profile 67% females, 33% males, 100% minorities, 10% international.

Music Faculty 3 undergraduate (full-time), 2 undergraduate (part-time). 33% of full-time faculty have terminal degrees.

Fisk University (continued)

Graduate students do not teach undergraduate courses. Undergraduate student–faculty ratio: 5:1.

Student Life Student groups/activities include Jubilee Singers, University Choir, Jazz Ensemble.

Expenses for 2005–2006 Application fee: $50. Comprehensive fee: $19,910 includes full-time tuition ($12,480), mandatory fees ($700), and college room and board ($6730). College room only: $3910. Full-time tuition and fees vary according to course load. Room and board charges vary according to board plan. Special program-related fees: $80–$200 per course for applied lesson fee.

Application Procedures Students admitted directly into the professional program freshman year. Deadline for freshmen and transfers: June 15. Required: essay, high school transcript, college transcript(s) for transfer students, 2 letters of recommendation, audition, SAT I or ACT test scores (minimum combined SAT I score of 900, minimum composite ACT score of 19), minimum 2.5 high school GPA. Recommended: interview, video, portfolio. Auditions held twice on campus; recorded music is permissible as a substitute for live auditions if a live audition is impossible and videotaped performances are permissible as a substitute for live auditions if a live audition is impossible. Portfolio reviews held 3 times on campus.

Web Site http://www.fisk.edu

Undergraduate Contact Dr. William Carter, Director of Admissions, Music Department, Fisk University, 1000 17th Avenue North, Nashville, Tennessee 37208; 615-329-8666, fax: 615-329-8774, e-mail address: admit@fisk.edu

Five Towns College

Dix Hills, New York

Independent, coed. Suburban campus. Total enrollment: 1,162. Music program established 1972.

Degrees Bachelor of Music in the areas of jazz/commercial music, music education. Majors and concentrations: audio recording technology, composition/songwriting, music business, music education, performance, video music. Graduate degrees offered: Master of Music in the areas of composition arranging, music history, music performance, audio recording technology. Doctor of Musical Arts in the areas of composition and arranging, music history and literature, music performance, music education. Program accredited by NCATE.

Enrollment 297 total; 248 undergraduate, 49 graduate.

Music Student Profile 48% females, 52% males, 14% minorities.

Music Faculty 18 total (full-time), 43 total (part-time). 42% of full-time faculty have terminal degrees. Graduate students do not teach undergraduate courses. Undergraduate student–faculty ratio: 13:1.

Student Life Student groups/activities include Music Theatre Production Society, Audio Recording Society, Music Educators National Conference Student Chapter.

Expenses for 2005–2006 Application fee: $35. Comprehensive fee: $24,350 includes full-time tuition ($14,100) and college room and board ($10,250). Room and board charges vary according to board plan and location. Special program-related fees: $10 per semester for piano lab fee, $50–$300 per semester for film/video lab , $675 per semester for private music instruction.

Financial Aid Program-specific awards: 80 Music Program Awards for musical performers ($1000–$7000), 25 Theatre Awards for theatre arts students ($3000–$4000).

Application Procedures Students admitted directly into the professional program freshman year. Deadline for freshmen and transfers: continuous. Required: essay, high school transcript, college transcript(s) for transfer students, minimum 2.0 high school GPA, 2 letters of recommendation, audition, SAT I or ACT test scores (minimum combined SAT I score of 1400, minimum composite ACT score of 19), personal statement. Recommended: minimum 3.0 high school GPA, interview. Auditions held on an individual basis on campus; recorded music is permissible as a substitute for live auditions for international applicants or when distance is prohibitive and videotaped performances are permissible as a substitute for live auditions when distance is prohibitive.

Web Site http://www.ftc.edu

Undergraduate Contact Jerry Cohen, Dean of Enrollment, Five Towns College, 305 North Service Road, Dix Hills, New York 11746; 631-424-7000 ext. 2110, fax: 631-424-7008.

Graduate Contact Dr. Alfred Townsend, Chair of Graduate Program, Music Division, Five Towns College, 305 North Service Road, Dix Hills, New York 11746; 631-424-7000 ext. 2142, fax: 631-656-2172.

More About the College

Nestled on nearly 40 rolling acres at Dix Hills, Long Island, New York, Five Towns College is a comprehensive institution of higher education with a well-rounded music, media, and performing arts environment. Through its five major divisions—Music, Business, Liberal Arts, Fine Arts, and Childhood Education—the College offers more than thirty different programs of study leading to associate, bachelor's, master's and doctoral degrees.

The College awards a Bachelor of Music degree in jazz/commercial music, with major areas of concentration in performance, composition/songwriting, musical theater, and audio recording technology and music business. These programs are designed for students pursuing careers as professional performers, composers, recording engineers, music business executives, or producers.

The College also offers a Bachelor of Music degree program in music education. The Music Education Program is designed for students interested in a career as a teacher of music in a public or private school and leads to New York State Certification. In addition, the College offers a master's degree program (grades K–12) leading to a Master of Music (M.M.) in jazz/commercial music or music education as well as a Doctor of Musical Arts (D.M.A.).

Five Towns College offers the Bachelor of Fine Arts (B.F.A.) degree program in theater, with major areas of concentration in acting and musical theater. The theater program is designed for students who are interested in a career in the performing arts field as an actor, entertainer, director, stage manager, lighting or sound engineer, or any other related aspect of the entertainment industry.

For students interested in nonperforming careers in the music industry, Five Towns College offers the Bachelor of Professional Studies (B.P.S.) degree program in business management, with major areas of concentration in audio recording technology and music business. A Bachelor of Fine Art degree (B.F.A.) in film/video is also available to those interested in pursuing filmmaking, commercial video production, and television production. These programs are designed for students planning to pursue careers in management, record labels, retail, and marketing with firms in the areas of record and music production, broadcasting, concert promotion, radio, television, theater, and communications. The program is intended for students who are interested in developing their business and technical expertise.

Five Towns College offers the Bachelor of Science (B.S.) degree in elementary education (grades 1–6), with areas of concentration in music and theater and elective offerings in a variety of fields. Students teach in neighboring school districts to gain experience. Upon completion of the program, students are licensed by the State of New York. A Bachelor of Science (B.S.) in mass communication is offered, with concentrations in broadcasting and journalism, and students are able to broadcast on the college radio station WFTU (AM/FM).

Students who attend Five Towns College benefit from the institution's excellent reputation for preparing students for entry into the entertainment industry. In addition to its highly qualified faculty, the College has facilities that are state-of-the-art. The College is also equipped with a film/video production facility and sound stages of various sizes. The Dix Hills Center for the Performing Arts has been described as "acoustically perfect." The Five Towns College library consists of more than 35,000 print and nonprint materials and has a significant collection of recorded music. The Five Towns College Living/Learning Center is a complex of four residence halls. Students reside in single- and double-occupancy rooms, each equipped with a private bathroom, high-speed Internet access, and satellite TV.

Five Towns College is fully accredited by the Middle States Association and the New York State Board of Regents.

Program Facilities Performance spaces include the Dix Hills Center for the Performing Arts (500 seats), the Student Center, and The Upbeat Café. In addition, the College is equipped with 16-, 24-, 48-, and 72-channel state-of-the-art recording studios as well as a MIDI technology laboratory. The College's film/video studios are equipped with both linear and nonlinear digital-editing suites as well as AVID nonlinear editing suites. The College operates WFTU, a 1,000-watt commercial radio station, and Radio Five Towns, a low-power on-campus radio station.

Faculty, Resident Artists, and Alumni The many gifted and talented musicians and educators who compose the Five Towns College faculty bring a vast array of backgrounds and experiences to campus. The faculty is exemplary in both their academic and performance credentials. Artists-in-residence include the Township Theatre Group, Wes Belcamp, and Peter Rogine. Representative visiting artists include the Sea Cliff Chamber Players, the Sound Symphony Orchestra, and the Gilbert & Sullivan Light Opera Theatre Company of Long Island. John Sebastian, Ian McDonald, Steve Howe, Arvell Shaw, J.Geils, Jimmy Vivino, Sal Salvador, Arlen Roth, Tuck and Patti, and Special EFX are just a few of the artists/clinicians who appeared at the College the past few seasons. Alumni work throughout the music industry in numerous capacities, such as musicians, business managers, audio recording engineers, and music educators.

Student Performance Students have the opportunity to perform in ensembles of every size and instrumentation. The most popular ensembles include the Concert Choir, Stage Band, Guitar Ensemble, and Percussion Ensemble. Students are invited to participate in any of the major theatrical productions produced on campus each year by the Play Production Workshop and the Light Opera Company. These include musicals, operettas, comedies, dramas, and children's theater productions. The Upbeat Café and the Student Center provide informal venues for students to gather, perform, and collaborate each afternoon.

Special Programs The College is a member of the Phi Sigma National Honor Society and hosts a student chapter of the Music Educators National Conference (MENC). Numerous festivals and performances are held each year, including a Stage Band Festival and Music Industry Conference. Past events have included the Classic American Guitar Show, the Long Island Media Arts Show, and the Great American Songbook.

Dorothy F. Schmidt College of Arts and Letters
Florida Atlantic University
Boca Raton, Florida

State-supported, coed. Suburban campus. Total enrollment: 25,704. Music program established 1963.

Florida International University
Miami, Florida

State-supported, coed. Urban campus. Total enrollment: 36,904. Music program established 1973.

Florida Southern College
Lakeland, Florida

Independent, coed. Suburban campus. Total enrollment: 1,921.

Florida State University
Tallahassee, Florida

State-supported, coed. Suburban campus. Total enrollment: 39,146. Music program established 1900.

Degrees Bachelor of Music in the areas of performance, piano pedagogy, composition, music history/literature, music theory, music theater, music therapy; Bachelor of Music Education in the areas of instrumental music education, choral music education, general music education. Majors and concentrations: classical music, composition, jazz, music, music education, music history and literature, music theater, music theory, music therapy, piano/organ, stringed instruments, voice, wind and percussion instruments. Graduate degrees offered: Master of Arts in the area of arts administration; Master of Music in the areas of performance, accompanying, piano pedagogy, choral conducting, opera, instrumental conducting, jazz, theory, composition, ethnomusicology, historical musicology, music therapy; Master of Music Education in the areas of instrumental music education, choral music education, general music education. Doctor of Music in the areas of composition, performance; Doctor of Education in the area of music education; Doctor of Philosophy in the areas of music education, music theory, ethnomusicology, historical musicology. Cross-registration with Tallahassee Community College. Program accredited by NASM, NCATE.

Enrollment 1,142 total; 492 undergraduate, 430 graduate, 220 nonprofessional degree.

Music Student Profile 53% females, 47% males, 24% minorities, 7% international.

Music Faculty 90 total (full-time), 7 total (part-time). 80% of full-time faculty have terminal degrees. Graduate students teach about a quarter of undergraduate courses. Undergraduate student–faculty ratio: 8:1.

Student Life Student groups/activities include Collegiate Music Educators National Conference, American Choral Directors Association, American String Teachers Association. Special housing available for music students.

Expenses for 2005–2006 Application fee: $30. State resident tuition: $3208 full-time. Nonresident tuition: $16,340 full-time. Full-time tuition varies according to location. College room and board: $6778. College room only: $3600. Room and board charges vary according to board plan and housing facility. Special program-related fees: $30 per recital for student degree recital (staff and recording), $60 per recital for non-degree recital.

Financial Aid Program-specific awards: 72 out-of-state tuition waivers for program majors ($9525), 200 general scholarships for program majors ($250–$2500).

Application Procedures Students admitted directly into the professional program freshman year. Deadline for freshmen: March 1; transfers: July 1. Required: essay, high school transcript, college transcript(s) for transfer students, minimum 3.0 high school GPA, letter of recommendation, audition, SAT I or ACT test scores. Auditions held 4 times on campus; recorded music is permissible as a substitute for live auditions when distance is prohibitive.

Web Site http://www.music.fsu.edu

Undergraduate Contact Dr. Ted Stanley, Program Director for Undergraduate Studies, College of Music, Florida State University, Tallahassee, Florida 32306-1180; 850-644-4833, fax: 850-644-2033, e-mail address: tstanley@garnet.acns.fsu.edu

Graduate Contact Dr. Seth Beckman, Assistant Dean/Director of Graduate Studies, College of Music, Florida State University, Tallahassee, Florida 32306-1180; 850-644-5848, fax: 850-644-2033, e-mail address: sbeckman@mailer.fsu.edu

Fort Hays State University
Hays, Kansas

State-supported, coed. Small town campus. Total enrollment: 7,373. Music program established 1902.

Friends University
Wichita, Kansas

Independent, coed. Urban campus. Total enrollment: 3,190.

Friends University (continued)

Degrees Bachelor of Fine Arts; Bachelor of Music; Bachelor of Music Education. Majors and concentrations: instrumental music education, piano, vocal music education, voice. Program accredited by NASM.
Enrollment 400 total; all undergraduate.
Music Student Profile 50% females, 50% males, 30% minorities.
Music Faculty 9 total (full-time), 25 total (part-time). 75% of full-time faculty have terminal degrees. Graduate students do not teach undergraduate courses.
Student Life Student groups/activities include Mu Phi Epsilon, American Choral Directors Association, Music Educators National Conference.
Financial Aid Program-specific awards: 10 Miller Scholarships for program majors ($1000), 100 departmental scholarships for program majors ($1000–$1500).
Application Procedures Students admitted directly into the professional program freshman year. Deadline for freshmen: August 1; transfers: August 26. Required: high school transcript, college transcript(s) for transfer students, minimum 2.0 high school GPA, audition, SAT I or ACT test scores, minimum 3.0 high school GPA or ACT score of 20 for scholarship consideration. Auditions held by appointment on campus; recorded music is permissible as a substitute for live auditions if a campus visit is impossible.
Web Site http://www.friends.edu
Undergraduate Contact Dr. John Taylor, Director of Instrumental Music and Music Education, Division of Fine Arts, Friends University, 2100 University Drive, Wichita, Kansas 67213; 316-295-5535, fax: 316-295-5593, e-mail address: taylorj@friends.edu

Frost School of Music

See University of Miami

Furman University

Greenville, South Carolina

Independent, coed. Suburban campus. Total enrollment: 3,221.
Degrees Bachelor of Music in the areas of performance, church music, music education, music theory. Majors and concentrations: church music, music education, music theory, performance, piano/organ, stringed instruments, voice, wind and percussion instruments. Program accredited by NASM.
Enrollment 161 total; 119 undergraduate, 42 nonprofessional degree.
Music Student Profile 61% females, 39% males, 7% minorities.
Music Faculty 18 undergraduate (full-time), 18 undergraduate (part-time). 94% of full-time faculty have terminal degrees. Graduate students do not teach undergraduate courses. Undergraduate student–faculty ratio: 12:1.
Student Life Student groups/activities include Phi Mu Alpha, Sigma Alpha Iota.
Expenses for 2005–2006 Application fee: $40. Comprehensive fee: $33,264 includes full-time tuition ($25,888), mandatory fees ($464), and college room and board ($6912). College room only: $3712. Room and board charges vary according to board plan and housing facility. Special program-related fees: $50 per term for lab fee for private lessons, $198–$396 per term for private noncredit lessons.
Financial Aid Program-specific awards: 16 Daniel Scholarships for program majors ($1500–$2500), 12 Timmons Scholarships for program majors ($1000–$4000), 132 general music scholarships for program students ($1000–$8000), 6 Gunter Scholarships for program majors ($1500–$3000), 5 Lusby Scholarships for strings students ($4000–$6000).
Application Procedures Students admitted directly into the professional program freshman year. Deadline for freshmen and transfers: January 15. Notification date for freshmen: March 15. Required: essay, high school transcript, college transcript(s) for transfer students, SAT I or ACT test scores, audition for scholarship consideration, audition for ensembles and/or private lessons. Recommended: 2 letters of recommendation. Auditions held 4 times on campus; recorded music is permissible as a substitute for live auditions when distance is prohibitive and

videotaped performances are permissible as a substitute for live auditions when distance is prohibitive.
Web Site http://www.furman.edu
Undergraduate Contact Mr. Woody O'Cain, Admissions Director, Furman University, Greenville, South Carolina 29613; 864-294-2034, fax: 864-294-3127, e-mail address: woody.o'cain@furman.edu

George Mason University

Fairfax, Virginia

State-supported, coed. Suburban campus. Total enrollment: 29,728. Music program established 1972.

Georgetown College

Georgetown, Kentucky

Independent, coed. Suburban campus. Total enrollment: 1,904. Music program established 1840.

Georgia College & State University

Milledgeville, Georgia

State-supported, coed. Small town campus. Total enrollment: 5,659. Music program established 1935.
Degrees Bachelor of Arts in the area of music performance; Bachelor of Music Education in the areas of choral music, instrumental music, general music; Bachelor of Music Therapy. Majors and concentrations: choral music education, instrumental music education, music education, music therapy. Program accredited by NASM, NCATE, AMTA.
Enrollment 80 total; 66 undergraduate, 14 nonprofessional degree.
Music Student Profile 75% females, 25% males, 7% minorities, 2% international.
Music Faculty 10 undergraduate (full-time), 11 undergraduate (part-time). 100% of full-time faculty have terminal degrees. Graduate students do not teach undergraduate courses. Undergraduate student–faculty ratio: 7:1.
Student Life Student groups/activities include Music Educators National Conference Student Chapter, American Choral Directors Association Student Chapter, Phi Mu Alpha/Sigma Alpha Iota. Special housing available for music students.
Expenses for 2005–2006 Application fee: $25. State resident tuition: $3404 full-time. Nonresident tuition: $13,616 full-time. Mandatory fees: $738 full-time. Full-time tuition and fees vary according to location. College room and board: $6878. College room only: $3690. Room and board charges vary according to board plan and housing facility. Special program-related fees: $100 per course for applied music fees.
Financial Aid Program-specific awards: 6 Outstanding Student Scholarships for those demonstrating talent and academic achievement ($1500), 4–5 Max Noah Scholarships for music majors/minors ($600), 4–5 Foundation Scholarships for music majors/minors ($400).
Application Procedures Students apply for admission into the professional program by sophomore year. Deadline for freshmen and transfers: continuous. Required: high school transcript, college transcript(s) for transfer students, letter of recommendation, interview, audition, SAT I or ACT test scores (minimum combined SAT I score of 960, minimum composite ACT score of 21), completion of College Preparatory Curriculum (CPC) with no deficiencies, minimum 2.14 high school GPA. Recommended: minimum 3.0 high school GPA. Auditions held 3 times and by appointment on campus; recorded music is permissible as a substitute for live auditions on a case-by-case basis and videotaped performances are permissible as a substitute for live auditions on a case-by-case basis.
Web Site http://www.gcsu.edu/music
Undergraduate Contact Chairman, Department of Music and Theatre, Georgia College & State University, Box 066, Milledgeville, Georgia 31061; 478-445-4226, fax: 478-445-1633.

Georgia Southern University
Statesboro, Georgia

State-supported, coed. Total enrollment: 16,646. Music program established 1967.
Degrees Bachelor of Music. Majors and concentrations: composition, music education, performance. Graduate degrees offered: Master of Music in the areas of composition, music education, performance, music technology. Program accredited by NASM.
Enrollment 170 total; 140 undergraduate, 20 graduate, 10 nonprofessional degree.
Music Student Profile 50% females, 50% males, 25% minorities, 5% international.
Music Faculty 20 total (full-time), 6 total (part-time). 100% of full-time faculty have terminal degrees. Graduate students do not teach undergraduate courses. Undergraduate student–faculty ratio: 16:1.
Student Life Student groups/activities include Collegiate Music Educators National Conference, American Choral Directors Association, professional music fraternities and sororities.
Expenses for 2005–2006 Application fee: $50. State resident tuition: $2438 full-time. Nonresident tuition: $9754 full-time. Mandatory fees: $1024 full-time. Full-time tuition and fees vary according to degree level and location. College room and board: $6300. College room only: $3968. Room and board charges vary according to board plan and housing facility.
Financial Aid Program-specific awards: 12 endowed scholarships for music majors ($500–$4000), 40 Georgia Southern Foundation Music Scholarships for music majors demonstrating talent and academic merit ($800–$2000), 40 symphony service awards for symphony players ($250), 130 symphonic wind ensemble/marching band service awards for symphonic wind ensemble/marching band players ($150–$800), 15 jazz ensemble service awards for jazz ensemble players ($250–$1200), 37 choral service awards for members of Southern Chorale ($150–$1000).
Application Procedures Students admitted directly into the professional program freshman year. Deadline for freshmen and transfers: May 1. Required: high school transcript, college transcript(s) for transfer students, minimum 2.0 high school GPA, audition, SAT I or ACT test scores (minimum combined SAT I score of 980, minimum composite ACT score of 20). Auditions held 4 times and by appointment on campus; recorded music is permissible as a substitute for live auditions when distance is prohibitive and videotaped performances are permissible as a substitute for live auditions when distance is prohibitive.
Web Site http://class.georgiasouthern.edu/music
Undergraduate Contact Department of Music, Georgia Southern University, PO Box 8052, Statesboro, Georgia 30460-8052; 912-681-5396, fax: 912-681-0583, e-mail address: music@georgiasouthern.edu
Graduate Contact Dr. Greg Harwood, Director of Graduate Music Studies, Department of Music, Georgia Southern University, PO Box 8052, Statesboro, Georgia 30460-8052; 912-681-5396 ext. 5813, fax: 912-871-1295, e-mail address: gharwood@georgiasouthern.edu

Georgia State University
Atlanta, Georgia

State-supported, coed. Urban campus. Total enrollment: 25,945. Music program established 1958.
Degrees Bachelor of Music in the areas of music education, performance, jazz studies, composition, sound recording; Bachelor of Science in the area of music management. Majors and concentrations: composition, jazz studies, music education, music management, performance, sound recording technology. Graduate degrees offered: Master of Music in the areas of music education, performance, composition, jazz studies, music theory, conducting, piano pedagogy, sacred music. Doctor of Philosophy in the area of music education. Cross-registration with Georgia State University System, Emory University. Program accredited by NASM.
Enrollment 405 total; 320 undergraduate, 70 graduate, 15 nonprofessional degree.
Music Student Profile 50% females, 50% males, 15% minorities, 10% international.

Music Faculty 29 total (full-time), 34 total (part-time). 64% of full-time faculty have terminal degrees. Graduate students teach a few undergraduate courses. Undergraduate student–faculty ratio: 10:1.
Student Life Student groups/activities include Pi Kappa Lambda.
Expenses for 2005–2006 Application fee: $50. State resident tuition: $3638 full-time. Nonresident tuition: $14,552 full-time. Mandatory fees: $826 full-time. Full-time tuition and fees vary according to course load, degree level, and program. College room and board: $6980. College room only: $5380. Room and board charges vary according to board plan and housing facility. Special program-related fees: $10 for locker, $50 per semester for use of recording studios/equipment, $50 per recital for use of hall.
Financial Aid Program-specific awards: 1 The Charles Thomas Wurm Music Scholarship for program majors ($1000), 1 The Friends of Rick Bell Jazz Scholarship for jazz majors ($1000), 1 The Haskell Boyter Choral Scholarship for voice majors ($1000), 1 The Thomas M. Brumby Keyboard Scholarship for keyboard majors ($1000), 1 The Friends of Music Scholarship for program majors ($1000), 1 The Montgomery Music Scholarship for program majors ($1000), 1 The National Association for Recording Arts and Sciences Award for music technology majors ($1000), 1 The Presser Foundation Music Scholarship for program majors ($4000), 1 Bill Lowery Award for music management majors ($1000), 4 Alfredo Barili Awards for strings majors ($1000), 1 Charles and Rosemary Hall Scholarship for music management students ($1000).
Application Procedures Students admitted directly into the professional program freshman year. Deadline for freshmen: March 1; transfers: June 1. Required: high school transcript, college transcript(s) for transfer students, minimum 2.0 high school GPA, audition, SAT I test score only, portfolio review for composition applicants. Recommended: essay, minimum 3.0 high school GPA, 2 letters of recommendation, portfolio. Auditions held 3 times on campus; recorded music is permissible as a substitute for live auditions when distance is prohibitive and videotaped performances are permissible as a substitute for live auditions when distance is prohibitive. Portfolio reviews held 3 times on campus.
Web Site http://www.music.gsu.edu
Contact Dr. David Myers, Associate Director, School of Music, Georgia State University, PO Box 4097, Atlanta, Georgia 30302-4097; 404-651-3676, fax: 404-651-1583, e-mail address: dmyers@landgate.gsu.edu

Gordon College
Wenham, Massachusetts

Independent nondenominational, coed. Small town campus. Total enrollment: 1,650.

Grace College
Winona Lake, Indiana

Independent, coed. Small town campus. Total enrollment: 1,275. Music program established 1948.
Degrees Bachelor of Music. Majors and concentrations: music education. Program accredited by NASM.
Enrollment 21 total; 18 undergraduate, 3 nonprofessional degree.
Music Student Profile 60% females, 40% males.
Music Faculty 4 undergraduate (full-time), 19 undergraduate (part-time). 50% of full-time faculty have terminal degrees. Graduate students do not teach undergraduate courses. Undergraduate student–faculty ratio: 6:1.
Student Life Student groups/activities include Music Educators National Conference.
Expenses for 2005–2006 Application fee: $20. Comprehensive fee: $22,170 includes full-time tuition ($15,620), mandatory fees ($400), and college room and board ($6150). College room only: $3070. Room and board charges vary according to board plan and housing facility. Special program-related fees: $100 per credit hour for fee for accompanists, $100 per credit hour for studio fee for vocalists, $100 per credit hour for studio fee for instrumentalists.

Grace College (continued)

Financial Aid Program-specific awards: 2–3 Grace Honors Brass Scholarships for freshmen program majors ($2500–$3000), 2–3 Grace Honors Woodwind Scholarships for freshmen program majors ($2500–$3000), 4–5 Grace Honors String Scholarships for freshmen program majors ($2500–$3000), 8–10 music talent scholarships for freshmen program majors ($1500–$2500).

Application Procedures Students admitted directly into the professional program freshman year. Deadline for freshmen and transfers: August 1. Notification date for freshmen and transfers: continuous. Required: high school transcript, college transcript(s) for transfer students, minimum 2.0 high school GPA, 3 letters of recommendation, audition, SAT I or ACT test scores (minimum combined SAT I score of 950, minimum composite ACT score of 20). Recommended: essay. Auditions held 3 times on campus; recorded music is permissible as a substitute for live auditions when distance is prohibitive or scheduling is difficult and videotaped performances are permissible as a substitute for live auditions when distance is prohibitive.

Web Site http://www.musicatgrace.org

Undergraduate Contact Anecia Miller, Director of Admission/Registrar, Admissions Office, Grace College, 200 Seminary Drive, Winona Lake, Indiana 46590; 574-372-5100 ext. 6411, fax: 574-372-5144.

Grand Valley State University
Allendale, Michigan

State-supported, coed. Small town campus. Total enrollment: 22,565. Music program established 1968.

Degrees Bachelor of Music in the area of performance; Bachelor of Music Education in the areas of vocal music education, instrumental music education. Majors and concentrations: music education, piano/organ, stringed instruments, voice, wind and percussion instruments. Program accredited by NASM.

Enrollment 154 total; 125 undergraduate, 29 nonprofessional degree.

Music Student Profile 54% females, 46% males, 2% minorities, 3% international.

Music Faculty 20 undergraduate (full-time), 30 undergraduate (part-time). 80% of full-time faculty have terminal degrees. Graduate students do not teach undergraduate courses. Undergraduate student–faculty ratio: 8:1.

Student Life Student groups/activities include Music Educators National Conference, Mu Phi Epsilon.

Expenses for 2005–2006 Application fee: $30. State resident tuition: $6220 full-time. Nonresident tuition: $12,510 full-time. Full-time tuition varies according to course level, program, and student level. College room and board: $6360. Room and board charges vary according to board plan, housing facility, and location.

Financial Aid Program-specific awards: 2 Blodgett Piano Awards for pianists ($800–$1200), 3 Eitzen Voice Awards for vocalists ($800–$1200), 3 Arthur Hills Scholarships for musically talented juniors ($800–$1200), 12 music honors scholarships for performance and composition majors ($2000–$4000), 5 Brass Quintet scholarships for brass players ($4000), 6 out-of-state tuition waivers for music and dance students ($5000), 2 International Scholarships ($12,000).

Application Procedures Students admitted directly into the professional program freshman year. Deadline for freshmen and transfers: April 30. Required: high school transcript, college transcript(s) for transfer students, minimum 3.0 high school GPA, 2 letters of recommendation, interview, audition, SAT I or ACT test scores, theory placement examination. Recommended: essay. Auditions held 6 times on campus; recorded music is permissible as a substitute for live auditions when distance is prohibitive and videotaped performances are permissible as a substitute for live auditions when distance is prohibitive.

Web Site http://www.gvsu.edu

Undergraduate Contact Jodi Chycinski, Director of Admissions, Grand Valley State University, 1 Campus Drive, Allendale, Michigan 49401; 616-331-2025, e-mail address: go2gvsu@gvsu.edu

The Greatbatch School of Music
See Houghton College

Grove City College
Grove City, Pennsylvania

Independent Presbyterian, coed. Small town campus. Total enrollment: 2,341. Music program established 1876.

Harding University
Searcy, Arkansas

Independent, coed. Small town campus. Total enrollment: 5,744. Music program established 1934.

Degrees Bachelor of Music Education. Majors and concentrations: instrumental music, vocal music. Program accredited by NASM.

Enrollment 75 total; 40 undergraduate, 35 nonprofessional degree.

Music Student Profile 60% females, 40% males, 5% minorities, 5% international.

Music Faculty 8 undergraduate (full-time), 8 undergraduate (part-time). 63% of full-time faculty have terminal degrees. Graduate students do not teach undergraduate courses. Undergraduate student–faculty ratio: 8:1.

Student Life Student groups/activities include Collegiate Music Educators National Conference, American Choral Directors Association, National Association of Teachers of Singing.

Expenses for 2005–2006 Application fee: $35. Comprehensive fee: $16,512 includes full-time tuition ($10,800), mandatory fees ($400), and college room and board ($5312). College room only: $2636. Full-time tuition and fees vary according to course load. Room and board charges vary according to board plan and housing facility. Special program-related fees: $42 per semester hour for instrument rental, $218 per semester hour for private lessons.

Financial Aid Program-specific awards: 60–65 departmental scholarships for music majors ($1200).

Application Procedures Students apply for admission into the professional program by junior year. Deadline for freshmen and transfers: continuous. Required: high school transcript, college transcript(s) for transfer students, SAT I or ACT test scores. Recommended: minimum 2.0 high school GPA, interview, audition. Auditions held once on campus; recorded music is permissible as a substitute for live auditions when distance is prohibitive and videotaped performances are permissible as a substitute for live auditions when distance is prohibitive.

Web Site http://www.harding.edu/music/

Undergraduate Contact Mr. Mike Williams, Director of Admissions, Harding University, Box 12255, Searcy, Arkansas 72149-0001; 800-477-4407, fax: 501-279-4865.

Hardin-Simmons University
Abilene, Texas

Independent Baptist, coed. Urban campus. Total enrollment: 2,435. Music program established 1926.

Degrees Bachelor of Music in the areas of performance, music education, church music, music theory/composition. Majors and concentrations: church music, music business, music education, music performance, music theory and composition. Graduate degrees offered: Master of Music in the areas of performance, music education, music theory/composition, church music. Cross-registration with Abilene Christian University, McMurry University. Program accredited by NASM.

Enrollment 98 total; 71 undergraduate, 7 graduate, 20 nonprofessional degree.

Music Student Profile 56% females, 44% males, 7% minorities.

Music Faculty 17 total (full-time), 7 total (part-time). 71% of full-time faculty have terminal degrees. Graduate students do not teach undergraduate courses. Undergraduate student–faculty ratio: 10:1.

Student Life Student groups/activities include Music Educators National Conference Student Chapter, Phi Mu Alpha, Sigma Alpha Iota.

Expenses for 2006–2007 Application fee: $50. Comprehensive fee: $20,206 includes full-time tuition ($14,850), mandatory fees ($776), and college room and board ($4580). College room only: $2365. Special program-related fees: $15 per semester for music performance facilities fee, $125 per credit hour for private instruction.

Financial Aid Program-specific awards: 1 Irl Allison Award for pianists/returning students ($400), 6 Foreman Awards for cowboy band /returning students ($1890), 1 Hamilton Award for vocalists/returning students ($1600), 1 Lacewell Award for church music majors ($2500), 4 Reeves Awards for program majors ($2475), 1 Shaw Award for church music majors ($1400), 1 Presser Award for outstanding music majors ($4200).

Application Procedures Students admitted directly into the professional program freshman year. Deadline for freshmen and transfers: continuous. Required: high school transcript, college transcript(s) for transfer students, minimum 2.0 high school GPA, audition, SAT I or ACT test scores (minimum combined SAT I score of 860, minimum composite ACT score of 18), two letters of recommendation for scholarship consideration. Auditions held 4 times on campus; recorded music is permissible as a substitute for live auditions if a campus visit is impossible and videotaped performances are permissible as a substitute for live auditions if a campus visit is impossible.

Web Site http://www.hsutx.edu/academics/music/index.html

Undergraduate Contact Shane Davidson, Associate Vice President of Enrollment Services, Hardin-Simmons University, Box 16050, Abilene, Texas 79698-6050; 915-670-1207, fax: 915-670-1527.

Graduate Contact Dr. Leigh Anne Hunsaker, Program Director, School of Music, Hardin-Simmons University, Box 16230, Abilene, Texas 79698-6230; 915-670-1391, fax: 915-670-5873.

The Hartt School

See University of Hartford

Hartwick College

Oneonta, New York

Independent, coed. Total enrollment: 1,463.

Hastings College

Hastings, Nebraska

Independent Presbyterian, coed. Small town campus. Total enrollment: 1,189. Music program established 1882.

Degrees Bachelor of Music in the areas of performance, music education, piano pedagogy. Majors and concentrations: music, music education, piano pedagogy, piano/organ, stringed instruments, voice, wind and percussion instruments. Program accredited by NASM, NCATE.

Enrollment 80 total; 60 undergraduate, 20 nonprofessional degree.

Music Student Profile 56% females, 44% males, 2% minorities, 1% international.

Music Faculty 9 undergraduate (full-time), 8 undergraduate (part-time). 89% of full-time faculty have terminal degrees. Graduate students do not teach undergraduate courses. Undergraduate student–faculty ratio: 13:1.

Student Life Student groups/activities include Sigma Alpha Iota, Music Educators National Conference, Phi Mu Alpha Sinfonia.

Expenses for 2005–2006 Application fee: $20. Comprehensive fee: $22,218 includes full-time tuition ($16,578), mandatory fees ($690), and college room and board ($4950). College room only: $2116. Full-time tuition and fees vary according to course level and program. Room and board charges vary according to board plan and housing facility. Special program-related fees: $550 per semester for private lessons.

Financial Aid Program-specific awards: 150 music scholarships for vocalists and instrumentalists ($920).

Application Procedures Students apply for admission into the professional program by freshman year. Deadline for freshmen and transfers: August 20. Required: essay, high school transcript, college transcript(s) for transfer students, minimum 2.0 high school GPA, letter of recommendation, interview, audition, SAT I or ACT test scores (minimum composite ACT score of 24). Auditions held by request on campus and off campus in Denver, CO; Kansas City, MO; Omaha, NE; Lincoln, NE; recorded music is permissible as a substitute for live auditions when distance is prohibitive and videotaped performances are permissible as a substitute for live auditions when distance is prohibitive.

Web Site http://www.hastings.edu

Undergraduate Contact Mary Molliconi, Admissions Department, Hastings College, 7th and Turner, Hastings, Nebraska 68901; 402-461-7315, fax: 402-463-3002.

Heidelberg College

Tiffin, Ohio

Independent, coed. Small town campus. Total enrollment: 1,435. Music program established 1886.

Degrees Bachelor of Music in the areas of composition, performance, music industry, music education, music performance/pedagogy. Majors and concentrations: composition, music, music education, music industry, piano/organ, stringed instruments, voice, wind and percussion instruments. Program accredited by NASM.

Enrollment 68 total; 51 undergraduate, 15 nonprofessional degree.

Music Student Profile 50% females, 50% males, 3% minorities, 1% international.

Music Faculty 8 undergraduate (full-time), 15 undergraduate (part-time). 100% of full-time faculty have terminal degrees. Graduate students do not teach undergraduate courses. Undergraduate student–faculty ratio: 6:1.

Student Life Student groups/activities include Ohio Collegiate Music Educators National Conference, American Choral Directors Association, Tau Mu Sigma. Special housing available for music students.

Expenses for 2005–2006 Application fee: $25. Comprehensive fee: $23,242 includes full-time tuition ($15,740), mandatory fees ($394), and college room and board ($7108). College room only: $3296. Full-time tuition and fees vary according to course load, degree level, and location. Room and board charges vary according to board plan and housing facility.

Financial Aid Program-specific awards: 20–25 music scholarships for program majors ($2500–$3000), 10 endowed music awards for program majors ($500–$1000).

Application Procedures Students admitted directly into the professional program freshman year. Deadline for freshmen and transfers: continuous. Required: high school transcript, college transcript(s) for transfer students, minimum 2.0 high school GPA, 2 letters of recommendation, interview, audition, SAT I or ACT test scores. Recommended: essay. Auditions held 3 times and as needed on campus; recorded music is permissible as a substitute for live auditions when distance is prohibitive and videotaped performances are permissible as a substitute for live auditions when distance is prohibitive.

Web Site http://www.heidelberg.edu/

Undergraduate Contact Dr. Douglas McConnell, Chair, Department of Music, Heidelberg College, 310 East Market Street, Tiffin, Ohio 44883; 419-448-2073, fax: 419-448-2124, e-mail address: dmcconne@heidelberg.edu

Henderson State University

Arkadelphia, Arkansas

State-supported, coed. Small town campus. Total enrollment: 3,584.

Degrees Bachelor of Music in the areas of performance, music education, composition. Majors and concentrations: composition, music education, voice, wind and percussion instruments. Cross-registration with Ouachita Baptist University. Program accredited by NASM.

Henderson State University (continued)

Enrollment 125 total; 80 undergraduate, 45 nonprofessional degree.
Music Student Profile 47% females, 53% males, 1% minorities, 1% international.
Music Faculty 13 undergraduate (full-time), 4 undergraduate (part-time). 98% of full-time faculty have terminal degrees. Graduate students do not teach undergraduate courses. Undergraduate student–faculty ratio: 9:1.
Student Life Student groups/activities include Elementary Music Workshops, Phi Mu Alpha.
Expenses for 2005–2006 Application fee: $0. State resident tuition: $4050 full-time. Nonresident tuition: $8100 full-time. Mandatory fees: $575 full-time. Full-time tuition and fees vary according to course load and program. College room and board: $3888. Room and board charges vary according to board plan and housing facility. Special program-related fees: $40–$60 per credit hour for applied music fees.
Financial Aid Program-specific awards: 55–100 band scholarships for band members ($800–$2000), 30–50 music scholarships for program majors/non-majors ($1000–$1600).
Application Procedures Students admitted directly into the professional program freshman year. Deadline for freshmen and transfers: continuous. Required: high school transcript, college transcript(s) for transfer students, minimum 2.0 high school GPA, SAT I or ACT test scores (minimum composite ACT score of 19). Recommended: interview, audition. Auditions held continuously on campus and off campus in various schools in Arkansas; recorded music is permissible as a substitute for live auditions when distance is prohibitive and videotaped performances are permissible as a substitute for live auditions when distance is prohibitive; must have references.
Web Site http://www.hsu.edu/dept/mus
Undergraduate Contact Mr. Tom Gattin, Registrar, Admissions Office, Henderson State University, Box 7534, Arkadelphia, Arkansas 71999-0001; 870-230-5135, fax: 870-230-5144.

Holy Names University
Oakland, California

Independent Roman Catholic, coed, primarily women. Urban campus. Total enrollment: 1,093. Music program established 1880.
Degrees Bachelor of Music in the areas of piano performance, vocal performance, instrumental performance, piano pedagogy. Majors and concentrations: classical music, piano, piano pedagogy, voice. Graduate degrees offered: Master of Music in the areas of piano performance, piano pedagogy, vocal performance, music education with Kodály emphasis, vocal performance with pedagogy emphasis, piano pedagogy with Suzuki emphasis.
Enrollment 27 total; 12 undergraduate, 14 graduate, 1 nonprofessional degree.
Music Student Profile 78% females, 22% males, 19% minorities, 4% international.
Music Faculty 1 undergraduate (full-time), 4 undergraduate (part-time), 1 graduate (full-time), 3 graduate (part-time). 50% of full-time faculty have terminal degrees. Graduate students do not teach undergraduate courses. Undergraduate student–faculty ratio: 3:1.
Student Life Student groups/activities include Mu Phi Epsilon.
Expenses for 2006–2007 Application fee: $50. Tuition: $22,470 full-time. Mandatory fees: $240 full-time. Special program-related fees: $750 per semester for private music lessons.
Financial Aid Program-specific awards: 8 Distinguished Musician Scholarships for students demonstrating need and talent ($5000).
Application Procedures Students admitted directly into the professional program freshman year. Deadline for freshmen and transfers: continuous. Required: essay, high school transcript, college transcript(s) for transfer students, 2 letters of recommendation, audition, SAT I or ACT test scores, minimum TOEFL score of 490 score for international students, minimum 2.7 high school GPA, minimum 2.2 GPA in transferable college units for transfer students. Recommended: interview. Auditions held as needed

on campus; recorded music is permissible as a substitute for live auditions when distance is prohibitive and videotaped performances are permissible as a substitute for live auditions if of good quality.
Web Site http://www.hnu.edu
Undergraduate Contact Lonnie R. Morris Jr., Vice President for Enrollment Management, Holy Names University, 3500 Mountain Boulevard, Oakland, California 94619-1699; 510-436-1351, fax: 510-436-1325, e-mail address: lmorris@hnu.edu
Graduate Contact Kathleen Archambeau, Graduate Admissions Counselor, Holy Names University, 3500 Mountain Boulevard, Oakland, California 94619-1699; 510-436-1351, fax: 510-436-1325, e-mail address: archambeau@hnu.edu

Hope College
Holland, Michigan

Independent, coed. Small town campus. Total enrollment: 3,141. Music program established 1928.

The Greatbatch School of Music
Houghton College
Houghton, New York

Independent Wesleyan, coed. Rural campus. Total enrollment: 1,411. Music program established 1946.
Degrees Bachelor of Music in the areas of applied music, music education, composition. Majors and concentrations: brass, composition, guitar, music education, organ, piano, stringed instruments, voice, wind and percussion instruments. Graduate degrees offered: Master of Music in the areas of collaborative performance, composition, conducting, performance. Program accredited by NASM.
Enrollment 120 total; 100 undergraduate, 5 graduate, 15 nonprofessional degree.
Music Student Profile 60% females, 40% males, 5% minorities, 5% international.
Music Faculty 13 total (full-time), 22 total (part-time). 80% of full-time faculty have terminal degrees. Graduate students do not teach undergraduate courses. Undergraduate student–faculty ratio: 7:1.
Student Life Student groups/activities include Pi Kappa Lambda, New York State Music Educators Association, Music Educators National Conference. Special housing available for music students.
Expenses for 2005–2006 Application fee: $40. Comprehensive fee: $25,980 includes full-time tuition ($19,420) and college room and board ($6560). Full-time tuition varies according to class time, program, and reciprocity agreements. Room and board charges vary according to board plan and housing facility. Special program-related fees: $630 per hour for private lessons.
Financial Aid Program-specific awards: 20–30 performance grants for program majors ($1000–$8000), 1 Presidential Scholarship for program majors ($15,000).
Application Procedures Students admitted directly into the professional program freshman year. Deadline for freshmen and transfers: continuous. Required: essay, high school transcript, college transcript(s) for transfer students, minimum 2.0 high school GPA, 2 letters of recommendation, audition, SAT I or ACT test scores. Recommended: minimum 3.0 high school GPA, interview. Auditions held 7 times on campus; recorded music is permissible as a substitute for live auditions when distance is prohibitive and videotaped performances are permissible as a substitute for live auditions when distance is prohibitive.
Web Site http://campus.houghton.edu/orgs/music/
Undergraduate Contact Connie Van Slyke, Administrative Assistant, The Greatbatch School of Music, Houghton College, 1 Willard Avenue, Houghton, New York 14744; 585-567-9400, fax: 585-567-9517, e-mail address: music@houghton.edu
Graduate Contact Mindy Airhart, Graduate Communications Assistant, The Greatbatch School of Music, Houghton College, 1 Willard Avenue, Houston, New York 14744; 585-567-9400, fax: 585-567-9517, e-mail address: music@houghton.edu

Howard Payne University
Brownwood, Texas

Independent, coed. Small town campus. Total enrollment: 1,319. Music program established 1900.
Degrees Bachelor of Music in the areas of piano, organ, voice, instrumental music, piano pedagogy and accompanying, church music, choral music education, instrumental music education. Majors and concentrations: accompanying, choral music education, church music, instrumental music education, music, piano pedagogy, piano/organ, voice, wind and percussion instruments. Program accredited by NASM.
Enrollment 61 total; all undergraduate.
Music Student Profile 50% females, 50% males, 3% minorities, 4% international.
Music Faculty 9 undergraduate (full-time), 3 undergraduate (part-time). 60% of full-time faculty have terminal degrees. Graduate students do not teach undergraduate courses. Undergraduate student–faculty ratio: 5:1.
Student Life Student groups/activities include Music Educators National Conference, American Choral Directors Association, Southern Baptist Church Music Conference.
Expenses for 2005–2006 Special program-related fees: $100 per course for applied music fees, $100 per course for piano accompanying fees, $330 per semester for computer lab use.
Financial Aid Program-specific awards: 1 Turner Music Award for program majors ($1000), 1 Presser Award for program majors ($4000), 1 Schubert Music Award for program majors ($150), 100 music scholarships for program majors/minors ($400–$2000).
Application Procedures Students admitted directly into the professional program freshman year. Deadline for freshmen and transfers: continuous. Required: high school transcript, college transcript(s) for transfer students, interview, audition, SAT I or ACT test scores (minimum combined SAT I score of 910, minimum composite ACT score of 19). Recommended: minimum 3.0 high school GPA, letter of recommendation. Auditions held 4 times at student's convenience on campus; recorded music is permissible as a substitute for live auditions if a campus visit is impossible and videotaped performances are permissible as a substitute for live auditions if a campus visit is impossible.
Web Site http://www.hputx.edu
Undergraduate Contact Ms. Cheryl Mangrum, Director, Enrollment Services, Howard Payne University, 1000 Fisk Street, HPU Station 828, Brownwood, Texas 76801-2794; 915-649-8020, fax: 915-649-8901.

Howard University
Washington, District of Columbia

Independent, coed. Urban campus. Total enrollment: 10,623. Music program established 1902.
Degrees Bachelor of Music; Bachelor of Music Education. Majors and concentrations: composition, instrumental performance, jazz studies, music business, music education, music history, music therapy, voice performance. Graduate degrees offered: Master of Music in the areas of performance, jazz studies; Master of Music Education in the areas of vocal performance, instrumental performance. Cross-registration with Consortium of Universities of the Washington Metropolitan Area. Program accredited by NASM.
Enrollment 133 total; 127 undergraduate, 6 graduate.
Music Student Profile 50% females, 50% males, 90% minorities, 5% international.
Music Faculty 19 total (full-time), 14 total (part-time). 50% of full-time faculty have terminal degrees. Graduate students teach a few undergraduate courses. Undergraduate student–faculty ratio: 6:1.
Student Life Student groups/activities include Howard University Choir, Howard University Marching Band, Howard University Jazz Ensemble.
Expenses for 2005–2006 Application fee: $45. Comprehensive fee: $18,481 includes full-time tuition ($11,490), mandatory fees ($805), and college room and board ($6186). College room only: $3736. Room and board charges vary according to board plan and housing facility.

Financial Aid Program-specific awards: Special Talent Awards for program majors ($2500), Trustee Scholarships for program majors ($2500), grant/aid awards for program majors.
Application Procedures Students admitted directly into the professional program freshman year. Deadline for freshmen and transfers: continuous. Required: high school transcript, college transcript(s) for transfer students, 2 letters of recommendation, audition, SAT I or ACT test scores (minimum combined SAT I score of 940), GED (if applicable). Recommended: minimum 3.0 high school GPA. Auditions held by appointment on campus; recorded music is permissible as a substitute for live auditions when distance is prohibitive and videotaped performances are permissible as a substitute for live auditions when distance is prohibitive.
Web Site http://howard.edu
Contact Dr. Thomas A. Korth, Chair, Department of Music, Howard University, College of Arts and Sciences, Washington, District of Columbia 20059; 202-806-7087, fax: 202-806-9673, e-mail address: tkorth@howard.edu

Hugh A. Glauser School of Music
See Kent State University

Hugh Hodgson School of Music
See University of Georgia

Hunter College of the City University of New York
New York, New York

State and locally supported, coed. Urban campus. Total enrollment: 20,843. Music program established 1975.
Degrees Bachelor of Music in the area of performance. Majors and concentrations: classical music, composition, jazz, piano/organ, stringed instruments, voice, wind and percussion instruments. Graduate degrees offered: Master of Arts in the areas of music performance, music composition, music education, music theory, music history, ethnomusicology. Cross-registration with senior colleges of the City University of New York System.
Enrollment 260 total; 20 undergraduate, 80 graduate, 160 nonprofessional degree.
Music Student Profile 72% females, 28% males, 60% minorities, 30% international.
Music Faculty 12 total (full-time), 29 total (part-time). 100% of full-time faculty have terminal degrees. Graduate students teach a few undergraduate courses. Undergraduate student–faculty ratio: 18:1.
Student Life Student groups/activities include Music Theater Workshop, Hunter College Jazz Society, Collegium Musicum.
Expenses for 2006–2007 Application fee: $65. State resident tuition: $4000 full-time. Nonresident tuition: $10,800 full-time. Mandatory fees: $349 full-time. College room only: $3478. Special program-related fees: $20 per semester for practice room fee.
Financial Aid Program-specific awards: 20 alumni awards for students taking private lessons ($500), 10 Music Department Awards for students taking private lessons ($500).
Application Procedures Students admitted directly into the professional program freshman year. Deadline for freshmen: November 1; transfers: March 15. Notification date for freshmen and transfers: June 1. Required: high school transcript, college transcript(s) for transfer students, audition, minimum 2.2 high school GPA, minimum 2.0 college GPA for transfer students with 24 credits, minimum 2.7 college GPA for transfer students with 28 credits. Recommended: minimum 3.0 high school GPA. Auditions held 8 times on campus; recorded music is permissible as a substitute for live auditions for provisional admission and videotaped performances are permissible as a substitute for live auditions for provisional acceptance.
Web Site http://www.hunter.cuny.edu/music/
Undergraduate Contact Dr. Ruth DeFord, Director of Undergraduate Studies, Department of Music, Hunter College of the City

Hunter College of the City University of New York (continued)

University of New York, 695 Park Avenue, New York, New York 10021; 212-772-5537, fax: 212-772-5022, e-mail address: ruth.deford@hunter.cuny.edu

Graduate Contact Dr. L. Poundie Burstein, Director of Graduate Studies, Department of Music, Hunter College of the City University of New York, 695 Park Avenue, New York, New York 10021; 212-772-5152, fax: 212-772-5022, e-mail address: huntermust@aol.com

Huntington University

Huntington, Indiana

Independent, coed. Small town campus. Total enrollment: 1,019. Music program established 1897.

Degrees Bachelor of Music in the areas of music performance, music education, music composition. Majors and concentrations: church music, composition, music, music business, music education. Program accredited by NASM.

Enrollment 37 total; 28 undergraduate, 9 nonprofessional degree.

Music Student Profile 70% females, 30% males.

Music Faculty 5 undergraduate (full-time), 16 undergraduate (part-time). 100% of full-time faculty have terminal degrees. Graduate students do not teach undergraduate courses. Undergraduate student–faculty ratio: 6:1.

Expenses for 2006–2007 Application fee: $20. Comprehensive fee: $25,390 includes full-time tuition ($18,420), mandatory fees ($440), and college room and board ($6530). Special program-related fees: $240 per half-hour lesson for private instruction and practice room fee.

Financial Aid Program-specific awards: 25 performance grants for program majors/minors ($34,150).

Application Procedures Students admitted directly into the professional program freshman year. Deadline for freshmen and transfers: continuous. Required: high school transcript, college transcript(s) for transfer students, minimum 2.0 high school GPA, audition, SAT I or ACT test scores. Auditions held as needed on campus.

Web Site http://www.huntington.edu

Undergraduate Contact Mr. Jeffrey Berggren, Executive Director of Enrollment Management, Admissions Department, Huntington University, 2303 College Avenue, Huntington, Indiana 46750; 260-356-6000, fax: 260-356-9448.

Hurley School of Music

See Centenary College of Louisiana

Idaho State University

Pocatello, Idaho

State-supported, coed. Small town campus. Total enrollment: 13,977. Music program established 1940.

Degrees Bachelor of Music in the area of performance; Bachelor of Music Education. Majors and concentrations: guitar, music, music education, piano, stringed instruments, voice, wind and percussion instruments. Graduate degrees offered: Master of Education in the area of music education. Program accredited by NASM.

Enrollment 99 total; 72 undergraduate, 7 graduate, 20 nonprofessional degree.

Music Student Profile 60% females, 40% males, 2% minorities.

Music Faculty 12 undergraduate (full-time), 11 undergraduate (part-time). 67% of full-time faculty have terminal degrees. Graduate students do not teach undergraduate courses. Undergraduate student–faculty ratio: 6:1.

Student Life Student groups/activities include Music Educators National Conference Student Chapter, American Choral Directors Association Student Chapter.

Expenses for 2006–2007 Application fee: $40. One-time mandatory fee: $660. Nonresident tuition: $7700 full-time. Mandatory fees: $4000 full-time. College room and board: $5030. College room only: $2100. Special program-related fees: $145–$290 per lesson for applied music fee .

Financial Aid Program-specific awards: 80 ensemble scholarships for program majors/minors ($350–$1000), 2 Missal Band Scholarships for band majors ($1000), 7 Berryman Endowment Awards for program majors ($500–$600), 6 Phoenix Endowment Awards for program majors ($500–$600), 11 Department of Music Endowment Awards for program majors ($350–$500), 1 Anderson Vocal Scholarship for vocal majors ($1000–$1200), 75 marching band scholarships for instrumentalists ($500–$800), 20 vocal endowment awards for vocal majors ($500–$1000), 1 Kwiat Endowment Award for piano majors ($350).

Application Procedures Students apply for admission into the professional program by sophomore year. Deadline for freshmen: August 1; transfers: continuous. Notification date for freshmen and transfers: continuous. Required: high school transcript, college transcript(s) for transfer students, minimum 2.0 high school GPA, letter of recommendation, interview, audition, placement examinations in piano and theory, SAT I or ACT (ACT preferred). Recommended: essay, minimum 3.0 high school GPA. Auditions held 3-4 times on campus and off campus in various Idaho locations; recorded music is permissible as a substitute for live auditions when distance is prohibitive and videotaped performances are permissible as a substitute for live auditions when distance is prohibitive.

Web Site http://www.isu.edu/music

Undergraduate Contact Dr. Randy A. Earles, Chairman, Department of Music, Idaho State University, Box 8099, Pocatello, Idaho 83209-8099; 208-282-3636, fax: 208-282-4884, e-mail address: earlrand@isu.edu

Graduate Contact Dr. Randy A. Earles, Chairman, Music, Idaho State University, Box 8099, Pocutello, Idaho 83209-8099; 208-282-3636, fax: 208-282-4884, e-mail address: earlrand@isu.edu

Illinois State University

Normal, Illinois

State-supported, coed. Urban campus. Total enrollment: 20,653. Music program established 1913.

Degrees Bachelor of Arts in the area of musical theatre; Bachelor of Music in the areas of performance, music therapy, music composition; Bachelor of Music Education; Bachelor of Science in the area of music business. Majors and concentrations: classical guitar, classical music, composition, music, music business, music education, music theater, music therapy, piano/organ, stringed instruments, voice, wind and percussion instruments. Graduate degrees offered: Master of Music in the areas of performance, music composition, music therapy; Master of Music Education; Master of Science. Program accredited by NASM.

Enrollment 331 total; 266 undergraduate, 65 graduate.

Music Student Profile 57% females, 43% males, 12% minorities, 6% international.

Music Faculty 43 total (full-time). 65% of full-time faculty have terminal degrees. Graduate students teach a few undergraduate courses. Undergraduate student–faculty ratio: 6:1.

Student Life Student groups/activities include National Association of Music Therapy, Music Educators National Conference, Tau Beta Sigma. Special housing available for music students.

Expenses for 2005–2006 Application fee: $30. State resident tuition: $5400 full-time. Nonresident tuition: $11,280 full-time. Mandatory fees: $1691 full-time. Full-time tuition and fees vary according to course load. College room and board: $5748. College room only: $3010. Room and board charges vary according to board plan. Special program-related fees: $10 per semester for locker rental, $15 per degree for practice room usage.

Financial Aid Program-specific awards: 16 tuition waivers for program majors and minors ($300–$3700), 20 talent grants-in-aid for program majors and minors ($200–$2600), 20 endowed scholarships for enrolled music majors.

Application Procedures Students admitted directly into the professional program freshman year. Deadline for freshmen and transfers: March 1. Notification date for freshmen and transfers: April 15. Required: essay, high school transcript, college transcript(s) for transfer students, minimum 2.0 high school GPA, audition, SAT I or ACT test scores. Recommended: 3 letters of recommendation. Auditions held 6 times on campus; recorded music is permissible as a substitute for live auditions for

out-of-state applicants and videotaped performances are permissible as a substitute for live auditions for out-of-state applicants.
Web Site http://www.music.ilstu.edu
Undergraduate Contact Mrs. Janet Tulley, Assistant to the Director, School of Music, Illinois State University, Campus Box 5660, Normal, Illinois 61790-5660; 309-438-3566, fax: 309-438-5833, e-mail address: jatulle@ilstu.edu
Graduate Contact Dr. Joe Neisler, Graduate Music Admissions Director, School of Music, Illinois State University, Campus Box 5660, Normal, Illinois 61790-5660; 309-438-8960, fax: 309-438-5833, e-mail address: jneisle@ilstu.edu

Illinois Wesleyan University
Bloomington, Illinois

Independent, coed. Suburban campus. Total enrollment: 2,146. Music program established 1897.
Degrees Bachelor of Music in the areas of performance, composition; Bachelor of Music Education in the areas of vocal music education, instrumental music education. Majors and concentrations: brass instruments performance, classical music, composition, music, music education, piano, stringed instruments, voice, wind and percussion instruments. Program accredited by NASM.
Enrollment 189 total; 150 undergraduate, 39 nonprofessional degree.
Music Student Profile 56% females, 44% males, 7% minorities, 3% international.
Music Faculty 19 undergraduate (full-time), 31 undergraduate (part-time). 100% of full-time faculty have terminal degrees. Graduate students do not teach undergraduate courses. Undergraduate student–faculty ratio: 11:1.
Student Life Student groups/activities include Music Educators National Conference Student Chapter, Phi Mu Alpha/Delta Omicron, Sigma Alpha Iota. Special housing available for music students.
Expenses for 2006–2007 Application fee: $0. Comprehensive fee: $35,790 includes full-time tuition ($28,926), mandatory fees ($150), and college room and board ($6714). College room only: $4104. Special program-related fees: $290 per semester for private music lessons beyond curricular requirements.
Financial Aid Program-specific awards: 16–40 Music Talent Awards for program students ($6000–$22,900).
Application Procedures Students admitted directly into the professional program freshman year. Deadline for freshmen: March 1; transfers: April 1. Notification date for freshmen: April 1; transfers: May 1. Required: essay, high school transcript, college transcript(s) for transfer students, minimum 3.0 high school GPA, interview, audition, SAT I or ACT test scores (minimum combined SAT I score of 1100, minimum composite ACT score of 23), portfolio for composition majors. Recommended: 2 letters of recommendation. Auditions held by appointment on campus; recorded music is permissible as a substitute for live auditions when distance is prohibitive and videotaped performances are permissible as a substitute for live auditions when distance is prohibitive. Portfolio reviews held by appointment on campus.
Web Site http://www.iwu.edu
Undergraduate Contact Ms. Laura Dolan, Music Admissions Coordinator, School of Music, Illinois Wesleyan University, PO Box 2900, Bloomington, Illinois 61702; 309-556-3063, fax: 309-556-3411, e-mail address: ldolan@iwu.edu

Immaculata University
Immaculata, Pennsylvania

Independent Roman Catholic, coed, primarily women. Suburban campus. Total enrollment: 4,019. Music program established 1921.
Degrees Bachelor of Music. Majors and concentrations: music education, music therapy. Graduate degrees offered: Master of Arts in the area of music therapy. Cross-registration with . Program accredited by NASM, AMTA.
Enrollment 77 total; 28 undergraduate, 26 graduate, 23 nonprofessional degree.

Music Student Profile 81% females, 19% males, 9% minorities, 2% international.
Music Faculty 5 undergraduate (full-time), 25 undergraduate (part-time), 1 graduate (full-time), 2 graduate (part-time). 80% of full-time faculty have terminal degrees. Graduate students do not teach undergraduate courses. Undergraduate student–faculty ratio: 8:1.
Student Life Student groups/activities include Music Educators National Conference Student Chapter, American Music Therapy Association Student Chapter, Annual Institute for Music and Healing, chorale, symphony, madrigals.
Expenses for 2006–2007 Application fee: $35. Comprehensive fee: $29,910 includes full-time tuition ($20,575) and college room and board ($9335). College room only: $5010. Special program-related fees: $300–$590 per course for private music lessons.
Financial Aid Program-specific awards: music scholarships for music majors ($1000), 1 Borelli Award for program juniors or seniors ($500), 2 Almira Doutt Awards for program juniors or seniors ($1000), 30 Immaculata Talent Grants for music majors ($6000).
Application Procedures Students admitted directly into the professional program freshman year. Deadline for freshmen and transfers: continuous. Required: high school transcript, college transcript(s) for transfer students, minimum 2.0 high school GPA, letter of recommendation, audition, SAT I or ACT test scores. Recommended: essay, interview, video. Auditions held 8 times on campus; recorded music is permissible as a substitute for live auditions if a campus visit is impossible and videotaped performances are permissible as a substitute for live auditions if a campus visit is impossible.
Web Site http://www.immaculata.edu
Undergraduate Contact Mr. Michael Walden, Director of Admission, Immaculata University, 1145 King Road, Immaculata, Pennsylvania 19345; 610-647-4400 ext. 3046, fax: 610-251-1668, e-mail address: mwalden@immaculata.edu
Graduate Contact Dr. Brian Abrams, Chair, Graduate Music Therapy Program, Music Therapy Department, Immaculata University, PO Box 697, Immaculata, Pennsylvania 19345-0697; 610-647-4400 ext. 3490, fax: 610-251-1668, e-mail address: babrams@immaculata.edu

Indiana State University
Terre Haute, Indiana

State-supported, coed. Small town campus. Total enrollment: 10,679.
Degrees Bachelor of Arts in the areas of music theory, music history and literature, composition; Bachelor of Music in the area of performance; Bachelor of Music Education in the areas of instrumental/general, choral/general; Bachelor of Science in the area of music business. Majors and concentrations: composition, music education, music history and literature, music merchandising and business administration, music theory, piano, stringed instruments, voice, wind and percussion instruments. Graduate degrees offered: Master of Music in the areas of performance, composition, music education, music theory, music history and literature, wind conducting, choral conducting. Cross-registration with Saint Mary-of-the-Woods College, Rose-Hulman Institute of Technology. Program accredited by NASM.
Enrollment 265 total; 250 undergraduate, 15 graduate.
Music Student Profile 50% females, 50% males, 5% minorities, 4% international.
Music Faculty 26 total (full-time), 19 total (part-time). 88% of full-time faculty have terminal degrees. Graduate students teach a few undergraduate courses. Undergraduate student–faculty ratio: 8:1.
Student Life Student groups/activities include Music Educators National Conference, Music Industry Association, Music Teachers National Association. Special housing available for music students.
Expenses for 2005–2006 Application fee: $25. State resident tuition: $5756 full-time. Nonresident tuition: $12,752 full-time. Mandatory fees: $108 full-time. Full-time tuition and fees vary according to course load. College room and board: $5938. College room only: $3150. Room and board charges vary

Indiana State University (continued)

according to board plan, housing facility, and student level. Special program-related fees: $100 per contact hour for applied music fee.

Financial Aid Program-specific awards: 22 Creative and Performing Arts Scholarship s ($2000), departmental scholarships ($1000).

Application Procedures Students admitted directly into the professional program freshman year. Deadline for freshmen and transfers: June 1. Required: high school transcript, college transcript(s) for transfer students, minimum 2.0 high school GPA, audition, SAT I or ACT test scores, minimum 2.0 college GPA for transfer students, 1-2 letters of recommendation. Recommended: essay. Auditions held 8 times and by appointment on campus; recorded music is permissible as a substitute for live auditions when distance is prohibitive or for international applicants, reaudition upon arriving on campus and videotaped performances are permissible as a substitute for live auditions when distance is prohibitive or for international applicants, reaudition upon arriving on campus.

Web Site http://www.indstate.edu/music

Undergraduate Contact Dr. Todd Sullivan, Chairperson, Department of Music, Indiana State University, Terre Haute, Indiana 47809; 812-237-2771, fax: 812-237-3009.

Graduate Contact Dr. Linda Damer, Director of Graduate Studies, Department of Music, Indiana State University, Terre Haute, Indiana 47809; 812-237-2790, fax: 812-237-3009.

Indiana University Bloomington

Bloomington, Indiana

State-supported, coed. Small town campus. Total enrollment: 37,958. Music program established 1910.

Degrees Bachelor of Music in the area of performance; Bachelor of Music Education in the areas of choral-general teaching, instrumental teaching, choral and instrumental teaching area; Bachelor of Science in the areas of audio recording, opera scenic technique, ballet, music and an outside field. Majors and concentrations: audio recording technology, ballet, bassoon, cello, choral music education, clarinet, classical guitar, composition, double bass, early music, euphonium, flute, harp, horn, instrumental music education, jazz studies, oboe, opera scenic technique, organ, percussion, performance, piano, saxophone, trombone, trumpet, tuba, viola, violin, voice. Graduate degrees offered: Master of Arts in the areas of musicology, music theory; Master of Arts in Teaching in the area of music education; Master of Music in the areas of choral conducting, composition, early music, instrumental conducting, jazz studies, music theory, organ and church music, wind conducting, performance; Master of Music Education; Master of Science in the areas of ballet, music theater scenic techniques, stage direction for opera. Doctor of Music in the areas of choral conducting, composition, early music, instrumental conducting, organ and church music, wind conducting, performance, brass pedagogy; Doctor of Music Education; Doctor of Philosophy in the areas of music theory, musicology, music education. Program accredited by NASM.

Enrollment 1,633 total; 801 undergraduate, 818 graduate, 14 nonprofessional degree.

Music Student Profile 51% females, 49% males, 10% minorities, 20% international.

Music Faculty 148 total (full-time), 23 total (part-time). Graduate students teach about a quarter of undergraduate courses. Undergraduate student–faculty ratio: 18:1.

Student Life Student groups/activities include opera theater, choral ensembles, singing Hoosiers , instrumental ensembles (orchestra, band, jazz, chamber groups).

Expenses for 2005–2006 Application fee: $50. State resident tuition: $6291 full-time. Nonresident tuition: $18,687 full-time. Mandatory fees: $821 full-time. Full-time tuition and fees vary according to location, program, and student level. College room and board: $6240. College room only: $3760. Room and board charges vary according to board plan and housing facility. Special program-related fees: $10 per semester for locker rental, $35 per recital for recital recording, $35 per program for recital

program printing, $50 per course for electronic course, $150 per course for ballet therapy, $650 per semester for applied music fee.

Financial Aid Program-specific awards: School of Music Dean's Award for those demonstrating musical ability and scholastic achievement, minority scholarships for minority students demonstrating musical ability, scholastic achievement, and financial need, University Grants for those demonstrating musical ability, scholastic achievement, and financial need.

Application Procedures Students admitted directly into the professional program freshman year. Deadline for freshmen and transfers: December 1. Notification date for freshmen and transfers: May 1. Required: essay, high school transcript, college transcript(s) for transfer students, minimum 2.0 high school GPA, interview, video, audition, portfolio, SAT I or ACT test scores. Recommended: minimum 3.0 high school GPA. Auditions held 3 times on campus; recorded music is permissible as a substitute for live auditions and videotaped performances are permissible as a substitute for live auditions.

Web Site http://www.music.indiana.edu

Contact Music Admissions, School of Music, Indiana University Bloomington, 1201 East 3rd Street- MU 101, Bloomington, Indiana 47405; 812-855-7998, fax: 812-856-6086, e-mail address: musicadm@indiana.edu

Indiana University of Pennsylvania

Indiana, Pennsylvania

State-supported, coed. Small town campus. Total enrollment: 14,081.

Indiana University–Purdue University Fort Wayne

Fort Wayne, Indiana

State-supported, coed. Urban campus. Total enrollment: 11,795. Music program established 1967.

Degrees Bachelor of Music in the areas of piano, voice, orchestral instruments, interdisciplinary studies; Bachelor of Music Education in the area of choral and/or instrumental teaching; Bachelor of Science in Music Therapy in the area of music therapy. Majors and concentrations: interdisciplinary studies, music, music education, music therapy, piano/organ, stringed instruments, voice, wind and percussion instruments. Cross-registration with Taylor University, Manchester College. Program accredited by NASM, AMTA, NCATE.

Enrollment 125 total; all undergraduate.

Music Student Profile 55% females, 45% males, 9% minorities, 2% international.

Music Faculty 12 undergraduate (full-time), 32 undergraduate (part-time). 90% of full-time faculty have terminal degrees. Graduate students do not teach undergraduate courses. Undergraduate student–faculty ratio: 14:1.

Student Life Student groups/activities include Sigma Alpha Iota, Music Educators National Conference, American Choral Directors Association.

Expenses for 2005–2006 Application fee: $30. State resident tuition: $4523 full-time. Nonresident tuition: $11,142 full-time. Mandatory fees: $544 full-time. Full-time tuition and fees vary according to course load, location, and student level. College room only: $4750. Room charges vary according to housing facility.

Financial Aid Program-specific awards: 1–2 Ator Scholarships for instrumental majors ($800), 1–2 Loessi Scholarships for vocal/choral majors ($800), 6–8 Whitney Scholarships for program majors ($500), 20 departmental merit awards for program majors ($500).

Application Procedures Students admitted directly into the professional program freshman year. Deadline for freshmen and transfers: August 1. Notification date for freshmen and transfers: August 21. Required: high school transcript, college transcript(s) for transfer students, minimum 2.0 high school GPA, interview, audition, SAT I or ACT test scores, music theory placement exam. Auditions held continuously on campus;

recorded music is permissible as a substitute for live auditions if a campus visit is impossible and videotaped performances are permissible as a substitute for live auditions if a campus visit is impossible.
Web Site http://www.ipfw.edu/vpa
Undergraduate Contact Dr. Robert Bean, Chair, Department of Music, Indiana University–Purdue University Fort Wayne, 2101 Coliseum Boulevard East, Fort Wayne, Indiana 46805-1499; 219-481-6714, fax: 219-481-5422, e-mail address: beanr@ipfw.edu

Indiana University South Bend
South Bend, Indiana

State-supported, coed. Suburban campus. Total enrollment: 7,459. Music program established 1965.
Degrees Bachelor of Music in the areas of piano, orchestral instruments, guitar, composition, voice; Bachelor of Science in the area of music and an outside field. Majors and concentrations: brass, composition, guitar, piano/organ, stringed instruments, voice, wind and percussion instruments. Graduate degrees offered: Master of Music in the areas of piano, orchestral instruments, guitar, composition, voice. Cross-registration with Indiana University System, Bethel College.
Enrollment 79 total; 62 undergraduate, 17 graduate.
Music Student Profile 45% females, 55% males, 5% minorities, 10% international.
Music Faculty 10 total (full-time), 12 total (part-time). 100% of full-time faculty have terminal degrees. Graduate students teach a few undergraduate courses. Undergraduate student–faculty ratio: 8:1.
Expenses for 2005–2006 Application fee: $43. State resident tuition: $4583 full-time. Nonresident tuition: $12,002 full-time. Mandatory fees: $406 full-time. Full-time tuition and fees vary according to course load. Special program-related fees: $191 per semester for applied music fee.
Financial Aid Program-specific awards: 22 music scholarships for pianists and string instrumentalists ($3500).
Application Procedures Students admitted directly into the professional program freshman year. Deadline for freshmen and transfers: July 15. Notification date for freshmen and transfers: September 1. Required: high school transcript, college transcript(s) for transfer students, minimum 2.0 high school GPA, audition, SAT I or ACT test scores. Auditions held twice on campus; recorded music is permissible as a substitute for live auditions for international applicants and videotaped performances are permissible as a substitute for live auditions for international applicants.
Web Site http://www.iusb.edu/%7Emajors/music.shtml
Undergraduate Contact Dr. David Barton, Music Area Coordinator, School of the Arts, Indiana University South Bend, 1700 Mishawaka Avenue, PO Box 7111, South Bend, Indiana 46634; 574-520-4161, fax: 574-237-4317, e-mail address: dbarton@iusb.edu
Graduate Contact Dr. David Barton, Director of Graduate Studies, School of the Arts, Indiana University South Bend, 1700 Mishawaka Avenue, PO Box 7111, South Bend, Indiana 46634; 574-520-4161, e-mail address: dbarton@iusb.edu

Iowa State University of Science and Technology
Ames, Iowa

State-supported, coed. Suburban campus. Total enrollment: 25,741. Music program established 1967.
Degrees Bachelor of Music in the areas of music education, performance, composition; Bachelor of Music Education in the areas of vocal music education, instrumental music education. Majors and concentrations: composition, music, music education, piano/organ, stringed instruments, voice, wind and percussion instruments. Program accredited by NASM.
Enrollment 123 total; all undergraduate.
Music Student Profile 52% females, 48% males, 2% minorities, 2% international.

Music Faculty 24 undergraduate (full-time), 7 undergraduate (part-time). 77% of full-time faculty have terminal degrees. Graduate students do not teach undergraduate courses. Undergraduate student–faculty ratio: 4:1.
Student Life Student groups/activities include Phi Mu Alpha Sinfonia, Sigma Alpha Iota, Kappa Kappa Psi/Tau Beta Sigma.
Expenses for 2005–2006 Application fee: $30. State resident tuition: $4890 full-time. Nonresident tuition: $14,980 full-time. Mandatory fees: $744 full-time. Full-time tuition and fees vary according to class time, degree level, and program. College room and board: $6197. College room only: $3295. Room and board charges vary according to board plan and housing facility. Special program-related fees: $90–$130 per semester for applied music fee.
Financial Aid Program-specific awards: 45–50 departmental scholarships for program majors ($300–$2200).
Application Procedures Students admitted directly into the professional program freshman year. Deadline for freshmen and transfers: continuous. Required: high school transcript, college transcript(s) for transfer students, minimum 2.0 high school GPA, interview, audition, SAT I or ACT test scores (minimum composite ACT score of 24). Auditions held continuously on campus; recorded music is permissible as a substitute for live auditions if a campus visit is impossible and videotaped performances are permissible as a substitute for live auditions if a campus visit is impossible.
Web Site http://www.music.iastate.edu/
Undergraduate Contact Admissions Secretary, Department of Music, Iowa State University of Science and Technology, 149 Music Hall, Ames, Iowa 50011; 515-294-3831, fax: 515-294-6409, e-mail address: takrock@iastate.edu

Iowa Wesleyan College
Mount Pleasant, Iowa

Independent United Methodist, coed. Small town campus. Total enrollment: 849.
Degrees Bachelor of Music Education. Majors and concentrations: music education. Cross-registration with Southeastern Community College.
Enrollment 14 total; 13 undergraduate, 1 nonprofessional degree.
Music Faculty 4 undergraduate (full-time), 6 undergraduate (part-time). 75% of full-time faculty have terminal degrees. Graduate students do not teach undergraduate courses. Undergraduate student–faculty ratio: 3:1.
Student Life Student groups/activities include Music Educators National Conference Student Chapter, American Choral Directors Association Student Chapter.
Expenses for 2006–2007 Comprehensive fee: $23,330 includes full-time tuition ($17,800) and college room and board ($5530). College room only: $2280.
Financial Aid Program-specific awards: 5–8 Goodell Music Scholarships for incoming students ($3000–$6000).
Application Procedures Students apply for admission into the professional program by sophomore year. Deadline for freshmen and transfers: continuous. Required: essay, high school transcript, college transcript(s) for transfer students, minimum 2.0 high school GPA, letter of recommendation, SAT I or ACT test scores (minimum composite ACT score of 19), audition for scholarship consideration. Recommended: audition. Auditions held by appointment on campus; recorded music is permissible as a substitute for live auditions when distance is prohibitive (beyond 200-mile radius) and videotaped performances are permissible as a substitute for live auditions when distance is prohibitive.
Web Site http://www.iwc.edu
Undergraduate Contact Mr. Cary Owens, Director, Admissions Department, Iowa Wesleyan College, 601 North Main Street, Mount Pleasant, Iowa 52641; 319-385-6231, fax: 319-385-6296, e-mail address: admit@iwc.edu

Ithaca College
Ithaca, New York

Independent, coed. Small town campus. Total enrollment: 6,412. Music program established 1892.

Ithaca College (continued)

Degrees Bachelor of Music in the areas of composition, jazz studies, music education, performance, performance/music education, music theory, music in combination with an outside field, recording. Majors and concentrations: composition, guitar, jazz, music education, music theory, performance, piano/organ, recording arts and sciences, stringed instruments, voice, wind and percussion instruments. Graduate degrees offered: Master of Music in the areas of brasses, composition, conducting, music education, performance, strings, Suzuki pedagogy, woodwinds. Cross-registration with Cornell University, Wells College. Program accredited by NASM.

Enrollment 529 total; 460 undergraduate, 46 graduate, 23 nonprofessional degree.

Music Student Profile 57% females, 43% males, 6% minorities, 1% international.

Music Faculty 57 undergraduate (full-time), 36 undergraduate (part-time). 90% of full-time faculty have terminal degrees. Graduate students teach a few undergraduate courses. Undergraduate student–faculty ratio: 7:1.

Student Life Student groups/activities include American Choral Directors Association, Music Educators National Conference, American String Teachers Association.

Expenses for 2005–2006 Application fee: $55. Comprehensive fee: $35,144 includes full-time tuition ($25,194) and college room and board ($9950). College room only: $5120.

Financial Aid Program-specific awards: 14 Clinton B. Ford Music Scholarships for instrumentalists ($670–$2260), 16 Ithaca Premier Talent Scholarships for program majors ($10,000–$13,000), 15 Leo A. & Frances MacArthur Keilocker Scholarships for talented stringed instrumentalists ($5500), 20 Col. George S. Howard '25 Scholarships for talented wind instrumentalists ($300–$1330), 10 Iola Angood Taylor Scholarship for students from public school music programs ($1272–$1917), 9 Robert S. Boothroyd Scholarships for outstanding music students ($608–$1687), 4 Allan H. Treman Music Scholarships for outstanding music students ($1103), Gretchen Haller/Haenchen Music Scholarship for those demonstrating financial need (vocal performance preference), 4 James J. Whalen Young Artist Scholarships for freshmen music majors ($12,194–$15,194).

Application Procedures Students admitted directly into the professional program freshman year. Deadline for freshmen: February 1; transfers: March 1. Notification date for freshmen: April 15. Required: essay, high school transcript, college transcript(s) for transfer students, letter of recommendation, audition, SAT I or ACT test scores, two original music scores for composition applicants. Recommended: minimum 3.0 high school GPA, interview. Auditions held 12 times on campus and off campus in New York, NY; Washington, DC; Philadelphia, PA; Boston, MA; recorded music is permissible as a substitute for live auditions when distance is prohibitive or scheduling is difficult and videotaped performances are permissible as a substitute for live auditions when distance is prohibitive or scheduling is difficult (video preferred).

Web Site http://www.ithaca.edu/music

Undergraduate Contact Mr. Gerard Turbide, Acting Director, Admission, Ithaca College, 100 Job Hall, Ithaca, New York 14850-7020; 607-274-3124, fax: 607-274-1900, e-mail address: admission@ithaca.edu

Graduate Contact Dr. Gregory Woodward, Dean of Graduate Studies, Division of Graduate Studies, Ithaca College, 111 Towers Concourse, Ithaca, New York 14850-7142; 607-274-3527, fax: 607-274-1263.

More About the College

Since its founding in 1892 as a conservatory of music, Ithaca College has been nurturing and developing its musical character. The College remains dedicated to the goals of its founder, W. Grant Egbert, who said, "It is my plan to build a school of music second to none in the excellence of its faculty, the soundness of its educational ideals, and the superior quality of instruction."

As the conservatory evolved into a college with expanded academic offerings, the programs in music retained their position of prominence. Today, Ithaca's School of Music is counted among the nation's leading schools devoted primarily to undergraduate study. Students benefit from a blend of first-class faculty members, innovative programs, and outstanding facilities.

Students in the School of Music take about one quarter of their academic work in the liberal arts, primarily through the School of Humanities and Sciences. Additional electives from the Schools of Business, Communications, and Health Sciences and Human Performance are also available. The interaction between the schools is another advantage to an Ithaca education: physics majors can be found working in the electroacoustic music studios, television-radio majors may take courses such as Music and the Media, and music students play in the pit orchestra for theater productions and perform on sound tracks for student filmmakers. The planned studies option allows students to create their own degree programs that take advantage of the broad array of courses and majors—some 2,000 courses and more than 100 degree programs are offered.

Students who come to the Ithaca College School of Music are already dedicated to the idea of mastering voice, piano, guitar, organ, or any of the standard orchestral and band instruments. At Ithaca they continue their training under a faculty of performing professionals who are dedicated to teaching undergraduates. Students prepare for their musical performances through weekly private lessons and hour-long repertory classes with their major teachers and fellow students. Repertory classes provide opportunities for students to perform for each other, review performance techniques, and meet guest artists such as Vladimir Felstman, Midori, Emmanuel Ax, Richard Stoltzman, Ani Kavafiann, and the Guarneri String Quartet. As soloists and with ensembles, students become part of the rich musical life of the school, where more than 300 recitals, concerts, musicals, and operas are given each year.

All degree programs emphasize performance. Each year, some 500 undergraduate and 40 graduate students are involved in live performances—on campus, in the Ithaca community, throughout the northeastern United States, and at national and international concert venues. In addition, several ensembles tour annually and have won critical acclaim for their work in New York City at Lincoln Center, St. Patrick's Cathedral, and Carnegie Hall; throughout New England; in Washington, D.C., and other cities; and in international venues such as London's Royal Academy of Music and the University of Limerick in Ireland.

The city of Ithaca is one of the country's premier college towns, with about 26,000 students at Ithaca College and Cornell University. Surrounded by magnificent gorges, lakes, and countryside in the Finger Lakes region of New York State, Ithaca is a thriving cultural center. The community supports an impressive array of concerts, art galleries, movies, and theater productions. Among the artists who have performed in town recently are Ladysmith Black Mambazo, Itzhak Perlman, Arlo Guthrie, Branford Marsalis, Yo Yo Ma, and Janos Starker.

Ithaca College's combination of a resident faculty, an emphasis on undergraduate performance, and access to a wide spectrum of liberal arts courses makes it an excellent choice among the major music schools in the nation.

Program Facilities Performance spaces include Ford Hall Auditorium (735 seats), the Hockett Family Recital Hall (250 seats), and Nabenhauer Recital Hall (150 seats). Electroacoustic music studios, computer-assisted instruction facilities, a professionally equipped recording studio, and a full complement of practice instruments are available. Some ninety practice room spaces are open to students, and there are forty Steinway grand pianos included in the 167 pianos at the school. The library has extensive holdings of music and recordings. A recent 69,000-square-foot music building addition has nearly doubled the existing space and includes increased rehearsal space, a computer classroom and lab, and a music education resource center.

Faculty, Resident Artists, and Alumni Faculty members perform nationally and regionally; many are scholars in the fields of music education, theory, composition, and history. Resident faculty ensembles include the Ithaca Brass, Ithaca Wind Quintet, and Ariadne String Quartet. Alumni hold positions in major orchestras and opera companies, perform in many prestigious chamber ensembles, sing on Broadway, and are recognized jazz recording artists. They also hold teaching positions in secondary schools and universities and are successful in arts administration, music publishing, audio technology, and music business.

Student Performance Opportunities Every student is required to perform in a major ensemble each semester; many participate in more than one. There are more than twenty student ensembles, including symphony orchestra, chamber orchestra, wind ensemble, concert band, symphonic band, brass choir, percussion ensemble, guitar ensemble, choir, chorus, women's chorale, madrigal singers, vocal jazz ensemble, opera workshop, and jazz workshop, as well as other numerous chamber ensembles.

Special Programs Students may study abroad at the Ithaca College London Center or in one of nearly fifty affiliated programs worldwide. The Office of Career Services offers special assistance geared to music students, and alumni also actively serve as career opportunity resources.

Jackson State University
Jackson, Mississippi

State-supported, coed. Urban campus. Total enrollment: 8,351.
Degrees Bachelor of Music in the areas of piano performance, vocal and instrumental performance, church music, music technology; Bachelor of Music Education in the areas of instrumental music education, vocal music education, piano music education, jazz music education. Majors and concentrations: church music, jazz, music education, music technology, piano, stringed instruments, voice, wind and percussion instruments. Graduate degrees offered: Master of Music in the areas of performance, church music; Master of Music Education. Program accredited by NASM.
Enrollment 137 total; 125 undergraduate, 12 graduate.
Music Student Profile 45% females, 55% males, 3% international.
Music Faculty 7 graduate (full-time), 3 total (part-time). 55% of full-time faculty have terminal degrees. Graduate students do not teach undergraduate courses. Undergraduate student–faculty ratio: 5:1.
Student Life Student groups/activities include Music Educators National Conference, Music Teachers National Association, Tau Beta Sigma, Phi Mu Alpha Sinfonia.
Expenses for 2005–2006 Application fee: $0. State resident tuition: $3964 full-time. Nonresident tuition: $8872 full-time. College room and board: $5044. College room only: $2998. Room and board charges vary according to board plan.
Financial Aid Program-specific awards: 250 music scholarships for talented program majors ($1000).
Application Procedures Students admitted directly into the professional program freshman year. Deadline for freshmen and transfers: July 1. Required: high school transcript, audition, SAT I or ACT test scores (minimum composite ACT score of 16), minimum 2.5 high school GPA. Recommended: 3 letters of recommendation, video, portfolio. Auditions held 3 times on campus and off campus in St. Louis, MO; Chicago, IL; Detroit, MI; Atlanta, GA; Hattiesburg, MS; Clarksdale, MS; Memphis, TN; recorded music is permissible as a substitute for live auditions when distance is prohibitive and videotaped performances are permissible as a substitute for live auditions when distance is prohibitive.
Web Site http://www.jsums.edu
Undergraduate Contact Dr. Jimmie James Jr., Chair, Department of Music, Jackson State University, PO Box 17055, Jackson, Mississippi 39217; 601-979-2141, fax: 601-979-2568, e-mail address: jimmie.james@jsums.edu
Graduate Contact Dr. Johnny Anthony, Associate Professor, Department of Music, Jackson State University, PO Box 17055, Jackson, Mississippi 39217; 601-979-2141, fax: 601-979-2568, e-mail address: johnny.anthony@jsums.edu

Jacksonville State University
Jacksonville, Alabama

State-supported, coed. Small town campus. Total enrollment: 9,110. Music program established 1960.
Degrees Bachelor of Arts in the area of music education. Majors and concentrations: music, music education. Graduate degrees offered: Master of Arts in the area of music education. Program accredited by NASM.
Enrollment 250 total; 210 undergraduate, 25 graduate, 15 nonprofessional degree.
Music Student Profile 45% females, 55% males, 12% minorities, 5% international.
Music Faculty 15 undergraduate (full-time), 7 undergraduate (part-time), 4 graduate (full-time). 75% of full-time faculty have terminal degrees. Graduate students do not teach undergraduate courses. Undergraduate student–faculty ratio: 12:1.
Student Life Student groups/activities include Music Educators National Conference Student Chapter, Phi Mu Alpha Sinfonia, Sigma Alpha Iota. Special housing available for music students.
Expenses for 2005–2006 Application fee: $20. State resident tuition: $4040 full-time. Nonresident tuition: $8080 full-time. College room and board: $3258. College room only: $1680. Room and board charges vary according to board plan and housing facility. Special program-related fees: $5 per semester for class applied music fee, $25 per semester for individual applied music fee.
Financial Aid Program-specific awards: 75–100 band scholarships for wind and percussion majors ($200–$1600), 25–50 choral scholarships for vocal/choral majors ($200–$1600), 10–15 vocal scholarships for voice majors ($200–$1600), 10–15 piano scholarships for piano majors ($200–$1600), 10–15 jazz scholarships for jazz ensemble participants ($200–$1600).
Application Procedures Students admitted directly into the professional program freshman year. Deadline for freshmen and transfers: continuous. Required: high school transcript, college transcript(s) for transfer students, minimum 2.0 high school GPA, SAT I or ACT test scores. Recommended: interview, audition. Auditions held 4 times on campus; recorded music is permissible as a substitute for live auditions if a campus visit is impossible and videotaped performances are permissible as a substitute for live auditions if a campus visit is impossible.
Web Site http://music.jsu.edu/
Undergraduate Contact Ms. Kathy Cambron, Registrar, Office of Admissions and Records, Jacksonville State University, 700 Pelham Road North, Jacksonville, Alabama 36265; 256-782-5400.
Graduate Contact Dr. William Carr, Dean, College of Graduate Studies and Continuing Education, Jacksonville State University, 700 Pelham Road North, Jacksonville, Alabama 36265; 256-782-5329.

Jacksonville University
Jacksonville, Florida

Independent, coed. Suburban campus. Total enrollment: 2,948. Music program established 1958.
Degrees Bachelor of Music in the areas of performance, composition and theory; Bachelor of Music Education. Majors and concentrations: music, music education, music theory and composition, voice performance. Program accredited by NASM.
Enrollment 33 total; all undergraduate.
Music Student Profile 58% females, 42% males, 22% minorities, 3% international.
Music Faculty 12 undergraduate (full-time), 3 undergraduate (part-time). 33% of full-time faculty have terminal degrees. Graduate students do not teach undergraduate courses. Undergraduate student–faculty ratio: 2:1.
Student Life Student groups/activities include Mu Phi Epsilon, Florida National Music Educators Conference Student Chapter, Pi Kappa Lambda.
Expenses for 2005–2006 Application fee: $30. Comprehensive fee: $26,430 includes full-time tuition ($19,970) and college room and board ($6460). College room only: $3030.
Financial Aid Program-specific awards: 52 music awards for those demonstrating need and talent ($750–$7000), 4 Phillips Scholar-

Jacksonville University (continued)

ships for those demonstrating exceptional talent ($1000–$4000), 1 orchestra award for those demonstrating need and talent ($3000), 1 band award for those demonstrating need and talent ($3000), 1 Larson Scholarship for those demonstrating exceptional talent ($4000), 1 Warren Scholarship for those demonstrating exceptional talent ($1000), 2 Sheldon Bryan Scholarships for those demonstrating exceptional talent ($2000–$6000).

Application Procedures Students admitted directly into the professional program freshman year. Deadline for freshmen and transfers: continuous. Notification date for freshmen and transfers: continuous. Required: high school transcript, college transcript(s) for transfer students, minimum 2.0 high school GPA, audition, SAT I or ACT test scores (minimum combined SAT I score of 800). Recommended: essay, minimum 3.0 high school GPA, 2 letters of recommendation. Auditions held 5 times and by appointment on campus; recorded music is permissible as a substitute for live auditions if a campus visit is impossible and videotaped performances are permissible as a substitute for live auditions if a campus visit is impossible.

Web Site http://www.ju.edu

Undergraduate Contact Ms. Miriam King, Vice President of Enrollment Management, Jacksonville University, 2800 University Boulevard North, Jacksonville, Florida 32211; 904-256-7000, fax: 904-256-7012, e-mail address: admissions@ju.edu

James Madison University
Harrisonburg, Virginia

State-supported, coed. Small town campus. Total enrollment: 16,938. Music program established 1934.

Degrees Bachelor of Music in the areas of music industry, music education, performance, composition, music theatre. Majors and concentrations: accompanying, composition, music business, music education, music theater, piano, stringed instruments, voice, wind and percussion instruments. Graduate degrees offered: Master of Music in the areas of performance, music education, conducting, music theory/composition. Program accredited by NASM.

Enrollment 383 total; 365 undergraduate, 18 graduate.

Music Student Profile 50% females, 50% males, 8% minorities, 1% international.

Music Faculty 39 total (full-time), 10 total (part-time). 74% of full-time faculty have terminal degrees. Graduate students do not teach undergraduate courses. Undergraduate student–faculty ratio: 13:1.

Student Life Student groups/activities include Music Educators National Conference, Kappa Kappa Psi, Sigma Alpha Iota, Pi Kappa Lambda.

Expenses for 2005–2006 Application fee: $40. State resident tuition: $5886 full-time. Nonresident tuition: $15,322 full-time. College room and board: $6372. College room only: $3278. Room and board charges vary according to board plan and housing facility.

Financial Aid Program-specific awards: 50 music performance awards for program majors ($2000).

Application Procedures Students admitted directly into the professional program freshman year. Deadline for freshmen: January 15; transfers: February 1. Notification date for freshmen: March 25; transfers: April 1. Required: essay, high school transcript, college transcript(s) for transfer students, minimum 2.0 high school GPA, 3 letters of recommendation, audition, SAT I or ACT test scores, music aptitude test, piano placement test, SAT II verbal test. Recommended: minimum 3.0 high school GPA, interview. Auditions held 3 times on campus; recorded music is permissible as a substitute for live auditions when distance is prohibitive and videotaped performances are permissible as a substitute for live auditions when distance is prohibitive.

Web Site http://www.jmu.edu/music/

Undergraduate Contact Dr. Michele M. Kirkdorffer, Music Admissions, School of Music, James Madison University, MSC 7301, Harrisonburg, Virginia 22807; 540-568-6197, fax: 540-568-7819, e-mail address: music_admit@jmu.edu

Graduate Contact Dr. Mary Jean Speare, Director of Graduate Studies, School of Music, James Madison University, MSC 7301,

Harrisonburg, Virginia 22807; 540-568-6197, fax: 540-568-7819, e-mail address: spearemj@jmu.edu

John M. Long School of Music
See Troy University

Peabody Conservatory of Music
The Johns Hopkins University
Baltimore, Maryland

Independent, coed. Urban campus. Total enrollment: 6,025.

Degrees Bachelor of Music in the areas of composition, performance, recording arts and sciences, music education, jazz performance, computer music. Majors and concentrations: composition, computer music, jazz performance, music education, performance, recording arts and sciences. Graduate degrees offered: Master of Arts in the area of acoustical studies; Master of Music in the areas of composition, performance, conducting, music education, musicology, computer music, theory pedagogy, performance pedagogy. Doctor of Musical Arts in the areas of composition, performance, conducting. Cross-registration with Maryland Institute College of Art, Loyola College. Program accredited by NASM.

Enrollment 701 total; 347 undergraduate, 354 graduate.

Music Student Profile 51% females, 49% males, 13% minorities, 25% international.

Music Faculty 77 total (full-time), 82 total (part-time). 37% of full-time faculty have terminal degrees. Graduate students do not teach undergraduate courses. Undergraduate student–faculty ratio: 15:1.

Student Life Special housing available for music students.

Expenses for 2006–2007 Application fee: $60. Comprehensive fee: $45,022 includes full-time tuition ($33,900), mandatory fees ($500), and college room and board ($10,622). College room only: $6096. Special program-related fees: $150 per year for technology fee.

Financial Aid Program-specific awards: performance scholarships for talented applicants ($1000–$15,000), institutional grants and aid for applicants demonstrating financial need ($500–$15,000).

Application Procedures Students admitted directly into the professional program freshman year. Deadline for freshmen and transfers: April 15. Notification date for freshmen and transfers: June 10. Required: essay, high school transcript, college transcript(s) for transfer students, minimum 3.0 high school GPA, 3 letters of recommendation, audition, SAT I test score only (minimum combined SAT I score of 1010), TOEFL score for international students. Recommended: interview. Auditions held 12 times on campus and off campus in New York, NY; Boston, MA; Atlanta, GA; Chicago, IL; San Francisco, CA; Los Angeles, CA; recorded music is permissible as a substitute for live auditions when distance is prohibitive (beyond 300-mile radius).

Web Site http://www.peabody.jhu.edu/

Contact Mr. David Lane, Director of Admissions, Peabody Conservatory of Music, The Johns Hopkins University, 1 East Mount Vernon Place, Baltimore, Maryland 21202; 410-659-8110, e-mail address: admissions@peabody.jhu.edu

More About the Conservatory

The Admissions office at the Peabody Institute understands how daunting the college search process can be to an aspiring artist. Students are likely to be clicking on Web sites and collecting literature from many colleges, conservatories, and universities. The college viewbooks they receive generally paint a wholly appealing picture of life at the school—no scheduling problems, an exquisite campus, incredibly talented students, and understanding faculty members—one could imagine that a Carnegie Hall debut is only a step away. How does a student make a wise choice and separate the fantasies from realities?

As the Director of Admissions at Peabody has said, "If a student and I do our jobs well, it is likely he or she will be happy with the final school selected. We need to see if what Peabody has to offer fits a student's needs."

Of course, Peabody has much to offer. The school was founded in 1857 but did not actually open its doors until 1866. The advantage of this age is that Peabody has been turning out top quality musicians for more than a century, and the music world has come to assume that anyone who graduates from Peabody is a good performer. When students are asked how they heard about the school, they often reply, "I don't know. I think I've always known about Peabody."

Peabody is one of the schools of The Johns Hopkins University. Therefore, Peabody students have access to the resources of the University. A shuttle bus runs hourly between the campuses. Double degrees, music minors, etc., can be shared with the schools of Arts and Sciences and Engineering. Thus, Peabody graduates are simultaneously graduates of JHU. If the Carnegie Hall fantasy doesn't work out, a Peabody/Hopkins diploma is a powerful credential to have on a resume.

The focus of Peabody's student body, which is made up of about 640 students, is classical music and Jazz. All Peabody undergraduates—even those majoring in music education or recording arts and sciences—must complete the same performance curriculum as those majoring in performance.

Students can write or call Peabody for application materials, or to learn details about the school's philosophy, audition requirements, faculty members, and the financial side of things. In any case, the Peabody Institute wishes every student planning to pursue a music career the best of luck in finding the right school.

Jordan College of Fine Arts
See Butler University

Juilliard Jazz
See The Juilliard School

The Juilliard School
New York, New York

Independent, coed. Urban campus. Total enrollment: 808. Music program established 1905.
Degrees Artist's Diploma; Bachelor of Music in the area of music performance. Majors and concentrations: bassoon, clarinet, composition, double bass, flute, French horn, harp, harpsichord, horn, oboe, organ, percussion, piano, trombone, trumpet, tuba, viola, violin, violoncello, voice. Graduate degrees offered: Master of Music. Doctor of Musical Arts. Cross-registration with Columbia University, Barnard College.
Enrollment 609 total; 318 undergraduate, 291 graduate.
Music Student Profile 46% females, 54% males, 44% minorities, 33% international.
Music Faculty 84 total (full-time), 108 total (part-time). Graduate students teach a few undergraduate courses. Undergraduate student–faculty ratio: 2:1.
Student Life Student groups/activities include orchestra and symphony concerts around Manhattan, mainstage opera productions, chamber music concerts. Special housing available for music students.
Expenses for 2005–2006 Application fee: $100. Comprehensive fee: $34,500 includes full-time tuition ($24,330), mandatory fees ($600), and college room and board ($9570). Room and board charges vary according to housing facility.
Financial Aid Program-specific awards: merit and/or need-based aid for program majors ($24,982).
Application Procedures Students admitted directly into the professional program freshman year. Deadline for freshmen and transfers: December 1. Notification date for freshmen and transfers: April 1. Required: essay, high school transcript, college transcript(s) for transfer students, letter of recommendation, interview, audition, TOEFL score for non-native English speakers, pre-screening audio tape for composition, flute, percussion, piano, violin, cello, and voice. Auditions held once on campus.
Web Site http://www.juilliard.edu

Contact Ms. Lee Cioppa, Associate Dean for Admissions, The Juilliard School, 60 Lincoln Center Plaza, New York, New York 10023-6588; 212-799-5000 ext. 223, fax: 212-769-6420, e-mail address: admissions@juilliard.edu

Juilliard Jazz
The Juilliard School
New York, New York

Independent, coed. Urban campus. Total enrollment: 808. Music program established 2003.
Degrees Artist's Diploma; Bachelor of Music. Majors and concentrations: jazz studies. Cross-registration with Barnard College and Columbia College (Columbia University).
Enrollment 27 total; 11 undergraduate, 16 graduate.
Music Student Profile 11% females, 89% males, 57% minorities, 11% international.
Music Faculty 7 total (full-time), 12 total (part-time). Graduate students do not teach undergraduate courses.
Student Life Student groups/activities include Juilliard Jazz Orchestra and Ensemble, composer-performer collaboration, tour opportunities and bookings in metro area clubs, International Association for Jazz Education. Special housing available for music students.
Expenses for 2005–2006 Application fee: $100. Comprehensive fee: $34,500 includes full-time tuition ($24,330), mandatory fees ($600), and college room and board ($9570). Room and board charges vary according to housing facility.
Financial Aid Program-specific awards: 11 merit and/or need-based aid for program majors ($32,343).
Application Procedures Students admitted directly into the professional program freshman year. Deadline for freshmen: December 1. Notification date for freshmen: April 1. Required: essay, high school transcript, college transcript(s) for transfer students, letter of recommendation, audition, pre-audition audio performance tape, TOEFL for all students for whom English is not a native language. Auditions held once on campus.
Web Site http://www.juilliard.edu
Contact Ms. Lee Cioppa, Associate Dean for Admissions, The Juilliard School, 60 Lincoln Center Plaza, New York, New York 10023-6588; 212-799-5000 ext. 223, fax: 212-769-6420, e-mail address: admissions@juilliard.edu

More About the School

The Juilliard School, located in Manhattan's Lincoln Center, represents 100 years of the finest performing arts education in North America. Each year, Juilliard presents more than 700 performances in dance, drama, and music. Juilliard's central mission is to educate talented performing musicians, dancers, and actors so that they may achieve the highest artistic standards as well as become leaders in their professions.

The Dance Division, founded in 1951, aims to create true contemporary dancers—trained equally in classical ballet and modern dance. The Dance Division's four-year course of study offers students the choice of pursuing a Bachelor of Fine Arts degree or a diploma. In addition to daily technique classes, dancers refine their skills in focused study of repertory, pas de deux, pointe or men's class, dance composition, anatomy, acting, dance history, stagecraft, production, music theory, and elements of performing. The dancers work in an enormous variety of repertory styles and techniques. Also offered are electives such as voice, tap, and jazz. All dancers have the opportunity to work with living choreographers on newly commissioned works, established repertory, and their own compositions.

Since 1968, the Drama Division has become one of the most respected training programs for actors in the English-speaking world. The classical theater training program offers students the choice of pursuing a Bachelor of Fine Arts degree or a diploma. Each of the drama classes, numbering around 20 students, moves as a group through the four years of the program, whose major emphasis is on dramatic interpretation—the students' ability to bring their bodies and voices into harmony with the characters

The Juilliard School (continued)

being portrayed. The training integrates the whole artist—voice, body, mind, and emotion—to become characters from any tradition, classical to contemporary. Actors refine the tools of their craft in acting, Alexander technique, comedy, mask, music, singing, and speech classes. Acting classes and rehearsal projects focus on the styles, conventions, and inner worlds of plays. Students learn and explore how they may transform their total selves into living characters in those worlds. All the hard work and excitement culminate in the fourth year, as students again act in four full-scale productions in different styles.

The Music Division offers a four-year undergraduate program leading to a Bachelor of Music degree, or a three year diploma program. Graduate-level degree programs lead to the Master of Music or Doctor of Musical Arts degrees. Graduate-level programs concentrating exclusively on performance include the graduate diploma and the artist diploma. With individualized instruction from members of a superb faculty and with continual performance opportunities at the school, around the city, the country, and the world, Juilliard helps its music students transform their passions and skills into artistic maturity. Students of orchestral instruments have ample opportunities to play in large ensembles, including the Juilliard Orchestra and Juilliard Symphony. Juilliard orchestras perform at the finest venues in New York: Alice Tully Hall, Avery Fisher Hall, and Carnegie Hall. Those interested in twentieth and twenty-first century music can play in the New Juilliard Ensemble or in the multidisciplinary Electric Ensemble@Juilliard. At any given time, some 120 separate chamber ensembles are also at work at Juilliard. Student musicians form their own groups, audition for faculty coaches, then attend weekly coaching sessions that culminate each semester in performances around the building and beyond.

The Vocal Arts Department offers a comprehensive training program for singers at all stages of development. In addition to private lessons, voice majors receive professional vocal coaching, a process that combines musical instruction with guidance in diction, language and text, movement, and character development. In performances for the Juilliard community and the public, vocalists explore the entire spectrum of concert and art song repertoire. The advanced Juilliard Opera Center accepts artists who have already completed their formal education and who demonstrate a significant potential for careers as operatic performers. This program offers singers performance experience and an intensive course of practical study that helps provide a successful transition from an academic to a professional environment.

In 2001, Juilliard married America's greatest indigenous art form with the same standards of training and performance set by the classical division. Juilliard now offers a four-year Jazz Studies Bachelor of Music program, as well as graduate-level Master of Music, graduate diploma, and artist diploma programs. Courses include jazz improvisation, jazz history, composition and arranging, and the business of jazz. The Jazz Orchestra often opens for Jazz at Lincoln Center and presents two programs a year of student and faculty compositions and arrangements. Students perform regularly at local clubs such as Birdland, Triad, Swing 46, Blue Note, and the new Jazz at Lincoln Center's Dizzy's Club Coca-Cola, and they have traveled nationally and internationally, including to Costa Rica and Japan.

Aspiring artists in all divisions obtain an education that is truly unique, with a long-standing tradition of excellence that is reflected in the achievements of alumni; a world-class faculty; an institution based in New York City at Lincoln Center, with contacts in the performing arts all around the city, the nation, and the world; and an institutional philosophy that nurtures the complete artist and the complete human being.

J. William Fulbright College of Arts and Sciences

See University of Arkansas

Kansas State University
Manhattan, Kansas

State-supported, coed. Suburban campus. Total enrollment: 23,182.
Degrees Bachelor of Music in the areas of performance, composition, music theater; Bachelor of Music Education. Majors and concentrations: composition, music, music education, music theater, piano/organ, stringed instruments, voice, wind and percussion instruments. Graduate degrees offered: Master of Music in the areas of music education, performance, music history and literature, composition. Program accredited by NASM.
Enrollment 165 total; 130 undergraduate, 15 graduate, 20 nonprofessional degree.
Music Student Profile 55% females, 45% males, 5% minorities, 5% international.
Music Faculty 26 total (full-time), 2 total (part-time). 92% of full-time faculty have terminal degrees. Graduate students teach a few undergraduate courses.
Student Life Student groups/activities include Music Educators National Conference Student Chapter, American Choral Directors Association, music fraternities and sororities.
Expenses for 2005–2006 Application fee: $30. State resident tuition: $4560 full-time. Nonresident tuition: $13,890 full-time. Mandatory fees: $564 full-time. College room and board: $5772. Room and board charges vary according to board plan.
Financial Aid Program-specific awards: 50 Music Service Guild Awards for freshmen program majors ($500).
Application Procedures Students admitted directly into the professional program freshman year. Deadline for freshmen and transfers: continuous. Required: high school transcript, SAT I or ACT test scores (minimum composite ACT score of 21). Recommended: audition. Auditions held 3 times on campus; recorded music is permissible as a substitute for live auditions if a campus visit is impossible and videotaped performances are permissible as a substitute for live auditions if a campus visit is impossible.
Undergraduate Contact Dr. Paul Hunt, Head, Music Department, Kansas State University, McCain 109, Manhattan, Kansas 66506; 785-532-5740, fax: 785-532-6899, e-mail address: music@ksu.edu
Graduate Contact Dr. Alfred Cochran, Director of Graduate Studies, Music Department, Kansas State University, McCain 109, Manhattan, Kansas 66506; 785-532-3807, fax: 785-532-6899, e-mail address: cochalw@ksu.edu

Keene State College
Keene, New Hampshire

State-supported, coed. Small town campus. Total enrollment: 4,846. Music program established 1971.

Kennesaw State University
Kennesaw, Georgia

State-supported, coed. Suburban campus. Total enrollment: 18,556. Music program established 1984.
Degrees Bachelor of Music in the areas of performance, music education. Majors and concentrations: classical guitar, music education, piano, stringed instruments, voice, wind and percussion instruments. Cross-registration with University System of Georgia. Program accredited by NASM.
Enrollment 154 total; 113 undergraduate, 41 nonprofessional degree.
Music Student Profile 45% females, 55% males, 6% minorities, 4% international.
Music Faculty 11 undergraduate (full-time), 23 undergraduate (part-time). 100% of full-time faculty have terminal degrees.

Graduate students do not teach undergraduate courses. Undergraduate student–faculty ratio: 17:1.

Student Life Student groups/activities include Music Educators National Conference Student Chapter, Pi Kappa Lambda, Music Teachers National Association Student Chapter. Special housing available for music students.

Expenses for 2005–2006 Application fee: $40. State resident tuition: $2438 full-time. Nonresident tuition: $9754 full-time. Mandatory fees: $606 full-time. College room only: $5880. Room charges vary according to housing facility. Special program-related fees: $150 per semester for composition lessons, $150 per semester for applied music techniques fee, $150 per semester for applied music fee.

Financial Aid Program-specific awards: 1–2 Gibson Scholarships for voice/piano majors ($500), 1 Sullivan Scholarship for voice majors ($500), 1–2 Miller and Wilhoit Scholarships for program majors ($1100), 15–20 Kennesaw State College Foundation Scholarships for program majors ($300), 3–6 Cobb County Music Teachers Awards for program majors ($300–$1500), 1 Hollingsworth Scholarship for program majors ($1000), 1 H. F. Rodenhausen Scholarship for program majors ($500), 1 J. Watkins Scholarship for piano students ($500).

Application Procedures Students admitted directly into the professional program freshman year. Deadline for freshmen and transfers: May 27. Required: high school transcript, college transcript(s) for transfer students, minimum 2.0 high school GPA, interview, audition, SAT I or ACT test scores (minimum combined SAT I score of 950), immunization record. Auditions held 4 times and by arrangement on campus; videotaped performances are permissible as a substitute for live auditions with approval from the department.

Web Site http://www.kennesaw.edu/music

Undergraduate Contact Mr. Peter Witte, Chair, Department of Music, Kennesaw State University, 1000 Chastain Road #3201, Kennesaw, Georgia 30144; 770-423-6151, fax: 770-423-6368, e-mail address: pwitte@kennesaw.edu

Hugh A. Glauser School of Music
Kent State University
Kent, Ohio

State-supported, coed. Suburban campus. Total enrollment: 23,622. Music program established 1913.

Kentucky State University
Frankfort, Kentucky

State-related, coed. Small town campus. Total enrollment: 2,386.

Kentucky Wesleyan College
Owensboro, Kentucky

Independent Methodist, coed. Suburban campus. Total enrollment: 755. Music program established 1958.

Degrees Bachelor of Music in the area of music performance; Bachelor of Music Education in the area of music education. Majors and concentrations: brass instruments performance, guitar, organ, percussion, piano, voice, wind instruments. Cross-registration with Brescia University.

Enrollment 46 total; 21 undergraduate, 25 nonprofessional degree.

Music Student Profile 58% females, 42% males, 4% minorities, 2% international.

Music Faculty 2 undergraduate (full-time), 5 undergraduate (part-time). 100% of full-time faculty have terminal degrees. Graduate students do not teach undergraduate courses. Undergraduate student–faculty ratio: 8:1.

Student Life Student groups/activities include Kentucky Wesleyan Band, Kentucky Wesleyan Singers, Kentucky Wesleyan Players.

Expenses for 2006–2007 Application fee: $0. Comprehensive fee: $19,350 includes full-time tuition ($13,200), mandatory fees

($400), and college room and board ($5750). College room only: $2600. Special program-related fees: $50 per credit hour for applied music fee.

Financial Aid Program-specific awards: 30–35 music scholarships for program majors ($2000).

Application Procedures Students admitted directly into the professional program freshman year. Deadline for freshmen and transfers: continuous. Required: high school transcript, college transcript(s) for transfer students, minimum 2.0 high school GPA, audition, SAT I or ACT test scores. Recommended: essay, minimum 3.0 high school GPA, 3 letters of recommendation, interview. Auditions held 4 times and by appointment on campus and off campus in various cities by special arrangement; recorded music is permissible as a substitute for live auditions and videotaped performances are permissible as a substitute for live auditions.

Web Site http://www.kwc.edu

Undergraduate Contact Dr. Diane K. Earle, Director of Music Program, Music Department, Kentucky Wesleyan College, 3000 Frederica Street, Owensboro, Kentucky 42302-1039; 270-852-3617, fax: 270-926-3196, e-mail address: dearle@kwc.edu

Lakehead University
Thunder Bay, Ontario, Canada

Province-supported, coed. Suburban campus. Total enrollment: 7,558. Music program established 1988.

Degrees Honors Bachelor of Arts in the area of music; Honors Bachelor of Music in the area of music. Majors and concentrations: classical music. Program accredited by CUMS.

Enrollment 55 total; all undergraduate.

Music Student Profile 50% females, 50% males, 5% minorities.

Music Faculty 3 undergraduate (full-time), 20 undergraduate (part-time). 100% of full-time faculty have terminal degrees. Graduate students do not teach undergraduate courses. Undergraduate student–faculty ratio: 4:1.

Student Life Student groups/activities include ensembles concerts (chamber, vocal, new music), student recitals, Lakehead University Music Association (student group).

Expenses for 2005–2006 Application fee: $105 Canadian dollars. Canadian resident tuition: $4140 full-time. Mandatory fees: $531 full-time. College room and board: $6569. College room only: $4980. International student tuition: $10,000 full-time.

Financial Aid Program-specific awards: 1 Munro Family Memorial Prize for program majors ($725), 5 A. L. Musselman Awards for program majors ($297–$800), 1 Westlake Music Scholarship for continuing students ($450), 1 Ranta Entrance Award for incoming students ($300), 1 Lakehead University Music Festival Scholarship for incoming students ($1226), 1 Westlake Music Scholarship for incoming students ($450), 1 Canadian Scholars Press Music Bursary for program majors ($500), 1 Westlake Music Bursary for continuing students ($750), 2 Wilma C. Ayre Memorial Bursaries for continuing students ($300), 10 William H. Buset Memorial Bursaries for program majors ($1000).

Application Procedures Students admitted directly into the professional program freshman year. Deadline for freshmen and transfers: continuous. Required: high school transcript, college transcript(s) for transfer students, minimum 2.0 high school GPA, interview, audition, music theory entrance test. Auditions held by appointment on campus; recorded music is permissible as a substitute for live auditions for out-of-town applicants and videotaped performances are permissible as a substitute for live auditions for out-of-town applicants.

Web Site http://www.lakeheadu.ca

Undergraduate Contact Office of Admissions, Lakehead University, 955 Oliver Road, Thunder Bay, Ontario P7B 5E1, Canada; 807-343-8500, fax: 807-343-8156, e-mail address: admissions@lakeheadu.ca

Lamar University
Beaumont, Texas

State-supported, coed. Suburban campus. Total enrollment: 10,595. Music program established 1953.

Lamar University (continued)

Degrees Bachelor of Music in the areas of performance, composition, music education. Majors and concentrations: composition, music education, piano, stringed instruments, voice, wind and percussion instruments. Graduate degrees offered: Master of Music in the area of performance; Master of Music Education. Program accredited by NASM.
Enrollment 140 total; 130 undergraduate, 10 graduate.
Music Student Profile 50% females, 50% males, 20% minorities.
Music Faculty 13 total (full-time), 7 total (part-time). 70% of full-time faculty have terminal degrees. Graduate students do not teach undergraduate courses. Undergraduate student–faculty ratio: 8:1.
Student Life Student groups/activities include Delta Omicron, Phi Mu Alpha Sinfonia, Pi Kappa Lambda.
Expenses for 2005–2006 Application fee: $0. State resident tuition: $2880 full-time. Nonresident tuition: $9504 full-time. College room and board: $5254. College room only: $3600. Room and board charges vary according to board plan and housing facility. Special program-related fees: $5–$20 per class for class fee, $50 per hour for applied music fee ($150 maximum).
Financial Aid Program-specific awards: 45–50 band scholarships for band students ($300–$3000), 20–25 choir scholarships for choir students ($300–$3000), 5–10 orchestra scholarships for orchestra students ($700–$2000), 20–30 endowed scholarships for program majors ($300–$3000).
Application Procedures Students admitted directly into the professional program freshman year. Deadline for freshmen and transfers: continuous. Required: high school transcript, college transcript(s) for transfer students, audition, SAT I or ACT test scores, THEA scores. Recommended: interview. Auditions held continuously on campus; recorded music is permissible as a substitute for live auditions when distance is prohibitive and videotaped performances are permissible as a substitute for live auditions when distance is prohibitive.
Web Site http://www.lamar.edu
Undergraduate Contact Dr. Harry Bulow, Chair, Department of Music, Theatre & Dance, Lamar University, PO Box 10044, Beaumont, Texas 77710; 409-880-8144, fax: 409-880-8143.
Graduate Contact Dr. Robert M. Culberson Jr., Director of Graduate Studies in Music, Department of Music, Theatre & Dance, Lamar University, PO Box 10044, Beaumont, Texas 77710; 409-880-8073, fax: 409-880-8143, e-mail address: culbertsrm@hal.lamar.edu

Lambuth University
Jackson, Tennessee

Independent United Methodist, coed. Urban campus. Total enrollment: 805. Music program established 1924.
Degrees Bachelor of Music in the area of music. Majors and concentrations: church music, performance. Cross-registration with Union University, Freed-Hardeman University.
Enrollment 26 total; all undergraduate.
Music Student Profile 58% females, 42% males, 8% minorities, 3% international.
Music Faculty 4 undergraduate (full-time), 3 undergraduate (part-time). 75% of full-time faculty have terminal degrees. Graduate students do not teach undergraduate courses. Undergraduate student–faculty ratio: 10:1.
Student Life Student groups/activities include musicians for theater performances, jazz band.
Expenses for 2006–2007 Application fee: $25. Comprehensive fee: $23,090 includes full-time tuition ($15,980), mandatory fees ($400), and college room and board ($6710). College room only: $3195. Special program-related fees: $100–$200 per semester for applied music lesson fee.
Financial Aid Program-specific awards: 20–25 endowed music majors awards for program majors ($250), 50–75 student musician awards for band/choir majors ($200–$2000).
Application Procedures Students admitted directly into the professional program freshman year. Deadline for freshmen and transfers: continuous. Required: essay, high school transcript, college transcript(s) for transfer students, minimum 2.0 high school GPA, 2 letters of recommendation, SAT I or ACT test scores. Recommended: audition. Auditions held 3 times and by

appointment on campus; recorded music is permissible as a substitute for live auditions when distance is prohibitive and videotaped performances are permissible as a substitute for live auditions when distance is prohibitive.
Web Site http://www.lambuth.edu
Undergraduate Contact Ms. Lisa Warmath, Director of Admissions, Lambuth University, 705 Lambuth Boulevard, Jackson, Tennessee 38301; 731-425-3332, fax: 731-988-4600, e-mail address: admit@lambuth.edu

Lamont School of Music
See University of Denver

Lander University
Greenwood, South Carolina

State-supported, coed. Small town campus. Total enrollment: 2,703. Music program established 1872.
Degrees Bachelor of Science in the areas of instrumental music education, vocal music education. Majors and concentrations: instrumental music, keyboard, music education, voice. Cross-registration with University of Plymouth (England). Program accredited by NASM.
Enrollment 42 total; all undergraduate.
Music Student Profile 69% females, 31% males, 24% minorities, 1% international.
Music Faculty 6 undergraduate (full-time), 8 undergraduate (part-time). 80% of full-time faculty have terminal degrees. Graduate students do not teach undergraduate courses. Undergraduate student–faculty ratio: 11:1.
Student Life Student groups/activities include Music Educators National Conference.
Expenses for 2005–2006 Application fee: $35. State resident tuition: $6108 full-time. Nonresident tuition: $13,528 full-time. Mandatory fees: $560 full-time. Full-time tuition and fees vary according to degree level. College room and board: $5468. College room only: $3360. Room and board charges vary according to board plan and housing facility. Special program-related fees: $40 per semester for applied music fee.
Financial Aid Program-specific awards: 1 Kerhoulas Award for incoming students ($500), 1 White Award for instrumentalists ($1500), 1 Hutto Award for voice majors ($150), 2 Lenti Awards for piano majors ($900), 1 Scofield Scholarship for voice majors ($300), 1 Wilkins Scholarship for concert band/jazz ensemble members ($150), 1 Lenna Clifford Scholarship for violin or piano majors ($1000–$2000).
Application Procedures Students admitted directly into the professional program freshman year. Deadline for freshmen and transfers: continuous. Required: high school transcript, college transcript(s) for transfer students, letter of recommendation, audition, SAT I or ACT test scores, music theory test, minimum 2.5 high school GPA. Recommended: minimum 3.0 high school GPA, interview, standing in top 50% of graduating class. Auditions held 2-3 times on campus; recorded music is permissible as a substitute for live auditions when distance is prohibitive and videotaped performances are permissible as a substitute for live auditions when distance is prohibitive.
Web Site http://www.lander.edu
Undergraduate Contact Mr. Jonathan Reece, Director of Admissions, Lander University, 320 Stanley Avenue, Greenwood, South Carolina 29649; 864-388-8307, fax: 864-388-8890, e-mail address: jreece@lander.edu

Lawrence University
Appleton, Wisconsin

Independent, coed. Small town campus. Total enrollment: 1,450. Music program established 1874.
Degrees Bachelor of Arts/Bachelor of Music in the areas of liberal arts in combination with music performance, music education, theory-composition; Bachelor of Music in the areas of music education, music theory-composition, performance. Majors and concentrations: choral music, classical guitar, classical music,

harpsichord, instrumental music, jazz, music, music education, music theory and composition, performance, piano/organ, stringed instruments, voice, wind and percussion instruments. Program accredited by NASM.

Enrollment 1,405 total; 295 undergraduate, 1,110 nonprofessional degree.

Music Student Profile 54% females, 46% males, 8% minorities, 10% international.

Music Faculty 38 undergraduate (full-time), 26 undergraduate (part-time). 96% of full-time faculty have terminal degrees. Graduate students do not teach undergraduate courses. Undergraduate student–faculty ratio: 6:1.

Student Life Student groups/activities include Phi Mu Alpha Sinfonia, Sigma Alpha Iota, WLFM-FM (campus radio station).

Expenses for 2006–2007 Application fee: $40. Comprehensive fee: $35,979 includes full-time tuition ($29,376), mandatory fees ($222), and college room and board ($6381). College room only: $2934.

Financial Aid Program-specific awards: 20–30 performance awards for top auditions ($2000–$7500), 10–12 Trustee Awards for top auditions ($10,000), Institutional Grants for those demonstrating need ($21,000), 5–10 music education scholarships for those demonstrating potential during participation in on-campus workshop ($5000), 1–5 theory/composition scholarships for those selected by faculty based on portfolios ($5000).

Application Procedures Students admitted directly into the professional program freshman year. Deadline for freshmen: January 15; transfers: May 15. Notification date for freshmen: April 1; transfers: June 1. Required: essay, high school transcript, college transcript(s) for transfer students, 3 letters of recommendation, audition. Recommended: minimum 3.0 high school GPA, interview. Auditions held 14 times on campus and off campus in New York, NY; Washington, D.C.; Boston, MA; Denver, CO; Interlochen, MI; Los Angeles, CA; San Francisco, CA; Portland, OR; Seattle, WA; Dallas, TX; recorded music is permissible as a substitute for live auditions when distance is prohibitive to campus or a regional site (over 350 miles) and videotaped performances are permissible as a substitute for live auditions when distance is prohibitive to campus or a regional site (over 350 miles).

Web Site http://www.lawrence.edu

Undergraduate Contact Jacob Allen, Assistant Director of Conservatory Admissions, Lawrence University, PO Box 599, Appleton, Wisconsin 54912-0599; 920-832-6889, fax: 920-832-6782, e-mail address: jacob.g.allen@lawrence.edu

More About the University

The Lawrence Conservatory of Music is a nationally recognized conservatory devoted exclusively to the education of undergraduate musicians within a college of the liberal arts and sciences.

The faculty of performers, composers, scholars, and pedagogues provide individual attention and guidance to the more than 350 music majors and the many college students who participate in the Conservatory's activities.

Music facilities are housed within three adjoining buildings: the Music-Drama Center, the Memorial Chapel, and the Ruth Harwood Shattuck Hall of Music. The music library, located in the Media Center of the University library, holds more than 32,000 recordings and scores as well as music reference works.

Music students choose from five degree programs: the Bachelor of Music degree in performance, the Bachelor of Music degree in music education (instrumental; general; choral/general; instrumental/general; choral/general/instrumental), the Bachelor of Music degree in theory-composition, the Bachelor of Arts degree in music, and the double degree. The Lawrence five-year double-degree program permits students to earn a Bachelor of Music degree and a Bachelor of Arts degree in a discipline other than music. The combined degree program provides both professional-level study of music and a rigorous academic program of study. In addition, students may design their own majors or pursue a double major within the Bachelor of Music degree. The curriculum in the Conservatory of Music seeks to ensure that all music students, regardless of their major, graduate

with a thorough and firm grounding in music theory and analysis, music history and literature, and both solo and ensemble performance.

At Lawrence, music is not isolated from the other disciplines. All music majors complete a core curriculum in the college in addition to their Conservatory course work. Conservatory students live in the same residence halls and dine with college students, taking full advantage of the residential nature of the liberal arts institution. While the degree curriculum within the Conservatory is intense and focused in music, it allows students to explore the liberal arts and sciences through an array of courses taught by an accomplished faculty. The study of music at Lawrence occurs within the context of the liberal arts, thereby providing a well-rounded, broad-based understanding of music.

This preparation and training have allowed Lawrence's students and ensembles to receive national and international awards; major ensembles have performed at regional and national music conferences and have recorded CDs for national distribution; students have placed as finalists and winners in the Metropolitan Opera auditions, the Concert Artists Guild Competition, the MTNA Solo and Chamber Music Competitions, the Grace Vamos Competition, and *Down Beat* magazine's Outstanding Jazz Big Band Award and Outstanding Jazz Composition Award competitions, among others. Each summer, conservatory students continue their studies at festivals such as Tanglewood and Aspen.

Lawrence University is committed to the development of intellect and talent, the acquisition of knowledge and understanding, and the cultivation of judgment and values. The University prepares students for lives of service, achievement, leadership, and personal fulfillment. Lawrence Conservatory graduates are counted not only among the ranks of professional orchestras and opera companies, Grammy Award winners, university faculties, elementary and high school teachers, college administrators, and composers, but also among authors, medical and law professionals, and public servants.

Program Facilities The Conservatory's facilities include the Memorial Chapel (concert hall of 1,250 seats); Harper Recital Hall (250 seats); Miller Hall (150 seats/choral rehearsal hall); an orchestral rehearsal hall (315 seats); a jazz rehearsal/recording studio; percussion studios; a recording studio that includes a 16-track digital system with compact disk recording, editing, and production capabilities; a Macintosh-based computer lab, offering MIDI technology in conjunction with Finale, Symphony, and Vivace programs; Cloak Theatre (experimental black box); Stansbury Theatre (proscenium theater of 500 seats); an outdoor amphitheater; WLFM campus radio station affiliated with Wisconsin Public Radio; historical instruments, such as the forty-one-stop mechanical action organ by John Brombaugh, an 1815 Broadwood piano, and a Guarneri violin.

Faculty and Resident Artists There are 38 full-time faculty members and 23 part-time faculty members. Artists-in-residence include faculty chamber ensembles and baritone Dale Duesing. Recent visiting artists include Emanuel Ax, Midari, The Saint Paul Chamber Orchestra, Wayne Shorter, Wynton Marsalis, Diane Reeves, the American Brass Quintet, and the Vermeer String Quartet.

Student Performance Opportunities Ensembles include Symphony Orchestra, Chamber Orchestra, Collegium Musicum, Wind Ensemble, Symphonic Band, Jazz Ensemble, Percussion Ensemble, African and Brazilian Drumming Ensembles, Cello Ensemble, Low Brass Choir, Horn Choir, Concert Choir, Lawrence Chorale Opera Theatre, Music Theatre, Jazz Singers, and numerous chamber ensembles and small jazz groups.

Special Programs The Conservatory also offers a five-year double-degree (B.A./B.Mus.) program; music education certification (K–12); fifty-five off-campus programs, both domestic and international; academic advising; residence hall life; a counseling

Lawrence University (continued)

center; a career center; a writing skills lab; more than 100 campus clubs and organizations; twenty-three varsity sports; and numerous club and intramural sports.

Lebanon Valley College

Annville, Pennsylvania

Independent United Methodist, coed. Small town campus. Total enrollment: 1,915. Music program established 1932.

Degrees Bachelor of Music in the area of music recording technology; Bachelor of Science in the area of music education. Majors and concentrations: music education, music technology. Program accredited by NASM.

Enrollment 275 total; 223 undergraduate, 52 nonprofessional degree.

Music Student Profile 43% females, 57% males, 3% minorities.

Music Faculty 14 undergraduate (full-time), 25 undergraduate (part-time). 70% of full-time faculty have terminal degrees. Graduate students do not teach undergraduate courses. Undergraduate student–faculty ratio: 16:1.

Student Life Student groups/activities include Audio Engineering Society, Music Educators National Conference Student Chapter.

Expenses for 2005–2006 Application fee: $30. Comprehensive fee: $31,700 includes full-time tuition ($24,210), mandatory fees ($650), and college room and board ($6840). College room only: $3340. Room and board charges vary according to board plan and housing facility. Special program-related fees: $120 per unit for private instruction.

Financial Aid Program-specific awards: 4 Carmean String Scholarships for string players ($1000), 6 Carmean Talent Awards for musically talented students ($1000).

Application Procedures Students apply for admission into the professional program by sophomore year. Deadline for freshmen and transfers: May 2. Required: high school transcript, college transcript(s) for transfer students, audition, SAT I or ACT test scores. Recommended: essay, 2 letters of recommendation, interview. Auditions held by appointment on campus; recorded music is permissible as a substitute for live auditions for international applicants or when distance is prohibitive and videotaped performances are permissible as a substitute for live auditions for international applicants or when distance is prohibitive.

Web Site http://www.lvc.edu

Undergraduate Contact Mr. Barry Hill, Director, Music Recording Technology, Department of Music, Lebanon Valley College, Blair Music Center, Annville, Pennsylvania 17003; 717-867-6285, fax: 717-867-6390, e-mail address: hill@lvc.edu

Lee University

Cleveland, Tennessee

Independent, coed. Small town campus. Total enrollment: 3,930.

Degrees Bachelor of Arts in the area of church music; Bachelor of Music in the area of performance; Bachelor of Music Education in the areas of vocal/general music education, instrumental music education, keyboard; Bachelor of Science in the area of music business emphasis. Majors and concentrations: applied music, church music, music business, piano, stringed instruments, voice, wind and percussion instruments. Graduate degrees offered: Master of Church Music; Master of Music in the area of music education. Program accredited by NASM.

Enrollment 254 total; 128 undergraduate, 23 graduate, 103 nonprofessional degree.

Music Student Profile 56% females, 44% males, 14% minorities, 8% international.

Music Faculty 22 total (full-time), 33 total (part-time). 40% of full-time faculty have terminal degrees. Graduate students do not teach undergraduate courses. Undergraduate student–faculty ratio: 14:1.

Student Life Student groups/activities include Music Drama Workshop, Choral Union.

Expenses for 2005–2006 Application fee: $25. Comprehensive fee: $14,780 includes full-time tuition ($9400), mandatory fees

($210), and college room and board ($5170). College room only: $2680. Full-time tuition and fees vary according to program. Room and board charges vary according to board plan and housing facility. Special program-related fees: $125 per semester for accompanist fee, $200 per semester for practice room rental, lesson fee.

Financial Aid Program-specific awards: 27 endowed scholarships for program majors ($1250), 245 performance scholarships for ensemble members ($705).

Application Procedures Students apply for admission into the professional program by sophomore year. Deadline for freshmen and transfers: continuous. Required: high school transcript, college transcript(s) for transfer students, audition, SAT I or ACT test scores. Recommended: 3 letters of recommendation, interview. Auditions held 4 times on campus; recorded music is permissible as a substitute for live auditions when distance is prohibitive and videotaped performances are permissible as a substitute for live auditions when distance is prohibitive.

Web Site http://flame.leeuniversity.edu/music/

Undergraduate Contact Ms. Dawn Andrews, Assistant to the Dean, School of Music, Lee University, PO Box 3450, Cleveland, Tennessee 37320-3450; 423-614-8240, fax: 423-614-8242, e-mail address: dandrews@leeuniversity.edu

Graduate Contact Dr. Jim Burns, Director of Graduate Studies, School of Music, Lee University, PO Box 3450, Cleveland, Tennessee 37320-3450; 423-614-8240, fax: 423-614-8242, e-mail address: jburns@leeuniversity.edu

Lehman College of the City University of New York

Bronx, New York

State and locally supported, coed. Urban campus. Total enrollment: 10,615.

Degrees Bachelor of Science in the area of music. Majors and concentrations: composition, instrumental performance, voice. Graduate degrees offered: Master of Arts in Teaching in the area of music education. Cross-registration with City University of New York colleges.

Enrollment 59 total; 20 undergraduate, 39 graduate.

Music Student Profile 71% females, 29% males, 79% minorities, 3% international.

Music Faculty 11 total (full-time), 12 total (part-time). 100% of full-time faculty have terminal degrees. Graduate students do not teach undergraduate courses.

Student Life Student groups/activities include stage band, chorus, ensembles.

Expenses for 2006–2007 Application fee: $50. State resident tuition: $4000 full-time. Nonresident tuition: $10,800 full-time. Mandatory fees: $288 full-time.

Financial Aid Program-specific awards: Bellezeller Scholarship for music students.

Application Procedures Students admitted directly into the professional program freshman year. Deadline for freshmen and transfers: continuous. Required: high school transcript, college transcript(s) for transfer students, minimum 2.0 high school GPA, interview, audition. Recommended: essay, portfolio, SAT I or ACT test scores. Auditions held by appointment on campus; recorded music is permissible as a substitute for live auditions at the discretion of the chair and videotaped performances are permissible as a substitute for live auditions at the discretion of the chair. Portfolio reviews held by appointment on campus.

Web Site http://www.lehman.cuny.edu

Undergraduate Contact Clarence Wilkes, Director of Admissions, Lehman College of the City University of New York, 250 Bedford Park Boulevard West, Shuster Hall 155, Bronx, New York 10468; 718-960-8706, fax: 718-960-8712.

Graduate Contact Office of Graduate Admissions, Lehman College of the City University of New York, Shuster Hall, Room 150, Bronx, New York 10468; 718-960-8702, fax: 718-960-8713.

Leigh Gerdine College of Fine Arts

See Webster University

Lenoir-Rhyne College
Hickory, North Carolina

Independent Lutheran, coed. Small town campus. Total enrollment: 1,579. Music program established 1900.

Liberty University
Lynchburg, Virginia

Independent nondenominational, coed. Suburban campus. Total enrollment: 12,458. Music program established 1971.
Degrees Bachelor of Music in the areas of choral music, instrumental music, instrumental music education, choral music education; Bachelor of Science in the area of worship and music ministry. Majors and concentrations: music, music education. Program accredited by NCATE.
Enrollment 100 total; all undergraduate.
Music Student Profile 51% females, 49% males, 10% minorities, 2% international.
Music Faculty 15 undergraduate (full-time), 4 undergraduate (part-time). 72% of full-time faculty have terminal degrees. Graduate students do not teach undergraduate courses. Undergraduate student–faculty ratio: 10:1.
Student Life Student groups/activities include Music Educators National Conference, American Choral Directors Association.
Expenses for 2006–2007 Application fee: $35. Comprehensive fee: $20,750 includes full-time tuition ($14,400), mandatory fees ($950), and college room and board ($5400). Special program-related fees: $30 per semester for practice room rental, $150 per year for concert band tour.
Financial Aid Program-specific awards: 11 Fine Arts Scholarships for program majors ($500–$1000), 80–100 marching band service awards for marching band members ($200–$500), 40–50 Concert Band Service Awards for concert band members ($300–$500).
Application Procedures Students apply for admission into the professional program by sophomore year. Deadline for freshmen and transfers: August 1. Required: high school transcript, college transcript(s) for transfer students, 3 letters of recommendation, audition, SAT I test score only. Recommended: interview. Auditions held 4 times on campus; recorded music is permissible as a substitute for live auditions when distance is prohibitive and videotaped performances are permissible as a substitute for live auditions when distance is prohibitive.
Web Site http://www.liberty.edu/academics/finearts
Undergraduate Contact Dr. John Hugo, Chairman, Department of Fine Arts, Liberty University, 1971 University Boulevard, Lynchburg, Virginia 24502-2269; 804-582-2318, fax: 804-582-2891, e-mail address: finearts@liberty.edu

Lincoln University
Jefferson City, Missouri

State-supported, coed. Small town campus. Total enrollment: 3,180. Music program established 1951.

Lionel Hampton School of Music

See University of Idaho

Lock Haven University of Pennsylvania
Lock Haven, Pennsylvania

State-supported, coed. Rural campus. Total enrollment: 5,283.

Long Island University, C.W. Post Campus
Brookville, New York

Independent, coed. Suburban campus. Total enrollment: 8,472. Music program established 1956.

Degrees Bachelor of Music. Majors and concentrations: music education. Graduate degrees offered: Master of Arts in the areas of history and literature, theory and composition; Master of Science in the area of music education.
Enrollment 163 total; 119 undergraduate, 44 graduate.
Music Student Profile 50% females, 50% males, 15% minorities, 10% international.
Music Faculty 8 total (full-time), 80 total (part-time). 20% of full-time faculty have terminal degrees. Graduate students do not teach undergraduate courses. Undergraduate student–faculty ratio: 12:1.
Student Life Student groups/activities include Music Educators National Conference, American Choral Directors Association, international and domestic concert tours. Special housing available for music students.
Expenses for 2005–2006 Application fee: $30. Comprehensive fee: $31,930 includes full-time tuition ($22,100), mandatory fees ($1130), and college room and board ($8700). College room only: $5730. Full-time tuition and fees vary according to program. Room and board charges vary according to board plan and housing facility. Special program-related fees: $200 per semester for studio and piano expenses.
Financial Aid Program-specific awards: 140 music scholarships for music students ($2500).
Application Procedures Students admitted directly into the professional program freshman year. Deadline for freshmen: continuous. Notification date for freshmen: continuous. Required: high school transcript, college transcript(s) for transfer students, interview, audition, SAT I test score only. Auditions held twice or by appointment on campus; recorded music is permissible as a substitute for live auditions if a live audition is impossible and videotaped performances are permissible as a substitute for live auditions if a live audition is impossible.
Web Site http://www.liu.edu/~svpa/music/
Undergraduate Contact Nancy Urbanas, Advisor, Undergraduate Admissions, Long Island University, C.W. Post Campus, 720 Northern Boulevard, Brookville, New York 11548; 516-299-2459.
Graduate Contact John Meschi, Graduate Advisor, Department of Music, Long Island University, C.W. Post Campus, 720 Northern Boulevard, Brookville, New York 11548; 516-299-2105.

Longwood University
Farmville, Virginia

State-supported, coed. Total enrollment: 4,289.
Degrees Bachelor of Music in the areas of performance, education, piano pedagogy. Majors and concentrations: brass, music education, piano, piano pedagogy, voice, wind and percussion instruments. Cross-registration with Hampden-Sydney College. Program accredited by NASM.
Enrollment 61 undergraduate, 4 nonprofessional degree.
Music Student Profile 60% females, 40% males, 10% minorities.
Music Faculty 7 undergraduate (full-time), 9 undergraduate (part-time). 86% of full-time faculty have terminal degrees. Graduate students do not teach undergraduate courses. Undergraduate student–faculty ratio: 9:1.
Student Life Student groups/activities include Music Educators National Conference, Sigma Alpha Iota, Phi Mu Alpha.
Expenses for 2005–2006 Application fee: $40. State resident tuition: $3586 full-time. Nonresident tuition: $10,270 full-time. Mandatory fees: $3434 full-time. College room and board: $5586. College room only: $3288. Room and board charges vary according to board plan. Special program-related fees: $178 per semester for applied music fee.
Financial Aid Program-specific awards: 4 Hull Scholarships for music majors ($1455), 1 Haga Scholarship for junior and senior music majors ($1000), 2 Holiday Dinner Scholarships for music majors ($500–$1000), 7 Foundation Scholarships for music majors ($500), 7 Cole Scholarships for music majors ($750–$1500), 1 Pauline Boehm Haga Scholarship for music education majors with highest GPA ($861), 3 Roy Clark Scholarships for music majors ($985), 1 Mary Pucket Asher King Scholarship for music majors ($543).
Application Procedures Students admitted directly into the professional program freshman year. Deadline for freshmen and transfers: March 1. Required: essay, high school transcript,

Longwood University (continued)

college transcript(s) for transfer students, minimum 2.0 high school GPA, interview, audition, SAT I or ACT test scores (minimum combined SAT I score of 980). Recommended: 2 letters of recommendation. Auditions held 6 times and by appointment on campus; recorded music is permissible as a substitute for live auditions for out-of-state applicants and videotaped performances are permissible as a substitute for live auditions for out-of-state applicants.
Web Site http://web.longwood.edu/music
Undergraduate Contact Dr. Patricia Lust, Chair, Department of Music, Longwood University, 201 High Street, Wygal Building, Farmville, Virginia 23909; 434-395-2049, fax: 434-395-2149, e-mail address: lustpd@longwood.edu

Louisiana College
Pineville, Louisiana

Independent Southern Baptist, coed. Small town campus. Total enrollment: 1,085.

Louisiana State University and Agricultural and Mechanical College
Baton Rouge, Louisiana

State-supported, coed. Urban campus. Total enrollment: 31,264.
Degrees Bachelor of Music in the areas of performance, composition; Bachelor of Music Education in the areas of instrumental music education, vocal music education. Majors and concentrations: composition, harp, music education, organ, piano, piano pedagogy, stringed instruments, voice, wind and percussion instruments. Graduate degrees offered: Master of Music in the areas of performance, theory, musicology, music education, piano pedagogy, conducting. Doctor of Musical Arts in the areas of performance, conducting; Doctor of Philosophy in the areas of music education, musicology, music theory, composition. Cross-registration with Southern University and Agricultural and Mechanical College, Baton Rouge Community College. Program accredited by NASM.
Enrollment 482 total; 299 undergraduate, 182 graduate, 1 nonprofessional degree.
Music Student Profile 47% females, 53% males, 20% minorities, 10% international.
Music Faculty 49 total (full-time), 8 total (part-time). 100% of full-time faculty have terminal degrees. Graduate students teach a few undergraduate courses. Undergraduate student–faculty ratio: 10:1.
Student Life Student groups/activities include music fraternities and sororities, student chapters of American Choral Directors Association, Music
Educators National Conference, Music Teachers National Association.
Expenses for 2005–2006 Application fee: $40. State resident tuition: $2981 full-time. Nonresident tuition: $11,281 full-time. Mandatory fees: $1438 full-time. College room and board: $6330. College room only: $3930. Room and board charges vary according to board plan and housing facility. Special program-related fees: $10 per year for locker rental fee, $75 for senior recital fee.
Financial Aid Program-specific awards: 100 School of Music Scholarships for talented students ($1000–$9675).
Application Procedures Students admitted directly into the professional program freshman year. Deadline for freshmen and transfers: April 15. Required: high school transcript, college transcript(s) for transfer students, minimum 3.0 high school GPA, audition, SAT I or ACT test scores (minimum composite ACT score of 19). Recommended: 2 letters of recommendation, essay (for full scholarship consideration). Auditions held 3 times and by appointment on campus; recorded music is permissible as a substitute for live auditions if a live audition is impossible and videotaped performances are permissible as a substitute for live auditions if a live audition is impossible.
Web Site http://www.music.lsu.edu

Undergraduate Contact Dr. Sara Lynn Baird, Associate Dean, School of Music, Louisiana State University and Agricultural and Mechanical College, 102 School of Music, Baton Rouge, Louisiana 70803; 225-578-3261, fax: 225-578-2562, e-mail address: sbaird@lsu.edu
Graduate Contact Dr. Bill Grimes, Director of Graduate Studies, School of Music, Louisiana State University and Agricultural and Mechanical College, 102 School of Music, Baton Rouge, Louisiana 70803; 225-578-3261, fax: 225-578-2562, e-mail address: bgrimes@lsu.edu

Louisiana Tech University
Ruston, Louisiana

State-supported, coed. Small town campus. Total enrollment: 11,691. Music program established 1959.
Degrees Bachelor of Arts in the area of music education; Bachelor of Music in the areas of voice, keyboard, instruments of symphony orchestra or band. Majors and concentrations: guitar, instrumental music, keyboard, voice. Cross-registration with Grambling State University. Program accredited by NASM.
Enrollment 47 total; all undergraduate.
Music Student Profile 55% females, 45% males, 15% minorities, 3% international.
Music Faculty 11 total (full-time), 2 total (part-time). 60% of full-time faculty have terminal degrees. Graduate students do not teach undergraduate courses. Undergraduate student–faculty ratio: 5:1.
Student Life Student groups/activities include Phi Mu Alpha, Sigma Alpha Iota, Music Educators National Conference.
Expenses for 2005–2006 Application fee: $20. State resident tuition: $3914 full-time. Nonresident tuition: $8819 full-time. Mandatory fees: $461 full-time. College room and board: $4035. College room only: $2130.
Financial Aid Program-specific awards: 40–60 departmental scholarships for program majors ($100–$5200), out-of-state fee waivers for academically qualified students ($4400), 10 Dorm Scholarships for program majors ($650–$1300), out-of-state fee waivers for qualified performers ($4400).
Application Procedures Students admitted directly into the professional program freshman year. Deadline for freshmen and transfers: August 2. Required: high school transcript, college transcript(s) for transfer students, minimum 2.0 high school GPA, interview, audition, SAT I or ACT test scores (minimum composite ACT score of 22), standing in top 35% of high school class. Recommended: letter of recommendation, resume. Auditions held as needed on campus and off campus in high schools of prospective students; recorded music is permissible as a substitute for live auditions when distance is prohibitive and videotaped performances are permissible as a substitute for live auditions when distance is prohibitive.
Web Site http://performingarts.latech.edu
Undergraduate Contact Jan Albritton, Director of Admissions, Louisiana Tech University, PO Box 3178 Tech Station, Ruston, Louisiana 71272; 318-257-3036, e-mail address: jalbritton@lteman.latech.edu

Loyola University New Orleans
New Orleans, Louisiana

Independent Roman Catholic (Jesuit), coed. Urban campus. Total enrollment: 5,423. Music program established 1932.
Degrees Bachelor of Music in the areas of performance, piano pedagogy, jazz studies, theory, composition, music business; Bachelor of Music Education; Bachelor of Music Therapy. Majors and concentrations: composition, guitar performance, instrumental performance, jazz studies, keyboard performance, music business, music education, music theory, music therapy, piano pedagogy, voice performance. Graduate degrees offered: Master of Music in the area of performance; Master of Music Education; Master of Music Therapy. Cross-registration with Xavier University of Louisiana, Tulane University, Notre Dame Seminary, Southern University at New Orleans. Program accredited by NASM.
Enrollment 353 total; 327 undergraduate, 26 graduate.

Music Student Profile 49% females, 51% males, 15% minorities, 3% international.

Music Faculty 24 total (full-time), 37 total (part-time). 62% of full-time faculty have terminal degrees. Graduate students do not teach undergraduate courses. Undergraduate student–faculty ratio: 6:1.

Student Life Student groups/activities include Loyola Association of Music Therapy Students, Music Educators National Conference Student Chapter, Loyola University Community Action Program.

Expenses for 2005–2006 Application fee: $20. Comprehensive fee: $33,558 includes full-time tuition ($24,410), mandatory fees ($836), and college room and board ($8312). College room only: $5166. Room and board charges vary according to board plan and housing facility. Special program-related fees: $100 for student teaching fee.

Financial Aid Program-specific awards: 52 music scholarships for music majors ($4500).

Application Procedures Students admitted directly into the professional program freshman year. Deadline for freshmen and transfers: May 1. Notification date for freshmen and transfers: May 1. Required: essay, high school transcript, college transcript(s) for transfer students, minimum 2.0 high school GPA, 2 letters of recommendation, audition, SAT I or ACT test scores (minimum combined SAT I score of 990, minimum composite ACT score of 21), portfolio for composition and music business majors. Auditions held 3 times on campus; recorded music is permissible as a substitute for live auditions when distance is prohibitive and videotaped performances are permissible as a substitute for live auditions when distance is prohibitive. Portfolio reviews held 3 times on campus.

Web Site http://www.music.loyno.edu

Contact Dr. Anthony Decuir, Associate Dean, College of Music, Loyola University New Orleans, 6363 Saint Charles Avenue, New Orleans, Louisiana 70118; 504-865-3037, fax: 504-865-2852, e-mail address: decuir@loyno.edu

Lynn University

Boca Raton, Florida

Independent, coed. Suburban campus. Total enrollment: 2,747. Music program established 1991.

Manhattan School of Music

New York, New York

Independent, coed. Urban campus. Total enrollment: 891. Music program established 1917.

Degrees Bachelor of Music in the areas of classical performance, classical composition, jazz/jazz composition. Majors and concentrations: classical guitar, classical music, composition, jazz, piano, stringed instruments, voice, wind and percussion instruments. Graduate degrees offered: Master of Music in the areas of classical performance, classical composition, jazz/jazz composition, orchestral performance. Doctor of Musical Arts in the areas of classical performance, classical composition, jazz arts advancement. Cross-registration with Barnard College .

Enrollment 418 undergraduate, 477 graduate.

Music Student Profile 52% females, 48% males, 15% minorities, 40% international.

Music Faculty 70 total (full-time), 126 total (part-time). 20% of full-time faculty have terminal degrees. Graduate students teach a few undergraduate courses. Undergraduate student–faculty ratio: 10:1.

Student Life Student groups/activities include orchestra, opera studio. Special housing available for music students.

Expenses for 2006–2007 Application fee: $100. Comprehensive fee: $42,760 includes full-time tuition ($27,400), mandatory fees ($2560), and college room and board ($12,800). College room only: $8400.

Financial Aid Program-specific awards available.

Application Procedures Students admitted directly into the professional program freshman year. Deadline for freshmen and transfers: December 1. Notification date for freshmen and transfers: April 1. Required: essay, high school transcript, college transcript(s) for transfer students, minimum 2.0 high school GPA, letter of recommendation, audition, pre-screen tape/CD for voice, flute, jazz, cello, violin composition applicants, list of performance experience. Recommended: minimum 3.0 high school GPA, interview, SAT I or ACT test scores. Auditions held twice on campus; videotaped performances are permissible as a substitute for live auditions for applicants living outside North America and for cello, double bass, and tuba applicants.

Web Site http://www.msmnyc.edu

Contact Ms. Amy A. Anderson, Assistant Dean of Admission and Financial Aid, Manhattan School of Music, 120 Claremont Avenue, New York, New York 10027-4698; 212-749-2802 ext. 4501, fax: 212-749-3025, e-mail address: admission@msmnyc.edu

More About the School

Since 1917, Manhattan School of Music (MSM) has prepared gifted young musicians to assume their place on the world's stages.

In selecting MSM, students choose to work with faculty members who are themselves performers with international reputations. They choose to be with students from around the world who come together to create an environment remarkable not just for its intensity, but for genuine friendliness and cooperation. And, of course, they choose New York itself, a major center of music and art in America.

While many fine music conservatories are acknowledged for their ability to develop talents and skills, MSM has a particular combination of strengths that make it an excellent place from which to launch a career.

With extensive performance opportunities on campus as well as the chance to freelance and begin to develop a network of professional contacts, students undergo remarkable changes here: they start to function as professional musicians while they are still in school. It is this powerful convergence of opportunity and training that gives students the chance to go as far as their talent, intelligence, and courage can take them.

Alumni are the School's best examples of this training. Here are just a few of MSM alumni from 1970 to the present: Laura Albeck, Metropolitan Opera Orchestra; Robert Anderson, Minnesota Orchestra; Gerald Appleman, New York Philharmonic; Karen Beardsley, soprano, New York City Opera; Elizabeth Burkhardt, Atlanta Symphony; John Carabella, New York Philharmonic; Ron Carter, jazz bassist; Harry Connick Jr., singer; Todd Coolman, jazz bassist; Alison Dalton, Chicago Symphony; Jacqui Danilow, Metropolitan Opera Orchestra; Garry Dial, jazz pianist; James Dooley, San José Symphony; Don Ehrlich, San Francisco Symphony; Desiree Elsevier, Metropolitan Opera Orchestra; Mary Ewing, New York Philharmonic; Lauren Flannigan, soprano, Metropolitan Opera; Anna Garzuly, Gewandhaus Orchestra (Leipzig); Susan Graham, mezzo-soprano, Metropolitan Opera; Andrea Gruber, soprano, Metropolitan Opera; Laura Hamilton, Metropolitan Opera Orchestra; Herbie Hancock, jazz pianist; Stefon Harris, jazz vibraphonist; Louella Hasbun, San José Symphony; Douglas Hedwig, Metropolitan Opera Orchestra; Frank Hosticka, Metropolitan Opera Orchestra; Simon James, Seattle Symphony; Richard Jensen, Cincinnati Symphony; Henry Kao, New Jersey Symphony; Gilad Karni, Bamburger Sinfoniker; Kemal Khan, conductor; Christopher Komer, New Jersey Symphony; Dawn Kotoski, soprano, Metropolitan Opera; Morris Lang, New York Philharmonic; Michael Leonhart, Grammy Award winner; Igor Leschishin, Kennedy Center Opera Orchestra; Roy Lewis, Manhattan String Quartet; Douglas Lindsay, Cincinnati Symphony; George Manahan, Music Director, New York City Opera; Marvis Martin, soprano, Metropolitan Opera; Kerri McDermott, New York Philharmonic; Peter McGinnis, jazz trombonist; Sharon Meekins, Metropolitan Opera Orchestra; Warren Mok, tenor, Berlin Opera; Jane Monheit, jazz vocalist; Jason Moran, jazz pianist; Frank Morelli, Orpheus Chamber Orchestra; June Morganstern, Chicago Lyric Opera Orchestra; Elmar Oliveira, concert violinist; Susan Quittmeyer, mezzo-soprano, Metropolitan Opera; Max Roach, jazz artist; Tatiana Ruhland, Dresden Philharmonic; Bruce Smith, Detroit Symphony;

Manhattan School of Music (continued)

Dawn Stahler, Dallas Symphony; James Stubbs, Metropolitan Opera Orchestra; Stewart Taylor, Israel Philharmonic; Dawn Upshaw, soprano, Metropolitan Opera; Roland Vasquez, jazz drummer; Rosa Vento, soprano, Vienna State Opera; Geraldine Walther, San Francisco Symphony; Bing Wang, Los Angeles Philharmonic; Mark Wells, Canadian Opera Orchestra; Virginia Chen Wells, Toronto Symphony; Thomas Wetzel, Milwaukee Symphony; Timothy Wilson, San Francisco Opera Orchestra; Carol Wincenc, concert flutist; Naomi Youngstein, New Jersey Symphony; and Dolora Zajick, mezzo-soprano, Metropolitan Opera.

Manhattanville College

Purchase, New York

Independent, coed. Suburban campus. Total enrollment: 2,806. Music program established 1937.

The New School: A University
Mannes College The New School for Music

New York, New York

Independent, coed. Urban campus. Total enrollment: 366. Music program established 1916.
Degrees Bachelor of Music in the areas of orchestral instruments, piano, voice, composition, music theory, orchestral and choral conducting, guitar; Bachelor of Science in the areas of orchestral instruments, piano, harpsichord, voice, classical guitar, orchestral conducting, choral conducting, composition, theory. Majors and concentrations: classical guitar, composition, conducting, guitar, harpsichord, music theory, performance, piano, stringed instruments, voice, wind and percussion instruments. Graduate degrees offered: Master of Music in the areas of orchestral instruments, piano, voice, composition, music theory, orchestral and choral conducting, guitar. Cross-registration with The New School.
Enrollment 294 total; 136 undergraduate, 158 graduate.
Music Student Profile 57% females, 43% males, 22% minorities, 45% international.
Music Faculty 8 total (full-time), 135 total (part-time). Graduate students do not teach undergraduate courses. Undergraduate student–faculty ratio: 4:1.
Student Life Special housing available for music students.
Expenses for 2005–2006 Application fee: $100. Comprehensive fee: $37,880 includes full-time tuition ($25,560), mandatory fees ($570), and college room and board ($11,750). College room only: $8750. Full-time tuition and fees vary according to degree level and program. Room and board charges vary according to board plan.
Financial Aid Program-specific awards: merit scholarships for above-average students.
Application Procedures Students admitted directly into the professional program freshman year. Deadline for freshmen and transfers: December 1. Notification date for freshmen and transfers: April 15. Required: essay, high school transcript, college transcript(s) for transfer students, letter of recommendation, interview, audition, TOEFL for international students for whom English is a second language. Recommended: minimum 2.0 high school GPA. Auditions held twice on campus.
Web Site http://www.mannes.edu
Undergraduate Contact Ms. Georgia Schmidt, Assistant Director of Admissions, Mannes College The New School for Music, 150 West 85th Street, New York, New York 10024; 212-580-0210 ext. 4805, fax: 212-580-1738, e-mail address: schmittg@newschool.edu
Graduate Contact Ms. Georgia Schmitt, Assistant Director of Admissions, Mannes College The New School for Music, 150

West 85th Street, New York, New York 10024; 212-580-0210 ext. 4805, fax: 212-580-1738, e-mail address: schmittg@newschool.edu

More About the College

For students at Mannes College The New School for Music, music is a part of life both in and out of the classroom. The instruction they receive allows students both to benefit from and to contribute to New York City's rich musical and cultural life. And from its location on Manhattan's Upper West Side, students can walk to world-renowned cultural institutions like Lincoln Center, Carnegie Hall, and the Metropolitan Museum of Art.

Training the complete classical musician is the main activity at Mannes. Small classes and a small student body (fewer than 300 students) ensure that each student receives personalized instruction and has close interaction with faculty and staff members, administrators, and peers. Mannes guides students toward the highest professional standards. For aspiring musicians, there is no substitute for the experience gained by performing. Through ensembles and other public appearances, and by helping students develop connections outside the school, Mannes offers numerous ways for students to perform both at school and in the New York music community.

As part of the curriculum, performance courses are balanced with techniques of music courses to give students solid training in the language of music. Through ear training, dictation, keyboard skills, theory, and analysis courses, students deepen their understanding of the role the performer plays in the art of music. In addition, students receive private lessons with one of the school's 150 distinguished faculty members and study a curriculum that is tailored to meet their particular needs. Students may also earn a Bachelor of Science degree in all majors by completing the Bachelor of Music curriculum and taking or transferring 30 additional academic credits from another approved institution.

Students at Mannes have access to everything aspiring musicians need. The Federal-style building Mannes calls home offers classrooms, practice rooms, a state-of-the-art computer lab, and the Scherman Music Library, which features a collection that includes 8,000 books, 30,000 scores, 9,000 recordings, 300 video recordings, many music-related periodicals, specialized databases,

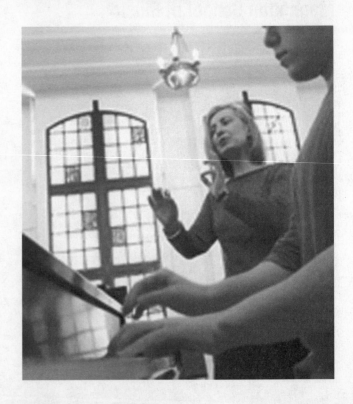

and electronic resources, as well as study carrels, computers, and a complete music and listening library. The New School also offers the facilities of the Fogelman Social Science and Humanities Library, located on the downtown campus, and, through a consortium known as the Research Library Association of South Manhattan, the Bobst Library at New York University and the consortium's online catalog, Bobcat, are accessible on the Internet.

The pursuit of instrumental and vocal mastery is complemented by classes in literature, history, and liberal arts. Degree candidates have access to The New School's broad liberal arts curriculum, and Mannes students share resources with The New School's other divisions: The New School for General Studies, The New School for Social Research, Milano The New School for Management and Urban Policy, Parsons The New School for Design, Eugene Lang College The New School for Liberal Arts, The New School for Drama, and The New School for Jazz and Contemporary Music.

To connect students to the professional world, Mannes utilizes a variety of channels, including faculty members, guest artists, and artists-in-residence. Students also have access to a network of thousands of successful alumni who are putting their training to work on stages around the world. Alumni of Mannes have distinguished themselves in many leading orchestras and opera companies, from the Metropolitan Opera and L'Orchestre de Paris to the Chicago Lyric Opera and the Hong Kong Sinfonietta, and have participated in and enriched the lives of the people in the communities where they perform, live, and work. Mannes's distinguished alumni include Frederica von Stade, Richard Goode, Murray Perahia, JoAnn Falletta, and Kaori Sato. For more information about Mannes, students should visit http://www.mannes. newschool.edu.

Mansfield University of Pennsylvania
Mansfield, Pennsylvania

State-supported, coed. Small town campus. Total enrollment: 3,390. Music program established 1880.
Degrees Bachelor of Music in the areas of music education, music therapy, performance, elective studies in business. Majors and concentrations: music, music business, music education, music performance, music therapy, piano, stringed instruments, voice, wind and percussion instruments. Graduate degrees offered: Master of Arts in the areas of music education, instrumental conducting, choral conducting. Program accredited by NASM.
Enrollment 282 total; 225 undergraduate, 32 graduate, 25 nonprofessional degree.
Music Student Profile 60% females, 40% males, 4% minorities, 1% international.
Music Faculty 18 total (full-time), 4 total (part-time). 94% of full-time faculty have terminal degrees. Graduate students do not teach undergraduate courses. Undergraduate student–faculty ratio: 12:1.
Student Life Student groups/activities include Music Educators National Conference Student Chapter, Mid-Atlantic Regional Association of Music Therapy Students, American Choral Directors Association.
Expenses for 2005–2006 Application fee: $25. State resident tuition: $4906 full-time. Nonresident tuition: $12,266 full-time. Mandatory fees: $1502 full-time. College room and board: $5868. Room and board charges vary according to board plan. Special program-related fees: $25 for recording and program fee, $30 per course for instrument rental fee for all techniques courses.
Financial Aid Program-specific awards: 5 Kreuscher Awards for program majors ($1000), 1 Darrin-Dye Award for freshmen program majors ($1000), 1 Doud Award for freshmen program majors ($3400), 2 Music Department Scholarships for freshmen program majors ($1000–$2000), 5 Jones Awards for voice program majors ($2000), 1 Frances Award for freshman program majors ($1000), 1 Ruc Scholarship for upper class students from Pennsylvania ($1000).
Application Procedures Students admitted directly into the professional program freshman year. Deadline for freshmen and

transfers: February 28. Required: high school transcript, college transcript(s) for transfer students, minimum 2.0 high school GPA, 2 letters of recommendation, interview, audition, SAT I or ACT test scores, theory placement test, piano proficiency test, aural skills test. Recommended: essay, minimum 3.0 high school GPA. Auditions held 8 times on campus; recorded music is permissible as a substitute for live auditions when distance is prohibitive and without editing and videotaped performances are permissible as a substitute for live auditions when distance is prohibitive and without editing.
Web Site http://www.mnsfld.edu
Contact Dr. Adam F. Brennan, Chairperson, Department of Music, Mansfield University of Pennsylvania, Butler Center 110, Mansfield, Pennsylvania 16933; 570-662-4710, fax: 570-662-4114.

Margaret E. Petree College of Music and Performing Arts
See Oklahoma City University

Mariam Cannon Hayes School of Music
See Appalachian State University

Marshall University
Huntington, West Virginia

State-supported, coed. Urban campus. Total enrollment: 13,988. Music program established 1980.

Mars Hill College
Mars Hill, North Carolina

Independent Baptist, coed. Small town campus. Total enrollment: 1,378. Music program established 1952.

Marygrove College
Detroit, Michigan

Independent Roman Catholic, coed, primarily women. Urban campus. Total enrollment: 3,591. Music program established 1927.
Degrees Bachelor of Music in the areas of performance (voice, organ or piano), piano pedagogy, music education, sacred music (choral or piano emphasis), theory and composition. Majors and concentrations: electronic music, music education, music theory and composition, performance, piano pedagogy, sacred music. Cross-registration with University of Detroit Mercy.
Enrollment 33 total; 29 undergraduate, 4 nonprofessional degree.
Music Student Profile 75% females, 25% males, 75% minorities, 1% international.
Music Faculty 4 undergraduate (full-time), 7 undergraduate (part-time). 100% of full-time faculty have terminal degrees. Graduate students do not teach undergraduate courses. Undergraduate student–faculty ratio: 9:1.
Student Life Student groups/activities include Music Teachers National Association Student Chapter, Marygrove College Chorale, Lyric Theatre Program.
Expenses for 2005–2006 Application fee: $25. Comprehensive fee: $19,335 includes full-time tuition ($12,800), mandatory fees ($335), and college room and board ($6200). Special program-related fees: $25 per semester for choir fee, $65 per credit hour for private lessons.
Financial Aid Program-specific awards: 2–4 music scholarships for talented students ($500–$1000), Distinguished Student Awards for talented students ($2000–$9000), Admissions Talent Awards for talented students ($3000–$9000).
Application Procedures Students admitted directly into the professional program freshman year. Deadline for freshmen and transfers: continuous. Required: high school transcript, college

Marygrove College (continued)

transcript(s) for transfer students, SAT I or ACT test scores, minimum 2.7 high school GPA, minimum 2.0 college GPA for transfer applicants, audition for scholarship consideration. Recommended: interview, audition. Auditions held twice on campus; recorded music is permissible as a substitute for live auditions for international applicants and videotaped performances are permissible as a substitute for live auditions for international applicants.
Web Site http://www.marygrove.edu
Undergraduate Contact Sally Janacek, Director of Admissions, Marygrove College, 8425 West McNichols Road, Detroit, Michigan 48221; 313-927-1570, fax: 313-864-6670, e-mail address: adm@marygrove.edu

Marylhurst University
Marylhurst, Oregon

Independent Roman Catholic, coed. Suburban campus. Total enrollment: 1,268. Music program established 1972.
Degrees Bachelor of Music Therapy. Majors and concentrations: music therapy. Program accredited by NASM, AMTA.
Enrollment 61 total; 36 undergraduate, 25 nonprofessional degree.
Music Student Profile 75% females, 25% males, 20% minorities, 5% international.
Music Faculty 1 undergraduate (full-time), 24 undergraduate (part-time). 100% of full-time faculty have terminal degrees. Graduate students do not teach undergraduate courses. Undergraduate student–faculty ratio: 6:1.
Expenses for 2005–2006 Application fee: $20. Tuition: $13,860 full-time. Mandatory fees: $360 full-time. Full-time tuition and fees vary according to course load. Special program-related fees: $30 per course for music therapy practicum, $100 per course for private music lessons.
Financial Aid Program-specific awards: 6 departmental scholarships for music therapy majors ($1000–$3000), 2–4 departmental scholarships for music majors ($300–$1000).
Application Procedures Students admitted directly into the professional program freshman year. Deadline for freshmen and transfers: continuous. Required: essay, high school transcript, college transcript(s) for transfer students, minimum 3.0 high school GPA, letter of recommendation, interview, audition, SAT I or ACT test scores (minimum combined SAT I score of 900, minimum composite ACT score of 19). Auditions held as needed on campus; recorded music is permissible as a substitute for live auditions when distance is prohibitive or in special circumstances and videotaped performances are permissible as a substitute for live auditions when distance is prohibitive or in special circumstances.
Web Site http://www.marylhurst.edu/
Undergraduate Contact Christine Korb, Director of Music Therapy Program, Music Department, Marylhurst University, PO Box 261, Marylhurst, Oregon 97036-0261; 503-636-8141 ext. 3361, fax: 503-636-9526, e-mail address: musictherapy@marylhurst.edu

The Mary Pappert School of Music
See Duquesne University

Maryville College
Maryville, Tennessee

Independent Presbyterian, coed. Suburban campus. Total enrollment: 1,146.

Marywood University
Scranton, Pennsylvania

Independent Roman Catholic, coed. Suburban campus. Total enrollment: 3,127. Music program established 1915.

Mason Gross School of the Arts
New Brunswick, New Jersey

State-supported, coed. Small town campus. Music program established 1976.
Degrees Bachelor of Music in the areas of music education, jazz, performance. Majors and concentrations: classical music, jazz, music education. Graduate degrees offered: Master of Music in the areas of performance, jazz, music education, collaborative piano, instrumental, choral, and orchestral conducting. Doctor of Musical Arts in the areas of performance, music education, collaborative piano, instrumental, choral, and orfhestral conducting. Program accredited by NASM.
Enrollment 445 total; 192 undergraduate, 203 graduate, 50 nonprofessional degree.
Music Student Profile 40% females, 60% males, 10% minorities, 15% international.
Music Faculty 43 total (full-time), 52 total (part-time). 100% of full-time faculty have terminal degrees. Graduate students teach about a quarter of undergraduate courses. Undergraduate student–faculty ratio: 3:1.
Student Life Student groups/activities include National Association of Teachers.
Financial Aid Program-specific awards: 10 Benefit Series Awards for those with artistic merit ($500–$3500), 10 Marryott Scholarships for those with artistic merit ($500–$4000), 12 Douglass Noe Awards for those with artistic merit ($500–$2500), 2 Douglass Shaw Awards for those with artistic merit ($500–$1500), 5 Douglass Waksman Awards for those with artistic merit ($500–$2000), Lockfeld Awards in Jazz for those with artistic merit ($1000), 2 Jean Hooper Awards for those with artistic merit ($2500), 17 W. Robert and Leone Schare Scholarships for those with artistic merit ($500–$1700).
Application Procedures Students admitted directly into the professional program freshman year. Deadline for freshmen: continuous; transfers: March 15. Notification date for freshmen and transfers: May 1. Required: high school transcript, college transcript(s) for transfer students, minimum 2.0 high school GPA, interview, audition, SAT I or ACT test scores. Auditions held 4 times on campus; recorded music is permissible as a substitute for live auditions when distance is prohibitive or scheduling is difficult and videotaped performances are permissible as a substitute for live auditions when distance is prohibitive or scheduling is difficult.
Web Site http://www.rutgers.edu
Undergraduate Contact Dr. Rufus Hallmark, Chairman, Music Department, Rutgers, The State University of New Jersey, Mason Gross School of the Arts, Marryott Music Building, New Brunswick, New Jersey 08901; 732-932-8860, fax: 732-932-1517.
Graduate Contact Dr. Richard Chrisman, Graduate Director, Music Department, Rutgers, The State University of New Jersey, Mason Gross School of the Arts, Marryott Music Building, New Brunswick, New Jersey 08901; 732-932-9272, fax: 732-932-1517, e-mail address: chrisman@rci.rutgers.edu

McGill University
Montreal, Quebec, Canada

Province-supported, coed. Urban campus. Total enrollment: 30,333. Music program established 1921.
Degrees Bachelor of Music. Majors and concentrations: composition, early music, jazz performance, music education, music history, music technology, music theory, performance. Graduate degrees offered: Master of Arts in the areas of music education, music technology, musicology, theory; Master of Music in the areas of composition, performance, sound recording. Doctor of Music in the areas of composition, performance; Doctor of Philosophy in the areas of music education, music technology, musicology, theory. Cross-registration with any Quebec university. Program accredited by CUMS.

Enrollment 746 total; 462 undergraduate, 240 graduate, 44 nonprofessional degree.
Music Student Profile 51% females, 49% males, 12% international.
Music Faculty 55 total (full-time), 100 total (part-time). 44% of full-time faculty have terminal degrees. Graduate students teach about a quarter of undergraduate courses. Undergraduate student–faculty ratio: 10:1.
Student Life Student groups/activities include performance at various campus functions.
Expenses for 2006–2007 Application fee: $60 Canadian dollars. Special program-related fees: $700 per 30 credits for instruments, practice rooms, ensemble music, society fee.
Financial Aid Program-specific awards: 8–10 faculty special scholarships for freshmen with exceptional musical skills ($10,000), 2–5 McGill Major Awards for freshmen with high academic standing ($5000–$8000), 12 music entrance scholarships for freshmen with exceptional musical skills ($2000), 2 Lloyd Carr-Harris String Scholarships for freshmen string players with exceptional musical skills ($10,000).
Application Procedures Students admitted directly into the professional program freshman year. Deadline for freshmen and transfers: January 15. Notification date for freshmen and transfers: March 30. Required: high school transcript, college transcript(s) for transfer students, minimum 2.0 high school GPA, letter of recommendation, audition, statement of intent, portfolio for composition majors, screening tape for all jazz instruments, piano, and female voice, music education letter in support of suitability. Recommended: minimum 3.0 high school GPA. Auditions held once on campus; recorded music is permissible as a substitute for live auditions when distance is prohibitive or a scheduling conflict exists (students not eligible for scholarships if audition is taped or video) and videotaped performances are permissible as a substitute for live auditions when distance is prohibitive or a scheduling conflict exists (students not eligible for scholarships if audition is taped or video). Portfolio reviews held twice on campus.
Web Site http://www.mcgill.ca/music
Contact Patrick O'Neill, Admissions Officer, Schulich School of Music, McGill University, 555 Sherbrooke Street West, Montreal, Quebec H3A 1E3, Canada; 514-398-4546, fax: 514-398-8061, e-mail address: undergradadmissions.music@mcgill.ca

More About the University

The Schulich School of Music is part of McGill University, an internationally recognized University renowned for its high standard of education and research. The pursuit of excellence is central to the University's mission and is reflected in the accomplishments of its faculty, the quality of its facilities, and its commitment to teaching and learning.

Founded as the Conservatorium of Music in 1904 and later incorporated as a faculty in 1920, the Schulich School of Music of McGill University (formerly known as the Faculty of Music) has enjoyed steady growth from a handful of students to its present

position as the largest music school in Canada. Building on a strong base of studio and classroom teaching, the Faculty is renowned for its orchestral, opera, jazz, chamber, and early music programs and for its award-winning creative and research work in composition, theory, musicology, music education, and music technology.

Campus and Surroundings McGill is uniquely positioned in the world of musical culture and education. Its location in the heart of downtown Montreal, provides links to one of the most vibrant cultural scenes in the world. The Schulich School of Music of McGill University provides musical arts leadership in the context of one of the world's great educational and research institutions.

Program Facilities High-quality digital composition studios, music technology laboratories, recording studios, and a library (the major resource for research in music in eastern Canada), together with its performance opportunities and facilities, make McGill Canada's premier school of music. To accommodate the more than 650 annual events presented by staff members, students, and guests, the Schulich School of Music of McGill University supports several performance facilities. Pollack Concert Hall seats 600 and is one of the most prominent concert venues in Montreal. It has an orchestra pit for opera productions and is fitted with an elaborate speaker system that produces optimal sound quality for electroacoustic concerts. Redpath Hall, with a capacity of 320, provides a more intimate performing environment. This atmosphere, together with its magnificent French classical organ, has made it the preferred concert venue for early music and chamber music groups. The Tanna Schulich Hall, which seats 187, is the School's newest hall and an excellent venue for solo and small ensemble performances. The smaller Clara Lichtenstein Recital Hall provides a third venue for recitals and symposia and may be booked by students wishing to present less formal concerts or to arrange recording sessions for their work. The Marvin Duchow Music Library, located in the New Music Building, opened on September 30, 2005. It provides a state-of-the-art working environment for academic studies and has one of the largest collections of music books, scores, and recordings in Canada. It provides students with ready computer access to electronic databases all over the world. Rapidly increasing acquisitions of interactive CD-ROMs and laser discs have put users in touch with exciting new ways to learn about music. The library's subscriptions to well over 200 music journals and magazines allow readers to keep abreast of developments in every field of music. Of particular note among the library's several special collections is the David Edelbert Collection, the largest collection of sound recordings of Handel in the world.

McGill is at the forefront of new developments in high-definition video and multichannel audio Internet transmission. The Schulich School of Music of McGill University is home to CIRMMT ("kermit"), the Centre for Interdisciplinary Research in Music Media and Technology. CIRMMT is attracting a dynamic team of international researchers in sound recording, music technology, computer and electrical engineering, neuroscience, and cognition to create a leadership environment where musicians and scientists work together to transform the nature of musical training and research. A $50-million addition to the School's historic Strathcona Building, which opened in 2005, houses the Marvin Duchow Music Library, the 200-seat Tanna Schulich recital hall, CIRMMT research labs, an opera rehearsal room, the Wirth Opera Studio, recording studios and control rooms, and a full symphonic scoring stage/research laboratory.

Faculty, Resident Artists, and Alumni The reputation of its professors—55 full-time and more than 100 part-time—attracts some 840 students annually from around the world. The Concerts and Publicity Office produces guest, staff, and student concerts both on and off campus, many of which are recorded by CBC and Société Radio-Canada for national broadcast. In addition, a number of concerts are Web broadcast. McGill ensembles and soloists are also recorded by the Recording Studio.

McGill University (continued)

Student Performance Opportunities McGill ensembles tour extensively and have earned praise from critics in North America and Europe for their performances and recordings. The McGill Symphony Orchestra has performed in Carnegie Hall, the National Arts Centre in Ottawa, the Grand Théâtre de Québec, Montreal's Place des Arts, and Roy Thomson Hall in Toronto. The McGill Jazz Ensemble, recently declared the best university stage band in North America, has won numerous awards for its recordings and has played in London, Paris, and Dublin and at prestigious international jazz festivals. Opera McGill provides students with the rigorous discipline and stage experience required to become professional singers through its noted productions of operas, such as Mozart's *The Magic Flute* and Britten's *A Midsummer Night's Dream*. This year's performance was Bernstein's *Candide*. McGill is renowned for its strengths in early music and contemporary music through such high-profile ensembles as the McGill Baroque Orchestra and the McGill Contemporary Music Ensemble. Participation in large ensemble and chamber music training are integral to all programs; students benefit from many coaching sessions and performance opportunities.

Special Programs The Faculty regularly hosts distinguished musical visitors from around the globe. Recent guests include Ida Haendel, Jane Eaglen, Franz-Paul Decker, Sandy Pearlman, and Joni Mitchell. The McGill Summer Organ Academy is a biennial event that takes advantage of the great instruments in the Montreal area. McGill is a leading partner in "Montréal Nouvelles Musiques," an international biennial festival of contemporary music that alternates with McGill's "MusiMars." The Faculty regularly hosts major international conferences and festivals.

McLean School of Music

See Middle Tennessee State University

McNeese State University

Lake Charles, Louisiana

State-supported, coed. Suburban campus. Total enrollment: 8,785. Music program established 1939.

Meadows School of the Arts/Division of Music

See Southern Methodist University

Mercer University

Macon, Georgia

Independent Baptist, coed. Suburban campus. Total enrollment: 7,154. Music program established 1978.
Degrees Bachelor of Music in the area of performance; Bachelor of Music Education. Majors and concentrations: composition, guitar, harpsichord, music education, music theory, piano/organ, stringed instruments, voice, wind and percussion instruments. Graduate degrees offered: Master of Music in the areas of church music, performance with an emphasis in church music. Program accredited by NASM.
Enrollment 70 total; 35 undergraduate, 35 nonprofessional degree.
Music Student Profile 50% females, 50% males, 12% minorities.
Music Faculty 13 undergraduate (full-time), 15 undergraduate (part-time). 100% of full-time faculty have terminal degrees. Graduate students do not teach undergraduate courses. Undergraduate student–faculty ratio: 5:1.

Student Life Student groups/activities include Music Educators National Conference Student Chapter, American Choral Directors Association Student Chapter, Mu Phi Epsilon.
Expenses for 2005–2006 Application fee: $50. Comprehensive fee: $30,873 includes full-time tuition ($23,460) and college room and board ($7413). College room only: $3570. Full-time tuition varies according to class time, course load, and location. Room and board charges vary according to board plan, housing facility, and location. Special program-related fees: $218 per semester for lesson fee.
Financial Aid Program-specific awards: 40 music scholarships for music majors ($1000–$6000).
Application Procedures Students apply for admission into the professional program by sophomore year. Deadline for freshmen and transfers: continuous. Notification date for freshmen and transfers: continuous. Required: high school transcript, college transcript(s) for transfer students, minimum 2.0 high school GPA, letter of recommendation, audition, SAT I or ACT test scores, list of extracurricular activities. Auditions held 4 times and by appointment on campus; recorded music is permissible as a substitute for live auditions when distance is prohibitive and videotaped performances are permissible as a substitute for live auditions when distance is prohibitive.
Web Site http://www.mercer.edu/music/
Undergraduate Contact Director of Admissions, Mercer University, 1400 Coleman Avenue, Macon, Georgia 31207; 478-301-2650, fax: 478-301-4120.

The D'Angelo School of Music
Mercyhurst College

Erie, Pennsylvania

Independent Roman Catholic, coed. Suburban campus. Total enrollment: 4,120. Music program established 1987.

Meredith College

Raleigh, North Carolina

Independent, Urban campus. Total enrollment: 2,168. Music program established 1899.
Degrees Bachelor of Music in the areas of performance, music education. Majors and concentrations: classical music, composition, music, music education, piano pedagogy, piano/organ, stringed instruments, voice, wind and percussion instruments. Graduate degrees offered: Master of Music in the area of performance/pedagogy. Cross-registration with North Carolina State University and Cooperating Raleigh Colleges Consortium. Program accredited by NASM.
Enrollment 100 total; 60 undergraduate, 10 graduate, 30 nonprofessional degree.
Music Student Profile 100% females, 5% international.
Music Faculty 9 total (full-time), 25 total (part-time). 100% of full-time faculty have terminal degrees. Graduate students do not teach undergraduate courses. Undergraduate student–faculty ratio: 5:1.
Student Life Student groups/activities include Sigma Alpha Iota, Pi Kappa Lambda, Collegiate Music Educators National Conference.
Expenses for 2006–2007 Application fee: $40. Comprehensive fee: $27,140 includes full-time tuition ($21,150), mandatory fees ($50), and college room and board ($5940). Special program-related fees: $150–$300 per semester for applied music fee, $380 per semester for professional accompanist fee (if applicable).
Financial Aid Program-specific awards: 1 Excellence in Music Scholarship for incoming freshmen ($7500), 1 Robert H. Lewis Award for incoming freshmen ($6000), 3 music talent scholarships for incoming freshmen ($500–$1500), 1 Mary Perry Beddingfield Award for incoming freshmen ($1000).
Application Procedures Students admitted directly into the professional program freshman year. Deadline for freshmen and transfers: continuous. Required: high school transcript, college transcript(s) for transfer students, minimum 2.0 high school GPA, 2 letters of recommendation, interview, audition, SAT I test score only. Recommended: essay. Auditions held at various times on

campus; recorded music is permissible as a substitute for live auditions when distance is prohibitive or scheduling is difficult and videotaped performances are permissible as a substitute for live auditions when distance is prohibitive or scheduling is difficult.
Web Site http://www.meredith.edu
Undergraduate Contact Ms. Heidi Flebcher, Director, Office of Admissions, Meredith College, 3800 Hillsborough Street, Raleigh, North Carolina 27607-5298; 800-637-3348, fax: 919-760-2348, e-mail address: admissions@meredith.edu
Graduate Contact Director, John E. Weems Graduate School, Meredith College, 3800 Hillsborough Street, Raleigh, North Carolina 27607-5298; 919-760-8423, fax: 919-760-2898, e-mail address: gradmusic@meredith.edu

Metropolitan State College of Denver
Denver, Colorado

State-supported, coed. Urban campus. Total enrollment: 20,761. Music program established 1965.
Degrees Bachelor of Music in the areas of music performance, composition; Bachelor of Music Education in the areas of choral music education, instrumental music education. Majors and concentrations: composition, music education, music performance. Cross-registration with University of Colorado at Denver. Program accredited by NASM.
Enrollment 390 total; 300 undergraduate, 90 nonprofessional degree.
Music Student Profile 55% females, 45% males, 7% minorities, 3% international.
Music Faculty 10 undergraduate (full-time), 42 undergraduate (part-time). 100% of full-time faculty have terminal degrees. Graduate students do not teach undergraduate courses. Undergraduate student–faculty ratio: 27:1.
Student Life Student groups/activities include Music Activities Committee, Colorado Collegiate Music Educators, American Choral Directors Association.
Expenses for 2005–2006 Application fee: $25. State resident tuition: $2283 full-time. Nonresident tuition: $9366 full-time. Mandatory fees: $576 full-time. Full-time tuition and fees vary according to course load and location. Special program-related fees: $15 per semester for ensemble fee.
Financial Aid Program-specific awards: 80 Colorado Scholars Music Talent Awards for music students ($500).
Application Procedures Students admitted directly into the professional program freshman year. Deadline for freshmen and transfers: continuous. Required: high school transcript, college transcript(s) for transfer students, audition, SAT I or ACT test scores. Auditions held twice on campus.
Web Site http://www.mscd.edu/~music
Undergraduate Contact William Hathaway-Clark, Director, Admissions, Metropolitan State College of Denver, PO Box 173362, Campus Box 58, Denver, Colorado 80217; 303-556-3993, fax: 303-556-6345, e-mail address: hathaway@mscd.edu

Miami University
Oxford, Ohio

State-related, coed. Small town campus. Total enrollment: 16,338. Music program established 1929.
Degrees Bachelor of Music in the areas of performance, music education. Majors and concentrations: harp, music, music education, piano/organ, stringed instruments, voice, wind and percussion instruments. Graduate degrees offered: Master of Music in the areas of performance, music education. Program accredited by NASM, NCATE.
Enrollment 250 total; 225 undergraduate, 25 graduate.
Music Student Profile 50% females, 50% males, 5% minorities, 1% international.
Music Faculty 31 total (full-time), 12 total (part-time). 50% of full-time faculty have terminal degrees. Graduate students teach a few undergraduate courses. Undergraduate student–faculty ratio: 6:1.

Student Life Student groups/activities include Music Educators National Conference, American Choral Directors Association, professional music fraternities and sororities.
Expenses for 2005–2006 Application fee: $45. State resident tuition: $19,877 full-time. Nonresident tuition: $19,877 full-time. Mandatory fees: $1610 full-time. College room and board: $7610. College room only: $3860. Room and board charges vary according to board plan and housing facility. Ohio residents receive a minimum of $10,000 in resident scholarships. Special program-related fees: $85 per semester for fee for 1/2 hour lesson, $135 per semester for fee for hour lesson.
Financial Aid Program-specific awards: 40 music talent awards for music majors ($4000).
Application Procedures Students admitted directly into the professional program freshman year. Deadline for freshmen: January 31; transfers: May 1. Notification date for freshmen: March 15; transfers: June 1. Required: essay, high school transcript, college transcript(s) for transfer students, minimum 2.0 high school GPA, audition, SAT I or ACT test scores. Recommended: minimum 3.0 high school GPA, 3 letters of recommendation, interview. Auditions held 15 times on campus; recorded music is permissible as a substitute for live auditions when distance is prohibitive and videotaped performances are permissible as a substitute for live auditions when distance is prohibitive.
Web Site http://www.muohio.edu/music/
Undergraduate Contact Barbara Wright, Administrative Assistant, Department of Music, Miami University, 119 Center for the Performing Arts, Oxford, Ohio 45056; 513-529-3014, fax: 513-529-3027, e-mail address: wrightbk@muohio.edu
Graduate Contact Dr. Claire Boge, Director of Graduate Studies, Department of Music, Miami University, 119 Center for the Performing Arts, Oxford, Ohio 45056; 513-529-3014, fax: 513-529-3027, e-mail address: bogecl@muohio.edu

Michigan State University
East Lansing, Michigan

State-supported, coed. Suburban campus. Total enrollment: 45,166. Music program established 1929.

McLean School of Music
Middle Tennessee State University
Murfreesboro, Tennessee

State-supported, coed. Total enrollment: 22,554. Music program established 1911.
Degrees Bachelor of Music in the areas of music education, performance, music industry, music theory/composition, jazz studies. Majors and concentrations: instrumental music education, instrumental performance, jazz studies, music education, music industry, music theory and composition, vocal music education, voice performance. Graduate degrees offered: Master of Arts in the area of music. Program accredited by NASM.
Enrollment 287 total; 257 undergraduate, 30 graduate.
Music Student Profile 47% females, 53% males, 10% minorities, 2% international.
Music Faculty 34 undergraduate (full-time), 30 undergraduate (part-time), 20 graduate (full-time), 6 graduate (part-time). 65% of full-time faculty have terminal degrees. Graduate students teach a few undergraduate courses. Undergraduate student–faculty ratio: 8:1.
Student Life Student groups/activities include American Guild of Organists, Music Educators National Conference Student Chapter, International Association for Jazz Education Student Chapter.
Expenses for 2005–2006 Application fee: $25. State resident tuition: $3678 full-time. Nonresident tuition: $12,990 full-time. Mandatory fees: $922 full-time. College room and board: $5626. College room only: $3478. Room and board charges vary according to board plan and housing facility. Special program-related fees: $150 per credit hour for lab fee.
Financial Aid Program-specific awards: 140 music scholarships for program majors and non-majors ($1000).

Middle Tennessee State University (continued)

Application Procedures Students admitted directly into the professional program freshman year. Deadline for freshmen and transfers: continuous. Required: high school transcript, college transcript(s) for transfer students, minimum 2.0 high school GPA, audition, SAT I or ACT test scores (minimum composite ACT score of 21), theory placement test. Auditions held 4 times and by appointment on campus; recorded music is permissible as a substitute for live auditions if a campus visit is impossible and videotaped performances are permissible as a substitute for live auditions if a campus visit is impossible.

Web Site http://www.mtsu.edu/~music

Undergraduate Contact Ms. Connie Bowrey, Music Admissions, McLean School of Music, Middle Tennessee State University, Box 47, Murfreesboro, Tennessee 37132; 615-898-2469, fax: 615-898-5037.

Graduate Contact Dr. Stephen Shearon, Coordinator of Graduate Studies, McLean School of Music, Middle Tennessee State University, Box 47, Murfreesboro, Tennessee 37132; 615-898-5984, fax: 615-898-5037.

Midwestern State University

Wichita Falls, Texas

State-supported, coed. Urban campus. Total enrollment: 6,279. Music program established 1954.

Degrees Bachelor of Music in the areas of performance, teacher certification. Majors and concentrations: guitar, music, music education, piano/organ, voice, wind and percussion instruments. Program accredited by NASM.

Enrollment 70 total; all undergraduate.

Music Student Profile 60% females, 40% males, 5% minorities, 5% international.

Music Faculty 9 undergraduate (full-time), 5 undergraduate (part-time). 80% of full-time faculty have terminal degrees. Graduate students do not teach undergraduate courses. Undergraduate student–faculty ratio: 10:1.

Student Life Student groups/activities include Mu Phi Epsilon, Kappa Kappa Psi, Tau Beta Sigma.

Expenses for 2006–2007 Application fee: $25. State resident tuition: $1500 full-time. Nonresident tuition: $9750 full-time. Mandatory fees: $3066 full-time. College room and board: $5220. College room only: $2660. Special program-related fees: $70 per course for private lesson fee.

Financial Aid Program-specific awards: 50 music scholarships for program majors ($1000–$1600).

Application Procedures Students admitted directly into the professional program freshman year. Deadline for freshmen and transfers: continuous. Notification date for freshmen and transfers: August 15. Required: high school transcript, minimum 2.0 high school GPA, audition, SAT I or ACT test scores. Recommended: 3 letters of recommendation, interview. Auditions held by appointment on campus; recorded music is permissible as a substitute for live auditions when distance is prohibitive and videotaped performances are permissible as a substitute for live auditions when distance is prohibitive.

Web Site http://www.mwsu.edu/htmldocs/departments/fine_arts/

Undergraduate Contact Dr. Ronald Hough, Scholarship Coordinator, Music Program, Midwestern State University, 3410 Taft Boulevard, Wichita Falls, Texas 76308; 940-397-4260, fax: 940-397-4511, e-mail address: ron.hough@mwsu.edu

Millersville University of Pennsylvania

Millersville, Pennsylvania

State-supported, coed. Small town campus. Total enrollment: 7,998. Music program established 1947.

Millikin University

Decatur, Illinois

Independent, coed. Suburban campus. Total enrollment: 2,641. Music program established 1901.

Degrees Bachelor of Music in the areas of performance, music education, commercial music, music business. Majors and concentrations: commercial music, instrumental music education, keyboard, music business, orchestral instruments, vocal music education, voice. Program accredited by NASM.

Enrollment 314 total; 274 undergraduate, 40 nonprofessional degree.

Music Student Profile 54% females, 46% males, 9% minorities.

Music Faculty 22 undergraduate (full-time), 35 undergraduate (part-time). 87% of full-time faculty have terminal degrees. Graduate students do not teach undergraduate courses. Undergraduate student–faculty ratio: 5:1.

Student Life Student groups/activities include Music Educators National Conference Student Chapter, music fraternity and sorority, Music and Entertainment Industry Educators Association. Special housing available for music students.

Expenses for 2005–2006 Application fee: $0. One-time mandatory fee: $75. Comprehensive fee: $27,834 includes full-time tuition ($20,696), mandatory fees ($425), and college room and board ($6713). College room only: $3763. Full-time tuition and fees vary according to course load. Room and board charges vary according to board plan and housing facility.

Financial Aid Program-specific awards: 128 talent awards for those passing audition evaluations ($1000–$9000), 31 Young Artist Awards for top 5% of auditionees ($10,000–$18,000).

Application Procedures Students admitted directly into the professional program freshman year. Deadline for freshmen and transfers: continuous. Required: high school transcript, college transcript(s) for transfer students, interview, audition, SAT I or ACT test scores, standing in top half of graduating class. Auditions held 8 times on campus; recorded music is permissible as a substitute for live auditions when distance is prohibitive (instrumentalists only) and videotaped performances are permissible as a substitute for live auditions when distance is prohibitive (instrumentalists only).

Web Site http://www.millikin.edu/music

Undergraduate Contact Nancy Freeman, Audition Coordinator, School of Music, Millikin University, 1184 West Main Street, Decatur, Illinois 62522; 800-373-7733, fax: 217-420-6652, e-mail address: som@mail.milikin.edu

Minnesota State University Mankato

Mankato, Minnesota

State-supported, coed. Small town campus. Total enrollment: 14,335.

Degrees Bachelor of Music in the areas of voice, piano, winds, strings, percussion, organ; Bachelor of Science in the areas of music education (instrumental, choral/vocal), music industry. Majors and concentrations: music, music education, music industry, piano/organ, stringed instruments, voice, wind and percussion instruments. Graduate degrees offered: Master of Music in the areas of performance, music education, choral conducting, wind band conducting. Program accredited by NASM.

Enrollment 110 total; 90 undergraduate, 10 graduate, 10 nonprofessional degree.

Music Student Profile 60% females, 40% males, 8% minorities, 4% international.

Music Faculty 14 total (full-time), 8 total (part-time). 91% of full-time faculty have terminal degrees. Graduate students do not teach undergraduate courses. Undergraduate student–faculty ratio: 10:1.

Student Life Student groups/activities include Music Educators National Conference, American Choral Directors Association, International Association for Jazz Education.

Expenses for 2005–2006 Application fee: $20. State resident tuition: $5104 full-time. Nonresident tuition: $10,932 full-time. Mandatory fees: $742 full-time. Full-time tuition and fees vary according to course load and reciprocity agreements. College room and board: $5083. Room and board charges vary according to board plan. Special program-related fees: $10–$35 per term for instrument rental.

Financial Aid Program-specific awards: 1 Stewart Ross Band Scholarship for band instrumentalists ($600), 1 Nancy Cora Williams Scholarship for music education majors ($500), 1 Van

Sickle Endowment Award for string or voice majors ($600), 1 Een Endowment Award for program majors ($470), 16 talent grants for incoming freshmen ($600), 7 Stein Scholarships for music majors ($350), 7 Music Foundation Awards for music majors ($450), 4 Mankato Symphony Awards for orchestra students ($1250), 2 Kiyo Suyematsu Scholarships for music majors ($1500), 1 Lindberg Woodwind Scholarship for woodwind players (especially double reeds) ($1000).

Application Procedures Students apply for admission into the professional program by freshman year. Deadline for freshmen and transfers: continuous. Required: high school transcript, college transcript(s) for transfer students, minimum 2.0 high school GPA, 3 letters of recommendation, interview, audition, SAT I or ACT test scores. Recommended: minimum 3.0 high school GPA. Auditions held as needed on campus; recorded music is permissible as a substitute for live auditions when distance is prohibitive and videotaped performances are permissible as a substitute for live auditions when distance is prohibitive. Portfolio reviews held twice on campus.

Web Site http://www.intech.mnsu.edu/music

Undergraduate Contact Dr. John Lindberg, Chair, Music Department, Minnesota State University Mankato, PAC 202, Mankato, Minnesota 56002-8400; 507-389-2118, fax: 507-389-2922, e-mail address: john.lindberg@mankato.msus.edu

Graduate Contact Dr. David Dickau, Graduate Coordinator, Music Department, Minnesota State University Mankato, PAC 202, Mankato, Minnesota 56002-8400; 507-389-5546, fax: 507-389-2922.

Mississippi College
Clinton, Mississippi

Independent Southern Baptist, coed. Suburban campus. Total enrollment: 3,905. Music program established 1948.

Mississippi State University
Mississippi State, Mississippi

State-supported, coed. Total enrollment: 16,101. Music program established 1957.

Mississippi University for Women
Columbus, Mississippi

State-supported, coed, primarily women. Small town campus. Total enrollment: 2,328. Music program established 1935.

Degrees Bachelor of Music. Majors and concentrations: music education. Cross-registration with Mississippi State University. Program accredited by NASM, NCATE.

Enrollment 26 total; 5 undergraduate, 21 nonprofessional degree.

Music Student Profile 60% females, 40% males, 8% minorities, 4% international.

Music Faculty 5 undergraduate (full-time), 2 undergraduate (part-time). 60% of full-time faculty have terminal degrees. Graduate students do not teach undergraduate courses. Undergraduate student–faculty ratio: 1:1.

Student Life Student groups/activities include Music Educators National Conference.

Financial Aid Program-specific awards: 30 service awards for ensemble performers ($400), 12 scholarships for program majors ($750).

Application Procedures Students admitted directly into the professional program freshman year. Deadline for freshmen and transfers: continuous. Required: high school transcript, college transcript(s) for transfer students, ACT test score only (minimum composite ACT score of 18). Recommended: minimum 2.0 high school GPA, interview, audition. Auditions held 4 times and by appointment on campus.

Web Site http://www.muw.edu/fine_arts

Undergraduate Contact Director of Admissions, Office of Admissions, Mississippi University for Women, W-1613, Columbus, Mississippi 39701; 662-329-7106, fax: 662-241 - 7481, e-mail address: admissions@muw.edu

Mississippi Valley State University
Itta Bena, Mississippi

State-supported, coed. Small town campus. Total enrollment: 3,165.

Missouri State University
Springfield, Missouri

State-supported, coed. Suburban campus. Total enrollment: 18,928. Music program established 1908.

Montana State University
Bozeman, Montana

State-supported, coed. Small town campus. Total enrollment: 12,166. Music program established 1967.

Degrees Bachelor of Arts in the area of music; Bachelor of Music Education. Majors and concentrations: music education, piano/organ, stringed instruments, studio teaching, voice, wind and percussion instruments. Program accredited by NASM.

Enrollment 89 total; all undergraduate.

Music Student Profile 52% females, 48% males.

Music Faculty 11 undergraduate (full-time), 9 undergraduate (part-time). 100% of full-time faculty have terminal degrees. Graduate students do not teach undergraduate courses. Undergraduate student–faculty ratio: 6:1.

Student Life Student groups/activities include Kappa Kappa Psi (Beta), Collegiate Music Educators National Conference, American Choral Directors Association.

Expenses for 2005–2006 Application fee: $30. State resident tuition: $5221 full-time. Nonresident tuition: $14,945 full-time. Full-time tuition varies according to course load. College room and board: $6150. Room and board charges vary according to board plan and housing facility. Special program-related fees: $3 per course for music, $15 per course for lab fee/instrument maintenance, $75 per semester for applied music fee.

Financial Aid Program-specific awards: 30 fee waivers for program majors ($2067), 6 Intermountain Opera Awards for state resident program majors ($1200), 49 music performance awards for program majors ($100–$1500).

Application Procedures Students admitted directly into the professional program freshman year. Deadline for freshmen and transfers: continuous. Required: high school transcript, audition for scholarship consideration. Auditions held continuously on campus; recorded music is permissible as a substitute for live auditions when distance is prohibitive and videotaped performances are permissible as a substitute for live auditions when distance is prohibitive.

Web Site http://www.montana.edu/wwwmusic

Undergraduate Contact Ms. Carole Oeschger, Administrative Officer, Department of Music, Montana State University, PO Box 173420, Bozeman, Montana 59717-0342; 406-994-1911, fax: 406-994-6656, e-mail address: oeschger@montana.edu

Montclair State University
Upper Montclair, New Jersey

State-supported, coed. Suburban campus. Total enrollment: 16,063. Music program established 1963.

Degrees Bachelor of Arts in the areas of music education, music therapy; Bachelor of Music in the areas of performance, music theory/composition, musical theater. Majors and concentrations: classical music, music, music education, music theater, music theory and composition, music therapy, performance, piano/organ, stringed instruments, voice, wind and percussion instruments. Graduate degrees offered: Master of Arts in the areas of performance, theory/composition, music education, music therapy. Program accredited by NASM.

Enrollment 320 total; 240 undergraduate, 50 graduate, 30 nonprofessional degree.

Music Student Profile 60% females, 40% males, 30% minorities, 15% international.

Montclair State University (continued)

Music Faculty 16 total (full-time), 52 total (part-time). 100% of full-time faculty have terminal degrees. Graduate students do not teach undergraduate courses. Undergraduate student–faculty ratio: 3:1.

Student Life Student groups/activities include Sigma Alpha Iota, Phi Mu Alpha Sinfonia, Music Educators National Conference.

Expenses for 2005–2006 Application fee: $55. State resident tuition: $5581 full-time. Nonresident tuition: $10,029 full-time. Mandatory fees: $2128 full-time. College room and board: $8618. College room only: $5768. Room and board charges vary according to board plan and housing facility. Special program-related fees: $50 per semester for instrument rental, $100 per recital for recital recording fee, $400 per semester for applied music fees.

Financial Aid Program-specific awards: 1–10 Griffiths Piano Scholarships for piano majors ($100–$500), 1–10 Ravina Strings Awards for strings majors ($100–$500), 1–10 Howe Scholarships for music majors ($100–$500), 1 Hooper Scholarship for instrumental majors ($5000).

Application Procedures Students apply for admission into the professional program by sophomore year. Deadline for freshmen: March 1; transfers: May 1. Notification date for freshmen and transfers: continuous. Required: high school transcript, college transcript(s) for transfer students, interview, audition, SAT I test score only, portfolio for theory/composition applicants. Recommended: essay, 2 letters of recommendation. Auditions held 5 times on campus; recorded music is permissible as a substitute for live auditions when distance is prohibitive and videotaped performances are permissible as a substitute for live auditions when distance is prohibitive. Portfolio reviews held 5 times and by appointment on campus.

Web Site http://www.montclair.edu/music

Contact Admissions Chairperson, Department of Music, Montclair State University, 1 Normal Avenue, Montclair, New Jersey 07043; 973-655-7610, fax: 973-655-5279, e-mail address: music@mail.montclair.edu

Moores School of Music

See University of Houston

Moravian College
Bethlehem, Pennsylvania

Independent, coed. Suburban campus. Total enrollment: 2,030. Music program established 1982.

Degrees Bachelor of Music in the areas of performance, composition, music education, sacred music. Majors and concentrations: composition, instrumental music, jazz, music education, performance, sacred music, voice. Cross-registration with Lehigh University, Lafayette College, Muhlenberg College, DeSales University, Cedar Crest College. Program accredited by NASM.

Enrollment 62 total; 47 undergraduate, 15 nonprofessional degree.

Music Student Profile 68% females, 32% males, 7% minorities.

Music Faculty 6 undergraduate (full-time), 45 undergraduate (part-time). 83% of full-time faculty have terminal degrees. Graduate students do not teach undergraduate courses. Undergraduate student–faculty ratio: 8:1.

Student Life Student groups/activities include Music Educators National Conference, Delta Omicron, American Choral Directors Association.

Expenses for 2005–2006 Application fee: $40. One-time mandatory fee: $100. Comprehensive fee: $32,793 includes full-time tuition ($24,813), mandatory fees ($450), and college room and board ($7530). College room only: $4230. Room and board charges vary according to board plan and housing facility. Special program-related fees: $160 for set of lessons (electives) beyond degree requirement.

Financial Aid Program-specific awards: 15 Ina Love Thursby Scholarships for those demonstrating need ($1000), 9 Arthur Hugo Awards for incoming freshmen demonstrating need and talent ($3000), 1 Richard and Monica Shantz Award for seniors demonstrating need ($1000), 1 John H. Reimers Music Scholar-

ship for junior and senior music majors demonstrating excellence in performance and academics ($500).

Application Procedures Students admitted directly into the professional program freshman year. Deadline for freshmen: September 1; transfers: continuous. Required: essay, high school transcript, college transcript(s) for transfer students, minimum 2.0 high school GPA, 3 letters of recommendation, audition, SAT I or ACT test scores. Recommended: interview. Auditions held last weekend in January on campus; recorded music is permissible as a substitute for live auditions if distance is prohibitive and videotaped performances are permissible as a substitute for live auditions if distance is prohibitive.

Web Site http://www.moravian.edu/academics/departments/music/index.htm

Undergraduate Contact Mr. James Earl Barnes, Chair, Music Department, Moravian College, 1200 Main Street, Bethlehem, Pennsylvania 18018; 610-861-1672, fax: 610-861-1657, e-mail address: mejeb01@moravian.edu

Morehead State University
Morehead, Kentucky

State-supported, coed. Small town campus. Total enrollment: 9,062. Music program established 1937.

Degrees Bachelor of Music in the areas of performance, jazz studies; Bachelor of Music Education. Majors and concentrations: jazz, music education, piano/organ, stringed instruments, voice, wind and percussion instruments. Graduate degrees offered: Master of Music in the areas of performance, music education. Program accredited by NASM, NCATE.

Enrollment 221 total; 200 undergraduate, 15 graduate, 6 nonprofessional degree.

Music Student Profile 60% females, 40% males, 6% minorities, 8% international.

Music Faculty 27 undergraduate (full-time), 8 undergraduate (part-time), 13 graduate (full-time). 63% of full-time faculty have terminal degrees. Graduate students do not teach undergraduate courses. Undergraduate student–faculty ratio: 14:1.

Student Life Student groups/activities include concerts, recitals, master classes (guest artists). Special housing available for music students.

Expenses for 2005–2006 Application fee: $0. State resident tuition: $4320 full-time. Nonresident tuition: $11,480 full-time. Full-time tuition varies according to course load and reciprocity agreements. College room and board: $4830. Room and board charges vary according to board plan and housing facility. Special program-related fees: $10–$20 per semester for instrument rental, $30–$90 per semester for private lessons.

Financial Aid Program-specific awards: 60 music scholarships for program majors and minors ($2000).

Application Procedures Students admitted directly into the professional program freshman year. Deadline for freshmen and transfers: June 15. Notification date for freshmen: August 1. Required: high school transcript, college transcript(s) for transfer students, minimum 2.0 high school GPA, SAT I or ACT test scores. Recommended: minimum 3.0 high school GPA, 2 letters of recommendation, interview, video, audition. Auditions held 4 times on campus; recorded music is permissible as a substitute for live auditions when distance is prohibitive and videotaped performances are permissible as a substitute for live auditions when distance is prohibitive.

Web Site http://www.moreheadstate.edu/music

Undergraduate Contact Dr. M. Scott McBride, Chair, Department of Music, Morehead State University, Baird Music Hall #106, Morehead, Kentucky 40351-1689; 606-783-2473, fax: 606-783-5447, e-mail address: s.mcbride@moreheadstate.edu

Graduate Contact Dr. Robert Pritchard, Graduate Studies Coordinator, Department of Music, Morehead State University, Baird Music Hall #302, Morehead, Kentucky 40351-1689; 606-783-2493, fax: 606-783-5447, e-mail address: r.pritch@moreheadstate.edu

Morningside College

Sioux City, Iowa

Independent, coed. Suburban campus. Total enrollment: 1,440. Music program established 1900.

Mount Allison University

Sackville, New Brunswick, Canada

Province-supported, coed. Small town campus. Total enrollment: 2,369. Music program established 1874.

Degrees Bachelor of Music. Majors and concentrations: music. Program accredited by CUMS.

Enrollment 87 total; 73 undergraduate, 14 nonprofessional degree.

Music Student Profile 70% females, 30% males.

Music Faculty 11 undergraduate (full-time), 5 undergraduate (part-time). 81% of full-time faculty have terminal degrees. Graduate students do not teach undergraduate courses. Undergraduate student–faculty ratio: 7:1.

Student Life Student groups/activities include symphonic band, choral society, chamber orchestra, chamber choir (female), instrumental jazz ensemble, Garnet and Gold, Ethel Peak Music Society. Special housing available for music students.

Expenses for 2005–2006 Application fee: $50 Canadian dollars. Tuition, fee, and room and board charges are reported in Canadian dollars. Province resident tuition: $6100 full-time. Mandatory fees: $242 full-time. Full-time tuition and fees vary according to course load. College room and board: $6630. College room only: $3430. Room and board charges vary according to board plan. International student tuition: $12,200 full-time.

Financial Aid Program-specific awards: Blakie Scholarships for freshmen program majors, Blair Scholarship for freshmen program majors, Robert Marsh Scholarship for freshmen program majors, Gladys Muttart Scholarship for freshmen program majors, Pickard Scholarships for freshmen program majors, Howard Brown Scholarship for freshmen program majors.

Application Procedures Students admitted directly into the professional program freshman year. Deadline for freshmen and transfers: February 15. Required: high school transcript, college transcript(s) for transfer students, minimum 3.0 high school GPA, interview, audition, music theory examination, completion of college preparatory courses. Recommended: 2 letters of recommendation. Auditions held 3 times and by appointment on campus; recorded music is permissible as a substitute for live auditions if a campus visit is impossible and videotaped performances are permissible as a substitute for live auditions if a campus visit is impossible.

Web Site http://www.mta.ca/music/

Undergraduate Contact Head, Department of Music, Mount Allison University, 134 Main Street, Sackville, New Brunswick E4L 1A6, Canada; 506-364-2374, fax: 506-364-2376, e-mail address: musdept@mta.ca

Mount Union College

Alliance, Ohio

Independent United Methodist, coed. Suburban campus. Total enrollment: 2,205. Music program established 1896.

Murray State University

Murray, Kentucky

State-supported, coed. Small town campus. Total enrollment: 10,266. Music program established 1930.

Musicians Institute

Hollywood, California

Proprietary, coed. Total enrollment: 650 (2004). Music program established 1994.

Degrees Bachelor of Music in the area of commercial music. Majors and concentrations: bass, guitar, keyboard, percussion, voice. Mandatory cross-registration with Los Angeles City College. Program accredited by NASM.

Enrollment 55 total; all undergraduate.

Music Faculty 20 total (full-time), 20 total (part-time). 75% of full-time faculty have terminal degrees. Graduate students do not teach undergraduate courses.

Student Life Student groups/activities include recording sessions, clinics, live concerts.

Expenses for 2005–2006 Application fee: $100. Tuition: $16,800 full-time. Mandatory fees: $400 full-time. Full-time tuition and fees vary according to degree level and program. Special program-related fees: $50–$200 per quarter for lab fees.

Financial Aid Program-specific awards: 5 partial scholarships ($500–$2000), 3 Stanley Clark Awards ($2500–$5000).

Application Procedures Students admitted directly into the professional program freshman year. Deadline for freshmen and transfers: July 15. Required: essay, high school transcript, college transcript(s) for transfer students, minimum 2.0 high school GPA, 2 letters of recommendation, video, audition, SAT I or ACT test scores (minimum combined SAT I score of 1500, minimum composite ACT score of 21), minimum TOEFL score of 500 for international applicants, recorded music performance. Recommended: interview. Portfolio reviews held continuously on campus.

Web Site http://www.mi.edu

Undergraduate Contact Steve Lunn, Director of Admissions, Admissions, Musicians Institute, 1655 North McCadden Place, Hollywood, California 90028; 323-462-1384, fax: 323-462-1575.

Nazareth College of Rochester

Rochester, New York

Independent, coed. Suburban campus. Total enrollment: 3,120. Music program established 1924.

Degrees Bachelor of Music in the area of music. Majors and concentrations: music education, music history, music theater, music theory, music therapy, performance. Graduate degrees offered: Master of Science in the area of education (music). Cross-registration with Rochester Area Colleges Inter-Institutional Undergraduate Student Enrollment Program. Program accredited by NASM, AAMT.

Enrollment 225 total; 185 undergraduate, 40 graduate.

Music Student Profile 78% females, 22% males, 3% minorities, 2% international.

Music Faculty 10 undergraduate (full-time), 38 undergraduate (part-time). 90% of full-time faculty have terminal degrees. Graduate students do not teach undergraduate courses. Undergraduate student–faculty ratio: 10:1.

Student Life Student groups/activities include Music Educators National Conference Student Chapter, Music Therapy Club, Pi Kappa Lambda Honor Society: Theta Lambda Chapter.

Expenses for 2005–2006 Application fee: $40. Comprehensive fee: $28,234 includes full-time tuition ($19,214), mandatory fees ($660), and college room and board ($8360). College room only: $4680. Room and board charges vary according to board plan and housing facility. Special program-related fees: $35 per course for music therapy clinic fee, $160 per course for group lessons, $160 per course for voice or instrument lessons for minors, $300 per course for voice or instrument lessons for majors.

Financial Aid Program-specific awards: 8 Honors Music Scholarships for incoming freshmen passing audition evaluations ($2000–$6000), 5 Gerald Wilmot Music Scholarships for honors juniors or seniors ($1000–$2500), 2 Lewis Dollinger Scholarships for honors juniors or seniors ($1000), 1 Presser Scholarship for seniors ($4000).

Application Procedures Students apply for admission into the professional program by sophomore year. Deadline for freshmen and transfers: continuous. Required: essay, high school transcript, college transcript(s) for transfer students, minimum 2.0 high school GPA, 2 letters of recommendation, interview, audition, SAT I or ACT test scores. Auditions held 9 times on campus and off campus in Albany, NY; recorded music is permissible as a substitute for live auditions and videotaped

Nazareth College of Rochester (continued)

performances are permissible as a substitute for live auditions when distance is prohibitive or in special circumstances.
Web Site http://www.naz.edu/dept/music/
Undergraduate Contact Mr. Tom DaRin, Vice President for Enrollment Management, Nazareth College of Rochester, 4245 East Avenue, Rochester, New York 14618; 585-389-2860, fax: 585-389-2939.
Graduate Contact Dr. Mary Carlson, Program Director for Graduate and Undergraduate Music Education, Music Department, Nazareth College of Rochester, 4245 East Avenue, Rochester, New York 14618; 585-389-2697, fax: 585-389-2939, e-mail address: mccarlso@naz.edu

Nebraska Wesleyan University
Lincoln, Nebraska

Independent United Methodist, coed. Suburban campus. Total enrollment: 2,016.
Degrees Bachelor of Arts in the area of music; Bachelor of Music in the areas of performance, music education. Majors and concentrations: music education, music performance. Program accredited by NASM.
Enrollment 48 total; all undergraduate.
Music Student Profile 54% females, 46% males.
Music Faculty 7 undergraduate (full-time), 14 undergraduate (part-time). 86% of full-time faculty have terminal degrees. Graduate students do not teach undergraduate courses. Undergraduate student–faculty ratio: 10:1.
Student Life Student groups/activities include Mu Phi Epsilon, Music Educators National Conference, Nebraska Music Educators Association.
Expenses for 2005–2006 Application fee: $20. Comprehensive fee: $23,425 includes full-time tuition ($18,100), mandatory fees ($310), and college room and board ($5015). Room and board charges vary according to board plan and housing facility.
Financial Aid Program-specific awards: 16 music scholarships for program majors ($500–$3500), 10 ensemble participation grants for non-music majors ($300).
Application Procedures Students admitted directly into the professional program freshman year. Deadline for freshmen and transfers: continuous. Required: high school transcript, college transcript(s) for transfer students, audition, ACT test score only, must be in top half of high school graduating class or have ACT of 21 or better. Recommended: interview. Auditions held 6 times on campus; recorded music is permissible as a substitute for live auditions if a campus visit is impossible and videotaped performances are permissible as a substitute for live auditions if a campus visit is impossible.
Web Site http://music.nebrwesleyan.edu/
Undergraduate Contact Ms. Patricia Karthauser, Vice President for Enrollment and Marketing, Nebraska Wesleyan University, 5000 St. Paul Avenue, Lincoln, Nebraska 68504-2794; 402-465-2551, fax: 402-465-2179, e-mail address: pkart@nebrwesleyan.edu

Newberry College
Newberry, South Carolina

Independent Evangelical Lutheran, coed. Small town campus. Total enrollment: 841. Music program established 1933.

New England Conservatory of Music
Boston, Massachusetts

Independent, coed. Urban campus. Total enrollment: 801. Music program established 1867.
Degrees Bachelor of Music in the areas of composition, historical performance, music history, music theory, performance. Majors and concentrations: classical music, composition, contemporary improvisation, historical performance, jazz, music history, music theory, performance, piano, piano/organ, stringed instruments, voice, wind and percussion instruments. Graduate degrees offered: Master of Music in the areas of composition, historical performance, music history, music theory, collaborative piano,

conducting, musicology, vocal pedagogy, performance. Doctor of Musical Arts in the areas of performance, composition. Cross-registration with Northeastern University, Tufts University, Simmons College, Harvard University. Program accredited by NASM.
Enrollment 789 total; 403 undergraduate, 386 graduate.
Music Student Profile 53% females, 47% males, 14% minorities, 26% international.
Music Faculty 84 total (full-time), 117 total (part-time). Graduate students teach a few undergraduate courses. Undergraduate student–faculty ratio: 4:1.
Student Life Special housing available for music students.
Expenses for 2006–2007 Application fee: $100. Comprehensive fee: $40,389 includes full-time tuition ($29,000), mandatory fees ($300), and college room and board ($11,089). Special program-related fees: $60 per year for practice room fee for percussion majors, $100 per semester for registration fee for any electronic music course, $120 per year for practice room fee for collaborative piano, piano, and harpsichord majors only.
Application Procedures Students admitted directly into the professional program freshman year. Deadline for freshmen and transfers: continuous. Notification date for freshmen and transfers: April 1. Required: essay, high school transcript, college transcript(s) for transfer students, 2 letters of recommendation, audition, SAT I or ACT test scores, portfolio for composition majors, resume, repertoire listing, minimum 2.75 high school GPA. Auditions held 35 times on campus; recorded music is permissible as a substitute for live auditions when distance is prohibitive and videotaped performances are permissible as a substitute for live auditions when distance is prohibitive. Portfolio reviews held as needed on campus.
Web Site http://www.newenglandconservatory.edu
Contact Mr. Tom Novak, Director of Admissions and Financial Aid, New England Conservatory of Music, 290 Huntington Avenue, Boston, Massachusetts 02115; 617-585-1101, fax: 617-585-1115, e-mail address: tnovak@newenglandconservatory.edu

More About the Conservatory

New England Conservatory (NEC) promotes the power of music to enrich lives, drawing on its depth and breadth as a music school that houses the diverse, rich influences of classical, jazz, and world music traditions. NEC's renowned faculty members challenge students to master their art in a supportive environment that focuses on excellence and encourages creativity. Musicians trained at NEC go on to craft successful careers as inspired performers, dynamic teachers, and innovative leaders.

NEC is the most enduring independent school of music in the United States, founded in 1867 by educational maverick Eben Tourjée, and making history ever since with jazz instruction and professional chamber music programs, to name a few milestones. Opening its doors in 1903, Jordan Hall is literally at the heart of NEC's main building and is renowned for its wonderful acoustics. It serves as the stage for both NEC student concerts and the world's leading concert artists.

NEC's performance-focused curriculum provides a wealth of solo and ensemble experiences for students, including required recitals and participation in four orchestras, three choruses, two wind ensembles, large and small jazz ensembles, new music groups, and a wide variety of chamber music groups. Additionally, the opera department presents two full-length staged operas with orchestra each year as well as several programs of opera scenes.

As seasoned concert soloists, orchestra and chamber musicians, veterans of the world's premier opera stages, and jazz legends, NEC's diverse faculty members form a musical network that spans the globe and enhances the careers of graduates. In the past few years, some of the foremost performer/teachers in the world have joined the faculty, including conductor Joseph Silverstein; Donald Weilerstein and Miriam Fried, violin; Kim Kashkashian and Matha Katz, viola; Paul Katz, cello; Paula Robison, flute; John Ferrillo, oboe; Bruce Brubaker and Alexander Korsantia, piano; Vinson Cole, Delores Ziegler, Lorraine Nubar, Luretta Bybee, Heidi Skok, James McDonald, and Patricia Misslin, voice; and jazz musicians Billy Hart, Dave Holland, and Brad Shepik. The addition of these teachers to the existing strong faculty has created an incomparable music-training program. NEC faculty members and alumni make up almost half of the Boston Symphony Orchestra and have been honored with Grammy Awards, MacArthur Fellowships, and Naumburg Awards.

Boston itself is one of the world's great music centers and is a capital of higher education. NEC students have the opportunity to benefit from cross-registration for classes at Tufts University, Northeastern University, and Simmons College, as well as to apply to a five-year, double-degree program offered with Tufts. In addition, New England Conservatory and Harvard University now enroll a very select number of exceptional students to earn both a Bachelor of Arts degree from Harvard and a Master of Music degree from NEC. NEC's thriving Performance Outreach program provides performance opportunities for students in the Boston area and beyond and helps young musicians develop the skills to communicate with audiences of all ages and backgrounds. Performance sites include social, civic, cultural, and educational organizations that have forged partnerships with NEC. The Music Referral Service brokers professional engagements for students in the city and surrounding area. The Career Services Center also provides comprehensive information on summer festivals, competitions, private teaching referrals, and resume and career counseling—all the essential materials needed to expand a musician's horizons.

NEC alumni are renowned as soloists—with singer Denyce Graves, today's Carmen of choice, and jazz clarinetist Don Byron currently at the top of their respective fields. Many are also extending their art form: in the classical world, violinist Lara St. John; and in the jazz world, all three members of Medeski, Martin & Wood. Alumni are principals or section players in professional orchestras in the United States and around the world, teach at major music schools, and influence the future of music in other ways. Three such notable alums are Los Angeles Philharmonic Executive Director Deborah Borda, St. Paul Chamber Orchestra President and Managing Director Bruce Coppock, and Curtis Institute's new director, Roberto Diaz. Alumni composers Richard Danielpour, Michael Gandolfi, and Lee Hyla write music that is being avidly performed—and the last two also teach at NEC. Students and alumni have also enjoyed impressive successes at international competitions in recent years, including the Metropolitan Opera National Auditions, Naumburg Award, William Kapell International Piano Competition, Young Concert Artists International Auditions, Concert Artists Guild Auditions, Fischoff National Chamber Music Competition, Irving M. Klein International String Competition, and Italy's Paolo Borciani Chamber Music Competition.

New Mexico State University

Las Cruces, New Mexico

State-supported, coed. Suburban campus. Total enrollment: 16,072. Music program established 1905.
Degrees Bachelor of Music in the areas of performance, piano pedagogy, music business; Bachelor of Music Education in the areas of vocal music education, instrumental music education. Majors and concentrations: music, music business, music education, piano, piano pedagogy, stringed instruments, voice performance, wind and percussion instruments. Graduate degrees offered: Master of Music in the areas of accompanying, performance, music education, conducting. Program accredited by NASM.
Enrollment 32 total; 23 undergraduate, 9 graduate.
Music Student Profile 46% females, 54% males, 61% minorities, 1% international.
Music Faculty 17 total (full-time), 8 total (part-time). 94% of full-time faculty have terminal degrees. Graduate students teach a few undergraduate courses. Undergraduate student–faculty ratio: 14:1.
Student Life Student groups/activities include Sigma Alpha Iota, Music Educators National Conference Student Chapter.
Expenses for 2005–2006 Application fee: $15. State resident tuition: $2868 full-time. Nonresident tuition: $12,156 full-time.

Mandatory fees: $1050 full-time. College room and board: $5332. College room only: $3072. Room and board charges vary according to board plan and gender.
Financial Aid Program-specific awards: 1 Theodore Presser Scholarship for junior program majors ($1500), 1 Vivien B. Head Scholarship for program majors, 1 Ray Tross Scholarship for woodwind majors, band, choir, and orchestra service grants for musically talented performers, 1 Ruthena C. King Memorial Award for music majors residing in Otero County, 1 Elenore Ward Memorial Scholarship for instrumentalists, music majors, 1 Frederick and Norma Sell Scholarship for instrumentalists, 1 Wooten Scholarship for music majors, 1 8va Scholarship for music majors, trumpet.
Application Procedures Students admitted directly into the professional program freshman year. Deadline for freshmen and transfers: April 15. Notification date for freshmen and transfers: July 1. Required: high school transcript, college transcript(s) for transfer students, audition, SAT I or ACT test scores. Recommended: minimum 3.0 high school GPA, 3 letters of recommendation, interview. Auditions held continuously on campus and off campus in various New Mexico cities; recorded music is permissible as a substitute for live auditions.
Web Site http://www.nmsu.edu/~music
Contact Dr. Greg Fant, Head, Music Department, New Mexico State University, MSC 3F, Las Cruces, New Mexico 88003; 505-646-2421, fax: 505-646-8199, e-mail address: music@nmsu.edu

The New School: A University
See Mannes College The New School for Music

The New School: A University
See The New School for Jazz and Contemporary Music

The New School: A University
The New School for Jazz and Contemporary Music
New York, New York

Independent, coed. Total enrollment: 287. Music program established 1986.
Degrees Bachelor of Arts/Bachelor of Fine Arts in the area of liberal arts/jazz; Bachelor of Fine Arts in the area of jazz. Majors and concentrations: composition, jazz, jazz performance.
Enrollment 287 total; all undergraduate.
Music Student Profile 20% females, 80% males, 31% minorities, 19% international.
Music Faculty 2 undergraduate (full-time), 124 undergraduate (part-time). 33% of full-time faculty have terminal degrees. Graduate students do not teach undergraduate courses. Undergraduate student–faculty ratio: 6:1.
Student Life Student groups/activities include Jazz Student Council, University Committees.
Expenses for 2006–2007 Comprehensive fee: $38,600 includes full-time tuition ($27,600) and college room and board ($11,000). Special program-related fees: $5–$15 for cassette tapes, reading materials.
Financial Aid Program-specific awards: 97 jazz scholarships for those demonstrating talent/ability ($8000), 15 University Scholar Awards for minority students ($3500).
Application Procedures Students admitted directly into the professional program freshman year. Deadline for freshmen and transfers: January 1. Notification date for freshmen and transfers: April 1. Required: high school transcript, college transcript(s) for transfer students, minimum 2.0 high school GPA, letter of recommendation, audition, TOEFL score for international applicants, personal statement. Auditions held 15 times on campus and off campus in selected high schools; recorded music is permissible as a substitute for live auditions when distance is prohibitive.
Web Site http://www.newschool.edu/jazz

The New School for Jazz and Contemporary Music (continued)

Undergraduate Contact Ms. Teri Lucas, Director of Admissions, The New School for Jazz and Contemporary Music, 55 West 13th Street, New York, New York 10011; 212-229-5896 ext. 4589, fax: 212-229-8936, e-mail address: jazzadm@newschool.edu

More About the School

At The New School for Jazz and Contemporary Music, art, life, and education are fused to produce a new breed of musician—one who is artistically, professionally, and academically ready to take on the world. Based on the tradition of artist-as-mentor, the curriculum is taught by a faculty of professional artists drawn from New York City's renowned jazz community, with significant ties to the evolution of jazz, blues, pop, and new genres. With their help, the emerging performers, composers, and arrangers at New School Jazz learn to develop an individual creative voice and an appreciation for high standards. Students benefit from the expert training associated with a conservatory as well as the generative spirit and vigor of jazz that flows through the School. This environment extends past the walls of the School and into the streets and studios, clubs, and concert halls of New York City—the jazz capital of the world.

With a large percentage of the student body from outside the United States, New School Jazz is a truly multicultural universe, thanks to the widely varied backgrounds of both students and instructors as well as the depth of the curriculum. The New School for Jazz and Contemporary Music has received international recognition as a leading center of arts education today. The school's mission is "respecting tradition, embracing innovation." Bachelor of Fine Arts students do the core of their work in classrooms and in private studios with exceptional musician-educators. They gain direct exposure to modern music's traditions and practices in an intellectual context that encourages both exploration and innovation.

No aspiring musician can expect to make it in this highly competitive industry without real-world performance experience. In addition to the strong curriculum, students at New School Jazz have ample opportunities to perform at school and in professional venues with their peers, as well as with current stars of the jazz world. Indeed, many well-known alumni started their careers while they were undergraduates. Students perform each semester in a variety of ensembles and venues. Ensembles include the Thelonious Monk Ensemble, the Electric Miles Ensemble, Rhythm Section and Vocal accompaniment, the Charlie Parker Ensemble, the Afro–Cuban Jazz Orchestra, and the Art Blakey Ensemble. In addition, each Monday night at Sweet Rhythm, a well-known Greenwich Village jazz club, students get to display their talents in a professional club setting with a variety of professional and student-organized ensembles. All seniors are required to offer a recital the semester they graduate. Students also perform at various independent and school-sponsored events through the New School Jazz Outreach Project, which features a gig office and jazz industry internships. This program provides hands-on experience, develops networking skills, and creates job opportunities.

The New School for Jazz and Contemporary Music is one of eight schools that make up The New School, and students can take advantage of everything the university has to offer. There are numerous opportunities for cross-registration, and students can enroll in everything from humanities courses at Eugene Lang College The New School for Liberal Arts to art and design courses at Parsons The New School for Design and classical music instruction at Mannes College The New School for Music. To take further advantage of the university setting, The New School for Jazz and Contemporary Music and Eugene Lang College The New School for Liberal Arts have structured a five-year curriculum in which students simultaneously complete two degrees, the music B.F.A. and the liberal arts B.A. Outside the curriculum, students are encouraged to participate in artistic collaborations and performances with the other schools. For more information, students should visit http://www.jazz.newschool.edu.

Location New York City is the unqualified capital of the jazz world, and the School is located in one of the city's most exciting neighborhoods—Greenwich Village—where New York history, the arts, politics, and commerce come together. Whether it is historic performance venues like the Village Vanguard or the Blue Note, the wealth of jazz artists in the area, or just the fast-paced urban environment, at The New School for Jazz and Contemporary Music, inspiration is pervasive.

Program Facilities The School's 20,000-square-foot state-of-the-art facility on West 13th Street was designed specifically to help young artists realize their goal of becoming effective music professionals. The facility offers administrative, classroom, practice, and rehearsal space—all constructed with the highest quality and attention to acoustics, soundproofing, and aesthetics. All classrooms are fully dedicated with Yamaha grand pianos, drum kits, amplifiers, vocal PA systems, and full-component stereo systems. Specialized instrumental practice and teaching rooms are offered, as well as an MP3 listening library and keyboard/MIDI labs. Concert and recording needs are served in an intimate and beautiful performance space seating 120, with full capacity for professional sound, lighting, and recording. A second studio is used for additional recording and engineering, with both studios connected to the university's server and Internet sites. Additional university performance facilities within a two-block radius include a 170-seat auditorium and an excellent and acoustically balanced concert hall with a capacity of 500.

Alumni New School Jazz alumni include Lucien Ban, Miri Ben-Ari, Peter Bernstein, Walter Blanding Jr., Avashi Cohen, Jesse Davis, John Ellis, Rebecca Coupe Franks, Robert Glasper, Aaron Goldberg, Larry Goldings, Roy Hargrove, Susie Ibarra, Ali Jackson, Ori Kaplan, Gregoire Maret, Virginia Mayhew, Carlos McKinney, Brad Mehldau, Shedrick Mitchell, Vickie Natale, Bilal Oliver, John Popper, Jaz Sawyer, Woody Shaw III, Alex Skolnick, E. J. Strickland, Marcus Strickland, Manuel Valera, and Sam Yahel.

Faculty Faculty members at New School Jazz include Ahmed Abdullah, trumpet; Junko Arita, voice; Jane Ira Bloom, saxophone; Richard Boukas, guitar; Joanne Brackeen, piano; Cecil Bridgewater, trumpet; Brian Camelio, guitar; Jeff Carney, bass; Joe Chambers, drums; Haim Cotton, piano; Andrew Cyrille, drums; Gerard D'Angelo, piano; Elijah Dixon, voice; Armen Donelian, piano; Mario Escalera, woodwinds; Chico Freeman, saxophone; Ray Gallon, piano; Hal Galper, piano; George Garzone, saxophone; David Glasser, saxophone; Dan Greenblatt, saxophone; Chico Hamilton, drums; Billy Harper, saxophone; Richard Harper, Voice, trombone; Gerry Hemingway, percussion; Adam Holzman, keyboard; Satoshi Inoue, guitar; Sonia Jacobsen, saxophone; Vic Juris, guitar; Michael Karn, saxophone; Bill Kirchner, woodwinds; Janet Lawson, voice; Lee Ann Ledgerwood, piano; Elisabeth Lohninger, voice; Amy London, voice; David Lopato, piano; Arun Luthra, saxophone; Ed MacEachen, guitar; Junior Mance, piano; Abdourahmane Mboup, percussion; Andy McKee, bass; Andy Milne, piano; Kirk Nurock, piano; Jimmy Owens, trumpet; Charli Persip, drums; Ron Petrides, guitar; Benny Powell, trombone; Robert Sadin, composition; Bobby Sanabria, percussion; David Schnitter, saxophone; Kenneth Kamal Scott, voice; Harel Shachal, saxophones; Rich Shemaria, piano; Jim Snidero, saxophone; Joan Stiles, piano; Rory Stuart, guitar; Francesca Tanksley, piano; Charles Tolliver, trumpet; Johannes Wallmann, piano; Johannes Weidenmueller, bass; Buster Williams, bass; Reggie Workman, bass; Peter Zak, piano; Amir Ziv, drums; Rachel Z, piano.

New World School of the Arts
Miami, Florida

State-supported, coed. Urban campus. Total enrollment: 371. Music program established 1988.
Degrees Bachelor of Music in the areas of instrumental studies, vocal studies, composition/electronic music. Majors and concen-

trations: bass, bassoon, cello, clarinet, composition, flute, French horn, guitar, oboe, percussion, piano, saxophone, trombone, trumpet, tuba, viola, violin, voice. Mandatory cross-registration with Miami-Dade Community College, University of Florida. Program accredited by NASM.

Enrollment 45 total; all undergraduate.

Music Student Profile 58% females, 42% males, 76% minorities, 16% international.

Music Faculty 5 undergraduate (full-time), 12 undergraduate (part-time). 85% of full-time faculty have terminal degrees. Graduate students do not teach undergraduate courses. Undergraduate student–faculty ratio: 3:1.

Student Life Student groups/activities include Student Government, opera ensemble, chamber orchestra.

Expenses for 2005–2006 Application fee: $0. State resident tuition: $12,000 full-time. Nonresident tuition: $17,000 full-time.

Financial Aid Program-specific awards: 25–30 NWSA Music Scholarships for talented music students ($2000).

Application Procedures Students admitted directly into the professional program freshman year. Deadline for freshmen and transfers: continuous. Required: essay, high school transcript, college transcript(s) for transfer students, 2 letters of recommendation, audition. Recommended: minimum 2.0 high school GPA, interview, SAT I or ACT test scores. Auditions held by appointment on campus; recorded music is permissible as a substitute for live auditions when distance is prohibitive or if a campus visit is impossible and videotaped performances are permissible as a substitute for live auditions when distance is prohibitive or if a campus visit is impossible.

Web Site http://www.mdc.edu/nwsa

Undergraduate Contact Pamela Neumann, Recruitment and Admissions Coordinator, Student Services, New World School of the Arts, 300 North East 2nd Avenue, Miami, Florida 33132; 305-237-7007, fax: 305-237-3794, e-mail address: nwsaadm@mdc.edu

New York University Steinhardt School
New York University
New York, New York

Independent, coed. Urban campus. Total enrollment: 40,004.

Degrees Bachelor of Music in the areas of performance (instrumental and voice), theory and composition, music business, music technology, music education, voice. Majors and concentrations: instrumental performance, music business, music education, music performance, music technology, music theory and composition, voice performance. Graduate degrees offered: Master of Arts in the areas of music performance and composition, music education, music therapy, music business; Master of Music in the area of music technology. Doctor of Education in the area of music education; Doctor of Philosophy in the areas of music performance and composition, music education. Program accredited by AMTA.

Enrollment 1,057 total; 621 undergraduate, 436 graduate.

Music Student Profile 46% females, 54% males, 19% minorities, 9% international.

Music Faculty 19 total (full-time), 300 total (part-time). 100% of full-time faculty have terminal degrees. Graduate students teach a few undergraduate courses. Undergraduate student–faculty ratio: 2:1.

Student Life Student groups/activities include various performance venues on campus and throughout New York City (ensembles, orchestra, concert, band, choirs), internships.

Expenses for 2005–2006 Application fee: $65. Comprehensive fee: $43,170 includes full-time tuition ($29,890), mandatory fees ($1800), and college room and board ($11,480). Full-time tuition and fees vary according to program. Room and board charges vary according to board plan and housing facility. Special program-related fees: $75 for recital fee, $90 for music and music education private instruction fee.

Financial Aid Program-specific awards: 5–10 talent awards for performance students.

Application Procedures Students admitted directly into the professional program freshman year. Deadline for freshmen: January 15; transfers: April 1. Notification date for freshmen: April 1;

transfers: continuous. Required: essay, high school transcript, college transcript(s) for transfer students, 3 letters of recommendation, interview, audition, portfolio, SAT I or ACT test scores, strong high school GPA. Auditions held 12 times on campus; recorded music is permissible as a substitute for live auditions when distance is prohibitive and videotaped performances are permissible as a substitute for live auditions when distance is prohibitive. Portfolio reviews held continuously on campus.

Web Site http://www.steinhardt.nyu.edu/go-now

Undergraduate Contact Ms. Candice MacLusky, Assistant Director of Undergraduate Admissions, New York University, 22 Washington Square North, New York, New York 10011-9191; 212-998-4500, fax: 212-995-4902.

Graduate Contact Mr. John Myers, Director of Enrollment Services, Office of Graduate Admissions, The Steinhardt School of Education, New York University, 82 Washington Square East, 2nd Floor, New York, New York 10003-6680; 212-998-5030, fax: 212-995-4328, e-mail address: ed.gradadmissions@nyu.edu

More About the University

Facilities and resources for the Department of Music and Performing Arts Professions include private practice rooms, ensemble rehearsal rooms, teaching studios, the Frederick Loewe Theatre, two recital rooms, the Black Box recital theatre, and the newly restored Provincetown Playhouse; twelve computer music and recording studios (Mac-based computer music, audio for video, and film music studios); multimedia laboratories using IBM, SBI, and Mac computers; digital recording and editing rooms featuring Digidesign Pro Tools and Sonic Solutions multitrack systems; a multitrack facility featuring analog and digital recording, automated inline console, outboard effects, and MIDI processing for live and studio performance; Village Records (a full-service NYU-based record company providing experience in all aspects of record production and promotion); the Nordoff-Robbins Center for Music Therapy (an international outreach and training center for music therapists); the NYU Arts and Media Studio (advanced hardware platforms for computer music, graphics, and animation); and the Elmer Holmes Bobst Library (open stack; more than 3.4 million volumes), which includes the Avery Fisher Center for Music and Media. The new Kimmel Center for University Life includes a 900-seat state-of-the-art theater, a second 540-seat theater, a 150-seat recital room, and additional ensemble rehearsal rooms and private practice rooms.

Faculty, Resident Artists, and Alumni Faculty members are internationally acclaimed artists, composers, scholars, industry executives, and members of such renowned music organizations as the New York Philharmonic and the Metropolitan Opera. They include Robin Eubanks, Bryan Lynch, Chris Potter, John Scofield, and Kenny Werner (jazz); Martin Canin, Eduardus Halim, Miyoko Lotto, and Seymour Bernstein (piano); Stanley Drucker and Esther Lamneck (clarinet); Pamela Frank, Anton Miller, and Martin Beaver (violin); and David Elliott (music education).

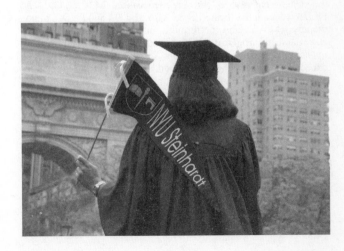

New York University (continued)

Currently in residence: Combo Nuvo, the New Hudson Saxophone Quartet, the NYU Music Theatre Repertory Ensemble, the NYU New Music Ensemble, and the Quintet of the Americas. Composers in residence have included George Perle, Milton Babbitt, Ned Rorem, Roger Reynolds, Lukas Foss, Emil Sein, Morton Subotnik, and George Crumb.

Student Performance Opportunities Student composers and performers are involved in national and international tours and are regularly featured in concerts and recitals at NYU, Carnegie Recital Hall, Merkin Hall, Lincoln Center, and landmark jazz clubs and new music venues in Greenwich Village and SoHo. Performance ensembles include string trio-to-quintet chamber music ensembles and brass and woodwind chamber music ensembles, chamber symphony, two symphony orchestras, concert wind ensemble, Washington Square Woodwind Ensemble, trio-to-septet jazz ensembles, two big band concert ensembles, new music and dance ensemble, percussion ensembles, Choral Arts Society, Women's Choir, opera workshop, music theater ensemble, All-University Gospel Choir, University Singers, Jazz Choir, and Composers Ensemble. An active NYU composers' forum features visiting composers and provides ongoing opportunities for students' work to be performed. Several mainstage and workshop musical theater and opera productions are presented each year.

Added to this are the excitement and opportunities of New York City that enable students to build important career alliances and professional opportunities. World-class artists regularly provide seminars and master classes and often join students in performances on- and off-campus. Music business and technology students as well as performance and composition majors gain hands-on experience through internships at leading recording companies, publishing houses, and concert management and public relations firms. Students in music education gain the finest student experiences in the country's largest public school system.

Special Programs Interactive Arts Performance Series; Stephen F. Temmer Tonmeister Studies (advanced recording technology); annual summer composer's seminar; summer musical theater at Washington Square; summer Kodály Workshop for music educators; summer string quartet, woodwind quintet and woodwind chamber music, and jazz guitar performance institutes; and summer musical theater, new music, and dance in Genoa, Italy, a summer study-abroad program that includes participation in an international music festival and study with distinguished NYU faculty members and Italian performers and composers.

The Department of Music and Performing Arts Professions at New York University's Steinhardt School of Education offers degree programs in music performance (B.M., M.A., and Ph.D.), music composition (B.M., M.A., and Ph.D.), music business (B.M. and M.A.), music technology (B.M. and M.M.), and music therapy (M.A.). Alongside the music programs described above, the department also offers dance education (M.A., Ed.D., and Ph.D.), educational theater (B.S., M.A., Ed.D., and Ph.D.), drama therapy (M.A.), and performing arts administration (M.A.). Baccalaureate programs combine intense professional training in music performance, composition, technology, music business, dance, or theater with a solid liberal arts core in the humanities and the social and natural sciences. In seminars, master classes, and selected classes, undergraduate students join advanced graduate students and faculty members in a collaborative environment that fosters creativity of the highest order.

For those interested in careers in the visual arts, the Department of Art and Art Professions at NYU's Steinhardt School of Education offers studio art (B.F.A., M.F.A., and M.A.), including painting, drawing, sculpture, printmaking, photography, and art in media (digital, photography, and video); art education (M.A. and Ph.D.); a dual B.F.A. studio art/M.A. art education program; visual arts administration, including not-for-profit studies (M.A.); visual culture (M.A.), including theory and costume studies; and art therapy (M.A.). The M.A. Program in

Studio Art: Art in Media is an academic-year program that includes course offerings in conjunction with the International Center for Photography; the M.A. Program in Studio Art for other studio areas is a three-summer-only program offered in New York City and Venice.

The department's classrooms, studios, galleries, educational resource center, offices, and auditorium are all housed in a six-story, turn-of-the-century, Beaux Arts–style building on an historic block just east of NYU's main campus. Faculty members are first-rate artists, educators, and professionals recognized nationally and internationally for their expertise and accomplishments. Faculty artists show extensively worldwide and represent broadly diverse approaches to content and media. Faculty arts professionals influence arts policy and practice. A wide range of programming, including lectures, performances, panels, symposia, and video screenings, enhances knowledge gained in the classroom and studios. Students participate in top internship experiences with unparalleled networking potential. Study-abroad opportunities are available. Undergraduates are encouraged to enroll in one of several excellent University-based programs in Berlin, Florence, Ghana, London, Madrid, Paris, Prague, and Shanghai, while graduate students may participate in the department's Summer Studio Art Program in Venice or the Visual Arts Administration Program in the Netherlands, Vienna, and Paris. All of these elements combine to provide an intense and challenging learning environment dedicated solely to the visual arts within a stimulating urban landscape. NYU attracts talented high achievers from across the country and around the world. The diverse course offerings of NYU's fourteen schools and colleges provide unparalleled opportunities to pursue many academic interests.

New York University Steinhardt School
See New York University

Nicholls State University
Thibodaux, Louisiana

State-supported, coed. Small town campus. Total enrollment: 7,525. Music program established 1967.
Degrees Bachelor of Arts in the area of music; Bachelor of Music Education in the areas of instrumental music, vocal music. Majors and concentrations: instrumental music education, vocal music education. Cross-registration with Loyola University New Orleans. Program accredited by NASM.
Enrollment 60 total; all undergraduate.
Music Student Profile 55% females, 45% males, 7% minorities.
Music Faculty 9 undergraduate (full-time), 2 undergraduate (part-time). 51% of full-time faculty have terminal degrees. Graduate students do not teach undergraduate courses. Undergraduate student–faculty ratio: 7:1.
Student Life Student groups/activities include Phi Mu Alpha Sinfonia, Sigma Alpha Iota.
Expenses for 2005–2006 Application fee: $20. State resident tuition: $2230 full-time. Nonresident tuition: $7679 full-time. Mandatory fees: $1159 full-time. College room and board: $3720. College room only: $1900. Special program-related fees: $10–$150 per course for laboratory fees.
Financial Aid Program-specific awards: 265 band service awards for instrumental ensemble members ($500), 28 choir service awards for choir members ($200), 25 Division of Music Awards for program majors ($600), 30 academic scholarships for program majors ($500).
Application Procedures Students admitted directly into the professional program freshman year. Deadline for freshmen and transfers: continuous. Notification date for freshmen and transfers: August 15. Required: high school transcript, college transcript(s) for transfer students, audition, ACT test score only (minimum composite ACT score of 20). Recommended: 3 letters of recommendation. Auditions held 4 times on campus;

recorded music is permissible as a substitute for live auditions if a campus visit is impossible and videotaped performances are permissible as a substitute for live auditions if a campus visit is impossible.
Web Site http://www.nicholls.edu/perform/
Undergraduate Contact Dr. Carol Britt, Director, School of Fine Arts, Nicholls State University, PO Box 2017, Thibodaux, Louisiana 70310; 985-448-4600, fax: 985-448-4674, e-mail address: mus-cdb@nicholls.edu

Norfolk State University
Norfolk, Virginia

State-supported, coed. Urban campus. Total enrollment: 6,096. Music program established 1952.
Degrees Bachelor of Music in the areas of media, music education. Majors and concentrations: music education, music media, piano/organ, stringed instruments, voice, wind and percussion instruments. Graduate degrees offered: Master of Music in the areas of performance, theory and composition, music education. Cross-registration with Old Dominion University. Program accredited by NASM.
Enrollment 160 total; 150 undergraduate, 10 graduate.
Music Student Profile 40% females, 60% males, 90% minorities, 1% international.
Music Faculty 22 total (full-time), 6 total (part-time). 47% of full-time faculty have terminal degrees. Graduate students do not teach undergraduate courses. Undergraduate student–faculty ratio: 3:1.
Student Life Student groups/activities include Music Educators National Conference, American Choral Directors Association, Intercollegiate Music Association.
Expenses for 2006–2007 Application fee: $25. State resident tuition: $4670 full-time. Nonresident tuition: $14,480 full-time. College room and board: $6474. College room only: $4110. Special program-related fees: $35 per applied lesson for miscellaneous music fees.
Financial Aid Program-specific awards: 100 band scholarships for band students ($500–$1000), 20 choir scholarships for choir students ($500), 20 jazz ensemble scholarships for jazz players ($500).
Application Procedures Students admitted directly into the professional program freshman year. Deadline for freshmen and transfers: August 1. Required: high school transcript, college transcript(s) for transfer students, minimum 2.0 high school GPA, audition, SAT I or ACT test scores. Auditions held 4 times on campus.
Undergraduate Contact Mr. O'Neill Sanford, Head, Department of Music, Norfolk State University, 700 Park Avenue, Norfolk, Virginia 23504; 757-823-8544, fax: 757-823-2605.
Graduate Contact Ernest Brown, Coordinator, Department of Music, Norfolk State University, 700 Park Avenue, Norfolk, Virginia 23504; 757-823-8582, fax: 757-823-2605.

North Carolina School of the Arts
Winston-Salem, North Carolina

State-supported, coed. Urban campus. Total enrollment: 827. Music program established 1965.
Degrees Bachelor of Music in the area of music performance. Majors and concentrations: classical music, composition, guitar, harp, performance, piano/organ, saxophone, stringed instruments, voice, wind and percussion instruments. Graduate degrees offered: Master of Music in the areas of music performance, opera, voice performance.
Enrollment 168 total; 99 undergraduate, 38 graduate, 31 nonprofessional degree.
Music Student Profile 40% females, 60% males, 10% minorities, 8% international.
Music Faculty 28 total (full-time), 6 total (part-time). 90% of full-time faculty have terminal degrees. Graduate students do not teach undergraduate courses. Undergraduate student–faculty ratio: 4:1.
Student Life Special housing available for music students.

Expenses for 2005–2006 Application fee: $50. State resident tuition: $2755 full-time. Nonresident tuition: $14,035 full-time. Mandatory fees: $1551 full-time. Full-time tuition and fees vary according to program. College room and board: $5700. College room only: $3035. Room and board charges vary according to board plan and housing facility. Special program-related fees: $135 per year for educational and technology fee, $160 for music course fee.
Financial Aid Program-specific awards: 91 talent/need scholarships for those demonstrating talent and/or need ($3178).
Application Procedures Students admitted directly into the professional program freshman year. Deadline for freshmen and transfers: continuous. Required: high school transcript, 2 letters of recommendation, interview, audition, portfolio for composition applicants. Recommended: SAT I or ACT test scores. Auditions held several times on campus and off campus in various cities in the U.S.; recorded music is permissible as a substitute for live auditions for provisional acceptance and videotaped performances are permissible as a substitute for live auditions for provisional acceptance. Portfolio reviews held several times on campus.
Web Site http://www.ncarts.edu
Contact Ms. Sheeler Lawson, Director of Admissions, North Carolina School of the Arts, 1533 South Main Street, Winston-Salem, North Carolina 27117-2189; 336-770-3291, fax: 336-770-3370, e-mail address: admissions@ncarts.edu

Northern Arizona University
Flagstaff, Arizona

State-supported, coed. Small town campus. Total enrollment: 18,779.
Degrees Bachelor of Arts in the area of music; Bachelor of Music in the area of performance; Bachelor of Music Education. Majors and concentrations: choral music education, instrumental music education, instrumental performance, piano, piano accompanying, voice performance. Graduate degrees offered: Master of Music in the areas of performance, music education, music history/musicology, music theory/composition, conducting. Program accredited by NASM.
Enrollment 360 total; 300 undergraduate, 60 graduate.
Music Faculty 28 total (full-time), 19 total (part-time). 90% of full-time faculty have terminal degrees. Graduate students teach a few undergraduate courses. Undergraduate student–faculty ratio: 13:1.
Student Life Student groups/activities include music fraternities and sororities, Music Educators National Conference Student Chapter, American Choral Directors Association.
Expenses for 2005–2006 Application fee: $25. State resident tuition: $4223 full-time. Nonresident tuition: $12,853 full-time. Mandatory fees: $170 full-time. Full-time tuition and fees vary according to program. College room and board: $5960. College room only: $3256. Room and board charges vary according to board plan and housing facility. Special program-related fees: $74 per semester for private lessons.
Financial Aid Program-specific awards: 60–90 tuition waiver scholarships for program majors and minors ($1300–$5516).
Application Procedures Students admitted directly into the professional program freshman year. Deadline for freshmen and transfers: continuous. Required: high school transcript, college transcript(s) for transfer students, minimum 2.0 high school GPA, audition, SAT I or ACT test scores. Recommended: 3 letters of recommendation. Auditions held 3 times and by request on campus; recorded music is permissible as a substitute for live auditions when distance is prohibitive and videotaped performances are permissible as a substitute for live auditions when distance is prohibitive.
Web Site http://www.cal.nau.edu/music
Undergraduate Contact Dr. Mary Anne Bruner, Student Services Coordinator, School of Music, Northern Arizona University, PO Box 6040, Flagstaff, Arizona 86011-6040; 928-523-2018, fax: 928-523-5111, e-mail address: maryanne.bruner@nau.edu
Graduate Contact Lisa Perkins, Administrative Assistant, School of Music, Northern Arizona University, PO Box 6040, Flagstaff, Arizona 86011-6040; 928-523-2770, fax: 928-523-5111, e-mail address: lisa.perkins@nau.edu

Northern Illinois University

De Kalb, Illinois

State-supported, coed. Small town campus. Total enrollment: 25,208.

Degrees Bachelor of Music in the areas of performance, music education, composition, jazz studies. Majors and concentrations: composition, jazz, music education, piano/organ, stringed instruments, voice, wind and percussion instruments. Graduate degrees offered: Master of Music in the areas of performance, music education, individualized studies. Program accredited by NASM.

Enrollment 520 total; 380 undergraduate, 140 graduate.

Music Student Profile 44% females, 56% males, 10% minorities, 8% international.

Music Faculty 35 total (full-time), 20 total (part-time). 100% of full-time faculty have terminal degrees. Graduate students do not teach undergraduate courses. Undergraduate student–faculty ratio: 5:1.

Student Life Student groups/activities include professional fraternities and sororities, Music Educators National Conference, International Association for Jazz Education. Special housing available for music students.

Expenses for 2005–2006 State resident tuition: $5061 full-time. Nonresident tuition: $10,123 full-time. Mandatory fees: $1378 full-time. Full-time tuition and fees vary according to course load. College room and board: $5950. Room and board charges vary according to board plan and housing facility. Special program-related fees: $20–$50 for applied fees.

Financial Aid Program-specific awards: 80 scholarships for program majors ($300–$3400).

Application Procedures Students admitted directly into the professional program freshman year. Deadline for freshmen: August 1; transfers: July 15. Required: high school transcript, college transcript(s) for transfer students, audition, SAT I or ACT test scores. Auditions held 4 times on campus; recorded music is permissible as a substitute for live auditions by request and videotaped performances are permissible as a substitute for live auditions by request.

Web Site http://www.niu.edu/music

Undergraduate Contact Ms. Lynn Slater, Coordinator of Undergraduate Admissions, School of Music, Northern Illinois University, De Kalb, Illinois 60115; 815-753-1546, fax: 815-753-1759, e-mail address: lslater@niu.edu

Graduate Contact Dr. C. T. Blickhan, Assistant Director and Coordinator of Graduate Studies, School of Music, Northern Illinois University, De Kalb, Illinois 60115-2889; 815-753-7975, fax: 815-753-1759, e-mail address: blickhan@niu.edu

Northern Kentucky University

Highland Heights, Kentucky

State-supported, coed. Suburban campus. Total enrollment: 13,908. Music program established 1969.

Degrees Bachelor of Music in the areas of performance, music education. Majors and concentrations: guitar, music education, piano, piano pedagogy, stringed instruments, voice, wind and percussion instruments. Cross-registration with Greater Cincinnati Consortium of Colleges and Universities. Program accredited by NASM.

Enrollment 137 total; 96 undergraduate, 41 nonprofessional degree.

Music Student Profile 50% females, 50% males, 1% minorities, 5% international.

Music Faculty 22 undergraduate (full-time), 18 undergraduate (part-time). 100% of full-time faculty have terminal degrees. Graduate students do not teach undergraduate courses. Undergraduate student–faculty ratio: 12:1.

Student Life Student groups/activities include Sigma Alpha Iota, Phi Mu Alpha, Music Educators National Conference Student Chapter.

Expenses for 2005–2006 Application fee: $30. State resident tuition: $4968 full-time. Nonresident tuition: $9696 full-time. Full-time tuition varies according to location. College room and board: $4660. College room only: $2580. Room and board

charges vary according to board plan, housing facility, and location. Special program-related fees: $350 per semester for private music lessons.

Financial Aid Program-specific awards: 18 University Scholarships for musically talented students ($1500), 10 private scholarships for musically talented students ($3000).

Application Procedures Students apply for admission into the professional program by sophomore year. Deadline for freshmen and transfers: August 1. Required: high school transcript, college transcript(s) for transfer students, SAT I or ACT test scores, audition, music theory test, and music history test for transfers. Recommended: 2 letters of recommendation, audition. Auditions held 4 times on campus; recorded music is permissible as a substitute for live auditions and videotaped performances are permissible as a substitute for live auditions if a live audition is impossible.

Web Site http://www.nku.edu/~music

Undergraduate Contact David Dunevant, Assistant Chair, Department of Music, Northern Kentucky University, Fine Arts Center, Room 253, Highland Heights, Kentucky 41099-1005; 859-572-6399, fax: 859-572-6076, e-mail address: dunevantd@nku.edu

Northern Michigan University

Marquette, Michigan

State-supported, coed. Small town campus. Total enrollment: 9,379. Music program established 1969.

Degrees Bachelor of Music Education. Majors and concentrations: choral music education, instrumental music education. Program accredited by NASM.

Enrollment 60 total; all undergraduate.

Music Student Profile 55% females, 45% males, 3% international.

Music Faculty 11 undergraduate (full-time). 90% of full-time faculty have terminal degrees. Graduate students do not teach undergraduate courses. Undergraduate student–faculty ratio: 5:1.

Student Life Student groups/activities include Music Educators National Conference, Marquette Symphony Orchestra, Marquette Chorale Society.

Expenses for 2005–2006 Application fee: $30. One-time mandatory fee: $150. State resident tuition: $5328 full-time. Nonresident tuition: $9072 full-time. Mandatory fees: $630 full-time. College room and board: $6013. Room and board charges vary according to board plan and housing facility.

Financial Aid Program-specific awards: 20 scholarships for talented program majors ($1000).

Application Procedures Students apply for admission into the professional program by freshman year. Deadline for freshmen and transfers: continuous. Required: high school transcript, college transcript(s) for transfer students, SAT I or ACT test scores (minimum combined SAT I score of 800, minimum composite ACT score of 20), minimum 2.7 high school GPA. Recommended: letter of recommendation, audition. Auditions held as needed for voice and instrumental applicants on campus; recorded music is permissible as a substitute for live auditions if a campus visit is impossible and videotaped performances are permissible as a substitute for live auditions if a campus visit is impossible.

Web Site http://www.nmu.edu/departments/music/

Undergraduate Contact Dr. Donald Grant, Head, Music Department, Northern Michigan University, 1401 Presque Isle Avenue, Marquette, Michigan 49855; 906-227-2563, fax: 906-227-2165.

Northern State University

Aberdeen, South Dakota

State-supported, coed. Small town campus. Total enrollment: 2,631. Music program established 1940.

Degrees Bachelor of Arts in the area of music; Bachelor of Music Education in the areas of instrumental music, vocal music, composite (instrumental and vocal). Majors and concentrations: instrumental music, piano/organ, stringed instruments, voice. Program accredited by NASM.

Enrollment 93 total; 90 undergraduate, 3 nonprofessional degree.

Music Student Profile 60% females, 40% males.

Music Faculty 12 undergraduate (full-time), 1 undergraduate (part-time). 75% of full-time faculty have terminal degrees. Graduate students do not teach undergraduate courses. Undergraduate student–faculty ratio: 8:1.

Student Life Student groups/activities include Music Educators National Conference, Sigma Alpha Iota, Phi Mu Alpha Sinfonia. Special housing available for music students.

Expenses for 2005–2006 Application fee: $15. State resident tuition: $2290 full-time. Nonresident tuition: $7278 full-time. Mandatory fees: $2409 full-time. Full-time tuition and fees vary according to course level, course load, and reciprocity agreements. College room and board: $3980. College room only: $2023. Room and board charges vary according to board plan.

Financial Aid Program-specific awards: 35 music scholarships for incoming freshmen/transfers ($600).

Application Procedures Students admitted directly into the professional program freshman year. Deadline for freshmen and transfers: August 15. Notification date for freshmen and transfers: continuous. Required: high school transcript, college transcript(s) for transfer students, minimum 2.0 high school GPA, audition, SAT I or ACT test scores. Recommended: 3 letters of recommendation. Auditions held once and by appointment on campus and off campus in Sioux Falls, Rapid City, and Pierre, SD; recorded music is permissible as a substitute for live auditions when distance is prohibitive and videotaped performances are permissible as a substitute for live auditions when distance is prohibitive.

Web Site http://www.northern.edu

Undergraduate Contact Admissions Office, Northern State University, Dacotah Hall Room 101, 1200 South Jay Street, Aberdeen, South Dakota 57401-7198; 605-626-2544, fax: 605-626-2587, e-mail address: admissions@northern.edu

North Park University
Chicago, Illinois

Independent, coed. Urban campus. Total enrollment: 2,181 (2004). Music program established 1960.

Degrees Bachelor of Music in the area of performance; Bachelor of Music Education. Majors and concentrations: brass, music education, piano, stringed instruments, voice, wind instruments. Graduate degrees offered: Master of Music in the area of vocal performance. Program accredited by NASM.

Enrollment 45 total; 24 undergraduate, 5 graduate, 16 nonprofessional degree.

Music Student Profile 71% females, 29% males, 2% international.

Music Faculty 5 undergraduate (full-time), 27 undergraduate (part-time), 4 graduate (part-time). 100% of full-time faculty have terminal degrees. Graduate students do not teach undergraduate courses. Undergraduate student–faculty ratio: 10:1.

Student Life Student groups/activities include Student Performance Awards Competition, Chicago-area competitions.

Expenses for 2005–2006 Application fee: $20. Comprehensive fee: $21,240 includes full-time tuition ($13,900), mandatory fees ($60), and college room and board ($7280). College room only: $3800. Full-time tuition and fees vary according to program. Room and board charges vary according to board plan, housing facility, and student level.

Financial Aid Program-specific awards: 15 music scholarships for freshmen and transfer students ($1000–$4000), 14 named music scholarships for continuing students ($300–$1500).

Application Procedures Students apply for admission into the professional program by sophomore year. Deadline for freshmen and transfers: continuous. Required: essay, high school transcript, college transcript(s) for transfer students, letter of recommendation, interview, SAT I or ACT test scores (minimum combined SAT I score of 800, minimum composite ACT score of 17), audition for scholarship consideration. Recommended: minimum 2.0 high school GPA, audition. Auditions held 3 times and by appointment on campus; recorded music is permissible as a substitute for live auditions if a campus visit is impossible and videotaped performances are permissible as a substitute for live auditions if a campus visit is impossible.

Web Site http://www.northpark.edu

Undergraduate Contact Mr. Joseph Lill, Admissions Coordinator, School of Music, North Park University, 3225 West Foster Avenue, Chicago, Illinois 60625; 773-244-5634, fax: 773-244-5230, e-mail address: jlill@northpark.edu

Graduate Contact Mr. Joseph Lill, Graduate Admissions Coordinator, School of Music, North Park University, 3225 West Foster Avenue, Chicago, Illinois 60625; 773-244-5634, fax: 773-244-5230, e-mail address: jlill@northpark.edu

Northwestern Oklahoma State University
Alva, Oklahoma

State-supported, coed. Small town campus. Total enrollment: 2,102.

Northwestern State University of Louisiana
Natchitoches, Louisiana

State-supported, coed. Small town campus. Total enrollment: 9,847. Music program established 1883.

Degrees Bachelor of Music in the areas of performance, sacred music; Bachelor of Music Education in the areas of instrumental music education, vocal music education, piano music education. Majors and concentrations: music, music education, piano/organ, sacred music, voice, wind and percussion instruments. Graduate degrees offered: Master of Music in the areas of instrumental music, vocal music, piano, music education. Cross-registration with Louisiana State University in Shreveport, Louisiana State University and Agricultural and Mechanical College. Program accredited by NASM.

Enrollment 191 total; 176 undergraduate, 15 graduate.

Music Student Profile 40% females, 60% males, 10% minorities, 1% international.

Music Faculty 21 total (full-time), 11 total (part-time). 80% of full-time faculty have terminal degrees. Graduate students teach a few undergraduate courses. Undergraduate student–faculty ratio: 8:1.

Student Life Student groups/activities include professional fraternities and sororities, Music Educators National Conference. Special housing available for music students.

Expenses for 2005–2006 Application fee: $20. State resident tuition: $2240 full-time. Nonresident tuition: $8318 full-time. Mandatory fees: $1153 full-time. Full-time tuition and fees vary according to course load. College room and board: $3626. College room only: $2050. Room and board charges vary according to board plan, housing facility, and location.

Financial Aid Program-specific awards: 300 band awards for incoming freshmen ($800–$1200), 100 music awards for incoming freshmen ($800–$1200), 20 Deer Scholarships for music majors ($2000), 20 Magale Scholarships for music majors ($200–$1200), 30 orchestra awards for music majors ($1000–$3000), 10 keyboard awards for music majors ($1000–$3000).

Application Procedures Students admitted directly into the professional program freshman year. Deadline for freshmen and transfers: August 15. Notification date for freshmen: August 15. Required: high school transcript, college transcript(s) for transfer students, minimum 2.0 high school GPA, 3 letters of recommendation, audition, SAT I or ACT test scores. Recommended: interview, video, portfolio. Auditions held by appointment on campus; recorded music is permissible as a substitute for live auditions with approval from the department and videotaped performances are permissible as a substitute for live auditions with approval from the department. Portfolio reviews held by appointment on campus.

Web Site http://www.nsula.edu/capa/

Undergraduate Contact Ms. Jana Lucky, Director, Office of Admissions, Northwestern State University of Louisiana, College Avenue, Natchitoches, Louisiana 71497; 318-357-4503, fax: 318-357-5906.

Northwestern State University of Louisiana *(continued)*

Graduate Contact Dr. Kathleen Byrd, Dean, Graduate Studies, Northwestern State University of Louisiana, College Avenue, Natchitoches, Louisiana 71497; 318-357-5851, fax: 318-357-5019, e-mail address: byrd@nsula.edu

Northwestern University

Evanston, Illinois

Independent, coed. Suburban campus. Total enrollment: 17,004. Music program established 1895.

Degrees Bachelor of Arts/Bachelor of Music in the area of music and liberal arts; Bachelor of Music in the areas of composition, music history, music education, music technology, percussion, piano, strings, music theory, voice, winds, jazz studies, music cognition, music academic studies; Bachelor of Music/Bachelor of Science in the area of music and engineering; Bachelor of Music/Master of Science in Journalism in the area of mucic and journalism. Majors and concentrations: classical music, composition, jazz studies, music, music academic studies, music cognition, music education, music history and literature, music technology, music theory, piano, stringed instruments, voice and opera, wind and percussion instruments. Graduate degrees offered: Master of Music in the areas of composition, conducting, musicology, jazz pedagogy, music education, music technology, percussion, piano, strings, music theory, voice, winds, piano pedagogy, string pedagogy, music education and string pedagogy, piano pedagogy. Doctor of Music in the areas of composition, conducting, percussion, piano, strings, voice, winds, music technology and new media; Doctor of Philosophy in the areas of music education, musicology, music theory, music cognition. Program accredited by NASM.

Enrollment 672 total; 418 undergraduate, 254 graduate.

Music Student Profile 52% females, 48% males, 29% minorities, 11% international.

Music Faculty 73 total (full-time), 100 total (part-time). 88% of full-time faculty have terminal degrees. Graduate students teach a few undergraduate courses. Undergraduate student–faculty ratio: 3:1.

Student Life Student groups/activities include Phi Mu Alpha Sinfonia, Sigma Alpha Iota, Pi Kappa Lambda. Special housing available for music students.

Expenses for 2006–2007 Application fee: $65. Comprehensive fee: $43,825 includes full-time tuition ($33,408), mandatory fees ($151), and college room and board ($10,266). College room only: $5835.

Financial Aid Program-specific awards: 5 Eckstein Scholars Prizes for top auditioning students ($2500), 5–7 music scholarships for outstanding auditions ($5000).

Application Procedures Students admitted directly into the professional program freshman year. Deadline for freshmen: January 1; transfers: May 1. Notification date for freshmen: April 15; transfers: July 1. Required: essay, high school transcript, college transcript(s) for transfer students, minimum 3.0 high school GPA, letter of recommendation, audition, SAT I or ACT test scores (minimum combined SAT I score of 1100, minimum composite ACT score of 23), portfolio for composition, music education, music theory, music history, music technology, music cognition. Recommended: interview, SAT II, 1 additional letter of recommendation from music teacher. Auditions held 26 times on campus and off campus in Los Angeles, CA; San Francisco, CA; Denver, CO; Boston, MA; Seattle, WA; Minneapolis, MN; New York, NY; Cleveland, OH; Orlando, FL; Houston, TX; Dallas, TX; recorded music is permissible as a substitute for live auditions when distance is prohibitive (beyond a 250-mile radius) and videotaped performances are permissible as a substitute for live auditions when distance is prohibitive (beyond a 250-mile radius). Portfolio reviews held once on campus.

Web Site http://music.northwestern.edu

Undergraduate Contact Ms. Angela B. Taylor, Coordinator of Music Admission and Financial Aid, School of Music, Northwestern University, 711 Elgin Road, Evanston, Illinois 60208-1200; 847-491-3141, fax: 847-491-7440, e-mail address: a-taylor8@northwestern.edu

Graduate Contact Mr. Cory D. Wikan, Coordinator of Music Admission and Financial Aid, School of Music, Northwestern University, 711 Elgin Road, Evanston, Illinois 60208-1200; 847-491-3141, fax: 847-491-7440, e-mail address: c.wikan@northwestern.edu

More About the University

Established in 1895, the School of Music ranks among the nation's most prestigious music schools, providing an environment in which musicians can dedicate themselves to their art. Committed to educating students toward highly proficient performance coupled with comprehensive musicianship, the School has developed distinctive programs that meet the artistic and professional needs of those seeking careers in classical, jazz, and music theater performance; education; composition; conducting; music theory; music history; technology; criticism; arts administration; and other fields requiring specialized knowledge of music. These programs are responsive to new directions, recognizing that a thriving curriculum should preserve the riches of tradition while encouraging the exploration and advancement of practices to produce the music of the future.

School of Music faculty members endeavor to expand musical knowledge through research and scholarship; to prepare students meticulously as performers, composers, teachers, scholars, and audience members; and to enrich their communities through their own artistry. Undergraduate programs give students a comprehensive musical grounding through an education centered on musical production, informed by scholarly study of theory and history, and complemented by broad study in the humanities. Graduate programs emphasize scholarly performance and include concentrated work and research in specific fields of interest, producing informed performers, independent scholars, and inspired teachers. Besides providing instruction in voice and all principal instruments and academic areas of music, the School supports a variety of large and small ensembles and staged musical productions that give students high-quality experience in all areas of musical expression. Being part of an eminent research university, the School of Music offers students the unique advantage of pursuing academic study outside music through a variety of courses with distinguished faculty members in all disciplines.

Several celebrated artists visit the School each year. Guests have included Pierre Boulez, Grace Bumbry, John Cage, Janina Fialkowska, Eliot Fisk, Renee Fleming, James Galway, Erich Leinsdorf, Witold Lutoslowski, Wynton Marsalis, Bobby McFerrin, Sherrill Milnes, James Moody, Angel Romero, Dmitri Shostakovich, Sir Georg Solti, and Pinchas Zukerman. Three annual performing arts series present artists such as these in concerts, recitals, and master classes. The School also is uniquely situated to allow excellent opportunities for professional associations in the Chicago metropolitan area.

The School of Music occupies six buildings on Northwestern's lakefront campus: the Music Administration Building, Regenstein Hall, Pick-Staiger Concert Hall, the Practice Hall, Lutkin Hall, and the Deering Music Library. These facilities provide classrooms, offices, computer labs, an electronic music studio, a computer music studio, numerous practice rooms, and three recital halls. Pick-Staiger Concert Hall, an acoustically superb 1,000-seat concert hall, offers the campus and surrounding community top-level student and professional performances year-round. Deering Music Library, recognized internationally for its contemporary music collection, is also a leader in library automation. Housed within the Cambridge-inspired structure are a multimedia listening center; holdings of 142,000 books, musical scores, journals, and microforms as well as 53,000 discs and tapes; a manuscript collection documenting contemporary notation compiled by John Cage for use in his book, *Notations*; holograph scores, sketches, and letters of musicians; the Fritz Reiner Library; and other rare printed resources.

Notre Dame de Namur University

Belmont, California

Independent Roman Catholic, coed. Suburban campus. Total enrollment: 1,588. Music program established 1851.

Degrees Bachelor of Fine Arts in the area of music theater; Bachelor of Music in the area of performance. Majors and concentrations: brass, harp, harpsichord, music theater, piano/organ, stringed instruments, voice, wind and percussion instruments. Graduate degrees offered: Master of Music in the areas of performance, pedagogy. Cross-registration with Trinity College, Emmanuel College. Program accredited by NASM.
Enrollment 57 total; 30 undergraduate, 12 graduate, 15 nonprofessional degree.
Music Student Profile 79% females, 21% males, 50% international.
Music Faculty 2 total (full-time), 14 total (part-time). 100% of full-time faculty have terminal degrees. Graduate students do not teach undergraduate courses. Undergraduate student–faculty ratio: 9:1.
Expenses for 2006–2007 Application fee: $40. Comprehensive fee: $34,230 includes full-time tuition ($23,650), mandatory fees ($200), and college room and board ($10,380). College room only: $7000. Special program-related fees: $510 per semester for private applied lessons.
Financial Aid Program-specific awards: 6 Brooks Memorial Scholarships for those demonstrating need/talent ($1400), 21 music assistance grants for those demonstrating need/talent ($700), 1 La Ratta Scholarship for those demonstrating need/talent ($840), Presidential Scholarships for those demonstrating academic excellence, 1 Sr. Anthony Marie Herzo Scholarship for musically talented students ($2500), 1 Asbjorn Finess Scholarship for string students ($4000).
Application Procedures Students admitted directly into the professional program freshman year. Deadline for freshmen and transfers: continuous. Required: essay, high school transcript, college transcript(s) for transfer students, letter of recommendation, audition, SAT I or ACT test scores, minimum TOEFL score of 450 for international students. Recommended: minimum 3.0 high school GPA. Auditions held twice on campus and off campus in Carmel, CA; Sacramento, CA; recorded music is permissible as a substitute for live auditions when distance is prohibitive and videotaped performances are permissible as a substitute for live auditions when distance is prohibitive.
Web Site http://www.music.ndnu.edu
Undergraduate Contact Katy Murphy, Director of Undergraduate Admissions, Notre Dame de Namur University, 1500 Ralston Avenue, Belmont, California 94002-1997; 650-508-3525, fax: 650-637-0493.
Graduate Contact Barbara Sterner, Assistant Dean of Graduate Admissions, Graduate Office, Notre Dame de Namur University, 1500 Ralston Avenue, Belmont, California 94002-1997; 650-508-3527, fax: 650-637-0493, e-mail address: grad.admit@ndnu.edu

Nyack College

Nyack, New York

Independent, coed. Suburban campus. Total enrollment: 3,000. Music program established 1947.
Degrees Bachelor of Music in the areas of performance, music education, composition; Bachelor of Sacred Music in the area of church music. Majors and concentrations: church music, classical music, composition, music, music education, piano/organ, stringed instruments, voice, wind and percussion instruments. Cross-registration with Rockland Community College. Program accredited by NASM.
Enrollment 105 total; 75 undergraduate, 30 nonprofessional degree.
Music Student Profile 65% females, 35% males, 35% minorities, 5% international.
Music Faculty 6 undergraduate (full-time), 25 undergraduate (part-time). 60% of full-time faculty have terminal degrees. Graduate students do not teach undergraduate courses. Undergraduate student–faculty ratio: 15:1.
Student Life Student groups/activities include Music Educators National Conference, American Guild of Organists, American Choral Directors Association.
Expenses for 2006–2007 Application fee: $25. Comprehensive fee: $23,000 includes full-time tuition ($15,400) and college room and board ($7600). Special program-related fees: $260 per credit for private lessons.

Financial Aid Program-specific awards: 45 music achievement grants for talented performers ($1000–$10,000).
Application Procedures Students admitted directly into the professional program freshman year. Deadline for freshmen and transfers: continuous. Notification date for freshmen: continuous. Required: essay, high school transcript, college transcript(s) for transfer students, 3 letters of recommendation, interview, audition, SAT I or ACT test scores (minimum combined SAT I score of 920), portfolio for composition majors. Recommended: minimum 2.0 high school GPA. Auditions held 4 times and by appointment on campus; recorded music is permissible as a substitute for live auditions when distance is prohibitive (beyond a 200-mile radius) and videotaped performances are permissible as a substitute for live auditions when distance is prohibitive (beyond a 200-mile radius). Portfolio reviews held continuously on campus.
Web Site http://www.nyackcollege.edu
Undergraduate Contact Mr. Miguel Sanchez, Head, Admissions Office, Nyack College, 1 South Boulevard, Nyack, New York 10960; 800-366-9225 ext. 350, fax: 845-358-3047, e-mail address: sanchezm@nyack.edu

Oakland City University

Oakland City, Indiana

Independent General Baptist, coed. Rural campus. Total enrollment: 1,900.
Degrees Bachelor of Arts in the areas of church music, music performance, general studies; Bachelor of Music Education in the area of vocal/general music education. Majors and concentrations: church music, music, music education, music performance, piano/organ, voice.
Enrollment 25 total; 18 undergraduate, 7 nonprofessional degree.
Music Student Profile 95% females, 5% males.
Music Faculty 3 undergraduate (full-time), 2 undergraduate (part-time). 50% of full-time faculty have terminal degrees. Graduate students do not teach undergraduate courses. Undergraduate student–faculty ratio: 5:1.
Student Life Student groups/activities include Music Educators National Conference, Music Club (honorary).
Expenses for 2006–2007 Application fee: $35. Comprehensive fee: $19,620 includes full-time tuition ($13,860), mandatory fees ($360), and college room and board ($5400). College room only: $1760. Special program-related fees: $75 for piano maintenance.
Financial Aid Program-specific awards: 1 Neva Barnard Music Scholarship for outstanding voice students, 1 Tri Kappa Music Scholarship for outstanding instrumental students, 1 Keys Piano Scholarship for outstanding piano students, 2–3 Bradbury Music Scholarships for music students demonstrating need and improvement in studies, 2–3 Dufford Music Scholarships for music majors demonstrating need and potential for improvement in studies.
Application Procedures Students admitted directly into the professional program freshman year. Deadline for freshmen and transfers: continuous. Notification date for freshmen and transfers: continuous. Required: high school transcript, college transcript(s) for transfer students, audition, SAT I or ACT test scores. Recommended: minimum 2.0 high school GPA, 3 letters of recommendation, interview, video, resume. Auditions held by appointment on campus; recorded music is permissible as a substitute for live auditions when distance is prohibitive and videotaped performances are permissible as a substitute for live auditions when distance is prohibitive.
Web Site http://www.oak.edu
Undergraduate Contact Dr. Jean Cox, Associate Professor, Department of Music, Oakland City University, 143 Lucretia Street, Oakland City, Indiana 47660; 812-749-1254.

Oakland University

Rochester, Michigan

State-supported, coed. Suburban campus. Total enrollment: 17,339. Music program established 1972.
Degrees Bachelor of Music in the areas of performance, composition, education. Majors and concentrations: composi-

Oakland University (continued)

tion, instrumental performance, keyboard, music education, voice. Graduate degrees offered: Master of Music in the areas of music education, conducting, performance, composition, pedagogy. Program accredited by NASM.
Enrollment 400 total; 200 undergraduate, 60 graduate, 140 nonprofessional degree.
Music Student Profile 77% females, 23% males, 7% minorities.
Music Faculty 12 total (full-time), 60 total (part-time). 82% of full-time faculty have terminal degrees. Graduate students do not teach undergraduate courses. Undergraduate student–faculty ratio: 19:1.
Student Life Student groups/activities include MENC-The National Association for Music Education, ensembles.
Expenses for 2005–2006 Application fee: $40. State resident tuition: $6443 full-time. Nonresident tuition: $14,869 full-time. Full-time tuition varies according to program and student level. College room and board: $6080. Room and board charges vary according to housing facility. Special program-related fees: $13–$85 per credit for applied music lessons or classes.
Financial Aid Program-specific awards: music scholarships for talented students ($750–$2000).
Application Procedures Students admitted directly into the professional program freshman year. Deadline for freshmen and transfers: July 15. Required: high school transcript, audition, SAT I or ACT test scores, minimum 2.5 high school GPA. Auditions held 3 times on campus; recorded music is permissible as a substitute for live auditions if a campus visit is impossible and videotaped performances are permissible as a substitute for live auditions if a campus visit is impossible.
Web Site http://www.otus.oakland.edu/mtd
Undergraduate Contact John-Paul White, Director of Undergraduate Music Education, Department of Music, Theatre, and Dance, Oakland University, 315 Varner Hall, Rochester, Michigan 48309; 248-370-2030, fax: 248-370-2041.
Graduate Contact Jackie Wiggins, Department of Music, Theatre, and Dance, Oakland University, 211 Varner Hall, Rochester, Michigan 48309; 248-370-2030, fax: 248-370-2041, e-mail address: jwiggins@oakland.edu

Oberlin College
Oberlin, Ohio

Independent, coed. Small town campus. Total enrollment: 2,864. Music program established 1865.
Degrees Bachelor of Music in the areas of performance, music education, composition, music history, electronic and computer music, jazz studies, music theory, accompanying. Majors and concentrations: accompanying, brass, composition, electronic music, historical performance, jazz, music education, music theory, musicology, piano/organ, stringed instruments, voice, wind and percussion instruments. Graduate degrees offered: Master of Music in the areas of historical performance, opera theater, conducting; Master of Music Education. Program accredited by NASM.
Enrollment 584 total; 572 undergraduate, 12 graduate.
Music Student Profile 52% females, 48% males, 16% minorities, 13% international.
Music Faculty 70 total (full-time), 21 total (part-time). 90% of full-time faculty have terminal degrees. Graduate students do not teach undergraduate courses. Undergraduate student–faculty ratio: 7:1.
Expenses for 2005–2006 Application fee: $100. Comprehensive fee: $40,904 includes full-time tuition ($32,524), mandatory fees ($200), and college room and board ($8180). College room only: $4300. Full-time tuition and fees vary according to course load. Room and board charges vary according to board plan and housing facility.
Financial Aid Program-specific awards: 220 Oberlin College Scholarships for those demonstrating need ($2000–$34,000), 200 Oberlin Conservatory Dean's Scholarships for those demonstrating talent and academic achievement ($2000–$26,000), 10 Oberlin College Prize Funds for those with academic merit ($50–$4000), 15 Oberlin Conservatory/Aspen-John H. Stern Scholarships for enrolled students ($1500), 220 work-study awards for program majors ($500–$1600).

Application Procedures Students admitted directly into the professional program freshman year. Deadline for freshmen and transfers: December 1. Notification date for freshmen and transfers: April 1. Required: essay, high school transcript, college transcript(s) for transfer students, 2 letters of recommendation, audition, SAT I or ACT test scores, transfer release form (for transfer applicants). Recommended: minimum 3.0 high school GPA, interview, video. Auditions held 28 times on campus and off campus in Atlanta, GA; Boston, MA; Chicago, IL; Denver, CO; Houston, TX; Interlochen, MI; Los Angeles, CA; Minneapolis, MN; New York, NY; Portland, OR; San Diego, CA; San Francisco, CA; Seattle, WA; Washington, DC; Bangkok, Hong Kong; Seoul, Singapore, Taipei; recorded music is permissible as a substitute for live auditions if of good quality and videotaped performances are permissible as a substitute for live auditions if of good quality.
Web Site http://www.oberlin.edu/con
Contact Mr. Michael Manderen, Director of Conservatory Admissions, Conservatory of Music, Oberlin College, 39 West College Street, Oberlin, Ohio 44074; 440-775-8413, fax: 440-775-6972, e-mail address: conservatory.admissions@oberlin.edu

More About the College

Within the Conservatory, which is housed in a modern complex designed by Minoru Yamasaki, are ensemble rehearsal rooms, two excellent concert halls, and 153 individual practice rooms. The Conservatory houses one of the largest collection of Steinway pianos in the world, and the campus is also home to twenty-five organs. Other features include numerous instrument collections, seven acoustically isolated and optimized electronic music studios, and a library that rivals those in the nation's largest university music schools.

The Conservatory of Music and the College of Arts and Sciences share the same campus. As a result, Conservatory students can take courses in both the College and the Conservatory in the same semester and can simultaneously pursue majors in both divisions, completing majors leading to both the B.Mus. and the B.A. degrees after five years. Twenty-five to 30 percent of the Conservatory's students are in the Double Degree Program. Additionally, the Conservatory offers four dual-degree programs, open only to Oberlin's own undergraduates, which combine bachelor's degree study in performance or music education with graduate study leading to the master's degree in conducting, opera theater, music education, or music teaching.

The Oberlin Conservatory is one of the few major music schools in the country devoted primarily to the education of undergraduate musicians. As a division of Oberlin College, the Conservatory is also recognized for being paired with a preeminent college of the liberal arts and sciences. These factors allow the conservatory to offer its students the essential components of excellent musical training: an accomplished faculty, outstanding facilities, an extensive curriculum drawing on both divisions of Oberlin College, and an active cultural life centered on campus and drawing on Cleveland as well.

"You're at Oberlin? What do you play?" Every Oberlinian has heard this question even though the Conservatory of Music is but one fourth the size of its partner, the College of Arts and Sciences. Yet it is natural that the name Oberlin should evoke thoughts of music. Built up by an amateur cellist (Charles Grandison Finney) and funded mainly by a former piano student (Charles Martin Hall), Oberlin College created America's first professorship in music in 1835. Oberlin's Conservatory of Music, established in 1865, is the country's first continuously operating conservatory. Even before the Civil War, a visitor, Thomas Hastings, pronounced the Oberlin choir "the finest in the land." A century later, Igor Stravinsky was similarly effusive over the Conservatory's young instrumentalists.

Oberlin has been the source of much innovation in American musical education. It established the country's first full-time chair in music history (1892), offered the country's first four-year degree program in public school music (1921), introduced to the United States the renowned Suzuki method of string pedagogy (1958), pioneered a program in electronic music (1969), and created the American-Soviet Youth Orchestra, composed of 100 young musicians from the United States and the former U.S.S.R., the first arts exchange produced jointly by the two countries (1988).

Conservatory alumni include well-known composers, conductors, performers, and teachers. Some, like David Zinman, conductor, have gained public renown. Others, like jazz pioneer Will Marion Cook—whom Duke Ellington called "my conservatory"—are revered mainly by specialists. Today's Oberlin graduates are to be found in virtually every major American orchestra as well as in international orchestras from Berlin to Hong Kong. Its singers and pianists are no less ubiquitous, as are Oberlinians in the many new allied fields of music.

The Oberlin Conservatory of Music has taken great pains to both educate and train its students. More than ever, technical proficiency is essential to success in music; however, the day when a pianist could simply perfect a limited repertoire of classics in order to launch a career is past. Increasingly, musicians need to master worlds of sound that were scarcely imaginable when they were students. Only the most well-educated minds can attain such flexibility. Oberlin is committed to providing its students a balanced combination of professional training and comprehensive education.

Ohio Northern University

Ada, Ohio

Independent, coed. Small town campus. Total enrollment: 3,542. Music program established 1871.
Degrees Bachelor of Music. Majors and concentrations: composition, music and business, music education, music performance. Program accredited by NASM, NCATE.
Enrollment 84 total; 70 undergraduate, 14 nonprofessional degree.
Music Student Profile 65% females, 35% males, 4% minorities.
Music Faculty 8 undergraduate (full-time), 18 undergraduate (part-time). 63% of full-time faculty have terminal degrees. Graduate students do not teach undergraduate courses. Undergraduate student–faculty ratio: 3:1.
Student Life Student groups/activities include Ohio Music Education Association, National Association of Teachers of Singing, National Federation of Music Clubs.
Expenses for 2006–2007 Application fee: $30. Comprehensive fee: $35,340 includes full-time tuition ($28,050), mandatory fees ($210), and college room and board ($7080). College room only: $3540. Special program-related fees: $50 per quarter for private lessons.
Financial Aid Program-specific awards: 30 Snyder Scholarships for top musicians ($8000–$10,000), 30 Dean's Talent Awards for top musicians ($5000–$8000).
Application Procedures Students admitted directly into the professional program freshman year. Deadline for freshmen and transfers: continuous. Required: high school transcript, college transcript(s) for transfer students, minimum 2.0 high school GPA, audition, SAT I or ACT test scores. Auditions held 5 times on campus; recorded music is permissible as a substitute for live auditions for out-of-state applicants and videotaped performances are permissible as a substitute for live auditions for out-of-state applicants.
Web Site http://www.onu.edu
Undergraduate Contact Dr. Edwin L. Williams, Chairman, Music Department, Ohio Northern University, 525 South Main Street, Ada, Ohio 45810; 419-772-2151, fax: 419-772-2488, e-mail address: e-williams@onu.edu

The Ohio State University

Columbus, Ohio

State-supported, coed. Total enrollment: 50,504. Music program established 1921.

Ohio University

Athens, Ohio

State-supported, coed. Small town campus. Total enrollment: 20,396. Music program established 1946.
Degrees Bachelor of Music in the areas of performance, composition, theory, history, education, therapy. Majors and concentrations: music education, music history and literature, music theory and composition, music therapy, piano/organ, stringed instruments, voice, wind and percussion instruments. Graduate degrees offered: Master of Music in the areas of performance, composition, theory, history, education, therapy, conducting, and pedagogy. Program accredited by NASM.
Enrollment 282 total; 230 undergraduate, 52 graduate.
Music Student Profile 46% females, 54% males, 4% minorities, 3% international.
Music Faculty 33 total (full-time), 11 total (part-time). 70% of full-time faculty have terminal degrees. Graduate students do not teach undergraduate courses. Undergraduate student–faculty ratio: 12:1.
Student Life Student groups/activities include Music Educators National Conference Student Chapter, American Association of Music Therapy Student Chapter, honorary music fraternities.
Expenses for 2005–2006 Application fee: $45. State resident tuition: $8235 full-time. Nonresident tuition: $17,199 full-time. College room and board: $7686. College room only: $3855. Room and board charges vary according to board plan. Special program-related fees: $25 per quarter for methods classes, $100 per quarter for applied music lesson fee.
Financial Aid Program-specific awards: 15–20 talent scholarships for artistically talented students ($1000–$7000).
Application Procedures Students admitted directly into the professional program freshman year. Deadline for freshmen and transfers: February 1. Notification date for freshmen and transfers: March 15. Required: high school transcript, college transcript(s) for transfer students, minimum 2.0 high school GPA, letter of recommendation, audition, portfolio for composition majors, interview for music education and music therapy majors. Recommended: minimum 3.0 high school GPA, interview, SAT I or ACT test scores. Auditions held 4-6 times on campus; recorded music is permissible as a substitute for live auditions if a campus visit is impossible and videotaped performances are permissible as a substitute for live auditions when distance is prohibitive if a campus visit is impossible. Portfolio reviews held once on campus.
Web Site http://www.ohiou.edu/music
Undergraduate Contact Dr. Sylvester Young, Associate Director, School of Music, Ohio University, Music Building, Athens, Ohio 45701-2979; 740-593-4244, fax: 740-593-1429, e-mail address: youngs@ohio.edu
Graduate Contact Dr. Meryl Mantione, Director, School of Music, Ohio University, Music Building, Athens, Ohio 45701-2979; 740-593-4244, fax: 740-593-1429, e-mail address: mantione@ohio.edu

Ohio Wesleyan University

Delaware, Ohio

Independent United Methodist, coed. Small town campus. Total enrollment: 1,976. Music program established 1877.
Degrees Bachelor of Music in the areas of performance, music education. Majors and concentrations: music education, music performance, piano/organ, stringed instruments, voice, wind and percussion instruments. Program accredited by NASM.
Music Faculty 8 undergraduate (full-time), 8 undergraduate (part-time). 100% of full-time faculty have terminal degrees. Graduate students do not teach undergraduate courses.
Student Life Student groups/activities include Mu Phi Epsilon Student Chapter, Music Educators National Conference Student Chapter.
Expenses for 2005–2006 Application fee: $35. Comprehensive fee: $35,830 includes full-time tuition ($27,920), mandatory fees ($360), and college room and board ($7550). College room only: $3750. Room and board charges vary according to board plan.
Financial Aid Program-specific awards: Ruth Wilson Music Scholarships for program majors, Edward D. and Laura Rich Cleary

Ohio Wesleyan University (continued)

Music Education Memorial Scholarship for music education majors, Edith Mahon Davis Music Education Scholarship for music education majors, Ohio Wesleyan University Merit Scholarships for program majors, Edith M. Keller Scholarship in Music Education for music education majors, Col. George Howard Instrumental Music Scholarship for instrumental majors.
Application Procedures Students admitted directly into the professional program freshman year. Deadline for freshmen and transfers: March 1. Required: essay, high school transcript, college transcript(s) for transfer students, letter of recommendation, audition, SAT I or ACT test scores. Recommended: interview, video. Auditions held 6 scheduled times and by appointment on campus; recorded music is permissible as a substitute for live auditions when distance is prohibitive and videotaped performances are permissible as a substitute for live auditions when distance is prohibitive.
Web Site http://www.owu.edu/~musicd
Undergraduate Contact Admissions, Ohio Wesleyan University, Slocum Hall, 61 South Sandusky Street, Delaware, Ohio 43015; 740-368-2000, fax: 740-368-3314.

Oklahoma Baptist University

Shawnee, Oklahoma

Independent Southern Baptist, coed. Total enrollment: 1,883 (2004). Music program established 1917.
Degrees Bachelor of Music in the areas of voice/keyboard, music performance, church music, theory/composition; Bachelor of Music Education in the areas of vocal music education, instrumental music education. Majors and concentrations: music education, music theory and composition, piano, sacred music, stringed instruments, voice, wind and percussion instruments. Cross-registration with St. Gregory's University. Program accredited by NASM.
Enrollment 100 total; 84 undergraduate, 16 nonprofessional degree.
Music Student Profile 55% females, 45% males, 8% minorities, 2% international.
Music Faculty 16 undergraduate (full-time), 7 undergraduate (part-time). 65% of full-time faculty have terminal degrees. Graduate students do not teach undergraduate courses. Undergraduate student–faculty ratio: 9:1.
Student Life Student groups/activities include Music Educators National Conference, Sigma Alpha Iota, Phi Mu Alpha Sinfonia.
Expenses for 2005–2006 Application fee: $25. Comprehensive fee: $17,986 includes full-time tuition ($12,924), mandatory fees ($922), and college room and board ($4140). College room only: $1840. Full-time tuition and fees vary according to course load. Room and board charges vary according to board plan and housing facility. Special program-related fees: $900 per course for applied music fees.
Financial Aid Program-specific awards: 82 music scholarships for program majors ($1092).
Application Procedures Students admitted directly into the professional program freshman year. Deadline for freshmen and transfers: continuous. Required: high school transcript, college transcript(s) for transfer students, minimum 2.0 high school GPA, audition, SAT I or ACT test scores. Auditions held 4 times on campus; recorded music is permissible as a substitute for live auditions when distance is prohibitive and videotaped performances are permissible as a substitute for live auditions when distance is prohibitive.
Web Site http://www.okbu.edu
Undergraduate Contact Mr. Trent Argo, Dean of Admissions, Oklahoma Baptist University, Box 61173, 500 West University, Shawnee, Oklahoma 74804; 800-654-3285, fax: 405-878-2046, e-mail address: trent.argo@okbu.edu

Oklahoma Christian University

Oklahoma City, Oklahoma

Independent, coed. Suburban campus. Total enrollment: 2,058. Music program established 1972.

Margaret E. Petree College of Music and Performing Arts

Oklahoma City University

Oklahoma City, Oklahoma

Independent United Methodist, coed. Urban campus. Total enrollment: 3,688. Music program established 1904.
Degrees Bachelor of Music in the areas of performance, music theater, composition, piano pedagogy, instrumental, vocal, guitar, piano, organ, music business; Bachelor of Music Education in the areas of vocal music education, instrumental music education. Majors and concentrations: composition, music, music business, music education, music theater, piano/organ, stringed instruments, voice, wind and percussion instruments. Graduate degrees offered: Master of Music in the areas of performance, composition, music theater, opera performance, conducting. Program accredited by NASM.
Enrollment 270 total; 221 undergraduate, 49 graduate.
Music Student Profile 52% females, 48% males, 13% minorities, 6% international.
Music Faculty 24 total (full-time), 31 total (part-time). 42% of full-time faculty have terminal degrees. Graduate students do not teach undergraduate courses. Undergraduate student–faculty ratio: 14:1.
Student Life Student groups/activities include American String Teachers Association, Sigma Alpha Iota, Music Educators National Conference.
Expenses for 2005–2006 Application fee: $30. Comprehensive fee: $23,863 includes full-time tuition ($16,700), mandatory fees ($913), and college room and board ($6250). College room only: $3050. Full-time tuition and fees vary according to program. Room and board charges vary according to board plan and housing facility. Special program-related fees: $150 per credit hour for applied music fee, $250 per semester for facilities fee, $300 per semester for accompanist fee (vocal only).
Financial Aid Program-specific awards: 175 general music scholarships for program majors and performers ($4500).
Application Procedures Students admitted directly into the professional program freshman year. Deadline for freshmen and transfers: continuous. Notification date for freshmen and transfers: August 22. Required: essay, high school transcript, college transcript(s) for transfer students, minimum 2.0 high school GPA, audition, SAT I or ACT test scores (minimum combined SAT I score of 1030, minimum composite ACT score of 22), minimum 2.5 high school GPA, standing in top 50% of graduating class, portfolio for composition majors. Recommended: minimum 3.0 high school GPA. Auditions held 6 times on campus; recorded music is permissible as a substitute for live auditions if a campus visit is impossible and videotaped performances are permissible as a substitute for live auditions if a campus visit is impossible.
Web Site http://www.okcu.edu/music
Undergraduate Contact Ms. Mary Mowry, Coordinator of Student Services, College of Performing Arts, School of Music, Oklahoma City University, 2501 North Blackwelder, Oklahoma City, Oklahoma 73106; 405-521-5980, fax: 405-521-5971, e-mail address: mamowry@okcu.edu
Graduate Contact Dr. David Steffens, Graduate Studies Advisor, College of Performing Arts, School of Music, Oklahoma City University, 2501 North Blackwelder, Oklahoma City, Oklahoma 73106; 405-521-5981, fax: 405-521-5791, e-mail address: dsteffens@okcu.edu

Oklahoma State University

Stillwater, Oklahoma

State-supported, coed. Small town campus. Total enrollment: 23,461. Music program established 1902.
Degrees Bachelor of Music in the areas of performance, music education, music business. Majors and concentrations: music business, music education, piano/organ, stringed instruments, voice, wind and percussion instruments. Graduate degrees offered: Master of Music in the area of pedagogy and performance. Program accredited by NASM.

Enrollment 139 total; 116 undergraduate, 13 graduate, 10 nonprofessional degree.
Music Student Profile 44% females, 56% males, 17% minorities, 4% international.
Music Faculty 21 total (full-time), 9 total (part-time). 52% of full-time faculty have terminal degrees. Graduate students teach a few undergraduate courses. Undergraduate student–faculty ratio: 5:1.
Student Life Student groups/activities include professional music fraternities and sororities.
Expenses for 2005–2006 Application fee: $40. State resident tuition: $3099 full-time. Nonresident tuition: $11,122 full-time. Mandatory fees: $1266 full-time. Full-time tuition and fees vary according to program and student level. College room and board: $5848. College room only: $2848. Room and board charges vary according to board plan, housing facility, and location. Special program-related fees: $10 per credit for organ rental, $15 per credit for class piano fee, $25 per credit for ensemble enrollment fee, $25 per credit for applied lessons.
Financial Aid Program-specific awards: 200–250 music scholarships for program majors and musicians ($50–$2500).
Application Procedures Students admitted directly into the professional program freshman year. Deadline for freshmen and transfers: continuous. Required: high school transcript, college transcript(s) for transfer students, minimum 3.0 high school GPA, audition, ACT test score only (minimum composite ACT score of 22). Auditions held continuously on campus and off campus in various locations in Oklahoma; recorded music is permissible as a substitute for live auditions if a campus visit is impossible and videotaped performances are permissible as a substitute for live auditions if a campus visit is impossible.
Web Site http://music.okstate.edu
Undergraduate Contact Prof. Julia C. Combs, Head, Department of Music, Oklahoma State University, 132 Seretean Center, Stillwater, Oklahoma 74078-4077; 405-744-6133, fax: 405-744-9324, e-mail address: lawsojl@okstate.edu
Graduate Contact Dr. Gerald D. Frank, Graduate Program Coordinator, Department of Music, Oklahoma State University, 132 Seretean Center, Stillwater, Oklahoma 74078-4077; 405-744-8985, fax: 405-744-9324, e-mail address: fgerald@okstate.edu

Old Dominion University
Norfolk, Virginia

State-supported, coed. Urban campus. Total enrollment: 21,274. Music program established 1950.

Oral Roberts University
Tulsa, Oklahoma

Independent interdenominational, coed. Urban campus. Total enrollment: 4,086. Music program established 1963.
Degrees Bachelor of Music in the areas of sacred music, composition, performance, composition/technology; Bachelor of Music Education in the areas of vocal music education, instrumental music education. Majors and concentrations: composition, music education, piano, sacred music, stringed instruments, voice, wind and percussion instruments. Program accredited by NASM.
Enrollment 68 total; all undergraduate.
Music Student Profile 52% females, 48% males, 13% minorities, 5% international.
Music Faculty 14 undergraduate (full-time), 25 undergraduate (part-time). 59% of full-time faculty have terminal degrees. Graduate students do not teach undergraduate courses. Undergraduate student–faculty ratio: 3:1.
Student Life Student groups/activities include opera and musical productions, Family Christmas Concert, oratorio presentations.
Expenses for 2005–2006 Application fee: $35. Comprehensive fee: $22,650 includes full-time tuition ($15,400), mandatory fees ($480), and college room and board ($6770). College room only: $3280. Room and board charges vary according to board plan and housing facility. Special program-related fees: $40 per course for music ensemble fee, $55 per course for music equipment, $250 per semester for applied music lesson fee.

Financial Aid Program-specific awards: 188 talent awards for music majors, minors, or participants ($500–$5000), 40 special awards ($500–$2000).
Application Procedures Students admitted directly into the professional program freshman year. Deadline for freshmen and transfers: continuous. Required: essay, high school transcript, college transcript(s) for transfer students, minimum 2.0 high school GPA, 2 letters of recommendation, audition, SAT I or ACT test scores (minimum combined SAT I score of 990, minimum composite ACT score of 20). Auditions held by appointment on campus; recorded music is permissible as a substitute for live auditions when distance is prohibitive and videotaped performances are permissible as a substitute for live auditions when distance is prohibitive. Portfolio reviews held as needed on campus.
Web Site http://www.oru.edu
Undergraduate Contact Mrs. Stacey Lehwald, Secretary, Music Department, Oral Roberts University, 7777 South Lewis Avenue, Tulsa, Oklahoma 74171; 918-495-7500, fax: 918-495-7502, e-mail address: slehwald@oru.edu

Otterbein College
Westerville, Ohio

Independent United Methodist, coed. Suburban campus. Total enrollment: 3,094. Music program established 1847.
Degrees Bachelor of Fine Arts in the area of musical theater; Bachelor of Music in the area of performance; Bachelor of Music Education in the area of vocal and instrumental music education. Majors and concentrations: classical music, music, music education, music theater, piano/organ, stringed instruments, voice, wind and percussion instruments. Cross-registration with Ohio State University, Capital University, Columbus State Community College. Program accredited by NASM.
Enrollment 140 total; 80 undergraduate, 60 nonprofessional degree.
Music Student Profile 55% females, 45% males, 2% minorities, 5% international.
Music Faculty 10 undergraduate (full-time), 40 undergraduate (part-time). 90% of full-time faculty have terminal degrees. Graduate students do not teach undergraduate courses. Undergraduate student–faculty ratio: 3:1.
Student Life Student groups/activities include Ohio Student Music Educators Association, Delta Omicron, Music and Entertainment Industry Students Association.
Expenses for 2005–2006 Application fee: $25. Comprehensive fee: $28,986 includes full-time tuition ($22,518) and college room and board ($6468). College room only: $2994. Full-time tuition varies according to course load and program. Room and board charges vary according to housing facility. Special program-related fees: $750–$1500 per year for private applied music lessons.
Financial Aid Program-specific awards: 20–30 Music Talent Awards for program majors ($1000–$6000).
Application Procedures Students admitted directly into the professional program freshman year. Deadline for freshmen and transfers: continuous. Required: high school transcript, college transcript(s) for transfer students, minimum 2.0 high school GPA, audition, SAT I or ACT test scores. Recommended: interview. Auditions held continuously on campus and off campus; recorded music is permissible as a substitute for live auditions when distance is prohibitive and videotaped performances are permissible as a substitute for live auditions when distance is prohibitive.
Web Site http://www.otterbein.edu/admission/music.html
Undergraduate Contact Debbie Byrne, Admission Counselor/Arts Recruiter, Admissions Office, Otterbein College, Westerville, Ohio 43081; 614-823-1219, fax: 614-823-1200, e-mail address: dbyrne@otterbein.edu

Bernice Young Jones School of Fine Arts
Ouachita Baptist University
Arkadelphia, Arkansas

Independent Baptist, coed. Small town campus. Total enrollment: 1,499. Music program established 1886.

Pacific Lutheran University
Tacoma, Washington

Independent, coed. Suburban campus. Total enrollment: 3,680. Music program established 1891.
Degrees Bachelor of Music in the area of performance; Bachelor of Musical Arts in the area of music combined with an outside field; Bachelor of Music Education in the areas of choral music, band, orchestra. Majors and concentrations: composition, music education, performance. Program accredited by NASM.
Enrollment 164 total; all undergraduate.
Music Student Profile 60% females, 40% males, 8% minorities, 5% international.
Music Faculty 15 undergraduate (full-time), 35 undergraduate (part-time). 60% of full-time faculty have terminal degrees. Graduate students do not teach undergraduate courses. Undergraduate student–faculty ratio: 15:1.
Student Life Student groups/activities include Music Educators National Conference, American Choral Directors Association, Mu Phi Epsilon.
Expenses for 2005–2006 Application fee: $40. Comprehensive fee: $28,805 includes full-time tuition ($22,040) and college room and board ($6765). College room only: $3330. Full-time tuition varies according to course load. Room and board charges vary according to board plan and housing facility. Special program-related fees: $100–$650 per year for ensemble tours (domestic), $180–$360 per semester for private lessons.
Financial Aid Program-specific awards: 100–120 music scholarships for incoming freshmen demonstrating need and talent ($1000–$5000), 150 music scholarships for continuing program students ($1000–$5000).
Application Procedures Students admitted directly into the professional program freshman year. Deadline for freshmen and transfers: continuous. Required: essay, high school transcript, college transcript(s) for transfer students, 2 letters of recommendation, SAT I or ACT test scores, minimum 2.5 high school GPA, audition for scholarship consideration. Auditions held once on campus; recorded music is permissible as a substitute for live auditions and videotaped performances are permissible as a substitute for live auditions.
Web Site http://www.plu.edu/
Undergraduate Contact Nita Muir, Administrative Assistant, Department of Music, Pacific Lutheran University, Tacoma, Washington 98447; 253-535-7603, fax: 253-535-8669.

Pacific Union College
Angwin, California

Independent Seventh-day Adventist, coed. Rural campus. Total enrollment: 1,518. Music program established 1967.
Degrees Bachelor of Music in the areas of music education, performance. Majors and concentrations: music education, piano/organ, stringed instruments, voice, wind and percussion instruments. Program accredited by NASM.
Enrollment 38 total; 10 undergraduate, 28 nonprofessional degree.
Music Student Profile 60% females, 40% males, 80% minorities, 10% international.
Music Faculty 6 undergraduate (full-time), 4 undergraduate (part-time). 67% of full-time faculty have terminal degrees. Graduate students do not teach undergraduate courses. Undergraduate student–faculty ratio: 1:1.
Student Life Student groups/activities include California Music Educators Association, Pi Kappa Lambda.
Expenses for 2005–2006 Application fee: $30. Comprehensive fee: $24,555 includes full-time tuition ($18,990), mandatory fees

($135), and college room and board ($5430). College room only: $3312. Full-time tuition and fees vary according to course load.
Financial Aid Program-specific awards: 6 Proficiency in Performance Scholarships for ensemble participants ($1000), 6 Loye Scholarships for organists ($1000–$3000), 1–2 Mayes Music Ministry Scholarships for organ/voice majors ($500–$1000), 1–2 Coltrin Lewis Scholarships for musicians ($500–$1000), 1–2 Edward Mackett Scholarships for brass musicians ($500–$1000).
Application Procedures Students admitted directly into the professional program freshman year. Deadline for freshmen and transfers: continuous. Required: high school transcript, college transcript(s) for transfer students, 2 letters of recommendation, audition, SAT I or ACT test scores, minimum 2.3 high school GPA. Recommended: video. Auditions held 3 times on campus; recorded music is permissible as a substitute for live auditions when distance is prohibitive and videotaped performances are permissible as a substitute for live auditions when distance is prohibitive.
Web Site http://www.puc.edu
Undergraduate Contact Mr. Sean Kootsey, Admissions Director, Enrollment Services, Pacific Union College, 1 Angwin Avenue, Angwin, California 94508; 707-965-6425, fax: 707-965-6432, e-mail address: skootsey@puc.edu

Palm Beach Atlantic University
West Palm Beach, Florida

Independent nondenominational, coed. Urban campus. Total enrollment: 3,171. Music program established 1994.
Degrees Bachelor of Music in the areas of performance, church music, music education, music composition. Majors and concentrations: church music, composition, instrumental performance, keyboard performance, music education, voice performance. Program accredited by NASM.
Enrollment 81 total; 55 undergraduate, 26 nonprofessional degree.
Music Student Profile 67% females, 33% males, 14% minorities, 1% international.
Music Faculty 10 undergraduate (full-time), 22 undergraduate (part-time). 50% of full-time faculty have terminal degrees. Graduate students do not teach undergraduate courses. Undergraduate student–faculty ratio: 5:1.
Student Life Student groups/activities include Collegiate Music Educators National Conference, National Association of Teachers of Singing (local chapter).
Expenses for 2005–2006 Application fee: $25. Comprehensive fee: $24,030 includes full-time tuition ($17,130), mandatory fees ($220), and college room and board ($6680). College room only: $3350. Full-time tuition and fees vary according to course load, degree level, program, and reciprocity agreements. Room and board charges vary according to board plan and housing facility. Special program-related fees: $75–$265 per course for applied fees.
Financial Aid Program-specific awards: 50–80 music scholarships for program majors ($2000–$3000), 1 Brown Vargas Scholarship for music theater students ($400), 1 Arrigo Dodge Piano Scholarship for piano students ($2000).
Application Procedures Students admitted directly into the professional program freshman year. Deadline for freshmen and transfers: continuous. Required: essay, high school transcript, college transcript(s) for transfer students, minimum 2.0 high school GPA, 2 letters of recommendation, audition, SAT I or ACT test scores (minimum combined SAT I score of 970). Recommended: minimum 3.0 high school GPA, interview, video. Auditions held continuously on campus; videotaped performances are permissible as a substitute for live auditions when distance is prohibitive.
Web Site http://www.pba.edu
Undergraduate Contact Mr. Buckley A. James, Dean, Admissions Department, Palm Beach Atlantic University, PO Box 24708, West Palm Beach, Florida 33416; 800-238-3998, fax: 561-803-2115, e-mail address: admit@pba.edu

Peabody Conservatory of Music
See The Johns Hopkins University

The Pennsylvania State University University Park Campus

University Park, Pennsylvania

State-related, coed. Small town campus. Total enrollment: 40,709. Music program established 1929.

Degrees Bachelor of Music in the areas of performance, composition; Bachelor of Musical Arts in the area of performance; Bachelor of Science in the area of music education. Majors and concentrations: classical music, composition, music education, music history, music theory, piano/organ, stringed instruments, voice, wind and percussion instruments. Graduate degrees offered: Master of Arts in the areas of theory and history (integrative), theory, musicology; Master of Music in the areas of performance, conducting, piano pedagogy and performance, voice pedagogy and performance, composition/theory; Master of Music Education. Doctor of Philosophy in the area of music education. Program accredited by NASM.

Enrollment 330 total; 255 undergraduate, 75 graduate.

Music Faculty 45 total (full-time), 10 total (part-time). 45% of full-time faculty have terminal degrees. Graduate students teach a few undergraduate courses. Undergraduate student–faculty ratio: 6:1.

Expenses for 2005–2006 Application fee: $50. State resident tuition: $11,024 full-time. Nonresident tuition: $21,260 full-time. Mandatory fees: $484 full-time. College room and board: $6530. College room only: $3430. Special program-related fees: $150–$200 per semester for applied music lesson fee.

Financial Aid Program-specific awards: 107 music scholarships for program majors ($2000).

Application Procedures Students admitted directly into the professional program freshman year. Deadline for freshmen: November 30; transfers: June 1. Notification date for freshmen and transfers: continuous. Required: high school transcript, college transcript(s) for transfer students, minimum 2.0 high school GPA, audition, SAT I or ACT test scores. Recommended: interview. Auditions held 5 times on campus; recorded music is permissible as a substitute for live auditions when distance is prohibitive and videotaped performances are permissible as a substitute for live auditions when distance is prohibitive.

Web Site http://www.music.psu.edu/

Undergraduate Contact Ms. Irene Kohute, Staff Assistant V, School of Music, The Pennsylvania State University University Park Campus, 233 Music Building, University Park, Pennsylvania 16802-1503; 814-863-0418, fax: 814-865-6785, e-mail address: music-ug-adm@psu.edu

Graduate Contact Ms. Lisa Stamm, Graduate Admissions Secretary, School of Music, The Pennsylvania State University University Park Campus, 233 Music Building, University Park, Pennsylvania 16802; 814-865-1052, fax: 814-865-6785, e-mail address: music-gr-adm@psu.edu

Philadelphia Biblical University

Langhorne, Pennsylvania

Independent nondenominational, coed. Suburban campus. Total enrollment: 1,439. Music program established 1969.

Degrees Bachelor of Music in the areas of performance, music education, church music, composition. Majors and concentrations: church music, composition, guitar, music education, piano/organ, stringed instruments, voice, wind and percussion instruments. Program accredited by NASM.

Enrollment 64 total; all undergraduate.

Music Student Profile 59% females, 41% males, 15% minorities, 13% international.

Music Faculty 7 undergraduate (full-time), 24 undergraduate (part-time). 86% of full-time faculty have terminal degrees. Graduate students do not teach undergraduate courses. Undergraduate student–faculty ratio: 9:1.

Student Life Student groups/activities include Music Educators National Conference, American Choral Directors Association, Pennsylvania Music Teachers Association.

Expenses for 2006–2007 Application fee: $25. Comprehensive fee: $22,425 includes full-time tuition ($15,555), mandatory fees

($320), and college room and board ($6550). College room only: $3400. Special program-related fees: $20–$30 for junior/senior recital fees, $25 per credit for instrumental rental fee for class brass, strings, woodwinds, percussion , $270 per credit for summer private lessons.

Financial Aid Program-specific awards: 63 music scholarships for freshmen ($600–$3000).

Application Procedures Students admitted directly into the professional program freshman year. Deadline for freshmen and transfers: continuous. Required: high school transcript, college transcript(s) for transfer students, minimum 2.0 high school GPA, 3 letters of recommendation, interview, audition, SAT I or ACT test scores (minimum combined SAT I score of 920, minimum composite ACT score of 19). Auditions held 5 times on campus; recorded music is permissible as a substitute for live auditions when distance is prohibitive (beyond 300-mile radius) and videotaped performances are permissible as a substitute for live auditions when distance is prohibitive (beyond 300-mile radius).

Web Site http://www.pbu.edu

Undergraduate Contact Dr. Paul Isensee, Dean, School of Music and Performing Arts, Philadelphia Biblical University, 200 Manor Avenue, Langhorne, Pennsylvania 19047; 215-702-4322, fax: 215-702-4342, e-mail address: pisensee@pbu.edu

Pittsburg State University

Pittsburg, Kansas

State-supported, coed. Small town campus. Total enrollment: 6,628. Music program established 1914.

Degrees Bachelor of Music in the areas of classical, music performance; Bachelor of Music Education in the area of instrumental and vocal music education (grades K-12). Majors and concentrations: music education, piano/organ, stringed instruments, voice, wind and percussion instruments. Graduate degrees offered: Master of Music in the areas of performance, vocal music education, instrumental music education, instrumental conducting, choral conducting. Program accredited by NASM, NCATE.

Enrollment 88 total; 80 undergraduate, 8 graduate.

Music Student Profile 55% females, 45% males, 10% minorities, 10% international.

Music Faculty 15 total (full-time), 5 total (part-time). 75% of full-time faculty have terminal degrees. Graduate students do not teach undergraduate courses. Undergraduate student–faculty ratio: 6:1.

Student Life Student groups/activities include Music Educators National Conference Student Chapter, International Association for Jazz Education, Phi Mu Alpha.

Expenses for 2005–2006 Application fee: $30. State resident tuition: $2850 full-time. Nonresident tuition: $9732 full-time. Mandatory fees: $712 full-time. College room and board: $4550. Room and board charges vary according to board plan and housing facility.

Financial Aid Program-specific awards: 100 music scholarships for program majors and minors ($300–$2000).

Application Procedures Students admitted directly into the professional program freshman year. Deadline for freshmen and transfers: continuous. Required: high school transcript, college transcript(s) for transfer students, minimum 2.0 high school GPA, audition. Recommended: SAT I or ACT test scores. Auditions held continuously on campus; recorded music is permissible as a substitute for live auditions when distance is prohibitive and videotaped performances are permissible as a substitute for live auditions when distance is prohibitive.

Web Site http://www.pittstate.edu/music/

Undergraduate Contact Ms. Ange Peterson, Director, Admission Office, Pittsburg State University, Horace Mann Building, Room 107, 1701 South Broadway, Pittsburg, Kansas 66762; 620-235-4251, fax: 620-235-6003, e-mail address: psuadmit@pittstate.edu

Graduate Contact Dr. Russell Jones, Director, Graduate Studies in Music, Department of Music, Pittsburg State University, 1701 South Broadway, Pittsburg, Kansas 66762; 620-235-4466, fax: 620-235-4468, e-mail address: rjones@pittstate.edu

Portland State University

Portland, Oregon

State-supported, coed. Urban campus. Total enrollment: 24,120. Music program established 1954.

Potter College of Arts, Humanities, and Social Sciences

See Western Kentucky University

Prairie View A&M University

Prairie View, Texas

State-supported, coed. Small town campus. Total enrollment: 7,912. Music program established 1920.

Degrees Bachelor of Music in the areas of applied music, music education. Majors and concentrations: music, music education, piano, voice, wind and percussion instruments.

Enrollment 91 total; 82 undergraduate, 9 nonprofessional degree.

Music Student Profile 50% females, 50% males, 99% minorities.

Music Faculty 12 undergraduate (full-time), 7 undergraduate (part-time). 50% of full-time faculty have terminal degrees. Graduate students do not teach undergraduate courses. Undergraduate student–faculty ratio: 10:1.

Student Life Student groups/activities include Music Educators National Conference Student Chapter, Kappa Kappa Psi, Tau Beta Sigma.

Expenses for 2005–2006 Application fee: $25. State resident tuition: $1500 full-time. Nonresident tuition: $9780 full-time. Mandatory fees: $3406 full-time. Full-time tuition and fees vary according to course load and degree level. College room and board: $6204. Room and board charges vary according to board plan and housing facility. Special program-related fees: $10 per semester for lab fees, $12 per semester for applied music fees.

Financial Aid Program-specific awards: 3 University Talent Scholarships for program majors ($1000–$2500), 1 Bobby J. Baldwin Scholarship for piano majors ($500–$3000), 100 marching band scholarships ($200–$3000), 5 choir scholarships for University Chorale participants ($100–$500).

Application Procedures Students admitted directly into the professional program freshman year. Deadline for freshmen and transfers: June 1. Notification date for freshmen and transfers: August 1. Required: high school transcript, college transcript(s) for transfer students, minimum 2.0 high school GPA, letter of recommendation, interview, audition, SAT I or ACT test scores. Auditions held 4 times on campus and off campus in various cities in Texas including Dallas, Houston, Fort Worth, San Antonio; recorded music is permissible as a substitute for live auditions when distance is prohibitive and videotaped performances are permissible as a substitute for live auditions when distance is prohibitive.

Undergraduate Contact Director of Admissions, Prairie View A&M University, PO Box 3089, Prairie View, Texas 77446; 936-857-2618.

Purchase College, State University of New York

Purchase, New York

State-supported, coed. Small town campus. Total enrollment: 3,826.

Degrees Bachelor of Music in the areas of performance, composition. Majors and concentrations: bass, cello, classical guitar, classical music, composition, historical performance, horn, jazz, opera, percussion, piano/organ, production, stringed instruments, studio composition, trombone, trumpet, tuba, viola, violin, voice, wind instruments. Graduate degrees offered: Master of Music in the areas of performance, composition. Program accredited by NASM.

Enrollment 398 total; 314 undergraduate, 84 graduate.

Music Student Profile 32% females, 68% males, 15% minorities, 6% international.

Music Faculty 75 total. 90% of full-time faculty have terminal degrees. Graduate students do not teach undergraduate courses. Undergraduate student–faculty ratio: 10:1.

Student Life Student groups/activities include Ballet and Arts in Education performances, performances in the community.

Expenses for 2006–2007 Application fee: $40. State resident tuition: $4350 full-time. Nonresident tuition: $10,610 full-time. Mandatory fees: $1258 full-time. College room and board: $8466. College room only: $5378. Special program-related fees: $50 for audition, $1900 per year for applied music fees.

Financial Aid Program-specific awards: 130 music scholarships/awards ($2500).

Application Procedures Students admitted directly into the professional program freshman year. Deadline for freshmen and transfers: June 1. Notification date for freshmen and transfers: July 1. Required: high school transcript, college transcript(s) for transfer students, audition, SAT I or ACT test scores, minimum TOEFL score of 550 for international applicants, portfolio for composition majors. Recommended: essay, minimum 3.0 high school GPA, 2 letters of recommendation, interview. Auditions held 4 times on campus; recorded music is permissible as a substitute for live auditions when distance is prohibitive or in special circumstances and videotaped performances are permissible as a substitute for live auditions when distance is prohibitive or in special circumstances. Portfolio reviews held 4 times on campus.

Web Site http://www.purchase.edu/music

Undergraduate Contact James Gibson, Admissions Counselor, Conservatory of Theatre Arts and Film, Purchase College, State University of New York, 735 Anderson Hill Road, Purchase, New York 10577-1400; 914-251-6305, fax: 914-251-6314.

Graduate Contact Ms. Sabrina Johnson, Counselor, Conservatory of Music, Purchase College, State University of New York, 735 Anderson Hill Road, Purchase, New York 10577-1400; 914-251-6479, fax: 914-251-6739.

More About the College

The Conservatory of Music at Purchase College offers a comprehensive musical education at both the undergraduate and graduate levels for gifted students who wish to pursue the art of music at a professional level. All students who enter the Conservatory of Music have been admitted as the result of an audition process. Purchase is an intimate community of approximately 425 students studying with distinguished and dedicated faculty members who are as committed to their teaching as they are to their own careers as performers, composers, and scholars.

The Conservatory of Music offers the following degrees and programs: Bachelor of Music, Performer's Certificate, Master of Music, and the Artist's Diploma. Areas of study include performance: brass (trumpet, horn, trombone, tuba), classical guitar, harp, percussion, piano (also organ/harpsichord), strings (violin, viola, cello, bass), voice, and woodwinds (flute, oboe, clarinet, bassoon); jazz studies; composition; studio composition; and studio production.

The core undergraduate curriculum for the Bachelor of Music degree is similar throughout the four years for all areas of study: students take private or small-group study; ensemble; a series of courses in music theory, history, and musicianship; and courses specific to their primary area of study. All students perform here—early, classical, contemporary, jazz, electro-acoustic, and commercial—and the opportunities to perform are numerous.

The 30-credit general education program in the liberal arts and sciences supports the Conservatory curriculum and provides a broad education that enhances the musical education and better prepares the students to function successfully as thoughtful, responsible, and contributive members to society.

The Master of Music degree is an intensive program designed to provide advanced training for students seeking professional careers in music. Other training opportunities include the one- or two-year Performer's Certificate postbaccalaureate program and the Artist's Diploma postgraduate program.

The Conservatory of Music provides the serious, developing musician an educational experience that encourages excellence within the context of a nurturing and supportive learning environment. Instruction in the classroom and studio is significantly enhanced by a regular series of concerts, including faculty and guest artist recitals, master classes, workshops and special events. Among those who have offered their musical gifts and special insights to the Conservatory of Music community are Emanuel Ax, Colorado Quartet, Misha Dichter, Emerson Quartet, Vladimir Feltsman, Guarneri Quartet, Jimmy Heath, Freddie Hubbard, Marilyn Horne, Juilliard Quartet, Jennifer Larmore, Midori, New Millenium Ensemble, Charles Niedich, Garrick Ohlssohn, Orpheus, Frederic Rzewski, Clark Terry, Tokyo Quartet, and Yo-Yo Ma.

The Conservatory of Music at Purchase College is one of the few conservatories in the nation producing fully mounted opera productions predominantly for undergraduates. The jazz curriculum is performance-driven and includes both large and small ensemble work. The majority of the studio production and composition students work professionally while still at Purchase because of the contacts and opportunities offered to them by the faculty. The other major areas of study also provide similar intensive training and resources in support of professional development.

Aaron Copland School of Music
Queens College of the City University of New York
Flushing, New York

State and locally supported, coed. Urban campus. Total enrollment: 17,638. Music program established 1937.
Degrees Bachelor of Music in the area of performance. Majors and concentrations: brass, composition, piano/organ, stringed instruments, voice, wind and percussion instruments. Graduate degrees offered: Master of Arts in the areas of performance, composition, musicology, music theory, jazz performance, jazz composition, conducting; Master of Science in the area of music education.
Enrollment 350 total; 250 undergraduate, 100 graduate.
Music Student Profile 50% females, 50% males, 50% minorities, 35% international.
Music Faculty 26 total (full-time), 44 total (part-time). 90% of full-time faculty have terminal degrees. Graduate students teach a few undergraduate courses. Undergraduate student–faculty ratio: 15:1.
Student Life Student groups/activities include Music Educators National Conference, Music Students Association.
Expenses for 2006–2007 Application fee: $65. State resident tuition: $4000 full-time. Nonresident tuition: $10,800 full-time. Mandatory fees: $377 full-time.
Financial Aid Program-specific awards: 1–3 Boris Schwarz Scholarships for string majors ($250–$500), 2 Zatkin Scholarships-Opera Awards for voice majors ($250–$500), 1 Edward Downes Scholarship for voice majors ($250–$500), 25 departmental scholarships for those demonstrating talent/financial need ($200–$1000), 2 Castellini Awards for string majors ($1000), 2 Rosenfeld Awards for string majors ($1000), 1–2 Novack Scholarships for theory students ($500–$1000), 5–10 LeFrak Scholarships for performance majors ($200–$1000).
Application Procedures Students admitted directly into the professional program freshman year. Deadline for freshmen and transfers: March 15. Notification date for freshmen and transfers: continuous. Required: essay, high school transcript, college transcript(s) for transfer students, minimum 3.0 high school GPA, 3 letters of recommendation, audition. Recommended: portfolio, SAT I or ACT test scores. Auditions held twice on campus; recorded music is permissible as a substitute for live auditions when distance is prohibitive and videotaped performances are permissible as a substitute for live auditions when distance is prohibitive. Portfolio reviews held twice on campus.
Web Site http://www.qc.edu
Undergraduate Contact Dr. Jonathan Irving, Special Assistant to the Director, Aaron Copland School of Music, Queens College of the

City University of New York, 65-30 Kissena Boulevard, Flushing, New York 11367; 718-997-3802, fax: 718-997-3849, e-mail address: jonathan_irving@qc.edu
Graduate Contact Prof. William Rothstein, Graduate Advisor, Aaron Copland School of Music, Queens College of the City University of New York, 65-30 Kissena Boulevard, Flushing, New York 11367; 718-997-3863, fax: 817-997-3849, e-mail address: wrothste@qcunix1.qc.edu

Queens University of Charlotte
Charlotte, North Carolina

Independent Presbyterian, coed. Suburban campus. Total enrollment: 2,113. Music program established 1857.
Degrees Bachelor of Music in the areas of music therapy, applied music performance. Majors and concentrations: guitar, harp, music therapy, piano/organ, stringed instruments, voice, wind and percussion instruments. Cross-registration with 13 member colleges of the Charlotte Area Educational Consortium. Program accredited by NASM, AMTA.
Enrollment 41 total; 28 undergraduate, 13 nonprofessional degree.
Music Student Profile 97% females, 3% males, 3% minorities.
Music Faculty 6 undergraduate (full-time), 16 undergraduate (part-time). 66% of full-time faculty have terminal degrees. Graduate students do not teach undergraduate courses. Undergraduate student–faculty ratio: 4:1.
Student Life Student groups/activities include Music Therapy Club, Drama Club.
Expenses for 2006–2007 Application fee: $40. Comprehensive fee: $26,430 includes full-time tuition ($19,450) and college room and board ($6980). Special program-related fees: $25 per credit hour for accompanist fee, $100 per semester credit hour for private music instruction.
Financial Aid Program-specific awards: music major awards for program majors ($500–$3000), music minor awards for program minors ($500–$1000), 1–3 Stegner Music Scholarships for music majors ($500–$3000), 1 Lammers Music Scholarship for music majors ($5000), 1 Kennedy Scholarship for music majors ($500), 1–2 O'Quinn Scholarships for music majors ($2500).
Application Procedures Students admitted directly into the professional program freshman year. Deadline for freshmen and transfers: continuous. Required: essay, high school transcript, college transcript(s) for transfer students, minimum 2.0 high school GPA, 2 letters of recommendation, interview, audition, SAT I or ACT test scores (minimum combined SAT I score of 750). Recommended: portfolio. Auditions held 3 times and by appointment on campus; videotaped performances are permissible as a substitute for live auditions if student has already visited the campus or when distance is prohibitive. Portfolio reviews held twice a year (minimum) on campus.
Web Site http://www.queens.edu
Undergraduate Contact Mr. Brian Ralph, Vice President of Enrollment Management, CAS Admissions, Queens University of Charlotte, 1900 Selwyn Avenue, Charlotte, North Carolina 28274; 800-849-0202, fax: 704-337-2503, e-mail address: ralphb@queens.edu

Radford University
Radford, Virginia

State-supported, coed. Small town campus. Total enrollment: 9,552.
Degrees Bachelor of Music. Majors and concentrations: music business, music education, music therapy. Graduate degrees offered: Master of Science in the area of music therapy. Program accredited by NASM.
Enrollment 109 total; 90 undergraduate, 19 graduate.
Music Student Profile 51% females, 49% males, 11% minorities, 4% international.
Music Faculty 16 total (full-time), 12 total (part-time). 44% of full-time faculty have terminal degrees. Graduate students teach a few undergraduate courses. Undergraduate student–faculty ratio: 3:1.

Radford University (continued)

Student Life Student groups/activities include Music Therapy Club, Music Educators National Conference Student Chapter, Arts and Entertainment Association. Special housing available for music students.

Expenses for 2005–2006 Application fee: $35. State resident tuition: $3235 full-time. Nonresident tuition: $10,473 full-time. Mandatory fees: $1895 full-time. College room and board: $6120. College room only: $3300. Room and board charges vary according to board plan and housing facility.

Financial Aid Program-specific awards: 2–4 Arts Society Awards for freshmen ($4000), 3 Ingram-Lee Awards for program majors ($1200), 1 Presser Award for seniors ($4000), 1 May Award for program majors ($850), 1 Vickers Award for program majors ($1000), 1 Grabeal Award for program majors ($750), 1 Jason Rooker Memorial Award for music therapy majors ($500), 1 Bondurant Award for music business majors ($500).

Application Procedures Students apply for admission into the professional program by freshman year. Deadline for freshmen: April 1; transfers: June 1. Notification date for freshmen and transfers: continuous. Required: high school transcript, college transcript(s) for transfer students, minimum 2.0 high school GPA, audition, SAT I or ACT test scores. Recommended: essay, minimum 3.0 high school GPA. Auditions held continuously by appointment on campus; recorded music is permissible as a substitute for live auditions if unedited and videotaped performances are permissible as a substitute for live auditions if unedited.

Web Site http://www.radford.edu/~musc-web/

Undergraduate Contact Mr. David Kraus, Director, Office of Admissions, Radford University, PO Box 6903, Radford, Virginia 24142; 540-831-5371, fax: 540-831-5138, e-mail address: dwkraus@radford.edu

Graduate Contact Ms. Sharon Gunter, Admissions Coordinator, College of Graduate and Extended Education, Radford University, PO Box 6928, Radford, Virginia 24142; 540-831-5724, e-mail address: gradcoll@radford.edu

Rhode Island College

Providence, Rhode Island

State-supported, coed. Suburban campus. Total enrollment: 8,871. Music program established 1967.

Shepherd School of Music
Rice University

Houston, Texas

Independent, coed. Urban campus. Total enrollment: 5,258. Music program established 1974.

Degrees Bachelor of Music in the areas of performance, music theory, composition, musicology. Majors and concentrations: composition, music, music history, music theory, piano/organ, stringed instruments, voice, wind and percussion instruments. Graduate degrees offered: Master of Music in the areas of performance, music theory, composition, musicology, conducting. Doctor of Musical Arts in the areas of performance, composition.

Enrollment 300 total; 120 undergraduate, 180 graduate.

Music Student Profile 54% females, 46% males, 5% minorities, 20% international.

Music Faculty 32 total (full-time), 23 total (part-time). 99% of full-time faculty have terminal degrees. Graduate students teach a few undergraduate courses. Undergraduate student–faculty ratio: 5:1.

Student Life Student groups/activities include Symphony Orchestra, Chamber Ensembles, Opera.

Expenses for 2005–2006 Application fee: $50. Comprehensive fee: $32,726 includes full-time tuition ($23,310), mandatory fees ($436), and college room and board ($8980). College room only: $5700. Full-time tuition and fees vary according to student level. Room and board charges vary according to board plan.

Financial Aid Program-specific awards: merit awards for program majors ($1000).

Application Procedures Students admitted directly into the professional program freshman year. Deadline for freshmen: January 2; transfers: March 15. Notification date for freshmen: April 1; transfers: May 15. Required: essay, high school transcript, college transcript(s) for transfer students, 2 letters of recommendation, interview, audition, portfolio, SAT I or ACT test scores, two SAT II scores, portfolio for composition students, ACT (writing component). Recommended: minimum 3.0 high school GPA. Auditions held on campus; recorded music is permissible as a substitute for live auditions if a live audition is impossible and videotaped performances are permissible as a substitute for live auditions if a live audition is impossible. Portfolio reviews held on campus.

Web Site http://www.rice.edu/music

Undergraduate Contact Mr. Matthew Loden, Director of Music Admissions, Shepherd School of Music, Rice University, PO Box 1892, Houston, Texas 77251; 713-348-3032, fax: 713-348-5317, e-mail address: mloden@rice.edu

Graduate Contact Ms. Suzanne Taylor, Admissions Assistant, Shepherd School of Music, Rice University, PO Box 1892, Houston, Texas 77251; 713-348-3578, fax: 713-348-5317, e-mail address: sctaylor@rice.edu

Rider University

See Westminster Choir College of Rider University

Chicago College of Performing Arts - The Music Conservatory
Roosevelt University

Chicago, Illinois

Independent, coed. Urban campus. Total enrollment: 7,234. Music program established 1867.

Degrees Bachelor of Music in the areas of jazz performance, classical performance, music education, composition. Majors and concentrations: composition, jazz performance, music education, stringed instruments, voice, wind and percussion instruments. Graduate degrees offered: Master of Music in the areas of classical performance, theory, composition, musicology, orchestral studies. Cross-registration with School of the Art Institute of Chicago. Program accredited by NASM.

Enrollment 382 total; 268 undergraduate, 100 graduate, 14 nonprofessional degree.

Music Student Profile 50% females, 50% males, 47% minorities, 30% international.

Music Faculty 25 total (full-time), 70 total (part-time). 52% of full-time faculty have terminal degrees. Graduate students do not teach undergraduate courses. Undergraduate student–faculty ratio: 11:1.

Student Life Student groups/activities include Music Educators National Conference, Mu Phi Epsilon (music honorary fraternity).

Expenses for 2005–2006 Application fee: $25. Comprehensive fee: $22,420 includes full-time tuition ($14,180), mandatory fees ($250), and college room and board ($7990). College room only: $5800. Full-time tuition and fees vary according to course load and program. Room and board charges vary according to board plan, housing facility, and location.

Financial Aid Program-specific awards: 200 music scholarships for music majors ($5000).

Application Procedures Students admitted directly into the professional program freshman year. Deadline for freshmen and transfers: January 15. Notification date for freshmen and transfers: April 1. Required: essay, high school transcript, college transcript(s) for transfer students, minimum 2.0 high school GPA, audition, SAT I or ACT test scores (minimum combined SAT I score of 1000, minimum composite ACT score of 20), interview (for music education). Recommended: minimum 3.0 high school GPA, letter of recommendation. Auditions held 10 times on campus; recorded music is permissible as a substitute for live auditions when distance is prohibitive and videotaped performances are permissible as a substitute for live auditions when distance is prohibitive.

Web Site http://ccpa.roosevelt.edu
Undergraduate Contact Amy White, Assistant Dean for Enrollment and Student Services, Chicago College of Performing Arts, Room 918, Roosevelt University, 430 South Michigan Avenue, Chicago, Illinois 60605; 312-341-3789, fax: 312-341-6358, e-mail address: music@roosevelt.edu

Graduate Contact Amy White, Assistant Dean for Enrollment and Student Services, Chicago College of Performing Arts, Room 918, Roosevelt University, 430 South Michigan Avenue, Chicago, Illinois 60605; 312-341-3789, fax: 312-341-6358, e-mail address: music@roosevelt.edu

More About the Conservatory

The Music Conservatory at Roosevelt University's Chicago College of Performing Arts provides professional training and education within the context of a vibrant university in a world-class city. It is a place where musical genres from classical to jazz are valued, where the energies of one discipline spill over to enliven other artistic endeavors, where preparing to be a teacher is as important as preparing to be a performer or scholar, and where students come to enhance their unique talents and polish them to perfection.

The Music Conservatory is well situated on the top floors of the historic landmark Auditorium Building, designed by world-famous architects Dankmar Adler and Louis Sullivan. The building includes the 3,800-seat Auditorium Theatre, renowned for its beauty and exquisite acoustics. Located on the corner of Michigan Avenue and Congress Parkway, this edifice is now an integral part of the "educational corridor" of more than 50,000 students enrolled in various institutions in the famous downtown Loop. Across the street are the Pritzker Music Pavilion of Millennium Park, the magnificent Buckingham Fountain, and the sparkling beauty of Lake Michigan. The new state-of-the-art residence hall, the University Center of Chicago, is located just one block away on the corner of State Street and Congress Parkway.

Within walking distance are many of the city's major cultural institutions, including Symphony Center, home of the Chicago Symphony Orchestra; the Lyric Opera; the Jazz Showcase; the Goodman, Chicago, Oriental, and Cadillac theaters; the Art Institute; the Field Museum of Natural History; and the "Magnificent Mile" of shops and galleries. This ideal location provides opportunities for learning from some of the most accomplished musicians in the world, from principals in the Chicago Symphony to Grammy-nominated jazz artists.

Faculty *Violin:* Shmuel Ashkenasi (First Violin, Vermeer Quartet); Robert Chen (Co-Concertmaster, Chicago Symphony); Nathan Cole (Chicago Symphony); Cyrus Forough; Vadim Gluzman (Concert Artist); Robert Hanford (Concertmaster, Lyric Opera of Chicago); Stefan Hersh (Former Principal Second Violin, Minnesota Orchestra/Former violinist, Chicago String Quartet); Yang Liu (Concert Artist); Laura Park Chen (Lyric Opera of Chicago); *Viola:* Li-Kuo Chang (Chicago Symphony); Roger Chase (Former Guest Principal, Berlin Philharmonic); Lawrence Neuman (Chicago Symphony); *Cello:* Tanya Carey (Former Assistant Principal, Milwaukee Symphony); Barbara Haffner (Assistant Principal, Lyric Opera of Chicago); Richard Hirschl (Chicago Symphony); Ken Olsen (Chicago Symphony); John Sharp (Principal, Chicago Symphony); *Bass:* Michael Hovnanian (Chicago Symphony); Stephen Lester (Chicago Symphony); *Harp:* Sarah Bullen (Principal, Chicago Symphony); *Flute:* Dionne Hansen-Jackson (Lyric Opera of Chicago); Donald Peck (former Principal, Chicago Symphony); *Oboe/English Horn:* Eugene Izotov (Principal, Chicago Symphony); Peggy Michel (Music of the Baroque); Grover Schiltz (English Horn, Chicago Symphony); *Clarinet:* Gregory Smith (Chicago Symphony); Carolee Smith; John Bruce Yeh (Chicago Symphony); *Bassoon:* Dennis Michel (Chicago Symphony); Theodore Soluri (Milwaukee Symphony); *Saxophone:* Jan Berry; *Horn:* Dale Clevenger (Principal, Chicago Symphony); Alice Render; *Trumpet:* Tage Larsen (Chicago Symphony); Channing Philbrick (Lyric Opera of

Chicago); Mark Ridenour (Assistant Principal, Chicago Symphony); *Trombone:* Jay Friedman (Principal, Chicago Symphony); *Tuba:* Gene Pokorny, masterclasses (Principal, Chicago Symphony); Charles Schuchat (Former Principal, Israel Philharmonic); *Percussion:* Edward Harrison (Principal Timpanist, Lyric Opera of Chicago); Vadim Karpinos (Chicago Symphony); *Orchestral Seminar:* Henry Fogel (President, American Symphony Orchestra League); *Piano:* Emilio del Rosario; Ani Gogova; Kuang-Hao Huang; Ludmila Lazar; Meng-Chieh Liu; Solomon Mikowsky; Jorge Federico Osorio; Graham Scott; *Guitar:* Denis Azabagic; Paul Henry; Pamela Kimmel; *Voice:* Michael Best, Mark Crayton; Christine Flasch; Judith Haddon; David Holloway; Jonita Lattimore; Elizabeth Norman; Samuel Ramey; Roger Scanlan; Richard Stilwell; Tracy Watson; Dana Brown, (vocal coach); Giulio Favario, (vocal coach); Stephen Hargreaves (vocal coach); *Music Education:* Charles Groeling; Mary Jo Ferneding; Cheryl Frazes Hill; Mark Taylor; *Composition:* Stacy Garrop; Kyong-Mee Choi; *Jazz Studies:* Neal Alger, guitar; Jackie Allen, voice; Rob Amster, bass; Steve Berry, trombone; John Blane, trombone; Linda Clifford, voice; Jo Ann Daugherty, piano; Carey Deadman, trumpet; Jerry DiMuzio, saxophone; Andy Distel, voice; Jim Gailloreto, saxophone; Tom Garling, trombone; Phil Gratteau, drum set; Roger Harris, piano; Laurence Hobgood, piano; Art Hoyle, trumpet; Roger Ingram, trumpet; Henry Johnson, guitar; Scott Mason, bass; John McLean, guitar; Paul Mertens, saxophone; Michael Molloy, voice; Jeff Morrow, voice; Dave Onderdonk, guitar; Rob Parton, trumpet; Judy Roberts, voice; Marlene Rosenberg, bass; Ron Ruvio, trumpet; Fred Simon, piano; Mike Smith, saxophone; Colleen Timler, voice; Jim Trompeter, piano; Paul Wertico, drum set; and Brad Wheeler, saxophone.

Student Performance Opportunities There are more than 200 concerts, recitals, operas, and theater performances presented each year. Ensembles include Symphony Orchestra, Chamber Orchestra, Conservatory Chorus, Wind Ensemble, Women's Chorus, Opera, Jazz Ensembles, Chamber Music, New Music Ensemble, Guitar Ensemble, and Collegium Musicum.

Programs and Additional Information The Bachelor of Music degree is offered in performance (including orchestral studies), composition, jazz studies, and music education. The Master of Music degree is offered in performance (including orchestral studies), composition, music theory, and musicology. A Performance Diploma is available in performance (classical), including a joint program in opera with the Chicago Opera Theater, and orchestral studies.

There is a diverse student body from forty states and twenty-three other countries. Roosevelt University offers exclusive ESL preparation. The Music Scholarship program is open to both U.S. and international applicants.

Rowan University
Glassboro, New Jersey

State-supported, coed. Small town campus. Total enrollment: 9,762. Music program established 1958.

Degrees Bachelor of Music in the areas of applied music, jazz, music education, composition. Majors and concentrations: composition, jazz, music education, performance. Graduate degrees offered: Master of Arts in the area of music education; Master of Music in the areas of applied music, jazz, composition. Program accredited by NASM.

Enrollment 174 undergraduate, 31 graduate.

Music Student Profile 60% females, 40% males, 18% minorities, 5% international.

Music Faculty 19 total (full-time), 40 total (part-time). 80% of full-time faculty have terminal degrees. Graduate students do not teach undergraduate courses. Undergraduate student–faculty ratio: 7:1.

Student Life Student groups/activities include Music Educators National Conference Student Chapter, Pi Kappa Lambda, Phi Mu Alpha.

Rowan University (continued)

Expenses for 2005–2006 Application fee: $50. State resident tuition: $6294 full-time. Nonresident tuition: $12,588 full-time. Mandatory fees: $2313 full-time. Full-time tuition and fees vary according to degree level. College room and board: $8242. Room and board charges vary according to board plan and housing facility. Special program-related fees: $6 per credit for lab fees, $15 per quarter for instrument rental.
Financial Aid Program-specific awards: 20 Department of Music Scholarships for music students ($4000).
Application Procedures Students admitted directly into the professional program freshman year. Deadline for freshmen: March 15; transfers: April 15. Notification date for freshmen: May 1. Required: high school transcript, college transcript(s) for transfer students, letter of recommendation, audition, SAT I or ACT test scores, portfolio for composition applicants. Auditions held 5 times on campus; recorded music is permissible as a substitute for live auditions when distance is prohibitive and videotaped performances are permissible as a substitute for live auditions when distance is prohibitive. Portfolio reviews held throughout the year on campus.
Web Site http://www.rowan.edu
Undergraduate Contact Dr. Robert Rawlins, Chair, Department of Music, Rowan University, 201 Mullica Hill Road, Glassboro, New Jersey 08028-1702; 856-256-4557, fax: 856-256-4644, e-mail address: rawlinsr@rowan.edu
Graduate Contact Bryan Appleby-Wineberg, Assistant Professor, Department of Music, Rowan University, 201 Mullica Hill Road, Glassboro, New Jersey 08028-1702; 856-256-4500 ext. 3526, fax: 856-256-4644, e-mail address: applebywineberg@rowan.edu

The Rudi E. Scheidt School of Music

See University of Memphis

Rutgers, The State University of New Jersey

See Mason Gross School of the Arts

St. Cloud State University

St. Cloud, Minnesota

State-supported, coed. Suburban campus. Total enrollment: 15,964. Music program established 1869.
Degrees Bachelor of Arts in the area of music; Bachelor of Music in the areas of performance, piano pedagogy; Bachelor of Science in the area of music education. Majors and concentrations: jazz, music education, music theory and composition, performance, piano pedagogy. Graduate degrees offered: Master of Music in the areas of education, conducting, piano pedagogy. Program accredited by NASM.
Enrollment 155 total; 110 undergraduate, 45 graduate.
Music Student Profile 50% females, 50% males, 3% minorities, 4% international.
Music Faculty 18 total (full-time), 8 total (part-time). 90% of full-time faculty have terminal degrees. Graduate students do not teach undergraduate courses. Undergraduate student–faculty ratio: 18:1.
Student Life Student groups/activities include Sigma Alpha Iota, Music Educators National Conference Student Chapter, American Choral Directors Association Student Chapter.
Expenses for 2005–2006 Application fee: $20. State resident tuition: $4760 full-time. Nonresident tuition: $10,332 full-time. Mandatory fees: $562 full-time. Full-time tuition and fees vary according to course load and reciprocity agreements. College room and board: $4688. College room only: $3340. Room and board charges vary according to board plan and housing facility. Special program-related fees: $55 per credit for private lessons, $60 per year for instrument rental .
Financial Aid Program-specific awards: 20 Endowed/Foundation Scholarships for talented students ($1500), 7 David Swenson Memorial Awards for percussion students ($3500).

Application Procedures Students apply for admission into the professional program by freshman year. Deadline for freshmen and transfers: continuous. Required: high school transcript, college transcript(s) for transfer students, minimum 2.0 high school GPA, ACT test score only (minimum composite ACT score of 25), audition for scholarship consideration. Auditions held twice on campus; recorded music is permissible as a substitute for live auditions by arrangement with department and videotaped performances are permissible as a substitute for live auditions by arrangement with department.
Web Site http://www.stcloudstate.edu/music
Undergraduate Contact Ms. Pat Krueger, Associate Director of Admissions, Admissions, St. Cloud State University, 720 4th Avenue South, St. Cloud, Minnesota 56301-4498; 320-308-3981, fax: 320-308-2243, e-mail address: scsu4u@stcloudstate.edu
Graduate Contact Mr. Dennis Nunes, Dean, School of Graduate Studies, St. Cloud State University, 720 4th Avenue South, St. Cloud, Minnesota 56301-4498; 320-308-2113, fax: 320-308-5371.

St. Francis Xavier University

Antigonish, Nova Scotia, Canada

Independent Roman Catholic, coed. Small town campus. Total enrollment: 4,969.
Degrees Bachelor of Music in the areas of jazz performance, jazz composition/arranging. Majors and concentrations: bass, brass, jazz guitar, piano, voice, wind and percussion instruments.
Enrollment 83 total.
Music Student Profile 25% females, 75% males, 3% minorities, 1% international.
Music Faculty 9 undergraduate (full-time), 4 undergraduate (part-time). 100% of full-time faculty have terminal degrees. Graduate students do not teach undergraduate courses. Undergraduate student–faculty ratio: 9:1.
Student Life Student groups/activities include Nova Scotia Music Educators Association, Music Society, Big Band.
Expenses for 2006–2007 Application fee: $40 Canadian dollars. Tuition, fee, and room and board charges are reported in Canadian dollars. Comprehensive fee: $13,615 includes full-time tuition ($5975), mandatory fees ($1145), and college room and board ($6495). International student tuition: $10,875 full-time.
Financial Aid Program-specific awards: 3 music scholarships for program majors ($1000), 8 music bursaries for program majors ($250–$500).
Application Procedures Students apply for admission into the professional program by sophomore year. Deadline for freshmen and transfers: August 1. Notification date for freshmen and transfers: August 15. Required: high school transcript, college transcript(s) for transfer students, audition. Recommended: 2 letters of recommendation. Auditions held continuously on campus; recorded music is permissible as a substitute for live auditions if certified by a teacher and videotaped performances are permissible as a substitute for live auditions if certified by a teacher.
Web Site http://www.stfx.ca/academic/music
Undergraduate Contact Director of Admissions, St. Francis Xavier University, PO Box 5000, Antigonish, Nova Scotia B2G 2W5, Canada; 902-867-2219, fax: 902-867-2329.

Saint Mary's College

Notre Dame, Indiana

Independent Roman Catholic, women only. Suburban campus. Total enrollment: 1,397. Music program established 1894.
Degrees Bachelor of Music in the area of music. Majors and concentrations: music education, piano performance, voice performance. Cross-registration with University of Notre Dame. Program accredited by NASM, NCATE.
Enrollment 20 total; 10 undergraduate, 10 nonprofessional degree.
Music Student Profile 100% females.
Music Faculty 5 undergraduate (full-time), 20 undergraduate (part-time). 100% of full-time faculty have terminal degrees. Graduate students do not teach undergraduate courses. Undergraduate student–faculty ratio: 4:1.

Student Life Student groups/activities include Music Educators National Conference Student Chapter, Madrigal Dinners/Opera/Musical Theater, National Association of Teachers of Singing competitions.

Expenses for 2006–2007 Application fee: $30. Comprehensive fee: $34,005 includes full-time tuition ($25,030), mandatory fees ($550), and college room and board ($8425). College room only: $5190. Special program-related fees: $215 per half hour for private lessons, $360 per 50 minutes for private lessons.

Financial Aid Program-specific awards: 4 Moreau Music Scholarships for exceptionally talented singers and pianists ($4000).

Application Procedures Students admitted directly into the professional program freshman year. Deadline for freshmen and transfers: continuous. Required: essay, high school transcript, college transcript(s) for transfer students, minimum 3.0 high school GPA, letter of recommendation, audition, SAT I or ACT test scores, minimum 3.0 college GPA for transfer students. Recommended: interview. Auditions held continuously on campus; recorded music is permissible as a substitute for live auditions when distance is prohibitive and videotaped performances are permissible as a substitute for live auditions when distance is prohibitive.

Web Site http://www.saintmarys.edu/~music/

Undergraduate Contact Dr. Nancy Menk, Chair, Department of Music, Saint Mary's College, 313 Moreau Center for the Arts, Notre Dame, Indiana 46556-5001; 574-284-4632 ext. 4633, fax: 574-284-4884, e-mail address: nmenk@saintmarys.edu

St. Norbert College

De Pere, Wisconsin

Independent Roman Catholic, coed. Suburban campus. Total enrollment: 2,050.

St. Olaf College

Northfield, Minnesota

Independent Lutheran, coed. Small town campus. Total enrollment: 3,058. Music program established 1895.

Degrees Bachelor of Music in the areas of performance, music education, church music, theory/composition. Majors and concentrations: church music, music education, music theory and composition, piano/organ performance, stringed instruments, voice performance, wind and percussion instruments. Cross-registration with Carleton College. Program accredited by NASM.

Enrollment 291 total; 124 undergraduate, 167 nonprofessional degree.

Music Student Profile 56% females, 44% males, 6% minorities, 2% international.

Music Faculty 28 undergraduate (full-time), 33 undergraduate (part-time). 85% of full-time faculty have terminal degrees. Graduate students do not teach undergraduate courses. Undergraduate student–faculty ratio: 11:1.

Student Life Student groups/activities include Music Educators National Conference, Phi Kappa Lampda, American Choral Directors Association.

Expenses for 2006–2007 Application fee: $35. Comprehensive fee: $35,600 includes full-time tuition ($28,200) and college room and board ($7400). College room only: $3450.

Financial Aid Program-specific awards: 30 honors music scholarships for music and non-music majors ($6000), 60 music achievement and recognition scholarships for music and non-music majors ($1500–$3000), performance study scholarships for music majors ($640–$1280).

Application Procedures Students admitted directly into the professional program freshman year. Deadline for freshmen: December 1; transfers: February 15. Notification date for freshmen: February 1; transfers: May 1. Required: essay, high school transcript, college transcript(s) for transfer students, 2 letters of recommendation, audition, SAT I or ACT test scores. Recommended: minimum 3.0 high school GPA, portfolio for theory/composition applicants. Auditions held once on campus; recorded music is permissible as a substitute for live auditions for provisional acceptance and videotaped performances are permis-

sible as a substitute for live auditions if a live audition is impossible. Portfolio reviews held by request on campus.

Web Site http://www.stolaf.edu/depts/music/

Undergraduate Contact Ms. Mary Hakes, Music Admissions Coordinator, Department of Music, St. Olaf College, 1520 St. Olaf Avenue, Northfield, Minnesota 55057-1098; 507-646-3297, fax: 507-646-3527, e-mail address: music@stolaf.edu

Saint Xavier University

Chicago, Illinois

Independent Roman Catholic, coed. Urban campus. Total enrollment: 5,705. Music program established 1847.

Degrees Bachelor of Music in the areas of performance, music education. Majors and concentrations: music education, piano, stringed instruments, voice, wind and percussion instruments. Program accredited by NASM.

Enrollment 33 total; 28 undergraduate, 5 nonprofessional degree.

Music Student Profile 70% females, 30% males, 15% minorities.

Music Faculty 5 undergraduate (full-time), 10 undergraduate (part-time). 60% of full-time faculty have terminal degrees. Graduate students do not teach undergraduate courses. Undergraduate student–faculty ratio: 6:1.

Student Life Student groups/activities include Collegiate Music Educators National Conference.

Expenses for 2005–2006 Application fee: $25. Comprehensive fee: $25,598 includes full-time tuition ($18,350), mandatory fees ($170), and college room and board ($7078). College room only: $4428. Full-time tuition and fees vary according to course load. Room and board charges vary according to board plan and housing facility. Special program-related fees: $100 per credit per semester for accompanist fee.

Financial Aid Program-specific awards: 3 Sinon Catherine O'Donohue Keyboard Scholarships for keyboard students ($2000), 2 Sister Gabrielle McShane Awards for vocalists/instrumentalists ($2000), 20 ensemble awards for ensemble performers ($750–$5000), 8 talent awards for voice/band/orchestra participants ($1000–$7000).

Application Procedures Students apply for admission into the professional program by sophomore year. Deadline for freshmen and transfers: continuous. Required: essay, high school transcript, college transcript(s) for transfer students, minimum 2.0 high school GPA, letter of recommendation, interview, audition, SAT I or ACT test scores. Auditions held 4-5 times and by appointment on campus; recorded music is permissible as a substitute for live auditions and videotaped performances are permissible as a substitute for live auditions for out-of-state and international applicants.

Web Site http://www.sxu.edu

Undergraduate Contact Dr. Greg Coutts, Chair, Music Department, Saint Xavier University, 3700 West 103rd Street, Chicago, Illinois 60655; 773-298-3424, fax: 773-779-9061, e-mail address: coutts@sxu.edu

Salem College

Winston-Salem, North Carolina

Independent Moravian, Urban campus. Total enrollment: 1,109. Music program established 1879.

Degrees Bachelor of Music. Majors and concentrations: flute, music education, music performance, organ, piano, voice. Cross-registration with Wake Forest University. Program accredited by NASM.

Enrollment 30 total; 10 undergraduate, 20 nonprofessional degree.

Music Student Profile 100% females, 25% minorities, 12% international.

Music Faculty 4 undergraduate (full-time), 5 undergraduate (part-time). 100% of full-time faculty have terminal degrees. Graduate students do not teach undergraduate courses. Undergraduate student–faculty ratio: 7:1.

Student Life Student groups/activities include Pierrette's Players (drama club).

Expenses for 2005–2006 Application fee: $30. Comprehensive fee: $26,441 includes full-time tuition ($16,975), mandatory fees

Salem College (continued)

($215), and college room and board ($9251). Special program-related fees: $230 per semester for private lessons.

Financial Aid Program-specific awards: 3 Dunford Scholarships for program majors ($2500–$3000), 3 Christian Gregor Awards for program majors ($5000–$6000), 5 Vardell Music Scholarships for program majors ($1000–$1500), 1 Mueller Scholarship for organ majors ($3000), 1 Pfohl Scholarship for program majors ($5000), 1 Maud Hawks Scholarship for program major ($16,000).

Application Procedures Students admitted directly into the professional program freshman year. Deadline for freshmen and transfers: continuous. Required: essay, high school transcript, college transcript(s) for transfer students, 2 letters of recommendation, audition, SAT I or ACT test scores, minimum 2.0 college GPA for transfer applicants. Recommended: interview. Auditions held once in February and by appointment on campus; recorded music is permissible as a substitute for live auditions if a campus visit is impossible and videotaped performances are permissible as a substitute for live auditions if a campus visit is impossible.

Web Site http://www.salem.edu

Undergraduate Contact Dana Evans, Dean of Admissions and Financial Aid, Salem College, PO Box 10548, Winston-Salem, North Carolina 27108; 336-721-2621, fax: 336-917-5572, e-mail address: evans@salem.edu

Samford University

Birmingham, Alabama

Independent Baptist, coed. Suburban campus. Total enrollment: 4,507. Music program established 1949.

Degrees Bachelor of Music in the areas of performance, church music, music theory/composition, music education, musical theatre. Majors and concentrations: church music, music education, music theater, music theory and composition, piano/organ, stringed instruments, voice, wind and percussion instruments. Graduate degrees offered: Master of Music in the areas of church music, music education. Program accredited by NASM.

Enrollment 117 total; 95 undergraduate, 6 graduate, 16 nonprofessional degree.

Music Student Profile 55% females, 45% males, 3% minorities, 1% international.

Music Faculty 17 total (full-time), 14 total (part-time). 75% of full-time faculty have terminal degrees. Graduate students do not teach undergraduate courses. Undergraduate student–faculty ratio: 8:1.

Student Life Student groups/activities include Phi Mu Alpha Sinfonia, Delta Omicron, Music Educators National Conference Student Chapter.

Expenses for 2005–2006 Application fee: $35. Comprehensive fee: $20,258 includes full-time tuition ($14,642) and college room and board ($5616). College room only: $2860. Full-time tuition varies according to course load. Room and board charges vary according to board plan and housing facility. Special program-related fees: $45 per credit hour for applied music fee.

Financial Aid Program-specific awards: 55 music scholarships for program majors ($1000–$3000), 35 band scholarships for band members ($500–$1500).

Application Procedures Students admitted directly into the professional program freshman year. Deadline for freshmen and transfers: March 1. Notification date for freshmen and transfers: May 1. Required: essay, high school transcript, college transcript(s) for transfer students, 2 letters of recommendation, audition, SAT I or ACT test scores, music theory placement exam, piano proficiency exam. Recommended: minimum 3.0 high school GPA. Auditions held 4 times in February on campus; videotaped performances are permissible as a substitute for live auditions in special circumstances and when scheduling is difficult.

Web Site http://www.samford.edu/schools/music/music.html

Undergraduate Contact Dr. Billy Strickland, Assistant Dean for Undergraduate Studies, Division of Music, Samford University, PO Box 292242, 800 Lakeshore Drive, Birmingham, Alabama 35229; 205-726-2826, fax: 205-726-2165, e-mail address: bjstrick@samford.edu

Graduate Contact Dr. Paul Richardson, Assistant Dean for Graduate Studies, Division of Music, Samford University, PO Box 292242,

800 Lakeshore Drive, Birmingham, Alabama 35229; 205-726-2496, fax: 205-726-2165, e-mail address: parichar@samford.edu

Sam Houston State University

Huntsville, Texas

State-supported, coed. Small town campus. Total enrollment: 15,000. Music program established 1938.

Degrees Bachelor of Music in the areas of performance, music theory/composition, music literature, music therapy, teacher certification. Majors and concentrations: music, music education, music literature, music theory and composition, music therapy, piano/organ, stringed instruments, voice, wind and percussion instruments. Graduate degrees offered: Master of Music in the areas of performance, music theory/composition, conducting, musicology, Kodály pedagogy; Master of Music Education. Program accredited by NASM.

Enrollment 335 total; 261 undergraduate, 19 graduate, 55 nonprofessional degree.

Music Student Profile 56% females, 44% males, 35% minorities, 2% international.

Music Faculty 23 total (full-time), 27 total (part-time). 72% of full-time faculty have terminal degrees. Graduate students do not teach undergraduate courses. Undergraduate student–faculty ratio: 7:1.

Student Life Student groups/activities include American Association of Music Therapy Student Chapter, Sigma Alpha Iota, Kappa Kappa Psi.

Expenses for 2005–2006 Application fee: $35. State resident tuition: $3822 full-time. Nonresident tuition: $9728 full-time. Full-time tuition varies according to course load. College room and board: $5002. College room only: $2826. Room and board charges vary according to board plan and housing facility. Special program-related fees: $20 for recital recording fee, $30 for recital hall rental fee.

Financial Aid Program-specific awards: 82 scholarships for program students ($200–$2000).

Application Procedures Students admitted directly into the professional program freshman year. Deadline for freshmen and transfers: continuous. Required: high school transcript, college transcript(s) for transfer students, 3 letters of recommendation, interview, audition, SAT I or ACT test scores. Recommended: minimum 2.0 high school GPA. Auditions held 4 times on campus; recorded music is permissible as a substitute for live auditions with permission of the chair and videotaped performances are permissible as a substitute for live auditions when distance is prohibitive.

Web Site http://www.shsu.edu/~music

Undergraduate Contact Dr. Rodney M. Cannon, Director, School of Music, Sam Houston State University, PO Box 2208, Huntsville, Texas 77341-2208; 936-294-1360, fax: 936-294-3765, e-mail address: mus_rmc@shsu.edu

Graduate Contact Dr. Scott Plugge, Graduate Student Advisor, School of Music, Sam Houston State University, PO Box 2208, Huntsville, Texas 77341-2208; 936-294-1360, fax: 936-294-3765, e-mail address: mus_sdp@shsu.edu

San Diego State University

San Diego, California

State-supported, coed. Urban campus. Total enrollment: 32,936. Music program established 1898.

Degrees Bachelor of Music in the areas of performance, jazz studies, composition, general music, music education. Majors and concentrations: classical music, composition, guitar, jazz, music, music education, piano/organ, stringed instruments, voice, wind and percussion instruments, world music instruments. Graduate degrees offered: Master of Arts in the areas of music, piano pedagogy, ethnomusicology, theory, musicology; Master of Music in the areas of performance, jazz studies, composition, conducting. Cross-registration with University of California, San Diego.

Enrollment 340 total; 250 undergraduate, 50 graduate, 40 nonprofessional degree.

Music Student Profile 55% females, 45% males, 40% minorities, 5% international.
Music Faculty 20 total (full-time), 34 total (part-time). 60% of full-time faculty have terminal degrees. Graduate students teach a few undergraduate courses. Undergraduate student–faculty ratio: 17:1.
Student Life Student groups/activities include Phi Mu Alpha, Kappa Kappa Psi, Sigma Alpha Iota.
Expenses for 2005–2006 Application fee: $55. State resident tuition: $0 full-time. Nonresident tuition: $10,170 full-time. Mandatory fees: $3155 full-time. Full-time tuition and fees vary according to degree level. College room and board: $9849. Room and board charges vary according to board plan and housing facility. Special program-related fees: $20 per semester for equipment use fee, $20 per semester for instrument use fee, $20 per semester for piano practice room.
Financial Aid Program-specific awards: 40–50 scholarships for music majors ($500–$3000).
Application Procedures Students admitted directly into the professional program freshman year. Deadline for freshmen and transfers: November 30. Notification date for freshmen and transfers: April 1. Required: high school transcript, college transcript(s) for transfer students, minimum 3.0 high school GPA, audition, SAT I or ACT test scores. Auditions held twice on campus; videotaped performances are permissible as a substitute for live auditions when distance is prohibitive.
Web Site http://www.musicdance.sdsu.edu
Undergraduate Contact Mrs. Sandra Konar, Music and Dance Student Coordinator, School of Music and Dance, San Diego State University, San Diego, California 92182-7902; 619-594-6032, fax: 619-594-1692, e-mail address: music.dance@sdsu.edu
Graduate Contact Prof. Martin Chambers, Graduate Advisor - Music, School of Music and Dance, San Diego State University, San Diego, California 92182-7902; 619-594-6031, fax: 619-594-1692, e-mail address: music.dance@sdsu.edu

San Francisco Conservatory of Music
San Francisco, California

Independent, coed. Urban campus. Music program established 1917.
Degrees Bachelor of Music in the areas of classical guitar, composition, keyboard instruments, orchestral instruments, voice. Majors and concentrations: classical guitar, composition, piano/organ, stringed instruments, voice, wind and percussion instruments. Graduate degrees offered: Master of Music in the areas of chamber music, classical guitar, composition, conducting, keyboard instruments, orchestral instruments, piano accompanying, voice. Program accredited by NASM.
Enrollment 315 total; 157 undergraduate, 158 graduate.
Music Student Profile 60% females, 40% males, 22% minorities, 23% international.
Music Faculty 25 total (full-time), 72 total (part-time). 50% of full-time faculty have terminal degrees. Graduate students do not teach undergraduate courses. Undergraduate student–faculty ratio: 5:1.
Student Life Student groups/activities include Student Government Organization.
Financial Aid Program-specific awards: 120 Conservatory Scholarships for undergraduates ($12,000).
Application Procedures Students admitted directly into the professional program freshman year. Deadline for freshmen and transfers: December 15. Notification date for freshmen and transfers: April 1. Required: high school transcript, college transcript(s) for transfer students, minimum 2.0 high school GPA, 2 letters of recommendation, audition, minimum TOEFL score of 500/173 or minimum of 61 on TOEFL iBT for students for whom English is not the first language. Recommended: essay, SAT I or ACT test scores. Auditions held 5 times: January, February, March, May, and November on campus and off campus in Boston, MA; New York, NY; Chicago, IL; Interlochen, MI; Houston, TX; Oberlin, OH; Idyllwild, CA; videotaped performances are permissible as a substitute for live auditions for non-voice applicants residing outside of northern California and international applicants.
Web Site http://www.sfcm.edu

Contact Ms. Chris Daly, Assistant Director of Admission, San Francisco Conservatory of Music, 50 Oak Street, San Francisco, California 94102; 800-899-7326, fax: 415-503-6299, e-mail address: admit@sfcm.edu

More About the Conservatory

The San Francisco Conservatory of Music (SFCM), founded in 1917, is a nationally prominent conservatory with an international reputation and student body. Enrollment is kept small (335 total students) to ensure close student-faculty interaction and frequent and regular performance opportunities for every student throughout the program. Significant personal attention for each student and a collaborative and intimate atmosphere guarantee that students receive intense and rigorous preparation for careers in music.

The Bay Area's public transportation provides quick access to downtown San Francisco and the Civic Center, the city's cultural center and the site of the Conservatory's new, state-of-the-art facility, which opens in fall 2006. From its new location at Civic Center, the Conservatory will strengthen ties with the San Francisco Symphony, the Opera, and other arts and educational organizations, further developing its intellectual and musical collaborations. Students already enjoy free tickets to the symphony, the ballet, the opera, and various theatrical offerings. Museums, galleries, and the remarkable physical beauty of San Francisco—its parks, beaches, views, and neighborhoods—provide much to explore and enjoy.

Performing is a major aspect of student life at SFCM. Students not only present their required solo and chamber recitals but also participate actively in the major ensembles, collaborate with classmates and faculty members in performances, and have positions with Bay Area choirs, orchestras, and other ensembles.

Every year, the Conservatory's Community Service Program sends students into the community, both as soloists and ensembles, to perform at hospitals, senior centers, schools, and other institutions. The popular Music To Go Program offers some 1,000 paid-performance opportunities each year to students who audition to be on call for private and corporate events throughout the Bay Area. Outside the Conservatory, students augment their study as members of regional opera companies, orchestras, chamber music ensembles, and choruses; this also allows students to make important professional connections while they are still students. Alumni are counted among the members of national and international arts organizations, including the Chicago Symphony, Glyndebourne Festival Opera, Israel Philharmonic, Los Angeles Philharmonic, Metropolitan Opera, Minnesota Orchestra, National Symphony Orchestra, San Francisco Opera and Opera Orchestra and Ballet Orchestra, Peabody Trio, Tokyo Philharmonic Orchestra, and Stuttgart Staatsoper.

San Francisco's Conservatory of Music students receive instruction from a world-class faculty in an atmosphere that is at

San Francisco Conservatory of Music (continued)

once intense and informal. From the studio to the classroom, SFCM faculty members are passionately committed to the development of the individual, both artistically and intellectually. Personal attention is a hallmark of an SFCM education.

Program Facilities New facilities include Concert Hall (435 seats), sure to be one of the finest concert halls of its size in California; a Recital Hall (130 seats); the Osher Salon (100 seats), a multiuse performance/teaching space; a new, roof-top library, offering more than 40,000 volumes, scores, and periodicals and more than 10,000 recordings; a Computer Center and the Electronic Composition Studio; two professional recording studios; a roof garden; forty-two practice rooms; forty-four teaching studios; fourteen classrooms; a student lounge; and café.

Faculty, Visiting Artists, and Alumni SFCM faculty members are past and present members of the San Francisco Symphony, San Francisco Ballet Orchestra, San Francisco Opera and Opera Orchestra, Philharmonia Baroque Orchestra, Smithson Quartet, Francesca Trio, and others and perform internationally as soloists and chamber musicians. Recent master classes have been presented by Elmar Oliveira, Ned Roremy, Marilyn Horne, Lynn Harrell, Jerry Hadley, Thomas Hampson, Richard Goode, Leon Fleisher, Yo-Yo Ma, Mstislav Rostropovich, Menachem Pressler, Gil Kalish, and Frederica von Stade. Nationally known alumni include pianist-conductor Jeffrey Kahane, pianist Robin Sutherland, Pulitzer Prize–winning composer Aaron Jay Kernis, guitarist David Tanenbaum, and Naumburg Award–winning cellist Hai-Ye Ni. Yehudi Menuhin and Isaac Stern studied at the Conservatory as children.

Student Performance Opportunities Approximately 400 events are presented at the Conservatory each year, featuring solo and chamber recitals by students and faculty members, small ensembles, fully staged operas, and symphonic programs. Conservatory ensembles include the Orchestra, Opera Theatre, Opera Workshop, Musical Theatre Workshop, Baroque Ensemble, Guitar Ensemble, Percussion Ensemble, New Music Ensemble, and a host of other smaller, specialized groups. Chamber music, especially for strings and piano, is a signature program at SFCM.

San Francisco State University
San Francisco, California

State-supported, coed. Urban campus. Total enrollment: 28,950. Music program established 1930.

San Jose State University
San Jose, California

State-supported, coed. Urban campus. Total enrollment: 29,975. Music program established 1847.
Degrees Bachelor of Arts; Bachelor of Music in the areas of performance, composition. Majors and concentrations: composition, instrumental music, jazz studies, music education, voice. Graduate degrees offered: Master of Arts in the area of music. Program accredited by NASM.
Enrollment 275 total; 225 undergraduate, 50 graduate.
Music Student Profile 57% females, 43% males, 47% minorities.
Music Faculty 17 undergraduate (full-time), 38 undergraduate (part-time). 90% of full-time faculty have terminal degrees. Graduate students teach a few undergraduate courses. Undergraduate student–faculty ratio: 4:1.
Student Life Student groups/activities include Music Educators National Conference Student Chapter, Mu Phi Epsilon, American Choral Directors Association Student Chapter.
Expenses for 2005–2006 Application fee: $55. Nonresident tuition: $10,170 full-time. Mandatory fees: $3292 full-time. Full-time tuition and fees vary according to course load. College room and board: $8718. College room only: $5412. Room and board charges vary according to board plan and housing facility.

Special program-related fees: $30 per semester for equipment use fee, $125 per semester for applied lesson.
Financial Aid Program-specific awards: 50 music scholarships for freshmen and transfer students ($200–$1000).
Application Procedures Students admitted directly into the professional program freshman year. Deadline for freshmen and transfers: February 1. Notification date for freshmen: October 1; transfers: March 16. Required: essay, high school transcript, college transcript(s) for transfer students, minimum 2.0 high school GPA, audition, SAT I or ACT test scores, TOEFL score for international applicants. Auditions held 3 times on campus; recorded music is permissible as a substitute for live auditions when distance is prohibitive and videotaped performances are permissible as a substitute for live auditions when distance is prohibitive.
Web Site http://www.sjsu.edu/depts/music_dance
Undergraduate Contact Director of Admissions, San Jose State University, 1 Washington Square, San Jose, California 95192-0009; 408-924-2550, fax: 408-924-2050, e-mail address: contact@anrnet.sjsu.edu
Graduate Contact Director of Admissions, Graduate Admissions and Program Evaluation, San Jose State University, 1 Washington Square, San Jose, California 95192-0025; 408-924-2480, fax: 408-924-2477.

Schulich School of Music
See McGill University

Schwob School of Music
See Columbus State University

Setnor School of Music
See Syracuse University

Seton Hall University
South Orange, New Jersey

Independent Roman Catholic, coed. Suburban campus. Total enrollment: 9,637. Music program established 1968.
Degrees Bachelor of Arts in the area of music; Bachelor of Science in the area of music education. Majors and concentrations: applied music, music education.
Enrollment 25 total; all undergraduate.
Music Student Profile 50% females, 50% males, 10% minorities, 1% international.
Music Faculty 3 undergraduate (full-time), 10 undergraduate (part-time). 100% of full-time faculty have terminal degrees. Graduate students do not teach undergraduate courses. Undergraduate student–faculty ratio: 10:1.
Student Life Student groups/activities include Theatre in the Round.
Expenses for 2006–2007 Application fee: $55. Comprehensive fee: $35,186 includes full-time tuition ($22,770), mandatory fees ($1950), and college room and board ($10,466). College room only: $6664.
Financial Aid Program-specific awards: 10–15 Pep Band Grants for all participants ($500), 10–15 Choir Grants for all participants ($500–$2000).
Application Procedures Students admitted directly into the professional program freshman year. Deadline for freshmen and transfers: continuous. Required: essay, high school transcript, minimum 2.0 high school GPA, 3 letters of recommendation, interview, audition, SAT I or ACT test scores. Auditions held by appointment on campus; recorded music is permissible as a substitute for live auditions for out-of-state applicants and videotaped performances are permissible as a substitute for live auditions for out-of-state applicants.
Web Site http://www.shu.edu/
Undergraduate Contact Prof. Jeanette Hile, Chair, Department of Art and Music, Seton Hall University, 400 South Orange Avenue,

South Orange, New Jersey 07079; 973-761-9417, fax: 973-275-2368, e-mail address: hilejean@shu.edu

Seton Hill University
Greensburg, Pennsylvania

Independent Roman Catholic, coed. Small town campus. Total enrollment: 1,863. Music program established 1918.

Degrees Bachelor of Music in the areas of performance, music education, sacred music, music therapy. Majors and concentrations: music education, music performance, music therapy, sacred music. Cross-registration with Saint Vincent College. Program accredited by NASM, AMTA.

Enrollment 81 total; 70 undergraduate, 11 nonprofessional degree.

Music Student Profile 60% females, 40% males, 3% minorities, 3% international.

Music Faculty 5 undergraduate (full-time), 19 undergraduate (part-time). 80% of full-time faculty have terminal degrees. Graduate students do not teach undergraduate courses. Undergraduate student–faculty ratio: 10:1.

Student Life Student groups/activities include Music Educators National Conference, Pennsylvania Music Educators Association Student Chapter, American Guild of Organists.

Expenses for 2005–2006 Application fee: $35. Comprehensive fee: $29,020 includes full-time tuition ($21,870), mandatory fees ($120), and college room and board ($7030). Room and board charges vary according to board plan and housing facility. Special program-related fees: $15 for large ensembles, $15–$50 for music education methods course fee, $130 for private instruction on a secondary instrument, $260 for private instruction on a major instrument.

Financial Aid Program-specific awards: 2 Gabriel Burda Scholarships for incoming students ($4000), 4 string quartet scholarships for string players ($1500), 1 Highberger Scholarship for incoming students ($1000), 1 Choral Society Scholarship for incoming students ($500), 1 symphonic winds scholarship for incoming students ($1000), 1–4 Mildred Gardner Music Scholarships for incoming students from Westmoreland County (PA) ($1000–$4000).

Application Procedures Students admitted directly into the professional program freshman year. Deadline for freshmen and transfers: continuous. Notification date for freshmen and transfers: continuous. Required: high school transcript, college transcript(s) for transfer students, minimum 2.0 high school GPA, audition, SAT I or ACT test scores. Recommended: essay, minimum 3.0 high school GPA, letter of recommendation, interview. Auditions held by appointment on campus; recorded music is permissible as a substitute for live auditions if a campus visit is impossible and videotaped performances are permissible as a substitute for live auditions if a campus visit is impossible.

Web Site http://www.setonhill.edu

Undergraduate Contact Ms. Mary Kay Cooper, Director, Admissions Office, Seton Hill University, College Avenue, Greensburg, Pennsylvania 15601; 724-838-4255, fax: 724-830-4611, e-mail address: mcooper@setonhill.edu

Shenandoah Conservatory
See Shenandoah University

Shenandoah Conservatory
Shenandoah University
Winchester, Virginia

Independent United Methodist, coed. Total enrollment: 2,998.

Degrees Bachelor of Music in the areas of church music, commercial music, composition, jazz studies, music education, performance, piano accompanying, music with elective studies, music theater accompanying; Bachelor of Music Therapy; Bachelor of Science in the area of arts management. Majors and concentrations: arts management, church music, commercial music, composition, jazz, music education, music theater accompanying, music therapy, music with elective studies, performance, piano accompanying, piano/organ, stringed instruments, voice, wind and percussion instruments. Graduate degrees offered: Master of Music in the areas of composition, conducting, performance, church music, dance accompanying, piano accompanying, pedagogy; Master of Music Education; Master of Music Therapy; Master of Science in the areas of arts administration, music. Doctor of Musical Arts in the areas of music education, performance. Program accredited by NASM.

Enrollment 472 total; 285 undergraduate, 180 graduate, 7 nonprofessional degree.

Music Student Profile 59% females, 41% males, 6% minorities, 10% international.

Music Faculty 41 total (full-time), 49 total (part-time). 63% of full-time faculty have terminal degrees. Graduate students teach a few undergraduate courses. Undergraduate student–faculty ratio: 5:1.

Student Life Student groups/activities include music fraternities and sororities, Music Educators National Conference Student Chapter, Student Association of Music Therapy.

Expenses for 2005–2006 Application fee: $30. Comprehensive fee: $27,600 includes full-time tuition ($19,900), mandatory fees ($150), and college room and board ($7550). Full-time tuition and fees vary according to course load and program. Room and board charges vary according to board plan. Special program-related fees: $125 per half-hour lesson for private voice and piano lessons, $250 per one-hour lesson for private music lessons for majors.

Financial Aid Program-specific awards: 194 talent and academic scholarships for program students ($5331).

Application Procedures Students admitted directly into the professional program freshman year. Deadline for freshmen and transfers: continuous. Required: high school transcript, college transcript(s) for transfer students, minimum 2.0 high school GPA, interview, video, audition, SAT I or ACT test scores, portfolio for composition majors. Recommended: letter of recommendation, portfolio. Auditions held 10 times on campus and off campus in various cities; recorded music is permissible as a substitute for live auditions if a campus visit is impossible and videotaped performances are permissible as a substitute for live auditions if a campus visit is impossible. Portfolio reviews held 10 times on campus and off campus in various cities.

Web Site http://www.su.edu

Contact Mr. David Anthony, Dean, Admissions Office, Shenandoah University, 1460 University Drive, Winchester, Virginia 22601-5195; 540-665-4581, fax: 540-665-4627, e-mail address: admit@su.edu

Shepherd School of Music
See Rice University

Shorter College
Rome, Georgia

Independent Baptist, coed. Small town campus. Total enrollment: 967.

Silver Lake College
Manitowoc, Wisconsin

Independent Roman Catholic, coed. Rural campus. Total enrollment: 913. Music program established 1960.

Simon Fraser University
Burnaby, British Columbia, Canada

Province-supported, coed. Suburban campus. Total enrollment: 20,187. Music program established 1992.

Degrees Bachelor of Fine Arts. Majors and concentrations: music. Graduate degrees offered: Master of Fine Arts in the area of interdisciplinary studies.

Enrollment 46 total.

Simon Fraser University (continued)

Music Faculty 5 total (full-time). 100% of full-time faculty have terminal degrees. Graduate students do not teach undergraduate courses. Undergraduate student–faculty ratio: 11:1.

Student Life Student groups/activities include Standing Wave.

Expenses for 2006–2007 Application fee: $100 Canadian dollars. Tuition and fee charges are reported in Canadian dollars.

Financial Aid Program-specific awards: 5 Adaline May Clark Scholarships for program majors ($100–$500), 1 Murray Farr Award for program majors ($500), 3 Bice Caple Awards for students in SCA ($1000), 2 SFU Service Awards for students in SCA ($250), 1 Sean McLeod Memorial Bursary for program majors ($500), 1 Marcia Scholarship in Electroacoustics for program majors ($250).

Application Procedures Students admitted directly into the professional program freshman year. Deadline for freshmen and transfers: April 30. Required: high school transcript, college transcript(s) for transfer students, minimum 3.0 high school GPA, interview. Recommended: audition. Auditions held twice on campus; recorded music is permissible as a substitute for live auditions for international applicants and students who live outside the lower mainland.

Web Site http://www.sfu.ca/sca

Undergraduate Contact Linda Hegland, Undergraduate Advisor, School for the Contemporary Arts, Simon Fraser University, 8888 University Drive, Burnaby, British Columbia V5A 1S6, Canada; 604-291-3363, fax: 604-291-5907, e-mail address: ca@sfu.ca

Graduate Contact Noni Fidler, Graduate Secretary, MFA Program, School for the Contemporary Arts, Simon Fraser University, 8888 University Drive, Burnaby, British Columbia V5A 1S6, Canada; 604-291-3724, fax: 604-291-5907, e-mail address: mfagrad@sfu.ca

Simpson College

Indianola, Iowa

Independent United Methodist, coed. Small town campus. Total enrollment: 2,035. Music program established 1900.

Degrees Bachelor of Music in the areas of classical music, piano/organ, voice, winds and percussion music, vocal music education, instrumental music education. Majors and concentrations: brass, classical guitar, classical music, music education, piano/organ, voice, wind and percussion instruments. Program accredited by NASM.

Enrollment 105 total; 95 undergraduate, 10 nonprofessional degree.

Music Student Profile 60% females, 40% males, 4% minorities, 1% international.

Music Faculty 13 undergraduate (full-time), 15 undergraduate (part-time). 75% of full-time faculty have terminal degrees. Graduate students do not teach undergraduate courses. Undergraduate student–faculty ratio: 7:1.

Student Life Student groups/activities include Phi Mu Alpha Sinfonia, Mu Phi Epsilon, Music Educators National Conference.

Expenses for 2005–2006 Application fee: $0. Comprehensive fee: $26,833 includes full-time tuition ($20,693), mandatory fees ($218), and college room and board ($5922). College room only: $2842. Room and board charges vary according to board plan and housing facility. Special program-related fees: $50 per semester for recital fee, $50 per semester for accompanist fee, $225 per credit hour for lesson fee.

Financial Aid Program-specific awards: 70–80 music scholarships for program majors ($2000–$5000).

Application Procedures Students apply for admission into the professional program by sophomore year. Deadline for freshmen and transfers: August 1. Notification date for freshmen and transfers: June 30. Required: essay, high school transcript, college transcript(s) for transfer students, minimum 2.0 high school GPA, letter of recommendation, audition, SAT I or ACT test scores (minimum composite ACT score of 21). Recommended: minimum 3.0 high school GPA, interview, video. Auditions held twice plus special auditions on campus; recorded music is permissible as a substitute for live auditions if a campus visit is impossible and videotaped performances are permissible as a substitute for live auditions if a campus visit is impossible.

Web Site http://www.simpson.edu

Undergraduate Contact Dr. Maria DiPalma, Chairperson, Department of Music, Simpson College, 701 North Street, Indianola, Iowa 50125-1297; 515-961-1637, fax: 515-961-1498, e-mail address: dipalma@simpson.edu

More About the College

The Simpson College Conservatory of Music was founded in 1891. In 1940, it became the Music Department at Simpson and has developed and maintained a position of preeminence among schools offering serious musical training in the Midwest.

Simpson combines the atmosphere of a fine small liberal arts college with a distinguished program in music education and music performance. Students at Simpson are given the opportunity of working with superior teachers in private study and in small classes and are given extraordinary opportunities for both ensemble and solo performance. Here, every student is an individual and treated as such, often having the opportunity for upper-division directed studies in such areas as conducting, vocal repertory, ethnomusicology, Kodaly and Orff techniques, and opera coaching.

The Middle Ages, the Renaissance, the great operatic repertory of the nineteenth century, and the vitality of twentieth-century musical thought and American jazz are living, breathing, exciting, and viable entities in the music department. Visiting artists such as Chanticleer, soprano Evelyn Lear, and jazz great Maynard Ferguson give recitals and master classes. Alumni artists like John Osborn, a tenor who is performing internationally at the Metropolitan Opera, Vienna Stadsoper, National Opera, and Glimmerglass; Kimm Julian, well-known baritone with regional opera companies and in Europe; and Beverly O'Reagan Thiele, soprano who sings with many regional companies, the New York City Opera, and the Metropolitan Opera, also return for recitals and master classes. Distinguished music educators on the national scene appear regularly to participate in the music education workshop series for students and area teachers.

Indianola and the Blank Performing Arts Center are the home of the Des Moines Metro Opera, one of America's leading regional opera companies, and a number of students become a part of its staff each summer.

Simpson is a remarkable place for a young musician to watch, listen, and grow. It is a place where each student is challenged to develop his or her musical and artistic gifts to the fullest and counseled carefully on realistic career goals and the steps to be taken beyond the Simpson years.

Slippery Rock University of Pennsylvania

Slippery Rock, Pennsylvania

State-supported, coed. Rural campus. Total enrollment: 8,105. Music program established 1960.

Degrees Bachelor of Music in the area of performance; Bachelor of Science in the areas of music education, music therapy. Majors and concentrations: band, music education, music therapy, orchestral instruments, piano, voice. Program accredited by NASM, AMTA.
Enrollment 117 total; 108 undergraduate, 9 nonprofessional degree.
Music Student Profile 60% females, 40% males, 1% international.
Music Faculty 13 undergraduate (full-time), 5 undergraduate (part-time). 38% of full-time faculty have terminal degrees. Graduate students do not teach undergraduate courses. Undergraduate student–faculty ratio: 9:1.
Student Life Student groups/activities include Pennsylvania Collegiate Music Educators Association, National Association of Music Therapy Regional Association Student Chapter, Mu Phi Epsilon. Special housing available for music students.
Expenses for 2006–2007 Application fee: $25. State resident tuition: $4906 full-time. Nonresident tuition: $7360 full-time. Mandatory fees: $1369 full-time. College room and board: $4796. College room only: $2688. Special program-related fees: $25 per semester for accompanist fee.
Financial Aid Program-specific awards: 1 Swope Scholarship for sophomores and juniors ($500), 10 Madrigal Scholarships for vocal majors ($400), 1 Winder Scholarship for freshmen ($500), 1 Chapin Scholarship for flutists ($500), 1 Williamson Scholarship for vocal majors ($500), 1 Kevin Woods Memorial Scholarship for sophomore, junior, or senior instrumental majors ($500), 1 Dwight Baker Memorial Scholarship for instrumental majors ($250), 3 Kate Brennan Scholarships for upperclassmen music education majors ($250), 1 Sue Shuttleworth Scholarship for upperclassmen music therapy majors ($250), 1 Terry Steele Jazz Scholarship for freshmen ($200).
Application Procedures Students admitted directly into the professional program freshman year. Deadline for freshmen and transfers: June 1. Required: college transcript(s) for transfer students, minimum 2.0 high school GPA, interview, audition, Seashore Musical Aptitude Test. Auditions held 5 times and by appointment on campus; recorded music is permissible as a substitute for live auditions when distance is prohibitive or scheduling is difficult and videotaped performances are permissible as a substitute for live auditions when distance is prohibitive or scheduling is difficult.
Web Site http://www.sru.edu
Undergraduate Contact Stacey Steele, Audition Committee Chair, Department of Music, Slippery Rock University of Pennsylvania, Swope Music Hall, Slippery Rock, Pennsylvania 16057; 724-738-2440, fax: 724-738-4469, e-mail address: stacey.steele@sru.edu

Southeastern Louisiana University

Hammond, Louisiana

State-supported, coed. Small town campus. Total enrollment: 15,472. Music program established 1946.
Degrees Bachelor of Music in the areas of instrumental music, vocal music, keyboard; Bachelor of Music Education in the areas of instrumental music education, vocal music education. Majors and concentrations: band, guitar, music education, piano, strings, voice. Graduate degrees offered: Master of Music in the areas of theory, performance. Cross-registration with Southern University and Agricultural and Mechanical College. Program accredited by NASM, NCATE.
Enrollment 177 total; 161 undergraduate, 16 graduate.
Music Student Profile 42% females, 58% males, 18% minorities, 10% international.
Music Faculty 18 total (full-time), 19 total (part-time). 75% of full-time faculty have terminal degrees. Graduate students teach a few undergraduate courses. Undergraduate student–faculty ratio: 4:1.
Student Life Student groups/activities include Phi Mu Alpha Sinfonia, Music Educators National Conference, Delta Omicron. Special housing available for music students.
Expenses for 2005–2006 Application fee: $20. State resident tuition: $3341 full-time. Nonresident tuition: $8669 full-time. Full-time tuition varies according to course load. College room and board: $5180. College room only: $3150. Room and board charges vary according to board plan and housing facility.

Financial Aid Program-specific awards: 200 performance grants for music majors ($1000).
Application Procedures Students apply for admission into the professional program by sophomore year. Deadline for freshmen and transfers: continuous. Required: high school transcript, college transcript(s) for transfer students, minimum 2.0 high school GPA, audition, ACT test score only (minimum composite ACT score of 20), minimum ACT score of 20 or standing in top 50% of high school class. Auditions held 10 times on campus and off campus in various locations; recorded music is permissible as a substitute for live auditions when distance is prohibitive and videotaped performances are permissible as a substitute for live auditions when distance is prohibitive.
Web Site http://www.selu.edu/music
Undergraduate Contact Dr. David Evenson, Head, Department of Music and Dramatic Arts, Southeastern Louisiana University, SLU Box 10815, Hammond, Louisiana 70402; 985-549-2184, fax: 985-549-2892, e-mail address: devenson@selu.edu
Graduate Contact Dr. Bryan DePoy, Graduate Coordinator, Department of Music and Dramatic Arts, Southeastern Louisiana University, SLU Box 10815, Hammond, Louisiana 70402; 985-549-2184, fax: 985-549-2892, e-mail address: bdepoy@selu.edu

Southeastern Oklahoma State University

Durant, Oklahoma

State-supported, coed. Small town campus. Total enrollment: 4,075. Music program established 1978.

Southeast Missouri State University

Cape Girardeau, Missouri

State-supported, coed. Small town campus. Total enrollment: 10,292.

Southern Adventist University

Collegedale, Tennessee

Independent Seventh-day Adventist, coed. Small town campus. Total enrollment: 2,522.
Degrees Bachelor of Music. Majors and concentrations: music education. Program accredited by NASM.
Enrollment 53 total; 19 undergraduate, 34 nonprofessional degree.
Music Student Profile 62% females, 38% males, 26% minorities, 7% international.
Music Faculty 7 undergraduate (full-time), 15 undergraduate (part-time). 29% of full-time faculty have terminal degrees. Graduate students do not teach undergraduate courses. Undergraduate student–faculty ratio: 4:1.
Student Life Student groups/activities include student ensembles, opera scenes and musical theater, solo and small ensemble performances at religious services.
Expenses for 2006–2007 Application fee: $25. Comprehensive fee: $19,388 includes full-time tuition ($14,300), mandatory fees ($484), and college room and board ($4604). College room only: $2604. Special program-related fees: $150–$300 per semester for private lesson fee.
Financial Aid Program-specific awards: 28 symphony scholarships for string, wind, and percussion students ($1700), 15 band scholarships for wind and percussion students ($800), 19 choral/vocal scholarships for vocal students ($420), 5 keyboard awards for organ/piano students ($500).
Application Procedures Students apply for admission into the professional program by freshman year. Deadline for freshmen and transfers: continuous. Required: high school transcript, college transcript(s) for transfer students, audition, SAT I or ACT test scores. Auditions held twice on campus; recorded music is permissible as a substitute for live auditions when distance is prohibitive and videotaped performances are permissible as a substitute for live auditions when distance is prohibitive.
Web Site http://www.southern.edu

Southern Adventist University (continued)

Undergraduate Contact Marc Grundy, Director of Enrollment Services, Southern Adventist University, PO Box 370, Collegedale, Tennessee 37315; 800-768-8437, fax: 423-238-3005.

Southern Arkansas University–Magnolia

Magnolia, Arkansas

State-supported, coed. Small town campus. Total enrollment: 3,057.

Degrees Bachelor of Music Education. Majors and concentrations: music education. Program accredited by NASM.

Enrollment 34 total; all undergraduate.

Music Student Profile 59% females, 41% males, 27% minorities, 4% international.

Music Faculty 7 undergraduate (full-time), 4 undergraduate (part-time). 68% of full-time faculty have terminal degrees. Graduate students do not teach undergraduate courses. Undergraduate student–faculty ratio: 19:1.

Expenses for 2005–2006 State resident tuition: $3900 full-time. Nonresident tuition: $5910 full-time. Mandatory fees: $390 full-time. Full-time tuition and fees vary according to course load. College room and board: $3790. College room only: $1960. Special program-related fees: $40 per 1 semester hour for applied music fee, $60 per 2 semester hours for applied music fee.

Financial Aid Program-specific awards: 105 departmental scholarships for music majors/minors and participants in music activities ($2369).

Application Procedures Students admitted directly into the professional program freshman year. Deadline for freshmen and transfers: August 15. Required: high school transcript, college transcript(s) for transfer students, ACT test score only (minimum composite ACT score of 19), audition for scholarship consideration. Recommended: minimum 2.0 high school GPA, interview, audition. Auditions held by appointment on campus.

Web Site http://www.saumag.edu/music/

Undergraduate Contact Dr. Dan Dykame, Chair, Music Department, Southern Arkansas University–Magnolia, 100 East University, Magnolia, Arkansas 71753-5000; 870-235-4247, fax: 870-235-5005, e-mail address: dhdykema@saumag.edu

Southern Illinois University Carbondale

Carbondale, Illinois

State-supported, coed. Rural campus. Total enrollment: 21,441.

Degrees Bachelor of Music in the areas of performance, piano pedagogy, music theory/composition, music education. Majors and concentrations: classical music, guitar, music business, music education, music theater, music theory and composition, opera, piano pedagogy, piano/organ, stringed instruments, voice, wind and percussion instruments. Graduate degrees offered: Master of Music in the areas of performance, piano pedagogy, music theory/composition, music history/literature, opera/music theater, music education. Program accredited by NASM.

Enrollment 270 total; 170 undergraduate, 40 graduate, 60 nonprofessional degree.

Music Student Profile 45% females, 55% males, 5% minorities, 18% international.

Music Faculty 26 total (full-time), 3 total (part-time). 85% of full-time faculty have terminal degrees. Graduate students do not teach undergraduate courses. Undergraduate student–faculty ratio: 7:1.

Student Life Student groups/activities include Collegiate Music Educators National Conference, Phi Mu Alpha Sinfonia, Mu Phi Epsilon. Special housing available for music students.

Expenses for 2005–2006 Application fee: $30. State resident tuition: $5310 full-time. Nonresident tuition: $13,275 full-time. Mandatory fees: $1521 full-time. Full-time tuition and fees vary according to course load and student level. College room and board: $5560. College room only: $3058. Room and board

charges vary according to board plan and housing facility. Special program-related fees: $20 per semester for instrument rental.

Financial Aid Program-specific awards: 20–30 music scholarships for musically talented students ($300–$2000).

Application Procedures Students admitted directly into the professional program freshman year. Deadline for freshmen and transfers: continuous. Notification date for freshmen: August 15. Required: high school transcript, college transcript(s) for transfer students, audition, ACT test score only (minimum composite ACT score of 18). Auditions held 3 times and by appointment on campus; recorded music is permissible as a substitute for live auditions for out-of-state applicants and videotaped performances are permissible as a substitute for live auditions for international applicants and out-of-state applicants.

Web Site http://www.siu.edu/~music

Undergraduate Contact Dr. Jeanine Wagner, Undergraduate Advisor, School of Music, Southern Illinois University Carbondale, Mailcode 4302, Carbondale, Illinois 62901-4302; 618-453-5815, fax: 618-453-5808, e-mail address: jwagner@siu.edu

Graduate Contact Dr. Frank Stemper, Graduate Advisor, School of Music, Southern Illinois University Carbondale, Mailcode 4302, Carbondale, Illinois 62901-4302; 618-536-8742, fax: 618-453-5808, e-mail address: fstemp@siu.edu

Southern Illinois University Edwardsville

Edwardsville, Illinois

State-supported, coed. Suburban campus. Total enrollment: 13,460. Music program established 1958.

Degrees Bachelor of Music in the areas of performance, music education, jazz performance, musical theater, theory/composition, music merchandising. Majors and concentrations: jazz, music education, music history and literature, music merchandising, music theater, music theory and composition, performance. Graduate degrees offered: Master of Music in the areas of music education, performance. Program accredited by NASM.

Enrollment 235 total; 175 undergraduate, 35 graduate, 25 nonprofessional degree.

Music Student Profile 55% females, 45% males, 16% minorities, 5% international.

Music Faculty 22 total (full-time), 20 total (part-time). 68% of full-time faculty have terminal degrees. Graduate students teach a few undergraduate courses. Undergraduate student–faculty ratio: 5:1.

Student Life Student groups/activities include Sigma Alpha Iota, Phi Mu Alpha Sinfonia, Music Educators National Conference. Special housing available for music students.

Expenses for 2005–2006 Application fee: $50. State resident tuition: $4320 full-time. Nonresident tuition: $10,800 full-time. Mandatory fees: $859 full-time. Full-time tuition and fees vary according to course load. College room and board: $5819. College room only: $3389. Room and board charges vary according to board plan and housing facility. Special program-related fees: $10 for music methods fee, $20 per course for private applied lessons, $30 for ensemble fee.

Financial Aid Program-specific awards: 20–40 Music Talent Awards for those demonstrating talent and academic achievement ($100–$1000), 20 Provost Scholarships for those demonstrating talent and academic achievement ($2000).

Application Procedures Students admitted directly into the professional program freshman year. Deadline for freshmen and transfers: April 1. Notification date for freshmen and transfers: August 19. Required: high school transcript, college transcript(s) for transfer students, audition, SAT I or ACT test scores, minimum 2.5 high school GPA. Recommended: letter of recommendation. Auditions held 3 times and by appointment on campus; recorded music is permissible as a substitute for live auditions when distance is prohibitive and videotaped performances are permissible as a substitute for live auditions when distance is prohibitive.

Web Site http://www.siue.edu/MUSIC/

Undergraduate Contact Music Department, Southern Illinois University Edwardsville, Box 1771, Edwardsville, Illinois 62026-1771; 618-650-3900, fax: 618-692-5988, e-mail address: admis@siue.edu

Graduate Contact Darryl Coan, Director of Graduate Studies, Department of Music, Southern Illinois University Edwardsville, Box 1771, Edwardsville, Illinois 62026-1771; 618-650-3900, fax: 618-692-5988.

Meadows School of the Arts/Division of Music
Southern Methodist University
Dallas, Texas

Independent, coed. Suburban campus. Total enrollment: 11,152.
Degrees Bachelor of Music in the areas of performance, music education, composition, music therapy. Majors and concentrations: bassoon, cello, clarinet, composition, double bass, flute, French horn, guitar, harp, harpsichord, music education, music therapy, oboe, organ, percussion, piano, saxophone, trombone, trumpet, tuba, viola, violin. Graduate degrees offered: Master of Music in the areas of performance, music education, music theory, composition, music history, piano performance and pedagogy; Master of Sacred Music in the area of sacred music (jointly with Perkins School of Theology). Program accredited by NASM.
Enrollment 292 total; 121 undergraduate, 139 graduate, 32 nonprofessional degree.
Music Student Profile 53% females, 47% males, 15% minorities, 20% international.
Music Faculty 34 undergraduate (full-time), 40 undergraduate (part-time), 34 graduate (full-time), 40 graduate (part-time). 94% of full-time faculty have terminal degrees. Graduate students teach a few undergraduate courses. Undergraduate student–faculty ratio: 5:1.
Student Life Student groups/activities include Music Educators National Conference, National Association of Music Therapy, Music Teachers National Association. Special housing available for music students.
Expenses for 2006–2007 Application fee: $50. Comprehensive fee: $38,325 includes full-time tuition ($25,400), mandatory fees ($3230), and college room and board ($9695). College room only: $5775. Special program-related fees: $22 per term for concert fee, $25 per term for practice room fee, $50 per rental course for recital recording fee.
Financial Aid Program-specific awards: 160 Meadows Artistic Scholarships for talented program majors ($2000–$10,000).
Application Procedures Students apply for admission into the professional program by freshman year. Deadline for freshmen and transfers: April 1. Notification date for freshmen: May 1; transfers: June 1. Required: essay, high school transcript, college transcript(s) for transfer students, letter of recommendation, audition, SAT I or ACT test scores. Recommended: interview. Auditions held 15 times on campus and off campus in various locations; recorded music is permissible as a substitute for live auditions if a live audition is impossible and videotaped performances are permissible as a substitute for live auditions if a live audition is impossible.
Undergraduate Contact Tommy Newton, Director of Recruitment, Meadows School of the Arts, Southern Methodist University, PO Box 750356, Dallas, Texas 75275-0356; 214-768-3217, fax: 214-768-3272, e-mail address: tnewton@smu.edu
Graduate Contact Ms. Jean Cherry, Director of Graduate Admissions and Records, Meadows School of the Arts, Southern Methodist University, PO Box 750356, Dallas, Texas 75275-0356; 214-768-3765, fax: 214-768-3272, e-mail address: jcherry@mail.smu.edu

Southern University and Agricultural and Mechanical College
Baton Rouge, Louisiana

State-supported, coed. Suburban campus. Total enrollment: 9,941. Music program established 1937.

Degrees Bachelor of Music in the area of performance; Bachelor of Music Education. Majors and concentrations: instrumental music, music education, piano, voice, wind and percussion instruments. Cross-registration with Louisiana State University, Southeastern Louisiana University. Program accredited by NASM.
Enrollment 135 total.
Music Student Profile 26% females, 74% males, 99% minorities, 1% international.
Music Faculty 9 undergraduate (full-time), 8 undergraduate (part-time). 22% of full-time faculty have terminal degrees. Graduate students do not teach undergraduate courses. Undergraduate student–faculty ratio: 10:1.
Student Life Student groups/activities include Phi Mu Alpha Sinfonia, Mu Phi Epsilon/Sigma Iota.
Expenses for 2005–2006 Application fee: $20. State resident tuition: $3592 full-time. Nonresident tuition: $9384 full-time. Full-time tuition varies according to course load and location. College room and board: $4646. College room only: $2816. Room and board charges vary according to board plan and housing facility.
Financial Aid Program-specific awards: 12 choir/vocal awards for choir singers ($100–$500), 10–15 music awards for program majors ($100–$500), 6 transfer scholarships for transfer students ($1000).
Application Procedures Students admitted directly into the professional program freshman year. Deadline for freshmen and transfers: continuous. Notification date for freshmen and transfers: continuous. Required: high school transcript, college transcript(s) for transfer students, audition, SAT I or ACT test scores, medical history, good conduct letter. Auditions held twice and by appointment on campus; recorded music is permissible as a substitute for live auditions for out-of-state applicants and videotaped performances are permissible as a substitute for live auditions for out-of-state applicants.
Web Site http://www.subr.edu
Undergraduate Contact Mrs. Velva Thomas, Director of Admissions, Southern University and Agricultural and Mechanical College, PO Box 9901, Southern University Station, Baton Rouge, Louisiana 70813; 225-771-2430.

Southwestern Oklahoma State University
Weatherford, Oklahoma

State-supported, coed. Small town campus. Total enrollment: 4,841.
Degrees Bachelor of Music in the areas of music therapy, music theory/composition, performance/instrumental, vocal, keyboard, music with elective studies in business; Bachelor of Music Education in the areas of instrumental music education, vocal/keyboard music education. Majors and concentrations: composition, music, music and business, music education, music theory, music therapy, performance, piano/organ, stringed instruments, voice, wind and percussion instruments. Graduate degrees offered: Master of Music in the area of performance and music education. Program accredited by NASM, AMTA.
Enrollment 150 total; 140 undergraduate, 10 graduate.
Music Student Profile 60% females, 40% males, 5% minorities, 5% international.
Music Faculty 13 total (full-time), 6 total (part-time). 64% of full-time faculty have terminal degrees. Graduate students teach a few undergraduate courses. Undergraduate student–faculty ratio: 10:1.
Student Life Student groups/activities include music fraternities and sororities, American Music Therapy Association, Music Educators National Conference.
Expenses for 2005–2006 Special program-related fees: $50 per credit hour for applied lessons fee.
Financial Aid Program-specific awards: ensemble music scholarships for ensemble performers, music scholarships for those passing audition evaluations.
Application Procedures Students admitted directly into the professional program freshman year. Deadline for freshmen and transfers: continuous. Required: high school transcript, college transcript(s) for transfer students, SAT I or ACT test scores

Southwestern Oklahoma State University (continued)

(minimum composite ACT score of 19), audition for transfer students. Recommended: audition. Auditions held continuously by appointment on campus; recorded music is permissible as a substitute for live auditions when distance is prohibitive and videotaped performances are permissible as a substitute for live auditions when distance is prohibitive.
Web Site http://www.swosu.edu
Undergraduate Contact Ms. Marla Russ, Secretary, Department of Music, Southwestern Oklahoma State University, 100 Campus Drive, Weatherford, Oklahoma 73096; 580-774-3708, fax: 580-774-3714, e-mail address: marla.russ@swosu.edu
Graduate Contact Dr. Dennis Widen, Assistant Professor, Department of Music, Southwestern Oklahoma State University, 100 Campus Drive, Weatherford, Oklahoma 73096; 580-774-3216, fax: 580-774-3714, e-mail address: dennis.widen@swosu.edu

Southwestern University

Georgetown, Texas

Independent Methodist, coed. Suburban campus. Total enrollment: 1,309.

State University of New York at Binghamton

Binghamton, New York

State-supported, coed. Suburban campus. Total enrollment: 14,018.
Degrees Bachelor of Music in the area of performance. Majors and concentrations: organ, piano, stringed instruments, voice, wind and percussion instruments. Graduate degrees offered: Master of Music in the areas of performance, composition, conducting, music history. Program accredited by NASM.
Enrollment 86 total; 6 undergraduate, 30 graduate, 50 nonprofessional degree.
Music Faculty 9 total (full-time), 25 total (part-time). 75% of full-time faculty have terminal degrees. Graduate students do not teach undergraduate courses.
Expenses for 2005–2006 Application fee: $40. State resident tuition: $4350 full-time. Nonresident tuition: $10,610 full-time. Mandatory fees: $1488 full-time. College room and board: $8150. College room only: $4970. Room and board charges vary according to board plan and housing facility. Special program-related fees: $15 per year for practice room fee.
Financial Aid Program-specific awards: 9 endowed scholarships for music majors ($500–$2500).
Application Procedures Students apply for admission into the professional program by freshman year. Deadline for freshmen and transfers: January 15. Required: essay, high school transcript, college transcript(s) for transfer students, audition, SAT I or ACT test scores. Auditions held as needed on campus.
Web Site http://music.binghamton.edu/
Undergraduate Contact Dr. Colleen Reardon, Director of Undergraduate Studies, Department of Music, State University of New York at Binghamton, PO Box 6000, Binghamton, New York 13902-6000; 607-777-2530, fax: 607-777-4425, e-mail address: reardon@binghamton.edu
Graduate Contact Dr. Jonathan Biggers, Director of Graduate Studies, Department of Music, State University of New York at Binghamton, PO Box 6000, Binghamton, New York 13902-6000; 607-777-2595, fax: 607-777-4425, e-mail address: biggers@binghamton.edu

State University of New York at Buffalo

Buffalo, New York

State-supported, coed. Total enrollment: 27,220. Music program established 1958.

The Crane School of Music
State University of New York College at Potsdam

Potsdam, New York

State-supported, coed. Total enrollment: 4,329. Music program established 1886.
Degrees Bachelor of Music in the areas of music education, musical studies, performance, business of music. Majors and concentrations: classical music, guitar, harp, keyboard, music, music and business, music education, musical studies, piano/organ, stringed instruments, voice, wind and percussion instruments. Graduate degrees offered: Master of Music in the areas of music education, performance, composition, music theory, music history. Cross-registration with State University of New York College of Technology at Canton, St. Lawrence University, Clarkson College. Program accredited by NASM.
Enrollment 625 total; 550 undergraduate, 50 graduate, 25 nonprofessional degree.
Music Student Profile 54% females, 46% males, 4% minorities, 1% international.
Music Faculty 63 undergraduate (full-time), 8 undergraduate (part-time). 95% of full-time faculty have terminal degrees. Graduate students do not teach undergraduate courses. Undergraduate student–faculty ratio: 12:1.
Student Life Student groups/activities include Music Educators National Conference, Phi Mu Alpha Sinfonia, Sigma Alpha Iota.
Expenses for 2005–2006 Application fee: $40. State resident tuition: $4350 full-time. Nonresident tuition: $10,610 full-time. Mandatory fees: $939 full-time. College room and board: $7670. College room only: $4420. Room and board charges vary according to board plan and housing facility. Special program-related fees: $30–$60 per year for community performance series fee, $150 per semester for instrument maintenance.
Financial Aid Program-specific awards: 100 endowed scholarships for program students ($851).
Application Procedures Students admitted directly into the professional program freshman year. Deadline for freshmen and transfers: March 1. Notification date for freshmen and transfers: April 1. Required: high school transcript, college transcript(s) for transfer students, audition, SAT I or ACT test scores, 80% average out of 100% in high school. Auditions held 9 times on campus and off campus in Albany, NY; Rochester, NY; locations on Long Island; recorded music is permissible as a substitute for live auditions for out-of-state and international applicants and videotaped performances are permissible as a substitute for live auditions for out-of-state and international applicants.
Web Site http://www.potsdam.edu/crane/
Undergraduate Contact Thomas W. Nesbitt, Director, Admissions Office, State University of New York College at Potsdam, Potsdam, New York 13676; 315-267-2180.
Graduate Contact Dr. Glenn Guiles, Associate Dean, The Crane School of Music, State University of New York College at Potsdam, 44 Pierrepont Avenue, Potsdam, New York 13676; 315-267-2775, fax: 315-267-2413.

State University of New York, Fredonia

Fredonia, New York

State-supported, coed. Small town campus. Total enrollment: 5,432. Music program established 1931.
Degrees Bachelor of Fine Arts in the area of music theater; Bachelor of Music in the areas of music education, performance, composition; Bachelor of Science in the areas of sound recording technology, music therapy. Majors and concentrations: brass, composition, guitar, music education, music therapy, piano, sound recording technology, stringed instruments, voice, wind and percussion instruments. Graduate degrees offered: Master of Music in the areas of music education, performance, theory/composition. Program accredited by NASM, AMTA.
Enrollment 555 total; 475 undergraduate, 60 graduate, 20 nonprofessional degree.

Music Student Profile 50% females, 50% males, 6% minorities, 5% international.

Music Faculty 38 total (full-time), 35 total (part-time). 90% of full-time faculty have terminal degrees. Graduate students teach a few undergraduate courses. Undergraduate student–faculty ratio: 10:1.

Student Life Student groups/activities include Music Educators National Conference Student Chapter, National Association of Music Therapy Student Chapter, professional music fraternities.

Expenses for 2005–2006 Application fee: $40. State resident tuition: $4350 full-time. Nonresident tuition: $10,610 full-time. Mandatory fees: $1091 full-time. College room and board: $6940. College room only: $4350. Room and board charges vary according to board plan and housing facility. Special program-related fees: $200 per semester for comprehensive music fee (all majors).

Financial Aid Program-specific awards: 40–50 Hillman Foundation Awards for program majors ($500–$1500), 10–15 piano scholarships for program majors ($500–$2000).

Application Procedures Students admitted directly into the professional program freshman year. Deadline for freshmen and transfers: continuous. Required: high school transcript, college transcript(s) for transfer students, 2 letters of recommendation, audition, SAT I or ACT test scores. Auditions held 6 times on campus and off campus in Suffolk County, Long Island; recorded music is permissible as a substitute for live auditions when distance is prohibitive and videotaped performances are permissible as a substitute for live auditions when distance is prohibitive.

Web Site http://www.fredonia.edu/som/

Undergraduate Contact Mr. Barry Kilpatrick, Assistant Director (Admissions), School of Music, State University of New York, Fredonia, Mason Hall, Fredonia, New York 14063; 716-673-3153, fax: 716-673-3154, e-mail address: barry.kilpatrick@fredonia.edu

Graduate Contact Ms. Patricia Corron, Graduate Advisor, School of Music, State University of New York, Fredonia, Mason Hall, Fredonia, New York 14063; 716-673-4636, fax: 716-673-3154, e-mail address: patricia.corron@fredonia.edu

Stephen F. Austin State University
Nacogdoches, Texas

State-supported, coed. Small town campus. Total enrollment: 11,435. Music program established 1923.

Degrees Bachelor of Music in the areas of performance, composition, music education. Majors and concentrations: music education, music theory and composition, orchestral instruments, piano pedagogy, piano/organ, voice, wind and percussion instruments. Graduate degrees offered: Master of Arts in the areas of music education, music; Master of Music in the areas of performance, conducting, accompanying. Program accredited by NASM.

Enrollment 279 total; 256 undergraduate, 23 graduate.

Music Student Profile 48% females, 52% males, 18% minorities, 1% international.

Music Faculty 28 total (full-time), 6 total (part-time). 75% of full-time faculty have terminal degrees. Graduate students teach a few undergraduate courses. Undergraduate student–faculty ratio: 12:1.

Student Life Student groups/activities include Texas Music Educators Association, National Association of Teachers of Singing, Music Teachers National Association.

Expenses for 2005–2006 Application fee: $25. State resident tuition: $4718 full-time. Nonresident tuition: $12,998 full-time. Full-time tuition varies according to course load. College room and board: $5459. Room and board charges vary according to board plan and housing facility. Special program-related fees: $15 per class for elementary music education fee, $15 per class for computer lab fee, $15 per class for ensemble materials fees, $15 for recital fee, $20 per credit hour for applied music lesson fee, $61 per credit hour for accompanist, keyboard maintenance.

Financial Aid Program-specific awards: 12 Young Artists Scholarship Awards for incoming freshmen ($5000–$12,000), 75 music activity scholarships for program students ($600–$8000).

Application Procedures Students admitted directly into the professional program freshman year. Deadline for freshmen and transfers: continuous. Notification date for freshmen and transfers: continuous. Required: high school transcript, college transcript(s) for transfer students, audition, SAT or ACT (scores required vary according to high school rank). Auditions held as needed on campus; recorded music is permissible as a substitute for live auditions when distance is prohibitive and videotaped performances are permissible as a substitute for live auditions when distance is prohibitive.

Web Site http://www.music.sfasu.edu

Contact Dr. Ronald E. Anderson, Chair, Department of Music, Stephen F. Austin State University, Box 13043, SFA Station, Nacogdoches, Texas 75962; 936-468-4602, fax: 936-468-5810, e-mail address: randerson@sfasu.edu

Stetson University
DeLand, Florida

Independent, coed. Small town campus. Total enrollment: 3,665. Music program established 1883.

Susquehanna University
Selinsgrove, Pennsylvania

Independent, coed. Suburban campus. Total enrollment: 1,989. Music program established 1899.

Degrees Bachelor of Music in the areas of performance, music education, church music. Majors and concentrations: brass, church music, music education, performance, piano/organ, stringed instruments, voice, wind and percussion instruments. Program accredited by NASM.

Enrollment 98 total; 74 undergraduate, 24 nonprofessional degree.

Music Student Profile 61% females, 39% males, 1% minorities.

Music Faculty 11 undergraduate (full-time), 18 undergraduate (part-time). 90% of full-time faculty have terminal degrees. Graduate students do not teach undergraduate courses. Undergraduate student–faculty ratio: 10:1.

Student Life Student groups/activities include Music Educators National Conference Student Chapter, Phi Mu Alpha Sinfonia, Sigma Alpha Iota.

Expenses for 2005–2006 Application fee: $35. Comprehensive fee: $33,465 includes full-time tuition ($26,265) and college room and board ($7200).

Financial Aid Program-specific awards: 1 Isaacs Scholarship for program majors ($10,000), music scholarships for program majors ($2000–$5000), performance grants for program majors and non-majors ($1000–$1500).

Application Procedures Students admitted directly into the professional program freshman year. Deadline for freshmen: March 1; transfers: continuous. Notification date for freshmen: continuous. Required: essay, high school transcript, college transcript(s) for transfer students, 2 letters of recommendation, audition, SAT I or ACT test scores. Recommended: interview. Auditions held 5 times on campus; recorded music is permissible as a substitute for live auditions in special circumstances and videotaped performances are permissible as a substitute for live auditions in special circumstances.

Web Site http://www.susqu.edu/music/

Undergraduate Contact Ms. Heather Loomis, Administrative Assistant, Department of Music, Susquehanna University, 514 University Avenue, Selinsgrove, Pennsylvania 17870; 570-372-4309, fax: 570-372-2789, e-mail address: musicdept@susqu.edu

The Swinney Conservatory of Music
See Central Methodist University

Sybil B. Harrington College of Fine Arts and Humanities
See West Texas A&M University

Setnor School of Music
Syracuse University
Syracuse, New York

Independent, coed. Urban campus. Total enrollment: 17,266. Music program established 1877.

Degrees Bachelor of Arts in the area of music; Bachelor of Music in the areas of music composition, music education, music industry, performance. Majors and concentrations: composition, music, music business, music education, performance. Graduate degrees offered: Master of Music in the areas of music composition, music education, organ, percussion, piano, strings, voice, wind instruments. Program accredited by NASM.

Enrollment 222 total; 198 undergraduate, 24 graduate.

Music Student Profile 68% females, 32% males, 6% minorities.

Music Faculty 19 total (full-time), 51 total (part-time). 92% of full-time faculty have terminal degrees. Graduate students teach a few undergraduate courses. Undergraduate student–faculty ratio: 9:1.

Student Life Student groups/activities include Sigma Alpha Iota, Music Educators National Conference, Pi Kappa Lambda.

Expenses for 2005–2006 Application fee: $60. Comprehensive fee: $38,655 includes full-time tuition ($27,210), mandatory fees ($1075), and college room and board ($10,370). College room only: $5620. Room and board charges vary according to board plan and housing facility. Special program-related fees: $15 per course for practice room fee (piano), $36–$72 per course for practice room fee (organ), $200–$400 per semester for private lessons.

Financial Aid Program-specific awards: 36 Special Music Awards for talented program majors ($18,000).

Application Procedures Students admitted directly into the professional program freshman year. Deadline for freshmen and transfers: January 1. Notification date for freshmen: March 1; transfers: August 15. Required: essay, high school transcript, college transcript(s) for transfer students, minimum 3.0 high school GPA, 2 letters of recommendation, audition, SAT I or ACT test scores, high school counselor evaluation. Recommended: interview. Auditions held 10 times on campus and off campus in New York, NY; videotaped performances are permissible as a substitute for live auditions if a live audition is impossible.

Web Site http://vpa.syr.edu/

Undergraduate Contact Director, CVPA Recruitment and Admissions, College of Visual and Performing Arts, Syracuse University, 202P Crouse College, Syracuse, New York 13244-1010; 315-443-2769, fax: 315-443-1935, e-mail address: admissu@syr.edu

Graduate Contact Graduate School, Syracuse University, Suite 303 Bowne Hall, Syracuse, New York 13244; 315-443-3028, fax: 315-443-3423, e-mail address: gradschl@syr.edu

More About the University

The Setnor School of Music at Syracuse University (SU) encourages students to reach their musical and intellectual potential through preparation as performers, composers, arrangers, music educators, and music industry professionals. Students are a part of a vibrant creative environment led by faculty members who are absorbed in music making both on and off campus.

Although part of a large university, the Setnor School of Music enjoys an intimate atmosphere that allows each student to receive the individual attention and opportunity for regular performance that every serious young musician requires. In this inclusive program with a classical basis, students are also exposed to contemporary music and world music of many genres. Students are immersed in music in many contexts: private lessons, ensemble rehearsals, recitals, guest artists, master classes, and performances. Qualified composition, music education, music industry, and B.A. music students may participate in a performance honors program that allows them to pursue a high level of proficiency on their instrument.

A wide array of ensembles provides ample variety for performance opportunities. All students in the Setnor School of Music are required to be involved in one of the School's ensembles every semester, although many participate in several groups. This experience helps students develop the important skill of functioning in group situations and complements the many hours every dedicated musician spends in solitary practice. A required weekly convocation provides a forum for music students and faculty members to convene as a community and features a lively mix of student, faculty, and guest performances. Academic electives, which provide a liberal arts component to the curriculum, can be selected from the broad range of courses offered at the University.

Students benefit from a faculty of active professionals who are members of the Syracuse Symphony Orchestra, composers whose works have been performed nationally and internationally, and recitalists who have won competitions worldwide and have performed with internationally known orchestras and ensembles. They are dedicated to challenging, inspiring, and encouraging students to explore all of their musical and intellectual potential.

The creative activities of the Setnor School of Music are an integral part of the College of Visual and Performing Arts. The College serves as the center of SU's cultural life on a campus whose lively and diverse schedule of events could only be found at a large university.

The city of Syracuse itself offers a rich culture: it is home to the Syracuse Symphony Orchestra, the Syracuse Opera, the Society for New Music, and Syracuse Stage. Syracuse is also a regular stop for touring companies of Broadway's most popular musical comedies, experimental theater troupes, nationally known comedians, rock groups, and dance companies. Nestled between the Finger Lakes and the Adirondacks, in central New York State, Syracuse is within a day's drive of New York City, Boston, Cleveland, Pittsburgh, Philadelphia, Toronto, and Montreal.

Program Facilities Crouse College houses the acoustically rich Setnor Auditorium (665 seats); the 3,823-pipe Holtkamp organ; classrooms, practice rooms, and studios; a digital electronic music studio with equipment for sampling sound processing and recording and MIDI-based programming using Macintosh computers; and the Music Education Resource Center. Belfer Audio Archive (a newly refurbished studio that offers study in sound archiving and digital multitrack and live acoustic recording) is located in the Syracuse University Library.

Faculty, Resident Artists, and Alumni Included in the faculty are members of the Syracuse Symphony Orchestra, active recitalists and performers, published authors, and widely performed composers. Recent visiting artists have included the Kronos Quartet, Joshua Bell, the Cassatt String Quartet, the Boston Brass, and the California EAR Unit. Alumni perform worldwide and are active in many areas of the music industry.

Student Performances Formal groups include chamber groups and small ensembles, Men's Chorale, Women's Choir, Instrumental Jazz Ensemble, Contemporary Music Ensemble, Opera Workshop, Orange Opus (new music ensemble that performs works by SU student composers), Oratorio Society, Pride of the Orange Marching Band, Sour Sitrus Society (basketball pep band), Symphony Band, University Orchestra, University Singers, Brazilian Music Ensemble, Wind Ensemble, and Windjammer (vocal jazz).

Special Programs Guest artists perform and hold lectures and master classes on a regular basis. Internships—local or national—are available in many areas of the music industry, and merit scholarships are available for exceptionally qualified students. Other special programs include a performance honors program for nonperformance music majors, study abroad in Strasbourg through SU Abroad, and an honors program for students who desire a rigorous academic challenge.

Taylor University
Upland, Indiana

Independent interdenominational, coed. Rural campus. Total enrollment: 1,865. Music program established 1970.

Degrees Bachelor of Arts in the area of music; Bachelor of Music in the areas of performance, composition; Bachelor of Music

Education in the area of music education; Bachelor of Science in the areas of management, marketing. Majors and concentrations: composition, guitar, music education, piano/organ, stringed instruments, theater arts/drama, voice, wind and percussion instruments. Cross-registration with Taylor University-Fort Wayne Campus. Program accredited by NASM.
Enrollment 60 total; 40 undergraduate, 20 nonprofessional degree.
Music Student Profile 52% females, 48% males, 5% minorities, 5% international.
Music Faculty 8 undergraduate (full-time), 20 undergraduate (part-time). 100% of full-time faculty have terminal degrees. Graduate students do not teach undergraduate courses. Undergraduate student–faculty ratio: 15:1.
Student Life Student groups/activities include Music Educators National Conference, National Association of Schools of Singing, Marion Philharmonic Orchestra.
Expenses for 2005–2006 Application fee: $25. Comprehensive fee: $26,376 includes full-time tuition ($20,520), mandatory fees ($226), and college room and board ($5630). College room only: $2732. Full-time tuition and fees vary according to course load. Room and board charges vary according to housing facility. Special program-related fees: $180 per semester for applied lesson fee.
Financial Aid Program-specific awards: 10 music scholarships for music majors ($3000–$5200), 20 music merit awards for music majors ($1500–$3000), 20 applied music awards for music majors ($1000–$1500).
Application Procedures Students admitted directly into the professional program freshman year. Deadline for freshmen and transfers: February 1. Notification date for freshmen and transfers: continuous. Required: essay, high school transcript, college transcript(s) for transfer students, minimum 3.0 high school GPA, 3 letters of recommendation, interview, audition, SAT I or ACT test scores. Auditions held 4 times on campus; recorded music is permissible as a substitute for live auditions when distance is prohibitive and videotaped performances are permissible as a substitute for live auditions when distance is prohibitive.
Web Site http://www.tayloru.edu
Undergraduate Contact Mr. Steve Mortland, Admissions Department, Taylor University, 236 West Reade Avenue, Upland, Indiana 46989; 317-998-5206, e-mail address: stmortlan@tayloru.edu

Esther Boyer College of Music
Temple University
Philadelphia, Pennsylvania

State-related, coed. Urban campus. Total enrollment: 33,693. Music program established 1962.

Tennessee Technological University
Cookeville, Tennessee

State-supported, coed. Small town campus. Total enrollment: 9,313. Music program established 1948.
Degrees Bachelor of Music. Majors and concentrations: music education, performance. Program accredited by NASM.
Enrollment 147 total; all undergraduate.
Music Student Profile 50% females, 50% males, 3% minorities.
Music Faculty 24 undergraduate (full-time), 6 undergraduate (part-time). 43% of full-time faculty have terminal degrees. Graduate students do not teach undergraduate courses. Undergraduate student–faculty ratio: 6:1.
Student Life Student groups/activities include Collegiate Music Educators National Conference, American Choral Directors Association Student Chapter, music therapy student organization.
Expenses for 2006–2007 Application fee: $15. State resident tuition: $4660 full-time. Nonresident tuition: $14,620 full-time. College room and board: $6650. College room only: $3096. Special program-related fees: $25 for recital fee, $100 per credit hour for private lesson fees.

Financial Aid Program-specific awards: 197 studio and ensemble scholarships for those demonstrating talent ($960).
Application Procedures Students admitted directly into the professional program freshman year. Deadline for freshmen and transfers: continuous. Required: high school transcript, college transcript(s) for transfer students, minimum 2.0 high school GPA, SAT I or ACT test scores (minimum composite ACT score of 19). Recommended: audition. Auditions held 3 times on campus; recorded music is permissible as a substitute for live auditions when distance is prohibitive and videotaped performances are permissible as a substitute for live auditions when distance is prohibitive.
Web Site http://www.tntech.edu/music
Undergraduate Contact Prof. Jonathan Good, Chairperson, Department of Music and Art, Tennessee Technological University, Box 5045, Cookeville, Tennessee 38505; 931-372-3161 ext. 6089, fax: 931-372-6279.

Tennessee Wesleyan College
Athens, Tennessee

Independent United Methodist, coed. Small town campus. Total enrollment: 815. Music program established 1955.

Texas A&M University–Commerce
Commerce, Texas

State-supported, coed. Small town campus. Total enrollment: 8,787. Music program established 1917.
Degrees Bachelor of Music in the areas of performance, piano pedagogy; Bachelor of Science in the area of music education. Majors and concentrations: music education, piano, piano pedagogy, voice, wind and percussion instruments. Graduate degrees offered: Master of Music in the areas of performance, music education. Program accredited by NASM.
Enrollment 160 total; 130 undergraduate, 30 graduate.
Music Student Profile 46% females, 54% males, 16% minorities, 3% international.
Music Faculty 15 total (full-time), 10 total (part-time). 53% of full-time faculty have terminal degrees. Graduate students do not teach undergraduate courses. Undergraduate student–faculty ratio: 10:1.
Student Life Student groups/activities include Phi Mu Alpha, professional fraternities and sororities, Mu Phi Epsilon.
Expenses for 2005–2006 Application fee: 25. State resident tuition: $3834 full-time. Nonresident tuition: $11,574 full-time. Mandatory fees: $990 full-time. Full-time tuition and fees vary according to course load. College room and board: $5740. Room and board charges vary according to board plan and housing facility. Special program-related fees: $100 per semester for applied music fees.
Financial Aid Program-specific awards: 120 music scholarships for program students ($1000).
Application Procedures Students admitted directly into the professional program freshman year. Deadline for freshmen and transfers: August 1. Required: high school transcript, college transcript(s) for transfer students, audition, SAT I or ACT test scores (minimum combined SAT I score of 920, minimum composite ACT score of 20). Recommended: letter of recommendation, interview. Auditions held 5 times and by appointment on campus; recorded music is permissible as a substitute for live auditions if a campus visit is impossible, if unedited, and if of good quality and videotaped performances are permissible as a substitute for live auditions if a campus visit is impossible, if unedited, and if of good quality.
Web Site http://www.TAMU-Commerce.edu
Undergraduate Contact Randy McDonald, Director of Admissions, Texas A&M University–Commerce, 2600 Neal Street, Commerce, Texas 75429; 903-886-5102.
Graduate Contact Dr. Allan Headley, Dean of Graduate School, Texas A&M University–Commerce, Commerce, Texas 75429; 903-886-5163.

Texas A&M University–Corpus Christi

Corpus Christi, Texas

State-supported, coed. Suburban campus. Total enrollment: 8,227. Music program established 1972.

Degrees Bachelor of Music in the areas of performance, music education. Majors and concentrations: classical guitar, keyboard, music education, voice, wind and percussion instruments. Program accredited by NASM.

Enrollment 80 total; 49 undergraduate, 31 nonprofessional degree.

Music Student Profile 42% females, 58% males, 48% minorities, 2% international.

Music Faculty 8 undergraduate (full-time), 10 undergraduate (part-time). 76% of full-time faculty have terminal degrees. Graduate students do not teach undergraduate courses. Undergraduate student–faculty ratio: 5:1.

Expenses for 2005–2006 Application fee: $20. State resident tuition: $3348 full-time. Nonresident tuition: $11,628 full-time. Mandatory fees: $1168 full-time. Full-time tuition and fees vary according to course load. College room and board: $7800. College room only: $5400. Room and board charges vary according to housing facility. Special program-related fees: $40 per semester for applied music fee.

Financial Aid Program-specific awards: 70 music scholarships for program students ($200–$8000).

Application Procedures Students apply for admission into the professional program by sophomore year. Deadline for freshmen and transfers: July 3. Notification date for freshmen and transfers: continuous. Required: high school transcript, college transcript(s) for transfer students, minimum 2.0 high school GPA, audition, SAT I or ACT test scores, theory assessment examination, Texas Academic Skills Proficiency test. Recommended: 3 letters of recommendation, essay (for scholarship applicants). Auditions held 3 times (spring) on campus; recorded music is permissible as a substitute for live auditions when distance is prohibitive and videotaped performances are permissible as a substitute for live auditions when distance is prohibitive.

Web Site http://www.tamucc.edu/~aandh/musicweb/index.htm

Undergraduate Contact Dr. Sam Logsdon, Academic Advisor, Department of Music, Texas A&M University–Corpus Christi, 6300 Ocean Drive, Unit 5720, Corpus Christi, Texas 78412; 361-825-2761, fax: 361-827-6097, e-mail address: sam.logsden@mail.tamucc.edu

Texas A&M University–Kingsville

Kingsville, Texas

State-supported, coed. Small town campus. Total enrollment: 7,126. Music program established 1930.

Texas Christian University

Fort Worth, Texas

Independent, coed. Suburban campus. Total enrollment: 8,749. Music program established 1873.

Texas Southern University

Houston, Texas

State-supported, coed. Urban campus. Total enrollment: 11,903. Music program established 1947.

Texas State University-San Marcos

San Marcos, Texas

State-supported, coed. Suburban campus. Total enrollment: 27,129. Music program established 1903.

Degrees Bachelor of Music in the areas of performance, sound recording technology, music education, jazz performance. Majors and concentrations: brass, classical music, composition, electronic composition, guitar, jazz, music education, piano/organ, sound recording technology, stringed instruments, voice, wind and percussion instruments. Graduate degrees offered: Master of Music in the areas of music education, performance, theory/composition, conducting. Program accredited by NASM.

Enrollment 475 total; 375 undergraduate, 50 graduate, 50 nonprofessional degree.

Music Student Profile 40% females, 60% males, 40% minorities, 1% international.

Music Faculty 31 total (full-time), 31 total (part-time). 50% of full-time faculty have terminal degrees. Graduate students teach a few undergraduate courses. Undergraduate student–faculty ratio: 6:1.

Student Life Student groups/activities include Music Educators National Conference Student Chapter, American Choral Directors Association Student Chapter, professional music fraternities.

Expenses for 2005–2006 Application fee: $40. State resident tuition: $3780 full-time. Nonresident tuition: $12,060 full-time. Mandatory fees: $1472 full-time. Full-time tuition and fees vary according to course load. College room and board: $5610. College room only: $3524. Room and board charges vary according to board plan and housing facility. Special program-related fees: $18 per credit hour for private lesson fee.

Financial Aid Program-specific awards: 5–10 Schneider Scholarships for Victoria, TX area students ($500–$1000), 50–100 music scholarships for music majors ($1000–$3000).

Application Procedures Students admitted directly into the professional program freshman year. Deadline for freshmen and transfers: July 1. Notification date for freshmen and transfers: July 15. Required: essay, high school transcript, college transcript(s) for transfer students, 3 letters of recommendation, audition, SAT I or ACT test scores (minimum combined SAT I score of 920, minimum composite ACT score of 20). Recommended: minimum 2.0 high school GPA. Auditions held 5 times on campus; recorded music is permissible as a substitute for live auditions when distance is prohibitive or scheduling is difficult and videotaped performances are permissible as a substitute for live auditions when distance is prohibitive or scheduling is difficult.

Web Site http://www.finearts.swt.edu/music/music.html

Undergraduate Contact Lucy Bloor, Academic Advisor, School of Music, Texas State University-San Marcos, 601 University Drive, San Marcos, Texas 78666-4616; 512-245-7928, fax: 512-245-8181.

Graduate Contact Dr. Russell Riepe, Coordinator of Graduate Studies, School of Music, Texas State University-San Marcos, 601 University Drive, San Marcos, Texas 78666-4616; 512-245-2651, fax: 512-245-8181.

Texas Tech University

Lubbock, Texas

State-supported, coed. Urban campus. Total enrollment: 28,001. Music program established 1923.

Degrees Bachelor of Music in the areas of performance, composition, music theory, music education. Majors and concentrations: composition, music, music education, music theory, piano/organ, stringed instruments, voice, wind and percussion instruments. Graduate degrees offered: Master of Music in the areas of performance, music history and literature, music theory, pedagogy, composition; Master of Music Education. Doctor of Musical Arts in the areas of performance, conducting, composition, piano pedagogy; Doctor of Philosophy in the areas of performance, music theory, music history, music education, composition, music administration. Cross-registration with South Plains College. Program accredited by NASM.

Enrollment 487 total; 345 undergraduate, 95 graduate, 47 nonprofessional degree.

Music Student Profile 45% females, 55% males, 24% minorities, 17% international.

Music Faculty 51 total (full-time), 2 total (part-time). 66% of full-time faculty have terminal degrees. Graduate students teach a few undergraduate courses.

Student Life Student groups/activities include Texas Music Educators Conference Student Chapter, Music Educators National Conference Student Chapter, Texas Music Educators Association Student Chapter. Special housing available for music students.

Expenses for 2005–2006 Application fee: $50. State resident tuition: $3870 full-time. Nonresident tuition: $12,150 full-time.

Mandatory fees: $2282 full-time. Full-time tuition and fees vary according to course load, program, and reciprocity agreements. College room and board: $6875. College room only: $3663. Room and board charges vary according to board plan and housing facility. Special program-related fees: $10 per semester for locker rental, $15 per semester per instrument for instrument rental, $15 per semester hour for private music lessons.
Financial Aid Program-specific awards: 200 endowed scholarships for program majors ($200–$3000).
Application Procedures Students admitted directly into the professional program freshman year. Deadline for freshmen and transfers: continuous. Required: essay, high school transcript, college transcript(s) for transfer students, minimum 2.0 high school GPA, letter of recommendation, interview, audition, SAT I or ACT test scores, portfolio for composition applicants. Recommended: minimum 3.0 high school GPA, video. Auditions held 4 times and by request on campus; recorded music is permissible as a substitute for live auditions when distance is prohibitive and videotaped performances are permissible as a substitute for live auditions when distance is prohibitive. Portfolio reviews held on campus.
Web Site http://www.music.ttu.edu
Undergraduate Contact Dr. Lisa Rogers, Associate Director for Undergraduate Studies, School of Music, Texas Tech University, Box 42033, Lubbock, Texas 79409-2033; 806-742-2270 ext. 250, fax: 806-742-2294.
Graduate Contact Dr. Michael Stoune, Associate Director for Graduate Studies, School of Music, Texas Tech University, Box 42033, Lubbock, Texas 79409-2033; 806-742-2270 ext. 255, fax: 806-742-2294, e-mail address: grad.music@ttu.edu

Towson University
Towson, Maryland

State-supported, coed. Suburban campus. Total enrollment: 18,011. Music program established 1966.
Degrees Bachelor of Music in the areas of music performance, music composition, jazz studies; Bachelor of Science in the area of music education. Majors and concentrations: commercial jazz, composition, jazz composition, jazz performance, music education, performance. Graduate degrees offered: Master of Music in the areas of music performance, music composition; Master of Science in the area of music education. Program accredited by NASM.
Enrollment 430 total; 240 undergraduate, 155 graduate, 35 nonprofessional degree.
Music Student Profile 57% females, 43% males, 20% minorities, 10% international.
Music Faculty 26 total (full-time), 47 total (part-time). 90% of full-time faculty have terminal degrees. Graduate students do not teach undergraduate courses. Undergraduate student–faculty ratio: 18:1.
Student Life Student groups/activities include Kappa Kappa Psi (band fraternity), Opera Club, American Choral Directors Association.
Expenses for 2005–2006 Application fee: $45. State resident tuition: $5180 full-time. Nonresident tuition: $14,114 full-time. Mandatory fees: $1916 full-time. Full-time tuition and fees vary according to course load. College room and board: $6828. College room only: $3968. Room and board charges vary according to board plan and housing facility. Special program-related fees: $75 per semester for instrument rental, $100–$260 per credit for private lessons.
Financial Aid Program-specific awards: 10 Music Department Tuition Waiver Scholarships for Maryland residents ($5200), 3 Dean's Awards in the Fine Arts for program students ($2000), 15 Music Department Awards in the Fine Arts for program students ($1000), 1–2 double reed scholarships for bassoon/oboe players, 1 May Diekmann Scholarship for oboe majors, 1 cello scholarship for cello majors, marching band scholarships for marching band participants.
Application Procedures Students admitted directly into the professional program freshman year. Deadline for freshmen: February 1; transfers: March 1. Required: high school transcript, college transcript(s) for transfer students, minimum 3.0 high school GPA, 2 letters of recommendation, audition, SAT I or ACT test scores

(minimum combined SAT I score of 1100), portfolio for composition majors, minimum 3.0 high school GPA, interview for vocalists. Recommended: essay. Auditions held 4 times on campus; videotaped performances are permissible as a substitute for live auditions on a case-by-case basis. Portfolio reviews held twice on campus.
Web Site http://www.towson.edu/music
Undergraduate Contact Mary Ann Criss, Assistant to the Chair, Department of Music, Towson University, 8000 York Road, Towson , Maryland 21252; 410-704-2836, fax: 410-704-2841, e-mail address: mcriss@towson.edu
Graduate Contact Graduate Coordinator, Department of Music, Towson University, 8000 York Road, Towson, Maryland 21252; 410-704-2839, fax: 410-704-2841.

Trinity University
San Antonio, Texas

Independent, coed. Urban campus. Total enrollment: 2,756. Music program established 1975.
Degrees Bachelor of Music in the areas of performance, composition, music education. Majors and concentrations: choral music education, composition, guitar, harpsichord, instrumental music education, piano/organ, stringed instruments, voice, wind and percussion instruments. Program accredited by NASM.
Enrollment 50 total; 10 undergraduate, 40 nonprofessional degree.
Music Student Profile 65% females, 35% males, 10% minorities, 3% international.
Music Faculty 11 undergraduate (full-time), 18 undergraduate (part-time). 100% of full-time faculty have terminal degrees. Graduate students do not teach undergraduate courses. Undergraduate student–faculty ratio: 10:1.
Student Life Student groups/activities include Opera Workshop/ Musical Theater, Pep Band.
Expenses for 2005–2006 Application fee: $50. Comprehensive fee: $30,307 includes full-time tuition ($21,432), mandatory fees ($150), and college room and board ($8725). College room only: $5815. Full-time tuition and fees vary according to course load. Room and board charges vary according to board plan. Special program-related fees: $200 per semester for individual instruction.
Financial Aid Program-specific awards: 100 music awards for program students ($800–$10,000).
Application Procedures Students apply for admission into the professional program by sophomore year. Deadline for freshmen and transfers: February 25. Notification date for freshmen and transfers: April 1. Required: essay, high school transcript, college transcript(s) for transfer students, minimum 2.0 high school GPA, audition, SAT I or ACT test scores. Recommended: minimum 3.0 high school GPA, 2 letters of recommendation, interview. Auditions held 4 times on campus; recorded music is permissible as a substitute for live auditions if a campus visit is impossible and videotaped performances are permissible as a substitute for live auditions if a campus visit is impossible.
Web Site http://www.trinity.edu/departments/public_relations/ Academic/fact_sheets/music.htm#
Undergraduate Contact Dr. Kenneth Greene, Chairman, Department of Music, Trinity University, 1 Trinity Place, San Antonio, Texas 78212-7200; 210-999-8212, fax: 210-999-8170.

John M. Long School of Music
Troy University
Troy, Alabama

State-supported, coed. Small town campus. Total enrollment: 26,880. Music program established 1965.
Degrees Bachelor of Science. Majors and concentrations: choral music education, instrumental music education, music industry. Graduate degrees offered: Master of Science in the areas of music education, conducting. Program accredited by NASM.
Enrollment 136 total; 124 undergraduate, 11 graduate, 1 nonprofessional degree.

Troy University (continued)

Music Student Profile 33% females, 67% males, 21% minorities, 2% international.

Music Faculty 14 total (full-time), 10 total (part-time). 36% of full-time faculty have terminal degrees. Graduate students teach a few undergraduate courses. Undergraduate student–faculty ratio: 10:1.

Student Life Student groups/activities include Collegiate Music Educators National Conference, Phi Mu Alpha Sinfonia, Sigma Alpha Iota.

Expenses for 2005–2006 Application fee: $20. State resident tuition: $4004 full-time. Nonresident tuition: $8008 full-time. Mandatory fees: $674 full-time. College room and board: $4964. College room only: $2300. Room and board charges vary according to board plan and housing facility. Special program-related fees: $60 per semester for private lessons.

Financial Aid Program-specific awards: 80–100 band scholarships for instrumental majors ($300–$2000), 25–30 choral scholarships for singers or pianists ($200–$2000).

Application Procedures Students admitted directly into the professional program freshman year. Deadline for freshmen and transfers: continuous. Required: high school transcript, college transcript(s) for transfer students, minimum 2.0 high school GPA, audition, SAT I or ACT test scores (minimum combined SAT I score of 870, minimum composite ACT score of 18), minimum 2.0 college GPA for transfer students. Recommended: letter of recommendation, interview. Auditions held 3 times and by appointment on campus; recorded music is permissible as a substitute for live auditions if a campus visit is impossible and videotaped performances are permissible as a substitute for live auditions if a campus visit is impossible.

Web Site http://www.tsumusic.troyst.edu

Undergraduate Contact Dr. William Denison, Director, John M. Long School of Music, Troy University, Smith Hall 112, University Avenue, Troy, Alabama 36082; 334-670-3322, fax: 334-670-3858.

Graduate Contact Mr. James Smith, Graduate Music Coordinator, John M. Long School of Music, Troy University, Long Hall 10, Troy, Alabama 36082; 334-670-3283, fax: 334-670-3858, e-mail address: jsmith@troy.edu

Truman State University

Kirksville, Missouri

State-supported, coed. Small town campus. Total enrollment: 5,803. Music program established 1940.

Degrees Bachelor of Music in the area of performance. Majors and concentrations: brass, piano, stringed instruments, voice, wind and percussion instruments. Graduate degrees offered: Master of Arts in the areas of performance, research, composition; Master of Art Education. Program accredited by NASM.

Enrollment 188 total; 142 undergraduate, 16 graduate.

Music Student Profile 59% females, 41% males, 1% minorities, 1% international.

Music Faculty 19 total (full-time), 6 total (part-time). 99% of full-time faculty have terminal degrees. Graduate students teach a few undergraduate courses. Undergraduate student–faculty ratio: 10:1.

Student Life Student groups/activities include Phi Mu Alpha, Sigma Alpha Iota, Collegiate Music Educators National Conference.

Expenses for 2005–2006 Application fee: $0. One-time mandatory fee: $150. State resident tuition: $5740 full-time. Nonresident tuition: $9920 full-time. Mandatory fees: $72 full-time. College room and board: $5380. Room and board charges vary according to housing facility. Special program-related fees: $40–$80 per semester for private lessons.

Financial Aid Program-specific awards: 21 endowed scholarships for program majors ($300–$1500), 100 service scholarships for program majors and non-majors ($300–$1500).

Application Procedures Students admitted directly into the professional program freshman year. Deadline for freshmen and transfers: May 1. Notification date for freshmen: December 5. Required: essay, high school transcript, college transcript(s) for transfer students, audition, SAT I or ACT test scores. Recommended: portfolio. Auditions held continuously on campus and off campus in Kansas City, MO; St. Louis, MO; Chicago, IL; Des Moines, IA; recorded music is permissible as a substitute for live auditions with approval from the department and videotaped performances are permissible as a substitute for live auditions with approval from the department.

Web Site http://www.truman.edu

Undergraduate Contact Mr. Dan Peterson, Director of Bands, Division of Fine Arts, Truman State University, 100 East Normal, Ophelia Parrish 1101, Kirksville, Missouri 63501; 660-785-4417, fax: 660-785-7463, e-mail address: pete@truman.edu

Graduate Contact Dr. Warren Gooch, Associate Professor of Music, Division of Fine Arts, Truman State University, 100 East Normal, Ophelia Parrish 1101, Kirksville, Missouri 63501; 660-785-4417, fax: 660-785-7463, e-mail address: wgooch@truman.edu

Union University

Jackson, Tennessee

Independent Southern Baptist, coed. Small town campus. Total enrollment: 2,866. Music program established 1920.

Degrees Bachelor of Music in the areas of performance, music education, church music, music in combination with an outside field, music theory. Majors and concentrations: choral music education, church music, instrumental music education, music and business, music and communication studies, music and religion, music theory, performance, piano/organ, voice. Cross-registration with Lambuth University, Freed-Hardeman University. Program accredited by NASM.

Enrollment 78 total.

Music Student Profile 60% females, 40% males, 3% minorities.

Music Faculty 11 undergraduate (full-time), 12 undergraduate (part-time). 91% of full-time faculty have terminal degrees. Graduate students do not teach undergraduate courses. Undergraduate student–faculty ratio: 8:1.

Student Life Student groups/activities include Phi Mu Alpha Sinfonia, Sigma Alpha Iota, Pi Kappa Lambda (national music honor society).

Expenses for 2005–2006 Application fee: $25. Comprehensive fee: $21,920 includes full-time tuition ($15,900), mandatory fees ($550), and college room and board ($5470). College room only: $3290. Full-time tuition and fees vary according to class time, course load, location, and program. Room and board charges vary according to board plan and location. Special program-related fees: $50 per semester for class piano/voice fee, $125–$225 per semester for private lessons.

Financial Aid Program-specific awards: 65 talent scholarships for program majors ($1000–$4000), 20 vocal ensemble scholarships for musically qualified students ($1300–$1700), 30 instrumental ensemble scholarships for musically qualified students ($300–$1500).

Application Procedures Students admitted directly into the professional program freshman year. Deadline for freshmen and transfers: continuous. Required: essay, high school transcript, college transcript(s) for transfer students, interview, audition, SAT I or ACT test scores. Auditions held 4 times and individually by arrangement on campus; recorded music is permissible as a substitute for live auditions when distance is prohibitive and videotaped performances are permissible as a substitute for live auditions when distance is prohibitive.

Web Site http://www.uu.edu/dept/music/

Undergraduate Contact Robbie Graves, Director of Enrollment Services, Union University, 1050 Union University Drive, Jackson, Tennessee 38305; 800-338-8646, fax: 731-661-5175, e-mail address: rgraves@uu.edu

The University of Alabama

Tuscaloosa, Alabama

State-supported, coed. Suburban campus. Total enrollment: 21,835. Music program established 1905.

Degrees Bachelor of Music in the areas of performance, music theory, composition, music therapy. Majors and concentrations: composition, music performance, music theory, music therapy. Graduate degrees offered: Master of Music in the areas of

performance, composition, musicology/ethnomusicology theory, choral conducting, wind conducting, organ performance. Program accredited by NASM.
Enrollment 307 total; 122 undergraduate, 75 graduate, 110 nonprofessional degree.
Music Student Profile 47% females, 53% males, 15% minorities, 4% international.
Music Faculty 34 total (full-time), 9 total (part-time). 88% of full-time faculty have terminal degrees. Graduate students teach a few undergraduate courses. Undergraduate student–faculty ratio: 3:1.
Student Life Student groups/activities include Community Music School, University Bands, Music education program.
Expenses for 2005–2006 Application fee: $30. State resident tuition: $4864 full-time. Nonresident tuition: $13,516 full-time. Full-time tuition varies according to course load. College room and board: $5024. College room only: $3120. Room and board charges vary according to board plan and housing facility. Special program-related fees: $100 per semester for fee for applied lessons (voice, instruments).
Financial Aid Program-specific awards: 1 Binnie Pulliam Coasts-Montgomery Music Study Club Scholarship for program students ($2200), 1 Carleton K. Butler Endowed Scholarship for members of Million Dollar Band; program students ($1700), 1 David and Janet McElroy Endowed Support Fund for program students ($1500), 1 David Thomas Hughey Memorial Endowed Scholarship for program students ($2068), 13 Georges Ryken Trust Scholarships for program students ($48,162), 5 Gilbert W. Norwood Endowed Scholarships in the School of Music for program students ($18,526), 1 Helen Johnson Crow Endowed Scholarship in the School of Music for program students ($2068), 1 Henry C. Miller, Jr. Endowed Scholarship in Clarinet for program students ($4456), 4 Henry C. Miller, Jr. Endowed Scholarships in Jazz for program students ($2750), 1 Herbert Shaddix Endowed Scholarship for Piano for program students ($450), 13 Huxford Endowed Support Fund for the University of Alabama Symphony Orchestra for Huxford Symphony Orchestra members ($78,878), 1 Louise Rogers McAllister Scholarship for program students ($1000), 1 Lucille Devere Maxwell Bettis Scholarship-Tuscaloosa Music Club for program students ($400), 1 Matthew Locke McCorkle Scholarship Fund for students with great potential in music ($4134), 12 Million Dollar Band Association Endowed Scholarships for members Million Dollar band ($8750), 1 Peyton Norvell Wiggins Memorial Endowed Music Scholarship Fund for program students ($1500), 1 Presser Foundation Scholarship for program students ($4000), 1 Stella Searcy Harris Scholarship-Tuscaloosa Music Club for program students ($600), 1 Wilbur H. Rowand Scholarship for program students ($1000), 1 William Steven Memorial Endowed Voice Scholarship Fund for program students ($3000).
Application Procedures Students apply for admission into the professional program by sophomore year. Deadline for freshmen and transfers: continuous. Required: high school transcript, college transcript(s) for transfer students, minimum 2.0 high school GPA, audition, SAT I or ACT test scores. Auditions held 3 times on campus; recorded music is permissible as a substitute for live auditions follow same format as live auditions and must be recorded on CD/audio cassette or VHS tape with completed audition application and videotaped performances are permissible as a substitute for live auditions.
Web Site http://www.music.ua.edu
Undergraduate Contact Ms. Mary K. Spiegel, Director, Undergraduate Admissions, The University of Alabama, Box 870132, Tuscaloosa, Alabama 35487; 205-348-8197, fax: 205-348-9046, e-mail address: mary.spiegel@ua.edu
Graduate Contact Dr. Carl F. Williams, Director, Graduate Admissions and Recruitment, The University of Alabama, PO Box 870118, Tuscaloosa, Alabama 35487; 205-348-5921, fax: 205-348-0400, e-mail address: cwilliam@aalan.ua.edu

University of Alaska Anchorage
Anchorage, Alaska

State-supported, coed. Urban campus. Total enrollment: 16,261.
Degrees Bachelor of Music in the areas of performance, music education. Majors and concentrations: classical music, music,

music education, piano/organ, stringed instruments, voice, wind and percussion instruments. Program accredited by NASM.
Enrollment 68 total; 48 undergraduate, 20 nonprofessional degree.
Music Student Profile 60% females, 40% males, 10% minorities.
Music Faculty 7 undergraduate (full-time), 20 undergraduate (part-time). 50% of full-time faculty have terminal degrees. Graduate students do not teach undergraduate courses. Undergraduate student–faculty ratio: 3:1.
Student Life Student groups/activities include Music Educators National Conference Student Chapter.
Expenses for 2005–2006 Application fee: $40. State resident tuition: $2952 full-time. Nonresident tuition: $9048 full-time. Mandatory fees: $513 full-time. Full-time tuition and fees vary according to course level. College room and board: $7810. College room only: $4710. Room and board charges vary according to board plan and housing facility.
Financial Aid Program-specific awards: 1 music scholarship for incoming students ($2400).
Application Procedures Students admitted directly into the professional program freshman year. Deadline for freshmen and transfers: July 1. Required: high school transcript, college transcript(s) for transfer students. Recommended: minimum 2.0 high school GPA.
Web Site http://www.uaa.alaska.edu/music
Undergraduate Contact Mr. Mike Turner, Counseling Coordinator, Advising and Counseling Department, University of Alaska Anchorage, 3211 Providence Drive, Anchorage, Alaska 99508; 907-786-4500, fax: 907-786-4519, e-mail address: afmtt@uaa.alaska.edu

University of Alaska Fairbanks
Fairbanks, Alaska

State-supported, coed. Small town campus. Total enrollment: 8,230.

University of Alberta
Edmonton, Alberta, Canada

Province-supported, coed. Urban campus. Total enrollment: 35,443. Music program established 1947.
Degrees Bachelor of Music in the areas of school music, performance, music theory and composition, music history and literature, world music; Bachelor of Music/Bachelor of Education in the area of secondary music education. Majors and concentrations: classical music, composition, guitar, harp, music education, music history and literature, music theory and composition, piano/organ, stringed instruments, voice, wind and percussion instruments, world music. Graduate degrees offered: Master of Arts in the areas of music (ethnomusicology, musicology, theory); Master of Music in the areas of applied music, composition, choral conducting. Doctor of Music in the areas of keyboard performance, choral conducting, composition; Doctor of Philosophy in the areas of music, ethnomusicology, musicology, theory. Cross-registration with Grant MacEwan Community College. Program accredited by CUMS.
Enrollment 379 total; 129 undergraduate, 50 graduate, 200 nonprofessional degree.
Music Student Profile 60% females, 40% males, 10% minorities, 4% international.
Music Faculty 21 total (full-time), 33 total (part-time). 100% of full-time faculty have terminal degrees. Graduate students teach a few undergraduate courses. Undergraduate student–faculty ratio: 9:1.
Expenses for 2006–2007 Application fee: $100 Canadian dollars. Tuition, fee, and room and board charges are reported in Canadian dollars. Canadian resident tuition: $4,537 full-time. Mandatory fees: $498 full-time. College room and board: $4712. College room only: $2032. International student tuition: $15,091 full-time. Special program-related fees: $10–$20 per year for lockers and keys.
Financial Aid Program-specific awards: 1 Alberta Baroque Music Society Scholarship for academically and artistically talented students ($1250), 10–35 Beryl Barns Memorial Awards for

University of Alberta (continued)

academically and artistically talented students ($500–$2000), 2 Richard Eaton Scholarships in Music and Voice for academically and artistically talented students ($2000–$4000), 1 Abigal Edith Condell Memorial Scholarship in Music for academically and artistically talented students ($1500), 1 Edmonton Musical Club Scholarship in Music for academically and artistically talented students ($1500), 2 FM105 Easy Rock Prizes for academically and artistically talented students ($1000), 1 John Newman Memorial Scholarship for Performance of Contemporary Music for academically and artistically talented students ($1250), 9 Peace River Pioneer Memorial Scholarships in Music for academically and artistically talented students ($750–$1500), 1 Mary Stinson Prize in Piano Accompaniment for academically and artistically talented students ($1000), 4–5 Universiade '83 Scholarships for academically and artistically talented students ($3000), 1 Margo Fraser Memorial Scholarship for academically and artistically talented students ($2000), 1 Edmonton Composer's Concert Society Scholarship for academically and artistically talented students ($500), 1 Edmonton Opera Guild Award for academically and artistically talented students ($2000), 1 Edna and John Bullock Memorial Scholarship for academically and artistically talented students ($1250), 1 Ernesto B. Lejano Scholarship in Piano Performance for academically and artistically talented students ($1000), 1 Lois Field Scholarship in Music Education for academically and artistically talented students ($1000).
Application Procedures Students admitted directly into the professional program freshman year. Deadline for freshmen and transfers: May 1. Notification date for freshmen and transfers: June 15. Required: high school transcript, college transcript(s) for transfer students, minimum 2.0 high school GPA, audition, music rudiments exam, aural skills exam, portfolio for composition applicants. Recommended: minimum 3.0 high school GPA, interview. Auditions held twice on campus; recorded music is permissible as a substitute for live auditions when distance is prohibitive and videotaped performances are permissible as a substitute for live auditions when distance is prohibitive. Portfolio reviews held continuously on campus.
Web Site http://www.ualberta.ca/music
Undergraduate Contact Ms. Donna Maskell, Executive Assistant, Department of Music, University of Alberta, FAB 3-82, Edmonton, Alberta T6G 2C9, Canada; 780-492-0603, fax: 780-492-9246.
Graduate Contact Dr. Henry Klumpenhouwer, Graduate Coordinator, Department of Music, University of Alberta, FAB 3-82, Edmonton, Alberta T6G 2C9, Canada; 780-492-2238, fax: 780-492-9246.

The University of Arizona
Tucson, Arizona

State-supported, coed. Urban campus. Total enrollment: 37,036. Music program established 1893.

J. William Fulbright College of Arts and Sciences
University of Arkansas
Fayetteville, Arkansas

State-supported, coed. Suburban campus. Total enrollment: 17,821. Music program established 1952.
Degrees Bachelor of Music in the areas of performance, music education, composition, music theory. Majors and concentrations: composition, guitar, music education, music theory, piano/organ, stringed instruments, voice, wind and percussion instruments. Graduate degrees offered: Master of Music in the areas of performance, music education, composition, music history, music theory, conducting. Program accredited by NASM.
Enrollment 380 total; 300 undergraduate, 30 graduate, 50 nonprofessional degree.
Music Student Profile 60% females, 40% males, 10% minorities, 5% international.
Music Faculty 29 undergraduate (full-time), 29 graduate (full-time), 10 total (part-time). 95% of full-time faculty have

terminal degrees. Graduate students teach a few undergraduate courses. Undergraduate student–faculty ratio: 9:1.
Student Life Student groups/activities include drama department productions, North Arkansas Symphony Orchestra, North Arkansas Symphony Chorus.
Expenses for 2005–2006 Application fee: $40. State resident tuition: $4361 full-time. Nonresident tuition: $12,089 full-time. Mandatory fees: $1133 full-time. College room and board: $6365. College room only: $3782. Room and board charges vary according to board plan and housing facility.
Financial Aid Program-specific awards: 102 music scholarships for music major and non-major ensemble members ($1200–$3500), 215 band scholarships for music major and non-major ensemble members ($1200–$3500), 25 Inspirational Singers Awards for gospel choir members ($1200–$2500).
Application Procedures Students apply for admission into the professional program by sophomore year. Deadline for freshmen and transfers: May 1. Required: essay, high school transcript, minimum 3.0 high school GPA, audition, SAT I or ACT test scores, minimum 3.0 high school GPA. Auditions held by appointment on campus; recorded music is permissible as a substitute for live auditions when distance is prohibitive and videotaped performances are permissible as a substitute for live auditions when distance is prohibitive.
Web Site http://www.uark.edu/depts/uamusic
Contact Dr. Ronda Mains, Associate Chair, Department of Music, University of Arkansas, 201 Music Building, Fayetteville, Arkansas 72701; 479-575-4701, fax: 479-575-5409, e-mail address: rmains@uark.edu

University of Arkansas at Monticello
Monticello, Arkansas

State-supported, coed. Small town campus. Total enrollment: 2,875 (2004). Music program established 1935.
Degrees Bachelor of Music Education in the areas of vocal music, piano, instrumental. Majors and concentrations: music education, piano, voice, wind and percussion instruments. Program accredited by NASM.
Enrollment 45 total; all undergraduate.
Music Student Profile 29% females, 71% males, 4% minorities.
Music Faculty 7 undergraduate (full-time), 5 undergraduate (part-time). 43% of full-time faculty have terminal degrees. Graduate students do not teach undergraduate courses. Undergraduate student–faculty ratio: 6:1.
Student Life Student groups/activities include Music Educators National Conference Student Chapter, Kappa Kappa Psi, Pi Kappa Lambda.
Expenses for 2005–2006 Special program-related fees: $40–$55 per course for applied lessons in voice, piano, or wind/percussion instruments.
Financial Aid Program-specific awards: 125 band performance scholarships for band players ($375–$1500), 48 choir performance scholarships for choir singers ($375–$1500), 6 piano performance scholarships for pianists ($375–$1500), 9 endowed departmental scholarships for program majors demonstrating talent and academic achievement ($600–$1000).
Application Procedures Students admitted directly into the professional program freshman year. Deadline for freshmen and transfers: August 15. Required: high school transcript, college transcript(s) for transfer students, minimum 2.0 high school GPA, audition, ACT test score only. Auditions held 3 times on campus and off campus in various high schools; recorded music is permissible as a substitute for live auditions for out-of-state applicants and videotaped performances are permissible as a substitute for live auditions for out-of-state applicants.
Web Site http://www.uamont.edu
Undergraduate Contact Ms. Mary Whiting, Director of Admissions, University of Arkansas at Monticello, PO Box 3600, Monticello, Arkansas 71656; 870-460-1026, fax: 870-460-1922.

University of Bridgeport
Bridgeport, Connecticut

Independent, coed. Urban campus. Total enrollment: 3,626.

Degrees Bachelor of Music. Majors and concentrations: jazz studies, music education, performance.
Enrollment 28 total; all undergraduate.
Music Student Profile 43% females, 57% males, 50% minorities, 21% international.
Music Faculty 2 undergraduate (full-time), 11 undergraduate (part-time). 100% of full-time faculty have terminal degrees. Graduate students do not teach undergraduate courses. Undergraduate student–faculty ratio: 8:1.
Expenses for 2005–2006 Application fee: $25. Comprehensive fee: $29,595 includes full-time tuition ($19,200), mandatory fees ($1395), and college room and board ($9000). College room only: $4600. Full-time tuition and fees vary according to program. Room and board charges vary according to board plan and student level. Special program-related fees: $425 per credit hour for private lessons.
Financial Aid Program-specific awards: 5–20 Music Department Scholarships for music majors ($3500–$19,310).
Application Procedures Students admitted directly into the professional program freshman year. Deadline for freshmen and transfers: continuous. Required: essay, high school transcript, college transcript(s) for transfer students, audition, SAT I or ACT test scores. Recommended: minimum 2.0 high school GPA, 2 letters of recommendation, interview. Auditions held as needed on campus; recorded music is permissible as a substitute for live auditions when distance is prohibitive and videotaped performances are permissible as a substitute for live auditions when distance is prohibitive.
Web Site http://www.bridgeport.edu
Undergraduate Contact Ms. Barbara L. Maryak, Dean of Admissions, University of Bridgeport, 126 Park Avenue, Wahlstrom Library, Bridgeport, Connecticut 06604; 800-EXCEL-UB, fax: 203-576-4941, e-mail address: admit@bridgeport.edu

The University of British Columbia
Vancouver, British Columbia, Canada

Province-supported, coed. Urban campus. Total enrollment: 42,427. Music program established 1959.
Degrees Bachelor of Music in the areas of composition, general studies, elementary education stream, secondary education stream, guitar, music scholarship, opera, orchestral instruments, organ, piano, voice. Majors and concentrations: composition, guitar, harpsichord, music, music education, music scholarship, opera, orchestral instruments, piano/organ, voice. Graduate degrees offered: Master of Arts in the areas of ethnomusicology, musicology, music theory; Master of Music in the areas of composition, piano, organ, voice, orchestral instruments, opera, guitar, harpsichord, choral conducting. Doctor of Musical Arts in the areas of composition, piano, voice, orchestral instruments; Doctor of Philosophy in the areas of ethnomusicology, musicology, music theory. Program accredited by CUMS.
Enrollment 368 total; 257 undergraduate, 111 graduate.
Music Student Profile 61% females, 39% males, 5% international.
Music Faculty 28 total (full-time), 56 total (part-time). 70% of full-time faculty have terminal degrees. Graduate students teach a few undergraduate courses. Undergraduate student–faculty ratio: 3:1.
Student Life Student groups/activities include student ensembles, opera productions, musical theatre.
Financial Aid Program-specific awards: scholarships for program students ($1000–$3000).
Application Procedures Students admitted directly into the professional program freshman year. Deadline for freshmen and transfers: March 31. Notification date for freshmen and transfers: May 6. Required: high school transcript, college transcript(s) for transfer students, 2 letters of recommendation, audition, music theory examination, original music scores for composition applicants, minimum 2.5 high school GPA, video audition for out-of-town applicants, original essay for music scholarship applicants. Auditions held once on campus; recorded music is permissible as a substitute for live auditions when distance is prohibitive and videotaped performances are permissible as a substitute for live auditions when distance is prohibitive. Portfolio reviews held once on campus.
Web Site http://www.music.ubc.ca

Contact Ms. Miriam Nechemia, Admissions Officer, School of Music, The University of British Columbia, 6361 Memorial Road, Vancouver, British Columbia V6T 1Z2, Canada; 604-822-5750, fax: 604-822-4884, e-mail address: miriamn@interchange.ubc.ca

University of Calgary
Calgary, Alberta, Canada

Province-supported, coed. Urban campus. Total enrollment: 27,928. Music program established 1967.
Degrees Bachelor of Music in the areas of music education, performance, music theory, composition, music history. Majors and concentrations: brass, classical music, music education, music history, music performance, music theory and composition, piano/organ, stringed instruments, voice, wind and percussion instruments. Graduate degrees offered: Master of Arts in the area of musicology; Master of Music in the areas of performance, composition, conducting, music education. Doctor of Philosophy in the areas of music education, composition, musicology. Cross-registration with Mount Royal College. Program accredited by CUMS.
Enrollment 180 total; 150 undergraduate, 30 graduate.
Music Student Profile 60% females, 40% males, 5% minorities, 10% international.
Music Faculty 17 total (full-time), 30 total (part-time). 90% of full-time faculty have terminal degrees. Graduate students teach a few undergraduate courses. Undergraduate student–faculty ratio: 12:1.
Student Life Student groups/activities include wind ensemble/symphonic band, symphony orchestra, choral ensembles.
Expenses for 2005–2006 Application fee: $130 Canadian dollars. Tuition and fee charges are reported in Canadian dollars. Special program-related fees: $100 per year for lab fee for recital, $300 per semester for lessons.
Financial Aid Program-specific awards: 47 music awards for students demonstrating high academic and musical achievement ($150–$3000).
Application Procedures Students admitted directly into the professional program freshman year. Deadline for freshmen and transfers: April 1. Notification date for freshmen and transfers: June 15. Required: high school transcript, college transcript(s) for transfer students, letter of recommendation, audition, proof of Royal Conservatory of Music grade III theory. Auditions held twice on campus; recorded music is permissible as a substitute for live auditions when distance is prohibitive and videotaped performances are permissible as a substitute for live auditions when distance is prohibitive.
Web Site http://www.ffa.ucalgary.ca
Contact Lynda McKay, Academic Advisor, Faculty of Fine Arts, University of Calgary, 2500 University Drive, NW, Calgary, Alberta T2N 1N4, Canada; 403-220-5383, fax: 403-282-6925, e-mail address: lhmckay@ucalgary.ca

Claire Trevor School of the Arts
University of California, Irvine
Irvine, California

State-supported, coed. Total enrollment: 24,362. Music program established 1965.
Degrees Bachelor of Arts in the area of music; Bachelor of Music in the areas of voice, piano, wind and percussion instruments, stringed instruments, jazz instrumental. Majors and concentrations: bassoon, clarinet, composition, double bass, flute, French horn, guitar, harp, jazz, lute, oboe, percussion, piano, saxophone, trombone, trumpet, tuba, viola, violin, violoncello, voice. Graduate degrees offered: Master of Fine Arts in the area of music. Cross-registration with University of California System.
Enrollment 145 total; 125 undergraduate, 20 graduate.
Music Student Profile 70% females, 30% males, 65% minorities, 10% international.
Music Faculty 12 total (full-time), 25 total (part-time). 100% of full-time faculty have terminal degrees. Graduate students do not teach undergraduate courses. Undergraduate student–faculty ratio: 12:1.

University of California, Irvine (continued)

Student Life Student groups/activities include Mu Phi Epsilon Delta Sigma Chapter, Kappa Kappa Psi Lambda Alpha Chapter. Special housing available for music students.

Expenses for 2006–2007 Application fee: $60. State resident tuition: $0 full-time. Nonresident tuition: $17,820 full-time. Mandatory fees: $6141 full-time. College room and board: $9875.

Financial Aid Program-specific awards: 4 Rawlins Scholarships for strings or piano majors ($5000), 3 Philharmonic Society of Orange County Scholarships for instrumental or voice majors ($2500), 1 Harry and Marjorie Slim Scholarship for instrumental or voice majors ($1000), 1 Tierney Scholarship for instrumental or voice majors ($4200), Artsbridge Scholarships for instrumental or voice majors ($2500), 10–12 music scholarships for instrumental or voice majors ($1000), 1 Winifred Smith Scholarship for cello (preferred), violin/piano students ($5000), 3 Alice Lowell Scholarships for instrumental or voice students ($2000), 1 Phyllis Kovach Vacca Scholarship for cello (preferred), piano students ($1500).

Application Procedures Students admitted directly into the professional program freshman year. Deadline for freshmen and transfers: November 30. Notification date for freshmen and transfers: continuous. Required: essay, high school transcript, college transcript(s) for transfer students, audition, SAT I or ACT test scores, minimum 3.0 college GPA for transfer students, SAT II. Recommended: minimum 3.0 high school GPA. Auditions held once on campus; recorded music is permissible as a substitute for live auditions when distance is prohibitive and videotaped performances are permissible as a substitute for live auditions when distance is prohibitive.

Web Site http://www.arts.uci.edu

Undergraduate Contact Ms. Amina El-Sadr, Admissions Counselor, Office of Admissions and Relations with Schools, University of California, Irvine, 206 Administration Building, Irvine, California 92697-1075; 949-824-4545, e-mail address: aelsadr@uci.edu

Graduate Contact Ms. Sally Avila, Administrative Assistant, Department of Music, University of California, Irvine, 303 Music and Media Building, 726, Irvine, California 92697-2775; 949-824-6615, fax: 949-824-4914, e-mail address: slavila@uci.edu

University of California, Santa Barbara

Santa Barbara, California

State-supported, coed. Suburban campus. Total enrollment: 21,016. Music program established 1976.

Degrees Bachelor of Music in the areas of composition, orchestral instruments, piano, voice. Majors and concentrations: accompanying, brass, composition, orchestral instruments, piano, stringed instruments, voice, wind and percussion instruments. Graduate degrees offered: Master of Music in the areas of piano accompanying, woodwinds and brass, keyboard, strings, voice. Doctor of Musical Arts in the areas of keyboard, strings, voice; Doctor of Philosophy in the areas of composition, ethnomusicology, musicology, theory.

Enrollment 190 total; 53 undergraduate, 72 graduate, 65 nonprofessional degree.

Music Student Profile 63% females, 37% males, 28% minorities, 10% international.

Music Faculty 18 total (full-time), 25 total (part-time). 100% of full-time faculty have terminal degrees. Graduate students teach a few undergraduate courses. Undergraduate student–faculty ratio: 3:1.

Student Life Student groups/activities include symphony orchestra, ensembles, Contemporary Music Festival (annual).

Expenses for 2005–2006 Application fee: $40. State resident tuition: $0 full-time. Nonresident tuition: $17,820 full-time. Mandatory fees: $6993 full-time. College room and board: $10,577. College room only: $8110.

Financial Aid Program-specific awards: 10 Excellence at Entrance Awards for incoming freshmen ($300–$1500), 15 grants-in-aid for continuing program majors demonstrating need, musical and academic excellence ($300–$1500), 3 quarterly performance

awards for outstanding performers ($500), 1 Carl Zytonski Vocal Scholarship for incoming voice students ($1500), 1 Erno Daniel Memorial Award for piano students ($200), 1 Carnzu Clark Award for all bachelors music students ($3000–$5000).

Application Procedures Students admitted directly into the professional program freshman year. Deadline for freshmen and transfers: November 30. Notification date for freshmen: March 15; transfers: April 1. Required: essay, high school transcript, college transcript(s) for transfer students, minimum 3.0 high school GPA, audition, SAT I or ACT test scores, portfolio for composition applicants. Auditions held once during last weekend in January on campus; recorded music is permissible as a substitute for live auditions when distance is prohibitive and videotaped performances are permissible as a substitute for live auditions when distance is prohibitive.

Web Site http://www.music.ucsb.edu/

Undergraduate Contact Ms. Marcia Campbell, Undergraduate Advisor, Department of Music, University of California, Santa Barbara, Santa Barbara, California 93106-6070; 805-893-5672, fax: 805-893-7194, e-mail address: mcampbel@music.ucsb.edu

Graduate Contact Mrs. Sandy Cummings, Graduate Program Advisor, Department of Music, University of California, Santa Barbara, Santa Barbara, California 93106; 805-893-4603, fax: 805-893-7194, e-mail address: cummings@music.ucsb.edu

University of Central Arkansas

Conway, Arkansas

State-supported, coed. Small town campus. Total enrollment: 11,375. Music program established 1908.

Degrees Bachelor of Music in the areas of performance, music education. Majors and concentrations: brass, music, music education, piano/organ, stringed instruments, voice, wind and percussion instruments. Graduate degrees offered: Master of Music in the areas of performance, music theory, music education, choral conducting, instrumental conducting. Program accredited by NASM.

Enrollment 155 total; 135 undergraduate, 20 graduate.

Music Student Profile 50% females, 50% males, 15% minorities, 10% international.

Music Faculty 27 total (full-time), 9 total (part-time). 77% of full-time faculty have terminal degrees. Graduate students do not teach undergraduate courses. Undergraduate student–faculty ratio: 6:1.

Student Life Student groups/activities include Music Teachers National Association competitions, Arkansas Symphony Orchestra.

Expenses for 2005–2006 Application fee: $0. State resident tuition: $4500 full-time. Nonresident tuition: $9000 full-time. Mandatory fees: $1164 full-time. College room and board: $4320. College room only: $1940. Room and board charges vary according to board plan and housing facility. Special program-related fees: $25–$40 per credit hour for practice room fees.

Financial Aid Program-specific awards: 143 music scholarships for wind, brass, percussion, orchestral, vocal, and keyboard students ($200–$2500).

Application Procedures Students apply for admission into the professional program by freshman year. Deadline for freshmen and transfers: continuous. Required: college transcript(s) for transfer students, 3 letters of recommendation, audition, SAT I or ACT test scores. Recommended: high school transcript, minimum 3.0 high school GPA, interview. Auditions held 3 times and by appointment on campus; recorded music is permissible as a substitute for live auditions when distance is prohibitive, in special circumstances, or for international applicants and videotaped performances are permissible as a substitute for live auditions when distance is prohibitive, in special circumstances, or for international applicants.

Web Site http://www.uca.edu/divisions/academic/music

Undergraduate Contact Ms. Jann Bryant, Instructor, Department of Music, University of Central Arkansas, UCA 201 Donaghey Avenue, Conway, Arkansas 72035-0001; 501-450-5755, fax: 501-450-5773, e-mail address: jannb@uca.edu

Graduate Contact Dr. Jane Dahlenburg, Graduate Advisor, Department of Music, University of Central Arkansas, UCA 201

Donaghey Avenue, Conway, Arkansas 72035-0001; 501-450-3301, fax: 501-450-5773, e-mail address: dahlen@uca.edu

University of Central Florida
Orlando, Florida

State-supported, coed. Suburban campus. Total enrollment: 44,953. Music program established 1968.

University of Central Oklahoma
Edmond, Oklahoma

State-supported, coed. Suburban campus. Total enrollment: 15,953. Music program established 1890.

University of Cincinnati

See University of Cincinnati College Conservatory of Music

University of Cincinnati

University of Cincinnati College Conservatory of Music
Cincinnati, Ohio

State-supported, coed. Urban campus. Total enrollment: 27,932. Music program established 1867.
Degrees Bachelor of Music in the areas of performance, music education, jazz, theory/history/composition. Majors and concentrations: classical guitar, composition, harpsichord, jazz, music, music education, music history, music theory, piano/organ, stringed instruments, voice, wind and percussion instruments. Graduate degrees offered: Master of Music in the areas of performance, music education, theory/history/composition, conducting, collaborative piano. Doctor of Musical Arts in the areas of performance, composition, conducting; Doctor of Philosophy in the areas of music theory, musicology. Cross-registration with Greater Cincinnati Consortium of Colleges and Universities. Program accredited by NASM.
Enrollment 1,015 total; 361 undergraduate, 654 graduate.
Music Student Profile 47% females, 53% males, 9% minorities, 16% international.
Music Faculty 100 total (full-time), 50 total (part-time). 80% of full-time faculty have terminal degrees. Graduate students teach a few undergraduate courses. Undergraduate student–faculty ratio: 7:1.
Student Life Student groups/activities include Student Artist Program, music fraternities and sororities. Special housing available for music students.
Expenses for 2005–2006 Application fee: $40. State resident tuition: $7458 full-time. Nonresident tuition: $21,210 full-time. Mandatory fees: $1425 full-time. Full-time tuition and fees vary according to course load, degree level, location, program, and reciprocity agreements. College room and board: $7890. College room only: $4680. Room and board charges vary according to board plan and housing facility.
Financial Aid Program-specific awards: 300 endowed scholarships for program majors ($1600–$4500), 185 Cincinnatus Awards for those in top 5% of graduating class with minimum 26 ACT score or minimum 1170 SAT score ($2000–$20,000).
Application Procedures Students admitted directly into the professional program freshman year. Deadline for freshmen and transfers: December 1. Notification date for freshmen and transfers: continuous. Required: high school transcript, college transcript(s) for transfer students, letter of recommendation, interview, audition, SAT I or ACT test scores. Recommended: minimum 3.0 high school GPA. Auditions held 15 times on campus and off campus in Atlanta, GA; Chicago, IL; Interlochen, MI; Los Angeles, CA; New York, NY; San Francisco, CA; recorded music is permissible as a substitute for live auditions with

approval from the department and videotaped performances are permissible as a substitute for live auditions with approval from the department.
Web Site http://www.ccm.uc.edu
Undergraduate Contact Mr. P.J. Woolston, Senior Admissions Officer, College-Conservatory of Music, University of Cincinnati, PO Box 210003, Cincinnati, Ohio 45221-0003; 513-556-9479, fax: 513-556-1028, e-mail address: pj.woolston@uc.edu
Graduate Contact Mr. Paul R. Hillner, Assistant Dean, College-Conservatory of Music, University of Cincinnati, PO Box 210003, Cincinnati, Ohio 45221-0003; 513-556-9478, fax: 513-556-1028, e-mail address: paul.hillner@uc.edu

More About the University

The University of Cincinnati College-Conservatory of Music (CCM) is the result of the merger of two distinguished schools of music—the Cincinnati Conservatory of Music, established in 1867, and the College of Music at Cincinnati, established in 1878. This merger in 1955, and subsequent union with the University of Cincinnati in 1962, brought together the professional training in the performing arts and media of a city long noted for its support in these areas.

Cited in the *New York Times* as one of the nation's leading conservatories, CCM is among the nation's most comprehensive performing arts schools, housing not only the standard disciplines of instrumental performance, voice, musicology, theory, and composition but also music education, conducting, musical theater, drama, opera, theater design and production (makeup, lighting, scene design, stage management, costuming, sound design, and theater production), electronic media, jazz and studio music, dance, arts administration, accompanying, opera coaching, and directing. (The last four programs listed are at the graduate level only.)

Performing groups are continually recognized for their outstanding achievements. The jazz ensemble has regularly won the *Down Beat* magazine award for the best student ensemble; the National Opera Association has honored the CCM opera program with thirty first-place awards in the past eighteen years; and the

University of Cincinnati College Conservatory of Music (continued)

wind department has been featured at major conventions and conferences in this country and in Japan and currently has more than twelve CDs on the market. Six additional outstanding CDs have been produced by the CCM Philharmonia Orchestra, the Faculty Jazz Ensemble, and the Ensemble for Eighteenth Century Music. All have been recorded commercially. The CCM Philharmonia Orchestra was the only U.S. orchestra invited to perform at the One Hundred Days Festival that preceded Expo 98 in Lisbon, Portugal. The Orchestra received rave reviews for these March 1998 performances.

The CCM Dance Division, the first music school in the United States to offer courses in classical ballet, is the founding institution and affiliate of the Cincinnati Ballet. Both the Cincinnati Ballet and the Cincinnati Opera Association offer numerous performance opportunities to dance majors. The Dance Division also offers continual ballet performance experience, featuring works by Division faculty members and guest choreographers, as well as the opportunity to work with notable guest artists, including Bart Cook, Vivi Flindt, Sean Curren, Adam Skulte, and Laura Alonzo, among others. Other opportunities exist in productions by the opera and musical theater areas of CCM.

Theater training offers a unique opportunity for CCM students because of the combination of instruction in vocal coaching, dance, opera, musical theater, drama, theater design and production, and arts administration within one division. Students have the opportunity to share in a wide-ranging scope of classes, major productions, workshop productions, master classes, and internships. This remarkable sharing of experiences among experts in all areas of theater and arts administration allows students exposure to a wealth of learning opportunities. In addition, the division manages CCM's major theater and concert venues. Technical facilities currently include a state-of-the-art computerized lighting control mechanism for the theaters. The technical-support area, which opened in 1997, includes an 8,500-square-foot scene shop; a 3,000-square-foot costume shop plus wig, make-up, and prosthetics studios; a 1,500-square-foot design/drafting studio; an 800-square-foot light lab; and CAD drafting stations. The United States Institute of Technical Theater (USITT) has honored these programs with more than thirty awards in the past ten years.

In addition to the strengths of the College-Conservatory of Music, students have the resources of a major university at their disposal. The libraries of the University constitute a nationally recognized research center, with holdings that include 3.2 million bound volumes and more than 40,000 serial subscriptions. They also offer access to an expanding number of libraries throughout the state via the OhioLINK online catalog.

Student-support offices serve the entire University population and offer academic counseling and tutoring, resume and interview skills training, psychological and personal counseling, student health clinics, day-care centers, special programming for ethnic groups and women, and a host of center activities, such as special-interest clubs, student government, and intramural sports.

The extensive physical facilities of the University provide residence halls for students; banking services; swimming, tennis, track, volleyball, basketball, racquetball/handball, and bowling; plus a movie theater and more than six restaurants ranging from fast food to table service. A state-of-the-art recreational facility opened in February 2006.

Cincinnati, "North America's most livable city" (*Places Rated Almanac*, 1993), is bordered on the south by the Ohio River and truly offers something for everyone. Nearby are Mt. Adams and the adjoining Eden Park, a stylish urban area perched on top of a hill with spectacular views of the city and the Ohio River and the home of the Playhouse in the Park, the Cincinnati Art Museum, and the Krohn Conservatory. Within walking distance is University Village, offering inexpensive restaurants and shops, and just beyond is the Ludlow Avenue of Clifton, with its boutiques, restaurants, and gaslit, tree-lined streets. At the heart of

downtown, just a 5-minute bus ride away, is Fountain Square—the place Cincinnatians go to celebrate, demonstrate, welcome hometown heroes, or bring in the new year. Also downtown are numerous and diverse cultural opportunities, including the Cincinnati Symphony Orchestra, the Pops, the Cincinnati Opera, the Cincinnati Ballet, Ensemble Theatre of Cincinnati, the Broadway Series, the Museum Center at Union Terminal, the Contemporary Art Center, the Taft Museum of Art, the National Underground Railroad Freedom Center, and more.

Both of CCM's founding schools, the Cincinnati Conservatory of Music and the College of Music of Cincinnati, were charter members of the National Association of Schools of Music (NASM), in which CCM continues to play a vital leadership role. Theater programs have received accreditation from the National Association of Schools of Theater (NAST) and the University/ Resident Theater Association (URTA), and the dance program holds accreditation from the National Association of Schools of Dance (NASD).

Program Facilities In 1999, CCM celebrated the grand opening of its campus village, a collection of renovated and new buildings that significantly enhance the College's teaching and performance capabilities. The complex stresses the synergy between the performing arts and electronic media and effectively accommodates nearly 1,000 performances each year that take place at CCM. With the help of its design architect, Henry N. Cobb, the College has produced a physical environment that truly reflects and advances its reputation as one of the finest and most comprehensive training centers for the performing arts and electronic media. The Corbett Center for the Performing Arts houses the elegant 738-seat Corbett Auditorium, the 380-seat Patricia Corbett Theater, the 140-seat Watson Recital Hall, the Cohen Family Studio Theater, three dance studios, and four large rehearsal rooms. CCM's Theater Production Wing includes the scene and costume shops, various design-oriented classrooms, labs, jazz studios, and ensemble rehearsal rooms. The Dieterle Vocal Arts Center is the home to the voice, opera, choral, and accompanying departments. It has nineteen faculty studios, three private coaching rooms, the Italo Tajo Archive Room, two warm-up rooms, the 100-seat choral rehearsal room, and the choral library. The Center is also the location of the Nippert Rehearsal Studio, a large, grand opera–scale rehearsal space with dressing rooms and technical support so that the space can double as a performance venue for workshops and concerts. Memorial Hall houses teaching studios for piano, harpsichord, strings, and winds, plus practice rooms, chamber music rehearsal rooms, and the electronic music studios. The computer music studio, used by composers, researchers, and performers, contains a Genelec multichannel audio system, workstations, and peripherals for sampling, editing, synthesis, signal processing, algorithmic composition, programming, and controller development. Mary Emery Hall, the home of the academic offices and the electronic media division, is the newest addition to the CCM Village. Highlights include the Bartlett Television Studio and the J. Ralph Corbett Audio Production Center, a master classroom, smart classrooms with audio/video link-up to the University library, and the stunning Robert J. Werner Recital Hall, a 300-seat intimate performing space for chamber music and solo recitals. The Gorno Memorial Music Library houses more than 155,000 volumes, including books, music scores, periodicals, and numerous special collections of rare books, music, and recordings.

Faculty, Resident Artists, and Alumni CCM has more than 150 faculty members including Kurt Sassmannshaus (violin), Masao Kawasaki (viola), Yehuda Hanani (violoncello), Al Laszlo (double bass), William Winstead (bassoon), Randy Gardner (horn), Mark Ostoich (oboe), Brad Garner (flute), Awadagin Pratt (piano), and James Tocco (piano and chamber music). Ensembles-In-Residence include The Percussion Group Cincinnati and the Pridonoff Piano Duo. Alumni continue to hold key positions in the performing and media arts. Numbered among them are American and European opera stars Kathleen Battle, Barbara Daniels,

Catherine Keen, David Malis, Stanford Olsen, and Mark Oswald; producers Earl Hamner (The Waltons and Falcon Crest) and Dan Guntzelman (Growing Pains); musical theater stars Faith Prince, Lee Roy Reams, Michele Pawk, Jason Graae, Jim Walton, and Vicki Lewis; prima ballerina Suzanne Farrell; jazz great Al Hirt; composers Albert Hague (*Plain and Fancy, Redhead, How the Grinch Stole Christmas*), Randy Edelman (*Last of the Mohicans, While You Were Sleeping*), Stephen Flaherty (*Once on This Island, Ragtime, Seussical*), theatrical producer Kevin McCollum (*Rent, Avenue Q., The Drowsy Chaperone*), and a host of international competition winners and instrumentalists who hold positions in the major orchestras, both in the United States and in Europe.

Student Performance Opportunities Nearly 1,000 performances a year take place at CCM by two large orchestras, three chamber orchestras, two wind ensembles, five choruses, more than forty chamber groups, dance productions and choreographers' workshops, jazz ensembles, early music ensembles, brass choir, and twenty-four mainstage and workshop productions in opera, musical theater, and drama.

University of Colorado at Boulder
Boulder, Colorado

State-supported, coed. Small town campus. Total enrollment: 31,068. Music program established 1920.
Degrees Bachelor of Music in the areas of composition, musicology, all major instruments, voice, voice theater; Bachelor of Music Education in the areas of instrumental music education, choral music education, general music. Majors and concentrations: brass, composition, music education, musicology, opera, performance, piano/organ, stringed instruments, voice, wind and percussion instruments. Graduate degrees offered: Master of Music in the areas of performance, composition, conducting, musicology, performance and pedagogy; Master of Music Education in the areas of general, instrumental (band), string, and vocal music. Doctor of Musical Arts in the areas of performance, composition, conducting, performance and pedagogy; Doctor of Philosophy in the areas of music education, musicology. Cross-registration with University of Colorado System. Program accredited by NASM.
Enrollment 510 total; 280 undergraduate, 230 graduate.
Music Student Profile 46% females, 54% males, 14% minorities, 8% international.
Music Faculty 58 total (full-time), 15 total (part-time). 75% of full-time faculty have terminal degrees. Graduate students teach a few undergraduate courses. Undergraduate student–faculty ratio: 6:1.
Student Life Student groups/activities include Sigma Alpha Iota, Phi Mu Alpha, Music Educators National Conference.
Expenses for 2005–2006 Application fee: $50. One-time mandatory fee: $108. State resident tuition: $4446 full-time. Nonresident tuition: $21,900 full-time. Mandatory fees: $926 full-time. Full-time tuition and fees vary according to program. College room and board: $7980. Room and board charges vary according to board plan, location, and student level. Special program-related fees: $15 per class for music course fees.
Financial Aid Program-specific awards: 200 music scholarships for program majors ($3500).
Application Procedures Students admitted directly into the professional program freshman year. Deadline for freshmen and transfers: February 1. Notification date for freshmen and transfers: July 1. Required: essay, high school transcript, college transcript(s) for transfer students, minimum 2.0 high school GPA, letter of recommendation, audition, SAT I or ACT test scores. Auditions held weekly in February and by appointment on campus; recorded music is permissible as a substitute for live auditions when distance is prohibitive and videotaped performances are permissible as a substitute for live auditions when distance is prohibitive.
Web Site http://www.colorado.edu/music
Undergraduate Contact Dr. Charles Wolzien, Associate Dean for Undergraduate Studies, College of Music, University of Colorado at Boulder, Campus Box 301, Boulder, Colorado 80309-0301; 303-492-6354, fax: 303-492-5619, e-mail address: ugradmus@colorado.edu

Graduate Contact Dr. David Pinkow, Associate Dean for Graduate Studies, College of Music, University of Colorado at Boulder, Campus Box 301, Boulder, Colorado 80309-0301; 303-492-2207, fax: 303-492-5619, e-mail address: gradmusc@colorado.edu

University of Colorado at Denver and Health Sciences Center - Downtown Denver Campus
Denver, Colorado

State-supported, coed. Urban campus. Total enrollment: 19,755. Music program established 1973.

University of Connecticut
Storrs, Connecticut

State-supported, coed. Rural campus. Total enrollment: 23,185.
Degrees Bachelor of Arts in the areas of music, jazz; Bachelor of Music in the areas of vocal performance, instrumental performance, music theory; Bachelor of Science in the area of music education. Majors and concentrations: music education, music history/theory, piano/organ, stringed instruments, voice, wind and percussion instruments. Graduate degrees offered: Master of Arts in the areas of music theory, musicology; Master of Music in the areas of performance, performance with conducting (instrumental, choral), music education. Doctor of Musical Arts in the areas of performance, conducting; Doctor of Philosophy in the areas of music theory and history, music education. Program accredited by NASM.
Enrollment 226 total; 158 undergraduate, 68 graduate.
Music Student Profile 56% females, 44% males, 9% minorities, 3% international.
Music Faculty 24 total (full-time), 26 total (part-time). 100% of full-time faculty have terminal degrees. Graduate students teach a few undergraduate courses. Undergraduate student–faculty ratio: 9:1.
Student Life Student groups/activities include Music Educators National Conference Student Chapter, American Choral Directors Association Student Chapter. Special housing available for music students.
Expenses for 2006–2007 Application fee: $70. State resident tuition: $6456 full-time. Nonresident tuition: $19,656 full-time. Mandatory fees: $1906 full-time. College room and board: $8266. College room only: $4350. Special program-related fees: $230 per course for applied music fee.
Financial Aid Program-specific awards: 1–2 Victor Borge Awards for those demonstrating talent and academic achievement ($1000–$3000), 1 Dean's Scholarship for those demonstrating talent and academic achievement ($2000), 20–25 departmental scholarships for program students ($1000–$4600).
Application Procedures Students admitted directly into the professional program freshman year. Deadline for freshmen: February 1; transfers: April 1. Notification date for freshmen and transfers: July 1. Required: high school transcript, college transcript(s) for transfer students, audition, SAT I test score only. Recommended: minimum 3.0 high school GPA. Auditions held 4 times on campus; recorded music is permissible as a substitute for live auditions when distance is prohibitive (beyond a 150-mile radius) and videotaped performances are permissible as a substitute for live auditions when distance is prohibitive (beyond a 150-mile radius).
Web Site http://www.sfa.uconn.edu
Undergraduate Contact Deborah Trahan, Administrative Assistant, Music Department, University of Connecticut, 1295 Storrs Road, Unit 1012, Storrs, Connecticut 06269-1012; 860-486-3728, fax: 860-486-3796, e-mail address: music@uconn.edu
Graduate Contact Dr. Richard Bass, Director of Graduate Studies, Music Department, University of Connecticut, 1295 Storrs Road, Unit 1012, Storrs, Connecticut 06269-1012; 860-486-4197, fax: 860-486-3796, e-mail address: richard.bass@uconn.edu

University of Dayton

Dayton, Ohio

Independent Roman Catholic, coed. Suburban campus. Total enrollment: 10,572.

Degrees Bachelor of Music; Bachelor of Music Education. Majors and concentrations: composition, music, music education, music therapy, performance. Graduate degrees offered: Master of Education in the area of music. Cross-registration with Southwestern Ohio Council for Higher Education. Program accredited by NASM, AMTA.

Enrollment 155 total; 110 undergraduate, 35 graduate, 10 nonprofessional degree.

Music Student Profile 65% females, 35% males, 1% minorities.

Music Faculty 15 undergraduate (full-time), 36 undergraduate (part-time). 75% of full-time faculty have terminal degrees. Graduate students do not teach undergraduate courses. Undergraduate student–faculty ratio: 15:1.

Student Life Student groups/activities include music fraternity and sorority, Ohio Collegiate Music Education Association, Music Therapy Club.

Expenses for 2005–2006 Application fee: $0. Comprehensive fee: $29,626 includes full-time tuition ($22,046), mandatory fees ($800), and college room and board ($6780). College room only: $4000. Full-time tuition and fees vary according to program. Room and board charges vary according to board plan, housing facility, and student level. Special program-related fees: $75 per course for pedagogy classes, $150–$250 per semester for lesson fees.

Financial Aid Program-specific awards: 10–13 Music Talent Awards for program students ($5000), 12–18 Reichard Awards for program students ($500), 12–18 band grants for band members.

Application Procedures Students admitted directly into the professional program freshman year. Deadline for freshmen and transfers: continuous. Notification date for freshmen and transfers: continuous. Required: essay, high school transcript, college transcript(s) for transfer students, minimum 2.0 high school GPA, 2 letters of recommendation, interview, audition, SAT I or ACT test scores, portfolio for composition applicants. Recommended: minimum 3.0 high school GPA. Auditions held 4 times and by appointment on campus; recorded music is permissible as a substitute for live auditions if a campus visit is impossible and videotaped performances are permissible as a substitute for live auditions if a campus visit is impossible. Portfolio reviews held once on campus.

Web Site http://www.udayton.edu/~music

Undergraduate Contact Mrs. Jeanie Smith, Coordinator, Music Admissions, Department of Music, University of Dayton, 300 College Park, Dayton, Ohio 45469-0290; 937-229-3936, fax: 937-229-3916, e-mail address: jean.smith@notes.udayton.edu

Graduate Contact Dr. Linda Hartley, Coordinator, Graduate Studies in Music Education, Department of Music, University of Dayton, 300 College Park, Dayton, Ohio 45469-0290; 937-229-3232, fax: 937-229-3916, e-mail address: lhartley@udayton.edu

University of Delaware

Newark, Delaware

State-related, coed. Small town campus. Total enrollment: 20,373. Music program established 1938.

Degrees Bachelor of Music in the areas of applied vocal and instrumental music, music theory and composition; Bachelor of Music Education in the areas of instrumental music education, choral music education. Majors and concentrations: classical music, music, music education, music theory and composition, piano, stringed instruments, voice, wind and percussion instruments. Graduate degrees offered: Master of Music in the areas of instrumental performance, teaching, voice, strings, instrumental conducting, composition. Program accredited by NASM.

Enrollment 217 total; 202 undergraduate, 15 graduate.

Music Student Profile 52% females, 48% males, 3% minorities, 1% international.

Music Faculty 30 total (full-time), 17 total (part-time). 80% of full-time faculty have terminal degrees. Graduate students teach a few undergraduate courses. Undergraduate student–faculty ratio: 4:1.

Student Life Student groups/activities include Sigma Alpha Iota, Phi Mu Alpha, Music Educators National Conference. Special housing available for music students.

Expenses for 2005–2006 Application fee: $60. State resident tuition: $6614 full-time. Nonresident tuition: $16,770 full-time. Mandatory fees: $704 full-time. College room and board: $6824. College room only: $3924. Room and board charges vary according to housing facility.

Financial Aid Program-specific awards: 10–12 Arts and Humanities Awards for state residents demonstrating need/talent ($1500–$3000), 10 Quigley Awards for female state residents ($1000–$3000), 30 Music Department Awards for talented majors in needed instruments ($1000–$12,000).

Application Procedures Students admitted directly into the professional program freshman year. Deadline for freshmen and transfers: March 1. Notification date for freshmen and transfers: April 15. Required: essay, high school transcript, college transcript(s) for transfer students, minimum 2.0 high school GPA, audition, SAT I or ACT test scores (minimum combined SAT I score of 1000), musicality test. Recommended: minimum 3.0 high school GPA, 2 letters of recommendation, interview. Auditions held 5 times on campus; recorded music is permissible as a substitute for live auditions when distance is prohibitive and videotaped performances are permissible as a substitute for live auditions when distance is prohibitive.

Web Site http://www.music.udel.edu

Undergraduate Contact Mr. Lou Hirsh, Associate Provost for Enrollment Services, University of Delaware, 116 Hullihen Hall, Newark, Delaware 19716; 302-831-8125, fax: 302-831-6905.

Graduate Contact Dr. James C. Prodan, Chair, Department of Music, University of Delaware, 209 Amy DuPont Music Building, Newark, Delaware 19716; 302-831-2577, fax: 302-831-3589.

Lamont School of Music

University of Denver

Denver, Colorado

Independent, coed. Total enrollment: 10,374. Music program established 1931.

Degrees Bachelor of Music in the areas of performance, jazz, composition, commercial music. Majors and concentrations: accordion, arranging, classical music, commercial music, composition, guitar, harp, jazz, music, music technology, piano/organ, stringed instruments, voice, wind and percussion instruments. Graduate degrees offered: Master of Arts in the areas of music theory, music history and literature; Master of Music in the areas of performance, composition, conducting, piano pedagogy, Suzuki pedagogy. Program accredited by NASM.

Enrollment 315 total; 235 undergraduate, 61 graduate, 19 nonprofessional degree.

Music Student Profile 50% females, 50% males, 10% minorities, 15% international.

Music Faculty 23 total (full-time), 28 total (part-time). 18% of full-time faculty have terminal degrees. Graduate students do not teach undergraduate courses. Undergraduate student–faculty ratio: 7:1.

Student Life Student groups/activities include professional music fraternities and sororities, ensemble groups. Special housing available for music students.

Expenses for 2005–2006 Application fee: $50. Comprehensive fee: $37,159 includes full-time tuition ($27,756), mandatory fees ($654), and college room and board ($8749). College room only: $5355. Full-time tuition and fees vary according to class time, course load, and program. Room and board charges vary according to board plan and housing facility. Special program-related fees: $85 per year for chamber music

Financial Aid Program-specific awards: 206 music activity grants for program majors ($15,400), 10 endowed awards for specific program majors ($27,756), 7 endowed full-tuition awards for program majors ($27,756).

Application Procedures Students admitted directly into the professional program freshman year. Deadline for freshmen: February 1; transfers: March 15. Required: essay, high school transcript, college transcript(s) for transfer students, 2 letters of recommen-

dation, interview, audition, SAT I or ACT test scores, pre-screening auditions for jazz studies and commercial music major application. Recommended: minimum 3.0 high school GPA, video. Auditions held 4 times on campus; recorded music is permissible as a substitute for live auditions if a campus visit is impossible and videotaped performances are permissible as a substitute for live auditions if a campus visit is impossible.
Web Site http://www.du.edu/lamont
Contact Mr. Malcolm Lynn Baker, Director of Admissions, Lamont School of Music, University of Denver, 2344 East Iliff Avenue, Denver, Colorado 80208; 303-871-6973, fax: 303-871-6382, e-mail address: mbaker@du.edu

University of Evansville
Evansville, Indiana

Independent, coed. Suburban campus. Total enrollment: 2,836. Music program established 1933.
Degrees Bachelor of Music in the areas of performance, performance (Suzuki violin emphasis), music therapy, music education, performance (sacred music emphasis); Bachelor of Science in the area of music management. Majors and concentrations: classical guitar, music education, music management, music therapy, piano/organ, stringed instruments, voice, wind and percussion instruments. Program accredited by NASM.
Enrollment 104 total; all undergraduate.
Music Student Profile 73% females, 27% males, 7% minorities, 2% international.
Music Faculty 18 undergraduate (full-time), 12 undergraduate (part-time). 100% of full-time faculty have terminal degrees. Graduate students do not teach undergraduate courses. Undergraduate student–faculty ratio: 4:1.
Student Life Student groups/activities include American Music Therapy Association Student Chapter, Music Educators National Conference Student Chapter, Phi Mu Alpha/Sigma Alpha Iota.
Expenses for 2005–2006 Application fee: $35. Comprehensive fee: $28,320 includes full-time tuition ($21,120), mandatory fees ($540), and college room and board ($6660). College room only: $3280. Room and board charges vary according to board plan and housing facility. Special program-related fees: $260 per credit hour for applied music fee.
Financial Aid Program-specific awards: 100 academic scholarships for those demonstrating talent and academic achievement ($8000).
Application Procedures Students admitted directly into the professional program freshman year. Deadline for freshmen: May 1; transfers: June 1. Required: essay, high school transcript, college transcript(s) for transfer students, minimum 2.0 high school GPA, audition, SAT I or ACT test scores. Recommended: minimum 3.0 high school GPA, 2 letters of recommendation. Auditions held 4 times on campus; recorded music is permissible as a substitute for live auditions when distance is prohibitive and videotaped performances are permissible as a substitute for live auditions when distance is prohibitive.
Web Site http://music.evansville.edu
Undergraduate Contact Eva Key, Music Admission Coordinator, Department of Music, University of Evansville, 1800 Lincoln Avenue, Evansville, Indiana 47722; 812-488-2742, fax: 812-488-2101, e-mail address: music@evansville.edu

University of Florida
Gainesville, Florida

State-supported, coed. Suburban campus. Total enrollment: 49,693.

Hugh Hodgson School of Music
University of Georgia
Athens, Georgia

State-supported, coed. Suburban campus. Total enrollment: 33,660. Music program established 1927.

Degrees Bachelor of Music in the areas of performance, composition, music therapy, music theory. Majors and concentrations: composition, music education, music theory, music therapy, piano/organ, stringed instruments, voice, wind and percussion instruments. Graduate degrees offered: Master of Music in the areas of musicology, composition, music literature, performance; Master of Music Education in the areas of music education, music therapy. Doctor of Musical Arts in the areas of performance, composition, music education, choral conducting; Doctor of Education in the area of music education; Doctor of Philosophy in the areas of musicology/ethnomusicology, music theory, music education. Cross-registration with University System of Georgia. Program accredited by NASM, NCATE, AMTA.
Enrollment 401 total; 96 undergraduate, 139 graduate, 166 nonprofessional degree.
Music Student Profile 51% females, 49% males, 14% minorities, 8% international.
Music Faculty 50 total (full-time), 12 total (part-time). 80% of full-time faculty have terminal degrees. Graduate students teach a few undergraduate courses. Undergraduate student–faculty ratio: 10:1.
Student Life Student groups/activities include Music Educators National Conference, Music Teachers National Association, American Music Therapy Association.
Expenses for 2005–2006 Application fee: $50. State resident tuition: $3638 full-time. Nonresident tuition: $15,858 full-time. Mandatory fees: $990 full-time. Full-time tuition and fees vary according to course load, location, program, and reciprocity agreements. College room and board: $6376. College room only: $3436. Room and board charges vary according to board plan and housing facility. Special program-related fees: $50 for stage managing and recording engineer for recital.
Financial Aid Program-specific awards: 95 music scholarships for performance majors ($1750).
Application Procedures Students admitted directly into the professional program freshman year. Deadline for freshmen: February 1; transfers: July 1. Notification date for freshmen and transfers: continuous. Required: high school transcript, college transcript(s) for transfer students, minimum 3.0 high school GPA, letter of recommendation, interview, audition, SAT I or ACT test scores (minimum combined SAT I score of 1060). Recommended: portfolio for composition applicants. Auditions held 4 times and by appointment on campus; recorded music is permissible as a substitute for live auditions when distance is prohibitive or scheduling is difficult and videotaped performances are permissible as a substitute for live auditions when distance is prohibitive or scheduling is difficult. Portfolio reviews held by appointment on campus.
Web Site http://www.music.uga.edu
Undergraduate Contact Ms. Suzanne Caruso, Administrative Coordinator, School of Music, University of Georgia, Music Building, Athens, Georgia 30602-3153; 706-542-2764, fax: 706-542-2773, e-mail address: scaruso@uga.edu
Graduate Contact Ms. Susan LeCroy, Administrative Coordinator, School of Music, University of Georgia, Music Building, Athens, Georgia 30602-3153; 706-542-2743, fax: 706-542-2773, e-mail address: shlecroy@uga.edu

The Hartt School
University of Hartford
West Hartford, Connecticut

Independent, coed. Suburban campus. Total enrollment: 7,260. Music program established 1920.
Degrees Bachelor of Arts in the areas of performing arts management, music; Bachelor of Music in the areas of performance, jazz studies, music management, composition, music history, music theory, music education, music production and technology, pre-cantorial studies. Majors and concentrations: composition, instrumental music, jazz, music education, music history, music management, music theory, performing arts management, pre-cantorial studies, production/technology, voice. Graduate degrees offered: Master of Music in the areas of performance, liturgical music, conducting, composition, music history, music theory, performance (Suzuki pedagogy), piano

University of Hartford (continued)

(accompanying or pedagogy emphasis); Master of Music Education in the areas of conducting (choral and instrumental) early childhood, performance, pedagogy, research, Kodály, technology. Doctor of Musical Arts in the areas of performance, composition, conducting, music education; Doctor of Philosophy in the area of music education. Cross-registration with Trinity College, Saint Joseph College, Hartford Seminary, Central Connecticut State University, University of Connecticut (Hartford Campus), Capitol Community College. Program accredited by NASM.
Enrollment 472 total; 361 undergraduate, 79 graduate, 32 nonprofessional degree.
Music Student Profile 55% females, 45% males, 10% minorities, 20% international.
Music Faculty 45 total (full-time), 75 total (part-time). 70% of full-time faculty have terminal degrees. Graduate students teach a few undergraduate courses. Undergraduate student–faculty ratio: 8:1.
Student Life Student groups/activities include Music Educators National Conference, American Choral Directors Association, Music and Entertainment Industry Student Association. Special housing available for music students.
Expenses for 2006–2007 Application fee: $35. Comprehensive fee: $35,688 includes full-time tuition ($24,576), mandatory fees ($1190), and college room and board ($9922). College room only: $6118.
Financial Aid Program-specific awards: 400 Performing Arts Scholarships for students passing audition evaluations ($7000).
Application Procedures Students admitted directly into the professional program freshman year. Deadline for freshmen and transfers: continuous. Notification date for freshmen and transfers: May 1. Required: essay, high school transcript, college transcript(s) for transfer students, minimum 2.0 high school GPA, 3 letters of recommendation, interview, audition, SAT I or ACT test scores, music aptitude profile test, theory placement test. Recommended: minimum 3.0 high school GPA. Auditions held 5 times on campus and off campus; recorded music is permissible as a substitute for live auditions if a campus visit is impossible or special requirements exist and videotaped performances are permissible as a substitute for live auditions when distance is prohibitive (video required of all performance majors).
Web Site http://www.hartford.edu/hartt
Undergraduate Contact Director of Admissions, The Hartt School, University of Hartford, 200 Bloomfield Avenue, West Hartford, Connecticut 06117-1500; 860-768-4465, fax: 860-768-4441, e-mail address: harttadm@hartford.edu
Graduate Contact Dr. Clark Saunders, Director of Graduate Studies, The Hartt School, University of Hartford, 200 Bloomfield Avenue, West Hartford, Connecticut 06117-1500; 860-768-5245, fax: 860-768-4441, e-mail address: clsaunder@hartford.edu

University of Hawaii at Manoa
Honolulu, Hawaii

State-supported, coed. Urban campus. Total enrollment: 20,644. Music program established 1947.

Moores School of Music
University of Houston
Houston, Texas

State-supported, coed. Urban campus. Total enrollment: 35,344. Music program established 1927.
Degrees Bachelor of Music in the areas of applied music, music with teaching certificate, music theory, composition, music with elective studies. Majors and concentrations: composition, music education, music theory, piano/organ, stringed instruments, voice, wind and percussion instruments. Graduate degrees offered: Master of Music in the areas of applied music, music theory, composition, music literature, music education, accompanying and chamber music, performance and pedagogy. Doctor

of Musical Arts in the areas of performance, conducting, composition, music education. Program accredited by NASM.
Enrollment 590 total; 316 undergraduate, 162 graduate, 112 nonprofessional degree.
Music Student Profile 47% females, 53% males, 31% minorities, 11% international.
Music Faculty 16 undergraduate (full-time), 30 undergraduate (part-time), 17 graduate (full-time), 12 graduate (part-time). 57% of full-time faculty have terminal degrees. Graduate students teach a few undergraduate courses. Undergraduate student–faculty ratio: 7:1.
Student Life Student groups/activities include Phi Mu Alpha Sinfonia, Sigma Alpha Iota, Kappa Kappa Psi.
Expenses for 2005–2006 Application fee: $50. State resident tuition: $3920 full-time. Nonresident tuition: $12,200 full-time. Mandatory fees: $2566 full-time. Full-time tuition and fees vary according to course level, course load, degree level, location, program, reciprocity agreements, and student level. College room and board: $6058. College room only: $3492. Room and board charges vary according to board plan and housing facility. Special program-related fees: $10–$55 per semester for some music courses, $10–$180 per semester for applied music courses, $210 per semester for piano use, $225 per semester for music major fee.
Financial Aid Program-specific awards: 384 music scholarships for program students ($2000), 220 band grants for program students ($500).
Application Procedures Students apply for admission into the professional program by junior year. Deadline for freshmen: April 2; transfers: May 1. Required: high school transcript, college transcript(s) for transfer students, minimum 2.0 high school GPA, audition, SAT I or ACT test scores. Recommended: minimum 3.0 high school GPA, 3 letters of recommendation, interview. Auditions held 3 times on campus; recorded music is permissible as a substitute for live auditions when distance is prohibitive or scheduling is difficult and videotaped performances are permissible as a substitute for live auditions when distance is prohibitive or scheduling is difficult.
Web Site http://www.uh.edu/music/
Undergraduate Contact Mr. John Benzer, Academic Advisor, Moores School of Music, University of Houston, Houston, Texas 77204-4017; 713-743-3172, fax: 713-743-3166, e-mail address: jbenzer@uh.edu
Graduate Contact Dr. Sharon Joy, Graduate Advisor, Moores School of Music, University of Houston, Houston, Texas 77204-4017; 713-743-3314, fax: 713-743-3166, e-mail address: gradmusic@orpheus.music.uh.edu

Lionel Hampton School of Music
University of Idaho
Moscow, Idaho

State-supported, coed. Small town campus. Total enrollment: 12,476. Music program established 1893.

University of Illinois at Urbana–Champaign
Champaign, Illinois

State-supported, coed. Small town campus. Total enrollment: 41,938. Music program established 1895.

The University of Iowa
Iowa City, Iowa

State-supported, coed. Small town campus. Total enrollment: 28,426. Music program established 1856.
Degrees Bachelor of Music in the areas of performance, composition, music therapy. Majors and concentrations: composition, music education, music performance, music therapy, piano/organ, stringed instruments, voice, wind and percussion instruments. Graduate degrees offered: Master of Arts in the

areas of performance, theory, composition, musicology, music education; Master of Fine Arts in the area of performance. Doctor of Musical Arts in the areas of performance, conducting; Doctor of Philosophy in the areas of composition, musicology, music education, theory, music literature. Program accredited by NASM.

Enrollment 445 total; 250 undergraduate, 195 graduate.

Music Student Profile 51% females, 49% males, 5% minorities, 11% international.

Music Faculty 52 total (full-time), 4 total (part-time). 99% of full-time faculty have terminal degrees. Graduate students teach about a quarter of undergraduate courses. Undergraduate student–faculty ratio: 9:1.

Student Life Student groups/activities include Pi Kappa Lambda, Music Educators National Conference, Sigma Alpha Iota. Special housing available for music students.

Expenses for 2006–2007 Application fee: $40. State resident tuition: $5110 full-time. Nonresident tuition: $17,334 full-time. Mandatory fees: $825 full-time. College room and board: $6912. Special program-related fees: $83–$150 per credit hour for applied music fee.

Financial Aid Program-specific awards: 50 music activities scholarships for composition and performance majors ($500–$4000).

Application Procedures Students admitted directly into the professional program freshman year. Deadline for freshmen and transfers: continuous. Required: high school transcript, college transcript(s) for transfer students, minimum 2.0 high school GPA, letter of recommendation, audition, SAT I or ACT test scores. Auditions held once in February and continuously by appointment on campus; recorded music is permissible as a substitute for live auditions if a campus visit is impossible and videotaped performances are permissible as a substitute for live auditions when distance is prohibitive.

Web Site http://www.uiowa.edu/~music/

Undergraduate Contact Carlos Rodriguez, Associate Director for Undergraduate Studies, School of Music, The University of Iowa, 1014 Voxman Music Building, Iowa City, Iowa 52242; 319-335-3030, fax: 319-335-2637, e-mail address: music-admissions@uiowa.edu

Graduate Contact Dr. Maurita Murphy Mead, Associate Director for Graduate Studies, School of Music, The University of Iowa, 1012 Voxman Music Building, Iowa City, Iowa 52242; 319-335-1603, fax: 319-335-2637, e-mail address: music-admissions@uiowa.edu

University of Kansas

Lawrence, Kansas

State-supported, coed. Total enrollment: 28,949. Music program established 1877.

Degrees Bachelor of Fine Arts in the area of theater/voice; Bachelor of Music in the areas of performance, music theory, history, composition, church music; Bachelor of Music Education in the areas of music education, music therapy. Majors and concentrations: church music, composition, music, music education, music history, music theater, music theory, music therapy, piano/organ, stringed instruments, voice, wind and percussion instruments. Graduate degrees offered: Master of Music in the areas of performance, musicology, music theory, composition, conducting, church music, opera; Master of Music Education in the areas of music education, music therapy. Doctor of Musical Arts in the areas of performance, composition, conducting, church music; Doctor of Philosophy in the areas of music theory, music education, music history, music therapy. Program accredited by NASM, AMTA.

Enrollment 525 total; 345 undergraduate, 180 graduate.

Music Student Profile 50% females, 50% males, 5% minorities, 15% international.

Music Faculty 55 total (full-time), 9 total (part-time). 100% of full-time faculty have terminal degrees. Graduate students teach a few undergraduate courses. Undergraduate student–faculty ratio: 10:1.

Student Life Student groups/activities include Kappa Kappa Psi, Tau Beta Sigma, Music Educators National Conference Student Chapter.

Expenses for 2005–2006 Application fee: $30. State resident tuition: $4824 full-time. Nonresident tuition: $13,277 full-time.

Mandatory fees: $589 full-time. Full-time tuition and fees vary according to program and reciprocity agreements. College room and board: $5502. College room only: $2752. Room and board charges vary according to board plan and housing facility. Special program-related fees: $15 per music credit hour for enhancement of student learning.

Financial Aid Program-specific awards: 70–80 music scholarships for those demonstrating talent ($2000).

Application Procedures Students admitted directly into the professional program freshman year. Deadline for freshmen and transfers: April 1. Required: high school transcript, college transcript(s) for transfer students, 3 letters of recommendation, audition, SAT I or ACT test scores, minimum 2.5 high school GPA. Recommended: interview. Auditions held at various times on campus; recorded music is permissible as a substitute for live auditions when distance is prohibitive and videotaped performances are permissible as a substitute for live auditions when distance is prohibitive.

Web Site http://www.music.ku.edu

Undergraduate Contact Department of Music and Dance, University of Kansas, 452 Murphy Hall, Lawrence, Kansas 66045; 785-864-3436, fax: 785-864-5387.

Graduate Contact Director of Graduate Studies, Department of Music and Dance, University of Kansas, 1530 Naismith Drive-452 Murphy Hall, Lawrence, Kansas 66045; 785-864-3436, fax: 785-864-5866.

University of Kentucky

Lexington, Kentucky

State-supported, coed. Urban campus. Total enrollment: 25,672. Music program established 1918.

University of Louisiana at Lafayette

Lafayette, Louisiana

State-supported, coed. Urban campus. Total enrollment: 17,075.

Degrees Bachelor of Music in the areas of performance, composition, media, jazz, theory, conducting; Bachelor of Music Education in the area of instrumental and vocal. Majors and concentrations: jazz studies, music education, music media, music theory and composition, performance, piano pedagogy. Graduate degrees offered: Master of Music in the areas of performance, conducting, music theory/composition; Master of Music Education. Program accredited by NASM.

Enrollment 243 total; 212 undergraduate, 31 graduate.

Music Faculty 21 total (full-time), 5 total (part-time). 75% of full-time faculty have terminal degrees. Graduate students teach a few undergraduate courses. Undergraduate student–faculty ratio: 10:1.

Student Life Student groups/activities include Music Educators National Conference, Sigma Alpha Iota, Phi Mu Alpha.

Expenses for 2005–2006 Application fee: $25. State resident tuition: $3324 full-time. Nonresident tuition: $9504 full-time. Full-time tuition varies according to course load. College room and board: $3478. Room and board charges vary according to board plan and housing facility. Special program-related fees: $30 per per credit hour for standard fees.

Financial Aid Program-specific awards: marching band stipend for all students in marching band ($500), 100 marching band housing awards for all students in marching band, 25 fellowships for all music students ($200).

Application Procedures Students admitted directly into the professional program freshman year. Deadline for freshmen and transfers: continuous. Required: high school transcript, college transcript(s) for transfer students, minimum 2.0 high school GPA, audition, SAT I or ACT test scores. Auditions held in February and March on campus; recorded music is permissible as a substitute for live auditions when distance is prohibitive or scheduling is difficult and videotaped performances are permissible as a substitute for live auditions when distance is prohibitive or scheduling is difficult.

Web Site http://music.louisiana.edu/

University of Louisiana at Lafayette (continued)

Undergraduate Contact Dr. A. C. Himes, Director, School of Music, University of Louisiana at Lafayette, Box 41207, Lafayette, Louisiana 70504-1207; 337-482-6016, fax: 337-482-5017, e-mail address: himes@louisiana.edu

Graduate Contact Dr. Andrea Loewy, Director of Graduate Studies, School of Music, University of Louisiana at Lafayette, Box 41207, Lafayette, Louisiana 70504-1207; 337-482-5214, fax: 337-482-5017, e-mail address: akloewy@aol.com

University of Louisiana at Monroe
Monroe, Louisiana

State-supported, coed. Urban campus. Total enrollment: 9,056. Music program established 1957.

Degrees Bachelor of Music in the areas of performance, pedagogy, music theory/composition, music history/literature, music theater; Bachelor of Music Education. Majors and concentrations: classical music, music, music education, music history and literature, music theater, music theory and composition, piano pedagogy, piano/organ, stringed instruments, voice, wind and percussion instruments. Graduate degrees offered: Master of Music in the areas of performance, music education, music theory/composition, conducting. Cross-registration with all 4 year public universities in Louisiana. Program accredited by NASM, NASM.

Enrollment 118 total; 104 undergraduate, 14 graduate.

Music Student Profile 55% females, 45% males, 10% minorities, 5% international.

Music Faculty 20 total (full-time), 2 total (part-time). 50% of full-time faculty have terminal degrees. Graduate students do not teach undergraduate courses. Undergraduate student–faculty ratio: 4:1.

Student Life Student groups/activities include Music Educators National Conference Student Chapter, music sorority, band fraternity and sorority. Special housing available for music students.

Expenses for 2005–2006 Application fee: $20. State resident tuition: $2334 full-time. Nonresident tuition: $8284 full-time. Mandatory fees: $1068 full-time. Full-time tuition and fees vary according to course load and program. College room and board: $4120. College room only: $2230. Room and board charges vary according to board plan and housing facility.

Financial Aid Program-specific awards: 220 Music Talent Grants for members of major ensembles ($900).

Application Procedures Students admitted directly into the professional program freshman year. Deadline for freshmen and transfers: continuous. Notification date for freshmen and transfers: continuous. Required: high school transcript, college transcript(s) for transfer students, minimum 2.0 high school GPA, audition, ACT test score only. Recommended: interview. Auditions held throughout the year on campus; recorded music is permissible as a substitute for live auditions when distance is prohibitive or scheduling is difficult and videotaped performances are permissible as a substitute for live auditions when distance is prohibitive or scheduling is difficult.

Web Site http://www.ulm.edu/music

Contact Dr. James Goodman, Director, School of Music, University of Louisiana at Monroe, 700 University Avenue, Monroe, Louisiana 71209-0380; 318-342-1570, fax: 318-342-1599, e-mail address: goodman@ulm.edu

University of Louisville
Louisville, Kentucky

State-supported, coed. Urban campus. Total enrollment: 20,734. Music program established 1932.

Degrees Bachelor of Music in the areas of performance, music history, music theory, composition, music education, music therapy. Majors and concentrations: music education, music history, music performance, music theory and composition, music therapy, piano pedagogy, piano/organ, stringed instruments, voice, wind and percussion instruments. Graduate degrees offered: Master of Arts in Teaching in the areas of instrumental music education, vocal music education; Master of Music in the areas of performance, music history, music theory/composition, jazz performance; Master of Music Education in the areas of instrumental music education, vocal music education. Cross-registration with Metroversity. Program accredited by NASM.

Enrollment 325 total; 174 undergraduate, 62 graduate, 89 nonprofessional degree.

Music Student Profile 47% females, 53% males, 12% minorities, 7% international.

Music Faculty 33 total (full-time), 38 total (part-time). 70% of full-time faculty have terminal degrees. Graduate students do not teach undergraduate courses. Undergraduate student–faculty ratio: 9:1.

Student Life Student groups/activities include Phi Mu Alpha Symphonic, Delta Omnicrom, Music Educators National Conference Student Chapter, International Association of Jazz Educators, American Musicological Society. Special housing available for music students.

Expenses for 2005–2006 Application fee: $30. State resident tuition: $5532 full-time. Nonresident tuition: $15,092 full-time. Full-time tuition varies according to reciprocity agreements. College room and board: $6036. College room only: $4490. Room and board charges vary according to board plan and housing facility. Special program-related fees: $5 per semester for practice room key/lock, $100 per semester for accompanist fee.

Financial Aid Program-specific awards: 1 Sister Cities Award for program majors ($12,000), 1 Presser Award for academically qualified applicants ($4000), 1 Babb Award for composition majors ($2000), 150 performance awards for music majors ($3200).

Application Procedures Students admitted directly into the professional program freshman year. Deadline for freshmen: June 2; transfers: July 2. Required: high school transcript, college transcript(s) for transfer students, minimum 2.0 high school GPA, 2 letters of recommendation, interview, audition, SAT I or ACT test scores (minimum composite ACT score of 21), minimum 2.75 high school GPA, essay for music history applicants, portfolio for composition and music theory applicants, video for piano pedagogy and conducting applicants. Auditions held 4-6 times on campus; recorded music is permissible as a substitute for live auditions when distance is prohibitive and videotaped performances are permissible as a substitute for live auditions when distance is prohibitive.

Web Site http://www.louisville.edu/music

Undergraduate Contact Amanda Boyd, Admissions Coordinator, School of Music, University of Louisville, Louisville, Kentucky 40292; 502-852-1623, fax: 502-852-0520, e-mail address: amanda.boyd@louisville.edu

Graduate Contact Dr. Jean Christensen, Director of Graduate Studies, School of Music, University of Louisville, Louisville, Kentucky 40292; 502-852-0540, fax: 502-852-0520, e-mail address: jmchri01@louisville.edu

University of Maine
Orono, Maine

State-supported, coed. Total enrollment: 11,435.

University of Manitoba
Winnipeg, Manitoba, Canada

Province-supported, coed. Suburban campus. Total enrollment: 27,599. Music program established 1964.

Degrees Bachelor of Music in the areas of performance, history, general music, composition; Bachelor of Music/Bachelor of Education. Majors and concentrations: composition, music, music education, music history, performance. Graduate degrees offered: Master of Music in the areas of performance, composition, choral and wind conducting.

Enrollment 249 total; 229 undergraduate, 20 graduate.

Music Student Profile 10% minorities, 5% international.

Music Faculty 20 total (full-time), 42 total (part-time). 55% of full-time faculty have terminal degrees. Graduate students do not teach undergraduate courses. Undergraduate student–faculty ratio: 4:1.

Student Life Student groups/activities include University Orchestra, Wind and Jazz Ensembles, University choirs.

Expenses for 2005–2006 Application fee: $35 Canadian dollars.

Financial Aid Program-specific awards: University of Manitoba Entrance Scholarships for entering students with 85.1 or higher in best five academic subjects combined with excellence in performance audition ($800–$2000), 28 Faculty of Music Scholarships for excellent auditions ($200–$2000), 7 Faculty of Music Bursaries for those demonstrating financial need ($150–$1500), 6 prizes for best performance in musical competitions ($100–$1000).

Application Procedures Students admitted directly into the professional program freshman year. Deadline for freshmen and transfers: April 1. Notification date for freshmen and transfers: June 1. Required: essay, high school transcript, college transcript(s) for transfer students, minimum 2.0 high school GPA, letter of recommendation, interview, audition, theory assessment, portfolios for composition applicants only. Recommended: minimum 3.0 high school GPA. Auditions held 7 times on campus and off campus in Calgary, AB; Camrose, AB; recorded music is permissible as a substitute for live auditions out-of-province applicants and videotaped performances are permissible as a substitute for live auditions out-of-province applicants. Portfolio reviews held on campus.

Web Site http://umanitoba.ca/music

Undergraduate Contact Susan Leeson, Registrar, Faculty of Music, University of Manitoba, 65 Dafoe Road, Winnipeg, Manitoba R3T 2N2, Canada; 204-474-9133, fax: 204-474-7546, e-mail address: sleeson@cc.umanitoba.ca

Graduate Contact Dr. Karen Jensen, Associate Dean, Faculty of Music, University of Manitoba, 65 DaFoe Road, Winnipeg, Manitoba R3T 2N2, Canada; 204-474-9536, fax: 204-474-7546, e-mail address: kjensen@cc.umanitoba.ac

University of Maryland, College Park
College Park, Maryland

State-supported, coed. Suburban campus. Total enrollment: 35,300. Music program established 1964.

Degrees Bachelor of Music in the areas of theory, composition, music performance, music education. Majors and concentrations: choral music education, composition, instrumental music education, music theory, piano, stringed instruments, voice, wind and percussion instruments. Graduate degrees offered: Master of Arts in the areas of ethnomusicology, music history and literature, music theory; Master of Music in the areas of performance, theory/composition, music education. Doctor of Musical Arts in the areas of performance, composition; Doctor of Philosophy in the areas of musicology, ethnomusicology, theory, music education. Cross-registration with University of Maryland System. Program accredited by NASM.

Enrollment 582 total; 243 undergraduate, 339 graduate.

Music Student Profile 55% females, 45% males, 30% minorities, 20% international.

Music Faculty 45 total (full-time), 49 total (part-time). 53% of full-time faculty have terminal degrees. Graduate students teach a few undergraduate courses. Undergraduate student–faculty ratio: 3:1.

Student Life Student groups/activities include Phi Mu Alpha, Sigma Alpha Iota, Pi Kappa Lambda.

Expenses for 2005–2006 Application fee: $55. State resident tuition: $6566 full-time. Nonresident tuition: $18,890 full-time. Mandatory fees: $1255 full-time. College room and board: $8075. College room only: $4784. Room and board charges vary according to board plan. Special program-related fees: $200 per semester for applied music fee.

Financial Aid Program-specific awards: 10 Creative and Performing Arts Scholarships for program majors ($7500), 35 Director's Scholarships for program majors ($1000–$10,000), 15 Endowed Funds Awards for program majors ($1000–$15,000).

Application Procedures Students admitted directly into the professional program freshman year. Deadline for freshmen: December 1; transfers: December 15. Notification date for freshmen and transfers: March 1. Required: essay, high school transcript, college transcript(s) for transfer students, minimum 3.0 high school GPA, 2 letters of recommendation, audition, SAT I or ACT test scores (minimum combined SAT I score of 1200), portfolio for composition applicants. Recommended: interview, record of co-curricular activities. Auditions held once on campus; recorded music is permissible as a substitute for live auditions when distance is prohibitive (beyond a 250-mile radius) and video-taped performances are permissible as a substitute for live auditions when distance is prohibitive (beyond a 250-mile radius). Portfolio reviews held as needed on campus.

Web Site http://www.music.umd.edu

Contact Mrs. Ashley Fleming, Director of Admissions, School of Music, University of Maryland, College Park, Clarice Smith Performing Arts Center, College Park, Maryland 20742-9504; 301-405-1313, fax: 301-314-7966, e-mail address: music-admissions@umail.umd.edu

University of Massachusetts Amherst
Amherst, Massachusetts

State-supported, coed. Total enrollment: 25,093. Music program established 1968.

Degrees Bachelor of Music. Majors and concentrations: jazz and African-American music, music education, music history, music theory and composition, performance. Graduate degrees offered: Master of Music in the areas of collaborative piano, composition, music education, musicology, jazz composition and arranging, music theory, performance, conducting. Doctor of Philosophy in the areas of music theory, music education. Cross-registration with Amherst College, Hampshire College, Mount Holyoke College, Smith College. Program accredited by NASM.

Enrollment 315 total; 176 undergraduate, 88 graduate, 51 nonprofessional degree.

Music Faculty 33 total (full-time), 28 total (part-time). 98% of full-time faculty have terminal degrees. Graduate students teach a few undergraduate courses. Undergraduate student–faculty ratio: 5:1.

Student Life Student groups/activities include Music Educators National Conference Student Chapter, Kappa Kappa Psi, Tau Beta Sigma.

Expenses for 2006–2007 Application fee: $40. State resident tuition: $2031 full-time. Nonresident tuition: $10,857 full-time. Mandatory fees: $7564 full-time.

Financial Aid Program-specific awards: Chancellor's Talent Awards for program majors, alumni scholarships for program majors.

Application Procedures Deadline for freshmen: January 15; transfers: April 1. Notification date for freshmen: April 1; transfers: June 15. Required: essay, high school transcript, college transcript(s) for transfer students, audition, SAT I test score only, minimum combined SAT I score of 1000 for in-state applicants; 1200 for out-of-state applicants. Auditions held 5 times and by request on campus; recorded music is permissible as a substitute for live auditions when distance is prohibitive and videotaped performances are permissible as a substitute for live auditions when distance is prohibitive.

Web Site http://www.umass.edu/music/

Undergraduate Contact Mr. Christopher T. Thornley, Director of Admissions, Department of Music and Dance, University of Massachusetts Amherst, 271 Fine Arts Center, Amherst, Massachusetts 01003-9330; 413-545-6048, fax: 413-545-2092, e-mail address: cthornley@music.umass.edu

Graduate Contact Denise Cuddeback, Graduate Secretary, Department of Music and Dance, University of Massachusetts Amherst, 273 Fine Arts Center, Box 32520, Amherst, Massachusetts 01003-2520; 413-545-0311, fax: 413-545-2092, e-mail address: gradstudies@music.umass.edu

University of Massachusetts Dartmouth

North Dartmouth, Massachusetts

State-supported, coed. Suburban campus. Total enrollment: 8,549. Music program established 1964.

Degrees Bachelor of Arts in the area of music. Majors and concentrations: music, music education, music technology, western music, world music. Cross-registration with University of Massachusetts System, Southeastern Association for Cooperation in Higher Education in Massachusetts.

Enrollment 69 total; all undergraduate.

Music Student Profile 39% females, 61% males, 13% minorities.

Music Faculty 5 total (full-time), 23 total (part-time). 100% of full-time faculty have terminal degrees. Graduate students do not teach undergraduate courses. Undergraduate student–faculty ratio: 6:1.

Student Life Student groups/activities include Kekeli African Drum and Dance, jazz, pep, and concert bands, chorus.

Expenses for 2005–2006 Application fee: $35, $55 for nonresidents. State resident tuition: $1417 full-time. Nonresident tuition: $8099 full-time. Mandatory fees: $6619 full-time. Full-time tuition and fees vary according to reciprocity agreements. College room and board: $7634. College room only: $4460. Room and board charges vary according to board plan and housing facility. Special program-related fees: $243 per semester for CVPA fee, $420 per course for applied music fee.

Financial Aid Program-specific awards: 1 Alda Alves and Bruce Yenawine Scholarship for CVPA students ($1000), 1 Lillian Telles Jenkins Scholarship for CVPA students ($400), 4 Ayuko Ito Scholarships for CVPA students ($1000), 1 Clement Yeager Scholarship for CVPA students ($700–$2500).

Application Procedures Students admitted directly into the professional program freshman year. Deadline for freshmen and transfers: continuous. Notification date for freshmen and transfers: continuous. Required: high school transcript, college transcript(s) for transfer students, minimum 2.0 high school GPA, audition, SAT I or ACT test scores. Recommended: essay, minimum 3.0 high school GPA, 3 letters of recommendation. Auditions held monthly from January to May on campus; videotaped performances are permissible as a substitute for live auditions (non-New England students should contact department for requirements).

Web Site http://www.umassd.edu/cvpa

Undergraduate Contact Mr. Steven T. Briggs, Director of Admissions, University of Massachusetts Dartmouth, 285 Old Westport Road, North Dartmouth, Massachusetts 02747-2300; 508-999-8606, fax: 508-999-8755, e-mail address: admissions@umassd.edu

More About the University

"A world of sound . . . a community of musicians."

All candidates for a Bachelor of Arts (B.A.) in music follow a standard core curriculum. Each student may also choose an option in Western music performance, composition, music education, world music, jazz studies, or music technology. The music curriculum meets the requirements for a well-rounded liberal arts education.

The performance/composition option gives students a thorough grounding in the performance and historical background of the Western music tradition. Graduates of this option may enter graduate school or pursue careers as active composers and performing musicians. The education program develops skillful teachers who are in demand throughout New England. Students are exposed to Western, African-American, and world music—allowing them to bring diverse experiences into the classroom. State-of-the-art facilities and course content in music technology enable students to function at the cutting-edge of today's music scene, from sound recording and manipulation to electronic composition and video scoring. Jazz and world music studios open students to the music and dance of the world's peoples, including the dynamic traditions of Africa, Asia, the Americas, and the African-American heritage. Through cultural studies and

ensemble experiences, graduates bring a fluency to their work as performers, teachers, composers, or graduate scholars.

Facilities and Equipment The music facilities of the College of Visual and Performing Arts (CVPA) include an 800-seat auditorium, an intimate 200-seat recital hall, computer-aided music stations, an electronic clavinova piano lab, two electronic music studios for electronic composition, recording technology and sound production capabilities, Steinway concert grand pianos, traditional and non-Western percussion instruments (Gamelan, steel drums), individual practice rooms, and a campus-wide computer network.

Faculty The performance faculty members are accomplished musicians who perform in recital halls and on concert stages, both internationally and in the United States. The composition and academic faculty members are noted for their publications, academic papers, creative work, and workshops.

Performance Opportunities Students have opportunities to perform in the following groups: University Chorus, Spinners Vocal Ensemble, Gospel Choir, Wind Ensemble, Concert Band, Large and Small Jazz Ensembles, Brass Ensemble, West African Drum and Dance Ensemble, Contemporary Jazz and Jazz Vocal Ensembles, Guitar Ensemble, and Percussion Ensemble. The Music Department presents a Guest Artist Recital Series, a Faculty Recital Series, a Guest Artist Lecture Series, and community concerts as well as student ensemble and solo recitals.

Career Opportunities Graduates have a variety of career options open to them from teaching and performing to electronic music (composition, sound design, and audio recording), advanced study, and careers in related fields.

Special Programs Music Minor: Students majoring in another field may pursue a minor in music, emphasizing performance, music theory, or jazz. A new minor in music therapy is designed for students who are interested in the therapeutic applications of music while majoring in related fields, such as education, nursing, geriatrics, and psychology.

Study Abroad: Students are encouraged to pursue fieldwork study and research abroad in a culture relevant to their area of concentration. This work may fulfill specific course requirements with prior approval. All study abroad should be planned in consultation with the student's faculty adviser and the Music Department chairperson.

Requirements for Admission All candidates must pass an entrance audition and take an advisory exam to assess background and determine potential. Candidates are expected to have some facility on their instrument and to have some preparation in fundamental concepts of music theory. All applicants must also follow the University of Massachusetts Dartmouth's admissions procedures that are detailed in the University Catalogue.

University of Massachusetts Lowell

Lowell, Massachusetts

State-supported, coed. Urban campus. Total enrollment: 10,666. Music program established 1894.

Degrees Bachelor of Music. Majors and concentrations: music business, performance, sound recording technology. Graduate degrees offered: Master of Music in the areas of performance, conducting, music education. Program accredited by NASM, NCATE.

Enrollment 326 total; 306 undergraduate, 20 graduate.

Music Student Profile 36% females, 64% males, 12% minorities, 10% international.

Music Faculty 12 total (full-time), 42 total (part-time). 100% of full-time faculty have terminal degrees. Graduate students do not teach undergraduate courses. Undergraduate student–faculty ratio: 13:1.

Student Life Student groups/activities include Society of Professional Audio Recording Services, Music Educators National Conference, Audio Engineering Society, Entertainment and Music Industry Association.

Expenses for 2005–2006 Application fee: $20. State resident tuition: $1454 full-time. Nonresident tuition: $8567 full-time. Mandatory fees: $6712 full-time. College room and board: $6311. College room only: $3810. Room and board charges vary according to board plan and housing facility.
Financial Aid Program-specific awards available.
Application Procedures Students apply for admission into the professional program by sophomore year. Deadline for freshmen and transfers: continuous. Required: high school transcript, college transcript(s) for transfer students, 2 letters of recommendation, audition, SAT I test score only (minimum combined SAT I score of 1000), minimum 3.0 for sound recording technology. Recommended: minimum 2.5 high school GPA. Auditions held 4 times on campus; recorded music is permissible as a substitute for live auditions when distance is prohibitive and videotaped performances are permissible as a substitute for live auditions when distance is prohibitive.
Web Site http://www.uml.edu
Undergraduate Contact Dr. William Moylan, Chair, Department of Music, University of Massachusetts Lowell, 35 Wilder Street, Suite 3, Lowell, Massachusetts 01854-3083; 978-934-3850, fax: 978-934-3034, e-mail address: william_moylan@uml.edu
Graduate Contact Dr. Nicholas Tobin, Graduate Coordinator, Department of Music, University of Massachusetts Lowell, 35 Wilder Street, Suite 3, Lowell, Massachusetts 01854-3083; 978-934-3879, fax: 978-934-3034, e-mail address: nicholas_tobin@uml.edu

The Rudi E. Scheidt School of Music
University of Memphis
Memphis, Tennessee

State-supported, coed. Urban campus. Total enrollment: 20,465. Music program established 1953.
Degrees Bachelor of Music in the areas of performance, composition, music history, music education, music business, recording technology, jazz/studio performance, jazz/studio composition and arranging. Majors and concentrations: composition, jazz composing and arranging, jazz performance, music business, music education, music history, performance, sound recording technology. Graduate degrees offered: Master of Music in the areas of performance, sacred music, music history, Orff-Schulwerk, pedagogy, music education, jazz/studio music, composition, conducting, music theory. Doctor of Musical Arts in the areas of composition, performance, conducting; Doctor of Philosophy in the areas of musicology, music education. Program accredited by NASM.
Enrollment 467 total; 343 undergraduate, 114 graduate, 10 nonprofessional degree.
Music Student Profile 41% females, 59% males, 28% minorities, 5% international.
Music Faculty 42 undergraduate (full-time), 16 undergraduate (part-time), 42 graduate (full-time). 60% of full-time faculty have terminal degrees. Graduate students teach a few undergraduate courses. Undergraduate student–faculty ratio: 8:1.
Student Life Student groups/activities include Music Educators National Conference Student Chapter, Music Entertainers and Industry Student Association, American String Teachers Association Student Chapter.
Expenses for 2005–2006 Application fee: $25. State resident tuition: $4216 full-time. Nonresident tuition: $14,030 full-time. Mandatory fees: $868 full-time. Full-time tuition and fees vary according to program and reciprocity agreements. College room and board: $6069. College room only: $2950. Room and board charges vary according to housing facility. Special program-related fees: $150 per one-hour lesson for applied lessons fee.
Financial Aid Program-specific awards: 275 School of Music Awards for talented music students ($3200).
Application Procedures Students admitted directly into the professional program freshman year. Deadline for freshmen and transfers: June 1. Required: high school transcript, college transcript(s) for transfer students, minimum 2.0 high school GPA, 2 letters of recommendation, audition, SAT I or ACT test scores (minimum combined SAT I score of 930, minimum composite ACT score of 20). Auditions held continuously by appointment

on campus; recorded music is permissible as a substitute for live auditions when distance is prohibitive and videotaped performances are permissible as a substitute for live auditions when distance is prohibitive.
Web Site http://music.memphis.edu/
Undergraduate Contact Ms. Kay Yager, Admissions Director, School of Music, University of Memphis, 3775 Central Avenue, Memphis, Tennessee 38152; 901-678-3766, fax: 901-678-3096, e-mail address: kayyager@memphis.edu
Graduate Contact Dr. John D. Peterson, Associate Director for Graduate Studies, School of Music, University of Memphis, 3775 Central Avenue, Memphis, Tennessee 38152; 901-678-3769, fax: 901-678-0708, e-mail address: jdpete@memphis.edu

Frost School of Music
University of Miami
Coral Gables, Florida

Independent, coed. Suburban campus. Total enrollment: 15,674. Music program established 1926.
Degrees Bachelor of Arts; Bachelor of Music; Bachelor of Science. Majors and concentrations: composition, composition/commercial music and production, instrumental performance, keyboard performance, music, music business and entertainment, music education, music engineering technology, music theater, music therapy, performance, studio music and jazz, vocal performance. Graduate degrees offered: Master of Music in the areas of accompanying and chamber music, conducting, electronic music, jazz performance, jazz pedagogy, keyboard performance and pedagogy, media writing/production, music education, theory, composition, music therapy, music business and entertainment industries, musicology, studio jazz writing, performance; Master of Science in the area of music engineering. Doctor of Musical Arts in the areas of accompanying and chamber music, composition, jazz composition, conducting, keyboard performance and pedagogy, performance, jazz performance. Program accredited by NASM.
Enrollment 716 total; 529 undergraduate, 187 graduate.
Music Student Profile 46% females, 54% males, 30% minorities, 10% international.
Music Faculty 58 total (full-time), 56 total (part-time). 80% of full-time faculty have terminal degrees. Graduate students teach a few undergraduate courses. Undergraduate student–faculty ratio: 7:1.
Student Life Student groups/activities include Phi Mu Alpha Sinfonia, Sigma Alpha Iota, Pi Kappa Lambda.
Expenses for 2005–2006 Application fee: $65. Comprehensive fee: $37,926 includes full-time tuition ($29,020) and college room and board ($8906). College room only: $5224. Full-time tuition varies according to course load, location, and program. Room and board charges vary according to board plan and housing facility.
Financial Aid Program-specific awards: 160 Music Scholarships for those demonstrating talent ($2000–$31,288), 75 Academic Scholarships for those demonstrating academic talent ($5200–$15,000), need-based grants, loans for those demonstrating need ($2000–$15,000).
Application Procedures Students admitted directly into the professional program freshman year. Deadline for freshmen and transfers: February 1. Notification date for freshmen and transfers: April 1. Required: essay, high school transcript, college transcript(s) for transfer students, 3 letters of recommendation, audition, SAT I or ACT test scores, portfolio for music theory/composition. Recommended: minimum 3.0 high school GPA. Auditions held 4 times on campus and off campus in Atlanta, GA; Boston, MA; Chicago, IL; Dallas, TX; Houston, TX; New York, NY; Philadelphia, PA; Washington, DC; Interlochen, MI; recorded music is permissible as a substitute for live auditions when distance is prohibitive and videotaped performances are permissible as a substitute for live auditions when distance is prohibitive.
Web Site http://www.music.miami.edu
Undergraduate Contact Mrs. Catherine Tanner, Director of Admission and Recruitment, Frost School of Music, University of

University of Miami (continued)

Miami, PO Box 248165, Coral Gables, Florida 33124; 305-284-2241, fax: 305-284-6475, e-mail address: ctanner@miami.edu
Graduate Contact Dr. Edward P. Asmus, Associate Dean, Frost School of Music, University of Miami, PO Box 248165, Coral Gables, Florida 33124; 305-284-2241, fax: 305-284-6475, e-mail address: ed.asmus@miami.edu

More About the University

Each year, students from across the United States and approximately forty countries pursue undergraduate and graduate study at the Frost School of Music at the University of Miami. The Frost School enjoys a reputation as a comprehensive and innovative music school, with more than three dozen degree, certificate, diploma, and international exchange program options available.

Since its founding in 1926 and accreditation in 1939 by the National Association of Schools of Music, the Frost School of Music has become one of the largest schools of its kind in a private institution of higher learning in the United States. The Frost School pioneered innovative programs in music business and entertainment industries, music engineering, and studio music and jazz. Since its inception, strong programs in composition/theory, performance, and music education have been a part of the curriculum. Flexible, well-rounded music instruction, designed to give graduates a professional edge, remains a hallmark of the Frost School.

More than 58 full-time faculty members and 56 adjunct faculty members are active in the classroom and as dedicated music professionals. The diverse nature of the programs in the Frost School of Music has attracted a faculty with a broad outlook in its approach to music education, and its members impart and encourage diversity in the music classroom.

Students choosing the Frost School of Music are focused and serious about their studies and are eager for the academic and performance opportunities available to them at the University of Miami. The low ratio of students to faculty members fosters close academic bonding. Every music student enjoys one-on-one studio instruction.

Many of the more than 4,500 students who have graduated from the Frost School of Music have distinguished themselves professionally. Alumni provide a veritable "Who's Who" of both performance and related musical careers. Frost School of Music graduates perform with major orchestras, operas, and jazz ensembles. Their compositions range from orchestral and operatic music to film and video scores. Some graduates are among the top solo performing artists in the country; others excel as arrangers, recording engineers, editors, therapists, teachers, publishers, distributors, and retailers.

The Frost School of Music is situated on the University's Coral Gables campus, minutes from the city of Miami, where students enjoy a delightful climate that lends itself to a wide range of activities. All the cultural advantages of a metropolitan center are available to Frost School of Music students. In addition to being the home of the New World Symphony and the Florida Grand Opera, the Miami area is regularly included in concert tours of major symphonies, concert artists, jazz performers, and opera companies. Music students are able to participate in master classes given frequently by visiting artists performing in the greater Miami area.

Facilities The music complex includes a 600-seat concert hall and 150-seat recital hall, five rehearsal halls, two state-of-the-art recording studios, two computer/MIDI keyboard labs, two multimedia classrooms, instructional studios, practice rooms, and classrooms.

The Marta and Austin Weeks Music Library and Technology Center, the newest and largest branch of the University of Miami Libraries, showcases a wide range of resources. Among the nationally known collections housed in the 22,500-square-foot facility are sound recordings, musical theater archives, musical scores, musical manuscripts, research collections, and a wealth of e-resources. This state-of-the-art research facility was built at a cost of $9.9 million.

The 5,200-square-foot Music Technology Center houses a Music Engineering Lab, two Keyboard/Computer Labs, a Multimedia Instruction and Learning Lab (MILL), an Electronic Music Lab, and a Media-Writing and Production Lab. All of the labs contain computers with flat-panel displays, sophisticated software packages for program-specific work, 5.1 Surround Sound™ monitoring, audio/video playback systems, and video projection capabilities.

Faculty and Alumni There are more than 114 faculty members. Faculty members perform with the Florida Grand Opera, Miami City Ballet Orchestra, the Naples Philharmonic, and various jazz ensembles. Academic faculty members are widely published and recognized in their various fields. Alumni include Grammy winners Bruce Hornsby and Jon Secada; opera stars Marvis Martin and Sandra Lopez; television star Dawnn Lewis; Keith Buterbaugh, Raoul in *Phantom of the Opera;* Gary Fry, arranger and producer of more than 1,800 commercials; Sam Pilafian, founder of the Empire Brass Quintet and Travelin' Light; and Matt Pierson, Senior Vice President/General Manager Jazz for Warner Brothers Records.

Performance The Frost School of Music serves as a major cultural resource for the Greater Miami area, presenting more than 300 musical events annually. Complementing on-campus recitals and concerts by students and faculty members are programs by guest artists, composers, conductors, and lecturers from virtually every corner of the world. Festival Miami, a monthlong international music festival held each fall, typically features performances by an array of faculty and guest artists, student ensembles, composers, and conductors, including many premiere performances of new compositions. Several of the Frost School's more than fifty ensembles have performed in tours around the United States and the world.

University of Michigan
Ann Arbor, Michigan

State-supported, coed. Suburban campus. Total enrollment: 39,993. Music program established 1984.
Degrees Bachelor of Fine Arts in the area of musical theatre. Majors and concentrations: musical theater.
Enrollment 80 total; all undergraduate.
Music Student Profile 50% females, 50% males, 20% minorities.
Music Faculty 9 total undergraduate. Graduate students do not teach undergraduate courses. Undergraduate student–faculty ratio: 9:1.
Expenses for 2005–2006 Application fee: $40. State resident tuition: $9213 full-time. Nonresident tuition: $27,602 full-time. Mandatory fees: $187 full-time. Full-time tuition and fees vary according to course load, degree level, location, program, and student level. College room and board: $7374. Room and board charges vary according to board plan and housing facility.
Financial Aid Program-specific awards available.
Application Procedures Students admitted directly into the professional program freshman year. Deadline for freshmen and transfers: December 1. Required: essay, high school transcript, college transcript(s) for transfer students, minimum 3.0 high school GPA, 2 letters of recommendation, audition, SAT I or ACT test scores (minimum combined SAT I score of 1100, minimum composite ACT score of 24), typed resumé (bring to audition), recent photograph (bring to audition), brief personal statement (bring to audition). Auditions held 10 times on campus and off campus in Chicago, IL; New York, NY.
Web Site http://www.music.umich.edu
Undergraduate Contact Ms. Laura Strozeski, Assistant Dean for Enrollment Management and Student Services, Office of Admissions and Student Services, University of Michigan, 2290 Moore Building, 1100 Baits Drive, Ann Arbor, Michigan 48109-2085; 734-764-0593, fax: 734-763-5097, e-mail address: music.admissions@umich.edu

University of Michigan
Ann Arbor, Michigan

State-supported, coed. Suburban campus. Total enrollment: 39,993. Music program established 1880.

Degrees Bachelor of Fine Arts in the areas of performing arts technology, jazz and improvisation, jazz studies, jazz and contemplative studies, design, production; Bachelor of Music in the areas of composition, music and technology, music education, music history, music theory, performance; Bachelor of Musical Arts in the areas of composition, jazz studies, music history, music theory, performance; Bachelor of Science in the area of sound engineering. Majors and concentrations: composition, jazz, music education, music history, music technology, music theory, performing arts technology, piano/organ, stringed instruments, theater design and production, voice, wind and percussion instruments. Graduate degrees offered: Master of Arts in the areas of composition, media arts, musicology, music theory; Master of Music in the areas of arts administration, church music, composition, conducting, improvisation, piano pedagogy and performance, collaborative piano, chamber music, early keyboard instruments, music education, performance: strings, voice, winds and percussion. Doctor of Musical Arts in the areas of collaborative piano, composition, conducting, organ performance, harpsichord performance, piano pedagogy and performance, piano performance, string instruments, voice, wind instruments; Doctor of Philosophy in the areas of music education, music theory, composition, musicology and music theory. Program accredited by NASM.

Enrollment 1,106 total; 812 undergraduate, 294 graduate.

Music Student Profile 52% females, 48% males, 17% minorities, 7% international.

Music Faculty 140 total (full-time), 35 total (part-time). 45% of full-time faculty have terminal degrees. Graduate students teach a few undergraduate courses. Undergraduate student–faculty ratio: 8:1.

Student Life Student groups/activities include Music Educators National Conference, Pi Kappa Lambda, Sigma Alpha Iota/Phi Mu Alpha.

Expenses for 2005–2006 Application fee: $40. State resident tuition: $9213 full-time. Nonresident tuition: $27,602 full-time. Mandatory fees: $187 full-time. Full-time tuition and fees vary according to course load, degree level, location, program, and student level. College room and board: $7374. Room and board charges vary according to board plan and housing facility.

Financial Aid Program-specific awards: 163 merit awards for program students ($7067).

Application Procedures Students admitted directly into the professional program freshman year. Deadline for freshmen and transfers: December 1. Required: essay, high school transcript, college transcript(s) for transfer students, minimum 3.0 high school GPA, 2 letters of recommendation, audition, SAT I or ACT test scores (minimum combined SAT I score of 1100, minimum composite ACT score of 24), portfolio for composition and performing arts technology students, interview for music education and technology applicants. Auditions held 15 times on campus and off campus in New York, NY; Los Angeles, CA; Houston, TX; Chicago, IL; recorded music is permissible as a substitute for live auditions in some programs when distance is prohibitive and videotaped performances are permissible as a substitute for live auditions when distance is prohibitive. Portfolio reviews held continuously on campus.

Web Site http://www.music.umich.edu

Contact Ms. Laura Strozeski, Assistant Dean for Enrollment Management and Student Services, School of Music, University of Michigan, 1100 Baits Drive, Ann Arbor, Michigan 48109-2085; 734-764-0593, fax: 734-763-5097, e-mail address: music.admissions@umich.edu

More About the University

The University of Michigan School of Music, founded in 1880, is one of the oldest and largest schools of music in the United States. A Michigan education means much more than having access to one of the finest faculties in the country and a wide range of degree programs. It is the opportunity to experience a wealth of cultural opportunities that is almost unparalleled in the United States. The School of Music, as a component of a major university, offers its students a strong combination of breadth and depth of both an artistic and intellectual nature. Students in the School of Music benefit from the personal contact possible in a small unit of 1,000 students while at the same time taking advantage of the many opportunities and resources available at a major research university.

An extensive array of degree programs enables each student to choose the curriculum that best meets individual interests and career goals. The Bachelor of Music degree offers intensive professional training in music, while the Bachelor of Fine Arts program provides professional training in dance, jazz, theater, music technology, or musical theater. The Bachelor of Musical Arts and Bachelor of Theatre Arts degrees are designed for students who want a greater emphasis on the liberal arts. The Bachelor of Science in Sound Engineering allows students to explore state-of-the-art performing arts technology while pursuing a rigorous engineering curriculum. It is also possible for undergraduate students to pursue liberal arts academic minors and dual-degree programs with other colleges within the University, such as the College of Engineering or the College of Literature, Science, and the Arts. Although many members of the Michigan faculty are highly active professionally, they all participate in the life of the School and are in every sense a resident faculty. Notable figures in today's musical world come to the School to present lecture-demonstrations, teach master classes, or meet informally with students to expand their contact with major performing artists. The School enjoys extraordinary facilities and the University and Ann Arbor both provide a rich extracurricular environment with an abundance of performance opportunities. Graduates of the School of Music have distinguished themselves in all areas of performance, composition, conducting, directing, choreography, scholarship, teaching, and arts administration.

Program Facilities Performance venues: Hill Auditorium (3,700 seats), Power Center for the Performing Arts (1,500 seats), Rackham Auditorium (1,100 seats), Recital Hall, Lydia Mendelssohn Theatre, Trueblood Theatre, McIntosh Theatre, Blanche Anderson Moore Hall, Pease Studio Theatre (dance), and the new Walgreen Drama Center and Arthur Miller Theatre. Practice/study rooms: 135 practice rooms with pianos; ten organ practice rooms; special facilities for harp, harpsichord, carillon, and percussion; Rehearsal Hall for ensembles; listening room with ninety stations. The School has two professional-quality Electronic Music Studios, a Microcomputer and Synthesizer Laboratory, and one of the foremost music libraries in the country.

Faculty, Guest Artists, and Alumni Faculty members are performers currently active on the international stage; highly experienced musicians who are current and former members of major orchestras, opera houses, and dance and theater companies; prize-winning composers; and scholars and theorists who are renowned leaders in their disciplines. Guest artists to visit the school recently include the Royal Shakespeare Company, Marilyn Horne, Audra McDonald, Edgar Meyer, Murray Perahia, Leonard Slatkin, James Starker, Andre Watts, and Ely Ameling. Well-known alumni include Jessye Norman, Roberta Alexander, George Crumb, Ashley Putnam, Marian Mercer, Bob McGrath, Andrew Lippa, and Michael Maguire.

Student Performance Opportunities Students and faculty members present more than 300 concerts, recitals, and staged performances each year. Student ensembles include the University Symphony and University Philharmonia Orchestras; Symphony, Concert, and Marching Bands; University Choir, Chamber Choir, and Orpheus Singers; Opera and Musical Theatre Productions; Digital Music Ensemble; Jazz Ensembles; Men's and Women's Glee Clubs; Percussion Ensemble; Creative Arts Orchestra; Javanese Gamelan; Early Music Ensemble; Contemporary Directions Ensemble; and Composers' Forum. Concerts are frequently presented out of town and occasionally on national and international tours.

University of Minnesota, Duluth
Duluth, Minnesota

State-supported, coed. Suburban campus. Total enrollment: 10,496. Music program established 1942.

Degrees Bachelor of Arts in the area of music; Bachelor of Music in the areas of jazz studies, performance, music education, theory-composition. Majors and concentrations: jazz studies, music education, music theory and composition, performance. Graduate degrees offered: Master of Music in the area of performance; Master of Music Education. Cross-registration with University of Wisconsin-Superior, College of St. Scholastica. Program accredited by NASM.

Enrollment 518 total; 156 undergraduate, 12 graduate, 350 nonprofessional degree.

Music Student Profile 53% females, 47% males, 5% minorities.

Music Faculty 18 total (full-time), 15 total (part-time). 100% of full-time faculty have terminal degrees. Graduate students do not teach undergraduate courses. Undergraduate student–faculty ratio: 7:1.

Student Life Student groups/activities include Music Educators National Conference, American Choral Directors Association, International Association for Jazz Education.

Expenses for 2005–2006 Application fee: $35. State resident tuition: $7170 full-time. Nonresident tuition: $18,270 full-time. Mandatory fees: $1758 full-time. Full-time tuition and fees vary according to course load, degree level, program, and reciprocity agreements. College room and board: $5546. Special program-related fees: $115–$230 per semester for lesson fees (music majors).

Financial Aid Program-specific awards: 1 Bernstein Jazz Scholarship for jazz players ($500), 1–3 Comella Scholarships for music education majors ($600), 1–3 Faricy Scholarships for trumpet players ($400), 1–3 Gauger Scholarships for keyboardists ($300), 3 Gendein Scholarships for state residents ($400), 2 Gershgol Scholarships for program majors ($800), 1–2 Oreck Scholarships for program majors ($500), 8 Gregg Johnson Scholarships for program majors ($400), 1 opera scholarship for voice performance majors ($300).

Application Procedures Students admitted directly into the professional program freshman year. Deadline for freshmen and transfers: continuous. Required: college transcript(s) for transfer students, interview, audition, SAT I or ACT test scores. Auditions held 3 times and by request on campus; recorded music is permissible as a substitute for live auditions when distance is prohibitive and videotaped performances are permissible as a substitute for live auditions when distance is prohibitive.

Web Site http://www.d.umn.edu/music/

Undergraduate Contact Dr. Mark Whitlock, Chair, Scholarship Committee, Department of Music, University of Minnesota, Duluth, 231 H, 1201 Ordean Court, Duluth, Minnesota 55812; 218-726-6124, fax: 218-726-8210, e-mail address: mwhitloc@d.umn.edu

Graduate Contact Dr. Judith Kritzmire, Head, Department of Music, University of Minnesota, Duluth, 231 H, 1201 Ordean Court, Duluth, Minnesota 55812; 218-726-8260, fax: 218-726-8210, e-mail address: jkritzmi@d.umn.edu

University of Minnesota, Twin Cities Campus
Minneapolis, Minnesota

State-supported, coed. Urban campus. Total enrollment: 51,175. Music program established 1902.

University of Mississippi
University, Mississippi

State-supported, coed. Small town campus. Total enrollment: 14,901. Music program established 1926.

Degrees Bachelor of Music in the areas of performance, music theory, instrumental music education, vocal music education, keyboard music education. Majors and concentrations: music education, music theory, piano/organ, stringed instruments, voice, wind and percussion instruments. Graduate degrees offered: Master of Music in the areas of performance, instrumental music education, vocal music education, choral conducting, music theory, keyboard music education. Doctor of Arts in the areas of music theory, music literature, performance pedagogy, music education. Program accredited by NASM.

Enrollment 233 total; 141 undergraduate, 62 graduate, 30 nonprofessional degree.

Music Student Profile 43% females, 57% males, 7% minorities, 3% international.

Music Faculty 24 total (full-time), 9 total (part-time). 75% of full-time faculty have terminal degrees. Graduate students do not teach undergraduate courses. Undergraduate student–faculty ratio: 8:1.

Student Life Student groups/activities include Music Educators National Conference, American Choral Directors Association.

Expenses for 2005–2006 Application fee: $25, $40 for nonresidents. State resident tuition: $4320 full-time. Nonresident tuition: $9744 full-time. College room and board: $5762. College room only: $2972. Room and board charges vary according to board plan and housing facility. Special program-related fees: $35 per semester hour for applied lesson fee.

Financial Aid Program-specific awards: 150 band scholarships for wind and percussion players ($1500), 25 orchestra scholarships for stringed instrument players ($500–$1500), 75 chorus scholarships for vocalists ($500–$1500), 15 piano scholarships for pianists ($1000–$2000), 4 special scholarships for music majors ($1000–$2000).

Application Procedures Students apply for admission into the professional program by sophomore year. Deadline for freshmen and transfers: April 1. Required: high school transcript, college transcript(s) for transfer students, minimum 2.0 high school GPA, interview, audition, SAT I or ACT test scores (minimum composite ACT score of 20). Recommended: 2 letters of recommendation. Auditions held by appointment on campus; recorded music is permissible as a substitute for live auditions with special permission and videotaped performances are permissible as a substitute for live auditions with special permission.

Web Site http://www.olemiss.edu/depts/music/

Undergraduate Contact Dr. Carol Dale, Undergraduate Coordinator, Music Department, University of Mississippi, 131 Scruggs Hall, University, Mississippi 38677; 662-915-7268, fax: 662-915-1230.

Graduate Contact Dr. Alan Spurgeon, Professor, Music Department, University of Mississippi, 162 Scruggs Hall, University, Mississippi 38677; 662-915-7268, fax: 662-915-1230.

University of Missouri–Columbia
Columbia, Missouri

State-supported, coed. Small town campus. Total enrollment: 27,985. Music program established 1912.

Degrees Bachelor of Music in the areas of performance, theory, history, composition; Bachelor of Science in the area of music education. Majors and concentrations: composition, music education, music history, music theory, piano, stringed instruments, voice, wind and percussion instruments. Graduate degrees offered: Master of Arts in the area of music history; Master of Education; Master of Music in the areas of band conducting, choral conducting, orchestra conducting, piano, strings, winds, percussion, voice, music theory, composition, accompanying, piano pedagogy. Doctor of Philosophy in the area of music education. Program accredited by NASM.

Enrollment 215 total; 155 undergraduate, 45 graduate, 15 nonprofessional degree.

Music Student Profile 53% females, 47% males, 10% minorities, 8% international.

Music Faculty 32 total (full-time), 5 total (part-time). 45% of full-time faculty have terminal degrees. Graduate students teach a few undergraduate courses. Undergraduate student–faculty ratio: 5:1.

Expenses for 2005–2006 Application fee: $35. State resident tuition: $6495 full-time. Nonresident tuition: $16,272 full-time. Mandatory fees: $1250 full-time. Full-time tuition and fees vary according to course load, program, and reciprocity agreements. College room and board: $6245. Room and board charges vary

according to board plan and housing facility. Special program-related fees: $152 per semester for applied music fee.
Financial Aid Program-specific awards: 80 music scholarships for band, orchestra, chorus participants ($800).
Application Procedures Students admitted directly into the professional program freshman year. Deadline for freshmen and transfers: April 1. Notification date for freshmen and transfers: continuous. Required: high school transcript, college transcript(s) for transfer students, minimum 2.0 high school GPA, audition, ACT test score only. Recommended: 2 letters of recommendation. Auditions held 4 times on campus; recorded music is permissible as a substitute for live auditions when distance is prohibitive and videotaped performances are permissible as a substitute for live auditions when distance is prohibitive.
Web Site http://www.missouri.edu/%7Emusicwww/
Contact Mr. Dan L. Willett, Director of Graduate and Undergraduate Studies in Music, School of Music, University of Missouri–Columbia, 138 Fine Arts, Columbia, Missouri 65211; 573-882-0933, fax: 573-884-7444, e-mail address: willettd@missouri.edu

University of Missouri–Kansas City
Kansas City, Missouri

State-supported, coed. Urban campus. Total enrollment: 14,310. Music program established 1907.
Degrees Bachelor of Arts in the area of music therapy; Bachelor of Music in the areas of composition, instrumental music, voice, piano pedagogy, music, applied music; Bachelor of Music Education in the areas of music education, music therapy. Majors and concentrations: composition, guitar, music education, music theory, music therapy, piano pedagogy, piano/organ, stringed instruments, studio music and jazz, voice, wind and percussion instruments. Graduate degrees offered: Master of Arts in the area of music therapy; Master of Music in the areas of composition, applied music, voice, conducting; Master of Music Education. Doctor of Musical Arts in the areas of performance, composition, conducting. Program accredited by NASM, AMTA.
Enrollment 625 total; 375 undergraduate, 225 graduate, 25 nonprofessional degree.
Music Student Profile 57% females, 43% males, 10% minorities, 12% international.
Music Faculty 48 total (full-time), 25 total (part-time). 80% of full-time faculty have terminal degrees. Graduate students teach a few undergraduate courses. Undergraduate student–faculty ratio: 12:1.
Student Life Student groups/activities include Collegiate Music Educators National Conference, Music Therapy Association, American Choral Directors Association.
Expenses for 2006–2007 Application fee: $35. State resident tuition: $6819 full-time. Nonresident tuition: $17,085 full-time. Special program-related fees: $175 per semester for applied lesson fee.
Financial Aid Program-specific awards: music awards for program majors ($500–$12,000).
Application Procedures Students admitted directly into the professional program freshman year. Deadline for freshmen and transfers: March 3. Required: high school transcript, college transcript(s) for transfer students, minimum 2.0 high school GPA, 3 letters of recommendation, audition, SAT I or ACT test scores, ACT score for state residents, SAT I or ACT score for out-of-state residents, portfolio for composition applicants. Recommended: minimum 3.0 high school GPA. Auditions held 5 times on campus; recorded music is permissible as a substitute for live auditions for provisional acceptance and videotaped performances are permissible as a substitute for live auditions for provisional acceptance. Portfolio reviews held continuously on campus.
Web Site http://www.umkc.edu/conservatory
Contact Dr. James Elswick, Associate Director of Admissions, UMKC Conservatory of Music, University of Missouri–Kansas City, 5227 Holmes Road, Kansas City, Missouri 64110; 816-235-2900, fax: 816-235-5264, e-mail address: cadmissions@umkc.edu

University of Missouri–St. Louis
St. Louis, Missouri

State-supported, coed. Suburban campus. Total enrollment: 15,561. Music program established 1965.

University of Mobile
Mobile, Alabama

Independent Southern Baptist, coed. Suburban campus. Total enrollment: 1,758. Music program established 1996.
Degrees Bachelor of Music; Bachelor of Science in Music Education. Majors and concentrations: church music, music education. Program accredited by NASM.
Enrollment 57 total; 39 undergraduate, 18 nonprofessional degree.
Music Student Profile 46% females, 54% males, 11% minorities.
Music Faculty 10 undergraduate (full-time), 13 undergraduate (part-time). 40% of full-time faculty have terminal degrees. Graduate students do not teach undergraduate courses. Undergraduate student–faculty ratio: 10:1.
Student Life Student groups/activities include Music Educators National Conference, Voices of Mobile, Christmas Spectacular, chamber singers, wind ensemble, Ram Corps, piano ensemble, opera workshop, university singers.
Expenses for 2005–2006 Application fee: $30. Comprehensive fee: $16,950 includes full-time tuition ($10,230), mandatory fees ($330), and college room and board ($6390). College room only: $2680. Full-time tuition and fees vary according to course load. Room and board charges vary according to housing facility.
Financial Aid Program-specific awards: 1 Cummings Performance Fund Award, 1 Tim Hudmon Music Scholarship, 1 Melvin Memorial Fund Award, 1 Murphry Memorial Fund Award, 1 Megginson Sinclair Scholarship for organ majors ($1000), 50 departmental scholarships for music students ($1500), 1 Bergdolt Scholarship for full-time music majors.
Application Procedures Students admitted directly into the professional program freshman year. Deadline for freshmen and transfers: continuous. Required: high school transcript, college transcript(s) for transfer students, minimum 2.0 high school GPA, interview, audition, SAT I or ACT test scores (minimum combined SAT I score of 890, minimum composite ACT score of 19). Auditions held weekly on campus. Portfolio reviews held weekly on campus.
Web Site http://www.umobile.edu
Undergraduate Contact Mrs. Joy Lockwood, Assistant to the Director, Center for Performing Arts, University of Mobile, PO Box 13220, Mobile, Alabama 36663-0220; 251-442-2320, fax: 251-442-2526, e-mail address: joyl@mail.umobile.edu

The University of Montana–Missoula
Missoula, Montana

State-supported, coed. Total enrollment: 13,602.
Degrees Bachelor of Music in the areas of performance, composition, music technology; Bachelor of Music Education. Majors and concentrations: composition, instrumental music, music education, music technology, piano/organ, voice. Graduate degrees offered: Master of Music in the areas of performance, theory, technology/composition, music education, musical theater. Program accredited by NASM.
Enrollment 235 total; 220 undergraduate, 15 graduate.
Music Student Profile 50% females, 50% males, 4% minorities, 2% international.
Music Faculty 22 total (full-time), 4 total (part-time). 100% of full-time faculty have terminal degrees. Graduate students teach a few undergraduate courses. Undergraduate student–faculty ratio: 11:1.
Student Life Student groups/activities include Collegiate Music Educators National Conference.
Expenses for 2006–2007 Application fee: $30. State resident tuition: $3739 full-time. Nonresident tuition: $13,246 full-time. Mandatory fees: $1291 full-time. College room and board:

The University of Montana–Missoula (continued)

$5860. College room only: $2660. Special program-related fees: $85 per semester for music fees.

Financial Aid Program-specific awards: 80 awards for music majors ($500–$4500).

Application Procedures Students admitted directly into the professional program freshman year. Deadline for freshmen and transfers: July 1. Required: high school transcript, college transcript(s) for transfer students, audition, SAT I or ACT test scores, minimum 2.5 high school GPA. Recommended: interview. Auditions held by appointment on campus; recorded music is permissible as a substitute for live auditions when distance is prohibitive.

Web Site http://www.sfa.umt.edu/music

Contact Dr. Stephen Kalm, Chair, Department of Music, The University of Montana–Missoula, Missoula, Montana 59812-7992; 406-243-6880, fax: 406-243-2441.

University of Montevallo
Montevallo, Alabama

State-supported, coed. Small town campus. Total enrollment: 2,999. Music program established 1924.

Degrees Bachelor of Music in the areas of performance, composition, instrumental music education, choral music education. Majors and concentrations: classical music, composition, guitar, music, music education, piano pedagogy, piano/organ, voice, wind and percussion instruments. Graduate degrees offered: Master of Music in the areas of performance, music education. Cross-registration with Samford University, Birmingham-Southern University, University of Alabama at Birmingham, Miles College. Program accredited by NASM.

Enrollment 99 total; 76 undergraduate, 4 graduate, 19 nonprofessional degree.

Music Student Profile 63% females, 37% males, 14% minorities.

Music Faculty 12 total (full-time), 13 total (part-time). 92% of full-time faculty have terminal degrees. Graduate students do not teach undergraduate courses. Undergraduate student–faculty ratio: 6:1.

Expenses for 2005–2006 Application fee: 25. State resident tuition: $5460 full-time. Nonresident tuition: $10,920 full-time. Mandatory fees: $204 full-time. Full-time tuition and fees vary according to course load. College room and board: $3966. Room and board charges vary according to board plan and housing facility. Special program-related fees: $65 per credit hour for applied music fees.

Financial Aid Program-specific awards: 40 College of Fine Arts Awards for talented students ($1000), 26 music awards for talented students ($850).

Application Procedures Students admitted directly into the professional program freshman year. Deadline for freshmen and transfers: July 29. Required: high school transcript, college transcript(s) for transfer students, minimum 2.0 high school GPA, interview, audition, SAT I or ACT test scores (minimum composite ACT score of 18), music theory entrance test, piano placement examination. Recommended: 2 letters of recommendation. Auditions held 3 times in February and March and by appointment on campus; videotaped performances are permissible as a substitute for live auditions with prior approval.

Web Site http://www.montevallo.edu/music

Undergraduate Contact Dr. Cynthia Jones, Interim Chair, Department of Music, University of Montevallo, Station 6670, Montevallo, Alabama 35115; 205-665-6670, fax: 205-665-6676, e-mail address: jonescp@montevallo.edu

Graduate Contact Dr. Lori Ardovino, Coordinator of Graduate Studies, Department of Music, University of Montevallo, Station 6670, Montevallo, Alabama 35115; 205-665-6670, fax: 205-665-6676, e-mail address: ardovinl@montevallo.edu

University of Nebraska at Kearney
Kearney, Nebraska

State-supported, coed. Small town campus. Total enrollment: 6,445. Music program established 1923.

University of Nebraska at Omaha
Omaha, Nebraska

State-supported, coed. Urban campus. Total enrollment: 14,093. Music program established 1918.

Degrees Bachelor of Music in the areas of music education, music performance, music composition, music technology. Majors and concentrations: classical music, composition, music, music education, music performance, music technology, piano/organ, stringed instruments, voice, wind and percussion instruments. Graduate degrees offered: Master of Music in the areas of music education, music performance, conducting. Cross-registration with University of Nebraska System, Metro Community College Omaha. Program accredited by NASM.

Enrollment 205 total; 170 undergraduate, 35 graduate.

Music Student Profile 51% females, 49% males, 19% minorities, 10% international.

Music Faculty 16 undergraduate (full-time), 24 undergraduate (part-time), 16 graduate (full-time), 24 graduate (part-time). 95% of full-time faculty have terminal degrees. Graduate students do not teach undergraduate courses. Undergraduate student–faculty ratio: 9:1.

Student Life Student groups/activities include Music Educators National Conference Student Chapter, Nebraska State Bandmasters Association Student Chapter, band professional sorority and fraternity, Music Teachers National Association, Student Chapter.

Expenses for 2005–2006 Application fee: $45. State resident tuition: $4133 full-time. Nonresident tuition: $12,180 full-time. Mandatory fees: $692 full-time. Full-time tuition and fees vary according to course load and student level. College room and board: $6140. College room only: $3690. Room and board charges vary according to board plan. Special program-related fees: $25 per semester for facilities fee (instrument use, piano tuning), $100 per credit hour for applied fee.

Financial Aid Program-specific awards: 150 Athletic Bands Scholarships for band participants ($250–$600), 30–40 music scholarships for program majors ($500–$7000), 125–150 ensemble scholarships for ensemble participants ($200–$800), 6–10 Jazz Program Scholarships for majors ($500–$1000).

Application Procedures Students admitted directly into the professional program freshman year. Deadline for freshmen and transfers: August 1. Required: high school transcript, college transcript(s) for transfer students, audition, ACT test score only (minimum composite ACT score of 20). Recommended: 2 letters of recommendation. Auditions held 5 times on campus; recorded music is permissible as a substitute for live auditions when distance is prohibitive and videotaped performances are permissible as a substitute for live auditions when distance is prohibitive.

Web Site http://music.unomaha.edu

Undergraduate Contact Dr. James R. Saker, Chair, Department of Music, University of Nebraska at Omaha, Strauss Performing Arts Center, Omaha, Nebraska 68182-0245; 402-554-2251, fax: 402-554-2252, e-mail address: jsaker@mail.unomaha.edu

Graduate Contact Dr. Roger Foltz, Chair, Graduate Program Committee, Department of Music, University of Nebraska at Omaha, Strauss Performing Arts Center, Omaha, Nebraska 68182-0245; 402-554-2474, fax: 402-554-2252, e-mail address: rfoltz@unomaha.edu

University of Nebraska–Lincoln
Lincoln, Nebraska

State-supported, coed. Urban campus. Total enrollment: 21,675. Music program established 1898.

Degrees Bachelor of Music; Bachelor of Music Education. Majors and concentrations: music education, performance. Graduate degrees offered: Master of Music in the areas of music theory, composition, performance, conducting, music education. Doctor of Musical Arts in the areas of performance, composition, conducting. Program accredited by NASM.

Enrollment 363 total; 210 undergraduate, 103 graduate, 50 nonprofessional degree.

Music Student Profile 49% females, 51% males, 8% minorities, 2% international.

Music Faculty 42 total (full-time), 8 total (part-time). 100% of full-time faculty have terminal degrees. Graduate students teach a few undergraduate courses. Undergraduate student–faculty ratio: 5:1.

Student Life Student groups/activities include Sigma Alpha Iota, Music Educators National Conference, Mu Phi Epsilon. Special housing available for music students.

Expenses for 2005–2006 Application fee: $45. State resident tuition: $4530 full-time. Nonresident tuition: $13,440 full-time. Mandatory fees: $1010 full-time. Full-time tuition and fees vary according to course load. College room and board: $6008. College room only: $3239. Room and board charges vary according to board plan and housing facility. Special program-related fees: $15 per instrument for instrument rental, $25 per semester for applied fees.

Financial Aid Program-specific awards: 150 endowed awards for music majors ($100–$6000).

Application Procedures Students admitted directly into the professional program freshman year. Deadline for freshmen and transfers: July 1. Required: high school transcript, college transcript(s) for transfer students, audition, ACT test score only. Auditions held 3 times on campus; recorded music is permissible as a substitute for live auditions for out-of-state applicants and videotaped performances are permissible as a substitute for live auditions for out-of-state applicants.

Web Site http://www.unl.edu/music/

Contact Ms. Susan Tribby, Admissions Coordinator, School of Music, University of Nebraska–Lincoln, 108 Westbrook Music Building, Lincoln, Nebraska 68588-0100; 402-472-6845, fax: 402-472-8962, e-mail address: stribby@unl.edu

University of Nevada, Las Vegas

Las Vegas, Nevada

State-supported, coed. Urban campus. Total enrollment: 27,344. Music program established 1968.

University of Nevada, Reno

Reno, Nevada

State-supported, coed. Urban campus. Total enrollment: 16,336.

University of New Hampshire

Durham, New Hampshire

State-supported, coed. Small town campus. Total enrollment: 14,564. Music program established 1923.

Degrees Bachelor of Music in the areas of music education, performance, music theory/composition. Majors and concentrations: guitar, music education, music theory, piano, stringed instruments, voice, wind and percussion instruments. Graduate degrees offered: Master of Arts in the areas of music education, music studies. Program accredited by NASM.

Enrollment 216 total; 148 undergraduate, 14 graduate, 54 nonprofessional degree.

Music Student Profile 48% females, 52% males, 4% minorities.

Music Faculty 20 total (full-time), 20 total (part-time). 100% of full-time faculty have terminal degrees. Graduate students do not teach undergraduate courses. Undergraduate student–faculty ratio: 7:1.

Student Life Student groups/activities include Music Educators National Conference, Music Teachers National Association.

Expenses for 2006–2007 Application fee: $45. State resident tuition: $8240 full-time. Nonresident tuition: $20,690 full-time. Mandatory fees: $2161 full-time. College room and board: $7584. College room only: $4606. Special program-related fees: $50 per semester for concert fee, $150 per credit hour for applied music fee.

Financial Aid Program-specific awards: 89 University Music Scholarships for program students ($3000).

Application Procedures Students admitted directly into the professional program freshman year. Deadline for freshmen: February 1; transfers: March 1. Notification date for freshmen and transfers: May 1. Required: essay, high school transcript, college transcript(s) for transfer students, letter of recommendation, audition, SAT I or ACT test scores. Recommended: portfolio for composition applicants. Auditions held 6 times and by appointment on campus; recorded music is permissible as a substitute for live auditions when distance is prohibitive and videotaped performances are permissible as a substitute for live auditions when distance is prohibitive. Portfolio reviews held continuously on campus.

Web Site http://www.unh.edu/music/index.html

Undergraduate Contact Isabel Gray, Program Coordinator, Department of Music, University of New Hampshire, PCAC 30 College Road, Durham, New Hampshire 03824; 603-862-2418, fax: 603-862-3155, e-mail address: igray@cisunix.unh.edu

Graduate Contact Dr. Robert Stibler, Graduate Coordinator, Department of Music, University of New Hampshire, PCAC 30 College Road, Durham, New Hampshire 03824; 603-862-2404, fax: 603-862-3155, e-mail address: rstibler@cisunix.unh.edu

University of New Mexico

Albuquerque, New Mexico

State-supported, coed. Urban campus. Total enrollment: 26,172.

Degrees Bachelor of Music in the areas of performance, music theory/composition; Bachelor of Music Education. Majors and concentrations: jazz studies, music, music education, music theory and composition, opera, piano/organ, string pedagogy, stringed instruments, voice, wind and percussion instruments. Graduate degrees offered: Master of Music in the areas of performance, conducting, music education, piano accompaniment, music theory/composition, music history and literature. Program accredited by NASM.

Enrollment 290 total; 200 undergraduate, 70 graduate, 20 nonprofessional degree.

Music Student Profile 60% females, 40% males, 10% minorities, 5% international.

Music Faculty 28 total (full-time), 25 total (part-time). 40% of full-time faculty have terminal degrees. Graduate students teach a few undergraduate courses. Undergraduate student–faculty ratio: 10:1.

Student Life Student groups/activities include Music Educators National Conference, Collegiate Chorale, Jazz Festival.

Expenses for 2005–2006 Application fee: $20. State resident tuition: $4108 full-time. Nonresident tuition: $13,438 full-time. College room and board: $6518. College room only: $3818. Room and board charges vary according to board plan and housing facility. Special program-related fees: $10–$50 per course for lab and visiting artists and clinicians fees, $25–$150 per 1-4 credit hours for applied fees.

Financial Aid Program-specific awards: 15 Friends of Music Awards for juniors and seniors ($1800), 7 music achievement awards for program students ($2000), 7 wind symphony awards for program students ($2000), 6 Jones Scholarships for program students ($1500), 1 orchestra scholarship for program students ($1400), 2 Anderson Awards for program students ($1250), 13 University Bands Awards for program students ($1200), 30 individual scholarships for program students ($500–$2000), 1 Presser Award for undergraduate senior ($4200).

Application Procedures Students admitted directly into the professional program freshman year. Deadline for freshmen and transfers: July 24. Notification date for freshmen and transfers: August 24. Required: essay, high school transcript, college transcript(s) for transfer students, minimum 2.0 high school GPA, 3 letters of recommendation, audition, SAT I or ACT test scores. Recommended: interview, video, portfolio for composition majors. Auditions held 3 times and by request on campus; recorded music is permissible as a substitute for live auditions when distance is prohibitive and videotaped performances are permissible as a substitute for live auditions when distance is prohibitive. Portfolio reviews held by request on campus.

Web Site http://www.unm.edu

Undergraduate Contact Mr. Keith Lemmons, Undergraduate Advisor, Department of Music, University of New Mexico, Fine Arts Center, Room 1105, Albuquerque, New Mexico 87131-1411; 505-277-4905, fax: 505-277-0708, e-mail address: klemmons@unm.edu

University of New Mexico (continued)

Graduate Contact Mr. Karl Hinterbichler, Graduate Coordinator, Department of Music, University of New Mexico, Fine Arts Center, Albuquerque, New Mexico 87131-1411; 505-277-4331, fax: 505-277-0708, e-mail address: khtbn@unm.edu

University of North Alabama

Florence, Alabama

State-supported, coed. Urban campus. Total enrollment: 6,415.

The University of North Carolina at Chapel Hill

Chapel Hill, North Carolina

State-supported, coed. Suburban campus. Total enrollment: 26,878.

The University of North Carolina at Charlotte

Charlotte, North Carolina

State-supported, coed. Suburban campus. Total enrollment: 20,772. Music program established 1990.
Degrees Bachelor of Music in the areas of performance, music education. Majors and concentrations: music education, piano/organ performance, stringed instrument performance, voice, wind and percussion instruments performance. Cross-registration with Charlotte Area Educational Consortium.
Enrollment 90 total; all undergraduate.
Music Student Profile 50% females, 50% males, 5% international.
Music Faculty 14 total (full-time), 15 total (part-time). 80% of full-time faculty have terminal degrees. Graduate students do not teach undergraduate courses. Undergraduate student–faculty ratio: 7:1.
Student Life Student groups/activities include Music Educators National Conference, Phi Mu Alpha Sinfonia, Sigma Alpha Iota.
Expenses for 2005–2006 Application fee: $50. State resident tuition: $2129 full-time. Nonresident tuition: $12,541 full-time. Mandatory fees: $1420 full-time. Full-time tuition and fees vary according to course load. College room and board: $5550. College room only: $2840. Room and board charges vary according to board plan and housing facility. Special program-related fees: $45 per credit hour for applied music courses.
Financial Aid Program-specific awards: 12 Music Department Scholarships for music majors ($1500), 12 Stone Scholarships for incoming freshmen ($2000), 1 Fleet-Green Jazz Scholarship for freshmen ($500), 1 Conboy Piano Scholarship for freshman music majors ($1000), 5 Robinson Scholarships for music majors ($2000), 5 Beck Scholarships for music majors ($2000).
Application Procedures Students admitted directly into the professional program freshman year. Deadline for freshmen and transfers: continuous. Required: high school transcript, college transcript(s) for transfer students, minimum 2.0 high school GPA, 3 letters of recommendation, audition, SAT I or ACT test scores, medical history, completed audition application form. Auditions held 6 times on campus; recorded music is permissible as a substitute for live auditions when distance is prohibitive and videotaped performances are permissible as a substitute for live auditions when distance is prohibitive.
Web Site http://www.uncc.edu/music
Undergraduate Contact Denise Shropshire, Administrative Secretary, Department of Music, The University of North Carolina at Charlotte, 9201 University City Boulevard, Rowe Arts 124, Charlotte, North Carolina 28223-0001; 704-687-2472, fax: 704-687-6806, e-mail address: dlshrops@email.uncc.edu

The University of North Carolina at Greensboro

Greensboro, North Carolina

State-supported, coed. Urban campus. Total enrollment: 16,060. Music program established 1892.

Degrees Bachelor of Music in the areas of performance, music education, composition. Majors and concentrations: classical music, composition, jazz, music education, piano/organ, stringed instruments, voice, wind and percussion instruments. Graduate degrees offered: Master of Music in the areas of performance, music education, composition, music theory, vocal pedagogy. Doctor of Musical Arts in the area of performance; Doctor of Philosophy in the area of music education. Cross-registration with Bennett College, Elon College, Greensboro College, Guilford College, High Point University, Guilford Technical Community College, North Carolina Agricultural and Technical State University. Program accredited by NASM.
Enrollment 576 total; 289 undergraduate, 197 graduate, 90 nonprofessional degree.
Music Student Profile 55% females, 45% males, 20% minorities, 1% international.
Music Faculty 52 total (full-time), 16 total (part-time). 81% of full-time faculty have terminal degrees. Graduate students teach a few undergraduate courses. Undergraduate student–faculty ratio: 8:1.
Student Life Student groups/activities include Collegiate Music Educators National Conference, Phi Mu Alpha Sinfonia, Mu Phi Epsilon.
Expenses for 2006–2007 Application fee: $45. State resident tuition: $2308 full-time. Nonresident tuition: $13,576 full-time. Mandatory fees: $1505 full-time. College room and board: $5706. College room only: $3232.
Financial Aid Program-specific awards: 150–175 music scholarships for program students ($1000–$6000).
Application Procedures Students admitted directly into the professional program freshman year. Deadline for freshmen and transfers: August 1. Notification date for freshmen and transfers: continuous. Required: high school transcript, college transcript(s) for transfer students, audition, SAT I or ACT test scores, minimum of 16 high school units. Auditions held 5 times and by appointment; recorded music is permissible as a substitute for live auditions and videotaped performances are permissible as a substitute for live auditions.
Web Site http://www.uncg.edu/mus/
Undergraduate Contact Ms. Dianna Carter, Director of Undergraduate Advising, School of Music, The University of North Carolina at Greensboro, PO Box 26170, Greensboro, North Carolina 27402-6170; 336-334-3638, fax: 336-334-5497, e-mail address: dtcarter@uncg.edu
Graduate Contact Dr. David Nelson, Associate Dean and Director of Academic Programs, School of Music, The University of North Carolina at Greensboro, PO Box 26170, Greensboro, North Carolina 27402-6170; 336-334-5789, fax: 336-334-5497.

The University of North Carolina at Pembroke

Pembroke, North Carolina

State-supported, coed. Rural campus. Total enrollment: 5,732. Music program established 1928.
Degrees Bachelor of Music in the areas of music education, music business, musical theater. Majors and concentrations: instrumental music education, keyboard, music business, music education, music theater, vocal music education. Graduate degrees offered: Master of Arts in the area of music education; Master of Arts in Teaching in the area of music. Program accredited by NASM.
Enrollment 90 total; 22 undergraduate, 12 graduate, 56 nonprofessional degree.
Music Student Profile 53% females, 47% males, 33% minorities.
Music Faculty 10 total (full-time), 20 total (part-time). 80% of full-time faculty have terminal degrees. Graduate students teach a few undergraduate courses. Undergraduate student–faculty ratio: 8:1.
Student Life Student groups/activities include Phi Mu Alpha, Music Educators National Conference, Sigma Alpha Iota.
Expenses for 2005–2006 Application fee: $40. State resident tuition: $1689 full-time. Nonresident tuition: $11,129 full-time. Mandatory fees: $1291 full-time. Full-time tuition and fees vary according to course load and location. College room and board:

$4890. College room only: $2700. Room and board charges vary according to board plan and housing facility.

Financial Aid Program-specific awards: 5–15 non-majors stipends for freshmen ensemble performers ($300), 10–20 majors scholarships for program majors ($600).

Application Procedures Students apply for admission into the professional program by sophomore year. Deadline for freshmen and transfers: continuous. Required: high school transcript, college transcript(s) for transfer students, minimum 2.0 high school GPA, 2 letters of recommendation, interview, audition, SAT I or ACT test scores. Auditions held 5 times and by arrangement on campus and off campus in various locations; recorded music is permissible as a substitute for live auditions when distance is prohibitive and videotaped performances are permissible as a substitute for live auditions when distance is prohibitive.

Web Site http://www.uncp.edu/music

Contact Dr. Janita Byars, Chair, Department of Music, The University of North Carolina at Pembroke, PO Box 1510, Pembroke, North Carolina 28372-1510; 910-522-5704, fax: 910-521-6390, e-mail address: janita.byars@uncp.edu

The University of North Carolina Wilmington
Wilmington, North Carolina

State-supported, coed. Urban campus. Total enrollment: 11,653. Music program established 1986.

Degrees Bachelor of Music in the areas of performance, music education. Majors and concentrations: instrumental music, jazz studies, keyboard, music education, vocal music. Cross-registration with Cape Fear Community College. Program accredited by NASM.

Enrollment 58 total; all undergraduate.

Music Student Profile 47% females, 53% males, 6% minorities.

Music Faculty 13 undergraduate (full-time), 13 undergraduate (part-time). 100% of full-time faculty have terminal degrees. Graduate students do not teach undergraduate courses. Undergraduate student–faculty ratio: 2:1.

Student Life Student groups/activities include pep band.

Expenses for 2005–2006 Application fee: $45. State resident tuition: $1928 full-time. Nonresident tuition: $11,863 full-time. Mandatory fees: $1767 full-time. Full-time tuition and fees vary according to course load. College room and board: $6412. Room and board charges vary according to board plan and housing facility.

Financial Aid Program-specific awards: 3 departmental awards for music majors ($500), Levent Chen Scholarship for viola majors ($500), 1 Johanna Rehder Scholarship for voice majors, jazz awards for jazz ensemble participants ($250–$500), 1 William F. Adcock Jr. Scholarship for rising senior music majors ($1500), 1 Cape Fear Jazz Appreciation Society Scholarship for jazz majors ($750), Outstanding Music Education Major Award.

Application Procedures Students apply for admission into the professional program by sophomore year. Deadline for freshmen: April 15; transfers: continuous. Required: essay, high school transcript, college transcript(s) for transfer students, minimum 3.0 high school GPA, 2 letters of recommendation, audition, SAT I or ACT test scores (minimum combined SAT I score of 1200). Recommended: interview, video. Auditions held 10 times on campus; recorded music is permissible as a substitute for live auditions when distance is prohibitive and videotaped performances are permissible as a substitute for live auditions when distance is prohibitive.

Web Site http://www.uncw.edu/music

Undergraduate Contact Dr. Frank Bongiorno, Chair, Department of Music, The University of North Carolina Wilmington, 601 South College Road, Wilmington, North Carolina 20403-3297; 910-962-3390, fax: 910-962-7106, e-mail address: uncwmus@uncwil.edu

University of North Dakota
Grand Forks, North Dakota

State-supported, coed. Small town campus. Total enrollment: 12,954. Music program established 1883.

Degrees Bachelor of Music in the areas of performance, music education, music therapy. Majors and concentrations: music education, music therapy, piano/organ, strings, voice, wind and percussion instruments. Graduate degrees offered: Master of Music in the areas of music education, composition, vocal performance, vocal pedagogy, keyboard performance, keyboard pedagogy, instrumental conducting, choral conducting. Doctor of Philosophy in the areas of teaching and learning, music education. Program accredited by NASM.

Enrollment 99 total; 40 undergraduate, 13 graduate, 46 nonprofessional degree.

Music Student Profile 50% females, 50% males, 2% minorities, 4% international.

Music Faculty 17 total (full-time), 9 total (part-time). 50% of full-time faculty have terminal degrees. Graduate students teach a few undergraduate courses. Undergraduate student–faculty ratio: 4:1.

Student Life Student groups/activities include Music Educators National Conference, American Choral Directors Association, Sigma Alpha Delta/Pi Kappa Lambda.

Expenses for 2005–2006 Application fee: $35. State resident tuition: $4390 full-time. Nonresident tuition: $11,722 full-time. Mandatory fees: $937 full-time. Full-time tuition and fees vary according to degree level, program, and reciprocity agreements. College room and board: $4787. College room only: $1979. Room and board charges vary according to board plan and housing facility. Special program-related fees: $50 per semester for applied music fees.

Financial Aid Program-specific awards: 77 music scholarships for program majors/minors/participants ($300–$1500).

Application Procedures Students admitted directly into the professional program freshman year. Deadline for freshmen and transfers: continuous. Required: high school transcript, college transcript(s) for transfer students, audition, ACT test score only. Auditions held 3 times on campus and off campus in various cities in North Dakota and Minnesota; recorded music is permissible as a substitute for live auditions when distance is prohibitive and videotaped performances are permissible as a substitute for live auditions when distance is prohibitive.

Web Site http://www.und.edu/dept/undmusic

Undergraduate Contact Dr. Gary Towne, Chair, Music Department, University of North Dakota, Box 7125, Grand Forks, North Dakota 58202; 701-777-2644, fax: 701-777-3320, e-mail address: gary_towne@und.nodak.edu

Graduate Contact Dr. James Popejoy, Director of Graduate Studies, Music Department, University of North Dakota, Box 7125, Grand Forks, North Dakota 58202; 701-777-2815, fax: 701-777-3320, e-mail address: james_popejoy@und.nodak.edu

University of Northern Colorado
Greeley, Colorado

State-supported, coed. Total enrollment: 13,156. Music program established 1895.

Degrees Bachelor of Music in the areas of instrumental performance, piano, music theory and composition, voice performance; Bachelor of Music Education in the areas of instrumental music education, piano music education, general music education. Majors and concentrations: classical music, composition, jazz studies, music, music education, piano/organ, stringed instruments, voice, wind and percussion instruments. Graduate degrees offered: Master of Music in the areas of choral conducting, instrumental performance, music history and literature, music theory and composition, wind/orchestral conducting, music education. Doctor of Arts in the areas of music, choral conducting, music history and literature, music theory, composition, wind/orchestral conducting, music education, jazz pedagogy, opera theater, performance/pedagogy. Program accredited by NASM.

Music Faculty 34 total (full-time), 5 total (part-time). 58% of full-time faculty have terminal degrees. Graduate students teach about a quarter of undergraduate courses. Undergraduate student–faculty ratio: 10:1.

Student Life Student groups/activities include Kappa Kappa Psi, National Association of Jazz Educators, Collegiate Music Educators National Conference.

University of Northern Colorado (continued)

Expenses for 2005–2006 Application fee: $40. State resident tuition: $3192 full-time. Nonresident tuition: $11,736 full-time. Mandatory fees: $645 full-time. College room and board: $6412. College room only: $3150. Room and board charges vary according to board plan and housing facility. Special program-related fees: $5 per credit hour for university technology fee, $20 per course for private lesson fee for non-majors, $20 per semester for music major fee.

Financial Aid Program-specific awards: Music Talent Awards for program majors, academic scholarships for program majors, Laure Kay Rushing Vocal Music Scholarship.

Application Procedures Students apply for admission into the professional program by sophomore year. Deadline for freshmen and transfers: continuous. Required: high school transcript, college transcript(s) for transfer students, interview, audition, SAT I or ACT test scores, minimum 2.8 high school GPA. Auditions held 5 times on campus; recorded music is permissible as a substitute for live auditions when distance is prohibitive and videotaped performances are permissible as a substitute for live auditions for conducting applicants when distance is prohibitive.

Web Site http://arts.unco.edu

Undergraduate Contact Dr. Rob Hallquist, Director, School of Music, University of Northern Colorado, Frasier 108, Greeley, Colorado 80639; 970-351-2679, fax: 970-351-2679.

Graduate Contact Dr. Robert C. Ehle, Graduate Coordinator, School of Music, University of Northern Colorado, Frasier 104, Greeley, Colorado 80639; 970-351-1922, fax: 970-351-2679, e-mail address: rehle@arts.unco.edu

University of Northern Iowa
Cedar Falls, Iowa

State-supported, coed. Small town campus. Total enrollment: 12,622. Music program established 1935.

University of North Florida
Jacksonville, Florida

State-supported, coed. Urban campus. Total enrollment: 15,234. Music program established 1972.

University of North Texas
Denton, Texas

State-supported, coed. Suburban campus. Total enrollment: 32,047.

University of Oklahoma
Norman, Oklahoma

State-supported, coed. Suburban campus. Total enrollment: 26,968. Music program established 1898.

University of Oregon
Eugene, Oregon

State-supported, coed. Urban campus. Total enrollment: 20,347. Music program established 1886.

Degrees Bachelor of Music in the areas of music composition, music education, music performance, jazz studies. Majors and concentrations: composition, jazz, music, music education, piano/organ, stringed instruments, voice, wind and percussion instruments. Graduate degrees offered: Master of Arts in the areas of music history, music theory; Master of Music in the areas of conducting, piano pedagogy, music composition, music performance, music education, jazz studies, intermedia music technology, string pedagogy. Doctor of Musical Arts in the area of music performance; Doctor of Philosophy in the areas of music composition, music education, music history, music theory. Program accredited by NASM.

Enrollment 486 total; 345 undergraduate, 141 graduate.

Music Student Profile 46% females, 54% males, 12% minorities, 11% international.

Music Faculty 46 total (full-time), 16 total (part-time). 95% of full-time faculty have terminal degrees. Graduate students teach a few undergraduate courses. Undergraduate student–faculty ratio: 8:1.

Student Life Student groups/activities include Oregon Bach Festival, Oregon Festival of American Music, Suzuki Strings Program. Special housing available for music students.

Expenses for 2005–2006 Application fee: $50. State resident tuition: $4164 full-time. Nonresident tuition: $15,996 full-time. Mandatory fees: $1449 full-time. Full-time tuition and fees vary according to class time, course level, course load, degree level, program, and reciprocity agreements. College room and board: $7496. Room and board charges vary according to board plan and housing facility. Special program-related fees: $10–$50 per term for instrument rental, $20 per term for organ, harpsichord, or percussion fee, $20 per term for ensemble fee, $20 per term for music education class instrument fee, $35 per credit for private lessons, $50–$200 per term for accompanying fee, $75 per term for synthesizer lab fee, $100 per recital for recital and recording fee, $100 per term for music major fee, $125 per term for group lessons.

Financial Aid Program-specific awards: 1 Presser Scholarship for outstanding juniors and seniors ($4200), 2 Corbett Scholarships for Oregon students ($1750), 2 Stauffer Scholarships for male graduates of Oregon high schools ($1000), 2 Mu Phi Epsilon Patron Scholarships for program students ($1000), 4 Polastri Scholarships for voice majors ($2000), 30 Ruth Lorraine Close Scholarships for music majors ($1800), 1 Dorthy Pederson Fahlman Piano Scholarship for piano majors ($1000), 9 Virginia Whitfield Scholarships for music education majors ($700), 1 Bailey Vocal Scholarship for voice majors ($2000), 4 School of Music general scholarships for music ($1000), 1 Atwood Music Scholarship for music majors ($1000), 1 Robert and Leona Anderson DeArmond Scholarship for voice majors ($1000), 1 Robert and Margaret Guitteau Scholarship for music majors ($1500), 2 Maude and H.B. Densmore Memorial Scholarships for voice majors ($1500), 2 Mu Phi Epsilon Patrons Scholarships for music majors ($1500), 15 School of Music Dean's Scholarships ($3000).

Application Procedures Students admitted directly into the professional program freshman year. Deadline for freshmen: January 15; transfers: May 15. Notification date for freshmen and transfers: continuous. Required: high school transcript, college transcript(s) for transfer students, minimum 3.0 high school GPA, audition, SAT I or ACT test scores. Recommended: essay, 3 letters of recommendation. Auditions held once on campus; recorded music is permissible as a substitute for live auditions when distance is prohibitive and videotaped performances are permissible as a substitute for live auditions when distance is prohibitive.

Web Site http://music.uoregon.edu/

Undergraduate Contact Ms. Val Lawson, Undergraduate Secretary, School of Music, University of Oregon, 1225 University of Oregon, Eugene, Oregon 97403-1225; 541-346-1164, fax: 541-346-0723, e-mail address: audition@uoregon.edu

Graduate Contact Ms. Anne Merydith, Graduate Secretary, School of Music, University of Oregon, 1225 University of Oregon, Eugene, Oregon 97403-1225; 541-346-5664, fax: 541-346-0723, e-mail address: gradmus@uoregon.edu

University of Portland
Portland, Oregon

Independent Roman Catholic, coed. Urban campus. Total enrollment: 3,413. Music program established 1901.

Degrees Bachelor of Music Education. Majors and concentrations: music education. Cross-registration with Concordia University and other area universities. Program accredited by NASM.

Enrollment 27 total; 5 undergraduate, 22 nonprofessional degree.

Music Student Profile 58% females, 42% males, 6% minorities, 3% international.

Music Faculty 5 total (full-time), 22 total (part-time). 80% of full-time faculty have terminal degrees. Graduate students do not teach undergraduate courses. Undergraduate student–faculty ratio: 1:1.

Student Life Student groups/activities include Collegiate Music Educators National Conference, Music Club.

Expenses for 2005–2006 Application fee: $50. Comprehensive fee: $32,300 includes full-time tuition ($24,580), mandatory fees ($320), and college room and board ($7400). College room only: $3700. Full-time tuition and fees vary according to program. Room and board charges vary according to board plan and housing facility. Special program-related fees: $25 per year for practice room rental, $30 per semester for electronic music lab fees, $120 per semester for private lesson fee.

Financial Aid Program-specific awards: 1–3 Dean's Scholarships for performers ($2200), 1–3 Vance Scholarships for music education majors ($2200), 10–20 Talent Grants (Seegert Scholarships) for program majors and minors ($1700).

Application Procedures Students admitted directly into the professional program freshman year. Deadline for freshmen: February 1; transfers: June 1. Notification date for freshmen and transfers: continuous. Required: essay, high school transcript, college transcript(s) for transfer students, minimum 2.0 high school GPA, letter of recommendation, audition, SAT I or ACT test scores. Recommended: interview. Auditions held 4 times on campus; recorded music is permissible as a substitute for live auditions when distance is prohibitive or scheduling is difficult and videotaped performances are permissible as a substitute for live auditions when distance is prohibitive or scheduling is difficult.

Web Site http://www.up.edu/up_sub.asp?ctnt=353&mnu=40&chl=50&lvl=2

Undergraduate Contact Office of Admissions, University of Portland, 5000 North Willamette Boulevard, Portland, Oregon 97203; 503-943-7147, e-mail address: admissio@up.edu

University of Prince Edward Island
Charlottetown, Prince Edward Island, Canada

Province-supported, coed. Small town campus. Total enrollment: 3,912. Music program established 1969.

Degrees Bachelor of Music in the area of general music; Bachelor of Music Education. Majors and concentrations: classical music, guitar, music, music education, music history, music theory and composition, performance, piano/organ, voice, wind and percussion instruments. Program accredited by CUMS.

Enrollment 45 total; 44 undergraduate, 1 nonprofessional degree.

Music Student Profile 73% females, 27% males, 1% minorities, 1% international.

Music Faculty 6 undergraduate (full-time), 10 undergraduate (part-time). 85% of full-time faculty have terminal degrees. Graduate students do not teach undergraduate courses. Undergraduate student–faculty ratio: 6:1.

Student Life Student groups/activities include University of Prince Edward Island Music Society.

Expenses for 2005–2006 Application fee: $50 Canadian dollars. Tuition, fee, and room and board charges are reported in Canadian dollars. Province resident tuition: $4620 full-time. Mandatory fees: $1060 full-time. Full-time tuition and fees vary according to course load and degree level. College room and board: $7490. College room only: $4300. Room and board charges vary according to board plan and housing facility. International student tuition: $8430 full-time. Special program-related fees: $60 per year for instrument rental, locker, telephone, practice room rental, $125 for cost of sessional defraging applied music faculty.

Financial Aid Program-specific awards: 5–10 Mary O. Kinch Returning Scholarships for 2nd, 3rd, 4th, 5th year students ($500–$1500), 1 Tersteeg Music Scholarship for 3rd-5th year students ($350), 1 Bevan-MacRae Music Award for 3rd-5th year students ($250), 8 music alumni scholarships for freshmen ($200–$750), 3 Music Society Scholarships for sophomores, juniors, and seniors ($125), 2 Claude and Dr. Bernice Bell Awards for program students ($1000), 1 Elsie Cuthbertson Memorial Music Scholarship for program students ($250), 1 Frances Dindial Memorial Music Scholarship for freshmen ($600), 1 Eleanor Wheler Scholarship for entering students ($1000), 1 Carl Mathis Music Award for voice or horn majors ($250), 1 Reesor Music Award for organ majors ($300), 6–12 Mary O'Kinch Scholarships for entering students ($1600–$20,000), 2 Mary O. Kinch Music Education Scholarships for 5th year students ($800), 1 Florence

Simmons Award for organ majors ($500), 1 Christine Burdett Award for 2nd, 3rd, 4th, 5th year students ($750), 1 James A. Ready Scholarship for program studies ($1000), 1 Theresa (Zaat) Maloney Award for program students ($500).

Application Procedures Students admitted directly into the professional program freshman year. Deadline for freshmen and transfers: August 15. Notification date for freshmen and transfers: August 25. Required: high school transcript, college transcript(s) for transfer students, letter of recommendation, interview, audition, music theory test, ear test. Recommended: essay, minimum 3.0 high school GPA, resume. Auditions held 4 times on campus; recorded music is permissible as a substitute for live auditions when distance is prohibitive (with later audition on campus) and videotaped performances are permissible as a substitute for live auditions when distance is prohibitive (with later audition on campus).

Web Site http://www.upei.ca/music

Undergraduate Contact Ms. Gloria J. Jay, Audition Coordinator, Department of Music, University of Prince Edward Island, 550 University Avenue, Charlottetown, Prince Edward Island C1A 4P3, Canada; 902-566-0507, fax: 902-566-0777, e-mail address: gjay@upei.ca

University of Puget Sound
Tacoma, Washington

Independent, coed. Suburban campus. Total enrollment: 2,887. Music program established 1892.

Degrees Bachelor of Music in the areas of performance, music education, with elective studies in business. Majors and concentrations: classical music, harp, harpsichord, music, music business, music education, piano/organ, stringed instruments, voice, wind and percussion instruments. Program accredited by NASM.

Enrollment 625 total; 125 undergraduate, 500 nonprofessional degree.

Music Student Profile 54% females, 46% males, 12% minorities, 3% international.

Music Faculty 12 undergraduate (full-time), 24 undergraduate (part-time). 90% of full-time faculty have terminal degrees. Graduate students do not teach undergraduate courses. Undergraduate student–faculty ratio: 11:1.

Student Life Student groups/activities include Music Educators National Conference, Phi Mu Alpha Sinfonia, Sigma Alpha Iota. Special housing available for music students.

Expenses for 2005–2006 Application fee: $40. Comprehensive fee: $35,600 includes full-time tuition ($28,270), mandatory fees ($190), and college room and board ($7140). College room only: $3900. Full-time tuition and fees vary according to course load. Room and board charges vary according to board plan and housing facility. Special program-related fees: $195 per semester for applied music lessons.

Financial Aid Program-specific awards: 100 music scholarships for continuing students ($5000), 35 music scholarships for incoming students ($5000).

Application Procedures Students admitted directly into the professional program freshman year. Deadline for freshmen and transfers: February 1. Notification date for freshmen: June 1. Required: essay, high school transcript, college transcript(s) for transfer students, 3 letters of recommendation, audition, SAT I or ACT test scores. Recommended: minimum 3.0 high school GPA, interview. Auditions held once and by appointment on campus and off campus in Denver, CO; Minneapolis, MN; San Francisco, CA; recorded music is permissible as a substitute for live auditions when distance is prohibitive and videotaped performances are permissible as a substitute for live auditions when distance is prohibitive.

Web Site http://www.ups.edu/music/home.htm

Undergraduate Contact Mr. Chad Minnick, Music Admission Coordinator, School of Music, University of Puget Sound, 1500 North Warner Street, Tacoma, Washington 98416-1076; 253-879-3730, fax: 253-879-2906, e-mail address: cminnick@ups.edu

University of Redlands
Redlands, California

Independent, coed. Small town campus. Total enrollment: 2,454. Music program established 1907.

Degrees Bachelor of Music in the areas of performance, music education, composition. Majors and concentrations: composition, music education, piano/organ, stringed instruments, voice, wind and percussion instruments. Graduate degrees offered: Master of Music in the areas of performance, music education, composition. Program accredited by NASM.

Enrollment 154 total; 75 undergraduate, 18 graduate, 61 nonprofessional degree.

Music Student Profile 60% females, 40% males, 12% minorities, 3% international.

Music Faculty 11 total (full-time), 27 total (part-time). 86% of full-time faculty have terminal degrees. Graduate students do not teach undergraduate courses.

Student Life Student groups/activities include Sigma Alpha Iota, Phi Mu Alpha Sinfonia, Music Educators National Conference Student Chapter.

Expenses for 2005–2006 Application fee: $45. Comprehensive fee: $36,164 includes full-time tuition ($26,864), mandatory fees ($300), and college room and board ($9000). College room only: $5020. Room and board charges vary according to board plan and housing facility.

Financial Aid Program-specific awards: music merit awards for incoming freshmen, area specific awards for program students.

Application Procedures Students admitted directly into the professional program freshman year. Deadline for freshmen and transfers: May 1. Notification date for freshmen: September 1; transfers: August 1. Required: essay, high school transcript, college transcript(s) for transfer students, minimum 3.0 high school GPA, 2 letters of recommendation, audition, SAT I or ACT test scores (minimum combined SAT I score of 1150, minimum composite ACT score of 25), portfolio for composition majors. Recommended: interview. Auditions held 3 times on campus; recorded music is permissible as a substitute for live auditions when distance is prohibitive (beyond a 200-mile radius) and videotaped performances are permissible as a substitute for live auditions when distance is prohibitive (beyond a 200-mile radius). Portfolio reviews held continuously on campus.

Web Site http://www.redlands.edu/music

Contact Ms. Kimberley Wolf, Admissions Coordinator, School of Music, University of Redlands, 1200 East Colton Avenue, Box 3080, Redlands, California 92373; 909-335-4014, fax: 909-748-6343, e-mail address: music@redlands.edu

University of Regina
Regina, Saskatchewan, Canada

Province-supported, coed. Urban campus. Total enrollment: 12,670. Music program established 1968.

University of Rhode Island
Kingston, Rhode Island

State-supported, coed. Small town campus. Total enrollment: 15,095. Music program established 1933.

Degrees Bachelor of Arts in the areas of music, music history and literature, jazz studies, music and communication studies, music and psychology, music and elementary education; Bachelor of Arts/Bachelor of Science in the areas of music and business administration, music and computer science; Bachelor of Music in the areas of music education, music composition, music performance. Majors and concentrations: composition, jazz studies, music, music and business administration, music and communication studies, music and computer science, music and elementary education, music and psychology, music education, music history and literature, music performance. Graduate degrees offered: Master of Music in the areas of music education, performance. Program accredited by NASM, NCATE.

Enrollment 165 total; 120 undergraduate, 25 graduate, 20 nonprofessional degree.

Music Student Profile 50% females, 50% males, 8% minorities, 5% international.

Music Faculty 16 total (full-time), 22 total (part-time). 90% of full-time faculty have terminal degrees. Graduate students do not teach undergraduate courses. Undergraduate student–faculty ratio: 8:1.

Student Life Student groups/activities include Music Educators National Conference Student Chapter, Kappa Kappa Psi/Tau Beta Sigma, American Choral Directors Association Student Chapter.

Expenses for 2005–2006 Application fee: $50. State resident tuition: $5258 full-time. Nonresident tuition: $17,900 full-time. Mandatory fees: $2026 full-time. Full-time tuition and fees vary according to reciprocity agreements. College room and board: $8114. College room only: $4620. Room and board charges vary according to board plan and housing facility. Special program-related fees: $190 per semester for applied music lesson fee.

Financial Aid Program-specific awards: 45 music scholarships for program majors ($250–$4000), 4 Honors String Quartet Scholarships for top string players ($4577–$11,603), 25 University Centennial Scholarships for academically and musically talented students ($1000–$16,000).

Application Procedures Students admitted directly into the professional program freshman year. Deadline for freshmen and transfers: continuous. Notification date for freshmen and transfers: continuous. Required: high school transcript, college transcript(s) for transfer students, audition, SAT I or ACT test scores, minimum 2.5 college GPA for transfer students. Recommended: minimum 3.0 high school GPA, 2 letters of recommendation, interview, video. Auditions held 6 times on campus; recorded music is permissible as a substitute for live auditions with approval from the department and videotaped performances are permissible as a substitute for live auditions with approval from the department.

Web Site http://www.uri.edu/artsci/mus

Undergraduate Contact Mr. John Dempsey, Professor, Department of Music, University of Rhode Island, Fine Arts Center, Kingston, Rhode Island 02881; 401-874-2782, fax: 401-874-2772, e-mail address: music@etal.uri.edu

Graduate Contact Dr. Ronald T. Lee, Coordinator, Graduate Studies in Music, Department of Music, University of Rhode Island, Fine Arts Center, Kingston, Rhode Island 02881; 401-874-2431, fax: 401-874-2772, e-mail address: music@etal.uri.edu

Eastman School of Music of the University of Rochester
University of Rochester
Rochester, New York

Independent, coed. Suburban campus. Total enrollment: 8,588. Music program established 1921.

University of South Alabama
Mobile, Alabama

State-supported, coed. Suburban campus. Total enrollment: 13,122. Music program established 1965.

Degrees Bachelor of Fine Arts in the area of music theater; Bachelor of Music in the area of performance. Majors and concentrations: interdisciplinary studies, music education, music industry, music theater, performance. Program accredited by NASM, NCATE.

Enrollment 90 total.

Music Faculty 12 total (full-time), 12 total (part-time). 100% of full-time faculty have terminal degrees. Graduate students do not teach undergraduate courses. Undergraduate student–faculty ratio: 7:1.

Student Life Student groups/activities include Music Educators National Conference, Sigma Alpha Iota, Phi Mu Alpha.

Expenses for 2005–2006 Application fee: $25. State resident tuition: $3810 full-time. Nonresident tuition: $7620 full-time. Mandatory fees: $692 full-time. College room and board: $4428. College room only: $2468. Room and board charges vary

according to board plan, housing facility, and location. Special program-related fees: $60–$180 per semester for private lessons.
Financial Aid Program-specific awards: 85 music scholarships for ensemble performers ($200–$1000), 1 Theodore Presser Award for senior music majors ($4200), 2 Chester Piano Scholarships for enrolled piano students ($300–$500), 3 Laidlaw Scholarships for enrolled music majors ($1500–$2000), 1 Mike Bartels Award for percussion majors ($2500–$3500).
Application Procedures Students admitted directly into the professional program freshman year. Deadline for freshmen and transfers: August 10. Required: high school transcript, college transcript(s) for transfer students, minimum 2.0 high school GPA, audition, SAT I or ACT test scores. Auditions held 4 times on campus; recorded music is permissible as a substitute for live auditions when distance is prohibitive.
Web Site http://www.southalabama.edu/music/
Undergraduate Contact Dr. Greg Gruner, Chairman, Department of Music, University of South Alabama, Laidlaw Performing Arts Center, Room 1075, Mobile, Alabama 36688; 251-460-6136 ext. 6804, fax: 251-460-7328, e-mail address: ggruner@jaguar1.usouthal.edu

University of South Carolina
Columbia, South Carolina

State-supported, coed. Total enrollment: 27,065. Music program established 1937.
Degrees Bachelor of Music in the areas of performance, music education, music theory/composition, jazz studies. Majors and concentrations: guitar, jazz, music education, music theory and composition, piano/organ, stringed instruments, voice, wind and percussion instruments. Graduate degrees offered: Master of Music in the areas of composition, performance, piano pedagogy, music history, music theory, conducting, jazz studies, opera theater; Master of Music Education. Doctor of Musical Arts in the areas of composition, performance, piano pedagogy, conducting; Doctor of Philosophy in the area of music education. Program accredited by NASM, NCATE.
Enrollment 460 total; 336 undergraduate, 119 graduate, 5 nonprofessional degree.
Music Student Profile 42% females, 58% males, 16% minorities, 10% international.
Music Faculty 44 total (full-time), 12 total (part-time). 90% of full-time faculty have terminal degrees. Graduate students teach a few undergraduate courses. Undergraduate student–faculty ratio: 10:1.
Student Life Student groups/activities include Preparatory Program (applied instruction for community), String Project, Children's Music Development Center. Special housing available for music students.
Expenses for 2005–2006 Application fee: $50. State resident tuition: $6914 full-time. Nonresident tuition: $18,556 full-time. Full-time tuition varies according to program. College room and board: $6080. Room and board charges vary according to board plan, housing facility, and location. Special program-related fees: $45–$290 for applied music fee, $50 for recital fee.
Financial Aid Program-specific awards: 200 music scholarships for program majors and minors ($500–$4100).
Application Procedures Students admitted directly into the professional program freshman year. Deadline for freshmen: May 1; transfers: July 1. Notification date for freshmen and transfers: continuous. Required: high school transcript, college transcript(s) for transfer students, minimum 2.0 high school GPA, audition, SAT I or ACT test scores (minimum combined SAT I score of 1000, minimum composite ACT score of 24). Recommended: minimum 3.0 high school GPA. Auditions held 5 times on campus; recorded music is permissible as a substitute for live auditions when distance is prohibitive for provisional acceptance and videotaped performances are permissible as a substitute for live auditions when distance is prohibitive for provisional acceptance.
Web Site http://www.music.sc.edu/index.html
Undergraduate Contact Ms. Jean Smith, Administrative Assistant, School of Music, University of South Carolina, Columbia, South Carolina 29208; 803-777-4335, fax: 803-777-6508, e-mail address: ugmusic@mozart.sc.edu

Graduate Contact Ms. Trina Brooks, Administrative Assistant, School of Music, University of South Carolina, Columbia, South Carolina 29208; 803-777-4106, fax: 803-777-6508, e-mail address: gradmusic@mozart.sc.edu

The University of South Dakota
Vermillion, South Dakota

State-supported, coed. Small town campus. Total enrollment: 8,641. Music program established 1882.
Degrees Bachelor of Music in the areas of performance, music education. Majors and concentrations: brass, music education, piano/organ, stringed instruments, voice, wind and percussion instruments. Graduate degrees offered: Master of Music in the areas of music education, performance, music history, history of musical instruments. Cross-registration with South Dakota State University System . Program accredited by NASM.
Enrollment 142 total; 121 undergraduate, 21 graduate.
Music Student Profile 65% females, 35% males, 8% minorities, 6% international.
Music Faculty 17 total (full-time), 4 total (part-time). 90% of full-time faculty have terminal degrees. Graduate students teach a few undergraduate courses. Undergraduate student–faculty ratio: 14:1.
Student Life Student groups/activities include Music Educators National Conference.
Expenses for 2005–2006 Application fee: $20. State resident tuition: $2291 full-time. Nonresident tuition: $7278 full-time. Mandatory fees: $2538 full-time. Full-time tuition and fees vary according to course load and reciprocity agreements. College room and board: $4240. College room only: $2253. Room and board charges vary according to board plan and housing facility.
Financial Aid Program-specific awards: 100 music scholarships for program majors ($200–$4000).
Application Procedures Students admitted directly into the professional program freshman year. Deadline for freshmen and transfers: continuous. Required: high school transcript, college transcript(s) for transfer students, audition, SAT I or ACT test scores, 4 years of high school English (grade of C or above), 3 years of high school advanced math, social sciences and lab science, 1/2 year of fine arts, minimum 2.6 high school GPA. Auditions held twice on campus; recorded music is permissible as a substitute for live auditions when distance is prohibitive and videotaped performances are permissible as a substitute for live auditions when distance is prohibitive.
Web Site http://www.usd.edu/cfa/Music
Contact Dr. Larry Schou, Chair, Music Department, The University of South Dakota, CFA 114a, 414 East Clark Street, Vermillion, South Dakota 57069; 605-677-5274, fax: 605-677-5988, e-mail address: lschou@usd.edu

USC Thornton School of Music
University of Southern California
Los Angeles, California

Independent, coed. Urban campus. Total enrollment: 32,836. Music program established 1884.
Degrees Bachelor of Music in the areas of performance, composition, jazz studies, music industry, vocal arts. Majors and concentrations: classical guitar, composition, jazz studies, music, music industry, piano/organ/harpsichord, stringed instruments, studio/jazz guitar, voice, wind and percussion instruments. Graduate degrees offered: Master of Arts in the areas of music history and literature, early music, teaching music; Master of Music in the areas of choral music, sacred music, composition, jazz studies, music education, conducting, performance, keyboard collaborative arts, vocal arts; Master of Music Education. Doctor of Musical Arts in the areas of choral music, sacred music, music education, early music performance, performance, keyboard collaborative arts, vocal arts, jazz studies; Doctor of Philosophy in the area of historical musicology. Program accredited by NASM.
Enrollment 1,071 total; 589 undergraduate, 444 graduate, 38 nonprofessional degree.

University of Southern California (continued)

Music Student Profile 49% females, 51% males, 37% minorities, 14% international.
Music Faculty 70 total (full-time), 90 total (part-time). 80% of full-time faculty have terminal degrees. Graduate students teach a few undergraduate courses. Undergraduate student–faculty ratio: 6:1.
Student Life Student groups/activities include Music Industry Connection, Thornton Outreach Programs, Music Educators National Conference and Music Teachers National Association.
Expenses for 2005–2006 Application fee: $65. Comprehensive fee: $41,618 includes full-time tuition ($31,458), mandatory fees ($550), and college room and board ($9610). College room only: $5260. Full-time tuition and fees vary according to program. Room and board charges vary according to board plan and housing facility. Special program-related fees: $325 per course unit for individual instruction fees.
Financial Aid Program-specific awards: music scholarships for music performance majors.
Application Procedures Students admitted directly into the professional program freshman year. Deadline for freshmen: January 10; transfers: February 1. Notification date for freshmen: April 1. Required: essay, high school transcript, college transcript(s) for transfer students, minimum 3.0 high school GPA, 3 letters of recommendation, SAT I or ACT test scores, resume/repertoire list, three original scores for composition applicants, audition for most majors. Recommended: interview. Auditions held 6 times and by appointment on campus and off campus in San Francisco, CA; Seattle, WA; Chicago, IL; Interlochen, MI; Houston, TX; New York, NY; recorded music is permissible as a substitute for live auditions if a campus visit is impossible (except vocalists) and videotaped performances are permissible as a substitute for live auditions if a campus visit is impossible (except pianists).
Web Site http://www.usc.edu/music
Contact Mr. Phillip Placenti, Director of Admission and Financial Aid, USC Thornton School of Music, University of Southern California, University Park Campus-UUC 218, Los Angeles, California 90089-2991; 213-740-8986, fax: 213-740-8995, e-mail address: uscmusic@usc.edu

University of Southern Maine
Portland, Maine

State-supported, coed. Suburban campus. Total enrollment: 10,944. Music program established 1957.

University of Southern Mississippi
Hattiesburg, Mississippi

State-supported, coed. Suburban campus. Total enrollment: 15,030. Music program established 1938.

University of South Florida
Tampa, Florida

State-supported, coed. Urban campus. Total enrollment: 42,660. Music program established 1960.
Degrees Bachelor of Music in the areas of performance, composition, piano pedagogy, jazz studies; Bachelor of Science in the area of music education. Majors and concentrations: composition, jazz studies, music, music education, piano pedagogy. Graduate degrees offered: Master of Arts in the area of music education; Master of Music in the areas of jazz, performance, composition, piano pedagogy, theory, conducting. Doctor of Philosophy in the area of music education. Program accredited by NASM.
Enrollment 393 total; 293 undergraduate, 100 graduate.
Music Student Profile 55% females, 45% males, 15% minorities, 8% international.
Music Faculty 31 total (full-time), 17 total (part-time). 75% of full-time faculty have terminal degrees. Graduate students teach a few undergraduate courses. Undergraduate student–faculty ratio: 20:1.

Student Life Student groups/activities include Collegiate Music Educators National Conference, professional music fraternities, Taste of the Arts.
Expenses for 2005–2006 Application fee: $30. State resident tuition: $3310 full-time. Nonresident tuition: $16,076 full-time. Mandatory fees: $74 full-time. Full-time tuition and fees vary according to course level, course load, and location. College room and board: $6900. College room only: $3563. Room and board charges vary according to board plan, housing facility, and location. Special program-related fees: $10–$50 per course for materials fees.
Financial Aid Program-specific awards: 75 music scholarships for music students ($400–$1600).
Application Procedures Students admitted directly into the professional program freshman year. Deadline for freshmen and transfers: continuous. Required: high school transcript, college transcript(s) for transfer students, audition, portfolio, SAT I or ACT test scores (minimum combined SAT I score of 1000, minimum composite ACT score of 21). Recommended: 4 letters of recommendation. Auditions held 4 times on campus; recorded music is permissible as a substitute for live auditions if a campus visit is impossible and videotaped performances are permissible as a substitute for live auditions if a campus visit is impossible. Portfolio reviews held on campus.
Web Site http://music.arts.usf.edu
Contact Dr. William Hayden, Associate Director and Advisor, School of Music, University of South Florida, 4202 East Fowler Avenue FAH110, Tampa, Florida 33620-7350; 813-974-1753, fax: 813-974-8721.

The University of Tampa
Tampa, Florida

Independent, coed. Urban campus. Total enrollment: 5,202.

The University of Tennessee
Knoxville, Tennessee

State-supported, coed. Urban campus. Total enrollment: 31,157. Music program established 1947.
Degrees Bachelor of Music in the areas of music theory/composition, studio music and jazz, piano, organ, piano pedagogy and literature, sacred music, strings, voice, woodwind, brass, percussion instruments, instrumental and vocal music education. Majors and concentrations: jazz, music, music education, music theory and composition, piano pedagogy, piano/organ, sacred music, stringed instruments, voice, wind and percussion instruments. Graduate degrees offered: Master of Music in the areas of accompanying, choral conducting, composition, instrumental conducting, jazz, music education, music theory, musicology, organ, piano, piano literature and pedagogy, strings, voice, winds and percussion instruments. Program accredited by NASM.
Enrollment 392 total; 326 undergraduate, 66 graduate.
Music Student Profile 40% females, 60% males, 8% minorities, 4% international.
Music Faculty 40 total (full-time), 11 total (part-time). 90% of full-time faculty have terminal degrees. Graduate students teach a few undergraduate courses. Undergraduate student–faculty ratio: 6:1.
Student Life Student groups/activities include Sigma Alpha Iota, Phi Mu Alpha, MENC.
Expenses for 2005–2006 Application fee: $30. State resident tuition: $5290 full-time. Nonresident tuition: $16,360 full-time. Mandatory fees: $336 full-time. Full-time tuition and fees vary according to location and program. College room and board: $5560. College room only: $2890. Room and board charges vary according to board plan and housing facility. Special program-related fees: $60–$120 per semester for private lessons.
Financial Aid Program-specific awards: 200 music scholarships for high school seniors ($2000).
Application Procedures Students apply for admission into the professional program by freshman year. Deadline for freshmen and transfers: continuous. Required: high school transcript, college transcript(s) for transfer students, minimum 2.0 high

school GPA, audition, SAT I or ACT test scores. Auditions held 3 times on campus; recorded music is permissible as a substitute for live auditions when distance is prohibitive and videotaped performances are permissible as a substitute for live auditions when distance is prohibitive.
Web Site http://www.music.utk.edu
Undergraduate Contact Ms. Carolyn Anderson, Associate Director for Undergraduate Studies, School of Music, The University of Tennessee, Music Building, 1741 Volunteer Boulevard, Knoxville, Tennessee 37996-2600; 865-974-3241, fax: 865-974-1941, e-mail address: music@utk.edu
Graduate Contact Ms. Angela Batey, Associate Director for Graduate Studies, School of Music, The University of Tennessee, 211 Music Building, 1741 Volunteer Boulevard, Knoxville, Tennessee 37996-2600; 865-974-3241, fax: 865-974-1941, e-mail address: music@utk.edu

The University of Tennessee at Chattanooga
Chattanooga, Tennessee

State-supported, coed. Urban campus. Total enrollment: 8,656. Music program established 1933.
Degrees Bachelor of Music in the areas of performance, sacred music, music theory/composition, music education. Majors and concentrations: music education, music theory and composition, piano/organ, sacred music, stringed instruments, voice, wind and percussion instruments. Graduate degrees offered: Master of Music in the areas of music education, performance. Program accredited by NASM.
Enrollment 100 total; 76 undergraduate, 11 graduate, 13 nonprofessional degree.
Music Student Profile 65% females, 35% males, 10% minorities, 4% international.
Music Faculty 15 total (full-time), 18 total (part-time). 100% of full-time faculty have terminal degrees. Graduate students do not teach undergraduate courses. Undergraduate student–faculty ratio: 5:1.
Student Life Student groups/activities include Music Educators National Conference Student Chapter, Sigma Alpha Iota, Phi Mu Alpha Sinfonia.
Expenses for 2005–2006 Application fee: 25. State resident tuition: $4500 full-time. Nonresident tuition: $14,024 full-time. Mandatory fees: $900 full-time. College room and board: $6238. College room only: $3790. Room and board charges vary according to housing facility. Special program-related fees: $60–$120 per semester for applied music fee.
Financial Aid Program-specific awards: 70 performance grants for ensemble participants ($400–$2000).
Application Procedures Students admitted directly into the professional program freshman year. Deadline for freshmen and transfers: continuous. Required: high school transcript, college transcript(s) for transfer students, letter of recommendation, SAT I or ACT test scores, audition for scholarship consideration. Recommended: essay. Auditions held 3 times on campus; recorded music is permissible as a substitute for live auditions when distance is prohibitive.
Web Site http://www.utc.edu/academic/music
Undergraduate Contact Dr. Lee Harris, Acting Head, Music Department, The University of Tennessee at Chattanooga, 615 McCallie Avenue, Chattanooga, Tennessee 37403; 423-425-4601, fax: 423-425-4603, e-mail address: lee-harris@utc.edu
Graduate Contact Dr. Monte Coulter, Coordinator, Graduate Programs in Music, Music Department, The University of Tennessee at Chattanooga, 615 McCallie Avenue, Chattanooga, Tennessee 37403; 423-425-4601, fax: 423-425-4603, e-mail address: monte-coulter@utc.edu

The University of Tennessee at Martin
Martin, Tennessee

State-supported, coed. Small town campus. Total enrollment: 6,484. Music program established 1970.

The University of Texas at Arlington
Arlington, Texas

State-supported, coed. Urban campus. Total enrollment: 25,432.

The University of Texas at Austin
Austin, Texas

State-supported, coed. Urban campus. Total enrollment: 49,696. Music program established 1938.

The University of Texas at El Paso
El Paso, Texas

State-supported, coed. Urban campus. Total enrollment: 19,268.

The University of Texas at San Antonio
San Antonio, Texas

State-supported, coed. Suburban campus. Total enrollment: 27,337. Music program established 1975.
Degrees Bachelor of Music in the areas of performance, composition, music marketing, music education. Majors and concentrations: classical guitar, classical music, composition, music education, music marketing, piano/organ, stringed instruments, voice, wind and percussion instruments. Graduate degrees offered: Master of Music in the areas of performance, music education, conducting, piano pedagogy. Program accredited by NASM.
Enrollment 300 total; 270 undergraduate, 30 graduate.
Music Student Profile 50% females, 50% males, 50% minorities, 5% international.
Music Faculty 22 total (full-time), 32 total (part-time). 95% of full-time faculty have terminal degrees. Graduate students do not teach undergraduate courses. Undergraduate student–faculty ratio: 11:1.
Student Life Student groups/activities include Music Educators National Conference Student Chapter, Sigma Alpha Iota, Phi Mu Alpha Sinfonia.
Expenses for 2005–2006 Application fee: $30. State resident tuition: $3,968 full-time. Nonresident tuition: $12,248 full-time. Mandatory fees: $1890 full-time. College room and board: $7190. College room only: $4770. Special program-related fees: $100 per course for private lesson fee.
Financial Aid Program-specific awards: 90 Department of Music Scholarships for program majors ($1000).
Application Procedures Students admitted directly into the professional program freshman year. Deadline for freshmen and transfers: July 1. Notification date for freshmen: August 1. Required: high school transcript, college transcript(s) for transfer students, audition, SAT I or ACT test scores. Auditions held twice on campus; recorded music is permissible as a substitute for live auditions when distance is prohibitive and videotaped performances are permissible as a substitute for live auditions when distance is prohibitive.
Web Site http://music.utsa.edu
Undergraduate Contact Dr. Diana Allan, Associate Professor, Department of Music, The University of Texas at San Antonio, 6900 North Loop 1604 West, San Antonio, Texas 78249-1130; 210-458-4354, fax: 210-458-4381.
Graduate Contact Dr. Kasandra Keeling, Assistant Professor, Department of Music, The University of Texas at San Antonio, 6900 North Loop 1604 West, San Antonio, Texas 78249-1130; 210-458-4354, fax: 210-458-4381.

The University of Texas at Tyler
Tyler, Texas

State-supported, coed. Urban campus. Total enrollment: 5,748. Music program established 1978.

The University of the Arts
Philadelphia, Pennsylvania

Independent, coed. Total enrollment: 2,277. Music program established 1870.

Degrees Bachelor of Music in the areas of voice, composition, instrumental performance. Majors and concentrations: composition, instrumental performance, jazz studies, music education. Graduate degrees offered: Master of Arts in Teaching in the area of music education; Master of Music in the area of jazz studies. Program accredited by NASM.

Enrollment 217 total; 194 undergraduate, 23 graduate.

Music Student Profile 56% females, 44% males, 17% minorities, 3% international.

Music Faculty 4 undergraduate (full-time), 35 undergraduate (part-time), 6 graduate (full-time), 18 graduate (part-time). 60% of full-time faculty have terminal degrees. Graduate students do not teach undergraduate courses. Undergraduate student–faculty ratio: 5:1.

Student Life Student groups/activities include Music Educators National Conference, National Academy of Recording Arts and Sciences, International Association for Jazz Education. Special housing available for music students.

Expenses for 2006–2007 Application fee: $60. Tuition: $24,730 full-time. Mandatory fees: $950 full-time. College room only: $6300.

Financial Aid Program-specific awards: 45 merit scholarships for incoming students ($500–$8000).

Application Procedures Students admitted directly into the professional program freshman year. Deadline for freshmen and transfers: continuous. Notification date for freshmen and transfers: September 1. Required: essay, high school transcript, college transcript(s) for transfer students, minimum 2.0 high school GPA, letter of recommendation, audition, SAT I or ACT test scores, resume, audition repertoire. Recommended: minimum 3.0 high school GPA. Auditions held 9 times on campus and off campus in various locations in California; recorded music is permissible as a substitute for live auditions with approval from the department and videotaped performances are permissible as a substitute for live auditions with approval from the department.

Web Site http://www.uarts.edu

Contact Susan Gandy, Director of Admission, The University of the Arts, 320 South Broad Street, Philadelphia, Pennsylvania 19102; 800-616-ARTS ext. 6049, fax: 215-717-6045, e-mail address: admissions@uarts.edu

University of the Cumberlands
Williamsburg, Kentucky

Independent Kentucky Baptist, coed. Rural campus. Total enrollment: 1,843. Music program established 1968.

Degrees Bachelor of Music in the areas of music education, church music. Majors and concentrations: church music, instrumental music, piano, vocal music.

Enrollment 62 total; 50 undergraduate, 12 nonprofessional degree.

Music Student Profile 2% minorities, 2% international.

Music Faculty 8 undergraduate (full-time), 1 undergraduate (part-time). 50% of full-time faculty have terminal degrees. Graduate students do not teach undergraduate courses. Undergraduate student–faculty ratio: 9:1.

Student Life Student groups/activities include Collegiate Music Educators National Conference, American Choral Directors Association, National Association of Teachers of Singing competitions.

Expenses for 2006–2007 Application fee: $30. Comprehensive fee: $19,984 includes full-time tuition ($13,298), mandatory fees ($360), and college room and board ($6326). Special program-related fees: $5 per semester for locker rental, $50 for instrument maintenance, $75 per semester for applied lesson fee.

Financial Aid Program-specific awards: 10–15 music scholarships for program majors ($400–$5000).

Application Procedures Students admitted directly into the professional program freshman year. Deadline for freshmen and transfers: continuous. Required: essay, high school transcript, college transcript(s) for transfer students, minimum 2.0 high school GPA, 3 letters of recommendation, SAT I or ACT test scores. Recommended: interview, audition. Auditions held continuously on campus and off campus in Louisville, KY; recorded music is permissible as a substitute for live auditions when distance is prohibitive and videotaped performances are permissible as a substitute for live auditions when distance is prohibitive.

Undergraduate Contact Dr. Jeff Smoak, Chair, Music Department, University of the Cumberlands, 7525 College Station Drive, Williamsburg, Kentucky 40769; 606-539-4332, fax: 606-539-4332, e-mail address: jsmoak@cumberlandcollege.edu

University of the Incarnate Word
San Antonio, Texas

Independent Roman Catholic, coed. Urban campus. Total enrollment: 5,217. Music program established 1932.

Degrees Bachelor of Arts in the areas of composition, performance; Bachelor of Music Education; Bachelor of Music Therapy. Majors and concentrations: brass, composition, music, music education, music industry, music therapy, piano/organ, stringed instruments, voice, wind and percussion instruments. Cross-registration with Our Lady of the Lake University of San Antonio, St. Mary's University of San Antonio, Alamo Community Colleges. Program accredited by NASM.

Enrollment 40 total; all undergraduate.

Music Student Profile 65% females, 35% males, 60% minorities.

Music Faculty 6 undergraduate (full-time), 18 undergraduate (part-time). 83% of full-time faculty have terminal degrees. Graduate students do not teach undergraduate courses. Undergraduate student–faculty ratio: 6:1.

Student Life Student groups/activities include American Music Therapy Association.

Expenses for 2006–2007 Application fee: $20. One-time mandatory fee: $1500. Comprehensive fee: $24,747 includes full-time tuition ($17,400), mandatory fees ($872), and college room and board ($6475). College room only: $3800. Special program-related fees: $170 per semester for private lessons.

Financial Aid Program-specific awards: 1 Sarah Eliz Bell Endowed Scholarship for program majors ($1200), 1 Hortense Buchanan Award for program majors ($100), 1 Lamar Moreau Award for program majors ($100), 1 Sister Margaret Alacoque Colothan Endowed Scholarship for program majors ($700), 8 music scholarships for program majors ($500–$4000), 3 music minor scholarships for program minors ($500–$800).

Application Procedures Students apply for admission into the professional program by sophomore year. Deadline for freshmen and transfers: continuous. Required: high school transcript, college transcript(s) for transfer students, minimum 2.0 high school GPA, 2 letters of recommendation, interview, video, audition, SAT I or ACT test scores. Auditions held twice on campus; recorded music is permissible as a substitute for live auditions with 3 letters of recommendation and videotaped performances are permissible as a substitute for live auditions with 3 letters of recommendation.

Web Site http://www.uiw.edu

Undergraduate Contact William Gokelman, Chair of Music, Music Department, University of the Incarnate Word, 4301 Broadway, San Antonio, Texas 78209; 210-829-3848, fax: 210-829-3880, e-mail address: gokelman@universe.uiwtx.edu

University of the Pacific
Stockton, California

Independent, coed. Suburban campus. Total enrollment: 6,196. Music program established 1878.

Degrees Bachelor of Arts in the area of music; Bachelor of Music in the areas of performance, music education, music therapy, music composition, music history, music management. Majors and concentrations: brass, composition, music education, music history, music management, music therapy, piano, stringed instruments, voice, wind and percussion instruments. Graduate degrees offered: Master of Arts in the area of music therapy; Master of Music in the area of music education. Program accredited by NASM, AMTA.

Enrollment 180 total; 167 undergraduate, 11 graduate, 2 nonprofessional degree.

Music Faculty 23 total (full-time), 21 total (part-time). 65% of full-time faculty have terminal degrees. Graduate students do not teach undergraduate courses. Undergraduate student–faculty ratio: 8:1.

Student Life Student groups/activities include Music Educators National Conference Student Chapter, Music Therapy Association, professional music fraternities.

Expenses for 2005–2006 Application fee: $60. Comprehensive fee: $34,566 includes full-time tuition ($25,658), mandatory fees ($430), and college room and board ($8478). College room only: $5760. Room and board charges vary according to board plan and housing facility. Special program-related fees: $10–$15 per semester for practice room fee, $70–$125 per credit for applied music fee.

Financial Aid Program-specific awards: 118 music scholarships for those demonstrating talent and need ($3000–$15,000), 29 Conservatory Performance Scholarships for those demonstrating musical achievement ($1000–$9600).

Application Procedures Students admitted directly into the professional program freshman year. Deadline for freshmen and transfers: February 15. Required: essay, high school transcript, college transcript(s) for transfer students, letter of recommendation, interview, audition, SAT I or ACT test scores. Recommended: minimum 3.0 high school GPA. Auditions held 4 times on campus; recorded music is permissible as a substitute for live auditions if a campus visit is impossible and videotaped performances are permissible as a substitute for live auditions if a campus visit is impossible.

Web Site http://www.uop.edu/conservatory

Undergraduate Contact Mr. David Duggan, Coordinator of Student Services, Conservatory of Music, University of the Pacific, 3601 Pacific Avenue, Stockton, California 95211; 209-946-2418, fax: 209-946-2770, e-mail address: conservatory@pacific.edu

Graduate Contact Robin Lattin, Recruitment Administrator, Office of Research and Graduate Studies, University of the Pacific, 3601 Pacific Avenue, Stockton, California 95211; 209-946-2261, fax: 209-946-2858, e-mail address: gradschool@pacific.edu

The University of Toledo

Toledo, Ohio

State-supported, coed. Total enrollment: 19,480. Music program established 1948.

University of Tulsa

Tulsa, Oklahoma

Independent, coed. Urban campus. Total enrollment: 4,084.

Degrees Bachelor of Music in the areas of performance, composition, theory; Bachelor of Music Education in the areas of instrumental music education, vocal music education. Majors and concentrations: composition, music education, music theory, piano, stringed instruments, voice, wind and percussion instruments. Program accredited by NASM.

Enrollment 119 total.

Music Student Profile 55% females, 45% males, 10% minorities.

Music Faculty 14 total (full-time), 22 total (part-time). 100% of full-time faculty have terminal degrees. Graduate students do not teach undergraduate courses. Undergraduate student–faculty ratio: 6:1.

Student Life Student groups/activities include Sigma Alpha Iota, Phi Mu Alpha Sinfonia, Music Educators National Conference.

Expenses for 2006–2007 Application fee: $35. Comprehensive fee: $27,790 includes full-time tuition ($20,658), mandatory fees ($80), and college room and board ($7052). College room only: $3896.

Financial Aid Program-specific awards: 100 grants-in-aid for program students ($7000), 4 Kathleen C. Parriott Scholarships for music majors ($23,000), Roger P. Fenn Memorial Scholarship for string or wind music education majors ($750), 1 Presser

Scholarship for senior music education majors ($4000), 1 Fourjay Scholarship in music for program majors ($2500), 1 Gretchen Ninan Gaither Memorial Scholarship for string majors ($1000), 1 Michael Houghton Memorial Scholarship for music education majors ($3000), 1 Albert and Florence Lukken Memorial Scholarship for voice or piano majors ($1250), 1 Maude B. Pape Memorial Scholarship for voice majors ($3500), 1 Sigma Alpha Iota Patroness Scholarship for outstanding Sigma Alpha Iota members ($2000), 4 Marshall Scholarships for program majors ($3000).

Application Procedures Students admitted directly into the professional program freshman year. Deadline for freshmen and transfers: continuous. Required: essay, high school transcript, college transcript(s) for transfer students, minimum 3.0 high school GPA, letter of recommendation, interview, audition, SAT I or ACT test scores. Auditions held twice and by appointment on campus; recorded music is permissible as a substitute for live auditions when distance is prohibitive and videotaped performances are permissible as a substitute for live auditions when distance is prohibitive.

Web Site http://www.cas.utulsa.edu/music

Undergraduate Contact Dr. Frank Ryan, Director, School of Music, University of Tulsa, 600 South College Avenue, Tulsa, Oklahoma 74104-3189; 918-631-2262, fax: 918-631-3589, e-mail address: frank-ryan@utulsa.edu

University of Utah

Salt Lake City, Utah

State-supported, coed. Urban campus. Total enrollment: 29,012. Music program established 1908.

Degrees Bachelor of Arts in the area of music; Bachelor of Music in the areas of performance, music education, theory, composition, history and literature; Bachelor of Music Education in the areas of instrumental music, choral music. Majors and concentrations: brass, composition, harp, jazz, music education, music history and literature, music theory, organ, piano, stringed instruments, voice, wind and percussion instruments, woodwind instruments. Graduate degrees offered: Master of Arts in the area of musicology; Master of Music in the areas of composition, history/literature, performance, music education, conducting, theory, musicology, collaborative piano; Master of Music Education. Doctor of Philosophy in the areas of composition, music education. Program accredited by NASM.

Enrollment 433 total; 361 undergraduate, 72 graduate.

Music Student Profile 53% females, 47% males, 2% minorities, 5% international.

Music Faculty 30 total (full-time), 53 total (part-time). 80% of full-time faculty have terminal degrees. Graduate students teach a few undergraduate courses. Undergraduate student–faculty ratio: 5:1.

Student Life Student groups/activities include Music Educators National Conference, world-wide competitions.

Expenses for 2005–2006 Application fee: $35. State resident tuition: $3672 full-time. Nonresident tuition: $12,860 full-time. Mandatory fees: $670 full-time. Full-time tuition and fees vary according to course level, course load, degree level, and student level. College room and board: $5422. College room only: $2704. Room and board charges vary according to board plan and housing facility. Special program-related fees: $60 per year for practice rooms, $175–$350 per semester for private lessons.

Financial Aid Program-specific awards: 180–190 music scholarships for music majors ($500–$3300).

Application Procedures Students admitted directly into the professional program freshman year. Deadline for freshmen and transfers: July 1. Required: high school transcript, college transcript(s) for transfer students, minimum 2.0 high school GPA, audition, SAT I or ACT test scores. Recommended: essay, minimum 3.0 high school GPA, 3 letters of recommendation, interview, video, portfolio. Auditions held 2-3 times on campus; recorded music is permissible as a substitute for live auditions when distance is prohibitive and videotaped performances are permissible as a substitute for live auditions when distance is prohibitive. Portfolio reviews held as needed on campus.

Web Site http://www.music.utah.edu/

University of Utah (continued)

Undergraduate Contact Dr. David Power, Associate Director for Undergraduate Studies, School of Music, University of Utah, 204 DGH-1375 East Presidents Circle, Salt Lake City, Utah 84112-0030; 801-581-6762, fax: 801-581-5683.

Graduate Contact Dr. Robert Baldwin, Director for Graduate Studies, School of Music, University of Utah, 204 DGH-1375 East Presidents Circle, Salt Lake City, Utah 84112-0030; 801-581-6762, fax: 801-581-5683.

University of Vermont

Burlington, Vermont

State-supported, coed. Suburban campus. Total enrollment: 11,597. Music program established 1926.

University of Washington

Seattle, Washington

State-supported, coed. Urban campus. Total enrollment: 39,251. Music program established 1911.

University of West Georgia

Carrollton, Georgia

State-supported, coed. Small town campus. Total enrollment: 10,155. Music program established 1966.

Degrees Bachelor of Music in the areas of performance, composition, music education, music. Majors and concentrations: composition, music education, performance. Graduate degrees offered: Master of Music in the areas of music education, performance. Program accredited by NASM.

Enrollment 105 total; 85 undergraduate, 10 graduate, 10 nonprofessional degree.

Music Student Profile 48% females, 52% males, 19% minorities.

Music Faculty 8 total (full-time), 13 total (part-time). 100% of full-time faculty have terminal degrees. Graduate students do not teach undergraduate courses. Undergraduate student–faculty ratio: 10:1.

Student Life Student groups/activities include Music Educators National Conference Collegiate Chapter, Kappa Kappa Psi, Sigma Alpha Iota.

Expenses for 2005–2006 Application fee: $20. State resident tuition: $2438 full-time. Nonresident tuition: $9754 full-time. Mandatory fees: $832 full-time. Full-time tuition and fees vary according to course load. College room and board: $5568. College room only: $3540. Room and board charges vary according to board plan and housing facility. Special program-related fees: $38 per credit hour for applied music fee.

Financial Aid Program-specific awards: 34 music scholarships and service awards for music major and non-major ensemble members ($1000).

Application Procedures Students apply for admission into the professional program by freshman year. Deadline for freshmen and transfers: continuous. Notification date for freshmen and transfers: continuous. Required: high school transcript, college transcript(s) for transfer students, audition, SAT I or ACT test scores (minimum combined SAT I score of 840), minimum Freshman Index of 2050 (H.S. GPA x 500 + SAT). Recommended: letter of recommendation, interview, portfolio. Auditions held 4 times on campus; recorded music is permissible as a substitute for live auditions when distance is prohibitive and videotaped performances are permissible as a substitute for live auditions when distance is prohibitive. Portfolio reviews held 4 times on campus.

Web Site http://www.westga.edu/~musicdpt

Contact Dr. Kevin R. Hibbard, Chair, Department of Music, University of West Georgia, Carrollton, Georgia 30118-2210; 678-839-6516, fax: 678-839-6259, e-mail address: musicdpt@westga.edu

University of Wisconsin–Eau Claire

Eau Claire, Wisconsin

State-supported, coed. Urban campus. Total enrollment: 10,566. Music program established 1947.

University of Wisconsin–Green Bay

Green Bay, Wisconsin

State-supported, coed. Suburban campus. Total enrollment: 5,826. Music program established 1971.

Degrees Bachelor of Music in the areas of music education, performance. Majors and concentrations: bass, guitar, music education, piano/organ, voice, wind and percussion instruments. Program accredited by NASM.

Enrollment 99 total; 65 undergraduate, 34 nonprofessional degree.

Music Student Profile 65% females, 35% males, 5% minorities, 2% international.

Music Faculty 11 undergraduate (full-time), 10 undergraduate (part-time). 73% of full-time faculty have terminal degrees. Graduate students do not teach undergraduate courses. Undergraduate student–faculty ratio: 9:1.

Student Life Student groups/activities include American Choral Directors Association College Chapter, Music Educators National Conference Student Chapter, Jazz Society.

Expenses for 2005–2006 Application fee: $35. State resident tuition: $4277 full-time. Nonresident tuition: $14,323 full-time. Mandatory fees: $1148 full-time. Full-time tuition and fees vary according to reciprocity agreements. College room and board: $4698. College room only: $2772. Room and board charges vary according to board plan and housing facility. Special program-related fees: $25 per semester for instrument rental fee.

Financial Aid Program-specific awards: 3 jazz scholarships for program majors ($500), 2 piano accompanying awards for program majors ($500), 15 music merit scholarships ($750).

Application Procedures Students apply for admission into the professional program by sophomore year. Deadline for freshmen and transfers: continuous. Required: high school transcript, college transcript(s) for transfer students, 2 letters of recommendation, interview, audition, ACT test score only. Recommended: essay, minimum 3.0 high school GPA. Auditions held 3 times and by appointment on campus.

Undergraduate Contact Dr. Sarah Meredith, Chair, Music Program, University of Wisconsin–Green Bay, 2420 Nicolet Drive, Green Bay, Wisconsin 54311-7001; 920-465-2637, fax: 920-465-2890, e-mail address: meredits@uwgb.edu

University of Wisconsin–Madison

Madison, Wisconsin

State-supported, coed. Urban campus. Total enrollment: 41,480. Music program established 1895.

Degrees Bachelor of Music in the areas of performance, music education. Majors and concentrations: brass, composition, music education, piano/organ, stringed instruments, voice, wind and percussion instruments. Graduate degrees offered: Master of Musical Arts in the areas of brass instruments, choral conducting, composition, music education, ethnomusicology, musicology, instrumental conducting-orchestra, instrumental conducting-wind ensemble, opera, organ, percussion, piano, piano-accompanying, piano pedagogy/performance; Master of Music Education. Doctor of Musical Arts in the areas of brass instruments, choral conducting, composition, instrumental conducting-orchestra, instrumental conducting-wind ensemble, organ, piano, stringed instruments, voice, woodwind instruments. Program accredited by NASM.

Enrollment 450 total; 200 undergraduate, 175 graduate, 75 nonprofessional degree.

Music Student Profile 50% females, 50% males, 10% minorities, 7% international.

Music Faculty 51 total (full-time), 3 total (part-time). 50% of full-time faculty have terminal degrees. Graduate students teach a few undergraduate courses. Undergraduate student–faculty ratio: 9:1.

Student Life Student groups/activities include Sigma Alpha Iota/Phi Mu Alpha, Music Educators National Conference Student Chapter, Music Teachers National Association Student Chapter.

Expenses for 2005–2006 Application fee: $35. State resident tuition: $6284 full-time. Nonresident tuition: $20,284 full-time. Mandatory fees: $333 full-time. Full-time tuition and fees vary according to degree level and reciprocity agreements. College room and board: $6500. Room and board charges vary according to board plan, housing facility, and location. Special program-related fees: $30 per semester for recital recording, $40 per recital for non-required recital fee, $50 per fall/spring for locker rental, $60–$65 per semester for practice room.

Financial Aid Program-specific awards: 40–50 endowed scholarships for program majors ($500–$5000), 40 Music Clinic Scholarships for in-state program majors ($5000–$5500).

Application Procedures Students apply for admission into the professional program by freshman, sophomore year. Deadline for freshmen: February 1; transfers: March 1. Notification date for freshmen: March 10; transfers: April 30. Required: high school transcript, college transcript(s) for transfer students, 2 letters of recommendation, interview, audition, minimum 2.5 high school GPA. Recommended: minimum 3.0 high school GPA. Auditions held 3 times and by appointment on campus; recorded music is permissible as a substitute for live auditions when distance is prohibitive and videotaped performances are permissible as a substitute for live auditions in some cases when distance is prohibitive.

Web Site http://www.wisc.edu/music

Undergraduate Contact Prof. Marc Fink, Associate Director, School of Music, University of Wisconsin–Madison, 1621 Humanities, Madison, Wisconsin 53706; 608-263-3623, fax: 608-262-8876, e-mail address: mdfink@facstaff.wisc.edu

Graduate Contact Dr. Susan Cook, Director of Graduate Studies, School of Music, University of Wisconsin–Madison, 4531 Humanities, Madison, Wisconsin 53706; 608-262-9295, fax: 608-262-8876, e-mail address: sccook@facstaff.wisc.edu

University of Wisconsin–Milwaukee

Milwaukee, Wisconsin

State-supported, coed. Urban campus. Total enrollment: 27,502.

University of Wisconsin–Oshkosh

Oshkosh, Wisconsin

State-supported, coed. Suburban campus. Total enrollment: 10,997. Music program established 1952.

Degrees Bachelor of Music in the areas of performance, music therapy, music industry; Bachelor of Music Education in the areas of general music, choral music, instrumental music. Majors and concentrations: brass, music business/music industry, music education, piano, sound recording technology, stringed instruments, voice, wind and percussion instruments. Program accredited by NASM.

Enrollment 222 total; 210 undergraduate, 12 nonprofessional degree.

Music Student Profile 40% females, 60% males, 5% minorities, 5% international.

Music Faculty 20 undergraduate (full-time), 13 undergraduate (part-time). 85% of full-time faculty have terminal degrees. Graduate students do not teach undergraduate courses. Undergraduate student–faculty ratio: 12:1.

Student Life Student groups/activities include Music Educators National Conference Student Chapter, American Music Therapy Association Student Chapter, Oshkosh Recording Association. Special housing available for music students.

Expenses for 2005–2006 Application fee: $35. State resident tuition: $4,981 full-time. Nonresident tuition: $15,027 full-time. Full-time tuition varies according to reciprocity agreements. College room and board: $4884. College room only: $2784. Room and board charges vary according to board plan and housing facility.

Financial Aid Program-specific awards: 4 Willcockson Prizes in the Arts for incoming freshmen ($1000), 4–5 ensemble awards for music majors ($10,000), 1 Henry Pensis Award for double reed players ($300), 1 Stanley Linton Music Education Award for music education students ($300), 1 Roger Dennis Music Education Award for music education students ($300), 1 Richard K. Porter Vocal Performance Award for voice students ($150), 1 Patricia Radford Fell Award for piano students ($300), 13 music scholarships for music majors ($1000–$2000), 3 Thoma Awards for pianists ($1000).

Application Procedures Students admitted directly into the professional program freshman year. Deadline for freshmen and transfers: April 1. Required: high school transcript, audition, ACT test score only. Auditions held 4 times on campus; recorded music is permissible as a substitute for live auditions when distance is prohibitive and videotaped performances are permissible as a substitute for live auditions when distance is prohibitive.

Web Site http://www.uwosh.edu/departments/music

Undergraduate Contact Admissions Office, University of Wisconsin–Oshkosh, 800 Algoma Boulevard, Oshkosh, Wisconsin 54901; 920-424-0202, fax: 920-424-1207.

University of Wisconsin–River Falls

River Falls, Wisconsin

State-supported, coed. Suburban campus. Total enrollment: 5,950.

University of Wisconsin–Stevens Point

Stevens Point, Wisconsin

State-supported, coed. Small town campus. Total enrollment: 8,577. Music program established 1928.

Degrees Bachelor of Music. Majors and concentrations: jazz studies, music education, music literature, performance. Graduate degrees offered: Master of Music Education in the areas of instrumental music education, choral music education, jazz pedagogy, studio pedagogy, Suzuki talent education. Program accredited by NASM.

Enrollment 234 total; 186 undergraduate, 8 graduate, 40 nonprofessional degree.

Music Student Profile 60% females, 40% males, 3% minorities, 1% international.

Music Faculty 21 undergraduate (full-time), 4 undergraduate (part-time). 90% of full-time faculty have terminal degrees. Graduate students do not teach undergraduate courses. Undergraduate student–faculty ratio: 15:1.

Student Life Student groups/activities include Music Educators National Conference, American String Teachers Association.

Expenses for 2005–2006 Application fee: $35. State resident tuition: $4277 full-time. Nonresident tuition: $14,323 full-time. Mandatory fees: $785 full-time. Full-time tuition and fees vary according to course load and reciprocity agreements. College room and board: $4322. College room only: $2574. Room and board charges vary according to housing facility.

Financial Aid Program-specific awards: music scholarships for those demonstrating talent, academic achievement, and need.

Application Procedures Students apply for admission into the professional program by sophomore year. Deadline for freshmen: January 15; transfers: February 15. Required: high school transcript, college transcript(s) for transfer students, audition, SAT I or ACT test scores (minimum composite ACT score of 18). Recommended: 2 letters of recommendation. Auditions held 3 times and by appointment on campus; recorded music is permissible as a substitute for live auditions when distance is prohibitive and videotaped performances are permissible as a substitute for live auditions when distance is prohibitive.

Web Site http://www.uwsp.edu/music/

Undergraduate Contact Dr. Robert Kase, Chair, Music Department, University of Wisconsin–Stevens Point, Fine Arts Center, Stevens Point, Wisconsin 54481; 715-346-3107, fax: 715-346-2718, e-mail address: rkase@uwsp.edu

Graduate Contact Dr. Patricia Holland, Coordinator of Graduate Studies, Music Department, University of Wisconsin–Stevens

University of Wisconsin–Stevens Point (continued)

Point, Fine Arts Center, Stevens Point, Wisconsin 54481; 715-346-3119, fax: 715-346-2718, e-mail address: pholland@uwsp.edu

University of Wisconsin–Superior

Superior, Wisconsin

State-supported, coed. Small town campus. Total enrollment: 2,872. Music program established 1939.
Degrees Bachelor of Music in the areas of performance, composition, jazz performance; Bachelor of Music Education in the areas of choral music, instrumental music, general music. Majors and concentrations: composition, guitar, harpsichord, jazz performance, music education, piano/organ, stringed instruments, voice, wind and percussion instruments. Cross-registration with University of Minnesota, Duluth; College of St. Scholastica. Program accredited by NASM.
Enrollment 50 total; all undergraduate.
Music Student Profile 51% females, 49% males, 1% minorities, 1% international.
Music Faculty 7 undergraduate (full-time), 15 undergraduate (part-time). 85% of full-time faculty have terminal degrees. Graduate students do not teach undergraduate courses. Undergraduate student–faculty ratio: 8:1.
Student Life Student groups/activities include Music Educators National Conference Student Chapter, American Choral Directors Association Student Chapter.
Expenses for 2005–2006 Application fee: $35. State resident tuition: $4,427 full-time. Nonresident tuition: $14,473 full-time. Mandatory fees: $761 full-time. College room and board: $4422. College room only: $2552.
Financial Aid Program-specific awards: 1 NBC Keyboard Award for pianists and organists ($1000), 6 Foundation Awards for incoming freshmen ($500), 1 Rock Scholarship for junior and senior pianists ($1000), 1 McLean Award for pianists and violinists ($500), 1 string scholarship for string players ($600).
Application Procedures Students admitted directly into the professional program freshman year. Deadline for freshmen and transfers: continuous. Notification date for freshmen and transfers: August 5. Required: high school transcript, college transcript(s) for transfer students, interview, audition, ACT test score only, standing in top half of graduating class, minimum composite ACT score of 21 or standing in top third of class. Recommended: 2 letters of recommendation. Auditions held 3 times on campus; recorded music is permissible as a substitute for live auditions when distance is prohibitive and videotaped performances are permissible as a substitute for live auditions when distance is prohibitive.
Web Site http://www.uwsuper.edu/
Undergraduate Contact Dr. Greg Kehl Moore, Chair, Department of Music, University of Wisconsin–Superior, Box 2000, Superior, Wisconsin 54880-2898; 715-394-8116, fax: 715-394-8578, e-mail address: gmoore@uwsuper.edu

University of Wisconsin–Whitewater

Whitewater, Wisconsin

State-supported, coed. Small town campus. Total enrollment: 10,750. Music program established 1947.
Degrees Bachelor of Music in the areas of music education, performance, music history, music theory. Majors and concentrations: choral music education, instrumental music education, music, music history/theory, performance. Program accredited by NASM.
Enrollment 175 total; 160 undergraduate, 15 nonprofessional degree.
Music Student Profile 55% females, 45% males, 1% minorities, 1% international.
Music Faculty 19 undergraduate (full-time), 5 undergraduate (part-time). 84% of full-time faculty have terminal degrees. Graduate students do not teach undergraduate courses. Undergraduate student–faculty ratio: 8:1.

Student Life Student groups/activities include Music Educators National Conference Student Chapter, International Association for Jazz Education Student Chapter, music societies.
Expenses for 2005–2006 Application fee: $35. One-time mandatory fee: $100. State resident tuition: $4370 full-time. Nonresident tuition: $14,965 full-time. Mandatory fees: $710 full-time. Full-time tuition and fees vary according to degree level and reciprocity agreements. College room and board: $4210. College room only: $2460. Room and board charges vary according to board plan. Special program-related fees: $75 for recital production fee.
Financial Aid Program-specific awards: 25 music scholarships for program majors ($500–$3000).
Application Procedures Students admitted directly into the professional program freshman year. Deadline for freshmen and transfers: continuous. Notification date for freshmen and transfers: continuous. Required: essay, high school transcript, college transcript(s) for transfer students, letter of recommendation, audition, ACT test score only (minimum composite ACT score of 20), standing in top 60% of graduating class. Auditions held 6 times on campus; recorded music is permissible as a substitute for live auditions if a campus visit is impossible and videotaped performances are permissible as a substitute for live auditions if a campus visit is impossible.
Web Site http://academics.uww.edu/CAC/Music/index.htm
Undergraduate Contact Dr. Marr Sinschak, Audition Coordinator, Music Department, University of Wisconsin–Whitewater, 800 West Main Street, Whitewater, Wisconsin 53190; 262-472-1310, fax: 262-472-2808.

University of Wyoming

Laramie, Wyoming

State-supported, coed. Total enrollment: 13,126.
Degrees Bachelor of Music in the area of music performance; Bachelor of Music Education. Majors and concentrations: music education, music performance. Graduate degrees offered: Master of Music in the area of performance. Cross-registration with Wyoming community colleges. Program accredited by NASM.
Enrollment 161 total; 148 undergraduate, 9 graduate, 4 nonprofessional degree.
Music Student Profile 65% females, 35% males, 7% minorities, 5% international.
Music Faculty 15 undergraduate (full-time), 15 undergraduate (part-time), 9 graduate (full-time). 90% of full-time faculty have terminal degrees. Graduate students do not teach undergraduate courses. Undergraduate student–faculty ratio: 18:1.
Student Life Student groups/activities include Wyoming Music Educators Association, band fraternities, Kappa Kappa Psi, Tau Beta Sigma, marching band.
Expenses for 2005–2006 Application fee: $30. State resident tuition: $2760 full-time. Nonresident tuition: $9150 full-time. Mandatory fees: $666 full-time. Full-time tuition and fees vary according to course load, location, program, and reciprocity agreements. College room and board: $6240. College room only: $2709. Room and board charges vary according to board plan and housing facility. Special program-related fees: $35 per semester for practice room fees, $125–$250 per semester for lesson fees.
Financial Aid Program-specific awards: 20 private awards for music majors ($300–$500), 205 general scholarships for all students who participate in music ($200–$7000).
Application Procedures Students admitted directly into the professional program freshman year. Deadline for freshmen and transfers: August 28. Notification date for freshmen and transfers: continuous. Required: high school transcript, college transcript(s) for transfer students, minimum 2.0 high school GPA, 3 letters of recommendation, audition, SAT I or ACT test scores. Recommended: interview, portfolio. Auditions held twice and by appointment on campus; recorded music is permissible as a substitute for live auditions when distance is prohibitive and videotaped performances are permissible as a substitute for live auditions when distance is prohibitive. Portfolio reviews held once per semester and by appointment on campus.
Web Site http://www.uwyo.edu/music

Undergraduate Contact Office of Admissions, University of Wyoming, Department 3435, 1000 East University Avenue, Laramie, Wyoming 82071; 307-766-5160, fax: 307-766-4042.
Graduate Contact Dean, Graduate School, University of Wyoming, Department 3108, 1000 East University Avenue, Laramie, Wyoming 82071; 307-766-2287, fax: 307-766-4042.

USC Thornton School of Music

See University of Southern California

Utah State University
Logan, Utah

State-supported, coed. Urban campus. Total enrollment: 14,458. Music program established 1969.
Degrees Bachelor of Music in the areas of music education, performance, piano pedagogy; Bachelor of Science in the area of music therapy. Majors and concentrations: guitar performance, individualized major, music education, music therapy, organ performance, piano pedagogy, piano performance, stringed instrument performance, voice performance, wind and percussion instruments performance. Program accredited by NASM, AMTA.
Enrollment 353 total; all undergraduate.
Music Student Profile 70% females, 30% males, 3% minorities, 2% international.
Music Faculty 25 undergraduate (full-time), 35 undergraduate (part-time). 70% of full-time faculty have terminal degrees. Graduate students do not teach undergraduate courses. Undergraduate student–faculty ratio: 20:1.
Student Life Student groups/activities include Music Therapy Student Association, Kappa Kappa Psi (band fraternity), Tau Beta Sigma (band sorority), Music Education National Conference Student Chapter, American String Teacher Association, American Choral Directors Association.
Expenses for 2005–2006 Application fee: $40. State resident tuition: $3128 full-time. Nonresident tuition: $10,072 full-time. Mandatory fees: $544 full-time. Full-time tuition and fees vary according to course load and student level. College room and board: $4330. College room only: $1550. Room and board charges vary according to board plan and housing facility. Special program-related fees: $8 per semester for instrument locker rentals, $9–$25 per semester for keyboards, instrument rental, $45 per semester for piano/organ practice rooms, $208 per semester for private instruction (non-majors), $358 per semester for private instruction (majors).
Financial Aid Program-specific awards: scholarships for performance and education students, marching band members ($150–$2000).
Application Procedures Students apply for admission into the professional program by freshman year. Deadline for freshmen and transfers: continuous. Required: high school transcript, college transcript(s) for transfer students, interview, audition, ACT test score only, minimum 2.5 high school GPA. Recommended: minimum 3.0 high school GPA, video. Auditions held at various times on campus and off campus in Salt Lake City, UT; Rexburg, ID; recorded music is permissible as a substitute for live auditions when distance is prohibitive and videotaped performances are permissible as a substitute for live auditions when distance is prohibitive.
Web Site http://www.usu.edu/music/
Undergraduate Contact Dorothy Kent, Staff Assistant, Department of Music, Utah State University, 4015 Old Main Hill, Logan, Utah 84322-4015; 435-797-3036, fax: 435-797-1862, e-mail address: musicdep@cc.usu.edu

Valdosta State University
Valdosta, Georgia

State-supported, coed. Small town campus. Total enrollment: 10,503.

Valley City State University
Valley City, North Dakota

State-supported, coed. Small town campus. Total enrollment: 1,035. Music program established 1892.
Degrees Bachelor of Science. Majors and concentrations: music education. Program accredited by NASM.
Enrollment 30 total; 25 undergraduate, 5 nonprofessional degree.
Music Student Profile 65% females, 35% males, 5% minorities.
Music Faculty 5 undergraduate (full-time), 6 undergraduate (part-time). 60% of full-time faculty have terminal degrees. Graduate students do not teach undergraduate courses. Undergraduate student–faculty ratio: 6:1.
Student Life Student groups/activities include Music Educators National Conference, Music Teachers National Association, National Association of Teachers of Singing.
Expenses for 2005–2006 Application fee: $35. State resident tuition: $3656 full-time. Nonresident tuition: $9761 full-time. Mandatory fees: $1504 full-time. College room and board: $4694. College room only: $2080. Room and board charges vary according to board plan. Special program-related fees: $15 per semester for band instrument rental, $25–$100 per semester for accompanists, $50–$100 per credit for applied lessons.
Financial Aid Program-specific awards: 35 Friends of Music Scholarships for program majors, minors, participants ($150–$1600).
Application Procedures Students admitted directly into the professional program freshman year. Required: high school transcript, college transcript(s) for transfer students, interview, audition, theory placement exam, piano placement exam. Auditions held 3 times on campus; recorded music is permissible as a substitute for live auditions when distance is prohibitive and videotaped performances are permissible as a substitute for live auditions when distance is prohibitive.
Web Site http://www.vcsu.nodak.edu
Undergraduate Contact Dr. Diana Skroch, Chair, Department of Music, Valley City State University, 101 College Street SW, Valley City, North Dakota 58072; 800-532-8641 ext. 37273, fax: 701-845-7245, e-mail address: diana_skroch@mail.vcsu.nodak.edu

Valparaiso University
Valparaiso, Indiana

Independent, coed. Small town campus. Total enrollment: 3,864. Music program established 1925.
Degrees Bachelor of Music in the areas of church music, performance, composition; Bachelor of Music Education in the area of combined vocal and instrumental music. Majors and concentrations: church music, classical music, composition, music, music education, piano/organ, stringed instruments, voice, wind and percussion instruments. Program accredited by NASM.
Enrollment 138 total; 73 undergraduate, 65 nonprofessional degree.
Music Student Profile 57% females, 43% males, 5% minorities.
Music Faculty 10 undergraduate (full-time), 25 undergraduate (part-time). 100% of full-time faculty have terminal degrees. Graduate students do not teach undergraduate courses. Undergraduate student–faculty ratio: 12:1.
Student Life Student groups/activities include American Guild of Organists, Music Educators National Conference, Music Enterprises Student Association.
Expenses for 2005–2006 Application fee: $30. Comprehensive fee: $28,970 includes full-time tuition ($22,000), mandatory fees ($750), and college room and board ($6220). College room only: $3910. Room and board charges vary according to housing facility and student level. Special program-related fees: $300 per course for studio instruction fee.
Financial Aid Program-specific awards: 35–40 music scholarships for performers ($1000–$2400).
Application Procedures Students admitted directly into the professional program freshman year. Deadline for freshmen and transfers: continuous. Notification date for freshmen and transfers: August 15. Required: high school transcript, college

Valparaiso University (continued)

transcript(s) for transfer students, SAT I or ACT test scores, video or audition, theory diagnostic test. Recommended: essay, letter of recommendation, interview. Auditions held twice on campus; recorded music is permissible as a substitute for live auditions by arrangement with department and videotaped performances are permissible as a substitute for live auditions when distance is prohibitive or if a campus visit is impossible.
Web Site http://www.valpo.edu/music/
Undergraduate Contact Dr. Linda C. Ferguson, Chair, Department of Music, Valparaiso University, Center for the Arts, Valparaiso, Indiana 46383-6493; 219-464-5454, fax: 219-464-5244, e-mail address: linda.ferguson@valpo.edu

Blair School of Music

Vanderbilt University
Nashville, Tennessee

Independent, coed. Urban campus. Total enrollment: 11,481. Music program established 1986.
Degrees Bachelor of Music in the areas of performance, musical arts, composition/music theory; Bachelor of Music/Master of Education in the area of musical arts/education. Majors and concentrations: music education, music theory and composition, musical arts, performance. Program accredited by NASM.
Enrollment 180 total; all undergraduate.
Music Student Profile 55% females, 45% males, 10% minorities.
Music Faculty 30 undergraduate (full-time), 40 undergraduate (part-time). 32% of full-time faculty have terminal degrees. Graduate students do not teach undergraduate courses.
Student Life Student groups/activities include Pi Kappa Lambda/Sigma Alpha Iota, Voice Majors Association, Phi Mu Alpha Sinfonia, Sigma Alpha Iota Sorority, Music Educators National Conference.
Expenses for 2005–2006 Application fee: $50. Comprehensive fee: $41,986 includes full-time tuition ($30,920), mandatory fees ($780), and college room and board ($10,286). College room only: $6760.
Financial Aid Program-specific awards: 1 Harold Sterling Vanderbilt Scholarship for program majors ($21,930), 1–50 Blair Dean's Honor Scholarships for program majors ($1000–$10,000), Blair Help Loans for program majors ($500–$2400), 1 Frances Hampton Currey Music Scholarship for program majors ($22,900), 1 Laura Kemp Goad Honor Scholarship for program majors ($22,900), 1 Joel and Stella Hargrove Scholarship for program majors ($5000), 1 Rae S. Miller Piano Scholarship for piano majors ($5000), 1 Wilda and William Moennig Scholarship for program majors ($12,000), 1 Del Sawyer Trumpet Scholarship for trumpet majors ($22,900), 1 Wilma Ward Scholarship for voice majors ($22,900), 1 William and Saidee Jarrell Award for program majors ($4000).
Application Procedures Students admitted directly into the professional program freshman year. Deadline for freshmen and transfers: continuous. Notification date for freshmen and transfers: April 1. Required: essay, high school transcript, college transcript(s) for transfer students, 2 letters of recommendation, audition, SAT I or ACT test scores, portfolio for composition applicants. Recommended: minimum 3.0 high school GPA, video for voice majors. Auditions held 5 times on campus and off campus in Washington, DC; Interlochen, MI; Los Angeles, CA; Houston, TX; Dallas, TX, Boston, MA; recorded music is permissible as a substitute for live auditions for musical arts or performance majors (except in percussion); when distance is prohibitive and videotaped performances are permissible as a substitute for live auditions for percussion majors when distance is prohibitive. Portfolio reviews held by appointment on campus.
Web Site http://www.vanderbilt.edu
Undergraduate Contact Dr. Dwayne Sagen, Assistant Dean, Blair School of Music, Vanderbilt University, 2400 Blakemore Avenue, Nashville, Tennessee 37212-3499; 615-322-7679, fax: 615-343-0324, e-mail address: dwayne.p.sagen@vanderbilt.edu

VanderCook College of Music
Chicago, Illinois

Independent, coed. Urban campus. Music program established 1928.
Degrees Bachelor of Music Education. Majors and concentrations: choral music education, instrumental music education. Graduate degrees offered: Master of Music Education in the areas of instrumental music education, choral music education, music education with certification. Cross-registration with Illinois Institute of Technology. Program accredited by NASM.
Enrollment 282 total; 91 undergraduate, 191 graduate.
Music Student Profile 47% females, 53% males, 20% minorities, 2% international.
Music Faculty 11 total (full-time), 30 total (part-time). 30% of full-time faculty have terminal degrees. Graduate students do not teach undergraduate courses. Undergraduate student–faculty ratio: 3:1.
Student Life Student groups/activities include Music Educators National Conference Student Chapter, Phi Mu Alpha Sinfonia, Midwest Clinic.
Expenses for 2006–2007 Application fee: $35. Comprehensive fee: $25,940 includes full-time tuition ($17,120), mandatory fees ($770), and college room and board ($8050). Special program-related fees: $70 per class for techniques classes, $125 per semester for computer lab use.
Financial Aid Program-specific awards: 30 talent awards for voice and instrument majors ($2500), 4 tuition assistance grants for program majors ($500), 15 VCM Apprentice Grant for program majors ($1000), 15 academic awards for program majors ($1000).
Application Procedures Students admitted directly into the professional program freshman year. Deadline for freshmen and transfers: continuous. Notification date for freshmen and transfers: continuous. Required: essay, high school transcript, college transcript(s) for transfer students, minimum 3.0 high school GPA, 3 letters of recommendation, interview, audition, SAT I or ACT test scores (minimum combined SAT I score of 1000, minimum composite ACT score of 20), minimum TOEFL score of 500 for international applicants. Auditions held 7 times yearly and by appointment on campus; recorded music is permissible as a substitute for live auditions for out-of-state applicants or if a campus visit is impossible and videotaped performances are permissible as a substitute for live auditions for out-of-state applicants or if a campus visit is impossible.
Web Site http://www.vandercook.edu
Undergraduate Contact Ms. Tam Trutwin, Director of Student Recruitment, VanderCook College of Music, 3140 South Federal Street, Chicago, Illinois 60616; 800-448-2655 ext. 241, fax: 312-225-5211, e-mail address: ttrutwin@vandercook.edu
Graduate Contact Ms. Kelly Westergaard, Admissions Coordinator, VanderCook College of Music, 3140 South Federal Street, Chicago, Illinois 60616; 800-448-2655 ext. 230, fax: 312-225-5211, e-mail address: kwest@vandercook.edu

Virginia Commonwealth University
Richmond, Virginia

State-supported, coed. Urban campus. Total enrollment: 29,349.
Degrees Bachelor of Arts in the area of classical and jazz; Bachelor of Music in the areas of music education, performance, jazz studies. Majors and concentrations: guitar, jazz, music education, piano/organ, stringed instruments, voice, wind and percussion instruments. Graduate degrees offered: Master of Music in the area of music education. Program accredited by NASM.
Enrollment 302 total; 258 undergraduate, 26 graduate, 18 nonprofessional degree.
Music Student Profile 60% females, 40% males, 30% minorities, 2% international.
Music Faculty 20 total (full-time), 41 total (part-time). 56% of full-time faculty have terminal degrees. Graduate students teach a few undergraduate courses. Undergraduate student–faculty ratio: 10:1.
Student Life Student groups/activities include Ensembles.
Expenses for 2005–2006 Application fee: $30. State resident tuition: $5385 full-time. Nonresident tuition: $17,440 full-time.

College room and board: $7042. College room only: $4102. Room and board charges vary according to board plan. Special program-related fees: $30 per course for music course, $75–$265 per semester for arts major fee, $175–$335 for private music lessons.

Financial Aid Program-specific awards: Jessica McCain Memorial Scholarship for strings/music education students, Jesus Silva Merit Scholarship for guitar students, Sue Durden Scholarship in Music for full-time students, Waverly M. Cole Music Fund for organ students.

Application Procedures Students admitted directly into the professional program freshman year. Deadline for freshmen and transfers: continuous. Required: essay, high school transcript, college transcript(s) for transfer students, minimum 2.0 high school GPA, letter of recommendation, interview, audition, SAT I or ACT test scores (minimum combined SAT I score of 900). Auditions held 5 times and by appointment on campus; recorded music is permissible as a substitute for live auditions when distance is prohibitive and videotaped performances are permissible as a substitute for live auditions when distance is prohibitive.

Web Site http://www.vcumusic.org

Undergraduate Contact Calvin Sutton, Undergraduate Admissions Coordinator, Department of Music, Virginia Commonwealth University, 922 Park Avenue, PO Box 842004, Richmond, Virginia 23284-2004; 804-828-1166, fax: 804-827-0230, e-mail address: music@vcu.edu

Graduate Contact Ms. Linda Johnston, Administrative Coordinator, Department of Music, Virginia Commonwealth University, 922 Park Avenue, PO Box 842004, Richmond, Virginia 23284-2004; 804-828-8008, fax: 804-827-0230, e-mail address: gradmus@vcu.edu

Virginia State University

Petersburg, Virginia

State-supported, coed. Suburban campus. Total enrollment: 5,055. Music program established 1882.

Viterbo University

La Crosse, Wisconsin

Independent Roman Catholic, coed. Suburban campus. Total enrollment: 2,534. Music program established 1944.

Walla Walla College

College Place, Washington

Independent Seventh-day Adventist, coed. Small town campus. Total enrollment: 1,942. Music program established 1892.

Degrees Bachelor of Music in the areas of performance, music education. Majors and concentrations: bass, brass, cello, guitar, harp, harpsichord, music education, organ, percussion, piano, viola, violin, voice, wind instruments. Cross-registration with Whitman College. Program accredited by NASM.

Enrollment 25 total; 13 undergraduate, 12 nonprofessional degree.

Music Student Profile 58% females, 42% males, 3% minorities, 1% international.

Music Faculty 7 undergraduate (full-time), 13 undergraduate (part-time). 57% of full-time faculty have terminal degrees. Graduate students do not teach undergraduate courses.

Student Life Student groups/activities include Music Club, Pi Kappa Lambda.

Expenses for 2006–2007 Application fee: $40. Comprehensive fee: $24,489 includes full-time tuition ($19,725), mandatory fees ($192), and college room and board ($4572). College room only: $2472. Special program-related fees: $216 per credit hour per quarter for applied lessons.

Financial Aid Program-specific awards: 30 music lesson scholarships for program students ($3000), 1 Soper Award for program students ($2000).

Application Procedures Students apply for admission into the professional program by freshman year. Deadline for freshmen

and transfers: September 30. Notification date for freshmen and transfers: continuous. Required: high school transcript, college transcript(s) for transfer students, minimum 2.0 high school GPA, 3 letters of recommendation, audition, SAT I or ACT test scores. Auditions held once and by arrangement on campus; videotaped performances are permissible as a substitute for live auditions when distance is prohibitive.

Web Site http://music.wwc.edu

Undergraduate Contact Matthew James, Chair, Department of Music, Walla Walla College, 204 South College Avenue, College Place, Washington 99324-1198; 509-527-2561, fax: 509-527-2177, e-mail address: music_department@wwc.edu

Wartburg College

Waverly, Iowa

Independent Lutheran, coed. Small town campus. Total enrollment: 1,811. Music program established 1952.

Degrees Bachelor of Arts in the area of church music; Bachelor of Music in the areas of voice, keyboard, instrumental music; Bachelor of Music Education in the areas of vocal music education, instrumental music education; Bachelor of Music Education/Music Therapy. Majors and concentrations: brass, church music, guitar, music education, piano/organ, stringed instruments, voice, wind and percussion instruments. Program accredited by NASM, AMTA.

Enrollment 111 total; 94 undergraduate, 17 nonprofessional degree.

Music Student Profile 80% females, 20% males, 1% minorities, 4% international.

Music Faculty 13 undergraduate (full-time), 16 undergraduate (part-time). 92% of full-time faculty have terminal degrees. Graduate students do not teach undergraduate courses. Undergraduate student–faculty ratio: 10:1.

Student Life Student groups/activities include American Music Therapy Association, Music Educators National Conference, National Association of Teachers of Singing.

Expenses for 2005–2006 Application fee: $20. Comprehensive fee: $26,895 includes full-time tuition ($20,500), mandatory fees ($630), and college room and board ($5765). College room only: $2815. Room and board charges vary according to board plan and housing facility. Special program-related fees: $260 per semester for applied lesson fee.

Financial Aid Program-specific awards: 60 Meistersinger Music Scholarships for talented students ($1000–$4000), 30–50 fellowships for talented students ($400).

Application Procedures Students apply for admission into the professional program by freshman year. Deadline for freshmen and transfers: continuous. Notification date for freshmen and transfers: continuous. Required: high school transcript, college transcript(s) for transfer students, minimum 2.0 high school GPA, SAT I or ACT test scores, theory placement exam. Recommended: minimum 3.0 high school GPA, interview, audition, portfolio. Auditions held 4 times and by appointment on campus; recorded music is permissible as a substitute for live auditions when distance is prohibitive (beyond a 250-mile radius) and videotaped performances are permissible as a substitute for live auditions when distance is prohibitive (beyond a 250-mile radius). Portfolio reviews held on individual basis on campus; the submission of slides may be substituted for portfolios.

Web Site http://www.wartburg.edu//music

Undergraduate Contact Doug Bowman, Director of Admissions, Wartburg College, Whitehouse Business Center 201, 100 Wartburg Boulevard, Waverly, Iowa 50677-0903; 319-352-8264, fax: 319-352-8579.

Washburn University

Topeka, Kansas

City-supported, coed. Urban campus. Total enrollment: 7,261.

Degrees Bachelor of Music in the area of music performance; Bachelor of Music Education. Majors and concentrations: instrumental performance, keyboard, music, music education, piano/organ, stringed instruments, vocal music, voice, wind and percussion instruments. Program accredited by NASM.

Washburn University (continued)

Enrollment 98 total; 68 undergraduate, 30 nonprofessional degree.

Music Student Profile 52% females, 48% males, 10% minorities, 4% international.

Music Faculty 12 undergraduate (full-time), 20 undergraduate (part-time). 80% of full-time faculty have terminal degrees. Graduate students do not teach undergraduate courses. Undergraduate student–faculty ratio: 6:1.

Student Life Student groups/activities include Pep Band, Marching Band.

Expenses for 2005–2006 Application fee: $20. State resident tuition: $4920 full-time. Nonresident tuition: $11,130 full-time. Mandatory fees: $62 full-time. College room and board: $4752. College room only: $2772.

Financial Aid Program-specific awards: 60 music endowments for program majors ($200–$5000).

Application Procedures Students admitted directly into the professional program freshman year. Deadline for freshmen and transfers: continuous. Required: high school transcript, college transcript(s) for transfer students, audition, ACT test score only. Recommended: 2 letters of recommendation, interview. Auditions held 3 times on campus and off campus in Kansas City, KS; Wichita, KS; recorded music is permissible as a substitute for live auditions when distance is prohibitive and videotaped performances are permissible as a substitute for live auditions when distance is prohibitive.

Web Site http://www.washburn.edu/cas

Undergraduate Contact Ann Marie Snook, Scholarship Coordinator, Music Department, Washburn University, 1700 Southwest College, Topeka, Kansas 66621; 785-231-1010 ext. 1520, fax: 785-357-4168, e-mail address: annmarie.snook@washburn.edu

Washington State University
Pullman, Washington

State-supported, coed. Rural campus. Total enrollment: 23,544. Music program established 1904.

Wayland Baptist University
Plainview, Texas

Independent Baptist, coed. Small town campus. Total enrollment: 1,124. Music program established 1908.

Wayne State University
Detroit, Michigan

State-supported, coed. Urban campus. Total enrollment: 33,137. Music program established 1918.

Degrees Bachelor of Arts in the area of music; Bachelor of Music in the areas of jazz studies, music education, music technology, music management, performance. Majors and concentrations: jazz, music, music education, music management, music technology, music theory and composition, piano/organ, stringed instruments, voice, wind and percussion instruments. Graduate degrees offered: Master of Arts in the area of music; Master of Music in the areas of composition/theory, choral conducting, jazz performance, music education, performance. Program accredited by NASM.

Enrollment 323 total; 291 undergraduate, 32 graduate.

Music Student Profile 40% females, 60% males, 30% minorities, 5% international.

Music Faculty 16 total (full-time), 65 total (part-time). 70% of full-time faculty have terminal degrees. Graduate students do not teach undergraduate courses. Undergraduate student–faculty ratio: 20:1.

Student Life Student groups/activities include Delta Omicron, Phi Mu Alpha, Mu Phi Epsilon. Special housing available for music students.

Expenses for 2005–2006 Application fee: $30. State resident tuition: $5682 full-time. Nonresident tuition: $13,014 full-time. Mandatory fees: $757 full-time. Full-time tuition and fees vary according to student level. College room and board: $5350.

Room and board charges vary according to housing facility. Special program-related fees: $15–$75 per hour for studio time.

Financial Aid Program-specific: 34 talent scholarships for program majors ($1150–$2800), 148 activity awards for ensemble participants ($100–$1500), 27 awards for high academic and musical achievement ($500–$4200), 26 full scholarships for program majors ($2200–$5500).

Application Procedures Students admitted directly into the professional program freshman year. Deadline for freshmen and transfers: August 1. Required: high school transcript, college transcript(s) for transfer students, interview, audition, SAT I or ACT test scores (minimum combined SAT I score of 970, minimum composite ACT score of 21), minimum 2.75 high school GPA. Recommended: minimum 3.0 high school GPA, 2 letters of recommendation, portfolio. Auditions held twice and by appointment on campus; recorded music is permissible as a substitute for live auditions when distance is prohibitive and videotaped performances are permissible as a substitute for live auditions when distance is prohibitive.

Web Site http://www.music.wayne.edu

Undergraduate Contact Dr. Norah Duncan IV, Associate Chair, Department of Music, Wayne State University, 1321 Old Main, Detroit, Michigan 48202; 313-577-1795, fax: 313-577-5420.

Graduate Contact Dr. Mary Wischusen, Graduate Director, Department of Music, Wayne State University, 1321 Old Main, Detroit, Michigan 48202; 313-577-1795, fax: 313-577-5420.

Weber State University
Ogden, Utah

State-supported, coed. Urban campus. Total enrollment: 18,142. Music program established 1998.

Degrees Bachelor of Music in the areas of performance, pedagogy; Bachelor of Music Education. Majors and concentrations: music education, pedagogy, performance. Program accredited by NASM.

Enrollment 115 total; 97 undergraduate, 18 nonprofessional degree.

Music Student Profile 70% females, 30% males, 2% minorities, 2% international.

Music Faculty 12 total (full-time), 26 total (part-time). 100% of full-time faculty have terminal degrees. Graduate students do not teach undergraduate courses. Undergraduate student–faculty ratio: 8:1.

Student Life Student groups/activities include Music Educators National Conference, Music Teachers National Association, American String Teachers Association.

Expenses for 2005–2006 Application fee: $30. State resident tuition: $2547 full-time. Nonresident tuition: $9008 full-time. Mandatory fees: $591 full-time. College room and board: $6500. College room only: $3300. Room and board charges vary according to board plan and housing facility. Special program-related fees: $230 per semester for private music lessons (non-majors/minors), $320 per semester for private music lessons (majors/minors).

Financial Aid Program-specific awards: 90 activity waivers for participants in music groups ($1000–$2000), 1 Presser Scholarship for outstanding music students ($4200), 23 Donor Scholarships for music majors ($300–$1500).

Application Procedures Students admitted directly into the professional program freshman year. Deadline for freshmen and transfers: continuous. Required: high school transcript, college transcript(s) for transfer students, audition, ACT test score only. Recommended: minimum 3.0 high school GPA, at least one letter of recommendation. Auditions held twice on campus; recorded music is permissible as a substitute for live auditions when distance is prohibitive and videotaped performances are permissible as a substitute for live auditions when distance is prohibitive.

Web Site http://www.weber.edu

Undergraduate Contact Dr. Michael Palumbo, Chair, Department of Performing Arts, Weber State University, 1905 University Circle, Ogden , Utah 84408-1905; 801-626-6991, fax: 801-626-6811, e-mail address: mpalumbo@weber.edu

Leigh Gerdine College of Fine Arts
Webster University
St. Louis, Missouri

Independent, coed. Suburban campus. Total enrollment: 7,327. Music program established 1925.
Degrees Bachelor of Music in the areas of jazz studies, vocal performance, composition, piano performance, instrumental performance; Bachelor of Music Education in the areas of choral music education, instrumental music education, jazz studies. Majors and concentrations: classical music, composition, guitar, jazz performance, jazz/music technology, music, music education, piano/organ, stringed instruments, voice, wind and percussion instruments. Graduate degrees offered: Master of Music in the areas of piano, vocal performance, composition, music education, church music, orchestral performance. Cross-registration with various colleges in St. Louis. Program accredited by NASM.
Enrollment 155 total; 90 undergraduate, 50 graduate, 15 nonprofessional degree.
Music Student Profile 60% females, 40% males, 10% minorities, 5% international.
Music Faculty 11 total (full-time), 52 total (part-time). 75% of full-time faculty have terminal degrees. Graduate students teach a few undergraduate courses. Undergraduate student–faculty ratio: 10:1.
Student Life Student groups/activities include Music Educators National Conference, International Association for Jazz Education.
Expenses for 2005–2006 Application fee: $25. Comprehensive fee: $23,947 includes full-time tuition ($17,210) and college room and board ($6737). College room only: $3586. Full-time tuition varies according to program. Room and board charges vary according to board plan and housing facility. Special program-related fees: $200–$400 per course for applied music fee.
Financial Aid Program-specific awards: 14 Buder Scholarships for continuing students and transfers ($1000–$6000), 6 jazz awards for upperclassmen ($1000–$2500), 1 Opera Award for undergraduates ($1000), 12 Merit/Audition Awards for entering students ($1500).
Application Procedures Students admitted directly into the professional program freshman year. Deadline for freshmen and transfers: continuous. Required: essay, high school transcript, college transcript(s) for transfer students, 2 letters of recommendation, interview, audition, SAT I or ACT test scores, minimum 2.5 high school GPA, completion of candidacy examination at end of sophomore year. Auditions held 10 times on campus and off campus in Interlochen, MI; Dallas, TX; videotaped performances are permissible as a substitute for live auditions when distance is prohibitive.
Web Site http://www.webster.edu/depts/finearts/music/music.html
Undergraduate Contact Jennifer Andonoff, Auditions Coordinator, Office of Admissions, Webster University, 470 East Lockwood Avenue, St. Louis, Missouri 63119-3194; 314-968-7001, fax: 314-968-7115, e-mail address: andonoff@webster.edu
Graduate Contact Dr. Glen Bauer, Director of Graduate Studies in Music, Department of Music, Webster University, 470 East Lockwood Avenue, St. Louis, Missouri 63119-3194; 314-968-7037, fax: 314-963-6048, e-mail address: bauerga@webster.edu

West Chester University of Pennsylvania
West Chester, Pennsylvania

State-supported, coed. Suburban campus. Total enrollment: 12,988.

Western Carolina University
Cullowhee, North Carolina

State-supported, coed. Rural campus. Total enrollment: 8,665. Music program established 1952.

Degrees Bachelor of Music in the areas of performance, commercial and electronic music; Bachelor of Science in Education. Majors and concentrations: commercial and electronic music, music, music education, music theater, performance. Graduate degrees offered: Master of Music in the area of performance. Program accredited by NASM.
Enrollment 180 total; 126 undergraduate, 9 graduate, 45 nonprofessional degree.
Music Student Profile 41% females, 59% males, 2% minorities.
Music Faculty 21 total (full-time), 7 total (part-time). 86% of full-time faculty have terminal degrees. Graduate students do not teach undergraduate courses. Undergraduate student–faculty ratio: 10:1.
Student Life Student groups/activities include Kappa Kappa Psi, Phi Mu Alpha Sinfonia, Sigma Alpha Iota, Student Music Educators National Conference (NCMEA).
Expenses for 2006–2007 Application fee: $40.
Financial Aid Program-specific awards: 12 Chancellor's Scholarships for program students ($1000), 25 Gulley Music Awards for program students ($500), 15 University Music Friends Awards for program students ($400), 5 academic excellence awards for program students ($1000).
Application Procedures Students admitted directly into the professional program freshman year. Deadline for freshmen and transfers: continuous. Required: high school transcript, college transcript(s) for transfer students, letter of recommendation, audition, SAT I or ACT test scores. Auditions held once and as needed on campus; recorded music is permissible as a substitute for live auditions with prior approval and videotaped performances are permissible as a substitute for live auditions with prior approval.
Web Site http://music.wcu.edu
Undergraduate Contact Dr. Robert Kehrberg, Head, Department of Music, Western Carolina University, Cullowee, North Carolina 28723; 828-227-7242, fax: 828-227-7266, e-mail address: rkehrberg@wcu.edu
Graduate Contact Dr. Robert Kehrberg, Head, Department of Music, Western Carolina University, Cullowee, North Carolina 28723; 828-227-7242, fax: 828-227-7266, e-mail address: rkehrberg@wcu.edu

Western Connecticut State University
Danbury, Connecticut

State-supported, coed. Urban campus. Total enrollment: 5,907. Music program established 1903.

Western Illinois University
Macomb, Illinois

State-supported, coed. Small town campus. Total enrollment: 13,404. Music program established 1901.
Degrees Bachelor of Music. Majors and concentrations: applied music, jazz studies, music business, music education, music performance, music therapy, teacher certification. Graduate degrees offered: Master of Music in the areas of performance, piano pedagogy, music education, theory/composition, conducting, music history/literature. Program accredited by NASM, NCATE.
Enrollment 250 total; 230 undergraduate, 20 graduate.
Music Student Profile 55% females, 45% males, 5% minorities, 2% international.
Music Faculty 36 total (full-time), 6 total (part-time). 90% of full-time faculty have terminal degrees. Graduate students do not teach undergraduate courses. Undergraduate student–faculty ratio: 14:1.
Student Life Student groups/activities include Music Teachers National Association, National Association of Music Business Institutes, Music Educators National Conference. Special housing available for music students.
Expenses for 2005–2006 Application fee: $30. State resident tuition: $4968 full-time. Nonresident tuition: $7452 full-time. Mandatory fees: $1931 full-time. Full-time tuition and fees vary according to location and student level. College room and

Western Illinois University (continued)

board: $6143. College room only: $3693. Room and board charges vary according to housing facility and student level.
Financial Aid Program-specific awards: 100 talent grants for ensemble participants ($2500), 120 endowed scholarships for music majors ($1000).
Application Procedures Students admitted directly into the professional program freshman year. Deadline for freshmen and transfers: continuous. Required: high school transcript, college transcript(s) for transfer students, 3 letters of recommendation, audition, SAT I or ACT test scores, sight-reading, sight-singing, piano placement screening, theory placement screening, pitch matching. Auditions held 4 times on campus; recorded music is permissible as a substitute for live auditions when distance is prohibitive and videotaped performances are permissible as a substitute for live auditions when distance is prohibitive. Portfolio reviews held twice on campus.
Web Site http://www.wiu.edu/music
Undergraduate Contact Mrs. Yvonne Oliver, Auditions Coordinator, School of Music, Western Illinois University, 1 University Circle, Macomb, Illinois 61455; 309-298-1087, fax: 309-298-1968, e-mail address: yl-oliver@wiu.edu
Graduate Contact Dr. Elizabeth Wehrman, Director of Graduate Studies, School of Music, Western Illinois University, 1 University Circle, Macomb, Illinois 61455; 309-298-1544, fax: 309-298-1968, e-mail address: ea-wehrman@wiu.edu

Potter College of Arts, Humanities, and Social Sciences
Western Kentucky University
Bowling Green, Kentucky

State-supported, coed. Suburban campus. Total enrollment: 18,634. Music program established 1948.
Degrees Bachelor of Music in the areas of performance, music education (K-12). Majors and concentrations: guitar, music education, piano, stringed instruments, voice, wind and percussion instruments. Graduate degrees offered: Master of Arts in the area of music education. Program accredited by NASM.
Enrollment 165 total; 100 undergraduate, 25 graduate, 40 nonprofessional degree.
Music Student Profile 55% females, 45% males, 9% minorities, 1% international.
Music Faculty 20 total (full-time), 15 total (part-time). 55% of full-time faculty have terminal degrees. Graduate students do not teach undergraduate courses. Undergraduate student–faculty ratio: 10:1.
Student Life Student groups/activities include music fraternities and sororities, musical production sponsored by Theater Department.
Expenses for 2005–2006 Application fee: $35. State resident tuition: $5316 full-time. Nonresident tuition: $12,732 full-time. Full-time tuition varies according to course load, location, program, and reciprocity agreements. College room and board: $4876. College room only: $2800. Room and board charges vary according to board plan and housing facility. Special program-related fees: $50 per semester for applied lessons.
Financial Aid Program-specific awards: 70 talent grants for program majors ($1500), 18 scholarships for majors and minors ($300–$1500).
Application Procedures Students admitted directly into the professional program freshman year. Required: high school transcript, college transcript(s) for transfer students, minimum 2.0 high school GPA, audition, ACT test score only (minimum composite ACT score of 18). Recommended: minimum 3.0 high school GPA. Auditions held 3 times and by appointment on campus; recorded music is permissible as a substitute for live auditions for out-of-state applicants and videotaped performances are permissible as a substitute for live auditions for out-of-state applicants.
Web Site http://www.wku.edu/Dept/Academic/AHSS/Music/
Undergraduate Contact Office of Admissions, Western Kentucky University, 1 Big Red Way, Bowling Green, Kentucky 42101; 270-745-5422.

Graduate Contact Office of Graduate Studies and Research, Western Kentucky University, 1 Big Red Way, Bowling Green, Kentucky 42101; 800-896-6960, e-mail address: graduate.studies@wku.edu

Western Michigan University
Kalamazoo, Michigan

State-supported, coed. Urban campus. Total enrollment: 26,239. Music program established 1913.
Degrees Bachelor of Music in the areas of performance, music education, jazz studies, music therapy, music composition. Majors and concentrations: classical music, composition, jazz, music, music education, music therapy, piano/organ, stringed instruments, voice, wind and percussion instruments. Graduate degrees offered: Master of Music in the areas of performance, music education, composition, conducting, music therapy. Program accredited by NASM.
Enrollment 413 total; 349 undergraduate, 64 graduate.
Music Student Profile 50% females, 50% males, 9% minorities, 5% international.
Music Faculty 38 total (full-time), 20 total (part-time). 88% of full-time faculty have terminal degrees. Graduate students teach a few undergraduate courses. Undergraduate student–faculty ratio: 12:1.
Student Life Student groups/activities include Collegiate Music Educators National Conference, music fraternities, Student Music Therapists Association.
Expenses for 2005–2006 Application fee: $35. State resident tuition: $5826 full-time. Nonresident tuition: $15,204 full-time. Mandatory fees: $652 full-time. Full-time tuition and fees vary according to course load, location, and student level. College room and board: $6651. College room only: $3518. Room and board charges vary according to board plan. Special program-related fees: $7 per semester for applied music fee, $150 per semester for music major fee.
Financial Aid Program-specific awards: 80 School of Music Scholarships for program majors ($500–$7000).
Application Procedures Students admitted directly into the professional program freshman year. Deadline for freshmen and transfers: continuous. Required: high school transcript, college transcript(s) for transfer students, audition, SAT I or ACT test scores. Recommended: minimum 3.0 high school GPA, letter of recommendation. Auditions held 4 times on campus; recorded music is permissible as a substitute for live auditions when distance is prohibitive and videotaped performances are permissible as a substitute for live auditions when distance is prohibitive.
Web Site http://www.wmich.edu/music
Undergraduate Contact Ms. Margaret J. Hamilton, Assistant Director, School of Music, Western Michigan University, 1903 West Michigan Avenue, Kalamazoo, Michigan 49008-5434; 269-387-4672, fax: 269-387-1113, e-mail address: margaret.hamilton@wmich.edu
Graduate Contact Dr. Michael L. Miller, Coordinator of Graduate Studies, School of Music, Western Michigan University, 1903 West Michigan Avenue, Kalamazoo, Michigan 49008-5434; 269-387-4672, fax: 269-387-1113, e-mail address: music_grad@wmich.edu

Western State College of Colorado
Gunnison, Colorado

State-supported, coed. Small town campus. Total enrollment: 2,177. Music program established 1911.
Degrees Bachelor of Arts in the area of music (music education emphasis). Majors and concentrations: music education. Program accredited by NASM.
Enrollment 36 total; 16 undergraduate, 20 nonprofessional degree.
Music Student Profile 44% females, 56% males, 3% minorities.
Music Faculty 5 undergraduate (full-time), 4 undergraduate (part-time). 60% of full-time faculty have terminal degrees. Graduate students do not teach undergraduate courses. Undergraduate student–faculty ratio: 2:1.

Student Life Student groups/activities include choir, symphony band, orchestra.

Expenses for 2006–2007 Application fee: $30. State resident tuition: $2,411 full-time. Nonresident tuition: $10,968 full-time. Mandatory fees: $796 full-time. College room and board: $6976. College room only: $3794. Special program-related fees: $30 per semester credit for hardware/software upgrades, $50 per semester credit for maintenance and repair of instruments.

Application Procedures Students admitted directly into the professional program freshman year. Deadline for freshmen and transfers: continuous. Required: high school transcript, college transcript(s) for transfer students, minimum 2.0 high school GPA, letter of recommendation, SAT I or ACT test scores. Recommended: essay, minimum 3.0 high school GPA, interview, video, audition. Auditions held 5 times and by arrangement on campus; recorded music is permissible as a substitute for live auditions and videotaped performances are permissible as a substitute for live auditions.

Web Site http://www.western.edu/music

Undergraduate Contact Dr. Martha Violett, Director, Music Program, Department of Art and Music, Western State College of Colorado, 101 Quigley Hall, Gunnison, Colorado 81231; 970-943-3054, fax: 970-943-2329, e-mail address: mviolett@western.edu

Western Washington University

Bellingham, Washington

State-supported, coed. Small town campus. Total enrollment: 14,247. Music program established 1947.

Rider University

Westminster Choir College of Rider University

Princeton, New Jersey

Independent, coed. Small town campus. Music program established 1926.

Degrees Bachelor of Arts in the area of music; Bachelor of Music in the areas of sacred music, music education, theory and composition, organ performance, voice performance, music theater, piano. Majors and concentrations: music education, music theater, music theory and composition, organ performance, piano, sacred music, voice performance. Graduate degrees offered: Master of Arts in the area of teaching (music); Master of Music in the areas of sacred music, music education, choral conducting, piano pedagogy and performance, piano accompanying and coaching, composition, organ performance, voice pedagogy and performance, piano performance; Master of Music Education in the area of music education; Master of Voice Pedagogy in the area of voice pedagogy. Cross-registration with Princeton University, Princeton Ballet School, Rider University. Program accredited by NASM, NCATE.

Enrollment 454 total; 335 undergraduate, 119 graduate.

Music Student Profile 65% females, 35% males, 18% minorities, 9% international.

Music Faculty 35 total (full-time), 66 total (part-time). 83% of full-time faculty have terminal degrees. Graduate students do not teach undergraduate courses. Undergraduate student–faculty ratio: 7:1.

Student Life Student groups/activities include Music Teachers National Association, Music Educators National Conference, American Choral Directors Association, National Association of Teachers of Singing. Special housing available for music students.

Expenses for 2005–2006 Application fee: $45. One-time mandatory fee: $560. Comprehensive fee: $32,670 includes full-time tuition ($22,910), mandatory fees ($560), and college room and board ($9200). College room only: $4380. Room and board charges vary according to board plan. Special program-related fees: $125 per semester for senior student teaching.

Financial Aid Program-specific awards: 118 Rider Grant for undergraduates ($4229), 121 merit scholarships for undergraduates ($8007), 16 Leadership Scholarship for proven leaders

($2000), 3 Music Theatre Award for music theatre majors ($10,000), 110 endowed scholarships for qualifying students ($2811), 57 Recognition Awards for undergraduates ($3965).

Application Procedures Required: essay, high school transcript, college transcript(s) for transfer students, 2 letters of recommendation, audition, SAT I or ACT test scores, repertoire list, TOEFL score and certification of finances (international students only), internal music exam, interview for BA, music education, and sacred music applicants. Recommended: minimum 3.0 high school GPA, interview.

Web Site http://westminster.rider.edu

Contact Ms. Katherine Shields, Senior Associate Director of Admission, Office of Admissions, Westminster Choir College of Rider University, 101 Walnut Lane, Princeton, New Jersey 08540-3899; 609-921-7100 ext. 8103, fax: 609-921-2538, e-mail address: kshields@rider.edu

More About the School

Home of the famous Westminster Symphonic Choir, Westminster Choir College of Rider University integrates music study with professional choral performances conducted in concert with major symphony orchestras. Westminster Choir College offers outstanding music training in a stimulating yet friendly learning environment. Westminster appeals to students who seek excellent musical training and substantial performance experience to become well-rounded career musicians. The College attracts talented musicians from around the world for superb training and practical experience as performers, composers, conductors, teachers, and church musicians.

All Westminster students perform in professional concerts each year. The 200-voice Westminster Symphonic Choir sings and records on a regular basis with the New York Philharmonic under world-class conductors in Lincoln Center and Carnegie Hall. The Westminster Symphonic Choir has performed and recorded with conductors, including Bernstein, Ormandy, Masur, Toscanini, Walter, Leinsdorf, Mehta, Ozawa, and Muti. Students may also perform in seven additional choirs, including the Westminster Choir (Choir-in-Residence at the Spoleto Festival U.S.A.), the Westminster Kantori, Chapel Choir, Westminster Concert Bell Choir, Jubilee Singers (performing music of the African-American heritage), Williamson Voices, and Schola Cantorum. The Westminster choirs tour nationally and internationally. Westminster also offers students opportunities to perform in ensembles with pianists, organists, and the Westminster Conservatory Community Orchestra. Young composers' works are showcased on campus and in community concerts.

Westminster's scenic 23-acre campus, ideally situated in picturesque Princeton within walking distance of Princeton's Palmer Square, is an outstanding atmosphere for living, performing, and learning. Westminster's campus centers on elegant Williamson Hall in the original Georgian quadrangle, providing an intimate setting for recitals and chamber ensembles. Stately Bristol Chapel, housing a 50-rank Aeolian-Skinner organ, a 16-rank Fisk organ, a 14-rank Noack organ, and two 9-foot grand pianos, is a large recital facility for student, faculty, and guest performers. Nestled among the trees, the Playhouse/Opera Theatre offers a stage and two Steinway grand pianos. Beyond Bristol Chapel, Scheide Recital Hall showcases a 44-rank Casavant organ.

Westminster offers practice rooms in each of its three residence halls and has more than 120 pianos and twenty-one pipe organs, including practice organs by Flentrop, Holtkamp, Schantz, Moller, and Noack. The Yvonne Theater, located at Rider University's Lawrenceville, New Jersey, campus is also home to performance facilities.

The Talbott Library/Learning Center houses 65,000 books, scores, periodicals, and microforms. A single-copy reference file of 45,000 individual octavos is the largest collection of its type in the United States. The Performance Collection contains 5,400 titles in multiple copies for student study, class assignments, student teaching, and church choirs and 80,000 choral music reference files. Special collections include the Erik Routley

Westminster Choir College of Rider University (continued)

Collections of Books and Hymnals, D. DeWitt Wasson Reference Collection of Organ Music, and the Organ Historical Society's American Organ Archives. Voice students use a state-of-the-art voice laboratory, an invaluable resource for vocal pedagogy, for the scientific study of the vocal mechanism and singing. The Piano Department has a fully equipped piano laboratory in which an entire class of students can be instructed simultaneously. The Media Center contains more than 9,000 recordings and videos, with facilities for student playback. The Music Education Resource Collection contains 1,000 textbooks, recordings, film-strips, charts, and resource materials in addition to listening equipment and an electronic piano. The library also houses a state-of-the-art electronic music computer laboratory with fifteen Kurzweil synthesizers, sixteen Macintosh Power PCs running Finale and Performer, a multimedia center with CD-ROM and laser disc, computers customized for music theory and sight-singing programs, and 100 music fundamental programs.

Princeton, 40 miles from New York and Philadelphia, is within easy reach by train or bus, offering students a wealth of educational, cultural, and recreational activities. Princeton University, a short walk from Westminster, offers lectures, art exhibits, recitals, and concerts. Westminster students may enroll in courses at Princeton University and use the University's athletic and recreational facilities. Near Westminster, the Tony Award–winning McCarter Theatre stages several major productions each year and hosts guest artists and performers.

Westminster College
New Wilmington, Pennsylvania

Independent, coed. Small town campus. Total enrollment: 1,593. Music program established 1947.
Degrees Bachelor of Music. Majors and concentrations: music education, performance, sacred music. Program accredited by NASM.
Enrollment 70 total; 42 undergraduate, 28 nonprofessional degree.
Music Student Profile 64% females, 36% males.
Music Faculty 7 undergraduate (full-time), 19 undergraduate (part-time). 86% of full-time faculty have terminal degrees. Graduate students do not teach undergraduate courses.
Student Life Student groups/activities include Music Educators National Conference, Mu Phi Epsilon, American Choral Directors Association.
Expenses for 2006–2007 Application fee: $35. Comprehensive fee: $31,395 includes full-time tuition ($23,220), mandatory fees ($1105), and college room and board ($7070).
Financial Aid Program-specific awards: music scholarships for program majors ($800–$2500).
Application Procedures Students admitted directly into the professional program freshman year. Deadline for freshmen and transfers: May 1. Required: essay, high school transcript, college transcript(s) for transfer students, minimum 2.0 high school GPA, 2 letters of recommendation, SAT I or ACT test scores, audition on primary instrument or voice, sight singing, rhythmic reading. Recommended: minimum 3.0 high school GPA, interview. Auditions held 8 times on campus; recorded music is permissible as a substitute for live auditions when distance is prohibitive and videotaped performances are permissible as a substitute for live auditions when distance is prohibitive.
Web Site http://www.westminster.edu/acad/musi/
Undergraduate Contact Doug Swartz, Director, Admissions, Westminster College, 319 South Market Street, New Wilmington, Pennsylvania 16172-0001; 724-946-7100, fax: 724-946-6171.

Sybil B. Harrington College of Fine Arts and Humanities
West Texas A&M University
Canyon, Texas

State-supported, coed. Small town campus. Total enrollment: 8,667. Music program established 1916.

Degrees Bachelor of Music in the areas of performance, music therapy, composition, music with elective studies in business, music (all-level certification). Majors and concentrations: composition, music, piano/organ, stringed instruments, voice, wind and percussion instruments. Graduate degrees offered: Master of Arts in the area of music; Master of Music in the area of performance. Program accredited by NASM.
Enrollment 197 total; 187 undergraduate, 10 graduate.
Music Student Profile 50% females, 50% males, 10% minorities, 2% international.
Music Faculty 21 total (full-time), 8 total (part-time). 50% of full-time faculty have terminal degrees. Graduate students do not teach undergraduate courses. Undergraduate student–faculty ratio: 20:1.
Expenses for 2005–2006 Application fee: $25. State resident tuition: $2760 full-time. Nonresident tuition: $11,040 full-time. Mandatory fees: $996 full-time. College room and board: $4916. College room only: $2300. Special program-related fees: $60 per semester for applied music fee.
Financial Aid Program-specific awards available.
Application Procedures Students admitted directly into the professional program freshman year. Deadline for freshmen and transfers: February 1. Required: high school transcript, college transcript(s) for transfer students, 2 letters of recommendation, audition, SAT I or ACT test scores. Auditions held 3 times on campus; recorded music is permissible as a substitute for live auditions if a campus visit is impossible and videotaped performances are permissible as a substitute for live auditions if a campus visit is impossible.
Web Site http://www.wtamu.edu/academic/fah/mus
Undergraduate Contact Donna Flatt, Secretary, Department of Music and Dance, West Texas A&M University, WTAMU Box 60879, Canyon, Texas 79016; 806-651-2840, fax: 806-651-2958, e-mail address: tdubois@mail.wtamu.edu
Graduate Contact Dr. Douglas Morrison, Assistant Professor, Department of Music and Dance, West Texas A&M University, WTAMU Box 60879, Canyon, Texas 79016; 806-651-2830, fax: 806-651-2958.

West Virginia University
Morgantown, West Virginia

State-supported, coed. Small town campus. Total enrollment: 26,051. Music program established 1897.
Degrees Bachelor of Music in the areas of music history, composition, performance, music education. Majors and concentrations: brass, classical music, composition, jazz, music, music education, music history, music performance, piano/organ, stringed instruments, voice, wind and percussion instruments. Graduate degrees offered: Master of Music in the areas of performance, composition, music history, music education. Doctor of Musical Arts in the areas of piano, voice, organ, percussion/world music, orchestral instruments; Doctor of Philosophy in the area of music education. Program accredited by NASM.
Enrollment 340 total; 260 undergraduate, 80 graduate.
Music Student Profile 49% females, 51% males, 4% minorities, 8% international.
Music Faculty 34 total (full-time), 14 total (part-time). 95% of full-time faculty have terminal degrees. Graduate students teach a few undergraduate courses. Undergraduate student–faculty ratio: 8:1.
Student Life Student groups/activities include Music Educators National Conference, Music Teachers National Association. Special housing available for music students.
Expenses for 2005–2006 Application fee: $25. State resident tuition: $4164 full-time. Nonresident tuition: $12,874 full-time. Full-time tuition varies according to location, program, and reciprocity agreements. College room and board: $6342. College room only: $3348. Room and board charges vary according to board plan, housing facility, and location. Special program-related fees: $15 per semester for practice room fee, $150 per semester for music lessons.
Financial Aid Program-specific awards: 1–2 Carolyn and Clifford Brown Music Alumni Scholarships for music majors ($1000), 1 Frank E. and Margaret S. Lorince Scholarship for music majors

($2000), 6 Music Faculty Recognition Scholarships for music majors ($1000), 2–3 Eleanor Tucker Donley Memorial Scholarships for music majors ($1000), 12 Ida Cope Tait Music Scholarships for music majors ($500–$1000), 2 Edith Roberts Williams Music Scholarships for music majors ($1000), 5 Morgantown Music Club Scholarships for music majors ($500), 14 Loyalty Permanent Endowments Awards for music majors ($500–$1000), 56 fine arts scholarships for music majors, 20 performing arts scholarships for music majors ($1000).

Application Procedures Students admitted directly into the professional program freshman year. Deadline for freshmen and transfers: continuous. Notification date for freshmen and transfers: August 1. Required: high school transcript, college transcript(s) for transfer students, minimum 2.0 high school GPA, 2 letters of recommendation, audition, SAT I or ACT test scores. Recommended: interview. Auditions held 3 times and by appointment on campus; recorded music is permissible as a substitute for live auditions when distance is prohibitive and videotaped performances are permissible as a substitute for live auditions when distance is prohibitive.

Web Site http://www.wvu.edu/~music

Undergraduate Contact Dr. Peter Kolkay, Director, Undergraduate Admissions, Music Department, West Virginia University, College of Creative Arts, PO Box 6111, Morgantown, West Virginia 26506-6111; 304-293-5511 ext. 3151, fax: 304-293-7491, e-mail address: peter.kolkay@mail.wvu.edu

Graduate Contact Dr. Keith Jackson, Director of Graduate Studies, Music Department, West Virginia University, College of Creative Arts, PO Box 6111, Morgantown, West Virginia 26506-6111; 304-293-5511 ext. 3224, fax: 304-293-7491, e-mail address: keith.jackson@mail.wvu.edu

West Virginia Wesleyan College

Buckhannon, West Virginia

Independent, coed. Small town campus. Total enrollment: 1,408. Music program established 1937.

Degrees Bachelor of Music Education. Majors and concentrations: music education. Program accredited by NASM.

Enrollment 67 total; all undergraduate.

Music Student Profile 50% females, 50% males, 10% minorities, 3% international.

Music Faculty 6 undergraduate (full-time), 11 undergraduate (part-time). 83% of full-time faculty have terminal degrees. Graduate students do not teach undergraduate courses. Undergraduate student–faculty ratio: 10:1.

Student Life Student groups/activities include Music Educators National Conference Student Chapter, Sigma Alpha Iota/Phi Mu Alpha Sinfonia, Music Teachers National Association.

Expenses for 2005–2006 Application fee: $35. Comprehensive fee: $26,800 includes full-time tuition ($20,250), mandatory fees ($1000), and college room and board ($5550). Full-time tuition and fees vary according to course load. Room and board charges vary according to board plan and housing facility.

Financial Aid Program-specific awards: 25 music scholarships for incoming students ($1000–$6000), 25 Performing Arts Awards for incoming students ($1000–$6000).

Application Procedures Students apply for admission into the professional program by freshman year. Deadline for freshmen and transfers: continuous. Required: essay, high school transcript, college transcript(s) for transfer students, minimum 2.0 high school GPA, letter of recommendation, audition. Recommended: minimum 3.0 high school GPA, interview, video, SAT I or ACT test scores. Auditions held 6 times on campus and off campus in Washington, DC; recorded music is permissible as a substitute for live auditions if scheduling is difficult and videotaped performances are permissible as a substitute for live auditions if scheduling is difficult.

Web Site http://www.wvwc.edu

Undergraduate Contact Mr. Robert N. Skinner, Director of Admission, West Virginia Wesleyan College, 59 College Avenue, Buckhannon, West Virginia 26201; 800-722-9933, fax: 304-473-8108.

Wheaton Conservatory of Music
Wheaton College

Wheaton, Illinois

Independent nondenominational, coed. Suburban campus. Total enrollment: 2,932. Music program established 1882.

Degrees Bachelor of Music in the areas of performance, composition, music history/literature, elective studies; Bachelor of Music Education. Majors and concentrations: composition, media music studies, music education, music history and literature, pedagogy, piano/organ, stringed instruments, voice, wind and percussion instruments. Program accredited by NASM.

Enrollment 200 total; 190 undergraduate, 10 nonprofessional degree.

Music Student Profile 60% females, 40% males, 9% minorities, 10% international.

Music Faculty 20 undergraduate (full-time), 31 undergraduate (part-time). 100% of full-time faculty have terminal degrees. Graduate students do not teach undergraduate courses. Undergraduate student–faculty ratio: 7:1.

Student Life Student groups/activities include Music Educators National Conference, American Guild of Organists, National Association of Teachers of Singing.

Expenses for 2005–2006 Application fee: $50. Comprehensive fee: $27,700 includes full-time tuition ($21,100) and college room and board ($6600). College room only: $3900. Room and board charges vary according to board plan and housing facility. Special program-related fees: $25 per credit hour for music course fee, $125 per semester for ensemble fee, $245–$485 per semester for performance course.

Financial Aid Program-specific awards: 2 Cording Awards for those demonstrating talent ($2000), 8 Presidential Honor Awards for those demonstrating talent ($3000), 8 Special Achievement Awards for those demonstrating talent ($1000–$4000), 2 Schulteiss Awards for those demonstrating talent ($2000).

Application Procedures Students admitted directly into the professional program freshman year. Deadline for freshmen: February 15; transfers: March 1. Notification date for freshmen and transfers: April 1. Required: essay, high school transcript, college transcript(s) for transfer students, 4 letters of recommendation, audition, SAT I or ACT test scores, portfolio for composition applicants. Recommended: minimum 3.0 high school GPA, interview. Auditions held 6 times on campus; recorded music is permissible as a substitute for live auditions when distance is prohibitive and videotaped performances are permissible as a substitute for live auditions when distance is prohibitive.

Web Site http://www.wheaton.edu/Conservatory/index.html

Undergraduate Contact Ms. Debbie Rodgers, Admissions Counselor, Wheaton Conservatory of Music, Wheaton College, 501 East College Avenue, Wheaton, Illinois 60187; 800-222-2419 ext. 3, fax: 630-752-5341, e-mail address: music@wheaton.edu

More About the Conservatory

Wheaton College, founded in 1860, is an independent, nondenominational, Christian liberal arts college. The Conservatory of Music, established in 1882, exists to produce professional musicians equipped to pursue varied careers in music and the arts.

Wheaton's historic campus is located 25 miles west of Chicago. The city is only 45 minutes by train or car. Among Chicago's many cultural attractions are the Lyric Opera of Chicago, Chicago Symphony Orchestra, many theaters, art museums, and jazz and chamber music performances. Wheaton is a residential college with shopping, trains, and churches all within walking distance. Representing more than forty countries and all fifty states, 220 Conservatory students, 2,219 undergraduate liberal arts students, and 458 graduate students form the Wheaton College Community.

Program Facilities Wheaton's primary music facility is McAlister Hall, which houses teaching studios and practice rooms. Performances take place in Edman Memorial Chapel, with seating for 2,350; Pierce Chapel, with seating for 900; and the 500-seat Barrows Auditorium. The state-of-the-art Music Technol-

Wheaton College (continued)

ogy Lab features sixteen Macintosh workstations for sound synthesis and digital recording. There are more than eighty pianos on campus, including six concert grands. There are six pipe organs, including a new 50-stop, 70-rank, four-manual, dual-console mechanical action pipe organ built in 2001 by the Casavant Organ Company of Canada. The music library holds more than 28,000 items, including recordings, complete scores, and reference books.

Faculty, Alumni, and Visiting Artists One hundred percent of full-time Conservatory faculty members have doctoral degrees. Faculty artists are in demand as performers and lecturers across the nation and abroad. Choral conductor Mary Hopper led the Wheaton College Women's Chorale in its recent appearance at the American Choral Directors Association national convention in New York City. Baritone Gerard Sundberg performed recently in the United Kingdom and France, as well as regularly with the Atlanta Symphony Orchestra. Pianist William Phemister participated in an arts festival in North Korea. Violinist Lee Joiner led an international roster of faculty artists for the International Improvisation Institute—Music on the Fly in July 2003.

Alumni pursue varied careers in opera (Dr. Stephen Morscheck, Sylvia McNair and Wendy White), jazz (Deanna Witkowski), orchestral conducting (John Nelson, Ensemble Orchestral de Paris) and orchestral performance (Douglas Yeo, bass trombonist, Boston Symphony Orchestra and Eric Carlson, trombonist, Philadelphia Orchestra). In addition, alumni actively and successfully pursue careers in schools, churches, and contemporary music all over the world.

Recent visiting artists for performances and master classes include world-renowned musicians, such as Hungarian National Philharmonic Orchestra, Canadian Brass (2003), tenor Ben Heppner (2001 and 2002), Turtle Island String Quartet, Emerson String Quartet (2002), and soprano Kathleen Battle (2001).

Student Performance Opportunities Wheaton offers ten Conservatory Music Ensembles. Vocal and choral ensembles include Concert Choir, Men's Glee Club, Opera Music Theater, West Suburban Choral Union, and Women's Chorale. Instrumental ensembles include Jazz Ensemble, Pep Band, Percussion Ensemble, Symphony Orchestra, and Symphonic Band. In addition, chamber ensembles and soloists rehearse and perform regularly on campus, in the local community, and in Chicago. Large-scale productions, touring, and recording projects are a

regular part of the Conservatory schedule. Four annual competitions, the Concerto Competition (winning soloist performs with the Symphony Orchestra), the Chamber Music Competition, the Nordin Vocal Competition, and the Foster String Competition afford students additional opportunities to perform.

Special Programs Off-campus study opportunities include Arts in London, a four-week program offered on alternate years in May. Course selection may include but is not limited to art survey, English cathedral music, musical theater, pop Shakespeare, songwriting, and world music. The International Improvisation Institute is held every July at Wheaton's Black Hills, South Dakota Campus. Committed to teaching and developing the skill of improvisation, this weeklong program attracts many fine faculty artists and performers and is open to all musicians (high school juniors and above). Wheaton's Music Ensembles tour annually both nationally and regionally. International touring opportunities exist as well, including Music and Ministry in the Great Cities of Europe, a three-week trip offered on alternate years.

Wheaton Conservatory of Music
See Wheaton College

Wilfrid Laurier University
Waterloo, Ontario, Canada

Province-supported, coed. Urban campus. Total enrollment: 12,296 (2004). Music program established 1975.

Willamette University
Salem, Oregon

Independent United Methodist, coed. Urban campus. Total enrollment: 2,642. Music program established 1842.

Winters School of Music
William Carey College
Hattiesburg, Mississippi

Independent Southern Baptist, coed. Small town campus. Total enrollment: 2,758. Music program established 1966.

William Paterson University of New Jersey
Wayne, New Jersey

State-supported, coed. Suburban campus. Total enrollment: 10,970.

Wingate University
Wingate, North Carolina

Independent Baptist, coed. Small town campus. Total enrollment: 1,632. Music program established 1977.

Winters School of Music
See William Carey College

Winthrop University
Rock Hill, South Carolina

State-supported, coed. Suburban campus. Total enrollment: 6,480. Music program established 1886.

Wittenberg University
Springfield, Ohio

Independent, coed. Suburban campus. Total enrollment: 2,093. Music program established 1931.

Degrees Bachelor of Music in the areas of performance, church music, composition; Bachelor of Music Education in the areas of choral music education, instrumental music education. Majors and concentrations: church music, composition, music education, piano/organ, stringed instruments, voice, wind and percussion instruments. Cross-registration with Southwestern Ohio Consortium for Higher Education. Program accredited by NASM.

Enrollment 37 total; 23 undergraduate, 14 nonprofessional degree.

Music Student Profile 60% females, 40% males, 3% minorities, 4% international.

Music Faculty 10 undergraduate (full-time), 19 undergraduate (part-time). 100% of full-time faculty have terminal degrees. Graduate students do not teach undergraduate courses. Undergraduate student–faculty ratio: 14:1.

Student Life Student groups/activities include Ohio Collegiate Music Education Association, Wittenberg Series Events.

Expenses for 2006–2007 Application fee: $40. Comprehensive fee: $36,778 includes full-time tuition ($29,080), mandatory fees ($200), and college room and board ($7498). College room only: $3890.

Financial Aid Program-specific awards: 25 music alumni scholarships for incoming students ($540–$12,400), 10 Alida Atwell Smith Scholarships for those demonstrating need and talent ($3500), 10 Jan Bender Scholarships for those demonstrating need and talent ($3500), 10 Pavlik Scholarships for those demonstrating need and talent ($3500), 10 Sara Krieg Scholarships for those demonstrating need and talent ($600–$5000).

Application Procedures Students apply for admission into the professional program by freshman year. Deadline for freshmen and transfers: continuous. Notification date for freshmen: April 11; transfers: August 1. Required: essay, high school transcript, college transcript(s) for transfer students, minimum 2.0 high school GPA, 2 letters of recommendation, audition, SAT I or ACT test scores. Recommended: interview. Auditions held 3 times and by appointment on campus; recorded music is permissible as a substitute for live auditions when distance is prohibitive and videotaped performances are permissible as a substitute for live auditions when distance is prohibitive.

Web Site http://www4.wittenberg.edu/academics/music

Undergraduate Contact Mr. Evan Lipp, Associate Vice President, Enrollment Management, Wittenberg University, PO Box 720, Springfield, Ohio 45501-0720; 937-327-6314, fax: 937-327-6340, e-mail address: elipp@wittenberg.edu

Wright State University
Dayton, Ohio

State-supported, coed. Suburban campus. Total enrollment: 16,207. Music program established 1966.

Degrees Bachelor of Music in the areas of performance, music history and literature, music education. Majors and concentrations: music education, music history and literature, piano/organ, stringed instruments, voice, wind and percussion instruments. Graduate degrees offered: Master of Humanities in the area of music; Master of Music in the areas of music education, performance. Cross-registration with Southern Ohio Consortium of Higher Education. Program accredited by NASM.

Enrollment 200 total; 130 undergraduate, 20 graduate, 50 nonprofessional degree.

Music Student Profile 60% females, 40% males, 15% minorities, 5% international.

Music Faculty 16 total (full-time), 24 total (part-time). 71% of full-time faculty have terminal degrees. Graduate students teach a few undergraduate courses. Undergraduate student–faculty ratio: 3:1.

Student Life Student groups/activities include Collegiate Music Educators National Conference, American Choral Directors Association.

Expenses for 2006–2007 Application fee: $30. State resident tuition: $7278 full-time. Nonresident tuition: $14,004 full-time.

College room and board: $7180. Special program-related fees: $15 for instrument rental fee, $50 for junior, senior recital fee, $150–$300 per quarter for applied music lesson fee.

Financial Aid Program-specific awards: 5 string scholarships for string players ($1500), 45 music scholarships for program majors ($1500), 25 Arts Gala Scholarships for music majors from the Miami Valley ($1500).

Application Procedures Students admitted directly into the professional program freshman year. Deadline for freshmen and transfers: continuous. Required: essay, high school transcript, college transcript(s) for transfer students, minimum 2.0 high school GPA, 3 letters of recommendation, audition, SAT I or ACT test scores. Auditions held 4 times on campus; recorded music is permissible as a substitute for live auditions when distance is prohibitive and videotaped performances are permissible as a substitute for live auditions when distance is prohibitive.

Web Site http://www.wright.edu/music

Undergraduate Contact Victoria Chadbourne, Promotions and Outreach Coordinator, Department of Music, Wright State University, 3640 Colonel Glenn Highway, Dayton, Ohio 45435; 937-775-2787, fax: 937-775-3786, e-mail address: music@wright.edu

Graduate Contact Dr. Hank Dahlman, Graduate Studies in Music, Department of Music, Wright State University, 3640 Colonel Glenn Highway, Dayton, Ohio 45435; 937-775-3721, fax: 937-775-3786, e-mail address: hank.dahlman@wright.edu

Xavier University of Louisiana
New Orleans, Louisiana

Independent Roman Catholic, coed. Urban campus. Total enrollment: 4,121. Music program established 1925.

York University
Toronto, Ontario, Canada

Province-supported, coed. Urban campus. Total enrollment: 49,496. Music program established 1969.

Degrees Bachelor of Fine Arts in the areas of music performance, composition. Majors and concentrations: classical performance, composition, electronic music, improvisation, jazz, world music.

Enrollment 454 total; 352 undergraduate, 102 nonprofessional degree.

Music Student Profile 50% females, 50% males, 1% international.

Music Faculty 23 total (full-time), 48 total (part-time). 94% of full-time faculty have terminal degrees. Graduate students teach a few undergraduate courses. Undergraduate student–faculty ratio: 9:1.

Student Life Student groups/activities include York Music Students Association, Creative Arts Students Association.

Expenses for 2005–2006 Application fee: $90 Canadian dollars. Comprehensive fee: $10,981 includes full-time tuition ($4862) and college room and board ($6119). College room only: $3719. Full-time tuition varies according to course load, degree level, and program. Room and board charges vary according to board plan and housing facility. International student tuition: $14,862 full-time. Special program-related fees: $10–$40 per course for material fees.

Financial Aid Program-specific awards: 3 talent awards for applicants with outstanding auditions ($1000), 5 Harry Rowe Bursaries for demonstrated achievement or potential in artistic or scholarly work ($2000), 1 Oscar Peterson Scholarship for outstanding jazz performers ($2000), 1 Ella Fitzgerald Award for Jazz Performances for those demonstrating artistic excellence ($3000), 1 Sorbara Award for outstanding achievement in composition ($2500), 2 Nirvan Bhavan Foundation Scholarships for excellence in Indian studies ($3000), 21 IMASCO Performing Arts Awards for 2nd- or 3rd-year students demonstrating outstanding ability and sound academic standing ($3000), 1 Douglas Menzie Phillips Jazz Scholarship for outstanding achievement in jazz performance ($2500), 1 Nancy Scoular Underhill Piano Award for 2nd-year pianists who demonstrate exceptional promise/ability ($1000).

Application Procedures Students admitted directly into the professional program freshman year. Deadline for freshmen and

York University (continued)

transfers: February 1. Notification date for freshmen: June 16; transfers: continuous. Required: essay, high school transcript, college transcript(s) for transfer students, minimum 3.0 high school GPA, SAT I, ACT or Canadian equivalent, recording of performance, written critiques of music recordings (provided), taped audition. Recommended: 2 letters of recommendation. Auditions held on campus; recorded music is permissible as a substitute for live auditions.

Web Site http://www.finearts.yorku.ca/music/index.htm

Undergraduate Contact Pamela Persaud, Manager, Student and Academic Services, York University, 4700 Keele Street, 201 T Goldfarb Centre of Fine Arts, Toronto, Ontario M3J 1P3, Canada; 416-736-5135, fax: 416-736-5447, e-mail address: ask_ffa@yorku.ca

Dana School of Music
Youngstown State University
Youngstown, Ohio

State-supported, coed. Urban campus. Total enrollment: 12,809. Music program established 1941.

Degrees Bachelor of Music in the areas of performance, music education, applied music, composition, jazz studies. Majors and concentrations: classical music, jazz, music education, music theory and composition, piano/organ, stringed instruments, voice, wind and percussion instruments. Graduate degrees offered: Master of Music in the areas of performance, music education, music theory and composition, music history and literature, jazz studies. Program accredited by NASM.

Enrollment 310 total; 275 undergraduate, 35 graduate.

Music Student Profile 50% females, 50% males, 4% minorities, 1% international.

Music Faculty 12 undergraduate (full-time), 24 undergraduate (part-time), 13 graduate (full-time). 70% of full-time faculty have terminal degrees. Graduate students teach a few undergraduate courses. Undergraduate student–faculty ratio: 9:1.

Student Life Student groups/activities include New Music Society, Jazz Society, Ohio Collegiate Music Education Association.

Expenses for 2005–2006 Application fee: $30. State resident tuition: $6104 full-time. Nonresident tuition: $11,312 full-time. Mandatory fees: $229 full-time. Full-time tuition and fees vary according to course load. College room and board: $6280. Room and board charges vary according to board plan and housing facility. Special program-related fees: $55 per credit hour for applied music fee.

Financial Aid Program-specific awards: 50 Youngstown State University Foundation Music Awards for program students ($800), 2 University Grants-in-Aid for program students ($1800), 2 Monday Musical Awards for program students ($1000), 10 Showcase Awards for program students ($600), 12 named music scholarships for program students ($1000).

Application Procedures Students admitted directly into the professional program freshman year. Deadline for freshmen and transfers: continuous. Required: high school transcript, college transcript(s) for transfer students, letter of recommendation, audition, SAT I or ACT test scores. Recommended: minimum 3.0 high school GPA, interview. Auditions held 4 times on campus; recorded music is permissible as a substitute for live auditions when distance is prohibitive and videotaped performances are permissible as a substitute for live auditions when distance is prohibitive.

Web Site http://www.fpa.ysu.edu/music/index.html

Undergraduate Contact Meredith Young, Executive Director, Enrollment Management, Youngstown State University, 1 University Plaza, Youngstown, Ohio 44555; 330-941-2000, fax: 330-941-3674, e-mail address: emyoung@ysu.edu

Graduate Contact Dr. Darla Funk, Coordinator of Graduate Studies/Music, Dana School of Music, Youngstown State University, 1 University Plaza, Youngstown, Ohio 44555; 330-941-3636, fax: 330-941-1490, e-mail address: djfunk@ysu.edu

Theater Programs

Adelphi University

Garden City, New York

Independent, coed. Suburban campus. Total enrollment: 7,898. Theater program established 1974.

Degrees Bachelor of Fine Arts in the area of theater. Majors and concentrations: acting, technical theater. Program accredited by NAST.

Enrollment 137 total; all undergraduate.

Theater Student Profile 60% females, 40% males, 18% minorities, 2% international.

Theater Faculty 6 undergraduate (full-time), 11 undergraduate (part-time). 100% of full-time faculty have terminal degrees. Graduate students do not teach undergraduate courses. Undergraduate student–faculty ratio: 15:1.

Student Life Student groups/activities include INTERACT, Alpha Psi Omega (dramatic fraternity). Special housing available for theater students.

Expenses for 2005–2006 Application fee: $35. Comprehensive fee: $28,910 includes full-time tuition ($18,620), mandatory fees ($1100), and college room and board ($9190). College room only: $5990. Full-time tuition and fees vary according to course level, location, and program. Room and board charges vary according to board plan and housing facility.

Financial Aid Program-specific awards: 8–10 Barnes Scholarships for freshmen actors ($4000–$9000), 8–10 talent awards for actors, tech/design students ($2000–$9000).

Application Procedures Students admitted directly into the professional program freshman year. Deadline for freshmen and transfers: continuous. Required: essay, high school transcript, college transcript(s) for transfer students, minimum 2.0 high school GPA, 2 letters of recommendation, SAT I or ACT test scores (minimum combined SAT I score of 1000), portfolio for technical theater majors, audition for acting applicants. Auditions held 10 times on campus; videotaped performances are permissible as a substitute for live auditions when distance is prohibitive. Portfolio reviews held continuously on campus; the submission of slides may be substituted for portfolios when distance is prohibitive.

Web Site http://www.adelphi.edu

Undergraduate Contact Mr. Nicholas Petron, Chair, Department of Performing Arts, Adelphi University, Post Hall, Room 4, Garden City, New York 11530; 516-877-4930, fax: 516-877-4926, e-mail address: petron@adelphi.edu

More About the University

Adelphi University, the first liberal arts institution of higher education on Long Island, was chartered June 24, 1896, by the Board of Regents of the State of New York. The charter was one of the earliest granted by the Board of Regents to a coeducational college.

In keeping with its 110-year history, Adelphi University continues to make use of its rich resources to render significant service to Long Island, New York State, and the nation. The University serves as a national center for liberal learning by staging cultural events in the University Center and the Olmsted Theatre and by strengthening the ties between the professional schools and the community. Adelphi's most essential mission is the education of a new generation of leaders.

Today, Adelphi University reaffirms its commitment and dedication to providing excellence in education and to facing and surmounting the challenges of the twenty-first century with high standards and scholarship. As the nation's social fabric becomes increasingly complex, Adelphi remains committed to recognizing such change. In the face of the demands of rapid technological advances, the University draws on a rich tradition of scholarly knowledge and human values to empower students for future leadership as learned and cultivated men and women.

Performing arts majors may choose concentrations in acting, design/technical theater, or dance to prepare for a lifetime of practice in drama, music, and dramatic movement. Adelphi's programs offer a unique blend of theatrical practice—the skills, crafts, and attitudes necessary to succeed in the performing arts—with the tradition of liberal learning, through which each new generation of creators and critics reinterprets and revitalizes these arts. To this end, the Department of Performing Arts offers programs leading to a Bachelor of Fine Arts (B.F.A.) degree in dance and a B.F.A. degree in theater arts, with specializations in acting and design/technical theater.

The proximity of New York City is a constant resource for observation and career opportunities for all performing arts programs.

Albertus Magnus College

New Haven, Connecticut

Independent Roman Catholic, coed. Suburban campus. Total enrollment: 2,230. Theater program established 1971.

Degrees Bachelor of Fine Arts. Majors and concentrations: performance.

Enrollment 3 total; all undergraduate.

Theater Student Profile 66% females, 34% males, 28% minorities.

Theater Faculty 1 total (full-time). 100% of full-time faculty have terminal degrees. Graduate students do not teach undergraduate courses.

Student Life Student groups/activities include Non-Equity Professional Theatre/ACT 2 Theatre.

Expenses for 2005–2006 Application fee: $35. Comprehensive fee: $24,860 includes full-time tuition ($16,600), mandatory fees ($710), and college room and board ($7550). Full-time tuition and fees vary according to class time and program. Special program-related fees: $20–$100 per course for material fees for some studio classes.

Financial Aid Program-specific awards available.

Application Procedures Students apply for admission into the professional program by sophomore year. Deadline for freshmen and transfers: continuous. Required: high school transcript, college transcript(s) for transfer students, minimum 2.0 high school GPA, 2 letters of recommendation, SAT I or ACT test scores. Recommended: essay, interview.

Web Site http://www.albertus.edu

Undergraduate Contact Mr. Richard Lolatte, Dean of Admissions, Albertus Magnus College, 700 Prospect Street, New Haven, Connecticut 06511; 203-773-8501, fax: 203-773-5248, e-mail address: admissions@albertus.edu

American Academy of Dramatic Arts

New York, New York

Independent, coed. Urban campus. Total enrollment: 220. Theater program established 1884.

Degrees Associate in Occupational Studies in the areas of acting, dramatic arts; Certificate in the area of advanced studies in actor training. Majors and concentrations: acting. Program accredited by NAST.

Enrollment 220 total; all undergraduate.

Theater Student Profile 63% females, 37% males, 12% minorities, 18% international.

Theater Faculty 7 undergraduate (full-time), 19 undergraduate (part-time). 28% of full-time faculty have terminal degrees. Graduate students do not teach undergraduate courses. Undergraduate student–faculty ratio: 16:1.

American Academy of Dramatic Arts (continued)

Expenses for 2006–2007 Application fee: $50. Tuition: $16,900 full-time. Mandatory fees: $500 full-time. Special program-related fees: $400 per year for library and classroom materials.

Financial Aid Program-specific awards: 2–3 Spencer Tracy Scholarships for sophomores ($1000–$3000), 2–6 Greta Nissen Scholarships for female sophomores demonstrating need ($1500–$4000), 1–2 Julie Harris Scholarships for sophomores ($500–$1500), 2–4 Henrietta Alice Metcalf Memorial Scholarships for sophomores ($500–$3000), 1–2 Kirk Douglas Scholarships for sophomores ($1500–$2500), 1–3 Harryetta Peterka Scholarships for sophomores ($1000–$3000), 1–3 Samuel Freeman Scholarships for sophomores ($1000–$2000), 1–2 Princess Grace Scholarships for sophomores ($1000–$2000), 1–3 W.K. Hearst Scholarships for sophomores ($1000–$3000), 1–3 Neil Simon Scholarships for sophomores ($1000–$2000), 2–4 Dina Merrill Scholarships for sophomores ($1500–$3000).

Application Procedures Students admitted directly into the professional program freshman year. Deadline for freshmen and transfers: continuous. Required: essay, high school transcript, college transcript(s) for transfer students, 2 letters of recommendation, interview, audition. Recommended: minimum 2.0 high school GPA, SAT I or ACT test scores. Auditions held bi-weekly on campus and off campus in various cities in the U.S..

Web Site http://www.aada.org

Undergraduate Contact Ms. Karen Higginbotham, Director of Admissions, American Academy of Dramatic Arts, 120 Madison Avenue, New York, New York 10016-7004; 212-686-0620 ext. 315, fax: 212-696-1284, e-mail address: admissions-ny@aada.org

More About the Academy

Whether students aspire to the stages of Broadway or the soundstages of Burbank, the American Academy of Dramatic Arts (AADA) has both the location and the program to move them closer to their dream. Founded in 1884 as the first acting school in America, the Academy stresses practical, professional training for stage, film, and television. With campuses in both New York City and Los Angeles, the Academy offers the aspiring actor a stimulating, inspiring environment and a fertile ground for professional and personal growth.

The Academy has a full-time, two-year, college-accredited conservatory program; a third-year of advanced performance and professional showcase (Academy Company); and a six-week Summer Program. It also offers evening and Saturday programs for those unable to commit to full-time training. If students wish to continue their studies toward a B.A., a B.F.A., or advanced degrees, Academy credits are accepted at colleges throughout the United States, and the Academy offers a B.S. in Film and Television program through its affiliation with St. John's University and a B.A. in Theater program through its affiliation with Hunter College (CUNY). For more information, students should call the Admissions Office on the New York campus at 800-463-8990.

The Academy alumni list is an impressive one, with prominent names from all aspects of the entertainment industry, past and present, including 5 Kennedy Center honorees. AADA alumni have been nominated for a total of 72 Oscars, 205 Emmys, and 58 Tonys, with Cecil B. DeMille, Grace Kelly, Robert Redford, Kim Cattrall, Paul Rudd, and 2003 Oscar winner Adrien Brody among their ranks.

Academy students come from all parts of the United States, from Canada, and from other countries as well, extending to Europe and Asia and South America and involving such countries as Singapore and Azerbaijan. The Academy goes to great lengths to invite talent from around the world to enlarge its tradition and to integrate its work in the world community of artists. The Academy community is enriched by the cultures and contributions of talented actors from this country and the fellowship of actors that exists worldwide.

Fewer than half of the entering students are recent high school graduates. Others transfer to the Academy from traditional colleges to study acting in a more concentrated, professional environment. The program is highly structured, focusing on acting, voice and speech, and movement, with an emphasis on self-discipline, self-discovery, and, above all, individuality. At each stage of development, students' classroom knowledge is evaluated through performance projects, scene work, or onstage performances. Students who do extremely well in the program may be invited to join the Academy Company, which offers actors further performance opportunities, often in the presence of casting directors, agents, and other industry professionals.

Students invited to the second or third years may apply to transfer from one campus to the other.

In place of on-campus student housing, the AADA offers a variety of attractive off-campus options through special arrangements with a local housing resource for student housing or other types of housing services, depending upon the student's choice of location.

Scholarships are awarded on the basis of merit and need and may supplement other forms of financial aid. First Year scholarships are determined by the student's application and audition. Second Year and Academy Company students may apply for scholarships by writing to the Academy's Scholarship Committee.

Facilities AADA New York is housed in the six-story landmark Stanford White Building in the heart of midtown Manhattan. AADA Los Angeles is located in the heart of Hollywood, adjacent to the former Charlie Chaplin studios. Each site includes classrooms, rehearsal halls, movement studios, production and costume departments, a library/learning center, a video studio, and theaters.

Faculty The Academy's faculty is composed of seasoned instructors, trained by master teachers, and working professional guest directors, all well-trained within their own disciplines and examples of the excellence that the Academy hopes to instill in its students.

Student Performances Students perform roles in four first-year performance projects and at least three second-year projects and full productions. Academy Company performs, on average, twelve fully-mounted productions each year and a final showcase.

Career Advisement Seminars offered by career counselors provide the practical information actors need to initiate professional careers. The Academy also offers Q&A events with professional actors who generously share their experiences and advice. In addition, the Academy is host to SAG Foundation events that provide SAG members and Academy students the opportunity to participate in conversations with celebrities as well as career advice seminars.

American Academy of Dramatic Arts/ Hollywood
Hollywood, California

Independent, coed. Suburban campus. Total enrollment: 308 (2004). Theater program established 1974.

Arcadia University
Glenside, Pennsylvania

Independent, coed. Suburban campus. Total enrollment: 3,403. Theater program established 2002.

Arizona State University
Tempe, Arizona

State-supported, coed. Suburban campus. Total enrollment: 51,612. Theater program established 1963.

Arkansas State University
State University, Arkansas

State-supported, coed. Small town campus. Total enrollment: 10,414. Theater program established 1958.
Degrees Bachelor of Fine Arts. Majors and concentrations: acting, design technology, directing, music theater.
Enrollment 40 total; all undergraduate.
Theater Student Profile 60% females, 40% males, 5% minorities, 5% international.
Theater Faculty 6 undergraduate (full-time). 100% of full-time faculty have terminal degrees. Graduate students do not teach undergraduate courses. Undergraduate student–faculty ratio: 8:1.
Student Life Student groups/activities include Jonesboro Fine Arts Council, Imperial Theater, Paragould Fine Arts Council.
Expenses for 2005–2006 Application fee: $15. State resident tuition: $4260 full-time. Nonresident tuition: $10,965 full-time. Mandatory fees: $1180 full-time. Full-time tuition and fees vary according to course load, location, and program. College room and board: $4190. Room and board charges vary according to board plan and housing facility.
Financial Aid Program-specific awards: 17 theater arts scholarships for program majors ($250).
Application Procedures Students apply for admission into the professional program by freshman year. Deadline for freshmen and transfers: continuous. Required: high school transcript, SAT I or ACT test scores, minimum 2.3 high school GPA. Recommended: 2 letters of recommendation, interview and portfolio for production applicants, video and audition for performance applicants. Auditions held twice on campus and off campus in various sites in Arkansas; recorded music is permissible as a substitute for live auditions when distance is prohibitive and videotaped performances are permissible as a substitute for live auditions when distance is prohibitive. Portfolio reviews held once on campus; the submission of slides may be substituted for portfolios when distance is prohibitive.
Web Site http://www.astate.edu
Undergraduate Contact Mr. Bob W. Simpson, Chair, Department of Theatre, Arkansas State University, PO Box 2309, State University, Arkansas 72467; 870-972-2037, fax: 870-972-2830, e-mail address: bsimpson@astate.edu

Auburn University
Auburn University, Alabama

State-supported, coed. Small town campus. Total enrollment: 23,333. Theater program established 1945.

Avila University
Kansas City, Missouri

Independent Roman Catholic, coed. Suburban campus. Total enrollment: 1,697. Theater program established 1973.

Barry University
Miami Shores, Florida

Independent Roman Catholic, coed. Suburban campus. Total enrollment: 9,207. Theater program established 1948.

Baylor University
Waco, Texas

Independent Baptist, coed. Urban campus. Total enrollment: 13,975. Theater program established 1947.

Bernice Young Jones School of Fine Arts

See Ouachita Baptist University

The Boston Conservatory
Boston, Massachusetts

Independent, coed. Urban campus. Total enrollment: 537 (2004). Theater program established 1940.
Degrees Bachelor of Fine Arts in the area of musical theater. Majors and concentrations: music theater. Graduate degrees offered: Master of Music in the area of musical theater. Cross-registration with ProArts Consortium. Program accredited by NASM.
Enrollment 203 total; 188 undergraduate, 15 graduate.
Theater Student Profile 59% females, 41% males, 10% minorities, 2% international.
Theater Faculty 16 total (full-time), 20 total (part-time). Graduate students do not teach undergraduate courses. Undergraduate student–faculty ratio: 12:1.
Student Life Student groups/activities include Cabaret, Hoofers Dance Troupe. Special housing available for theater students.
Expenses for 2006–2007 Application fee: $105. Comprehensive fee: $42,155 includes full-time tuition ($26,400), mandatory fees ($1435), and college room and board ($14,320).
Financial Aid Program-specific awards: Conservatory Theater Scholarships for program majors.
Application Procedures Students admitted directly into the professional program freshman year. Deadline for freshmen and transfers: December 1. Notification date for freshmen and transfers: April 1. Required: essay, high school transcript, college transcript(s) for transfer students, 2 letters of recommendation, interview, audition, minimum TOEFL score of 550 for international applicants, artistic resumé, minimum 2.7 high school GPA. Auditions held during the months of January, February, and March on campus and off campus in Chicago, IL; Houston, TX; Los Angeles, CA; San Francisco, CA; New York, NY; Atlanta, GA; videotaped performances are permissible as a substitute for live auditions if a campus visit or regional audition is impossible.
Web Site http://www.bostonconservatory.edu
Contact Admissions Office, The Boston Conservatory, 8 The Fenway, Boston, Massachusetts 02215; 617-912-9153, fax: 617-247-3159, e-mail address: admissions@bostonconservatory.edu

More About the Conservatory

The Boston Conservatory trains exceptional young performing artists for careers that enrich and transform the human experience. Known for its multidisciplinary environment, the Conservatory offers fully accredited graduate and undergraduate programs in music, dance, theater, and music education and presents more than 200 performances each year by students, faculty members, and guest artists. The intimacy of the Conservatory's class settings provides a student-centered atmosphere that is uniquely intensive and supportive.

Since its founding in 1867, the Boston Conservatory has shared its talent and creativity with the city of Boston, the region, and the nation, and it continues to grow today as a vibrant community of artists and educators.

The Boston Conservatory was one of the first colleges to offer integrated training in theater encompassing acting, voice, and dance. Beginning as a full acting/drama program in the 1930s, the Theater Division now trains the "triple threat" actor/singer, offering a complete musical theater and acting curriculum coupled with music and voice study and a full range of dance (ballet, modern, tap, jazz, and styles). The B.F.A. program offers in-depth courses in theater academics and cultural liberal arts.

The Theater Division faculty is composed of experienced performers and teachers committed to bringing out the best each student has to offer. Potential is acknowledged and developed within a strong interactive musical theater curriculum. Frequent in-class performances with appropriate coaching and critique give guidance and constant evaluation of the student's work.

Performance opportunities are available throughout the year, from in-class and studio work to mainstage productions. All major productions are directed by faculty members or guest directors and have an open, professional casting policy in order for the most qualified person to get the role regardless of class standing.

The Boston Conservatory (continued)

Technical and stagecraft experience is provided, and production assistance is required for freshmen during major runs.

In addition to these opportunities, the studio theater offers small-scale productions throughout the year, directed by faculty members, graduate students, and senior directors.

The Boston Conservatory alumni can be seen performing on Broadway in *Les Misérables, 42nd Street,* and *The Phantom of the Opera;* in national tours of *Jesus Christ Superstar, Beauty and the Beast,* and *Miss Saigon;* at the Globe Theater in London; on television in *Law and Order, Judging Amy,* and *The Young and the Restless;* and as producers, directors, and creators of Broadway, touring, and television productions, such as *Forbidden Broadway* and *MADTV.*

The Boston area provides varied outside work in theater and dance as well as industrials. Regional theater productions often cast students in both lead and ensemble parts.

Boston is a major center of higher education in America, with more than fifty major colleges and universities. The city provides a diverse student population and an endless array of courses, lectures, concerts, and social opportunities. The Conservatory is a member of the Pro-Arts Consortium, in collaboration with five area colleges (Emerson College, Berklee College of Music, School of the Museum of Fine Arts, Massachusetts College of Art, and Boston Architectural Center), offering extensive cross-registration course possibilities to all students.

On-campus housing is provided for freshmen and to upperclassmen and graduates on a space-available basis, offering brownstone-style living accommodations just a few steps from the main training and rehearsal buildings. For those students interested in off-campus housing, Boston offers a wide range of architectural styles and rent prices in neighborhoods throughout the city, which are all within easy access to the school by public transportation.

The Boston Conservatory strives to meet each student's needs—musically and personally—and provides a nurturing, safe environment in which to study, learn, and grow. The supportive atmosphere of the college extends to student life areas as well. More than a dozen special-interest groups and organizations exist on campus, with new ones developing constantly as the student population grows and needs change. As part of the student services, a number of career seminars are given each year ranging from resume writing and audition anxiety to grant writing and tax laws for the performing artist. In addition, there is an active student government and a student-run newspaper.

Boston University
Boston, Massachusetts

Independent, coed. Urban campus. Total enrollment: 30,957. Theater program established 1950.
Degrees Bachelor of Fine Arts in the areas of acting, design, stage management, independent theater study. Majors and concentrations: acting, costume design, costume production, lighting design, set design, sound design, stage management, technical production, theater arts/drama. Graduate degrees offered: Master of Fine Arts in the areas of directing, theater education, scene design, technical production, costume design, costume production, lighting design.
Enrollment 230 total; 190 undergraduate, 40 graduate.
Theater Student Profile 67% females, 33% males, 7% minorities.
Theater Faculty 20 total (full-time), 7 total (part-time). Graduate students do not teach undergraduate courses.
Student Life Special housing available for theater students.
Expenses for 2005–2006 Application fee: $70. Comprehensive fee: $42,046 includes full-time tuition ($31,530), mandatory fees ($436), and college room and board ($10,080). College room only: $6450. Full-time tuition and fees vary according to class time and degree level. Room and board charges vary according to board plan and housing facility.
Financial Aid Program-specific awards: 12 grants/performance awards for program students ($2000–$8000).

Application Procedures Students admitted directly into the professional program freshman year. Deadline for freshmen: January 1; transfers: April 1. Notification date for freshmen: April 15. Required: essay, high school transcript, 2 letters of recommendation, audition, portfolio, SAT I or ACT test scores, audition for acting and independent theater study applicants, portfolio for design, technical production, and stage management applicants. Auditions held 20 times on campus and off campus in New York, NY; Chicago, IL; San Francisco, CA; Los Angeles, CA; Washington, DC. Portfolio reviews held 10 times on campus and off campus in New York, NY; Chicago, IL; San Francisco, CA; CA; Washington, DC; the submission of slides may be substituted for portfolios when distance is prohibitive.
Web Site http://www.bu.edu/cfa/theatre
Contact Mr. Paolo DiFabio, Associate Director for Theatre Performance, Theatre Arts Department, Boston University, 855 Commonwealth Avenue, Room 470, Boston, Massachusetts 02215; 617-353-3390, fax: 617-353-4363, e-mail address: pdifabio@bu.edu

More About the University

Boston University College of Fine Arts (CFA) is a small, conservatory-style school within a major university, offering outstanding professional training in music, the theater, and visual arts. The College was begun as the College of Music in 1873, and the School of Theater Arts was organized in 1950. The School of Theatre enrolls approximately 250 students and offers the Bachelor of Fine Arts (B.F.A.) and the Master of Fine Arts (M.F.A.). It is one of this country's leading institutions for the study of acting, theater arts, stage management, and design/production and for preparation for careers in all aspects of the entertainment industry.

Campus Surroundings Boston University—independent, coeducational, nonsectarian—is an internationally recognized center of higher education and research. The University is located in the heart of Boston, along the banks of the Charles River and adjacent to the historic Back Bay district of Boston. Boston University is perfectly situated to enjoy both the charm and beauty of the city and its cultural and recreational attractions. Students benefit from the many major theaters, musical organizations, and museums and galleries that make Boston a rich and varied cultural environment.

Program Facilities Performance spaces include the Boston University Theatre, an 850-seat proscenium house; Studio 210, a 100-seat black box space; and the Theatre Lab, a 100-seat proscenium studio. The Theatre is equipped with a computerized lighting system, shops for scenery and costume construction, and an electronic sound studio. There are three movement studios and six additional rehearsal studios.

Faculty, Resident Artists, and Alumni Faculty members are not only master teachers but are also accomplished professionals who maintain vital careers in the theater. Distinguished faculty members include Nicholas Martin, Artistic Director of the Huntington Theatre Company, and Jim Petosa, Director of the School of Theatre and Artistic Director of the Olney Theatre Center outside Washington, D.C. Guest artists have included actors Jason Alexander, Claire Bloom, and Campbell Scott, and designers Ralph Funicello and Desmond Heeley. Alumni include actors Geena Davis, Olympia Dukakis, Julianne Moore, and Alfre Woodard; Nina Tassler, President of CBS Television, Drama Division; playwright Martin Sherman; and stage and theater designer, Wynn P. Thomas, whose credits include *A Beautiful Mind* and *Analyze This.*

Student Performance Opportunities The School of Theatre produces six fully mounted productions each year as well as ten to twenty workshop productions directed by faculty members and graduate and undergraduate students. An annual festival of new plays provides a showcase for work by undergraduate playwrights.

Special Programs The Huntington Theatre Company, one of Boston's leading professional companies, is in residence at the Boston University Theatre. A variety of assistantships and internships are available for students in the areas of design, production, directing, stage management, and theater management. Advanced acting majors have the opportunity to audition for understudy assignments and supporting roles in Huntington Theatre productions. Through the Professional Theatre Initiative, School of Theatre students gain professional opportunities with the Huntingdon Theatre Company, the Boston Playwrights Theatre, the Williamstown Theatre Festival, and the Olney Theatre Center. In addition, students have the opportunity to study abroad at the London Academy of Music and Dramatic Arts (LAMDA) in their junior year. Post graduation, the Los Angeles Internship Program offers a semester of study and work in the heart of the film and television. The program provides an unparalleled hands-on introduction to the film and television industries and is appropriate for any student interested in an entertainment career. Students can also earn minors in dance, liberal arts, business, or communications.

Bradley University
Peoria, Illinois

Independent, coed. Urban campus. Total enrollment: 6,154. Theater program established 1978.
Degrees Bachelor of Arts in the areas of theater arts, performance, production; Bachelor of Science in the areas of theater performance, production, theater arts. Majors and concentrations: performance, production, theater arts/drama. Program accredited by NAST.
Enrollment 62 total; all undergraduate.
Theater Student Profile 63% females, 37% males, 5% minorities.
Theater Faculty 5 undergraduate (full-time), 2 undergraduate (part-time). 100% of full-time faculty have terminal degrees. Graduate students do not teach undergraduate courses. Undergraduate student–faculty ratio: 10:1.
Student Life Student groups/activities include Alpha Psi Omega, USitt, Met (lab theatre), Bar-be-que Kittens (improv).
Expenses for 2005–2006 Application fee: $35. Comprehensive fee: $25,280 includes full-time tuition ($18,700), mandatory fees ($130), and college room and board ($6450). College room only: $3700. Full-time tuition and fees vary according to program. Room and board charges vary according to board plan.
Financial Aid Program-specific awards: 21 theater scholarships for theater majors ($2000).
Application Procedures Students admitted directly into the professional program freshman year. Deadline for freshmen and transfers: continuous. Required: high school transcript, college transcript(s) for transfer students, minimum 2.0 high school GPA, audition, portfolio, SAT I or ACT test scores, portfolio and audition for scholarship consideration. Recommended: letter of recommendation. Auditions held 8 times on campus; recorded music is permissible as a substitute for live auditions when distance is prohibitive and videotaped performances are permissible as a substitute for live auditions when distance is prohibitive. Portfolio reviews held 8 times on campus; the submission of slides may be substituted for portfolios.
Web Site http://gcc.bradley.edu/theatre
Undergraduate Contact Ms. Nickie Roberson, Director of Admissions, Office of Undergraduate Admissions, Bradley University, Swords Hall, Peoria, Illinois 61625; 800-447-6460, fax: 309-677-2797, e-mail address: admissions@bradley.edu

Brenau University
Gainesville, Georgia

Independent, Small town campus. Total enrollment: 743. Theater program established 1979.
Degrees Bachelor of Fine Arts. Majors and concentrations: arts management, music theater. Mandatory cross-registration with Gainesville College.
Enrollment 39 total; 13 undergraduate, 26 nonprofessional degree.
Theater Student Profile 90% females, 10% males, 1% minorities.

Theater Faculty 3 undergraduate (full-time), 2 undergraduate (part-time). 100% of full-time faculty have terminal degrees. Graduate students do not teach undergraduate courses. Undergraduate student–faculty ratio: 10:1.
Student Life Student groups/activities include Gainesville Theatre Alliance, Alpha Psi Omega, Wonder Quest Children's Theatre. Special housing available for theater students.
Expenses for 2005–2006 Application fee: $35. Comprehensive fee: $24,990 includes full-time tuition ($16,440) and college room and board ($8550). Full-time tuition varies according to class time, location, and program. Room and board charges vary according to housing facility.
Financial Aid Program-specific awards: 20 talent scholarships for program majors ($1500–$5000).
Application Procedures Students admitted directly into the professional program freshman year. Deadline for freshmen and transfers: continuous. Required: essay, high school transcript, college transcript(s) for transfer students, minimum 2.0 high school GPA, audition, SAT I or ACT test scores (minimum combined SAT I score of 900, minimum composite ACT score of 19), health certificate. Recommended: minimum 3.0 high school GPA, interview, portfolio, 1-2 letters of recommendation. Auditions held 8 times and by appointment on campus; videotaped performances are permissible as a substitute for live auditions when distance is prohibitive. Portfolio reviews held upon request on campus; the submission of slides may be substituted for portfolios when distance is prohibitive.
Web Site http://www.brenau.edu
Undergraduate Contact Christina Jackson, Admissions Coordinator, Brenau University, 500 Washington Street, SE, Gainesville, Georgia 30501; 770-534-6100, fax: 770-538-4306, e-mail address: cjackson@lib.brenau.edu

Brigham Young University
Provo, Utah

Independent, coed. Suburban campus. Total enrollment: 34,067. Theater program established 1920.
Degrees Bachelor of Arts in the areas of theater arts education, theater arts studies, media arts studies; Bachelor of Fine Arts in the areas of music dance theater, acting. Majors and concentrations: acting, media arts, music theatre/dance, theater arts studies, theater education. Graduate degrees offered: Master of Arts in the area of theater and media arts; Master of Fine Arts in the area of production design. Program accredited by NAST.
Enrollment 310 total; 82 undergraduate, 6 graduate, 222 nonprofessional degree.
Theater Student Profile 57% females, 43% males.
Theater Faculty 18 undergraduate (full-time), 4 undergraduate (part-time), 5 graduate (full-time), 3 graduate (part-time). 87% of full-time faculty have terminal degrees. Graduate students teach a few undergraduate courses. Undergraduate student–faculty ratio: 10:1.
Expenses for 2005–2006 Application fee: $30. Comprehensive fee: $10,906 includes full-time tuition ($5116) and college room and board ($5790). Full-time tuition varies according to reciprocity agreements. Room and board charges vary according to board plan and housing facility.
Financial Aid Program-specific awards: 144 merit awards for program majors ($470).
Application Procedures Students apply for admission into the professional program by freshman year. Required: essay, high school transcript, college transcript(s) for transfer students, minimum 3.0 high school GPA, 3 letters of recommendation, audition, SAT I or ACT test scores. Auditions held twice on campus; recorded music is permissible as a substitute for live auditions if a campus visit is impossible and videotaped performances are permissible as a substitute for live auditions if a campus visit is impossible.
Web Site http://cfac.byu.edu/tma
Undergraduate Contact Roxanna Boyer, Department Assistant, Department of Theatre and Media Arts, Brigham Young University, D-581 HFAC, Provo, Utah 84602; 801-422-6242, fax: 801-422-0654, e-mail address: roxanna_boyer@byu.edu
Graduate Contact Darl Larson, Graduate Coordinator, Department of Graduate Studies, Brigham Young University, D-581-HFAC, Provo, Utah 84602; 801-422-9184, fax: 801-422-0654.

Brooklyn College of the City University of New York

Brooklyn, New York

State and locally supported, coed. Urban campus. Total enrollment: 15,281. Theater program established 1973.

Jordan College of Fine Arts - Department of Theatre
Butler University

Indianapolis, Indiana

Independent, coed. Urban campus. Total enrollment: 4,384.
Degrees Bachelor of Arts in the area of theatre; Bachelor of Science in the area of arts administration/theatre. Majors and concentrations: theater, theater arts administration. Cross-registration with Indianapolis Consortium for Urban Education. Program accredited by NAST.
Enrollment 78 total; all undergraduate.
Theater Student Profile 75% females, 25% males, 5% minorities.
Theater Faculty 6 undergraduate (full-time), 9 undergraduate (part-time). 100% of full-time faculty have terminal degrees. Graduate students do not teach undergraduate courses. Undergraduate student–faculty ratio: 5:1.
Student Life Student groups/activities include Study Abroad Partnership with Hong Kong Academy for Performing Arts and Flinders University, Australia, Alpha Psi Omega, Phoenix Theatre, Indiana Repertory Theatre.
Expenses for 2005–2006 Application fee: $35. Comprehensive fee: $31,944 includes full-time tuition ($23,530), mandatory fees ($244), and college room and board ($8170). College room only: $3980. Full-time tuition and fees vary according to program. Room and board charges vary according to housing facility.
Financial Aid Program-specific awards: talent audition awards.
Application Procedures Students admitted directly into the professional program freshman year. Deadline for freshmen and transfers: continuous. Required: high school transcript, college transcript(s) for transfer students, minimum 2.0 high school GPA, interview, audition, SAT I or ACT test scores, head shot photo, theatre application. Recommended: minimum 3.0 high school GPA, letter of recommendation, portfolio. Auditions held 6 times on campus.
Web Site http://www.butler.edu/theatre
Undergraduate Contact Ms. Kathy Lang, Admission Representative, Jordan College of Fine Arts, Butler University, Lilly Hall - 138B, 4600 Sunset Avenue, Indianapolis, Indiana 46208; 800-368-6852 ext. 9656, fax: 317-940-9658, e-mail address: klang@butler.edu

More About the University

Butler University is most proud of its tradition of excellence and innovation. Challenging and enabling students to meet their personal and professional goals has guided the University since 1855. Today, Butler is an independent, coeducational, nonsectarian university, with a total undergraduate enrollment of more than 3,800 students. The University is accredited by the North Central Association of Colleges and Schools.

Butler Theatre is an award-winning undergraduate program accredited by the National Association of Schools of Theatre (NAST). The Butler program offers a choice of two degrees: Bachelor of Arts (B.A.) in theater and Bachelor of Science (B.S.) in arts administration. The program fosters a creative environment where students develop practical and critical skills, create exciting work, and commit fully to the collaborative process of making theater. Through its professional ties in the Indiana Repertory Theatre, the program provides students regular interaction with professional theater artists, technicians, and administrators, and it facilitates professional experience through internships and contract employment.

Campus and Surroundings Indianapolis, Indiana's state capital and the twelfth-largest city in the nation, has a variety of cultural activities, including the Indiana Repertory Theatre, Phoenix Theatre, Indianapolis Symphony Orchestra, Dance Kaleidoscope,

the Indianapolis Museum of Art, and the world's largest children's museum. Citywide celebrations are plentiful, including ethnic festivals, art fairs, and outdoor music festivals.

Program Facilities The Lilly Hall Studio Theatre is the venue for most main stage productions. Robertson Studio 33 is the space used for classes in voice, acting, and directing and for student-directed productions and rehearsals. Butler's Clowes Memorial Hall is a 2,200-seat performance hall that hosts a variety of events, from community arts groups to national and international touring companies and many University performances. A new performing arts complex is currently under construction. The first phase of the complex, a 47,000-square-foot addition to Lilly Hall called the Courtyard Building, was completed in spring 2003. This new building houses a choral rehearsal hall, an instrumental rehearsal hall, dance studios, a theater studio, an electronic music lab, and a percussion studio. The second phase, the 140-seat Eidson-Duckwall Recital Hall, was completed in fall 2004. The third phase is a 450-seat performance hall/proscenium theater with adjustable acoustical features.

Special Programs Butler is committed to experiencing theater as a global art form, in theory and in practice. The University runs a comprehensive study-abroad program, which encourages students in their junior year to study at a university overseas for one semester. The following countries have emerged as the most popular destinations for theater majors: Australia, United Kingdom, Ireland, Spain, Germany, China (Hong Kong), and South America.

Created in 2002, Butler International Theatre Exchange (BITE) is an annual workshop for students, educators, and theater professionals in Indiana who are devoted to exploring transnational processes of creating live performances with master artists and theater companies from around the world. Each exchange is structured around a twelve-day intensive program of training, held during Butler's first summer session in May.

Cooperative Agreements Butler Theatre enjoys a creative partnership with the Indiana Repertory Theatre (IRT), Indiana's largest, fully professional regional theater located in the heart of the city of Indianapolis. The benefits of this partnership include a freshman orientation program that provides first-semester theater majors access to the artistic, administrative, and technical staff of the IRT as an introduction to professional theater practice; a stage management training program taught by the IRT's senior stage management team; and professional internships for juniors and seniors in all areas of the theater's operation. An increasing number of theater majors have made their professional acting debuts at the IRT during their four years of study.

Faculty/Alumni Butler's faculty members have expertise in stage directing, acting, performance theory, costume design, play analysis, stage lighting, arts administration, children's theater, technical direction, and auditioning and voice. *BeckettWorks* received ACF National Artistic Achievement Awards for Directing (Department Chair John Green) and Scenic Lighting and Design (Assistant Professor Madeleine Sobota.) Associate Professor Diane Timmerman had her 90-minute adaptations of five Shakespeare plays published by Smith and Krauss.

Butler alumni work in a range of theater careers, including an education assistant at the Chicago Shakespeare Theatre, a marketing manager at the Yale Repertory Theatre, an owner of a casting agency, and actors in Los Angeles and Chicago. Other alumni are technical directors, costumer designers, stage managers, and soundboard operators.

Student Performance Opportunities Butler Theater stages between fifteen and twenty shows each year, including four major productions directed by faculty members and guest artists, student-directed honors theses productions and independent projects, faculty and student-directed works in progress, and plays written by students.

In 2000 and 2003, the department was invited to tour Ireland with productions of plays by Samuel Beckett and W.B. Yeats. In

2004, the department went to Italy, and in 2005, it went to Australia. The department also went to St. Petersburg, Russia, in 2006.

Career Placement Services and Opportunities With a liberal arts education and practical experience, Butler graduates are prepared for success in many careers. Collaborative partnerships with professional theaters provide networking and internship opportunities for theater students. A sampling of internships include the following positions: production at the Phoenix Theatre; sound at the Indiana Repertory Theatre; stage manager for the Phoenix Theatre, Civic Theatre, and Edyvean Repertory Theatre; marketing for *Fosse* at the Shubert Theatre in Chicago; public relations for the Indiana Arts Commission; internships at Denver Center Theatre Academy and Steppenwolf Theatre in Chicago; and acting at venues around the country. Graduates often find employment at the venues where they served as interns.

California Institute of the Arts
Valencia, California

Independent, coed. Total enrollment: 1,327. Theater program established 1961.
Degrees Bachelor of Fine Arts in the areas of acting, design and production. Majors and concentrations: acting, costume design, lighting design, puppetry, set design, sound design, stage management, technical direction. Graduate degrees offered: Master of Fine Arts in the area of acting design and production. Program accredited by NAST.
Enrollment 286 total; 156 undergraduate, 130 graduate.
Theater Student Profile 54% females, 46% males, 32% minorities, 5% international.
Theater Faculty 31 total (full-time), 13 total (part-time). 80% of full-time faculty have terminal degrees. Graduate students do not teach undergraduate courses. Undergraduate student–faculty ratio: 6:1.
Student Life Student groups/activities include Community Arts Partnership (CAP). Special housing available for theater students.
Expenses for 2005–2006 Application fee: $65. Comprehensive fee: $35,422 includes full-time tuition ($27,260), mandatory fees ($465), and college room and board ($7697). College room only: $4095. Full-time tuition and fees vary according to course load. Room and board charges vary according to board plan, housing facility, and location. Special program-related fees: $475 per year for technology fee.
Financial Aid Program-specific awards: CalArts Scholarships for students demonstrating talent ($6000–$15,000).
Application Procedures Students admitted directly into the professional program freshman year. Deadline for freshmen and transfers: January 5. Required: essay, high school transcript, college transcript(s) for transfer students, audition for acting applicants, portfolio for design applicants. Recommended: 2 letters of recommendation, interview. Auditions held 15 times on campus and off campus in New York, NY; Chicago, IL. Portfolio reviews held continuously for design majors on campus; the submission of slides may be substituted for portfolios by arrangement with the Office of Admissions.
Web Site http://www.calarts.edu
Contact Ms. Jillian Rothschild, Assistant Director of Admissions, California Institute of the Arts, 24700 McBean Parkway, Valencia, California 91355; 661-255-1050 ext. 2716, fax: 661-253-7710, e-mail address: jroths@calarts.edu

More About the Institute

The California Institute of the Arts (CalArts) School of Theater trains students from a worldwide perspective and historical precedent while engaging them with the next, the new. The School's mission is to promote a cultural and aesthetic diversity of viewpoint, experience, and expression.

Programs of Study The School of Theater offers undergraduate degrees in the areas of Programs in Performance, including acting; costume, lighting, scene, sound design, management, and technical direction. Undergraduate programs lead to a Bachelor in Fine Arts (B.F.A.) degree.

The CalArts School of Theater supports and broadens the work of burgeoning artists from multiple disciplines. The School of Theater's relatively small size allows for a low student-faculty ratio (7:1), small classes, and one-on-one instruction. Every student works closely with his or her mentor, a faculty member who serves as that student's artistic and academic adviser. Students gain essential practical experience through full School of Theater productions and various other performances, including an annual New Works Festival.

Facilities On-campus performance spaces include four black box theaters, a thrust configuration stage, and a cabaret-style stage. Among them is the Walt Disney Modular Theater, or the MOD, which is a vast black box that can be arranged to support an unlimited range of stage and seating configurations. The School of Theater operates shops and labs for scenery, costumes, props, sound, lighting, and computers.

Off-campus, CalArts' dramatic performance space in downtown Los Angeles, REDCAT (Roy and Edna Disney/CalArts Theater), opened in 2003 as part of the Frank Gehry-designed Walt Disney Concert Hall complex. REDCAT provides numerous opportunities for School of Theater students, both as a performance venue for select productions and as a forum for acquiring professional experience in design, production, and management.

Faculty and Alumni Leading professional theater artists in every area of practice comprise the School of Theater faculty. Each member of the faculty is committed to fostering the ambitions of the next generation of theater artists. Students benefit from an intimate environment and one-on-one instruction. Faculty members include Jon Gottlieb, Marissa Chibas, Travis Preston, Erik Ehn, Carol Bixler, Fran Bennett, Martha Ferrara, Ellen McCartney, Christopher Barreca, Mary Heilman, Mary Lou Rosato, and Stephanie Young.

Faculty members are in constant contact with noted theater companies and current stage, film, and television productions, they are uniquely able to recommend students for valuable observerships and internships.

Special Programs The Center for New Performance at CalArts (CNP) is the professional producing arm of CalArts. Dedicated to the creation of adventurous projects that challenge and redefine the boundaries of contemporary performance, the Center for New Performance enables current students, faculty members, alumni, and guest artists to collaborate in producing new, vital, boundary-crossing performances.

Housed in the CalArts School of Theater, the Cotsen Center for the Puppetry of the Arts is an interdisciplinary laboratory for the study and exploration of puppets and performing objects in theater, film, dance, and art. It allows School of Theater students to incorporate the use of performing objects into their theatrical vocabularies, or concentrate on work centered on puppets and other performing objects.

CalArts champions cross-pollination in the arts. In addition to various collaborations within the School of Theater, students work with writers, musicians, composers, choreographers, filmmakers, animators, and visual artists throughout CalArts.

School of Theater students have access to valuable teaching and community engagement experience through Community Arts Partnership (CAP) workshops and classes at community art centers throughout Los Angeles.

Cooperative Agreements Most Center for New Theater projects are performed under the Actors Equity Association Contact with the University/Resident Theater Association (U/RTA); an employment agreement devised to develop and expand both professional theater and advance training laboratories. This agreement allows students to garner equity points toward participation in the Actors Equity Association.

California Institute of the Arts (continued)

The School of Theater features exchange programs with the Royal Scottish Academy of Music and Drama and the Toi Whakaari New Zealand Drama School. Graduate directors and stage managers may have internships with the Sundance Theater Laboratory.

Carnegie Mellon University

Pittsburgh, Pennsylvania

Independent, coed. Urban campus. Total enrollment: 10,017. Theater program established 1914.

Degrees Bachelor of Fine Arts in the area of drama. Majors and concentrations: acting, design, directing, music theater, performance technology and management, theater arts/drama. Graduate degrees offered: Master of Fine Arts in the area of drama. Cross-registration with University of Pittsburgh, Pittsburgh Filmmakers.

Enrollment 265 total; 210 undergraduate, 55 graduate.

Theater Student Profile 40% females, 60% males, 8% minorities, 5% international.

Theater Faculty 32 total (full-time), 10 total (part-time). 95% of full-time faculty have terminal degrees. Graduate students do not teach undergraduate courses. Undergraduate student–faculty ratio: 6:1.

Student Life Student groups/activities include Scotch 'n Soda (student-run theater group). Special housing available for theater students.

Expenses for 2006–2007 Application fee: $60. Comprehensive fee: $43,858 includes full-time tuition ($34,180), mandatory fees ($398), and college room and board ($9280). College room only: $5440. Special program-related fees: $20 per semester for class, script fees.

Application Procedures Students admitted directly into the professional program freshman year. Deadline for freshmen and transfers: January 1. Notification date for freshmen and transfers: April 1. Required: high school transcript, college transcript(s) for transfer students, minimum 2.0 high school GPA, 3 letters of recommendation, interview, audition, portfolio, SAT I or ACT test scores. Recommended: minimum 3.0 high school GPA. Auditions held once for acting, music theater, and directing applicants on campus and off campus in New York, NY; Chicago, IL; San Francisco, CA; Los Angeles, CA; Houston, TX; Miami, FL; Atlanta, GA. Portfolio reviews held once for design and production applicants on campus and off campus in New York, NY; Chicago, IL; San Francisco, CA; Los Angeles, CA; Houston, TX; Miami, FL; Atlanta, GA; the submission of slides may be substituted for portfolios if a campus visit is impossible.

Web Site http://www.cmu.edu/cfa/drama

Undergraduate Contact Ms. Rebecca Lombardi, Assistant Director of Admissions, Carnegie Mellon University, Warner Hall 100, Pittsburgh, Pennsylvania 15213; 412-268-2082, fax: 412-261-0281, e-mail address: rl3j@andrew.cmu.edu

Graduate Contact Mr. Dick Block, Associate Head/Graduate Admissions Coordinator, School of Drama, Carnegie Mellon University, Purnell Center for The Arts - 222, Pittsburgh, Pennsylvania 15213-3890; 412-268-7219, fax: 412-621-0281, e-mail address: rblock@andrew.cmu.edu

Catawba College

Salisbury, North Carolina

Independent, coed. Small town campus. Total enrollment: 1,288. Theater program established 1956.

Degrees Bachelor of Fine Arts. Majors and concentrations: acting and directing, costume design, lighting/sound design, music theater, scenic design, theater arts/drama, theater management.

Enrollment 96 total; 16 undergraduate, 80 nonprofessional degree.

Theater Student Profile 58% females, 42% males, 9% minorities.

Theater Faculty 7 undergraduate (full-time), 6 undergraduate (part-time). 100% of full-time faculty have terminal degrees. Graduate students do not teach undergraduate courses. Undergraduate student–faculty ratio: 2:1.

Student Life Student groups/activities include Alpha Psi Omega, Blue Masque Drama Club.

Expenses for 2005–2006 Application fee: $25. Comprehensive fee: $25,000 includes full-time tuition ($18,750) and college room and board ($6250). Full-time tuition varies according to class time.

Financial Aid Program-specific awards: 25 theater arts scholarships and academic awards for incoming freshmen and transfers ($1100).

Application Procedures Students apply for admission into the professional program by freshman year. Deadline for freshmen and transfers: continuous. Required: high school transcript, college transcript(s) for transfer students, minimum 3.0 high school GPA, 2 letters of recommendation, interview, audition, portfolio, SAT I or ACT test scores. Recommended: essay. Auditions held 5 times on campus and off campus in North Carolina Theatre Conference Meeting sites; recorded music is permissible as a substitute for live auditions and videotaped performances are permissible as a substitute for live auditions when distance is prohibitive. Portfolio reviews held 5 times on campus and off campus in North Carolina Theatre Conference Meeting sites; the submission of slides may be substituted for portfolios.

Web Site http://www.catawba.edu/academic/theatrearts/

Undergraduate Contact Dr. Woodrow Hood, Chair, Theatre Arts Department, Catawba College, 2300 West Innes Street, Salisbury, North Carolina 28144; 704-637-4771, fax: 704-637-4207, e-mail address: wbhood@catawba.edu

Central Connecticut State University

New Britain, Connecticut

State-supported, coed. Suburban campus. Total enrollment: 12,315. Theater program established 1973.

Degrees Bachelor of Fine Arts. Majors and concentrations: acting, dance, directing, educational theater, technical theater.

Enrollment 74 total; all undergraduate.

Theater Student Profile 55% females, 45% males, 13% minorities, 1% international.

Theater Faculty 7 undergraduate (full-time), 2 undergraduate (part-time). 100% of full-time faculty have terminal degrees. Graduate students do not teach undergraduate courses. Undergraduate student–faculty ratio: 16:1.

Student Life Student groups/activities include Theatre Unlimited (student producing organization), community outreach programs in children's theater and workshops.

Expenses for 2005–2006 Application fee: $50. State resident tuition: $3034 full-time. Nonresident tuition: $9820 full-time. Mandatory fees: $3130 full-time. Full-time tuition and fees vary according to course level, course load, and reciprocity agreements. College room and board: $7456. College room only: $4250. Room and board charges vary according to board plan.

Financial Aid Program-specific awards: 1 Thad Torp Memorial Scholarship for juniors ($3000), 1 acting scholarship for sophomores ($1000).

Application Procedures Students admitted directly into the professional program freshman year. Deadline for freshmen: May 1; transfers: continuous. Required: high school transcript, college transcript(s) for transfer students, letter of recommendation, SAT I test score only, audition for acting majors. Recommended: minimum 2.0 high school GPA, interview, portfolio. Auditions held once on campus. Portfolio reviews held as needed on campus; the submission of slides may be substituted for portfolios for executed design projects.

Web Site http://www.ccsu.edu

Undergraduate Contact Associate Director, Undergraduate Admissions, Office of Admissions, Central Connecticut State University, PO Box 4010, 1615 Stanley Street, New Britain, Connecticut 06050; 860-832-CCSU, fax: 860-832-2295, e-mail address: admissions@CCSU.edu

Central Missouri State University

Warrensburg, Missouri

State-supported, coed. Small town campus. Total enrollment: 10,604.

Chapman University
Orange, California

Independent, coed. Suburban campus. Total enrollment: 5,732.
Degrees Bachelor of Fine Arts. Majors and concentrations: performance.
Enrollment 141 total; 22 undergraduate, 119 nonprofessional degree.
Theater Student Profile 74% females, 26% males, 14% minorities.
Theater Faculty 5 undergraduate (full-time), 8 undergraduate (part-time). 60% of full-time faculty have terminal degrees. Graduate students do not teach undergraduate courses. Undergraduate student–faculty ratio: 5:1.
Student Life Student groups/activities include Shakespeare Orange County-Summer Professional Theaters, American Celebration, Performing Arts Society of Chapman.
Expenses for 2006–2007 Application fee: $55. Comprehensive fee: $41,248 includes full-time tuition ($29,900), mandatory fees ($848), and college room and board ($10,500). Special program-related fees: $75 per per course for introduction technology courses; materials fees, $75 per per course for introduction theater courses, theater tickets.
Financial Aid Program-specific awards: 40 talent awards for incoming students ($2000).
Application Procedures Students apply for admission into the professional program by sophomore year. Deadline for freshmen: January 31; transfers: March 15. Required: essay, high school transcript, college transcript(s) for transfer students, minimum 2.0 high school GPA, 2 letters of recommendation, audition, SAT I or ACT test scores, recent photograph, resume. Recommended: interview, video. Auditions held 4 times on campus; videotaped performances are permissible as a substitute for live auditions with permission of the Senior Department Secretary.
Web Site http://www.chapman.edu/comm/td/
Undergraduate Contact Ms. Bonnie Walker, Senior Department Secretary, Theatre and Dance Department, Chapman University, 1 University Drive, Orange, California 92866; 714-744-7087, fax: 714-744-7015, e-mail address: tdoffice@chapman.edu

Chicago College of Performing Arts - The Theatre Conservatory

See Roosevelt University

Clarion University of Pennsylvania
Clarion, Pennsylvania

State-supported, coed. Rural campus. Total enrollment: 6,338.

College of Santa Fe
Santa Fe, New Mexico

Independent, coed. Suburban campus. Total enrollment: 1,661. Theater program established 1965.
Degrees Bachelor of Fine Arts in the areas of theater, acting, design and technical theater, music theater. Majors and concentrations: acting, music theater, technical theater, theater, theater design/technology, theater management.
Enrollment 123 total; 23 undergraduate, 100 nonprofessional degree.
Theater Student Profile 63% females, 37% males, 24% minorities.
Theater Faculty 7 undergraduate (full-time), 15 undergraduate (part-time). 86% of full-time faculty have terminal degrees. Graduate students do not teach undergraduate courses. Undergraduate student–faculty ratio: 8:1.
Student Life Student groups/activities include Drama Council, Improv Troop, Technical Theatre Students Union.
Expenses for 2005–2006 Application fee: $35. Comprehensive fee: $28,978 includes full-time tuition ($21,530), mandatory fees ($746), and college room and board ($6702). College room only: $3204. Room and board charges vary according to board plan

and housing facility. Special program-related fees: $10–$25 per course for theater workshops, $240 per semester hour for private voice lessons.
Application Procedures Students apply for admission into the professional program by sophomore year. Deadline for freshmen and transfers: March 1. Notification date for freshmen and transfers: July 1. Required: essay, high school transcript, college transcript(s) for transfer students, minimum 2.0 high school GPA, 2 letters of recommendation, interview, audition, portfolio, SAT I or ACT test scores (minimum combined SAT I score of 1000, minimum composite ACT score of 21). Recommended: minimum 3.0 high school GPA, campus visit. Auditions held by appointment on campus and off campus in various cities in the U.S.; recorded music is permissible as a substitute for live auditions with approval from the department and videotaped performances are permissible as a substitute for live auditions with approval from the department. Portfolio reviews held by appointment on campus and off campus in various cities in the U.S..
Web Site http://www.csf.edu
Undergraduate Contact Mr. Thomas Salzman, Chair, Performing Arts Department, College of Santa Fe, 1600 Saint Michael's Drive, Santa Fe, New Mexico 87505; 505-473-6439, fax: 505-473-6016, e-mail address: jkilbourn@csf.edu

Columbia College Chicago
Chicago, Illinois

Independent, coed. Urban campus. Total enrollment: 10,842. Theater program established 1969.
Degrees Bachelor of Arts in the areas of acting, directing, theater design, music theater performance; Bachelor of Fine Arts in the areas of acting, directing, theatrical design. Majors and concentrations: acting, directing, music theater, playwriting, theater design.
Enrollment 719 total; all undergraduate.
Theater Student Profile 62% females, 38% males, 29% minorities, 1% international.
Theater Faculty 24 total (full-time), 42 total (part-time). 20% of full-time faculty have terminal degrees. Graduate students do not teach undergraduate courses. Undergraduate student–faculty ratio: 11:1.
Student Life Student groups/activities include Black Actor's Guild.
Expenses for 2006–2007 Application fee: $35. Comprehensive fee: $26,553 includes full-time tuition ($16,328), mandatory fees ($460), and college room and board ($9765). College room only: $8265. Special program-related fees: $10–$75 per course for class fees.
Financial Aid Program-specific awards: 1 Freshman Achievement in Theater Award for theater students ($1500), 1 Michael Merritt Scholarship for theater/stage design majors ($1000), 1 Betty Garrett Music Theater Scholarship for music theater majors ($1000).
Application Procedures Students admitted directly into the professional program freshman year. Deadline for freshmen and transfers: continuous. Notification date for freshmen and transfers: continuous. Required: essay, high school transcript, college transcript(s) for transfer students, letter of recommendation, students with less than a 2.0 GPA may be required to see an admissions counselor for a personal interview and may be required to attend an intensive remediation program, audition and portfolio for transfer students. Recommended: minimum 2.0 high school GPA, interview, SAT I or ACT test scores. Auditions held on campus. Portfolio reviews held on campus.
Web Site http://www.colum.edu
Undergraduate Contact Mr. Murphy Monroe, Director, Office of Admissions, Columbia College Chicago, 600 South Michigan Avenue, Chicago, Illinois 60605; 312-344-7133, fax: 312-344-8024, e-mail address: admissions@colum.edu

More About the College

Columbia College is the largest and most diverse private undergraduate and graduate arts, media, and communications college in the nation. Located in downtown Chicago, Columbia sits at the heart of the Midwest's arts and communications

Columbia College Chicago (continued)

industries. Columbia's faculty and student body comprise a widely diverse mix of cultures and backgrounds, creating a stimulating environment ideally suited to the pursuit of creative innovation. Intimate class settings (class sizes average only 16 students) facilitate personal attention and practical mentoring with a faculty of working professionals. An aggressive, wide-reaching internship program offers students the opportunity to gain on-site education in their areas of interest.

Columbia places a strong emphasis on each student's development of a professional body of work or portfolio in all disciplines across the college. Columbia's Portfolio Center is dedicated to helping graduating students present their body of work in the most professional way—the exact way employers want to see it. Faculty members work closely with students to help them refine and select appropriate pieces and samples for inclusion in their final portfolio.

Columbia College takes a hands-on, minds-on approach to learning that encourages students to fully explore their chosen field of interest. A required core series of liberal arts classes provides a broad and enriching academic foundation, and elective credit hours allow students to investigate a wide variety of different disciplines throughout the College.

The Theater Department equips its students with the skills needed to fully develop their careers. Run as a professional theater, Columbia's Theater Department provides rigorous, complete, one-on-one training for actors, directors, playwrights, designers, and stage technicians. Through their training, students are equipped with the best and broadest skills necessary to develop their careers fully. Students are immersed in a dynamic and challenging experience that prepares them for both the excitement of live performance and the challenges inherent in a professional life in the theater. Students' study takes place in the classroom, in workshops, and on the stages of the department. Classes in acting technique and craft, singing, dance, and construction are available in the major concentrations of acting, directing, musical theater performance, technical theater, and theater design. There are as many as forty fully staged and workshop performances presented each semester. A subscription season of mainstage plays is attended by individual ticket buyers, special groups, and the College community. The students learn to engage with the world as theater makers and collaborate with their fellow artists to produce engaging work for Chicago stages.

Students must complete all general study and major requirements in order to earn a degree. However, students are encouraged to enroll in other courses, and special workshops enrich their studies. New students are encouraged to start general study course requirements as well as beginning-level courses in the major in the first semester.

Campus and Surroundings Columbia students sit center stage to one of the most vibrant cities in the country; an urban canvas teeming with all the vitality, inspiration, and drama on which creative minds thrive. Located in the middle of the South Loop, Chicago's liveliest downtown district, students enjoy direct access to major theaters, museums, concert halls, restaurants, clubs, parks, galleries, recreational facilities, and Lake Michigan.

This puts Columbia right in the middle of Chicago's professional community, easily connecting students to the city's major corporations, ad agencies, television and radio stations, public relations firms, production houses, recording facilities, theaters, galleries, museums, design studios, and dance companies. Even before they graduate, students can explore all of the nuances of their future careers through internships and professional networking opportunities.

Program Facilities Columbia College consists of eighteen campus buildings located primarily in the historic South Loop neighborhood of downtown Chicago. The centers for dance, music, and theater are conveniently located and are designed for their specific performance needs, including individual and group rehearsal and specialized performance spaces. The Theater

Department has three theaters: the Getz Theater, a 400-seat Art Deco proscenium, and two black-box theaters.

The College's 200,000-volume library and instructional service center provide comprehensive information and study facilities. Reading/study rooms and special audiovisual equipment are available for use in individual projects and research. As a member of a statewide online computer catalog and resource-sharing network, Columbia's library provides students with access to the resources of forty-five academic institutions in Illinois, effectively creating an information base of several million volumes.

Faculty, Resident Artists, and Alumni The faculty is made up of professionals in their areas of expertise who work in the Chicago area. There are part-time faculty members, artists in residence, and full-time faculty members as well as occasional guest lecturers.

Student Performance Opportunities Currently enrolled students, from new freshmen to seniors, can audition for department productions. There is no precasting. Shows usually rehearse evenings and weekends. Students can audition for several shows during the year as long as there are no time conflicts involving scheduled auditions, rehearsals, performances, and classes. Class attendance and maintaining a good GPA are also important.

Senior Showcase is held each spring semester for students who have all the prerequisites. Invited guests include working professionals, directors, agents, producers, casting agents, and production managers.

In addition, students are encouraged to audition within Chicago's professional theater community, as long as it fits around their class schedules.

Concordia University
Montreal, Quebec, Canada

Province-supported, coed. Urban campus. Total enrollment: 31,042. Theater program established 1975.
Degrees Bachelor of Fine Arts in the areas of theatre, design for the theater, theater and development, theater performance, playwriting. Majors and concentrations: performance, playwriting, theater arts/drama, theater design, theatre and development. Cross-registration with any university in Quebec or other approved international institutions.
Enrollment 177 total; all undergraduate.
Theater Student Profile 4% international.
Theater Faculty 11 total (full-time), 17 total (part-time). Graduate students teach a few undergraduate courses. Undergraduate student–faculty ratio: 8:1.
Student Life Student groups/activities include Concordia Association for Students in Theater (CAST), Art Matters Festival, Fine Arts Student Alliance (FASA).
Expenses for 2005–2006 Application fee: $50 Canadian dollars. Tuition, fee, and room and board charges are reported in Canadian dollars. Province resident tuition: $1668 full-time. Canadian resident tuition: $4651 full-time. Mandatory fees: $979 full-time. Full-time tuition and fees vary according to program. College room and board: $6905. Room and board charges vary according to housing facility. International student tuition: $11,238 full-time. Special program-related fees: $50–$100 for various lab/materials fees.
Financial Aid Program-specific awards: Concordia University Entrance Scholarships for Canadian students ($2000).
Application Procedures Students admitted directly into the professional program freshman year. Deadline for freshmen and transfers: March 1. Notification date for freshmen and transfers: July 15. Required: high school transcript, college transcript(s) for transfer students, interview, audition, portfolio. Auditions held monthly from April through August on campus. Portfolio reviews held monthly from April through August on campus; the submission of slides may be substituted for portfolios for large works of art and three-dimensional pieces.
Web Site http://theatre.concordia.ca

Undergraduate Contact Ms. Jolanta Manowska, Communications Assistant, Office of Student Recruitment, Concordia University, 1455 de Maisonneuve Boulevard West, FB801, Montreal, Quebec H3G 1M8, Canada; 514-848-4772, fax: 514-848-2827.

Cornish College of the Arts
Seattle, Washington

Independent, coed. Urban campus. Total enrollment: 768. Theater program established 1914.

Degrees Bachelor of Fine Arts in the area of performance production. Majors and concentrations: costume design, lighting design, set design, sound design, stage management, technical direction.

Enrollment 45 total; all undergraduate.

Theater Student Profile 65% females, 35% males, 14% minorities, 4% international.

Theater Faculty 5 undergraduate (full-time), 4 undergraduate (part-time). 58% of full-time faculty have terminal degrees. Graduate students do not teach undergraduate courses. Undergraduate student–faculty ratio: 5:1.

Expenses for 2005–2006 Application fee: $35. Tuition: $21,200 full-time. Mandatory fees: $300 full-time. Special program-related fees: $150 per year for supplies.

Financial Aid Program-specific awards: Nellie Scholarships for new students, departmental scholarships for new and continuing students, Presidential Scholarships for continuing students.

Application Procedures Students admitted directly into the professional program freshman year. Deadline for freshmen and transfers: August 15. Notification date for freshmen and transfers: August 30. Required: essay, high school transcript, college transcript(s) for transfer students, minimum 2.0 high school GPA, interview, audition. Recommended: 2 letters of recommendation, portfolio, SAT I or ACT test scores. Auditions held 20 times on campus and off campus in Las Vegas, NV; videotaped performances are permissible as a substitute for live auditions when distance is prohibitive. Portfolio reviews held continuously on campus; the submission of slides may be substituted for portfolios when distance is prohibitive.

Web Site http://www.cornish.edu

Undergraduate Contact Eric Pedersen, Director of Admission, Cornish College of the Arts, 1000 Lenora, Seattle, Washington 98121; 800-726-ARTS, fax: 206-720-1011, e-mail address: epedersen@cornish.edu

Cornish College of the Arts
Seattle, Washington

Independent, coed. Urban campus. Total enrollment: 768. Theater program established 1914.

Degrees Bachelor of Fine Arts in the area of theater. Majors and concentrations: acting, original works, performing arts.

Enrollment 180 total; all undergraduate.

Theater Student Profile 65% females, 35% males, 14% minorities, 4% international.

Theater Faculty 16 undergraduate (full-time), 11 undergraduate (part-time). 58% of full-time faculty have terminal degrees. Graduate students do not teach undergraduate courses. Undergraduate student–faculty ratio: 9:1.

Expenses for 2005–2006 Application fee: $35. Tuition: $21,200 full-time. Mandatory fees: $300 full-time. Special program-related fees: $175 per year for supplies and studio rental.

Financial Aid Program-specific awards: Presidential Scholarships for continuing students, Nellie Scholarships for new students, departmental scholarships for new and continuing students.

Application Procedures Students admitted directly into the professional program freshman year. Deadline for freshmen and transfers: August 15. Notification date for freshmen and transfers: August 30. Required: essay, high school transcript, college transcript(s) for transfer students, minimum 2.0 high school GPA, audition. Recommended: minimum 3.0 high school GPA, 2 letters of recommendation, interview, SAT I or ACT test scores, current resumé/head shot. Auditions held 12 times on campus and off campus in Los Angeles, CA; San Francisco, CA;

Portland, OR; videotaped performances are permissible as a substitute for live auditions when distance is prohibitive.

Web Site http://www.cornish.edu

Undergraduate Contact Eric Pedersen, Director of Admission, Cornish College of the Arts, 1000 Lenora, Seattle, Washington 98121; 800-726-ARTS, fax: 206-720-1011, e-mail address: epedersen@cornish.edu

Culver-Stockton College
Canton, Missouri

Independent, coed. Rural campus. Total enrollment: 840. Theater program established 1855.

DePaul University
Chicago, Illinois

Independent Roman Catholic, coed. Urban campus. Total enrollment: 23,148. Theater program established 1925.

Dorothy F. Schmidt College of Arts and Letters

See Florida Atlantic University

Drake University
Des Moines, Iowa

Independent, coed. Suburban campus. Total enrollment: 5,277. Theater program established 1927.

East Carolina University
Greenville, North Carolina

State-supported, coed. Urban campus. Total enrollment: 23,164.

Degrees Bachelor of Fine Arts in the area of theatre arts. Majors and concentrations: acting, design production, music theater, stage management, theater education.

Enrollment 160 total; 150 undergraduate, 10 nonprofessional degree.

Theater Student Profile 55% females, 45% males, 1% minorities, 1% international.

Theater Faculty 19 undergraduate (full-time), 4 undergraduate (part-time). 95% of full-time faculty have terminal degrees. Graduate students do not teach undergraduate courses. Undergraduate student–faculty ratio: 10:1.

Student Life Student groups/activities include East Carolina Playhouse, East Carolina Summer Theatre, studio theater workshops.

Expenses for 2005–2006 Application fee: $50. State resident tuition: $2135 full-time. Nonresident tuition: $12,649 full-time. Mandatory fees: $1492 full-time. College room and board: $6840. College room only: $3790. Room and board charges vary according to board plan and housing facility.

Financial Aid Program-specific awards: 16 scholarships for program majors demonstrating merit ($800).

Application Procedures Students apply for admission into the professional program by sophomore year. Deadline for freshmen: March 15; transfers: April 15. Required: high school transcript, college transcript(s) for transfer students, audition, SAT I test score only. Recommended: minimum 2.0 high school GPA, 3 letters of recommendation. Auditions held once on campus.

Undergraduate Contact Undergraduate Admissions, East Carolina University, Wichard Building, Greenville, North Carolina 27858; 252-328-6640, e-mail address: admis@mail.ecu.edu

Eastern New Mexico University
Portales, New Mexico

State-supported, coed. Rural campus. Total enrollment: 4,033.

Elon University

Elon, North Carolina

Independent, coed. Suburban campus. Total enrollment: 4,956. Theater program established 1991.

Degrees Bachelor of Fine Arts. Majors and concentrations: acting, music theater.

Enrollment 121 total; 101 undergraduate, 20 nonprofessional degree.

Theater Student Profile 58% females, 42% males, 8% minorities, 2% international.

Theater Faculty 12 undergraduate (full-time), 10 undergraduate (part-time). 90% of full-time faculty have terminal degrees. Graduate students do not teach undergraduate courses. Undergraduate student–faculty ratio: 16:1.

Student Life Student groups/activities include Alpha Psi Omega, North Carolina Theatre Conference, Southeastern Theatre Conference. Special housing available for theater students.

Expenses for 2005–2006 Application fee: $40. Comprehensive fee: $25,371 includes full-time tuition ($18,699), mandatory fees ($250), and college room and board ($6422). Room and board charges vary according to board plan and housing facility.

Financial Aid Program-specific awards: 30 Perrine Scholarships for music theatre and theatre arts students ($500–$7000), 1 Clair Myers Award for outstanding music theatre seniors ($500), 1 Lynne Adams Award for outstanding freshmen program majors ($500).

Application Procedures Students admitted directly into the professional program freshman year. Deadline for freshmen and transfers: continuous. Required: essay, high school transcript, college transcript(s) for transfer students, audition, SAT I or ACT test scores, Counselor Evaluation Form, Deans' Evaluation Form (for transfers only), on-site audition/interview for all programs. Recommended: minimum 3.0 high school GPA. Auditions held 9 times on campus.

Web Site http://www.elon.edu/perarts/

Undergraduate Contact Kimberly Rippy, Audition Coordinator, Department of Performing Arts, Elon University, Campus Box 2800, Elon, North Carolina 27244; 366-278-5600, fax: 336-278-5609, e-mail address: krippy@elon.edu

Emerson College

Boston, Massachusetts

Independent, coed. Urban campus. Total enrollment: 4,326. Theater program established 1919.

Degrees Bachelor of Fine Arts in the area of performing arts. Majors and concentrations: acting, music theater, stage management, theater design/technology. Graduate degrees offered: Master of Arts in the area of theater education. Cross-registration with Boston Conservatory of Music, Massachusetts College of Art, Berklee College of Music, School of the Museum of Fine Arts, Boston Architectural Center.

Enrollment 575 total; 375 undergraduate, 200 nonprofessional degree.

Theater Student Profile 60% females, 40% males, 10% minorities, 5% international.

Theater Faculty 22 undergraduate (full-time), 45 undergraduate (part-time). 95% of full-time faculty have terminal degrees. Graduate students do not teach undergraduate courses.

Student Life Student groups/activities include Emerson Comedy Troupes, Musical Theatre Society, Mercutio Drama Ensemble, Rereworks.

Expenses for 2005–2006 Application fee: $60. Comprehensive fee: $35,042 includes full-time tuition ($24,064), mandatory fees ($558), and college room and board ($10,420). College room only: $6200.

Financial Aid Program-specific awards: Emerson Stage Scholarships for performing arts freshmen, Dean's Scholarships for performing arts freshmen, Trustee Scholarships for honors program admission students, Emerson Grants for those demonstrating financial need.

Application Procedures Students admitted directly into the professional program freshman year. Deadline for freshmen: February 1; transfers: March 1. Notification date for freshmen: April 1; transfers: May 1. Required: essay, high school transcript, college transcript(s) for transfer students, 2 letters of recommendation, interview, audition, portfolio, SAT I or ACT test scores, portfolio for design/technology applicants, minimum combined SAT I score of 1650. Recommended: minimum 3.0 high school GPA. Auditions held 25 times on campus and off campus in Seattle, WA; Los Angeles, CA; San Francisco, CA; Chicago, IL; Miami, FL; Atlanta, GA; New York, NY. Portfolio reviews held 10-14 times on campus and off campus in various locations; the submission of slides may be substituted for portfolios for design applicants.

Web Site http://www.emerson.edu

Undergraduate Contact Ms. Sara Ramirez, Director of Admission, Emerson College, 420 Boylston Street, Boston, Massachusetts 02116-4624; 617-824-8600, fax: 617-824-8609.

Graduate Contact Mr. Robert W. Colby, Graduate Program Director, Department of Performing Arts, Emerson College, 69 Brimmer Street, Boston, Massachusetts 02116-4624; 617-824-8780 ext. 8375, fax: 617-824-8799, e-mail address: robert_colby@emerson.edu

Emporia State University

Emporia, Kansas

State-supported, coed. Small town campus. Total enrollment: 6,288. Theater program established 1913.

Degrees Bachelor of Fine Arts. Majors and concentrations: theater.

Enrollment 85 total; all undergraduate.

Theater Student Profile 50% females, 50% males, 5% minorities, 2% international.

Theater Faculty 7 undergraduate (full-time), 3 undergraduate (part-time). 100% of full-time faculty have terminal degrees. Graduate students do not teach undergraduate courses. Undergraduate student–faculty ratio: 15:1.

Student Life Student groups/activities include Educational Theatre Company, Zoiks! - Improvisational Comedy Troupe.

Expenses for 2005–2006 Application fee: $30. State resident tuition: $2638 full-time. Nonresident tuition: $9990 full-time. Mandatory fees: $668 full-time. Full-time tuition and fees vary according to degree level. College room and board: $4787. College room only: $2363. Room and board charges vary according to board plan and housing facility.

Financial Aid Program-specific awards: 1 Anderson Scholarship for outstanding theater students ($1100), 1 Bruder Scholarship for outstanding theater students ($2500), 1 Wise Scholarship for outstanding theater students ($1600), 1 Pflaum Scholarship for outstanding theater students ($1300), 1 Karl Malden Scholarship for outstanding theater students ($2500), 1 Gilson Scholarship for future secondary teachers in theater ($600), 1 Halgedahl Scholarship for outstanding students in musical theater ($1200), 1 Frederickson Scholarship for outstanding theater students ($1100), 1 Matheny Scholarship for outstanding theater students ($1500), 1 Lehman Scholarship for outstanding new theater students ($1300), 1 Hill Scholarship for outstanding theater students ($1000).

Application Procedures Students admitted directly into the professional program freshman year. Deadline for freshmen and transfers: continuous. Required: high school transcript, college transcript(s) for transfer students, ACT test score only (minimum composite ACT score of 21). Recommended: 2 letters of recommendation, interview, audition, portfolio. Auditions held twice on campus; recorded music is permissible as a substitute for live auditions if a campus visit is impossible and videotaped performances are permissible as a substitute for live auditions if a campus visit is impossible. Portfolio reviews held twice on campus; the submission of slides may be substituted for portfolios if a campus visit is impossible.

Web Site http://www.emporia.edu/theatre

Undergraduate Contact Jim Bartrutt, Director of Theatre, Department of Communication and Theatre, Emporia State University, 1200 Commercial, Campus Box 4033, Emporia, Kansas 66801-5087; 620-341-5256, fax: 620-341-6031, e-mail address: bartrufj@emporia.edu

Fairleigh Dickinson University, College at Florham

Madison, New Jersey

Independent, coed. Suburban campus. Total enrollment: 3,481. Theater program established 2001.

Degrees Bachelor of Arts. Majors and concentrations: theater arts/drama.

Enrollment 25 undergraduate.

Theater Student Profile 60% females, 40% males, 15% minorities, 10% international.

Theater Faculty 4 undergraduate (full-time), 4 undergraduate (part-time). 80% of full-time faculty have terminal degrees. Graduate students do not teach undergraduate courses. Undergraduate student–faculty ratio: 15:1.

Student Life Student groups/activities include Playwrights Theatre of New Jersey, Main Stage Productions, Starshine (student-run drama club).

Expenses for 2005–2006 Application fee: $40. Comprehensive fee: $33,932 includes full-time tuition ($24,364), mandatory fees ($540), and college room and board ($9028). College room only: $5404. Room and board charges vary according to board plan and housing facility.

Financial Aid Program-specific awards: Col. Fairleigh Dickinson Awards for theater majors ($9000).

Application Procedures Students admitted directly into the professional program freshman year. Deadline for freshmen and transfers: continuous. Required: high school transcript, college transcript(s) for transfer students, 2 letters of recommendation, SAT I test score only (minimum combined SAT I score of 1100), minimum 2.8 high school GPA. Recommended: interview, audition. Auditions held once on campus.

Web Site http://fdu.edu

Undergraduate Contact Admissions Office, Fairleigh Dickinson University, College at Florham, 285 Madison Avenue, Madison, New Jersey 07940; 973-443-8900.

Feinstein College of Arts and Sciences

See Roger Williams University

Five Towns College

Dix Hills, New York

Independent, coed. Suburban campus. Total enrollment: 1,162. Theater program established 1999.

Degrees Bachelor of Fine Arts in the areas of theater arts, film/video production. Majors and concentrations: audio recording technology, film and video production, music business, music theater.

Enrollment 110 total; all undergraduate.

Theater Student Profile 65% females, 35% males, 11% minorities.

Theater Faculty 4 undergraduate (full-time), 1 undergraduate (part-time). Graduate students do not teach undergraduate courses. Undergraduate student–faculty ratio: 13:1.

Student Life Student groups/activities include drama workshop, opera workshop.

Expenses for 2005–2006 Application fee: $35. Comprehensive fee: $24,350 includes full-time tuition ($14,100) and college room and board ($10,250). Room and board charges vary according to board plan and location. Special program-related fees: $585 per semester for private music instruction (when applicable).

Financial Aid Program-specific awards: 25–35 scholarships ($2000–$5000).

Application Procedures Students admitted directly into the professional program freshman year. Deadline for freshmen and transfers: continuous. Required: high school transcript, college transcript(s) for transfer students, minimum 2.0 high school GPA, 2 letters of recommendation, interview, audition, SAT I or ACT test scores (minimum combined SAT I score of 1400), personal statement. Recommended: essay, minimum 3.0 high school GPA, video, portfolio. Auditions held by appointment on campus;

recorded music is permissible as a substitute for live auditions when distance is prohibitive and videotaped performances are permissible as a substitute for live auditions when distance is prohibitive. Portfolio reviews held annually on campus.

Web Site http://www.ftc.edu

Undergraduate Contact Jerry Cohen, Dean of Enrollment, Admissions Office, Five Towns College, 305 North Service Road, Dix Hills, New York 11746; 631-424-7000 ext. 2110, fax: 631-424-7008.

Dorothy F. Schmidt College of Arts and Letters

Florida Atlantic University

Boca Raton, Florida

State-supported, coed. Suburban campus. Total enrollment: 25,704. Theater program established 1972.

Degrees Bachelor of Arts. Majors and concentrations: acting, design/technical theater. Graduate degrees offered: Master of Fine Arts in the areas of acting, design technical.

Enrollment 134 total; 103 undergraduate, 31 graduate.

Theater Student Profile 65% females, 35% males, 30% minorities, 4% international.

Theater Faculty 9 undergraduate (full-time), 3 undergraduate (part-time), 9 graduate (full-time). 100% of full-time faculty have terminal degrees. Graduate students teach a few undergraduate courses. Undergraduate student–faculty ratio: 11:1.

Student Life Student groups/activities include Alpha Psi Omega, Coalition for the Advancement of Students in Theater.

Expenses for 2005–2006 Application fee: $30. State resident tuition: $2147 full-time. Nonresident tuition: $14,653 full-time. Mandatory fees: $1112 full-time. Full-time tuition and fees vary according to course load. College room and board: $7962. Room and board charges vary according to board plan and housing facility. Special program-related fees: $50 per course for lab fee for technical theater.

Financial Aid Program-specific awards: 20 Esther Griswold Awards for program majors ($1000–$2000), 3 Harold Burris-Meyer Scholarships for technical students ($500).

Application Procedures Students apply for admission into the professional program by sophomore year. Deadline for freshmen and transfers: June 1. Notification date for freshmen and transfers: July 1. Required: high school transcript, college transcript(s) for transfer students, minimum 3.0 high school GPA, 3 letters of recommendation, SAT I or ACT test scores (minimum combined SAT I score of 1000, minimum composite ACT score of 23). Recommended: interview, audition, portfolio. Auditions held 5 times on campus and off campus in Florida Theatre Conference sites and state thespian conference sites. Portfolio reviews held 10 times on campus and off campus in state thespian conference sites, Florida Theater Conference sites, University Resident Theater Association sites, Southeastern Theatre Conference sites; the submission of slides may be substituted for portfolios.

Web Site http://www.fau.edu/divdept/schmidt/theatre/index.htm

Contact Dr. Richard J. Gamble, Chair, Theatre Department, Florida Atlantic University, 777 Glades Road, Box 3091, Boca Raton, Florida 33431-6498; 561-297-3810, fax: 561-297-2180, e-mail address: gamble@fau.edu

Florida International University

Miami, Florida

State-supported, coed. Urban campus. Total enrollment: 36,904. Theater program established 1982.

Degrees Bachelor of Fine Arts in the area of theater. Majors and concentrations: acting, design. Cross-registration with Miami-Dade Community College. Program accredited by NAST.

Enrollment 100 total; 25 undergraduate, 75 nonprofessional degree.

Theater Student Profile 60% females, 40% males, 75% minorities, 20% international.

Theater Faculty 7 undergraduate (full-time), 6 undergraduate (part-time). 100% of full-time faculty have terminal degrees.

Florida International University (continued)

Graduate students do not teach undergraduate courses. Undergraduate student–faculty ratio: 10:1.

Student Life Student groups/activities include dance concerts/theater productions/showcase players, Youth Fair, senior projects (original 1-person shows). Special housing available for theater students.

Expenses for 2005–2006 Application fee: $25. State resident tuition: $3062 full-time. Nonresident tuition: $15,461 full-time. Mandatory fees: $252 full-time. Full-time tuition and fees vary according to course load. College room and board: $9102. College room only: $5518. Room and board charges vary according to housing facility.

Financial Aid Program-specific awards: 21 theater scholarships for program majors ($500–$1000), 2 Theatre Arts League Scholarships for junior/senior program majors ($500–$1000), 6 Dade County Youth Fair Scholarships for program majors ($1000).

Application Procedures Students admitted directly into the professional program freshman year. Deadline for freshmen: July 7; transfers: continuous. Required: high school transcript, college transcript(s) for transfer students, minimum 3.0 high school GPA, 2 letters of recommendation, interview, audition, SAT I or ACT test scores. Recommended: portfolio. Auditions held 5 times on campus and off campus in Florida Thespian Conference sites; Southeastern Theatre Conference sites. Portfolio reviews held 5 times on campus and off campus in Florida Thespian Conference sites; Southeastern Theatre Conference sites.

Web Site http://www.fiu.edu/~thedan/

Undergraduate Contact Wayne Robinson, Associate Professor, Department of Theatre and Dance, Florida International University, 11200 Southwest 8th Street, Miami, Florida 33199; 305-348-2895, fax: 305-348-1803, e-mail address: robinsonw@fiu.edu

Florida State University

Tallahassee, Florida

State-supported, coed. Suburban campus. Total enrollment: 39,146. Theater program established 1973.

Degrees Bachelor of Fine Arts. Majors and concentrations: acting, music theater. Graduate degrees offered: Master of Fine Arts in the areas of acting, costume design, directing, lighting design, scenic design, theater management, technical direction. Program accredited by NAST.

Enrollment 518 total; 85 undergraduate, 86 graduate, 347 nonprofessional degree.

Theater Student Profile 63% females, 37% males, 12% minorities, 1% international.

Theater Faculty 24 total (full-time). 90% of full-time faculty have terminal degrees. Graduate students teach a few undergraduate courses. Undergraduate student–faculty ratio: 14:1.

Student Life Student groups/activities include Florida Theatre Conference, Southeastern Theatre Conference, United Institute of Technical Theatre.

Expenses for 2005–2006 Application fee: $30. State resident tuition: $3208 full-time. Nonresident tuition: $16,340 full-time. Full-time tuition varies according to location. College room and board: $6778. College room only: $3600. Room and board charges vary according to board plan and housing facility.

Financial Aid Program-specific awards: 2 Presidential Scholarships for program students ($1500), 5 Patron's Scholarships for program students ($1000), 1 Hoffman Chair Scholarship for program students ($1000), 3 Fallon Scholarships for program students ($500), 1–9 School of Theatre Scholarships for program students ($500–$1000), 25 scholarships for program students ($750–$1000).

Application Procedures Students admitted directly into the professional program freshman year. Deadline for freshmen and transfers: continuous. Required: high school transcript, college transcript(s) for transfer students, 2 letters of recommendation, SAT I or ACT test scores, interview for design technology applicants, audition for acting and music theater applicants, portfolio for design technology applicants. Auditions held 11 times on campus and off campus in Florida Theatre Conference sites, United Auditions, Teens Educational Theatre Association,

Miami, FL. Portfolio reviews held 4-5 times on campus and off campus in Florida Theatre Conference sites.

Web Site http://theatre.fsu.edu

Contact Barbara Thomas, Program Assistant, School of Theatre, Florida State University, Fine Arts Building, Tallahassee, Florida 32306-1160; 850-644-7234, fax: 850-644-7246, e-mail address: sot-info@mailer.fsu.edu

The Hartt School

See University of Hartford

Hofstra University

Hempstead, New York

Independent, coed. Suburban campus. Total enrollment: 12,890. Theater program established 1956.

Degrees Bachelor of Fine Arts in the areas of performance, production. Majors and concentrations: acting, technical direction, theater arts/drama.

Enrollment 187 total; 45 undergraduate, 142 nonprofessional degree.

Theater Student Profile 70% females, 30% males, 2% minorities, 1% international.

Theater Faculty 7 total (full-time), 8 total (part-time). 100% of full-time faculty have terminal degrees. Graduate students do not teach undergraduate courses. Undergraduate student–faculty ratio: 10:1.

Student Life Student groups/activities include Alpha Psi Omega, Spectrum Players, Masquerade Musical Theater Organization.

Expenses for 2005–2006 Application fee: $50. Comprehensive fee: $30,830 includes full-time tuition ($20,500), mandatory fees ($1030), and college room and board ($9300). College room only: $6200. Full-time tuition and fees vary according to course load and program. Room and board charges vary according to board plan and housing facility.

Financial Aid Program-specific awards: 8–10 activity grants for freshmen ($2000–$3500).

Application Procedures Students apply for admission into the professional program by sophomore year. Deadline for freshmen and transfers: continuous. Required: high school transcript, college transcript(s) for transfer students, minimum 3.0 high school GPA, SAT I or ACT test scores (minimum combined SAT I score of 1050), portfolio for technical direction applicants, audition for scholarship consideration. Recommended: essay, interview, video. Auditions held once in March on campus; videotaped performances are permissible as a substitute for live auditions when distance is prohibitive. Portfolio reviews held once in March on campus; the submission of slides may be substituted for portfolios when distance is prohibitive.

Web Site http://www.hofstra.edu

Undergraduate Contact Admissions Office, Hofstra University, Holland House, Hempstead, New York 11549-1000; 516-463-6700, fax: 516-463-5100, e-mail address: hofstra@hofstra.edu

Howard University

Washington, District of Columbia

Independent, coed. Urban campus. Total enrollment: 10,623. Theater program established 1960.

Degrees Bachelor of Fine Arts. Majors and concentrations: acting, dance arts, music theater, pre-directing, theater arts administration, theater education, theater technology. Cross-registration with Consortium of Universities of the Washington Metropolitan Area. Program accredited by NAST.

Enrollment 175 total; all undergraduate.

Theater Student Profile 95% females, 5% males, 100% minorities.

Theater Faculty 12 undergraduate (full-time), 8 undergraduate (part-time). 100% of full-time faculty have terminal degrees. Graduate students do not teach undergraduate courses. Undergraduate student–faculty ratio: 25:1.

Student Life Student groups/activities include Student Play Festival, Fine Arts Festival.

Expenses for 2005–2006 Application fee: $45. Comprehensive fee: $18,481 includes full-time tuition ($11,490), mandatory fees ($805), and college room and board ($6186). College room only: $3736. Room and board charges vary according to board plan and housing facility.
Financial Aid Program-specific awards: Special Talent Awards for continuing students, Trustee Awards for continuing students.
Application Procedures Students admitted directly into the professional program freshman year. Deadline for freshmen and transfers: February 15. Notification date for freshmen and transfers: April 1. Required: essay, high school transcript, college transcript(s) for transfer students, minimum 2.0 high school GPA, 2 letters of recommendation, interview, audition, SAT I or ACT test scores (minimum combined SAT I score of 1000), resume. Auditions held once on campus.
Web Site http://www.howard.edu/collegefinearts/theatre
Undergraduate Contact Director, Office of Admissions, Howard University, 2400 6th Street, NW, Washington, District of Columbia 20059; 202-806-2700.

Idaho State University

Pocatello, Idaho

State-supported, coed. Small town campus. Total enrollment: 13,977. Theater program established 1924.
Degrees Bachelor of Arts in the area of theater; Bachelor of Fine Arts in the area of theater; Bachelor of Science in the area of theater. Majors and concentrations: acting and directing, costume design, costume production, theater arts/drama, theater design/technology, theater history.
Enrollment 53 total; 46 undergraduate, 7 graduate.
Theater Student Profile 57% females, 43% males, 10% minorities.
Theater Faculty 6 undergraduate (full-time), 3 undergraduate (part-time), 2 graduate (full-time). 75% of full-time faculty have terminal degrees. Graduate students teach a few undergraduate courses. Undergraduate student–faculty ratio: 5:1.
Student Life Student groups/activities include Alpha Psi Omega, summer theater.
Expenses for 2006–2007 Application fee: $40. One-time mandatory fee: $660. Nonresident tuition: $7700 full-time. Mandatory fees: $4000 full-time. College room and board: $5030. College room only: $2100. Special program-related fees: $10–$50 per course for studio space, costume.
Financial Aid Program-specific awards: Associated Students of ISU Awards for program students ($100–$1000), W. Jones Awards for program students ($100–$1000), Blomquist Award for theater majors ($100–$1000).
Application Procedures Students admitted directly into the professional program freshman year. Deadline for freshmen and transfers: August 1. Notification date for freshmen and transfers: August 10. Required: high school transcript, college transcript(s) for transfer students, minimum 2.0 high school GPA, 3 letters of recommendation, SAT I or ACT test scores (minimum combined SAT I score of 860, minimum composite ACT score of 18), portfolio, interview, and letters of recommendation for scholarship consideration. Videotaped performances are permissible as a substitute for live auditions. Portfolio reviews held twice.
Web Site http://www.isu.edu/departments/theadanc
Undergraduate Contact Dr. Sherri R. Dienstfrey, Chair, Department of Theatre and Dance, Idaho State University, Box 8006, Pocatello, Idaho 83209; 208-282-3173, fax: 208-282-6281, e-mail address: diensher@inu.edu
Graduate Contact Dr. Norm Schroder, Professor, Department of Theatre and Dance, Idaho State University, Box 8006, Pocatello, Idaho 83209; 208-282-3603, fax: 208-282-6281, e-mail address: diensher@inu.edu

Illinois State University

Normal, Illinois

State-supported, coed. Urban campus. Total enrollment: 20,653. Theater program established 1970.

Illinois Wesleyan University

Bloomington, Illinois

Independent, coed. Suburban campus. Total enrollment: 2,146. Theater program established 1948.
Degrees Bachelor of Arts in the area of theatre arts; Bachelor of Fine Arts in the areas of acting, music theatre, theatre design and technology. Majors and concentrations: acting, music theater, theater arts studies, theater design/technology.
Enrollment 113 total; 51 undergraduate, 62 nonprofessional degree.
Theater Student Profile 55% females, 45% males, 1% minorities.
Theater Faculty 8 undergraduate (full-time), 10 undergraduate (part-time). 100% of full-time faculty have terminal degrees. Graduate students do not teach undergraduate courses. Undergraduate student–faculty ratio: 12:1.
Student Life Student groups/activities include Comedy Improv Group, Sketch Comedy Group.
Expenses for 2006–2007 Application fee: $0. Comprehensive fee: $35,790 includes full-time tuition ($28,926), mandatory fees ($150), and college room and board ($6714). College room only: $4104. Special program-related fees: $40–$250 for course fees.
Financial Aid Program-specific awards: talent awards for entering freshmen ($5600–$10,000).
Application Procedures Required: essay, high school transcript, college transcript(s) for transfer students, minimum 3.0 high school GPA, SAT I or ACT test scores (minimum combined SAT I score of 1070, minimum composite ACT score of 23), portfolio for design applicants, audition for acting and music theater applicants, on-campus interview for BA applicants. Recommended: interview. Auditions held 4 times on campus; videotaped performances are permissible as a substitute for live auditions with special permission from School of Theatre Arts. Portfolio reviews held 4 times on campus; the submission of slides may be substituted for portfolios with special permission from School of Theatre Arts.
Web Site http://titan.iwu.edu/~theatre
Undergraduate Contact Ms. Bernadette Brennan, Recruitment Coordinator, Theatre Admission Office, Illinois Wesleyan University, PO Box 2900, Bloomington, Illinois 61702-2900; 309-556-3944, fax: 309-556-3558, e-mail address: theatre@titan.iwu.edu

More About the Programs

The School of Theatre Arts at Illinois Wesleyan University (IWU) offers Bachelor of Arts in Theatre Arts, Bachelor of Fine Arts in Acting, Bachelor of Fine Arts in Music Theatre, and Bachelor of Fine Arts in Theatre Design and Technology programs as well as minors in theater arts, theater dance, and arts management (offered with the Department of Business Administration).

Students in the Theatre Arts programs enjoy the low faculty-student ratio, which ensures close mentoring relationships with faculty members. Furthermore, because IWU is strictly an undergraduate institution, courses are never taught by graduate students.

Illinois Wesleyan University (continued)

Theater students are challenged to stretch themselves through opportunities to explore all aspects of theater—through course work and hands-on experiences, both on campus and off.

In addition to obtaining solid training in theater arts, the students are strengthened by the University's liberal arts curriculum, which ensures that they receive a broad education in a variety of disciplines across campus. Students graduate from these programs ready to succeed, having begun to develop their own network of contacts through alumni, internships, summer-stock job opportunities, and visitors who come to campus to deliver master classes or to serve as guest designers, directors, or choreographers. Students begin their careers with excellent resumes, a game plan in place, and a superior educational foundation.

The Bachelor of Arts in Theatre Arts program allows students a broad range of exploration and study of the theater, giving them the opportunity to become theater artists and scholars whose expertise spans more than one facet of the discipline. This degree track is especially well suited to the student who wants a broad education in theater and students who aspire to a professional career in directing, playwriting, dramaturgy, theater management, or other subdiscipline; students who intend to pursue graduate training as a theater scholar or who aspire to teach at the university level; students who wish to double-major; and students who intend to teach on the high-school level.

The Bachelor of Fine Arts in Acting program and the Bachelor of Fine Arts in Music Theatre program are for students who aspire to acting careers or performance careers in musical theater, respectively. These well-rounded preprofessional curricula include applied training in acting, movement, voice, and dance as well as academically oriented courses like dramatic theory, history, and literature. All students are also exposed to the technical and design areas through course work and production experiences. In addition to intensive course work, B.F.A. actors and music theater students often apply their craft on stage in the School's active production season.

The Bachelor of Fine Arts in Theatre Design and Technology program is for students who aspire to careers as designers or technicians. The curriculum includes applied training in drawing, rendering, stagecraft, construction, drafting, and painting as well as such academically oriented courses as dramatic theory, history, and literature. All design/tech students also receive some performance training and have the opportunity to audition for roles and to apply their crafts behind the scenes in the School's active production season.

Campus and Surroundings Illinois Wesleyan University is located on a parklike campus in Bloomington's historic northside residential district. The twin cities of Bloomington and Normal, with a combined population of more than 110,000, offer all the amenities and cultural activities one would expect in a major metropolitan area, including a wide variety of shopping venues and restaurants, museums, art galleries, and a ballet company. The cities are located midway between Chicago and St. Louis, which are easily accessed by car, train, or bus within 2 to 3 hours.

The campus atmosphere is relaxed and friendly. More than 80 percent of the students live on campus. Thirty-five states and twenty nations are represented. On-campus activities and organizations include an International Society, Model U.N., a student senate, professional and honorary societies, intramural and intercollegiate sports, national social fraternities and sororities, political and religious groups, service groups, activities in the arts, a radio station, and several publications.

Program Facilities The main facilities of the School of Theatre Arts are the McPherson Theatre; the E. Melba Johnson Kirkpatrick Lab Theater; dance studios; the Carriage House, which is a classroom and rehearsal space; the Theatre Annex, which provides classrooms and office space; the Phoenix, a student-run black-box theater; the Light Lab (a lighting classroom); and a complete costume shop and a fully operational scene shop.

Student Performance Opportunities The School of Theatre Arts produces one mainstage musical and two mainstage non-musicals annually. In addition, one faculty-directed lab show and one faculty-choreographed dance concert are produced on alternate years. On the alternating year, one Shakespeare mainstage and one lab musical are produced. Three student-directed, 50-minute lab productions are also added to the calendar—one in either the spring or fall semester and two during the May Term.

Special Programs In recent years, many students in the School of Theatre Arts have participated in preprofessional internship programs during their careers at Illinois Wesleyan. Some result from the School's affiliation with the Great Lakes College Association (GLCA), which places interns with professional theaters, television studios, casting agencies, and the like in New York City. Internships are available in design, performance, and management. Recent examples include one student who worked with the producer of *Starlight Express* and the casting agency for *Les Misérables* and *Phantom of the Opera;* another student combined two GLCA internships—one in a casting agency for several television shows and the other in an acting studio in New York. Internships can also be arranged in such theatrical centers as Chicago, Los Angeles, and San Francisco. Internships can be taken for academic credit during the academic year.

The AMC Chicago Arts Program is a semester that students spend immersed in the art scenes of Chicago instead of at IWU. Students live with a roommate in a studio apartment in downtown Chicago, work at an arts-related internship, take a couple of courses, and explore an area of the arts in an independent-study project. Students attend openings, plays, readings, concerts, screenings, rehearsals, recording sessions, installations, performances, and more. They meet the people who are making and presenting art in Chicago and learn about what they do, how they do it, and how they got where they are today.

In some years a Travel Seminar is arranged during Illinois Wesleyan's unique May Term. Under the guidance of a faculty member in the School of Theatre Arts, students attend as many as fifteen plays in New York City or London. Discussions with many prominent actors, directors, designers, producers, and playwrights form an integral part of each Travel Seminar.

Ithaca College
Ithaca, New York

Independent, coed. Small town campus. Total enrollment: 6,412. Theater program established 1927.

Degrees Bachelor of Fine Arts in the areas of acting, musical theater, theatrical production arts. Majors and concentrations: acting, music theater, theater design and production, theater production, theater technology. Cross-registration with Cornell University, Wells College. Program accredited by NAST.

Enrollment 243 total; 142 undergraduate, 101 nonprofessional degree.

Theater Student Profile 62% females, 38% males, 13% minorities, 1% international.

Theater Faculty 19 undergraduate (full-time), 9 undergraduate (part-time). 89% of full-time faculty have terminal degrees. Graduate students do not teach undergraduate courses. Undergraduate student–faculty ratio: 11:1.

Student Life Student groups/activities include American College Theatre Festival, No Bucks Theater, IC Triple Threat Theater.

Expenses for 2005–2006 Application fee: $55. Comprehensive fee: $35,144 includes full-time tuition ($25,194) and college room and board ($9950). College room only: $5120.

Financial Aid Program-specific awards: 2 Peter Bergstrom Scholarships for acting or musical theater majors ($2590), 4 Richard M. Clark Memorial Scholarships for talented program majors ($1400–$3836), 1 George Hoerner Memorial Scholarship for technical theater and scenic design majors ($1632), 1 Theater

Arts Alumni Memorial Scholarship for junior or senior theater arts majors ($2006), 25 Jane Woods Werly Memorial Scholarship for sophomore, junior, or senior musical theater majors ($1120–$3850), 10 Ithaca Premier Talent Scholarships for theater arts majors ($10,000–$13,000), 1 Cissy Cheskis Scholarship for theater arts majors ($584), 1 Laura Hinkley Hauer '21 Scholarship for theater arts majors ($642), 2 Friars Scholarships for theater arts majors ($2500), 1 Katherine B. "Toby" Clarey Memorial Scholarship for talented acting or musical theater majors ($1125).

Application Procedures Students admitted directly into the professional program freshman year. Deadline for freshmen: February 1; transfers: March 1. Notification date for freshmen: April 15. Required: essay, high school transcript, college transcript(s) for transfer students, letter of recommendation, SAT I or ACT test scores, audition for acting and musical theater applicants, portfolio and interview for production arts applicants. Recommended: minimum 3.0 high school GPA. Auditions held 15-20 times for acting and musical theater applicants on campus and off campus in New York, NY; Houston, TX; Dallas, TX; Washington, DC; Chicago, IL; San Francisco, CA; Los Angeles, CA; videotaped performances are permissible as a substitute for live auditions when distance is prohibitive. Portfolio reviews held 15-20 times and by appointment on campus and off campus in New York, NY; Houston, TX; Dallas, TX; Washington, DC; Chicago, IL; San Francisco, CA; Los Angeles, CA; the submission of slides may be substituted for portfolios when distance is prohibitive.

Web Site http://www.ithaca.edu/hs.php

Undergraduate Contact Mr. Gerard Turbide, Acting Director, Admission, Ithaca College, 100 Job Hall, Ithaca, New York 14850-7020; 607-274-3124, fax: 607-274-1900, e-mail address: admission@ithaca.edu

More About the College

The Department of Theatre Arts offers a powerful combination of intensive classroom and performance experience that has made it one of the most effective and highly respected training programs in the nation. The goal is to prepare students for careers in the theater and entertainment business. It is a highly selective program, taught by faculty members whose academic training and professional theater experience have prepared them for the focused, personalized instruction that is the key to successful theatrical training.

The Bachelor of Fine Arts programs in acting and musical theater are performance oriented, providing professional training and experience. The Bachelor of Fine Arts in theatrical production arts and the Bachelor of Science in theater arts management prepare students to enter the design, technical, and managerial areas of the theater and entertainment industry. As with other programs at Ithaca College, the emphasis is on learning by doing. Students pursuing the technology concentration in production, for example, are involved in scenic carpentry, costume construction, drafting, electrics, sound, properties, stage management, and technical direction. The theatrical design concentration provides instruction in scenic design, costume design, lighting design, figure drawing, rendering, and art history, in addition to the technical areas. Students pursuing a Bachelor of Science in theater arts management have the opportunity to develop knowledge in marketing, advertising, publicity, fundraising, grant writing, accounting, personnel management, and other areas. For students who elect the liberal arts–based drama degree, courses include directing, acting, theater history, stagecraft, dramatic literature, dance, stage management, dramaturgy, and playwriting.

In addition to the annual senior showcase for New York City agents and casting directors, students and faculty members travel to New York City to see plays and participate in special theater events. Faculty members advise students about summer stock opportunities, graduate program admission, and work after graduation, taking extra time with individual students to prepare them for auditions or interviews. Design, technical, and theater arts management students have an outstanding record of acceptance at some of the nation's finest graduate programs.

Students direct all No Bucks Theatre productions; seniors may also direct studio theater productions. Student playwrights are encouraged to submit their plays for production.

Theater students may take advantage of courses outside their major within the School of Humanities and Sciences or in the College's Schools of Business, Communications, Health Sciences and Human Performance, Music, and the new interdisciplinary division. A comprehensive college, Ithaca offers some 2,000 courses and more than 100 different degree programs. Theater students may be particularly interested in exploring communications courses in areas such as audio production or film directing.

The city of Ithaca is one of the country's premier college towns, with about 26,000 students at Ithaca College and Cornell University. Surrounded by magnificent gorges, lakes, and countryside in the Finger Lakes region of New York State, Ithaca is a thriving cultural center. The community supports an impressive array of concerts, gallery shows, and movies as well as theater productions mounted by two local theater companies.

The combination of excellent undergraduate theater programs, a vibrant community, and a beautiful location make Ithaca College an exceptional choice for talented and motivated young artists who wish to make the theater and entertainment business their profession.

Program Facilities Performance facilities at Ithaca include a 520-seat proscenium theater, a 280-seat flexible theater, and a small studio theater, all featuring state-of-the-art equipment. Modern studios for acting, dance, and design combine with shops and workrooms for scenery, costumes, sound, electrics, and props to create a stimulating environment for artistic work. The school is a fully accredited member of the National Association of Schools of Theatre.

Faculty, Resident Artists, and Alumni With 20 full-time theater faculty members and an extensive professional staff, the Department of Theatre Arts offers small classes and individualized instruction. Since there are no graduate students, many production opportunities in acting, directing, managing, technical direction, and design exist for the undergraduate student. Guest artists regularly visit campus, sharing their experience and insights and becoming valuable professional contacts. Ithaca alumni in the theater and entertainment world also actively provide career assistance.

Student Performance Opportunities The main-stage season includes six productions; the studio season, six to eight productions. The department, the College, and the local community offer many additional opportunities.

Special Programs One of the most popular options for theater students is a semester at Ithaca College's London Center. Students spend their time studying and seeing plays—as many as twenty-five productions in a semester. Senior theater majors have an opportunity to participate in a field study for a week in New York City. Ithaca alumni discuss the theater and entertainment business, and qualified acting and musical theater majors present their annual showcase for agents and casting directors at an off-Broadway theater.

Jacksonville University
Jacksonville, Florida

Independent, coed. Suburban campus. Total enrollment: 2,948.
Degrees Bachelor of Fine Arts in the area of theater arts. Majors and concentrations: theater arts studies.
Enrollment 12 total; all undergraduate.
Theater Student Profile 58% females, 42% males, 22% minorities, 3% international.
Theater Faculty 4 undergraduate (full-time). 75% of full-time faculty have terminal degrees. Graduate students do not teach undergraduate courses. Undergraduate student–faculty ratio: 13:1.
Student Life Student groups/activities include Alpha Psi Omega, Theater Productions, Performance Outreach to local schools.

Jacksonville University (continued)

Expenses for 2005–2006 Application fee: $30. Comprehensive fee: $26,430 includes full-time tuition ($19,970) and college room and board ($6460). College room only: $3030.

Financial Aid Program-specific awards: 7 Theater Scholarships for those demonstrating need/talent ($1000–$2000).

Application Procedures Students admitted directly into the professional program freshman year. Deadline for freshmen and transfers: continuous. Notification date for freshmen and transfers: continuous. Required: high school transcript, college transcript(s) for transfer students, minimum 2.0 high school GPA, audition, SAT I or ACT test scores (minimum combined SAT I score of 800). Recommended: essay, minimum 3.0 high school GPA, letter of recommendation. Auditions held by appointment on campus; videotaped performances are permissible as a substitute for live auditions if visit to campus is not possible.

Web Site http://www.ju.edu

Undergraduate Contact Miriam King, Vice President of Enrollment Management, Jacksonville University, 2800 University Boulevard North, Jacksonville, Florida 32211; 904-745-7000, fax: 904-745-7012.

Johnson State College
Johnson, Vermont

State-supported, coed. Rural campus. Total enrollment: 1,866. Theater program established 1982.

Degrees Bachelor of Arts. Majors and concentrations: music theater, theater arts/drama. Cross-registration with members of National Student Exchange Program, any school within the Vermont State College System.

Enrollment 83 total; all undergraduate.

Theater Student Profile 54% females, 46% males, 18% minorities.

Theater Faculty 100% of full-time faculty have terminal degrees. Graduate students do not teach undergraduate courses. Undergraduate student–faculty ratio: 8:1.

Student Life Student groups/activities include Children's Theatre, American College Theatre Festival, Campus Theatre Club.

Expenses for 2006–2007 Application fee: $35. State resident tuition: $6722 full-time. Nonresident tuition: $14,524 full-time. Mandatory fees: $184 full-time. College room and board: $6910. College room only: $6132.

Financial Aid Program-specific awards: 13 Arthur Dibden Talent Scholarships for program majors ($250–$500).

Application Procedures Students apply for admission into the professional program by sophomore year. Deadline for freshmen and transfers: continuous. Notification date for freshmen and transfers: continuous. Required: essay, high school transcript, college transcript(s) for transfer students, minimum 2.0 high school GPA, letter of recommendation, audition, SAT I or ACT test scores. Recommended: interview. Auditions held by appointment on campus; videotaped performances are permissible as a substitute for live auditions by prior arrangement.

Web Site http://www.johnsonstatecollege.edu

Undergraduate Contact Ms. Penny P. Howrigan, Associate Dean of Enrollment Services, Johnson State College, 337 College Hill, Johnson, Vermont 05656; 800-635-1219, fax: 802-635-1230, e-mail address: jscapply@jsc.vsc.edu

Jordan College of Fine Arts - Department of Theatre

See Butler University

The Juilliard School
New York, New York

Independent, coed. Urban campus. Total enrollment: 808. Theater program established 1968.

Degrees Artist's Diploma; Bachelor of Fine Arts in the area of drama. Majors and concentrations: theater arts/drama. Cross-registration with Barnard and Columbia Colleges (Columbia University).

Enrollment 79 total; 71 undergraduate, 8 graduate.

Theater Student Profile 40% females, 60% males, 38% minorities, 4% international.

Theater Faculty 21 total (full-time), 5 total (part-time). Graduate students do not teach undergraduate courses. Undergraduate student–faculty ratio: 3:1.

Student Life Student groups/activities include public drama performances, cabaret performance, collaboration between undergraduate actors and graduate playwrights. Special housing available for theater students.

Expenses for 2005–2006 Application fee: $100. Comprehensive fee: $34,500 includes full-time tuition ($24,330), mandatory fees ($600), and college room and board ($9570). Room and board charges vary according to housing facility.

Financial Aid Program-specific awards: 70 merit and need-based aid for program majors ($26,915).

Application Procedures Students admitted directly into the professional program freshman year. Deadline for freshmen: December 1. Notification date for freshmen: April 1. Required: essay, high school transcript, college transcript(s) for transfer students, letter of recommendation, audition, resumé, TOEFL for all non-native English speakers. Recommended: photo. Auditions held once on campus and off campus in Chicago, IL; San Francisco, CA.

Web Site http://www.juilliard.edu

Undergraduate Contact Ms. Lee Cioppa, Associate Dean for Admissions, The Juilliard School, 60 Lincoln Center Plaza, New York, New York 10023-6588; 212-799-5000 ext. 223, fax: 212-769-6420, e-mail address: admissions@juilliard.edu

Kent State University
Kent, Ohio

State-supported, coed. Suburban campus. Total enrollment: 23,622. Theater program established 1983.

Degrees Bachelor of Fine Arts in the areas of design/technology, musical theater. Majors and concentrations: design technology, entertainment arts, music theater, theater arts/drama. Graduate degrees offered: Master of Fine Arts in the areas of acting, design/technology. Program accredited by NAST, NASD.

Enrollment 244 total; 30 undergraduate, 14 graduate, 200 nonprofessional degree.

Theater Student Profile 56% females, 44% males, 12% minorities, 5% international.

Theater Faculty 18 total (full-time), 4 total (part-time). 94% of full-time faculty have terminal degrees. Graduate students teach a few undergraduate courses. Undergraduate student–faculty ratio: 15:1.

Student Life Student groups/activities include Alpha Psi Omega, United States Institute for Theatre Technology, Kent Dance Association. Special housing available for theater students.

Expenses for 2005–2006 Application fee: $30. State resident tuition: $7954 full-time. Nonresident tuition: $15,386 full-time. Full-time tuition varies according to course level, course load, degree level, location, program, reciprocity agreements, and student level. College room and board: $6640. College room only: $4040. Room and board charges vary according to board plan and housing facility. Special program-related fees: $25–$50 per semester for design technology courses (materials).

Financial Aid Program-specific awards: 12 Creative Arts Awards for program majors ($1800–$3300).

Application Procedures Students admitted directly into the professional program freshman year. Deadline for freshmen and transfers: continuous. Required: high school transcript, college transcript(s) for transfer students, minimum 2.0 high school GPA, audition, portfolio, SAT I or ACT test scores (minimum combined SAT I score of 980, minimum composite ACT score of 21), completion of college preparatory courses. Recommended: minimum 3.0 high school GPA, 3 letters of recommendation, interview. Auditions held twice on campus and off campus in Southeastern Theatre Conference sites, Ohio Theatre Alliance sites, United States Institute for Theatre Technology Conference sites. Portfolio reviews held twice on campus and off campus in Southeastern Theatre Conference sites, United States Institute for Theatre Technology Conference sites; the submission of slides may be substituted for portfolios when distance is prohibitive.

Web Site http://www.theatre.kent.edu
Undergraduate Contact Dr. John R. Crawford, Chair, School of Theatre and Dance, Kent State University, PO Box 5190, Kent, Ohio 44242-0001; 330-672-2082, fax: 330-672-2889, e-mail address: jcrawfo1@kent.edu
Graduate Contact Dr. Rosemarie K. Bank, Graduate Coordinator, School of Theatre and Dance, Kent State University, PO Box 5190, Kent, Ohio 44242; 330-672-2082, fax: 330-672-2889.

Lamar D. Fain College of Fine Arts

See Midwestern State University

Leigh Gerdine College of Fine Arts

See Webster University

Lindenwood University

St. Charles, Missouri

Independent Presbyterian, coed. Suburban campus. Total enrollment: 9,076.
Degrees Bachelor of Fine Arts in the area of theater. Majors and concentrations: acting, arts management, design, directing, music theater, technical theater, theater education. Graduate degrees offered: Master of Fine Arts in the area of theater. Cross-registration with Maryville University of St. Louis, Missouri Baptist College, Fontbonne University, Webster University, Missouri Valley College.
Theater Faculty 5 undergraduate (full-time), 3 undergraduate (part-time), 5 graduate (full-time), 3 graduate (part-time). 90% of full-time faculty have terminal degrees. Graduate students do not teach undergraduate courses.
Student Life Student groups/activities include mainstage and black box productions, dinner theater productions, musical theater productions.
Expenses for 2006–2007 Application fee: $30. Comprehensive fee: $18,240 includes full-time tuition ($12,000), mandatory fees ($240), and college room and board ($6000). College room only: $3000. Special program-related fees: $25–$65 per class for computer studio fees; make-up kit fees.
Financial Aid Program-specific awards: talent awards and scholarships for high school students, talent awards and scholarships for transfer students.
Application Procedures Students admitted directly into the professional program freshman year. Deadline for freshmen and transfers: continuous. Required: high school transcript, college transcript(s) for transfer students, minimum 2.0 high school GPA, interview, audition, ACT test score only. Recommended: essay, minimum 3.0 high school GPA, letter of recommendation. Auditions held continuously on campus and off campus in various locations; recorded music is permissible as a substitute for live auditions when distance is prohibitive and videotaped performances are permissible as a substitute for live auditions when distance is prohibitive. Portfolio reviews held continuously on campus and off campus in various locations; the submission of slides may be substituted for portfolios when distance is prohibitive.
Undergraduate Contact Mr. Ted Gregory, Director, Theatre Department, Lindenwood University, 209 South Kings Highway, St. Charles, Missouri 63301; 636-949-4966, fax: 636-949-4910, e-mail address: tgregory@lindenwood.edu

Long Island University, C.W. Post Campus

Brookville, New York

Independent, coed. Suburban campus. Total enrollment: 8,472.
Degrees Bachelor of Fine Arts in the area of theater. Majors and concentrations: acting, arts management, dance, film, production/design, theater arts/drama. Graduate degrees offered: Master of Arts in the area of theater.
Enrollment 127 total; 120 undergraduate, 7 graduate.

Theater Student Profile 59% females, 41% males, 30% minorities, 5% international.
Theater Faculty 9 total (full-time), 9 total (part-time). Graduate students do not teach undergraduate courses. Undergraduate student–faculty ratio: 7:1.
Student Life Student groups/activities include Post Theatre Students Association, American College Theatre Festival.
Expenses for 2005–2006 Application fee: $30. Comprehensive fee: $31,930 includes full-time tuition ($22,100), mandatory fees ($1130), and college room and board ($8700). College room only: $5730. Full-time tuition and fees vary according to program. Room and board charges vary according to board plan and housing facility. Special program-related fees: $40 per class for dance accompanists, $45 per semester for production materials.
Financial Aid Program-specific awards: 15 Theatre Department Awards for program majors ($1000–$2000).
Application Procedures Students apply for admission into the professional program by freshman year. Deadline for freshmen and transfers: continuous. Notification date for freshmen and transfers: continuous. Required: essay, high school transcript, college transcript(s) for transfer students, 2 letters of recommendation, interview, SAT I or ACT test scores, audition for acting applicants, portfolio for design production majors. Recommended: minimum 3.0 high school GPA. Auditions held by appointment on campus and off campus in Southeastern Theatre Conference sites, International Thespian Society sites, Texas Magnate Auditions; recorded music is permissible as a substitute for live auditions if a campus visit is impossible and videotaped performances are permissible as a substitute for live auditions if a campus visit is impossible. Portfolio reviews held on campus and off campus in International Thespian Society sites; the submission of slides may be substituted for portfolios.
Web Site http://www.liu.edu
Undergraduate Contact Gary Bergman, Associate Provost for Enrollment Services, Admissions, Long Island University, C.W. Post Campus, 720 Northern Boulevard, Brookville, New York 11548; 516-299-2900, fax: 516-299-2418, e-mail address: enroll@cwpost.liu.edu
Graduate Contact Dr. Cara Gargano, Chair, Department of Theatre, Film, and Dance, Long Island University, C.W. Post Campus, 720 Northern Boulevard, Brookville, New York 11548; 516-299-2353, fax: 516-299-3824.

Longwood University

Farmville, Virginia

State-supported, coed. Total enrollment: 4,289. Theater program established 1966.
Degrees Bachelor of Arts in the area of theatre; Bachelor of Fine Arts in the area of theatre. Majors and concentrations: performance, technical theater, theater education. Cross-registration with Hampden-Sydney College. Program accredited by NAST.
Enrollment 40 total; all undergraduate.
Theater Student Profile 56% females, 44% males, 2% minorities, 1% international.
Theater Faculty 4 undergraduate (full-time), 2 undergraduate (part-time). 100% of full-time faculty have terminal degrees. Graduate students do not teach undergraduate courses. Undergraduate student–faculty ratio: 12:1.
Student Life Student groups/activities include Alpha Psi Omega. Special housing available for theater students.
Expenses for 2005–2006 Application fee: $40. State resident tuition: $3586 full-time. Nonresident tuition: $10,270 full-time. Mandatory fees: $3434 full-time. College room and board: $5586. College room only: $3288. Room and board charges vary according to board plan.
Application Procedures Students apply for admission into the professional program by sophomore year. Deadline for freshmen and transfers: continuous. Notification date for freshmen and transfers: June 1. Required: essay, high school transcript, college transcript(s) for transfer students, SAT I or ACT test scores, minimum 2.3 college GPA for transfers, minimum 2.5 high school GPA. Recommended: minimum 3.0 high school GPA.
Web Site http://www.longwood.edu/theatre

Longwood University (continued)

Undergraduate Contact Dr. Gene Muto, Theatre Program Coordinator, Department of Communication Studies and Theatre, Longwood University, 201 High Street, Farmville, Virginia 23909-1899; 434-395-2643, fax: 434-395-2680, e-mail address: theatre@longwood.edu

Marshall University
Huntington, West Virginia

State-supported, coed. Urban campus. Total enrollment: 13,988. Theater program established 1933.

Mars Hill College
Mars Hill, North Carolina

Independent Baptist, coed. Small town campus. Total enrollment: 1,378. Theater program established 1980.
Degrees Bachelor of Arts in the areas of theater arts, theater education; Bachelor of Fine Arts in the area of musical theater. Majors and concentrations: music theater, theater arts/drama, theater education. Cross-registration with Warren Wilson College, University of North Carolina at Asheville. Program accredited by NAST.
Enrollment 33 total; all undergraduate.
Theater Student Profile 54% females, 46% males, 15% minorities.
Theater Faculty 3 undergraduate (full-time), 2 undergraduate (part-time). 80% of full-time faculty have terminal degrees. Graduate students do not teach undergraduate courses. Undergraduate student–faculty ratio: 9:1.
Student Life Student groups/activities include affiliation with Southern Appalachian Repertory Theatre.
Expenses for 2006–2007 Application fee: $25. Comprehensive fee: $24,378 includes full-time tuition ($17,950) and college room and board ($6428). College room only: $3268. Special program-related fees: $100 per course for graphic design fees, $100 per course for makeup fees.
Financial Aid Program-specific awards: 12–15 performance scholarships for program majors ($500–$1000).
Application Procedures Students admitted directly into the professional program freshman year. Deadline for freshmen and transfers: continuous. Required: high school transcript, college transcript(s) for transfer students, minimum 2.0 high school GPA, 2 letters of recommendation, interview, audition. Auditions held 4 times and by appointment on campus; recorded music is permissible as a substitute for live auditions when distance is prohibitive and videotaped performances are permissible as a substitute for live auditions when distance is prohibitive.
Web Site http://www.mhc.edu
Undergraduate Contact Neil St. Clair, Head, Department of Theatre Arts, Mars Hill College, Mars Hill, North Carolina 28754; 828-689-1462, fax: 828-689-1272.

Marymount Manhattan College
New York, New York

Independent, coed. Total enrollment: 2,007. Theater program established 1977.
Degrees Bachelor of Fine Arts. Majors and concentrations: acting. Cross-registration with Hunter College of the City University of New York.
Enrollment 450 total; 176 undergraduate, 274 nonprofessional degree.
Theater Student Profile 58% females, 42% males, 20% minorities, 6% international.
Theater Faculty 14 undergraduate (full-time), 50 undergraduate (part-time). 80% of full-time faculty have terminal degrees. Graduate students do not teach undergraduate courses. Undergraduate student–faculty ratio: 12:1.
Student Life Student groups/activities include STAM (Student Theatre at Marymount), MMC Shakespeare Company.
Expenses for 2006–2007 Application fee: $60. Comprehensive fee: $31,728 includes full-time tuition ($18,748), mandatory fees

($890), and college room and board ($12,090). College room only: $10,090. Special program-related fees: $15 per credit for studio/performance courses.
Financial Aid Program-specific awards: competitive merit scholarships for freshmen program majors ($500–$5000), transfer competitive merit scholarships for transfer program majors ($500–$5000).
Application Procedures Students admitted directly into the professional program freshman year. Deadline for freshmen and transfers: March 11. Notification date for freshmen and transfers: continuous. Required: high school transcript, college transcript(s) for transfer students, minimum 2.0 high school GPA, letter of recommendation, interview, audition, SAT I or ACT test scores, minimum 2.8 high school GPA. Recommended: essay, minimum 3.0 high school GPA. Auditions held 6 times on campus and off campus in Dallas, TX; Chicago, IL; San Francisco, CA; videotaped performances are permissible as a substitute for live auditions when distance is prohibitive.
Web Site http://marymount.mmm.edu
Undergraduate Contact Prof. David Mold, Director of Theater Admissions, Theatre Arts Department, Marymount Manhattan College, 221 East 71st Street, New York, New York 10021; 212-774-0767, fax: 212-774-0770, e-mail address: theatre@mmm.edu

Rutgers, The State University of New Jersey
Mason Gross School of the Arts
New Brunswick, New Jersey

State-supported, coed. Small town campus. Theater program established 1976.
Degrees Bachelor of Fine Arts in the area of theater arts. Majors and concentrations: acting, design, production and management specialties. Graduate degrees offered: Master of Fine Arts in the area of theater arts.
Enrollment 272 total; 122 undergraduate, 74 graduate, 76 nonprofessional degree.
Theater Student Profile 49% females, 51% males, 22% minorities.
Theater Faculty 16 total (full-time), 35 total (part-time). Graduate students do not teach undergraduate courses.
Student Life Special housing available for theater students.
Expenses for 2005–2006 Special program-related fees: $30–$100 per year for class supplies, models, transportation to museums, salon costumes, tickets, $3300 per year for professional acting program fee.
Application Procedures Students admitted directly into the professional program freshman year. Deadline for freshmen: continuous; transfers: March 15. Required: high school transcript, college transcript(s) for transfer students, minimum 2.0 high school GPA, SAT I or ACT test scores, audition for acting majors, portfolio for design majors, interview for production and design majors. Recommended: essay, 2 letters of recommendation. Auditions held one weekend late February on campus and off campus in New York, NY; Chicago, IL; San Francisco, CA; Los Angeles, CA; Miami, FL; videotaped performances are permissible as a substitute for live auditions when distance is prohibitive. Portfolio reviews held by appointment on campus; the submission of slides may be substituted for portfolios when distance is prohibitive.
Web Site http://mgsa.rutgers.edu/theater/thea.html
Undergraduate Contact Assistant Vice President for University Undergraduate Admissions, Rutgers, The State University of New Jersey, Mason Gross School of the Arts, PO Box 2101, New Brunswick, New Jersey 08901-8527; 732-445-3770, fax: 732-445-0237.
Graduate Contact Mr. Donald J. Taylor, Director of Graduate and Professional Admissions, Rutgers, The State University of New Jersey, Mason Gross School of the Arts, Van Nest Hall, Room 204, New Brunswick, New Jersey 08901-8527; 732-932-7711, fax: 732-932-8231.

Meadows School of the Arts

See Southern Methodist University

Lamar D. Fain College of Fine Arts

Midwestern State University

Wichita Falls, Texas

State-supported, coed. Urban campus. Total enrollment: 6,279.
Degrees Bachelor of Arts in the areas of theater, theater with teacher certification; Bachelor of Fine Arts in the areas of theater, theater with teacher certification. Majors and concentrations: performance, theater design/technology.
Enrollment 49 total.
Theater Faculty 4 undergraduate (full-time). 75% of full-time faculty have terminal degrees. Graduate students do not teach undergraduate courses. Undergraduate student–faculty ratio: 12:1.
Student Life Student groups/activities include Alpha Psi Omega.
Expenses for 2006–2007 Application fee: $25. State resident tuition: $1500 full-time. Nonresident tuition: $9750 full-time. Mandatory fees: $3066 full-time. College room and board: $5220. College room only: $2660.
Financial Aid Program-specific awards: 30 theater scholarships for program majors ($500–$2000).
Application Procedures Students admitted directly into the professional program freshman year. Deadline for freshmen and transfers: continuous. Required: high school transcript, college transcript(s) for transfer students, SAT I or ACT test scores, minimum 3.0 high school GPA, audition, interview, and/or portfolio for scholarship consideration. Recommended: minimum 3.0 high school GPA, interview, audition. Auditions held 5 times on campus and off campus in theater conference locations; recorded music is permissible as a substitute for live auditions when distance is prohibitive and videotaped performances are permissible as a substitute for live auditions when distance is prohibitive. Portfolio reviews held once on campus; the submission of slides may be substituted for portfolios whenever needed.
Web Site http://finearts.mwsu.edu/theatre
Undergraduate Contact Ms. Laura N. Jefferson, Chair, Theatre Program, Midwestern State University, 3410 Taft Boulevard, Fain Fine Arts Center, Wichita Falls, Texas 76308; 940-397-4395, fax: 940-397-4909.

Millikin University

Decatur, Illinois

Independent, coed. Suburban campus. Total enrollment: 2,641.

Missouri State University

Springfield, Missouri

State-supported, coed. Suburban campus. Total enrollment: 18,928.

Nebraska Wesleyan University

Lincoln, Nebraska

Independent United Methodist, coed. Suburban campus. Total enrollment: 2,016. Theater program established 1958.
Degrees Bachelor of Fine Arts in the area of theater. Majors and concentrations: acting, creative writing, directing, music theater, production management, theater design/technology, theater management. Cross-registration with University of Nebraska-Lincoln.
Enrollment 40 total; 25 undergraduate, 15 nonprofessional degree.
Theater Student Profile 52% females, 48% males, 5% minorities, 2% international.
Theater Faculty 5 undergraduate (full-time), 2 undergraduate (part-time). 100% of full-time faculty have terminal degrees. Graduate students do not teach undergraduate courses. Undergraduate student–faculty ratio: 4:1.
Student Life Student groups/activities include Theta Alpha Phi (theater honorary society), American College Theatre Festival, Plainsman Players (local honorary).

Expenses for 2005–2006 Application fee: $20. Comprehensive fee: $23,425 includes full-time tuition ($18,100), mandatory fees ($310), and college room and board ($5015). Room and board charges vary according to board plan and housing facility.
Financial Aid Program-specific awards: 10–15 theater scholarships for program majors ($1250).
Application Procedures Students admitted directly into the professional program freshman year. Deadline for freshmen and transfers: May 1. Notification date for freshmen and transfers: continuous. Required: essay, high school transcript, college transcript(s) for transfer students, minimum 3.0 high school GPA, 2 letters of recommendation, interview, SAT I or ACT test scores (minimum combined SAT I score of 920, minimum composite ACT score of 20). Recommended: audition, portfolio. Auditions held by appointment on campus; videotaped performances are permissible as a substitute for live auditions when distance is prohibitive. Portfolio reviews held by appointment on campus; the submission of slides may be substituted for portfolios.
Web Site http://www.nebrwesleyan.edu/depts/commta/
Undergraduate Contact Dr. Jay Scott Chipman, Director of Theatre, Communication and Theatre Arts Department, Nebraska Wesleyan University, 5000 St. Paul Avenue, Lincoln, Nebraska 68504; 402-465-2386, fax: 402-456-2179, e-mail address: jsc@nebrwesleyan.edu

New World School of the Arts

Miami, Florida

State-supported, coed. Urban campus. Total enrollment: 371. Theater program established 1988.
Degrees Bachelor of Fine Arts in the area of theater. Majors and concentrations: acting, music theater. Mandatory cross-registration with University of Florida, Miami-Dade Community College. Program accredited by NAST.
Enrollment 56 total; all undergraduate.
Theater Student Profile 57% females, 43% males, 46% minorities, 4% international.
Theater Faculty 5 undergraduate (full-time), 20 undergraduate (part-time). 90% of full-time faculty have terminal degrees. Graduate students do not teach undergraduate courses. Undergraduate student–faculty ratio: 2:1.
Student Life Student groups/activities include Florida Theatre Association, State Thespians, Florida Association of Theater Education.
Expenses for 2005–2006 Application fee: $0. State resident tuition: $12,000 full-time. Nonresident tuition: $17,000 full-time.
Financial Aid Program-specific awards: 1 Robert Brenner Merit Scholarship for music theater majors ($1000), 1 Annett Foosaner Merit Scholarship for program majors ($1000), 2 Donald Khan Merit Scholarships for program majors ($1000), 1 Betty Ann Merit Scholarship for program majors ($1000), 1 Douglas Fairbanks/Southern Bell Merit Scholarship for program majors ($1000), 1 Tommy Tune Merit Scholarship for music theater majors ($500), 1 George Abbott Merit Scholarship for music theater majors ($500), 4 Nations Bank Merit Scholarships for program majors ($2000), 25 Miami-Dade Community College Merit Scholarships for program majors ($1500).
Application Procedures Students admitted directly into the professional program freshman year. Deadline for freshmen and transfers: continuous. Notification date for freshmen and transfers: continuous. Required: essay, high school transcript, college transcript(s) for transfer students, 2 letters of recommendation, audition. Recommended: minimum 2.0 high school GPA, interview, SAT I or ACT test scores. Auditions held continuously on campus and off campus in Southeastern Theatre Conference sites and Florida Theatre Conference sites; videotaped performances are permissible as a substitute for live auditions for out-of-state applicants.
Web Site http://www.mdc.edu/nwsa
Undergraduate Contact Pamela Neumann, Recruitment and Admissions Coordinator, Student Services, New World School of the Arts, 300 North East 2nd Avenue, Miami, Florida 33132; 305-237-7007, fax: 305-237-3794, e-mail address: nwsaadm@mdc.edu

Tisch School of the Arts, Department of Drama
New York University
New York, New York

Independent, coed. Urban campus. Total enrollment: 40,004. Theater program established 1965.

Degrees Bachelor of Fine Arts in the area of drama. Majors and concentrations: acting, directing, music theater, technical production. Graduate degrees offered: Master of Fine Arts in the area of acting.

Enrollment 1,441 total; 1,388 undergraduate, 53 graduate.

Theater Student Profile 60% females, 40% males, 23% minorities, 3% international.

Theater Faculty 31 undergraduate (full-time), 53 undergraduate (part-time), 9 graduate (full-time), 12 graduate (part-time). 100% of full-time faculty have terminal degrees. Graduate students do not teach undergraduate courses. Undergraduate student–faculty ratio: 5:1.

Student Life Student groups/activities include Community Connections, Tisch Talent Guild, The Collective.

Expenses for 2005–2006 Application fee: $65. Comprehensive fee: $43,170 includes full-time tuition ($29,890), mandatory fees ($1800), and college room and board ($11,480). Full-time tuition and fees vary according to program. Room and board charges vary according to board plan and housing facility.

Financial Aid Program-specific awards available.

Application Procedures Students admitted directly into the professional program freshman year. Deadline for freshmen: January 15; transfers: April 1. Notification date for freshmen: April 1; transfers: May 15. Required: essay, high school transcript, college transcript(s) for transfer students, 2 letters of recommendation, interview, audition, portfolio, SAT I or ACT test scores. Recommended: minimum 3.0 high school GPA. Auditions held continuously from November 1 through March 15 on campus and off campus in Chicago, IL; San Francisco, CA; Atlanta, GA; Los Angeles, CA; Houston, TX; videotaped performances are permissible as a substitute for live auditions with approval from the department. Portfolio reviews held continuously from November 1 through March 15 on campus and off campus in Chicago, IL; San Francisco, CA; Atlanta, GA; Los Angeles, CA; Houston, TX.

Web Site http://drama.tisch.nyu.edu

Undergraduate Contact Mr. Andrew I. Uriarte, Director of Recruitment and Student Affairs, Tisch School of the Arts, New York University, 721 Broadway, 8th Floor, New York, New York 10003-6807; 212-998-1900, fax: 212-995-4060, e-mail address: andrew.uriarte@nyu.edu

Graduate Contact Mr. Dan Sanford, Director of Graduate Admissions, Tisch School of the Arts, New York University, 721 Broadway, 8th Floor, New York, New York 10003-6807; 212-998-1900, fax: 212-995-4060, e-mail address: dan.sandford@nyu.edu

Tisch School of the Arts, Rita and Burton Goldberg Department of Dramatic Writing
New York University
New York, New York

Independent, coed. Urban campus. Total enrollment: 40,004. Theater program established 1980.

Degrees Bachelor of Fine Arts. Majors and concentrations: dramatic writing. Graduate degrees offered: Master of Fine Arts in the area of dramatic writing.

Enrollment 250 total; 206 undergraduate, 44 graduate.

Theater Student Profile 49% females, 51% males, 16% minorities, 4% international.

Theater Faculty 14 undergraduate (full-time), 20 undergraduate (part-time), 15 graduate (full-time), 26 graduate (part-time). 100% of full-time faculty have terminal degrees. Graduate students teach a few undergraduate courses. Undergraduate student–faculty ratio: 5:1.

Student Life Student groups/activities include Community Connections, The Collective, Tisch Talent Guild.

Expenses for 2005–2006 Application fee: $65. Comprehensive fee: $43,170 includes full-time tuition ($29,890), mandatory fees ($1800), and college room and board ($11,480). Full-time tuition and fees vary according to program. Room and board charges vary according to board plan and housing facility.

Application Procedures Students admitted directly into the professional program freshman year. Deadline for freshmen: January 15; transfers: April 1. Notification date for freshmen: April 1; transfers: May 15. Required: essay, high school transcript, college transcript(s) for transfer students, 2 letters of recommendation, portfolio, SAT I or ACT test scores. Recommended: minimum 3.0 high school GPA.

Web Site http://ddw.tisch.nyu.edu

Undergraduate Contact Mr. Andrew I. Uriarte, Director of Recruitment and Student Affairs, Tisch School of the Arts, New York University, 721 Broadway, 8th Floor, New York, New York 10003-6807; 212-998-1900, fax: 212-995-4060, e-mail address: andrew.uriarte@nyu.edu

Graduate Contact Mr. Dan Sandford, Director of Graduate Admissions, Tisch School of the Arts, New York University, 721 Broadway, 8th Floor, New York, New York 10003-6807; 212-998-1900, fax: 212-995-4060, e-mail address: dan.sandford@nyu.edu

New York University Steinhardt School
New York University
New York, New York

Independent, coed. Urban campus. Total enrollment: 40,004.

Degrees Bachelor of Science in the area of educational theatre. Majors and concentrations: educational theater. Graduate degrees offered: Master of Arts in the areas of teachers of educational theatre (all grades), teachers of educational theatre (with English 7-12), educational theatre in colleges and communities. Doctor of Education in the area of educational theatre for teachers of college/higher education; Doctor of Philosophy in the area of educational theatre for teachers in college/higher eduction.

Enrollment 204 total; 41 undergraduate, 163 graduate.

Theater Student Profile 80% females, 20% males, 16% minorities, 4% international.

Theater Faculty 4 total (full-time), 15 total (part-time). 75% of full-time faculty have terminal degrees. Graduate students teach a few undergraduate courses. Undergraduate student–faculty ratio: 2:1.

Expenses for 2005–2006 Application fee: $65. Comprehensive fee: $43,170 includes full-time tuition ($29,890), mandatory fees ($1800), and college room and board ($11,480). Full-time tuition and fees vary according to program. Room and board charges vary according to board plan and housing facility.

Application Procedures Students admitted directly into the professional program freshman year. Deadline for freshmen: January 15; transfers: April 1. Notification date for freshmen: April 1; transfers: continuous. Required: essay, high school transcript, college transcript(s) for transfer students, 3 letters of recommendation, interview, audition, SAT I or ACT test scores, strong high school GPA. Auditions held continuously on campus; videotaped performances are permissible as a substitute for live auditions when distance is prohibitive.

Web Site http://www.steinhardt.nyu.edu/go-now

Undergraduate Contact Ms. Candice MacLusky, Assistant Director of Undergraduate Admissions, The Steinhardt School of Education, New York University, 22 Washington Square North, New York, New York 10011-9191; 212-998-4500, fax: 212-995-4902.

Graduate Contact Mr. John Myers, Director of Enrollment Services, Office of Graduate Admissions, The Steinhardt School of Education, New York University, 82 Washington Square East, 2nd Floor, New York, New York 10003-6680; 212-998-5030, fax: 212-995-4328, e-mail address: ed.gradadmissions@nyu.edu

New York University Steinhardt School

See New York University

Niagara University
Niagara University, New York

Independent, coed. Suburban campus. Total enrollment: 3,853. Theater program established 1981.
Degrees Bachelor of Fine Arts in the area of theater arts. Majors and concentrations: acting, music theater, technical theater, theater arts/drama.
Enrollment 113 total; all undergraduate.
Theater Student Profile 62% females, 38% males, 6% minorities, 1% international.
Theater Faculty 6 undergraduate (full-time), 11 undergraduate (part-time). 100% of full-time faculty have terminal degrees. Graduate students do not teach undergraduate courses. Undergraduate student–faculty ratio: 6:1.
Student Life Student groups/activities include NU Players, P.E.A.N. U.T.S. (outreach program in elementary schools).
Expenses for 2005–2006 Application fee: $30. Comprehensive fee: $28,250 includes full-time tuition ($19,000), mandatory fees ($800), and college room and board ($8450). Special program-related fees: $640 per year for lab fees.
Financial Aid Program-specific awards: 40 departmental scholarships for program majors.
Application Procedures Students admitted directly into the professional program freshman year. Deadline for freshmen and transfers: continuous. Required: high school transcript, college transcript(s) for transfer students, interview, SAT I or ACT test scores, audition for scholarship consideration. Recommended: minimum 3.0 high school GPA, audition. Auditions held once (usually in April) on campus.
Web Site http://www.niagara.edu
Undergraduate Contact Dr. Sharon O. Watkinson, Chair, Theater and Fine Arts Department, Niagara University, Niagara University, New York 14109; 800-462-2111, fax: 716-286-8710, e-mail address: admissions@niagara.edu

North Carolina Agricultural and Technical State University
Greensboro, North Carolina

State-supported, coed. Urban campus. Total enrollment: 11,103. Theater program established 1898.
Degrees Bachelor of Fine Arts. Majors and concentrations: acting, theater technology. Cross-registration with University of North Carolina System. Program accredited by NAST.
Enrollment 75 total; all undergraduate.
Theater Student Profile 60% females, 40% males, 98% minorities.
Theater Faculty 5 undergraduate (full-time), 1 undergraduate (part-time). 100% of full-time faculty have terminal degrees. Graduate students do not teach undergraduate courses. Undergraduate student–faculty ratio: 12:1.
Student Life Student groups/activities include American College Theatre Festival, University/Resident Theatre Association, Southeastern Theatre Conference.
Expenses for 2006–2007 Application fee: $45. State resident tuition: $1769 full-time. Nonresident tuition: $11,211 full-time. Mandatory fees: $1355 full-time. College room and board: $5254. College room only: $2954.
Financial Aid Program-specific awards: 5 Chancellor's Awards for freshmen ($1000), 3 tuition remissions for upperclass out-of-state students ($950), 1 D.E. Coffey Scholarship for theater majors interested in costuming ($1000), 1–4 departmental scholarships ($200–$500).
Application Procedures Students admitted directly into the professional program freshman year. Deadline for freshmen and transfers: July 1. Required: high school transcript, college transcript(s) for transfer students, minimum 2.0 high school GPA, interview, audition, portfolio, SAT I or ACT test scores, minimum combined SAT I score of 820 for in-state applicants; 920 for out-of-state applicants, minimum composite ACT score of 17 for in-state applicants; 21 for out-of-state applicants. Recommended: 2 letters of recommendation. Auditions held twice on campus and off campus in Southeastern Theatre Conference venues; recorded music is permissible as a substitute for live auditions if pianist is not available and videotaped performances are permissible as a substitute for live auditions for out-of-state applicants and those unable to make live auditions. Portfolio reviews held twice on campus.
Web Site http://www.ncat.edu
Undergraduate Contact Frankie Day, Program Chair/Executive Director of Theatre, Division of Theatre Arts, North Carolina Agricultural and Technical State University, 1601 East Market Street, Crosby 225-C, Greensboro, North Carolina 27411; 336-334-7852, fax: 336-334-4741, e-mail address: frankie@ncat.edu

North Carolina School of the Arts
Winston-Salem, North Carolina

State-supported, coed. Urban campus. Total enrollment: 827. Theater program established 1965.
Degrees Bachelor of Fine Arts in the areas of drama/acting, design and production. Majors and concentrations: acting, costume design, costume technology, lighting design, makeup and wig design, scene painting, scenic design, sound design, stage automation, stage management, technical direction. Graduate degrees offered: Master of Fine Arts in the area of design and production.
Enrollment 308 total; 223 undergraduate, 32 graduate, 53 nonprofessional degree.
Theater Student Profile 47% females, 53% males, 8% minorities, 2% international.
Theater Faculty 34 total (full-time). 50% of full-time faculty have terminal degrees. Graduate students do not teach undergraduate courses. Undergraduate student–faculty ratio: 8:1.
Student Life Special housing available for theater students.
Expenses for 2005–2006 Application fee: $50. State resident tuition: $2755 full-time. Nonresident tuition: $14,035 full-time. Mandatory fees: $1551 full-time. Full-time tuition and fees vary according to program. College room and board: $5700. College room only: $3035. Room and board charges vary according to board plan and housing facility. Special program-related fees: $135 per year for educational and technology fee, $150 per year for School of Drama fee.
Financial Aid Program-specific awards: 124 talent/need scholarships ($2493).
Application Procedures Students admitted directly into the professional program freshman year. Deadline for freshmen and transfers: March 1. Required: high school transcript, college transcript(s) for transfer students, 2 letters of recommendation, interview, audition, portfolio for design and production applicants. Recommended: SAT I or ACT test scores. Auditions held by request on campus and off campus in New York, NY; Seattle, WA; Houston, TX; Chicago, IL; Miami, FL; San Francisco, CA; Los Angeles, CA. Portfolio reviews held 10 times on campus.
Web Site http://www.ncarts.edu
Contact Ms. Sheeler Lawson, Director of Admissions, North Carolina School of the Arts, 1533 South Main Street, Winston-Salem, North Carolina 27117-2189; 336-770-3291, fax: 336-770-3370, e-mail address: admissions@ncarts.edu

North Dakota State University
Fargo, North Dakota

State-supported, coed. Total enrollment: 12,099. Theater program established 1907.

Northern Illinois University
De Kalb, Illinois

State-supported, coed. Small town campus. Total enrollment: 25,208.

Northern Kentucky University
Highland Heights, Kentucky

State-supported, coed. Suburban campus. Total enrollment: 13,908. Theater program established 1970.

Northern Kentucky University (continued)

Degrees Bachelor of Fine Arts. Majors and concentrations: acting and directing, dance, design technology, music theater, playwriting, stage management. Cross-registration with University of Cincinnati, Thomas More College, Xavier University.
Enrollment 160 total; 40 undergraduate, 120 nonprofessional degree.
Theater Student Profile 50% females, 50% males, 3% minorities, 2% international.
Theater Faculty 15 undergraduate (full-time), 12 undergraduate (part-time). 100% of full-time faculty have terminal degrees. Graduate students do not teach undergraduate courses. Undergraduate student–faculty ratio: 12:1.
Student Life Student groups/activities include Student Theater, Stage One-Student Service Organization, Tour Troupes.
Expenses for 2005–2006 Application fee: $30. State resident tuition: $4968 full-time. Nonresident tuition: $9696 full-time. Full-time tuition varies according to location. College room and board: $4660. College room only: $2580. Room and board charges vary according to board plan, housing facility, and location. Special program-related fees: $90 per semester for private lessons (optional).
Financial Aid Program-specific awards: 4 Corbett Scholarships for program majors ($2500), 13 Theater Department Scholarships for program majors ($2500).
Application Procedures Students apply for admission into the professional program by freshman, sophomore, junior year. Deadline for freshmen and transfers: continuous. Required: high school transcript, college transcript(s) for transfer students, audition, portfolio, SAT I or ACT test scores. Recommended: minimum 2.0 high school GPA, 3 letters of recommendation, interview. Auditions held twice on campus; videotaped performances are permissible as a substitute for live auditions if a campus visit is impossible and only for scholarship consideration, not BFA acceptance. Portfolio reviews held twice on campus.
Web Site http://www.nku.edu/start/
Undergraduate Contact Office of Admissions, Northern Kentucky University, Lucas Administrative Centre, 4th Floor, Highland Heights, Kentucky 41099; 859-572-5220, fax: 859-572-5566, e-mail address: admitnku@nku.edu

Northwestern State University of Louisiana
Natchitoches, Louisiana

State-supported, coed. Small town campus. Total enrollment: 9,847. Theater program established 1953.
Degrees Bachelor of Science in the area of theater. Majors and concentrations: music theater, theater design/technology. Program accredited by NAST.
Theater Student Profile 60% females, 40% males, 15% minorities, 1% international.
Theater Faculty Graduate students do not teach undergraduate courses. Undergraduate student–faculty ratio: 19:1.
Student Life Student groups/activities include Northwestern Theatre, Northwestern Summer Theatre, Tap Rep. Class-Act (Musical Theatre), Out-on-a-Limb (Improv). Special housing available for theater students.
Expenses for 2005–2006 Application fee: $20. State resident tuition: $2240 full-time. Nonresident tuition: $8318 full-time. Mandatory fees: $1153 full-time. Full-time tuition and fees vary according to course load. College room and board: $3626. College room only: $2050. Room and board charges vary according to board plan, housing facility, and location.
Financial Aid Program-specific awards: 92 performance scholarships ($500–$1000).
Application Procedures Students apply for admission into the professional program by freshman year. Deadline for freshmen and transfers: July 1. Required: high school transcript, college transcript(s) for transfer students, minimum 2.0 high school GPA, 3 letters of recommendation, interview, audition, portfolio, ACT test score only (minimum composite ACT score of 20). Recommended: minimum 3.0 high school GPA. Auditions held on campus and off campus in Dallas, TX; recorded music is

permissible as a substitute for live auditions and videotaped performances are permissible as a substitute for live auditions. Portfolio reviews held on campus and off campus in Dallas, TX; the submission of slides may be substituted for portfolios.
Web Site http://www.nsula.edu/theatre/

Ohio Northern University
Ada, Ohio

Independent, coed. Small town campus. Total enrollment: 3,542. Theater program established 1964.
Degrees Bachelor of Fine Arts. Majors and concentrations: music theater, production management, theater arts/drama. Cross-registration with Queen Margaret College (Scotland); Queensland University of Technology (Australia); New Zealand Academy of Art, Singing, and Dancing.
Enrollment 120 total; all undergraduate.
Theater Student Profile 65% females, 35% males, 5% minorities.
Theater Faculty 8 total (full-time), 2 total (part-time). 100% of full-time faculty have terminal degrees. Graduate students do not teach undergraduate courses. Undergraduate student–faculty ratio: 8:1.
Student Life Student groups/activities include Theta Alpha Phi, Touring Children's Company, Touring Broadway Revue.
Expenses for 2006–2007 Application fee: $30. Comprehensive fee: $35,340 includes full-time tuition ($28,050), mandatory fees ($210), and college room and board ($7080). College room only: $3540.
Financial Aid Program-specific awards: 10–12 talent awards for program majors ($2000–$10,000).
Application Procedures Students admitted directly into the professional program freshman year. Deadline for freshmen and transfers: continuous. Notification date for freshmen and transfers: continuous. Required: high school transcript, college transcript(s) for transfer students, interview, audition, portfolio, SAT I or ACT test scores, minimum 2.5 high school GPA, minimum 2.0 college GPA for transfer students, portfolio for technology students. Recommended: essay, minimum 3.0 high school GPA, 2 letters of recommendation, video. Auditions held by appointment on campus; videotaped performances are permissible as a substitute for live auditions if a campus visit is impossible. Portfolio reviews held by appointment on campus.
Web Site http://www.onu.edu
Undergraduate Contact Ms. Karen Condeni, Vice President and Dean of Admissions, Ohio Northern University, 525 South Main Street, Ada, Ohio 45810; 419-772-2260, fax: 419-772-2313, e-mail address: admissions-ug@onu.edu

Ohio University
Athens, Ohio

State-supported, coed. Small town campus. Total enrollment: 20,396. Theater program established 1890.
Degrees Bachelor of Fine Arts in the areas of performance, production, design and technology, theater arts/drama. Majors and concentrations: performance, playwriting, theater design and production, theater management, theater technology. Graduate degrees offered: Master of Arts in the areas of history and criticism, theater (general); Master of Fine Arts in the areas of professional actor training, professional director training, professional playwriting, production, design and technology. Program accredited by NAST.
Enrollment 212 total; 145 undergraduate, 67 graduate.
Theater Student Profile 57% females, 43% males, 5% minorities, 3% international.
Theater Faculty 21 total (full-time). 91% of full-time faculty have terminal degrees. Graduate students teach a few undergraduate courses. Undergraduate student–faculty ratio: 12:1.
Student Life Student groups/activities include Ohio Valley Summer Theater, Monomoy Theatre, Cincinnati Playhouse in the Park. Special housing available for theater students.
Expenses for 2005–2006 Application fee: $45. State resident tuition: $8235 full-time. Nonresident tuition: $17,199 full-time. College room and board: $7686. College room only: $3855. Room and board charges vary according to board plan.

Financial Aid Program-specific awards: 15–25 Provost Talent Scholarships for incoming freshmen ($1500), 29 Dean's Scholarships for continuing students ($1000–$1500), 1 Third Century Scholarship for incoming freshmen ($3500), 1 President's Scholarship for incoming freshmen ($2500), 17 departmental scholarships for continuing students ($500–$1500).

Application Procedures Students apply for admission into the professional program by freshman year. Deadline for freshmen: February 2; transfers: continuous. Required: high school transcript, college transcript(s) for transfer students, minimum 3.0 high school GPA, SAT I or ACT test scores (minimum combined SAT I score of 990, minimum composite ACT score of 21), audition for scholarship consideration, portfolio for production design/technology applicants for scholarship consideration, writing sample for playwriting applicants for scholarship consideration. Auditions held twice in the winter on campus. Portfolio reviews held twice in the winter on campus.

Web Site http://www.ohiou.edu/theater

Contact Ms. Vicki Hanson, Secretary, School of Theater, Ohio University, 307 Kantner Hall, Athens, Ohio 45701; 740-593-4818, fax: 740-593-4817, e-mail address: theater@ohio.edu

Otterbein College
Westerville, Ohio

Independent United Methodist, coed. Suburban campus. Total enrollment: 3,094.

Degrees Bachelor of Fine Arts. Majors and concentrations: acting, design technology, music theater, music theatre/dance. Cross-registration with members of the Higher Education Council of Columbus. Program accredited by NAST.

Enrollment 120 total; 95 undergraduate, 25 nonprofessional degree.

Theater Student Profile 60% females, 40% males, 13% minorities, 3% international.

Theater Faculty 10 undergraduate (full-time), 20 undergraduate (part-time). 90% of full-time faculty have terminal degrees. Graduate students do not teach undergraduate courses. Undergraduate student–faculty ratio: 4:1.

Student Life Student groups/activities include Cap and Dagger (local theater honorary).

Expenses for 2005–2006 Application fee: $25. Comprehensive fee: $28,986 includes full-time tuition ($22,518) and college room and board ($6468). College room only: $2994. Full-time tuition varies according to course load and program. Room and board charges vary according to housing facility. Special program-related fees: $500 per quarter for private voice lessons (one hour weekly).

Financial Aid Program-specific awards: 20–35 theater talent awards for program majors ($750–$4000).

Application Procedures Students admitted directly into the professional program freshman year. Deadline for freshmen and transfers: March 20. Notification date for freshmen and transfers: March 25. Required: high school transcript, college transcript(s) for transfer students, interview, audition, portfolio, SAT I or ACT test scores, 2 letters of recommendation for design/technology applicants. Recommended: minimum 2.5 high school GPA. Auditions held 12 times on campus and off campus in New York, NY; Chicago, IL; Los Angeles, CA; San Francisco, CA; Las Vegas, NV; videotaped performances are permissible as a substitute for live auditions for out-of-state applicants with approval from the department. Portfolio reviews held at student's convenience on campus and off campus in New York, NY; Chicago, IL; Los Angeles, CA; Seattle, WA; Las Vegas, NV; Dallas TX; Houston, TX; the submission of slides may be substituted for portfolios for out-of-state applicants with approval from the department.

Web Site http://www.otterbein.edu/dept/thr/index.html

Undergraduate Contact Debbie Byrne, Admission Counselor/Arts Recruiter, Office of Admission, Otterbein College, 1 Otterbein College, Westerville, Ohio 43081-2006; 800-488-8144, fax: 614-823-1200, e-mail address: dbyrne@otterbein.edu

Bernice Young Jones School of Fine Arts
Ouachita Baptist University
Arkadelphia, Arkansas

Independent Baptist, coed. Small town campus. Total enrollment: 1,499.

Pace University
New York, New York

Independent, coed. Total enrollment: 14,177. Theater program established 1988.

Degrees Bachelor of Fine Arts in the area of theater. Majors and concentrations: acting, directing, music theater, set design, technical theater, theater management.

Enrollment 127 total; 53 undergraduate, 74 nonprofessional degree.

Theater Student Profile 69% females, 31% males, 18% minorities, 1% international.

Theater Faculty 7 undergraduate (full-time), 8 undergraduate (part-time). 100% of full-time faculty have terminal degrees. Graduate students do not teach undergraduate courses. Undergraduate student–faculty ratio: 15:1.

Student Life Student groups/activities include Honors Program.

Expenses for 2005–2006 Application fee: $45. Comprehensive fee: $34,328 includes full-time tuition ($24,756), mandatory fees ($632), and college room and board ($8940). Full-time tuition and fees vary according to student level. Room and board charges vary according to board plan and housing facility.

Application Procedures Students admitted directly into the professional program freshman year. Deadline for freshmen and transfers: continuous. Required: essay, high school transcript, college transcript(s) for transfer students, minimum 2.0 high school GPA, 2 letters of recommendation, interview, audition, portfolio, SAT I or ACT test scores, audition for performance majors, portfolio for design/technical theater majors. Recommended: video. Auditions held continuously on campus; videotaped performances are permissible as a substitute for live auditions when distance is prohibitive. Portfolio reviews held continuously on campus; the submission of slides may be substituted for portfolios if campus visit is impossible.

Web Site http://appserv.pace.edu/execute/page.cfm?doc_id=9255

Undergraduate Contact Kimberly Johnson, Counselor, Pace University, Pace Plaza, New York, New York 10038; 212-346-1225, fax: 212-346-1821, e-mail address: kjohnson@pace.edu

The Pennsylvania State University University Park Campus
University Park, Pennsylvania

State-related, coed. Small town campus. Total enrollment: 40,709. Theater program established 1935.

Degrees Bachelor of Fine Arts. Majors and concentrations: design technology, music theater, stage management. Graduate degrees offered: Master of Fine Arts in the areas of acting, costume, scene design. Program accredited by NAST.

Enrollment 185 total; 71 undergraduate, 33 graduate, 81 nonprofessional degree.

Theater Student Profile 63% females, 37% males, 9% minorities, 1% international.

Theater Faculty 21 total (full-time), 5 total (part-time). 98% of full-time faculty have terminal degrees. Graduate students teach a few undergraduate courses. Undergraduate student–faculty ratio: 8:1.

Student Life Student groups/activities include University Park Ensemble, Minority Theatre Workshop, Drama Duo. Special housing available for theater students.

Expenses for 2005–2006 Application fee: $50. State resident tuition: $11,024 full-time. Nonresident tuition: $21,260 full-time. Mandatory fees: $484 full-time. College room and board: $6530. College room only: $3430.

Financial Aid Program-specific awards: 1 Mona Shibley Bird Scholarship for above-average students ($862), 2 Gallu Scholar-

The Pennsylvania State University University Park Campus (continued)

ships for freshmen ($820), 2 Lethbridge-Jackson Awards for outstanding achievement ($466), 25 Mabel Reed Knight Scholarships for those demonstrating financial need ($350–$1500), 2 Irene Richards Scholarships for sophomores demonstrating high academic achievement ($1609).

Application Procedures Students admitted directly into the professional program freshman year. Deadline for freshmen and transfers: March 1. Notification date for freshmen and transfers: continuous. Required: essay, high school transcript, college transcript(s) for transfer students, minimum 2.0 high school GPA, 2 letters of recommendation, interview, audition, portfolio, SAT I or ACT test scores. Auditions held 7-8 times on campus and off campus in Chicago, IL; Irvine, CA; New York, NY; videotaped performances are permissible as a substitute for live auditions if distance is prohibitive or scheduling is difficult. Portfolio reviews held 7-8 times on campus and off campus in Chicago, IL; New York, NY; San Francisco, CA; the submission of slides may be substituted for portfolios only if accompanied by an interview.

Web Site http://www.theatre.psu.edu

Undergraduate Contact Ms. Joane Stoneberg, Academic Counselor, School of Theatre, The Pennsylvania State University University Park Campus, 101B Arts Building, University Park, Pennsylvania 16802; 814-863-1451, fax: 814-865-5754, e-mail address: jrg3@psu.edu

Graduate Contact Ms. Sue Carson, Staff Assistant, School of Theatre, The Pennsylvania State University University Park Campus, 103 Arts Building, University Park, Pennsylvania 16802; 814-865-7586, fax: 814-865-5754, e-mail address: msc1@psu.edu

Point Park University
Pittsburgh, Pennsylvania

Independent, coed. Urban campus. Total enrollment: 3,407. Theater program established 1968.

Degrees Bachelor of Arts/Bachelor of Fine Arts in the area of theater arts. Majors and concentrations: acting, music theater, stage management, technical theatre/design. Graduate degrees offered: Master of Fine Arts in the area of acting. Cross-registration with Carnegie Mellon University, University of Pittsburgh, Chatham College, Robert Morris College, Duquesne University, Carlow College.

Enrollment 335 total; 329 undergraduate, 6 graduate.

Theater Student Profile 65% females, 35% males, 10% minorities, 5% international.

Theater Faculty 11 undergraduate (full-time), 23 undergraduate (part-time), 2 graduate (full-time), 1 graduate (part-time). 100% of full-time faculty have terminal degrees. Graduate students teach a few undergraduate courses. Undergraduate student–faculty ratio: 10:1.

Student Life Student groups/activities include American College Theatre Festival.

Expenses for 2005–2006 Application fee: $40. Comprehensive fee: $24,160 includes full-time tuition ($16,280), mandatory fees ($460), and college room and board ($7420). College room only: $3500. Full-time tuition and fees vary according to program. Room and board charges vary according to board plan. Special program-related fees: $450 per term for voice/piano private lessons.

Financial Aid Program-specific awards: 35 apprenticeships for those demonstrating talent ($500–$3000), 35 talent scholarships for those demonstrating academic achievement and talent ($500–$5000).

Application Procedures Students admitted directly into the professional program freshman year. Deadline for freshmen and transfers: May 1. Required: high school transcript, college transcript(s) for transfer students, minimum 2.0 high school GPA, 2 letters of recommendation, interview, ACT test score only, theater questionnaire and 2 photos, portfolio for technical theater and stage management applicants, audition for acting and musical theater applicants. Auditions held 8 times on campus and off campus in New York, NY; Louisville, KY; state conferences in Pennsylvania, Arizona, Maryland, Atlanta, Southeastern Theatre Conference sites; recorded music is permissible

as a substitute for live auditions if a live audition is impossible and videotaped performances are permissible as a substitute for live auditions by prior arrangement. Portfolio reviews held 8 times on campus and off campus in Louisville, KY; state conferences in Pennsylvania, Arizona, Maryland, and New York; the submission of slides may be substituted for portfolios whenever needed.

Web Site http://www.pointpark.edu

Undergraduate Contact Mr. Joseph McGoldrick, Director of Artistic Recruitment, Conservatory of Performing Arts, Point Park University, 201 Wood Street, Pittsburgh, Pennsylvania 15222-1984; 412-392-3450, fax: 412-391-2424, e-mail address: jmcgoldrick@pointpark.edu

More About the Program

The Conservatory of Performing Arts confers Bachelor of Arts and Bachelor of Fine Arts degrees in dance, dance pedagogy, and theater arts and offers conservatory training within a liberal arts context. Students receive intense training in their concentration as well as a thorough academic education. Because the faculty members believe that performing arts majors develop best in front of a live audience, the program offers varied performing opportunities for students at the Pittsburgh Playhouse of Point Park University.

Nationally renowned, the Pittsburgh Playhouse is the performance facility for the Conservatory of Performing Arts. Here students participate in live-theater/dance experiences before a subscription audience. Consisting of three working theaters, this 70-year-old facility is fully staffed by a production team of designers and artisans who train and supervise student apprentices in building, designing, lighting, and managing shows. The front-of-house staff members as well as the box office and public relations personnel engage all students in the business aspect of running a theater. The season, which features student actors, dancers, designers, and stage managers, consists of five Playhouse Jr. shows for children and five Conservatory Company dramas/musicals.

Dance students may perform in one of five Playhouse Dance Company productions and a Playhouse Jr. Children's Dance Show as well as a public school outreach program.

The Bachelor of Arts degree in cinema and digital arts is an innovatively designed program, with an emphasis on professional education and liberal arts—both in theory and in practice. Exploring the integration of media and the arts in society as well as the impact of technology on culture, the curriculum provides practical, professional training while developing a sound foundation in the arts and humanities. Theory and aesthetics are taught as an integral part of developing communication and production skills.

In the Conservatory of Performing Arts, it is the mission to educate, train, and artistically equip students with the skills necessary to compete in the commercial media industry. The degree offered is a four-year, 120-credit Bachelor of Arts in cinema and digital arts, with concentrations in cinematography, directing, editing and sound, producing, and screenwriting.

This well-rounded educational experience culminates with the annual Point Park Digital Film Festival presented to showcase graduating senior thesis production projects. Admission to the Film and Electronic Arts program is based on self-discipline, professional attitude, and a commitment to the craft as demonstrated through an interview with the Director of Film.

The B.F.A. degree in film and video production is offered in collaboration with Pittsburgh Filmmakers. Students take their academic courses at Point Park University and their film and video requirements at Pittsburgh Filmmakers' newly built facility in the Oakland section of Pittsburgh. Both institutions work together to ensure that students receive a challenging educational experience.

Conservatory faculty members are working professionals in acting, singing, dancing, writing, composing, painting, designing, choreography, and other specialties. Guest artists and master teachers in musical theater, voice and speech, and dance are regularly featured. Past guests include Chita Rivera, Michael Rupert, Jeff Shade, Rob Ashford, Sherry Zunker-Dow, Cicely Berry, Paul Gavert, Patricia Wilde, Albert Poland, Barbara Pontecorvo, Edward Villella, Maxine Sherman, Marshall Swiney, and Claire Bataille. The program also offers many workshops and collaborative efforts of an interdisciplinary nature with other University programs.

During the summer, the Conservatory offers an International Summer Dance program (open by audition) featuring renowned names in the world of dance. The International Summer Dance program offers training in jazz, ballet, and modern dance. The program culminates in a recital performance.

The community of Pittsburgh itself is an arts and education center with the Pittsburgh Symphony, Opera, Ballet, and Dance Council and the Pittsburgh Public Theaters supplemented by eight other institutions of higher learning within a 15-minute drive. The whole city is truly the campus of the programs.

Prospective applicants must apply and be accepted by the University. An audition for and an interview with faculty members is required for all prospective majors. Scholarships/apprenticeships from $1000 to $5000 are based on either talent or academics or both. Presidential and special academic full- and part-time awards are highly competitive.

Off-campus auditions are possible at Thespian State Conferences and dance auditions in Chicago; New York; Dayton, Ohio; and Louisville, Kentucky. Videotaped auditions are acceptable; prospective students should contact the Conservatory for procedures.

For more information and audition guidelines, interested students should contact Joseph McGoldrick, Director of Artistic Recruitment, Point Park University, 201 Wood Street, Pittsburgh, Pennsylvania 15222; jmcgoldrick@pointpark.edu; 800-321-0129 (toll-free).

Program Facilities and Features At the Conservatory of Performing Arts, facilities include ten dance studios as well as the three-theater complex at the Pittsburgh Playhouse of Point Park University, which offers performance opportunities for students in front of a subscription audience. In addition, students can take advantage of the on-site costume/set construction apprenticeships, 11 private singing and piano instructors; art and design classes; more than 100 dance classes per week, acting classes with a ratio of 1 instructor to 15 students, and the Point Park University Singers. Point Park University is central to many educational, arts, and entertainment activities, and it is within walking distance of boating, swimming, and parks.

Alumni The Conservatory has numerous graduates performing in touring companies, on Broadway, in dance companies, in movies, on TV, and in other theaters. Many more alumni are teaching in schools, on faculties, choreographing, writing, directing, and stage managing across the world. Broadway and national touring productions of *Contact, Cabaret, 42nd St.,* and *Kiss Me Kate* as well as movie and TV credits, including *Pulp Fiction, Inspector Gadget, Wonder Boys, NYPD Blue, Due South, The Guiding Light, Providence, CSI: NYC,* and *Leaving L.A.* are just a few of the vehicles showcasing Conservatory graduates of theater and dance.

Potter College of Arts, Humanities, and Social Sciences

See Western Kentucky University

Purchase College, State University of New York

Purchase, New York

State-supported, coed. Small town campus. Total enrollment: 3,826.

Degrees Bachelor of Fine Arts in the areas of acting, design technology, film, dramatic writing. Majors and concentrations: acting, costume construction, costume design, design technology, dramatic writing, film, lighting design, playwriting, scenic design, screenwriting, stage management, technical direction. Graduate degrees offered: Master of Fine Arts in the areas of theater design, theater technology. Program accredited by CUPTP.

Enrollment 313 total; 306 undergraduate, 7 graduate.

Theater Student Profile 47% females, 53% males, 18% minorities, 1% international.

Theater Faculty 11 undergraduate (full-time), 34 undergraduate (part-time). 100% of full-time faculty have terminal degrees. Graduate students do not teach undergraduate courses.

Expenses for 2006–2007 Application fee: $40. State resident tuition: $4350 full-time. Nonresident tuition: $10,610 full-time. Mandatory fees: $1258 full-time. College room and board: $8466. College room only: $5378.

Financial Aid Program-specific awards: 124 theater scholarships/awards ($1122).

Application Procedures Students admitted directly into the professional program freshman year. Deadline for freshmen and transfers: March 1. Notification date for freshmen: April 1; transfers: May 1. Required: high school transcript, essay for film applicants, audition for acting applicants, portfolio for design and technical theater applicants, minimum TOEFL score of 550 for international applicants. Recommended: letter of recommendation, picture and resume for acting applicants, interview for design, technical theater applicants. Auditions held on campus and off campus in various locations once per year; videotaped performances are permissible as a substitute for live auditions for international applicants or with approval from the department for domestic applicants. Portfolio reviews held at various times on campus and off campus in various locations; the submission of slides may be substituted for portfolios with some original work.

Web Site http://www.purchase.edu

Undergraduate Contact Ms. Shirley Williams, Admissions Counselor, Purchase College, State University of New York, 735 Anderson Hill Road, Purchase, New York 10577-1400; 914-251-6315, fax: 914-251-6314.

Graduate Contact Ms. Sabrina Johnston, Admissions Counselor, Purchase College, State University of New York, 735 Anderson Hill Road, Purchase, New York 10577; 914-251-6479, fax: 914-251-6314.

More About the College

Professional training for a professional career in acting, design/technology, dramatic writing, and film is the dominant goal of the program. Young artists are selected for the intensity of both their interest and potential in becoming professionals. The program offers focused and in-depth training in theater and film with a faculty that is itself working, creating, and succeeding in New York's professional world.

The community of students and faculty members are constantly enriched by the creative bustle and aesthetic influence of New York City, just 35 minutes away. They work and thrive together on the modern Purchase campus and Performing Arts Center located in Westchester County, a beautiful and elegant suburb of New York City.

All classes, rehearsals, productions, and filming are taught and supervised by men and women who are contributing participants in the professional artistic life of New York City, the United States, and the international arts communities. These artist-teachers have a common goal: to thoroughly train young artists so that the individual creativity of each student is preserved and augmented by the most strenuous and critical practice and performance standards possible. Practical learning and practical experience is the daily life for the student artist at Purchase. State-of-the-art equipment, theaters, and work spaces for every aspect of training abound in this woods-surrounded center of contemporary art and learning.

In addition to this serious concentration in the arts, each student fulfills a SUNY-mandated 30-credit core in liberal arts and

Purchase College, State University of New York (continued)

sciences. Life at Purchase consists of a rich social intermix of the performing and visual arts with the more traditional academic life of the liberal arts and sciences.

The student's life after graduation is a powerfully active concern of the training program. Therefore, as the student gains proficiency, his or her work has gradually been presented to the professional community, and, by the time of graduation when the work is formally introduced to that professional community— using New York City presentations of actors; internships, portfolio reviews, and faculty personal contacts for designers; and completed student films (for filmmakers), Purchase students find that an extraordinary number of doors open for them: agents, producers, theaters, film companies, and television producers are available for the next creative and working step of the Purchase graduate.

The Conservatory of Theatre Arts and Film is now graduating some of the most exciting and successful young actors, designers, technical directors, stage managers, and filmmakers in America. It is not only the flagship program of the State University of New York but also among the finest and most prestigious of the conservatory programs offered in the disciplines of theater and film in the United States.

The Purchase College Conservatory of Theatre Arts and Film is a member of the Consortium of Undergraduate Professional Theatre Training Programs.

Rockford College
Rockford, Illinois

Independent, coed. Suburban campus. Total enrollment: 1,376. Theater program established 1994.

Feinstein College of Arts and Sciences
Roger Williams University
Bristol, Rhode Island

Independent, coed. Total enrollment: 5,214. Theater program established 1972.
Degrees Bachelor of Arts in the area of theater. Majors and concentrations: acting, design.
Enrollment 31 total; all undergraduate.
Theater Student Profile 51% females, 49% males, 6% minorities, 2% international.
Theater Faculty 4 undergraduate (full-time), 3 undergraduate (part-time). Graduate students do not teach undergraduate courses. Undergraduate student–faculty ratio: 8:1.
Student Life Student groups/activities include Stage Company, theater performances.
Expenses for 2006–2007 Application fee: $50. Comprehensive fee: $34,759 includes full-time tuition ($22,932), mandatory fees ($1134), and college room and board ($10,693). College room only: $5569.
Application Procedures Students admitted directly into the professional program freshman year. Deadline for freshmen and transfers: continuous. Required: essay, high school transcript, college transcript(s) for transfer students, 2 letters of recommendation, SAT I or ACT test scores, audition by the end of first semester. Auditions held on campus.
Web Site http://www.rwu.edu
Undergraduate Contact Michelle L. Beauregard, Director of Freshman Admissions, Roger Williams University, 1 Old Ferry Road, Bristol, Rhode Island 02809; 401-254-3500, fax: 401-254-3557, e-mail address: admit@rwu.edu
Graduate Contact Matthew McDonough, Director of Graduate Admissions, Roger Williams University, 1 Old Ferry Road, Bristol, Rhode Island 02806; 401-254-3500, fax: 401-254-3557, e-mail address: mmcdonough@rwu.edu

Chicago College of Performing Arts - The Theatre Conservatory
Roosevelt University
Chicago, Illinois

Independent, coed. Urban campus. Total enrollment: 7,234. Theater program established 1988.
Degrees Bachelor of Fine Arts in the areas of theater, musical theatre. Majors and concentrations: acting, music theater. Graduate degrees offered: Master of Arts in the area of directing (fast-track summer program); Master of Fine Arts in the area of theatre.
Enrollment 160 total; 140 undergraduate, 20 graduate.
Theater Student Profile 50% females, 50% males, 20% minorities, 10% international.
Theater Faculty 12 total (full-time), 16 total (part-time). 100% of full-time faculty have terminal degrees. Graduate students do not teach undergraduate courses. Undergraduate student–faculty ratio: 12:1.
Expenses for 2005–2006 Application fee: $25. Comprehensive fee: $22,420 includes full-time tuition ($14,180), mandatory fees ($250), and college room and board ($7990). College room only: $5800. Full-time tuition and fees vary according to course load and program. Room and board charges vary according to board plan, housing facility, and location.
Financial Aid Program-specific awards: 150 theatre award scholarships ($1000–$7000).
Application Procedures Students admitted directly into the professional program freshman year. Deadline for freshmen and transfers: January 15. Notification date for freshmen and transfers: April 1. Required: essay, high school transcript, college transcript(s) for transfer students, minimum 2.0 high school GPA, 3 letters of recommendation, interview, audition, SAT I or ACT test scores, minimum 2.0 college GPA for transfer students. Recommended: minimum 3.0 high school GPA. Auditions held six times on campus and off campus in Los Angeles, CA; Chicago, IL; New York, NY; Las Vegas, NV; San Francisco, CA.
Web Site http://ccpa.roosevelt.edu/theatre
Contact Amy White, Assistant Dean for Enrollment and Student Services, Roosevelt University, 430 South Michigan Avenue, Chicago, Illinois 60605; 312-341-3789, fax: 312-341-6358, e-mail address: theatre@roosevelt.edu

More About the University

The Theatre Conservatory of the Chicago College of Performing Arts (CCPA) at Roosevelt University provides training and education within the context of a vibrant university in a world-class city. It is a place where the energies of one discipline spill over to enliven other artistic endeavors and where students come to enhance their unique talents and polish them to perfection. At CCPA, students experience a professional program of study with a faculty that is committed to a comprehensive theater education.

Chicago College of Performing Arts at Roosevelt University is well situated on the top floors of the historic landmark Auditorium Building, designed by world-famous architects Dankmar Adler and Louis Sullivan. The building includes the 3,800-seat Auditorium Theatre, renowned for its beauty and exquisite acoustics. Located on the corner of Michigan Avenue and Congress Parkway, this edifice is now an integral part of the "educational corridor" of more than 50,000 students enrolled in various institutions in the famous downtown Loop. Across the street are Pritzker Music Pavilion of Millennium Park, the magnificent Buckingham Fountain, and the sparkling beauty of Lake Michigan. The new state-of-the-art residence hall, the University Center of Chicago, is located just one block away on the corner of State Street and Congress Parkway.

Within walking distance are many of the city's major cultural institutions, including the Goodman, Chicago, Oriental, and Cadillac theaters; Symphony Center, home of the Chicago Symphony Orchestra; the Lyric Opera, the Jazz Showcase; the Art Institute; the Field Museum of Natural History; and the Magnificent Mile of shops and galleries. This ideal location provides opportunities for learning from some of the most accomplished actors in Chicago, as well as interning with some of the literally hundreds of small theater companies in the city.

Faculty Joel G. Fink (Director of the Theatre Conservatory/ Associate Dean); Christine Adaire (Assistant Professor of Theatre); June Compton (Associate Professor of Theatre); Adrian Danzig (Assistant Professor of Theatre); Ray Frewen (Assistant Professor of Theatre); Sean Ryan Kelley (Associate Professor of Theatre); Stephen Kruse (Technical Director); Michael Lasswell (Instructor of Theatre); Kestutis Nakas (Associate Professor of Theatre); Luis Perez (Assistant Professor of Theatre); Candace Taylor (Assistant Professor of Theatre); and Scott Ziemba (Production Coordinator).

Part-time professional faculty: Jane Alderman; Angela Bonacasa; Belinda Bremmer; Philip Caldwell; Sharon Carlson; Lou Conte Dance Studio Staff; Chuck Coyl; Tom Creamer; Joseph Drummond; Nadine Gomez; Matt Harding; Catherine Head; Ted Hoerl; Patrick Holland; Damon Kiely; Molly McGrath; Jerry Proffit; Meera Sanghani; Steve Scott; Carin Silkaitis; Jana Stauffer; and Dan Stetzel. There are additional voice faculty members for private voice lessons.

Student Performance Opportunities There are fourteen to sixteen productions each year. Freshmen present showcases in their first year, auditioning with the entire conservatory thereafter. As an integral part of students' training, the Theatre Conservatory encourages advanced students to work with professional theater companies through specially arranged internships. In the past two years, theaters have included: The Goodman Theatre; Steppenwolf Theatre Company; Chicago Shakespeare Theatre; Lookingglass Theatre, and Northlight Theatre. Students have interned in the areas of acting, directing, stage and arts management, design, theater technology, business and marketing, public relations, and development/front of house.

Programs and Additional Information Undergraduate degree programs include the B.F.A. in acting and B.F.A. in musical theatre. Graduate degree programs include the M.F.A. in acting and M.A. Fast Track in directing (summer program designed for high school theater teachers).

A 320-bed residence hall is connected to the main building, and a new eighteen-story facility opened in fall 2004.

Russell Sage College

Troy, New York

Independent, women only. Urban campus. Total enrollment: 838. Theater program established 1916.

Degrees Bachelor of Arts. Majors and concentrations: theater arts/drama. Program accredited by NASAD.

Enrollment 16 total; all undergraduate.

Theater Student Profile 100% females.

Theater Faculty 5 undergraduate (full-time), 2 undergraduate (part-time). 71% of full-time faculty have terminal degrees. Graduate students do not teach undergraduate courses. Undergraduate student–faculty ratio: 12:1.

Student Life Student groups/activities include New York State Theatre Institute.

Expenses for 2005–2006 Application fee: $30. Comprehensive fee: $31,060 includes full-time tuition ($22,650), mandatory fees ($870), and college room and board ($7540). College room only: $3650. Special program-related fees: $250 per one-time internship fee for internship with New York State Theatre Institute.

Application Procedures Students admitted directly into the professional program freshman year. Deadline for freshmen: August 1; transfers: continuous. Required: essay, high school transcript, college transcript(s) for transfer students, minimum 2.0 high school GPA, 2 letters of recommendation, SAT I or ACT test scores. Recommended: interview, audition, portfolio. Auditions held on individual basis on campus; recorded music is permissible as a substitute for live auditions and videotaped performances are permissible as a substitute for live auditions. Portfolio reviews held on individual basis on campus; the submission of slides may be substituted for portfolios.

Web Site http://www.sage.edu

Undergraduate Contact Kathy Rusch, Director of Admissions, Admissions, Russell Sage College, 45 Ferry Street, Troy, New York 12180; 518-244-2217, fax: 518-244-6880, e-mail address: rischk@ sage.edu

Rutgers, The State University of New Jersey

See Mason Gross School of the Arts

Salem State College

Salem, Massachusetts

State-supported, coed. Small town campus. Total enrollment: 9,863. Theater program established 1984.

Degrees Bachelor of Fine Arts in the area of theater. Majors and concentrations: acting, costume design, lighting design, set design, stage management, technical theater. Program accredited by NAST.

Enrollment 162 total; 48 undergraduate, 114 nonprofessional degree.

Theater Student Profile 75% females, 25% males, 2% minorities, 2% international.

Theater Faculty 9 undergraduate (full-time), 2 undergraduate (part-time). 75% of full-time faculty have terminal degrees. Graduate students do not teach undergraduate courses. Undergraduate student–faculty ratio: 10:1.

Student Life Student groups/activities include Student Theater Ensemble, Salem State Summer Theater, Repertory Dance Theater.

Expenses for 2005–2006 Application fee: $25. State resident tuition: $910 full-time. Nonresident tuition: $7050 full-time. Mandatory fees: $4,374 full-time. Full-time tuition and fees vary according to class time. College room and board: $7350. College room only: $5047. Room and board charges vary according to board plan and housing facility.

Financial Aid Program-specific awards: 5–7 Presidential Arts Scholarships for program majors ($1000), 1 Ettinger Scholarship for program majors ($500), 1 David Allen George Scholarship for program majors ($500).

Application Procedures Students apply for admission into the professional program by freshman year. Deadline for freshmen and transfers: continuous. Required: high school transcript, college transcript(s) for transfer students, minimum 3.0 high school GPA, SAT I or ACT test scores (minimum combined SAT I score of 1120, minimum composite ACT score of 24), audition for acting majors, portfolio for design/technical theater majors. Recommended: essay, 2 letters of recommendation, interview, video. Auditions held twice on campus; recorded music is permissible as a substitute for live auditions if applicant is outside of the New England five-state region and videotaped performances are permissible as a substitute for live auditions if applicant is outside of the New England five-state region. Portfolio reviews held twice on campus; the submission of slides may be substituted for portfolios if applicant is outside of the New England five-state region.

Web Site http://www.salemstate.edu

Undergraduate Contact Mr. James Fallon, Chairperson, Department of Theatre and Speech Communication, Salem State College, Salem, Massachusetts 01970; 978-542-7234, fax: 978-542-6291, e-mail address: james.fallon@salemstate.edu

Sarofim School of Fine Arts

See Southwestern University

Shenandoah Conservatory

See Shenandoah University

Shenandoah Conservatory
Shenandoah University
Winchester, Virginia

Independent United Methodist, coed. Total enrollment: 2,998.
Degrees Bachelor of Fine Arts in the areas of music theater, theater for youth. Majors and concentrations: acting, costume design, music theater, scenic design, theater for youth. Program accredited by NASM.
Enrollment 179 total; all undergraduate.
Theater Student Profile 63% females, 37% males, 3% minorities, 1% international.
Theater Faculty 9 undergraduate (full-time), 2 undergraduate (part-time). 89% of full-time faculty have terminal degrees. Graduate students do not teach undergraduate courses. Undergraduate student–faculty ratio: 16:1.
Student Life Student groups/activities include Alpha Psi Omega fraternity shows, special workshops, Children's Theater.
Expenses for 2005–2006 Application fee: $30. Comprehensive fee: $27,600 includes full-time tuition ($19,900), mandatory fees ($150), and college room and board ($7550). Full-time tuition and fees vary according to course load and program. Room and board charges vary according to board plan.
Financial Aid Program-specific awards: 135 talent and academic scholarships for program students ($4304).
Application Procedures Students admitted directly into the professional program freshman year. Deadline for freshmen and transfers: continuous. Required: high school transcript, college transcript(s) for transfer students, minimum 2.0 high school GPA, interview, video, audition, SAT I or ACT test scores, portfolio for design majors. Recommended: letter of recommendation, portfolio. Auditions held 10 times on campus and off campus in various cities; recorded music is permissible as a substitute for live auditions if a campus visit is impossible and videotaped performances are permissible as a substitute for live auditions if a campus visit is impossible. Portfolio reviews held 10 times on campus and off campus in various cities; the submission of slides may be substituted for portfolios as part of portfolio.
Web Site http://www.su.edu
Undergraduate Contact Mr. David Anthony, Dean, Admissions Office, Shenandoah University, 1460 University Drive, Winchester, Virginia 22601-5195; 540-665-4581, fax: 540-665-4627, e-mail address: admit@su.edu

Shorter College
Rome, Georgia

Independent Baptist, coed. Small town campus. Total enrollment: 967.
Degrees Bachelor of Fine Arts in the areas of theatre, Musical Theatre. Majors and concentrations: music theater, theater arts/drama. Program accredited by NASM.
Enrollment 40 total; all undergraduate.
Theater Student Profile 60% females, 40% males, 5% minorities.
Theater Faculty 3 undergraduate (full-time), 4 undergraduate (part-time). 100% of full-time faculty have terminal degrees. Graduate students do not teach undergraduate courses.
Student Life Student groups/activities include Shorter Players.
Expenses for 2005–2006 Application fee: $25. Comprehensive fee: $19,700 includes full-time tuition ($13,200), mandatory fees ($300), and college room and board ($6200). College room only: $3400. Full-time tuition and fees vary according to course load. Room and board charges vary according to board plan and housing facility.
Financial Aid Program-specific awards: 10–12 theater scholarships for theater majors ($500–$1250).
Application Procedures Students admitted directly into the professional program freshman year. Deadline for freshmen and transfers: continuous. Required: high school transcript, college transcript(s) for transfer students, interview, audition, SAT I or ACT test scores, two-minute monologue (video), dance audition. Recommended: 2 letters of recommendation. Auditions held 4 times on campus. Portfolio reviews held 4 times on campus.
Web Site http://shorter.edu

Undergraduate Contact Dr. Alan B. Wingard, Dean, School of the Arts, Shorter College, 315 Shorter Avenue, Rome, Georgia 30165; 706-233-7248, fax: 706-236-1517, e-mail address: awingard@shorter.edu

Simon Fraser University
Burnaby, British Columbia, Canada

Province-supported, coed. Suburban campus. Total enrollment: 20,187. Theater program established 1992.
Degrees Bachelor of Fine Arts in the area of theater. Majors and concentrations: performance, theater design and production. Graduate degrees offered: Master of Fine Arts in the area of interdisciplinary studies.
Enrollment 70 total.
Theater Faculty 5 total (full-time). 100% of full-time faculty have terminal degrees. Graduate students do not teach undergraduate courses. Undergraduate student–faculty ratio: 23:1.
Student Life Student groups/activities include Black Box Theater Company.
Expenses for 2006–2007 Application fee: $100 Canadian dollars. Tuition and fee charges are reported in Canadian dollars. Special program-related fees: $35 per course for materials fee.
Financial Aid Program-specific awards: 1 Murray Farr Award for program majors ($500), 5 Adaline May Clark Scholarships for program majors ($100–$500), 3 Bice Caple Awards for SCA students ($1000), 2 SFU Service Awards for SCA students ($250).
Application Procedures Students apply for admission into the professional program by sophomore year. Deadline for freshmen and transfers: April 30. Required: high school transcript, college transcript(s) for transfer students, minimum 3.0 high school GPA, interview, audition. Auditions held twice on campus.
Web Site http://www.sfu.ca/sca
Undergraduate Contact Linda Hegland, Undergraduate Advisor, School for the Contemporary Arts, Simon Fraser University, 8888 University Drive, Burnaby, British Columbia V5A 1S6, Canada; 604-291-3363, fax: 604-291-5907, e-mail address: ca@sfu.ca
Graduate Contact Noni Fidler, Graduate Secretary, MFA Program, School for the Contemporary Arts, Simon Fraser University, 8888 University Drive, Burnaby, British Columbia V5A 1S6, Canada; 604-291-3724, fax: 604-291-5907, e-mail address: mfagrad@sfu.ca

Meadows School of the Arts
Southern Methodist University
Dallas, Texas

Independent, coed. Suburban campus. Total enrollment: 11,152. Theater program established 1964.
Degrees Bachelor of Fine Arts in the area of theater. Majors and concentrations: acting, theater studies. Graduate degrees offered: Master of Fine Arts in the areas of acting, design, directing. Program accredited by NAST.
Enrollment 118 total; 97 undergraduate, 21 graduate.
Theater Student Profile 45% females, 55% males, 18% minorities, 1% international.
Theater Faculty 15 total (full-time), 8 total (part-time). 89% of full-time faculty have terminal degrees. Graduate students teach a few undergraduate courses. Undergraduate student–faculty ratio: 8:1.
Student Life Special housing available for theater students.
Expenses for 2006–2007 Application fee: $50. Comprehensive fee: $38,325 includes full-time tuition ($25,400), mandatory fees ($3230), and college room and board ($9695). College room only: $5775.
Financial Aid Program-specific awards: 20 Meadows Artistic Scholarships for talented program majors ($1000–$5000).
Application Procedures Students admitted directly into the professional program freshman year. Deadline for freshmen and transfers: March 2. Required: essay, high school transcript, college transcript(s) for transfer students, letter of recommendation, audition, SAT I or ACT test scores. Recommended: interview. Auditions held 20 times on campus and off campus in various locations.

Web Site http://www.smu.edu/~meadows/
Undergraduate Contact Cecil O'Neal, Professor, Division of Theatre, Southern Methodist University, Meadows School of the Arts, PO Box 750356, Dallas, Texas 75275-0356; 214-768-2545, fax: 214-768-1136, e-mail address: coneal@mail.smu.edu
Graduate Contact Jean Cherry, Graduate Advisor, MSA Graduate Admissions/Records, Southern Methodist University, Meadows School of the Arts, PO Box 750356, Dallas, Texas 75275-0356; 214-768-3765, fax: 214-768-1136, e-mail address: jcherry@mail.smu.edu

Southern Oregon University
Ashland, Oregon

State-supported, coed. Small town campus. Total enrollment: 4,977. Theater program established 1982.
Degrees Bachelor of Fine Arts in the area of theater arts. Majors and concentrations: acting, costume design, design, directing, performance, scenic design, stage management, technical theater, theater business management.
Enrollment 139 total; 27 undergraduate, 112 nonprofessional degree.
Theater Student Profile 56% females, 44% males.
Theater Faculty 8 undergraduate (full-time), 2 undergraduate (part-time). 100% of full-time faculty have terminal degrees. Graduate students do not teach undergraduate courses.
Expenses for 2006–2007 Application fee: $50. State resident tuition: $4986 full-time. Nonresident tuition: $14,691 full-time. College room and board: $6468.
Financial Aid Program-specific awards: 2 Angus Bowmer Theatre Arts Scholarships for acting, directing, and design majors ($500), 2 Beverly Bartell Scholarships for actors ($600), 1 Leon Mulling Scholarship for program majors ($500), departmental awards for program majors, Schneider Award for program majors, 2 E. Mulling Scholarships for program majors ($350), 1 Jeffrey Allen Staver Memorial Award for scenic design majors ($1000).
Application Procedures Students apply for admission into the professional program by sophomore year. Deadline for freshmen and transfers: continuous. Required: high school transcript, college transcript(s) for transfer students, minimum 3.0 high school GPA, 3 letters of recommendation, interview, audition, SAT I or ACT test scores. Recommended: portfolio. Auditions held once in fall and spring on campus. Portfolio reviews held twice on campus; the submission of slides may be substituted for portfolios for applicants in technical areas.
Web Site http://www.sou.edu/thtr
Undergraduate Contact Associate Director of Admissions, Southern Oregon University, 1250 Siskiyou Boulevard, Ashland, Oregon 97520; 541-552-6411, fax: 541-552-6329, e-mail address: admissions@sou.edu

Sarofim School of Fine Arts
Southwestern University
Georgetown, Texas

Independent Methodist, coed. Suburban campus. Total enrollment: 1,309.

State University of New York, Fredonia
Fredonia, New York

State-supported, coed. Small town campus. Total enrollment: 5,432. Theater program established 1970.
Degrees Bachelor of Fine Arts. Majors and concentrations: acting, music theater, production/design. Program accredited by NAST, NASM.
Enrollment 141 total; 81 undergraduate, 60 nonprofessional degree.
Theater Student Profile 55% females, 45% males, 3% minorities, 1% international.

Theater Faculty 9 undergraduate (full-time), 3 undergraduate (part-time). 100% of full-time faculty have terminal degrees. Graduate students do not teach undergraduate courses. Undergraduate student–faculty ratio: 12:1.
Student Life Student groups/activities include Performing Arts Company (student run), Walter Gloor Mainstage Series, Orchesis Dance (student run).
Expenses for 2005–2006 Application fee: $40. State resident tuition: $4350 full-time. Nonresident tuition: $10,610 full-time. Mandatory fees: $1091 full-time. College room and board: $6940. College room only: $4350. Room and board charges vary according to board plan and housing facility. Special program-related fees: $50 per course for audition techniques class accompanist, $90 per program for BFA music theater freshman/sophomore School of Music fee.
Financial Aid Program-specific awards: 6 Jack Cogdill Scholarships for program majors ($1250), 3 Gertrude Prushaw Maytum Scholarships for program majors ($1250).
Application Procedures Students admitted directly into the professional program freshman year. Deadline for freshmen and transfers: continuous. Required: high school transcript, college transcript(s) for transfer students, 2 letters of recommendation, interview, audition, portfolio, SAT I or ACT test scores, portfolio for production design applicants, audition for acting and music theater applicants. Recommended: minimum 3.0 high school GPA. Auditions held 8 times throughout the year by appointment on campus; videotaped performances are permissible as a substitute for live auditions if a live audition is impossible. Portfolio reviews held 4 times and throughout the year by appointment on campus; the submission of slides may be substituted for portfolios if a campus visit is impossible.
Web Site http://www.fredonia.edu
Undergraduate Contact Dr. James Ivey, Chair, Department of Theatre and Dance, State University of New York, Fredonia, Rockefeller Arts Center, Fredonia, New York 14063; 716-673-3596, fax: 716-673-3621, e-mail address: james.ivey@fredonia.edu

Stephen F. Austin State University
Nacogdoches, Texas

State-supported, coed. Small town campus. Total enrollment: 11,435. Theater program established 1972.
Degrees Bachelor of Fine Arts in the area of theater. Majors and concentrations: acting, design, directing, stage management. Cross-registration with Rose Bruford College (United Kingdom). Program accredited by NAST.
Enrollment 181 total; 40 undergraduate, 141 nonprofessional degree.
Theater Student Profile 65% females, 35% males, 3% minorities, 10% international.
Theater Faculty 9 total (full-time), 2 total (part-time). 80% of full-time faculty have terminal degrees. Graduate students do not teach undergraduate courses. Undergraduate student–faculty ratio: 18:1.
Student Life Student groups/activities include Beta Phi Chapter of Alpha Psi Omega.
Expenses for 2005–2006 Application fee: $25. State resident tuition: $4718 full-time. Nonresident tuition: $12,998 full-time. Full-time tuition varies according to course load. College room and board: $5459. Room and board charges vary according to board plan and housing facility. Special program-related fees: $5 for theater admission, $7–$15 per course for supplies.
Financial Aid Program-specific awards: 8–10 departmental scholarships for incoming students passing audition evaluations ($750–$1000), 1 Gray Scholarship for Nacogdoches County, TX residents ($500), 5–8 Stokes Foundation Scholarships for enrolled students ($600–$1000), 1 Cochran Scholarship for enrolled students ($700), 1 alumni scholarship for enrolled students ($500), 1 McGrath Scholarship for enrolled students ($700).
Application Procedures Students apply for admission into the professional program by sophomore year. Deadline for freshmen and transfers: continuous. Required: high school transcript, college transcript(s) for transfer students, minimum 2.0 high school GPA, interview, SAT I or ACT test scores, audition for acting applicants, portfolio for design/technology applicants.

Stephen F. Austin State University (continued)

Auditions held 4 times on campus and off campus in conjunction with Texas Educational Theatre Association Convention and other regional festivals; videotaped performances are permissible as a substitute for live auditions when distance is prohibitive. Portfolio reviews held 4 times for design and technology applicants on campus and off campus in Texas Educational Theatre Association Convention; the submission of slides may be substituted for portfolios if a campus visit is impossible.
Web Site http://www.sfasu.edu/theatre/
Undergraduate Contact Dr. Clarence W. Bahs, Chairman, Department of Theatre, Stephen F. Austin State University, PO Box 6090 SFA Station, Nacogdoches, Texas 75962-6090; 936-468-4003, fax: 936-468-7601, e-mail address: cbahs@sfasu.edu

Stephens College
Columbia, Missouri

Independent, Urban campus. Total enrollment: 824. Theater program established 1899.
Degrees Bachelor of Fine Arts in the area of theater arts. Majors and concentrations: acting, design, directing, music theatre/dance, technical theater, theater arts/drama, theater management. Cross-registration with Mid-Missouri Associated Colleges and Universities.
Enrollment 100 total; all undergraduate.
Theater Student Profile 99% females, 1% males, 17% minorities, 4% international.
Theater Faculty 10 undergraduate (full-time). 80% of full-time faculty have terminal degrees. Graduate students do not teach undergraduate courses. Undergraduate student–faculty ratio: 12:1.
Student Life Student groups/activities include Warehouse Theatre, Velvetones (vocal group).
Expenses for 2006–2007 Application fee: $25. Comprehensive fee: $28,475 includes full-time tuition ($20,500) and college room and board ($7975). College room only: $4760.
Financial Aid Program-specific awards: 2 musical theater awards for vocalists ($500–$1500), 1 Patricia Barry Award for actors ($1500), 1 Maude Adams Award for actors ($1000), Leadership Awards for program majors.
Application Procedures Students admitted directly into the professional program freshman year. Deadline for freshmen and transfers: July 31. Notification date for freshmen and transfers: continuous. Required: essay, high school transcript, college transcript(s) for transfer students, minimum 2.0 high school GPA, letter of recommendation, SAT I or ACT test scores, portfolio for design/technical applicants. Recommended: minimum 3.0 high school GPA, interview, video. Portfolio reviews held as needed on campus and off campus in various locations.
Web Site http://www.stephens.edu
Undergraduate Contact Office of Admission, Stephens College, Box 2121, Columbia, Missouri 65215; 800-876-7207, fax: 573-876-7237, e-mail address: apply@stephens.edu

Syracuse University
Syracuse, New York

Independent, coed. Urban campus. Total enrollment: 17,266. Theater program established 1921.
Degrees Bachelor of Fine Arts in the areas of drama, musical theater, design/technical theater, stage management; Bachelor of Science in the area of drama. Majors and concentrations: acting, design/technical theater, music theater, stage management.
Enrollment 297 total; all undergraduate.
Theater Student Profile 57% females, 43% males, 13% minorities.
Theater Faculty 15 total (full-time), 10 total (part-time). 77% of full-time faculty have terminal degrees. Graduate students do not teach undergraduate courses. Undergraduate student–faculty ratio: 14:1.
Student Life Student groups/activities include Danceworks, Black Box Players.

Expenses for 2005–2006 Application fee: $60. Comprehensive fee: $38,655 includes full-time tuition ($27,210), mandatory fees ($1075), and college room and board ($10,370). College room only: $5620. Room and board charges vary according to board plan and housing facility. Special program-related fees: $15 per semester for piano maintenance, $25 for performances and subscriptions, $350–$700 per credit hour for private music lessons.
Application Procedures Students admitted directly into the professional program freshman year. Deadline for freshmen and transfers: January 1. Notification date for freshmen: March 15; transfers: August 15. Required: essay, high school transcript, college transcript(s) for transfer students, minimum 3.0 high school GPA, 2 letters of recommendation, SAT I or ACT test scores, audition for acting and musical theater applicants, high school counselor evaluation, portfolio for design/technical theater and stage management applicants. Recommended: interview. Auditions held 10 times on campus and off campus in New York, NY; Washington, DC; Los Angeles CA; Chicago, IL; videotaped performances are permissible as a substitute for live auditions if a live audition is not possible. Portfolio reviews held 7 times on campus; the submission of slides may be substituted for portfolios if original work is not available or if a campus visit is impossible (for design/technical applicants only).
Web Site http://vpa.syr.edu/drama
Undergraduate Contact Director, CVPA Recruitment and Admissions, College of Visual and Performing Arts, Syracuse University, 202P Crouse College, Syracuse, New York 13244-1010; 315-443-2769, fax: 315-443-1935, e-mail address: admissu@syr.edu

More About the Program

The Department of Drama at Syracuse University (SU) offers students the chance to study acting, musical theater, stage management, or design/technical theater. Students nurture their creative abilities through a unique combination of active faculty members, diverse performance and staging opportunities, excellent facilities, and a liberal education. Students prepare for a professional career in theater beginning with the first semester; four years are spent in intensive work in the major along with academic course work taken in other areas of the University.

The first year is a nonperformance year that allows young actors to focus on developing their basic acting and musical theater skills. From the second year on, drama students compete for roles in the twenty to thirty productions produced each year by the Department of Drama, Syracuse Stage, the Black Box Players, and the cabaret series. Considered an extension of classroom work, mainstage drama department productions are reserved for drama majors only. In addition, drama majors may earn equity points by working in Syracuse Stage productions.

Design/technical theater and stage management majors at SU have a particular advantage: they can work as assistants to professional designers and stage managers on Syracuse Stage productions and as assistants to faculty designers on mainstage Drama Department productions. They may also create their own designs in the black box and cabaret shows. Junior and senior design majors can create their own designs for the department mainstage shows. In addition, a unique partnership with the School of Art and Design provides opportunities for design/technical theater freshmen to develop their drawing skills.

The Regent Theatre Complex, shared by the Department of Drama and Syracuse Stage, houses four performance spaces that provide a broad range of possibilities.

The department's affiliation with Syracuse Stage, one of the country's outstanding Equity theater companies, opens the world of professional theater to students. Faculty members are not only outstanding teachers and mentors but also successful theater professionals. Performance and studio classes for majors in acting, design, and musical theater are taught by full-time faculty members, including freshman courses.

The Tepper Center for Theatre Careers is a unique program designed to ease the transition of graduating seniors into the professional entertainment world. Activities include a professional practices class in the spring, a one- to two-week workshop in New

York City, and special guests and alumni who return to the campus to speak with the seniors.

Graduates of the Department of Drama are involved in every aspect of professional theater, from lead roles in Broadway plays, musicals, movies, and television dramas to casting directors, writers, and producers. Alumni return to campus each year for panel discussions and bring their professional experiences to students.

Through the University's Division of International Programs Abroad (DIPA), students can study drama for a semester in London. Acting, voice/verse, and movement classes are taught by master teachers at the prestigious Globe Theater in London.

The city of Syracuse itself offers rich culture; it is a regular stop for touring companies of popular Broadway musicals and experimental theater troupes and is home to the Syracuse Symphony Orchestra, the Syracuse Opera, and the Society for New Music. Nestled between the Finger Lakes and the Adirondacks, in central New York State, Syracuse is within a day's drive of New York City, Boston, Philadelphia, Toronto, and Montreal.

Program Facilities The Regent Theatre Complex includes the John D. Archbold Theatre (500 seats), Arthur Storch Theatre (200 seats), Black Box Theatre (60 seats), and Sutton Pavilion (75-seat cabaret space). Other facilities available are dance studios, seminar rooms, design labs with a CAD lab, lecture rooms, performance/rehearsal studios, music practice rooms, showers, and locker rooms.

Faculty, Resident Artists, and Alumni Many faculty members are members of the Actors' Equity Association; all are working artists as well as teachers. Several Syracuse Stage professionals, including the artistic director, teach in the drama program. Among the ranks of alumni are Tony and Emmy award winners, New York City talent and casting agents, actors on Broadway and television and in movies, playwrights, screenplay and movie writers, and artistic and managing directors of theater companies.

Student Theater Opportunities Students are able to participate in Department of Drama productions; also available are Syracuse Stage, the Black Box Players student group, cabaret, and improvisational theater.

Special Programs The Department of Drama's partnership with Syracuse Stage allows undergraduates to experience professional theater while in school. Some student actors have been cast in professional productions, and some understudy the professional actors. Equity points may be earned through work with Syracuse Stage. Study abroad in London is offered through SU Abroad. Internships at Syracuse Stage and in New York City or Los Angeles are available for credit or in a volunteer capacity. Each Wednesday, Drama Lab brings students together with visiting artists, alumni, agents, and union representatives or to perform scenes from class. All University activities are available to students in the Department of Drama. An honors program is available for students who desire a rigorous academic challenge.

The Tepper Semester is a unique program that offers undergraduate students in advanced levels of acting, musical theater, design, and stage management the opportunity to become immersed in a rigorous artistic training program in the culturally rich setting of New York City.

Students in the Tepper Semester work closely with an accomplished faculty of professional, working artists who nurture the students' creative, intellectual, and personal growth. The faculty members also help students gain an understanding of the business skills essential for a rewarding and successful career in the industry.

Residency in New York City is an integral part of the Tepper Semester experience. Students live and study in the heart of New York's theater district during the fall semester of their senior year, with studio classes a mere 10-minute walk from their accommodations at the New Yorker Hotel. Their artistic training is fueled by the cultural and educational resources of the city. In addition to being exposed to a broad range of theater, they can experience museums, libraries, and various entertainment venues.

Texas Southern University
Houston, Texas

State-supported, coed. Urban campus. Total enrollment: 11,903. Theater program established 1948.

Tisch School of the Arts, Department of Drama
See New York University

Tisch School of the Arts, Rita and Burton Goldberg Department of Dramatic Writing
See New York University

Tulane University
New Orleans, Louisiana

Independent, coed. Urban campus. Total enrollment: 12,691. Theater program established 1937.
Degrees Bachelor of Fine Arts. Majors and concentrations: acting, design/technical theater. Graduate degrees offered: Master of Fine Arts in the area of design/technical theater. Cross-registration with Loyola University New Orleans.
Enrollment 73 total; 3 undergraduate, 12 graduate, 58 nonprofessional degree.
Theater Student Profile 60% females, 40% males.
Theater Faculty 14 total (full-time), 10 total (part-time). 100% of full-time faculty have terminal degrees. Graduate students teach a few undergraduate courses. Undergraduate student–faculty ratio: 10:1.
Student Life Student groups/activities include American College Theatre Festival, United States Institute for Theatre Technology, Southeastern Theatre Conference.
Expenses for 2005–2006 Application fee: $55. Comprehensive fee: $41,357 includes full-time tuition ($30,350), mandatory fees ($2596), and college room and board ($8411). College room only: $4841. Special program-related fees: $25 per semester for design studio fee.
Application Procedures Students apply for admission into the professional program by sophomore year. Deadline for freshmen: January 15; transfers: June 1. Notification date for freshmen: April 1; transfers: continuous. Required: essay, high school transcript, college transcript(s) for transfer students, minimum 2.0 high school GPA, SAT I or ACT test scores, minimum 3.0 college GPA for transfer students, one recommendation from high school counselor, audition for acting applicants, portfolio for design/technical applicants. Recommended: 2 letters of recommendation, interview, SAT II. Auditions held twice on campus. Portfolio reviews held twice on campus and off campus in United States Institute for Theatre Technology locations, Southeastern Theatre Conference locations; the submission of slides may be substituted for portfolios when scheduling is difficult.
Web Site http://www.tulane.edu/~theatre
Undergraduate Contact Prof. Ron Gural, Theatre Coordinator, Department of Theatre and Dance, Tulane University, McWilliams Hall, New Orleans, Louisiana 70118; 504-862-8000 ext. 1757, fax: 504-865-6737, e-mail address: tori@tulane.edu
Graduate Contact Prof. Marty Sacks, Technical Director and Design Staff Head, Department of Theatre and Dance, Tulane University, McWilliams Hall, New Orleans, Louisiana 70118; 504-862-8000 ext. 7744, fax: 504-865-6737, e-mail address: msachs@tulane.edu

The University of Arizona
Tucson, Arizona

State-supported, coed. Urban campus. Total enrollment: 37,036. Theater program established 1936.

The University of British Columbia
Vancouver, British Columbia, Canada

Province-supported, coed. Urban campus. Total enrollment: 42,427. Theater program established 1951.
Degrees Bachelor of Arts in the areas of film production, theatre; Bachelor of Fine Arts in the areas of theater, creative writing. Majors and concentrations: acting, creative writing, design, film, technical theater. Graduate degrees offered: Master of Fine Arts in the areas of theater, creative writing, film.
Enrollment 232 total; 170 undergraduate, 62 graduate.
Theater Student Profile 70% females, 30% males, 3% international.
Theater Faculty 24 total (full-time), 36 total (part-time). 83% of full-time faculty have terminal degrees. Graduate students teach a few undergraduate courses. Undergraduate student–faculty ratio: 8:1.
Student Life Student groups/activities include Theatre at UBC, Brave New Play Rites, Persistence of Vision.
Expenses for 2005–2006 Special program-related fees: $1000–$5000 per year for film production costs.
Financial Aid Program-specific awards: 1 Sharon Yacowar Frohlinger Memorial Scholarship for theater students ($310), 1 Faculty Women's Club/Ida Green Scholarship for program students ($1800), 1 Michael McQueen Scholarship for design students ($340), 1 Jessie Richardson Scholarship for acting students ($350), 1 Beatrice Johnson Wood Scholarship for acting students ($1850), 1 Mr. and Mrs. G. E. Poole Award for theater students ($1450).
Application Procedures Students apply for admission into the professional program by sophomore year. Deadline for freshmen and transfers: February 28. Required: high school transcript, college transcript(s) for transfer students, interview, minimum 2.75 high school GPA, audition for acting majors, portfolio for design/technical theater and creative writing majors, video for film majors. Auditions held once on campus. Portfolio reviews held once on campus; the submission of slides may be substituted for portfolios.
Web Site http:////www.theatre.ubc.ca/
Contact Karen Tong, Secretary, Department of Theatre, Film, and Creative Writing, The University of British Columbia, 6354 Crescent Road, Vancouver, British Columbia V6T 1Z2, Canada; 604-822-3880, fax: 604-822-5985, e-mail address: fwtheatr@interchange.ubc.ca

University of California, Santa Barbara
Santa Barbara, California

State-supported, coed. Suburban campus. Total enrollment: 21,016. Theater program established 1984.
Degrees Bachelor of Fine Arts. Majors and concentrations: acting.
Enrollment 260 total; 60 undergraduate, 200 nonprofessional degree.
Theater Student Profile 55% females, 45% males, 30% minorities.
Theater Faculty 6 undergraduate (full-time). 33% of full-time faculty have terminal degrees. Graduate students do not teach undergraduate courses. Undergraduate student–faculty ratio: 20:1.
Expenses for 2005–2006 Application fee: $40. State resident tuition: $0 full-time. Nonresident tuition: $17,820 full-time. Mandatory fees: $6993 full-time. College room and board: $10,577. College room only: $8110.
Financial Aid Program-specific awards: 4–5 Drama and Dance Affiliate Scholarships for seniors ($200–$400), 1 Stanley Glenn Scholarship for program majors ($800), 1–2 Theodore Hatlen Scholarships for program majors ($1000), 1 Robert G. Egan Memorial Scholarship for program majors ($1500).

Application Procedures Students apply for admission into the professional program by sophomore year. Deadline for freshmen and transfers: November 30. Notification date for freshmen: March 15; transfers: April 1. Required: essay, high school transcript, college transcript(s) for transfer students, minimum 3.0 high school GPA, audition, SAT I or ACT test scores. Auditions held twice on campus.
Web Site http://www.dramadance.ucsb.edu
Undergraduate Contact Amy Runjavac, Undergraduate Advisor, Department of Dramatic Art and Division of Dance, University of California, Santa Barbara, Building 479, Santa Barbara, California 93106-7060; 805-893-3241, fax: 805-893-7029, e-mail address: runjavac@dramadance.ucsb.edu

University of Central Florida
Orlando, Florida

State-supported, coed. Suburban campus. Total enrollment: 44,953. Theater program established 1968.
Degrees Bachelor of Fine Arts. Majors and concentrations: acting, performance, stage management. Graduate degrees offered: Master of Fine Arts in the areas of acting, design, musical theatre, theatre for young audiences.
Enrollment 407 total; 224 undergraduate, 43 graduate, 140 nonprofessional degree.
Theater Student Profile 55% females, 45% males, 15% minorities.
Theater Faculty 34 total (full-time), 6 total (part-time). 100% of full-time faculty have terminal degrees. Graduate students teach a few undergraduate courses. Undergraduate student–faculty ratio: 10:1.
Student Life Student groups/activities include Alpha Psi Omega, Florida Theatre Association.
Expenses for 2005–2006 Application fee: $30. State resident tuition: $3141 full-time. Nonresident tuition: $16,272 full-time. Mandatory fees: $198 full-time. Full-time tuition and fees vary according to course load. College room and board: $7400. College room only: $4300. Room and board charges vary according to board plan and housing facility. Special program-related fees: $15 per credit hour for equipment; lab fee.
Financial Aid Program-specific awards: 32 talent grants for program majors ($1000), 24 Disney Scholarships for design/technology and stage management majors ($2200), 1 James Cali Award for BFA majors ($1500), 6 Florida Theatrical Awards for BFA majors ($1000).
Application Procedures Students admitted directly into the professional program freshman year. Deadline for freshmen and transfers: August 1. Notification date for freshmen and transfers: August 15. Required: high school transcript, college transcript(s) for transfer students, minimum 3.0 high school GPA, 3 letters of recommendation, interview, audition, portfolio, SAT I or ACT test scores. Auditions held 5 times on campus; videotaped performances are permissible as a substitute for live auditions when distance is prohibitive. Portfolio reviews held 6 times on campus; the submission of slides may be substituted for portfolios when distance is prohibitive.
Web Site http://www.cas.ucf.edu/theatre
Undergraduate Contact Office of Admissions, University of Central Florida, PO Box 160111, Orlando, Florida 32816; 407-823-3180, e-mail address: admission@mail.ucf.edu
Graduate Contact Dr. Julia Listengarten, Associate Professor, Department of Theatre, University of Central Florida, PO Box 162372, Orlando, Florida 32816; 407-823-3858, fax: 407-823-6446, e-mail address: jlisteng@mail.ucf.edu

University of Cincinnati
See University of Cincinnati College Conservatory of Music

University of Cincinnati

University of Cincinnati College Conservatory of Music

Cincinnati, Ohio

State-supported, coed. Urban campus. Total enrollment: 27,932. Theater program established 1970.

Degrees Bachelor of Fine Arts in the areas of musical theater, dramatic performance, theater design and production. Majors and concentrations: costume design, dramatic performance, lighting design, makeup, music theater, set design, sound design, stage management. Graduate degrees offered: Master of Fine Arts in the areas of directing, theater design and production. Cross-registration with Greater Cincinnati Consortium of Colleges and Universities. Program accredited by NAST, NASM, NASD.

Enrollment 215 total; 181 undergraduate, 34 graduate.

Theater Student Profile 49% females, 51% males, 7% minorities, 1% international.

Theater Faculty 15 total (full-time), 11 total (part-time). 95% of full-time faculty have terminal degrees. Graduate students teach a few undergraduate courses. Undergraduate student–faculty ratio: 7:1.

Student Life Student groups/activities include Student Artist Program. Special housing available for theater students.

Expenses for 2005–2006 Application fee: $40. State resident tuition: $7458 full-time. Nonresident tuition: $21,210 full-time. Mandatory fees: $1425 full-time. Full-time tuition and fees vary according to course load, degree level, location, program, and reciprocity agreements. College room and board: $7890. College room only: $4680. Room and board charges vary according to board plan and housing facility.

Financial Aid Program-specific awards: 86 honors awards for program majors ($3700), 21 Cincinnatus Awards for those in top 5% of graduating class with minimum 26 ACT score or minimum 1170 SAT score ($2000–$20,000).

Application Procedures Students admitted directly into the professional program freshman year. Deadline for freshmen and transfers: February 1. Notification date for freshmen and transfers: continuous. Required: high school transcript, college transcript(s) for transfer students, letter of recommendation, audition, SAT I or ACT test scores, portfolio, interview, essay, and 3 letters of recommendation for theater design and production applicants. Recommended: minimum 3.0 high school GPA. Auditions held 10 times on campus and off campus in Atlanta, GA; New York, NY; Chicago, IL; Los Angeles, CA; San Francisco, CA; Seattle, WA; Southeastern Theatre Conference sites. Portfolio reviews held 8 times for theater design and production applicants on campus and off campus in New York, NY; Chicago, IL; Los Angeles, CA; CA; Atlanta, GA; Seattle, WA; Southeastern Theatre Conference sites; the submission of slides may be substituted for portfolios with approval from the department.

Web Site http://www.ccm.uc.edu

Undergraduate Contact Ms. Kelly Hebblethwaite, Senior Admissions Officer, College-Conservatory of Music, University of Cincinnati, PO Box 210003, Cincinnati, Ohio 45221-0003; 513-556-9479, fax: 513-556-1028, e-mail address: kelly.hebblethwaite@uc.edu

Graduate Contact Mr. Paul R. Hillner, Assistant Dean, College-Conservatory of Music, University of Cincinnati, PO Box 210003, Cincinnati, Ohio 45221-0003; 513-556-9478, fax: 513-556-1028, e-mail address: paul.hillner@uc.edu

University of Colorado at Boulder

Boulder, Colorado

State-supported, coed. Small town campus. Total enrollment: 31,068. Theater program established 1962.

Degrees Bachelor of Fine Arts in the area of theater. Majors and concentrations: design/technical theater, music theater, performance. Graduate degrees offered: Doctor of Philosophy in the area of theater.

Enrollment 198 total; 38 undergraduate, 27 graduate, 133 nonprofessional degree.

Theater Student Profile 66% females, 34% males, 12% minorities, 2% international.

Theater Faculty 14 total (full-time), 3 total (part-time). 100% of full-time faculty have terminal degrees. Graduate students teach a few undergraduate courses. Undergraduate student–faculty ratio: 4:1.

Student Life Student groups/activities include On Stage, Colorado Shakespeare Festival. Special housing available for theater students.

Expenses for 2005–2006 Application fee: $50. One-time mandatory fee: $108. State resident tuition: $4446 full-time. Nonresident tuition: $21,900 full-time. Mandatory fees: $926 full-time. Full-time tuition and fees vary according to program. College room and board: $7980. Room and board charges vary according to board plan, location, and student level. Special program-related fees: $25 per course for instructional support in selected courses.

Financial Aid Program-specific awards: 14 Technical Assistant Awards for program students ($4400), 5 University Theatre Awards for production majors ($550), 2 University Theatre Awards for incoming freshmen ($1250), 1 David A. Busse Scholarship for upperclass design students ($450), 1 Dorothy and Anthony Riddle Scholarship for theater participants ($900), 1 Mabel Gaiser Borgmann Scholarship for female drama students ($700), 1 Bonnie Potts Memorial Scholarship for senior theater majors ($100), 2 Katherine J. Lamont Scholarships for junior and senior theater and dance majors ($1300).

Application Procedures Students apply for admission into the professional program by sophomore year. Deadline for freshmen: January 15; transfers: April 1. Required: essay, high school transcript, college transcript(s) for transfer students, SAT I or ACT test scores, audition for music theater applicants. Recommended: minimum 3.0 high school GPA. Auditions held once on campus.

Web Site http://www.colorado.edu/TheatreDance/

Undergraduate Contact Dr. Bud Coleman, Chair, Department of Theatre and Dance, University of Colorado at Boulder, CB 261, Boulder, Colorado 80309-0261; 303-492-2793, fax: 303-492-7722, e-mail address: bud.coleman@colorado.edu

Graduate Contact Michelle Gupner, Theater Studies Assistant, Department of Theatre and Dance, University of Colorado at Boulder, CB 261, Boulder, Colorado 80309-0261; 303-492-7356, fax: 303-492-7722, e-mail address: gupner@colorado.edu

University of Connecticut

Storrs, Connecticut

State-supported, coed. Rural campus. Total enrollment: 23,185. Theater program established 1960.

Degrees Bachelor of Fine Arts. Majors and concentrations: acting, design/technical theater, puppetry. Graduate degrees offered: Master of Arts in the area of production-puppetry; Master of Fine Arts in the areas of acting, design, puppetry, technical direction. Program accredited by NAST.

Enrollment 163 total; 121 undergraduate, 30 graduate, 12 nonprofessional degree.

Theater Student Profile 53% females, 47% males.

Theater Faculty 13 total (full-time), 10 total (part-time). 85% of full-time faculty have terminal degrees. Graduate students teach a few undergraduate courses. Undergraduate student–faculty ratio: 5:1.

Student Life Student groups/activities include Connecticut Repertory Theatre. Special housing available for theater students.

Expenses for 2006–2007 Application fee: $70. State resident tuition: $6456 full-time. Nonresident tuition: $19,656 full-time. Mandatory fees: $1906 full-time. College room and board: $8266. College room only: $4350. Special program-related fees: $60 for supplemental materials costs.

Financial Aid Program-specific awards: 15 University Drama Scholarships for incoming students ($1000).

Application Procedures Students admitted directly into the professional program freshman year. Deadline for freshmen and transfers: March 6. Notification date for freshmen and transfers: continuous. Required: essay, high school transcript, college transcript(s) for transfer students, interview, audition, portfolio, SAT I or ACT test scores, interview and portfolio for design/

University of Connecticut (continued)

technical theater applicants, audition for acting applicants, audition and interview for puppetry applicants. Recommended: 2 letters of recommendation. Auditions held 4 times by appointment for acting and puppetry majors on campus. Portfolio reviews held by appointment on campus; the submission of slides may be substituted for portfolios if a campus visit is impossible.

Web Site http://www.drama.uconn.edu

Undergraduate Contact Admissions Assistant, Department of Dramatic Arts, University of Connecticut, U-127, 802 Bolton Road, Storrs, Connecticut 06269-1127; 860-486-2281, fax: 860-486-3110, e-mail address: daoffice@uconn.edu

Graduate Contact Ms. Mary Tellier, Administrative Assistant, Department of Dramatic Arts, University of Connecticut, U-127, 802 Bolton Road, Storrs, Connecticut 06269-1127; 860-486-2281, fax: 860-486-3110, e-mail address: mary.tellier@uconn.edu

University of Evansville
Evansville, Indiana

Independent, coed. Suburban campus. Total enrollment: 2,836.

University of Florida
Gainesville, Florida

State-supported, coed. Suburban campus. Total enrollment: 49,693. Theater program established 1975.

Degrees Bachelor of Fine Arts in the areas of theater performance, acting, musical theater, theater production, costume design, costume technology, light design, scene design. Majors and concentrations: acting, costume design, lighting design, music theater, scenic design. Graduate degrees offered: Master of Fine Arts in the areas of theater performance, theater production. Cross-registration with Florida State University System. Program accredited by NAST.

Enrollment 177 total; 43 undergraduate, 37 graduate, 97 nonprofessional degree.

Theater Student Profile 70% females, 30% males, 20% minorities, 1% international.

Theater Faculty 14 total (full-time), 4 total (part-time). 100% of full-time faculty have terminal degrees. Graduate students teach a few undergraduate courses. Undergraduate student–faculty ratio: 7:1.

Student Life Student groups/activities include International Production Program, Florida Players, Theatre Strike Force. Special housing available for theater students.

Expenses for 2005–2006 Application fee: $30. State resident tuition: $3,094 full-time. Nonresident tuition: $17,222 full-time. College room and board: $6260. College room only: $3940. Room and board charges vary according to board plan and housing facility. Special program-related fees: $15–$45 for lab fees.

Financial Aid Program-specific awards: 5 Constans Theater and Dance Scholarships for program majors ($500), 5 Ingram Scholarships for program majors ($500), 2 Richardson Scholarships for program majors ($1000), 8 Stoughton Scholarships for program majors ($500), 3 Outstanding Senior Awards for graduating seniors ($500), Hubbell Scholarships for program majors ($1000), 1 Gator Tones Musical Theatre Award for musical theatre majors ($200).

Application Procedures Students admitted directly into the professional program freshman year. Deadline for freshmen: January 7; transfers: March 1. Required: essay, high school transcript, college transcript(s) for transfer students, minimum 2.0 high school GPA, audition, portfolio, SAT I or ACT test scores. Auditions held twice on campus and off campus in New York, NY; Chicago, IL; San Francisco, CA (MFA). Portfolio reviews held twice on campus and off campus in Southeastern Theatre Conference, American College Theatre Festival, University Resident Theatre Association; the submission of slides may be substituted for portfolios with permission from the school.

Web Site http://www.arts.ufl.edu/theatreanddance

Undergraduate Contact Prof. Kevin Marshall, Director, School of Theatre and Dance, University of Florida, PO Box 115900, Gainesville, Florida 32611-5900; 352-273-2930, fax: 352-392-5114, e-mail address: kmarshall@arts.ufl.edu

Graduate Contact Dr. David Shelton, Graduate Coordinator, School of Theatre and Dance, University of Florida, PO Box 115900, Gainesville, Florida 32611-5900; 352-273-0503, fax: 352-392-5114, e-mail address: dshelton@ufl.edu

The Hartt School
University of Hartford
West Hartford, Connecticut

Independent, coed. Suburban campus. Total enrollment: 7,260. Theater program established 1996.

Degrees Bachelor of Fine Arts. Majors and concentrations: music theater, theater arts/drama. Cross-registration with Trinity College, Saint Joseph College, Hartford Seminary, Central Connecticut State University, University of Connecticut (Hartford Campus), Capitol Community College. Program accredited by NAST.

Enrollment 125 total; all undergraduate.

Theater Student Profile 60% females, 40% males, 1% minorities, 1% international.

Theater Faculty 4 undergraduate (full-time), 8 undergraduate (part-time). 100% of full-time faculty have terminal degrees. Graduate students do not teach undergraduate courses.

Student Life Special housing available for theater students.

Expenses for 2006–2007 Application fee: $35. Comprehensive fee: $35,688 includes full-time tuition ($24,576), mandatory fees ($1190), and college room and board ($9922). College room only: $6118.

Financial Aid Program-specific awards: 25 Performing Arts Scholarships for students passing audition evaluations ($7000).

Application Procedures Students admitted directly into the professional program freshman year. Deadline for freshmen and transfers: continuous. Required: high school transcript, college transcript(s) for transfer students, minimum 2.0 high school GPA, 3 letters of recommendation, interview, audition, SAT I or ACT test scores, headshot photo, resume. Recommended: essay, minimum 3.0 high school GPA. Auditions held 6 times on campus and off campus in Hartford, CT; Boston, MA; New York, NY; Chicago, IL; Miami, FL; San Francisco, CA; videotaped performances are permissible as a substitute for live auditions when distance is prohibitive.

Web Site http://www.hartford.edu/hartt

Undergraduate Contact Director of Admissions, The Hartt School, University of Hartford, 200 Bloomfield Avenue, West Hartford, Connecticut 06117-1500; 860-768-4465, fax: 860-768-4441, e-mail address: harttadm@hartford.edu

University of Houston
Houston, Texas

State-supported, coed. Urban campus. Total enrollment: 35,344. Theater program established 1970.

Degrees Bachelor of Arts in the area of theater. Majors and concentrations: acting, dance, design, directing, music theater, playwriting. Graduate degrees offered: Master of Arts in the area of theater; Master of Fine Arts in the area of theater.

Enrollment 290 total; 237 undergraduate, 53 graduate.

Theater Student Profile 67% females, 33% males, 26% minorities, 2% international.

Theater Faculty 11 total (full-time), 4 total (part-time). 100% of full-time faculty have terminal degrees. Graduate students teach a few undergraduate courses. Undergraduate student–faculty ratio: 16:1.

Student Life Student groups/activities include Alpha Psi Omega.

Expenses for 2005–2006 Application fee: $50. State resident tuition: $3920 full-time. Nonresident tuition: $12,200 full-time. Mandatory fees: $2566 full-time. Full-time tuition and fees vary according to course level, course load, degree level, location, program, reciprocity agreements, and student level. College room and board: $6058. College room only: $3492. Room and board charges vary according to board plan and housing facility. Special program-related fees: $20–$50 per course for equipment maintenance and supplies fee.

Financial Aid Program-specific awards: 5 theater scholarships for all theater students ($750), 1 Trey Wilson Award for all theater students ($1000), 1 Robert Bullard Award for all theater students ($500), 1 Cecil Pickett Award for all theater students ($1000), 1 Joseph Michael Adamo Award for all theater students ($500), 1 Jose Quintero Award for all theater students ($1000).

Application Procedures Students admitted directly into the professional program freshman year. Deadline for freshmen and transfers: July 1. Required: high school transcript, college transcript(s) for transfer students, minimum 3.0 high school GPA, 3 letters of recommendation, SAT I test score only.

Web Site http://www.hfac.uh.edu/theatre/home.html

Undergraduate Contact Molly Dean, Academic Advisor, Admission Office, University of Houston, 4800 Calhoun, Wortham Theatre, Houston, Texas 77204-4016; 713-743-2913, fax: 713-749-1420, e-mail address: mcdean@uh.edu

Graduate Contact Dr. Sidney Berger, Director, School of Theatre, University of Houston, 4800 Calhoun, Wortham Theatre, Houston, Texas 77204-4016; 713-743-2930, fax: 713-749-4016, e-mail address: sberger@uh.edu

University of Idaho

Moscow, Idaho

State-supported, coed. Small town campus. Total enrollment: 12,476. Theater program established 1930.

University of Illinois at Urbana–Champaign

Champaign, Illinois

State-supported, coed. Small town campus. Total enrollment: 41,938. Theater program established 1969.

Degrees Bachelor of Fine Arts in the areas of acting, design, technology and management, theater studies. Majors and concentrations: acting, costume design, lighting design, performance studies, set design, sound design, stage management, theater technology. Graduate degrees offered: Master of Fine Arts in the areas of acting, design, technology and management. Doctor of Philosophy in the area of theater history and criticism. Cross-registration with Parkland College. Program accredited by NAST.

Enrollment 184 total; 133 undergraduate, 51 graduate.

Theater Student Profile 55% females, 45% males, 13% minorities, 5% international.

Theater Faculty 18 total (full-time), 14 total (part-time). 100% of full-time faculty have terminal degrees. Graduate students teach a few undergraduate courses. Undergraduate student–faculty ratio: 5:1.

Expenses for 2005–2006 Application fee: $40. State resident tuition: $7042 full-time. Nonresident tuition: $21,128 full-time. Mandatory fees: $1582 full-time. Full-time tuition and fees vary according to course load, program, and student level. College room and board: $7176. College room only: $2970. Room and board charges vary according to board plan and housing facility. Special program-related fees: $5–$15 per semester for CAD lab fee.

Financial Aid Program-specific awards: 50 talented student tuition waivers for program students ($500–$1000), 6 Bernard Gold Awards for program students ($1000).

Application Procedures Students admitted directly into the professional program freshman year. Deadline for freshmen and transfers: continuous. Notification date for freshmen and transfers: April 15. Required: high school transcript, college transcript(s) for transfer students, interview, SAT I or ACT test scores, audition for acting applicants, portfolio for design applicants, statement of purpose for theater studies applicants. Recommended: essay, letter of recommendation. Auditions held 6 times on campus and off campus in Chicago, IL; videotaped performances are permissible as a substitute for live auditions if a campus visit is impossible. Portfolio reviews held 6 times on campus; the submission of slides may be substituted for portfolios for international applicants.

Web Site http://www.theatre.uiuc.edu/

Undergraduate Contact Office of Admissions and Records, University of Illinois at Urbana–Champaign, 901 West Illinois Street, 506 South Wright, Urbana, Illinois 61801; 217-333-0302.

Graduate Contact Cindy Hall, Staff Secretary, Department of Theatre, University of Illinois at Urbana–Champaign, 4-122 Krannert Center for the Performing Arts, 500 South Goodwin Avenue, Urbana, Illinois 61801; 217-333-3538, fax: 217-244-1861, e-mail address: cindyh@uiuc.edu

University of Kentucky

Lexington, Kentucky

State-supported, coed. Urban campus. Total enrollment: 25,672. Theater program established 1928.

Degrees Bachelor of Arts in the area of theater; Bachelor of Fine Arts in the areas of acting, design and technology. Majors and concentrations: acting, theater arts/drama, theater design/technology. Cross-registration with University of Kentucky Community College System . Program accredited by NAST.

Enrollment 105 total; all undergraduate.

Theater Student Profile 46% females, 54% males, 10% minorities, 1% international.

Theater Faculty 10 undergraduate (full-time), 4 undergraduate (part-time). 100% of full-time faculty have terminal degrees. Graduate students do not teach undergraduate courses. Undergraduate student–faculty ratio: 10:1.

Student Life Student groups/activities include United States Institute for Theatre Technology, Southeastern Theatre Conference. Special housing available for theater students.

Expenses for 2005–2006 Application fee: $40. State resident tuition: $5162 full-time. Nonresident tuition: $12,148 full-time. Mandatory fees: $650 full-time. Full-time tuition and fees vary according to degree level, program, reciprocity agreements, and student level. College room and board: $5129. College room only: $3363. Room and board charges vary according to board plan and housing facility. Special program-related fees: $15–$75 per semester for materials fee for design courses.

Financial Aid Program-specific awards: 2 Wallace Briggs Freshman Scholarships for entering freshmen ($1000), John and Ruth Koch Scholarship for entering freshmen acting majors ($1000), Wallace and Olive Briggs Scholarship for entering freshmen ($4000), 5 Lolo Robinson Scholarships for sophomore, junior, and senior theater majors ($500), 2 Raymond A. Smith Scholarships for junior and senior theater majors ($500), Governor's School for the Arts Scholarship for entering freshmen who participated in the Kentucky Governor's School for the Arts ($1000), 1 Christopher Maier Memorial Scholarship for junior, senior, sophomore ($1000).

Application Procedures Students apply for admission into the professional program by freshman year. Deadline for freshmen and transfers: continuous. Required: high school transcript, college transcript(s) for transfer students, minimum 3.0 high school GPA, 2 letters of recommendation, interview, SAT I or ACT test scores (minimum combined SAT I score of 950, minimum composite ACT score of 22), audition for acting applicants, portfolio for design applicants. Auditions held twice on campus and off campus in Louisville, KY; videotaped performances are permissible as a substitute for live auditions with permission of the chair. Portfolio reviews held once on campus; the submission of slides may be substituted for portfolios with permission of the program director.

Web Site http://www.uky.edu/FineArts/Theatre

Undergraduate Contact Robert Haven, Director of Undergraduate Studies, Department of Theatre, University of Kentucky, 114 Fine Arts Building, Lexington, Kentucky 40506; 859-257-3297, fax: 859-257-3042.

University of Louisiana at Lafayette

Lafayette, Louisiana

State-supported, coed. Urban campus. Total enrollment: 17,075. Theater program established 1994.

University of Louisiana at Lafayette (continued)

University of Memphis
Memphis, Tennessee

State-supported, coed. Urban campus. Total enrollment: 20,465. Theater program established 1950.

Degrees Bachelor of Fine Arts in the area of theatre. Majors and concentrations: design/technical theater, performance. Graduate degrees offered: Master of Fine Arts in the area of theatre. Program accredited by NAST.

Enrollment 103 total; 89 undergraduate, 14 graduate.

Theater Student Profile 51% females, 49% males, 24% minorities.

Theater Faculty 1 undergraduate (full-time), 12 undergraduate (part-time), 12 graduate (full-time). 70% of full-time faculty have terminal degrees. Graduate students teach a few undergraduate courses. Undergraduate student–faculty ratio: 9:1.

Student Life Student groups/activities include Fred Mertz Student Activity Group.

Expenses for 2005–2006 Application fee: $25. State resident tuition: $4216 full-time. Nonresident tuition: $14,030 full-time. Mandatory fees: $868 full-time. Full-time tuition and fees vary according to program and reciprocity agreements. College room and board: $6069. College room only: $2950. Room and board charges vary according to housing facility. Special program-related fees: $100 for supplies for scenic painting.

Financial Aid Program-specific awards: 3 University Talent Scholarships for program majors ($3470–$10,858), 4–9 departmental talent scholarships for program majors ($100–$400).

Application Procedures Students apply for admission into the professional program by freshman, sophomore year. Deadline for freshmen and transfers: August 1. Notification date for freshmen and transfers: continuous. Required: high school transcript, college transcript(s) for transfer students, audition, SAT I or ACT test scores (minimum combined SAT I score of 930, minimum composite ACT score of 20), minimum 3.0 GPA for auto-admission, portfolio for design applicants. Auditions held twice on campus. Portfolio reviews held twice on campus.

Web Site http://www.memphis.edu/theatre

Undergraduate Contact Mr. Robert A. Hetherington, Chair, Department of Theatre and Dance, University of Memphis, 144 Theatre Communication Building, Memphis, Tennessee 38152-3150; 901-678-2523, fax: 901-678-4331, e-mail address: rhether@memphis.edu

Graduate Contact Ms. Gloria Baxter, Coordinator of Graduate Studies, Department of Theatre and Dance, University of Memphis, 144 Theatre Communication Building, Memphis, Tennessee 38152-3150; 901-678-2523, fax: 901-678-4331, e-mail address: theatrelib@memphis.edu

University of Miami
Coral Gables, Florida

Independent, coed. Suburban campus. Total enrollment: 15,674. Theater program established 1936.

Degrees Bachelor of Fine Arts in the area of theater arts. Majors and concentrations: design production, music theater, performance, stage management, theater management.

Enrollment 130 total; 60 undergraduate, 70 nonprofessional degree.

Theater Student Profile 60% females, 40% males, 17% minorities.

Theater Faculty 19 undergraduate (full-time), 2 undergraduate (part-time). 100% of full-time faculty have terminal degrees. Graduate students do not teach undergraduate courses. Undergraduate student–faculty ratio: 6:1.

Student Life Student groups/activities include Jerry Herman Ring Theatre, TAG-Theatre Action Group.

Expenses for 2005–2006 Application fee: $65. Comprehensive fee: $37,926 includes full-time tuition ($29,020) and college room and board ($8906). College room only: $5224. Full-time tuition varies according to course load, location, and program. Room and board charges vary according to board plan and housing facility.

Financial Aid Program-specific awards: 12 departmental scholarships for program majors demonstrating need/talent ($1000–$3000).

Application Procedures Students admitted directly into the professional program freshman year. Deadline for freshmen: February 15; transfers: continuous. Notification date for freshmen: May 1; transfers: continuous. Required: essay, high school transcript, college transcript(s) for transfer students, minimum 3.0 high school GPA, letter of recommendation, interview, audition, portfolio, SAT I or ACT test scores (minimum combined SAT I score of 1200, minimum composite ACT score of 24). Auditions held by appointment on campus and off campus in New York, NY; Chicago, IL; Southeastern Theatre Conference sites; International Thespian Conference sites; videotaped performances are permissible as a substitute for live auditions if a campus visit is impossible. Portfolio reviews held by appointment on campus and off campus in New York, NY; Chicago, IL; Southeastern Theatre Conference sites; International Thespian Conference sites; the submission of slides may be substituted for portfolios for design, production, management applicants.

Web Site http://www.miami.edu/tha/

Undergraduate Contact Ms. Linda R. Oglesby, Administrator, Department of Theatre Arts, University of Miami, PO Box 248273, Coral Gables, Florida 33124-4820; 305-284-4474, fax: 305-284-5702, e-mail address: loglesby@mail.as.miami.edu

University of Michigan
Ann Arbor, Michigan

State-supported, coed. Suburban campus. Total enrollment: 39,993. Theater program established 1915.

Degrees Bachelor of Fine Arts in the areas of theatre performance, acting or directing, theatre design and production; Bachelor in Theater Arts. Majors and concentrations: acting, directing, production/design, theater arts/drama.

Enrollment 147 total; 125 undergraduate, 22 nonprofessional degree.

Theater Student Profile 58% females, 42% males, 7% minorities.

Theater Faculty 17 total (full-time), 14 total (part-time). 80% of full-time faculty have terminal degrees. Graduate students do not teach undergraduate courses. Undergraduate student–faculty ratio: 5:1.

Student Life Student groups/activities include Basement Arts Productions, University Productions.

Expenses for 2005–2006 State resident tuition: $9213 full-time. Nonresident tuition: $27,602 full-time. Mandatory fees: $187 full-time. Full-time tuition and fees vary according to course load, degree level, location, program, and student level. College room and board: $7374. Room and board charges vary according to board plan and housing facility.

Financial Aid Program-specific awards: 16–18 merit awards for continuing students ($800–$5000), 25 scholarships for continuing students ($500–$12,000).

Application Procedures Students admitted directly into the professional program freshman year. Deadline for freshmen and transfers: December 1. Required: essay, high school transcript, college transcript(s) for transfer students, minimum 3.0 high school GPA, 2 letters of recommendation, interview, SAT I or ACT test scores (minimum combined SAT I score of 1100, minimum composite ACT score of 24), portfolio for design, production, and directing applicants, audition for acting applicants. Recommended: production photos for design and production applicants. Auditions held 10 times on campus and off campus in Chicago, IL; New York, NY; Los Angeles, CA; San Francisco, CA. Portfolio reviews held 11 times and by appointment on campus and off campus in Chicago, IL; Los Angeles, CA; New York, NY; San Francisco, CA; the submission of slides may be substituted for portfolios when distance is prohibitive.

Web Site http://www.music.umich.edu

Undergraduate Contact Ms. Laura Strozeski, Assistant Dean for Enrollment Management & Student Services, Office of Admissions and Student Services, University of Michigan, 1100 Baits Drive, Ann Arbor, Michigan 48109-2085; 734-764-0593, fax: 734-763-5097, e-mail address: music.admissions@umich.edu

University of Michigan–Flint

Flint, Michigan

State-supported, coed. Urban campus. Total enrollment: 6,423. Theater program established 1975.
Degrees Bachelor of Fine Arts. Majors and concentrations: performance.
Enrollment 60 total; 7 undergraduate, 53 nonprofessional degree.
Theater Student Profile 50% females, 50% males, 8% minorities.
Theater Faculty 6 undergraduate (full-time), 6 undergraduate (part-time). 100% of full-time faculty have terminal degrees. Graduate students do not teach undergraduate courses. Undergraduate student–faculty ratio: 9:1.
Student Life Student groups/activities include American College Theatre Festival.
Expenses for 2005–2006 Application fee: $30. State resident tuition: $6082 full-time. Nonresident tuition: $11,834 full-time. Mandatory fees: $316 full-time. Full-time tuition and fees vary according to program.
Financial Aid Program-specific awards: 3 Carl and Sarah Morgan Trust Awards for theater majors ($1000–$3300), 1 Jeffrey F. Garfield Scholarship for theater majors ($1000–$3300), 14 departmental awards for theater majors ($1000–$3300).
Application Procedures Students apply for admission into the professional program by sophomore year. Deadline for freshmen and transfers: continuous. Required: high school transcript, college transcript(s) for transfer students, minimum 3.0 high school GPA, interview, audition, portfolio, SAT I or ACT test scores, minimum 2.7 high school GPA in academic courses in grades 10-12. Recommended: letter of recommendation. Auditions held once in March on campus. Portfolio reviews held once on campus.
Web Site http://www.flint.umich.edu
Undergraduate Contact Dr. Lauren Friesen, Chair, Department of Theater, University of Michigan–Flint, 303 East Kearsley Street, Flint, Michigan 48502-1950; 810-762-3349, fax: 810-766-6630, e-mail address: lfriesen@umich.edu

University of Minnesota, Duluth

Duluth, Minnesota

State-supported, coed. Suburban campus. Total enrollment: 10,496.

University of Minnesota, Twin Cities Campus

Minneapolis, Minnesota

State-supported, coed. Urban campus. Total enrollment: 51,175. Theater program established 1999.
Degrees Bachelor of Fine Arts. Majors and concentrations: acting. Graduate degrees offered: Master of Fine Arts in the area of design and technology. Program accredited by NAST.
Enrollment 377 total; 63 undergraduate, 10 graduate, 304 nonprofessional degree.
Theater Student Profile 60% females, 40% males, 5% minorities, 5% international.
Theater Faculty 5 undergraduate (full-time), 6 undergraduate (part-time), 7 graduate (full-time), 1 graduate (part-time). 100% of full-time faculty have terminal degrees. Graduate students do not teach undergraduate courses. Undergraduate student–faculty ratio: 15:1.
Student Life Student groups/activities include partnership with Guthrie Theater. Special housing available for theater students.
Expenses for 2005–2006 Application fee: $45. State resident tuition: $7140 full-time. Nonresident tuition: $19,670 full-time. Mandatory fees: $1482 full-time. Full-time tuition and fees vary according to program and reciprocity agreements. College room and board: $6722. College room only: $3886. Room and board charges vary according to board plan, housing facility, and location.
Financial Aid Program-specific awards: department scholarships.

Application Procedures Students admitted directly into the professional program freshman year. Deadline for freshmen and transfers: continuous. Notification date for freshmen and transfers: April 15. Required: high school transcript, college transcript(s) for transfer students, audition, SAT I or ACT test scores. Recommended: minimum 3.0 high school GPA, 2 letters of recommendation. Auditions held once in each city in January and February on campus and off campus in New York, NY; Chicago, IL; San Francisco, CA.
Web Site http://theatre.umn.edu/
Undergraduate Contact Nikki Schultz, Undergraduate Studies Secretary, Department of Theatre Arts and Dance, University of Minnesota, Twin Cities Campus, 580 Rarig Center, 330 21st Avenue South, Minneapolis, Minnesota 55455; 612-624-9183, fax: 612-625-6334, e-mail address: theatre@tc.umn.edu
Graduate Contact Virginia Arons, Secretary for Graduate Studies, 580 Rarig Centre, University of Minnesota, Twin Cities Campus, 330 21st Avenue South, Minneapolis, Minnesota 55455; 612-625-5029, fax: 612-625-6334, e-mail address: theatre@tc.umn.edu

The University of Montana–Missoula

Missoula, Montana

State-supported, coed. Total enrollment: 13,602. Theater program established 1950.
Degrees Bachelor of Fine Arts in the area of theater. Majors and concentrations: acting, design technology. Graduate degrees offered: Master of Fine Arts in the area of theater. Program accredited by NAST.
Enrollment 218 total; 132 undergraduate, 14 graduate, 72 nonprofessional degree.
Theater Student Profile 59% females, 41% males, 1% minorities, 1% international.
Theater Faculty 15 total. 100% of full-time faculty have terminal degrees. Graduate students teach a few undergraduate courses. Undergraduate student–faculty ratio: 17:1.
Student Life Student groups/activities include Montana Repertory Theatre Company.
Expenses for 2006–2007 Application fee: $30. State resident tuition: $3739 full-time. Nonresident tuition: $13,246 full-time. Mandatory fees: $1291 full-time. College room and board: $5860. College room only: $2660. Special program-related fees: $20–$60 per course for class materials/performance tickets (selected classes).
Financial Aid Program-specific awards: 4 departmental scholarships for program majors ($100–$500), 1 Gordon Scholarship for program majors ($300), 9 Dean Awards for program majors ($400–$800), 2 Mary Carol Zeman Awards for program majors ($500), 2 Kliber Memorial Awards for program majors ($500), 1 William Gillespie Award for program majors ($900), 1 Mott Ranch Award for program majors ($1000).
Application Procedures Students admitted directly into the professional program freshman year. Deadline for freshmen and transfers: March 1. Notification date for freshmen and transfers: continuous. Required: high school transcript, college transcript(s) for transfer students, minimum 2.0 high school GPA, SAT I test score only.
Web Site http://www.sfa.umt.edu/drama
Contact Desiree Twigg, Administrative Assistant, Department of Drama/Dance, The University of Montana–Missoula, Missoula, Montana 59812-8136; 406-243-4481, fax: 406-243-5726, e-mail address: umtheatredance@umontana.edu

University of Montevallo

Montevallo, Alabama

State-supported, coed. Small town campus. Total enrollment: 2,999. Theater program established 1923.
Degrees Bachelor of Fine Arts in the area of theater. Majors and concentrations: acting, directing, music theater, technical theatre/design. Cross-registration with Birmingham Area Consortium for Higher Education (BACHE): Samford University, Birmingham-Southern College, Miles College, University of Alabama at Birmingham.
Enrollment 85 total; all undergraduate.

University of Montevallo (continued)

Theater Student Profile 54% females, 46% males, 10% minorities.
Theater Faculty 5 undergraduate (full-time), 2 undergraduate (part-time). 100% of full-time faculty have terminal degrees. Graduate students do not teach undergraduate courses. Undergraduate student–faculty ratio: 15:1.
Student Life Student groups/activities include Joint Music-Theatre Musicals, College of Fine Arts fundraising gala.
Expenses for 2005–2006 Application fee: 25. State resident tuition: $5460 full-time. Nonresident tuition: $10,920 full-time. Mandatory fees: $204 full-time. Full-time tuition and fees vary according to course load. College room and board: $3966. Room and board charges vary according to board plan and housing facility. Special program-related fees: $100–$150 per semester for dance shoes, make-up, and art supplies.
Financial Aid Program-specific awards: 4–10 Dean of Fine Arts Awards for talented students with high GPA ($1000), 15 endowed awards for talented students ($1000–$8500), 4 President's Scholarships for talented students with high GPA ($3600).
Application Procedures Students apply for admission into the professional program by sophomore year. Deadline for freshmen and transfers: August 15. Notification date for freshmen and transfers: continuous. Required: high school transcript, college transcript(s) for transfer students, minimum 2.0 high school GPA, audition, portfolio, SAT I or ACT test scores (minimum combined SAT I score of 870, minimum composite ACT score of 18). Recommended: 2 letters of recommendation, interview for acting, directing and technical theater applicants. Auditions held twice on campus. Portfolio reviews held twice on campus; the submission of slides may be substituted for portfolios as part of interview.
Web Site http://www.montevallo.edu/thea/
Undergraduate Contact Pam Lucas, Division Secretary, Communication Art Department, University of Montevallo, Station 6210, Montevallo, Alabama 35115; 205-665-6210, fax: 205-665-6211, e-mail address: lucasp@montevallo.edu

University of Nebraska–Lincoln

Lincoln, Nebraska

State-supported, coed. Urban campus. Total enrollment: 21,675. Theater program established 1900.
Degrees Bachelor of Fine Arts in the areas of design/technical theatre, film and new media. Majors and concentrations: film and new media, theater design/technology. Graduate degrees offered: Master of Fine Arts in the areas of acting, design/technical theater, directing for stage and screen. Program accredited by NAST.
Theater Faculty 14 total (full-time), 2 total (part-time). 100% of full-time faculty have terminal degrees. Graduate students teach a few undergraduate courses. Undergraduate student–faculty ratio: 7:1.
Student Life Student groups/activities include American College Theatre Festival, University/Resident Theatre Association.
Expenses for 2005–2006 Application fee: $45. State resident tuition: $4530 full-time. Nonresident tuition: $13,440 full-time. Mandatory fees: $1010 full-time. Full-time tuition and fees vary according to course load. College room and board: $6008. College room only: $3239. Room and board charges vary according to board plan and housing facility. Special program-related fees: $25–$100 per course for scene painting, CAD, combat, film and new media classes.
Financial Aid Program-specific awards: 1–2 Williams-H. Alice Howell Awards for upperclass program majors ($750–$1500), 1 Dame Judith Anderson Award for sophomores ($100), 4 Eunice Vivian Peterson Memorial Scholarships for freshmen ($400–$550), 1–2 Helen Hayes MacArthur Scholarships for upperclass program majors ($1000), 4 Felton-Alice Howell Awards for theater students ($2500), 1–2 Ann Keyser Rawley Scholarships for upperclass program majors ($500–$1500), 1–2 Louise E. Mundy Scholarships ($500–$1000), 3–4 Nelle Powley Hills and John Hills Scholarships ($500–$1250).
Application Procedures Students admitted directly into the professional program freshman year. Deadline for freshmen and

transfers: continuous. Notification date for freshmen and transfers: March 24. Required: essay, high school transcript, college transcript(s) for transfer students, interview, portfolio, SAT I or ACT test scores (minimum combined SAT I score of 1050, minimum composite ACT score of 22), audition for scholarship consideration, contact Admissions Coordinator for application packet. Recommended: minimum 3.0 high school GPA, 3 letters of recommendation, portfolio for design/technical theater applicants. Auditions held twice on campus and off campus in Chicago, IL; Los Angeles, CA; New York, NY. Portfolio reviews held twice on campus and off campus in Chicago, IL; Los Angeles, CA; New York, NY.
Web Site http://www.unl.edu/TheatreArts
Undergraduate Contact Todd Cuddy, Admissions Coordinator, Department of Theatre Arts, University of Nebraska–Lincoln, PO Box 880201, 215 Temple Building, Lincoln, Nebraska 68588-0201; 402-472-2072 ext. 1, fax: 402-472-9055, e-mail address: theatrearts@unl.edu
Graduate Contact Dr. Tice Miller, Chair, Graduate Committee, Department of Theatre Arts, University of Nebraska–Lincoln, PO Box 880201, 215 Temple Building, Lincoln, Nebraska 68588-0201; 402-472-1619, fax: 402-472-9055, e-mail address: tmiller1@unl.edu

University of Nevada, Reno

Reno, Nevada

State-supported, coed. Urban campus. Total enrollment: 16,336. Theater program established 1988.
Degrees Bachelor of Fine Arts. Majors and concentrations: design technology, performance.
Enrollment 40 total; 10 undergraduate, 30 nonprofessional degree.
Theater Student Profile 50% females, 50% males, 25% minorities, 13% international.
Theater Faculty 5 total (full-time), 3 total (part-time). 100% of full-time faculty have terminal degrees. Graduate students do not teach undergraduate courses. Undergraduate student–faculty ratio: 2:1.
Expenses for 2005–2006 Application fee: $60. State resident tuition: $3060 full-time. Nonresident tuition: $11,735 full-time. Mandatory fees: $210 full-time. Full-time tuition and fees vary according to course load. College room and board: $7785. College room only: $4190. Room and board charges vary according to board plan and housing facility.
Application Procedures Students apply for admission into the professional program by junior year. Deadline for freshmen and transfers: continuous. Notification date for freshmen and transfers: continuous. Required: high school transcript, college transcript(s) for transfer students, SAT I or ACT test scores, minimum 2.5 high school GPA, minimum 2.0 college GPA for transfer students.
Undergraduate Contact Dr. Jim Bernardi, Director, University of Nevada, Reno, Department of Theatre/ 228 UNR, Reno, Nevada 89557; 775-784-6659, e-mail address: bernardi@nevada.edu

The University of North Carolina at Greensboro

Greensboro, North Carolina

State-supported, coed. Urban campus. Total enrollment: 16,060. Theater program established 1953.
Degrees Bachelor of Fine Arts. Majors and concentrations: acting, design, technical theater, theater education. Graduate degrees offered: Master of Education in the area of drama; Master of Fine Arts in the areas of acting, design, directing, theater for youth. Program accredited by NAST.
Enrollment 282 total; 178 undergraduate, 26 graduate, 78 nonprofessional degree.
Theater Student Profile 63% females, 37% males, 15% minorities.
Theater Faculty 14 total (full-time), 6 total (part-time). 100% of full-time faculty have terminal degrees. Graduate students teach a few undergraduate courses. Undergraduate student–faculty ratio: 15:1.

Student Life Student groups/activities include Alpha Psi Omega, North Carolina Theatre for Young People, North Carolina Theatre Conference.

Expenses for 2006–2007 Application fee: $45. State resident tuition: $2308 full-time. Nonresident tuition: $13,576 full-time. Mandatory fees: $1505 full-time. College room and board: $5706. College room only: $3232.

Financial Aid Program-specific awards: 1 W. Raymond Taylor Scholarship for drama majors ($500).

Application Procedures Students apply for admission into the professional program by sophomore year. Deadline for freshmen and transfers: August 1. Notification date for freshmen and transfers: continuous. Required: high school transcript, minimum 2.0 high school GPA, SAT I test score only, portfolio review for design students, audition for acting students. Recommended: 3 letters of recommendation. Auditions held twice on campus and off campus in Southeastern Theatre Conference sites; videotaped performances are permissible as a substitute for live auditions if a campus visit is impossible. Portfolio reviews held twice on campus; the submission of slides may be substituted for portfolios when distance is prohibitive.

Web Site http://www.uncg.edu

Contact Tom Humphrey, Head, Department of Theatre, The University of North Carolina at Greensboro, 201 Taylor, Greensboro, North Carolina 27412; 336-334-5576, fax: 336-334-5100, e-mail address: twhumphrey@uncg.edu

University of North Dakota

Grand Forks, North Dakota

State-supported, coed. Small town campus. Total enrollment: 12,954.

University of Oklahoma

Norman, Oklahoma

State-supported, coed. Suburban campus. Total enrollment: 26,968. Theater program established 1923.

Degrees Bachelor of Fine Arts in the area of drama. Majors and concentrations: design, design technology, dramaturgy, performance, stage management. Graduate degrees offered: Master of Arts in the area of drama; Master of Fine Arts in the area of drama (directing or design). Program accredited by NAST.

Enrollment 175 total; 150 undergraduate, 25 graduate.

Theater Student Profile 55% females, 45% males, 10% minorities, 3% international.

Theater Faculty 11 total (full-time), 2 total (part-time). 100% of full-time faculty have terminal degrees. Graduate students teach a few undergraduate courses. Undergraduate student–faculty ratio: 15:1.

Student Life Student groups/activities include Drama and Dance Association.

Expenses for 2005–2006 Application fee: $40. State resident tuition: $2862 full-time. Nonresident tuition: $10,755 full-time. Mandatory fees: $1546 full-time. Full-time tuition and fees vary according to course load, location, program, and reciprocity agreements. College room and board: $6361. College room only: $3355. Room and board charges vary according to board plan and housing facility. Special program-related fees: $5–$95 per course for lab fees.

Financial Aid Program-specific awards: 55 departmental scholarships for program majors ($500–$1500), 10 assistantships for program majors ($3300).

Application Procedures Students admitted directly into the professional program freshman year. Deadline for freshmen and transfers: June 1. Required: high school transcript, college transcript(s) for transfer students, 3 letters of recommendation, interview, audition, SAT I or ACT test scores (minimum combined SAT I score of 1100, minimum composite ACT score of 24), minimum 2.5 high school GPA, portfolio for design applicants. Recommended: essay, minimum 3.0 high school GPA. Auditions held 3 times and as needed on campus and off campus in University Resident Theatre Association locations, Texas Educational Theatre Association locations, and various other theater association sites; videotaped performances are permissible as a

substitute for live auditions with permission of the director. Portfolio reviews held 3 times and as needed on campus and off campus in University Resident Theatre Association locations, Texas Educational Theatre Association locations, and various other theater association sites; the submission of slides may be substituted for portfolios (slides preferred).

Web Site http://www.ou.edu/finearts/drama

Undergraduate Contact Charlotte Chandler, Administrative Assistant, School of Drama, University of Oklahoma, 640 Parrington Oval, Room 121, Norman, Oklahoma 73019-0310; 405-325-4021, fax: 405-325-0400, e-mail address: cchandler@ou.edu

Graduate Contact Dr. Judith Midyett Pender, Graduate Liaison, School of Drama, University of Oklahoma, 640 Parrington Oval, Room 121, Norman, Oklahoma 73019-0310; 405-325-5328, fax: 405-325-0400, e-mail address: jmpender@ou.edu

University of Rhode Island

Kingston, Rhode Island

State-supported, coed. Small town campus. Total enrollment: 15,095. Theater program established 1966.

University of Saskatchewan

Saskatoon, Saskatchewan, Canada

Province-supported, coed. Urban campus. Total enrollment: 19,639. Theater program established 1946.

University of South Alabama

Mobile, Alabama

State-supported, coed. Suburban campus. Total enrollment: 13,122. Theater program established 1968.

The University of South Dakota

Vermillion, South Dakota

State-supported, coed. Small town campus. Total enrollment: 8,641. Theater program established 1935.

University of Southern California

Los Angeles, California

Independent, coed. Urban campus. Total enrollment: 32,836. Theater program established 1990.

Degrees Bachelor of Fine Arts. Majors and concentrations: acting, design, stage management, technical direction. Graduate degrees offered: Master of Fine Arts. Cross-registration with University of Kent (England), British American Drama Academy.

Enrollment 421 total; 95 undergraduate, 18 graduate, 308 nonprofessional degree.

Theater Student Profile 57% females, 43% males, 12% minorities, 2% international.

Theater Faculty 19 total (full-time), 22 total (part-time). 100% of full-time faculty have terminal degrees. Graduate students do not teach undergraduate courses. Undergraduate student–faculty ratio: 25:1.

Student Life Student groups/activities include community-based theater lab, Theatre for Youth, Theater Representative Council.

Expenses for 2005–2006 Application fee: $65. Comprehensive fee: $41,618 includes full-time tuition ($31,458), mandatory fees ($550), and college room and board ($9610). College room only: $5260. Full-time tuition and fees vary according to program. Room and board charges vary according to board plan and housing facility.

Financial Aid Program-specific awards: 3–5 Trustee Scholarships for program majors demonstrating talent and academic achievement ($24,000), 10–11 Dean's Scholarships for program majors demonstrating talent and academic achievement ($6000), 2 Jack Nicholson Awards for performers demonstrating talent and academic achievement ($8000), 2 Stanley Musgrove Awards for those demonstrating talent and academic achievement ($2500),

University of Southern California (continued)

2 John Blankenship/William C. White Awards for those demonstrating talent and academic achievement ($2000), 1 James Pendleton Award for program majors demonstrating talent and academic achievement ($2500), 3–5 Presidential Scholarships for program majors demonstrating talent and academic achievement ($12,000), David Dukes Memorial Scholarship.

Application Procedures Students admitted directly into the professional program freshman year. Deadline for freshmen and transfers: January 3. Notification date for freshmen and transfers: continuous. Required: essay, high school transcript, college transcript(s) for transfer students, minimum 3.0 high school GPA, 2 letters of recommendation, interview, audition, SAT I or ACT test scores, portfolio for stage management, technical and design applicants. Auditions held on campus and off campus in New York, NY; Seattle, WA; Chicago, IL; Houston, TX; Los Angeles, CA; videotaped performances are permissible as a substitute for live auditions. Portfolio reviews held on campus and off campus in New York, NY; Seattle, WA; Chicago, IL; Houston, TX; Los Angeles, CA.

Web Site http://theatre/usc.edu

Undergraduate Contact Phyllis Lemons, Admission Coordinator, Student Services, University of Southern California, University Park, DRC 116, Los Angeles, California 90089-0791; 213-740-1286, fax: 213-821-1193, e-mail address: plemons@usc.edu

Graduate Contact Lori Ray Fisher, Assistant Dean, Student Services, University of Southern California, University Park, DRC 116, Los Angeles, California 90089-0791; 213-740-1286, fax: 213-821-1193, e-mail address: lfisher@usc.edu

More About the University

The School of Theatre at the University of Southern California (USC) grew out of the Department of Drama, founded by playwright and director William De Mille in 1945. Today, the School of Theatre is ranked among the top five undergraduate theater programs in the nation and is internationally recognized as a leader in offering professional training in a university environment.

The School offers Bachelor of Arts (B.A.) and Bachelor of Fine Arts (B.F.A.) programs as well as Master of Fine Arts (M.F.A.) programs in acting and in dramatic writing. The B.F.A. offers a conservatory approach, while the B.A. offers more flexibility and the opportunity to double major or minor in another discipline. Classes are kept small to facilitate close interaction between students and the School's faculty of top theater professionals. All students have faculty mentors to guide their course selection and professional development throughout their time at USC.

The USC School of Theatre sits in the center of Los Angeles, the entertainment capital of the world. Because of its location, students at USC take advantage of the many opportunities offered by the city's thriving arts culture and vibrant theater community.

The School offers educational and performance opportunities overseas. Students study abroad at the British American Drama Academy (BADA) for course credit, working with leading actors and directors. The School of Theatre holds the distinction of having created the first American university theatrical troupe—Festival Theatre USC-USA—to be invited to perform at the prestigious Fringe of the International Theatre Festival in Edinburgh, Scotland.

On campus, performance opportunities abound. USC's School of Theatre produces more than twelve main stage shows each season as well as experimental works and full productions of M.F.A. dramatic writing students' scripts. The School also encourages independent student productions. Students participate in the Brand New Theatre, which presents plays written, produced, acted, and directed by students. The School's partnership with the USC School of Cinema–Television allows theater students the opportunity to collaborate with film students on a variety of projects.

A unique professional association with Center Theatre Group has been established to offer students internships, including performance opportunities. The Center Theater Group is a nationally recognized arts organization that runs the Tony Award–winning regional theaters the Mark Taper Forum and the Ahmanson Theatre at the Los Angeles Music Center and the new Kirk Douglas Theatre in Culver City.

The many performance and production opportunities, the quality of programs, and the lasting relationships students forge with faculty members and peers make USC a nurturing environment for developing theater skills and knowledge. Whether a student chooses to major or minor in theater, to pursue studies in acting, dance, theatrical design, or dramatic writing, a theater education at the University of Southern California is a unique and invaluable experience.

Program Facilities In addition to studio spaces, the School of Theatre's active production program utilizes three main facilities. The Bing Theatre is a traditional proscenium house with seating for 575. The Massman Theatre is a flexible performance space, comparable to Equity Waiver and off-off Broadway theaters, with seating for 50 to 75 individuals. The Scene Dock Theatre is also a flexible performance space, with seating for up to 99 people.

Faculty, Visiting Artists, and Alumni In addition to a distinguished faculty, the School attracts well-known theater professionals to teach seminars, mentor students, and participate in productions. Recent guest artists include Tony Award–winning actor Brian Stokes Mitchell, Tony and Emmy Award–winning choreographer Twyla Tharp, actress and Lecoq-method expert Gates McFadden, *Laramie Project* creator Moises Kaufman, Royal Shakespeare Company founder Sir Peter Hall, Oscar and Tony Award–winning writer Christopher Hampton, performance artist Danny Hoch, internationally acclaimed actress Fiona Shaw, director Peter Sellars, and Tony Award–winning composer Jason Robert Brown, who joined the faculty last year. Graduates of the School work professionally in all aspects of theater, film, and television. John Ritter, Swoosie Kurtz, Le Var Burton, Kyra Sedgewick, Anthony Edwards, Daryl Hannah, Grant Heslov, Ally Sheedy, and Forest Whitaker are just a few of the many School of Theatre alumni who have gone on to achieve success on stage and in film and television.

University of Southern Mississippi
Hattiesburg, Mississippi

State-supported, coed. Suburban campus. Total enrollment: 15,030. Theater program established 1956.

Degrees Bachelor of Fine Arts in the areas of performance, design and technology. Majors and concentrations: acting, design/technical theater. Graduate degrees offered: Master of Fine Arts in the areas of performance, design and technical theater, directing. Program accredited by NAST.

Enrollment 149 total; 50 undergraduate, 20 graduate, 79 nonprofessional degree.

Theater Student Profile 50% females, 50% males, 10% minorities, 1% international.

Theater Faculty 8 total (full-time). 88% of full-time faculty have terminal degrees. Graduate students teach a few undergraduate courses. Undergraduate student–faculty ratio: 7:1.

Student Life Student groups/activities include Southern Arena Theater, "At the Door" events.

Expenses for 2006–2007 Application fee: $0. State resident tuition: $4312 full-time. Nonresident tuition: $9742 full-time. Mandatory fees: $30 full-time. College room and board: $5800. College room only: $2620.

Financial Aid Program-specific awards: 15–20 service awards for talented students with high test scores ($300).

Application Procedures Students apply for admission into the professional program by sophomore year. Deadline for freshmen and transfers: August 15. Required: high school transcript, college transcript(s) for transfer students, minimum 2.0 high school GPA, SAT I or ACT test scores. Recommended: 2 letters of recommendation, audition, portfolio. Auditions held twice on campus; recorded music is permissible as a substitute for live auditions when no accompanist is available and videotaped performances are permissible as a substitute for live auditions if

a campus visit is impossible. Portfolio reviews held twice on campus; the submission of slides may be substituted for portfolios slides or discs preferred.
Web Site http://www.arts.usm.edu
Undergraduate Contact Mr. Louis Rackoff, Chair, Department of Theatre and Dance, University of Southern Mississippi, Box 5052, Hattiesburg, Mississippi 39406-5052; 601-266-4994, fax: 601-266-6423, e-mail address: louis.rackoff@usm.edu
Graduate Contact Mr. Louis Rackhoff, Chair, Department of Theatre and Dance, University of Southern Mississippi, Box 5052, Hattiesburg, Mississippi 39406-5052; 601-266-4994, fax: 601-266-6423, e-mail address: louis.rackoff@usm.edu

University of South Florida

Tampa, Florida

State-supported, coed. Urban campus. Total enrollment: 42,660.
Degrees Bachelor of Arts in the area of theater; Bachelor of Fine Arts in the area of theater design. Majors and concentrations: performance, theater arts studies, theater design, theater production. Cross-registration with . Program accredited by NAST.
Enrollment 200 total; all undergraduate.
Theater Student Profile 50% females, 50% males, 2% international.
Theater Faculty 12 undergraduate (full-time), 6 undergraduate (part-time). Graduate students do not teach undergraduate courses.
Student Life Student groups/activities include Honors Research Symposium, Taste of the Arts, theatre productions.
Expenses for 2005–2006 Application fee: $30. State resident tuition: $3310 full-time. Nonresident tuition: $16,076 full-time. Mandatory fees: $74 full-time. Full-time tuition and fees vary according to course level, course load, and location. College room and board: $6900. College room only: $3563. Room and board charges vary according to board plan, housing facility, and location.
Financial Aid Program-specific awards: 1–8 Diversity Enhancement Award for minority students ($150–$250), 1–2 Exceptionally Talented Black Student Award ($200–$1000), 1–6 Green and Gold Talent Scholarship for out of state students ($1500).
Application Procedures Students admitted directly into the professional program freshman year. Deadline for freshmen and transfers: April 15. Required: high school transcript, college transcript(s) for transfer students, SAT I or ACT test scores, audition for theater program scholarship. Recommended: 3 letters of recommendation. Auditions held by appointment for students applying for theatre scholarship; videotaped performances are permissible as a substitute for live auditions. the submission of slides may be substituted for portfolios (theatre design program).
Web Site http://www.arts.usf.edu/cvpa/theatredance.html
Undergraduate Contact Ms. Merry Lynn Morris, Academic Advisor, School of Theatre and Dance/Advising, University of South Florida, 4202 East Fowler Avenue, FAH 110, Tampa, Florida 33620; 813-974-1739, fax: 813-974-4165, e-mail address: mmorris@arts.usf.edu
Graduate Contact Ms. Merry Lynn Morris, Academic Advisor, Advising/School of Theatre and Dance, University of South Florida, 4202 East Fowler Avenue, FAH 110, Tampa, Florida 33620; 813-974-1739, fax: 813-974-4165, e-mail address: mmorris@arts.usf.edu

The University of Tennessee at Martin

Martin, Tennessee

State-supported, coed. Small town campus. Total enrollment: 6,484. Theater program established 1999.

The University of Texas at Austin

Austin, Texas

State-supported, coed. Urban campus. Total enrollment: 49,696. Theater program established 1938.

The University of the Arts

Philadelphia, Pennsylvania

Independent, coed. Total enrollment: 2,277. Theater program established 1983.
Degrees Bachelor of Fine Arts in the areas of acting, musical theater, applied theater arts, design technical theater. Majors and concentrations: acting, applied theater arts, design/technical theater, music theater.
Enrollment 229 total; all undergraduate.
Theater Student Profile 56% females, 44% males, 17% minorities, 3% international.
Theater Faculty 9 undergraduate (full-time), 31 undergraduate (part-time). 66% of full-time faculty have terminal degrees. Graduate students do not teach undergraduate courses. Undergraduate student–faculty ratio: 6:1.
Student Life Student groups/activities include Student Government. Special housing available for theater students.
Expenses for 2006–2007 Application fee: $60. Tuition: $24,730 full-time. Mandatory fees: $950 full-time. College room only: $6300.
Financial Aid Program-specific awards: 30 merit scholarships for incoming students ($500–$8000).
Application Procedures Students admitted directly into the professional program freshman year. Deadline for freshmen and transfers: continuous. Notification date for freshmen and transfers: September 1. Required: essay, high school transcript, college transcript(s) for transfer students, minimum 2.0 high school GPA, letter of recommendation, audition, SAT I or ACT test scores, resume and photograph. Recommended: minimum 3.0 high school GPA, interview. Auditions held 9 times on campus and off campus in various thespian festival locations and in California; videotaped performances are permissible as a substitute for live auditions when applicant lives more than 200 miles from Philadelphia.
Web Site http://www.uarts.edu
Undergraduate Contact Susan Gandy, Director of Admission, The University of the Arts, 320 South Broad Street, Philadelphia, Pennsylvania 19102; 800-616-ARTS ext. 6049, fax: 215-717-6045, e-mail address: admissions@uarts.edu

University of Utah

Salt Lake City, Utah

State-supported, coed. Urban campus. Total enrollment: 29,012. Theater program established 1947.
Degrees Bachelor of Fine Arts in the areas of actor training, teaching, design, stage management. Majors and concentrations: acting, design, stage management, theater education.
Enrollment 200 total; all undergraduate.
Theater Student Profile 55% females, 45% males, 5% minorities, 5% international.
Theater Faculty 10 total (full-time), 15 total (part-time). 100% of full-time faculty have terminal degrees. Graduate students do not teach undergraduate courses. Undergraduate student–faculty ratio: 12:1.
Student Life Student groups/activities include Theatre School for Youth, American College Theatre Festival, Utah Theater Association. Special housing available for theater students.
Expenses for 2005–2006 Application fee: $35. State resident tuition: $3672 full-time. Nonresident tuition: $12,860 full-time. Mandatory fees: $670 full-time. Full-time tuition and fees vary according to course level, course load, degree level, and student level. College room and board: $5422. College room only: $2704. Room and board charges vary according to board plan and housing facility.
Financial Aid Program-specific awards: 4 special departmental scholarships for resident incoming freshmen ($2000), 3 continuing student scholarships for continuing students ($1000), 30 endowed scholarship funds for continuing students ($750).
Application Procedures Students admitted directly into the professional program freshman year. Deadline for freshmen: August 1; transfers: continuous. Required: high school transcript, college transcript(s) for transfer students, minimum 2.0 high school GPA, 2 letters of recommendation, SAT I or ACT test scores, audition

University of Utah (continued)

for actor training program. Recommended: essay, minimum 3.0 high school GPA, interview, video, portfolio for design applicants. Auditions held twice on campus and off campus at National Unified Auditions (New York, NY; Chicago, IL; Las Vegas, NV; San Francisco, CA; Los Angeles, CA). Portfolio reviews held twice on campus.
Web Site http://www.theatre.utah.edu/
Contact Faye Barron, Administrative Assistant, Department of Theatre, University of Utah, 240 South 1500 East, Room 206, Salt Lake City, Utah 84112-0170; 801-581-6448, fax: 801-585-6154, e-mail address: faye.barron@m.cc.utah.edu

University of Windsor
Windsor, Ontario, Canada

Province-supported, coed. Urban campus. Total enrollment: 16,765. Theater program established 1958.
Degrees Bachelor of Arts in the area of drama in education and community; Bachelor of Fine Arts in the area of acting. Majors and concentrations: acting, drama in education and community.
Enrollment 405 total; 229 undergraduate, 176 nonprofessional degree.
Theater Student Profile 60% females, 40% males, 4% minorities, 1% international.
Theater Faculty 14 undergraduate (full-time), 8 undergraduate (part-time). 65% of full-time faculty have terminal degrees. Graduate students do not teach undergraduate courses. Undergraduate student–faculty ratio: 20:1.
Student Life Student groups/activities include University Players, Club Soda Playfest.
Expenses for 2006–2007 Application fee: $60 Canadian dollars. Tuition, fee, and room and board charges are reported in Canadian dollars. Area resident tuition: $4990 full-time. College room and board: $7124. International student tuition: $12,232 full-time.
Financial Aid Program-specific awards: 5 School of Dramatic Art Scholarships for top 5 GPA ($200), 1 Frances Hyland Entrance Award for acting majors ($1000), 1 Claire Kire Memorial Bursary for 2nd- or 3rd-year dramatic art students ($100), 1 Myrtle Kennedy Memorial Award for 2nd-year and dramatic art students, 1 Jessica Sue Rogers Pauze Award for drama in education majors ($100), 1 Theatre Alive Scholarship for upperclass acting majors ($1000), 1 Daniel Patrick Kelly Award in Dramatic Art for 4th-year dramatic art students, 1 University of Windsor Women's Auxiliary of Dramatic Art Fund Award for dramatic art students.
Application Procedures Students admitted directly into the professional program freshman year. Deadline for freshmen and transfers: continuous. Required: high school transcript, college transcript(s) for transfer students, minimum 2.0 high school GPA, 3 letters of recommendation, application form, resume, interview for drama in education and community applicants, audition for acting applicants. Recommended: minimum 3.0 high school GPA. Auditions held twice on campus and off campus in Toronto, ON; Halifax, NS; Vancouver, BC; videotaped performances are permissible as a substitute for live auditions when distance is prohibitive.
Web Site http://www.uwindsor.ca/drama
Undergraduate Contact Brenda Bourque, Secretary, School of Dramatic Art, University of Windsor, 401 Sunset Avenue, Windsor, Ontario N9B 3P4, Canada; 519-253-3000 ext. 2804, fax: 519-971-3629, e-mail address: drama@uwindsor.ca

University of Wisconsin–Milwaukee
Milwaukee, Wisconsin

State-supported, coed. Urban campus. Total enrollment: 27,502. Theater program established 1978.
Degrees Bachelor of Fine Arts in the area of theater. Majors and concentrations: acting, costume production, stage management, technical production.
Enrollment 175 total; 50 undergraduate, 5 graduate, 120 nonprofessional degree.

Theater Student Profile 50% females, 50% males, 5% minorities.
Theater Faculty 13 undergraduate (full-time). 60% of full-time faculty have terminal degrees. Graduate students do not teach undergraduate courses. Undergraduate student–faculty ratio: 7:1.
Student Life Student groups/activities include Players Guild. Special housing available for theater students.
Expenses for 2005–2006 Application fee: $35. State resident tuition: $5494 full-time. Nonresident tuition: $18,246 full-time. Mandatory fees: $730 full-time. Full-time tuition and fees vary according to location, program, and reciprocity agreements. College room and board: $4922. College room only: $2988. Room and board charges vary according to board plan and housing facility. Special program-related fees: $15 per credit for differential tuition.
Financial Aid Program-specific awards: 8–10 Corliss Philabaum Scholarships ($500–$1500).
Application Procedures Students apply for admission into the professional program by freshman year. Deadline for freshmen and transfers: April 1. Notification date for freshmen and transfers: April 15. Required: high school transcript, college transcript(s) for transfer students, minimum 2.0 high school GPA, 2 letters of recommendation, interview, audition, SAT I or ACT test scores. Recommended: essay, portfolio. Auditions held once a year (spring) on campus. Portfolio reviews held once in the spring on campus; the submission of slides may be substituted for portfolios upon request of student.
Web Site http://www.uwm.edu/psoa
Undergraduate Contact Department of Enrollment Services, University of Wisconsin–Milwaukee, PO Box 749, Milwaukee, Wisconsin 53201; 414-229-5932, fax: 414-229-6940, e-mail address: desadmin@uwm.edu

University of Wisconsin–Stevens Point
Stevens Point, Wisconsin

State-supported, coed. Small town campus. Total enrollment: 8,577. Theater program established 1985.
Degrees Bachelor of Fine Arts. Majors and concentrations: acting, design technology, music theater. Program accredited by NAST.
Enrollment 145 total; 65 undergraduate, 80 nonprofessional degree.
Theater Student Profile 60% females, 40% males, 5% minorities.
Theater Faculty 12 undergraduate (full-time), 1 undergraduate (part-time). 100% of full-time faculty have terminal degrees. Graduate students do not teach undergraduate courses. Undergraduate student–faculty ratio: 5:1.
Student Life Student groups/activities include Players, "The Dons" Improv Group.
Expenses for 2005–2006 Application fee: $35. State resident tuition: $4277 full-time. Nonresident tuition: $14,323 full-time. Mandatory fees: $785 full-time. Full-time tuition and fees vary according to course load and reciprocity agreements. College room and board: $4322. College room only: $2574. Room and board charges vary according to housing facility.
Financial Aid Program-specific awards: 6 theater scholarships for incoming students ($500–$1000), 1 First Nighters Award for performance majors ($2000).
Application Procedures Students admitted directly into the professional program freshman year. Deadline for freshmen: April 1; transfers: February 2. Notification date for freshmen and transfers: April 1. Required: essay, high school transcript, college transcript(s) for transfer students, minimum 3.0 high school GPA, 3 letters of recommendation, audition, portfolio, standing in top 25% of graduating class or minimum ACT score of 21 for Wisconsin residents, SAT or ACT score for non-Wisconsin residents. Auditions held once on campus; recorded music is permissible as a substitute for live auditions in special circumstances. Portfolio reviews held once on campus.
Web Site http://www.uwsp.edu/theatre-dance
Undergraduate Contact Kenneth W. Risch, Chair, Department of Theatre and Dance, University of Wisconsin–Stevens Point, Noel Fine Arts Center #161, 1800 Portage Street, Stevens Point, Wisconsin 54481; 715-346-4429, fax: 715-346-4794.

University of Wisconsin–Superior

Superior, Wisconsin

State-supported, coed. Small town campus. Total enrollment: 2,872. Theater program established 1952.

Degrees Bachelor of Fine Arts in the area of theater. Majors and concentrations: acting, directing, lighting/sound design, scenic/technical theater. Cross-registration with University of Minnesota–Duluth.

Enrollment 17 total; 13 undergraduate, 1 graduate, 3 nonprofessional degree.

Theater Faculty 1 total (full-time), 3 total (part-time). 100% of full-time faculty have terminal degrees. Graduate students do not teach undergraduate courses. Undergraduate student–faculty ratio: 12:1.

Student Life Student groups/activities include student-directed shows, drama honorary organization.

Expenses for 2005–2006 Application fee: $35. State resident tuition: $4,427 full-time. Nonresident tuition: $14,473 full-time. Mandatory fees: $761 full-time. College room and board: $4422. College room only: $2552.

Financial Aid Program-specific awards: 5 departmental scholarships for program students ($100–$1000).

Application Procedures Students apply for admission into the professional program by sophomore year. Deadline for freshmen and transfers: continuous. Notification date for freshmen and transfers: continuous. Required: high school transcript, college transcript(s) for transfer students, minimum 2.0 high school GPA, audition, portfolio, SAT I or ACT test scores. Auditions held once on campus. Portfolio reviews held on campus.

Web Site http://staff.uwsuper.edu/commarts/

Undergraduate Contact Dr. Martha Eingeson, Chair, Department of Communicating Arts, University of Wisconsin–Superior, Holden Fine Arts Building, Belknap and Catlin, Superior, Wisconsin 54880-4500; 715-394-8369, fax: 715-394-8065, e-mail address: splatner@uwsuper.edu

Graduate Contact Dr. Martha Einerson, Graduate Student Coordinator, Department of Communicating Arts, University of Wisconsin–Superior, Holden Fine Arts Building, Belknap and Catlin, Superior, Wisconsin 54880-4500; 715-394-8369, fax: 715-394-8065, e-mail address: splatner@uwsuper.edu

University of Wisconsin–Whitewater

Whitewater, Wisconsin

State-supported, coed. Small town campus. Total enrollment: 10,750.

University of Wyoming

Laramie, Wyoming

State-supported, coed. Total enrollment: 13,126. Theater program established 1972.

Degrees Bachelor of Fine Arts in the areas of theater, performance, design, theater/English, directing/playwriting. Majors and concentrations: acting, costume design, directing, lighting design, playwriting, set design, technical direction, theater/English.

Enrollment 100 total; 80 undergraduate, 20 nonprofessional degree.

Theater Student Profile 50% females, 50% males, 17% minorities.

Theater Faculty 13 undergraduate (full-time), 1 undergraduate (part-time). 90% of full-time faculty have terminal degrees. Graduate students do not teach undergraduate courses. Undergraduate student–faculty ratio: 10:1.

Student Life Student groups/activities include Associated Students of the Performing Arts.

Expenses for 2005–2006 Application fee: $30. State resident tuition: $2760 full-time. Nonresident tuition: $9150 full-time. Mandatory fees: $666 full-time. Full-time tuition and fees vary according to course load, location, program, and reciprocity agreements. College room and board: $6240. College room only: $2709. Room and board charges vary according to board plan and housing facility.

Financial Aid Program-specific awards: 21 departmental awards for program majors ($2575).

Application Procedures Students admitted directly into the professional program freshman year. Deadline for freshmen and transfers: August 31. Required: high school transcript, college transcript(s) for transfer students, SAT I or ACT test scores, audition for scholarship consideration, minimum 2.5 high school GPA. Recommended: letter of recommendation, interview, audition, portfolio. Auditions held twice on campus and off campus in Rocky Mountain Theatre Association Festival locations; recorded music is permissible as a substitute for live auditions and videotaped performances are permissible as a substitute for live auditions if a campus visit is impossible. Portfolio reviews held twice on campus and off campus in Rocky Mountain Theatre Association Festival locations, Wyoming State Drama Festival; the submission of slides may be substituted for portfolios if a campus visit is impossible.

Web Site http://www.uwyo.edu/th&d/homepage.htm

Undergraduate Contact Dr. Rebecca Hilliker, Head, Department of Theatre and Dance, University of Wyoming, Box 3951, Laramie, Wyoming 82071-3951; 307-766-2198, fax: 307-766-2197, e-mail address: hilliker@uwyo.edu

Utah State University

Logan, Utah

State-supported, coed. Urban campus. Total enrollment: 14,458. Theater program established 1967.

Degrees Bachelor of Fine Arts in the area of theater arts. Majors and concentrations: acting, design/technical theater, theater education. Graduate degrees offered: Master of Fine Arts in the area of theater arts. Cross-registration with other institutions in the Utah University System.

Enrollment 95 total; 83 undergraduate, 7 graduate, 5 nonprofessional degree.

Theater Student Profile 65% females, 35% males, 5% minorities.

Theater Faculty 10 undergraduate (full-time), 3 undergraduate (part-time). 100% of full-time faculty have terminal degrees. Graduate students teach a few undergraduate courses. Undergraduate student–faculty ratio: 8:1.

Student Life Student groups/activities include Utah State Theatre productions, UST Children's Theatre, Old Lyric Repertory Company (summer).

Expenses for 2005–2006 Application fee: $40. State resident tuition: $3128 full-time. Nonresident tuition: $10,072 full-time. Mandatory fees: $544 full-time. Full-time tuition and fees vary according to course load and student level. College room and board: $4330. College room only: $1550. Room and board charges vary according to board plan and housing facility. Special program-related fees: $15 per course for scene design, $23 per course for intermediate/advanced acting fees, $25 per course for makeup, $30 per course for stage and costume crafts, materials, $50 per course for teaching clinic.

Financial Aid Program-specific awards: 20 talent awards for program students ($1000), 25 tuition scholarships or awards for program students ($1810).

Application Procedures Students apply for admission into the professional program by freshman year. Deadline for freshmen and transfers: July 1. Required: high school transcript, college transcript(s) for transfer students, minimum 2.0 high school GPA, interview, SAT I or ACT test scores, audition/portfolio/interview for scholarship consideration at end of freshman year. Auditions held 4 times on campus and off campus in Rocky Mountain Theatre festival; American College Theatre Festival; regional United States Institute for Theatre Technology (USITT) locations; recorded music is permissible as a substitute for live auditions if a campus visit is not possible or in cases of hardship and videotaped performances are permissible as a substitute for live auditions if a campus visit is not possible or in cases of hardship. Portfolio reviews held as needed on campus and off campus in American College Theatre Festival Region VII; the submission of slides may be substituted for portfolios if a campus visit is not possible or in cases of hardship.

Web Site http://www.usu.edu/~theatre

Undergraduate Contact Dr. Colin Johnson, Head, Department of Theatre Arts, Utah State University, 4025 Old Main Hill, Logan,

Utah State University (continued)

Utah 84322-4025; 435-797-3046, fax: 435-797-0086, e-mail address: colin.johnson@wpo.hass.usu.edu
Graduate Contact Ms. Nancy Hills, Graduate Program Coordinator, Department of Theatre Arts, Utah State University, 4025 Old Main Hill, Logan, Utah 84322-4025; 435-797-3049, fax: 435-797-0086, e-mail address: nhills@hass.usu.edu

Valdosta State University

Valdosta, Georgia

State-supported, coed. Small town campus. Total enrollment: 10,503. Theater program established 1964.
Degrees Bachelor of Fine Arts. Majors and concentrations: dance, performance, production. Program accredited by NAST.
Enrollment 120 total; all undergraduate.
Theater Student Profile 60% females, 40% males, 10% minorities, 5% international.
Theater Faculty 9 undergraduate (full-time). 100% of full-time faculty have terminal degrees. Graduate students do not teach undergraduate courses. Undergraduate student–faculty ratio: 15:1.
Student Life Student groups/activities include College Theater, Georgia Theatre Conference, Alpha Psi Omega.
Expenses for 2005–2006 Application fee: $20. State resident tuition: $2438 full-time. Nonresident tuition: $9754 full-time. Mandatory fees: $840 full-time. College room and board: $5524. College room only: $2904. Room and board charges vary according to board plan and housing facility.
Financial Aid Program-specific awards: 20 theater scholarships for program students ($1000–$3000).
Application Procedures Students admitted directly into the professional program freshman year. Deadline for freshmen and transfers: continuous. Required: high school transcript, college transcript(s) for transfer students, SAT I or ACT test scores (minimum combined SAT I score of 850), audition/portfolio for scholarship consideration. Recommended: minimum 2.0 high school GPA, interview. Auditions held twice on campus and off campus in Atlanta, GA; recorded music is permissible as a substitute for live auditions when distance is prohibitive and videotaped performances are permissible as a substitute for live auditions when distance is prohibitive. Portfolio reviews held twice on campus and off campus in Atlanta, GA; the submission of slides may be substituted for portfolios when distance is prohibitive.
Web Site http://www.valdosta.edu/comarts/
Undergraduate Contact Mr. Walter Peacock, Director, Admissions Office, Valdosta State University, 1500 North Patterson Street, Valdosta, Georgia 31698; 800-618-1878.

Virginia Commonwealth University

Richmond, Virginia

State-supported, coed. Urban campus. Total enrollment: 29,349. Theater program established 1940.
Degrees Bachelor of Fine Arts in the areas of theater, theater education. Majors and concentrations: costume design, lighting design, performance, scenic design, stage management, theater education. Graduate degrees offered: Master of Fine Arts in the areas of theater pedagogy (with emphasis in stage movement, voice and speech, acting, directing, history and literature). Program accredited by NAST.
Enrollment 271 total; 227 undergraduate, 44 graduate.
Theater Student Profile 60% females, 40% males, 27% minorities.
Theater Faculty 14 total (full-time), 3 total (part-time). 100% of full-time faculty have terminal degrees. Graduate students teach a few undergraduate courses. Undergraduate student–faculty ratio: 20:1.
Student Life Student groups/activities include Four Main Stage Productions per academic year, Senior Showcase in NYC.
Expenses for 2005–2006 Application fee: $30. State resident tuition: $5385 full-time. Nonresident tuition: $17,440 full-time. College room and board: $7042. College room only: $4102. Room and board charges vary according to board plan. Special

program-related fees: $30 per course for theater course fee, $75–$265 per semester for art major fee.
Financial Aid Program-specific awards: 4 Bobby Chandlar Award in Theatre for outstanding seniors ($300), Theatre VCU Alumnae Scholarship for theatre majors.
Application Procedures Students admitted directly into the professional program freshman year. Deadline for freshmen: February 1; transfers: May 1. Notification date for freshmen and transfers: continuous. Required: essay, high school transcript, college transcript(s) for transfer students, minimum 2.0 high school GPA, letter of recommendation, interview, audition, portfolio, SAT I or ACT test scores, portfolio for design applicants, audition for performance and theater education applicants. Auditions held 6 times on campus and off campus in Southeastern Theatre Conference sites; Virginia Theater Association sites. Portfolio reviews held 6 times on campus and off campus in Chicago, IL; New York, NY; Virginia Theater Association sites; the submission of slides may be substituted for portfolios with some original work.
Web Site http://www.vcu.edu/artweb/Theatre
Undergraduate Contact Kiersten Ware, Administrator, Theatre Department, Virginia Commonwealth University, Box 842524, Richmond, Virginia 23284-2524; 804-828-1514, fax: 804-828-6741, e-mail address: kware3@vcu.edu
Graduate Contact Dr. Noreen Barnes, Director of Graduate Studies, Theatre Department, Virginia Commonwealth University, Box 842524, Richmond, Virginia 23284-2524; 804-827-1677, fax: 804-828-6741, e-mail address: nbarnesm@saturn.vcu.edu

Virginia Intermont College

Bristol, Virginia

Independent, coed. Small town campus. Total enrollment: 1,138.
Degrees Bachelor of Fine Arts. Majors and concentrations: theater arts/drama. Cross-registration with King College.
Enrollment 5 total; all undergraduate.
Theater Student Profile 75% females, 25% males.
Theater Faculty 1 undergraduate (full-time). 100% of full-time faculty have terminal degrees. Graduate students do not teach undergraduate courses. Undergraduate student–faculty ratio: 2:1.
Student Life Student groups/activities include Southeastern Theatre Conference, American College Theatre Festival, WETS Live Radio Theater.
Expenses for 2005–2006 Application fee: $15. Comprehensive fee: $22,200 includes full-time tuition ($15,500), mandatory fees ($950), and college room and board ($5750). College room only: $2750. Full-time tuition and fees vary according to class time and program. Room and board charges vary according to housing facility.
Financial Aid Program-specific awards: performance scholarships for program majors ($500–$1500), departmental scholarships for program majors ($1200).
Application Procedures Students admitted directly into the professional program freshman year. Deadline for freshmen and transfers: continuous. Notification date for freshmen and transfers: continuous. Required: high school transcript, college transcript(s) for transfer students, minimum 2.0 high school GPA, SAT I or ACT test scores, audition for scholarship consideration. Recommended: letter of recommendation, interview, video, audition. Auditions held twice and by request on campus.
Undergraduate Contact Mr. Craig Wesley, Vice President for Enrollment Management, Virginia Intermont College, Box D-460, Bristol, Virginia 24201; 276-466-7856, fax: 276-466-7855, e-mail address: viadmit@vic.edu

Viterbo University

La Crosse, Wisconsin

Independent Roman Catholic, coed. Suburban campus. Total enrollment: 2,534. Theater program established 1944.

Wayne State University

Detroit, Michigan

State-supported, coed. Urban campus. Total enrollment: 33,137. Theater program established 1967.

Degrees Bachelor of Fine Arts. Majors and concentrations: theater arts/drama. Graduate degrees offered: Master of Fine Arts in the areas of acting, lighting design, costuming design, management, scene design, stage management. Doctor of Arts in the areas of theater history, criticism. Program accredited by NAST.

Enrollment 292 total; 212 undergraduate, 80 graduate.

Theater Student Profile 42% females, 58% males, 10% minorities, 1% international.

Theater Faculty 13 total (full-time), 6 total (part-time). 90% of full-time faculty have terminal degrees. Graduate students teach a few undergraduate courses. Undergraduate student–faculty ratio: 16:1.

Expenses for 2005–2006 Application fee: $30. State resident tuition: $5682 full-time. Nonresident tuition: $13,014 full-time. Mandatory fees: $757 full-time. Full-time tuition and fees vary according to student level. College room and board: $5350. Room and board charges vary according to housing facility.

Financial Aid Program-specific awards: 10 freshman incentive awards for incoming freshmen ($1800).

Application Procedures Students apply for admission into the professional program by junior year. Deadline for freshmen and transfers: August 3. Notification date for freshmen and transfers: continuous. Required: college transcript(s) for transfer students, minimum 2.0 high school GPA. Recommended: minimum 3.0 high school GPA.

Web Site http://www.theatre.wayne.edu

Undergraduate Contact Undergraduate Admissions, Wayne State University, 42 West Warren, Suite 436, Detroit, Michigan 48202; 313-577-3577, fax: 313-577-7536.

Graduate Contact Blair Anderson, Chair, Department of Theatre, Wayne State University, 4841 Cass Avenue, Suite 3225, Detroit, Michigan 48202; 313-577-3511, fax: 313-577-0935, e-mail address: ad5298@wayne.edu

Leigh Gerdine College of Fine Arts

Webster University

St. Louis, Missouri

Independent, coed. Suburban campus. Total enrollment: 7,327. Theater program established 1967.

Degrees Bachelor of Arts in the area of directing; Bachelor of Fine Arts in the areas of theater, musical theater, design/tech, stage management. Majors and concentrations: costume design, directing, lighting design, makeup and wig design, music theater, performance, scene painting, scenic design, sound design, technical direction, technical production. Cross-registration with various colleges in St. Louis.

Enrollment 140 total; all undergraduate.

Theater Student Profile 50% females, 50% males, 10% minorities, 1% international.

Theater Faculty 12 undergraduate (full-time), 20 undergraduate (part-time). 100% of full-time faculty have terminal degrees. Graduate students do not teach undergraduate courses. Undergraduate student–faculty ratio: 12:1.

Student Life Student groups/activities include United States Institute for Theatre Technology.

Expenses for 2005–2006 Application fee: $25. Comprehensive fee: $23,947 includes full-time tuition ($17,210) and college room and board ($6737). College room only: $3586. Full-time tuition varies according to program. Room and board charges vary according to board plan and housing facility. Special program-related fees: $300 per year for technical theater materials.

Financial Aid Program-specific awards: 5 endowed scholarships for talented juniors and seniors ($1500).

Application Procedures Students admitted directly into the professional program freshman year. Deadline for freshmen and transfers: March 15. Notification date for freshmen and transfers: April 1. Required: essay, high school transcript, college

transcript(s) for transfer students, minimum 2.0 high school GPA, letter of recommendation, audition, portfolio, SAT I or ACT test scores (minimum composite ACT score of 21), minimum combined SAT Reasoning Score of 1400. Recommended: minimum 3.0 high school GPA. Auditions held 12 times on campus and off campus in New York, NY; San Francisco, CA; Los Angeles, CA; Chicago, IL. Portfolio reviews held by arrangement on campus and off campus in New York, NY; San Francisco, CA; Los Angeles, CA; Chicago, IL; the submission of slides may be substituted for portfolios when distance is prohibitive.

Web Site http://www.webster.edu

Undergraduate Contact Ms. Jennifer Andonoff, Auditions Coordinator, Office of Admissions, Webster University, 470 East Lockwood Avenue, St. Louis, Missouri 63119-3194; 314-968-7001, fax: 314-968-7115, e-mail address: andonoff@webster.edu

More About the University

The Conservatory of Theatre Arts is a four-year, sequential professional training program located within a strong liberal arts teaching university. The Conservatory is among the few undergraduate programs in the country that utilize on-campus performing organizations: The Repertory Theatre of Saint Louis and the Opera Theatre of Saint Louis. They present their seasons in Webster's newly expanded Loretto-Hilton Center for the Performing Arts, which is also the home for the Conservatory's six-play season of student-performed and student-designed productions.

Students are selected through a national audition/interview process for their academic strengths and perceived professional potential. It is important that potential participants in the program exhibit a positive interest in combining study in the liberal arts with the discipline that a significant professional program demands.

The graduating class presents an annual showcase in New York. Webster hosts the annual Mid-West Theatre Auditions that presents opportunities for employment in the summer and year-round professional theaters. A regularly updated list of alumni activities is available upon request.

The Conservatory's goal is to present to its students the best possible opportunities to be challenged and to excel in all of the disciplines of theater. Because the program demands hard work in an intense situation, students tend to be goal-oriented.

The Department of Music provides outstanding music training in both the classical and jazz studies areas that utilize the St. Louis region's outstanding musicians as regular contributing members of the faculty. The department enjoys significant relationships with the Opera Theatre of Saint Louis and the Saint Louis Symphony Orchestra. Both are nationally recognized. The department strives to provide performance opportunities for students at the highest attainable levels. The Jazz Studies Program uses the recognized cadre of jazz artists as its faculty and as leaders of the various groups in this combo-based process of development.

In 2005–06, the department presented more than 100 recitals, performances, and concerts that represented the work of students, faculty, and visiting artists. Performing organizations on campus included the Webster University Symphony, the Webster University Big Band, three choral ensembles, Voices St. Louis, the Webster Wind Ensemble, and the Opera Studio. Students have opportunities to work with their studio faculty members and are constantly challenged to reach the highest musical standards.

The primary focus of the Department of Music is on undergraduate experiences. While a significant part of a strong liberal arts teaching university, the College of Fine Arts is the leader in training of undergraduates for the St. Louis region. There are approximately 110 undergraduates in twenty majors that comprise those studying in a variety of musical fields. Excellence is expected and excellence is the tradition. Students find music education at Webster to be a challenging and exciting experience.

Western Carolina University

Cullowhee, North Carolina

State-supported, coed. Rural campus. Total enrollment: 8,665. Theater program established 1975.

Degrees Bachelor of Fine Arts in the area of theater arts. Majors and concentrations: acting, costume design, lighting design, music theater, scenic design, technical theater.

Enrollment 49 total; 7 undergraduate, 42 nonprofessional degree.

Theater Student Profile 60% females, 40% males.

Theater Faculty 4 undergraduate (full-time), 4 undergraduate (part-time). 100% of full-time faculty have terminal degrees. Graduate students do not teach undergraduate courses. Undergraduate student–faculty ratio: 7:1.

Student Life Student groups/activities include Alpha Psi Omega, University Players, Black Theatre Ensemble.

Expenses for 2006–2007 Application fee: $40.

Financial Aid Program-specific awards: Josephina Niggli Scholarships for those demonstrating talent and academic achievement.

Application Procedures Students apply for admission into the professional program by sophomore year. Deadline for freshmen and transfers: continuous. Required: essay, high school transcript, college transcript(s) for transfer students, 3 letters of recommendation, interview, audition, SAT I or ACT test scores. Auditions held 3-4 times on campus and off campus in Southeastern Theatre Conference sites, North Carolina Theatre Conference sites; videotaped performances are permissible as a substitute for live auditions with prior approval. Portfolio reviews held by appointment on campus; the submission of slides may be substituted for portfolios.

Web Site http://www.wcu.edu

Undergraduate Contact Dr. Richard J. Beam, Associate Professor, Department of Communication/Theatre Arts, Western Carolina University, Belk 381, Cullowhee, North Carolina 28723; 828-227-3800, fax: 828-227-7647.

Potter College of Arts, Humanities, and Social Sciences

Western Kentucky University

Bowling Green, Kentucky

State-supported, coed. Suburban campus. Total enrollment: 18,634. Theater program established 1987.

Degrees Bachelor of Fine Arts in the area of performing arts. Majors and concentrations: acting, directing, music theater, theater design/technology.

Enrollment 58 total; all undergraduate.

Theater Student Profile 54% females, 46% males, 2% minorities.

Theater Faculty 7 undergraduate (full-time), 5 undergraduate (part-time). 100% of full-time faculty have terminal degrees. Graduate students do not teach undergraduate courses. Undergraduate student–faculty ratio: 7:1.

Student Life Student groups/activities include Alpha Psi Omega.

Expenses for 2005–2006 Application fee: $35. State resident tuition: $5316 full-time. Nonresident tuition: $12,732 full-time. Full-time tuition varies according to course load, location, program, and reciprocity agreements. College room and board: $4876. College room only: $2800. Room and board charges vary according to board plan and housing facility.

Financial Aid Program-specific awards: 10 Governor's School of the Arts Awards for students who complete Governor's School of the Arts ($1130–$3050), 20 departmental awards for sophomores and juniors demonstrating merit ($100–$1000).

Application Procedures Students apply for admission into the professional program by sophomore year. Deadline for freshmen and transfers: June 1. Required: high school transcript, college transcript(s) for transfer students, SAT I or ACT test scores (minimum combined SAT I score of 930, minimum composite ACT score of 20), minimum 2.5 high school GPA.

Web Site http://www.wku.edu/Dept/Academic/AHSS/Theatre/

Undergraduate Contact Office of Admissions, Western Kentucky University, 101 Cravens Center, One Big Red Way, Bowling Green, Kentucky 42101-3576; 502-745-5422.

Western Michigan University

Kalamazoo, Michigan

State-supported, coed. Urban campus. Total enrollment: 26,239. Theater program established 1976.

West Virginia University

Morgantown, West Virginia

State-supported, coed. Small town campus. Total enrollment: 26,051. Theater program established 1970.

Wright State University

Dayton, Ohio

State-supported, coed. Suburban campus. Total enrollment: 16,207.

Degrees Bachelor of Fine Arts in the areas of acting, musical theatre, theatre design/technology/stage management. Majors and concentrations: acting, film production, music theater, stage management, theater arts/drama, theater design/technology.

Enrollment 340 total; all undergraduate.

Theater Student Profile 50% females, 50% males, 5% minorities, 5% international.

Theater Faculty 17 undergraduate (full-time), 10 undergraduate (part-time). 75% of full-time faculty have terminal degrees. Graduate students do not teach undergraduate courses.

Expenses for 2006–2007 Application fee: $30. State resident tuition: $7278 full-time. Nonresident tuition: $14,004 full-time. College room and board: $7180. Special program-related fees: $20–$40 per quarter for certification, etc., $100 for film lab fees, $190–$360 per quarter for private voice lessons.

Financial Aid Program-specific awards: theater arts talent awards for incoming program students ($500–$2000), Milton Augsburger and Francisco Estevez Scholarships for incoming program students ($500–$2000), Faculty Academic scholarships for out-of-state incoming program students ($6400), merit scholarships for continuing students, Rising Star Scholarships for incoming/continuing students ($500–$1000), Arts Gala Scholarships for incoming/continuing students ($500–$2000), Tom Hanks Scholarship and Visiting Artist Funds for incoming students.

Application Procedures Students admitted directly into the professional program freshman year. Deadline for freshmen and transfers: March 1. Required: high school transcript, college transcript(s) for transfer students, interview, SAT I or ACT test scores, photograph, video if unavailable to audition in person, audition for acting and musical theater applicants, portfolio for scholarship consideration. Auditions held 6-8 times on campus and off campus in Louisville, KY; Atlanta, GA; videotaped performances are permissible as a substitute for live auditions. Portfolio reviews held on campus.

Web Site http://www.wright.edu/

Undergraduate Contact Ms. Victoria Oleen, Managing Director, Department of Theatre Arts, Wright State University, 3640 Colonel Glenn Highway, T148 CAC, Dayton, Ohio 45435; 937-775-3072, fax: 937-775-3787, e-mail address: victoria.oleen@wright.edu

More About the University

Wright State University (WSU) is a dynamic and diverse institution, with nearly 15,000 students pursuing studies in more than 100 undergraduate majors and forty graduate and professional degree programs. Named after aviation pioneers Orville and Wilbur Wright, the University seeks excellence in all of its academic programs, many of which receive national recognition. The Department of Theatre, Dance, and Motion Pictures is recognized as one of the premier performing arts programs for undergraduate training and performance in the nation. The department has established a growing reputation for superior theatrical production of musicals and dramas and has been repeatedly spotlighted. Some of these spotlights include winning a record fourteen awards from the American College Theatre Festival (ACTF) in 1997 for *1913: The Great Dayton*

Flood; being the only university in a four-state region to take two productions to the XXI Kennedy Center ACTF regional competition in 1998; the department's design/technology area winning the USITT National Olympics in 1995, 1997, 1999, and 2002; and, in the area of film, winning awards at the Los Angeles Independence Film Festival and the Sundance Festival.

Campus and Surroundings Wright State campus is adjacent to downtown Dayton, which is home to the Dayton Contemporary Dance Company, Dayton Ballet, Victoria Theatre, Human Race Theatre Company, Benjamin & Marian Schuster Performing Arts Center, Dayton Opera, and others. Wright State is also within an hour of Columbus and Cincinnati, which have many performing arts organizations.

Program Facilities The Department of Theatre, Dance, and Motion Pictures is housed in a state-of-the-art facility that includes acting and dance studios, a movement studio, a lighting and graphics lab, and motion-picture production facilities. Main-stage theater productions are held in the newly renovated Festival Playhouse, a 380-seat proscenium theater. Studio productions are in a 100-seat black box theater, and a student-performance theater that seats 92. The department has access to a comprehensive collection of play scripts, musical theater scores and soundtracks, and a videotape library.

Faculty, Resident Artists, Guest Artists and Alumni Chair W. Stuart McDowell is the founder and former artistic director of the Riverside Shakespeare Company in New York City and director of numerous professional productions across the country. Faculty members have worked with leading theater and dance companies throughout the country. Guest artists have included Shirley Jones, Ricky Ian Gordon, Jason Robert Brown, and Michael-John LaChiusa. Current notable alumni include Brad Sherwood (*Whose Line Is It Anyway?*), Erik Bork (recipient of two Emmy Awards), Angela Kahle (Radio City Music Hall Rockette and national tour of *42nd Street*), Ryan Cutlip (lead role in national tour of *Cabaret*), Heather Douglas (*Chicago*-London), Martin Fahrer (Art Director, Nickelodeon Television), and Carrie Hill (Master Electrician, Court Theatre). There are numerous recent graduates on national tours. The winners of the first annual Roger Sturtevant Award, given by Actors Equity, were Meegan Midkiff (2001 WSU) and Nick Verina (2005). This national award was given to 1 female actor and 1 male actor who demonstrated outstanding abilities in musical theater.

Student Performance Opportunities Students may work on six main-stage and three studio productions as actors, designers, dancers, or technicians. Students are also offered directing, design, choreography, acting, and dance opportunities in student productions in the directing lab and studio theater. Students majoring in motion-picture production are required to complete a fully realized film prior to graduation.

In 2005, a Tom Hanks Scholarship and Guest Artist funds were established to enhance programs in the department.

Cooperative Agreements Performance opportunities are also offered with the Human Race Theatre Company, Dayton Opera, the Dayton Ballet, and the Dayton Contemporary Dance Company.

Career Placement Acting/Musical Theatre students may perform a "Showcase" in New York City. Auditions for professional companies are held on campus.

York University
Toronto, Ontario, Canada

Province-supported, coed. Urban campus. Total enrollment: 49,496. Theater program established 1969.
Degrees Bachelor of Fine Arts in the area of theater. Majors and concentrations: acting, design production, directing, playwriting. Graduate degrees offered: Master of Fine Arts in the area of theater.
Enrollment 436 total; 247 undergraduate, 18 graduate, 171 nonprofessional degree.
Theater Student Profile 71% females, 29% males, 2% international.
Theater Faculty 19 total (full-time), 9 total (part-time). 72% of full-time faculty have terminal degrees. Graduate students teach a few undergraduate courses. Undergraduate student–faculty ratio: 11:1.
Student Life Student groups/activities include Theatre Students Association, Creative Arts Students Association.
Expenses for 2005–2006 Application fee: $90 Canadian dollars. Comprehensive fee: $10,981 includes full-time tuition ($4862) and college room and board ($6119). College room only: $3719. Full-time tuition varies according to course load, degree level, and program. Room and board charges vary according to board plan and housing facility. International student tuition: $14,862 full-time. Special program-related fees: $10–$40 per course for materials and supplies.
Financial Aid Program-specific awards: 3 talent awards for applicants with outstanding auditions ($1000), 5 Harry Rowe Bursaries for those demonstrating achievement or potential in artistic or scholarly work ($2000), 20 Fine Arts Bursaries for academically qualified students demonstrating financial need ($200–$700), 1 Cheryl Rosen Bursary for upperclassmen demonstrating need ($300), 1 Fitzhenry-Weatherhead Theatre Award for 3rd- or 4th- year students demonstrating achievement in theater sound ($500), 4 Friends of Theatre Bursaries for those demonstrating need ($500), 2 Theatre Department Bursaries for those demonstrating need ($550), 1 Jean Gascon Award for 3rd- or 4th- year students demonstrating need and originality and creativity in acting ($500), 21 IMASCO Performing Arts Awards for 2nd- or 3rd-year students demonstrating outstanding ability and sound academic standing ($3000), 1 Kenneth Ford Award for 3rd- or 4th- year students demonstrating talent in production and financial need ($300).
Application Procedures Students apply for admission into the professional program by freshman year. Deadline for freshmen and transfers: February 1. Notification date for freshmen: June 16; transfers: continuous. Required: high school transcript, college transcript(s) for transfer students, minimum 3.0 high school GPA, 2 letters of recommendation, interview, audition, SAT I, ACT or Canadian equivalent. Recommended: essay, portfolio for theater production applicants. Auditions held 10 times, or as needed on campus and off campus; videotaped performances are permissible as a substitute for live auditions when distance is prohibitive. Portfolio reviews held by appointment on campus; the submission of slides may be substituted for portfolios when distance is prohibitive.
Web Site http://www.yorku.ca/finearts/theatre
Undergraduate Contact Pamela Persaud, Manager, Student and Academic Services, York University, 201T GCFA, Faculty of Fine Arts, Toronto, Ontario M3J 1P3, Canada; 416-736-5135, fax: 416-736-5447, e-mail address: ask_ffa@yorku.ca
Graduate Contact Erika Batdorf, Graduate Program Director, Department of Theatre, York University, 201T Goldfarb Centre of Fine Arts, Toronto, Ontario M3J 1P3, Canada; 416-736-5135, e-mail address: ask_ffa@yorku.ca

Appendixes

Summer Programs in the Performing Arts

ACTEEN

Acteen June Academy
Acteen July Academy
Acteen August Academy
Acteen Summer Saturday Academy

Rita Litton
Acteen Director
35 West 45th Street
New York, NY 10036
Phone: 212-391-5915
Fax: 212-768-8918
E-mail: rita@acteen.com
Web site: www.acteen.com

AMERICAN ACADEMY OF DRAMATIC ARTS

American Academy of Dramatic Arts Summer Program at Los Angeles, California

Dan Justin
Director of Admissions
1336 North LaBrea Avenue
Hollywood, CA 90028
Phone: 800-222-2867
Web site: www.aada.org

American Academy of Dramatic Arts Summer Program at New York

Ms. Karen Higginbotham
Director of Admissions
120 Madison Avenue
New York, NY 10016
Phone: 800-463-8990
Fax: 212-685-8093
E-mail: admissions-ny@aada.org
Web site: www.aada.org

AMERICAN CONSERVATORY THEATER (A.C.T.)

Summer Training Congress

Bruce Williams
Director
30 Grant Avenue
San Francisco, CA 94108
Phone: 415-439-2350
Fax: 415-834-3300
E-mail: bwilliams@act-sf.org
Web site: www.ACTactortraining.org

APPEL FARM ARTS AND MUSIC CENTER

Appel Farm Summer Arts Camp

Ms. Jennie Quinn
Camp Director
PO Box 888
Elmer, NJ 08318-0888
Phone: 856-358-2472
Fax: 856-358-6513
E-mail: appelcamp@aol.com
Web site: www.appelfarm.org

ATELIER DES ARTS

Francia Tobacman
Director
55 Bethune Street, B645
New York, NY 10014
Phone: 212-727-1756
Fax: 212-691-0631
E-mail: info@atelierdesarts.org
Web site: www.atelierdesarts.org

ATLANTA BALLET

Centre for Dance Education

Sharon Story
Dean
Midtown Centre
1400 W. Peachtree Street, NW
Atlanta, GA 30309
Phone: 404-873-5811
Fax: 404-874-7905
E-mail: sstory@atlantaballet.com
Web site: www.atlantaballet.com

THE BANFF CENTRE

Summer Arts Programs

Arts, Office of the Registrar
Box 1020
Banff, Alberta
Canada T1L 1H5
Phone: 800-565-9989
Fax: 403-762-6345
E-mail: arts_info@banffcentre.ca
Web site: www.banffcentre.ca

BELVOIR TERRACE

Summer Contact: Ms. Nancy S. Goldberg
Director
80 Cliffwood Street
Lenox, MA 01240
Phone: 413-637-0555
Fax: 413-637-4651
E-mail: belvoirt@aol.com
Web site: www.belvoirterrace.com

Winter Contact: Ms. Nancy S. Goldberg
Director
101 West 79th Street
New York, NY 10024
Phone: 212-580-3398
Fax: 212-579-7282
E-mail: info@belvoirterrace
Web site: www.belvoirterrace.com

BERKLEE COLLEGE OF MUSIC

Berklee Business of Music Program
Berklee College of Music Summer Performance Program
Berklee Gospel Workshop
Berklee in L.A. Summer Performance Program
Berklee Music Production Workshop
Berklee Percussion Festival
Berklee Summer Brass Lines Program
Berklee Summer Brass Weekend
Berklee Summer Guitar Sessions
Berklee Summer Saxophone Weekend
Berklee Summer Songwriting Workshop
Berklee Summer String Fling

Mr. Anthony Byrne
Office of Special Programs
1140 Boylston Street
MS-155 SP
Boston, MA 02215
Phone: 617-747-2245
Fax: 617-262-5419
E-mail: summer@berklee.edu
Web site: www.berklee.edu/summer/
musicbusiness.html

THE BOSTON CONSERVATORY

Summer Dance '06

Mr. Toby Hanchett
Summer Programs Coordinator
Dance Division
8 The Fenway
Boston, MA 02215
Phone: 617-912-9166
Fax: 617-912-9101
E-mail: thanchett@bostonconservatory.edu
Web site: www.bostonconservatory.edu

Vocal/Choral Institute

Mr. Toby Hanchett
Summer Programs Coordinator
8 The Fenway
Boston, MA 02215
Phone: 617-912-9166
Fax: 617-912-9101
E-mail: thanchett@bostonconservatory.edu
Web site: www.bostonconservatory.edu

BOSTON UNIVERSITY TANGLEWOOD INSTITUTE

Ms. Chung-Un Seo
Administrative Director
855 Commonwealth Avenue
Boston, MA 02215
Phone: 800-643-4796
Fax: 617-353-7455
E-mail: tanglewd@bu.edu
Web site: www.bu.edu/tanglewood

BRANT LAKE CAMP

Brant Lake Camp's Dance Centre

Ms. Kirstin Been Spielman
Director
7586 State Route 8
Brant Lake, NY 12815
Phone: 518-494-2406
Fax: 518-494-7372
E-mail: brantlakec@aol.com
Web site: www.blcdance.com

BRIANSKY SARATOGA BALLET

Summer Program at Skidmore College, Saratoga Springs, NY

Admissions
220 West 93rd Street
New York, NY 10025
Phone: 212-799-0341
Fax: 212-799-0341
E-mail: olegbriansky@msn.com
Web site: www.briansky.org

BUCK'S ROCK PERFORMING AND CREATIVE ARTS CAMP

Ms. Laura Morris
Director
59 Buck's Rock Road
New Milford, CT 06776
Phone: 860-354-5030
Fax: 860-354-1355
E-mail: bucksrock@bucksrockcamp.com
Web site: www.bucksrockcamp.com

CALIFORNIA STATE SUMMER SCHOOL FOR THE ARTS/ INNER SPARK

Summer Contact: Shelly Reyes
Office Assistant
1010 Hurley
Suite 185
Sacramento, CA 95825
Phone: 916-274-5815
Fax: 916-274-5814
E-mail: shelly@innerspark.us
Web site: www.innerspark.us

Winter Contact: Shelly Reyes
Office Assistant
PO Box 1077
Sacramento, CA 95812-1077
Phone: 916-274-5815
Fax: 916-274-5814
E-mail: shelly@innerspark.us
Web site: www.innerspark.us

CAPITOL REGION EDUCATION COUNCIL
Center for Creative Youth

Nancy Wolfe
Director
Wesleyan University
350 High Street
Middletown, CT 06459
Phone: 860-685-3307
Fax: 860-685-3311
E-mail: ccy@wesleyan.edu
Web site: www.crec.org/ccy

CAZADERO PERFORMING ARTS CAMP
Cazadero Music Camp

Jim Mazzaferro
Camp Director
9068 Shetland Court
Elk Grove, CA 95624
Phone: 916-685-3867
Fax: 916-681-7505
E-mail: jim@cazadero.org
Web site: www.cazadero.org

CHOATE ROSEMARY HALL
Choate Rosemary Hall Summer Arts Conservatory– Theater

Mrs. Randi J. Brandt
Admissions Director, Arts Conservatory
Paul Mellon Arts Center
333 Christian Street
Wallingford, CT 06492
Phone: 203-697-2423
Fax: 203-697-2396
E-mail: rbrandt@choate.edu
Web site: www.choate.edu/summerprograms

CIRCLE IN THE SQUARE THEATRE SCHOOL
Summer Workshop—Acting and Musical

Admissions
1633 Broadway at 50th Street
New York, NY 10019
Phone: 212-307-0388
Fax: 212-307-0257
E-mail: circleinthesquare@att.net
Web site: www.circlesquare.org

CROSSROADS SCHOOL FOR ARTS AND SCIENCES
Crossroads School–Jazz Workshop

Angela Smith
Director, Summer Program
1714 21st Street
Santa Monica, CA 90404
Phone: 310-829-7391 ext. 506
Fax: 310-828-8147
E-mail: summer@xrds.org
Web site: www.xrds.org

DUKE YOUTH PROGRAMS–DUKE UNIVERSITY CONTINUING STUDIES
Duke Drama Workshop

Program Director
203 Bishop's House
Box 90702
Durham, NC 27708
Phone: 919-684-6259
Fax: 919-681-8235
E-mail: youth@duke.edu
Web site: www.learnmore.duke.edu/youth

EASTERN U.S. MUSIC CAMP, INC. AT COLGATE UNIVERSITY

Summer Contact: Dr. Thomas A. Brown
Director
Dana Arts Center
Hamilton, NY 13346-1398
Phone: 315-228-7041
Fax: 315-228-7557
E-mail: summer@easternusmusiccamp.com
Web site: www.easternusmusiccamp.com

Winter Contact: Dr. Thomas A. Brown
Director
7 Brook Hollow Road
Ballston Lake, NY 12019
Phone: 866-777-7841
Fax: 518-877-4943
E-mail: eusmc@easternusmusiccamp.com
Web site: www.easternusmusiccamp.com

EASTMAN SCHOOL OF MUSIC
Programs for High School Students
Collegiate Institutes for High School Students

Admissions
26 Gibbs Street
Rochester, NY 14604
Phone: 800-246-4706
Fax: 585-274-1005
E-mail: summer@esm.rochester.edu
Web site: www.esm.edu/summer

EDUCATION UNLIMITED
Actor's Workshop by Education Unlimited

Mr. Andy Spear
Director
1700 Shattuck Avenue, #305
Berkeley, CA 94709
Phone: 800-548-6612
Fax: 510-548-0212
E-mail: camps@educationunlimited.com
Web site: www.educationunlimited.com

ENSEMBLE THEATRE COMMUNITY SCHOOL

Summer Contact: Seth Orbach
Associate Director
PO Box 188
Eagles Mere, PA 17731
Phone: 570-525-3043
Fax: 570-525-3548
E-mail: info@etcschool.org
Web site: www.etcschool.org

Winter Contact: Seth Orbach
Associate Director
43 Lyman Circle
Shaker Heights, OH 44122
Phone: 216-464-1688
E-mail: info@etcschool.org
Web site: www.etcschool.org

THE EXPERIMENT IN INTERNATIONAL LIVING

The Experiment in International Living–United Kingdom Theatre Program

Annie Thompson
Enrollment Director
Summer Abroad, Kipling Road
PO Box 676
Brattleboro, VT 05302-0676
Phone: 800-345-2929
Fax: 802-258-3428
E-mail: eil@worldlearning.org
Web site: www.usexperiment.org

HARAND CAMP OF THE THEATRE ARTS

Summer Contact: Sulie Harand
Director
Carthage on the Lake
2001 Alford Park Drive
Kenosha, WI 53140-1994
Phone: 920-885-4517
Fax: 920-885-4521
E-mail: harandcamp@aol.com
Web site: www.harandcamp.com

Winter Contact: Sulie Harand
Director
708 Church Street, #231
Evanston, IL 60201
Phone: 847-864-1500
Fax: 847-864-1588
E-mail: harandcamp@aol.com
Web site: www.harandcamp.com

HOLLINS UNIVERSITY

Hollinsummer

Ms. Julie Aavatsmark
Associate Director of Admissions
PO Box 9707
Roanoke, VA 24020
Phone: 800-456-9595
Fax: 540-362-6218
E-mail: jaavatsmark@hollins.edu
Web site: www.hollins.edu/

THE HOTCHKISS SCHOOL

Hotchkiss School Summer Music Studies

Christie Gurney Rawlings
Admission and Student Life Director
PO Box 800
Lakeville, CT 06039
Phone: 860-435-3173
Fax: 860-435-4413
E-mail: crawling@hotchkiss.org
Web site: www.hotchkiss.org/AboutHotchkiss/
    SummerProg.asp

HUMANITIES SPRING IN ASSISI

Ms. Jane R. Oliensis
Director
Santa Maria di Lignano, 2
Assisi 06081, Italy
Phone: 39-075-802400
Fax: 39-075-802400
E-mail: info@humanitiesspring.com
Web site: www.humanitiesspring.com

THE HUN SCHOOL OF PRINCETON

The Hun School of Princeton Summer Theatre Classics

Summer Contact: Ms. Julia Ohm
Summer Programs Office
176 Edgerstoune Road
Princeton, NJ 08540
Phone: 609-921-7600 ext. 2339
E-mail: summer@hunschool.org
Web site: www.hunschool.org

Winter Contact: Ms. Donna O'Sullivan
Coordinator of Summer Programs
176 Edgerstoune Road
Princeton, NJ 08540
Phone: 609-921-7600 ext. 2265
Fax: 609-924-2170
E-mail: summer@hunschool.org
Web site: www.hunschool.org

HYDE SCHOOL

Hyde School Summer Challenge Program–Bath, ME

Melissa Burroughs
Director of Admission
616 High Street
Bath, ME 04530-5002
Phone: 207-443-5584
Fax: 207-442-9346
E-mail: bath.admissions@hyde.edu
Web site: www.hyde.edu

Hyde School Summer Challenge Program–Woodstock, CT

Michael Dawes
Director of Admissions
PO Box 237
Woodstock, CT 06281-0237
Phone: 860-963-9096
Fax: 860-928-0612
E-mail: woodstock.admissions@hyde.edu
Web site: www.hyde.edu

IDYLLWILD ARTS FOUNDATION

Idyllwild Arts Summer Program–American Experience for International Students

Ms. Diane Dennis
Summer Program Registrar
PO Box 38
Idyllwild, CA 92549
Phone: 951-659-2171 ext. 2365
Fax: 951-659-4552
E-mail: summer@idyllwildarts.org
Web site: www.idyllwildarts.org

INTERLOCHEN CENTER FOR THE ARTS

Interlochen Arts Camp

Ms. Amy Packard
Director of Admissions
PO Box 199
Interlochen, MI 49643
Phone: 231-276-7472
Fax: 231-276-7464
E-mail: admissions@interlochen.org
Web site: www.interlochen.org/

INTERN EXCHANGE INTERNATIONAL, LTD.

IEI–Theatre Plus Programme

Nina Miller Glickman
Director
1858 Mallard Lane
Villanova, PA 19085
Phone: 610-527-6066
Fax: 610-527-5499
E-mail: info@internexchange.com
Web site: www.internexchange.com

ITHACA COLLEGE DIVISION OF CONTINUING EDUCATION AND SUMMER SESSIONS

Ithaca College Summer Piano Institute

Mr. E. Kimball Milling
Director of Continuing Education and Summer Sessions
120 Towers Concourse
Ithaca, NY 14850-7141
Phone: 607-274-3143
Fax: 607-274-1263
E-mail: cess@ithaca.edu
Web site: www.ithaca.edu/cess

JACOB'S PILLOW DANCE

Summer Programs

J. R. Glover
Director of Education
358 George Carter Road
Becket, MA 01223
Phone: 413-243-9919
Fax: 413-243-4744
E-mail: info@jacobspillow.org
Web site: www.jacobspillow.org

KINHAVEN MUSIC SCHOOL

Summer Contact: Ms. Nancy Bidlack
Director
PO Box 68
Weston, VT 05161
Phone: 802-824-4332
Fax: 802-824-4332
Web site: www.kinhaven.org

Winter Contact: Ms. Nancy Bidlack
Director
1704 Sycamore Street
Bethlehem, PA 18017
Phone: 610-868-9200
Fax: 610-868-9200
Web site: www.kinhaven.org

LEARNING THEATRE, INC.

Encore! Ensemble Theatre Workshop

Ms. Susan Burke
Program Administrator
4661 Sweetmeadow Circle
Sarasota, FL 34238
Phone: 941-926-3244
Fax: 941-926-3254
E-mail: susanb@learntheatre.org
Web site: www.learntheatre.org

THE LEE STRASBERG THEATRE INSTITUTE

Summer Intensive Program

Admissions
115 East 15th Street
New York, NY 10003
Phone: 212-533-5500
Fax: 212-473-1727
E-mail: theleeny@aol.com
Web site: www.strasberg.com

Summer Program

Admissions
7936 Santa Monica Boulevard
Los Angeles, CA 90046
Telephone: 323-650-7777
Fax: 323-650-7770
E-mail: admissionsla@strasberg.com
Web site: www.strasberg.com

LEYSIN AMERICAN SCHOOL IN SWITZERLAND

Summer in Switzerland

Mr. Paul E. Dyer
US Director of Admissions
PO Box 7154
Portsmouth, NH 03802
Phone: 603-431-7654
Fax: 603-431-1280
E-mail: admissions@las.ch
Web site: www.las.ch/summer

THE LIMÓN INSTITUTE

Summer Dance Workshop with the Limón Dance Company

Admissions
307 West 38th Street, Suite 1105
New York, NY 10018
Phone: 212-777-3353 ext.18
E-mail: info@limon.org
Web site: www.limon.org

Summer Dance Workshop at Skidmore College

Office of the Dean of Special Programs
Skidmore College
815 North Broadway
Saratoga Springs, NY 12866-1632
Phone: 518-580-5590
E-mail: mmccoll@skidmore.edu
Web site: www.skidmore.edu/summer

MERCERSBURG ACADEMY SUMMER AND EXTENDED PROGRAMS

Mercersburg Onstage! Young Actors Workshop

Mr. Rick Hendrickson
Director of Summer and Extended Programs
300 East Seminary Street
Mercersburg, PA 17236
Phone: 717-328-6225
Fax: 717-328-9072
E-mail: summerprograms@mercersburg.edu
Web site: www.mercersburg.edu

Mercersburg The World's A Stage Theatre Workshop

Mr. Rick Hendrickson
Director of Summer and Extended Programs
300 East Seminary Street
Mercersburg, PA 17236
Phone: 717-328-6225
Fax: 717-328-9072
E-mail: summerprograms@mercersburg.edu
Web site: www.mercersburg.edu

MICHIGAN TECHNOLOGICAL UNIVERSITY

Michigan Technological University Orchestra Fellowship Program

Peter Larsen
Youth Programs Coordinator
1400 Townsend Drive
Houghton, MI 49931-1295
Phone: 906-487-2219
Fax: 906-487-3101
E-mail: yp@mtu.edu
Web site: www.mtu.edu/

NEW YORK FILM ACADEMY

The New York Film Academy, Universal Studios, Hollywood, CA

Admissions
100 East 17th Street
New York, NY 10003
Phone: 212-674-4300
Fax: 212-477-1414
E-mail: film@nyfa.com
Web site: www.nyfa.com

NEW YORK UNIVERSITY, TISCH SCHOOL OF THE ARTS

Tisch School of the Arts–International High School Program–Dublin
Tisch School of the Arts–International High School Program–Paris
Tisch School of the Arts–Summer High School Programs

Mr. Josh Murray
Assistant Director of Recruitment
Special Programs
721 Broadway
12th Floor
New York, NY 10003
Phone: 212-998-1500
Fax: 212-995-4610
E-mail: tisch.special.info@nyu.edu
Web site: specialprograms.tisch.nyu.edu

OPERAFESTIVAL ROMA, INC.

Operafestival di Roma

Dr. William M. Welty
Managing Director
1445 Willow Lake Drive
Charlottesville, VA 22902
Phone: 434-984-4945
Fax: 434-984-5220
E-mail: operafest@aol.com
Web site: www.operafest.com

PERIDANCE CENTER

International Dance School

Admissions
132 Fourth Avenue, Second Floor
New York, NY 10003
Phone: 212-505-0886
Fax: 212-674-2239
E-mail: info@peridance.com
Web site: www. peridance.com

PERRY-MANSFIELD PERFORMING ARTS SCHOOL AND CAMP

June Lindenmayer
Executive Director
40755 Routt County Road 36
Steamboat Springs, CO 80487
Phone: 800-430-2787
Fax: 970-879-5823
E-mail: p-m@perry-mansfield.org
Web site: www.perry-mansfield.org

POWER CHORD ACADEMY
Power Chord Academy–New York City

Mr. Bryan J. Wrzesinski
7336 Santa Monica Boulevard, #107
Los Angeles, CA 90046
Phone: 800-897-6677
Fax: 775-306-7923
E-mail: info@powerchordacademy.com
Web site: www.powerchordacademy.com

POWER CHORD ACADEMY
Power Chord Academy–San Diego

Mr. Bryan J. Wrzesinski
7336 Santa Monica Boulevard, #107
Los Angeles, CA 90046
Phone: 800-897-6677
Fax: 775-306-7923
E-mail: info@powerchordacademy.com
Web site: www.powerchordacademy.com

THE PUTNEY SCHOOL
The Putney School Summer Arts Program

Maria Ogden
Administrative Coordinator
Elm Lea Farm
418 Houghton Brook Road
Putney, VT 05346
Phone: 802-387-6297
Fax: 802-387-6216
E-mail: summer@putneyschool.org
Web site: www.putneyschool.org/summer

PUTNEY STUDENT TRAVEL
Putney Student Travel–Cultural Exploration–Theatre in Britain

Jeffrey Shumlin
Director
345 Hickory Ridge Road
Putney, VT 05346
Phone: 802-387-5000
Fax: 802-387-4276
E-mail: info@goputney.com
Web site: www.goputney.com

SARAH LAWRENCE COLLEGE
Sarah Lawrence College Summer High School Programs

Liz Irmiter
Director of Special Programs
1 Mead Way
Bronxville, NY 10708
Phone: 914-395-2693
E-mail: specialprograms@sarahlawrence.edu
Web site: www.sarahlawrence.edu/summer

THE SCHOOL OF TORONTO DANCE THEATRE
Summer School in Contemporary Dance

Patricia Fraser
Director
80 Winchester Street
Toronto, Ontario
Canada M4X 1B2
Phone: 416-967-6887
Fax: 416-967-4379
E-mail: info@schooloftdt.org

SIGNATURE MUSIC CAMP
Signature Music Teen Camp
Signature Music Youth Camp

Dr. Richard W. Ford
Executive Director
138 Fellows Avenue
Syracuse, NY 13210
Phone: 315-478-7480
Fax: 315-478-0962
E-mail: director@signaturemusic.org
Web site: www.signaturemusiccamp.org

SPOLETO STUDY ABROAD

Jill Muti
Director
PO Box 99147
Raleigh, NC 27624-9147
Phone: 919-384-0031
E-mail: spoleto@mindspring.com
Web site: www.spoletostudyabroad.com

STAGEDOOR MANOR PERFORMING ARTS TRAINING CENTER/THEATRE AND DANCE CAMP

Summer Contact: Barbara Martin
Director
116 Karmel Road
Loch Sheldrake, NY 12759-5308
Phone: 888-STAGE 88
Fax: 888-STAGE 88
Web site: www.stagedoormanor.com

Winter Contact: Barbara Martin
Director
3658 Churchville Avenue
Churchville, VA 24421
Phone: 888-STAGE 88
Fax: 888-STAGE 88
E-mail: stagedoormanor@aol.com
Web site: www.stagedoormanor.com

STELLA ADLER STUDIO OF ACTING
Summer Teen Conservatory

Admissions
31 West 27th Street, 3rd Floor
New York, NY 10001
Phone: 800-270-6775
Fax: 212-689-6110
Web site: www.stellaadler.com

SUFFIELD ACADEMY
The Summer Academy at Suffield

Tony O'Shaughnessy
Director, Summer Academy Admissions
185 North Main Street
Suffield, CT 06078
Phone: 860-386-4475
Fax: 860-386-4476
E-mail: summer@suffieldacademy.org
Web site: www.suffieldsummer.org

SUMMER THEATRE INSTITUTE NEW YORK CITY
Summer Theatre Institute–2006

Ms. Allyn Sitjar
Artistic Director
23 Tomahawk Trail
Sparta, NJ 07871
Phone: 201-415-5329
Fax: 973-729-3654
E-mail: youththeatreallyn@yahoo.com
Web site: www.youththeatreinstitutes.org

SYRACUSE UNIVERSITY
Syracuse University Summer College

Jolynn Parker
Program Manager
111 Waverly Avenue
Suite 240
Syracuse, NY 13244-1270
Phone: 315-443-5297
Fax: 315-443-3976
E-mail: sumcoll@syr.edu
Web site: www.summercollege.syr.edu/

TANGLEWOOD INSTITUTE
Boston University Tanglewood Institute Summer Programs

College of Fine Arts
Boston University
855 Commonwealth Avenue
Boston, MA 02215.
Phone: 617-353-3350
E-mail: tanglwd@bu.edu
Web site: www.bu.edu/cfa/music/tanglewood/programs/htm

UCLA SUMMER SESSIONS AND SPECIAL PROGRAMS
UCLA Summer Experience: Institutes

Dr. Susan Pertel Jain
Director of Academic Program Development
Box 951418
Los Angeles, CA 90095
Phone: 310-825-4101
Fax: 310-825-1528
E-mail: spjain@summer.ucla.edu
Web site: www.summer.ucla.edu

UNIVERSITY OF MARYLAND, OFFICE OF SUMMER AND WINTER TERMS
The Arts! at Maryland

Terrie Hruzd
Program Manager, Office of Summer and Winter Terms
2103 Reckord Armory
College Park, MD 20742
Phone: 301-405-8588
Fax: 301-314-9572
E-mail: hruzd@umd.edu
Web site: www.summer.umd.edu/arts

UNIVERSITY OF PENNSYLVANIA
University of Pennsylvania–Penn Summer Theatre Workshop

Mr. Matthew Palmer
Summer Sessions Assistant
3440 Market Street, Suite 100
Philadelphia, PA 19104-3335
Phone: 215-746-6901
Fax: 215-573-2053
Web site: www.upenn.edu/summer

THE UNIVERSITY OF THE ARTS
Pre-College Summer Institute, The University of the Arts

Erin Elman
Director, Pre-College Programs
320 South Broad Street
Philadelphia, PA 19102
Phone: 215-717-6430
Fax: 215-717-6433
E-mail: precollege@uarts.edu
Web site: www.uarts.edu/precollege

WILDERNESS DANCE CAMP, INC.
Wilderness Dance Camp

Ms. Chandra Saign
Director
10251 Lyndale Avenue South
Bloomington, MN 55420
Phone: 952-884-6009
E-mail: info@dancecamp.org
Web site: www.dancecamp.org/

WORLD HORIZONS INTERNATIONAL
World Horizons International–United Kingdom

Mr. Stuart L. Rabinowitz
Executive Director
PO Box 662
Bethelem, CT 06751
Phone: 800-262-5874
Fax: 203-266-6227
E-mail: worldhorizons@att.net
Web site: www.world-horizons.com

WYOMING SEMINARY COLLEGE PREPARATORY SCHOOL
The Performing Arts Institute of Wyoming Seminary

Nancy Sanderson
Director, The Performing Arts Institute of Wyoming Seminary
201 North Sprague Avenue
Kingston, PA 18704
Phone: 570-270-2186
Fax: 570-270-2198
E-mail: onstage@wyomingseminary.org
Web site: www.wyomingseminary.org/pai

Scholarships for Performing Artists

ALPHA DELTA KAPPA FOUNDATION
http://www.alphadeltakappa.org
Apha Delta Kappa Foundation Fine Arts Grants

Dee Frost, Scholarships and Grants Coordinator
Alpha Delta Kappa Foundation
1615 West 92nd Street
Kansas City, MO 64114-3296
Phone: 816-363-5525
Fax: 816-363-4010
E-mail: headquarters@alphadeltakappa.org

AMERICAN COLLEGE OF MUSICIANS/NATIONAL GUILD OF PIANO TEACHERS
http://www.pianoguild.com
American College of Musicians/National Guild of Piano Teachers 200-Dollar Scholarships

Pat McCabe, Scholarship Coordinator, Scholarship Committee
American College of Musicians/National Guild of Piano Teachers
PO Box 1807, 808 Rio Grande
Austin, TX 78767-1807
Phone: 512-478-5775
E-mail: ngpt@aol.com

AMERICAN FOUNDATION FOR THE BLIND
http://www.afb.org/scholarships.asp
R.L. Gillette Scholarship

Alina Vayntrub, Departmental Assistant, Information Center
American Foundation for the Blind
11 Penn Plaza, Suite 300
New York, NY 10001
Phone: 212-502-7661
Fax: 212-502-7771
E-mail: afbinfo@afb.net

AMERICAN LEGION, DEPARTMENT OF KANSAS
http://www.ksamlegion.org
Music Committee Scholarship

Scholarship Administrator
American Legion, Department of Kansas
1314 Southwest Topeka Boulevard
Topeka, KS 66612-1886

AMERICAN MUSICOLOGICAL SOCIETY
http://www.ams-net.org
Minority Travel Fund Award

Martha Feldman, Chair of the Committee
American Musicological Society
201 South 34th Street
Philadelphia, PA 19104-6313
Phone: 215-573-3673
E-mail: rore@uchicago.edu

AMERICAN ORFF-SCHULWERK ASSOCIATION
http://www.aosa.org
American Orff-Schulwerk Association Research Grant

Cindi Wobig, Executive Director
American Orff-Schulwerk Association
PO Box 391089
Cleveland, OH 44139-8089
Phone: 440-543-5366
Fax: 440-543-2687
E-mail: aosahdq@msn.com

Gunild Keetman Assistance Fund

Cindi Wobig, Executive Director
American Orff-Schulwerk Association
PO Box 391089
Cleveland, OH 44139-8089
Phone: 440-543-5366
Fax: 440-543-2687
E-mail: aosahdq@msn.com

AMERICAN STRING TEACHERS ASSOCIATION
http://www.astaweb.com
National Solo Competition

Michael Carrera, ASTA National Solo Competition, Committee Chair
American String Teachers Association
4153 Chain Bridge Road
Fairfax, VA 22030
Phone: 703-279-2113
Fax: 703-279-2114
E-mail: carrera@ohio.edu

AMERICAN THEATRE ORGAN SOCIETY, INC.
http://www.atos.org

American Theatre Organ Society Organ Performance Scholarship

Carlton B. Smith, Chairperson, Scholarship Program
American Theatre Organ Society, Inc.
2175 North Irwin Street
Indianapolis, IN 46219-2220
Phone: 317-356-1270
Fax: 317-322-9379
E-mail: smith@atos.org

BEEM FOUNDATION FOR THE ADVANCEMENT OF MUSIC
http://www.beemfoundation.org

BEEM Foundation Scholarship

Bette Cox, President
BEEM Foundation for the Advancement of Music
3864 Grayburn Avenue
Los Angeles, CA 90008-1941
Phone: 323-291-7252
Fax: 323-291-7752
E-mail: bette.cox@beemfoundation.com

BMI FOUNDATION, INC.
http://www.bmi.com

BMI Student Composer Awards
John Lennon Scholarship Program
Peermusic Latin Scholarship

Mr. Ralph N. Jackson, President
BMI Foundation, Inc.
320 West 57th Street
New York, NY 10019
Phone: 212-586-2000
Fax: 212-245-8986
E-mail: classical@bmi.com

CALIFORNIA ALLIANCE FOR ARTS EDUCATION (CAAE)
http://www.artsed411.org

Emerging Young Artist Awards

Peggy Burt, Project Manager
California Alliance for Arts Education (CAAE)
495 East Colorado Boulevard
Pasadena, CA 91101
Phone: 626-578-9315 Ext. 102
Fax: 626-578-9894
E-mail: peggy@artsed411.org

CASE WESTERN RESERVE UNIVERSITY
http://www.cwru.edu/artsci/thtr

Marc A. Klein Playwright Award

John Orlock, Chair

CHOPIN FOUNDATION OF THE UNITED STATES
http://www.chopin.org

Chopin Foundation of the United States Scholarship

Jadwiga Gewert, Executive Director
Chopin Foundation of the United States
1440 79th Street Causeway, Suite 117
Miami, FL 33141
Phone: 305-868-0624
Fax: 305-865-5150
E-mail: info@chopin.org

CIRI FOUNDATION
http://www.thecirifoundation.org

(limited to Alaska Native beneficiaries)

CIRI Foundation Susie Qimmiqsak Bevins Endowment Scholarship Fund
Cultural Fellowship Grants

Phone: 907-263-5582
Fax: 907-263-5588
E-mail: tcf@ciri.com

CLARICE SMITH PERFORMING ARTS CENTER AT MARYLAND
http://www.claricesmithcenter.umd.edu

William Kapell International Piano Competition and Festival

Christopher Patton, Coordinator
Clarice Smith Performing Arts Center at Maryland
Suite 3800, University of Maryland
College Park, MD 20742-1625
Phone: 301-405-8174
Fax: 301-405-5977
E-mail: kapell@deans.umd.edu

COLLEGEBOUND FOUNDATION
http://www.collegeboundfoundation.org

Janet B. Sondheim Scholarship

April Bell, Associate Program Director
CollegeBound Foundation
300 Water Street, Suite 300
Baltimore, MD 21202
Phone: 410-783-2905 Ext. 208
Fax: 410-727-5786
E-mail: abell@collegeboundfoundation.org

COLUMBIA UNIVERSITY, DEPARTMENT OF MUSIC
http://www.music.columbia.edu

Joseph H. Bearns Prize in Music

Bearns Prize Committee
Columbia University, Department of Music
2960 Broadway, 621 Dodge Hall, MC# 1813
New York, NY 10027
Phone: 212-854-3825
Fax: 212-854-8191

COMMUNITY FOUNDATION OF CAPE COD
http://www.capecodfoundation.org

Richard and Ethel Koff Memorial Scholarship Fund

Pauline Greenberg, Scholarship Associate
Community Foundation of Cape Cod
259 Willow Street
Yarmouthport, MA 02675
Phone: 508-790-3040
Fax: 508-790-4069
E-mail: pgreenberg@capecodfoundation.org

CONCERT ARTISTS GUILD
http://www.concertartists.org

Concert Artists Guild Competition

Amy Frawley, Competition Manager
Concert Artists Guild
850 7th Avenue, Suite 1205
New York, NY 10019-5230
Phone: 212-333-5200 Ext. 14
Fax: 212-977-7149
E-mail: caguild@concertartists.org

CONGRESSIONAL BLACK CAUCUS SPOUSES PROGRAM
http://www.cbcfinc.org

Congressional Black Caucus Spouses Performing Arts Scholarship

Appropriate Congressional District Office
Phone: 202-263-2836

CONTEMPORARY RECORD SOCIETY
http://www.crsnews.org

Contemporary Record Society National Competition for Performing Artists

Contemporary Record Society National Festival for the Performing Arts Scholarship

National Competition for Composers' Recordings

Administrative Assistant
Contemporary Record Society
724 Winchester Road
Broomall, PA 19008
Phone: 610-544-5920
Fax: 610-544-5921
E-mail: crsnews@verizon.net

DAYTON FOUNDATION
http://www.daytonfoundation.org

Mu Phi Epsilon Scholarship Fund

Diane Timmons, Director Grants and Programs
Dayton Foundation
2300 Kettering Tower
Dayton, OH 45423
Phone: 937-225-9966
E-mail: dtimmons@daytonfoundation.org

DELTA OMICRON INTERNATIONAL MUSIC FRATERNITY/ DELTA OMICRON FOUNDATION, INC.
http://delta-omicron.org

Summer Music Scholarships
Michelle A. May, Chair, Rotating Grants and Summer
Scholarships
Delta Omicron International Music Fraternity/Delta
Omicron Foundation, Inc.
1635 West Boston Boulevard
Detroit, MI 48206
Phone: 313-865-1149
Fax: 313-965-0868
E-mail: maybiz@aol.com

DOMENIC TROIANO GUITAR SCHOLARSHIP
http://www.domenictroiano.com/

Domenic Troiano Guitar Scholarship
Clinton Somerton
Domenic Troiano Guitar Scholarship
c/o Metronome Canada Culture Heritage Foundation
118 Sherbourne Street
Toronto
Canada
Phone: 416-367-0162
Fax: 416-367-1569
E-mail: clinton@domenictroiano.com

DONNA REED FOUNDATION FOR THE PERFORMING ARTS
http://www.donnareed.org

Donna Reed Performing Arts Scholarships
Gwen Ecklund, Executive Director
Donna Reed Foundation for the Performing Arts
1305 Broadway
Denison, IA 51442
Phone: 712-263-3334
Fax: 712-263-8026
E-mail: gwen@donnareed.org

FORT COLLINS SYMPHONY ASSOCIATION
http://www.fcsymphony.org

Adeline Rosenberg Memorial Prize

Fort Collins Symphony Association Young Artist Competition, Junior Division
Sidney Thompson, Chairman of the competition
Fort Collins Symphony Association
PO Box 1963
Fort Collins, CO 80522
Phone: 970-482-4823
Fax: 970-482-4858
E-mail: note@fcsymphony.org

GENERAL FEDERATION OF WOMEN'S CLUBS OF MASSACHUSETTS
http://www.gfwcma.org/

Dorchester Women's Club Scholarship

General Federation of Women's Clubs of Massachusetts Music Scholarship
Virginia Williams, Chairman Music Program, GFWC
of MA
General Federation of Women's Clubs of Massachusetts
PO Box 679
Sudbury, MA 01776-0679
Phone: 978-443-4569
E-mail: dlvtwillialms@aol.com

GEORGE BIRD GRINNELL AMERICAN INDIAN FUND
http://www.grinnellfund.org/

Al Qoyawayma Award
Paula Mintzies, President
George Bird Grinnell American Indian Fund
PO Box 59033
Potomac, MD 20859
Phone: 301-424-2440
Fax: 301-424-8281

GINA BACHAUER INTERNATIONAL PIANO FOUNDATION
http://www.bachauer.com

Gina Bachauer International Artists Piano Competition Award
Paul Pollei, Artistic Director
Gina Bachauer International Piano Foundation
138 West Broadway Suite 220
Salt Lake City, UT 84101-1664
Phone: 801-297-4250
Fax: 801-521-9202
E-mail: gina@bachauer.com

GLENN MILLER BIRTHPLACE SOCIETY
http://www.glennmiller.org
Glenn Miller Instrumental Scholarship
Jack Pullan Memorial Scholarship
Ralph Brewster Vocal Scholarship

Arlene Leonard, Secretary
Glenn Miller Birthplace Society
107 East Main Street, PO Box 61
Clarinda, IA 51632-0061
Phone: 712-542-2461
Fax: 712-542-2461
E-mail: gmbs@heartland.net

GRAND RAPIDS COMMUNITY FOUNDATION
http://www.grfoundation.org
Gerald M. Crane Memorial Music Scholarship Fund
See Web site.

HAPCO MUSIC FOUNDATION, INC.
http://www.hapcopromo.org
Traditional Marching Band Extravaganza
Scholarship Award

HapCo Music Foundation, Inc.
PO Box 784581
Winter Garden, FL 34778
Phone: 407-877-2262
E-mail: hapcopromo@aol.com

HOUSTON SYMPHONY
http://www.houstonsymphony.org
Houston Symphony Ima Hogg Young Artist
Competition
Houston Symphony League Concerto Competition

Carol Wilson, Education Coordinator
Houston Symphony
615 Louisiana
Houston, TX 77002
Phone: 713-238-1447
Fax: 713-224-0453
E-mail: e&o@houstonsymphony.org

ILLUMINATING ENGINEERING SOCIETY OF NORTH
AMERICA
http://www.iesna.org
Robert W. Thunen Memorial Scholarships

Chairperson (Thunen Scholarship Committee)
Illuminating Engineering Society of North America
IESNA Golden Gate Section, 1514 Gibbons Drive
Alameda, CA 94501-4001
Phone: 510-864-0204
Fax: 510-864-8511
E-mail: mrcatisbac@aol.com

INTERNATIONALER MUSIKWETTBEWERB
http://www.ard-musikwettbewerb.de
International Music Competition of the ARD Munich

Ingeborg Krause, Head of Organization
Internationaler Musikwettbewerb
Bayerischer Rundfink
Munich 80300
Germany
Phone: 49-89-5900247
Fax: 49-89-5900357
E-mail: ard.musikwettbewerb@brnet.de

JACK J. ISGUR FOUNDATION
Jack J. Isgur Foundation Scholarship

Charles Jensen, Attorney at Law
Jack J. Isgur Foundation
c/o Charles F. Jensen, Stinson, Morrison, Hecker LLP
1201 Walnut Street, 28th Floor
Kansas City, MO 64106
Phone: 816-691-2760
Fax: 816-691-3495
E-mail: cjensen@stinsonmoheck.com

KOSCIUSZKO FOUNDATION
http://www.kosciuszkofoundation.org
Kosciuszko Foundation Chopin Piano Competition

Tom Pniewski, Director of Cultural Programs
Kosciuszko Foundation
15 East 65th Street
New York, NY 10021-6595
Phone: 212-734-2130
Fax: 212-628-4552
E-mail: tompkf@aol.com

KURT WEILL FOUNDATION FOR MUSIC
http://www.kwf.org
Lotte Lenya Competition for Singers

Carolyn Weber, Director of Program Administration
and Business Affairs
Kurt Weill Foundation for Music
7 East 20th Street
New York, NY 10003-1106
Phone: 212-505-5240
Fax: 212-353-9663

LIEDERKRANZ FOUNDATION
http://www.liederkranznycity.org
Liederkranz Foundation Scholarship Award for Voice

Cynthia M. Kessel, Administrative Assistant
Liederkranz Foundation
6 East 87th Street
New York, NY 10128
Phone: 212-534-0880
Fax: 212-828-5372

LOS ANGELES PHILHARMONIC
http://www.laphil.org
Bronislaw Kaper Awards for Young Artists

Education Department
Los Angeles Philharmonic
151 South Grand Avenue
Los Angeles, CA 90012
Phone: 213-972-0704
Fax: 213-972-7650
E-mail: education@laphil.org

MIDLAND COMMUNITY THEATER
http://www.mctmidland.org
Madeira Shaner Scholarship

Georganne Payne, Director of Business Operations
and Development
Midland Community Theater
2000 West Wadley
Midland, TX 79705
Phone: 432-682-2544 Ext. 3006
E-mail: georganne@mctmidland.org

NATIONAL ASSOCIATION OF PASTORAL MUSICIANS
http://www.npm.org
Dan Schutte Scholarship
Elaine Rendler-Rene Dosogne-Georgetown Chorale Scholarship
Funk Family Memorial Scholarship
GIA Publication Pastoral Musician Scholarship
MuSonics Scholarship
National Association of Pastoral Musicians Members' Scholarship
NPM Board of Directors Scholarship
NPM Composers and Authors Scholarship
NPM Koinonia/Board of Directors Scholarship
NPM Miami Valley Catholic Church Musicians Scholarship
NPM Perrot Scholarship
Oregon Catholic Press Scholarship
Paluch Family Foundation/World Library Publications Scholarship
Steven C. Warner Scholarship

Kathleen Haley, Scholarship Department
National Association of Pastoral Musicians
962 Wayne Avenue
Suite 210
Silver Spring, MD 20910-4461
Phone: 240-247-3000
Fax: 240-247-3001
E-mail: npmsing@npm.org

NATIONAL FOUNDATION FOR ADVANCEMENT IN THE ARTS
http://www.artsawards.org
Arts Recognition and Talent Search (ARTS)

Programs Department
National Foundation for Advancement in the Arts
444 Brickell Avenue, Suite R14
Miami, FL 33133
Phone: 800-970-2787
Fax: 305-377-1149
E-mail: nfaa@nfaa.org

Astral Career Grant

Programs Department
National Foundation for Advancement in the Arts
444 Brickell Avenue, Suite R14
Miami, FL 33133
Phone: 800-970-2787 Ext. 33
Fax: 305-377-1149
E-mail: nfaa@nfaa.org

NATIONAL GUILD OF COMMUNITY SCHOOLS OF THE ARTS
http://www.nationalguild.org
Young Composers Awards

Carissa Reddick, YCA Coordinator
National Guild of Community Schools of the Arts
The Hartt School Community Division, University of Hartford, 200 Bloomfield Avenue
West Hartford, CT 06117
Phone: 860-768-7768 Ext. 8558
Fax: 860-768-4777
E-mail: youngcomp@hartford.edu

NATIONAL OPERA ASSOCIATION
http://www.noa.org
NOA Vocal Competition/ Legacy Award Program

Robert Hansen, Executive Secretary
National Opera Association
PO Box 60869
Canyon, TX 79016-0869
Phone: 806-651-2857
Fax: 806-651-2958
E-mail: hansen@mail.wtamu.edu

NATIONAL SYMPHONY ORCHESTRA EDUCATION PROGRAM
http://www.kennedy-center.org
National Symphony Orchestra Young Soloists' Competition- Bill Cerri Scholarship/College Division

Sharyn L. Byer, Competition Administrator
National Symphony Orchestra Education Program
115 Gresham Place
Falls Church, VA 22046

National Symphony Orchestra Young Soloists' Competition- Bill Cerri Scholarship/High School Division

Sharyn L. Byer, Competition Administrator
National Symphony Orchestra Education Program
115 Gresham Place
Falls Church, VA 22046

OMAHA SYMPHONY GUILD
http://www.omahasymphony.org
Omaha Symphony Guild International New Music Competition

Tim Dickmeyer, Touring and Education Coordinator
Omaha Symphony Guild
1605 Howard Street
Omaha, NE 68102-2705
Phone: 402-342-3836 Ext. 107
Fax: 402-342-3819
E-mail: tdickmeyer@omahasymphony.org

ORANGE COUNTY COMMUNITY FOUNDATION
http://www.heef.org
Arts Scholarship Program

Rose Garris, Hispanic Education Endowment Fund
Orange County Community Foundation
30 Corporate Park, Suite 410
Irvine, CA 92606
Phone: 949-543-4202 Ext. 23
Fax: 949-553-4211

PI LAMBDA THETA, INC.
http://www.pilambda.org
Nadeen Burkeholder Williams Music Scholarship

Pam Todd, Manager, Member Services
Pi Lambda Theta, Inc.
4101 East 3rd Street, PO Box 6626
Bloomington, IN 47407-6626
Phone: 812-339-3411
Fax: 812-339-3462
E-mail: endowment@pilambda.org

POLISH ARTS CLUB OF BUFFALO SCHOLARSHIP FOUNDATION
http://pacb.bfn.org/about/constitution.html

Polish Arts Club of Buffalo Scholarship Foundation Trust

Ann Flansburg, Selection Chair
Polish Arts Club of Buffalo Scholarship Foundation
PO Box 1362
Williamsville, NY 14231-1362
Phone: 716-626-9083
E-mail: donflans123@aol.com

QUEEN ELISABETH INTERNATIONAL MUSIC COMPETITION OF BELGIUM
http://www.qeimc.be

Queen Elisabeth Competition

Michel-Etienne Van Neste, Secretary General
Queen Elisabeth International Music Competition of Belgium
Rue Aux Lanes 20
Brussels 1000
Belgium
Phone: 32-2-2134050
Fax: 32-2-5143297
E-mail: info@qeimc.be

RHODE ISLAND FOUNDATION
http://www.rifoundation.org

Bach Organ and Keyboard Scholarship Fund

Libby Monahan, Scholarship Coordinator
Rhode Island Foundation
1 Union Station
Providence, RI 02903
Phone: 401-274-4564
Fax: 401-272-1359

Constant Memorial Scholarship for Aquidneck Island Residents

Libby Monahan, Scholarship Coordinator
Rhode Island Foundation
1 Union Station
Providence, RI 02903
Phone: 401-274-4564
Fax: 401-272-1359
E-mail: libbym@rifoundation.org

SAN ANGELO SYMPHONY SOCIETY
http://www.sanangelosymphony.org

Sorantin Young Artist Award

Claire Simons
San Angelo Symphony Society
PO Box 5922
San Angelo, TX 76902-5922
Phone: 325-658-5877
Fax: 325-653-1045
E-mail: receptionist@sanangelosymphony.org

SIGMA ALPHA IOTA PHILANTHROPIES, INC.
http://www.sai-national.org

Sigma Alpha Iota Graduate Performance Awards

Dr. Emily White, Project Director
Sigma Alpha Iota Philanthropies, Inc.
One Tunnel Road
Asheville, NC 28805
Phone: 828-251-0606
Fax: 828-251-0644
E-mail: webmaster@sai-national.org

Sigma Alpha Iota Jazz Performance Awards

Margie Halinski, Director
Sigma Alpha Iota Philanthropies, Inc.
One Tunnel Road
Asheville, NC 28805
Phone: 828-251-0606
Fax: 828-251-0644
E-mail: mhalinski@yahoo.com

Sigma Alpha Iota Jazz Studies Scholarship

Margie Halinski, Project Director
Sigma Alpha Iota Philanthropies, Inc.
One Tunnel Road
Asheville, NC 28805
Phone: 828-251-0606
Fax: 828-251-0644
E-mail: mhalinski@yahoo.com

Sigma Alpha Iota Music Business/Technology Scholarship

Kim L. Wangler, Director
Sigma Alpha Iota Philanthropies, Inc.
One Tunnel Road
Asheville, NC 28805
Phone: 828-251-0606
Fax: 828-251-0644
E-mail: wanglerkl@appstate.edu

Sigma Alpha Iota Music Therapy Scholarship

Michelle Gaddis Kennemer, Director
Sigma Alpha Iota Philanthropies, Inc.
One Tunnel Road
Asheville, NC 28805
Phone: 828-251-0606
Fax: 828-251-0644
E-mail: jmichelle17@hotmail.com

Sigma Alpha Iota Philanthropies Undergraduate Performance Scholarships

Dr. Emily White, Director
Sigma Alpha Iota Philanthropies, Inc.
One Tunnel Road
Asheville, NC 28805
Phone: 828-251-0606
Fax: 828-251-0644
E-mail: hornstein1@aol.com

Sigma Alpha Iota Philanthropies Undergraduate Scholarships

Eleanor Tapscott, Project Director
Sigma Alpha Iota Philanthropies, Inc.
One Tunnel Road
Asheville, NC 28805
Phone: 828-251-0606
Fax: 828-251-0644
E-mail: webmaster@sai-national.org

Sigma Alpha Iota Summer Music Scholarships in the U.S. or abroad

Mary Jennings, Director
Sigma Alpha Iota Philanthropies, Inc.
One Tunnel Road
Asheville, NC 28805
Phone: 828-251-0606
Fax: 828-251-0644
E-mail: maryj10101@aol.com

Sigma Alpha Iota Visually Impaired Scholarship

Karen Louise Gearreald, Director
Sigma Alpha Iota Philanthropies, Inc.
One Tunnel Road
Asheville, NC 28805
Phone: 828-251-0606
Fax: 828-251-0644
E-mail: hadley@exis.net

SINFONIA FOUNDATION
http://www.sinfonia.org

Sinfonia Foundation Scholarship

Cheri Faith Spicer, Administrative Coordinator
Sinfonia Foundation
10600 Old State Road
Evansville, IN 47711-1399
Phone: 812-867-2433
E-mail: lyrecrest@sinfonia.org

UNICO NATIONAL, INC
http://www.unico.org

Theodore Mazza Scholarship

UNICO National, Inc
UNICO National, Inc
271 US Highway 46 West, Suite A-108
Fairfield, NJ 07004
Phone: 973-808-0035
Fax: 973-808-0043

VSA ARTS
http://www.vsarts.org

VSA arts-Panasonic Young Soloist Award

Elena Widder, Director of Performing Arts
VSA arts
818 Connecticut Avenue, NW, Suite 600
Washington, DC 20006
Phone: 800-933-8721
Fax: 202-737-0725
E-mail: info@vsarts.org

VSA arts-Rosemary Kennedy International Young Soloist Award

Elena Widder, Director of Performing Arts
VSA arts
818 Connecticut Avenue, NW, Suite 600
Washington, DC 20006
Phone: 800-933-8721
Fax: 202-737-0725
E-mail: info@vsarts.org

WAMSO-MINNESOTA ORCHESTRA VOLUNTEER ASSOCIATION
http://www.wamso.org

Young Artist Competition

YAC Chair
WAMSO-Minnesota Orchestra Volunteer Association
Orchestra Hall
1111 Nicollet Mall
Minneapolis, MN 55403-2477
Phone: 612-371-5654
Fax: 612-371-7176
E-mail: wamso@mnorch.org

WAVERLY COMMUNITY HOUSE, INC.
http://www.waverlycomm.com

F. Lammot Belin Arts Scholarship

Chairperson
Waverly Community House, Inc.
1115 North Abington Road
PO Box 142
Waverly, PA 18471
Phone: 570-586-8191
Fax: 570-586-0185
E-mail: info@waverlycomm.com

WOMEN BAND DIRECTORS INTERNATIONAL
http://www.womenbanddirectors.org

Charlotte Plummer Owen Memorial Scholarship

Gladys Stone Wright Scholarship

Helen May Bulter Memorial Scholarship

Music Technology Scholarship

Diane Gorzycki, WBDI Scholarship Chair
Women Band Directors International
292 Band Hall-Louisiana State University
Baton Rouge, LA 70803
E-mail: dgorzycki@austin.rr.com

Martha Ann Stark Memorial Scholarship

Volkwein Memorial Scholarship

Diane Gorzycki, WBDI Scholarship Chair
Women Band Directors International
7424 Whistlestop Drive
Austin, TX 78749
E-mail: dgorzycki@austin.rr.com

Additional Resources

AMERICAN SYMPHONY ORCHESTRA LEAGUE (ASOL)
New York Headquarters
33 West 60th Street, 5th Floor
New York, NY 10023-7905
Phone: 212-262-5161
Fax: 212-262-5198
E-mail: league@symphony.org
Web site: www.symphony.org

Washington Office
910 17th Street N.W.
Washington, D.C. 20006
Phone: 202-776-0215
Fax: 202-776-0224
E-mail: heatherw@symphony.org

ASSOCIATION FOR THEATRE IN HIGH EDUCATION (ATHE)
P.O. Box 1290
Boulder, CO 80306-1290
Phone: 888-284-3737
        303-530-2167
Fax: 303-530-2168
E-mail: info@athe.org
Web site: www.athe.org

EDUCATIONAL THEATER ASSOCIATION
2343 Auburn Avenue
Cincinnati, OH 45219
Phone: 513-421-3900
Web site: www.edta.org

NATIONAL ASSOCIATION FOR MUSIC EDUCATION (NAME)
1806 Robert Fulton Drive
Reston, VA 20191
Phone: 703-860-4000
        800-336-3768
Fax: 703-860-1531
Web site: www.menc.org

NATIONAL ASSOCIATION OF SCHOOLS OF DANCE
NATIONAL ASSOCIATION OF SCHOOLS OF MUSIC (NASM)
NATIONAL ASSOCIATION OF SCHOOLS OF THEATRE
11250 Roger Bacon Drive, Suite 21
Reston, VA 20190
Phone: 703-437-0700
Fax: 703-860-1531
E-mail: info@arts-accredit.org
Web site: http://nast.arts-accredit.org

NATIONAL DANCE EDUCATION ORGANIZATION
4948 St. Elmo Avenue, Suite 301
Bethesda, Maryland 20814
Phone: 301-657-2880 or 301-657-2881
Fax: 301-657-2882
E-mail: info@ndeo.org
Web site: www.ndeo.org

VISUAL AND PERFORMING ARTS COLLEGE FAIRS
NATIONAL ASSOCIATION FOR COLLEGE ADMISSION COUNSELING (NACAC)
1631 Prince Street
Alexandria, Virginia 22314
Phone: 703-836-2222 or 800/822-6285
Fax: 703-836-8015
E-mail: info@nacac.com
Web site: www.nacac.org

Indexes

Performing Arts

Majors and Concentrations

Dance

Ballet
Belhaven College 195
Cornish College of the Arts 200
East Carolina University 201
Friends University 201
Indiana University Bloomington 202
North Carolina School of the Arts 206
Point Park University 206
Purchase College, State University of New York 207
Roger Williams University 209
Southern Methodist University 210
Texas Christian University 211
The University of Arizona 212
University of Oklahoma 217
University of South Florida 218
The University of the Arts 218
University of Utah 219
University of Wyoming 219
York University 221

Choreography
Columbia College 199
Columbia College Chicago 199
Roger Williams University 209
University of California, Santa Barbara 212
University of South Florida 218

Choreography and performance
Cornish College of the Arts 200
George Mason University 202
University of Colorado at Boulder 213
University of Florida 213
University of Illinois at Urbana–Champaign 214
University of Michigan 215
The University of North Carolina at Greensboro 217
University of Southern Mississippi 218

Composition
Purchase College, State University of New York 207
York University 221

Contemporary dance
Concordia University 200
North Carolina School of the Arts 206

Dance
Adelphi University 195
The Boston Conservatory 195
California Institute of the Arts 197
Florida State University 201
Jacksonville University 202
The Juilliard School 203
Long Island University, C.W. Post Campus 204
Marymount Manhattan College 204
Montclair State University 205

New York University 205
Ohio University 206
Ryerson University 209
Shenandoah University 209
Simon Fraser University 209
Slippery Rock University of Pennsylvania 210
State University of New York College at Brockport 210
Temple University 211
Tulane University 212
The University of Iowa 214
University of Massachusetts Amherst 215
University of Minnesota, Twin Cities Campus 215
University of Missouri–Kansas City 216
The University of North Carolina at Greensboro 217
The University of Texas at Austin 218
The University of the Arts 218
Virginia Intermont College 220
Webster University 220
West Texas A&M University 220
Wright State University 221

Dance arts
University of Idaho 214

Dance education
Brenau University 196
Columbia College Chicago 199
East Carolina University 201
Kent State University 204
Shenandoah University 209
University of Hartford 213
The University of North Carolina at Greensboro 217
University of Southern Mississippi 218
The University of the Arts 218

Dance in medicine
University of Florida 213

Dance pedagogy
Butler University 196
Point Park University 206

Dance performance
Brenau University 196
Butler University 196
Columbia College 199
Eastern Michigan University 201
Kent State University 204
Towson University 211
University of Colorado at Boulder 213
University of South Florida 218

Dance studies
University of South Florida 218

Dance theater
University of Hawaii at Manoa 213

Dance therapy
Eastern Michigan University 201

Jazz
Roger Williams University 209

Jazz dance
East Carolina University 201
Southern Methodist University 210
The University of Arizona 212
The University of the Arts 218
University of Wyoming 219

Modern dance
Belhaven College 195
Cornish College of the Arts 200
East Carolina University 201
Point Park University 206
Purchase College, State University of New York 207
Roger Williams University 209
Rutgers, The State University of New Jersey, Mason Gross School of the Arts 204
Southern Methodist University 210
Texas Christian University 211
The University of Arizona 212
University of Colorado at Boulder 213
University of Michigan 215
University of Oklahoma 217
University of South Florida 218
The University of the Arts 218
University of Utah 219
University of Wyoming 219
Virginia Commonwealth University 220
York University 221

Music theater
Columbia College Chicago 199

Performance
Chapman University 198
Columbia College Chicago 199
New World School of the Arts 205
Purchase College, State University of New York 207
University of California, Santa Barbara 212
University of Hartford 213

Production
Purchase College, State University of New York 207

Studio management
Eastern Michigan University 201

Tap dance
Roger Williams University 209

Theater arts/drama
University of Florida 213

World dance
University of Florida 213

Music

Accompanying
Howard Payne University 265
James Madison University 272
Oberlin College 302
University of California, Santa Barbara 332

Accordion
The College of New Jersey 246
University of Denver 336

Acoustic recording
City College of the City University of New York 243

Applied music
Butler University 234
Lee University 278
Seton Hall University 316
Western Illinois University 367

Arranging
University of Denver 336

Arts management
Shenandoah University 317

Audio recording technology
Cleveland Institute of Music 244

Five Towns College 258
Indiana University Bloomington 268

Ballet
Indiana University Bloomington 268

Band
Slippery Rock University of Pennsylvania 318
Southeastern Louisiana University 319

Bass
Musicians Institute 291
New World School of the Arts 294

Music education (continued)

Cleveland State University 245
Coe College 245
Coker College 245
The College of New Jersey 246
The College of Wooster 247
Colorado Christian University 247
Colorado State University 247
Columbus State University 249
Concordia College 249
Conservatory of Music of Puerto Rico 250
Converse College 250
Cornell College 251
Culver-Stockton College 251
DePaul University 253
DePauw University 254
Duquesne University 254
East Carolina University 255
East Central University 255
Eastern Illinois University 255
Eastern Michigan University 256
East Tennessee State University 256
East Texas Baptist University 256
Elmhurst College 257
Emporia State University 257
Five Towns College 258
Florida State University 259
Furman University 260
Georgia College & State University 260
Georgia Southern University 261
Georgia State University 261
Grace College 261
Grand Valley State University 262
Hardin-Simmons University 262
Hastings College 263
Heidelberg College 263
Henderson State University 263
Houghton College 264
Howard University 265
Huntington University 266
Idaho State University 266
Illinois State University 266
Illinois Wesleyan University 267
Immaculata University 267
Indiana State University 267
Indiana University–Purdue University Fort
    Wayne 268
Iowa State University of Science and Technology
    269
Iowa Wesleyan College 269
Ithaca College 269
Jackson State University 271
Jacksonville State University 271
Jacksonville University 271
James Madison University 272
The Johns Hopkins University 272
Kansas State University 274
Kennesaw State University 274
Lamar University 275
Lander University 276
Lawrence University 276
Lebanon Valley College 278
Liberty University 279
Long Island University, C.W. Post Campus 279
Longwood University 279
Louisiana State University and Agricultural and
    Mechanical College 280
Loyola University New Orleans 280
Mansfield University of Pennsylvania 283
Marygrove College 283
McGill University 284
Mercer University 286
Meredith College 286
Metropolitan State College of Denver 287
Miami University 287
Middle Tennessee State University 287
Midwestern State University 288
Minnesota State University Mankato 288

Mississippi University for Women 289
Montana State University 289
Montclair State University 289
Moravian College 290
Morehead State University 290
Nazareth College of Rochester 291
Nebraska Wesleyan University 292
New Mexico State University 293
New York University 295
Norfolk State University 297
Northern Illinois University 298
Northern Kentucky University 298
North Park University 299
Northwestern State University of Louisiana 299
Northwestern University 300
Nyack College 301
Oakland City University 301
Oakland University 301
Oberlin College 302
Ohio Northern University 303
Ohio University 303
Ohio Wesleyan University 303
Oklahoma Baptist University 304
Oklahoma City University 304
Oklahoma State University 304
Oral Roberts University 305
Otterbein College 305
Pacific Lutheran University 306
Pacific Union College 306
Palm Beach Atlantic University 306
The Pennsylvania State University University Park
    Campus 307
Philadelphia Biblical University 307
Pittsburg State University 307
Prairie View A&M University 308
Radford University 309
Roosevelt University 310
Rowan University 311
Rutgers, The State University of New Jersey,
    Mason Gross School of the Arts 284
St. Cloud State University 312
Saint Mary's College 312
St. Olaf College 313
Saint Xavier University 313
Salem College 313
Samford University 314
Sam Houston State University 314
San Diego State University 314
San Jose State University 316
Seton Hall University 316
Seton Hill University 317
Shenandoah University 317
Simpson College 318
Slippery Rock University of Pennsylvania 318
Southeastern Louisiana University 319
Southern Adventist University 319
Southern Arkansas University–Magnolia 320
Southern Illinois University Carbondale 320
Southern Illinois University Edwardsville 320
Southern Methodist University 321
Southern University and Agricultural and
    Mechanical College 321
Southwestern Oklahoma State University 321
State University of New York College at Potsdam
    322
State University of New York, Fredonia 322
Stephen F. Austin State University 323
Susquehanna University 323
Syracuse University 324
Taylor University 324
Tennessee Technological University 325
Texas A&M University–Commerce 325
Texas A&M University–Corpus Christi 326
Texas State University-San Marcos 326
Texas Tech University 326
Towson University 327
University of Alaska Anchorage 329
University of Alberta 329
University of Arkansas 330

University of Arkansas at Monticello 330
University of Bridgeport 330
The University of British Columbia 331
University of Calgary 331
University of Central Arkansas 332
University of Cincinnati 333
University of Colorado at Boulder 335
University of Connecticut 335
University of Dayton 336
University of Delaware 336
University of Evansville 337
University of Georgia 337
University of Hartford 337
University of Houston 338
The University of Iowa 338
University of Kansas 339
University of Louisiana at Lafayette 339
University of Louisiana at Monroe 340
University of Louisville 340
University of Manitoba 340
University of Massachusetts Amherst 341
University of Massachusetts Dartmouth 342
University of Memphis 343
University of Miami 343
University of Michigan 345
University of Minnesota, Duluth 346
University of Mississippi 346
University of Missouri–Columbia 346
University of Missouri–Kansas City 347
University of Mobile 347
The University of Montana–Missoula 347
University of Montevallo 348
University of Nebraska at Omaha 348
University of Nebraska–Lincoln 348
University of New Hampshire 349
University of New Mexico 349
The University of North Carolina at Charlotte 350
The University of North Carolina at
    Greensboro 350
The University of North Carolina at Pembroke 350
The University of North Carolina Wilmington 351
University of North Dakota 351
University of Northern Colorado 351
University of Oregon 352
University of Portland 352
University of Prince Edward Island 353
University of Puget Sound 353
University of Redlands 354
University of Rhode Island 354
University of South Alabama 354
University of South Carolina 355
The University of South Dakota 355
University of South Florida 356
The University of Tennessee 356
The University of Tennessee at Chattanooga 357
The University of Texas at San Antonio 357
The University of the Arts 358
University of the Incarnate Word 358
University of the Pacific 358
University of Tulsa 359
University of Utah 359
University of West Georgia 360
University of Wisconsin–Green Bay 360
University of Wisconsin–Madison 360
University of Wisconsin–Oshkosh 361
University of Wisconsin–Stevens Point 361
University of Wisconsin–Superior 362
University of Wyoming 362
Utah State University 363
Valley City State University 363
Valparaiso University 363
Vanderbilt University 364
Virginia Commonwealth University 364
Walla Walla College 365
Wartburg College 365
Washburn University 365
Wayne State University 366
Weber State University 366
Webster University 367

Western Carolina University *367*
Western Illinois University *367*
Western Kentucky University *368*
Western Michigan University *368*
Western State College of Colorado *368*
Westminster Choir College of Rider
    University *369*
Westminster College *370*
West Virginia University *370*
West Virginia Wesleyan College *371*
Wheaton College *371*
Wittenberg University *373*
Wright State University *373*
Youngstown State University *374*

Music engineering and production
Berklee College of Music *228*

Music engineering technology
University of Miami *343*

Music history
Birmingham-Southern College *229*
Bowling Green State University *231*
Bucknell University *234*
California State University, Long Beach *237*
Converse College *250*
Dalhousie University *252*
Howard University *265*
McGill University *284*
Nazareth College of Rochester *291*
New England Conservatory of Music *292*
The Pennsylvania State University University Park
    Campus *307*
Rice University *310*
University of Calgary *331*
University of Cincinnati *333*
University of Hartford *337*
University of Kansas *339*
University of Louisville *340*
University of Manitoba *340*
University of Massachusetts Amherst *341*
University of Memphis *343*
University of Michigan *345*
University of Missouri–Columbia *346*
University of Prince Edward Island *353*
University of the Pacific *358*
West Virginia University *370*

Music history and literature
Baldwin-Wallace College *226*
Butler University *234*
The Catholic University of America *240*
The College of Wooster *247*
Florida State University *259*
Indiana State University *267*
Northwestern University *300*
Ohio University *303*
Southern Illinois University Edwardsville *320*
University of Alberta *329*
University of Louisiana at Monroe *340*
University of Rhode Island *354*
University of Utah *359*
Wheaton College *371*
Wright State University *373*

Music history/theory
University of Connecticut *335*
University of Wisconsin–Whitewater *362*

Music industry
Capital University *239*
Drexel University *254*
Heidelberg College *263*
Middle Tennessee State University *287*
Minnesota State University Mankato *288*
Troy University *327*
University of South Alabama *354*
University of Southern California *355*
University of the Incarnate Word *358*

Music instruction
Dalhousie University *252*

Music literature
Sam Houston State University *314*
University of Wisconsin–Stevens Point *361*

Music management
California State University, Sacramento *237*
Georgia State University *261*
University of Evansville *337*
University of Hartford *337*
University of the Pacific *358*
Wayne State University *366*

Music marketing
The University of Texas at San Antonio *357*

Music media
Capital University *239*
Norfolk State University *297*
University of Louisiana at Lafayette *339*

Music merchandising
Capital University *239*
Southern Illinois University Edwardsville *320*

**Music merchandising and business
administration**
Indiana State University *267*

Music performance
Augsburg College *225*
Capital University *239*
Concordia University *250*
Duquesne University *254*
Hardin-Simmons University *262*
Mansfield University of Pennsylvania *283*
Metropolitan State College of Denver *287*
Nebraska Wesleyan University *292*
New York University *295*
Oakland City University *301*
Ohio Northern University *303*
Ohio Wesleyan University *303*
Salem College *313*
Seton Hill University *317*
The University of Alabama *328*
University of Calgary *331*
The University of Iowa *338*
University of Louisville *340*
University of Nebraska at Omaha *348*
University of Rhode Island *354*
University of Wyoming *362*
Western Illinois University *367*
West Virginia University *370*

Music scholarship
The University of British Columbia *331*

Music synthesis
Berklee College of Music *228*

Music teaching
Brevard College *232*

Music technology
Ball State University *226*
California Institute of the Arts *235*
Capital University *239*
Central Missouri State University *242*
Duquesne University *254*
Jackson State University *271*
Lebanon Valley College *278*
McGill University *284*
New York University *295*
Northwestern University *300*
University of Denver *336*
University of Massachusetts Dartmouth *342*
University of Michigan *345*
The University of Montana–Missoula *347*
University of Nebraska at Omaha *348*
Wayne State University *366*

Music theater
Baldwin-Wallace College *226*
Belmont University *227*
The Catholic University of America *240*
East Carolina University *255*
Florida State University *259*
Illinois State University *266*

James Madison University *272*
Kansas State University *274*
Montclair State University *289*
Nazareth College of Rochester *291*
Notre Dame de Namur University *300*
Oklahoma City University *304*
Otterbein College *305*
Samford University *314*
Southern Illinois University Carbondale *320*
Southern Illinois University Edwardsville *320*
University of Kansas *339*
University of Louisiana at Monroe *340*
University of Miami *343*
The University of North Carolina at Pembroke *350*
University of South Alabama *354*
Western Carolina University *367*
Westminster Choir College of Rider
    University *369*

Music theater accompanying
Shenandoah University *317*

Music theory
Baldwin-Wallace College *226*
Belmont University *227*
Butler University *234*
Concordia College *249*
Florida State University *259*
Furman University *260*
Indiana State University *267*
Ithaca College *269*
Loyola University New Orleans *280*
Mannes College The New School for Music *282*
McGill University *284*
Mercer University *286*
Nazareth College of Rochester *291*
New England Conservatory of Music *292*
Northwestern University *300*
Oberlin College *302*
The Pennsylvania State University University Park
    Campus *307*
Rice University *310*
Southwestern Oklahoma State University *321*
Texas Tech University *326*
Union University *328*
The University of Alabama *328*
University of Arkansas *330*
University of Cincinnati *333*
University of Georgia *337*
University of Hartford *337*
University of Houston *338*
University of Kansas *339*
University of Maryland, College Park *341*
University of Michigan *345*
University of Mississippi *346*
University of Missouri–Columbia *346*
University of Missouri–Kansas City *347*
University of New Hampshire *349*
University of Tulsa *359*
University of Utah *359*

Music theory and composition
Boston University *230*
California State University, Sacramento *237*
Centenary College of Louisiana *241*
Central Michigan University *242*
Coe College *245*
Concordia University *250*
Converse College *250*
Dalhousie University *252*
East Carolina University *255*
Hardin-Simmons University *262*
Jacksonville University *271*
Lawrence University *276*
Marygrove College *283*
Middle Tennessee State University *287*
Montclair State University *289*
New York University *295*
Ohio University *303*
Oklahoma Baptist University *304*
St. Cloud State University *312*

Brigham Young University 233
Butler University 234
California Institute of the Arts 235
California State University, Long Beach 237
Cameron University 238
Central College 241
The College of New Jersey 246
Covenant College 251
Culver-Stockton College 251
DePaul University 253
Eastern Illinois University 255
East Tennessee State University 256
Emporia State University 257
Friends University 259
Holy Names University 264
Houghton College 264
Idaho State University 266
Illinois Wesleyan University 267
Indiana State University 267
Indiana University Bloomington 268
Jackson State University 271
James Madison University 272
The Juilliard School 273
Kennesaw State University 274
Kentucky Wesleyan College 275
Lamar University 275
Lee University 278
Longwood University 279
Louisiana State University and Agricultural and Mechanical College 280
Manhattan School of Music 281
Mannes College The New School for Music 282
Mansfield University of Pennsylvania 283
New England Conservatory of Music 292
New Mexico State University 293
New World School of the Arts 294
Northern Arizona University 297
Northern Kentucky University 298
North Park University 299
Northwestern University 300
Oklahoma Baptist University 304
Oral Roberts University 305
Prairie View A&M University 308
St. Francis Xavier University 312
Saint Xavier University 313
Salem College 313
Slippery Rock University of Pennsylvania 318
Southeastern Louisiana University 319
Southern Methodist University 321
Southern University and Agricultural and Mechanical College 321
State University of New York at Binghamton 322
State University of New York, Fredonia 322
Texas A&M University–Commerce 325
Truman State University 328
University of Arkansas at Monticello 330
University of California, Irvine 331
University of California, Santa Barbara 332
University of Delaware 336
University of Maryland, College Park 341
University of Missouri–Columbia 346
University of New Hampshire 349
University of the Cumberlands 358
University of the Pacific 358
University of Tulsa 359
University of Utah 359
University of Wisconsin–Oshkosh 361
Walla Walla College 365
Western Kentucky University 368
Westminster Choir College of Rider University 369

Piano accompanying
Bowling Green State University 231
Northern Arizona University 297
Shenandoah University 317

Piano pedagogy
Belmont University 227
Bowling Green State University 231

Butler University 234
Calvary Bible College and Theological Seminary 238
Central Missouri State University 242
Colorado State University 247
Columbus State University 249
Converse College 250
East Carolina University 255
Hastings College 263
Holy Names University 264
Howard Payne University 265
Longwood University 279
Louisiana State University and Agricultural and Mechanical College 280
Loyola University New Orleans 280
Marygrove College 283
Meredith College 286
New Mexico State University 293
Northern Kentucky University 298
St. Cloud State University 312
Southern Illinois University Carbondale 320
Stephen F. Austin State University 323
Texas A&M University–Commerce 325
University of Louisiana at Lafayette 339
University of Louisiana at Monroe 340
University of Louisville 340
University of Missouri–Kansas City 347
University of Montevallo 348
University of South Florida 356
The University of Tennessee 356
Utah State University 363

Piano performance
Calvary Bible College and Theological Seminary 238
East Texas Baptist University 256
Fisk University 257
Saint Mary's College 312
Utah State University 363

Piano/organ
Appalachian State University 223
Augusta State University 225
Baldwin-Wallace College 226
Baylor University 227
Berry College 229
Birmingham-Southern College 229
Bowling Green State University 231
Bucknell University 234
California State University, Fullerton 237
Carnegie Mellon University 239
Centenary College of Louisiana 241
Central Michigan University 242
Central Missouri State University 242
Chapman University 242
Cleveland Institute of Music 244
Cleveland State University 245
Coe College 245
The College of Wooster 247
Colorado Christian University 247
Colorado State University 247
Columbus State University 249
Concordia College 249
Converse College 250
The Curtis Institute of Music 252
Dalhousie University 252
Delta State University 252
DePauw University 254
East Carolina University 255
East Central University 255
Eastern Michigan University 256
Florida State University 259
Furman University 260
Grand Valley State University 262
Hastings College 263
Heidelberg College 263
Howard Payne University 265
Hunter College of the City University of New York 265
Illinois State University 266

Indiana University–Purdue University Fort Wayne 268
Indiana University South Bend 269
Iowa State University of Science and Technology 269
Ithaca College 269
Kansas State University 274
Lawrence University 276
Mercer University 286
Meredith College 286
Miami University 287
Midwestern State University 288
Minnesota State University Mankato 288
Montana State University 289
Montclair State University 289
Morehead State University 290
New England Conservatory of Music 292
Norfolk State University 297
North Carolina School of the Arts 297
Northern Illinois University 298
Northern State University 298
Northwestern State University of Louisiana 299
Notre Dame de Namur University 300
Nyack College 301
Oakland City University 301
Oberlin College 302
Ohio University 303
Ohio Wesleyan University 303
Oklahoma City University 304
Oklahoma State University 304
Otterbein College 305
Pacific Union College 306
The Pennsylvania State University University Park Campus 307
Philadelphia Biblical University 307
Pittsburg State University 307
Purchase College, State University of New York 308
Queens College of the City University of New York 309
Queens University of Charlotte 309
Rice University 310
Samford University 314
Sam Houston State University 314
San Diego State University 314
San Francisco Conservatory of Music 315
Shenandoah University 317
Simpson College 318
Southern Illinois University Carbondale 320
Southwestern Oklahoma State University 321
State University of New York College at Potsdam 322
Stephen F. Austin State University 323
Susquehanna University 323
Taylor University 324
Texas State University-San Marcos 326
Texas Tech University 326
Trinity University 327
Union University 328
University of Alaska Anchorage 329
University of Alberta 329
University of Arkansas 330
The University of British Columbia 331
University of Calgary 331
University of Central Arkansas 332
University of Cincinnati 333
University of Colorado at Boulder 335
University of Connecticut 335
University of Denver 336
University of Evansville 337
University of Georgia 337
University of Houston 338
The University of Iowa 338
University of Kansas 339
University of Louisiana at Monroe 340
University of Louisville 340
University of Michigan 345
University of Mississippi 346
University of Missouri–Kansas City 347

Theater

Alphabetical Listing of Schools

University of Kentucky, Lexington, KY *339, 411*
University of Louisiana at Lafayette, Lafayette, LA *215, 339, 411*
University of Louisiana at Monroe, Monroe, LA *340*
University of Louisville, Louisville, KY *340*
University of Maine, Orono, ME *340*
University of Manitoba, Winnipeg, MB, Canada *340*
University of Maryland, College Park, College Park, MD *341*
University of Massachusetts Amherst, Amherst, MA *215, 341*
University of Massachusetts Dartmouth, North Dartmouth, MA *342*
University of Massachusetts Lowell, Lowell, MA *342*
University of Memphis, Memphis, TN *343, 412*
University of Miami, Coral Gables, FL *343, 412*
University of Michigan, Ann Arbor, MI *215, 344, 345, 412*
University of Michigan–Flint, Flint, MI *413*
University of Minnesota, Duluth, Duluth, MN *346, 413*
University of Minnesota, Twin Cities Campus, Minneapolis, MN *215, 346, 413*
University of Mississippi, University, MS *346*
University of Missouri–Columbia, Columbia, MO *346*
University of Missouri–Kansas City, Kansas City, MO *216, 347*
University of Missouri–St. Louis, St. Louis, MO *347*
University of Mobile, Mobile, AL *347*
The University of Montana–Missoula, Missoula, MT *217, 347, 413*
University of Montevallo, Montevallo, AL *348, 413*
University of Nebraska at Kearney, Kearney, NE *348*
University of Nebraska at Omaha, Omaha, NE *348*
University of Nebraska–Lincoln, Lincoln, NE *348, 414*
University of Nevada, Las Vegas, Las Vegas, NV *349*
University of Nevada, Reno, Reno, NV *349, 414*
University of New Hampshire, Durham, NH *349*
University of New Mexico, Albuquerque, NM *349*
University of North Alabama, Florence, AL *350*
The University of North Carolina at Chapel Hill, Chapel Hill, NC *350*
The University of North Carolina at Charlotte, Charlotte, NC *350*
The University of North Carolina at Greensboro, Greensboro, NC *217, 350, 414*
The University of North Carolina at Pembroke, Pembroke, NC *350*
The University of North Carolina Wilmington, Wilmington, NC *351*
University of North Dakota, Grand Forks, ND *351, 415*
University of Northern Colorado, Greeley, CO *351*
University of Northern Iowa, Cedar Falls, IA *352*
University of North Florida, Jacksonville, FL *352*
University of North Texas, Denton, TX *352*
University of Oklahoma, Norman, OK *217, 352, 415*
University of Oregon, Eugene, OR *352*
University of Portland, Portland, OR *352*
University of Prince Edward Island, Charlottetown, PE, Canada *353*
University of Puget Sound, Tacoma, WA *353*

University of Redlands, Redlands, CA *354*
University of Regina, Regina, SK, Canada *354*
University of Rhode Island, Kingston, RI *354, 415*
University of Rochester, Rochester, NY *354*
University of Saskatchewan, Saskatoon, SK, Canada *415*
University of South Alabama, Mobile, AL *354, 415*
University of South Carolina, Columbia, SC *355*
The University of South Dakota, Vermillion, SD *355, 415*
University of Southern California, Los Angeles, CA *355, 415*
University of Southern Maine, Portland, ME *356*
University of Southern Mississippi, Hattiesburg, MS *218, 356, 416*
University of South Florida, Tampa, FL *218, 356, 417*
The University of Tampa, Tampa, FL *356*
The University of Tennessee, Knoxville, TN *356*
The University of Tennessee at Chattanooga, Chattanooga, TN *357*
The University of Tennessee at Martin, Martin, TN *357, 417*
The University of Texas at Arlington, Arlington, TX *357*
The University of Texas at Austin, Austin, TX *218, 357, 417*
The University of Texas at El Paso, El Paso, TX *357*
The University of Texas at San Antonio, San Antonio, TX *357*
The University of Texas at Tyler, Tyler, TX *357*
The University of the Arts, Philadelphia, PA *218, 358, 417*
University of the Cumberlands, Williamsburg, KY *358*
University of the Incarnate Word, San Antonio, TX *358*
University of the Pacific, Stockton, CA *358*
The University of Toledo, Toledo, OH *359*
University of Tulsa, Tulsa, OK *359*
University of Utah, Salt Lake City, UT *219, 219, 359, 417*
University of Vermont, Burlington, VT *360*
University of Washington, Seattle, WA *360*
University of West Georgia, Carrollton, GA *360*
University of Windsor, Windsor, ON, Canada *418*
University of Wisconsin–Eau Claire, Eau Claire, WI *360*
University of Wisconsin–Green Bay, Green Bay, WI *360*
University of Wisconsin–Madison, Madison, WI *360*
University of Wisconsin–Milwaukee, Milwaukee, WI *219, 361, 418*
University of Wisconsin–Oshkosh, Oshkosh, WI *361*
University of Wisconsin–River Falls, River Falls, WI *361*
University of Wisconsin–Stevens Point, Stevens Point, WI *361, 418*
University of Wisconsin–Superior, Superior, WI *362, 419*
University of Wisconsin–Whitewater, Whitewater, WI *362, 419*
University of Wyoming, Laramie, WY *219, 362, 419*
USC Thornton School of Music—See University of Southern California
Utah State University, Logan, UT *363, 419*

V
Valdosta State University, Valdosta, GA *363, 420*
Valley City State University, Valley City, ND *363*
Valparaiso University, Valparaiso, IN *363*
Vanderbilt University, Nashville, TN *364*
VanderCook College of Music, Chicago, IL *364*
Virginia Commonwealth University, Richmond, VA *220, 364, 420*
Virginia Intermont College, Bristol, VA *220, 420*
Virginia State University, Petersburg, VA *365*
Viterbo University, La Crosse, WI *365, 420*

W
Walla Walla College, College Place, WA *365*
Wartburg College, Waverly, IA *365*
Washburn University, Topeka, KS *365*
Washington State University, Pullman, WA *366*
Wayland Baptist University, Plainview, TX *366*
Wayne State University, Detroit, MI *366, 421*
Weber State University, Ogden, UT *366*
Webster University, St. Louis, MO *220, 367, 421*
West Chester University of Pennsylvania, West Chester, PA *367*
Western Carolina University, Cullowhee, NC *367, 422*
Western Connecticut State University, Danbury, CT *367*
Western Illinois University, Macomb, IL *367*
Western Kentucky University, Bowling Green, KY *368, 422*
Western Michigan University, Kalamazoo, MI *220, 368, 422*
Western State College of Colorado, Gunnison, CO *368*
Western Washington University, Bellingham, WA *369*
Westminster Choir College of Rider University, Princeton, NJ *369*
Westminster College, New Wilmington, PA *370*
West Texas A&M University, Canyon, TX *220, 370*
West Virginia University, Morgantown, WV *370, 422*
West Virginia Wesleyan College, Buckhannon, WV *371*
Wheaton College, Wheaton, IL *371*
Wheaton Conservatory of Music—See Wheaton College
Wichita State University, Wichita, KS *221*
Wilfrid Laurier University, Waterloo, ON, Canada *372*
Willamette University, Salem, OR *372*
William Carey College, Hattiesburg, MS *372*
William Paterson University of New Jersey, Wayne, NJ *372*
Wingate University, Wingate, NC *372*
Winters School of Music—See William Carey College
Winthrop University, Rock Hill, SC *372*
Wittenberg University, Springfield, OH *373*
Wright State University, Dayton, OH *221, 373, 422*

X
Xavier University of Louisiana, New Orleans, LA *373*

Y
York University, Toronto, ON, Canada *221, 373, 423*
Youngstown State University, Youngstown, OH *374*

NOTES

NOTES

NOTES

NOTES

Peterson's
Book Satisfaction Survey

Give Us Your Feedback

Thank you for choosing Peterson's as your source for personalized solutions for your education and career achievement. Please take a few minutes to answer the following questions. Your answers will go a long way in helping us to produce the most user-friendly and comprehensive resources to meet your individual needs.

When completed, please tear out this page and mail it to us at:

Publishing Department
PETERSON'S, A Nelnet Company
2000 Lenox Drive
Lawrenceville, NJ 08648

You can also complete this survey online at **www.petersons.com/booksurvey.**

1. **What is the ISBN of the book you have purchased? (The ISBN can be found on the book's back cover in the lower right-hand corner.)** _____

2. **Where did you purchase this book?**
   ❑ Retailer, such as Barnes & Noble
   ❑ Online reseller, such as Amazon.com
   ❑ Petersons.com
   ❑ Other (please specify) _____

3. **If you purchased this book on Petersons.com, please rate the following aspects of your online purchasing experience on a scale of 4 to 1 (4 = Excellent and 1 = Poor).**

	4	3	2	1
Comprehensiveness of Peterson's Online Bookstore page	❑	❑	❑	❑
Overall online customer experience	❑	❑	❑	❑

4. **Which category best describes you?**
   ❑ High school student
   ❑ Parent of high school student
   ❑ College student
   ❑ Graduate/professional student
   ❑ Returning adult student

   ❑ Teacher
   ❑ Counselor
   ❑ Working professional/military
   ❑ Other (please specify) _____

5. **Rate your overall satisfaction with this book.**

Extremely Satisfied	Satisfied	Not Satisfied
❑	❑	❑

6. Rate each of the following aspects of this book on a scale of 4 to 1 (4 = Excellent and 1 = Poor).

	4	3	2	1
Comprehensiveness of the information	❑	❑	❑	❑
Accuracy of the information	❑	❑	❑	❑
Usability	❑	❑	❑	❑
Cover design	❑	❑	❑	❑
Book layout	❑	❑	❑	❑
Special features *(e.g., CD, flashcards, charts, etc.)*	❑	❑	❑	❑
Value for the money	❑	❑	❑	❑

7. This book was recommended by:
- ❑ Guidance counselor
- ❑ Parent/guardian
- ❑ Family member/relative
- ❑ Friend
- ❑ Teacher
- ❑ Not recommended by anyone—I found the book on my own
- ❑ Other (please specify) _____

8. Would you recommend this book to others?

Yes	Not Sure	No
❑	❑	❑

9. Please provide any additional comments.

_____

_____

_____

_____

_____

Remember, you can tear out this page and mail it to us at:

Publishing Department
PETERSON'S, A Nelnet Company
2000 Lenox Drive
Lawrenceville, NJ 08648

or you can complete the survey online at **www.petersons.com/booksurvey**.

Your feedback is important to us at Peterson's, and we thank you for your time!

If you would like us to keep in touch with you about new products and services, please include your e-mail here: _____